## *About Island Press*

Island Press is the only nonprofit organization in the United States whose principal purpose is the publication of books on environmental issues and natural resource management. We provide solutions-oriented information to professionals, public officials, business and community leaders, and concerned citizens who are shaping responses to environmental problems.

In 2001, Island Press celebrates its seventeenth anniversary as the leading provider of timely and practical books that take a multidisciplinary approach to critical environmental concerns. Our growing list of titles reflects our commitment to bringing the best of an expanding body of literature to the environmental community throughout North America and the world.

Support for Island Press is provided by The Bullitt Foundation, The Mary Flagler Cary Charitable Trust, The Nathan Cummings Foundation, Geraldine R. Dodge Foundation, Doris Duke Charitable Foundation, The Charles Engelhard Foundation, The Ford Foundation, The George Gund Foundation, The Vira I. Heinz Endowment, The William and Flora Hewlett Foundation, W. Alton Jones Foundation, The John D. and Catherine T. MacArthur Foundation, The Andrew W. Mellon Foundation, The Charles Stewart Mott Foundation, The Curtis and Edith Munson Foundation, National Fish and Wildlife Foundation, The New-Land Foundation, Oak Foundation, The Overbrook Foundation, The David and Lucile Packard Foundation, The Pew Charitable Trusts, Rockefeller Brothers Fund, The Winslow Foundation, and other generous donors.

# The Wellbeing
of Nations

la vida buena es cara,
hay otra mas barata,
pero ya no es vida

[the good life is dear,
there's another that is cheaper,
but it's no life]

*Spanish maxim*

# The Wellbeing of Nations

A Country-by-Country Index
of Quality of Life and the Environment

**Robert Prescott-Allen**

*in cooperation with*
International Development Research Centre
IUCN–The World Conservation Union
International Institute for Environment and Development
Food and Agriculture Organization of the United Nations
Map Maker Ltd
UNEP World Conservation Monitoring Centre

**ISLAND PRESS**
Washington • Covelo • London

ISLAND PRESS is a trademark of The Center for Resource Economics.


Library of Congress Cataloging-in-Publication Data


Prescott-Allen, Robert, 1942–
    The wellbeing of nations : a country-by-country index of quality of
life and the environment / Robert Prescott-Allen.
        p. cm.
    Includes bibliographical references and index.
    ISBN 1-55963-830-3 (cloth : alk. paper) — ISBN 1-55963-831-1 (pbk.
: alk. paper)
    1. Environmental quality.  2.  Environmental indicators.  I.  Title.

GE140 .P74 2001
363.7—dc21
                                                        2001004282

Printed on recycled, acid-free paper

British Cataloguing-in-Publication Data available.

Manufactured in the United States of America
10 9 8 7 6 5 4 3 2 1

# Contents

## Appendix A. Monetary and physical accounts    269

## Appendix B. Wellbeing Assessment    277

# List of Maps, Figures, and Tables

## Maps

## *Figures*

# Data Sources

## Major Sources

Food and Agriculture Organization of the United Nations
Global Environmental Monitoring System
International Telecommunication Union
IUCN—The World Conservation Union
United Nations Development Programme
United Nations Educational, Scientific, and Cultural Organization
United Nations Environment Programme
UNEP World Conservation Monitoring Centre
United Nations Population Division
World Bank
World Health Organization

## Other Important Sources

BirdLife International
Carbon Dioxide Information Analysis Center
Conservation International
Freedom House
International Institute for Strategic Studies
International Labour Office
International Livestock Research Institute
International Monetary Fund
International Soil Reference and Information Centre
Inter-Parliamentary Union
Organisation for Economic Co-operation and Development
Transparency International
United Nations Children's Fund
United Nations Crime Prevention and Criminal Justice Division
United Nations Economic Commission for Europe
United Nations Energy Statistics Unit
World Energy Council
World Meteorological Organization
World Resources Institute
World Wildlife Fund (USA)

# *Acknowledgments*

I could not have written this book without the help of two people. First, Christine, my wife and super editor, who scrutinized each draft for clarity and readability, and wrote improvements. Any part of this book that is expressed compellingly I owe to her; any that is turgid or obscure is due to my obstinacy in the face of her counsel. Above all, she sustained me with love throughout the four years it has taken me to bring this labor of love to fruition.

Second, Eric Dudley, the extraordinary polymath who invented and continues to develop Map Maker, the GIS program I used for all the maps in this book. He gave me new versions of Map Maker, taught me to use it, wrote a subprogram so that I could manipulate land quality data, wrote the Combo program for calculating and combining indicator scores, and has been a regular source of sage advice.

Many people contributed intellectually to the Barometer of Sustainability and Wellbeing Assessment method used by the book. The Barometer of Sustainability was inspired by the Human Development Index, which was devised by the late Mahub ul Haq and his colleagues at the Human Development Report Office of the United Nations Development Programme. The Barometer's early development was helped by the experience of Albert Adriaanse with his Environmental Pressure Index, and by advice from my colleagues on the IUCN International Assessment Team: Ashoke Chatterjee, Eric Dudley, Alejandro Imbach, Tony Hodge, Diana Lee-Smith, and Adil Najam. Tony Hodge, Alejandro Imbach, and Diana Lee-Smith also made major contributions to the Wellbeing Assessment method. Two people at IUCN's Regional Office for Southern Africa made specific improvements: Carmel Lue-Mbizvo urged the inclusion of global as well as local impacts on the ecosystem; Emmanuel Guveya sim-plified the method of calculating indicator scores. I have benefited greatly from discussions with Edgar Gutiérrez-Espeleta, Director of the Development Observatory at the University of Costa Rica; Manuel Winograd at the Land Management Unit of the Centro Internacional de Agricultura Tropical (CIAT) in Colombia; Ali Qadir, IUCN Pakistan; and Alex Moiseev and Irene Gujit.

I learned much from Tony Hodge during our assessment of the sustainability of British Columbia, and Tony has continued to feed me ideas and information. I have been immeasurably helped by those who have tested the Barometer of Sustainability: Ashok Kumar and his colleagues at Development Alternatives in Karnataka, India (watershed assessment in Tumkur District); Isabel Adriana Gutiérrez Montes at the Centro Agronomico Tropical de Investigación y Enseñanza (CATIE) and the IUCN Regional Office for Meso America (rural sustainable development assessment in Nicaragua); Peter Hardi and Lazlo Pinter at the International Institute for Sustainable Development (IISD) (assessment of the Prairie Ecozone in Manitoba); Stephen Owen, Stuart Gale, Linda Hannah, Justin Longo, Linda Michaluk, and Risa Smith, who shared the assessment of British Columbia's sustainability; Misael Kokwe, Emmanuel Guveya, and Freddie Kachote at the IUCN Regional Office for Southern Africa (wellbeing assessment of Mangisai, Nyevera, and Sedeya communities in Zimuto communal lands, Zimbabwe); and the great team of people who worked on district environmental action plans in Zimbabwe—Sam Chimbuya, Elliot Mhaka, Cephas Chidenga, Douglas Chimhande, Joseph Chizororo, Peter Gambara, Davison Haukozi, Carmel Lue-Mbizvo, Zii Masiye, John Mbetu, Peter Mfumu, John Mupingo, Constantine Mushure, Aaron Tshabangu, and Unity Tshabangu.

I owe a special debt to Nancy MacPherson, who coordinated the IUCN/IDRC project on assessing progress toward sustainability and who gave me the invaluable opportunity to co-develop and test the Wellbeing Assessment method as part of that project; and to Diana Lee-Smith and Alejandro Imbach, with whom I worked closely for much of the project.

IDRC, IUCN, IIED, IISD, and Island Press arranged for previous drafts to be independently reviewed. The comments of the anonymous reviewers made for a much better book.

The organizations who generously gave data are listed under "Data Sources" and acknowledged specifically in the notes to chapters and tables. Many individuals helped me to obtain information and advised on how to use it:

Food and Agriculture Organization of the United Nations: Sustainable Development Department—H. Carsalade, Linda Collette, Dominique Lantieri, J. S. Latham, and in particular Jeff Tschirley and Stephanie Vertecchi; Fisheries Department—Serge M. Garcia, Richard J. R. Grainger, John F. Caddy, Purwito Martosubroto, H. C. F. Naeve, Rolf Willmann; Forestry Department— Lennart S. Ljungman, Christel Palmberg-Lerche, Robert R. Davis, R. Michael Martin, Froylan Castañeda, Klaus Janz, Christian Pilegaard Hansen, So Thirong Patrick, P. Vantomme; Land and Water Development Division—W. G. Sombroek, Jean-Marc Faurès, G. G. Appelgren, José Benites, Mathieu Bousquet, Arumugam Kandiah, A. P. Koohafkan, Freddy Nachtergaele; Animal Production and Health Division—Keith Hammond, Beate Scherf; Commodities and Trade Division—M. De Nigris, A. Gürkan; Statistics Division—Sam Zarqua, Giulia Cimino, E. D. Gillin, Richard Hoad, L. O. Larson, Jorge Mernies, L. Naiken, Martha Neundorfer, Jean Viseur; Information Division—Jean-Philippe Decraene, Tony Loftas.

Global Environmental Monitoring System: Andrew S. Fraser (National Water Research Institute, UNEP and WHO GEMS/Water Collaborating Centre).

International Telecommunication Union: Michael R. Minges, Dalia Mendiluce, Linda O'Driscoll.

IUCN–The World Conservation Union: Adrian Phillips, Wendy Strahm, Simon Stuart.

United Nations Development Programme: Sakiko Fukuda-Parr and Selim Jahan.

United Nations Educational, Scientific and Cultural Organization: Chu Shiu-Kee, Lynda Bellaiche, Karl Hochgesand, Takeo Jimbow, Geraldo Nascimento.

United Nations Environment Programme: G. M. Bankobeza, Franklin G. Cardy, Arthur Lyon Dahl, Michael Graber, Miriam Schomaker, Veerle Vandweerd.

UNEP World Conservation Monitoring Centre: Mark Collins, Gillian Bunting, Harriet Gillett, Michael J. B. Green, Brian Groombridge, Jeremy (Jerry) Harrison, James Paine, Julie Reay, Tony Turner.

United Nations Population Division: Joseph Chamie, Joseph-Alfred Grinblat, Mary Beth Weinberger.

World Bank: John Dixon, Abdolreza Farivari, M. H. Saeed Ordoudabi, William C. Prince.

World Health Organization: Monika Blössner, Tord Kjellström, Doris Ma Fat, Dieter Schwela, the late Sylvère Siméant.

BirdLife International: Colin Bibby, Martin Sneary, Alison Stattersfield.

Carbon Dioxide Information Analysis Center: Tom Boden and Karen Gibson.

Conservation International: Lee Hannah and Silvio Olivieri.

Freedom House: Charles Braybow.

International Institute for Strategic Studies: Digby Waller.

International Labour Office: Magali Imbert-Luccioni and Brigitte du Jeu.

International Monetary Fund: Tom Nordman.

International Soil Reference and Information Centre: Roel Oldeman and Hans van Baren.

Organisation for Economic Co-operation and Development: Joke Waller-Hunter and Christian Avérous.

United Nations Children's Fund: Gareth Jones.

United Nations Economic Commission for Europe: G. de Bellis, Radovan Chrást, Andreas Kahnert, Kit Prins.

United Nations Energy Statistics Unit: Eszter Horváth and Gordon Telesford.

World Energy Council: Julian Chisholm.

World Resources Institute: Dan Tunstall and Eric Rodenburg.

World Wildlife Fund (USA): William M. (Bill) Eichbaum and David M. Olson.

United Nations Centre for Human Settlements: Christine Auclair.

United Nations Statistics Division: Peter Bartelmus, Cristina Hannig, Jan W. van Tongeren.

Equilibrium: Nigel Dudley.

International Journal of Hydropower & Dams: Alan Manchester.

This book could not have been published in full color without generous contributions to the cost of doing so by the International Development Research Centre (IDRC), IUCN–The World Conservation Union, and the International Institute for Environment and Development (IIED). I am especially grateful for the support of:

IDRC: Maureen O'Neil, President; Pierre Beemans, David Brooks, Terry Smutylo, Bill Carman, and in particular Fred Carden.

IUCN: David McDowell, former Director General; Jeff McNeely, Javed Ahmad, Mark Halle, Elaine Shaughnessy, Estelle Viguet, John Waugh.

IIED: Richard Sandbrook, former Executive Director, and Nigel Cross, current Executive Director.

Last but not least, I acknowledge Tom Lovejoy, who encouraged Island Press to publish *The Wellbeing of Nations;* and to everyone involved at Island Press for doing so.

My heartfelt thanks to all.

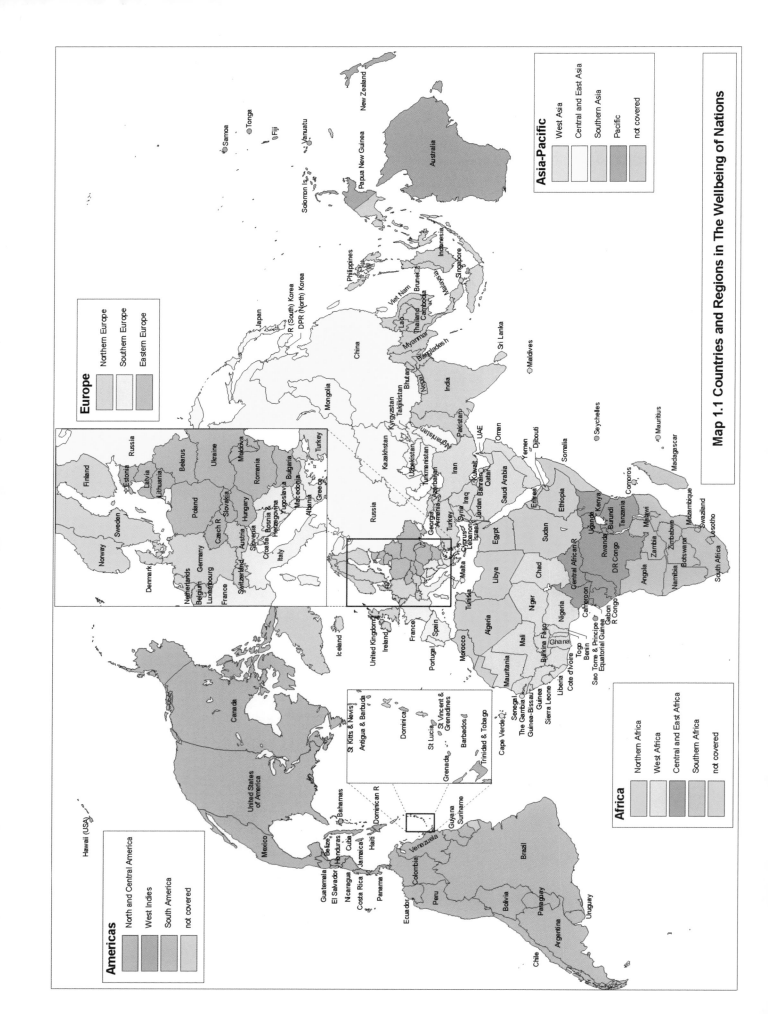

**Map 1.1 Countries and Regions in The Wellbeing of Nations**

**Americas**
- North and Central America
- West Indies
- South America
- not covered

**Europe**
- Northern Europe
- Southern Europe
- Eastern Europe

**Asia-Pacific**
- West Asia
- Central and East Asia
- Southern Asia
- Pacific
- not covered

**Africa**
- Northern Africa
- West Africa
- Central and East Africa
- Southern Africa
- not covered

# 1. The Quest for Wellbeing and Sustainability

## *How Far to the Good Life?*

The Chinese seek the five blessings of long life, riches, health, love of virtue, and a natural death in old age. The French desire liberty, equality, and fraternity. Indians aspire to power, pleasure, morality, and emancipation from the world. The English hope for health, wealth, and wisdom. Americans uphold life, liberty, and the pursuit of happiness.

However envisaged, the good life has always been a demanding goal. Today, it is becoming increasingly difficult to achieve for more than a minority and even harder to sustain. As human populations and economies have grown, it has become impossible to improve one's own wellbeing without affecting other people's. Through trade, money markets, and environmental change, the ripple of interactions, dependencies, and impacts among communities and nations has steadily widened. The scope of self-interest has expanded from the individual and his or her society to all societies. Our one Earth has become one world.

At the same time, people have become a shaping force in the planet's evolution, extending the scope of self-interest still further, from humanity to all life. Many views of the good life have regarded nature's bounty as a given. Today, pollution, resource shortages, and the declining diversity of plants and animals are signs that too much of that bounty is being taken. Henceforth, to sustain their own wellbeing, people need to look after the wellbeing of the ecosystem: the system of land, water, air, and living creatures that embraces and supports them.

This dramatic change in the human condition impels the growing concern for sustainable development. People still need ways of living that correspond to their views of the good life. But now these ways of life must also be equitable—both within and among societies and between present and future generations—and they must safeguard the diversity, productivity, and resilience of the ecosystem.

Nobody knows how to meet these new demands. There is no proven recipe for success. In fact, no one has a clear sense of what success would be. Making progress toward ways of living that are desirable, equitable, and sustainable is like going to a country we have never been to before with a sense of geography and the principles of navigation but without map or compass. We do not know what the destination will be like, we cannot tell how to get there, we are not even sure which direction to take.

However, if we had some navigational tools, we could define a starting point, check our position along the way, and so determine our direction. Then if we designed our actions so that we learned as we went along, we could make course corrections before going too far astray.

The most informative navigational aid is a wellbeing assessment that societies—from countries to communities—could undertake regularly. To enable each society to set a baseline, keep track of progress, and learn from its actions, the assessment would ask three questions:

- How well are people?

- How well is the ecosystem?

- How are people and the ecosystem affecting each other?

By exploring and measuring the three questions together, societies can learn what combinations of human and ecosystem wellbeing are sustainable, and make their own decisions about how to achieve them.

Until they do, the good life will recede into the unattainable distance. At present, no country is sustainable or even close. Nations with a high standard of living impose excessive pressure on the global environment. Nations with low demands on the ecosystem are desperately poor. No country knows how to be green without going into the red.

We have been unable to see this dichotomy so clearly before because there has been no way to compare human conditions with the state of the environment. To fill this gap, *The Wellbeing of Nations* presents a new method of measuring human and ecosystem wellbeing, together with a first assessment of 180 countries and four indices. The Human Wellbeing Index (HWI) and Ecosystem Wellbeing Index (EWI) are comprehensive measures of the quality of life and the environment. The Wellbeing Index (WI) juxtaposes them so that they can be compared. The Wellbeing/Stress Index (WSI) shows how much human wellbeing each nation obtains for the amount of ecosystem stress it causes. In the majority of countries, ecosystem stress is higher than human wellbeing, a clear sign that most people's efforts to improve their lot are inefficient and overexploit the environment.

The 180 countries are ranked in terms of the HWI, EWI, WI, and WSI. The first two rankings differ significantly from equivalents produced by other methods due to differences in scope, choice of issues and indicators, and the way in which the indicators are combined. The other two indices are unique to the Wellbeing Assessment method used in *The Wellbeing of Nations*.

The rankings themselves are not as important as what the indices say about each country and what they reveal about the strengths and weaknesses of the various methods as measures of performance. To explore the differences, the HWI is compared with the Human Development Index, and the EWI with the Ecological Footprint.[1]

## Why New Indices?

The four indices, and the Wellbeing Assessment method that produces them, provide several essentials for improving human and environmental conditions:

- A clearly stated goal.
- A way of measuring progress toward the goal.
- An analytical tool for deciding priority actions.
- A process to keep the goal constantly in mind and to help people learn how to reach it.

The first two essentials go together. A measurable goal is a more attainable goal. If gross domestic product (GDP) and its constituent indicators did not exist, the world would lack both a measurement of the market economy and a sense of economic growth as a realizable goal. The goal and the measurement emerged together, each reinforcing the other. The goal made the index significant, a measurement worth paying attention to. The index made the goal possible since no one will adopt an objective whose achievement cannot be recognized.

The same goes for equitable and sustainable ways of living. The HWI, EWI, WI, and WSI are the means by which societies can measure the overall conditions of people and the environment, thereby making it possible for them to adopt better human and ecosystem wellbeing as an achievable goal. The four indices act as beacons, signaling a society's wellbeing and sustainability and reminding it of the need to reach them.

By breaking down the indices into major components (e.g., land, water, air, biological diversity, energy, health, wealth, knowledge, community, equity), societies can identify the factors most responsible for their current levels of human and ecosystem wellbeing. This is the starting point for analyzing policies realistically and deciding which actions to take first.

It is fairly easy to forge consensus around the vague idea of sustainable development. It is much harder to get competing interest groups to agree on specific policies on (for instance) carbon dioxide emissions or terms of trade. Wellbeing assessments can facilitate consensus building by providing a logical progression from the goal, through objectives for particular themes or sectors, to standards of achievement for indicators. They also provide a much-needed mental bridge between the short term and the long term. The hurly burly of immediate demands and sudden events can overwhelm long-term goals and sharply reduce their influence over the daily decisions of households, businesses, and governments. Wellbeing assessments can offset this danger (to some extent at least) by providing a mechanism to link the practical realities of the present to people's vision of a desirable future.

## The Wellbeing Assessment Difference

The two main approaches to measuring sustainability are accounts and assessments. Accounts are constructed from raw data and are designed to be as complete as possible. Hence they excel at tracking the economy or the flow of materials and energy because these fields produce abundant statistics.

The most widely used method of measuring progress is the System of National Accounts, which records the transactions of national economies and sums them into monetary indicators such as the GDP. The GDP is enormously influential and is relied on by politicians, the business community, the media, and the public as a sign of prosperity and wellbeing. It is nothing of the kind. GDP measures the output of the market economy and is not designed to do anything more. Its narrow focus neglects completely many aspects of the economy (from income distribution to unpaid work and the black economy) and all nonmonetary contributors to human fulfillment (including health, education, freedom, security, and peace). It ignores the state of the ecosystem and either omits environmental and social costs (such as pollution, resource depletion, cancer, and crime) or counts them as benefits if they cause money to change hands.

Attempts at less distorted accounts include the System of Integrated Environmental and Economic Accounting, the Index of Sustainable Economic Welfare (or Genuine Progress Indicator), and the World Bank's estimates of national wealth and genuine saving. These green accounts are unlikely to provide a satisfactory measure of wellbeing because they use money as their measure, and money cannot measure everything. No matter how meticulous the calculation, dollars trivialize much of what people value most: fresh air, a species' existence, good health, security, a human life, or freedom. The price of liberty is eternal vigilance, not $4.99. (For more on accounts, see Appendix A.)

Assessments make no attempt to be complete but rely instead on measuring representative aspects, or indicators. Because they can be selective, they are better equipped than accounts to cover the wide array of issues necessary for an adequate portrayal of human and environmental conditions. Stimulated by the World Commission on Environment and Development's call for sustainable development in 1987 and the United Nations Conference on Environment and Development in 1992, major innovations in methods of assessing sustainable development have been made in the last decade or so. They include the pressure-state-response framework for environmental indicators, the Human Development Index, the Environmental Pressure Index, and the Ecological Footprint.[2]

Despite these advances, assessments continue to lag behind accounts in influencing national policies. They have yet to cover the full extent of human and environmental concerns and distill them into an index as power-

ful as the GDP. Among the major global assessments (Table 1.1), few combine their indicators into an index, so it is extremely difficult to extract the big picture from the details. Almost all of them focus either on people or on the environment. Few cover both, and none treats them as equals.

By contrast, the main features of *The Wellbeing of Nations* and the Wellbeing Assessment method are that they:

- Cover both people and the ecosystem, and give them equal weight.

- Assess the condition of people and the environment through a broad range of indicators chosen to represent widely shared values and key properties of human societies and the ecosystem.

- Combine the indicators into four indices.

The HWI is a more realistic measure of socioeconomic conditions than narrowly monetary indicators such as the GDP and covers more aspects of human wellbeing than the Human Development Index. The EWI is an equally broad measure of the state of the environment,

**Table 1.1. Global assessments and reports, showing their coverage of people and the ecosystem (✓ = major, ✗ = minor) and whether they combine indicators into an index (✓ = yes, ✗ = no).** Agenda 21 refers to the set of sustainable development indicators of the United Nations Commission on Sustainable Development (United Nations 1996). Ecological Footprint: Wackernagel et al. (2000). Environmental Sustainability Index: Global Leaders for Environment Tomorrow Task Force (2001). Global Environment Outlook: United Nations Environment Programme (1999). Human Development Report (includes the human development index): United Nations Development Programme (1990–1999). Living Planet Report: Loh et al. (1999). State of the World's Children: UNICEF (1999b). World Development Report: World Bank (2000a). World Resources Report: World Resources Institute et al. (1998).

| Assessment or Report | People | Ecosystem | Index |
|---|---|---|---|
| *Wellbeing of Nations* | ✓ | ✓ | ✓ |
| Agenda 21 | ✓ | ✓ | ✗ |
| Ecological Footprint | ✗ | ✓ | ✓ |
| Environmental Sustainability Index | ✗ | ✓ | ✓ |
| Global Environment Outlook | ✗ | ✓ | ✗ |
| Human Development Report | ✓ | ✗ | ✓ |
| Living Planet Report | ✗ | ✓ | ✓ |
| State of the World's Children | ✓ | ✗ | ✗ |
| World Development Report | ✓ | ✗ | ✗ |
| World Resources Report | ✗ | ✓ | ✗ |

with a fuller treatment of national conditions than other global indices except the Environmental Sustainability Index, which (unlike the EWI) is muddled by the inclusion of human indicators. The WI and WSI break new ground in measuring people and the ecosystem together to compare their conditions, show the impact of one on the other, and shine a spotlight on the improvement of both.

## Guide to This Book

*The Wellbeing of Nations* assesses 180 independent countries for which data could be obtained on at least half the indicators.[3] The countries are organized into 4 continental groups and 14 regions (Map 1.1):

### Americas (35 countries)
North and Central America (10 countries)
West Indies (13 countries)
South America (12 countries)

### Africa (53 countries)
Northern Africa (10 countries)
West Africa (17 countries)
Central and East Africa (13 countries)
Southern Africa (13 countries)

### Europe (37 countries)
Northern Europe (13 countries)
Southern Europe (12 countries)
Eastern Europe (12 countries)

### Asia–Pacific (55 countries)
West Asia (18 countries)
Russia, Central and East Asia (12 countries)
Southern Asia (17 countries)
Pacific (8 countries)

Chapter 2 assesses human wellbeing and Chapter 3 ecosystem wellbeing for all the countries. Each chapter is divided into six sections. The first section presents the HWI (Chapter 2) or EWI (Chapter 3). The remaining sections show how the index was obtained. Each section covers a dimension, or set of major features of wellbeing. Every dimension section starts with an overview of the elements that make up the dimension and a synthesis and index of the state of that dimension. Then the elements and their indicators are covered in turn. World maps for each index and most indicators summarize the performance of all the countries.

The map projection is the Dudley equal area projec-

tion, chosen because it shows countries' true areas with little distortion of their shapes and makes very efficient use of space. Its sole disadvantage is that north is not always straight up the page, so the orientation of some countries is unusual. Antarctica has been omitted to save space.[4]

Chapter 4 combines the results into the overall WI and WSI. It examines the patterns of national performance that the indices reveal and analyzes the scope for improvement. It discusses the relationships between ecosystem stress and human wellbeing, income, and resource consumption. Finally, it suggests the main changes needed for countries to progress toward satisfying and sustainable ways of life.

The rest of this chapter discusses why people and the ecosystem are treated equally and explains enough of the method for readers to follow the other chapters. A full description of the Wellbeing Assessment method is given in Appendix B.

## Equal Treatment of People and the Ecosystem

The underlying hypothesis of Wellbeing Assessment is that sustainable development is a combination of human wellbeing and ecosystem wellbeing (defined in Box 1.1). Human wellbeing is a requirement for sustainability because no rational person would want to perpetuate a low standard of living. Ecosystem wellbeing is a requirement because the ecosystem supports life and makes possible any standard of living. Although trade-offs between the needs of people and the needs of the ecosystem are unavoidable, they must be limited. For a while, human progress may be won at the expense of the natural environment. It may be necessary to turn forests and wetlands into farms, and farms into towns. But people will not prosper or even survive for long unless the ecosystem is healthy, productive, and diverse. At the same time, it does not matter how well the ecosystem is if people cannot meet their needs. A robust economy and flourishing community are as vital for people's health, wealth, and happiness as a rich and resilient ecosystem. Ultimately, human and ecosystem wellbeing are equally important, and a sustainable society needs to achieve both together.

The hypothesis is expressed in the metaphor of the Egg of Wellbeing (Figure 1.1). The ecosystem surrounds and supports people much as the white of an egg surrounds and supports the yolk. Just as an egg can be good only if both the yolk and white are good, so a society can be well and sustainable only if both people and the ecosystem are well.

To compare human development and ecosystem conservation and to keep the focus on improving both, the wellbeing of people and the ecosystem are considered together but measured separately. Information is organized into two subsystems: people (human communities, economies, and artifacts) and ecosystem (ecological communities, processes, and resources). Interactions between the two are recorded under the receiving subsystem. Human stresses on the ecosystem (such as pollution and resource depletion)—as well as benefits to it from conservation—are recorded under *ecosystem.* Benefits from the ecosystem to people (from the supply of resources to spiritual comfort) are recorded under *people,* along with environmental stresses on people (such as the effects of natural disasters). For example, the impact of agriculture and fisheries on the land, water, air, and organisms is measured as part of ecosystem wellbeing; their impact on food supply, incomes, employment, health, and community stability is measured as part of human wellbeing.

**Choosing What to Measure**

Since it is impossible to measure human or ecosystem wellbeing directly, assessments must select indicators of the main features of each. (An indicator is something that represents a particular attribute, characteristic, or property of a system.[5]) Knowing the essential role of indicators, it is tempting to jump right in and choose them at once. However, it is seldom clear at the start of an assessment how well a given set of indicators represents a desirable combination of human and environmental conditions, what aspects are left out, how much the indicators overlap, or how they relate to each other. Since indicators require the collection and analysis of often large amounts of data, choosing the wrong ones can be a costly mistake.

Consequently, it is necessary first to take apart the concepts of human and ecosystem wellbeing to identify the features that need to be measured and then to unpack each feature to reveal aspects that are both representative and measurable.

Wellbeing Assessment does this by going down the hierarchy in Figure 1.2, which provides a series of increasingly specific stepping stones from system and goal to indicators and performance criteria (standards of achievement).

The system is whatever is being assessed, and the goals provide the basis for deciding what will be measured. In *The Wellbeing of Nations,* the system is the people and ecosystem of 180 countries, and the proposed goal for the system is sustainable and equitable combinations of human and ecosystem wellbeing. Goals for people and the ecosystem are defined in Chapters 2 and 3.

Five human dimensions and five ecosystem dimensions have been identified to provide a common framework for all assessments using the Wellbeing Assessment method (Figure 1.3). The dimensions are designed to combine a wide range of topics into a few major groups of roughly equal importance. They are

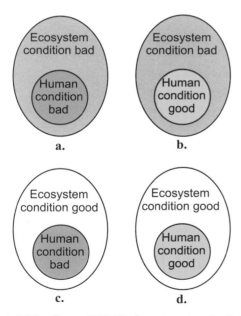

**Figure 1.1. The Egg of Wellbeing.** A society is obviously unwell and unsustainable if people are suffering and the ecosystem is degraded (a). It is also unwell and unsustainable if either the ecosystem condition is bad (b) or the human condition is bad (c). Only condition (d) is sustainable.

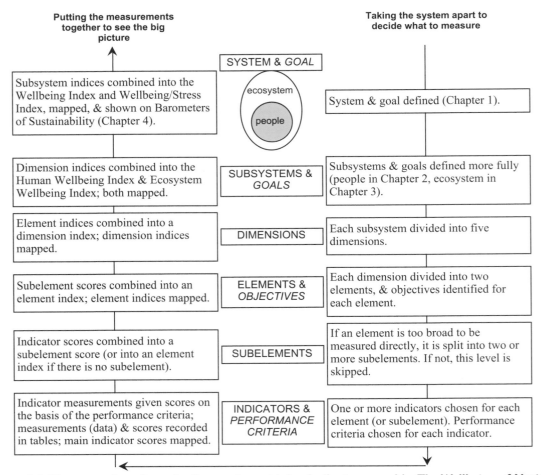

**Putting the measurements together to see the big picture**

**Taking the system apart to decide what to measure**

SYSTEM & *GOAL*

ecosystem

people

Subsystem indices combined into the Wellbeing Index and Wellbeing/Stress Index, mapped, & shown on Barometers of Sustainability (Chapter 4).

System & goal defined (Chapter 1).

SUBSYSTEMS & *GOALS*

Dimension indices combined into the Human Wellbeing Index & Ecosystem Wellbeing Index; both mapped.

Subsystems & goals defined more fully (people in Chapter 2, ecosystem in Chapter 3).

DIMENSIONS

Element indices combined into a dimension index; dimension indices mapped.

Each subsystem divided into five dimensions.

ELEMENTS & *OBJECTIVES*

Subelement scores combined into an element index; element indices mapped.

Each dimension divided into two elements, & objectives identified for each element.

SUBELEMENTS

Indicator scores combined into a subelement score (or into an element index if there is no subelement).

If an element is too broad to be measured directly, it is split into two or more subelements. If not, this level is skipped.

INDICATORS & *PERFORMANCE CRITERIA*

Indicator measurements given scores on the basis of the performance criteria; measurements (data) & scores recorded in tables; main indicator scores mapped.

One or more indicators chosen for each element (or subelement). Performance criteria chosen for each indicator.

**Figure 1.2. The procedure for selecting and combining indicators used in *The Wellbeing of Nations*.**

comprehensive enough to accommodate most of the concerns of most societies: any issue regarded as significant for wellbeing and sustainable development has a place in one of them. The remaining levels of the hierarchy (from elements and objectives through indicators and performance criteria) may vary from assessment to assessment.

The dimensions are subdivided into elements: key subjects or concerns that must be considered to get an adequate sense of the condition of people or the ecosystem. (If an element is too broad to measure directly, it is split into subelements; otherwise, the subelement level is skipped.) For example, I have divided the wealth dimension into two elements—household wealth and national wealth—and household wealth into two subelements: needs and income (Figure 1.4). An objective is defined for each element to aid the selection of indicators and performance criteria. The objective for household wealth

is "enough material goods and income to secure basic needs and decent livelihoods."

One or more indicators are chosen for each element (or subelement) on the basis of how fully the indicator represents the element or subelement concerned and how reliable and feasible it is (Box 1.2). *The Wellbeing of Nations* relies entirely on indicators for which data can be obtained from international sources. If an otherwise suitable indicator has insufficient data, a substitute is used. If none can be found, the indicator, subelement, or element is excluded, in which case its absence is clearly shown. For example, several indicators of food sufficiency are used because none is available for all countries, but there is no indicator of shelter because the data are too sparse (Figure 1.4). The details of choosing indicators are discussed in Appendix B.

Performance criteria are then chosen for each indicator. Their purpose is explained next.

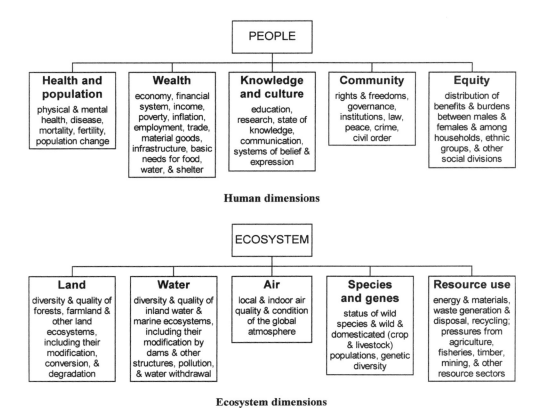

**Human dimensions**

**Ecosystem dimensions**

**Figure 1.3. Common framework of dimensions.** The dimensions (in **bold**) are fixed, but the elements covered under each dimension may change depending on the assessment. The lists here are examples to illustrate the scope of the dimensions. The elements identified for *The Wellbeing of Nations* are described in Chapters 2 (people) and 3 (ecosystem).

## Combining the Measurements

A large number of indicators is inevitable, given the broad scope of human and ecosystem wellbeing, but presents an enormous communication problem. Every indicator sends a signal. The more indicators, the more signals—a perplexing cacophony of good, bad, and somewhere-in-between news. Moreover, each indicator conveys information about the particular element or subelement it represents but not about the system as a whole.

The problem is overcome by combining the indicators into indices. How to do this raises other obstacles, however, because a typical set of indicators is a mess of incompatible measurements: land condition in hectares, water pollution in milligrams per liter, carbon dioxide emissions in metric tons of carbon, species diversity in percentages of threatened species, health in years of life expectancy and death rates, income in money, education in school enrollment rates, freedom in the observation of rights, and so on.

Combining such different indicators mixes apples and oranges. To do this successfully requires finding a common unit that does not distort their qualities as apples or oranges ("citrus units" would favor oranges, "pome units"

---

**Box 1.2. The ideal indicator is ...**

**Representative:** it covers the most important aspects of the element concerned; and shows trends over time and differences between places and groups of people.

**Reliable:** it directly reflects how far the objective concerned is met; and is well founded, accurate, and measured in a standardized way with sound and consistent sampling procedures.

**Feasible:** it depends on data that are readily available or obtainable at reasonable cost.

Indicator selection is often a matter of balancing these qualities.

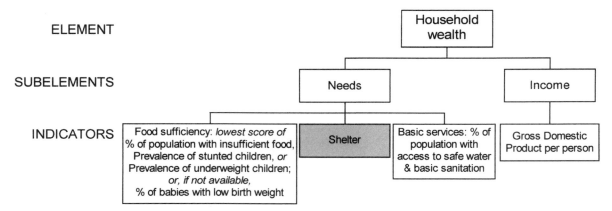

**Figure 1.4. Indicator chart for household wealth.** The absence of an indicator for shelter is shown by the shaded box.

would favor apples). The common unit may be a physical unit, money, or a performance score. Wellbeing Assessment uses performance scores.

Physical units can combine only a limited range of things. Materials can be combined on the basis of their weight, but this does not account for their different impacts: a ton of arsenic is more of a problem than a ton of old lace. Pollutants with similar effects can be combined according to their potential for that effect: greenhouse gas emissions can be combined according to the contribution of each gas to global warming, and heavy metals on the basis of their toxicity. But pollutants with different effects cannot be combined in this way.

Money is standard in all economic accounts, but it too has serious weaknesses. It reflects the market price of apples and oranges, not their taste, nutritional content, or cultural value. It can measure the value of things that are traded in the market, but it distorts the value of anything that is not traded. The less tradable the item, the greater the distortion. Since most items in an assessment of wellbeing and sustainability have no market price, nonmarket values have to be estimated from contingent values (asking people how much they would pay for a benefit or how much compensation they would accept if deprived of the benefit) or from expenditures on avoiding and treating damage. Using these methods together is like combining real apples (market values), fake apples (contingent values), real oranges (actual expenditures), and fake oranges (hypothetical expenditures).

The advantage of a performance score is that it measures how good an orange is at being an orange and how good an apple is as an apple—the distance between a standard level of performance and the actual performance recorded by an indicator measurement. On a 0–100 scale, best performance is 100 and worst 0. A given apple or orange would receive a score according to how good it was in relation to best and worst. Performance criteria for apples and oranges may be very different, but because their scores are calculated in the same way on the same scale, the scores can be combined.

Wellbeing Assessment uses the Barometer of Sustainability (Figure 1.5) because it is the only performance scale designed to measure human and ecosystem wellbeing together without submerging one in the other. The Barometer's unique features are:

- Two axes: one for human wellbeing, the other for ecosystem wellbeing. This enables each set of indicators to be combined independently, keeping them separate to allow analysis of people–ecosystem interactions.

- The axis with the lower score overrides the other axis. This prevents a high score for human wellbeing from offsetting a low score for ecosystem wellbeing (or vice versa), reflecting the view that people and the ecosystem are equally important and that sustainable development must improve and maintain the wellbeing of both.

- Each axis is divided into five bands. This allows users to define not just the end points of the scale but intermediate points as well, for greater flexibility and control of the scale.

The performance criteria enable indicator measurements to be given a score by converting them to the scale

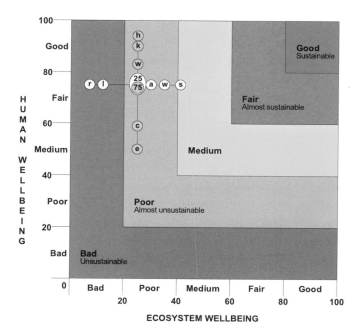

**Figure 1.5. Barometer of Sustainability.** The Wellbeing Index (WI) of a hypothetical country is shown on the Barometer. The Human Wellbeing Index (HWI) is in the yolk of the egg. The Ecosystem Wellbeing Index (EWI) is in the white. The WI is where the HWI and EWI intersect. Yellow circles (vertical axis) show the points on the scale of the human dimensions: c = community, e = equity, h = health and population, k = knowledge, w = wealth. White circles (horizontal axis) show the points of the ecosystem dimensions: a = air, l = land, r = resource use, s = species and genes, w = water.

of the Barometer. They define the rate of exchange between the indicator and the scale—the level of performance that is worth a given number of points (Table 1.2).

Performance criteria require a great deal of thought. They are guided by the range of actual performance, the objective of the element that the indicator represents, and

**Table 1.2. The five bands of the Barometer of Sustainability.**

| Band | Points Range | Top | Definition |
|---|---|---|---|
| Good | 100–81 | 100 | Desirable performance, objective fully met |
| Fair | 80–61 | 80 | Acceptable performance, objective almost or barely met |
| Medium | 60–41 | 60 | Neutral or transitional performance |
| Poor | 40–21 | 40 | Undesirable performance |
| Bad | 20–1 | 20 | Unacceptable performance |
| Base | 0 | 0 | Base of scale |

**Table 1.3 Performance criteria for food sufficiency indicators.** Performance is good (81–100 points) if less than 10% of the population lacks enough food.

| Band | Top Point on Scale | % of Population with Insufficient Food |
|---|---|---|
| Good | 100 | 0 |
| Fair | 80 | 10 |
| Medium | 60 | 20 |
| Poor | 40 | 35 |
| Bad | 20 | 50 |
| Base | 0 | 100 |

factors such as estimated sustainable rates, observed thresholds, international standards or targets, expert opinion, and the performance criteria of related indicators. For example, the World Health Organization has set international targets for three of the four food sufficiency indicators: less than 20% for prevalence of stunting in children, no more than 10% for prevalence of underweight children, and no more than 10% for babies with low birth weight. These targets strongly influenced my definition of good performance in food sufficiency as less than 10% of population undernourished, fair as 10–19%, and bad performance as 50% or more (Table 1.3 and Figure 1.6).

Performance criteria are displayed graphically on maps of the indicators, given in full in the tables in the Data section, and summarized in Appendix C. The technicalities of choosing them are discussed in Appendix B, which also explains the straightforward procedure for calculating scores.

To prevent high scores resulting merely from lack of data, a good score is allowed only if it is based on all applicable components (e.g., data in an indicator, indicators in an element, elements in a dimension) and a fair score only if it is based on at least half the components. Potentially good scores based on more than half but not all the applicable components are reduced to 80 (the top of fair). Potentially good or fair scores based on fewer than half the applicable components are reduced to 60 (the top of medium). For example, the needs score has two components: food sufficiency and basic services (Figure 1.4). Malta has a score of 88 (good) for food sufficiency but no data on basic services, so its score for needs is not 88 but 80.

The main indicators are mapped on the basis of their scores. Maps and analyses are in Chapters 2 and 3, and indicator measurements and scores are given in the Data section.

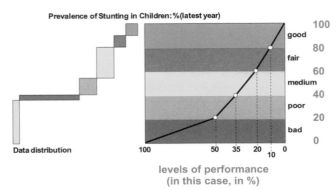

**Figure 1.6 How performance criteria are graphically displayed in this book.** In the square graphic on the right, the vertical axis is the scale of the Barometer of Sustainability and never changes: 0 is the base of the scale, and 20, 40, 60, 80, and 100 are the top points of, respectively, the bad, poor, medium, fair, and good bands. The horizontal axis shows levels of performance. It is specific to the indicator in question and is expressed in the measurement units of the indicator (in this case, percentages). The numbers along this axis represent levels of performance, from worst (on the left) to best (on the right). In this example, 100% corresponds to the base of the scale, 50% to the top point of the bad band, 35% to the top of poor, 20% to the top of medium, 10% to the top of fair, and 0% to the top of good. Note that the labels in red do not appear in the usual picture but are shown here to assist explanation. The staircase graphic on the left is explained in the text.

Throughout *The Wellbeing of Nations,* performance is mapped by color, the colors matching the bands of the Barometer of Sustainability (Figure 1.5): green always represents good performance; blue, fair; yellow, medium; pink, poor; and red, bad. Gray stands for no data. Seven territories excluded for general lack of data are also mapped in gray.[6]

Every indicator map includes a pair of graphics: a square graphic (explained in the caption to Figure 1.6) showing the performance criteria used to convert the indicator measurements to a score, and a staircase graphic showing the distribution of the data.

In the staircase graphic, the height of each step represents the number of countries whose performance (scored on the basis of the criteria specified in the square graphic) falls within that band. In the example of the prevalence of stunting in children (Figure 1.6), the largest number of countries has no data (gray), followed by medium (yellow) performance, then poor (pink), then fair (blue), then good (green), then bad (red).

The width of each step in the staircase graphic represents the proportion of the performance scale that falls within that band. In stunting in children, the good (green) and fair (blue) steps are narrowest because they include spans of only 10 percentage points. The bad (red) step is widest, comprising a 50-point spread. In between are the medium (yellow) and poor (pink) steps, each covering 15 percentage points.

Once the indicators have been given a score, they can be combined back up the hierarchy (Figure 1.2), from indicators to system: indicator scores are combined into a subelement score, subelement scores into an element index, element indices into a dimension index, and dimension indices into a subsystem index. Combining involves taking either the average or the lower of the scores. In Figure 1.4, for example, the needs (subelement) score is the lower score of the food sufficiency and basic services indicators; the household wealth (element) index is the average of the needs score and the income score. Dimensions are given equal weight, but elements, subelements, and indicators are sometimes given different weights: for example, the knowledge (element) index is the average of the education and communication scores, with education given twice the weight of communication.

The combining procedure used is stated in a panel at the start of each section of Chapters 2 and 3. A full description of combining procedures is given in Appendix B, and all index calculations are summarized in Appendix D.

## A Disclaimer and an Invitation

It is extremely difficult to take a clear and easily communicated snapshot of something as complex and poorly understood as human societies, the ecosystem, and interactions between them. There is no perfect or even best way to do it. All methods entail hard choices about what to focus on and are bound to omit aspects that somebody considers important. Problems of data quality and conflicting values mean that crucial parts of the picture are blurred and open to alternative interpretations.

Hence no method can provide a definitive assessment, and Wellbeing Assessment is no exception. Rather, the method provides a framework for reflection and debate about the relationship between people and the ecosystem, the factors that are crucial for ecosystem wellbeing and human wellbeing, the indicators that best represent these factors, and performance criteria for each indicator. The Wellbeing Assessment method is meant to be easy to use and is fully described in Appendix B. All data, assumptions, and judgments are in the tables and Appendices C and D. They are there so that readers with different views on the elements, indicators, and performance criteria may test them for themselves.

*The Wellbeing of Nations* is offered as both a contribution to the debate and a first approximation of national conditions. Because international statistics take several years to collect and process, global reviews are always a few years behind the times. Most of the data for this review are for 1996–1999. They provide a perspective of where countries were at the end of one millennium and a baseline so that they can assess their progress from 2001 onward. The data record national averages, which mask the often great differences that exist among groups and places within countries. I hope that countries and communities will expose and explore these differences themselves by using the method to undertake their own more detailed assessments.

## Notes

1. Human Development Index: United Nations Development Programme (1990–2000). Ecological Footprint: Wackernagel et al. (2000).
2. World Commission on Environment and Development (1987). United Nations Conference on Environment and Development: United Nations (1992). Pressure–state–response framework: Organisation for Economic Co-operation and Development (1994). Environmental Pressure Index: Adriaanse (1993) and Appendix B. The Human Development Index (United Nations Development Programme 1990–2000) is described in Chapter 2 and Appendix B. The Ecological Footprint (Wackernagel & Rees 1996) is described in Chapter 3 and Table 9 in the Data section.
3. The following countries and territories were excluded for lack of data. *Americas:* Anguilla, Aruba, Bermuda, British Virgin Islands, Cayman Islands, Falkland Islands (Malvinas), French Guiana, Greenland, Guadeloupe, Martinique, Montserrat, Netherlands Antilles, Puerto Rico, St Pierre and Miquelon, Turks and Caicos Islands, United States Virgin Islands. *Africa:* Mayotte, Réunion, St Helena and dependencies, Western Sahara. *Europe:* Andorra, Channel Islands, Faeroe Islands, Liechtenstein, Isle of Man, San Marino. *Asia–Pacific:* American Samoa, Cook Islands, East Timor, French Polynesia, Guam, Kiribati, Marshall Islands, Micronesia, Nauru, New Caledonia, Niue, Northern Mariana Islands, Palau, Palestine (Gaza Strip and West Bank), Tokelau, Tuvalu, Wallis and Futuna Islands.
4. All maps were made with Map Maker Pro, described in Appendix E.
5. Gallopín (1997).
6. Falkland Islands (Malvinas), French Guiana, Greenland, Guadeloupe, Martinique, New Caledonia, and Western Sahara.

# 2. Human Wellbeing

## Human Wellbeing Index

### Human Wellbeing Index (HWI) (Map 2.1)

**What it is:** Average of indices of health and population, wealth, knowledge, community, and equity *or* average of indices of health and population, wealth, knowledge, and community, *whichever is lower.*

**Country results:** 3 good (2%), 34 fair (19%), 52 medium (29%), 51 poor (28%), 40 bad (22%).

**Highlights:**

- Two-thirds of the world's people live in countries with a poor or bad HWI, and less than one-sixth in countries with a fair or good HWI.

- The gap between the best and worst off is huge: the median HWI of the top 10% of countries is almost eight times that of the bottom 10%.

- Even the top performers need to do better. Only Norway, Denmark, and Finland have a good HWI. The rest are merely fair, pulled down by flaws (such as debt, unemployment, and crime) and inequities—10 countries have a standard of living as high as the top three's but not as evenly shared.

## *Measuring Human Wellbeing*

Human wellbeing is a condition in which all members of society are able to determine and meet their needs and have a large range of choices and opportunities to fulfill their potential.

This definition builds on the idea of human development promoted by the United Nations Development Programme (UNDP) in its *Human Development Report:* that development is a process of enlarging choices. A long and healthy life, education, and an adequate income are essential features of this process, and UNDP includes them in its Human Development Index (HDI). Other features are self-respect, opportunities for being creative and productive, security against crime and violence, guaranteed human rights, and political, economic, and social freedom. UNDP excludes these from the HDI largely because they are hard to measure.[1] They also spark disagreement over the balance between personal and community interests and between material and nonmaterial values.

Yet people are both spiritual and physical, social and individual. Assessments of human wellbeing must include all these aspects, despite the technical and political challenges they pose. To ensure that as many as possible of the main features are covered, Wellbeing Assessment divides human wellbeing into 5 dimensions, which I have further split into 10 elements (Figure 2.1). They are described in the remaining sections of this chapter, and distilled into a short statement here:

| | |
|---|---|
| Health | People enjoy long lives in good health |
| Population | while keeping their numbers within the bounds of human and natural resources. |
| Household wealth | Individuals and households have the material goods and income to secure basic needs and decent livelihoods, |
| National wealth | and the community has the resources to support enterprise and maintain prosperity. |
| Knowledge | People have the knowledge to innovate and cope with change, live well and sustainably, and fulfill their potential, |
| Culture | with avenues for spiritual growth, creativity, and self-expression. |

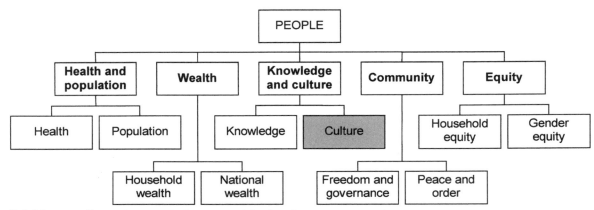

**Figure 2.1. Human dimensions and elements.** The five dimensions are in **bold**, the 10 elements in normal type. Culture (shaded box) is not covered due to lack of a suitable indicator.

| | |
|---|---|
| **Freedom and governance** | Human rights are fully respected, and individuals are free to choose how decisions are made and who should make them. Decision-making bodies are open, clean, and effective. |
| **Peace and order** | Communities coexist peacefully and protect their members from crime and violence. |
| **Household equity** | Benefits and burdens are shared fairly among households and groups |
| **Gender equity** | and between males and females. |

The resulting Human Wellbeing Index (HWI) measures progress toward a proposed goal of a high level of human wellbeing, based on all of these elements except culture (for which I could not identify a suitable indicator).

## Few Nations Well, Many Unwell

*The HWI of all countries is shown in Map 2.1. Table 2.1 gives a regional summary. Figure 2.2 displays patterns of performance. Full scores are in Table 1, and rankings in Table 25, in the Data section.*

To achieve a good HWI, a country must perform well in all dimensions. Only Norway, Denmark and Finland manage to do this. Norway enjoys a life expectancy of 79 years including 72 in full health, a fertility rate just below replacement, gross domestic product (GDP) per person over $26,000 (all dollars are international purchasing parity dollars),[2] inflation below 3%, unemployment below 4%, public debt down to a third of GDP, 100% enrollment through secondary school, a large university population, well-developed communications, strong political rights and civil liberties, and negligible corruption. Even in its weakest

**Table 2.1. Human Wellbeing Index (HWI), showing the number of countries at each level by continental group and region.** Most of the Americas has a medium HWI. The widest gaps are in the West Indies (Barbados with a fair HWI, Haiti with a bad HWI). Africa and Europe are the reverse of each other: Africa with poor or bad HWIs except for five countries with a medium HWI (Tunisia, Cape Verde, Seychelles, Mauritius, South Africa); Europe with good, fair, or medium HWIs except for Albania and Bosnia and Herzegovina (poor). Asia–Pacific has mainly poor or medium HWIs, but differences in performance are extreme within Asian regions.

| Region and Continental Group | Fair or Good | Medium | Poor | Bad | Total |
|---|---|---|---|---|---|
| North and Central America | 2 | 4 | 4 | 0 | 10 |
| West Indies | 1 | 10 | 1 | 1 | 13 |
| South America | 1 | 9 | 2 | 0 | 12 |
| *Americas* | *4* | *23* | *7* | *1* | *35* |
| Northern Africa | 0 | 1 | 4 | 5 | 10 |
| West Africa | 0 | 1 | 4 | 12 | 17 |
| Central and East Africa | 0 | 1 | 1 | 11 | 13 |
| Southern Africa | 0 | 2 | 7 | 4 | 13 |
| *Africa* | *0* | *5* | *16* | *32* | *53* |
| Northern Europe | 13 | 0 | 0 | 0 | 13 |
| Southern Europe | 7 | 3 | 2 | 0 | 12 |
| Eastern Europe | 7 | 5 | 0 | 0 | 12 |
| *Europe* | *27* | *8* | *2* | *0* | *37* |
| West Asia | 1 | 8 | 7 | 2 | 18 |
| Russia, Central and East Asia | 2 | 2 | 7 | 1 | 12 |
| Southern Asia | 1 | 4 | 8 | 4 | 17 |
| Pacific | 2 | 2 | 4 | 0 | 8 |
| *Asia-Pacific* | *6* | *16* | *26* | *7* | *55* |
| WORLD | 37 | 52 | 51 | 40 | 180 |

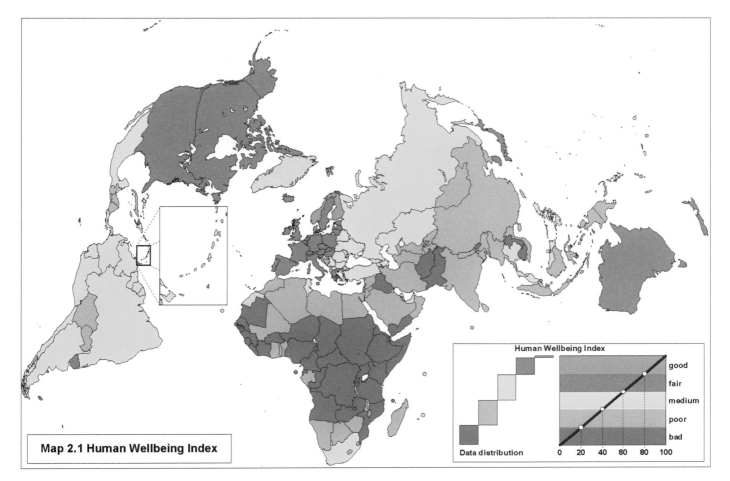

Map 2.1 Human Wellbeing Index

areas—crime, peace, and gender equity—Norway does better than most: over 180 assaults per 100,000 people (but low murder and rape rates), little more than 2% of the budget spent on the military, no less than one-third of parliamentary seats held by women, and school enrollment of males only 9% lower than that of females.

Thirty-four countries with 16% of the world population enjoy a fair HWI. Most deny themselves a good HWI by subpar showings in equity and one other dimension. The stellar economy of the United States is offset by the high incidence of violent crime and a wide gap between rich and poor. In other countries, the weakest areas (besides equity) are unemployment and debt, followed by inflation, crime, and peace.

Fifty-two countries—the largest group, with the second biggest share of the global population (17%)—have a medium HWI. Their performance is a bewildering mixture of highs, lows, and in between, unlike the predominantly fair scores of countries in the groups above them or mainly poor scores of those below. Russia's strongest area is education, but it is overwhelmed by corruption, war in Chechnya, high inflation and unemployment, and

a life expectancy of only 61 years, seven of which are lost to ill health.

Several medium countries are prevented from rising to a fair HWI or falling to a poor one by an especially high or low score in one dimension. Bulgaria does moderately well in knowledge and health and population, and could attain

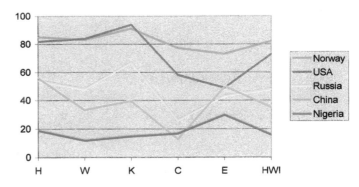

Figure 2.2 Comparison of five countries at each level of the Human Wellbeing Index (HWI) (green = good, blue = fair, yellow = medium, pink = poor, red = bad) and for each dimension (H = health and population, W = wealth, K = knowledge, C = community, E = equity).

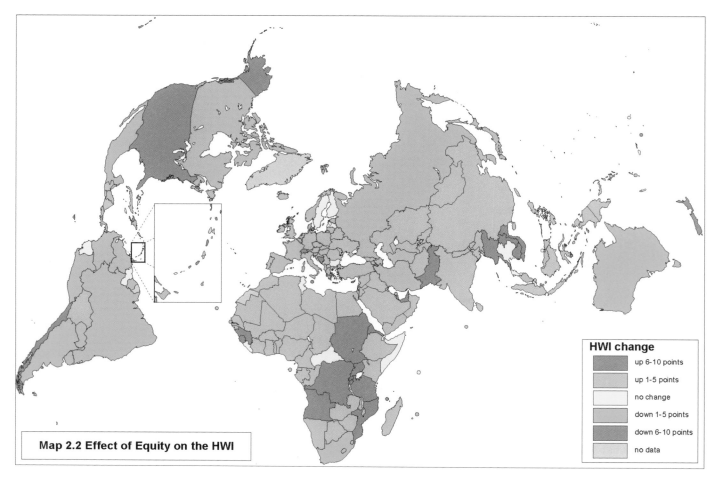

**Map 2.2 Effect of Equity on the HWI**

HWI change

- up 6-10 points
- up 1-5 points
- no change
- down 1-5 points
- down 6-10 points
- no data

a fair HWI but for its low income of $4,810 per person, double-digit inflation and unemployment, and burdensome external debt. By contrast, South Africa's 95% enrollment through secondary school offsets the declining health (life expectancy 49 years and dropping) and persistent violence that otherwise would reduce it to a poor HWI.

Fifty-one countries, with 54% of the world's people, have a poor HWI. They tend to have bright spots overshadowed by bigger areas of deficient performance. China's plusses are health (life expectancy of 70 years, much reduced child and maternal mortality rates), a subreplacement fertility rate, low unemployment (around 3%), moderate debt, and a low violent crime rate (at least officially). But its minuses are widespread poverty (34% of children are stunted by lack of food, only 24% of people have basic sanitation, and GDP per person is only $3,105), inadequate tertiary education, primitive communications (under nine main telephone lines and mobile phones per 100 people), denial of political rights and civil liberties, high levels of corruption, armed conflict in Xinjiang, and more than 5% of the budget spent on the military.

The 40 countries with a bad HWI represent 12$\frac{1}{2}$%

of the world population. All have poor or bad scores for health and population, wealth, knowledge, and (except for Burkina Faso) community. They are trapped in the vicious synergy of underdevelopment as illness and illiteracy cripple livelihoods, debt stifles the economy, and governments fail to lead. Nigeria has emerged from 16 years of military dictatorship with life expectancy a mere 50 years, a fertility rate of five children per woman, 43% of children stunted, half the households without safe water, GDP per person under $800, and institutions in ruins.

### The Equity Effect

*The effect of equity on the HWI is illustrated in Map 2.2 and Figure 2.3 and summarized in Table 2.2. Full details are in Table 1 in the Data section.*

Equity is *included* in the HWIs of 65 countries (36%) where it lowers the HWI. The high standard of living revealed by the other dimensions is unevenly distributed. Equity is therefore included to give a more realistic picture of national conditions. With the inclusion of equity,

Qatar's HWI drops from medium to poor, Chile's from fair to medium, and Switzerland's from good to fair. Nine other countries (Australia, Austria, Belgium, Canada, Iceland, Ireland, Luxembourg, Japan, and Netherlands) also fall from a good to a fair HWI. Nations with the biggest reductions in HWI are concentrated in the West Indies, West Asia and Northern Europe.

Conversely, equity is *excluded* from the HWI of 96 countries (53%) where its inclusion would have raised the HWI. Many of them are in Africa. In all but one of these countries (Slovakia), human development is inadequate throughout society, so what is being shared is misery. Accordingly, equity is excluded to avoid making conditions look rosier than they are. Haiti's HWI is thereby prevented from rising from bad to poor, and Libya's from poor to medium.

Equity has no effect on the HWIs of 19 countries (11%), such as Thailand and Samoa.[3]

## It's the Economy, and It's Not

Four of the five human dimensions—health and population, wealth, knowledge, and community—are highly correlated with the HWI, and the fifth (equity) is moderately correlated. Health and population, wealth, and knowledge are also strongly linked with each other and to a lesser extent community, especially freedom and gover-

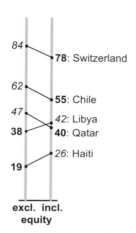

84
78: Switzerland
62
55: Chile
47
42: Libya
38
40: Qatar
26: Haiti
19

excl.  incl.
equity

**Figure 2.3. The equity effect: HWIs excluding and including equity.** The final HWI is the lower score (in **bold**).

nance. The close matches among dimensions and between dimensions and the HWI are probably due to two factors. First, health, wealth, knowledge, and freedom and governance reinforce each other, good performance in one fostering good performance in the others. Second, income plays a crucial role in them all, paying for health services and material necessities; for research, education and communication; and for such ingredients of freedom as free and fair elections, an honest and efficient judiciary and police force, and a clean and competent bureaucracy.

Not surprisingly, therefore, income is highly correlated both with the HWI and with health and knowledge. All of the 25 richest economies have a good or fair HWI, except for Israel, Kuwait, and United Arab Emirates (with medium HWIs), and Qatar (poor HWI). At the other end of the scale, all of the 25 poorest economies have a poor or bad HWI. Among countries with a good or fair HWI, Latvia's GDP per person of $5,730 is the lowest, but in 84% of the group it is above $10,000. While the income of countries with a poor or bad HWI ranges from $460 (Sierra Leone) to $20,985 (Qatar), in 91% it is below $5,000.

Income is not the only building block of a high standard of living. Health, population stability, education, and freedom and good governance are just as important. All but four countries with a good or fair HWI have high scores for all these elements (the exceptions are Estonia, Latvia, and Lithuania, with subpar health; and Singapore, with a medium rating for freedom and governance).[4]

## How Far from Having Nothing—Or How Close to Having It All?

*The Human Development Index (HDI), the only other international index of human wellbeing currently produced, is shown in Map 2.3 and compared with the HWI in Table 2.3. Full details are in Table 1 in the Data section.*

The HDI is consistently higher than the HWI.[5] Taking the 173 countries they have in common,

- 44 countries have a good HDI; only three a good HWI.

- Twice as many countries have a fair HDI as have a fair HWI.

**Table 2.2. Number of countries whose HWI is changed by the inclusion of equity, according to size of change and level of the HWI before the inclusion of equity.**

| HWI Change | Good | Fair | Medium | Poor | Bad | Total |
|---|---|---|---|---|---|---|
| Up 6–10 points | 0 | 0 | 0 | 3 | 16 | 19 |
| Up 1–5 points | 0 | 1 | 12 | 41 | 20 | 74 |
| UP SUBTOTAL | 0 | 1 | 12 | 44 | 36 | 93 |
| NO CHANGE | 1 | 2 | 11 | 1 | 4 | 19 |
| Down 1–5 points | 10 | 18 | 22 | 3 | 0 | 53 |
| Down 6–10 points | 2 | 6 | 6 | 1 | 0 | 15 |
| DOWN SUBTOTAL | 12 | 24 | 28 | 4 | 0 | 68 |
| TOTAL | 13 | 27 | 51 | 49 | 40 | 180 |

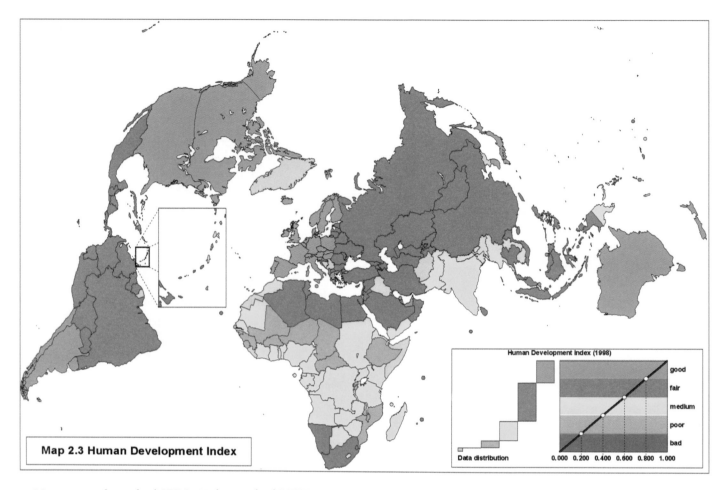

**Map 2.3 Human Development Index**

Human Development Index (1998)

good
fair
medium
poor
bad

Data distribution    0.000  0.200  0.400  0.600  0.800  1.000

- No country has a bad HDI; 37 have a bad HWI.

- Individual country scores are from 10 points (Denmark) to 51 points (Maldives) higher in the HDI than in the HWI.

These differences are due to contrasting aims and approaches. The two poles of human aspiration are escape from deprivation and fulfillment of potential. The primary aim of the HDI is to measure distance from deprivation: how far societies are from having nothing. The HWI tries to measure distance from fulfillment: how close societies are to the good life. This is not to pander to greed but to recognize that people have a wide range of needs whose satisfaction is a legitimate and compelling goal.

Because the HWI measures progress toward a high level of human wellbeing, it cannot omit such major concerns as freedom, violence, or equity. It therefore covers 9 elements represented by 36 indicators. The HDI, with the less onerous task of showing progress away from poverty, need address only a few issues, and thus is based on three elements represented by four indicators: health (life expectancy), wealth (income), and knowledge (literacy and school enrollment). It is easier for countries to do well on three elements than on nine.

However, with so few indicators, the HDI is more susceptible to distortion by missing data, forcing its compilers to provide their own estimates. For example,

**Table 2.3. Performance of 173 countries rated by the Human Wellbeing Index (HWI) and the Human Development Index (HDI).**

| Band | HWI | HDI |
|------|-----|-----|
| Good | 3 | 44 |
| Fair | 34 | 76 |
| Medium | 51 | 38 |
| Poor | 48 | 15 |
| Bad | 37 | 0 |
| Total | 173 | 173 |

in 22 developed countries where adult literacy is not measured, they assume the rate to be 99%, further elevating those countries' scores. With its larger number of indicators, the HWI is robust enough for missing data to be left blank.

Consistent with its less demanding goal, the performance criteria chosen for each indicator are less stringent for the HDI than for the HWI. Consequently, an income of $12,000 receives a score of 80 in the HDI, 64 in the HWI; a life expectancy of 55 years scores 50 in the HDI, 33 in the HWI.

The HDI also conveys a sense of international equity that the HWI contradicts:

- In the HDI, the score of top-ranked Canada (93) is almost 4 times that of bottom-ranked Sierra Leone (25). In the HWI, the score of first-place Norway (82) is more than 27 times that of last-place Somalia (3).

- In the HDI, the median score of the top 10% of countries (92) is about two and a half times that of the bottom 10% (37). In the HWI, the median score of the top 10% of countries (78) is almost eight times that of the bottom 10% (10).

Again, these discrepancies are due to scope and performance criteria. As one of four indicators, life expectancy has a much stronger influence on the HDI than on the HWI (where it is one of 36). In addition, its inherently restricted range—the longest life expectancy is little more than double the shortest—also limits any separation between rich and poor. The HDI further narrows the gap between haves and have-nots by compressing the span of scores for income: in the HDI, $5,000 scores 65 and $20,000 scores 88, a difference of only 23 points; in the HWI, they score 40 and 80 respectively, a 40-point difference.

The HDI and HWI present two contrasting views of the world. According to the HDI, most countries are pretty well off, and disparities among them are modest. From the HWI's perspective, a fortunate few are close to the good life (albeit with economic and social flaws), and the gap between them and the rest of the world is enormous.

# Health and Population

## Health and Population Index (Map 2.4)

**What it is:** Lower of health index and population index.

**Country results:** 26 good (14%), 22 fair (12%), 49 medium (27%), 34 poor (19%), 49 bad (27%).

A sustainable society would provide its members with the conditions for a long and healthy life. At the same time, its members would freely choose to limit family size so that their longevity and health did not result in population growth.

A long life is widely valued because it increases a person's opportunity to pursue goals, develop abilities, and fulfill potential. This is all the more so if the life can be lived in excellent health, with diseases and accidents few and far between and with an effective health service to overcome them when they occur.

As people's health improves and life spans lengthen, populations grow. Most people want children, and

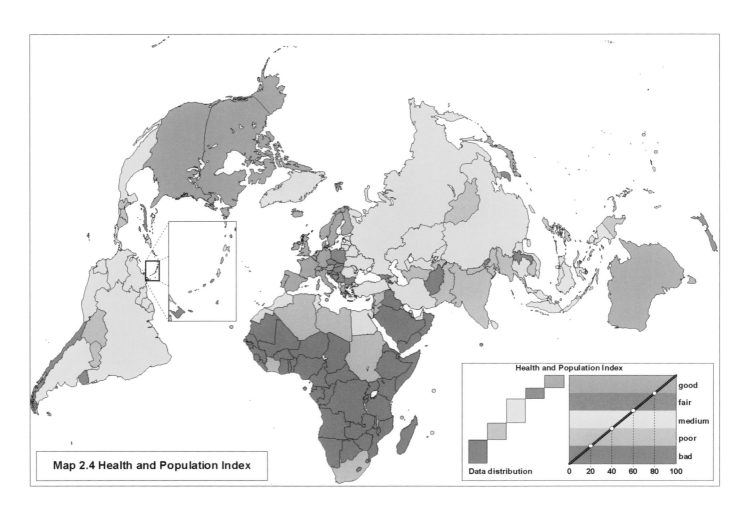

Map 2.4 Health and Population Index

more people mean more workers and consumers, so some regard population growth as an unambiguous good. But large populations, especially if they consume a lot, place enormous demands on the ecosystem. Rapidly growing populations also impose pressures on economies, infrastructure, and institutions, straining a society's capacity to provide adequate education, health services, and jobs.

Since good health does not compensate for high population growth or low fertility for poor health, the health and population index was obtained from whichever element (health or population) had the lower score.

Countries with a good index have populations that are long-lived, healthy, and stable or declining. The best performer is Japan, with an index of 91. Most countries with a fair index have good scores for population but merely fair scores for health (the rest have fair scores for both). By contrast, the majority of countries with a poor or bad health and population index have poor or bad scores for both elements. Most African and some Asian nations are typical of this group, including the worst performer, Sierra Leone (with an index of 2).

The largest gaps between high population and lower health scores are in Eastern Europe, Russia, North Korea, Myanmar, China, Thailand, and Seychelles. In the last three countries, they may mean only that health programs lag behind successful population policies. Elsewhere, they are signs of trouble. The health scores of Russia and Eastern Europe stem from a fall in living standards, a rise in alcoholism in men, and the decay of health services, which cut life expectancies in the late 1980s and early 1990s; their population scores reflect very low fertility rates, perhaps because of pessimism about the future. Despair may also be the cause of low fertility in North Korea and Myanmar. North Korea's low health score is due to famine, which doubled death rates between 1995 and 1997; Myanmar's, to spreading AIDS, malaria, and malnutrition.[6]

West Asia has the biggest gaps between high health and lower population scores. For example, Saudi Arabia has a health score of 62 but a population score of 16 due to a high total fertility rate of 5.6 children per woman. Improved health has failed to influence fertility patterns because one or both of two other essential factors are missing: economic security and access by women to education and wealth.

*For all data and scores for health and population, together with details of the indicators, performance criteria, and combining procedures, see Table 2 in the Data section.*

## Health

---

### Health Index (Map 2.5)

**What it is:** One indicator, healthy life expectancy at birth (Figure 2.4).

**Objective:** Long lives in good health.

**Country results:** 27 good (15%), 32 fair (18%), 59 medium (33%), 31 poor (17%), 31 bad (17%).

---

The health index measures healthy life expectancy at birth: the average number of years that a child born in a given year—in this case, 1999—could expect to live in good health. Total life expectancy at birth takes account of all causes of death, and the death rates from those causes, that a typical person would be exposed to in his or her lifetime. *Healthy* life expectancy is total life expectancy at birth adjusted for the number of years likely to be lost to disease and injury. The number is based on estimates of the prevalence, duration, and severity of communicable and noncommunicable illnesses, neuropsychiatric disorders, and intentional and unintentional injuries. As such it serves as an indicator of overall health, the healthfulness of living conditions (diet, clean water, sanitation, and clean air), and the availability and effectiveness of health services.

World average total life expectancy at birth (both sexes combined) in 1999 was 64.5 years, a rise of almost six years over the last two decades. Progress has not been uniform, however, and the gap between the longest and shortest life spans has widened. People in the top five countries (Japan, Sweden, Australia, Switzerland, France) live more than twice as long as

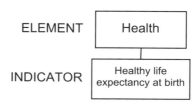

**Figure 2.4. Indicator chart for health.**

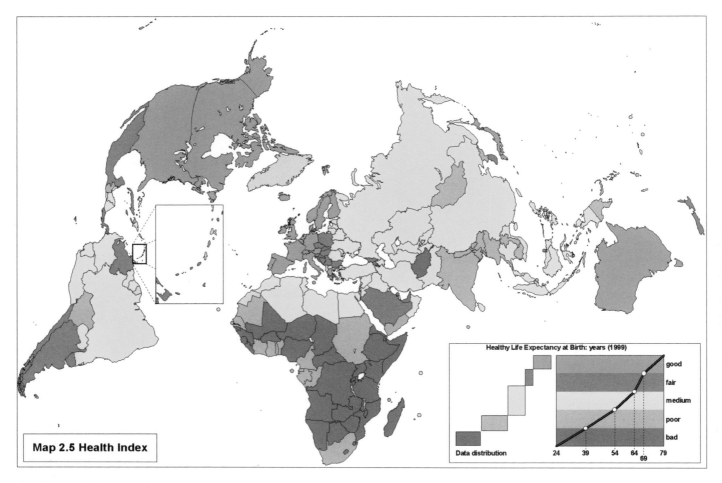

**Map 2.5 Health Index**

Healthy Life Expectancy at Birth: years (1999)

good
fair
medium
poor
bad

Data distribution    24    39    54    64    79
69

people in the bottom five (Botswana, Niger, Zambia, Malawi, Sierra Leone). Disparities in child survival (child death rates below 1% in industrialized countries, above 10% in Africa) are compounded by even greater disparities in adult survival, chiefly due to HIV/AIDS, which has cut life expectancies by 1–10 years in 39 countries (32 in Africa, four in the Americas, three in Asia) and by 11–20 years in Botswana, Lesotho, Kenya, Namibia, Swaziland, Zambia, and Zimbabwe. AIDS killed 300,000 Africans in 1989, 2.2 million in 1999. Where it is most prevalent, 55–60% of survivors to age 15 will die before age 60.

World average healthy life expectancy at birth in 1999 was 56.8 years, 7.7 years lower than total life expectancy. Although people who live longer have a greater opportunity to acquire nonfatal disabilities as they grow older, they spend less of their lives in ill health than people with short life spans. Years of disability account for 9% of life expectancy in countries with average life spans longer than 75 years; 18% in those with average life spans of 60 years or less. The

spread among healthy life expectancies is even wider than among total life expectancies: 46.6 years separate the total life expectancies of 80.9 years in Japan and 34.3 years in Sierra Leone; 48.6 years separate their healthy life expectancies of 74.5 and 25.9 years.

Patterns of disease also differ greatly. Among countries with a good health index, the top four causes of loss of healthy life expectancy are ischemic heart disease, depression (especially among women), cerebrovascular disease, and alcohol dependence. Among those with a bad health index, the top four causes are HIV/AIDS, malaria, acute lower respiratory infections, and diarrhoeal diseases.[7]

United Nations' targets are that all countries should have total life expectancies of at least 60 years by 2000, more than 70 years by 2005, and more than 75 years by 2015. I lowered these by six years to provide corresponding targets for healthy life expectancy—respectively, 54, 64, and 69 years—which define the top points of the poor, medium, and fair bands (as shown in the performance graph in Map 2.5).[8]

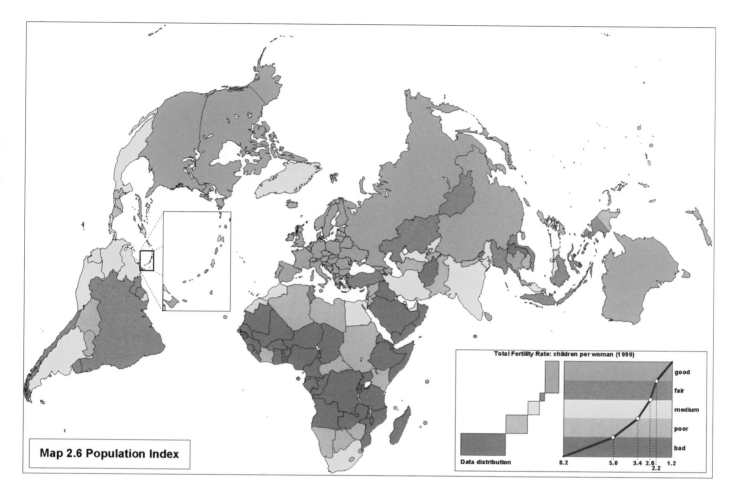

Map 2.6 Population Index

## Population

### Population Index (Map 2.6)

**What it is:** One indicator, total fertility rate (Figure 2.5).

**Objective:** A stable population.

**Country results:** 60 good (33%), 16 fair (9%), 27 medium (15%), 35 poor (19%), 42 bad (23%).

The total fertility rate (TFR) is the average number of children born alive by a woman in her lifetime. It is an indicator of family size, birth rates, birth control practices and services, and other factors that act together to determine family size (such as family income and security, women's status in society, and religious and cultural influences).

Because it directly reflects choices about family size, TFR is a good indicator of population stability. (Population growth rate may be a more direct measure, but because it includes migration it is not as clear a sign of what is going on within the society.)

TFRs range from 7.4 children per woman (Yemen) to 1.1 children (Spain). A sustainable rate would be the replacement rate, which (with average sex ratios) is 2.1.[9] The good band was therefore defined as 2.1 or below, and the fair band as less than half a child above replacement (see the performance graph in Map 2.6).

Rates below replacement are not sustainable, but the excessively high scores they get have little effect on the health and population index because they are usually offset by lower health scores. For example, although countries with a TFR of 1.1 or 1.2 receive a score of 100 for

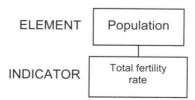

**Figure 2.5. Indicator chart for population.**

population, their health and population index ranges from 87 (Italy and Spain) to as low as 57 (Romania) due to their lower health scores.

Countries with a good population index (fertility rates at or below replacement) include 44% of the world's people. They cover all Europe (except Albania) and major parts of Asia and the Americas. The populations of half these countries—including Germany, Russia, and Japan—will fall between 1998 and 2050, their declines ranging from 1% of the 1998 population in Yugoslavia to 35% in Estonia. The populations of the other half—including the United States, China, and Thailand—will continue to rise due to immigration and higher proportions of young people. Regionally, the sharpest declines will be in Eastern and Southern Europe, which by 2050 will be reduced to, respectively, 18% and 20% of their 1998 sizes.

Countries with a fair or medium population index (slightly to moderately above replacement) represent respectively 10% and 28% of the global population, mostly in the Americas and Southern Asia.

Nations with a poor or bad population index have TFRs well above replacement and account for 20% of the world's people. The majority are in Africa (47

countries), followed by Asia–Pacific (22). These fast-growing populations place an increasingly heavy strain on environmental resources and on their abilities to lift themselves out of poverty.

Even so, falling populations are becoming almost as much of a concern as growing ones. In many developed countries fertility has stayed below replacement levels for at least 20 years. A generation ago a TFR of 1.3 children or below was considered highly unlikely. Now it is found in 11 countries. The chief worry is that declining fertility coupled with longer life expectancy is aging the world's population. In Europe the proportions of children (below 15 years) and elders (60 years or over) were roughly equal in 1998. By 2050, elders are expected to outnumber children by two and a half times, and one in every three people will be 60 years or older. Higher proportions of the elderly could mean that a smaller labor force has a larger body of retired people to support and a bigger health care bill to pay. But as elders look forward to more years of active life, retirement patterns are beginning to change. In Japan, for instance, older people are returning to work to seek new sources of personal growth as well as income to supplement inadequate pensions.[10]

# Wealth

**Wealth Index (Map 2.7)**

**What it is:** Average of household wealth index and national wealth index.

**Country results:** 8 good (4%), 29 fair (16%), 45 medium (25%), 48 poor (27%), 50 bad (28%).

Wealth is the material component of human wellbeing: the goods and income that enable people to survive and develop opportunities. The wealth index measures whether individuals and households can meet basic needs and gain secure livelihoods and whether the nation has the resources to support enterprise and maintain prosperity.

The richest economies—those with a good wealth index (United States, Denmark, Iceland, Luxembourg, Netherlands, Norway, Switzerland, and Singapore)—meet the basic needs of almost all their people and have incomes above $20,000 per person, low rates of inflation and unemployment, and limited debt.

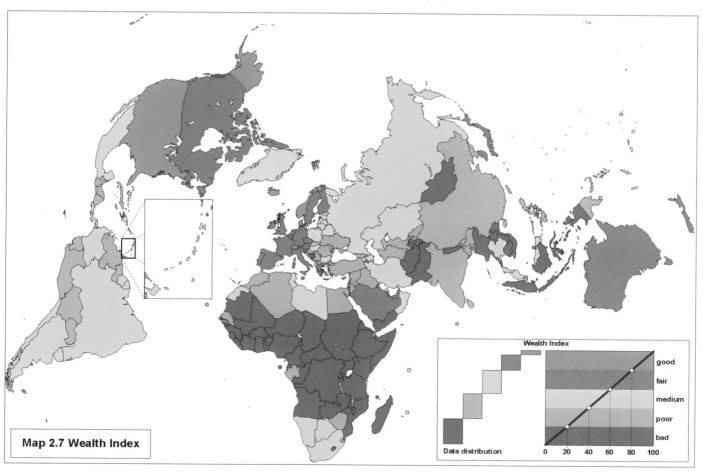

**Map 2.7 Wealth Index**

Wealth Index

good
fair
medium
poor
bad

Data distribution

0 20 40 60 80 100

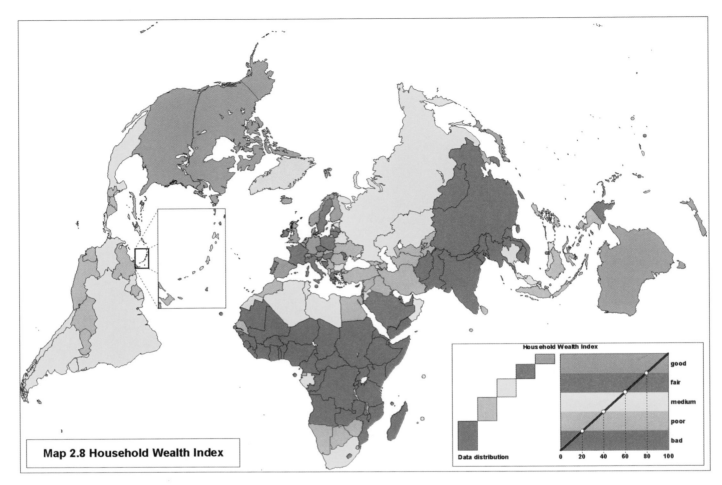

**Map 2.8 Household Wealth Index**

In general, countries with a fair wealth index (mainly in Northern and Southern Europe and West Asia) have lower incomes. A few have incomes as high as the top economies but are not as strong in other aspects (such as public debt in Belgium and unemployment in France).

Countries with a medium index are concentrated in South America, the West Indies, and Eastern Europe. They tend to have moderately healthy household economies but weaker national economies.

Most economies with a poor index are in Asia–Pacific, with clusters in Northern Africa, Eastern Europe, and Central America. Indonesia is typical: 42% of children are stunted by poor diet, little more than half the population has basic sanitation, income per person is $2,650, and the economy is struggling to recover from its collapse in 1997.

In countries with a bad index, almost entirely in Africa and Southern Asia, households are desperately poor and national economies crippled by debt.

*For all data and scores, together with details of the indicators, performance criteria, and combining procedures, see Table 3 (wealth index, household wealth) and Table 4 (national wealth) in the Data section.*

## Household Wealth

### Household Wealth Index (Map 2.8)

**What it is:** Average of needs and income scores (Figure 2.6).

**Objective:** Enough material goods and income to secure basic needs and decent livelihoods.

**Country results:** 19 good (11%), 27 fair (15%), 34 medium (19%), 44 poor (24%), 56 bad (31%).

The household wealth index is partly a poverty index, showing the extent to which people lack the essentials for survival. Needs include food, safe water, and basic sanita-

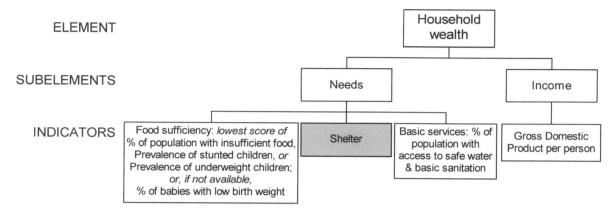

**Figure 2.6. Indicator chart for household wealth.** Shelter (shaded box) is not covered because of lack of a suitable indicator.

tion (shelter could not be covered due to data deficiencies). Income provides the resources required to meet these needs, provide a degree of security, acquire conveniences, and enjoy leisure.

At least half the population is acutely poor in countries with a bad index and at least a third in those with a poor index. In countries with a medium index, poverty afflicts more than a fifth of the population. A tenth to a fifth of the population is poor in countries with a fair or good index, possibly less in some of the latter. (However, poverty measurements change radically depending on the indicator, and the ones used here give only a rough approximation.)

## Needs

> ### Needs (Map 2.9)
> **What it is:** The lower score of a food sufficiency indicator (Map 2.10) and a basic services indicator (Map 2.11). The latter is based on water or sanitation, whichever is less available.
> **Country results:** 16 good (9%), 47 fair (26%), 31 medium (17%), 23 poor (13%), 58 bad (32%), 5 no data (3%).

Food and basic services (water and sanitation) are essential for health and survival, and people's needs are not met if they lack either. Hence the needs score is based on whichever is in shorter supply. For the same reason, the basic services score is based on water or sanitation, depending on which is less available. For example, North

Korea's needs score reflects food sufficiency, Zambia's water, and Moldova's sanitation (Figure 2.7). A good score for needs indicates that more than 90% of the population has adequate food, water and sanitation (e.g., Tonga); a fair score means that all are available to more than 80%. Conversely, a bad score means that 50% or more of the population lacks at least one of these necessities, be it food or either of the basic services.

In most countries, fewer people have access to basic services than to enough food: 65 countries have a good score for food but only 23 for water and sanitation; 19 countries have a bad score for food, 52 for basic services (Figure 2.8). These numbers explain why so few countries have a good score for needs and so many a bad score. Of

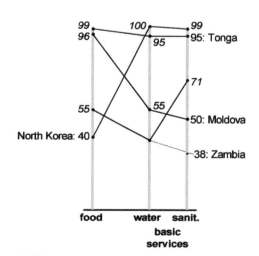

**Figure 2.7. Percentages of the population with sufficient food and basic services (water and sanitation).** The needs score is based on the lowest percentage.

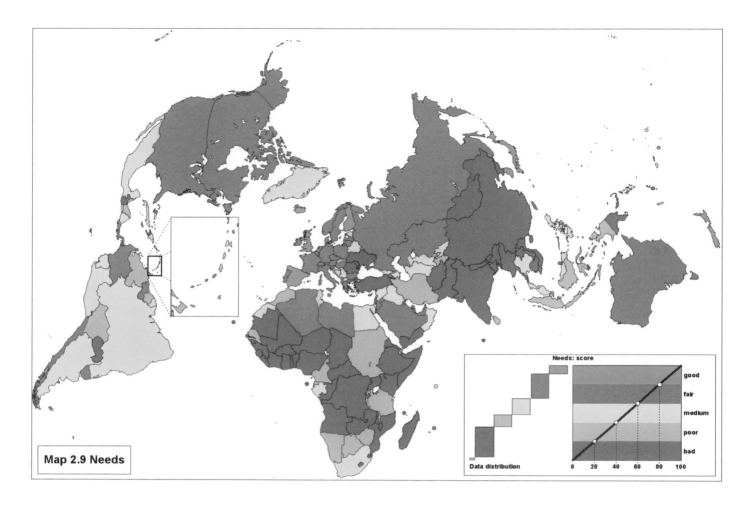

**Map 2.9 Needs**

Needs: score

good
fair
medium
poor
bad

Data distribution

0   20   40   60   80   100

those with a high score for food, only 16 rate as well for basic services. Most are like Moldova, where 96% of the people have enough food but many fewer (only 50%) have access to basic services. Lack of water or sanitation is also the sole or main contributing factor in all but six of the countries with a bad score for needs.

Within basic services, sanitation is more neglected than water supply. In two out of three countries, fewer people have access to adequate sanitation than to safe water, casting doubt on how safe the water really is. Of the 52 countries with a bad score for basic services, access to both services is the deficient factor in 20, water in 9, and sanitation in 23. Zambia is unusual in providing more people with sanitation than with clean water or sufficient food (Figure 2.7).

The information required to assess needs is often missing or suspect. Food sufficiency is represented by one of four indicators because none covers all countries. The most direct is the percentage of the population that is undernourished, but the survey

covers only the bigger developing countries. Of the alternatives—percentage of children who are stunted (short for their age), percentage of underweight children, and percentage of babies with low birth weight—the first two are preferable because they are less influ-

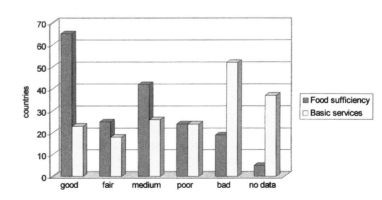

**Figure 2.8. Country performance for food sufficiency and basic services.**

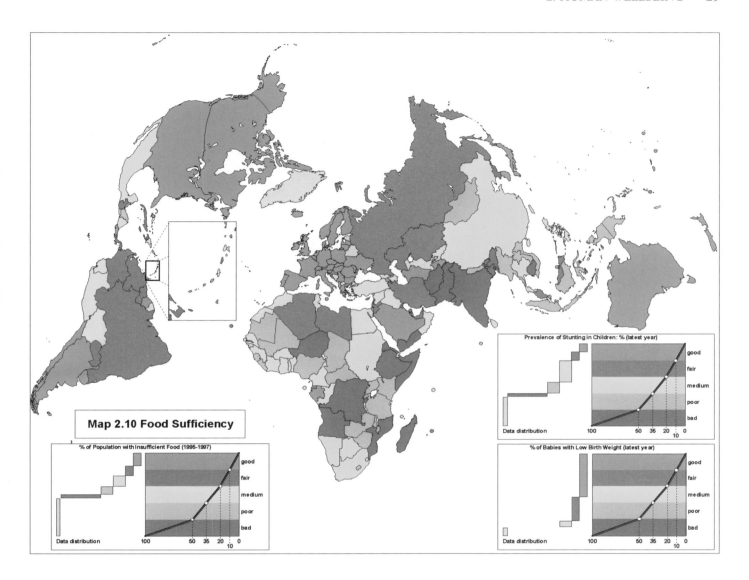

Map 2.10 Food Sufficiency

enced by factors other than prolonged lack of food (such as malaria).

Statistics on water and sanitation are available for fewer countries (Figure 2.4), and they are not as trustworthy. Government reports are sometimes more sanitized than the water, and surveys vary widely in thoroughness of coverage and standards of water safety, adequacy of sanitation, and accessibility. Accessible water may come from a standpipe at the far end of the street, and the sanitation may be as basic as a poorly maintained outhouse.

Relying on the most conservative of several indicators can offset these deficiencies to some extent. Independent estimates of food sufficiency in North Korea (40%) probably give a more realistic sense of the overall satisfaction of needs than official reports on basic services (99%).

The World Health Organization has set targets of less than 20% for prevalence of stunting in children and no more than 10% for prevalence of low birth weight babies and underweight children (no target exists for the percentage of the population that is undernourished). The United Nations' target for access to safe water and basic sanitation is 100%. These targets were used to define the good and fair bands of all the indicators. Performance on food sufficiency ranges from 73% of the population with not enough food (Afghanistan) to 1% (South Korea) and from 64% of children stunted (Ethiopia) to 1% (Croatia and Tonga). Performance on basic services ranges from 3% of the population with safe water and basic sanitation (Malawi) to 100% (several countries, including Barbados, Finland, Cyprus, and Singapore).[11]

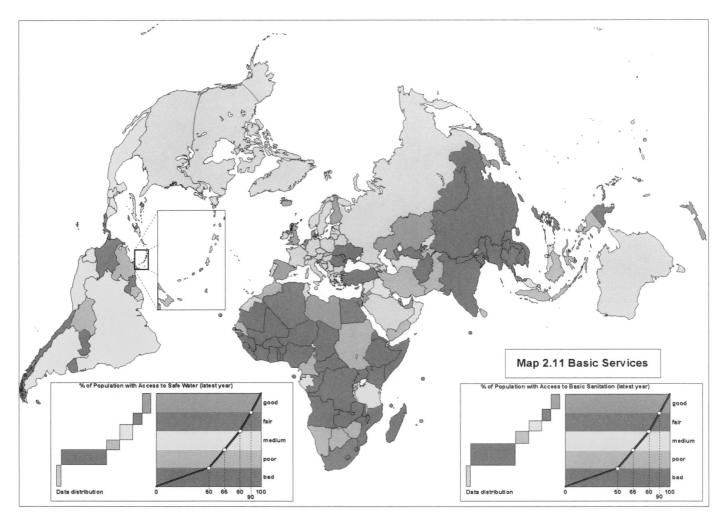

## Income/Size of Economy

> ### Income/Size of Economy (Map 2.12)
>
> **What it is:** One indicator, gross domestic product (GDP) per person (in international purchasing power parity dollars)—"income," for short.[12] The indicator is counted twice: under household wealth (income) and under national wealth (size of economy).
>
> **Country results:** 21 good (12%), 19 fair (11%), 35 medium (19%), 47 poor (26%), 58 bad (32%).

Most countries with incomes that are good (above $20,000) or fair (above $10,000) are in Europe (21), followed by Asia–Pacific (12, largely in West Asia), the Americas (6), and Africa (Seychelles).

The definitions of good and fair incomes beg the question, How much money is enough? The answer is that small increases in income are sufficient to escape from poverty, but it takes much more money to acquire the resources associated with high levels of human wellbeing. It is possible for countries to provide more than 90% of the people with adequate food and basic services at incomes as low as $4,280 (Tonga). But only at incomes above $10,000 (for food) and $14,000 (for basic services) do countries that meet 90% of their people's needs outnumber those that do not.

**Figure 2.9. Number of countries with good, fair, medium, poor, or bad scores for a combination of health and population, knowledge, and community at different income levels ($000s).**

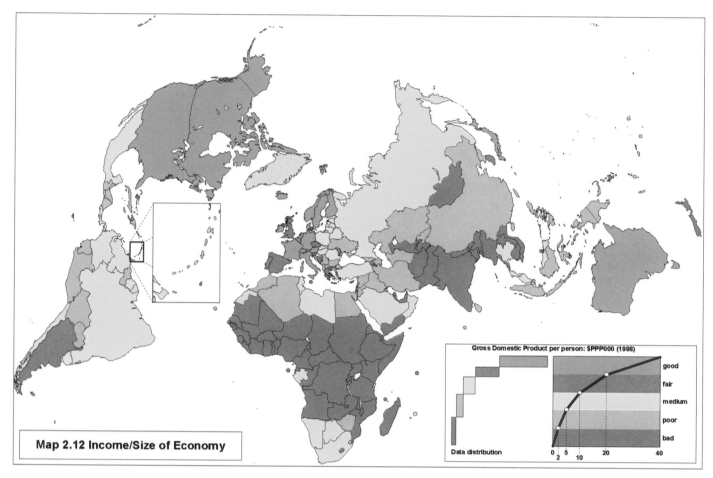

**Map 2.12 Income/Size of Economy**

Gross Domestic Product per person: $PPP000 (1998)

good
fair
medium
poor
bad

Data distribution

Securing the added benefits of human wellbeing takes higher incomes, as shown by comparing income with a combined score for health and population, knowledge, and community (Figure 2.9). Good scores predominate among countries with incomes above $20,000, fair scores above $10,000, and medium scores above $5,000. Only nine countries (five of which are in West Asia) have incomes above $10,000 but scores below fair. Almost all nations with incomes of $2,000 or less have poor or bad scores.[13]

## National Wealth

---

### National Wealth Index (Map 2.13)

**What it is:** Weighted average scores for three subelements [weights in brackets]: size of economy [2], inflation and unemployment [1], and debt [1] (Figure 2.10).

**Objective:** Sufficient resources to promote enterprise and maintain prosperity.

**Country results:** 6 good (3%), 23 fair (13%), 47 medium (26%), 54 poor (30%), 50 bad (28%).

---

Size of economy (GDP per person) is the main indicator of national wealth. Inflation was included to show whether real incomes are being eroded by rising prices, unemployment to measure the social impact of policies to control inflation, and debt to indicate if countries are living within their means. These additional indicators produce some dramatic shifts, demoting some countries from good to fair (high public debt and unemployment in Italy), fair to medium (the same in Greece and Argentina), and medium to poor (high inflation and public and external debt in Turkey); and promoting others from bad to poor (low inflation and unemployment in Bangladesh; moderate external and public debt in Bhutan) and poor to medium (low inflation and unemployment and moderate external debt in China). (Growth is not a separate indicator but can be measured by annual changes in the size of economy indicator or in the national wealth index.)

The financial crisis that blitzed Pacific Asia in 1997 and spread to Russia, South Africa, and Latin America in 1998 demonstrated that institutional and social factors are just as vital for a strong economy as strictly economic

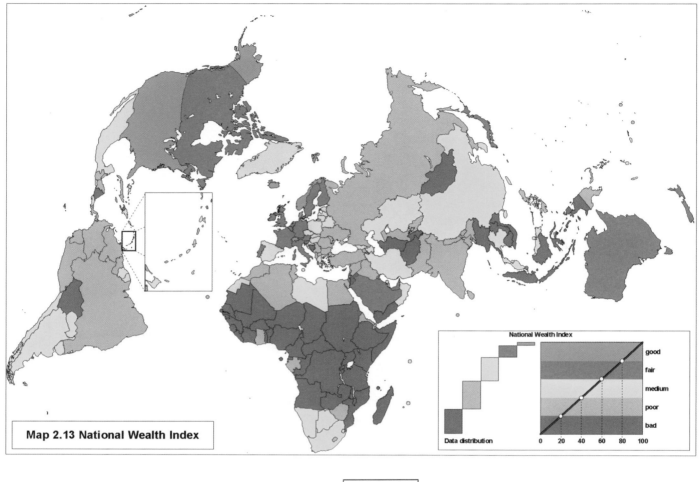

Map 2.13 National Wealth Index

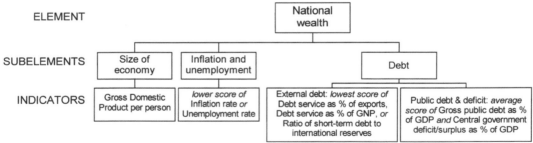

**Figure 2.10. Indicator chart for national wealth.**

ones: adequate regulation of the financial sector, separation of big business and government, open decision making and a free and vigilant press to give people confidence in markets and regulatory bodies, an education and research system that equips people to innovate, and a political system that can maintain social harmony while coping with economic shocks. To the extent possible, these are covered later in this chapter, under the dimensions of knowledge and community.

## Inflation and Unemployment

### Inflation and Unemployment (Map 2.14)

**What it is:** Lower score of inflation rate and unemployment rate.

**Country results:** 13 good (7%), 19 fair (11%), 29 medium (16%), 28 poor (16%), 13 bad (7%), 78 no data (43%).

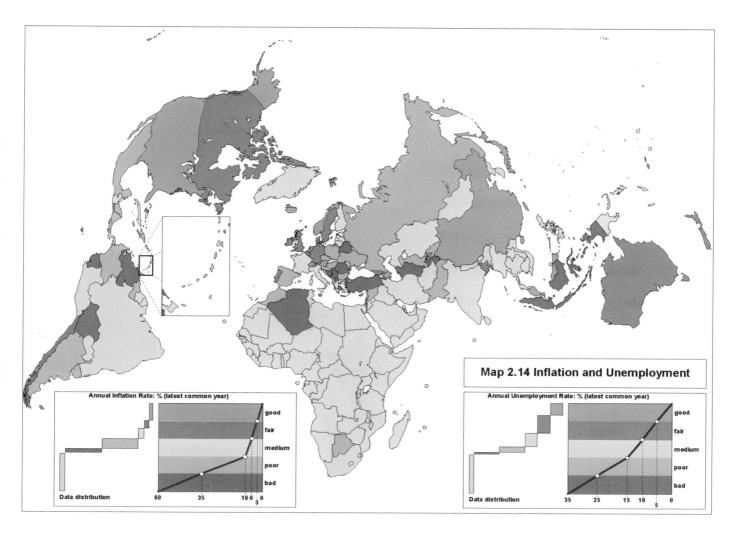

**Map 2.14 Inflation and Unemployment**

Annual Inflation Rate: % (latest common year)

good
fair
medium
poor
bad

Data distribution    60    35    10 6   0
                                      3

Annual Unemployment Rate: % (latest common year)

good
fair
medium
poor
bad

Data distribution    35    25    15   10    0
                                            5

In countries that record both, the annual inflation rate in the late 1990s ranged from 1,005% (Turkmenistan) to –0.8% (Azerbaijan and China) and the annual unemployment rate from 72.5% (Bosnia and Herzegovina) to 0.4% (Uzbekistan).

High inflation causes uncertainty about the future, which reduces investment and the real return on saving, shrinking future growth. Double-digit inflation is unquestionably harmful. Low inflation provides a predictable economic environment for households and businesses. However, negative inflation (deflation) signals a contracting economy, and even extremely low inflation (below 1%) may increase unemployment. Although economists debate how low inflation should be, central bank targets are from 3% to 0%.

Unemployment causes hardship, undermines self-esteem, wastes potential, and is socially divisive. Rates above 10% are generally regarded as undesirable, but rates much below 3% are probably impossible to sustain without driving up prices.

Inflation and unemployment used to be thought of as ends of a seesaw: if one goes down, the other goes up. But the worst of both worlds is possible (high inflation producing high unemployment, as in Ecuador and Russia), and so is the best: low inflation can stabilize output and jobs. Low inflation plus low unemployment are most likely when output is both potentially and actually high (as in the United States during the 1990s). Excluding deflationary economies (such as Azerbaijan), Luxembourg has the best combination of low inflation (1.0%) and low unemployment (2.5%), followed by Switzerland, Norway, Cyprus, and the United States.[14]

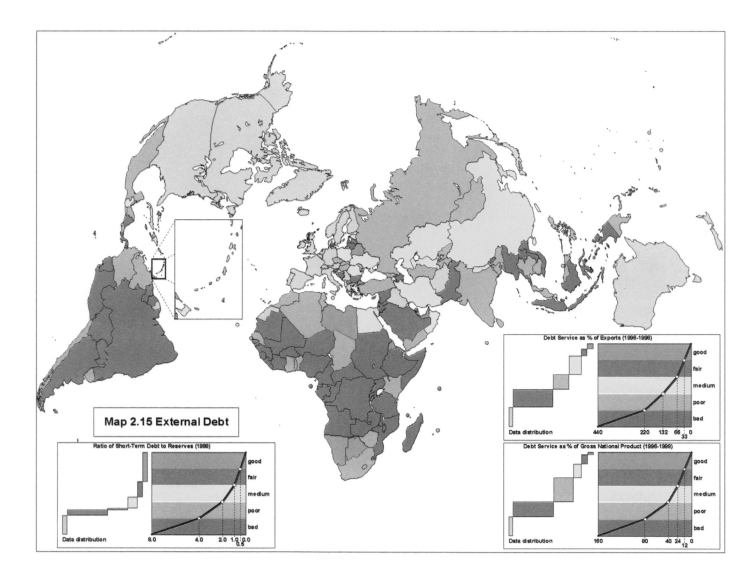

Map 2.15 External Debt

## Debt

### Debt (Maps 2.15 and 2.16)

**What it is:** Lower score of external debt indicator and public debt and deficit indicator; the external debt indicator (Map 2.15) is the lowest score of debt service as a percentage of exports, debt service as a percentage of GNP, and short-term debt as a percentage of international reserves; the public debt and deficit indicator (Map 2.16) is the weighted average score [weights in brackets] of gross public debt (general government gross financial liabilities) as a percentage of GDP [2] and annual central government deficit or surplus as a percentage of GDP [1].

**Country results:** 2 good (1%), 31 fair (17%), 34 medium (19%), 48 poor (27%), 58 bad (32%), 7 no data (4%).

Of the 58 countries with a bad score, 54 are for external debt, 3 for public debt and deficit (Malta, Lebanon, and Mongolia), and 1 for both (Brazil).

External debt is public and private debt to other countries or to international bodies. It is not recorded for industrialized countries. Debt service as percentages of exports and gross national product (GNP) compare a country's outstanding obligations with its power to pay for them. They are the two main indicators used by the World Bank to classify indebtedness, and the poor and bad performance bands match the World Bank's definitions of moderately and severely indebted, respectively.

The ratio of short-term debt to international reserves emerged during the Asian financial crisis as a key sign of a country's vulnerability to creditor panic. When the ratio exceeds 1.0, international creditors are inclined to

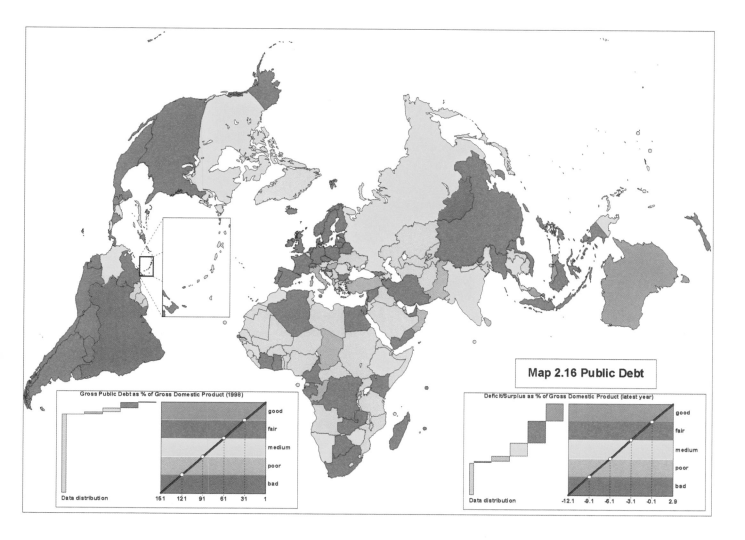

Map 2.16 Public Debt

Gross Public Debt as % of Gross Domestic Product (1998)

Deficit/Surplus as % of Gross Domestic Product (latest year)

bolt, which in Pacific Asia led to the runaway depletion of foreign exchange reserves. Short-term debt is more likely to be a practical problem for countries (such as South Korea) that borrow heavily from private sources than for those (such as Cameroon) where most of the debt is owed to much less skittish governments and international bodies. Since economies with open and well regulated access to global capital markets can manage ratios of short-term debt to reserves that are higher than 1.0, some of the more open economies (such as the Bahamas and Singapore) may be unduly penalized by this indicator.

Of the 55 countries with a bad score for external debt, 43 (mostly in Africa) received it for debt service, 6 for short-term debt, and 6 for both.[15]

Public debt consists of the gross financial liabilities of governments and is compiled only for industrialized countries. The public deficit indicator records the central government budget balance and is collected for a variety of countries. The bottom of the fair band corresponds to the standards for an acceptable public debt (60% of GDP) and deficit (3% of GDP) set by the European Union's Treaty of Maastricht.[16]

Of the 33 countries with a good or fair score for debt, 17 were rated for public debt and deficit (the United States, Australia, New Zealand, and 14 European nations), 7 for external debt and public deficit, and 9 for external debt alone.[17]

# Knowledge and Culture

## Knowledge Index (Map 2.17)

**What it is:** Weighted average [weights in brackets] of education score [2] and communication score [1] (Figure 2.11).

**Objective:** Better knowledge to equip people to innovate and cope with change, live well and sustainably, and fulfill their potential.

**Country results:** 24 good (13%), 26 fair (14%), 56 medium (31%), 24 poor (13%), 50 bad (28%).

*Culture (a society's systems of belief and expression) could not be covered here for lack of a suitable indicator.*

Knowledge helps people to lead more fulfilling and satisfying lives, deepening their understanding and enjoyment of the world and equipping them with the information and skills required to live well and sustainably. Knowledge is now the most important means of production in post-industrial economies, in the form of knowledge assets (discoveries, patents, and licenses) and market information (what to produce and how, what to sell and when), and as

Map 2.17 Knowledge Index

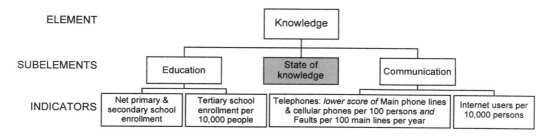

**Figure 2.11. Indicator chart for knowledge.** State of knowledge (shaded box) is not covered because of lack of a suitable indicator.

the resource of such growth industries as electronics, finance, medicine, communication, and entertainment.[18]

In the absence of a satisfactory way to measure the state of knowledge, the knowledge index gauges education and communication—the formal and informal means of transmitting and sharing knowledge. Countries with a good index have high levels of education and well-developed, widely shared communication systems. Those with a poor or bad index have medium or low scores for education and even lower ones for communication. The performance of countries with a fair or medium index is more mixed. Most (such as Kazakhstan) have a moderately to highly educated population but an underachieving communication sector. A few (such as United Arab Emirates) have an advanced communication system but not the education to make it fully productive.

*For all data and scores, together with details of the indicators, performance criteria, and combining procedures, see Table 5 (knowledge) in the Data section.*

## Education

---

### Education (Map 2.18)

**What it is:** Average score of two indicators: primary and secondary school enrollment (average score of the net primary and net secondary school enrollment rates) and tertiary school enrollment (students per 10,000 people; Figure 2.11). (The net enrollment rate is the percentage of children of primary or secondary school age who are enrolled in school at the level appropriate for their age.)

**Country results:** 27 good (15%), 52 fair (29%), 36 medium (20%), 21 poor (12%), 30 bad (17%), 14 no data (8%).

---

All countries with a good education score have primary enrollment rates above 95%, all but five (Belarus, Esto-nia, Iceland, Portugal, and Russia) have secondary enrollment rates above 90%, and all but three (Czech Republic, Germany, and Libya) have tertiary enrollment rates above 280 students per 10,000 people. High enrollment rates from primary school to university are signs not just of participation in education but also of educational attainment. Although it is possible for semiliterate individuals to reach and graduate from university, the percentages of children who enter secondary school and then a college or university are a reasonably reliable measure of successful completion of the levels below.

A more direct guide to a nation's level of education would be functional literacy: the ability to understand and use the information required to function effectively in a knowledge-dependent society. This includes the capacity to understand and use information from printed texts, to locate and use information in different formats (such as maps, tables, and charts), and to use and calculate numbers. However, functional literacy has been measured in few countries: one of the most thorough assessments, the International Adult Literacy Survey (IALS), covers only 12. The widely available adult literacy rate is an unsuitable gauge of educational attainment because its reliability is questionable and it does not measure functional literacy. Often the censuses and other household surveys that obtain the data merely ask people whether they are literate (or household heads how many in the household are literate). Literacy is usually defined in its narrowest sense, as the ability to read and write a simple statement about everyday life. Consequently, the adult literacy rate can show how many people are on the literacy ladder but not how far up they have gone. Thus Poland's adult literacy rate is reported to be 99.7%, although the IALS found that a mere 57.4% of the adult population has a level of prose literacy adequate for reading the dosage on a medicine bottle (i.e., above level 1 in Figure 2.12).[19]

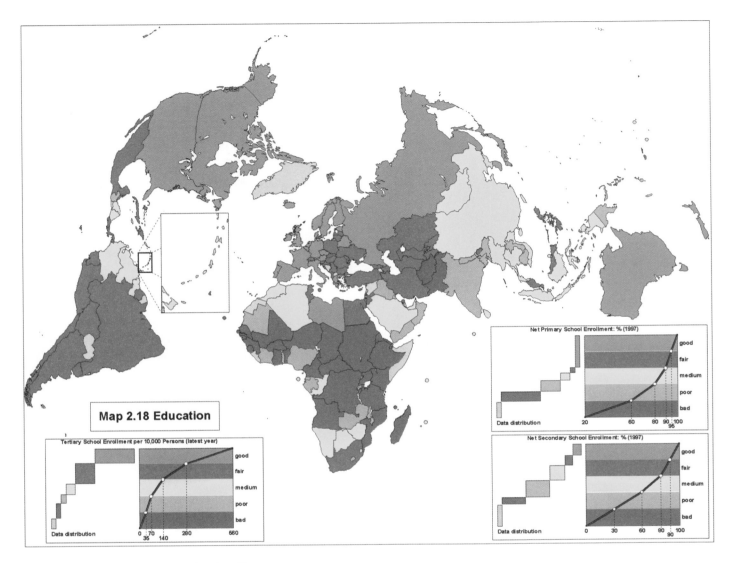

**Map 2.18 Education**

Without assessing different levels of literacy, it is impossible to tell what proportions of the so-called literate population are scarcely literate, highly literate, or in between. The IALS found that the percentages at each literacy level vary greatly: Poland has a high percentage of scarcely literate (42.6%) and a low percentage of highly literate (3.1%); Sweden the reverse (7.5% and 32.4%, respectively); Germany has low percentages of both (14.4% and 13.4%); the United States high percentages of both (20.7% and 21.1%).

Net primary school enrollment ranges from 13% (Bhutan) to almost 100% (50 countries), net secondary enrollment from 8% (Rwanda) to virtually 100% (eight countries), and tertiary enrollment from 3 students per 10,000 people (Djibouti) to 611 students (South Korea). Enrollment drops—often sharply—from primary to secondary school in all countries except the Republic of Congo, where it rises from 78% to 84%, and the eight countries

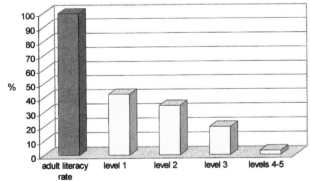

**Figure 2.12. Poland's adult literacy rate (blue) compared with levels of functional literacy (yellow).** Level 1 = scarcely literate (may be unable to read the dosage on a medicine bottle); level 2 = borderline literate (can deal only with simple messages); level 3 = adequately literate (minimum desirable threshold in many countries); levels 4 and 5 = highly literate (able to integrate several sources of information or solve more complex problems).

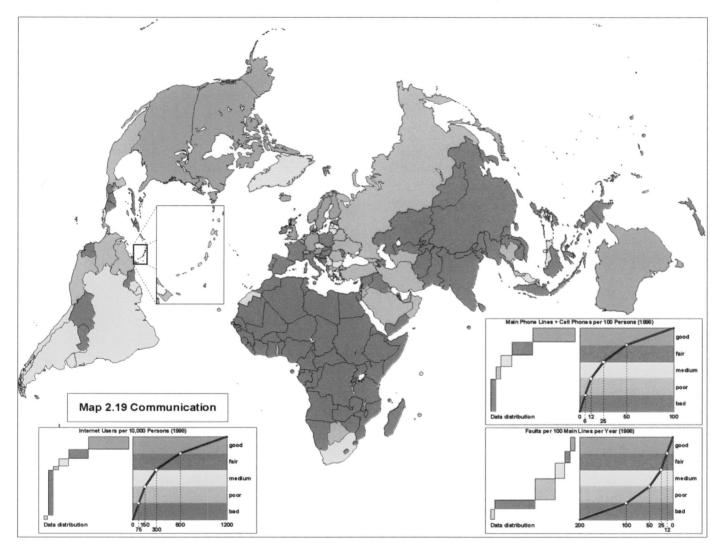

**Map 2.19 Communication**

Internet Users per 10,000 Persons (1998)

Data distribution

good
fair
medium
poor
bad

0  150  300  600  1200
   75

Main Phone Lines + Cell Phones per 100 Persons (1998)

Data distribution

good
fair
medium
poor
bad

0  12  25  50  100
  6

Faults per 100 Main Lines per Year (1998)

Data distribution

good
fair
medium
poor
bad

200  100  50  25  0
              12

with almost 100% in both. Tertiary enrollment seldom matches the primary and secondary rates. This is partly because the former is measured as a proportion of the total population and the latter as percentages of the primary and secondary school-age populations. But large discrepancies reflect real differences in the numbers of children who go on from high school to university. They are much lower than expected in Southern Africa and Southern Asia (Mauritius has a 68% secondary enrollment rate but only 57 tertiary students per 10,000 people; Cambodia, a 39% secondary enrollment rate and a mere eight tertiary students per 10,000 people) and much higher than expected in Central America (Panama has 302 tertiary students per 10,000 people, despite a 71% secondary enrollment rate).

The performance criteria for the indicators reflect United Nations' targets for universal primary education and literacy (interpreting the latter as functional literacy). The countries with the largest proportions of highly literate adults (Sweden, Canada, and the United States) have tertiary enrollment rates of 312, 595, and 534 students per 10,000 people, respectively. The good band for tertiary enrollment was set to include the lowest of these rates.[20]

## Communication

### Communication (Map 2.19)

**What it is:** Average score of telephone indicator and Internet users per 10,000 persons; the telephone indicator is the lower score of main telephone lines and cellular phone subscribers per 100 persons and faults per 100 main lines per year.

**Country results:** 20 good (11%), 20 fair (11%), 23 medium (13%), 26 poor (14%), 91 bad (51%).

Communication includes all media from puppet shows to books. But the focus here is on the telephone and Internet because together they provide people with an independent means of talking to each other, revolutionary access to information, and a cheap and convenient way to tell their stories and sell their wares.

Not surprisingly, telecommunication development and Internet use go together. Countries with a good communication score have advanced and reliable telephone systems and large numbers of Internet users. Those with a bad score have meager and unreliable phone systems and few people on the Internet. The number of countries with a bad score rises from 78 based on the telephone indicators alone to 91 including Internet use (more than for any other indicator), suggesting that the knowledge revolution is widening the gap between the haves and have-nots. Most of Africa and much of Southern Asia have under three main lines and mobile phone subscribers per 100 people, and fewer than 10 Internet users per 10,000.

The 69 countries with neither a good nor bad score have contradictory mixtures of performance. Internet use is lower than expected from the medium to fair state of the phone network in 19 countries (such as Barbados and Hungary) and higher than expected, given the frustrations of faulty lines, in 20 (such as Uruguay and Latvia).[21]

# Community

## Community Index (Map 2.20)

**What it is:** Lower of freedom and governance index and peace and order index.

**Country results:** 2 good (1%), 47 fair (26%), 32 medium (18%), 51 poor (28%), 48 bad (27%).

A desirable community upholds the freedom and rights of its members, has an open and clean government, is peaceful, and is safe from violence and crime. Only

Switzerland and Austria seem able to find the required balance of personal autonomy and social harmony and have a good community index. The rest of the world falls short in one aspect or another—a little in countries with a fair index, a lot in those with a poor or bad index.

Countries with a fair index fall into three groups, represented by Japan, Canada, and Benin (Figure 2.13). Japan (and Hungary, Malta, and Slovakia) are just as peaceful as Switzerland and Austria but not as free or as unblemished by corruption. Canada (along

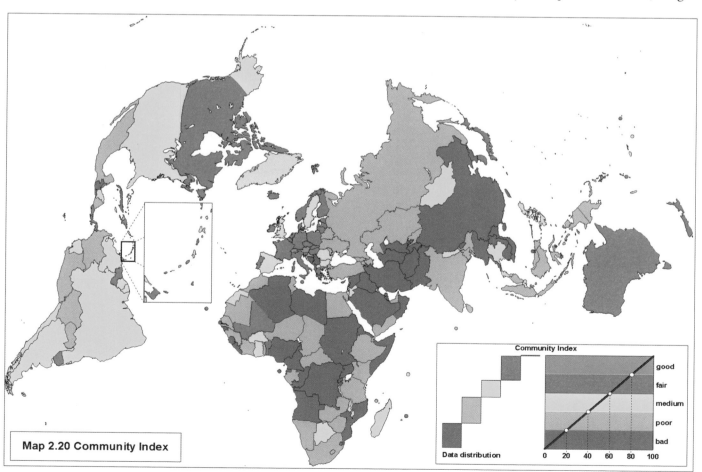

Map 2.20 Community Index

Community Index

good
fair
medium
poor
bad

Data distribution

0   20   40   60   80   100

**Figure 2.13. Community indices from medium to good.**
The index is the lower of the two scores (medium = 41–60, fair = 61–80, good = 81–100).

with Australia, New Zealand, and much of Northern Europe) are as free and well governed but have lower scores for peace and order. Benin (and the remaining fair index countries) have fair scores for both elements.

Countries with a medium index also fall into three groups, represented by Sweden, Madagascar, and Venezuela. Most have a high score for peace and order but a medium grade for freedom and governance due to corruption (the majority), limited civil liberties (e.g., Madagascar), or a restricted press (e.g., Nepal). Some have the reverse, their flaws being high crime rates (Sweden, the United States, Chile, Bahamas, Jamaica, Botswana) or armed conflict (Spain and the United Kingdom). Venezuela (and Ecuador, Suriname, Israel, Philippines, and Tonga) have medium scores for both elements.

Countries with a poor or bad index have almost uniformly low scores for both elements. Only 23 of the 100 have a fair score for peace and order—and half of these have no data on crime, so their high ratings may be false. A mere six (Bolivia, St Vincent and Grenadines, Namibia, São Tomé and Principe, South Africa, and Papua New Guinea) have a fair score for freedom and governance. More than a third (37) endure wretched mixtures of oppression, corruption, and violence, with poor or bad ratings across the board. Most (32) are in Africa and Asia, including all of Northern Africa, almost all of Central and East Africa, and West and Central Asia.

*For all data and scores, together with details of the indicators, performance criteria, and combining procedures, see Table 6 (community index, freedom and governance, peace) and Table 7 (crime) in the Data section.*

## Freedom and Governance

Freedom and governance are strongest in Northern Europe (all countries good or fair), followed by North and Central America and the Pacific (all countries good, fair, or medium). Close behind are the West Indies, South America, Eastern and Southern Europe, and Southern Africa, where only a handful of countries have a poor or bad index—in contrast to the rest of Africa and all Asia, where they are still in the majority.

The four indicators overlap to some extent but together produce more consistent results than if any were omitted. Freedom House's political rights rating (PRR) and civil liberties rating (CLR) provide comprehensive measurements of freedom. The PRR assesses

**Figure 2.14. Indicator chart for freedom and governance.**

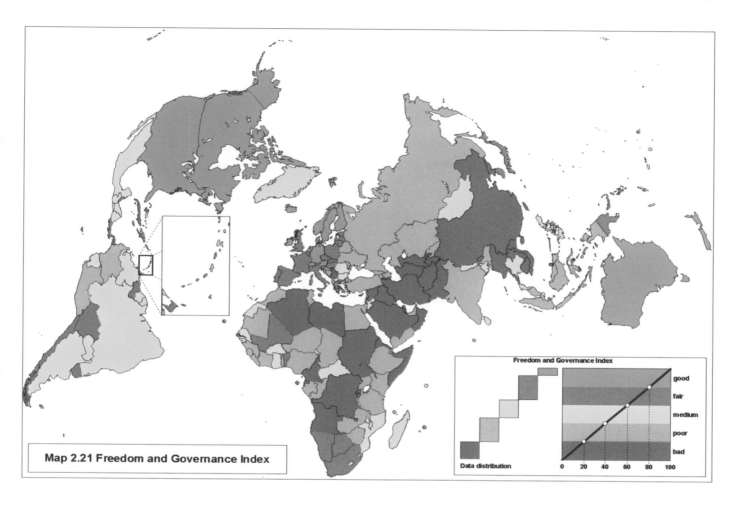

**Map 2.21 Freedom and Governance Index**

Freedom and Governance Index

good
fair
medium
poor
bad

Data distribution

0   20   40   60   80   100

whether all members of society have the right to choose their decision-making system and select who makes decisions. The CLR measures the practice of economic freedoms (e.g., secure property rights and free collective bargaining), freedoms of belief and expression (including religious tolerance and freedom of assembly), personal freedoms (such as freedom of movement and residence), and the rule of law (an independent judiciary, equal treatment under the law, fair and public hearings, direct civilian control of the police, and protection from political terror, unjustified imprisonment, exile, or torture).

All countries with a good or fair index are electoral democracies, as are 80% of those with a medium index but only a quarter of those with a poor index and none with a bad. Of the 70 countries with undemocratic regimes, 35 have a higher CLR than PRR, but civil liberties are higher only because political rights are so low.

Among the 100 electoral democracies, only 6 (Australia, Cyprus, St Vincent and Grenadines, and the struggling democracies of Indonesia, Nigeria, and Paraguay) have a higher CLR than PRR. This reflects both their more consistent commitment to political rights and the difficulty of upholding the complex array of civil liberties to the fullest extent. Even the most democratic societies are tested by antidemocratic forces: hostility is growing toward immigrants in Norway, anti-Semitism persists in Switzerland (an estimated tenth of the population is against Jews), Nazis are welcome in Austria's Freedom Party, and neo-Nazi groups exploit Denmark's tradition of tolerance.

The other two indicators—Freedom House's press freedom rating (PFR) and Transparency International's corruption perceptions index (CPI)—focus on a specific aspect of freedom and governance, respectively. The PFR (Map 2.22) gauges legal, administrative, political, and

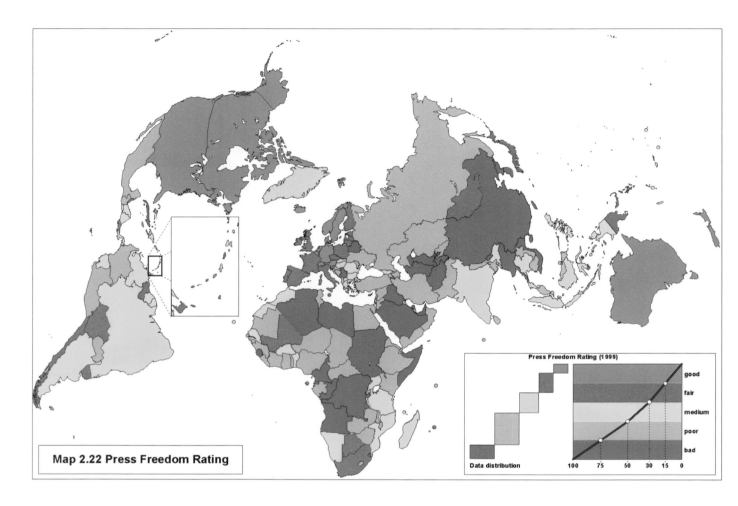

**Map 2.22 Press Freedom Rating**

Press Freedom Rating (1999)

good
fair
medium
poor
bad

Data distribution    100  75  50  30  15  0

economic influences on media content, as well as violations of press freedoms, such as censorship, harassment, assaults, and murder. The CPI (Map 2.23) measures the level of corruption (the abuse of public office for private gain) among public officials and politicians within a country, as perceived by businesspeople, risk analysts, and the general public.

Press freedom ranges from the total restrictions of Myanmar (where two journalists were tortured to death after their newspaper published an article critical of a military officer) and North Korea (where criticism of the regime or its head may be punished by imprisonment in a labor camp or execution) to the almost unfettered openness of Norway (with a variety of independent national and local newspapers and broadcasting stations, no government interference in the editorial content of state radio and television, and many newspapers subsidized by the state to promote political pluralism).

Among the 100 countries rated between 1997 and 2000, Nigeria and Yugoslavia are the most corrupt and Finland and Denmark the least. A free press is one of the forces that keeps a nation honest, and countries with the freest media usually have the cleanest governments. Most countries with a good or fair PFR also have a good or fair CPI, and most with a poor or bad CPI also have a poor or bad PFR. True to form, the media criticize the government freely and with impunity in Denmark, while journalists in Nigeria are regularly harassed, assaulted, and threatened with death. But there are some striking exceptions. Singapore is one of the least corrupt countries in the world (with the best CPI in Asia–Pacific after New Zealand), but the government tightly controls the media, censors Internet use, and does not tolerate reports of such corruption that exists. In South Korea, corruption is pervasive, although press freedom is growing and news broadcasting in particular is increasingly independent and diverse.[22]

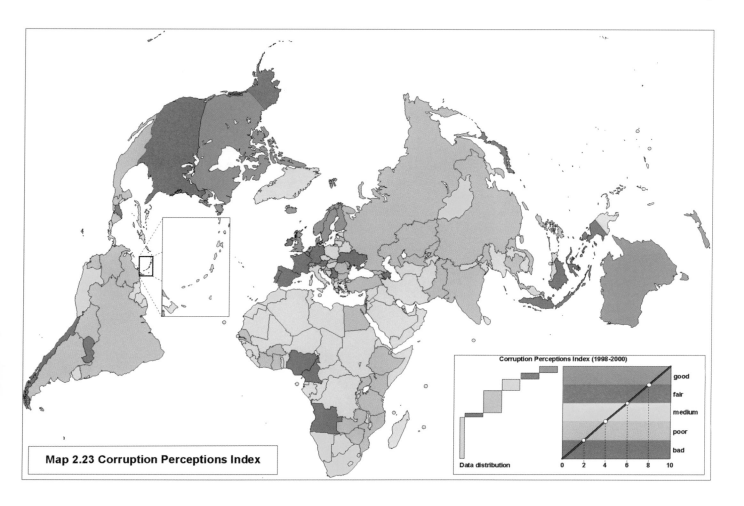

**Map 2.23 Corruption Perceptions Index**

## Peace and Order

### Peace and Order Index (Map 2.24)

**What it is:** Average of peace score and crime score (Figure 2.15).

**Objective:** Peaceful communities, protected from crime and violence.

**Country results:** 7 good (4%), 77 fair (43%), 36 medium (20%), 30 poor (17%), 25 bad (14%), 5 no data (3%).

A good or fair peace and order index should mean that the country is not engaged in any armed conflict (apart from peacekeeping missions), military expenditure is a small percentage of GDP, and the violent crime rate is low. This is probably true of countries with a good index, which were assessed on all these aspects. But 33 of those with a fair index may not merit it. Four (St Kitts and Nevis, Maldives, Samoa, and Vanuatu) had no peace data, and the rest could not be rated on crime: 15 in Africa (all except Egypt, Mauritius, Morocco, and Seychelles), 7 in the Americas (Argentina, Antigua and Barbuda, Belize, Brazil, Dominican Republic, Guyana, and Honduras), 6 in Asia–Pacific (Lao, Mongolia, Turkmenistan, Viet Nam, Fiji, and New Zealand), and Ireland. Europe has the most countries with a good or fair index based on both peace and crime (5 good, 22 fair).

### Peace

### Peace (Map 2.25)

**What it is:** Lower score of deaths from armed conflicts per year and military expenditure as a percentage of gross domestic product.

**Country results:** 39 good (22%), 36 fair (20%), 16 medium (9%), 36 poor (20%), 40 bad (22%), 13 no data (7%).

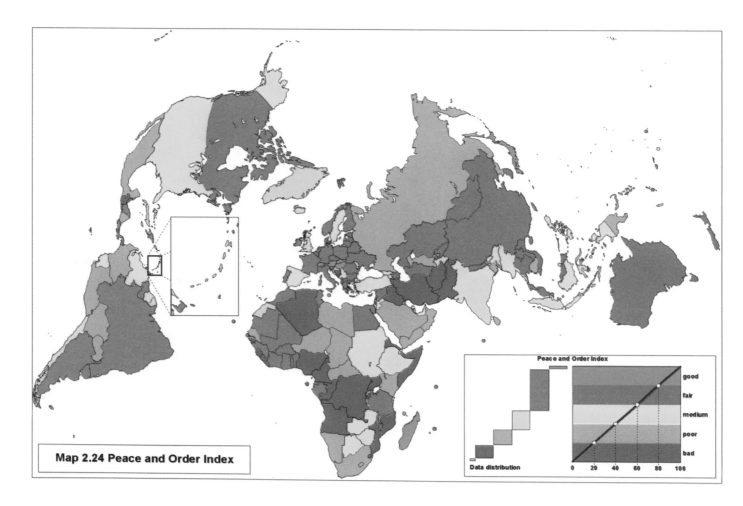

**Map 2.24 Peace and Order Index**

None of the countries with a good, fair, or medium score for peace is involved in armed conflict (other than international peacekeeping). They differ only in the amount of GDP they devote to the military.

All countries with a bad score and all but six with a poor score have incurred deaths from border and territorial conflicts, internal conflicts, or terrorism between 1995 and 1999. The exceptions (Armenia, Kuwait, Oman, Qatar, Saudi Arabia, and North Korea) have a poor score because their military expenditure exceeds 8% of GDP.

Although required for national defense, military expenditure—which ranges from 0.5% of GDP (Barbados) to 36% of GDP (Eritrea)—is a potentially destructive use of resources that competes with health, education, and other essentials for a prosperous peace. A country isn't necessarily bellicose if it buys guns and pays people to shoot them, but the likelihood of warfare rises with the priority given to fighting: the proportion of countries engaged in conflict increases from 29% (of those spending less than 2% of GDP) to 33% (2–3.9% of GDP) to 61% (4% and above).

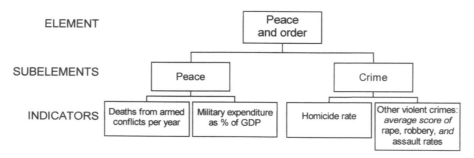

**Figure 2.15. Indicator chart for peace and order.**

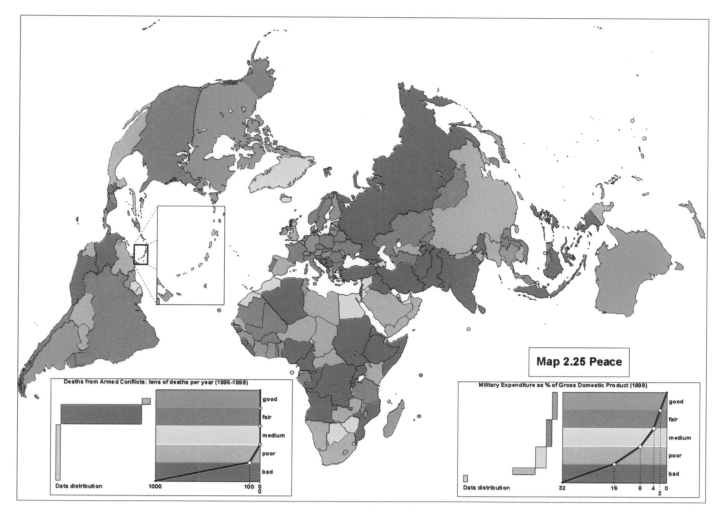

Average annual military and civilian deaths from armed conflicts range from 10 or below in countries subject to sporadic terrorism (such as Paraguay and Uzbekistan) to 84,000 in Rwanda, which has been at war internally since 1990 and in neighboring Democratic Republic of Congo since 1998. Even if a cease fire or peace accord is now in force (such as in Mozambique), all conflicts that occurred in any year between 1995 and 1999 were counted. Average death rates were estimated from the year each conflict started.[23]

## Crime

### Crime (Map 2.26)

**What it is:** Average of scores for homicide rate and for other violent crimes (average score for rape, robbery, and assault rates).

**Country results:** 23 good (13%), 42 fair (23%), 21 medium (12%), 7 poor (4%), 3 bad (2%), 84 no data (47%).

The focus here is on violent crimes because they are more harmful than other offenses and are recorded less erratically. Homicide is further distinguished from the other violent crimes because it is the most serious and is reported more consistently. Crime statistics reflect a combination of actual crime rates and the diligence of the police. If the justice system is weak, records will show unrealistically low rates. This problem is evident in the international data, which for several countries show utopian crime rates.

Homicide rates range from 142 per 100,000 people (São Tomé and Principe) to 0.4 (Madagascar), robbery rates from 688 (Bahrain) to 0.1 (Ethiopia and Syria), and assault rates from 1,487 (Trinidad and Tobago) to 0.2 (Egypt). The rates for rape range from 199 per 100,000 people (Estonia) to essentially 0 (Egypt). However, since women are often blamed if they are raped, victimized by the justice system, and ostracized by their communities, rape is commonly underreported. The data undoubtedly reflect this.

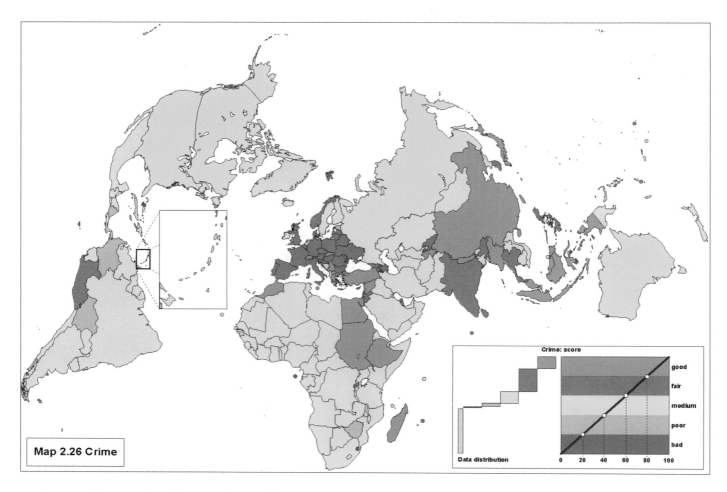

Map 2.26 Crime

In general, countries with a good score for crime report consistently low violent crime rates: homicides below 5 per 100,000 people (except Ethiopia, 7.6, and Yugoslavia, 5.5), rapes below 10, robberies below 40 (except Qatar, 66), and assaults below 80 (except Cyprus, 133). The performance of countries with a fair or medium score is often mixed. Sweden has medium homicide, rape, and robbery rates but a very high assault rate (611). Canada has the widest gap between its scores for homicides (94) and for other violent crimes (18) because it has one of the lowest homicide rates (1.8) but rape and assault rates of 84 and 737, respectively. Bahrain has the highest robbery rate but the fourth lowest homicide rate, and Kuwait has the fifth highest homicide rate but the third lowest rape rate. While almost all countries with a poor or bad score have homicide rates above 20 and robbery rates above 80, their rape and assault rates vary.[24]

# Equity

## Equity Index (Map 2.27)

**What it is:** Average of household equity index and gender equity index.

**Country results:** 0 good (0%), 20 fair (11%), 91 medium (51%), 56 poor (31%), 11 bad (6%), 2 no data (1%).

The equity index measures the distribution of wealth and other benefits within the general population of a country (household equity) and between males and females (gender equity). Since health, wealth, knowledge, freedom, peace, and other goods are widely valued, it is right that they be widely shared. The cost of achieving them should also be fairly shared. A society is not well if only a few groups in it enjoy power, privilege, and high levels of the opportunities and benefits that make up wellbeing, while others are weak, disadvantaged, and poor. Large disparities are both unjust and destabilizing.

Of all the human dimensions, equity is unique in having no country with a good index and the fewest with a bad index. The majority of the 69 countries assessed on gender equity alone have medium or poor

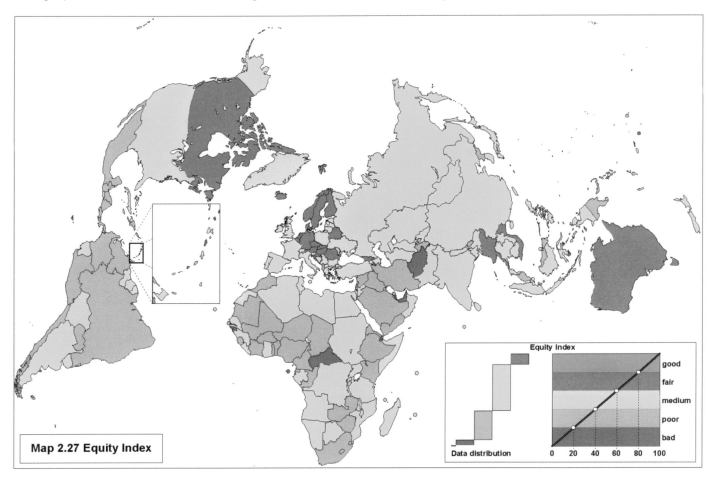

Map 2.27 Equity Index

49

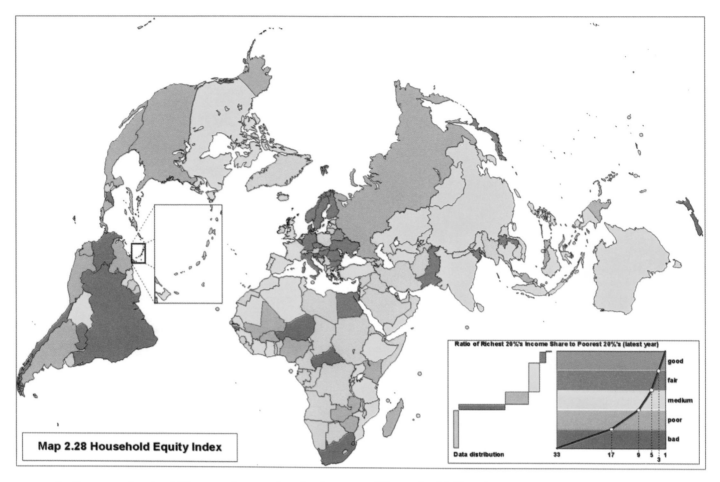

**Map 2.28 Household Equity Index**

Ratio of Richest 20%'s Income Share to Poorest 20%'s (latest year)

good
fair
medium
poor
bad

Data distribution    33    17    9  5  1
                                      3

scores. Performance by the 109 countries rated on both gender and household equity is more erratic. A mere 8 (all in Europe) achieve good or fair scores in both, and 14 (mostly in Africa) get poor or bad scores in both.[25] Most of the rest do markedly worse in one than in the other.

The household divide is wider than the gender gap by more than 5 points in 43 countries, including much of the Americas and Southern Africa: South Africa has a 52-point difference between fair gender and bad household equity, and Colombia a 41-point gap (gender medium, household bad). Gender discrimination exceeds inter-household disparities by more than 5 points in another 43 countries, including much of Northern Africa, Eastern Europe, and Southern Asia: in Egypt, Bangladesh, and Pakistan, household equity is at least 30 points higher than gender equity.

*For all data and scores for equity, together with details of the indicators, performance criteria, and combining procedures, see Table 8 in the Data section.*

## *Household Equity*

### Household Equity Index (Map 2.28)

**What it is:** One indicator, ratio of richest 20%'s income share to poorest 20%'s (Figure 2.16).

**Objective:** Equitable distribution of benefits and burdens among households and societal groups.

**Country results:** 2 good (1%), 20 fair (11%), 52 medium (29%), 24 poor (13%), 11 bad (6%), 71 no data (39%).

The ratio of the income share of the richest fifth of the population to that of the poorest fifth shows how much more money the rich get than the poor. Because the data are gathered by national surveys, which tend to miss the poorest households, the reported ratios are likely to be underestimates. They range from 32.5:1 in the Central African Republic to 2.6:1 in Slovakia. Average national incomes have no effect on the gap between rich and poor. Yemen and Zambia both have incomes per person of $720,

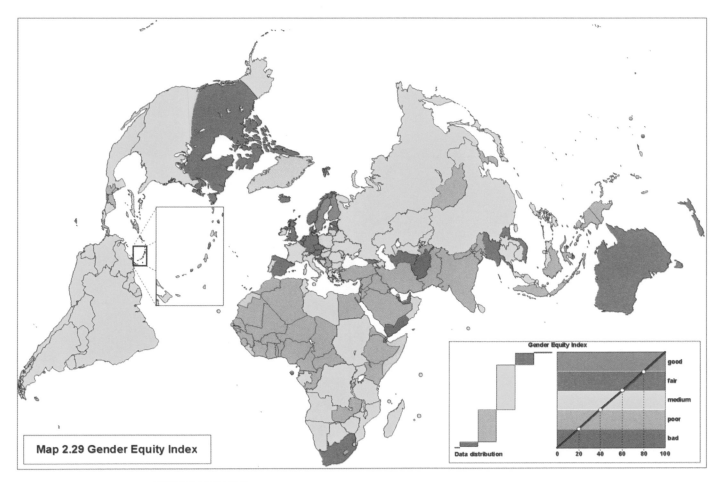

Map 2.29 Gender Equity Index

| ELEMENT | Household equity |
| INDICATOR | Ratio of richest 20%'s income to poorest 20%'s |

**Figure 2.16. Indicator chart for household equity.**

but Yemen's ratio is 8:1, Zambia's 13:1. Viet Nam and France, with the same ratios of 5.6:1, have incomes of $1,690 and $21,175, respectively.

Poor and bad ratios are mainly in the Americas and West and Southern Africa; medium and fair in Europe, Asia, and Northern Africa. Income disparities have risen in most Eastern European countries since their embrace of capitalism, so Belarus and Slovakia, the only countries in the good band, may not be there for long. During the 1990s, the income gap between rich and poor also widened in the Bahamas, China, and Thailand but narrowed in Jamaica and Brazil.[26]

Income share is the best available indicator of

household equity but does not necessarily reflect other areas of potential disparity such as health, knowledge, power, or freedom. Ideally, the index would cover these as well.

## Gender Equity

### Gender Equity Index (Map 2.29)

**What it is:** Average of gender and wealth, gender and knowledge, and gender and community scores (Figure 2.17).

**Objective:** Equal distribution of benefits and burdens between males and females.

**Country results:** 2 good (1%), 22 fair (12%), 84 medium (47%), 60 poor (33%), 10 bad (6%), 2 no data (1%).

Maps 2.30–2.32 show that the number of countries with major inequities increases sharply from wealth (income) to knowledge (education) to community (government). Almost half the countries have a medium gender equity

Map 2.30 Gender and Wealth

Ratio of Male Income to Female Income (latest year)

good
fair
medium
poor
bad

Data distribution          9.0      5.0    3.0  2.0  1.0
                                                   1.5

ELEMENT                Gender
                       equity

SUBELEMENTS   Gender and    Gender and    Gender and    Gender and
              health        wealth        knowledge     community

INDICATORS              Ratio of male income   Difference between   % of women in
                        to female income       male & female school  parliament
                                               enrollment rates

**Figure 2.17. Indicator chart for gender equity.** Gender and health (shaded box) is not covered due to lack of a suitable indicator (difference between male and female life expectancy is not used because it is hard to tell whether greater equality means men are doing better or women worse).

index, often because gains in wealth or knowledge are offset by subpar scores for community. Sweden, Finland, and only three of the countries with a fair index (Denmark, Germany, and Norway) have good or fair scores across the board. Others with a fair index are inconsistent. The door to gender parity opens in one room only to shut in another, and in countries with a poor or bad index most doors are still locked.

## Gender and Wealth

### Gender and Wealth (Map 2.30)

**What it is:** One indicator, ratio of male income to female income.

**Country results:** 16 good (9%), 68 fair (38%), 54 medium (30%), 22 poor (12%), 3 bad (2%), 17 no data (9%).

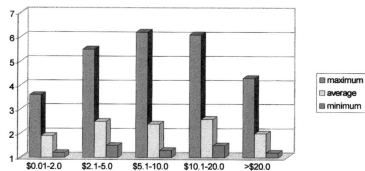

**Figure 2.18. Maximum, average, and minimum ratios of male income to female income in each of five GDP groups ($000s per person).**

## Gender and Knowledge

> ### Gender and Knowledge (Map 2.31)
>
> **What it is:** One indicator, difference between male and female school enrollment rates (average of net primary, net secondary, and tertiary differences).
>
> **Country results:** 27 good (15%), 37 fair (21%), 40 medium (22%), 32 poor (18%), 24 bad (13%), 20 no data (11%).

Males earn more than females everywhere, and income differences are wide, ranging from negligible (1.2:1 in Sweden and Cambodia) to more than six times (6.2:1 in Oman). The size of the difference is unrelated to a country's gross domestic product per person, except that it is smallest in both the richest and poorest countries (Figure 2.18). Income share between the sexes is least equal where average incomes are between $2,100–$20,000 per person, with males earning on average two and a half times as much as females. Once incomes are below $2,000 or above $20,000, the incomes of males are about double those of females.

The best-performing regions are Eastern Europe, where all countries have good or fair scores (men's income less than double women's), and Central and East Asia, where two-thirds do. The worst are West Asia, where almost two-thirds (61%) have bad or poor scores (men's income at least triple women's), and South America (42% with a poor score). Lower ratios in these regions, such as Turkey's 1.7:1 and Colombia's 2.0:1, demonstrate that such blatant inequities are avoidable.

The indicator does not show if women have equal access to high-paying jobs or are paid the same rate as equally qualified men. It also ignores situations in which men dominate wage earning but women maintain the unpaid economy, running the home, growing food, and fetching fuel and water.[27]

Education is essential for personal and economic development, and makes a crucial contribution to overall gender equity. Therefore the United Nations target is for all countries to achieve 0% difference in school enrollment and literacy by 2005.

Taking only those countries with data on all three levels (primary, secondary, and tertiary), the average difference in enrollment ranges from more than double (United Arab Emirates) to near parity (Australia). The smallest differences are in the Americas and Europe; the biggest are in Africa and West and Southern Asia.

While males always have more wealth and power than females, they sometimes have less education. Male enrollment is higher in about 60% of countries, especially in Africa and Southern Asia. Female enrollment is higher in the other 40%, notably in South America and Southern and Eastern Europe.

Inequality between male and female enrollment tends to shrink as overall enrollment improves (Figure 2.19). Of 77 countries with good or fair education scores, 20 have good

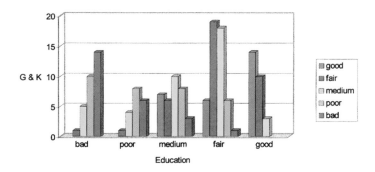

**Figure 2.19. Gender parity is high (good or fair gender and knowledge [G and K] scores) where overall enrollment is high (good or fair education scores) and low where overall enrollment is low.** Scale shows number of countries.

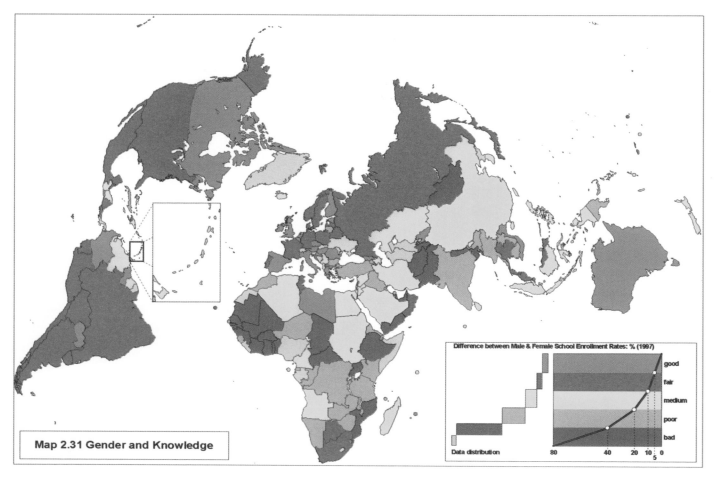

**Map 2.31 Gender and Knowledge**

Difference between Male & Female School Enrollment Rates: % (1997)

good
fair
medium
poor
bad

Data distribution    80    40    20  10  0
                                       5

equity scores (female–male enrollment differences below 5%), and 29 have fair scores (differences below 10%). By contrast, of 49 countries with poor or bad education scores, 38 get poor or bad equity scores (differences of 20% or more).[28]

## Gender and Community

### Gender and Community (Map 2.32)

**What it is:** One indicator, percentage of seats in the national parliament held by women.

**Country results:** 1 good (1%), 6 fair (3%), 19 medium (11%), 53 poor (29%), 87 bad (48%), 14 no data (8%).

The proportion of seats held by women in national parliaments is a sign of the opportunities open to women for political office and of society's willingness to be represented by them. It ranges from 0% (Djibouti, Jordan, Kuwait, United Arab Emirates, Tonga, and Vanuatu) to

42.7% (Sweden). In almost half the countries it is no higher than 10%.

Sweden and the 6 countries with a fair score (parliaments with more than 30% women) are also among the 16 freest and most democratic nations. But 4 of the others with good a freedom and governance index (Austria, Switzerland, Australia, and New Zealand) have only 21–30% parliamentary representation by women, and the rest (Canada, United States, Ireland, Portugal, and Luxembourg) fail to reach even this level. More than a third of countries with a fair freedom and governance index get a bad score for the percentage of women in parliament, including Greece (6.3%), Japan (4.6%), Papua New Guinea (1.8%), and Vanuatu (0%).

On the other side of the aisle, having women in parliament is no guarantee of freedom: five undemocratic regimes (Cuba, China, Lao, Turkmenistan, and Viet Nam) have parliaments with more than 20% women.

Low representation in parliament tends to translate into smaller percentages of ministerial or subministerial

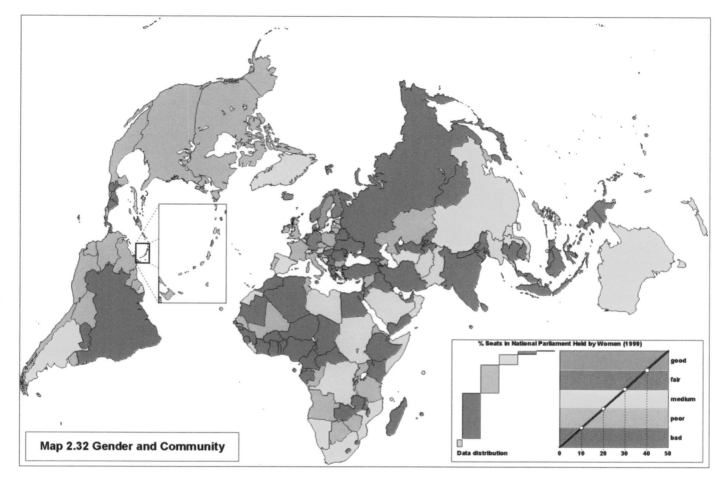

**Map 2.32 Gender and Community**

% Seats in National Parliament Held by Women (1999)

good
fair
medium
poor
bad

Data distribution    0    10    20    30    40    50

posts in government, although the data are less current and not strictly comparable. In half the countries, women have roughly the same proportions of senior posts as parliamentary seats. In just under a third, they have many fewer, as in Iceland (34.9% in parliament, 8.2% in government) and Turkmenistan (26% in parliament, 2.2% in government). Only in about a fifth do women have many more ministerial positions, as in the United States (13.3% in parliament, 33.1% women in government) and Haiti (3.6% in parliament, 22.2% in government).[29]

## Notes

1. United Nations Development Programme (1990). In other years, UNDP experimented with a human freedom index—a modification of Charles Humana's *World Human Rights Guide* (Humana 1992)—and proposed a political freedom index (United Nations Development Programme 1991, 1992).

2. International purchasing power parity dollars (PPP$) avoid distortion by exchange rates and national differences in purchasing power. PPP$ are estimated from the local costs of a common set of goods and services. Essentially they are U.S. dollars adjusted for the difference in cost of living between the United States and the country concerned.

3. Equity is an integral part of the Human Wellbeing Index because its inclusion provides a more realistic portrayal of conditions. It is treated as a separate dimension, rather than integrated into the other dimensions, to reveal clearly the impact of equity on each country's overall performance. By comparison, the World Bank's estimates of national wealth and genuine saving acknowledge the importance of distribution but do not cover it (Kunte et al. 1998; World Bank staff 1997). The Genuine Progress Indicator fully incorporates equity by adjusting its figure for personal consumption expenditure to reflect disparities in income (Cobb, Halstead, & Rowe 1995a). Since 1995, UNDP has published a gender-related development index (GDI) and a gender empowerment measure (GEM). It prefers to keep the GDI and GEM separate from the Human Development Index (HDI) to maintain the continuity of the HDI and show clearly the differences between it and the gender-adjusted indicators (United Nations

Development Programme 1995). UNDP has also experimented with a distribution-adjusted HDI (United Nations Development Programme 1991, 1992, 1993).

4. These findings support the thesis of Landes (1999) that good governance and freedom to innovate and to own the fruits of one's labor are key conditions for wealth.

5. The HDI is for 1998 and is from United Nations Development Programme (2000). The HDI was converted to a score by multiplying it by 100 and rounding to the nearest whole number.

6. Russia, Eastern Europe, North Korea, Myanmar: Lopez et al. (2000); Mathers et al. (2000).

7. Indicator description and data: Lopez et al. (2000); Mathers et al. (2000); World Health Organization (2000).

8. UN targets are from the International Conference on Population and Development, Cairo, 1994, and the World Summit for Social Development, Copenhagen, 1995 (United Nations Population Division 1997; Office of the UN System Support and Services 1996). The reduction by six years lowers the targets for healthy life expectancy from 7.1% to 20.0% below those for life expectancy, close to the range of the percentages of lifespan lost to disability (from 7.0% in Greece to 25.1% in Niger). See also Table 2.

9. Indicator description: United Nations (1996); United Nations Population Division (1998a). Data: UNICEF (1999b); United Nations Population Division, personal communication (1998).

10. Fertility decline and aging: United Nations Population Division (1998a). At present the oldest country in the world is Italy, with 1.6 elders per child. By 2050 it will be Spain, with 3.6 elders per child. Africa is the youngest continent, with 43% children and 4% elders in 1998. By 2050 it will still be the youngest, but with only twice as many children as elders. Uganda is the world's youngest country, with only one in every 31 persons aged 60 or over.

11. Undernourished percentage of population (does not have enough food to meet minimum daily energy requirements), indicator description: Food and Agriculture Organization of the United Nations (1996a); data: Food and Agriculture Organization of the United Nations (1999b). Stunting and underweight children, indicator descriptions and targets: Onis & Blössner (1997), Visschedjik & Siméant (1998); World Health Organization (1998b); data: Onis & Blössner (1997), UNICEF (1999b). Percentage of babies with low birth weight: indicator description and target, United Nations (1996); data: UNICEF (1999b), World Health Organization (1996–1998a).

    Safe water and basic sanitation, indicator descriptions and limitations: United Nations (1996); data: UNICEF (1999b), World Health Organization (1996–1998a). UN target is from the International Conference on Population

and Development, Cairo, 1994; the World Summit for Social Development, Copenhagen, 1995; the Fourth World Conference on Women, Beijing, 1995; and the Second World Conference on Human Settlements (Habitat II), Istanbul, 1996 (United Nations Population Division 1997; Office of the UN System Support and Services 1996).

12. Purchasing power parity dollars: see note 2.

13. Income data: United Nations Development Programme (2000). Relationships of income to provision of needs and to health and population, knowledge, and community: analysis of Tables 2, 4, 6, and 7, summarized in Table 3b in the Data section. The nine countries with incomes above $10,000 but scores below fair are Bahamas, St Kitts and Nevis, Seychelles, Brunei Darussalam, Bahrain, Kuwait, Qatar, Saudi Arabia, and United Arab Emirates.

14. Inflation data: International Monetary Fund (2000); International Institute for Strategic Studies (1999a). Indicator method: Table 4. Central bank inflation targets (central banks of Australia, Canada, England, the Euro area, New Zealand, and Sweden) (*The Economist* 1999). Unemployment data: International Labour Office (2000). Indicator method: Table 4.

15. External debt indicator description: United Nations (1996). External debt service data and World Bank classification of indebtedness, World Bank (1999b, 2000b). Impact of short-term debt ratio to international reserves: Sachs & Woo (1999). Description of reverse indicator, ratio of international reserves to short-term debt: IMF Policy Development and Review Department (2000). Data on short-term debt and international reserves: BIS/IMF/OECD/World Bank (2000).

16. Public debt indicator description: World Bank (1999a). Public debt data: Eurostat (2000); International Institute for Strategic Studies (1999a); World Bank (1999a, 2000a). Treaty of Maastricht standards: Black (1997).

17. Countries with fair debt scores not rated for public debt: Paraguay, Botswana, Belarus, Latvia, Lithuania, Bhutan, and United Arab Emirates. Countries with fair debt scores not rated for public debt and deficit (rated for external debt only): Antigua and Barbuda, Suriname, Eritrea, Libya, Swaziland, Slovenia, Saudi Arabia, Solomon Islands, and Vanuatu.

18. Knowledge in postindustrial economies: Chichilnisky (1997, 1998).

19. Adult literacy rate indicator description and limitations: United Nations (1996); data: UNESCO (1999a). International Adult Literacy Survey (IALS), including IALS data in figure and following paragraph: Organisation for Economic Co-operation and Development, Human Resources Development Canada & Statistics Canada (1997).

20. School enrollment indicator description: United Nations (1996); data: UNESCO (1999b, 1999c); UN target from the World Summit for Social Development, Copenhagen, 1995, and the Fourth World Conference on Women, Beijing, 1995: United Nations Population Division (1997); Office of the UN System Support and Services (1996).

21. Indicator descriptions: International Telecommunication Union (1997); data: International Telecommunication Union (1997, 1998, 1999, 2000). The number of main lines and cellular phones per 100 persons ranges from less than 0.1 (Democratic Republic of Congo) to 113.8 (Sweden). Luxembourg has the highest density of main lines (69.2) and Finland of mobile phone subscribers (57.2), who now outnumber main lines. Faults per 100 main telephone lines per year range from 761.0 (Tonga) to 1.1 (United Arab Emirates). The number of Internet users per 10,000 people ranges from almost 0 (Somalia) to 3,953 (Sweden).

22. Political rights rating, civil liberties rating, and press freedom rating descriptions and data: Freedom House (1999b, 2000a, 2000b). Corruption perceptions index description and data: Transparency International (1999, 2000).

23. Indicator description and data: International Institute for Strategic Studies (1999a, 1999b).

24. Indicator definitions and data: United Nations Crime Prevention and Criminal Justice Division (1997, 1999).

25. Good or fair scores in both household and gender equity: Belgium, Croatia, Czech Republic, Denmark, Finland, Germany, Norway, and Sweden. Poor or bad scores in both: Dominican Republic, Honduras, Panama, St Lucia, Burkina Faso, Central African Republic, Gambia, Guinea–Bissau, Kenya, Mali, Niger, Nigeria, Zambia, and Papua New Guinea.

26. Indicator description and data: World Bank (1998, 2000a).

27. Indicator description and data: United Nations Development Programme (1999, 2000). Dollars are purchasing power parity dollars (see note 2).

28. Indicator description: United Nations (1996); data: UNESCO (1999a, 1999b). UN target from the World Summit for Social Development, Copenhagen, 1995, and the Fourth World Conference on Women, Beijing, 1995: United Nations Population Division (1997); Office of the UN System Support and Services (1996).

29. Indicator description and data: Inter-Parliamentary Union (2000).

# 3. Ecosystem Wellbeing

## Ecosystem Wellbeing Index

### Ecosystem Wellbeing Index (EWI) (Map 3.1)

**What it is:** Average of indices of land, water, air, species and genes, and resource use, *or* average of indices of land, water, air, and species and genes, *whichever is lower.*

**Country results:** 0 good (0%), 27 fair (15%), 81 medium (45%), 68 poor (38%), 4 bad (2%).

**Highlights:**

- Countries with a poor or bad EWI cover almost half (48.4%) of the planet's land and inland water surface; those with a medium EWI, 43%. Countries with a fair EWI occupy a mere 8.6%.

- Many countries with a fair or medium EWI would probably have lower ratings if their environments were better monitored. Air quality, water quality, and the state of aquatic ecosystems are especially neglected.

- The way for most countries to raise their EWI is to restore and maintain habitats, expand protected areas, conserve agricultural diversity, and improve water quality. Industrialized countries also need to cut greenhouse gases.

## *Measuring Ecosystem Wellbeing*

Ecosystem wellbeing is a condition in which the ecosystem maintains its diversity and quality—and thus its capacity to support people and the rest of life—and its potential to adapt to change and provide a wide range of choices and opportunities for the future.

The global ecosystem consists of layers of smaller ecosystems: communities of plants, animals, and other creatures, together with their physical environments.

These are the building blocks of life. They maintain the planet's chemical balance and such life-supporting processes as the capture, storage, and transfer of energy and the cycling of nutrients and water. They moderate climate, filter and neutralize pollutants, and renew soil. They provide the resources that keep people alive and sustain economies, and their beauty and intricacy enrich mind and spirit.

Diversity includes the pattern (or type, size, and distribution) of these communities in the landscape and seascape, their species composition, the size and structure of component populations, and the connections and interactions among and within communities. The apparent overabundance—even redundancy and inefficiency—of this diversity is necessary to provide a range of responses to change (so that if one fails others can take its place) and to give people plenty of choices for the future.[1]

The quality of ecosystems includes their capacity to maintain themselves through cycles of growth, maturity, death, and renewal; their productivity; and the chemical and physical integrity of soil, water, and the atmosphere.

The opposite condition to ecosystem wellbeing is ecosystem stress, in which the ecosystem loses its diversity and quality and so becomes less able to support people and other life. The five main pressures people place on the ecosystem are:

- *Conversion and occupation of ecosystems.* Land ecosystems are converted to farmland and pasture or replaced by built systems, such as settlements, infrastructure, and mines. Dams and dikes alter the flow of rivers. Docks, jetties, breakwaters, and quays restructure coasts and shores. Habitat destruction due to ecosystem conversion is by far the biggest cause of losses of diversity (followed by resource extraction, translocation of species, and pollution).[2]

- *Resource extraction.* Plant and animal products, water, fossil fuels, and minerals are taken from the ecosystem, reducing the size of stocks and populations and modifying ecosystems; for instance, logging and grazing change the structure of vegetation, and fishing alters the structure of fish stocks by leaving fewer individuals of breeding age. The collapse of fisheries, such as Atlantic cod, throws people out of work and denies many their only source of income (other than social assistance). Reductions in fuelwood supplies add to the time and effort women must expend to seek fuel and carry it home. Exhaustion of accessible and easily extracted oil, gas, and ore increases the cost of producing energy and minerals.

- *Translocation of species.* Organisms are moved from their native habitat to new habitats, both deliberately (as in the stocking of nonnative fishes for recreational fishing and aquaculture) and accidentally (as in the entry of many diseases, pests, and weeds as stowaways on ships and imported farm produce). Such introduced species prey on native species or compete with them for food and space and are the agents of major outbreaks of disease among crops, livestock, and people.

- *Emissions and waste disposal.* Much of the material extracted from the ecosystem is returned to it as physical, chemical, and biological waste and pollution, usually in forms and at rates to which it is not adapted. The consequences include increased disease and death rates, lowered air and water quality, and disrupted atmosphere and climate.

- *Soil degradation.* Cultivation, grazing, and logging often degrade soils through erosion (above natural rates), loss of nutrients and organic matter, salinization, and physical damage such as compaction. This reduces the productivity of the land and harms aquatic ecosystems, polluting water, silting up reservoirs and channels, and smothering habitats such as coral reefs.

Singly and in concert these pressures reduce diversity and carrying capacity (the capacity of an ecosystem to support healthy organisms while maintaining its productivity, adaptability, and capability of renewal). Humans use energy, industry, and agriculture to enlarge their share of this capacity, but in doing so they encroach on the share of other species, shrinking diversity even more. As a result, people now consume, destroy, or control a quarter of the planet's terrestrial and aquatic plant energy, the ultimate source of food for virtually all nonplant life.[3]

The implications of reduced carrying capacity are that the Earth will support fewer people well, or more people less well, or a world of sharply increased disparities (a few people well, a great many poorly). It is also likely that climatic and environmental events will become more capricious, leading to a rise in so-called natural disasters: more frequent and severe storms, floods, droughts, and plagues.

To ensure full coverage of the diversity and quality of the ecosystem and of the main pressures on them, Wellbeing Assessment divides ecosystem wellbeing into 5 dimensions, which I have further split into 10 elements (Figure 3.1). They are described in the remaining sections of this chapter and distilled into a short statement here:

| | |
|---|---|
| **Land diversity** | All major land ecosystems are maintained or restored in large units with minimal loss of the habitats and communities within them. |
| **Land quality** | Soil degradation on cultivated and modified lands is kept close to degradation rates on natural lands. |
| **Inland waters** | All major aquatic ecosystems, both inland and |
| **Sea** | marine, are maintained or restored in large units with minimal loss of the communities and habitats within them and minimal stress from pollution and water uses. |
| **Global atmosphere** | Pollutants that disrupt the chemical balance of the global atmosphere are eliminated or substantially reduced. |
| **Local air quality** | Local air pollutants are below levels that affect people or the ecosystem. |
| **Wild diversity** | All native wild species are maintained, and extinctions are reduced to background rates. |
| **Domesticated diversity** | As much as possible of the heritage of crop varieties and livestock breeds is maintained. |
| **Energy and materials** | Consumption of energy and materials and |
| **Resource sectors** | extraction and production of resources are within the carrying capacity of the ecosystem. |

**Figure 3.1. Ecosystem dimensions and elements.** The 5 dimensions are in **bold**; the 10 elements are in normal type. Sea (shaded box) is not covered due to lack of adequate data.

The resulting Ecosystem Wellbeing Index (EWI) measures progress toward the proposed goal of a high level of ecosystem wellbeing, based on all these elements except the sea (on which data are inadequate). The goal might be stated better as a low level of ecosystem stress since we know more about the pressures that cause ecosystem stress than we do about the levels of diversity and quality required for ecosystem wellbeing.

The pressures a country places on the ecosystem often extend well beyond its borders. Pollutants are carried over long distances by winds and currents. Greenhouse gases and the chemicals that deplete the stratospheric ozone layer damage the atmosphere, which spans the entire planet. Dams and water withdrawals from rivers can have impacts all the way downstream. Importers of raw materials and processed goods reap the benefits while exporters incur the ecosystem stress caused by their extraction and manufacture. I have tried to account for such cross-border effects by:

- Including issues that portray global impacts (global atmosphere, energy and materials) and giving them the same weight as the corresponding national issues (local air quality, resource sectors).

- Factoring in the proportion of national food supply that is met by domestic production.

- Adding imports to domestic timber production and summing them as a percentage of national supply.

Thus, as far as possible, the EWI measures each country's stress on the ecosystem as a whole, not just on the area within the country's jurisdiction.

### Most of the Planet is Poor or Mediocre

*The EWI of all countries is shown in Map 3.1. Table 3.1 gives a regional summary. Figure 3.2 displays patterns of performance. Full scores are in Table 9, and rankings in Table 25, in the Data section.*

To achieve a good EWI, a country must perform well in all dimensions. None does so. Twenty-seven countries, occupying less than 9% of Earth's land and inland water surface, have a fair EWI, but not one of them was assessed on water quality or local air quality. Had they been, it is likely that many would have dropped to a medium EWI. Benin's EWI of 71 (the second highest, after the Republic of Congo's 72) is partly due to its low impact on inland waters and the global atmosphere: its rivers are largely undammed, it uses only 1.5% of its water supply, and it emits negligible amounts of the chemicals that damage the atmosphere. Not being rated on water quality or local air quality (factors that contribute to the poor EWI of nearby Ghana), its scores for water and air are high. These are buttressed by fairly low threats to wild and domesticated species: as far as is known, 4% of the country's mammals—but less than 1% of its flowering plants and no birds or livestock breeds—are at risk of extinction. Benin does moderately well even in its weakest element, land quality, with soil degradation

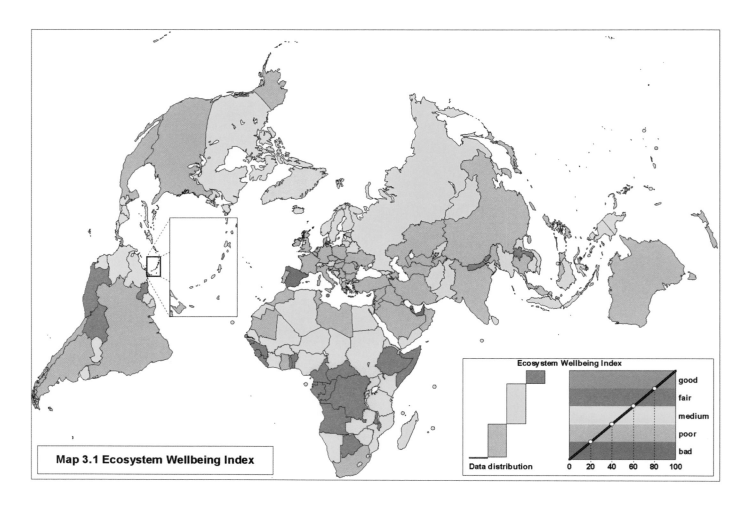

**Map 3.1 Ecosystem Wellbeing Index**

Ecosystem Wellbeing Index

good
fair
medium
poor
bad

Data distribution    0  20  40  60  80  100

affecting no more than 19% of its cultivated and modified land area.

Eighty-one countries, covering 43% of the planet's land and inland water surface, have a medium EWI. Colombia's performance is a typical mixture of strength in some aspects and weakness in others. Only about 10% of its land area has been converted to settlements and cultivation and 29% modified by logging, ranching, or other human activities. Although almost a third of the cultivated and modified area is degraded, most of the degradation is light and easily remedied. Water quality is a different story: the Magdalena, the country's largest river basin, is heavily contaminated with nutrients and fecal coliforms. Emissions to the global atmosphere are low (local air quality was not rated), and pressure from energy use, farming, and logging is also low. Despite this and the positive state of the land, many of Colombia's wild species are threatened, notably 10% of its mammals and 55% of its gymnosperms (plants such as conifers).

The 68 countries with a poor EWI occupy 48% of the Earth's land and inland water area. They tend to be better monitored than countries with a fair or medium

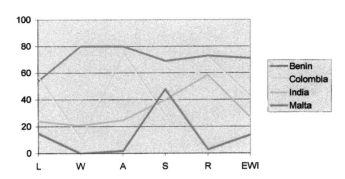

**Figure 3.2. Comparison of four countries at each level of the Ecosystem Wellbeing Index (EWI)** (blue = fair, yellow = medium, pink = poor, red = bad) and for each dimension (L = land, W = water, A = air, S = species and genes, R = resource use).  No country has a good EWI.

**Table 3.1. Ecosystem Wellbeing Index (EWI), showing the number of countries at each level by continental group and region.** Most of the Americas has a medium or poor EWI. Asia–Pacific is similar, except that more countries have a poor EWI, especially in West Asia. As with the Human Wellbeing Index, Africa and Europe are the reverse of each other, except in this case Africa is the better performer: most EWIs are poor in Europe, medium or fair in Africa. In Central and East Africa, the strongest region, all countries have a fair or medium EWI.

| Region and Continental Group | Fair | Medium | Poor | Bad | Total |
|---|---|---|---|---|---|
| North and Central America | 1 | 6 | 3 | 0 | 10 |
| West Indies | 1 | 7 | 5 | 0 | 13 |
| South America | 3 | 6 | 3 | 0 | 12 |
| *Americas* | *5* | *19* | *11* | *0* | *35* |
| Northern Africa | 2 | 5 | 3 | 0 | 10 |
| West Africa | 7 | 8 | 2 | 0 | 17 |
| Central and Eastern Africa | 6 | 7 | 0 | 0 | 13 |
| Southern Africa | 3 | 9 | 1 | 0 | 13 |
| *Africa* | *18* | *29* | *6* | *0* | *53* |
| Northern Europe | 0 | 6 | 7 | 0 | 13 |
| Southern Europe | 0 | 3 | 7 | 2 | 12 |
| Eastern Europe | 0 | 3 | 9 | 0 | 12 |
| *Europe* | *0* | *12* | *23* | *2* | *37* |
| West Asia | 0 | 3 | 13 | 2 | 18 |
| Russia, Central and East Asia | 0 | 5 | 7 | 0 | 12 |
| Southern Asia | 3 | 9 | 5 | 0 | 17 |
| Pacific | 1 | 4 | 3 | 0 | 8 |
| *Asia–Pacific* | *4* | *21* | *28* | *2* | *55* |
| WORLD | 27 | 81 | 68 | 4 | 180 |

EWI and to show a pattern of satisfactory results in a few elements but subpar performance in most. India has lost 98% of its natural land, more than 40% of its cultivated and modified land is degraded, rivers and even groundwater are polluted with nutrients and bacteria, city air is dense with particulates, and 8% of the country's flowering plants, 6% of its birds, and 24% of its mammals are at risk of extinction. India's best dimension is resource use, with moderate pressure from farming and fisheries balanced by low rates of energy consumption.

The four countries with a bad EWI—Spain, Malta, Bahrain, and United Arab Emirates (UAE)—cover 0.4% of the planet's land and inland water area. Spain has high proportions of threatened species and livestock breeds. The others have bad scores for water, air, and resource use, consuming many times their renewable supplies of water (Malta 3 times, UAE 14 times, Bahrain 60 times) and large amounts of ozone-depleting substances, and depending heavily on other countries for food and timber.

## The Resource Use Effect

*The effect of resource use on the EWI is illustrated in Map 3.2 and Figure 3.3 and summarized in Table 3.2. Full details are in Table 9 in the Data section.*

The resource use indicators measure parts of the consumption process whose impacts on the ecosystem may not be adequately covered by the other dimensions. Also, by factoring in imports, they may reveal pressures on the global ecosystem omitted by the mainly national indicators of land, water, air, and species and genes. If the other dimensions do not account for these pressures, resource use will lower the EWI and so is included to ensure that the EWI better reflects the actual state of the ecosystem. If they do account for them, resource use will leave the EWI unchanged or will increase it, and so is excluded to prevent double-counting. In 32 countries (18%), resource use lowers the EWI and is *included*. As a consequence, Lesotho's EWI falls from fair to medium. Resource use is *excluded* from the EWI of 138 countries (77%) where inclusion would have raised it. Spain's EWI is thereby prevented from rising from bad to poor, the EWIs of Panama and 11 other countries from poor to medium, and those of Cambodia and six others from medium to fair. Resource use has no effect on the EWIs of 10 countries (6%) such as Belize and Austria.

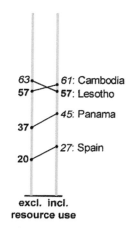

**Figure 3.3. The resource use effect: EWIs excluding and including resource use.** The final EWI is the lower score (in **bold**).

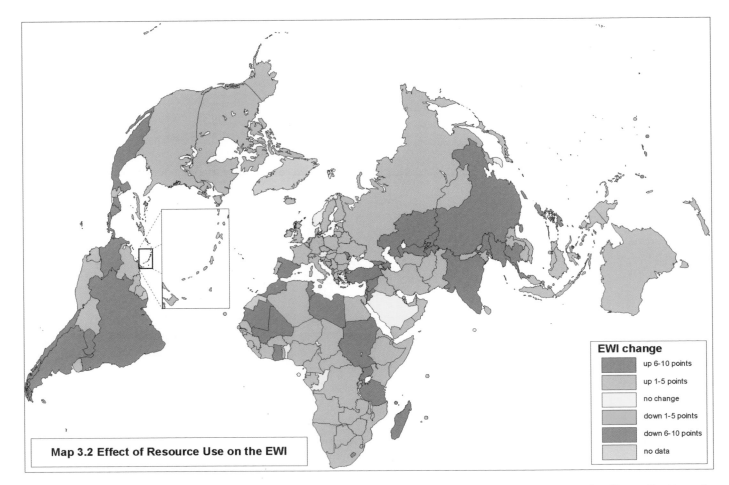

**Map 3.2 Effect of Resource Use on the EWI**

EWI change
- up 6-10 points
- up 1-5 points
- no change
- down 1-5 points
- down 6-10 points
- no data

**Table 3.2. Number of countries whose EWI is changed by the inclusion of resource use, according to size of change and level of the EWI before the inclusion of resource use.**

| EWI Change | Fair | Medium | Poor | Bad | Total |
|---|---|---|---|---|---|
| Up 6–10 points | 0 | 17 | 24 | 1 | 42 |
| Up 1–5 points | 23 | 45 | 28 | 0 | 96 |
| UP SUBTOTAL | 23 | 62 | 52 | 1 | 138 |
| NO CHANGE | 3 | 5 | 2 | 0 | 10 |
| Down 1–5 points | 1 | 13 | 13 | 3 | 30 |
| Down 6–10 points | 1 | 0 | 1 | 0 | 2 |
| DOWN SUBTOTAL | 2 | 13 | 14 | 3 | 32 |
| Total | 28 | 80 | 68 | 4 | 180 |

## Biodiversity and Environmental Quality

The five ecosystem dimensions are much less closely matched with the EWI or with each other than are human dimensions with the HWI. Only two, water and air, are highly correlated with the EWI. Resource use and land are moderately related to it (land much less so than resource use) and species and genes hardly at all. Air and resource use are strongly associated with each other, primarily due to the close link between energy consumption and carbon emissions. By the same token, local air quality and pressure on the global atmosphere are inversely correlated, rich countries controlling urban air pollution better than poor ones, but emitting more carbon dioxide.

Ecosystem dimensions are weakly linked because ecosystem wellbeing is more complex than human wellbeing, reflecting both the interplay of ecological processes and human impacts on them. Hence, representative indicators are more difficult to identify and reliable data harder to obtain.

Biodiversity (the diversity of ecological communities, species, and genetic variants) and environmental quality are the keys to ecosystem wellbeing. Indicators of the former are in the land, water, and species and genes dimensions; indicators of the latter are in the land, water, and air dimensions. Botswana is the one country that performs well across the board, with good or fair scores for all biodiversity components and for the two environmen-

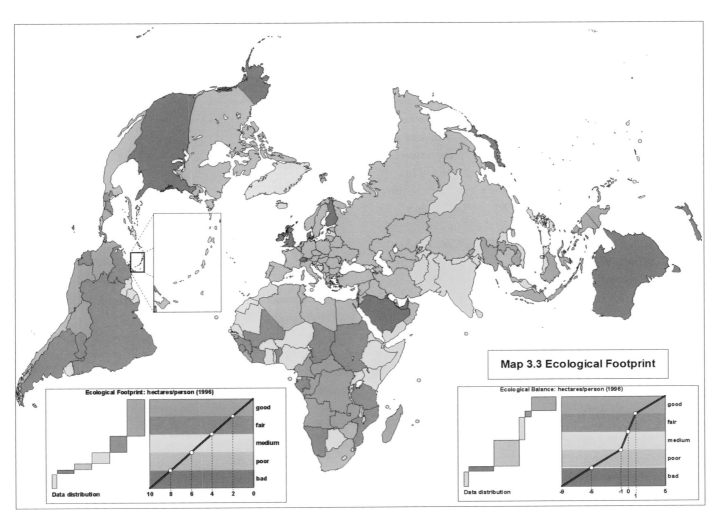

**Map 3.3 Ecological Footprint**

Ecological Footprint: hectares/person (1996)

Data distribution

good
fair
medium
poor
bad

10  8  6  4  2  0

Ecological Balance: hectares/person (1996)

Data distribution

good
fair
medium
poor
bad

-9  -5  -1 0 1  5

tal quality indicators on which it reports (land degradation and global atmosphere). Benin, Republic of Congo, and Namibia are the only other countries with good or fair scores for a majority of the indicators. Benin has no bad or poor scores. The others have one or two flaws (land protection in the Congo, animal breeds and inland water quality in Namibia).

Globally (excluding "no data" countries), the strongest performance areas, with the highest proportions of good or fair scores and the lowest of poor or bad scores, are river conversion (by dams), land quality, and global atmosphere. The weakest, with the fewest high scores and most low scores, are inland water quality, animal species, animal breeds, and land protection.

Among the 40 countries that could be rated on all biodiversity and environmental quality components, Sweden has the highest EWI (49), followed by Cuba (45), Finland and Lithuania (44), Canada, Norway, and Switzerland (43), and Austria (42). The EWIs of the rest

are poor. The group's strengths and weaknesses match those of the global set, except that due to the predominance of developed countries, local air quality is a strength and global atmosphere a major weakness.

Hence the way for most countries to raise their EWI is to restore and maintain habitats, increase the area of protected ecosystems, conserve agricultural diversity, improve water quality, and (chiefly industrialized countries) reduce greenhouse gases.

### The Size of the Foot—or Where It's Put?

*No environmental equivalent of the Human Development Index exists with which to compare the EWI. The Environmental Sustainability Index is compromised as a measurement of the state of the environment because it includes human indicators and indicators of environmental policies and practices (rather than of actual environmental stresses and conditions). The Ecological Footprint (EF), an index of consumption pressure, provides a more informative contrast. It is shown in Map 3.3 and compared with the EWI in Table 3.3. Full details are in Table 9 in the Data section.*

The EF combines the quantities of energy and renewable resources (minerals excluded) a society consumes by converting them to a common unit of area: the area of productive land and sea required to supply the resources and absorb the carbon dioxide from fossil fuels. This area is a society's ecological footprint. Of the 151 countries covered by the EF and the EWI, 73 have a footprint that exceeds the world average share of productive capacity of 2.2 hectares per person. The EF also estimates a country's ecological balance: if its footprint is bigger than its national area of productive land and sea, it has a deficit; if it is smaller, it has a surplus. In translating the EF into a score, I have defined the good band as a footprint smaller than both the world average share of productive capacity and the national productive area. The EF score is the lower of the footprint score and the balance score.

Eighteen countries have an EF score that is more than 10 points lower than the EWI. Forty-seven have an EF score that is more than 10 points higher. The main reason for these differences is that the EWI attempts to measure the actual state of the ecosystem, whereas the EF is a gauge of pressures whose effect on the ecosystem depends on how they are applied and where. A liter of gasoline burned without pollution controls in a confined space contaminates the air more than a liter of clean fuel burned in the open.[4]

Singapore has a footprint of 12.3 hectares per person and an ecological deficit of 13.8 hectares per person,

**Table 3.3. Performance of 151 countries rated by the Ecosystem Wellbeing Index (EWI) and the Ecological Footprint (EF).**

| Band | EWI | EF |
|---|---|---|
| Good | 0 | 19 |
| Fair | 22 | 19 |
| Medium | 65 | 43 |
| Poor | 62 | 55 |
| Bad | 2 | 15 |
| Total | 151 | 151 |

reflecting its small size and booming consumption. The EWI reflects these factors as well, with bad scores for air and resource use and a poor score for land. But it also takes account of mitigating performance: less than 4% of animal species and less than 2% of plant species threatened. Indonesia has a footprint of 1.5 hectares per person and an ecological surplus of 1.5 hectares per person. In line with this low pressure, the EWI includes fair scores for global atmosphere and resource use. But forest loss, high percentages of threatened mammals and birds, and severe water pollution reduce its overall EWI to medium.

To the extent that they are comparable, the gap between the EF and the EWI is the difference between the expected stress (EF) and the actual stress (EWI) caused by the consumption process. One is the size of the foot, the other what the foot treads on. Singapore and others with an EF score lower than the EWI damage the ecosystem less than expected from the amount they consume. Indonesia and others with a higher EF score harm it more than expected.

# Land

## Land Index (Map 3.4)

**What it is:** Lower of land diversity index and land quality index.

**Country results:** 0 good (0%), 11 fair (6%), 63 medium (35%), 88 poor (49%), 18 bad (10%).

To achieve a good or fair land index, a country must conserve or restore the diversity of its natural land ecosystems and maintain the quality of the ecosystems it develops. Land diversity matters because it is the foundation of

ecosystem health: loss, fragmentation, or structural modification of natural land ecosystems changes nutrient and water cycles, alters the chemistry of the atmosphere, menaces the survival of species, provokes outbreaks of pests and diseases, and reduces the ability of the environment to recover from disturbances.[5] Land quality—keeping cultivated and modified land in good heart—is vital to sustain yields of crops, livestock, and timber. Land diversity and land quality are quite different conditions, and success in one does not compensate for failure in the other. Diversity loss determines the index of most countries in all regions

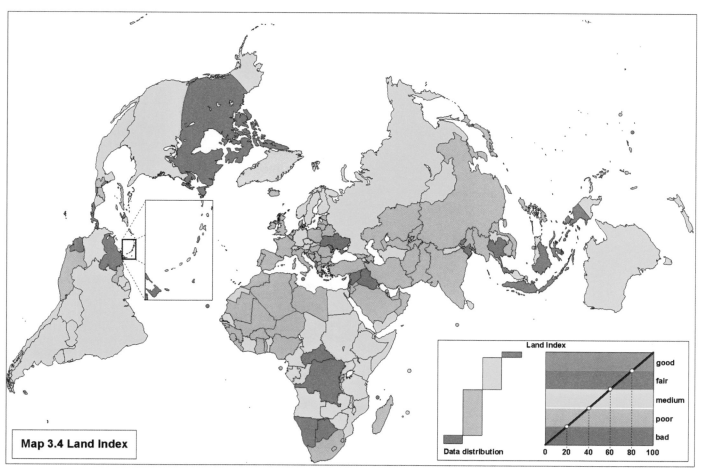

Map 3.4 Land Index

67

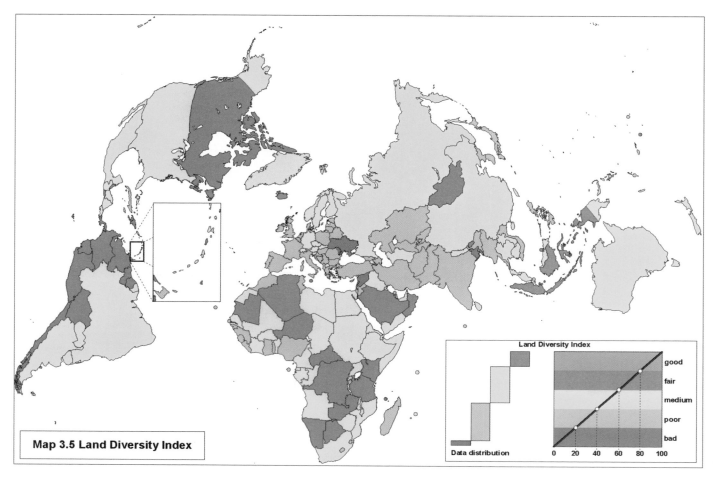

**Map 3.5 Land Diversity Index**

except North, Central, and South America, where land degradation is the more frequent determinant (Figure 3.4).

*For all data and scores, together with details of the indicators, performance criteria, and combining procedures, see Table 10 (land index, basic data, native forest change), Table 11 (natural, modified, cultivated, and built land), Table 12 (land protection), and Table 13 (land quality) in the Data section.*

## Land Diversity

### Land Diversity Index (Map 3.5)

**What it is:** Weighted average [weights in brackets] of land modification and conversion score [2] and land protection score [1] (Figure 3.5).

**Objective:** All major land ecosystems maintained or restored in large units with minimal loss of the habitats and communities within them.

**Country results:** 0 good (0%), 30 fair (17%), 69 medium (38%), 70 poor (39%), 11 bad (6%).

The land diversity index measures how much land has been converted to cultivated and built areas, how much of the unconverted remainder is natural (negligibly to lightly human-influenced), and how much of the land is protected.[6]

The proportions of the land that are converted, modified (moderately to heavily human-influenced but not

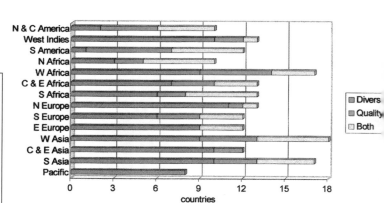

**Figure 3.4. Number of countries whose land index is determined by land diversity, land quality, or both.** Both elements are considered determinants if their scores are in the same performance band.

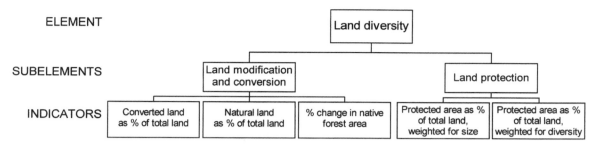

**Figure 3.5. Indicator chart for land diversity.**

cultivated or built), and natural reveal the scale and rate of a society's overall impact on the ecosystem, both within and beyond its borders. A nation that conserves its natural and modified lands is an ecological donor, helping to maintain the support system of the entire planet. A nation whose territory is largely cultivated and built is an ecological debtor, dependent on other countries for the services that natural and modified areas provide.

The select club of ecological donors—countries with a fair land diversity index—is a motley group, ranging in land area from 922-million-hectare Canada to 75,000-hectare-Dominica and in income per person from $25,110 Iceland to $480 Tanzania. One explanation of their performance is low population pressure: 83% of them (all except Dominica, Dominican Republic, Kenya, Brunei Darussalam, and Indonesia) have a land availability (land area divided by population) of 2 hectares or more per person, compared with 19% of those with a poor or bad land diversity index. Another explanation is low agricultural pressure: only six (20%) of the countries (Canada, Chile, Colombia, Guyana, Panama, and Venezuela) meet much of their needs from their land, achieving good or fair scores for both food sufficiency and food production as a percentage of supply. The others depend heavily on imports for food, are ill fed, or (in the cases of Mauritania and Mongolia) both.

Yet the American countries show that it is possible to maintain land diversity while producing enough from the land to meet most domestic needs. Chile's performance is particularly impressive. Less than 10% of its land is converted, 50% is still natural, and more than 18% is protected. At the same time, the country produces 85% of its food supply and meets the food needs of 95% of its people. Even Dominica, whose land availability is a globally more typical 1.1 hectares per person (compared

with Chile's 4.9), performs fairly well on both fronts. Although a quarter of the island's land area has been converted, almost 43% is still natural, 9% is protected, and the area of native forest is stable. The island produces 63% of its food supply (not enough, but respectable for its size) and achieves a fair score for food sufficiency.

The vastly more numerous ecological debtors (countries with a poor or bad land diversity index) tend to have a long history of land transformation and little land per person. Even in the best circumstances, restoring natural conditions would take many centuries. It is feasible only in nations with large proportions of unconverted land and land availability that is high (say 4 hectares or more per person) or, if low, stable or increasing.

None of the countries with a bad index qualifies. Among those with a poor index, more than half the land is unconverted in 53 of them, but only 17 meet the other criteria. Kazakhstan, Kyrgyzstan, Solomon Islands, and Vanuatu have 4 hectares or more per person; Trinidad and Tobago, Azerbaijan, Georgia, and 10 countries in Europe have less (from 0.4 to 3.0 hectares per person), but land availability is stable or increasing.[7]

Most countries with a poor index are burdened with large proportions of converted land, high population densities, or high growth rates. They will be lucky to hang onto the scraps of natural area they have left. If they fail to do so, their only way to offset their ecological debt will be to perform correspondingly better in other ecosystem elements, such as global atmosphere and species and genes.

Countries with a medium land diversity index are lesser debtors and could improve their positions fairly easily. All but Mauritius, Rwanda, and the Czech Republic have converted less than half their land

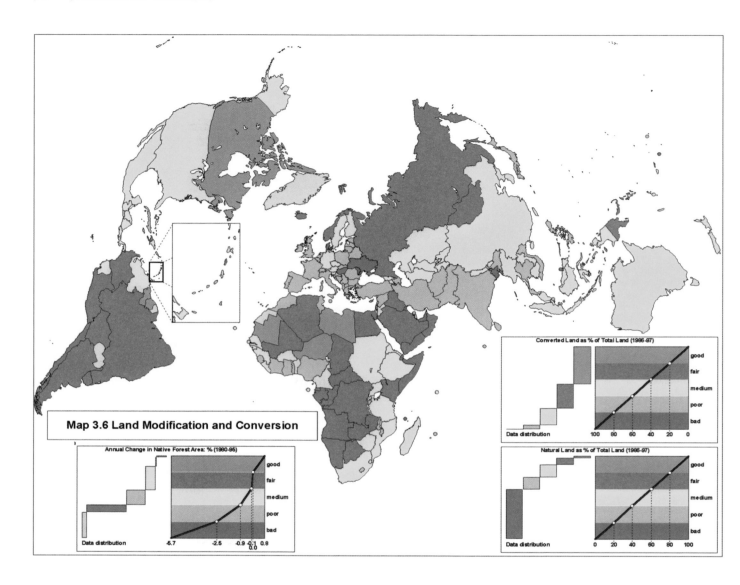

**Map 3.6 Land Modification and Conversion**

area. Land availability is over 4 hectares per person in 23 of them; among the 46 with less land, it is rising or stable in St Kitts and Nevis, Austria, Slovakia, and Slovenia.

The best way to maintain or restore a high percentage of natural land is to expand the system of protected areas. A large proportion of protected land shows a society's commitment to conserving its heritage of different landscapes. However, because protected designations may not be upheld in practice, the protection score was given half the weight of the modification and conversion score. Hence the land diversity index approximates the latter score, except where protection is much stronger or much weaker. In 21 countries, stronger protection raises the index to a higher performance band: Belize, Dominican Republic,

Ecuador, Panama, Venezuela, Tanzania, Bhutan, and Indonesia go from medium to fair; 11 countries from poor to medium (4 in Africa, 3 each in Europe and Asia, and St Lucia); and Denmark and Hungary go from bad to poor. In 53 countries, weaker protection drops the index to a lower band: Canada, Guyana, Suriname, Niger, and Mauritania go from good to fair; Libya from good to medium; 19 countries from fair to medium (9 in Africa, 5 in Asia–Pacific, 3 in South America, Norway, and Russia); 23 from medium to poor (13 in Asia–Pacific, 8 in Africa, 2 in the Americas); and Barbados, El Salvador, Malta, Lebanon, and Syria go from poor to bad.

Note that this index shows not how diverse each country is but how well it maintains the diversity it has. Some of the poor scorers—including India,

Nicaragua, and Madagascar—are also among the world's most biologically diverse.[8] They may have more land diversity left than some of the fair scorers (such as Iceland, Algeria, and Mongolia) that are less varied naturally.

## Land Modification and Conversion

---

### Land Modification and Conversion (Map 3.6)

**What it is:** Average of scores for converted land as percentage of total land, natural land as percentage of total land, and percentage average annual change in native forest area.

**Country results:** 6 good (3%), 36 fair (20%), 69 medium (38%), 61 poor (34%), 8 bad (4%).

---

In most countries with a good or fair score, no more than 10% of the land has been converted to cultivated and built areas, and more than 40% of the land is natural. However, the area of native (nonplanted) forest is stable in only nine (Canada, Dominica, Djibouti, Libya, Mauritania, Niger, Iraq, Mongolia, and Yemen). The rest—except Iceland and Norway (no data) and Egypt, Kuwait, Oman, and United Arab Emirates (no forest)—are losing their native forests to agriculture, settlement, and infrastructure. The majority of nations with a poor or bad score have converted more than 30% of their land, less than 5% remains natural, and native forests are shrinking in all but one (Mauritius) of the 32 countries with data.

Overall, the percentage of converted land ranges from 75.4% (Bangladesh) to 0.6% (Suriname), and of natural land from 0% (several countries) to 94% (Suriname). Annual change in native forest area ranges from a decline of 7.4% (Jamaica) to an increase (through natural regeneration) of 0.7% (Dominican Republic). The percentages of converted and natural land are correlated with each other but, surprisingly, not with forest change—probably because the data were derived in incompatible ways, often requiring leaps of extrapolation. All three indicators are influenced by land availability: 76% of the good and fair scores occur above 4 hectares per person (86% above 2 hectares per person); all the poor and bad scores are below 4 hectares per person (93% below 2 hectares per person).[9]

## Land Protection

---

### Land Protection (Map 3.7)

**What it is:** Weighted average [weights in brackets] of protected area size score [2] and protected area diversity score [1].

**Country results:** 9 good (5%), 39 fair (22%), 45 medium (25%), 27 poor (15%), 60 bad (33%).

---

Good and fair scores go to countries that keep substantial proportions of their various land and inland water ecosystems in large totally protected areas. The international target is full protection of 10% of each biome or major ecological region. Totally protected areas score higher than partially protected areas because they are likely to support a wider range of ecological communities. Within the totally protected category, large areas score higher than small ones because the bigger the area, the more it can buffer human activities and allow ecological communities to persist and evolve "naturally."[10] Areas qualify as large on a sliding scale depending on the size of the country: an 8,000-hectare protected area in a 75,000-hectare country (such as Dominica) is just as valuable as an 8-million-hectare protected area in a 75-million-hectare country (such as Zambia). Although protecting a country's ecosystem diversity matters as much as the size of the protected areas, the diversity score was given less weight because the indicator is less reliable. Note that both indicators measure protection on paper, not necessarily on the ground.

Only in North and Central America and Central and East Africa do more countries have good or fair scores than poor or bad. Performance is unrelated to land availability or to biological diversity: Central African Republic and Gabon are similar in both respects, but the former fully protects 5% of its land (4.5% in million-hectare areas), the latter 0.1%. Among countries with good or fair scores, 15 have less than a hectare of land per person; among those with bad scores, 11 have more than 4 hectares per person. Of the 45 countries with the most plant and animal species, 19 have a good or fair score, and 13 have a bad or poor score.[11]

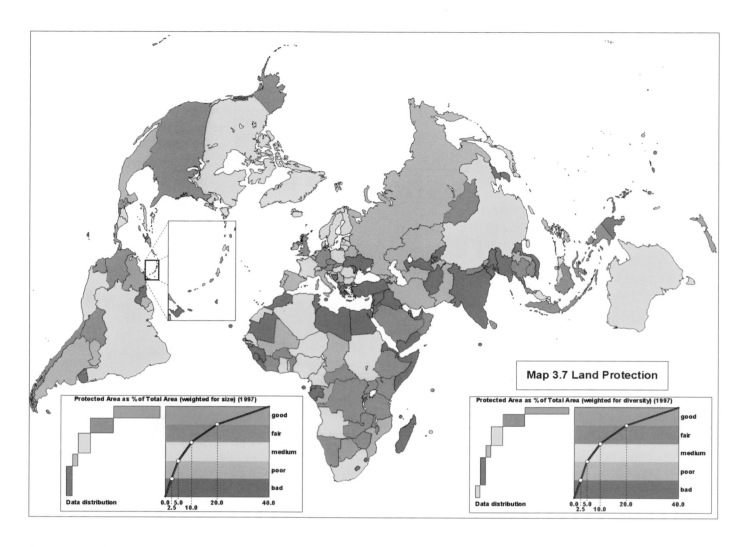

## Land Quality

### Land Quality Index (Map 3.8)

**What it is:** One indicator, degraded land as percentage of cultivated and modified land, weighted according to the severity of degradation (Figure 3.6).

**Objective:** Soil degradation close to background rates.

**Country results:** 37 good (21%), 39 fair (22%), 44 medium (24%), 38 poor (21%), 9 bad (5%), 13 no data (7%).

sion is a natural phenomenon; only human-caused erosion above background or natural rates is counted here as degradation.

In some of the countries with poor or bad scores, much of the productive land is arid or semiarid and highly vulnerable to degradation (66% in Mexico, 99% in Pakistan, and 100% in Cape Verde, Eritrea, Libya, Niger, and Tunisia). In others, such as China, large areas are naturally erosive, and high rates of soil loss are extremely hard to prevent. Excessive production and pro-

Production of crops, livestock, and timber depends on the quality of cultivated and modified land but can impair it through erosion, depletion of nutrients and organic matter, salinization, and physical deterioration (such as compaction). Soils may also be degraded by acid rain and chemical pollution. Ero-

**Figure 3.6. Indicator chart for land quality.**

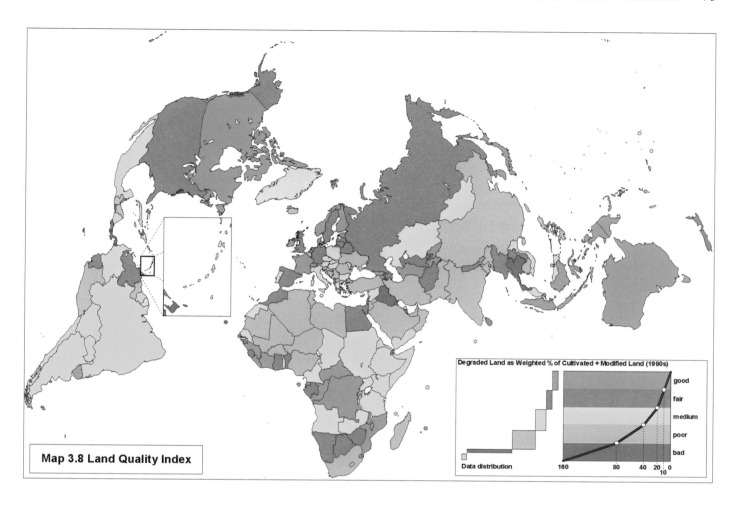

**Map 3.8 Land Quality Index**

Degraded Land as Weighted % of Cultivated + Modified Land (1990s)

good
fair
medium
poor
bad

Data distribution    160    80    40    20    0
                                          10

duction of unsuitable crops are also factors: in Thailand, cassava raised for export as livestock feed has reduced nutrient levels on many small farms.

Except for East and Southern Asia, the estimates of degradation come from a large-scale review (the Global Assessment of Soil Degradation), which may be inaccu-rate for countries smaller than 10 million hectares (the size of Iceland): too high for some small countries with bad scores (such as Costa Rica, Haiti, Panama, Cape Verde, and Albania) and too low for others with good scores (such as Bahamas, Liberia, Malawi, Denmark, Georgia, Israel, Lebanon, and Fiji).[12]

# Water

## Inland Waters Index (Map 3.9)

**What it is:** Lowest of river conversion, water quality, and water withdrawal scores (Figure 3.7).

**Objective:** All major aquatic ecosystems maintained or restored in large units with minimal loss of the communities and habitats within them and minimal stress from pollution and water uses.

**Country results:** 0 good (0%), 46 fair (26%), 42 medium (23%), 32 poor (18%), 52 bad (29%), 8 no data (4%).

*The sea could not be covered here for lack of adequate data.*

This index measures the three main threats to inland water ecosystems: river conversion, pollution, and water withdrawal. River conversion—the construction of dams, banks, channels, dikes, and embankments—destroys habitats or degrades them by disrupting flows. Pollution harms people and aquatic life: so much wastewater enters rivers each year that its adequate dilution takes two-thirds of the world's reliable runoff. Water withdrawal, by reducing flow volumes, can intensify the effects of conversion and pollution.[13]

Rivers and lakes are even less well monitored than

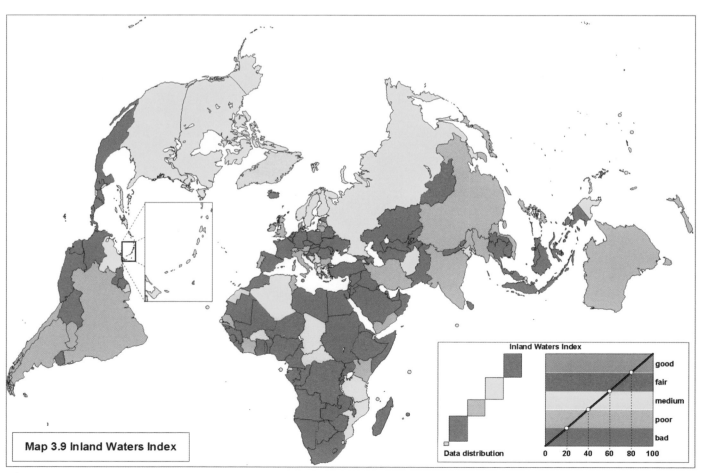

Map 3.9 Inland Waters Index

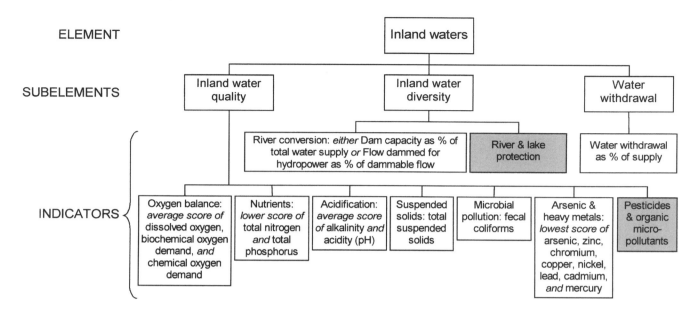

**Figure 3.7. Indicator chart for inland waters.** River and lake protection and pesticides and organic micropollutants (shaded boxes) are not covered due to lack of data.

land ecosystems but are probably in worse shape. Water quality is the weakest aspect, with data on a mere 72 countries, most of which do badly or poorly (Figure 3.8). No country with a fair index and only 11 with a medium index (Canada, Cuba, United States, Tanzania, Finland, Greece, Norway, Sweden, Russia, Bangladesh, and Papua New Guinea) could be rated on water quality. But it was the determining factor in two-thirds of the countries with a poor or bad index.

*For all data and scores, together with details of the indicators, performance criteria, and combining procedures, see Table 14 (water index, river conversion, water withdrawal), Table 15 (inland water quality: score, oxygen balance, nutrients, and acidification), and Table 16 (inland water quality: suspended solids, microbial pollution, and arsenic and heavy metals) in the Data section. The classification of drainage basins used to organize water quality data is in Appendix F.*

## Inland Water Quality

> ### Inland Water Quality (Map 3.10)
>
> **What it is:** Average score of drainage basins in each country, each basin score being the lowest score of six indicators: oxygen balance, nutrients, acidification, suspended solids, microbial pollution, and arsenic and heavy metals.
>
> **Country results:** 0 good (0%), 0 fair (0%), 12 medium (7%), 26 poor (14%), 34 bad (19%), 108 no data (60%).

Deliberately or inadvertently, societies still treat water bodies as the ultimate receptacles for most of their wastes. Consequently, water quality is neither good nor fair in any country. In most, it is bad or poor.

The water quality indicator includes six major pollution concerns. *Oxygen balance* is critical for aquatic life and the biogeochemical processes that reduce pollutant loads in rivers. *Nutrients* (nitrogen and phosphorus) from farmland and municipal waste pollute drinking water, contaminate fisheries, reduce diversity, and stimulate blooms of algae that consume oxygen when they rot. *Acidification* by sulfuric and nitric acids, originating largely from fossil fuel combustion, reduces aquatic productivity and diversity. *Sus-*

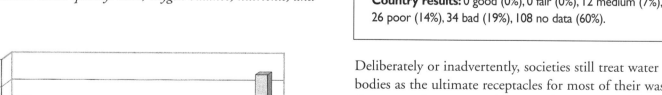

**Figure 3.8. Number of countries by performance band for water withdrawal, river conversion, and water quality.**

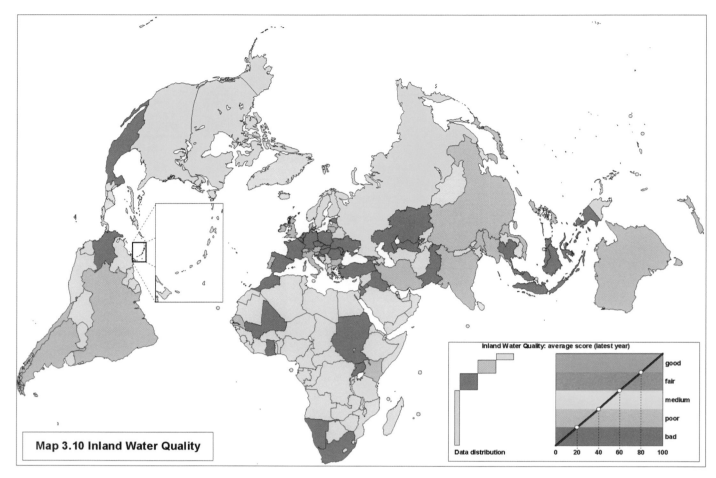

**Map 3.10 Inland Water Quality**

Inland Water Quality: average score (latest year)

Data distribution

good
fair
medium
poor
bad

0   20   40   60   80   100

*pended solids* (particles carried in the water column, mostly from erosion) can destroy fish habitat, limit light penetration, reduce reservoir life through sedimentation, and are the main carriers of pollutants that accumulate in the food chain. *Microbial pollutants* (human and animal feces) carry pathogens that cause 5 million human deaths a year worldwide. *Arsenic and heavy metals* (cadmium, chromium, copper, lead, mercury, nickel, and zinc) are highly toxic and can kill or deform people and aquatic life.[14]

To be healthy, rivers and lakes must be well oxygenated, sparingly nourished (not excessively enriched with nutrients), close to neutral in acidity, only lightly burdened with suspended solids and bacteria, and negligibly contaminated by poisons such as heavy metals. Failure to meet any of these criteria is cause for concern. Thus the River Kiso in Japan was rated on the basis of its poor score for fecal coliforms, despite medium to good scores for oxygen balance, nutrients, acidity, suspended solids, and heavy metals.

Nutrients are the leading cause of low water quality scores in all regions except Southern Asia (where fecal coliforms figure as frequently) and South America

(where heavy metals are the main culprit). The next most common cause of low scores is heavy metals in West Africa, Northern Europe, and Central and East

**Table 3.4. Countries reporting on most indicators for most basins.** Number of basins (total); number with at least one report on oxygen balance ($O_2$), nutrients (NP), acidification (pH), suspended solids (SS), fecal coliforms (FC), arsenic and heavy metals (HM); and mean percentage (%).

| Country | Total | $O_2$ | NP | pH | SS | FC | HM | % |
|---|---|---|---|---|---|---|---|---|
| Bangladesh | 3 | 3 | 2 | 3 | 3 | 3 | 0 | 78 |
| Hungary | 2 | 1 | 2 | 2 | 1 | 2 | 1 | 75 |
| Morocco | 4 | 3 | 3 | 3 | 2 | 3 | 3 | 71 |
| Japan | 10 | 7 | 7 | 7 | 7 | 7 | 7 | 70 |
| United Kingdom | 6 | 5 | 5 | 5 | 5 | 0 | 5 | 69 |
| Ghana | 3 | 2 | 2 | 2 | 2 | 2 | 2 | 67 |
| Belgium | 3 | 2 | 2 | 2 | 2 | 2 | 2 | 67 |
| Poland | 4 | 2 | 3 | 3 | 2 | 2 | 2 | 58 |
| Finland | 4 | 3 | 3 | 3 | 2 | 0 | 2 | 54 |
| Mexico | 12 | 7 | 7 | 7 | 7 | 7 | 2 | 51 |

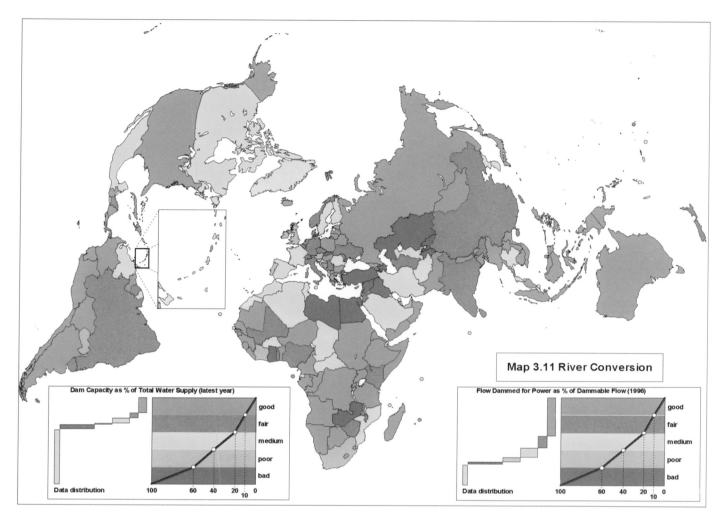

**Map 3.11 River Conversion**

Dam Capacity as % of Total Water Supply (latest year)

Data distribution    good fair medium poor bad

Flow Dammed for Power as % of Dammable Flow (1996)

Data distribution    good fair medium poor bad

Asia, and fecal coliforms in the Americas and Northern Africa.

A problem with measuring national water quality is how to translate data from an economical number of monitoring stations into a reading that is valid for the whole country. My approach was to divide the world into basins (Appendix F), defining a basin as an area of at least 100,000 square kilometers drained by a single river system or a group of smaller drainages. I chose a station at the mouth or downstream frontier of each country-basin (the part of a basin within one country) since a downstream point is fairly representative of the area that drains to that point. If possible, additional stations were chosen for large basins where conditions can change dramatically from one subbasin to another and for long coasts fed by many short rivers (as in Norway and New Zealand). Groundwater was treated as one basin. The number of country-basins so defined ranges from 32 in Russia to 2 in small islands and nations drained by one river system, such as Hungary (drained by the Danube).

No country reports on all indicators for all its basins. Table 3.4 lists the few with more than 50% coverage. They include only 2 (Bangladesh and Finland) of the 12 countries with medium scores. Bangladesh's omission of arsenic casts doubt on its score because high levels of arsenic have been found in its groundwater.[15] Inferior coverage reduces the reliability of other medium scores, notably those of Cuba, Tanzania, Albania, Norway, and Papua New Guinea, where coverage is especially sparse.

## River Conversion

### River Conversion (Map 3.11)

**What it is:** Dam capacity as percentage of total water supply or, if unavailable, flow dammed for hydropower as percentage of dammable flow.

**Country results:** 78 good (43%), 29 fair (16%), 24 medium (13%), 11 poor (6%), 12 bad (7%), 26 no data (14%).

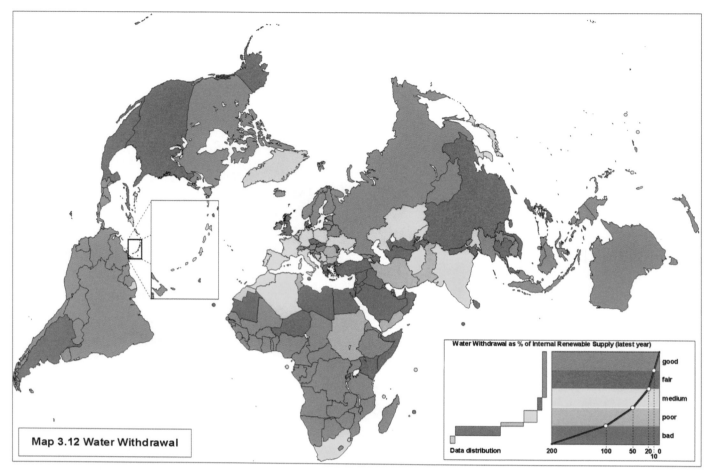

Map 3.12 Water Withdrawal

Water Withdrawal as % of Internal Renewable Supply (latest year)

good
fair
medium
poor
bad

Data distribution          200          100     50    20   0
                                                         10

Much as for the land, the proportions of rivers that are natural, modified, or built (dammed, embanked, or channeled) reveal a society's overall impact on aquatic ecosystems. Dams and dikes can harm species, habitats, fisheries, and people by drowning some areas, denying water to others, changing the timing and volume of flow, increasing the salinity of coastal waters, trapping sediments, and starving downstream wetlands of nutrients and silt.[16] As flow control increases, wild rivers are converted into a series of artificial lakes.

Dams affect less than 20% of river flow in more than half the countries surveyed. Countries where 40% or more of the flow is controlled by dams are largely in regions that are arid (Northern Africa, Southern Africa, West Asia) or densely populated (Europe).

Most countries in Africa and Asia were assessed on the basis of dam capacity as percentage of total water supply. Other countries were assessed on the basis of the hydropower indicator, which can result in underestimates since it omits dams used exclusively for water storage and irrigation.

Both indicators would give different results if they measured each country's basins and subbasins separately

rather than treating them as a single homogeneous entity. Zambia gets a bad score because its dam capacity is almost double its total water supply. But the dams are concentrated on the Kafue River, one of six major subbasins (four of the Zambezi, two of the Congo). The other subbasins are largely undammed, and the entire upper Zambezi above Victoria Falls is essentially wild. An average of the six subbasins would be more meaningful.[17]

## Water Withdrawal

### Water Withdrawal (Map 3.12)

**What it is:** One indicator, water withdrawal as a percentage of internal renewable supply. (Withdrawal is the total gross volume of ground and surface water extracted annually for domestic, agricultural, and industrial uses, including losses during transport. Internal renewable supply is the amount of water available each year from precipitation.)

**Country results:** 88 good (49%), 26 fair (14%), 24 medium (13%), 8 poor (4%), 19 bad (11%), 15 no data (8%).

Water withdrawal as a percentage of supply shows pressure on water bodies, the degree of water scarcity, and the likelihood of competition and conflict among different water uses and users. High rates of water withdrawal threaten aquatic species and ecosystems. Increases in water withdrawal, especially in dry lands and coastal areas, add to salinization and other water quality problems. In many countries, overuse of groundwater has led to land sinkage, salt water intrusion, or reduced river flow.

Water withdrawal ranges from 54,000% of internal renewable supply in Kuwait to close to 0% in eight countries. Countries with poor or bad scores are in dry regions of Africa and Asia or at the downstream end of rivers in Europe, where competition is high. A poor score means that the country uses at least half the internal renewable supply; a bad score that it uses all of it or more. The former situation puts great pressure on freshwater ecosystems. The latter is obviously unsustainable since water must be obtained from river flows of other countries (making the supply vulnerable to damming, pollution, and removal by upstream users), from fossil groundwater supplies (which are nonrenewable and eventually will disappear), or from desalinization.[18]

Good scores are good for the ecosystem but may be bad for the people. In Africa and Asia, they are often a sign that water use is too low to meet domestic and agricultural needs. Gabon is the only African country with a good score for water withdrawal that does not have a bad or poor score for food sufficiency or basic services (water and sanitation). And Brunei Darussalam and Malaysia are alone in Southern Asia to win on low water use without losing on basic needs.

# Air

## Air Index (Map 3.13)

**What it is:** Lower of global atmosphere index and local air quality index.

**Country results:** 0 good (0%), 82 fair (46%), 27 medium (15%), 42 poor (23%), 28 bad (16%); 1 no data (1%).

The global atmosphere provides essential conditions for the existence of life as we know it today. It regulates climate and the distribution of solar energy, maintaining the moisture and temperature regimes to which humans and other organisms are adapted. It lets in enough sunlight for plant production while blocking harmful solar and cosmic rays. It cleanses itself and prevents the ecosystem from suffocating in its own wastes by destroying the wastes or converting them to a form that the ecosystem can reuse. Rising levels of greenhouse gases, the weakening ozone shield, and reductions in the atmosphere's cleansing capacity are signs that human activities are disrupting the chemical balance on which these functions depend.[19]

Local air pollution damages human health, economic resources, and the ecosystem on a wide scale. Many cities

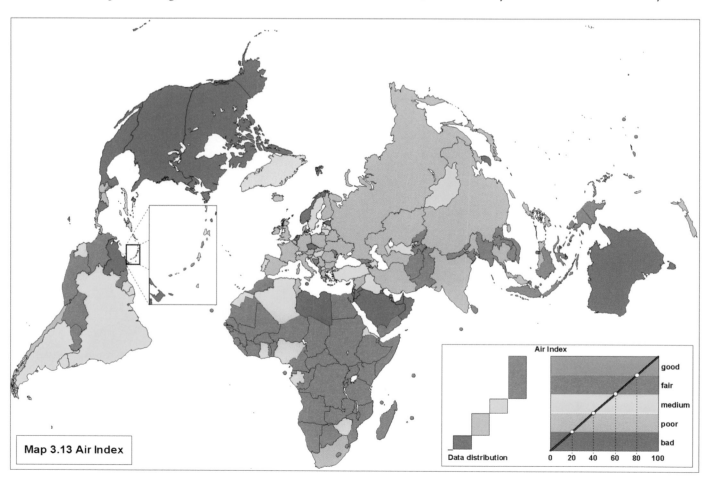

Map 3.13 Air Index

Air Index

good
fair
medium
poor
bad

Data distribution

0 20 40 60 80 100

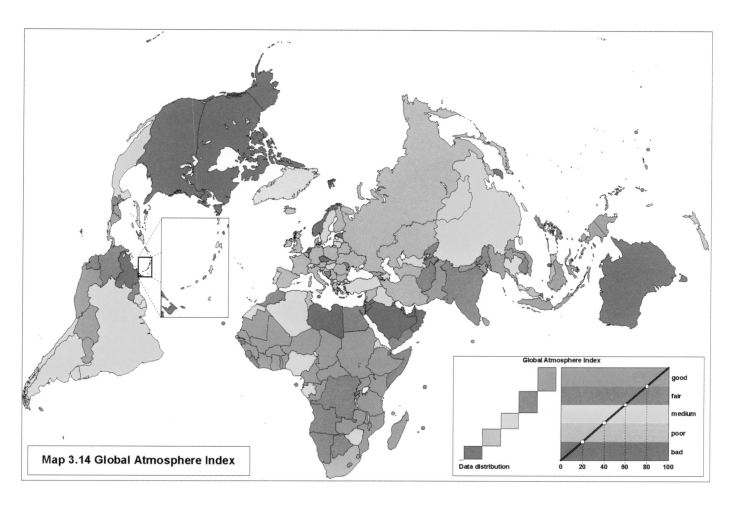

**Map 3.14 Global Atmosphere Index**

often choke in vehicle emissions. Smoke from burning vegetation is a major blight in rural areas that spreads into city air as well.

Because of a lack of data on local air quality, all countries with a fair air index and 15 with a medium index were assessed on global atmosphere alone (Argentina, Brazil, Cuba, Ecuador, Ghana, Croatia, Hungary, Lithuania, Portugal, Sweden, Switzerland, and Turkey were assessed on both). Among countries with a poor or bad index, 29 were rated only on global atmosphere, 41 on both elements. Among the latter, the weaker element is global atmosphere in South Africa, South Korea, and 25 industrialized nations; local air quality in 10 developing countries in the Americas and Asia. Panama, Italy, Bulgaria, and Kuwait have poor or bad scores for both.

*For all data and scores, together with details of the indicators, performance criteria, and combining procedures, see Table 17 (air index; global atmosphere) and Table 18 (local air quality) in the Data section.*

## Global Atmosphere

### Global Atmosphere Index (Map 3.14)

**What it is:** Lower of greenhouse gases score and ozone depleting substances score (Figure 3.9).

**Objective:** Elimination or sharp reduction of pollutants that disrupt the chemical balance of the atmosphere.

**Country results:** 46 good (26%), 43 fair (24%), 30 medium (17%), 34 poor (19%), 26 bad (14%), 1 no data (1%).

Greenhouse gases are so called because they allow the sun's rays to reach the Earth but prevent much of the heat from radiating away. The effects of rising concentrations of these gases are likely to include changes in rainfall patterns and in the timing and length of seasons, more frequent and severe storms, flooding of low-lying islands and coastal areas, the spread of insect-borne diseases, major disruptions to food supplies, and global warming. Global annual temperatures increased between 1910 and

**Map 3.15 Greenhouse Gases**

**Figure 3.9. Indicator chart for global atmosphere.**

1940 and stabilized until 1980. From then on they have risen rapidly, bringing the 11 warmest years since 1860.[20]

Ozone in the stratosphere filters out ultraviolet-B (UVB) rays from the sun. UVB rays reduce the productivity of the seas, damage crops and other plants, suppress human immunity to disease, and cause eye damage and skin cancer. Globally, in each decade since 1979, the stratospheric ozone layer has become 4–6% thinner in middle latitudes and 10–12% thinner in higher latitudes.[21]

Countries with a good index do well on both indicators. Those with a fair index include 24 (over half in Africa) rated on only one of the indicators. Among countries with a poor or bad index, carbon dioxide was the determining factor in

27, ozone depletion in 11, and 21 had poor or bad scores for both (Kazakhstan was not assessed on ozone depletion).

## Greenhouse Gases

### Greenhouse Gases (Map 3.15)

**What it is:** One indicator, carbon dioxide emissions per person.

**Country results:** 79 good (44%), 20 fair (11%), 29 medium (16%), 34 poor (19%), 15 bad (8%), 3 no data (2%).

This indicator is limited to carbon dioxide ($CO_2$) because it is the most important greenhouse gas, accounting for 64% of the increased greenhouse effect (methane accounts for 19%, nitrous oxide 6%, and halocarbons 11%). The chief human sources of $CO_2$ are burning of fossil fuels (coal, oil, and gas), cement manufacture, gas flaring, burning of wood and vegetation, and forest loss.[22]

The scientific consensus is that dangerous climate change will probably occur if the concentration of $CO_2$ in

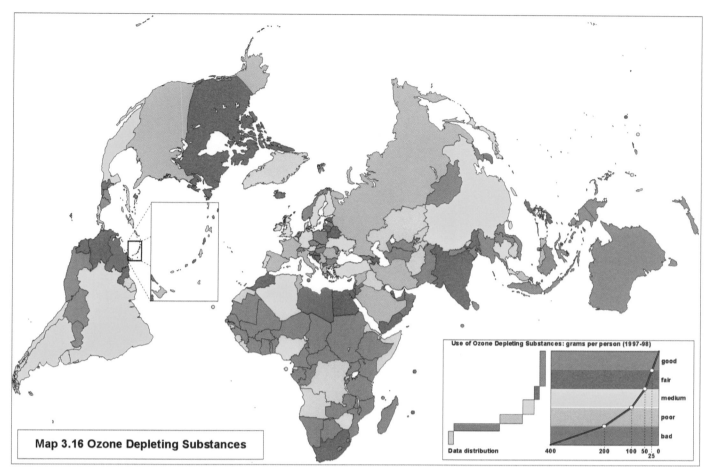

**Map 3.16 Ozone Depleting Substances**

the atmosphere rises to more than twice the preindustrial level. To stay below this level, global emissions would have to be cut from 6.6 billion metric tons of carbon in 1997 to between 3.7 and 4.9 billion metric tons. If the intermediate amount of 4.3 billion were shared equally by the world population of 10.8 billion projected for 2050 (United Nations medium variant projection), each person would have an emissions allowance of just under 400 kilograms.[23]

Countries with a good score achieve this target—but as a side effect of a low standard of living: only Botswana, Costa Rica, and St Lucia have a gross domestic product (GDP) above $5,000 per person; and only 14 have a medium HWI, the rest being poor or bad. Countries with a fair score emit up to twice the target amount and tend to be better off. Nine have medium incomes (GDP per person of $5,100–$10,000), and 11 low incomes ($5,000 or less). Eleven have a medium HWI; 8 a poor or bad HWI. Uniquely, Uruguay has both a fair score for $CO_2$ emissions and a fair HWI. At the other end of the spectrum, all countries with incomes above $20,000 have poor or bad

scores for $CO_2$ (except Switzerland), as do all countries with a fair HWI except for Uruguay, Barbados, Hungary, Latvia, Malta, Portugal, Sweden, and Switzerland.

Until the links between economic performance, transport, and fossil fuel consumption can be broken, countries will continue to balk at limiting—let alone substantially cutting—greenhouse gas emissions.

## Ozone Depleting Substances

### Ozone Depleting Substances (Map 3.16)

**What it is:** One indicator, use of ozone depleting substances per person (use is production or consumption, whichever is higher).

**Country results:** 67 good (37%), 27 fair (15%), 28 medium (16%), 17 poor (9%), 15 bad (8%), 26 no data (14%).

The protective stratospheric ozone shield is being weakened by gases known as ozone depleting substances (ODSs), such as chlorofluorocarbons (CFCs). They are

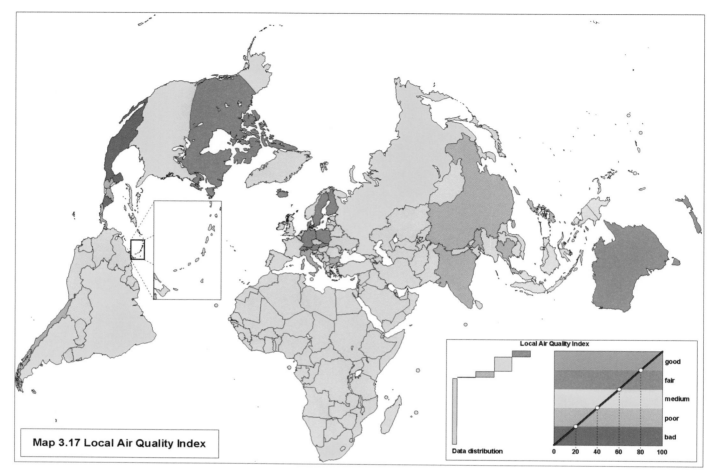

Map 3.17 Local Air Quality Index

produced exclusively by people for use in air conditioners, refrigerators, fire extinguishers, solvents, and plastic foams and as aerosol propellants.[24]

Most countries have agreed to phase out and eventually end ODS emissions. However, even if international targets are met, the ozone shield will take more than a century to recover. CFCs are likely to persist in the atmosphere for up to 50 years after emissions cease. Since the late 1980s, ODS consumption has dropped sharply in all industrialized countries and in Argentina, Brazil, Colombia, Egypt, South Africa, and Singapore. But it continues to rise in many developing countries, such as Venezuela, Nigeria, and India. In addition, phaseouts of production by the United States and Europe are being partly offset by illegal imports.

Since the aim is to eliminate use of ODSs, the best performance is 0 grams per person. Countries with a good score are within striking distance of this target. While most in this group are poor, they include a number with midrange incomes (largely in Eastern Europe) and four with high incomes (Norway, Switzerland, Australia, and New Zealand).

All countries were rated on consumption, except for those where production exceeds consumption (Mexico,

United States, Venezuela, France, Greece, Italy, Netherlands, Spain, United Kingdom, Russia, China, India, Israel, and Japan). These countries were rated on production because consumption data understate their reliance on ODSs and also ignore the problem of illegal trade. All have a poor or bad score except for India (fair) and Mexico, United Kingdom, China, and Japan (medium). Poor and bad scores among nonproducing countries are concentrated in West Asia.[25]

## Local Air Quality

### Local Air Quality Index (Map 3.17)

**What it is:** Average score of cities in each country, each city score being the lowest score of six indicators—sulfur dioxide, nitrogen dioxide, ground-level ozone, carbon monoxide, particulates (tiny solid or liquid particles that damage health and reduce visibility), and lead (Figure 3.10).

**Objective:** Minimal air pollution.

**Country results:** 0 good (0%), 12 fair (7%), 27 medium (15%), 12 poor (7%), 2 bad (1%), 127 no data (71%).

ELEMENT

Figure 3.10. Indicator chart for local air quality.

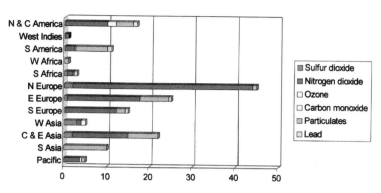

Figure 3.11. Number of cities covered in each region, and the determining pollutant for their air quality scores.

All six pollutants included in the local air quality index are hazards to health. Sulfur dioxide, nitrogen dioxide, and ozone also damage vegetation and aquatic life. Of the 160 cities analyzed, nitrogen dioxide determined the air quality score of 103 (64%) and particulates of 40 (25%). The former is the dominant pollutant in five of the seven regions where at least 10 cities were assessed, the latter in the other two regions—South America and Southern Asia (Figure 3.11). The main source of these contaminants is road transport, which needs to be better regulated everywhere.

The fair scores should be treated cautiously since none reflects measurement of all six pollutants in a representative sample of cities.[26]

# Species and Genes

## Species and Genes Index (Map 3.18)

**What it is:** Weighted average [weights in brackets] of wild diversity index [2] and domesticated diversity index [1].

**Country results:** 0 good (0%), 19 fair (11%), 89 medium (49%), 60 poor (33%), 12 bad (7%).

*Wild* diversity is the linchpin of natural and modified ecosystems, the basis of their resilience and adaptability. Wild species have intrinsic worth and are the source of all biological wealth, supplying food, raw materials, medicines, recreation, and a store of other goods and services worth many billions of dollars per year. Although it is natural for species to come and go, the background (or natural) rate of extinction is extremely low (less than 0.01% per century). The rising number of plant and animal species threatened with extinction foretells an irreparable and unprecedented loss. Wild species are more threatened today than since the extinction of the dinosaurs 65 million years ago.[27]

*Domesticated* diversity is the key to sustainable use of

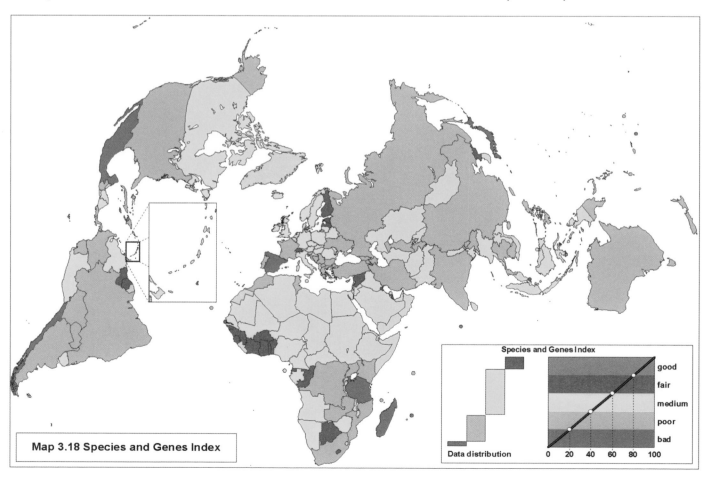

Map 3.18 Species and Genes Index

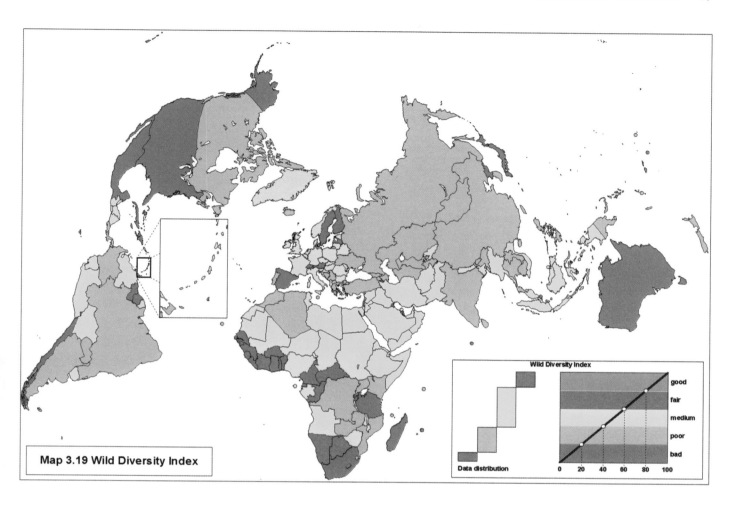

Map 3.19 Wild Diversity Index

modified and cultivated ecosystems. Many heirloom crops and ancient breeds represent centuries of selection to harmonize cultural preferences with ecosystem capacities. Locally adapted strains of livestock produce food, fiber, and income from places that are too cold, dry, wet, or barren to grow crops. The genetic material within crop varieties, livestock breeds, and domesticated strains of microorganisms provides essential traits for improving food and fiber production and developing biotechnologies. These traits—including yield, disease resistance, hardiness, marketability, and culturally desirable qualities such as flavor and color—are constantly in demand to cope with changing markets and environmental conditions.

Since the extinction of an entire species is more drastic than the loss of a breed or variety, wild diversity was given more weight than domesticated diversity. As a result, the species and genes index stays in the same performance band as the wild diversity rating in all but 36 countries. In 19 (such as Turkmenistan), high scores for domesticated diversity raise the index; in the other 17

(such as Austria), domesticated diversity is much more at risk than wild diversity and lowers the index.

*For all data and scores, together with details of the indicators, performance criteria, and combining procedures, see Table 19 (species and genes index, wild species rank, wild plant species), Table 20 (wild animal species, domesticated diversity), and Table 21 (domesticated diversity continued) in the Data section.*

## Wild Diversity

### Wild Diversity Index (Map 3.19)

**What it is:** Average of wild plant species score and wild animal species score (Figure 3.12).

**Objective:** Maintenance of all native wild species and reduction of extinctions to background rates.

**Country results:** 0 good (0%), 28 fair (16%), 77 medium (43%), 55 poor (31%), 20 bad (11%).

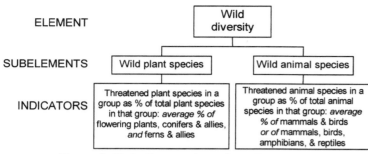

**Figure 3.12. Indicator chart for wild diversity.**

Most countries with a fair wild diversity index are modestly endowed with plant and animal species. Only four—Guyana, Suriname, Cameroon, and Côte d'Ivoire—rank among the top 45 nations in numbers of species. By contrast, 23 countries with a poor or bad index are in the top 45, including China, Mexico, Australia, and Madagascar.[28]

A species is threatened with extinction when it is reduced to a few small populations or restricted to such a small area that it could be wiped out by habitat change, disease outbreak, fire, pollution accident, building development, series of bad weather years, or other catastrophe. The aim is to maintain viable populations of all wild species, but since it is impossible to identify all species, let alone track what is happening to them, the indicators focus on groups whose numbers have been estimated and whose status is monitored.

Assessing species diversity maintenance on the basis of the percentage of threatened species per class (or other large group) accomplishes two things. First, it makes the numbers more meaningful: knowing that Rwanda and Mauritius both have nine threatened bird species says little about the performance of these countries without the information that Rwanda is home to 513 breeding bird species and Mauritius to 27. Second, it recognizes that

**Table 3.5. The species hierarchy.** Genetic loss increases up the hierarchy.

Kingdom (e.g., Animals [Animalia])
 Phylum (e.g., chordates [Chordata])
  Class (e.g., mammals [Mammalia])
   Order (e.g., even-toed ungulates [Artiodactyla])
    Family (e.g., antelope, buffalos, cattle, goats, and sheep [Bovidae])
     Genus (e.g., banteng, cattle, gaur, kouprey, yak [*Bos*])
      Species (e.g., cattle [*Bos primigenius*])
       Subspecies, type (e.g., humpless cattle)
        Breed group (e.g., Brown Swiss group)
         Breed (e.g., Braunvieh, Brune des Alpes, Rendena)

the higher an extinction is in the species hierarchy (Table 3.5), the more serious the genetic loss. Knowing only that 9% of Haiti's mammals, birds, reptiles, and amphibians are threatened masks the most alarming aspect: that all of its mammals are threatened, boding the disappearance of an entire class.

Habitat destruction is the main threat to species, so there ought to be a link between the land diversity index (LDI), which measures how much land is converted, natural, or protected, and the wild diversity index (WDI). Yet in only 57 countries (32%) do performances in the two indices fall in the same band: 4 fair (Suriname, Botswana, Central African Republic, and Namibia), 31 medium, 20 poor, and 2 bad (Haiti and Tonga).

In 40 countries (22%), the LDI and WDI differ by as much as two performance bands, with the WDI lower in 13 and higher in 27. Countries where the WDI is markedly lower tend to be medium-sized to large: all except Bhutan and Dominican Republic have a land area of more than 10 million hectares. The mismatch between the WDI and LDI may be due to the uneven occurrence of species: some parts of a country may have many species and others few. The species-rich habitats may be small or rare, whereas large or common habitats may be species-poor. In Chile, which has the most extreme spread between a bad WDI of 16 and a fair LDI of 67, the greatest number of species is concentrated in just 2 of the country's 12 ecoregions: the winter rain forests and the matorral (Mediterranean climate zone scrub). These also happen to be the most modified and least protected ecoregions. In Algeria (with a poor WDI of 34 and a fair LDI of 67), 83% of the natural land and 12% of the protected area is species-poor desert. The richest nondesert remnants are precisely the areas at greatest risk of conversion or modification. Thus the LDI can be an effective predictor of threats to species only if it is differentiated by ecoregion or major habitat, which at present it is not.[29]

Most (70%) of the countries where the WDI is much higher than the LDI are smaller than 10 million hectares. In the smallest, Barbados (with a fair WDI of 66 and a bad LDI of 17), 58% of the land area has been converted to settlements and cultivation, only 9% is natural or seminatural, and a mere 40 hectares is protected. Its most endangered animal group is reptiles, with two species threatened out of nine. But none of its mammal, breeding bird, or amphibian

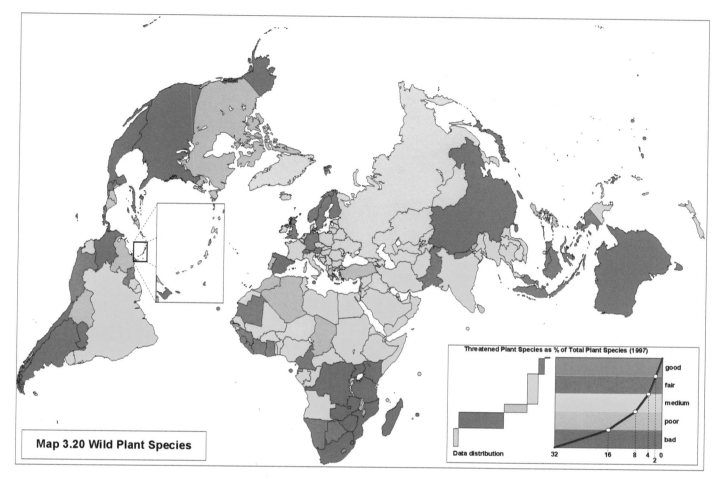

**Map 3.20 Wild Plant Species**

Threatened Plant Species as % of Total Plant Species (1997)

good
fair
medium
poor
bad

Data distribution

32    16    8  4  2  0

---

species is threatened, and only 2 (0.4%) of the 542 flowering plant species are at risk. One explanation may be that the main impact of land conversion and modification was in the past, and mostly common and resilient species remain. Another may be that concentrations of species are as easy to maintain as they are to lose.

## Wild Plant Species

---

### Wild Plant Species (Map 3.20)

**What it is:** Score of threatened plant species in a group as percentage of total species in that group (average percentage of three groups: flowering plants, gymnosperms [conifers, cycads, gnetophytes], and ferns and allies).

**Country results:** 2 good (1%), 31 fair (17%), 61 medium (34%), 18 poor (10%), 32 bad (18%), 36 no data (20%).

---

The plant species results are strongly influenced by the distribution of gymnosperms. Although they never make up more than 2% of the plant species in a country, the

percentage of gymnosperms that is threatened is generally high—up to 100%—compared with flowering plants (up to 51%) and ferns (up to 28%). High percentages (8% or above) of gymnosperms are threatened in 58 of the 64 countries for which there are data, but few countries have high percentages of threatened flowering plants or ferns (Figure 3.13). Among countries with a poor or bad score

**Figure 3.13. Number of countries with various percentages of threatened flowering plants, gymnosperms, and ferns and allies.**

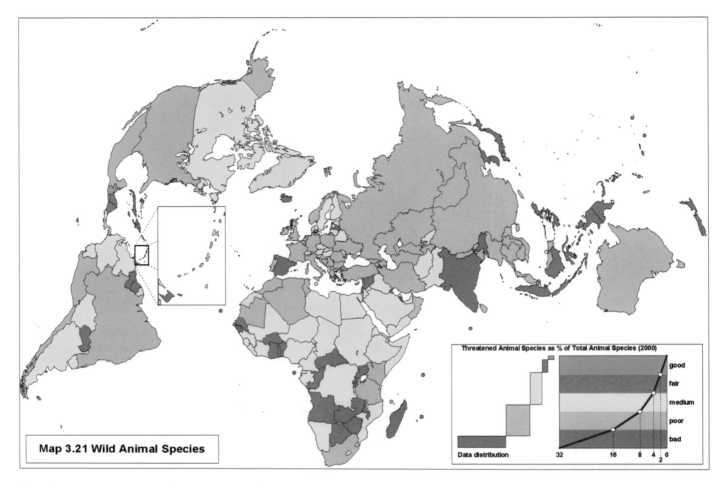

**Map 3.21 Wild Animal Species**

for plants, Canada, United States, Portugal, Spain, Japan, and Australia have high proportions of threatened species in all three groups. The rest have high percentages of threatened gymnosperms, except for Burkina Faso, Guinea–Bissau, Niger, and Mauritius, which lack these species, and Chad, Turkey, and Sri Lanka, which were not assessed on them.

The definition of a good percentage of threatened species (below 2%) is based on the estimated natural rate of extinction of less than 0.01% per century.

Coverage is fairly complete for flowering plants but much less for gymnosperms and ferns (Figure 3.13). Countries with no information on the status of gymnosperms, including 16 with a fair score and 47 with a medium score, may look better than they are. In fact, missing data probably distort the results of many more. A mere 46 countries cover all their plant groups, none of them in Northern Africa, Northern Europe, or West Asia and just one each in West Africa and Southern Asia. The only regions where coverage is complete for more than a third of the countries are North and Central America (80%), South America

(67%), Pacific (62%), Southern Africa (54%), and West Indies (46%). Significantly, these regions have the highest percentages of countries with bad or poor scores: 100%, 50%, 38%, 62%, and 46%, respectively.[30]

## Wild Animal Species

### Wild Animal Species (Map 3.21)

**What it is:** Score of threatened animal species in a group as percentage of total species in that group (average percentage of either two groups [mammals and birds] or four [mammals, birds, reptiles, and amphibians]).

**Country results:** 3 good (2%), 22 fair (12%), 54 medium (30%), 73 poor (41%), 28 bad (16%).

Mammal and bird data are more reliable than the data on reptiles and amphibians, and ideally the indicator would be based on these two classes alone. However, information on reptiles and amphibians is no worse than on plants, and excluding them would give misleadingly high

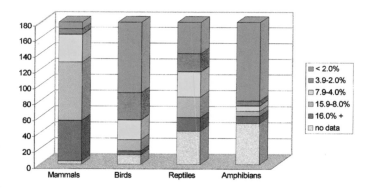

**Figure 3.14. Number of countries with various percentages of threatened mammals, birds, reptiles, and amphibians.**

scores to several countries. For example, Antigua and Barbuda and St Kitts and Nevis have no threatened mammals and only one threatened bird (2.7% and 3.1%, respectively, of their native bird species), but a third of their reptiles are threatened. Scores are based on mammals and birds alone in 160 countries, and on the four classes in 20 (10 in the Americas, 4 in Asia, 4 in Europe, and 2 in Africa).

High percentages (8% or above) of mammals are threatened in 107 countries, many more than the other classes (Figure 3.14). The mammals exclude ocean-dwelling whales and dolphins because they cannot be assigned to particular countries. The birds include only breeding species because of widely differing standards in recording vagrants, accidentals, and irregular migrants.

All countries with a bad score are islands, reflecting a high incidence of endemic species (species found nowhere else). The only islands with a fair score are Trinidad and Tobago.[31]

## Domesticated Diversity

### Domesticated Diversity Index (Map 3.22)

**What it is:** Average score of two indicators—number of not-at-risk breeds per million head of a species and ratio of threatened breeds to not-at-risk breeds of a species—based on three livestock species (Figure 3.15).

**Objective:** Maintenance of as much as possible of the heritage of livestock breeds.

**Country results:** 2 good (1%), 22 fair (12%), 78 medium (43%), 36 poor (20%), 13 bad (7%), 29 no data (16%).

Good and fair scores mean that domesticated animal stocks consist of a variety of different breeds, few of which are at risk of extinction. Poor and bad scores indicate that livestock diversity is low, many breeds are threatened, or both. As far as possible, only established breeds have been counted, excluding recent imports, experimental lines, and breeds under development. Nations were rated on the basis of up to three livestock species: the most numerous—cattle and kin (Bali cattle, mithun, yak) in 49 countries, sheep in 49, pig in 31, goat in 22—and the next most numerous or most fully assessed of these species plus water buffalo, Bactrian camel, dromedary, ass, horse, llama, and alpaca. Few countries have assessed their livestock species comprehensively. With better knowledge, they may prove to be more diverse and to have higher or lower proportions of threatened breeds.[32]

The two nations with a good score are Togo and the Republic of Congo. The latter has few breeds in total but many in relation to its livestock numbers: one breed per 285,000 goats (3.5 per million), one per 115,000 sheep (8.7 per million), and two per 75,000 head of cattle (26.7 per million). None is threatened, giving it an average of 13 not-at-risk breeds per million head, the highest of all countries rated on three species.

The lowest diversity is 0.1 breeds per million head, found in Argentina, Brazil, Mexico, Paraguay, Madagascar, and Saudi Arabia. Brazil's not-at-risk breeds are extremely few in relation to its vast stocks: 13 per 163 million cattle, 1 per 27 million pigs, and 3 per 18 million sheep. Four breeds of cattle, seven of pigs, and two of sheep are threatened. They include Crioulo Lageano cattle (noted for being good mothers) and the Canastrão pig of Rio de Janeiro and Minas Gerais, a fat Celtic type that once contributed to feijoada and dobradinha, pork dishes emblematic of those states.[33]

The most common threat to breeds is population decline, due to replacement by more popular types, industrialization of farming, abandonment of marginal lands, and war. The Holstein–Friesian, which accounts for more than a third of the world's dairy cows, has ousted many low-maintenance local breeds solely because of its unrivalled ability to fill up milk buckets. Intensive production systems leave free-range virtuosos out in the cold. As a result, formerly abundant breeds are now rare, such as the British Gloucester Old Spot, a pig capable of yielding excellent meat from foraging on windfall apples and being served low-cost feed such as whey. Sheep and

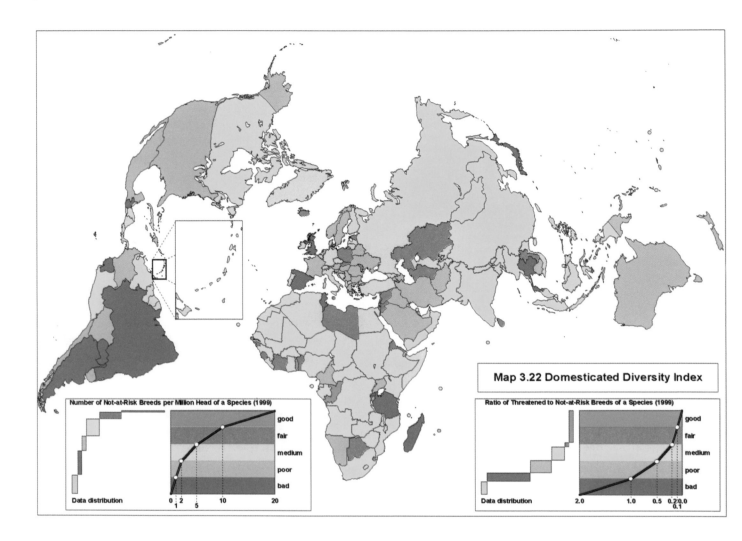

cattle breeds adapted to mountains, marshes, and semi-desert have been abandoned as the people who raised them died out or fled to the cities. Wars slaughter livestock as well as people and are decimating African cattle breeds such as the Serere of Uganda and the Bashi of the Democratic Republic of Congo.[34]

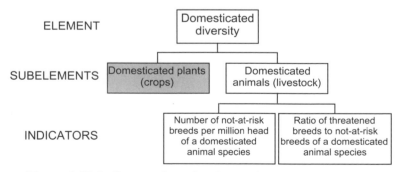

**Figure 3.15. Indicator chart for domesticated diversity.**
Crops (shaded box) are not covered due to lack of data.

The other major threats are deliberate crossbreeding and accidental interbreeding, which swamp a breed with the genes of another, obliterating its distinctive characteristics. They account for 30% of the risk to Europe's threatened cattle and horses and contribute to the endangerment of 32 of Africa's 43 threatened cattle breeds. Namibia's Damara cattle breed has become less Damara-like, losing its beautifully arched and twisted horns; and the Manjaca cattle breed of Guinea–Bissau has been entirely absorbed by the more abundant N'dama. Bolivia's Criollo goat has so much exotic blood that it is no longer recognizable as Criollo. Pakistan's sheep and goat diversity is being eroded as local breeds mate and merge with the flocks of refugees from Afghanistan.[35]

If breeds disappear, so will their unique combinations of genes. The genes provide both the adaptations necessary for production in diverse environments and the raw material required to meet the constant and changing demands of breeding programs. For example, China's highly prolific Taihu breeds are being used by the pork industry to increase the number of young produced by European pigs. The technology does not exist today, nor will it in the foreseeable future, to create these evolving genetic packages artificially.[36]

Local breeds are part of a country's cultural heritage. Navajo Churro sheep are integral to Navajo life in the arid southwestern United States, providing the people with milk, meat, and a two-textured, naturally colored wool esteemed by tribal rug and blanket weavers. Several of Tanzania's zebu cattle breeds are named for the tribes that raise them and the colors they favor: Iringa Red, Mkalama Dun, Singida White, and Ugogo Grey (the first three are threatened). Local breeds are also well attuned to the vagaries of their environments, and despite their often limited production potential they provide more secure sources of food and income than do nonlocal breeds.[37]

It is possible to reap the benefits of breeding without losing breeds, conserving domesticated diversity while increasing agricultural productivity. Kenya raises both indigenous Boran cattle and Improved Boran, upgraded by selection rather than with exotic blood. Denmark continues to use crossbreeding to better its Danish Red and Danish Friesian dairy cattle but also maintains purebred lines to preserve the traditional types. Financial incentives to raise local breeds can be boosted by linking the breeds to value-added products such as premium cheeses and meats. In Spain, for example, Ibérica pigs are the source of prestigious dried hams. In Italy, Pecorino Sardo cheese is produced specifically from the milk of Sarda sheep and Fontina cheese from the milk of three Valdostana cattle breeds.[38]

# Resource Use

All people stress the ecosystem by producing and consuming goods and services. The consumption process uses materials throughout and is fueled by energy: the more energy and materials consumed, the heavier the pressure on the environment. Resource sectors (primarily agriculture, fisheries, timber, mining, oil, and gas) are a more specific source of pressure: the greater their demands on arable land, the seas, inland waters, forests, and mineral deposits, the higher the risk of their depleting resources, degrading habitats, and threatening species.

The resource use index reflects energy consumption (materials use could not be assessed) more than the performance of resource sectors. Countries with a good index have a good score for energy and a good or fair score for resource sectors. Of those with a fair index, all

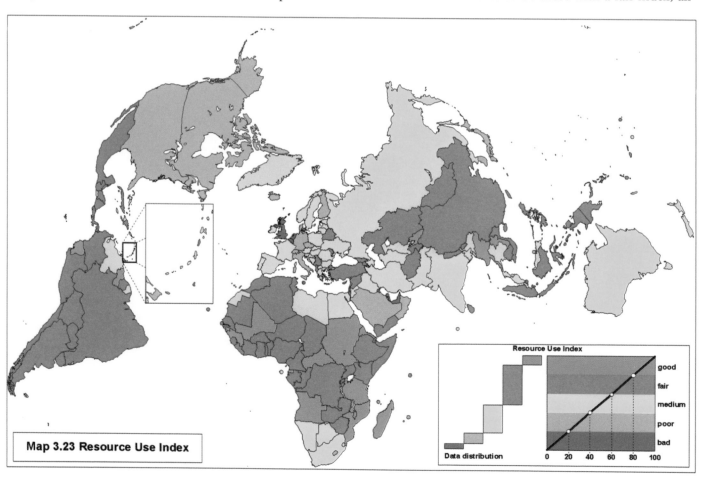

Map 3.23 Resource Use Index

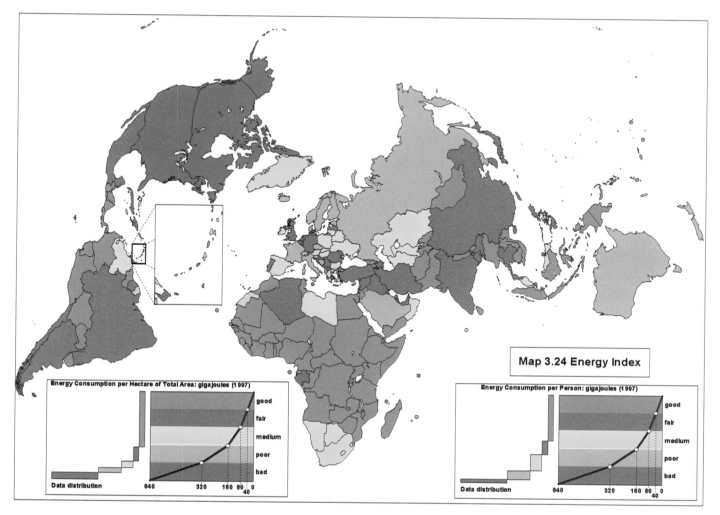

Map 3.24 Energy Index

except Kazakhstan have a good or fair energy score, but their scores for resource sectors range from fair (28 countries) through medium (41) to poor (Djibouti, Gambia, Niger, Nigeria, Rwanda, Somalia, and Yemen). Among nations with a poor or bad index, all except Lesotho, Cyprus, and Oman have a poor or bad energy score.

The pressures on the ecosystem summed in the resource use index are a direct result of the material benefits measured by the wealth index (Map 2.7). Most countries that do well in one do poorly in the other: of the 94 nations with a good or fair resource use index, 77 have a poor or bad wealth index and 17 a medium wealth index. Of the 37 with a good or fair wealth index, the resource use index is bad or poor in 24, medium in 13.

*For all data and scores, together with details of the indicators, performance criteria, and combining procedures, see Table 22 (resource use index, energy, timber), Table 23*

*(agriculture, fish and seafood self-reliance), and Table 24 (fisheries) in the Data section.*

## Energy and Materials

### Energy Index (Map 3.24)

**What it is:** Lower score of annual energy consumption per hectare of total area and annual energy consumption per person (Figure 3.16).

**Objective:** Energy consumption within the carrying capacity of the ecosystem.

**Country results:** 81 good (45%), 32 fair (18%), 30 medium (17%), 19 poor (11%), 18 bad (10%).

Energy consumption includes commercial energy (solid fuels, liquid fuels, gases, and electricity) and traditional fuels such as fuelwood, charcoal, and animal and plant waste. Although energy use is undoubtedly a source of

**Figure 3.16. Indicator chart for energy and materials.**
Materials (shaded box) are not covered due to lack of data on total material requirement and waste generation.

environmental pressure (because of its central role in the consumption of all goods and services), no one knows how much pressure can be attributed to it alone. Hence it is not known what level of use might be sustainable or even what would be the most appropriate measure of pressure from energy use. Energy consumption per hectare of total area is valid if the effects of a country's energy use are absorbed largely by the ecosystems within its borders. Energy consumption per person is more defensible if national energy use has a global impact. Since either may be the case, both indicators are employed here.

All countries with a good index use low amounts of energy, however measured. Among those with a fair index, 13 do better per hectare than per person, 8 the reverse, and 11 have fair scores for both. Only 13 of the medium, poor, and bad scorers are in the same performance band for both indicators. Canada has the biggest discrepancy: 10 gigajoules (GJ) per hectare (score of 95), 344 GJ per person (score of 18).

Energy is essential for human wellbeing, but how much is enough? Among countries with a good or fair

Human Wellbeing Index, consumption per hectare ranges from 6 GJ (Australia) to 16,726 GJ (Singapore), and consumption per person from 36 GJ (Uruguay) to 350 GJ (United States). Austria, France, Hungary, Portugal, Slovakia, and Slovenia have roughly the same levels of consumption per hectare and per person. The rest show wide differences between the two, with use per person higher in large countries and use per hectare higher in small or densely populated nations.

Portugal has the best combination of high human wellbeing (HWI of 72) and moderate energy use, both per hectare (75 GJ) and per person (70 GJ). As such it provides the benchmark for the fair performance band. Ireland, Spain, and Cyprus have similar levels of achievement: HWIs of 76, 73, and 67, respectively; fair scores for energy use per hectare; and medium scores for energy use per person.[39]

## Resource Sectors

---

**Resource Sectors Index (Map 3.25)**

**What it is:** Average of agriculture, fisheries, and timber scores (Figure 3.17).

**Objective:** Resource production within the carrying capacity of the ecosystem.

**Country results:** 3 good (2%), 53 fair (29%), 76 medium (42%), 36 poor (20%), 12 bad (7%).

---

Sustainable resource production means that crops, livestock, fish, and timber are produced in ways that limit ecosystem conversion and modification, maintain the resources on which production depends (soil, fish stocks, and forests), and have low impacts on the rest of the

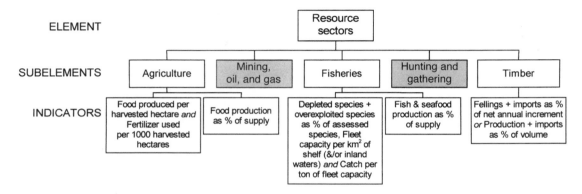

**Figure 3.17. Indicator chart for resource sectors.** Mining, oil, and gas and hunting and gathering (shaded boxes) are not covered due to lack of suitable indicators.

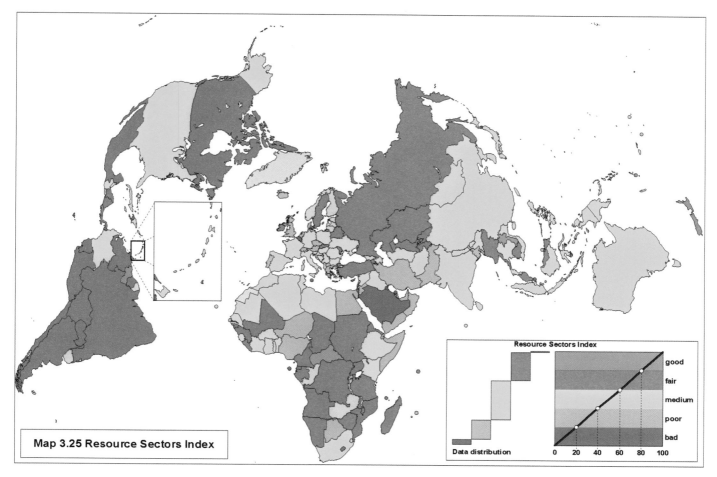

Map 3.25 Resource Sectors Index

ecosystem. Some of these factors are measured by other ecosystem indices, such as the land diversity index, the land quality index, and the domesticated diversity index. The resource sectors index should be interpreted in conjunction with them.

The three resource sectors tend to counterbalance each other. Only the countries with a good index (Guyana, Central African Republic, and Lao), and eight countries with a fair index (Costa Rica, Ecuador, Angola, Guinea, Madagascar, Malawi, Mozambique, and Tanzania) have high scores for all sectors. Only three countries with a poor index (St Lucia, Mauritius, and United Kingdom) and five with a bad index (Barbados, Lesotho, Malta, Kuwait, and Saudi Arabia) have low scores for all sectors.

Medium scores predominate in agriculture, poor and bad scores in fisheries, and good and fair scores in the timber sector (Figure 3.18). The fisheries results are not unexpected because excessively large and powerful fleets are chasing after declining stocks of fish. However, the absence of good performance in agriculture is surprising, and the timber picture looks too good to be true. Yet

both portrayals may fairly reflect what the indicators are intended to measure. The agriculture indicators measure productivity and self-reliance, which tend to offset each other because many of the most self-reliant countries are only moderately productive. The timber indicator measures the pressure of logging on wood supply, not its impact on the diversity and quality of forests or the loss of forests to agriculture and settlement (included in the land diversity index).

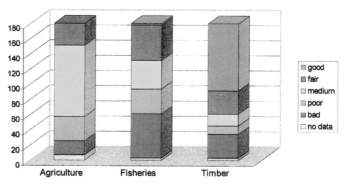

**Figure 3.18. Number of countries by performance band for agriculture, fisheries, and timber.**

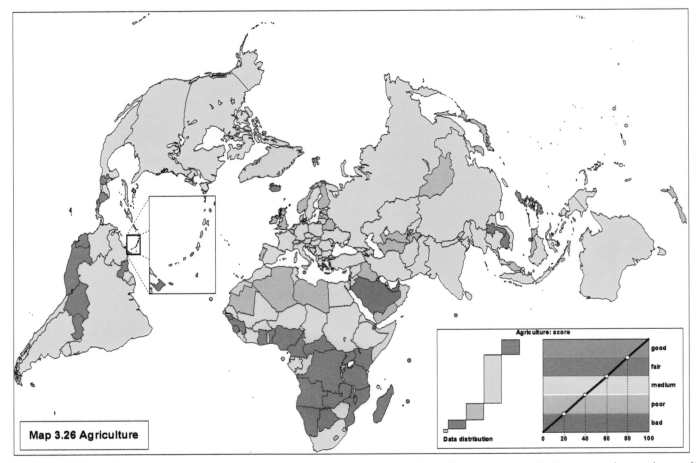

Map 3.26 Agriculture

## Agriculture

> ### Agriculture (Map 3.26)
>
> **What it is:** Lower of agricultural productivity score and agricultural self-reliance score. Agricultural productivity (not shown as a separate map) is the average score of food produced per harvested hectare and fertilizer used per 1,000 harvested hectares. Agricultural self-reliance (Map 3.27) is one indicator, food production as percentage of supply.
>
> **Country results:** 0 good (0%), 29 fair (16%), 94 medium (52%), 32 poor (18%), 18 bad (10%), 7 no data (4%).

High productivity per unit of land helps to prevent agriculture from putting natural and seminatural habitats to the plow. Land productivity can be increased by more efficient techniques, better control of pests and diseases, and the addition of fertilizer. High productivity per unit of fertilizer curbs excessive reliance on chemical inputs, which can pollute water and hurt the health of humans and other species.

High productivity is key to agricultural self-reliance, which matters for several reasons. First, it increases the security of the food supply, including control over the quality and safety of food and the manner in which it is produced. Second, it reduces the risk of environmental damage due to transport. Third, it ensures that countries bear the ecosystem stress resulting from food production rather than shift it to others.

The self-reliance indicator was calculated as the mean of eight food groups: cereals, starchy roots, sugar and sweeteners, plant oils and nuts, pulses and vegetables, fruit, meat and eggs, and dairy products. This checks distortion by surpluses of a few export crops. For example, Barbados produces a surplus of sugar but only 3% of its cereals; Botswana, a surplus of meat but less than half its supply of any other food group.[40]

The picture presented in Map 3.26 largely reflects the productivity score, which determined the agriculture rating in all countries in the fair band and 81 of those in the medium band.[41] Poor scores are a mixture: 16 were determined by self-reliance, 10 by productivity, and 6 by both factors.[42] All bad ratings reflect the self-reliance score, except for Namibia's (where productivity is bad and self-reliance poor).

Low food production (no more than 2 metric tons) per harvested hectare is the more common type of inferior pro-

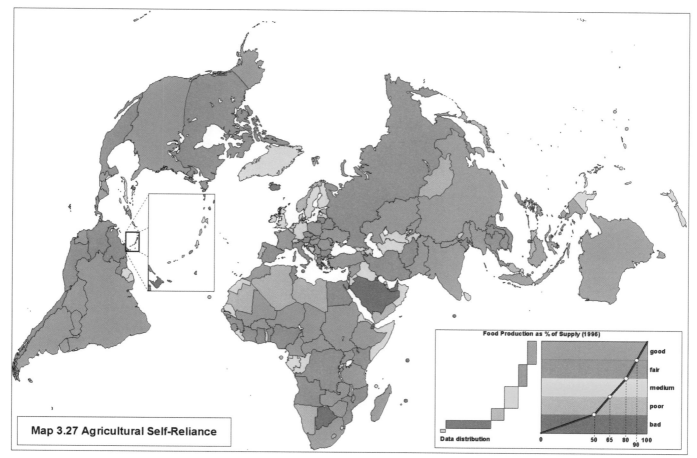

**Map 3.27 Agricultural Self-Reliance**

ductivity in Africa (especially West Africa) and Central Asia. High fertilizer use (at least 80 metric tons of fertilizer per 1,000 harvested hectares) is the more frequent culprit in North and South America, Europe (notably Northern Europe), East Asia, and the developed Pacific. Excess fertilizer usually ends up in rivers, lakes, and the sea. Of 30 countries with high rates of fertilizer use that were also assessed on water quality, 20 have a poor or bad water quality score wholly or largely due to nutrient pollution. They include China, Japan, South Korea, Australia, New Zealand, eight countries in Northern Europe, four in Eastern Europe, and three in Southern Europe.[43]

All countries with a bad score for self-reliance and most with a poor score have small harvested areas in relation to their population (less than a quarter of a hectare per person). The exceptions produce scant amounts from their harvested area (St Vincent and Grenadines, São Tomé and Principe, Portugal, Malaysia, and Solomon Islands) or depend heavily on fertilizer (Dominica). The one inexplicable case is Estonia, which has almost a third of a hectare of harvested area per person and is moderately productive yet grows only 60% of its food supply.

The countries with a fair agriculture score—18 African, 8 American, and 3 Asian—place little agricultural pressure on the ecosystem, producing more than 80% of their food supply using modest amounts of land and fertilizer. However, the food supply is generally too small to meet the nutritional needs of their

**Figure 3.19. Regional breakdown of the 89 countries with a good or fair score for agricultural self-reliance by performance band for food sufficiency.**

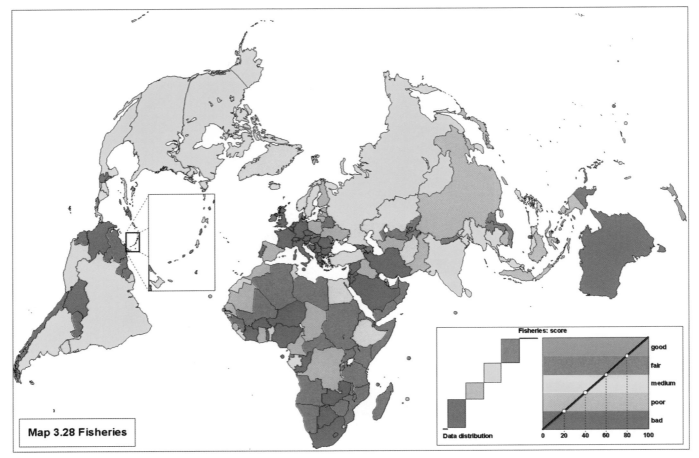

**Map 3.28 Fisheries**

Fisheries: score

good
fair
medium
poor
bad

Data distribution

0  20  40  60  80  100

people: only Costa Rica, Guyana, and Paraguay have high scores for food sufficiency, while Guatemala, Afghanistan, Cambodia, Lao, and 13 African countries have poor or bad scores (see the Wealth section in Chapter 2). In fact, self-reliance is consistently matched by food sufficiency only in Europe (Figure 3.19). In Africa and much of Asia, self-reliance often means a lack of money to buy desperately needed imports.

To what extent productivity and self-reliance affect actual ecosystem and human conditions depends on ecological practice and social policy, as the Philippines and Malaysia illustrate. The two countries are about the same size and have similar climates, but their performances are dramatically different. The Philippines' scores for productivity and self-reliance are both fair. Its land productivity is a modest 3.8 metric tons (mt) per hectare, but its fertilizer use is a respectably low 33.1 mt per 1,000 hectares. It produces surpluses of plant oils and fruit and more than 90% of its supply of all other food groups except cereals (88%) and dairy products (2%). Malaysia has a medium score for productivity and a poor score for self-reliance. High fertilizer productivity (only 12.2 mt of fertilizer used per 1,000 hectares) is negated by exceptionally low food production

per hectare (a scant 0.7 mt), perhaps due to the dominance of oil palm. Like the Philippines, it produces surpluses of plant oils and fruit but only half of its supply of starchy roots, a third of its vegetables, and a quarter of its cereals.

Theoretically, agriculture in the Philippines should have less of an impact on the land, and the people should be better fed than in Malaysia. Not so. A third of the Philippines' land area has been converted to cultivation, a quarter of Malaysia's. Land quality is poor in Malaysia but even worse in the Philippines, where soil degradation is extensive and severe. Almost a quarter (22%) of the population of the Philippines lacks sufficient food, compared with 2% in Malaysia, where undernutrition among children is also lower.

## Fisheries

### Fisheries (Map 3.28)

**What it is:** Lower of fishing pressure score and fish and seafood self-reliance score.

**Country results:** 2 good (1%), 47 fair (26%), 38 medium (21%), 32 poor (18%), 58 bad (32%), 3 no data (2%).

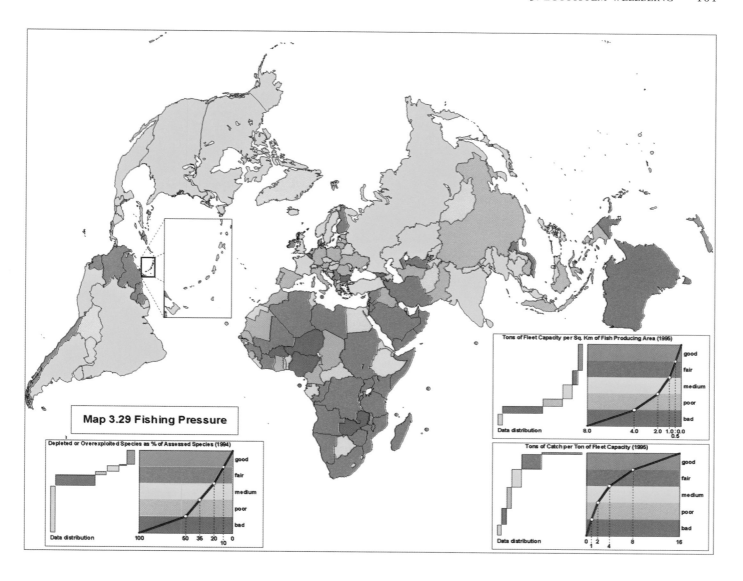

**Map 3.29 Fishing Pressure**

The two good scorers—Maldives and New Zealand—put little pressure on fisheries while producing their entire supply of seafood. Countries with a fair score produce more than 80% of their supply without imposing excessive stress on the fisheries. The rest perform modestly to badly in one aspect or the other.

Poor and bad scores are determined by fishing pressure in 31 countries (especially in West Africa, Eastern Europe, and Southern Asia), low self-reliance in 41 (particularly in the West Indies, Southern Africa, and West Asia), and both factors in 18 (notably in Southern and Northern Europe). Australia and 14 other countries dive from fair scores for pressure to bad scores for self-reliance. But Belize takes the biggest plunge, from good (self-reliance) to bad (pressure).

---

### Fishing Pressure (Map 3.29)

**What it is:** Average score of three indicators: depleted and overexploited species as percentage of assessed species, fish-catching capacity per unit of fish-producing area, and weight of catch per unit of fish-catching capacity.

**Country results:** 2 good (1%), 55 fair (31%), 51 medium (28%), 38 poor (21%), 11 bad (6%), 23 no data (13%).

---

Together, the three indicators provide an adequate if rough measure of fishing pressure. None can do so alone. Data on the first indicator (depleted and overexploited species) are available for a minority of the marine species fished by just 80 countries. Moreover, some species classified as depleted succumb to other stresses besides overfishing. In the Black Sea, for example, stocks of anchovy and sprats failed because of predation by an introduced ctenophore (a jellyfish-like animal); shads and sturgeons declined because of rising salt levels in estuaries as dams and water withdrawals reduced river flows; and turbot fisheries collapsed because excessive nutrients from the Danube and other rivers cut oxygen levels in seawater.

Fishing has exacerbated these changes. Thirteen of the species fished by Ukraine are well enough known for the Food and Agriculture Organization of the United Nations (FAO) to assess their condition: nine are lightly to fully exploited, and four are depleted or overexploited, including three Black Sea species (Pontic shad, Azov Sea sprat, and European sprat).[44]

Countries are disposed to overfish if their fleet can catch more than their national waters can produce. The second indicator—catching capacity (the total tonnage of a country's fishing fleet) per unit of fish-producing area—measures this relationship. The fish-producing area is the country's continental shelf for marine fisheries and its inland water area for freshwater fisheries. Eighteen land-locked countries were rated on the basis of their fresh-water fisheries, 93 countries on their marine fisheries, and 46 (where marine and inland water fleets could not be distinguished) on both.

Countries that concentrate their fishing on their own areas tend to do better with this indicator than those with large distant water fleets. Turkey fishes only the Black Sea and Mediterranean and has a low 0.9 tons of fleet capacity per square kilometer of shelf. Ukraine's fleet has a very high 5.5 tons of capacity for every square kilometer of shelf because its fleet is active both in the Black Sea and in every ocean but the Arctic.[45]

The second indicator takes no account of differences in productivity and so may penalize countries with small but rich fish-producing areas. The third indicator, catch per unit of catching capacity, corrects this distortion by comparing the fishing power of the fleet with the amount of fish it catches. For example, Peru's fleet is large for its narrow shelf (1.5 tons per square kilometer). But highly productive upwellings, which bring nutrients from the ocean depths to the surface, support an exceptionally bountiful fishery. As a result, Peru catches a phenomenally high 44 tons of fish per ton of capacity.

Because of weak data, the second and third indica-

tors seldom accord with the first. Of 33 countries where 35% or more of assessed species are depleted or overexploited, only 18 have a correspondingly low score for capacity per area or catch per capacity. The indicators match in most of Northern and West Africa, Southern and Eastern Europe, and West Asia but in none of South America or Central Africa. Allowing for this flaw, pressure is highest in Eastern Europe (all assessed countries have poor or bad scores), Southern Europe (60% poor or bad), and West Africa (53%). Pressure is lowest in Southern Africa (82% have fair scores; few species are overexploited or depleted), East Africa (67% fair), and West Asia (53% fair).

---

**Fish and Seafood Self-Reliance (Map 3.30)**

**What it is:** One indicator, fish and seafood production as a percentage of supply.

**Country results:** 82 good (46%), 15 fair (8%), 15 medium (8%), 9 poor (5%), 50 bad (28%), 9 no data (5%).

---

Countries that produce more than 90% of their supply of fish and seafood are in a position to control the stress their consumption puts on fisheries. Those producing 50% or less are not. The most self-reliant regions, with the highest proportions of good scores, are North and Central America, Central and East Asia, and Southern Asia. The least self-reliant, with the highest frequency of bad scores, are Southern Europe, West Indies, and Northern Europe. Few self-reliant countries live up to their promise, however. Only 34 with high (good or fair) scores also have high marks for fishing pressure. The strongest regions are Southern Africa, where seven of the eight nations with high scores for self-reliance have high marks for pressure as well (Zambia is the exception); and East Africa and South America, each having five countries with high scores for both.[46]

Eighty countries perform consistently, achieving either good or fair, medium, or poor or bad scores in both fish and seafood and agricultural self-reliance. In the other 91, scores differ widely. Among the 59 nations with good or fair grades in both types of self-reliance, only 17 also have high ratings for food self-sufficiency: 6 in South America, 4 in North and Central America, 4 in Eastern Europe, and Croatia, Russia, and Kazakhstan.[47]

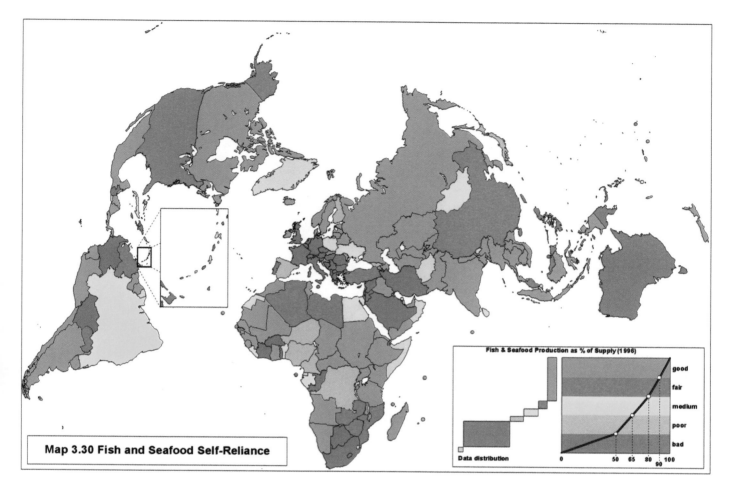

**Map 3.30 Fish and Seafood Self-Reliance**

## Timber

The timber indicator shows whether countries are extracting wood within the forest's rate of renewal. It does not show whether logging is sustainable because it does not cover impacts on forest diversity and quality.

Europe, Canada, the United States, Russia, Japan, Kazakhstan, Tajikistan, Turkmenistan, Australia, New Zealand, and six West Asian countries—52 countries in all—were assessed with the first indicator: fellings plus imports as a percentage of net annual increment (NAI,

the amount the forest grows each year, less natural losses).[48] At 100% of NAI or less, logging is within the forest's rate of renewal; at 80% or less it is well within it. At more than 100%, the stock is being depleted. The 30 countries with a good score obtained from this indicator are using forests conservatively, and the 8 with a fair score are using them close to but within their rate of renewal. Three medium, 1 poor, and 10 bad scorers are putting slight to severe pressure on their own timber resources or those of other countries.

The rest of the world was assessed with the other indicator. This is much less reliable because the relationship between the volume of wood in a forest and its NAI depends on its age, species composition, and productivity. The 59 countries with a good score are probably using forests within their rate of renewal, and the 22 with fair scores are possibly doing so.

Imports are added to fellings or production because some countries relieve pressure on their own forests by importing timber. Belgium, Denmark, Luxembourg,

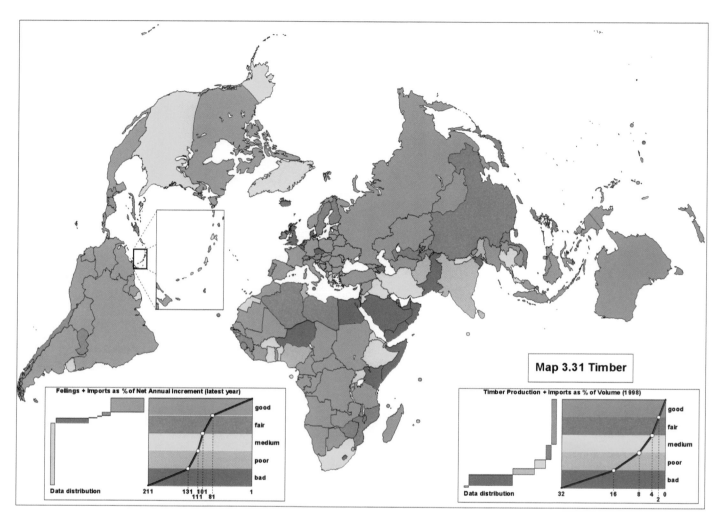

Netherlands, United Kingdom, Cyprus, and Israel could achieve fair scores by keeping fellings at current rates and cutting imports. Eight other countries with poor or bad scores could achieve medium scores by limiting imports.[49]

## Notes

1. Holling (1995).
2. Collar, Crosby, & Stattersfield (1994); World Conservation Monitoring Centre (1992).
3. This amounts to almost 40% if just land plant energy is considered (Vitousek et al. 1986). Ecosystem conversion accounts for about 37% of the plant energy that is destroyed or consumed, use of converted (cultivated and built) ecosystems for 29%, resource extraction and ecosystem modification for 26%, and soil degradation for 8% (my analysis of Vitousek et al. 1986 in Annex 1 of IUCN/UNEP/WWF 1991). IUCN/UNEP/WWF (1991) is also the source of the definition of carrying capacity.
4. Ecological Footprint description: Wackernagel et al. (2000). Data are for 1996 and are from Wackernagel et al. (2000). Seven of the eighteen countries with an EF score more than 10 points lower than the EWI are in Northern Europe, 3 are in West Asia, and the others are Canada, United States, Gambia, Zimbabwe, Belarus, Singapore, Australia, and New Zealand. Nineteen of the 47 countries with an EF score more than 10 points higher than the EWI are in Africa, 13 are in the Americas, and 9 in Southern Asia; the others are Bosnia and Herzegovina, Croatia, Georgia, Syria, China, and Papua New Guinea.
5. Levin (1995); O'Neill et al. (1995).
6. Ideally, the index would be differentiated by major ecosystem (rather than treating each country's land area as ecologically homogeneous) and would also measure how much each ecosystem has been fragmented into separate patches, but this information is not available.
7. The 10 European countries are Albania, Belarus, Croatia, Estonia, France, Greece, Latvia, Spain, United Kingdom, and Yugoslavia.
8. Based on the average of separate ranks for total species of

flowering plants, gymnosperms, pteridophytes, mammals, breeding birds, reptiles, and amphibians (see Table 19).

9. Indicator description: Table 11. Data: many sources (see Tables 11 and 12). Estimates of natural, modified, and converted land areas came from several sources, which often differed greatly. Many were derived from global and regional maps, resulting in large errors when translated into national statistics, and some were extrapolations.

10. Reid & Miller (1989).

11. Indicator description: United Nations (1996). Data: IUCN World Commission on Protected Areas & World Conservation Monitoring Centre (1998); World Conservation Monitoring Centre (1997); Iremonger, Ravilious, & Quinton (1997). The international target comes from IUCN/UNEP/WWF (1991) and Recommendation 16 of the 4th World Congress on National Parks and Protected Areas (McNeely 1993).

12. Indicator description: Oldeman (1993); van Lynden & Oldeman (1997). Data from GLASOD: Oldeman (1993); Oldeman, Hakkeling, & Sombroek (1991); UNEP/ISRIC (1990). Data from other studies: Baitullin & Bekturova (1997); FAO, UNDP, & UNEP (1994); van Lynden & Oldeman (1997).

13. Shiklomanov (1997).

14. Water quality concerns: National Water Research Institute (1996); Shiklomanov (1997). An additional major concern is salinization, not covered due to lack of data. Indicator descriptions: Table 15; National Water Research Institute (1996). Data: Eurostat et al. (1995); National Water Research Institute (1996); Organisation for Economic Co-operation and Development (1997, 1999); UNEP & WHO GEMS/Water Collaborating Centre (1988–1990, 1991–1993, 1999); OECD Centre for Co-operation with the Economies in Transition (1996). Performance criteria: United Nations Economic Commission for Europe (1990).

15. Arsenic in Bangladesh: Bangladesh Bureau of Statistics (1999).

16. Pernetta & Elder (1993); Welcomme (1985).

17. Indicator description: Table 14. Data: Food and Agriculture Organization of the United Nations (1995a, 1997b, 1997c, 1997d, 1999c, 2000b); World Energy Council (1999).

18. Impacts of water withdrawal: Shiklomanov (1997). Indicator description: United Nations (1996). Data: Eurostat, European Commission, & the European Environment Agency (1998); Food and Agriculture Organization of the United Nations (1995a, 1997b, 1997c, 1997d, 1999c, 2000b); Instituto Nacional de Estadística, Geografía e Informática (1998); Organisation for Economic Co-operation and Development (1999); World Resources Institute et al. (1998); Shiklomanov (1997).

19. Andreae & Dickinson (1995).

20. Intergovernmental Panel on Climate Change, Working Group 1 (1996).

21. World Meteorological Organization (1995).

22. Intergovernmental Panel on Climate Change, Working Group 1 (1996). The indicator is limited to burning of fossil fuels (coal, oil, gas), cement manufacture, and gas flaring because they are measured consistently for almost all countries, whereas forest loss and burning of wood and vegetation are not.

23. Indicator description: United Nations (1996). Data: Marland et al. (2000). Need to cut global $CO_2$ emissions by 60–80% of 1990 level (3.7–4.9 billion metric tons): Corner House (1997). Projected world population in 2050: United Nations Population Division (1998b).

24. World Meteorological Organization (1995); Ozone Secretariat, United Nations Environment Programme (1997).

25. Illegal trade: United Nations Environment Programme (1996); World Resources Institute et al. (1998). Indicator description: United Nations (1996). Data: Ozone Secretariat, United Nations Environment Programme (1999); United Nations Environment Programme (1998).

26. Health and environmental effects: World Health Organization (1998c); World Resources Institute et al. (1998). Indicator description: World Health Organization (1998c). Data: World Health Organization (1998c); Organisation for Economic Co-operation and Development (1999). Performance criteria: World Health Organization (1998d); Junker & Schwela (1998).

27. Background extinction rate: Reid & Miller (1989). Species more threatened today than since the dinosaurs: IUCN/UNEP/WWF (1991).

28. The top 45 countries are Indonesia, China, Mexico, Colombia, Brazil, Peru, India, United States, Ecuador, Venezuela, Australia, Papua New Guinea, Bolivia, Thailand, South Africa, Malaysia, Panama, Argentina, Tanzania, Democratic Republic of the Congo, Guatemala, Myanmar, Costa Rica, Kenya, Nicaragua, Viet Nam, Philippines, Angola, Uganda, Honduras, Cameroon, Nepal, Zimbabwe, Paraguay, Russia, Guyana, Suriname, Mozambique, Sudan, Nigeria, Japan, Ethiopia, Côte d'Ivoire, Malawi, and Madagascar (Table 19).

29. Chile: Dinerstein et al. (1995). Algeria: my analysis.

30. Indicator description: United Nations (1996). Data: World Conservation Monitoring Centre (1998a).

31. Indicator description: United Nations (1996). Data: IUCN Species Survival Commission (2000); BirdLife International (2000); World Conservation Monitoring Centre (1998b).

32. Also excluded are wild relatives, which are covered by the wild animal species indicator, and feral populations (descendants of domesticated stock now living in the wild)

because they are often a threat to wild species and natural ecosystems. Poultry were dropped because assessments include high proportions of nonestablished breeds. Indicator description: Table 20. Data: FAO Initiative for Domesticated Animal Diversity (1998, 1999); Rege (1999).

33. Characteristics of Crioulo Lageano cattle and Canastrão pig: FAO Initiative for Domesticated Animal Diversity (1998); Porter (1993). Pork dishes of Rio de Janeiro and Minas Gerais: Leroux (1980).

34. Holstein–Friesian cattle: Cunningham & Syrstad (1987). Gloucester Old Spot pig: Alderson (1989). War and African cattle breeds: Rege (1999); Rege & Tawah (1999).

35. Impact of crossbreeding and interbreeding on European cattle and horses: Simon (1999). African cattle: Rege (1999); Rege, Aboagye, & Tawah (1994); Rege & Tawah (1999). The Criollo goat: FAO Initiative for Domesticated Animal Diversity (1998). Pakistan's sheep and goats: Hasnain (1985).

36. Taihu pigs: Porter (1993).

37. Navajo Churro sheep: Bixby et al. (1994). Tanzanian cattle: Rege (1999); Rege & Tawah (1999).

38. Kenyan Boran cattle: Porter (1991); Rege & Tawah (1999). Danish Red and Danish Friesian cattle: FAO Initiative for Domesticated Animal Diversity (1998). Ibérica pigs: FAO Initiative for Domesticated Animal Diversity (1998); Porter (1993). Pecorino Sardo: Accademia Italiana della Cucina (1995). Fontina: Associazione Nazionale Allevatori Bovini Razza Valdostana (1995).

39. Indicator description: United Nations (1996). Data: United Nations Energy Statistics Unit (2000).

40. Data for all agricultural indicators: FAO (1998a).

41. Inferior self-reliance reduced 13 relatively productive countries to a medium rating (Belize, Cuba, Jamaica, Republic of Congo, Gabon, Rwanda, Comoros, Swaziland, Albania, Bosnia and Herzegovina, Fiji, Papua New Guinea, and Vanuatu).

42. Self-reliance was sole determinant of poor scores in Dominica, Grenada, St Vincent and Grenadines, Algeria, Gambia, Lesotho, Mauritania, Estonia, Portugal, Armenia, Japan, Malaysia, Mongolia, Yemen, Samoa, and Tonga; productivity in Finland, Ireland, United Kingdom, Belarus, Latvia, Iraq, Tajikistan, Turkmenistan, Uzbekistan, and New Zealand; and both factors in Libya, Cape Verde, São Tomé and Principe, Norway, South Korea, and Solomon Islands.

43. Northern Europe: Austria, Belgium, Denmark, Germany, Ireland, Luxembourg, Switzerland, United Kingdom. Eastern Europe: Czech Republic, Latvia, Lithuania, Poland. Southern Europe: Croatia, France, Slovenia.

44. Indicator description and data, including examples in this and previous paragraph: FAO Marine Resources Service, Fishery Resources Division (1997).

45. Second and third indicators (capacity per area and catch per capacity), description: Table 24. Data: FAO (1998b); FAO Fishery Information, Data and Statistics Unit (1998); FAO Fishery Resources Division, personal communication (1996).

46. Indicator data: FAO (1998a).

47. South America: Argentina, Chile, Guyana, Paraguay, Uruguay, and Venezuela. North and Central America: Canada, Costa Rica, Panama, and United States. Eastern Europe: Bulgaria, Lithuania, Moldova, and Slovakia.

48. The six West Asian countries are Armenia, Azerbaijan, Cyprus, Georgia, Israel, and Turkey.

49. Indicator data: FAO (1993, 1995c, 2000a); Pandey (1995); UNECE & FAO (2000). The eight countries that could achieve medium scores by cutting imports are St Lucia, Iceland, Mauritius, Kuwait, Saudi Arabia, Singapore, United Arab Emirates, and Yemen.

# 4. Combining Human and Ecosystem Wellbeing

## Distances to Sustainability

*This section introduces the Wellbeing Index (WI) and Wellbeing/Stress Index (WSI), two indices that combine human and ecosystem wellbeing, and then discusses the main combinations.*

---

### Highlights

- No country is sustainable or even close to sustainability.

- The leaders—Sweden, Finland, Norway, Iceland, and Austria—have good or fair human wellbeing but only medium ecosystem wellbeing.

- 37 *ecosystem deficit* countries (including the five leaders) have high standards of living but excessive impacts on the global environment.

- 27 *human deficit* countries have fairly low demands on the ecosystem but are desperately poor.

- The remaining 116 are *double deficit* countries, combining weak environmental performance and inadequate development.

- In 141 countries, ecosystem stress is higher than human wellbeing, a clear sign that most people's efforts to improve their lot are inefficient and overexploit the environment.

- A high quality of life can be attained for a low environmental price. Increases in human wellbeing do not necessarily result in greater impacts on the environment, which are less the product of the *level* of human wellbeing than of the *way* human wellbeing is pursued.

- The key conditions for combining high human wellbeing and low ecosystem stress are freedom, sound governance, and education.

---

## Wellbeing Index

### Wellbeing Index (WI)
### (Figure 4.1 and Map 4.1)

**What it is:** The point on the Barometer of Sustainability where the Human Wellbeing Index (HWI) and the Ecosystem Wellbeing Index (EWI) intersect.

**Country results:** 0 good (0%), 5 fair (3%), 86 medium (48%), 89 poor (49%), 0 bad (0%).

---

*The main combinations of human and ecosystem wellbeing that make up the WI are shown in Figure 4.1 (examples) and Map 4.1 (all countries). The WI of all countries is given in Table 25 in the Data section. Nations **bold** in the text are shown in Figure 4.1.*

The Wellbeing Index (WI) displays the HWI and EWI together, combining the quality of human life and the environment without submerging one in the other (Figure 4.1). The closer a country is to the top right corner of the Barometer, the nearer it is to achieving a high quality of life for a low environmental price. A single number does not do justice to the WI, whether it be the lower of the HWI and EWI or the average. The lower number ignores half the picture: either the state of the environment or the condition of people. For example, **Australia, China,** and **Gabon** would end up with identical scores of 28, despite Australia's much higher human wellbeing and Gabon's superior ecosystem wellbeing. The average also masks differences in human and ecosystem wellbeing: **Croatia, Russia,** and **Gabon** have the same average of 45.0, although Croatia is impeded by poor ecosystem wellbeing, Gabon by inferior human wellbeing, and Russia is weak in both.

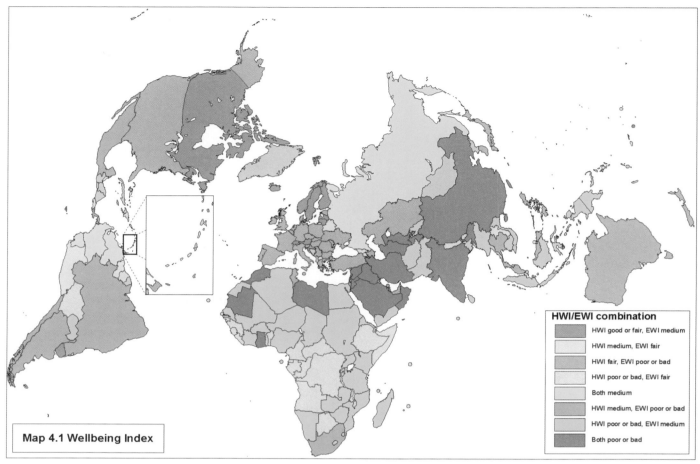

**Map 4.1 Wellbeing Index**

**HWI/EWI combination**

- HWI good or fair, EWI medium
- HWI medium, EWI fair
- HWI fair, EWI poor or bad
- HWI poor or bad, EWI fair
- Both medium
- HWI medium, EWI poor or bad
- HWI poor or bad, EWI medium
- Both poor or bad

**Figure 4.1. Main combinations of human and ecosystem wellbeing.** The Human Wellbeing Index (HWI) is in the yolk of the egg, the Ecosystem Wellbeing Index (EWI) in the white. The Wellbeing Index (WI), expressed as the average of the HWI and EWI, is next to the name of the country.

The merit of the average is that it expresses the distance a society has to go to achieve sustainability: Croatia, Russia, and Gabon are equally far from a sustainable WI of 81.0. Hence, when a single number is needed (such as to rank countries), the average is used. But it should be borne in mind that the true WI is the juxtaposition of human and ecosystem wellbeing shown on the Barometer of Sustainability.

A sustainable WI would combine a good HWI and a good EWI. In a close to sustainable WI, both parts would be fair or a mixture of good and fair. No country has achieved either. Instead, the 180 nations fall into eight combinations of human and ecosystem wellbeing in three major sets:

### Ecosystem deficit (HWI good or fair, EWI below fair): 37 countries

Moderate ecosystem deficit (HWI good or fair, EWI medium), 10 countries: 6 in Northern Europe (e.g.,

Sweden with the highest WI in the world); 2 in Eastern Europe; Canada; Uruguay.

High ecosystem deficit (HWI fair, EWI poor or bad), 27 countries: 7 each in Northern and Southern Europe; 5 in Eastern Europe; 2 in Central and East Asia; 2 in the Pacific (e.g., **Australia**); **United States**; Barbados; Cyprus; Singapore.

## Human deficit (HWI below fair, EWI fair): 27 countries

Moderate human deficit (HWI medium, EWI fair), 4 countries: Belize; Dominica; Guyana and **Peru.**

High human deficit (HWI poor or bad, EWI fair), 23 countries: 7 in West Africa; 6 in Central and East Africa (e.g., **Gabon**); 3 each in Southern Africa and Southern Asia; 2 in Northern Africa; Bolivia; Solomon Islands.

## Double deficit (HWI and EWI both below fair): 116 countries

Moderate double deficit (HWI and EWI both medium), 21 countries: 5 in the West Indies; 4 in South America; 2 each in West Asia and the Pacific; Costa Rica; Cape Verde; Seychelles; Mauritius; FYR Macedonia; Belarus; **Russia;** Brunei Darussalam.

High double deficit, ecosystem worse (HWI medium, EWI poor or bad), 27 countries: 6 in West Asia; 4 each in the West Indies and Eastern Europe; 3 each in South America and Southern Asia; 2 in North and Central America; 2 in Southern Europe (e.g., **Croatia**); Tunisia; South Africa; Kazakhstan.

High double deficit, people worse (HWI poor or bad, EWI medium), 50 countries: 8 each in Southern Africa (e.g., **Mozambique**) and Southern Asia; 7 in West Africa; 6 in Central and East Africa; 5 in Northern Africa; 4 in North and Central America; 4 in Central and East Asia; 2 each in the West Indies, Southern Europe, and the Pacific; Paraguay; Yemen.

Extreme double deficit (HWI and EWI both poor or bad), 18 countries: 8 in West Asia (e.g., **Iraq** with

the lowest WI in the world); 4 in Central and East Asia (e.g., **China**); 2 each in Northern Africa and West Africa; India; Tonga.

In general, human deficits are more pronounced than ecosystem deficits. As a result, human deficit nations tend to have lower WIs and to be farther from sustainability than their ecosystem deficit counterparts. In addition, their environmental ratings may not be as fair as they seem, since they do not include the quality of inland waters and local air. If they did, the countries might have lower EWIs and drop to double deficits.

## *Wellbeing/Stress Index*

---

### Wellbeing/Stress Index (WSI) (Map 4.2)

**What it is:** The ratio of human wellbeing to ecosystem stress (derived by subtracting the EWI from 100 to obtain an Ecosystem Stress Index [ESI] and then dividing the HWI by the ESI). (Ecosystem stress is the opposite of ecosystem wellbeing, and the ESI is the reverse of the EWI.)

**Country results:** 0 good (0%), 0 fair (0%), 37 medium (21%), 84 poor (47%), 59 bad (33%).

---

*The WSI and WSI score of all countries are given in Table 25 in the Data section.*

Combining high levels of human and ecosystem wellbeing calls for an economy that gets a bigger buck for the bang. The buck is income, jobs, and other benefits. The bang is pressure on the ecosystem: the quantity of resources extracted, the amount and effect of wastes returned, the extent and degree of modification of the land, and impacts on biodiversity.

The Wellbeing/Stress Index (WSI) compares the socioeconomic benefits of development with its environmental costs, showing how much human wellbeing a society obtains for the amount of stress it places on the environment. A country with an HWI and EWI of 81 would have a WSI above 4.0, a level of human wellbeing more than four times higher than its level of ecosystem stress. Hence a good WSI is more than 4.0 and a fair

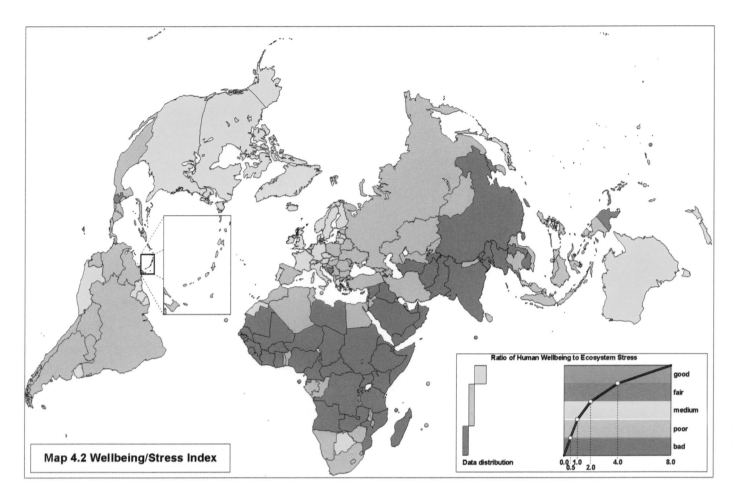

**Map 4.2 Wellbeing/Stress Index**

WSI more than 2.0 (human wellbeing twice the amount of ecosystem stress).

No country comes close. Among those rated on all human and ecosystem subelements, Sweden has the highest WSI: 1.55. Only 37 nations, more than half of them in Europe, have WSIs above 1.0 (that is, higher human wellbeing than ecosystem stress); 17 of the 37 edge above 1.0 by less than a tenth of a point (Table 4.2).

The Netherlands and Armenia head the poor scorers with WSIs of exactly 1.0, human wellbeing equaling ecosystem stress. In the other 141 nations, ecosystem stress is greater than human wellbeing, exceeding it by double or more in the 59 with a bad score—all in Africa and Asia–Pacific except for Guatemala, Haiti, and Bosnia and Herzegovina. Somalia has the lowest WSI (0.08), its limited impact on the environment far outweighed by the severity of human deprivation.

**Table 4.1. Number of countries in each performance group.** HW/EW combination = combination of human and ecosystem wellbeing. 1 through 5 are combinations of the Wellbeing Index (WI) and Wellbeing/Stress Index (WSI): 1 = fair WI/medium WSI; 2 = medium WI/medium WSI; 3 = medium WI/poor or bad WSI; 4 = poor WI/poor WSI; 5 = poor WI/bad WSI.

| | WI/WSI Group | | | | |
|---|---|---|---|---|---|
| HW/EW Combination | 1 | 2 | 3 | 4 | 5 |
| Moderate ecosystem deficit | 5 | 5 | | | |
| Moderate human deficit | | 4 | | | |
| Moderate double deficit | | 4 | 17 | | |
| High ecosystem deficit | | 18 | 9 | | |
| High human deficit | | 1 | 9 | | 13 |
| High double deficit, ecosystem worse | | | 10 | 16 | 1 |
| High double deficit, people worse | | | 9 | 9 | 32 |
| Extreme double deficit | | | | 6 | 12 |
| TOTAL | 5 | 32 | 54 | 31 | 58 |

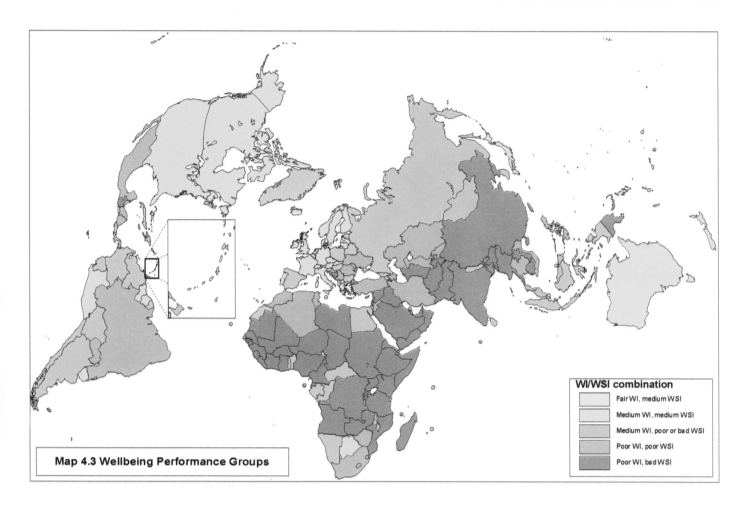

**Map 4.3 Wellbeing Performance Groups**

**WI/WSI combination**
- Fair WI, medium WSI
- Medium WI, medium WSI
- Medium WI, poor or bad WSI
- Poor WI, poor WSI
- Poor WI, bad WSI

## Wellbeing Performance Groups

---

### Wellbeing Performance Groups (Map 4.3)

**What they are:** Combinations of Wellbeing Index (WI) and Wellbeing/Stress Index (WSI).

**Country results:** 5 fair WI/medium WSI (3%), 32 medium WI/medium WSI (18%), 54 medium WI/poor or bad WSI (30%), 31 poor WI/poor WSI (17%), 58 poor WI/bad WSI (32%).

---

*The main performance groups are shown in Map 4.3, summarized in Table 4.1, and given in detail in Table 26 in the Data section. The top countries, ranked by WI, are in Table 4.2; all countries, in Table 27 in the Data section.*

Together the WI and WSI show how well and sustainable societies are overall, revealing a world that is largely unwell and unsustainable, much of it severely so. Only 37 countries, with WIs above 50.0 and WSIs above 1.0, have gone more than half the distance toward sustainability. The other 143 have a much longer road ahead.

The five leaders—Sweden, Finland, Norway, Iceland, and Austria—are all moderate ecosystem deficit countries with fair WIs and medium WSIs. They enjoy high human wellbeing but at the cost of low-medium ecosystem wellbeing. Their clear priority is to raise the latter to fair.

The 32 runners-up, with medium WIs and medium WSIs, are a mixture of ecosystem deficit, human deficit, and double deficit countries. In the ecosystem deficit group, Canada, Switzerland, Uruguay, Latvia, and Lithuania have medium EWIs and moderate deficits; the rest have poor EWIs and high deficits. While the priority for this group is the same as for the leaders—to better environmental conditions—Uruguay, Latvia, and Lithuania, with barely acceptable human wellbeing, also need to ele-

**Table 4.2. The 37 countries with a Wellbeing Index (WI) above 50.0.** HWI = Human Wellbeing Index, EWI = Ecosystem Wellbeing Index, ESI = Ecosystem Stress Index, WSI = Wellbeing/Stress Index. Countries with the same WI were ranked by WSI. Those with the same three-digit WSI were differentiated by taking the WSI to four digits. * Country not rated on all 30 human and ecosystem subelements. *Countries in italics were rated on less than two-thirds of the human or ecosystem indicators.*

| Rank | Country | HWI | EWI | ESI | WI | WSI |
|------|---------|-----|-----|-----|------|------|
| 1 | Sweden | 79 | 49 | 51 | 64.0 | 1.55 |
| 2 | Finland | 81 | 44 | 56 | 62.5 | 1.45 |
| 3 | Norway | 82 | 43 | 57 | 62.5 | 1.44 |
| 4 | Iceland* | 80 | 43 | 57 | 61.5 | 1.40 |
| 5 | Austria* | 80 | 42 | 58 | 61.0 | 1.38 |
| 6 | *Dominica** | 56 | 65 | 35 | 60.5 | 1.60 |
| 7= | Canada | 78 | 43 | 57 | 60.5 | 1.37 |
| 7= | Switzerland | 78 | 43 | 57 | 60.5 | 1.37 |
| 9 | Belize* | 50 | 64 | 36 | 57.0 | 1.39 |
| 10 | Guyana* | 51 | 63 | 37 | 57.0 | 1.38 |
| 11 | Uruguay* | 61 | 52 | 48 | 56.5 | 1.27 |
| 12 | Germany | 77 | 36 | 64 | 56.5 | 1.20 |
| 13 | Denmark | 81 | 31 | 69 | 56.0 | 1.17 |
| 14 | New Zealand* | 73 | 38 | 62 | 55.5 | 1.18 |
| 15 | Suriname* | 52 | 58 | 42 | 55.0 | 1.24 |
| 16 | Latvia* | 62 | 46 | 54 | 54.0 | 1.15 |
| 17 | Ireland* | 76 | 32 | 68 | 54.0 | 1.12 |
| 18 | Australia | 79 | 28 | 72 | 53.5 | 1.10 |
| 19 | Peru* | 44 | 62 | 38 | 53.0 | 1.16 |
| 20 | Slovenia* | 71 | 35 | 65 | 53.0 | 1.09 |
| 21 | *St Kitts and Nevis** | 52 | 53 | 47 | 52.5 | 1.11 |
| 22 | Lithuania | 61 | 44 | 56 | 52.5 | 1.09 |
| 23 | Cyprus* | 67 | 38 | 62 | 52.5 | 1.08 |
| 24 | Japan | 80 | 25 | 75 | 52.5 | 1.07 |
| 25 | *St Lucia** | 53 | 51 | 49 | 52.0 | 1.08 |
| 26 | *Grenada** | 55 | 49 | 51 | 52.0 | 1.08 |
| 27 | United States | 73 | 31 | 69 | 52.0 | 1.06 |
| 28 | Italy | 74 | 30 | 70 | 52.0 | 1.06 |
| 29 | France | 75 | 29 | 71 | 52.0 | 1.06 |
| 30= | Czech Republic* | 70 | 33 | 67 | 51.5 | 1.04 |
| 30= | Greece | 70 | 33 | 67 | 51.5 | 1.04 |
| 32 | Portugal | 72 | 31 | 69 | 51.5 | 1.04 |
| 33 | United Kingdom | 73 | 30 | 70 | 51.5 | 1.04 |
| 34 | Belgium | 80 | 23 | 77 | 51.5 | 1.04 |
| 35 | Botswana* | 34 | 68 | 32 | 51.0 | 1.06 |
| 36 | Slovakia* | 61 | 40 | 60 | 50.5 | 1.02 |
| 37 | Luxembourg* | 77 | 24 | 76 | 50.5 | 1.01 |

vate their HWIs. The human deficit countries (Belize, Dominica, Guyana, Peru, and Botswana) face the task of lifting their standard of living while maintaining ecosystem quality and diversity, more so in Botswana (poor HWI) than in the others (medium HWIs). The double deficit nations (Grenada, St Kitts and Nevis, St Lucia, and Suriname) need to improve on both fronts.

Twenty of the 37 leaders and runners-up were not rated on all 30 human and ecosystem subelements and might fall to a lower rank if they were.

The middle of the pack consists of the 54 countries with medium WIs but poor WSIs (or in one case, Central African Republic, a bad WSI). They are similar to the runners-up, except that all human or ecosystem deficits are high (none is moderate), as are more than half the double deficits. Hence they have the same targets as the runners-up, but are further from achieving them.

At the back of the pack are the 89 countries with poor WIs and poor or bad WSIs. Thirteen (Bhutan and 12 in Africa) have high human deficits and need to greatly improve their HWIs, all of which are well below 20. The rest have high or extreme double deficits— moderately to heavily stressed environments without the development to show for it. Theirs is the most demanding challenge: both to accelerate development and to upgrade the ecosystem.

## Human Wellbeing and Ecosystem Stress: Signs of a Way Forward

*Correlations and other supporting data are in Table 25 in the Data section.*

A striking feature of the pattern of deficits is that countries with higher human than ecosystem wellbeing generally have a higher WI than those where human conditions are worse than the state of the environment. For example, the average WI of the moderate ecosystem deficit countries (which include the five leaders) is 59.6, compared with 56.9 among the moderate human deficit countries. The separation is still greater between the two high-deficit groups: an average WI of 50.9 for the high ecosystem deficit countries and 41.3 for the high human deficit countries. A similar disparity is found among high double deficit countries.[1]

Underlying these patterns are differences in the ratio of human wellbeing to ecosystem stress. Among

**Figure 4.2. Ecosystem stress is only moderately related to human wellbeing.** The Ecosystem Stress Index (ESI) rises less steeply than the Human Wellbeing Index (HWI), and individual country performance often is much better or worse than the trendline. The 180 countries are in ascending order of HWI. Where an ESI is below the HWI, human wellbeing exceeds ecosystem stress. Where an ESI is above the HWI, ecosystem stress exceeds human wellbeing.

and ecosystem stress is due to the contrasting characteristics of each. Human wellbeing is consistent and predictable: several human elements (health, population, wealth, education, communication, and freedom and governance) reinforce each other, have similar scores, and are highly correlated with the HWI (Chapter 2, page 17). Ecosystem stress is much less consistent or predictable: only air and water are highly correlated with the EWI, and only air and resource use with each other (Chapter 3, page 64).

Income plays a major role in many more human than ecosystem elements and corresponds much more closely to the HWI than to the ESI. While the impact of rising incomes on human wellbeing is generally positive, on ecosystem wellbeing it may be negative (energy consumption tends to increase and pressure on the global atmosphere to worsen) or positive (local air quality tends to improve).

The inconsistency of ecosystem stress and the vari-

ecosystem deficit countries, the WSI is medium in 28, poor in 9, bad in none. Among human deficit countries, the WSI is medium in 5, poor in 8, bad in 14. Among high double deficit countries, all but one (United Arab Emirates) have a poor WSI where the ecosystem is worse off, most (64%) a bad WSI where people are worse off.

These differences reflect two aspects of the relationship between human wellbeing and ecosystem stress. One is that even when countries with a bad or poor HWI put little pressure on the ecosystem, that pressure is high in relation to the benefits they derive from it. The other, more broadly significant aspect is that the state of the environment is only moderately tied to human conditions: ecosystem stress rises with human wellbeing, but not as much, and many countries perform much better or worse than the trendline (Figure 4.2). Some of this variation is due to disparities in indicator coverage, but when countries are grouped by completeness of coverage, the conclusions are the same for each group:

- Increases in human wellbeing do not necessarily result in greater ecosystem stress.

- One country can achieve the same quality of life for a smaller environmental price than another (Figure 4.3).

The flexibility of the link between human wellbeing

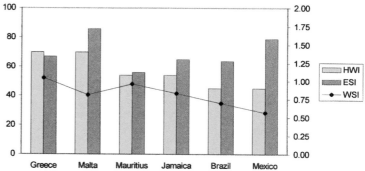

**Figure 4.3. Same quality of life, different environmental price.** Each pair of countries has the same Human Wellbeing Index (HWI), but the country on the left has a lower Ecosystem Stress Index (ESI) and hence a better Wellbeing/Stress Index (WSI). HWI and ESI scale on the left; WSI scale on the right.

able role of income result from the different effects of three factors. The first is consumption dependency. Higher incomes are more likely to increase ecosystem stress if they rely heavily on the consumption of energy and other resources. Among the country pairs in Figure 4.3, Estonia is more consumption dependent than Latvia—consuming 35.2 gigajoules of energy per $1,000 of income, in contrast to Latvia's 19.7 gigajoules—and has a bigger environmental impact.[2]

The second factor is ecological vulnerability. Some countries' environments are inherently more vulnerable than others. Densely populated areas are more likely to lose their ecosystems to settlements, infrastructure, and cultivation. Densely speciated areas—regions rich in species and habitats—are harder to develop without reducing diversity. Malta, with 12.16 people and 30.34 species per hectare, is ecologically more vulnerable than Greece (0.81 people and 0.41 species per hectare), and its level of ecosystem stress is higher.[3]

Consumption dependency and ecological vulnerability act in different ways. The former tends to influence environmental quality, the latter biodiversity (notably the diversity of land ecosystems and species and genes). But their indicators (energy/income, population/area, species/area) are approximate and may counteract each other. All three conform with the level of ecosystem stress in two of the six pairs in Figure 4.3 (Austria–Belgium and Brazil–Mexico), but in the others, one or two of the indicators are contradictory: Greece is more consumption dependent than Malta, Estonia has slightly fewer people per hectare than Latvia, species density is higher in Indonesia than in China, and both human and species densities are higher in Mauritius than in Jamaica.

Such contradictions undoubtedly reflect the third factor: the individual, local, and national decisions people make about their goals and how to achieve them. It is clear from the patterns revealed by this global assess-ment that the environmental price of development is not fixed, and much of the relationship between human wellbeing and ecosystem stress is a matter of choice. Ecosystem stress is a result not so much of the *level* of human wellbeing but of the *way* in which human well-being is pursued. A country's ecological vulnerability determines the minimum possible level of ecosystem stress. Consumption dependency and people's decisions determine how close the actual level of stress is to that minimum.

The opportunity and capacity to make sound decisions is crucial. Significantly, the WSI is highly correlated with the combination of freedom and governance plus education (more than with either of these alone or with income). This makes sense because the combination of freedom, good governance, and education provides people with both the opportunity and the capacity to make decisions that promote sus-tainability. Attaining high levels of human and ecosys-tem wellbeing requires organization, consensus, the rule of law, knowledge, and an awareness of being part of a wider community (extending beyond the confines of ethnic group, corporation, or nation, and ahead to future generations). These conditions do not guarantee that decisions will be right, but if they are made in ignorance, usurped by a minority, cloaked in secrecy, or influenced by bribes, decisions are much more likely to be wrong.

At present, all levels of human wellbeing cause too much damage to the environment, but they need not do so. High human wellbeing and low ecosystem stress—a win–no lose rather than a win–win situation—is an attainable combination. Countries with high standards of living can lead the way by reducing and eventually elimi-nating their ecosystem deficits. The rest of the world may feel that development is challenge enough without both-ering with conservation—but for all societies, real progress depends on both.

# Regional Reviews

*This section explores national performance patterns in the 14 regions, identifying common features and steps toward wellbeing and sustainability.*

## Highlights

- Northern Europe is the strongest region, with 12 countries in the top 40, including the 5 leaders.

- West Asia is the weakest, with 9 countries in the bottom 40 and the most with high or extreme double deficits.

- In the West Indies, South America, Northern and Eastern Europe, and West and Southern Asia, particularly wide differences in ecosystem wellbeing occur among nations with similar levels of human wellbeing.

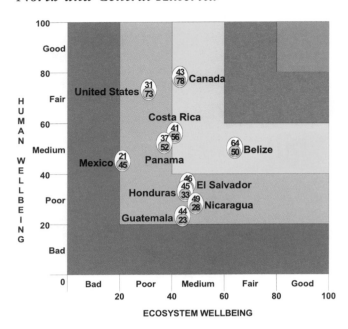

**Figure 4.4. Wellbeing of North and Central America.**
Human Wellbeing Index (HWI) in yolk of egg, Ecosystem
Wellbeing Index (EWI) in white. El Salvador's HWI is 36 and
EWI 46.

**Table 4.3. North and Central America:** Wellbeing Index
(WI), Wellbeing/Stress Index (WSI), performance group, and
number (#) of subelements covered (out of 30). 1 = fair
WI/medium WSI; 2 = medium WI and WSI; 3 = medium
WI/poor WSI; 4 = poor WI and WSI; 5 = poor WI/bad WSI;
mod. = moderate; def. = deficit, e = ecosystem worse; p = people
worse. Country order is by performance group and then by WI.

| Country | WI | WSI | Performance Group | # |
|---------|------|------|-------------------|-----|
| Canada | 60.5 | 1.37 | 2: mod. ecosystem def. | 30 |
| Belize | 57.0 | 1.39 | 2: mod. human def. | 24 |
| United States | 52.0 | 1.06 | 2: high ecosystem def. | 30 |
| Costa Rica | 48.5 | 0.95 | 3: mod. double def. | 28 |
| Panama | 44.5 | 0.83 | 3: high double def. e | 28 |
| El Salvador | 41.0 | 0.67 | 3: high double def. p | 26 |
| Honduras | 39.0 | 0.60 | 4: high double def. p | 27 |
| Nicaragua | 38.5 | 0.55 | 4: high double def. p | 28 |
| Mexico | 33.0 | 0.57 | 4: high double def. e | 29 |
| Guatemala | 33.5 | 0.41 | 5: high double def. p | 26 |

Most of North and Central America (Figure 4.4 and Table
4.3) shows the backward climb (from the bottom right to
the top left of the Barometer) of conventional development:
ecosystem wellbeing declines as human wellbeing improves,
from Nicaragua's poor HWI and medium EWI to the
United States' fair HWI and poor EWI. Mexico and
Guatemala are extreme examples of this tendency, with

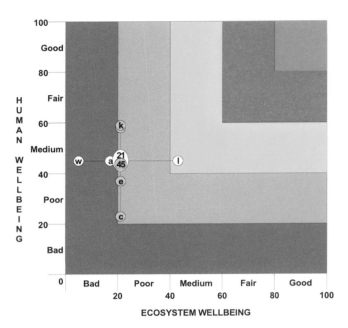

**Figure 4.5. Structure of wellbeing: Mexico.** Yellow circles
show the points on the scale of the human dimensions: c = community; e = equity; h = health and population; k = knowledge;
w = wealth. White circles show the points of the ecosystem
dimensions: a = air; l = land; r = resource use; s = species and
genes; w = water. Some dimensions are hidden by the egg
(wealth, species and genes) or behind another dimension (health
and population is behind knowledge). Mexico's EWI excludes
resource use, which otherwise would have increased it artificially.

Guatemala's very poor HWI and low-medium EWI reversed
into Mexico's very poor EWI and low-medium HWI.

Canada and Belize seem to have broken out of the
trap and to be moving toward the top right corner of the
Barometer. However, Belize may not be in as sound a
position as it looks since it was not assessed on crime,
household equity, river conversion, water quality, local air
quality, or domesticated diversity. If Belize had the Central American average score for local air quality (30) and
the same score as Mexico for water quality (5), its EWI
would fall to 37. In fact, none of the Central American
countries was rated for water quality. Fuller assessments
would probably reduce their scores for the environment
and shift their ecosystem positions on the Barometer
toward Mexico. However, it is unlikely that their human
positions would change significantly because coverage of
human indicators is fairly complete.

Thus, while Mexico bridges North and Central America geographically, in terms of wellbeing it is entirely Central American. Its weakest human dimensions are community, equity, and wealth (Figure 4.5). The poor score for
community (only El Salvador's and Guatemala's are worse)
is due to conflicts in the states of Chiapas and Guerrero,

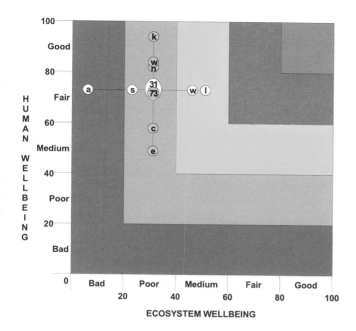

**Figure 4.6. Structure of wellbeing: United States.** See Figure 4.5 for key. The United States' EWI excludes resource use, which otherwise would have increased it artificially.

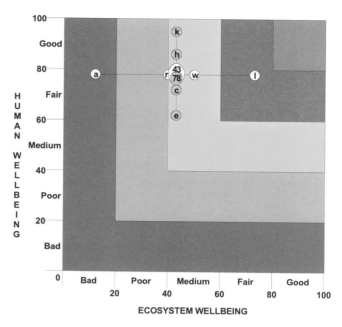

**Figure 4.7. Structure of wellbeing: Canada.** See Figure 4.5 for key. Some dimensions are hidden by the egg (wealth, species and genes, resource use).

which have caused an average of 830 deaths a year since 1994. Underlying such conflicts is the wide gap between a well-educated middle- and upper-class minority and a largely rural majority living in poverty (71% of the population),[4] a gap reflected in the poor score for equity. Inequities are exacerbated by corruption, a weak and politicized judicial system, and repression and human rights abuses in poor urban areas and throughout the countryside.

Political freedom has steadily increased since 1997, and the 2000 presidential election was the fairest in Mexico's history. This progress could provide the momentum to build the social infrastructure of human wellbeing: establishing the rule of law, professionalizing the bureaucracy, and extending economic and educational opportunities to rural areas.

These measures are also needed to increase ecosystem wellbeing. After Canada and the United States, Mexico is the least ecologically vulnerable country in the region,[5] yet it has the highest percentages of threatened wild species (10% of mammals and breeding birds, 36% of plants), and (apart from El Salvador) the lowest percentage of protected area—hence the poor score for species and genes and the low-medium score for land. Only stronger habitat protection coupled with improved rural living conditions can turn this around. And only better physical and social infrastructure, including societywide respect for regulations, can end the severe pollution of rivers, groundwater, and urban air behind the bad scores for air and water.

If human wellbeing were assessed solely on health and

population, wealth, and knowledge, the United States (Figure 4.6) and Canada (Figure 4.7) would have the same HWI. Their knowledge ratings are close, and the stronger economy of the United States offsets Canada's longer life spans and better health. Instead, community and equity make the difference. Canada has better scores for both elements of community: freedom and governance because corruption is lower; peace and order because it spends less on the military (1.1% of GDP versus 3.2%) and has lower homicide and robbery rates (but not lower rape or assault rates). The United States' equity score is lower largely because the income share of the richest households is nine times the share of the poorest (in Canada, it is five times).

The United States has a more pronounced ecosystem deficit than Canada, with lower scores for all dimensions (though in water only by a drop). The structure (pattern of dimensions) of each deficit is similar, however, and the same program is called for to reduce it: raise the scores for air and resource use by reducing carbon emissions and energy consumption; improve the species and genes rating by expanding habitat protection for wild species (in Canada 15% of plant species are threatened; in the United States 28% of plant species and 9% of animal species) and conserving agricultural diversity; and increase the water score by enhancing water quality and restoring the diversity of aquatic ecosystems. Probably the easiest elements to boost quickly are agricultural diversity (currently given scant support) and water quality.

## West Indies

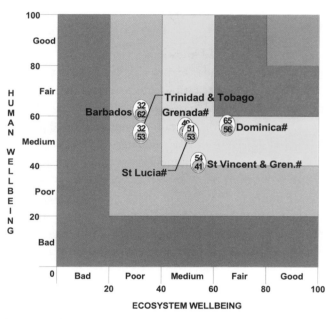

**Figure 4.8. Wellbeing of the West Indies: northern islands above, southern islands below.** Human Wellbeing Index (HWI) in yolk of egg, Ecosystem Wellbeing Index (EWI) in white. Jamaica's HWI is 54 and EWI 35; Grenada's HWI is 55 and EWI 49. # Dominica and Grenada were assessed on less than two-thirds of the human subelements; St Kitts and Nevis, St Lucia, and St Vincent and Grenadines on less than two-thirds of the ecosystem subelements.

In general, the smaller island states (under 100,000 hectares) seem to be closer to sustainability than the larger ones (Figure 4.8 and Table 4.4). Five of the top six countries in the region are small islands; the bottom seven, except for Antigua and Barbuda, are relatively

**Table 4.4. West Indies:** Wellbeing Index (WI), Wellbeing/Stress Index (WSI), performance group, and number (#) of subelements covered (out of 30). 1 = fair WI/medium WSI; 2 = medium WI and WSI; 3 = medium WI/poor WSI; 4 = poor WI and WSI; 5 = poor WI/bad WSI; mod. = moderate; def. = deficit; e = ecosystem worse; p = people worse. Country order is by performance group and then by WI. *Countries in italics were rated on less than two-thirds of the human or ecosystem subelements.*

| Country | WI | WSI | Performance Group | # |
|---|---|---|---|---|
| *Dominica* | *60.5* | *1.60* | *2: mod. human def.* | *19* |
| *St Kitts and Nevis* | *52.5* | *1.11* | *2: mod. double def.* | *19* |
| *St Lucia* | *52.0* | *1.08* | *2: mod. double def.* | *20* |
| *Grenada* | *52.0* | *1.08* | *2: mod. double def.* | *19* |
| Dominican Republic | 47.5 | 0.91 | 3: mod. double def. | 27 |
| *St Vincent and Grenadines* | *47.5* | *0.89* | *3: mod. double def.* | *19* |
| Barbados | 47.0 | 0.91 | 3: high ecosystem def. | 25 |
| Antigua and Barbuda | 44.5 | 0.82 | 3: high double def. e | 20 |
| Jamaica | 44.5 | 0.83 | 3: high double def. e | 27 |
| Bahamas | 43.0 | 0.79 | 3: high double def. e | 26 |
| Trinidad and Tobago | 42.5 | 0.78 | 3: high double def. e | 27 |
| Cuba | 42.5 | 0.73 | 3: high double def. p | 26 |
| Haiti | 31.0 | 0.33 | 5: high double def. p | 24 |

large. Unfortunately, apart from Barbados, the ratings of the small islands are marred by numerous data gaps. This is especially tantalizing because small island states face the same problem of sustainable development as cities—how to have a high quality of life without living beyond the ecological means of a restricted area—but the flow of people, goods, and services in and out of an independent country is easier to monitor. Some of the islands rated on the basis of the same indicators already show interesting differences. Dominica, for example, has an HWI 1 point higher than Grenada's but an EWI 12 points higher, probably helped by its lower ecological vulnerability (0.95 people and 17.44 species per hectare versus Grenada's 2.76 people and 33.88 species) and lower consumption dependency (3.3 gigajoules of energy per $1,000 of gross domestic product, half Grenada's 6.6 gigajoules).

Barbados (Figure 4.9) has the highest scores in the region for health, population, education, basic needs, and peace, and among the highest for freedom and governance. Its chief human weaknesses are crime (668 assaults and 130 robberies per 100,000 people), unemployment (almost 17%), and a riskily high (4.96) ratio of short-term debt to foreign exchange reserves. The lackluster equity rating is due

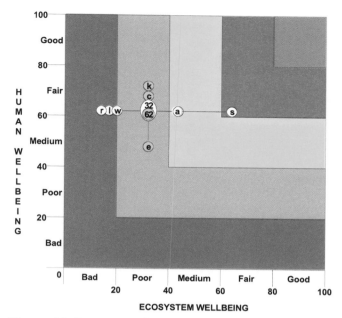

**Figure 4.9. Structure of wellbeing: Barbados.** Yellow circles show the points on the scale of the human dimensions: c = community; e = equity; h = health and population; k = knowledge; w = wealth. White circles show the points of the ecosystem dimensions: a = air; l = land; r = resource use; s = species and genes; w = water. Some dimensions are hidden by the egg (community, health and population, wealth).

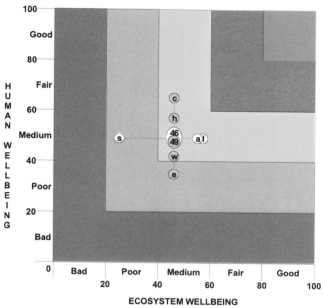

**Figure 4.10. Structure of wellbeing: Dominican Republic.** See Figure 4.9 for key. Some dimensions are hidden by the egg (knowledge, water) or behind another dimension (land is behind air). The Dominican Republic's EWI excludes resource use, which otherwise would have increased it artificially.

to underrepresentation of males in tertiary school and females in primary and secondary schools and in politics (women hold less than 11% of the seats in parliament).

Barbados has the highest population density in the region (6.28 people per hectare), which partly accounts for its extremely low scores for land, water, and resource use. Over half of its land area is either built or cultivated, less than a tenth is still more or less natural, and only 40 hectares are protected. Water withdrawal equals the renewable supply, the country depends on imports for food and timber, and its exploitation of fisheries is intense. Despite the evident pressure on land and water, few species are threatened: under 1% of plants and no mammals, breeding birds, amphibians, or land reptiles (two marine turtle species are at risk). Barbados could raise its EWI to medium by maintaining wild and domesticated diversity, increasing land protection, accelerating the phaseout of ozone depleting substances (consumption of which accounts for the low-medium score for air), holding energy use at current levels, increasing domestic food production without degrading the environment, and reducing fishing pressure.

Among the larger countries (Bahamas, Cuba, Dominican Republic, Haiti, Jamaica, and Trinidad and Tobago), the Dominican Republic (Figure 4.10) ranks fourth in human wellbeing, first in ecosystem wellbeing, and first

overall. Its strongest human dimension is community (surpassed only by Trinidad and Tobago): freedoms of expression, organization, and religion are generally respected, but elections are marred by violence and the judiciary is corrupt (crime was not rated). Its fair grade for education (only the Bahamas is better) is offset by mute communications: nine main telephone lines and three mobile phone subscribers per 100 people and even fewer Internet users (weaknesses shared by all countries in the group except the Bahamas). Incomes under $5,000 per person, and inflation and unemployment rates of 8% and 16%, reduce its wealth to low-medium, albeit the highest in the group after the Bahamas. With the Bahamas, its equity is the lowest: men have three times the income of women but less education (male enrollment drops from 95% of female enrollment at primary level to barely 80% at tertiary level).

On the environmental side, the Dominican Republic is the opposite of Barbados, with medium grades for land and water yet a poor score for species and genes. Its rates of land conversion and degradation are moderate, and 25% of the land is protected, including 14% in strictly protected areas bigger than 100,000 hectares. Yet, as in all the larger countries, many of its wild species are threatened: 20% of its mammals, 15% of the plants, and 10% of its reptiles and breeding birds. Since a major threat to many of the species is habitat loss, these percentages imply that land protection is better on paper than in practice.

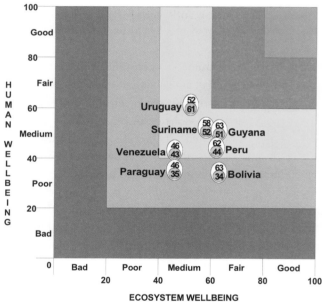

**Figure 4.11. Wellbeing of South America.** Human Wellbeing Index (HWI) in yolk of egg, Ecosystem Wellbeing Index (EWI) in white. The countries in the upper Barometer are the most fully assessed. Those in the lower Barometer were rated on fewer subelements (see Table 4.5).

South America provides several contrasting combinations of human and ecosystem wellbeing (Figure 4.11 and Table 4.5). Among the less fully assessed countries (lower Barometer of Figure 4.11), Peru and Venezuela have virtually the same HWI but quite different EWIs. Peru, with 0.20 people and 0.16 species per hectare against Venezuela's 0.27 people and 0.25 species, is somewhat less vulnerable ecologically. This advantage is borne out by a

**Table 4.5. South America:** Wellbeing Index (WI), Wellbeing/Stress Index (WSI), performance group, and number (#) of subelements covered (out of 30). 1 = fair WI/medium WSI; 2 = medium WI and WSI; 3 = medium WI/poor WSI; 4 = poor WI and WSI; 5 = poor WI/bad WSI; mod. = moderate; def. = deficit; e = ecosystem worse; p = people worse. Country order is by performance group and then by WI.

| Country | WI | WSI | Performance Group | # |
|---|---|---|---|---|
| Guyana | 57.0 | 1.38 | 2: mod. human def. | 27 |
| Peru | 53.0 | 1.16 | 2: mod. human def. | 28 |
| Uruguay | 56.5 | 1.27 | 2: mod. ecosystem def. | 27 |
| Suriname | 55.0 | 1.24 | 2: mod. double def. | 25 |
| Ecuador | 49.5 | 0.98 | 3: mod. double def. | 29 |
| Venezuela | 44.5 | 0.80 | 3: mod. double def. | 28 |
| Colombia | 42.5 | 0.74 | 3: mod. double def. | 29 |
| Bolivia | 48.5 | 0.92 | 3: high human def. | 28 |
| Argentina | 47.5 | 0.92 | 3: high double def. e | 29 |
| Chile | 42.5 | 0.79 | 3: high double def. e | 30 |
| Brazil | 40.5 | 0.70 | 4: high double def. e | 29 |
| Paraguay | 40.5 | 0.65 | 4: high double def. p | 27 |

higher score for species and genes and much lower rates of land conversion and forest loss. However, Venezuela fully protects 21% of its land area, compared with Peru's 2%; and only a tenth of its modified and cultivated land is moderately to strongly degraded, versus two-fifths in Peru. These differences raise Venezuela's land score to 71 and cut Peru's to 38. Peru ends up with a higher EWI because of superior performance in water and air, specifically river conversion and the global atmosphere (neither country was rated on inland water or local air quality). The decisive factor is Venezuela's greater consumption dependency: it consumes over three times more energy per dollar of GDP than Peru, has dammed a much higher proportion of its hydropower capacity (24% versus less than 1%), and emits 6 times more carbon dioxide and 19 times more ozone depleting substances per person. Reducing consumption dependency is clearly the key to raising Venezuela's EWI and would also improve its HWI by boosting economic efficiency.

Uruguay and Guyana have almost identical average WIs but trade places in almost every respect. Uruguay has fair human and medium ecosystem wellbeing, Guyana the reverse. Uruguay has the highest human wellbeing in the region—thanks to fair performance in health and population, knowledge, and community—and leads Guyana in every human dimension except community (it is penalized for high robbery and assault rates, whereas Guyana was not assessed on crime). Guyana has one of the two best EWIs in the region—with fair performance

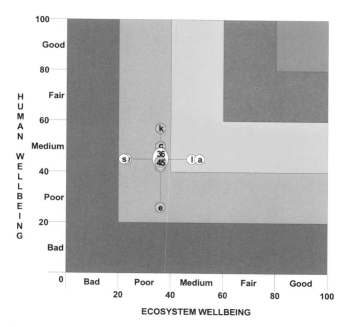

**Figure 4.12. Structure of wellbeing: Brazil.** Yellow circles show the points on the scale of the human dimensions: c = community; e = equity; h = health and population; k = knowledge; w = wealth. White circles show the points of the ecosystem dimensions: a = air; l = land; r = resource use; s = species and genes; w = water. Some dimensions are hidden by the egg (wealth) or behind another dimension (health and population is behind community, water behind species and genes). Brazil's EWI excludes resource use, which otherwise would have increased it artificially.

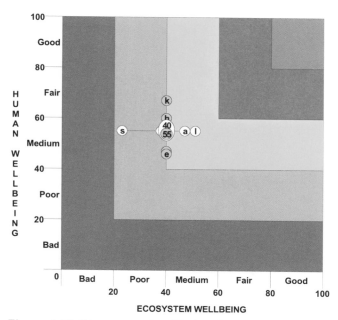

**Figure 4.13. Structure of wellbeing: Argentina.** See Figure 4.12 for key. Some dimensions are hidden by the egg (community, water) or behind another dimension (wealth is behind equity). Argentina's EWI excludes resource use, which otherwise would have increased it artificially.

in water, air, and species and genes—and is ahead of Uruguay in every ecosystem dimension except land (its cultivated land area, though much smaller, is more degraded). Uruguay's consumption dependency and species density are lower than Guyana's, and it could match the latter's EWI by greatly increasing the protected area (currently a tiny 0.3%), improving conservation of wild and domesticated diversity, and reducing consumption of ozone depleting substances. Guyana needs major improvements in income, health, education, and communication to equal Uruguay's HWI.

Of the countries in the upper Barometer of Figure 4.11, only Argentina, Brazil, and Chile were rated on air and water quality (Colombia lacks data on local air quality, Ecuador on water quality). If Ecuador had the average water quality of the other four countries, its EWI would fall to 42; if Colombia had the average air quality of the other four, its EWI would drop to 34.

Brazil (Figure 4.12) and Argentina (Figure 4.13) provide a more reliable contrast. Argentina is within reach of a fair HWI, but Brazil needs as big an effort to achieve a high-medium HWI. In both countries, the priority dimensions are wealth, equity, and community. Both are mired in debt and plagued by high unemployment, and

in both a quarter of the population lacks clean water and basic sanitation. Incomes are much lower in Brazil ($6,625 per person versus Argentina's $12,015) and even less fairly shared: in Argentina, the richest fifth of the population has 11 times the income share of the poorest fifth; in Brazil, 26 times. Rights and freedoms are more fully upheld in Argentina, but the judicial system is venal and inefficient. Brazil's is worse, and its police are among the world's most violent and corrupt. Brazil also trails Argentina in health and education.

Both countries could achieve an EWI above 50 by raising their medium scores in land and air to fair and their poor scores in water and species and genes to medium. The former would entail stabilizing land conversion, expanding the protected area system (more so in Argentina), making moderate improvements in the quality of cultivated land and urban air, and cutting ozone depleting substances. Brazil would also need to hold the line on carbon emissions, and Argentina (which emits more than twice as much per person) to reduce them. Water and species and genes present a tougher problem. Attaining medium scores requires cleaning up pollution (notably in Argentina's Paraná basin and the coastal drainages of Brazil), greatly enhancing species protection (better protected areas would help to secure the 24% of Argentina's plant species and 20% of Brazil's mammals at risk), and conserving domesticated diversity.

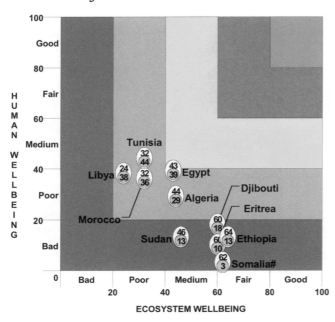

**Figure 4.14. Wellbeing of Northern Africa.** Human Wellbeing Index (HWI) in yolk of egg, Ecosystem Wellbeing Index (EWI) in white. Eritrea's EWI is 60. # Somalia was assessed on less than two-thirds of the human subelements.

**Table 4.6. Northern Africa:** Wellbeing Index (WI), Wellbeing/Stress Index (WSI), performance group, and number (#) of subelements covered (out of 30). 1 = fair WI/medium WSI; 2 = medium WI and WSI; 3 = medium WI/poor WSI; 4 = poor WI and WSI; 5 = poor WI/bad WSI; mod. = moderate; def. = deficit; e = ecosystem worse; p = people worse. Within each subregion, country order is by performance group and then by WI. *Somalia was rated on less than two-thirds of the human subelements.*

| Country | WI | WSI | Performance Group | # |
|---|---|---|---|---|
| *Northeast Africa* | | | | |
| Ethiopia | 38.5 | 0.36 | 5: high human def. | 27 |
| *Somalia* | *32.5* | *0.08* | *5: high human def.* | *19* |
| Djibouti | 39.0 | 0.45 | 5: high double def. p | 23 |
| Eritrea | 35.0 | 0.25 | 5: high double def. p | 22 |
| Sudan | 29.5 | 0.24 | 5: high double def. p | 26 |
| *North Africa* | | | | |
| Egypt | 41.0 | 0.68 | 3: high double def. p | 28 |
| Algeria | 36.5 | 0.52 | 4: high double def. p | 27 |
| Tunisia | 38.0 | 0.65 | 4: high double def. e | 26 |
| Morocco | 34.0 | 0.53 | 4: extreme double def. | 29 |
| Libyan Arab J | 31.0 | 0.50 | 5: extreme double def. | 24 |

In Northeast Africa, ecosystem stress is more than double the level of human wellbeing because living standards are so low (Figure 4.14 and Table 4.6). Ethiopia (Figure 4.15) is typical in almost every human dimension: life expectancy 42 years, healthy life expectancy 33.5 years, rapid population growth (6.2 children per woman), less than half the popula-

**Figure 4.15. Structure of wellbeing: Ethiopia.** Yellow circles show the points on the scale of the human dimensions: c = community; e = equity; h = health and population; k = knowledge; w = wealth. White circles show the points of the ecosystem dimensions: a = air; l = land; r = resource use; s = species and genes; w = water. Some dimensions are hidden by the egg (health and population) or behind another dimension (knowledge is behind wealth, water behind air). Ethiopia's HWI excludes equity and its EWI excludes resource use, which otherwise would have increased them artificially.

tion with enough food, less than a fifth with adequate water and sanitation, GDP per person $575, debt service payments bigger than GDP and nine times the value of exports, a mere third of primary-age children in primary school and a quarter of secondary-age children in secondary school, less than one main telephone line per 100 people, and a solitary Internet user per 100,000 people.

Despite these abysmal conditions, Ethiopia and its neighbors waste themselves on war: Djibouti, Somalia, and Sudan spend 5% of their GDP on the military, Ethiopia 6%, and Eritrea 36%. In the late 1990s, all but Djibouti have battled each other (border disputes among Eritrea, Ethiopia, and Sudan, between Ethiopia and Somalia, and between Sudan and Uganda) and internally (Somalia, northern and southern Sudan, and the Oromo area of Ethiopia). These conflicts have killed an average of 52,000 people a year since they began, and reveal a persistent refusal to set aside differences in favor of better lives for their people. (Ethiopia's score for community would be as bad as its co-combatants' but is lifted to poor by an astonishingly low reported crime rate.)

Endemic conflict also bodes ill for ecosystem wellbeing, which requires as great a commitment to the good

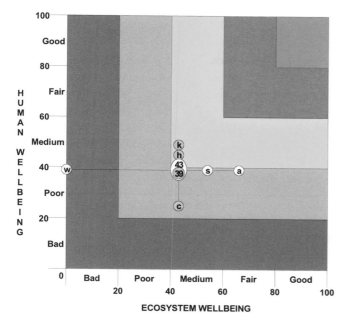

**Figure 4.16. Structure of wellbeing: Egypt.** See Figure 4.15 for key. Some dimensions are hidden by the egg (wealth) or behind another dimension (land is behind species and genes). Egypt's HWI excludes equity and its EWI excludes resource use, which otherwise would have increased them artificially.

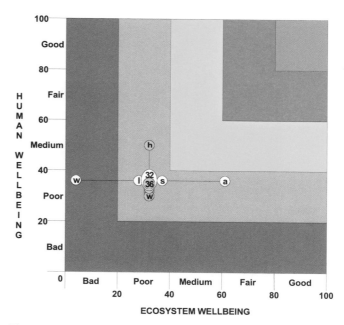

**Figure 4.17. Structure of wellbeing: Morocco.** See Figure 4.15 for key. Some dimensions are hidden by the egg (community, knowledge). Morocco's HWI excludes equity and its EWI excludes resource use, which otherwise would have increased them artificially.

of the community as does progress in health and education. The real EWIs of Ethiopia and its eastern neighbors are probably closer to Sudan's since it alone includes water quality (bad; in the Khartoum area, both the Blue and White Nile are bloated with heavy loads of nutrients). The chief concerns (besides water pollution) are land degradation, habitat loss, and the declining diversity of livestock breeds.

Human conditions are better in North Africa, but the state of the ecosystem is worse. Although the ratio of human wellbeing to ecosystem stress is higher than in Northeast Africa, the drift to the left of the Barometer is an ominous sign that the region is regressing environmentally almost as much as it is developing socioeconomically.

This need not be. Egypt, Morocco, and Libya have similar HWIs but quite dissimilar EWIs, showing that the environmental price of the quality of life is as flexible in North Africa as anywhere else. Egypt gets a zero score for water (Figure 4.16) because it extracts 80% of the flow of the Nile and 30 times more water than it receives from rain. Yet it manages to achieve a medium EWI, thanks to medium grades for land and species and genes and a fair rating for air (based on global atmosphere only). Morocco's water score also plumbs the depths (Figure 4.17): it takes a more frugal 37% of its supply (all from rainfall) but then fouls rivers and groundwater with nutrients, fecal coliforms, and heavy

metals. Its air score is close to Egypt's (and also does not count local air quality). Where it lags behind is in land and species and genes: 30% of land built or cultivated (Egypt 7%) and 13% of plant species threatened (Egypt 4%). Morocco could boost its EWI by cleaning up its water, curbing threats to wild and domesticated diversity, and expanding protected areas (which cover less than 1% of the land). Egypt's water problems are harder to fix, but it could raise its EWI further by strengthening habitat protection (its protected area coverage is also less than 1%).

Egypt's weakest human dimension is community, followed by wealth and health and population. Progress in one depends on advances in the others: Open and accountable government is needed to encourage enterprise, enterprise to raise incomes, economic opportunity and education (especially for females) to lower fertility rates, and population stability to relieve pressure on social services and the labor market.

Morocco also rates poorly in community, but corruption is lower than in Egypt, press freedom is higher, and attention is being paid to judicial reform and human rights. However, wealth and knowledge warrant just as much attention. The main needs are to extend safe water and sanitation to all, increase employment and incomes, cut external debt, and enhance access to primary and secondary education.

## West Africa

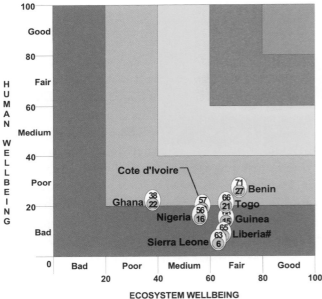

**Figure 4.18. Wellbeing of West Africa: Sahelian West Africa above, Coastal West Africa below.** Human Wellbeing Index (HWI) in yolk of egg, Ecosystem Wellbeing Index (EWI) in white. The HWI of Burkina Faso (BF) is 17; Chad's HWI is 14 and EWI 60; Côte d'Ivoire's HWI is 20; Guinea's EWI is 66; Liberia's HWI is 9. # Liberia was assessed on less than two-thirds of the human subelements.

Sahelian West Africa consists of the member countries of the Permanent Inter-State Committee to Combat Drought in the Sahel.[6] Coastal West Africa includes the remaining countries, which are generally less arid (although parts extend into the geographical Sahel).

**Table 4.7. West Africa:** Wellbeing Index (WI), Wellbeing/Stress Index (WSI), performance group, and number (#) of subelements covered (out of 30). 1 = fair WI/medium WSI; 2 = medium WI and WSI; 3 = medium WI/poor WSI; 4 = poor WI and WSI; 5 = poor WI/bad WSI; mod. = moderate; def. = deficit; e = ecosystem worse; p = people worse. Within each sub-region, country order is by performance group and then by WI. *Liberia was rated on less than two-thirds of the human subelements.*

| Country | WI | WSI | Performance Group | # |
|---|---|---|---|---|
| **Sahelian** | | | | |
| Cape Verde | 47.0 | 0.89 | 3: mod. double def. | 23 |
| Guinea-Bissau | 39.5 | 0.38 | 5: high human def. | 25 |
| Gambia | 39.0 | 0.42 | 5: high human def. | 25 |
| Burkina Faso | 37.5 | 0.40 | 5: high double def. p | 25 |
| Senegal | 37.0 | 0.43 | 5: high double def. p | 27 |
| Chad | 36.0 | 0.32 | 5: high double def. p | 24 |
| Niger | 33.5 | 0.25 | 5: high double def. p | 25 |
| Mali | 32.5 | 0.38 | 5: high double def. p | 27 |
| Mauritania | 28.5 | 0.28 | 5: extreme double def. | 26 |
| **Coastal** | | | | |
| Benin | 49.0 | 0.93 | 3: high human def. | 25 |
| Togo | 43.5 | 0.62 | 3: high human def. | 25 |
| Guinea | 40.5 | 0.44 | 5: high human def. | 26 |
| *Liberia* | *37.0* | *0.26* | *5: high human def.* | *21* |
| Sierra Leone | 34.5 | 0.16 | 5: high human def. | 25 |
| Côte d'Ivoire | 38.5 | 0.47 | 5: high double def. p | 26 |
| Nigeria | 36.0 | 0.36 | 5: high double def. p | 25 |
| Ghana | 30.0 | 0.35 | 5: extreme double def. | 28 |

The Sahelian group crowds the bottom of the Barometer, with Cape Verde a clear standout (Figure 4.18 and Table 4.7). It leads in every human dimension—performing especially well in education, freedom and governance, and peace—to achieve an HWI 26 points higher than the next highest (Mali). Its medium EWI omits several subelements and is much less meaningful.

Mali (Figure 4.19) is, with Senegal, the best assessed. Its HWI is pulled up by community and down by the other dimensions. In the 1990s, Malians chose their national and local governments freely and fairly, and political debate is open. The human rights record is positive overall but marred by violent clashes between communities and instances of police brutality and torture by security forces. Press freedom is the highest in Africa after Mauritius and South Africa: state-run media, 40 independent newspapers, and 60 independent radio and television stations provide a variety of viewpoints in all regional languages.[7]

In all other respects, Malians are poorly served: GDP

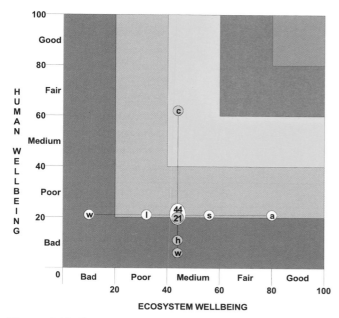

**Figure 4.19. Structure of wellbeing: Mali.** Yellow circles show the points on the scale of the human dimensions: c = community; e = equity; h = health and population; k = knowledge; w = wealth. White circles show the points of the ecosystem dimensions: a = air; l = land; r = resource use; s = species and genes; w = water. One dimension is behind another (knowledge is behind wealth). Mali's HWI excludes equity and its EWI excludes resource use, which otherwise would have increased them artificially.

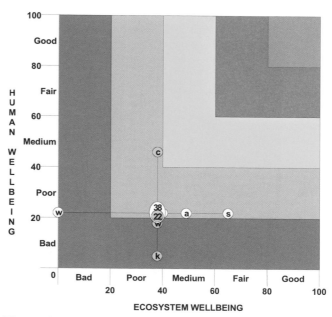

**Figure 4.20. Structure of wellbeing: Ghana.** See Figure 4.19 for key. Some dimensions are hidden by the egg (health and population, wealth, land). Ghana's HWI excludes equity and its EWI excludes resource use, which otherwise would have increased them artificially.

per person is $680 and falling, only 6% of the population has adequate sanitation, 30% of children are stunted and 40% underweight from lack of food, and the child mortality rate is an appalling 236 per 1,000 live births. The knowledge revolution is a mirage: just 38% of primary-age children attend primary school, 18% of secondary-age children attend secondary school, and a mere 0.3% of the population has a main line or cell phone. Similarly, most of the other Sahelian countries combine low levels of health and population, wealth, and knowledge with better performance in community—from a little better but still poor in Chad, Mauritania, Niger, and Senegal to a lot better (medium) in Burkina Faso.

Raising Mali's standard of living is hampered by pressures on the ecosystem, particularly on water and land, which undermine the environmental foundations of health and wealth. Nutrient levels are dangerously high in groundwater and the Niger River. And although only 7% of the land is cultivated or built, barely 3% is protected, while 1% of forest is lost every year. Most seriously, 40% of the cultivated and modified land area is moderately to strongly degraded, risking declines in the already low agricultural productivity.

Coastal West Africa also crowds the floor of the

Barometer (Figure 4.18). Benin is separated from the pack by its human performance, lifted by a standard of freedom and governance higher than Mali's. Ghana (Figure 4.20) stands out for its inferior state of environment—but Ghana is also alone in being rated on all ecosystem subelements. Its poor land and fair species and genes scores are close to those of most of the other coastal countries: 28% of the land is cultivated or built, not much (5%) is protected, the forest is shrinking fast, but the threatened proportion of the inadequately assessed flora and fauna seems to be fairly small. However, Ghana's medium rating for air, which includes the air quality of Accra, is well below the fair and good grades of the rest of West Africa (except Nigeria), which count only pressure on the global atmosphere. So is its low mark for water, a result of severe pollution by heavy metals and the impact of dams on the Volta River—a degree of river conversion much greater than anywhere else in the region.

The pattern of human wellbeing on the Coast is the same as in the Sahel: very poor health and population, wealth, and knowledge; marginally better community in Côte d'Ivoire, Guinea, Niger, and Togo; much better community in Ghana, although nowhere near the level of Benin, where political rights are more fully observed and the press is freer.

Community levels in Benin, Mali, and Cape Verde show that high standards are achievable in West Africa. The rest of the region needs to match them, and all countries to make equivalent progress in health, education, income, and environmental quality.

# Central and East Africa

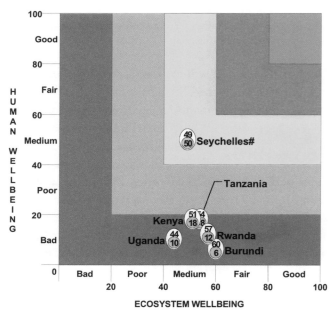

**Figure 4.21. Wellbeing of Central and East Africa: Central Africa above, East Africa below.** Human Wellbeing Index (HWI) in yolk of egg, Ecosystem Wellbeing Index (EWI) in white. Cameroon's HWI is 15 and EWI 64; the HWI of the Central African Republic (CAR) is 16; Tanzania's HWI is 18 and EWI 54. # São Tomé and Principe was assessed on less than two-thirds of the human subelements, Seychelles on less than two-thirds of the ecosystem subelements.

All but one of the Central African countries have high human deficits, combining fair ecosystem wellbeing and poor or bad (mostly bad) human wellbeing. By contrast, all but one of the East African countries have high double

**Table 4.8. Central and East Africa:** Wellbeing Index (WI), Wellbeing/Stress Index (WSI), performance group, and number (#) of subelements covered (out of 30). 1 = fair WI/medium WSI; 2 = medium WI and WSI; 3 = medium WI/poor or bad WSI; 4 = poor WI and WSI; 5 = poor WI/bad WSI; mod. = moderate; def. = deficit; e = ecosystem worse; p = people worse. Within each subregion, country order is by performance group and then by WI. *São Tomé and Principe was rated on less than two-thirds of the human subelements, Seychelles on less than two-thirds of the ecosystem subelements.*

| Country | WI | WSI | Performance Group | # |
|---|---|---|---|---|
| *Central Africa* | | | | |
| Gabon | 45.0 | 0.74 | 3: high human def. | 24 |
| Congo, R | 43.5 | 0.54 | 3: high human def. | 25 |
| Central African R | 41.0 | 0.47 | 3: high human def. | 25 |
| Cameroon | 39.5 | 0.42 | 5: high human def. | 25 |
| Equatorial Guinea | 38.5 | 0.39 | 5: high human def. | 23 |
| Congo, DR | 36.0 | 0.20 | 5: high human def. | 24 |
| *São Tomé and* | | | | |
| *Principe* | *31.5* | *0.21* | *5: high double def. p* | *19* |
| *East Africa* | | | | |
| *Seychelles* | *47.0* | *0.90* | *3: mod. double def.* | *20* |
| Tanzania | 36.0 | 0.39 | 5: high double def. p | 27 |
| Kenya | 35.5 | 0.40 | 5: high double def. p | 27 |
| Rwanda | 34.5 | 0.28 | 5: high double def. p | 24 |
| Burundi | 33.0 | 0.15 | 5: high double def. p | 24 |
| Uganda | 27.0 | 0.18 | 5: high double def. p | 27 |

deficits, combining medium ecosystem wellbeing and bad human wellbeing (Figure 4.21 and Table 4.8). Central Africa's environment scored better partly because it was less fully assessed and partly because more land is still natural or seminatural, less land is degraded, smaller percentages of wild species are threatened, and domesticated diversity is less at risk.

Gabon's air score (Figure 4.22) is relatively low because, like other oil producers, it uses fuel carelessly and emits large amounts of carbon. In most other environmental respects, Gabon is fairly typical of Central Africa. Just 4% of the land has been converted to farms and settlements, and 65% remains in a natural or seminatural state. Forest loss is well below 1% a year, and only 8% of cultivated and modified land is moderately degraded. Small percentages of flowering plant species (1.4%) and mammal and bird species (3.5%) are threatened. But the status of wild and domesticated diversity is poorly known, and the protected area system covers just 2.7% of the land area. The other countries in the subregion depart from this picture in different ways: Cameroon has much less natural land, land degradation

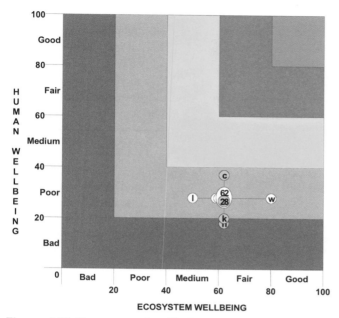

**Figure 4.22. Structure of wellbeing: Gabon.** Yellow circles show the points on the scale of the human dimensions: c = community; e = equity; h = health and population; k = knowledge; w = wealth. White circles show the points of the ecosystem dimensions: a = air; l = land; r = resource use; s = species and genes; w = water. Some dimensions are hidden by the egg (air, species and genes) or behind another dimension (health and population is behind knowledge, wealth is behind community). Gabon's HWI excludes equity and its EWI excludes resource use, which otherwise would have increased them artificially.

**Figure 4.23. Structure of wellbeing: Tanzania.** See Figure 4.22 for key. Some dimensions are hidden by the egg (health and population) or behind another dimension (land is behind water). Tanzania's HWI excludes equity and its EWI excludes resource use, which otherwise would have increased them artificially.

is extensive, and its heritage of livestock breeds is both better known and greatly at risk; the Central African Republic has an adequate system of protected areas; in the Democratic Republic of Congo 22% of plant species are threatened; and São Tomé and Principe has lost all but a patch of its natural land and is in danger of losing 26% of its mammals and birds.

Like much of East Africa, Tanzania (Figure 4.23) has retained a fair amount (40%) of natural land, but almost 13% of its cultivated and modified land is moderately to strongly degraded. The high point of its land performance is the system of parks and reserves, which cover an impressive 27% of the land—3% in strictly protected areas bigger than a million hectares. Inland water quality, while apparently almost fair, is erratically monitored. The weakest dimension is species and genes: a third of Tanzania's plant species is threatened, and almost two-thirds of its cattle breeds are at risk. Elsewhere in East Africa, land degradation is more widespread and severe (except possibly in the Seychelles, which lacks data); Burundi, Rwanda, and Seychelles have negligible natural land, and only scraps of Burundi are protected; livestock diversity is less at risk in

Kenya; and water pollution is worse in Kenya and Uganda (the only other countries where it was assessed).

Human conditions are virtually the same in Central and East Africa. All countries have poor or medium scores for equity (except Central African Republic and São Tomé and Principe, bad) and bad or poor scores for the other dimensions (except Seychelles, medium). Gabon's oil earnings translate into a regionally high GDP of $6,355 per person and higher percentages of people whose basic needs are met than anywhere else in the region except Seychelles (92% with enough food, 67% with safe water and basic sanitation) but not into better health or education. A high ratio (32.6) of short-term debt to reserves reduces its wealth score to poor.

Tanzania's knowledge, wealth, and health and population scores are bad because under half of primary-age children attend primary school; telecommunications barely function (more faults than main lines and cell phones combined); 40% of the population lacks sufficient food, 34% safe water; the economy is weak and heavily indebted; life expectancy at birth is 45 years, healthy life expectancy 36 years; and the total fertility rate exceeds five children per woman. Rapid improvements in these conditions depend on raising community standards from poor to medium or better: at present, corruption is rampant, the judiciary politically controlled, press freedom restricted, and elections tainted by fraud.

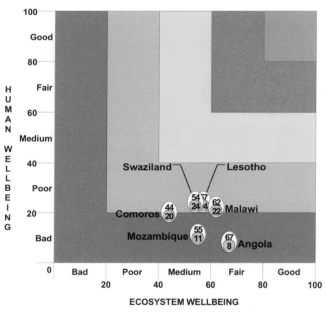

**Figure 4.24. Wellbeing of Southern Africa.** Human Wellbeing Index (HWI) in yolk of egg, Ecosystem Wellbeing Index (EWI) in white. The countries in the upper Barometer are the most fully assessed. Those in the lower Barometer were rated on fewer subelements (see Table 4.9). Lesotho's HWI is 24 and EWI 57.

Southern Africa is in a better position to advance toward sustainability than the other African regions (Figure 4.24 and Table 4.9). It has more countries with a WI above 40.0 (four) apart from Central and East Africa (also four); more with a WSI above 0.50 (eight), including the only one (Botswana) with a WSI above 1.00; more coun-

**Table 4.9. Southern Africa:** Wellbeing Index (WI), Wellbeing/Stress Index (WSI), performance group, and number (#) of subelements covered (out of 30). 1 = fair WI/medium WSI; 2 = medium WI and WSI; 3 = medium WI/poor WSI; 4 = poor WI and WSI; 5 = poor WI/bad WSI; mod. = moderate; def. = deficit; e = ecosystem worse; p = people worse. Country order is by performance group and then by WI.

| Country | WI | WSI | Performance Group | # |
|---|---|---|---|---|
| Botswana | 51.0 | 1.06 | 2: high human def. | 27 |
| Mauritius | 49.0 | 0.96 | 3: mod. double def. | 28 |
| Namibia | 44.0 | 0.74 | 3: high double def. p | 26 |
| Malawi | 42.0 | 0.58 | 3: high human def. | 25 |
| Lesotho | 40.5 | 0.56 | 3: high double def. p | 25 |
| Swaziland | 39.0 | 0.52 | 4: high double def. p | 25 |
| Zimbabwe | 39.0 | 0.51 | 4: high double def. p | 27 |
| South Africa | 35.0 | 0.59 | 4: high double def. e | 29 |
| Angola | 37.5 | 0.24 | 5: high human def. | 25 |
| Madagascar | 37.0 | 0.48 | 5: high double def. p | 27 |
| Mozambique | 33.0 | 0.24 | 5: high double def. p | 26 |
| Comoros | 32.0 | 0.36 | 5: high double def. p | 21 |
| Zambia | 29.5 | 0.28 | 5: high double def. p | 27 |

tries with fair or medium education (six: Botswana, Mauritius, Namibia, South Africa, Swaziland, and Zimbabwe); and more with fair or medium freedom and governance (eight: Botswana, Lesotho, Madagascar, Malawi, Mauritius, Mozambique, Namibia, and South Africa).

Botswana (Figure 4.25) enjoys medium scores for wealth and community, thanks to a GDP per person of $6,105, one of the lightest debt loads in the world, limited corruption (the least among the African countries rated by Transparency International), the longest continuous multiparty democracy in Africa (governments have been freely and fairly elected since independence in 1966), and a start to restoring the land rights of the Basarwa ("Bushmen").

All is not well, however. GDP per person is falling (down from $7,690 the previous year), and poverty is widespread: 45% of the population lacks basic sanitation and 25% enough food. Primary and secondary school enrollment rates are quite high, but few children go on to university (59 per 10,000 people), and although more people have access to telephones and the Internet than in most other countries in Africa, they are still a small minority. But the main drag on the HWI is the poor score for health and population, largely due to HIV/AIDS. Currently infecting one of every four adults, AIDS has sliced life expectancy to 39 years and healthy life expectancy to 32 years.

Environmentally, Botswana has much to build on. Air, water, land, and species and genes are fair (but the first

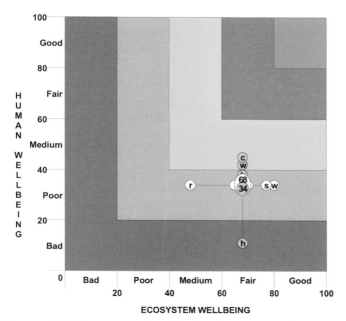

**Figure 4.25. Structure of wellbeing: Botswana.** Yellow circles show the points on the scale of the human dimensions: c = community; e = equity; h = health and population; k = knowledge; w = wealth. White circles show the points of the ecosystem dimensions: a = air; l = land; r = resource use; s = species and genes; w = water. Some dimensions are hidden by the egg (knowledge, air, land). Botswana's HWI excludes equity, which otherwise would have increased it artificially.

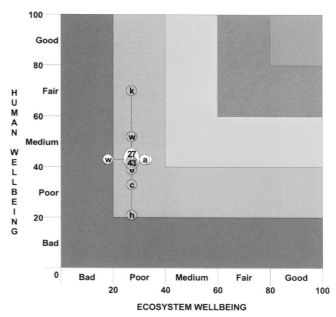

**Figure 4.26. Structure of wellbeing: South Africa.** See Figure 4.25 for key. Some dimensions are hidden by the egg (equity, species and genes) or behind another dimension (health and population is behind community, land is behind air). South Africa's EWI excludes resource use, which otherwise would have increased it artificially.

two do not include water quality or local air pollution). The main land concern is soil degradation (almost 14% of the modified and cultivated land area is moderately to strongly degraded), but more than 40% of the total land area is undisturbed, and more than 18% is protected, mostly in units of a million hectares or more. Few species are threatened (3% of mammals, 1% of breeding birds, 0.3% of flowering plants), and apparently little of the country's livestock diversity is at risk (except that local cattle types are lumped into the Tswana "breed" and may be disappearing). However, this modest pressure on the land may be a side effect of low self-reliance: Botswana imports most of its food, growing only a third of its supply of cereals and roots (hence the medium score for resource use).

South Africa's clear strength is knowledge (Figure 4.26): primary school enrollment virtually 100%, secondary enrollment 95%, 184 tertiary students per 10,000 people, and a moderately developed communication system (Africa's best along with those of Mauritius and the Seychelles). Wealth signals are mixed: GDP per person $8,490 and growing, but short-term debt more than double foreign exchange reserves; a low (for Africa) 13% of the population without safe water and basic sanitation, but 23% of children stunted by lack of food. The most

pressing weaknesses are health (as in the rest of the region, AIDS is whittling life expectancy) and community. South Africa's transition to democracy is being consolidated, the press has been unshackled, and the judiciary and other institutions that enforce the highly progressive constitution and protect human rights have established their independence. But these advances are compromised by a plague of violence, fueled by inequities and thwarted expectations: for example, the richest fifth of the population has 22 times the income share of the poorest fifth.

South Africa's struggle to spread the benefits of development is bound up with the state of the environment. More than a third of its extraordinarily rich plant diversity and 13% of its mammal species are at risk. Carbon dioxide emissions are high (2,232 kg per person), and dams control half the national water flow. Severe soil loss—accounting for both the poor score for land and the bad score for water—reduces the productivity of almost 40% of cultivated and modified land and burdens the waters of the Orange River basin (covering 47% of the country) with heavy loads of silt. One answer is to enhance habitat protection; another is to increase the resource efficiency of the economy. But improving the living conditions of the rural poor is also vital since much of the degraded area is land they depend on for survival.

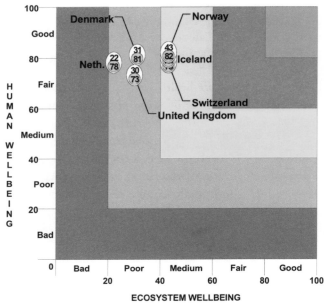

**Figure 4.27. Wellbeing of Northern Europe.** Human Wellbeing Index (HWI) in yolk of egg; Ecosystem Wellbeing Index (EWI) in white. Lux. = Luxembourg; Neth. = Netherlands. Finland's HWI is 81 and EWI 44; Luxembourg's HWI is 77 and EWI 24; Iceland's HWI is 80 and EWI 43; Switzerland's HWI is 77 and EWI 43.

Northern Europe spreads across the upper left eighth of the Barometer (Figure 4.27 and Table 4.10), with moderate ecosystem deficit countries to the right of high ecosystem deficit ones. HWIs are within 10 points of each other, and scores are similar for health and population (all good), wealth (good or high fair), and knowledge (good except for Luxembourg, capped at high fair because of lack of data).

**Table 4.10. Northern Europe:** Wellbeing Index (WI), Wellbeing/Stress Index (WSI), performance group, and number (#) of subelements covered (out of 30). 1 = fair WI/medium WSI; 2 = medium WI and WSI; 3 = medium WI/poor WSI; 4 = poor WI and WSI; 5 = poor WI/bad WSI; mod. = moderate; def. = deficit; e = ecosystem worse; p = people worse. Country order is by performance group and then by WI and WSI.

| Country | WI | WSI | Performance Group | # |
|---|---|---|---|---|
| Sweden | 64.0 | 1.55 | 1: mod. ecosystem def. | 30 |
| Finland | 62.5 | 1.45 | 1: mod. ecosystem def. | 30 |
| Norway | 62.5 | 1.44 | 1: mod. ecosystem def. | 30 |
| Iceland | 61.5 | 1.40 | 1: mod. ecosystem def. | 26 |
| Austria | 61.0 | 1.38 | 1: mod. ecosystem def. | 29 |
| Switzerland | 60.5 | 1.37 | 2: mod. ecosystem def. | 30 |
| Germany | 56.5 | 1.20 | 2: high ecosystem def. | 30 |
| Denmark | 56.0 | 1.17 | 2: high ecosystem def. | 30 |
| Ireland | 54.0 | 1.12 | 2: high ecosystem def. | 28 |
| United Kingdom | 51.5 | 1.04 | 2: high ecosystem def. | 30 |
| Belgium | 51.5 | 1.04 | 2: high ecosystem def. | 30 |
| Luxembourg | 50.5 | 1.01 | 2: high ecosystem def. | 28 |
| Netherlands | 50.0 | 1.00 | 3: high ecosystem def. | 30 |

However, community performance ranges from good (Switzerland and Austria) to medium (Sweden and the United Kingdom; Sweden is hampered by relatively high crime rates, especially assaults, and the United Kingdom by the conflict in Northern Ireland) and equity from high fair (Sweden, Norway, Finland, Denmark, Belgium) to medium (Switzerland, Luxembourg, Ireland, United Kingdom).

While there is still room to improve human wellbeing, the more pressing need is to eliminate ecosystem deficits. This will be easier for Sweden (Figure 4.28), with no poor or bad dimension; harder for the other moderate-deficit countries and Germany and Ireland, with one to three weak dimensions; and most demanding for the remaining high-deficit countries (including the Netherlands, Figure 4.29), which have low scores for four dimensions. Countries could go far by emulating the regional leaders in land protection (Austria and Germany), land quality (Ireland and Norway), local air quality (Sweden), fisheries (Ireland), and timber (Germany and Norway), but they also need to advance dramatically in the other elements.

*Species & genes* (Finland and Switzerland fair; the rest medium). The status of wild mammal and bird species goes from bad in Iceland (27.3% threatened) to medium in Switzerland (4.3%). That of wild plant species seems to be good (from 1.8% threatened in Ireland to 0.1% in Belgium and the Netherlands), but no country reports on all plant groups.[8] Livestock breeds are more at risk, especially in Austria and the United Kingdom, where threat-

**Figure 4.28. Structure of wellbeing: Sweden.** Yellow circles show the points on the scale of the human dimensions: c = community; e = equity; h = health and population; k = knowledge; w = wealth. White circles show the points of the ecosystem dimensions: a = air; l = land; r = resource use; s = species and genes; w = water. Some dimensions are hidden by the egg (equity, wealth, land, water, resource use).

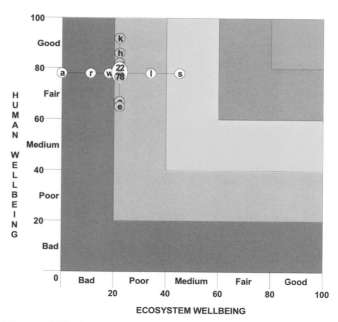

**Figure 4.29. Structure of wellbeing: Netherlands.** See Figure 4.28 for key. Some dimensions are hidden by the egg (wealth) or behind another dimension (community is behind equity).

ened breeds outnumber those whose survival is secure. The United Kingdom has pioneered livestock conservation but has the most breeds (120) to conserve.

*Land* (Austria, Finland, Germany, Norway, Sweden, and Switzerland medium; the rest poor). Finland, Norway, Sweden, Iceland, Austria, and Switzerland have converted less than a quarter of their land to buildings and cultivation, and the first four retain large tracts of natural land. Elsewhere, settlements and farmland occupy from 36% of the country in Ireland to 71% in Denmark, and natural land is scarce. Native forests are expanding in Austria and Germany, which also lead the region by protecting 28% and 25% of their respective land areas. Land quality is good or fair, except in Austria and Belgium (medium) and Iceland (poor due to overgrazing and plant removal).

*Water* (Iceland fair; Finland, Norway, and Sweden medium; the rest poor or bad). Iceland's fair score omits water quality, which is no better than medium in Finland, Norway, and Sweden (the latter two report patchily). Elsewhere, it is bad or poor, largely due to pollution by nutrients and heavy metals. Additional pressures on inland waters are high rates of extraction in Belgium (58% of rainfall) and Germany (41%) and dams in Austria, Ireland, Luxembourg, and the United Kingdom.

*Air* (Sweden and Switzerland medium; Luxembourg, Netherlands, and Norway bad; the rest poor). Local air

quality, which drops from Sweden's breathable 73 score to the United Kingdom's almost acceptable 55 score, is way above the grades for global atmosphere. Sweden and Switzerland, the region's lowest emitters of carbon dioxide, respectively discharge 1,462 and 1,531 kg of carbon per person, almost double the level that would get a fair score (below 800 kg). Most emit two to four times this amount, Norway exceeds it more than fivefold, and Luxembourg more than sixfold. Ozone depleting substances (ODSs) are a problem only where they are produced. Switzerland has cut consumption to an exemplary 1 gram per person. European Union members (all but Switzerland, Norway, and Iceland) consume 55 grams per person, but this is dwarfed by the almost 1,100 grams per person produced by the Netherlands, Europe's biggest manufacturer of ODSs.

*Resource use* (Austria, Ireland, Norway, and Sweden medium; the rest poor or bad). All countries consume too much energy, Belgium and the Netherlands the most (per hectare), Austria and Ireland the least. Many also consume more than their sustainable supply of farm produce (Iceland, Norway), seafood (Belgium, Germany), or timber (Netherlands, United Kingdom). Denmark and Ireland are self-reliant in seafood, and their fishing capacities are commensurate with their catches and fish-producing areas. Germany, Norway, Sweden, Finland, and Ireland keep their timber fellings plus imports well below the annual increment of their domestic forests (from 90% in Ireland to as low as 65% in Germany).

## Southern Europe

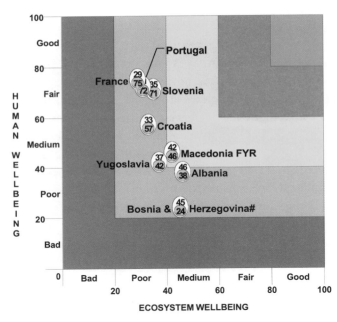

**Figure 4.30. Wellbeing of Southern Europe.** Human Wellbeing Index (HWI) in yolk of egg, Ecosystem Wellbeing Index (EWI) in white. Macedonia FYR = the Former Yugoslav Republic of Macedonia. Greece's EWI is 33; Portugal's HWI is 72 and EWI 31; Slovenia's HWI is 71 and EWI 35. # Bosnia and Herzegovina was assessed on less than two-thirds of the human subelements.

In Southern as in Northern Europe, most countries have high ecosystem deficits, clustering in the top left of the Barometer (Figure 4.30 and Table 4.11). A minority, consisting of Albania and the former Yugoslav republics except Slovenia, has double deficits. Those of Albania, Bosnia and Herzegovina, Macedonia, and Yugoslavia may

**Table 4.11. Southern Europe:** Wellbeing Index (WI), Wellbeing/Stress Index (WSI), performance group, and number (#) of subelements covered (out of 30). 1 = fair WI/medium WSI; 2 = medium WI and WSI; 3 = medium WI/poor WSI; 4 = poor WI and WSI; 5 = poor WI/bad WSI; mod. = moderate; def. = deficit, e = ecosystem worse; p = people worse. Country order is by performance group and then by WI. *Bosnia and Herzegovina was rated on less than two-thirds of the human subelements.*

| Country | WI | WSI | Performance Group | # |
|---|---|---|---|---|
| Slovenia | 53.0 | 1.09 | 2: high ecosystem def. | 28 |
| Italy | 52.0 | 1.06 | 2: high ecosystem def. | 30 |
| France | 52.0 | 1.06 | 2: high ecosystem def. | 30 |
| Greece | 51.5 | 1.04 | 2: high ecosystem def. | 30 |
| Portugal | 51.5 | 1.04 | 2: high ecosystem def. | 30 |
| Spain | 46.5 | 0.91 | 3: high ecosystem def. | 30 |
| Malta | 42.0 | 0.83 | 3: high ecosystem def. | 26 |
| Macedonia, FYR | 44.0 | 0.79 | 3: mod. double def. | 24 |
| Croatia | 45.0 | 0.85 | 3: high double def. e | 29 |
| Albania | 42.0 | 0.70 | 3: high double def. p | 27 |
| Yugoslavia | 39.5 | 0.67 | 4: high double def. e | 24 |
| *Bosnia and Herzegovina* | *34.5* | *0.44* | *5: high double def. p* | *20* |

be worse than shown: Albania's EWI does not include local air quality, and the EWIs of the others omit water quality and water withdrawal as well.

Croatia (Figure 4.31) leads the five double deficit countries in all human dimensions except community, falling well behind Macedonia in freedom and governance (medium in Macedonia, bad in Yugoslavia, poor in the rest). It is healthier (healthy life expectancy drops from 66.9 years in Croatia to 59.9 years in Albania), wealthier, and has better developed education and communication systems than the others. Land is in a sorry state in all five countries: natural land has almost entirely disappeared, and large areas of modified and cultivated land are moderately to strongly degraded (from 41% in Macedonia to 72% in Albania). Croatia's water quality is bad (nutrients). Albania consumes less energy and emits less carbon dioxide than the other countries and has fewer threatened animal species (2.4% of mammals and birds, versus 6.6% in Croatia and 13–14% in the others).

The seven high ecosystem deficit countries enjoy levels of human wellbeing far above the double deficit group's and show the rewards of better governance and commitment to peace and democracy. Their human dimension scores are as high as Northern Europe's except for health and population in Slovenia; wealth in Greece, Malta, and Slovenia; knowledge in Greece, Malta, and Portugal; and community in Spain. Slovenia has the lowest healthy life expectancy in the group (68.4 years), and

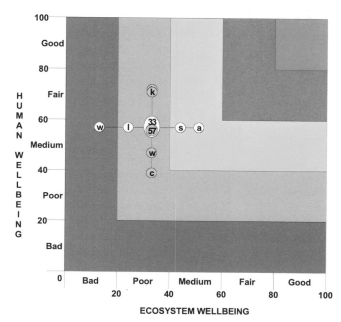

**Figure 4.31. Structure of wellbeing: Croatia.** Yellow circles show the points on the scale of the human dimensions: c = community; e = equity; h = health and population; k = knowledge; w = wealth. White circles show the points of the ecosystem dimensions: a = air; l = land; r = resource use; s = species and genes; w = water. One dimensions is behind another (health and population is behind knowledge). Croatia's HWI excludes equity and its EWI excludes resource use, which otherwise would have increased them artificially.

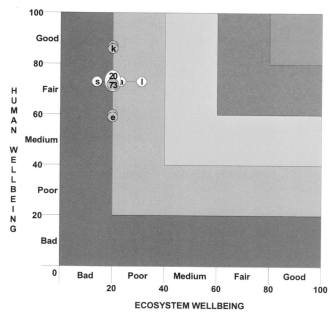

**Figure 4.32. Structure of wellbeing: Spain.** See Figure 4.31 for key. Some dimensions are hidden by the egg (wealth, air) or behind another dimension (community is behind equity, health and population behind knowledge, water behind species and genes). Spain's EWI excludes resource use, which otherwise would have increased it artificially.

its economy is sapped by inflation. Greece is the least prosperous (GDP per person $13,945), and its communication system needs upgrading; so does Portugal's. Malta's economy is flawed by high budget deficits, and it has the lowest education performance in the group. Spain's score for community is reduced by Basque separatist terrorism. Mediocre equity drags down the HWIs of all seven. Improving these aspects is the clear human priority.

Ecosystem stress is severe in all the high ecosystem deficit countries but especially in Malta and Spain, where it is higher than human wellbeing. Malta consumes more water, ozone depleting substances (ODSs), energy, food, and timber than its small, arid, and densely populated ecosystem can support. Spain has more room (room for almost 1,600 Maltas) but still causes an unusual degree of environmental damage, mostly to water, air, and species and genes (Figure 4.32).

Water quality is bad in Spain (nutrients and cadmium) and France (nutrients, heavy metals, and fecal coliforms), poor in Portugal, Slovenia, and Italy, medium in Greece (Malta not rated). Local air quality is medium except in Italy (poor) and Slovenia and Malta (not rated). However, all but Portugal have poor scores for global

atmosphere (and hence for air) because of their carbon dioxide emissions (over twice the amount of carbon that would qualify for a fair score), and four of them (Spain, France, Italy, and Greece) make large quantities of ODSs. Portugal does not produce ODSs, uses less energy (per person, hectare, and dollar of GDP), and emits a medium-scoring 1,370 kg of carbon per person.

Spain has the only bad score for species and genes (poor in France, Greece, Portugal, and Slovenia; medium in Italy and Malta). Despite having the fewest people and (after France) species per hectare, it has the most threatened plants (20%), mammals (29%), and breeding birds (2.2%). Like France and Italy, Spain has a rich heritage of livestock breeds, much of which has been lost already. While many of the survivors are in danger of disappearing in all three countries, more are on the brink in Spain: for every breed not at risk, almost two are threatened (compared with 0.75 each in France and Italy). Land scores are poor throughout (except Malta, bad) because of widespread loss of natural land and inadequate protection.

As in Northern Europe, a practical strategy for environmental progress in Southern Europe would be to emulate the regional leaders in some aspects (France in land quality, Portugal in energy) and to raise the bar in others (land protection, water quality, global atmosphere, local air quality, and wild and domesticated diversity).

133

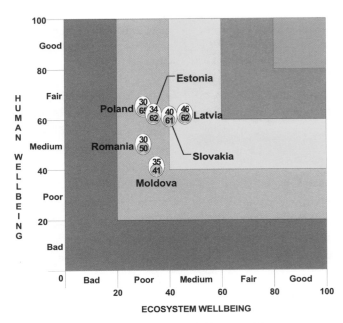

**Figure 4.33. Wellbeing of Eastern Europe.** Human Wellbeing Index (HWI) in yolk of egg, Ecosystem Wellbeing Index (EWI) in white. Hungary's EWI is 33.

**Table 4.12. Eastern Europe:** Wellbeing Index (WI), Wellbeing/Stress Index (WSI), performance group, and number (#) of subelements covered (out of 30). 1 = fair WI/medium WSI; 2 = medium WI and WSI; 3 = medium WI/poor WSI; 4 = poor WI and WSI; 5 = poor WI/bad WSI; mod. = moderate; def. = deficit; e = ecosystem worse; p = people worse. Country order is by performance group and then by WI.

| Country | WI | WSI | Performance Group | # |
|---|---|---|---|---|
| Latvia | 54.0 | 1.15 | 2: mod. ecosystem def. | 28 |
| Lithuania | 52.5 | 1.09 | 2: mod. ecosystem def. | 30 |
| Czech R | 51.5 | 1.04 | 2: high ecosystem def. | 29 |
| Slovakia | 50.5 | 1.02 | 2: high ecosystem def. | 29 |
| Hungary | 49.0 | 0.97 | 3: high ecosystem def. | 30 |
| Estonia | 48.0 | 0.94 | 3: high ecosystem def. | 28 |
| Poland | 47.5 | 0.93 | 3: high ecosystem def. | 30 |
| Belarus | 48.0 | 0.92 | 3: mod. double def. | 27 |
| Bulgaria | 44.5 | 0.84 | 3: high double def. e | 30 |
| Romania | 40.0 | 0.71 | 4: high double def. e | 30 |
| Moldova | 38.0 | 0.63 | 4: high double def. e | 28 |
| Ukraine | 36.5 | 0.64 | 4: high double def. e | 28 |

and Poland have HWIs within 4 points of each other but EWIs separated by up to 16 points.

The leaders in human wellbeing (Czech Republic, Hungary, Poland, Estonia, Latvia, Lithuania, and Slovakia) have a median HWI of 62, well below the Southern European vanguard's 72 and Northern Europe's 79 but well above the rest of Eastern Europe's 46. The leaders need to improve all human dimensions (except equity) to catch up with Northern Europe, and the laggards need to do likewise to catch up with their regional leaders. Healthy life expectancy at birth ranges from 61.5 years in Moldova to 68 years in the Czech Republic (in Northern Europe from 69 to 73 years). GDP per person rises from $1,945 in Moldova to $12,360 in the Czech Republic, far below Northern Europe's range of $20,335 to $33,505. Eastern European economies are also prone to high inflation, unemployment, or both and are more indebted. While all of Northern Europe (except Ireland) has a good score for communication, the most wired countries in Eastern Europe (Estonia, Slovakia, Hungary, and Poland) are no better than fair, although they are chatterboxes compared with Ukraine, Moldova, and Romania (19 main phone lines and cell phones per 100 people) and Belarus (7 Internet users per 10,000). The leaders with fair HWIs have fair scores for freedom and governance, falling short of the good scores of their northern neighbors (apart from Belgium and the United Kingdom), mainly because of greater corruption and restrictions on civil liberties. Freedoms are more limited in Bulgaria and Romania and still more so in Ukraine, Moldova, and authoritarian Belarus.

Eastern Europe clearly shows the breakability of the link between human wellbeing and ecosystem stress (Figure 4.33 and Table 4.12). The state of the environment is poor in 9 of the 12 countries, but development levels slide from comfortably fair in the Czech Republic, Hungary, and Poland to barely medium in Moldova. By the same token, nations with similar standards of living differ widely in ecosystem wellbeing: Belarus performs better than Ukraine; and Latvia, Lithuania, Slovakia, Estonia,

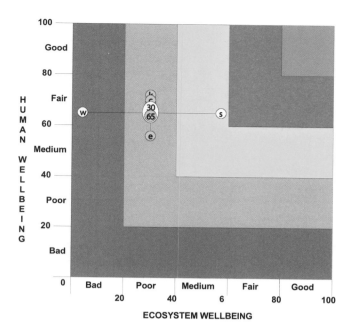

**Figure 4.34. Structure of wellbeing: Poland.** Yellow circles show the points on the scale of the human dimensions: c = community; e = equity; h = health and population; k = knowledge; w = wealth. White circles show the points of the ecosystem dimensions: a = air; l = land; r = resource use; s = species and genes; w = water. Some dimensions are hidden by the egg (air, land) or behind another dimension (health and population is behind community, wealth is behind equity). Poland's EWI excludes resource use, which otherwise would have increased it artificially.

The state of the environment is better in Belarus than Ukraine in almost every respect. Less land has been converted to cultivation and settlement (35% versus 72%); less of the cultivated and modified land is degraded (3% moderately versus 34% moderately and 3% extremely); less of the water supply is controlled by dams or extracted (5% and 7% versus 13% and 49%); and fewer bird and mammal species are threatened (4% versus 9%). Belarus's local air quality is medium, Ukraine's water quality bad (neither was rated on both). Agriculture is the one aspect in which Ukraine outperforms Belarus, being both more productive and more self-reliant, advantages that will vanish unless soil quality is restored.

Latvia and Estonia, by contrast, have almost identical scores for land and species and genes. What separates them is their impacts on water and air. Latvia's rivers are overloaded with nutrients, but Estonia's are even more burdened. Estonia also emits 3,559 kg of carbon per person, almost four times Latvia's 904 kg (neither was assessed on local air quality). The pair's economic and social performance also differs, but not enough to explain the environmental discrepancies. Estonia's education and communication systems are stronger, but Latvia has a

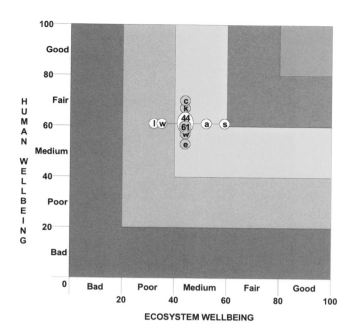

**Figure 4.35. Structure of wellbeing: Lithuania.** See Figure 4.34 for key. One dimension is hidden by the egg (health and population). Lithuania's EWI excludes resource use, which otherwise would have increased it artificially.

higher community rating because of fewer violent crimes. Latvia has the better score for wealth (57 versus 50) because of lower debt, but incomes are higher in Estonia (GDP per person $7,680 versus $5,730). Estonia also consumes over twice as much energy (per person) and uses it less efficiently, requiring 35 gigajoules (GJ) per $1,000 of GDP, compared with Latvia's 20 GJ. (While all of Eastern Europe uses energy inefficiently, only Ukraine is more profligate than Estonia.)

Poland (Figure 4.34) and Lithuania (Figure 4.35) share similar levels and patterns of human wellbeing; the chief differences are that healthy life expectancy in Poland is two years longer and its knowledge score is slightly higher. Yet they diverge environmentally along the same lines as Estonia and Latvia: scores are practically the same for land and species and genes; dramatically different for water and air. Poland grossly contaminates rivers and groundwater with nutrients, fecal coliforms, and heavy metals. In Lithuania, nutrient and heavy metal pollution of inland waters is also serious but not as extreme. Local air quality is medium in both countries, but Poland's carbon dioxide emissions are more than double Lithuania's even though they use almost the same amount of energy per person and Poland is more efficient (17 versus 24 GJ per $1,000 of GDP). The difference is that Lithuania consumes mostly liquid fuels, which are low in carbon compared with the coal that Poland burns in huge quantities.

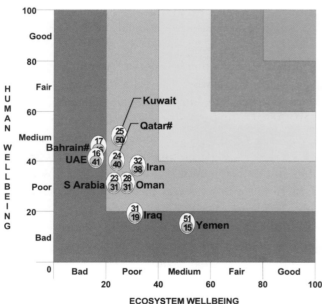

**Figure 4.36. Wellbeing of West Asia: northwest above, southwest below.** Human Wellbeing Index (HWI) in yolk of egg, Ecosystem Wellbeing Index (EWI) in white. Azerbaijan's HWI is 42 and EWI 28. Jordan's EWI is 28. Bahrain's HWI is 46. # Bahrain and Qatar were assessed on less than two-thirds of the ecosystem subelements.

West Asia presents the bleakest picture: most countries cluster in the bottom left corner of the Barometer (Figure 4.36), and it has the highest proportion of nations with high or extreme double deficits—all except Cyprus, Armenia, and Georgia—reflecting the widespread combination of environmental degradation, resource depletion, and depressed living standards (Table 4.13).

**Table 4.13. West Asia:** Wellbeing Index (WI), Wellbeing/Stress Index (WSI), performance group, and number of subelements covered (out of 30). 1 = fair WI/medium WSI; 2 = medium WI and WSI; 3 = medium WI/poor WSI; 4 = poor WI and WSI; 5 = poor WI/bad WSI; mod. = moderate; def. = deficit; e = ecosystem worse; p = people worse. Within each subregion, country order is by performance group and then by WI. *Bahrain and Qatar were rated on less than two-thirds of the ecosystem subelements.*

| Country | WI | WSI | Performance Group | # |
|---|---|---|---|---|
| *Northwest Asia* | | | | |
| Cyprus | 52.5 | 1.08 | 2: high ecosystem def. | 27 |
| Armenia | 50.0 | 1.00 | 3: mod. double def. | 26 |
| Georgia | 44.5 | 0.81 | 3: mod. double def. | 26 |
| Israel | 42.0 | 0.79 | 3: high double def. e | 27 |
| Turkey | 36.5 | 0.63 | 4: high double def. e | 30 |
| Azerbaijan | 35.0 | 0.58 | 4: high double def. e | 26 |
| Lebanon | 38.5 | 0.63 | 4: extreme double def. | 25 |
| Jordan | 33.0 | 0.53 | 4: extreme double def. | 28 |
| Syrian Arab R | 26.5 | 0.37 | 5: extreme double def. | 27 |
| *Southwest Asia* | | | | |
| Kuwait | 37.5 | 0.67 | 4: high double def. e | 25 |
| *Bahrain* | *31.5* | *0.55* | *4: high double def. e* | *20* |
| Iran | 35.0 | 0.56 | 4: extreme double def. | 26 |
| *Qatar* | *32.0* | *0.53* | *4: extreme double def.* | *20* |
| Yemen | 33.0 | 0.31 | 5: high double def. p | 26 |
| United Arab Emirates | 28.5 | 0.49 | 5: high double def. e | 23 |
| Oman | 29.5 | 0.43 | 5: extreme double def. | 23 |
| Saudi Arabia | 27.0 | 0.40 | 5: extreme double def. | 24 |
| Iraq | 25.0 | 0.28 | 5: extreme double def. | 24 |

The region is sharply divided between rich and poor: Incomes range from $720 per person in Yemen to more than $25,000 per person in Kuwait. Scores for wealth are poor for just under half the countries (Georgia, Iraq, Jordan, Lebanon, Syria, Turkey, and Yemen), fair for most of the other half (Cyprus, Israel, Kuwait, Qatar, Saudi Arabia, and United Arab Emirates). Armenia, Azerbaijan, Bahrain, Iran, and Oman have medium levels of wealth.

All but two countries have poor or bad ratings for freedom and governance, preventing their citizens from freely choosing how and by whom they will be governed, denying basic human rights, and shackling the press. Israel's score is medium, the average of a fair score in Israel proper (no better than fair because Arab Israelis are second-class citizens in education, housing, and social services) and poor in the West Bank and East Jerusalem. Cyprus is fair (rather than good) because of the division between Greek and Turkish Cypriots and limited political rights in Turkish Cyprus. Most nations also have poor or bad scores for peace, some because of ongoing conflicts

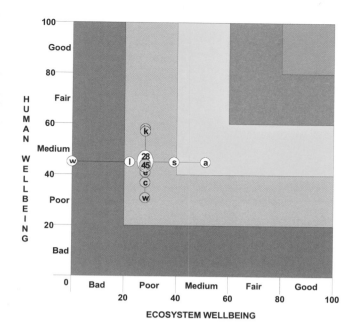

**Figure 4.37. Structure of wellbeing: Turkey.** Yellow circles show the points on the scale of the human dimensions: c = community; e = equity; h = health and population; k = knowledge; w = wealth. White circles show the points of the ecosystem dimensions: a = air; l = land; r = resource use; s = species and genes; w = water. Some dimensions are hidden by the egg (equity) or behind another dimension (health and population is behind knowledge). Turkey's EWI excludes resource use, which otherwise would have increased it artificially.

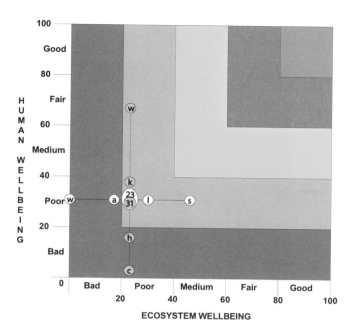

**Figure 4.38. Structure of wellbeing: Saudi Arabia.** See Figure 4.37 for key. One dimension is hidden by the egg (resource use). Saudi Arabia's HWI excludes equity, which otherwise would have increased it artificially.

with neighbors or groups inside their borders (Georgia, Iran, Iraq, Lebanon, Turkey, and Yemen), others because they devote 8% or more of their GDP to the military (Armenia, Kuwait, Oman, Qatar, and Saudi Arabia), Israel because of both.

Wealth is generally higher in Southwest Asia, but health and population, knowledge, and overall human wellbeing are higher in Northwest Asia. Turkey (Figure 4.37) and Saudi Arabia (Figure 4.38) typify their regions in this respect. Turkey's low wealth is due to inadequate infrastructure (only half the population has safe water), feverish inflation rates, and reckless deficits. Saudi Arabia's inferior health and population score reflects a fertility rate of almost six children per woman; its low grade for knowledge results from poor primary and secondary school attendance (a scant 63% of boys and 56% of girls) and negligible access to the Internet (one person in a thousand).

Damage to land, air, and water are widespread symptoms of wasteful consumption and disregard for the public good. The countries with fair scores for wealth emit excessive amounts of carbon dioxide and ozone depleting substances (ODSs). Several poorer nations (Iran, Jordan, Lebanon, and Syria) are heavy

users of ODSs. Yet Turkey sets an example with moderate impacts on the global atmosphere and medium local air quality. Eleven countries extract more than their renewable water supply: Azerbaijan, Israel, Jordan, and Syria in Northwest Asia, and all of Southwest Asia except Iran and Yemen (which use 55% and 72%, respectively). Turkey withdraws a restrained 18% but dams more than its total supply and severely pollutes rivers with nutrients, lead, and cadmium.

Turkey has the same HWI as Armenia, but Armenia's EWI is higher (by 27 points), partly because it was not rated on water quality, use of ODSs, or local air quality, but also because—despite being more densely populated—it is better at conserving land. Turkey has converted 46% of its land to buildings and cultivation, and the area of fairly natural land has shrunk to 2%. Armenia has converted 30%, and an estimated 13% is natural. Turkey protects less than 2%, Armenia 7%. As much as 42% of Turkey's agricultural land is moderately to strongly degraded, compared with 5% of Armenia's. However, scores for species and genes are almost identical because, although Turkey has higher percentages of threatened wild species (12% of plants, 15% of mammals), its livestock breeds are less at risk. Assuming Armenia's water quality is as bad as Georgia's (19 score) and its local air quality and ODS consumption are the same as Turkey's, Armenia would still have an EWI of 39 (11 points above Turkey's).[9]

## Russia and Central and East Asia

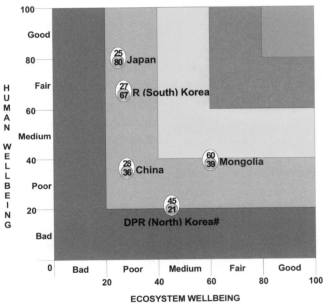

**Figure 4.39. Wellbeing of Russia and Central and East Asia: Russia and Central Asia above, East Asia below.** Human Wellbeing Index (HWI) in yolk of egg, Ecosystem Wellbeing Index (EWI) in white. Turkmenistan's EWI is 30. # Afghanistan and North Korea (DPR = Democratic People's Republic) were assessed on less than two-thirds of the human subelements.

**Table 4.14. Russia and Central and East Asia:** Wellbeing Index (WI), Wellbeing/Stress Index (WSI), performance group, and number (#) of subelements covered (out of 30). 1 = fair WI/medium WSI; 2 = medium WI and WSI; 3 = medium WI/poor WSI; 4 = poor WI and WSI; 5 = poor WI/bad WSI; mod. = moderate; def. = deficit; e = ecosystem worse; p = people worse. Within each subregion, country order is by performance group and then by WI. *Afghanistan and DPR Korea were rated on less than two-thirds of the human subelements.*

| Country | WI | WSI | Performance Group | # |
|---|---|---|---|---|
| *Russia* | | | | |
| Russian Federation | 45.0 | 0.83 | 3: mod. double def. | 29 |
| *Central Asia* | | | | |
| Kyrgyzstan | 40.0 | 0.66 | 3: high double def. p | 27 |
| Kazakhstan | 37.5 | 0.63 | 4: high double def. e | 28 |
| Uzbekistan | 33.0 | 0.51 | 4: extreme double def. | 26 |
| *Afghanistan* | *27.0* | *0.12* | *5: high double def. p* | *20* |
| Tajikistan | 33.5 | 0.46 | 5: extreme double def. | 26 |
| Turkmenistan | 31.0 | 0.46 | 5: extreme double def. | 25 |
| *East Asia* | | | | |
| Japan | 52.5 | 1.07 | 2: high ecosystem def. | 30 |
| Mongolia | 49.5 | 0.98 | 3: high double def. p | 26 |
| Korea, R | 47.0 | 0.92 | 3: high ecosystem def. | 30 |
| *Korea, DPR* | *33.0* | *0.38* | *5: high double def. p* | *18* |
| China | 32.0 | 0.50 | 5: extreme double def. | 30 |

Taliban, which shirks the duties of government but ruthlessly imposes religious dogma. The result: one of the world's worst records for disease, poverty, illiteracy, and abuse of women. Life is not nearly as grim elsewhere, but only Kazakhstan achieves medium scores for all human dimensions except community (poor). Ecosystem conditions are poor (the medium EWIs of Afghanistan and Kyrgyzstan are misleading since they do not count air and water quality), the main defects being skimpy land protection (all countries), massive river conversion (Kazakhstan, Kyrgyzstan, and Tajikistan) and overconsumption of water (Turkmenistan and Uzbekistan).

Continent-sized, sparsely populated Russia (Figure 4.40) has converted just 10% of its land to buildings and cultivation, and an estimated 66% is still natural. This includes 94% of native forest that is claimed to be undisturbed, implying that logging has affected a tree-huggingly small 6%.[10] Assuming that large tracts of natural forest do remain, they will not for long unless rampant cutting is curbed and the protected area (a meager 3%) is at least quadrupled. Rivers are extremely polluted in places—such as the Irtysh at Krasnyi Jar and the Kuban where it enters the Azov Sea—but on average water quality is medium. The main problems are acidification, heavy metals, and

Central Asian nations (Figure 4.39 and Table 4.14) differ in their ills, but oppression is common to all. In the most democratic, Kyrgyzstan, freedoms of expression and organization are upheld capriciously, and elections are tainted by ballot box stuffing and inflation of voter turnouts. In the least, Turkmenistan is ruled by a dictator, and Afghanistan is 10% fought over and 90% run by the

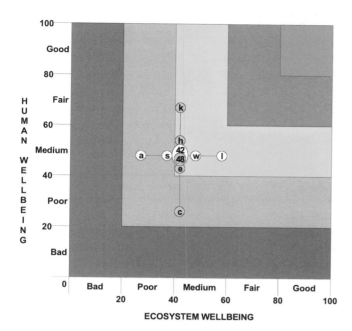

**Figure 4.40. Structure of wellbeing: Russia.** Yellow circles show the points on the scale of the human dimensions: c = community; e = equity; h = health and population; k = knowledge; w = wealth. White circles show the points of the ecosystem dimensions: a = air; l = land; r = resource use; s = species and genes; w = water. One dimension is hidden by the egg (wealth). Russia's EWI excludes resource use, which otherwise would have increased it artificially.

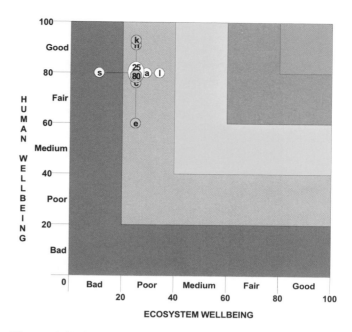

**Figure 4.41. Structure of wellbeing: Japan.** See Figure 4.40 for key. Some dimensions are hidden by the egg (community, wealth, water) or behind another dimension (health and population is behind knowledge). Japan's EWI excludes resource use, which otherwise would have increased it artificially.

excess nutrients, although this last lessened during the 1990s as agriculture stagnated and fertilizer use declined. Average local air quality is also medium, but Russia's air rating is poor because of high outputs of carbon dioxide and ozone depleting substances.

The chief obstacle to improving the environment is poor governance. The state has randomized into an arbitrary force, moved largely by corruption, that uses its power more to intimidate the media, coerce the judiciary, and make war on Chechnya than to create a fair arena for enterprise, provide high-quality social services, and uphold the rule of law. While education is still good, communications are backward, health is deteriorating, and infrastructure decaying. The economy is overdependent on consumption (38 gigajoules of energy per $1,000 of GDP) and short-changes citizens with double-digit unemployment, rising prices, and mediocre incomes (GDP $6,460 per person).

China's strength is health and population—a healthy life expectancy of 62 years and a fertility rate of 1.8 children per woman—but it is weak in most other aspects. Incomes are low (GDP $3,105 per person), three-quarters of the population lacks basic sanitation, university education is limited to a small minority, corruption is rife, and civil and political rights are ignored. The ecosystem is respected even less: 21% of farmland is moderately to strongly degraded;

rivers are laden with bacteria, toxics, and silt; and 17% of plants and 13% of mammals and birds are at risk.

In North Korea and Mongolia, almost half the people lack sufficient food. North Korea is poorer than China in all human dimensions; Mongolia, in all but community (thanks to huge advances in democracy). Their EWIs are better because neither was rated on air or water quality, both have less degraded land, and much of Mongolia's land is still fairly natural.

Japan (Figure 4.41) is among the world's leaders in every human dimension except equity (flawed by the obstacles women face in business and government). However, it needs to greatly improve every ecosystem dimension. Rivers and groundwater are polluted with nutrients, fecal coliforms, and heavy metals. Energy consumption is high, and carbon dioxide emissions three times the level that would get a fair score. The country's fisheries produce only 55% of its seafood supply, yet overexploit a fourth of major fish species. Well over half the land is built or cultivated, but less than 9% is protected—not enough to secure agricultural diversity or the 20% of plants and 18% of birds and mammals that are threatened.

South Korea has fewer species and livestock breeds at risk but protects less land and pollutes rivers as much and the global atmosphere more. Its task is to raise its EWI while elevating every human dimension except knowledge to catch up with Japan.

139

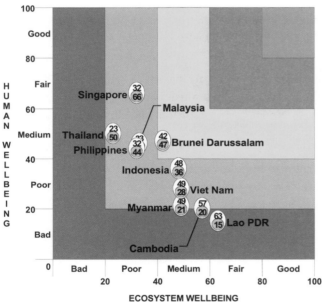

**Figure 4.42. Wellbeing of Southern Asia: South Asia above, Southeast Asia below.** Human Wellbeing Index (HWI) in yolk of egg, Ecosystem Wellbeing Index (EWI) in white. Lao PDR = Lao People's Democratic Republic. Maldives' HWI is 22 and EWI 47. Malaysia's HWI is 46 and EWI 33. # Maldives was assessed on less than two-thirds of the ecosystem subelements.

Most of South Asia is strung across the bottom of the Barometer, separated more by environmental than by socioeconomic performance (Figure 4.42 and Table 4.15). The exception is Sri Lanka, with a markedly higher quality of life thanks to superior health and population (Figure 4.43). Its healthy life expectancy of 62.8 years is well above the subregion's span of 49.4 years in Nepal to 55.9 years in

**Table 4.15. Southern Asia:** Wellbeing Index (WI), Wellbeing/Stress Index (WSI), performance group, and number (#) of subelements covered (out of 30). 1 = fair WI/medium WSI; 2 = medium WI and WSI; 3 = medium WI/poor WSI; 4 = poor WI and WSI; 5 = poor WI/bad WSI; mod. = moderate; def. = deficit; e = ecosystem worse; p = people worse. Within each subregion, country order is by performance group and then by WI. *Maldives was rated on less than two-thirds of the ecosystem subelements.*

| Country | WI | WSI | Performance Group | # |
|---|---|---|---|---|
| *South Asia* | | | | |
| Sri Lanka | 48.5 | 0.93 | 3: high double def. p | 28 |
| Nepal | 46.0 | 0.78 | 3: high human def. | 27 |
| Bhutan | 40.5 | 0.42 | 5: high human def. | 23 |
| Bangladesh | 36.5 | 0.50 | 5: high double def. p | 28 |
| *Maldives* | *34.5* | *0.42* | *5: high double def. p* | *19* |
| Pakistan | 31.0 | 0.32 | 5: high double def. p | 27 |
| India | 29.0 | 0.42 | 5: extreme double def. | 29 |
| *Southeast Asia* | | | | |
| Singapore | 49.0 | 0.97 | 3: high ecosystem def. | 24 |
| Brunei Darussalam | 44.5 | 0.81 | 3: mod. double def. | 22 |
| Indonesia | 42.0 | 0.69 | 3: high double def. p | 29 |
| Malaysia | 39.5 | 0.69 | 4: high double def. e | 29 |
| Philippines | 38.0 | 0.65 | 4: high double def. e | 30 |
| Thailand | 36.5 | 0.65 | 4: high double def. e | 30 |
| Viet Nam | 38.5 | 0.55 | 4: high double def. p | 27 |
| Lao PDR | 39.0 | 0.41 | 5: high human def. | 25 |
| Cambodia | 38.5 | 0.47 | 5: high double def. p | 25 |
| Myanmar | 35.0 | 0.41 | 5: high double def. p | 26 |

Pakistan, and its replacement-level fertility rate of 2.1 children per woman is well below the 3.0 of India and Bhutan's 5.4. These advances partly compensate for the depressed wealth, knowledge, and community that Sri Lanka shares with the rest of South Asia. GDP per person ranges from $1,155 in Nepal to $4,085 in the Maldives (Sri Lanka $2,980), and many in each nation go without the essentials for survival: 37% lack enough food in Bangladesh, 43% safe water in Sri Lanka, 84% basic sanitation in Nepal. Many are also deprived of the basic tools for intellectual development and economic betterment: primary school enrollment drops from 100% of primary-age children in Sri Lanka to 13% in Bhutan, tertiary enrollment from a low 64 per 10,000 people in India to 30 in Pakistan (47 in Sri Lanka); extremely small minorities have phones and access to the Internet. Restricted freedom, corruption, violence, armed conflict, or a mixture of these reduce community scores, which are medium in Nepal, bad in Bhutan and Pakistan, and poor in the rest—the key failing in Sri Lanka's case being the civil war with the Tamils.

The wide range of EWIs, from India's 27 to Bhutan's

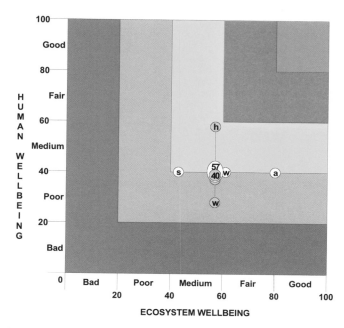

**Figure 4.43. Structure of wellbeing: Sri Lanka.** Yellow circles show the points on the scale of the human dimensions: c = community; e = equity; h = health and population; k = knowledge; w = wealth. White circles show the points of the ecosystem dimensions: a = air; l = land; r = resource use; s = species and genes; w = water. Some dimensions are hidden by the egg (community, knowledge) or behind another dimension (land is behind species and genes). Sri Lanka's HWI excludes equity and its EWI excludes resource use, which otherwise would have increased them artificially.

67, is due to two factors. First, differences in land diversity: lowest where most of the land is built or cultivated (Bangladesh and India), 5% or less is protected (Bangladesh, India, Maldives, and Pakistan), or forest loss is more than 2% a year (Bangladesh and Pakistan); highest where much of the land is natural (Nepal 21%, Bhutan 71%). Second, differences in coverage: local air quality was rated only in India, water quality in Bangladesh, India, and Pakistan. Sri Lanka's air score would be 25 if its city air is as poor as India's, its water score 29 if its rivers are as polluted as India's Coromandel Coast.

Southeast Asia climbs backwards from the bad HWI and fair EWI of Lao to the fair HWI and poor EWI of Singapore. Singapore could raise its HWI further by opening itself to political diversity and the free flow of information, giving women greater access to positions of power, and improving primary and secondary education. Cutting resource use is the key to boosting its EWI: energy consumption is the world's highest per hectare and ninth highest per person; carbon dioxide emissions are eight times the maximum fair level and rising fast.

While Thailand tackles its economic debt, its social and

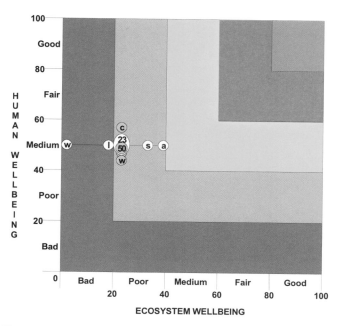

**Figure 4.44. Structure of wellbeing: Thailand.** See Figure 4.43 for key. Some dimensions are hidden by the egg (equity, health and population, knowledge). Thailand's EWI excludes resource use, which otherwise would have increased it artificially.

ecosystem deficits are mounting (Figure 4.44). Incomes have fallen since the Asian financial crisis (GDP per person is $5,455), poverty has spread (24% lack enough food), and disparities have sharpened (the richest fifth has nine times the income share of the poorest). Efforts to increase wealth are impoverishing the environment. Air quality is poor, rivers are clogged with nutrients and fecal coliforms, almost 80% of farm and grazing land is moderately degraded, and 8% of mammals and birds are at risk, along with much agricultural diversity. Feeding people sustainably and boosting health depend on protecting diversity and restoring land, air, and water quality. Combining this with building the economy requires better education, communication, and governance: freedoms are generally respected, and elections are being cleaned up, but corruption is common among officials, the police, and the judiciary.

The three next best assessed countries have lower HWIs and higher EWIs. Malaysia is wealthier, with better-developed communications, but its fertility rate is higher and it is only partly free. The Philippines is more educated, but fertility, poverty, and corruption are higher. Indonesia is weaker in all human dimensions. On the environmental side, Malaysia has less degraded land and fewer threatened species; the Philippines has less extreme land degradation and water pollution; Indonesia is stronger in all ecosystem dimensions except water, which is just as contaminated.

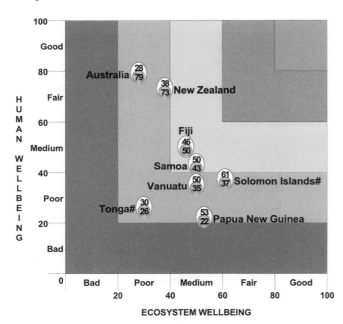

**Figure 4.45. Wellbeing of the Pacific.** Human Wellbeing Index (HWI) in yolk of egg, Ecosystem Wellbeing Index (EWI) in white. # Tonga was assessed on less than two-thirds of the human and ecosystem subelements; Solomon Islands on less than two-thirds of the human subelements.

**Table 4.16. Pacific:** Wellbeing Index (WI), Wellbeing/Stress Index (WSI), performance group, and number (#) of subelements covered (out of 30). 1 = fair WI/medium WSI; 2 = medium WI and WSI; 3 = medium WI/poor WSI; 4 = poor WI and WSI; 5 = poor WI/bad WSI; mod. = moderate; def. = deficit; e = ecosystem worse; p = people worse. Country order is by performance group and then by WI. *Tonga was rated on less than two-thirds of the human and ecosystem subelements, Solomon Islands on less than two-thirds of the human subelements.*

| Country | WI | WSI | Performance Group | # |
|---|---|---|---|---|
| New Zealand | 55.5 | 1.18 | 2: high ecosystem def. | 29 |
| Australia | 53.5 | 1.10 | 2: high ecosystem def. | 30 |
| *Solomon Islands* | *49.0* | *0.95* | *3: high human def.* | *22* |
| Fiji | 48.0 | 0.96 | 3: mod. double def. | 26 |
| Samoa | 46.5 | 0.86 | 3: mod. double def. | 22 |
| Vanuatu | 42.5 | 0.70 | 3: high double def. p | 21 |
| Papua New Guinea | 37.5 | 0.47 | 5: high double def. p | 27 |
| *Tonga* | *28.0* | *0.37* | *5: extreme double def.* | *18* |

Papua New Guinea (PNG) and the small island nations of the Pacific face the challenge of creating prosperous, democratic societies that protect their environments and respect their cultural traditions (Figure 4.45 and Table 4.16). Although PNG is better endowed with resources than its

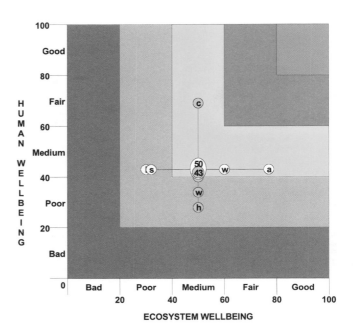

**Figure 4.46. Structure of wellbeing: Samoa.** Yellow circles show the points on the scale of the human dimensions: c = community; e = equity; h = health and population; k = knowledge; w = wealth. White circles show the points of the ecosystem dimensions: a = air; l = land; r = resource use; s = species and genes; w = water. Some dimensions are hidden by the egg (equity, knowledge) or behind another dimension (land is behind species and genes). Samoa's EWI excludes resource use, which otherwise would have increased it artificially.

smaller colleagues, it performs poorly in all human dimensions. Fiji is wealthier, more educated, and has a lower fertility rate than the others, but healthy lifespans are longer in Samoa and Tonga, and Fiji has yet to establish a political system that satisfies both indigenous and Indian Fijians. Underachievement in several dimensions pulls down the HWIs of the others, despite Tonga's medium scores for community and wealth and fair scores for community by Vanuatu, the Solomon Islands, and Samoa (Figure 4.46).

Samoa's community score reflects low rates of violent crime (except assaults) and acceptable, if flawed, freedom and governance. Its mixture of parliamentary democracy, chiefs, and village councils balances community norms and individual freedoms fairly well. However, corruption is growing, and the independent press has been victimized for exposing it. Incomes are low (GDP per person $3,830), 32% of the population lacks safe water, and the fertility rate exceeds 4 children per woman. Education, wealth, and power are also poorly shared in Samoa: fewer boys than girls have a secondary education, and women earn less than a third of the income and occupy just 8% of the seats in parliament.

The EWIs of PNG and its small island colleagues are distorted by lack of data on air and water quality. Land

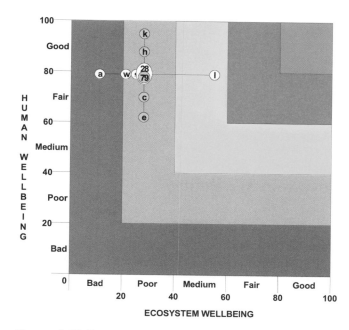

**Figure 4.47. Structure of wellbeing: Australia.** See Figure 4.46 for key. Some dimensions are hidden by the egg (wealth, species and genes). Australia's EWI excludes resource use, which otherwise would have increased it artificially.

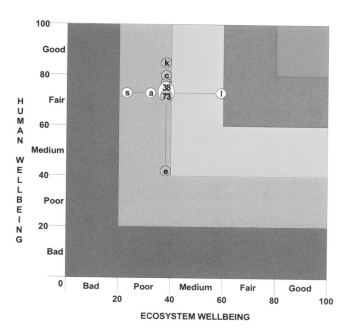

**Figure 4.48. Structure of wellbeing: New Zealand.** See Figure 4.46 for key. Some dimensions are hidden by the egg (wealth, water) or behind another dimension (health and population is behind community). New Zealand's EWI excludes resource use, which otherwise would have increased it artificially.

and species and genes paint a more realistic picture. In Samoa, half the land is built or cultivated, natural land has shrunk to scraps, barely over 4% is protected, and 57% of mammals and birds face extinction. Elsewhere, the converted area ranges from 74% in Tonga to 2% in PNG, the natural area from 0% (Tonga) to 63% (PNG). The percentages of mammals and birds at risk are high throughout—58% in Fiji, 54% in Tonga, 26% in the Solomons, 22% in Vanuatu, 16% in PNG—and protected area coverage is tiny (from 0% in the Solomons and Tonga to 2% in PNG). Since communities will not give up their land, conservation depends on setting up protected areas that provide opportunities for development and are community owned.

Australia (Figure 4.47) and New Zealand (Figure 4.48) enjoy Northern European levels of human wellbeing. New Zealand's health and population and knowledge scores are below Australia's due to a shorter healthy life expectancy (69 versus 73 years), lower tertiary enrollment, and an unreliable telephone system (Australia does not report its phone line faults). Australia's lesser score for community includes crime; New Zealand's does not. The latter's subpar equity rating reflects large disparities in wealth: the richest fifth of the population has 17 times the income share of the poorest fifth (compared with 7 times in Australia).

New Zealand's better EWI reflects differences in

water (inland water quality) and air (global atmosphere)—poor in New Zealand, worse in Australia. New Zealand reports on oxygen balance, nutrient levels, and acidity in all large and many smaller rivers: phosphorus levels are high in most of them, probably because of inefficient use of fertilizers. Australia reports on just three rivers (Murray–Darling, Burdekin, and Derwent), which carry extreme loads of silt and nutrients. While both countries have dramatically cut their use of ozone depleting substances, they emit increasing amounts of carbon dioxide: New Zealand 2,258 kg and Australia 4,709 kg of carbon per person, respectively almost three and six times the maximum level defined as fair. Fossil fuel consumption is excessive, with solid fuels the main culprit in Australia, liquid fuels in New Zealand.

Scores for land and species and genes are close. Although New Zealand has converted more of its land to buildings and cultivation (25% versus Australia's 8%), it also protects more (20% versus 8%). Domesticated diversity is low in both countries, and very high percentages of wild species are threatened: 19% of plants and 15% of birds and mammals in Australia, 7% of plants and 61% of birds and mammals in New Zealand.

Better management of transport and industry is needed to curb fossil fuel use, and of land outside protected areas to conserve wild species, increase agricultural diversity, and restore water quality.

# Aiming for Human and Ecosystem Wellbeing

## Highlights

- The main reasons why no country combines high levels of human and ecosystem wellbeing are that it is inherently difficult to do and, more importantly, no country is committed to doing it.

- Six initiatives are needed for countries to achieve ways of living that are desirable, equitable, and sustainable:

  ♦ Commitment to human and ecosystem wellbeing as a national goal

  ♦ Regular wellbeing assessments to build support for the goal, analyze how to achieve it, and track progress

  ♦ National information systems on human and ecosystem wellbeing and coverage of all aspects of wellbeing by the news media

  ♦ Replacement of most, if not all, existing taxes with taxes on energy and materials

  ♦ Wellbeing areas (Slow Zones) to maintain cultural heritage, wild and domesticated biodiversity, and a high quality of life in mixed built–cultivated–wild landscapes

  ♦ Regional wellbeing alliances, so that existing and new groups of nations can harmonize their efforts to achieve sustainability; and partnerships between rich ecosystem deficit and poor human deficit countries to exchange development support for ecosystem capacity

## Commitment to Human and Ecosystem Wellbeing

The combination of even fair levels of human and ecosystem wellbeing is obviously difficult to achieve, but the degree of difficulty is unknown because no society has consciously aimed for it.

The widespread espousal of international and national sustainable development agendas has not translated into equal commitments to raise the quality of human life and secure the quality and diversity of the environment. It is one thing to insert sustainability into policy documents and quite another to make the sweeping changes that the term implies. All aspects of wellbeing must be addressed together, but many—such as equity, the global atmosphere, and biodiversity—are poorly understood and fail to command more than fleeting political attention. The grand idea of people and the ecosystem in unison is reduced to pages of discrete prescriptions that tend to reflect the limited and often contradictory objectives of particular interest groups, from expanding trade to saving wilderness. These aims could contribute to sustainability if balanced by the other constituents of wellbeing but will obstruct it if pursued alone. Countries would have a better chance of forging them into a coherent agenda for sustainability if they made an explicit commitment to high levels of both human and ecosystem wellbeing as a national goal.

## Regular Wellbeing Assessments

National and local wellbeing assessments provide three essentials for transforming the vision of sustainable development into reality:

- A means of making the goal achievable and measuring progress toward it.

- An analytical tool for deciding priority actions.

- A process to keep the goal constantly in mind and to help people learn how to reach it.

As noted in Chapter 1, a goal that is measurable is attainable. The HWI, EWI, WI, and WSI provide the means by which societies can measure the overall conditions of people and the environment, thereby making it possible for them to adopt better human and ecosystem wellbeing as an achievable goal. Each society can then set targets for itself, deciding how much it wants to raise its

HWI and EWI (and hence its WI and WSI) in a given period.

By breaking down the indices into major components, societies can identify the factors most responsible for their current levels of human and ecosystem wellbeing. The regional reviews illustrated how the Barometer of Sustainability shows instantly what dimensions of wellbeing most need attention. These dimensions can be examined in detail to determine critical features and their relationships with other socioeconomic and environmental factors. Then on the basis of this analysis, societies can consider practical policy options and decide priority actions.

Wellbeing assessments can facilitate the task of building consensus on (or at least majority support for) policies and actions by providing a logical progression from the goal, through objectives for particular elements or sectors, to performance criteria for indicators. They also provide a much-needed mental bridge between the short term and the long term. The hurly-burly of immediate demands and sudden events can overwhelm long-term goals and sharply reduce their influence over the daily decisions of households, businesses, and governments. Wellbeing assessments can offset this danger (to some extent at least) by providing a mechanism to link the practical realities of the present to people's vision of a desirable future.

Sustainable development is fraught with uncertainty. What is a desirable human condition? What makes a resilient and supportive ecosystem? What combinations of human and ecosystem wellbeing would be equitable and durable? Regular wellbeing assessments provide a means of learning from experience, testing the assumptions behind policies and programs, analyzing their impacts, and providing the information needed to do better.

## Information and Communication on Human and Ecosystem Wellbeing

Most countries suffer from a glut of data but a dearth of understanding of human and environmental conditions and interactions. Tsunamis of facts, suppositions, opinions, and beliefs swamp the flow of useful information for decision making. Technologies to disseminate data have outstripped the capacities of societies to assemble and analyze the wide range of information needed to combine high levels of human and ecosystem wellbeing.

These capacities are often fragmented between a statistical agency and many usually tiny and underresourced departmental units responsible for monitoring and reporting on the economy, individual sectors, and international agreements. Such fragmentation has three consequences. First, data on the same topic may be gathered by more than one organization, using different methods and measurements and yielding incompatible results. Second, data are hard to find and are sometimes lost. Third, information is used inefficiently—assembled and analyzed for a particular purpose (say, for an impact assessment), then forgotten or poorly stored, then reassembled and reanalyzed for some other purpose (such as reporting on a treaty).

Lack of data prevented *The Wellbeing of Nations* from covering culture, the seas, and several subelements (state of knowledge, crop diversity, and consumption of materials). Other elements were limited to a small minority of countries or were marred by inferior indicators and inconsistent and unreliable data. Table 4.17 summarizes an informal evaluation of the quality of data on 30 elements and subelements, based on how well the data represented the element (or subelement) concerned, their reliability, and the number of countries for which the data were available. Only 9 of these elements and subelements had adequate data (good or fair rating); for 16, the data were poor or bad.

Environmental information lags well behind data on human conditions. While figures are regularly compiled on many aspects of health, education, and the economy, no one produces equivalent statistics on the status of ecosystems, species, or populations. Adequate environmental monitoring is difficult and expensive but would be far advanced if half the labor and money spent on ad hoc reports, one-time surveys, university theses, and conservation publicity were spent on systematic classification, mapping, and assessment of major ecosystems and groups of species and populations. Publicly and privately funded environmental projects and impact assessments could also contribute substantially to building a wellbeing information system in the countries concerned by standardizing and sharing their data and analyses.

Each country needs an information system on human and ecosystem wellbeing to ensure that essential data for decision making, education, and communication are collected, stored, analyzed, and shared efficiently. The system would turn existing information units into a network, fill the main information gaps, and organize data to facilitate assessments.

**Table 4.17. Informal evaluation of the quality of data on human and ecosystem elements and subelements reviewed for *The Wellbeing of Nations*.** Elements are in CAPITALS; subelements are in lowercase. *Elements and subelements dropped for lack of data are listed in italics.*

| Rating | Human Wellbeing Number and Names of ELEMENTS and Subelements | Ecosystem Wellbeing Number and Names of ELEMENTS and Subelements |
|---|---|---|
| Good | 3: POPULATION, income and size of economy, peace | 0 |
| Fair | 3: HEALTH, debt, education | 3: water withdrawal, global atmosphere, energy |
| Medium | 4: inflation and unemployment, communication, FREEDOM AND GOVERNANCE, GENDER EQUITY | 1: land protection |
| Poor | 3: needs, crime, HOUSEHOLD EQUITY | 5: LAND QUALITY, inland water quality, WILD DIVERSITY, domesticated animals, RESOURCE SECTORS |
| Bad | 2: *state of knowledge,* CULTURE | 6: land modification and conversion, inland water diversity, *SEA,* local air quality, *domesticated plants, materials* |
| Total | 15 | 15 |

At the same time, wellbeing needs to be fully and widely communicated. Television, radio, magazines, newspapers, and the Internet are the main sources of information about what is happening outside a person's immediate family, neighborhood, and workplace. What people hear and read inevitably conditions their concerns and influences political priorities. If news media reported regularly on the wellbeing of their society and fully covered all aspects of human life and the state of the environment, they would expand the set of issues that citizens and their governments feel compelled to address.

## Sustainable Wealth

Practical action hinges on wealth: how to gain enough of it for human wellbeing, how to spend it to enhance human wellbeing, and how to gain and spend it in ways that are compatible with ecosystem wellbeing. Wealth generation, resource use, and trade have the biggest impacts on human and environmental conditions, and the pace of progress toward high levels of wellbeing depends on the development of sustainable forms of these activities. One imperative is to equip the poorest societies to support themselves and obtain greater wealth from their local ecosystem in ways that restore the ecosystem's productivity and diversity. Another is for wealthier societies both to consume less and to pay more of the costs of consumption. Key steps:

- Take full account of the environmental and social costs of energy and resource production. Encourage the production methods that cost least and discourage those that cost most, if necessary by subsidizing the former and taxing (or removing subsidies from) the latter. Apply similar incentives to adopt technologies that increase the productivity of energy and materials. Many examples are brilliantly described in the book *Factor Four: Doubling Wealth, Halving Resource Use.*[11]

- Replace value-added (goods and services) taxes, sales taxes, and possibly income taxes with taxes on energy and raw materials. This step would increase the amount of value obtained from resources, raise economic efficiency, reduce consumption dependency, and reward enterprises that produce the greatest benefit for the least amount of damage to the environment. (Value-added taxes do the opposite—penalizing timber companies, for instance, for increasing the income from a log rather than rewarding them for using less wood.) Energy and raw materials taxes would be cheaper to collect than other taxes, and as long as the other taxes were cut by the same amount would not increase the total tax burden.

- Incorporate wellbeing assessments and conservation programs in resource production (food and agriculture, timber and forests, water and hydropower, energy and transport) strategies. This would provide resource sectors with a mechanism for increasing or maintaining the socioeconomic benefits of their activities while reducing their environmental costs.

- Protect ecologically sound products and practices from competition by ecologically damaging ones. Countries have the right and duty to ensure that their resources and environment are used sustainably and to protect responsible traders from being undercut by competitors whose prices do not include the full costs of production. This would be easier to achieve (and would not constitute a restraint of trade) by adopting energy and materials taxes and applying them equally to domestically produced goods and services and to imports.

- Provide consumers with simply expressed and quickly grasped statements of the social and environmental impacts of products and services so that they can make informed choices.

## Wellbeing Areas (Slow Zones)

Nature reserves and other strictly protected areas are unlikely to cover more than a small proportion of each country—too small to secure its wild diversity. Moreover, they are not designed to maintain domesticated diversity or mixed built–cultivated–wild landscapes that express long-lived but vulnerable marriages between a society and its ecosystem. Wellbeing areas are proposed to fill this gap. They would be dedicated to maintaining cultural and biological diversity, including wildlife habitats; food production methods that respect land and water and maintain local crop varieties and livestock breeds; cities, towns, and villages that provide decent and attractive living spaces and maintain architectural heritage; and transport systems that ease the movement of people and goods without bludgeoning the landscape or clogging towns with noise and pollutants.

Wellbeing areas would be protected landscapes, with an emphasis on maintaining genetic as well as landscape diversity, urban as well as rural heritage, and practices that express the bond between a society and its ecosystem (such as local cuisines and sustainable use of local resources). I call them Slow Zones after the Italian concepts of Slow Cities (towns that provide a quality of life in harmony with their environment) and Slow Food (food produced, cooked, and eaten with respect for nature and culture, in opposition to fast food). Each would be managed by the residents of the area, in ways that reflect its particular social and environmental context, within a common framework of standards.

## Wellbeing Alliances and Partnerships

In almost all regions, countries differ in size, population, cultures, environments, and human and ecosystem conditions. These differences bring their own sets of advantages and disadvantages. For example, Singapore has the highest human wellbeing in Southeast Asia but, being small and crowded, will find it harder than, say, Indonesia to improve its low ecosystem wellbeing. Groups of nations could pool their wellbeing by forming regional sustainable development blocs, possibly based on existing economic and political alliances, such as the Association of Southeast-Asian Nations, the Economic Community of West African States, the European Union, Mercosur (the common market of southern South America), and the North American Free Trade Agreement.

Countries with relatively diverse ecosystems could serve as reservoirs of diversity for countries whose environments are already heavily altered. In return, countries with stronger human development could assist in raising their environmental partners' standard of living.

Similarly, the practice of twinning municipalities could be expanded to twinning wealthy ecosystem deficit states or provinces with poor human deficit states or provinces (or even countries), exchanging development support for ecosystem capacity. This would supplement, not replace, good faith efforts by the well off to reduce ecosystem stress and by the disadvantaged to improve human conditions.

Regional groups of countries could also help each other by harmonizing their efforts to achieve sustainability. They could share information and expertise, adopt common legislation and incentive programs, and avoid any unfair competition that might arise if some countries act more slowly than others.

Wealthy countries have won much of their high human wellbeing at the cost of stress on the environments of other countries (via trade) or on the global ecosystem (notably impacts on the global atmosphere). Since they leave such a large ecological footprint, they should help to look after the places where they tread.

High human deficit and high and extreme double deficit countries will need a lot of help, including:

- Removal of tariffs on any goods they produce sustainably.

- Debt relief.

- Increased assistance with social and economic development and environmental protection.

This support should be extended to countries that commit themselves to improving human wellbeing (especially health, education, water and sanitation, equity, and democratic institutions) and ecosystem wellbeing. Attaching conditions to aid may be politically incorrect, but donors do it all the time, and it is necessary to ensure that the support gets results.

Several of these actions are on every do-gooder's wish list. Little is done about them because the constituencies that demand them are small and badly organized. This amplifies the importance of wellbeing assessments, for by engaging people in evaluations of their own conditions and prospects they can help to build constituencies for a high quality of life and a diverse and healthy environment. When we know what's going on, we can do something about it.

## Notes

1. High double deficit countries have an average WI of 39.3 where the state of the environment is worse, 36.6 where human conditions are worse.

2. Energy consumption is a fairly reliable guide to resource consumption in general. The correlation between energy consumption per person and the more comprehensive Ecological Footprint (pages 65–66 and Table 9 in the Data section) is high: 0.922.

3. Species per hectare was calculated on the basis of the esti-

mated total number of species of higher plants (angiosperms, gymnosperms, and pteridophytes), mammals, breeding birds, reptiles, and amphibians, and the total surface area (land and inland waters) of the country.

4. Boltvinik & Hernández Laos (1999).

5. Mexico has 0.50 people and 0.14 species per hectare.

6. Comité Permanent Inter-Etats de Lutte Contre la Sécheresse au Sahel (CILSS).

7. Freedom House (2000a, 2000b).

8. Percentages of threatened species are lower than those reported in Organisation for Economic Co-operation and Development (1999) and elsewhere (e.g., Eurostat 1997) because national reports are not consistent with each other or with the international standards of IUCN-The World Conservation Union. Some count subspecies as species, and most include species that are nationally threatened regardless of their global status, whereas IUCN counts only full species that are globally at risk.

9. Armenia's EWI would then be the same as Georgia's, except that Georgia's ODS use and local air quality were not assessed either. If they, too, are the same as Turkey's, Georgia's EWI would be 34.

10. The estimated 66% natural is close to the 69% of ecologically similar Canada. But only 51% of Canada's native forest is estimated to be undisturbed (UNECE & FAO 2000).

11. Weizsäcker, Lovins, & Lovins (1997).

# Data Tables

The following tables contain the data and scores for the indicators and indices used in *The Wellbeing of Nations:*

Countries are in alphabetical order within continental groups (the Russian Federation is treated as a continent). The sequence of groups is roughly west to east: Americas, Africa, Europe, Russian Federation, Asia, Pacific. Notes at the end of each table explain the data, performance criteria and combining procedures, and give sources.
-- = no data

# Table 1. Human Wellbeing Index

| Country | Health & pop | Wealth | Know-ledge | Com-munity | Equity | HWI + equity | HWI - equity | Equity diff | HWI | HDI | HDI score | HDI diff |
|---|---|---|---|---|---|---|---|---|---|---|---|---|
| AMERICAS | | | | | | | | | | | | |
| Antigua & Barbuda | 67 | 68 | 51 | 50 | 11 | 49 | 59 | -10 | 49 | 0.833 | 83 | 34 |
| Argentina | 60 | 47 | 67 | 55 | 46 | 55 | 57 | -2 | 55 | 0.837 | 84 | 29 |
| Bahamas | 50 | 58 | 71 | 54 | 39 | 54 | 58 | -4 | 54 | 0.844 | 84 | 30 |
| Barbados | 64 | 60 | 72 | 68 | 48 | 62 | 66 | -4 | 62 | 0.858 | 86 | 24 |
| Belize | 39 | 32 | 65 | 74 | 40 | 50 | 52 | -2 | 50 | 0.777 | 78 | 28 |
| Bolivia | 30 | 22 | 48 | 37 | 43 | 36 | 34 | 2 | 34 | 0.643 | 64 | 30 |
| Brazil | 50 | 42 | 57 | 50 | 26 | 45 | 50 | -5 | 45 | 0.747 | 75 | 30 |
| Canada | 86 | 77 | 95 | 72 | 62 | 78 | 82 | -4 | 78 | 0.935 | 93 | 16 |
| Chile | 70 | 55 | 62 | 60 | 30 | 55 | 62 | -7 | 55 | 0.826 | 83 | 28 |
| Colombia | 58 | 46 | 48 | 25 | 36 | 43 | 44 | -1 | 43 | 0.764 | 76 | 33 |
| Costa Rica | 55 | 49 | 61 | 74 | 40 | 56 | 60 | -4 | 56 | 0.797 | 80 | 24 |
| Cuba | 78 | 35 | 44 | 2 | 51 | 42 | 40 | 2 | 40 | 0.783 | 78 | 38 |
| Dominica | 81 | 43 | 58 | 80 | 19 | 56 | 65 | -9 | 56 | 0.793 | 79 | 23 |
| Dominican R | 57 | 42 | 47 | 65 | 35 | 49 | 53 | -4 | 49 | 0.729 | 73 | 24 |
| Ecuador | 50 | 28 | 50 | 46 | 43 | 43 | 43 | 0 | 43 | 0.722 | 72 | 29 |
| El Salvador | 48 | 42 | 43 | 12 | 42 | 37 | 36 | 1 | 36 | 0.696 | 70 | 34 |
| Grenada | 38 | 50 | 53 | 79 | 53 | 55 | 55 | 0 | 55 | 0.785 | 78 | 23 |
| Guatemala | 23 | 30 | 28 | 11 | 35 | 25 | 23 | 2 | 23 | 0.619 | 62 | 39 |
| Guyana | 52 | 34 | 43 | 74 | 53 | 51 | 51 | 0 | 51 | 0.709 | 71 | 20 |
| Haiti | 26 | 16 | 8 | 28 | 51 | 26 | 19 | 7 | 19 | 0.440 | 44 | 25 |
| Honduras | 31 | 27 | 32 | 45 | 29 | 33 | 34 | -1 | 33 | 0.653 | 65 | 32 |
| Jamaica | 70 | 39 | 49 | 57 | 53 | 54 | 54 | 0 | 54 | 0.735 | 73 | 19 |
| Mexico | 58 | 47 | 59 | 23 | 37 | 45 | 47 | -2 | 45 | 0.784 | 78 | 33 |
| Nicaragua | 29 | 26 | 33 | 24 | 38 | 30 | 28 | 2 | 28 | 0.631 | 63 | 35 |
| Panama | 60 | 42 | 54 | 70 | 32 | 52 | 56 | -4 | 52 | 0.776 | 78 | 26 |
| Paraguay | 31 | 34 | 43 | 40 | 25 | 35 | 37 | -2 | 35 | 0.736 | 74 | 39 |
| Peru | 51 | 35 | 59 | 36 | 40 | 44 | 45 | -1 | 44 | 0.737 | 74 | 30 |
| St Kitts & Nevis | 55 | 63 | 56 | 61 | 27 | 52 | 59 | -7 | 52 | 0.798 | 80 | 28 |
| St Lucia | 64 | 48 | 44 | 80 | 30 | 53 | 59 | -6 | 53 | 0.728 | 73 | 20 |
| St Vincent & Grenadines | 70 | 42 | 47 | 37 | 10 | 41 | 49 | -8 | 41 | 0.738 | 74 | 33 |
| Suriname | 57 | 42 | 58 | 59 | 46 | 52 | 54 | -2 | 52 | 0.766 | 77 | 25 |
| Trinidad & Tobago | 62 | 42 | 50 | 70 | 43 | 53 | 56 | -3 | 53 | 0.793 | 79 | 26 |
| United States | 82 | 84 | 94 | 58 | 49 | 73 | 79 | -6 | 73 | 0.929 | 93 | 20 |
| Uruguay | 70 | 52 | 66 | 66 | 53 | 61 | 63 | -2 | 61 | 0.825 | 82 | 22 |
| Venezuela | 53 | 34 | 49 | 43 | 34 | 43 | 45 | -2 | 43 | 0.770 | 77 | 34 |
| AFRICA | | | | | | | | | | | | |
| Algeria | 36 | 39 | 43 | 0 | 41 | 32 | 29 | 3 | 29 | 0.683 | 68 | 39 |
| Angola | 10 | 13 | 6 | 4 | 56 | 18 | 8 | 10 | 8 | 0.405 | 40 | 33 |
| Benin | 16 | 13 | 13 | 65 | 36 | 29 | 27 | 2 | 27 | 0.411 | 41 | 14 |
| Botswana | 11 | 42 | 38 | 45 | 51 | 37 | 34 | 3 | 34 | 0.593 | 59 | 25 |
| Burkina Faso | 11 | 11 | 4 | 42 | 37 | 21 | 17 | 4 | 17 | 0.303 | 30 | 13 |
| Burundi | 13 | 7 | 4 | 0 | 49 | 15 | 6 | 9 | 6 | 0.321 | 32 | 26 |
| Cameroon | 19 | 15 | 14 | 13 | 38 | 20 | 15 | 5 | 15 | 0.528 | 53 | 38 |
| Cape Verde | 39 | 27 | 49 | 74 | 51 | 48 | 47 | 1 | 47 | 0.688 | 69 | 22 |
| Central African R | 16 | 10 | 7 | 30 | 17 | 16 | 16 | 0 | 16 | 0.371 | 37 | 21 |
| Chad | 14 | 11 | 5 | 22 | 28 | 16 | 13 | 3 | 13 | 0.367 | 37 | 24 |
| Comoros | 24 | 13 | 8 | 37 | 46 | 26 | 20 | 6 | 20 | 0.510 | 51 | 31 |
| Congo, DR | 12 | 6 | 11 | 0 | 47 | 15 | 7 | 8 | 7 | 0.430 | 43 | 36 |
| Congo, R | 14 | 9 | 29 | 9 | 39 | 20 | 15 | 5 | 15 | 0.507 | 51 | 36 |
| Côte d'Ivoire | 21 | 14 | 19 | 27 | 40 | 24 | 20 | 4 | 20 | 0.420 | 42 | 22 |
| Djibouti | 18 | 21 | 4 | 30 | 16 | 18 | 18 | 0 | 18 | 0.447 | 45 | 27 |
| Egypt | 45 | 37 | 49 | 25 | 50 | 41 | 39 | 2 | 39 | 0.623 | 62 | 23 |
| Equatorial Guinea | 17 | 18 | 18 | 6 | 29 | 18 | 15 | 3 | 15 | 0.555 | 55 | 41 |
| Eritrea | 16 | 19 | 7 | 0 | 39 | 16 | 10 | 6 | 10 | 0.408 | 41 | 31 |
| Ethiopia | 13 | 5 | 5 | 30 | 38 | 18 | 13 | 5 | 13 | 0.309 | 31 | 18 |
| Gabon | 18 | 37 | 20 | 37 | 44 | 31 | 28 | 3 | 28 | 0.592 | 59 | 31 |
| Gambia | 19 | 16 | 13 | 18 | 33 | 20 | 16 | 4 | 16 | 0.396 | 40 | 24 |
| Ghana | 20 | 18 | 5 | 46 | 48 | 27 | 22 | 5 | 22 | 0.556 | 56 | 34 |
| Guinea | 18 | 15 | 6 | 23 | 41 | 21 | 15 | 6 | 15 | 0.394 | 39 | 24 |
| Guinea-Bissau | 16 | 7 | 11 | 20 | 18 | 14 | 13 | 1 | 13 | 0.331 | 33 | 20 |
| Kenya | 20 | 15 | 14 | 22 | 38 | 22 | 18 | 4 | 18 | 0.508 | 51 | 33 |
| Lesotho | 17 | 19 | 19 | 40 | 35 | 26 | 24 | 2 | 24 | 0.569 | 57 | 33 |
| Liberia | 13 | 7 | 0 | 18 | -- | 9 | 9 | 0 | 9 | -- | -- | -- |
| Libyan Arab J | 36 | 58 | 54 | 3 | 58 | 42 | 38 | 4 | 38 | 0.760 | 76 | 38 |
| Madagascar | 17 | 9 | 10 | 59 | 43 | 28 | 24 | 4 | 24 | 0.483 | 48 | 24 |
| Malawi | 7 | 6 | 25 | 50 | 42 | 26 | 22 | 4 | 22 | 0.385 | 38 | 16 |

| Country | Health & pop | Wealth | Know-ledge | Com-munity | Equity | HWI + equity | HWI - equity | Equity diff | HWI | HDI | HDI score | HDI diff |
|---|---|---|---|---|---|---|---|---|---|---|---|---|
| Mali | 11 | 6 | 6 | 62 | 35 | 24 | 21 | 3 | 21 | 0.380 | 38 | 17 |
| Mauritania | 18 | 13 | 15 | 24 | 39 | 22 | 17 | 5 | 17 | 0.451 | 45 | 28 |
| Mauritius | 57 | 54 | 43 | 72 | 46 | 54 | 56 | -2 | 54 | 0.761 | 76 | 22 |
| Morocco | 50 | 30 | 32 | 33 | 38 | 37 | 36 | 1 | 36 | 0.589 | 59 | 23 |
| Mozambique | 13 | 8 | 5 | 17 | 50 | 19 | 11 | 8 | 11 | 0.341 | 34 | 23 |
| Namibia | 15 | 41 | 40 | 40 | 49 | 37 | 34 | 3 | 34 | 0.632 | 63 | 29 |
| Niger | 7 | 7 | 2 | 30 | 25 | 14 | 11 | 3 | 11 | 0.293 | 29 | 18 |
| Nigeria | 19 | 12 | 15 | 17 | 30 | 19 | 16 | 3 | 16 | 0.439 | 44 | 28 |
| Rwanda | 12 | 12 | 14 | 12 | 57 | 21 | 12 | 9 | 12 | 0.382 | 38 | 26 |
| São Tomé & Principe | 13 | 12 | 7 | 9 | 18 | 12 | 10 | 2 | 10 | 0.547 | 55 | 45 |
| Senegal | 18 | 22 | 12 | 30 | 41 | 25 | 20 | 5 | 20 | 0.416 | 42 | 22 |
| Seychelles | 50 | 49 | 50 | 53 | 47 | 50 | 50 | 0 | 50 | 0.786 | 79 | 29 |
| Sierra Leone | 2 | 3 | 7 | 12 | 36 | 12 | 6 | 6 | 6 | 0.252 | 25 | 19 |
| Somalia | 6 | 7 | 0 | 0 | -- | 3 | 3 | 0 | 3 | -- | -- | -- |
| South Africa | 21 | 52 | 70 | 33 | 39 | 43 | 44 | -1 | 43 | 0.697 | 70 | 27 |
| Sudan | 25 | 13 | 10 | 4 | 45 | 19 | 13 | 6 | 13 | 0.477 | 48 | 35 |
| Swaziland | 19 | 36 | 36 | 6 | 30 | 25 | 24 | 1 | 24 | 0.655 | 65 | 41 |
| Tanzania | 16 | 10 | 6 | 39 | 48 | 24 | 18 | 6 | 18 | 0.415 | 41 | 24 |
| Togo | 14 | 16 | 28 | 27 | 25 | 22 | 21 | 1 | 21 | 0.471 | 47 | 26 |
| Tunisia | 55 | 43 | 50 | 29 | 45 | 44 | 44 | 0 | 44 | 0.703 | 70 | 26 |
| Uganda | 8 | 12 | 7 | 14 | 47 | 18 | 10 | 8 | 10 | 0.409 | 41 | 31 |
| Zambia | 8 | 8 | 15 | 35 | 35 | 20 | 16 | 4 | 16 | 0.420 | 42 | 26 |
| Zimbabwe | 12 | 24 | 31 | 25 | 34 | 25 | 23 | 2 | 23 | 0.555 | 55 | 33 |
| EUROPE | | | | | | | | | | | | |
| Albania | 52 | 39 | 45 | 18 | 40 | 39 | 38 | 1 | 38 | 0.713 | 71 | 33 |
| Austria | 85 | 79 | 91 | 81 | 66 | 80 | 84 | -4 | 80 | 0.908 | 91 | 11 |
| Belarus | 55 | 43 | 64 | 22 | 67 | 50 | 46 | 4 | 46 | 0.781 | 78 | 32 |
| Belgium | 85 | 74 | 90 | 78 | 71 | 80 | 82 | -2 | 80 | 0.925 | 92 | 13 |
| Bosnia & Herzegovina | 64 | 15 | 16 | 0 | 57 | 30 | 24 | 6 | 24 | -- | -- | -- |
| Bulgaria | 62 | 45 | 70 | 57 | 56 | 58 | 58 | 0 | 58 | 0.772 | 77 | 19 |
| Croatia | 72 | 47 | 71 | 39 | 69 | 60 | 57 | 3 | 57 | 0.795 | 79 | 23 |
| Czech R | 76 | 61 | 76 | 70 | 69 | 70 | 71 | -1 | 70 | 0.843 | 84 | 14 |
| Denmark | 81 | 83 | 89 | 74 | 76 | 81 | 82 | -1 | 81 | 0.911 | 91 | 10 |
| Estonia | 58 | 50 | 81 | 62 | 60 | 62 | 63 | -1 | 62 | 0.801 | 80 | 18 |
| Finland | 83 | 80 | 93 | 70 | 77 | 81 | 81 | 0 | 81 | 0.917 | 92 | 11 |
| France | 88 | 75 | 86 | 69 | 58 | 75 | 79 | -4 | 75 | 0.917 | 92 | 17 |
| Germany | 83 | 76 | 85 | 75 | 64 | 77 | 80 | -3 | 77 | 0.911 | 91 | 14 |
| Greece | 87 | 66 | 79 | 63 | 54 | 70 | 74 | -4 | 70 | 0.875 | 87 | 18 |
| Hungary | 61 | 58 | 75 | 69 | 61 | 65 | 66 | -1 | 65 | 0.817 | 82 | 17 |
| Iceland | 82 | 84 | 86 | 80* | 70 | 80 | 83 | -3 | 80 | 0.927 | 93 | 13 |
| Ireland | 81 | 78 | 85 | 80 | 55 | 76 | 81 | -5 | 76 | 0.907 | 91 | 15 |
| Italy | 87 | 71 | 84 | 69 | 60 | 74 | 78 | -4 | 74 | 0.903 | 90 | 16 |
| Latvia | 56 | 57 | 68 | 67 | 60 | 62 | 62 | 0 | 62 | 0.771 | 77 | 15 |
| Lithuania | 60 | 57 | 67 | 70 | 53 | 61 | 63 | -2 | 61 | 0.789 | 79 | 18 |
| Luxembourg | 84 | 89 | 80* | 78 | 55 | 77 | 83 | -6 | 77 | 0.908 | 91 | 14 |
| Macedonia, FYR | 59 | 28 | 48 | 50 | 50 | 47 | 46 | 1 | 46 | 0.763 | 76 | 30 |
| Malta | 83 | 68 | 73 | 80 | 45 | 70 | 76 | -6 | 70 | 0.865 | 86 | 16 |
| Moldova | 55 | 24 | 52 | 34 | 53 | 44 | 41 | 3 | 41 | 0.700 | 70 | 29 |
| Netherlands | 86 | 82 | 92 | 67 | 65 | 78 | 82 | -4 | 78 | 0.925 | 92 | 15 |
| Norway | 85 | 83 | 91 | 77 | 73 | 82 | 84 | -2 | 82 | 0.934 | 93 | 11 |
| Poland | 69 | 56 | 72 | 70 | 56 | 65 | 67 | -2 | 65 | 0.814 | 81 | 16 |
| Portugal | 81 | 72 | 79 | 71 | 56 | 72 | 76 | -4 | 72 | 0.864 | 86 | 14 |
| Romania | 57 | 32 | 55 | 56 | 63 | 53 | 50 | 3 | 50 | 0.770 | 77 | 27 |
| Slovakia | 70 | 45 | 69 | 61 | 69 | 63 | 61 | 2 | 61 | 0.825 | 82 | 22 |
| Slovenia | 78 | 68 | 81 | 71 | 59 | 71 | 74 | -3 | 71 | 0.861 | 86 | 15 |
| Spain | 87 | 71 | 86 | 60 | 59 | 73 | 76 | -3 | 73 | 0.899 | 90 | 17 |
| Sweden | 88 | 78 | 92 | 60 | 78 | 79 | 79 | 0 | 79 | 0.926 | 93 | 14 |
| Switzerland | 87 | 81 | 82 | 85 | 53 | 78 | 84 | -6 | 78 | 0.915 | 91 | 13 |
| Ukraine | 58 | 31 | 62 | 38 | 54 | 49 | 47 | 2 | 47 | 0.744 | 74 | 27 |
| United Kingdom | 85 | 80 | 90 | 52 | 59 | 73 | 77 | -4 | 73 | 0.918 | 92 | 19 |
| Yugoslavia | 69 | 27 | 56 | 18 | 44 | 43 | 42 | 1 | 42 | -- | -- | -- |
| RUSSIAN FEDERATION | 54 | 48 | 67 | 26 | 43 | 48 | 49 | -1 | 48 | 0.771 | 77 | 29 |
| ASIA | | | | | | | | | | | | |
| Afghanistan | 9 | 6 | 8 | 3 | 14 | 8 | 6 | 2 | 6 | -- | -- | -- |
| Armenia | 71 | 41 | 40 | 31 | 42 | 45 | 46 | -1 | 45 | 0.721 | 72 | 27 |
| Azerbaijan | 59 | 43 | 46 | 21 | 52 | 44 | 42 | 2 | 42 | 0.722 | 72 | 30 |
| Bahrain | 58 | 60 | 70 | 12 | 29 | 46 | 50 | -4 | 46 | 0.820 | 82 | 36 |
| Bangladesh | 35 | 24 | 15 | 36 | 44 | 31 | 27 | 4 | 27 | 0.461 | 46 | 19 |

| Country | Health & pop | Wealth | Know-ledge | Com-munity | Equity | HWI + equity | HWI - equity | Equity diff | HWI | HDI | HDI score | HDI diff |
|---|---|---|---|---|---|---|---|---|---|---|---|---|
| Bhutan | 18 | 24 | 2 | 11 | 40 | 19 | 14 | 5 | 14 | 0.483 | 48 | 34 |
| Brunei Darussalam | 58 | 68 | 44 | 17 | 47 | 47 | 47 | 0 | 47 | 0.848 | 85 | 38 |
| Cambodia | 26 | 13 | 23 | 20 | 47 | 26 | 20 | 6 | 20 | 0.512 | 51 | 31 |
| China | 56 | 34 | 40 | 13 | 50 | 39 | 36 | 3 | 36 | 0.706 | 71 | 35 |
| Cyprus | 82 | 74 | 69 | 69 | 41 | 67 | 73 | -6 | 67 | 0.886 | 89 | 22 |
| Georgia | 69 | 35 | 53 | 35 | 61 | 51 | 48 | 3 | 48 | 0.762 | 76 | 28 |
| India | 39 | 21 | 26 | 39 | 44 | 34 | 31 | 3 | 31 | 0.563 | 56 | 25 |
| Indonesia | 51 | 20 | 42 | 31 | 48 | 38 | 36 | 2 | 36 | 0.670 | 67 | 31 |
| Iran | 53 | 42 | 49 | 19 | 29 | 38 | 41 | -3 | 38 | 0.709 | 71 | 33 |
| Iraq | 19 | 32 | 25 | 1 | 22 | 20 | 19 | 1 | 19 | 0.583 | 58 | 39 |
| Israel | 60 | 62 | 81 | 43 | 51 | 59 | 61 | -2 | 59 | 0.883 | 88 | 29 |
| Japan | 91 | 79 | 93 | 76 | 60 | 80 | 85 | -5 | 80 | 0.924 | 92 | 12 |
| Jordan | 24 | 34 | 52 | 42 | 43 | 39 | 38 | 1 | 38 | 0.721 | 72 | 34 |
| Kazakhstan | 45 | 48 | 54 | 25 | 50 | 44 | 43 | 1 | 43 | 0.754 | 75 | 32 |
| Korea, DPR | 38 | 29 | 16 | 0 | 40 | 25 | 21 | 4 | 21 | -- | -- | -- |
| Korea, R | 64 | 67 | 93 | 63 | 49 | 67 | 72 | -5 | 67 | 0.854 | 85 | 18 |
| Kuwait | 55 | 78 | 52 | 37 | 27 | 50 | 55 | -5 | 50 | 0.836 | 84 | 34 |
| Kyrgyzstan | 44 | 33 | 47 | 28 | 52 | 41 | 38 | 3 | 38 | 0.706 | 71 | 33 |
| Lao PDR | 16 | 14 | 18 | 14 | 59 | 24 | 15 | 9 | 15 | 0.484 | 48 | 33 |
| Lebanon | 53 | 29 | 59 | 19 | 40 | 40 | 40 | 0 | 40 | 0.735 | 73 | 33 |
| Malaysia | 48 | 54 | 59 | 33 | 38 | 46 | 48 | -2 | 46 | 0.772 | 77 | 31 |
| Maldives | 19 | 31 | 13 | 24 | 42 | 26 | 22 | 4 | 22 | 0.727 | 73 | 51 |
| Mongolia | 40 | 18 | 39 | 60 | 47 | 41 | 39 | 2 | 39 | 0.628 | 63 | 24 |
| Myanmar | 37 | 13 | 34 | 0 | 62 | 29 | 21 | 8 | 21 | 0.585 | 58 | 37 |
| Nepal | 29 | 16 | 21 | 46 | 43 | 31 | 28 | 3 | 28 | 0.474 | 47 | 19 |
| Oman | 16 | 55 | 36 | 18 | 46 | 34 | 31 | 3 | 31 | 0.730 | 73 | 42 |
| Pakistan | 21 | 20 | 13 | 17 | 47 | 24 | 18 | 6 | 18 | 0.522 | 52 | 34 |
| Philippines | 39 | 35 | 57 | 46 | 48 | 45 | 44 | 1 | 44 | 0.744 | 74 | 30 |
| Qatar | 38 | 71 | 59 | 20 | 13 | 40 | 47 | -7 | 40 | 0.819 | 82 | 42 |
| Saudi Arabia | 16 | 67 | 38 | 3 | 36 | 32 | 31 | 1 | 31 | 0.747 | 75 | 44 |
| Singapore | 81 | 81 | 79 | 44 | 46 | 66 | 71 | -5 | 66 | 0.881 | 88 | 22 |
| Sri Lanka | 58 | 28 | 37 | 39 | 49 | 42 | 40 | 2 | 40 | 0.733 | 73 | 33 |
| Syrian Arab R | 34 | 28 | 44 | 7 | 34 | 29 | 28 | 1 | 28 | 0.660 | 66 | 38 |
| Tajikistan | 33 | 19 | 49 | 12 | 30 | 29 | 28 | 1 | 28 | 0.663 | 66 | 38 |
| Thailand | 52 | 44 | 47 | 57 | 51 | 50 | 50 | 0 | 50 | 0.745 | 74 | 24 |
| Turkey | 58 | 31 | 57 | 37 | 41 | 45 | 46 | -1 | 45 | 0.732 | 73 | 28 |
| Turkmenistan | 39 | 28 | 56 | 4 | 55 | 36 | 32 | 4 | 32 | 0.704 | 70 | 38 |
| United Arab Emirates | 43 | 73 | 60 | 21 | 8 | 41 | 49 | -8 | 41 | 0.810 | 81 | 40 |
| Uzbekistan | 43 | 31 | 57 | 13 | 52 | 39 | 36 | 3 | 36 | 0.686 | 69 | 33 |
| Viet Nam | 48 | 16 | 37 | 11 | 67 | 36 | 28 | 8 | 28 | 0.671 | 67 | 39 |
| Yemen | 5 | 13 | 17 | 24 | 29 | 18 | 15 | 3 | 15 | 0.448 | 45 | 30 |
| PACIFIC | | | | | | | | | | | | |
| Australia | 88 | 80 | 95 | 70 | 62 | 79 | 83 | -4 | 79 | 0.929 | 93 | 14 |
| Fiji | 51 | 45 | 49 | 56 | 47 | 50 | 50 | 0 | 50 | 0.769 | 77 | 27 |
| New Zealand | 80 | 77 | 85 | 80 | 42 | 73 | 80 | -7 | 73 | 0.903 | 90 | 17 |
| Papua New Guinea | 26 | 22 | 19 | 22 | 32 | 24 | 22 | 2 | 22 | 0.542 | 54 | 32 |
| Samoa | 28 | 34 | 43 | 69 | 40 | 43 | 43 | 0 | 43 | 0.711 | 71 | 28 |
| Solomon Is | 24 | 34 | 10 | 80 | 44 | 38 | 37 | 1 | 37 | 0.614 | 61 | 24 |
| Tonga | 33 | 49 | 2 | 48 | 0 | 26 | 33 | -7 | 26 | -- | -- | -- |
| Vanuatu | 30 | 30 | 21 | 65 | 29 | 35 | 36 | -1 | 35 | 0.623 | 62 | 27 |

**Notes**

The Human Wellbeing Index (**HWI**) is the lower of the HWI including equity (HWI + equity) and the HWI excluding equity (HWI – equity). The former is the unweighted average of indices of health and population, wealth, knowledge, community, and equity. The latter is the unweighted average of indices of health and population, wealth, knowledge, and community. Taking the lower version of the HWI prevents equity from offsetting poor performance in the other human dimensions.

Health & pop = health and population index (Table 2).

Wealth = wealth index (Table 3).

Knowledge = knowledge index (Table 5).

Community = community index (Table 6).

Equity = equity index (Table 8).

HWI + equity = HWI including equity.

HWI - equity = HWI excluding equity.

Equity diff = equity difference = difference in points between the HWI excluding equity and the HWI including equity (minus means that inclusion of equity lowers the HWI).

HDI = Human Development Index for 1998 (United Nations Development Programme 2000).

HDI score = HDI score obtained by placing the HDI directly on the Barometer scale (multiplying the HDI by 100 and rounding to the nearest whole number).

HDI diff = difference between the HDI score and the HWI.

Correlations between the HWI, its main components (dimensions and elements) and income are shown in Table 1a.

| | HWI | income | health | pop | Health & pop | h'hold wealth | national wealth | Wealth | Know-ledge | freedom & gov | peace & order | Com-munity | Equity |
|---|---|---|---|---|---|---|---|---|---|---|---|---|---|
| HWI | 1 | | | | | | | | | | | | |
| income | 0.824 | 1 | | | | | | | | | | | |
| health | 0.902 | 0.749 | 1 | | | | | | | | | | |
| population | 0.851 | 0.598 | 0.827 | 1 | | | | | | | | | |
| Health & population | 0.925 | 0.740 | 0.940 | 0.927 | 1 | | | | | | | | |
| household wealth | 0.895 | 0.880 | 0.851 | 0.712 | 0.815 | 1 | | | | | | | |
| national wealth | 0.871 | 0.901 | 0.811 | 0.684 | 0.782 | 0.895 | 1 | | | | | | |
| Wealth | 0.903 | 0.914 | 0.852 | 0.712 | 0.816 | 0.977 | 0.968 | 1 | | | | | |
| Knowledge | 0.948 | 0.795 | 0.868 | 0.816 | 0.879 | 0.871 | 0.835 | 0.874 | 1 | | | | |
| freedom & governance | 0.740 | 0.571 | 0.545 | 0.507 | 0.583 | 0.585 | 0.565 | 0.583 | 0.593 | 1 | | | |
| peace & order | 0.560 | 0.366 | 0.405 | 0.433 | 0.450 | 0.388 | 0.390 | 0.395 | 0.444 | 0.471 | 1 | | |
| Community | 0.782 | 0.556 | 0.577 | 0.554 | 0.613 | 0.590 | 0.573 | 0.589 | 0.609 | 0.908 | 0.705 | 1 | |
| Equity | 0.531 | 0.358 | 0.412 | 0.528 | 0.495 | 0.324 | 0.364 | 0.345 | 0.508 | 0.315 | 0.325 | 0.363 | 1 |

**Table 1a. Correlations between the HWI, human dimensions and elements, and income (GDP per person).** Correlations of 0.8 and above are shown in **bold**; those between 0.6 and 0.8 are shown in *italic*.

\* A score with an asterisk has been reduced in accordance with the insufficient data rule. To prevent high scores resulting merely from lack of data, a good score is allowed only if it is based on all applicable components (data in an indicator, indicators in an index), and a fair score only if it is based on at least half the components. Good and fair scores (100-61) based on fewer than half the applicable components have been reduced to 60. Good scores (100-81) based on more than half but not all the applicable components have been reduced to 80.

# Table 2. Health and Population

| Country | Pop. (000s) | Child mort./k | Disabled % LE | | | Female | | | Male | | | Average | | | H score | TFR | P score | H&P index |
|---|---|---|---|---|---|---|---|---|---|---|---|---|---|---|---|---|---|---|
| | | | F | M | ave. | LE | yrsdis | HLE | LE | yrsdis | HLE | LE | yrsdis | HLE | | | | |
| AMERICAS | | | | | | | | | | | | | | | | | | |
| Antigua & Barbuda | 68 | c 20 | 11.1 | 11.2 | 11.1 | 76.8 | 8.5 | 68.3 | 71.4 | 8.0 | 63.4 | 74.10 | 8.25 | 65.85 | 67 | 1.7 | 90 | 67 |
| Argentina | 37032 | 25 | 10.6 | 9.6 | 10.1 | 77.8 | 8.2 | 69.6 | 70.6 | 6.8 | 63.8 | 74.20 | 7.50 | 66.70 | 71 | 2.6 | 60 | 60 |
| Bahamas | 307 | 18 | 16.3 | 15.4 | 15.9 | 73.6 | 12.0 | 61.6 | 67.0 | 10.3 | 56.7 | 70.30 | 11.15 | 59.15 | 50 | 2.6 | 60 | 50 |
| Barbados | 270 | 14 | 13.1 | 14.2 | 13.6 | 77.8 | 10.2 | 67.6 | 72.7 | 10.3 | 62.4 | 75.25 | 10.25 | 65.00 | 64 | 1.5 | 94 | 64 |
| Belize | 241 | 37 | 15.5 | 15.9 | 15.7 | 74.9 | 11.6 | 63.3 | 69.6 | 11.1 | 58.5 | 72.25 | 11.35 | 60.90 | 54 | 3.5 | 39 | 39 |
| Bolivia | 8329 | 88 | 13.1 | 13.6 | 13.3 | 62.2 | 8.1 | 54.1 | 60.8 | 8.3 | 52.5 | 61.50 | 8.20 | 53.30 | 39 | 4.2 | 30 | 30 |
| Brazil | 170115 | 48 | 12.3 | 13.3 | 12.8 | 71.7 | 8.8 | 62.9 | 63.7 | 8.5 | 55.2 | 67.70 | 8.65 | 59.05 | 50 | 2.2 | 80 | 50 |
| Canada | 31147 | 7 | 9.6 | 8.1 | 8.9 | 81.8 | 7.8 | 74.0 | 76.2 | 6.2 | 70.0 | 79.00 | 7.00 | 72.00 | 86 | 1.6 | 92 | 86 |
| Chile | 15211 | 15 | 10.8 | 10.1 | 10.4 | 79.9 | 8.6 | 71.3 | 73.4 | 7.4 | 66.0 | 76.65 | 8.00 | 68.65 | 79 | 2.4 | 70 | 70 |
| Colombia | 42321 | 39 | 11.6 | 11.5 | 11.5 | 74.1 | 8.6 | 65.5 | 68.1 | 7.8 | 60.3 | 71.10 | 8.20 | 62.90 | 58 | 2.7 | 58 | 58 |
| Costa Rica | 4023 | 15 | 13.7 | 12.1 | 12.9 | 78.9 | 10.8 | 68.1 | 74.2 | 9.0 | 65.2 | 76.55 | 9.90 | 66.65 | 71 | 2.8 | 55 | 55 |
| Cuba | 11201 | 12 | 10.3 | 8.4 | 9.4 | 77.4 | 8.0 | 69.4 | 73.6 | 6.2 | 67.4 | 75.50 | 7.10 | 68.40 | 78 | 1.6 | 92 | 78 |
| Dominica | 71 | c 20 | 10.0 | 9.2 | 9.6 | 80.3 | 8.0 | 72.3 | 74.0 | 6.8 | 67.2 | 77.15 | 7.40 | 69.75 | 81 | 1.9 | 86 | 81 |
| Dominican R | 8495 | 46 | 13.6 | 12.9 | 13.3 | 72.8 | 9.9 | 62.9 | 71.3 | 9.2 | 62.1 | 72.05 | 9.55 | 62.50 | 57 | 2.7 | 58 | 57 |
| Ecuador | 12646 | 60 | 11.6 | 11.1 | 11.4 | 70.3 | 8.2 | 62.1 | 67.4 | 7.5 | 59.9 | 68.85 | 7.85 | 61.00 | 54 | 3.0 | 50 | 50 |
| El Salvador | 6276 | 41 | 11.6 | 12.4 | 12.0 | 73.0 | 8.5 | 64.5 | 66.9 | 8.3 | 58.6 | 69.95 | 8.40 | 61.55 | 55 | 3.1 | 48 | 48 |
| Grenada | 94 | c 28 | 9.7 | 9.7 | 9.7 | 75.9 | 7.4 | 68.5 | 69.1 | 6.7 | 62.4 | 72.50 | 7.05 | 65.45 | 66 | 3.6 | 38 | 38 |
| Guatemala | 11385 | 61 | 12.8 | 13.4 | 13.1 | 64.7 | 8.3 | 56.4 | 60.2 | 8.1 | 52.1 | 62.45 | 8.20 | 54.25 | 40 | 4.8 | 23 | 23 |
| Guyana | 861 | 78 | 12.3 | 12.9 | 12.6 | 72.2 | 8.9 | 63.3 | 65.5 | 8.4 | 57.1 | 68.85 | 8.65 | 60.20 | 52 | 2.3 | 75 | 52 |
| Haiti | 8222 | 105 | 17.8 | 16.2 | 17.0 | 55.0 | 9.8 | 45.2 | 50.6 | 8.2 | 42.4 | 52.80 | 9.00 | 43.80 | 26 | 4.3 | 29 | 26 |
| Honduras | 6485 | 49 | 12.0 | 12.0 | 12.0 | 70.8 | 8.5 | 62.3 | 68.2 | 8.2 | 60.0 | 69.50 | 8.35 | 61.15 | 54 | 4.1 | 31 | 31 |
| Jamaica | 2583 | 27 | 12.3 | 11.2 | 11.7 | 77.4 | 9.5 | 67.9 | 75.2 | 8.4 | 66.8 | 76.30 | 8.95 | 67.35 | 73 | 2.4 | 70 | 70 |
| Mexico | 98881 | 38 | 12.4 | 12.2 | 12.3 | 77.2 | 9.6 | 67.6 | 71.0 | 8.6 | 62.4 | 74.10 | 9.10 | 65.00 | 64 | 2.7 | 58 | 58 |
| Nicaragua | 5074 | 58 | 13.0 | 13.0 | 12.9 | 68.8 | 8.9 | 59.9 | 64.8 | 8.4 | 56.4 | 66.80 | 8.65 | 58.15 | 48 | 4.3 | 29 | 29 |
| Panama | 2856 | 28 | 11.4 | 10.7 | 11.0 | 75.8 | 8.6 | 67.2 | 72.7 | 7.8 | 64.9 | 74.25 | 8.20 | 66.05 | 68 | 2.6 | 60 | 60 |
| Paraguay | 5496 | 48 | 11.8 | 12.9 | 12.3 | 74.1 | 8.8 | 65.3 | 69.6 | 8.9 | 60.7 | 71.85 | 8.85 | 63.00 | 58 | 4.1 | 31 | 31 |
| Peru | 25662 | 65 | 11.9 | 11.6 | 11.7 | 69.0 | 8.2 | 60.8 | 65.6 | 7.6 | 58.0 | 67.30 | 7.90 | 59.40 | 51 | 2.9 | 53 | 51 |
| St Kitts & Nevis | 38 | c 37 | 9.5 | 9.7 | 9.6 | 71.2 | 6.8 | 64.4 | 65.0 | 6.3 | 58.7 | 68.10 | 6.55 | 61.55 | 55 | 2.4 | 70 | 55 |
| St Lucia | 154 | c 21 | 9.8 | 9.4 | 9.6 | 74.9 | 7.3 | 67.6 | 68.9 | 6.5 | 62.4 | 71.90 | 6.90 | 65.00 | 64 | 2.3 | 75 | 64 |
| St Vincent & Grenadines | 114 | c 23 | 9.8 | 9.5 | 9.7 | 75.2 | 7.4 | 67.8 | 71.8 | 6.8 | 65.0 | 73.50 | 7.10 | 66.40 | 70 | 1.9 | 86 | 70 |
| Suriname | 417 | 33 | 11.3 | 11.6 | 11.4 | 73.5 | 8.3 | 65.2 | 68.1 | 7.9 | 60.2 | 70.80 | 8.10 | 62.70 | 57 | 2.2 | 80 | 57 |
| Trinidad & Tobago | 1295 | 16 | 9.5 | 8.5 | 9.1 | 73.4 | 7.0 | 66.4 | 68.7 | 5.9 | 62.8 | 71.05 | 6.45 | 64.60 | 62 | 1.6 | 92 | 62 |
| United States | 278357 | 9 | 8.8 | 8.6 | 8.7 | 79.6 | 7.0 | 72.6 | 73.8 | 6.3 | 67.5 | 76.70 | 6.65 | 70.05 | 82 | 2.0 | 84 | 82 |
| Uruguay | 3337 | 20 | 10.2 | 9.1 | 9.6 | 77.8 | 7.9 | 69.9 | 70.5 | 6.4 | 64.1 | 74.15 | 7.15 | 67.00 | 72 | 2.4 | 70 | 70 |
| Venezuela | 24170 | 25 | 11.8 | 11.4 | 11.6 | 76.1 | 9.0 | 67.1 | 71.0 | 8.1 | 62.9 | 73.55 | 8.55 | 65.00 | 64 | 2.9 | 53 | 53 |
| AFRICA | | | | | | | | | | | | | | | | | | |
| Algeria | 31471 | 51 | 11.7 | 8.4 | 10.1 | 68.8 | 8.1 | 60.7 | 68.2 | 5.7 | 62.5 | 68.50 | 6.90 | 61.60 | 55 | 3.7 | 36 | 36 |
| Angola | 12878 | 208 | 20.7 | 20.0 | 20.4 | 49.1 | 10.2 | 38.9 | 46.3 | 9.3 | 37.0 | 47.70 | 9.75 | 37.95 | 19 | 6.6 | 10 | 10 |
| Benin | 6097 | 133 | 20.1 | 18.4 | 19.2 | 53.3 | 10.7 | 42.6 | 51.3 | 9.4 | 41.9 | 52.30 | 10.05 | 42.25 | 24 | 5.7 | 16 | 16 |
| Botswana | 1622 | 107 | 18.0 | 18.2 | 18.1 | 39.3 | 7.1 | 32.2 | 39.5 | 7.2 | 32.3 | 39.40 | 7.15 | 32.25 | 11 | 4.2 | 30 | 11 |
| Burkina Faso | 11937 | 171 | 21.9 | 19.9 | 20.9 | 45.7 | 10.0 | 35.7 | 44.1 | 8.8 | 35.3 | 44.90 | 9.40 | 35.50 | 15 | 6.4 | 11 | 11 |
| Burundi | 6695 | 179 | 21.1 | 19.9 | 20.5 | 43.8 | 9.2 | 34.6 | 43.2 | 8.6 | 34.6 | 43.50 | 8.90 | 34.60 | 14 | 6.1 | 13 | 13 |
| Cameroon | 15085 | 114 | 17.3 | 16.9 | 17.1 | 52.0 | 9.0 | 43.0 | 49.9 | 8.4 | 41.5 | 50.95 | 8.70 | 42.25 | 24 | 5.2 | 19 | 19 |
| Cape Verde | 428 | 64 | 15.5 | 15.0 | 15.3 | 71.8 | 11.2 | 60.6 | 64.2 | 9.6 | 54.6 | 68.00 | 10.40 | 57.60 | 47 | 3.5 | 39 | 39 |
| Central African R | 3615 | 157 | 18.7 | 17.7 | 18.3 | 44.9 | 8.4 | 36.5 | 43.3 | 7.7 | 35.6 | 44.10 | 8.05 | 36.05 | 16 | 4.8 | 23 | 16 |
| Chad | 7651 | 174 | 19.8 | 18.4 | 19.1 | 50.1 | 9.9 | 40.2 | 47.3 | 8.7 | 38.6 | 48.70 | 9.30 | 39.40 | 20 | 5.9 | 14 | 14 |
| Comoros | 694 | 106 | 18.3 | 17.7 | 18.0 | 58.1 | 10.6 | 47.5 | 56.0 | 9.9 | 46.1 | 57.05 | 10.25 | 46.80 | 30 | 4.7 | 24 | 24 |
| Congo, DR | 51654 | 139 | 22.1 | 19.3 | 20.7 | 46.5 | 10.3 | 36.2 | 45.1 | 8.7 | 36.4 | 45.80 | 9.50 | 36.30 | 16 | 6.3 | 12 | 12 |
| Congo, R | 2943 | 132 | 16.9 | 17.4 | 17.1 | 55.2 | 9.3 | 45.9 | 53.6 | 9.3 | 44.3 | 54.40 | 9.30 | 45.10 | 28 | 5.9 | 14 | 14 |
| Côte d'Ivoire | 14786 | 136 | 10.3 | 10.8 | 10.6 | 48.3 | 5.0 | 43.3 | 47.3 | 5.1 | 42.2 | 47.80 | 5.05 | 42.75 | 25 | 4.9 | 21 | 21 |
| Djibouti | 638 | 174 | 15.5 | 16.2 | 15.9 | 45.1 | 7.0 | 38.1 | 45.0 | 7.3 | 37.7 | 45.05 | 7.15 | 37.90 | 18 | 5.2 | 19 | 18 |
| Egypt | 68470 | 65 | 11.4 | 8.8 | 10.1 | 65.8 | 7.5 | 58.3 | 64.2 | 5.6 | 58.6 | 65.00 | 6.55 | 58.45 | 49 | 3.2 | 45 | 45 |
| Equatorial Guinea | 453 | 177 | 17.9 | 16.7 | 17.3 | 55.3 | 9.9 | 45.4 | 51.4 | 8.6 | 42.8 | 53.35 | 9.25 | 44.10 | 27 | 5.5 | 17 | 17 |
| Eritrea | 3850 | 146 | 20.6 | 17.5 | 19.1 | 46.5 | 9.6 | 36.9 | 46.7 | 8.2 | 38.5 | 46.60 | 8.90 | 37.70 | 18 | 5.6 | 16 | 16 |
| Ethiopia | 62565 | 184 | 22.1 | 19.1 | 20.6 | 43.0 | 9.5 | 33.5 | 41.4 | 7.9 | 33.5 | 42.20 | 8.70 | 33.50 | 13 | 6.2 | 13 | 13 |
| Gabon | 1226 | 135 | 14.8 | 14.6 | 14.7 | 57.5 | 8.5 | 49.0 | 54.6 | 8.0 | 46.6 | 56.05 | 8.25 | 47.80 | 32 | 5.3 | 18 | 18 |
| Gambia | 1305 | 203 | 16.1 | 15.7 | 15.9 | 58.9 | 9.5 | 49.4 | 56.0 | 8.8 | 47.2 | 57.45 | 9.15 | 48.30 | 32 | 5.1 | 19 | 19 |
| Ghana | 20212 | 101 | 17.2 | 16.9 | 17.1 | 55.6 | 9.6 | 46.0 | 54.2 | 9.2 | 45.0 | 54.90 | 9.40 | 45.50 | 29 | 5.0 | 20 | 20 |
| Guinea | 7430 | 207 | 21.2 | 19.9 | 20.6 | 48.9 | 10.4 | 38.5 | 46.2 | 9.2 | 37.0 | 47.55 | 9.80 | 37.75 | 18 | 5.4 | 18 | 18 |
| Guinea-Bissau | 1213 | 203 | 20.2 | 18.1 | 19.2 | 47.0 | 9.5 | 37.5 | 45.0 | 8.2 | 36.8 | 46.00 | 8.85 | 37.15 | 17 | 5.6 | 16 | 16 |
| Kenya | 30080 | 104 | 17.6 | 17.7 | 17.7 | 48.1 | 8.5 | 39.6 | 47.4 | 8.4 | 39.0 | 47.75 | 8.45 | 39.30 | 20 | 4.2 | 30 | 20 |

| Country | Pop. (000s) | Child mort./k | Disabled % LE F | M | ave. | Female LE | yrsdis | HLE | Male LE | yrsdis | HLE | Average LE | yrsdis | HLE | H score | TFR | P score | H&P index |
|---|---|---|---|---|---|---|---|---|---|---|---|---|---|---|---|---|---|---|
| Lesotho | 2153 | 130 | 17.7 | 17.0 | 17.4 | 45.2 | 8.0 | 37.2 | 44.1 | 7.5 | 36.6 | 44.65 | 7.75 | 36.90 | 17 | 4.7 | 24 | 17 |
| Liberia | 3154 | 174 | 23.8 | 20.4 | 22.2 | 44.9 | 10.7 | 34.2 | 42.5 | 8.7 | 33.8 | 43.70 | 9.70 | 34.00 | 13 | 6.2 | 13 | 13 |
| Libyan Arab J | 5605 | 32 | 12.1 | 8.2 | 10.2 | 67.0 | 8.1 | 58.9 | 65.0 | 5.3 | 59.7 | 66.00 | 6.70 | 59.30 | 51 | 3.7 | 36 | 36 |
| Madagascar | 15942 | 116 | 22.9 | 19.0 | 20.9 | 47.7 | 10.9 | 36.8 | 45.0 | 8.5 | 36.5 | 46.35 | 9.70 | 36.65 | 17 | 5.3 | 18 | 17 |
| Malawi | 10925 | 220 | 23.3 | 21.3 | 22.5 | 38.4 | 9.0 | 29.4 | 37.3 | 8.0 | 29.3 | 37.85 | 8.50 | 29.35 | 7 | 6.6 | 10 | 7 |
| Mali | 11234 | 236 | 23.8 | 21.0 | 22.5 | 44.0 | 10.5 | 33.5 | 41.3 | 8.7 | 32.6 | 42.65 | 9.60 | 33.05 | 12 | 6.4 | 11 | 11 |
| Mauritania | 2670 | 148 | 19.7 | 18.8 | 19.3 | 53.0 | 10.5 | 42.5 | 49.5 | 9.3 | 40.2 | 51.25 | 9.90 | 41.35 | 23 | 5.4 | 18 | 18 |
| Mauritius | 1158 | 18 | 10.4 | 11.6 | 10.9 | 74.0 | 7.7 | 66.3 | 66.7 | 7.7 | 59.0 | 70.35 | 7.70 | 62.65 | 57 | 1.9 | 86 | 57 |
| Morocco | 28351 | 68 | 11.0 | 9.8 | 10.5 | 66.8 | 7.4 | 59.4 | 65.1 | 6.4 | 58.7 | 65.95 | 6.90 | 59.05 | 50 | 2.9 | 53 | 50 |
| Mozambique | 19680 | 183 | 20.3 | 19.3 | 19.8 | 44.0 | 8.9 | 35.1 | 41.8 | 8.1 | 33.7 | 42.90 | 8.50 | 34.40 | 14 | 6.1 | 13 | 13 |
| Namibia | 1726 | 122 | 17.7 | 17.4 | 17.5 | 43.0 | 7.6 | 35.4 | 43.3 | 7.5 | 35.8 | 43.15 | 7.55 | 35.60 | 15 | 4.8 | 23 | 15 |
| Niger | 10730 | 190 | 25.8 | 24.3 | 25.1 | 40.6 | 10.5 | 30.1 | 37.1 | 9.0 | 28.1 | 38.85 | 9.75 | 29.10 | 7 | 6.7 | 9 | 7 |
| Nigeria | 111506 | 147 | 20.2 | 18.5 | 19.4 | 48.1 | 9.7 | 38.4 | 46.8 | 8.7 | 38.1 | 47.45 | 9.20 | 38.25 | 19 | 5.0 | 20 | 19 |
| Rwanda | 7733 | 202 | 22.6 | 20.3 | 21.5 | 42.3 | 9.6 | 32.7 | 41.3 | 8.4 | 32.9 | 41.80 | 9.00 | 32.80 | 12 | 6.0 | 14 | 12 |
| São Tomé & Principe | 147 | c 77 | 15.5 | 16.1 | 15.8 | 64.9 | 10.1 | 54.8 | 62.1 | 10.0 | 52.1 | 63.50 | 10.05 | 53.45 | 39 | 6.1 | 13 | 13 |
| Senegal | 9481 | 115 | 18.8 | 18.7 | 18.8 | 56.2 | 10.6 | 45.6 | 53.5 | 10.0 | 43.5 | 54.85 | 10.30 | 44.55 | 27 | 5.4 | 18 | 18 |
| Seychelles | 77 | c 18 | 11.9 | 13.0 | 12.4 | 70.5 | 8.4 | 62.1 | 64.8 | 8.4 | 56.4 | 67.65 | 8.40 | 59.25 | 50 | 2.0 | 84 | 50 |
| Sierra Leone | 4854 | 263 | 26.7 | 22.4 | 24.6 | 35.5 | 9.5 | 26.0 | 33.2 | 7.4 | 25.8 | 34.35 | 8.45 | 25.90 | 2 | 5.9 | 14 | 2 |
| Somalia | 10097 | 204 | 17.4 | 18.6 | 18.0 | 44.7 | 7.8 | 36.9 | 44.1 | 8.2 | 35.9 | 44.40 | 8.00 | 36.40 | 16 | 7.2 | 6 | 6 |
| South Africa | 40377 | 87 | 17.6 | 18.4 | 18.0 | 49.8 | 8.8 | 41.0 | 47.3 | 8.7 | 38.6 | 48.55 | 8.75 | 39.80 | 21 | 3.2 | 45 | 21 |
| Sudan | 29490 | 112 | 20.5 | 19.8 | 20.1 | 54.7 | 11.2 | 43.5 | 53.1 | 10.5 | 42.6 | 53.90 | 10.85 | 43.05 | 25 | 4.5 | 26 | 25 |
| Swaziland | 1008 | 100 | 17.9 | 17.5 | 17.7 | 46.8 | 8.4 | 38.4 | 45.8 | 8.0 | 37.8 | 46.30 | 8.20 | 38.10 | 19 | 4.6 | 25 | 19 |
| Tanzania | 33517 | 130 | 20.8 | 19.1 | 20.0 | 45.6 | 9.5 | 36.1 | 44.4 | 8.5 | 35.9 | 45.00 | 9.00 | 36.00 | 16 | 5.3 | 18 | 16 |
| Togo | 4629 | 129 | 18.6 | 18.2 | 18.4 | 50.8 | 9.4 | 41.4 | 48.9 | 8.9 | 40.0 | 49.85 | 9.15 | 40.70 | 22 | 5.9 | 14 | 14 |
| Tunisia | 9586 | 37 | 10.6 | 7.4 | 9.0 | 67.9 | 7.2 | 60.7 | 67.0 | 5.0 | 62.0 | 67.45 | 6.10 | 61.35 | 55 | 2.5 | 65 | 55 |
| Uganda | 21778 | 173 | 23.4 | 21.4 | 22.4 | 42.4 | 9.9 | 32.5 | 41.9 | 9.0 | 32.9 | 42.15 | 9.45 | 32.70 | 12 | 7.0 | 8 | 8 |
| Zambia | 9169 | 147 | 21.3 | 21.1 | 21.2 | 39.0 | 8.3 | 30.7 | 38.0 | 8.0 | 30.0 | 38.50 | 8.15 | 30.35 | 8 | 5.4 | 18 | 8 |
| Zimbabwe | 11669 | 117 | 18.9 | 18.4 | 18.7 | 40.0 | 7.6 | 32.4 | 40.9 | 7.5 | 33.4 | 40.45 | 7.55 | 32.90 | 12 | 3.7 | 36 | 12 |
| **EUROPE** | | | | | | | | | | | | | | | | | | |
| Albania | 3113 | 43 | 12.8 | 13.3 | 13.0 | 72.7 | 9.3 | 63.4 | 65.1 | 8.6 | 56.5 | 68.90 | 8.95 | 59.95 | 52 | 2.4 | 70 | 52 |
| Austria | 8211 | 7 | 7.4 | 7.5 | 7.5 | 80.4 | 6.0 | 74.4 | 74.4 | 5.6 | 68.8 | 77.40 | 5.80 | 71.60 | 85 | 1.4 | 96 | 85 |
| Belarus | 10236 | 28 | 9.9 | 9.9 | 9.9 | 74.5 | 7.3 | 67.2 | 62.4 | 6.2 | 56.2 | 68.45 | 6.75 | 61.70 | 55 | 1.4 | 96 | 55 |
| Belgium | 10161 | 8 | 8.2 | 7.8 | 8.0 | 81.3 | 6.7 | 74.6 | 74.5 | 5.8 | 68.7 | 77.90 | 6.25 | 71.65 | 85 | 1.6 | 92 | 85 |
| Bosnia & Herzegovina | 3972 | 17 | 11.5 | 11.0 | 11.3 | 75.0 | 8.6 | 66.4 | 71.3 | 7.9 | 63.4 | 73.15 | 8.25 | 64.90 | 64 | 1.4 | 96 | 64 |
| Bulgaria | 8225 | 20 | 9.4 | 9.3 | 9.4 | 74.8 | 7.1 | 67.7 | 67.5 | 6.3 | 61.2 | 71.15 | 6.70 | 64.45 | 62 | 1.2 | 100 | 62 |
| Croatia | 4473 | 12 | 8.6 | 8.7 | 8.6 | 77.2 | 6.6 | 70.6 | 69.3 | 6.0 | 63.3 | 73.25 | 6.30 | 66.95 | 72 | 1.6 | 92 | 72 |
| Czech R | 10244 | 8 | 9.5 | 8.8 | 9.2 | 78.3 | 7.5 | 70.8 | 71.5 | 6.3 | 65.2 | 74.90 | 6.90 | 68.00 | 76 | 1.2 | 100 | 76 |
| Denmark | 5293 | 9 | 8.4 | 7.9 | 8.1 | 78.1 | 6.6 | 71.5 | 72.9 | 5.7 | 67.2 | 75.50 | 6.15 | 69.35 | 81 | 1.7 | 90 | 81 |
| Estonia | 1396 | 25 | 9.5 | 9.8 | 9.7 | 75.3 | 7.2 | 68.1 | 64.4 | 6.3 | 58.1 | 69.85 | 6.75 | 63.10 | 58 | 1.3 | 98 | 58 |
| Finland | 5176 | 6 | 8.6 | 8.4 | 8.6 | 80.7 | 7.0 | 73.7 | 73.4 | 6.2 | 67.2 | 77.05 | 6.60 | 70.45 | 83 | 1.7 | 90 | 83 |
| France | 59080 | 8 | 8.0 | 7.5 | 7.8 | 83.6 | 6.7 | 76.9 | 74.9 | 5.6 | 69.3 | 79.25 | 6.15 | 73.10 | 88 | 1.7 | 90 | 88 |
| Germany | 82220 | 6 | 8.3 | 8.6 | 8.4 | 80.1 | 6.6 | 73.5 | 73.7 | 6.3 | 67.4 | 76.90 | 6.45 | 70.45 | 83 | 1.3 | 98 | 83 |
| Greece | 10645 | 9 | 7.4 | 6.7 | 7.0 | 80.5 | 5.9 | 74.6 | 75.5 | 5.0 | 70.5 | 78.00 | 5.45 | 72.55 | 87 | 1.3 | 98 | 87 |
| Hungary | 10036 | 12 | 9.6 | 9.0 | 9.3 | 75.1 | 7.2 | 67.9 | 66.3 | 5.9 | 60.4 | 70.70 | 6.55 | 64.15 | 61 | 1.3 | 98 | 61 |
| Iceland | 281 | 6 | 10.0 | 9.0 | 9.5 | 80.4 | 8.1 | 72.3 | 76.0 | 6.8 | 69.2 | 78.20 | 7.45 | 70.75 | 83 | 2.1 | 82 | 82 |
| Ireland | 3730 | 8 | 8.4 | 8.0 | 8.2 | 78.3 | 6.6 | 71.7 | 73.3 | 5.8 | 67.5 | 75.80 | 6.20 | 69.60 | 81 | 1.9 | 86 | 81 |
| Italy | 57298 | 8 | 8.2 | 7.1 | 7.7 | 82.1 | 6.7 | 75.4 | 75.4 | 5.4 | 70.0 | 78.75 | 6.05 | 72.70 | 87 | 1.2 | 100 | 87 |
| Latvia | 2357 | 25 | 9.9 | 10.2 | 10.1 | 74.6 | 7.4 | 67.2 | 63.6 | 6.5 | 57.1 | 69.10 | 6.95 | 62.15 | 56 | 1.3 | 98 | 56 |
| Lithuania | 3670 | 24 | 13.3 | 9.5 | 11.6 | 77.9 | 10.4 | 67.5 | 67.0 | 6.4 | 60.6 | 72.45 | 8.40 | 64.05 | 60 | 1.4 | 96 | 60 |
| Luxembourg | 431 | 8 | 8.8 | 8.7 | 8.8 | 81.4 | 7.2 | 74.2 | 74.5 | 6.5 | 68.0 | 77.95 | 6.85 | 71.10 | 84 | 1.7 | 90 | 84 |
| Macedonia, FYR | 2024 | 26 | 11.5 | 11.4 | 11.5 | 74.1 | 8.5 | 65.6 | 69.8 | 8.0 | 61.8 | 71.95 | 8.25 | 63.70 | 59 | 2.1 | 82 | 59 |
| Malta | 389 | 9 | 10.3 | 9.6 | 10.0 | 80.8 | 8.3 | 72.5 | 75.7 | 7.3 | 68.4 | 78.25 | 7.80 | 70.45 | 83 | 1.9 | 86 | 83 |
| Moldova | 4380 | 32 | 10.3 | 9.7 | 10.0 | 71.9 | 7.4 | 64.5 | 64.8 | 6.3 | 58.5 | 68.35 | 6.85 | 61.50 | 55 | 1.7 | 90 | 55 |
| Netherlands | 15786 | 8 | 8.2 | 7.2 | 7.8 | 81.1 | 6.7 | 74.4 | 75.0 | 5.4 | 69.6 | 78.05 | 6.05 | 72.00 | 86 | 1.5 | 94 | 86 |
| Norway | 4465 | 6 | 9.2 | 8.4 | 8.8 | 82.2 | 7.6 | 74.6 | 75.1 | 6.3 | 68.8 | 78.65 | 6.95 | 71.70 | 85 | 1.9 | 86 | 85 |
| Poland | 38765 | 16 | 8.5 | 8.2 | 8.4 | 76.6 | 6.5 | 70.1 | 67.9 | 5.6 | 62.3 | 72.25 | 6.05 | 66.20 | 69 | 1.5 | 94 | 69 |
| Portugal | 9875 | 11 | 8.6 | 8.4 | 8.5 | 79.5 | 6.8 | 72.7 | 72.0 | 6.1 | 65.9 | 75.75 | 6.45 | 69.30 | 81 | 1.4 | 96 | 81 |
| Romania | 22326 | 33 | 10.4 | 9.8 | 10.1 | 73.4 | 7.6 | 65.8 | 65.2 | 6.4 | 58.8 | 69.30 | 7.00 | 62.30 | 57 | 1.2 | 100 | 57 |
| Slovakia | 5387 | 13 | 9.1 | 7.8 | 8.5 | 76.7 | 7.0 | 69.7 | 68.9 | 5.4 | 63.5 | 72.80 | 6.20 | 66.60 | 70 | 1.4 | 96 | 70 |
| Slovenia | 1986 | 8 | 9.6 | 9.4 | 9.5 | 79.5 | 7.6 | 71.9 | 71.6 | 6.7 | 64.9 | 75.55 | 7.15 | 68.40 | 78 | 1.3 | 98 | 78 |
| Spain | 39630 | 8 | 7.7 | 7.3 | 7.6 | 82.1 | 6.4 | 75.7 | 75.3 | 5.5 | 69.8 | 78.70 | 5.95 | 72.75 | 87 | 1.1 | 100 | 87 |
| Sweden | 8910 | 6 | 8.5 | 7.7 | 8.1 | 81.9 | 7.0 | 74.9 | 77.1 | 5.9 | 71.2 | 79.50 | 6.45 | 73.05 | 88 | 1.6 | 92 | 88 |
| Switzerland | 7386 | 9 | 9.1 | 8.1 | 8.6 | 83.0 | 7.5 | 75.5 | 75.6 | 6.1 | 69.5 | 79.30 | 6.80 | 72.50 | 87 | 1.5 | 94 | 87 |
| Ukraine | 50456 | 25 | 9.3 | 9.1 | 9.2 | 74.4 | 6.9 | 67.5 | 64.3 | 5.8 | 58.5 | 69.35 | 6.35 | 63.00 | 58 | 1.4 | 96 | 58 |
| United Kingdom | 58830 | 8 | 7.5 | 6.7 | 7.1 | 79.7 | 6.0 | 73.7 | 74.7 | 5.0 | 69.7 | 77.20 | 5.50 | 71.70 | 85 | 1.7 | 90 | 85 |
| Yugoslavia | 10640 | 26 | 10.8 | 10.6 | 10.7 | 76.3 | 8.2 | 68.1 | 71.8 | 7.6 | 64.2 | 74.05 | 7.90 | 66.15 | 69 | 1.8 | 88 | 69 |

| Country | Pop. (000s) | Child mort./k | Disabled % LE | | | Female | | | Male | | | Average | | | *H* score | TFR | *P* score | H&P index |
|---|---|---|---|---|---|---|---|---|---|---|---|---|---|---|---|---|---|---|
| | | | F | M | ave. | LE | yrsdis | HLE | LE | yrsdis | HLE | LE | yrsdis | HLE | | | | |
| RUSSIAN FEDERATION | 146934 | 22 | 10.3 | 10.5 | 10.4 | 74.0 | 7.6 | 66.4 | 62.7 | 6.6 | 56.1 | 68.35 | 7.10 | 61.25 | 54 | 1.4 | 96 | 54 |
| ASIA | | | | | | | | | | | | | | | | | | |
| Afghanistan | 22720 | 257 | 17.9 | 18.9 | 18.3 | 47.1 | 8.4 | 38.7 | 45.2 | 8.5 | 36.7 | 46.15 | 8.45 | 37.70 | 18 | 6.7 | 9 | 9 |
| Armenia | 3520 | 33 | 11.4 | 10.1 | 10.8 | 77.1 | 8.8 | 68.3 | 72.3 | 7.3 | 65.0 | 74.70 | 8.05 | 66.65 | 71 | 1.7 | 90 | 71 |
| Azerbaijan | 7734 | 50 | 11.4 | 10.6 | 11.0 | 75.3 | 8.6 | 66.7 | 67.8 | 7.2 | 60.6 | 71.55 | 7.90 | 63.65 | 59 | 2.0 | 84 | 59 |
| Bahrain | 617 | 22 | 11.8 | 9.7 | 10.7 | 73.6 | 8.7 | 64.9 | 70.7 | 6.8 | 63.9 | 72.15 | 7.75 | 64.40 | 62 | 2.7 | 58 | 58 |
| Bangladesh | 129155 | 111 | 14.3 | 12.9 | 13.6 | 58.1 | 8.3 | 49.8 | 57.5 | 7.4 | 50.1 | 57.80 | 7.85 | 49.95 | 35 | 3.0 | 50 | 35 |
| Bhutan | 2124 | 96 | 14.2 | 13.8 | 14.0 | 60.9 | 8.7 | 52.2 | 59.6 | 8.2 | 51.4 | 60.25 | 8.45 | 51.80 | 37 | 5.4 | 18 | 18 |
| Brunei Darussalam | 328 | 11 | 18.0 | 14.6 | 16.4 | 79.7 | 14.3 | 65.4 | 74.3 | 10.9 | 63.4 | 77.00 | 12.60 | 64.40 | 62 | 2.7 | 58 | 58 |
| Cambodia | 11168 | 134 | 14.2 | 15.8 | 15.1 | 55.4 | 7.9 | 47.5 | 52.2 | 8.3 | 43.9 | 53.80 | 8.10 | 45.70 | 29 | 4.5 | 26 | 26 |
| China | 1284958 | 48 | 11.2 | 10.2 | 10.7 | 71.3 | 8.0 | 63.3 | 68.1 | 6.9 | 61.2 | 69.70 | 7.45 | 62.25 | 56 | 1.8 | 88 | 56 |
| Cyprus | 786 | 9 | 10.0 | 8.2 | 9.1 | 78.8 | 7.9 | 70.9 | 74.8 | 6.1 | 68.7 | 76.80 | 7.00 | 69.80 | 82 | 2.0 | 84 | 82 |
| Georgia | 4968 | 23 | 9.5 | 9.1 | 9.3 | 76.7 | 7.3 | 69.4 | 69.4 | 6.3 | 63.1 | 73.05 | 6.80 | 66.25 | 69 | 1.9 | 86 | 69 |
| India | 1013662 | 89 | 12.5 | 11.3 | 12.0 | 61.2 | 7.7 | 53.5 | 59.6 | 6.8 | 52.8 | 60.40 | 7.25 | 53.15 | 39 | 3.0 | 50 | 39 |
| Indonesia | 212107 | 63 | 12.2 | 11.7 | 11.9 | 69.0 | 8.4 | 60.6 | 66.6 | 7.8 | 58.8 | 67.80 | 8.10 | 59.70 | 51 | 2.5 | 65 | 51 |
| Iran | 67702 | 52 | 11.9 | 8.2 | 10.1 | 67.9 | 8.1 | 59.8 | 66.8 | 5.5 | 61.3 | 67.35 | 6.80 | 60.55 | 53 | 2.7 | 58 | 53 |
| Iraq | 23115 | 116 | 12.2 | 10.0 | 11.2 | 62.8 | 7.7 | 55.1 | 61.6 | 6.2 | 55.4 | 62.20 | 6.95 | 55.25 | 42 | 5.1 | 19 | 19 |
| Israel | 6217 | 10 | 10.4 | 9.3 | 9.9 | 79.9 | 8.3 | 71.6 | 76.3 | 7.1 | 69.2 | 78.10 | 7.70 | 70.40 | 83 | 2.6 | 60 | 60 |
| Japan | 126714 | 6 | 8.4 | 7.3 | 7.9 | 84.3 | 7.1 | 77.2 | 77.6 | 5.7 | 71.9 | 80.95 | 6.40 | 74.55 | 91 | 1.4 | 96 | 91 |
| Jordan | 6669 | 31 | 12.1 | 8.4 | 10.3 | 67.5 | 8.2 | 59.3 | 66.3 | 5.6 | 60.7 | 66.90 | 6.90 | 60.00 | 52 | 4.7 | 24 | 24 |
| Kazakhstan | 16223 | 41 | 12.4 | 12.3 | 12.4 | 69.9 | 8.7 | 61.2 | 58.7 | 7.2 | 51.5 | 64.30 | 7.95 | 56.35 | 45 | 2.2 | 80 | 45 |
| Korea, DPR | 24039 | 26 | 12.5 | 11.3 | 12.0 | 60.7 | 7.6 | 53.1 | 58.0 | 6.6 | 51.4 | 59.35 | 7.10 | 52.25 | 38 | 2.0 | 84 | 38 |
| Korea, R | 46844 | 13 | 10.9 | 9.3 | 10.2 | 76.0 | 8.3 | 67.7 | 68.7 | 6.4 | 62.3 | 72.35 | 7.35 | 65.00 | 64 | 1.7 | 90 | 64 |
| Kuwait | 1972 | 15 | 15.8 | 12.4 | 14.1 | 75.3 | 11.9 | 63.4 | 71.9 | 8.9 | 63.0 | 73.60 | 10.40 | 63.20 | 58 | 2.8 | 55 | 55 |
| Kyrgyzstan | 4699 | 50 | 14.3 | 13.3 | 13.9 | 69.0 | 9.9 | 59.1 | 61.6 | 8.2 | 53.4 | 65.30 | 9.05 | 56.25 | 44 | 3.1 | 48 | 44 |
| Lao PDR | 5433 | 150 | 16.7 | 16.6 | 16.7 | 56.6 | 9.5 | 47.1 | 54.0 | 9.0 | 45.0 | 55.30 | 9.25 | 46.05 | 29 | 5.6 | 16 | 16 |
| Lebanon | 3282 | 35 | 10.7 | 7.7 | 9.2 | 67.3 | 7.2 | 60.1 | 66.3 | 5.1 | 61.2 | 66.80 | 6.15 | 60.65 | 53 | 2.6 | 60 | 53 |
| Malaysia | 22244 | 15 | 11.9 | 9.4 | 10.6 | 69.9 | 8.3 | 61.6 | 67.6 | 6.3 | 61.3 | 68.75 | 7.30 | 61.45 | 55 | 3.1 | 48 | 48 |
| Maldives | 286 | 66 | 14.9 | 14.0 | 14.5 | 62.6 | 9.3 | 53.3 | 63.3 | 8.9 | 54.4 | 62.95 | 9.10 | 53.85 | 40 | 5.2 | 19 | 19 |
| Mongolia | 2662 | 73 | 13.1 | 13.0 | 13.1 | 64.8 | 8.5 | 56.3 | 59.0 | 7.7 | 51.3 | 61.90 | 8.10 | 53.80 | 40 | 2.5 | 65 | 40 |
| Myanmar | 45611 | 113 | 12.4 | 12.1 | 12.3 | 59.3 | 7.4 | 51.9 | 58.5 | 7.1 | 51.4 | 58.90 | 7.25 | 51.65 | 37 | 2.3 | 75 | 37 |
| Nepal | 23930 | 117 | 14.3 | 13.7 | 14.1 | 57.8 | 8.3 | 49.5 | 57.3 | 7.9 | 49.4 | 57.55 | 8.10 | 49.45 | 34 | 4.3 | 29 | 29 |
| Oman | 2542 | 30 | 13.1 | 12.2 | 12.7 | 73.8 | 9.7 | 64.1 | 70.4 | 8.6 | 61.8 | 72.10 | 9.15 | 62.95 | 58 | 5.7 | 16 | 16 |
| Pakistan | 156483 | 106 | 12.6 | 12.1 | 12.4 | 65.0 | 8.2 | 56.8 | 62.6 | 7.6 | 55.0 | 63.80 | 7.90 | 55.90 | 44 | 4.9 | 21 | 21 |
| Philippines | 75966 | 44 | 12.5 | 11.0 | 11.8 | 69.4 | 8.7 | 60.7 | 64.2 | 7.1 | 57.1 | 66.80 | 7.90 | 58.90 | 50 | 3.5 | 39 | 39 |
| Qatar | 599 | 23 | 15.8 | 10.3 | 13.1 | 74.6 | 11.8 | 62.8 | 71.6 | 7.4 | 64.2 | 73.10 | 9.60 | 63.50 | 59 | 3.6 | 38 | 38 |
| Saudi Arabia | 21607 | 27 | 12.0 | 8.2 | 10.1 | 72.7 | 8.7 | 64.0 | 70.9 | 5.8 | 65.1 | 71.80 | 7.25 | 64.55 | 62 | 5.6 | 16 | 16 |
| Singapore | 3567 | 6 | 11.8 | 10.2 | 11.1 | 80.8 | 9.6 | 71.2 | 75.1 | 7.7 | 67.4 | 77.95 | 8.65 | 69.30 | 81 | 1.7 | 90 | 81 |
| Sri Lanka | 18827 | 21 | 9.7 | 9.9 | 9.8 | 73.4 | 7.1 | 66.3 | 65.8 | 6.5 | 59.3 | 69.60 | 6.80 | 62.80 | 58 | 2.1 | 82 | 58 |
| Syrian Arab R | 16125 | 40 | 12.3 | 8.9 | 10.6 | 67.1 | 8.2 | 58.9 | 64.6 | 5.8 | 58.8 | 65.85 | 7.00 | 58.85 | 50 | 3.9 | 34 | 34 |
| Tajikistan | 6188 | 81 | 15.2 | 15.5 | 15.3 | 70.0 | 10.6 | 59.4 | 65.2 | 10.1 | 55.1 | 67.60 | 10.35 | 57.25 | 46 | 4.0 | 33 | 33 |
| Thailand | 61399 | 35 | 11.8 | 11.6 | 11.7 | 70.4 | 8.3 | 62.1 | 66.0 | 7.6 | 58.4 | 68.20 | 7.95 | 60.25 | 52 | 1.7 | 90 | 52 |
| Turkey | 66591 | 60 | 11.6 | 8.2 | 9.9 | 69.9 | 8.1 | 61.8 | 69.7 | 5.7 | 64.0 | 69.80 | 6.90 | 62.90 | 58 | 2.4 | 70 | 58 |
| Turkmenistan | 4459 | 77 | 13.2 | 14.9 | 14.0 | 65.3 | 8.6 | 56.7 | 61.0 | 9.1 | 51.9 | 63.15 | 8.85 | 54.30 | 41 | 3.5 | 39 | 39 |
| United Arab Emirates | 2441 | 19 | 13.0 | 10.0 | 11.6 | 75.6 | 9.8 | 65.8 | 72.3 | 7.3 | 65.0 | 73.95 | 8.55 | 65.40 | 66 | 3.3 | 43 | 43 |
| Uzbekistan | 24318 | 63 | 12.6 | 11.7 | 12.1 | 71.2 | 8.9 | 62.3 | 65.7 | 7.7 | 58.0 | 68.45 | 8.30 | 60.15 | 52 | 3.3 | 43 | 43 |
| Viet Nam | 79832 | 56 | 13.3 | 12.3 | 12.9 | 68.8 | 9.2 | 59.6 | 64.7 | 8.0 | 56.7 | 66.75 | 8.60 | 58.15 | 48 | 2.5 | 65 | 48 |
| Yemen | 18112 | 113 | 14.3 | 13.2 | 13.8 | 58.0 | 8.3 | 49.7 | 57.3 | 7.6 | 49.7 | 57.65 | 7.95 | 49.70 | 34 | 7.4 | 5 | 5 |
| PACIFIC | | | | | | | | | | | | | | | | | | |
| Australia | 18886 | 7 | 8.1 | 7.8 | 8.0 | 82.2 | 6.7 | 75.5 | 76.8 | 6.0 | 70.8 | 79.50 | 6.35 | 73.15 | 88 | 1.8 | 88 | 88 |
| Fiji | 817 | 23 | 11.7 | 9.8 | 10.8 | 69.2 | 8.1 | 61.1 | 64.0 | 6.3 | 57.7 | 66.60 | 7.20 | 59.40 | 51 | 2.7 | 58 | 51 |
| New Zealand | 3862 | 8 | 10.2 | 9.2 | 9.7 | 79.3 | 8.1 | 71.2 | 73.9 | 6.8 | 67.1 | 76.60 | 7.45 | 69.15 | 80 | 2.0 | 84 | 80 |
| Papua New Guinea | 4807 | 84 | 14.3 | 14.7 | 14.5 | 56.6 | 8.1 | 48.5 | 53.3 | 7.8 | 45.5 | 54.95 | 7.95 | 47.00 | 31 | 4.5 | 26 | 26 |
| Samoa | 180 | 27 | 11.9 | 10.2 | 11.1 | 70.7 | 8.4 | 62.3 | 65.4 | 6.7 | 58.7 | 68.05 | 7.55 | 60.50 | 53 | 4.4 | 28 | 28 |
| Solomon Is | 444 | 27 | 13.7 | 12.2 | 12.9 | 64.0 | 8.7 | 55.3 | 62.0 | 7.5 | 54.5 | 63.00 | 8.10 | 54.90 | 42 | 4.7 | 24 | 24 |
| Tonga | 99 | c 23 | 11.8 | 10.0 | 10.9 | 72.9 | 8.6 | 64.3 | 68.2 | 6.8 | 61.4 | 70.55 | 7.70 | 62.85 | 58 | 4.0 | 33 | 33 |
| Vanuatu | 190 | 48 | 13.7 | 12.7 | 13.1 | 63.0 | 8.6 | 54.4 | 58.7 | 7.4 | 51.3 | 60.85 | 8.00 | 52.85 | 38 | 4.2 | 30 | 30 |

**Notes**

The health and population index (**H&P index**) is the lower of a health index (*H score*) and a population index (*P score*). The lower score was chosen to avoid a high score for population offsetting a low score for health, and vice versa.

The health index is represented by a single indicator: healthy life expectancy at birth. All data are for 1999 and are from World Health Organization (2000), except for the child mortality data. Life expectancy at birth is one of four basic indicators of health endorsed by the United Nations Statistical Commission for its "minimum national social data set" (United Nations Statistical Division 1997). (The other three are the infant mortality rate, child mortality rate, and maternal mortality rate.) *Healthy* life expectancy at birth (HLE)—or disability-adjusted life expectancy at birth (DALE)—is a better indicator of a long and healthy life but until recently was compiled in only a few countries. In 2000, the World Health Organization adopted DALE as its sole indicator of the overall health of a population, and published estimates of DALE for 191 countries (Mathers *et al.* 2000; World Health Organization 2000). Life expectancy at birth is the average number of years that a child born in a given year could expect to live. It is calculated from the death rates of specific age groups—commonly 0-1, 1-5, and then 5-year groups for ages above 5. It reflects all the causes of death (including vehicle and other travel accidents, murders and suicides), and the death rates from those causes, that a typical person would be exposed to as she or he passes through each age group. HLE/DALE is life expectancy at birth minus the number of years that the new-born child could expect to live with various degrees of disability. It incorporates the likely incidence, duration and severity of disability. Disability includes a wide range of diseases and injuries, including neuro-psychiatric disorders. As such HLE/DALE is an excellent indicator of overall health, the healthfulness of living conditions, and the availability and effectiveness of health services. Nevertheless, it is subject to large uncertainties (actual HLE may be several years higher or lower than estimated HLE). Uncertainty ranges for each country are given in Mathers *et al.* (2000) and World Health Organization (2000).

Pop 000s = population estimates for the year 2000 in thousands of persons. Data are from United Nations Population Division (1998b).

Child mort./k = child mortality rate = deaths of children under 5 years of age per 1000 live births. Data are estimates and projections for 1995-2000 by United Nations Population Division (1998b), unless marked "c" which are for 1998 and are from UNICEF (1999b). Data and performance criteria (Table 2a) are given here as background information. The top of the medium band matches the UN target set by the International Conference on Population and Development (Cairo, 1994) and the World Summit for Social Development (Copenhagen, 1995) that all countries should have a child mortality rate below 45 per 1,000 live births by 2015 (United Nations Population Division 1997; Office of the UN System Support and Services 1996).

Disabled % LE = expected percentage of lifespan lived with disability:
    F = females
    M = males
    ave = average
Female/Male/Average:
    LE = life expectancy at birth in years
    yrsdis = expectation of disability at birth in years
    HLE = healthy life expectancy (LE minus yrsdis) in years

*H score* = health index, the score for healthy life expectancy. The performance criteria are shown in Table 2a. They are derived from performance criteria for life expectancy at birth unadjusted for disability. The base of the scale (24 years) and the top point of the good band (79 years) encompass the current range of healthy life expectancy (from 25.8 years for males in Sierra Leone to 77.2 years for females in Japan), and are six years below the corresponding points for unadjusted life expectancy (for which the range is from 33.2 years for males in Sierra Leone to 80.9 years for females in Japan). The top points of the poor, medium and fair bands for healthy life expectancy (HLE) were set at six points below the corresponding points for unadjusted life expectancy (LE). The latter were based on United Nations targets adopted by the International Conference on Population and Development (Cairo, 1994) and the World Summit for Social Development (Copenhagen, 1995) that all countries should have life expectancies of at least 60 years by 2000, more than 70 years by 2005, and more than 75 years by 2015 (United Nations Population Division 1997; Office of the UN System Support and Services 1996). These targets defined the top points of, respectively, the poor, medium, and fair bands for LE. Performance criteria for HLE are from 7.1% to 20.0% lower than those for LE, close to the range of percentages of lifespan lost to disability (7.0% to 25.1%).

The population index is represented by a single indicator: the total fertility rate—the average number of children born alive by a woman in her lifetime—derived from age-specific fertility rates (or sometimes surveys) (United Nations 1996, United Nations Population Division 1998a).

TFR = total fertility rate. Data are for 1999 and are from World Health Organization (2000).

*P score* = population index, the score for the total fertility rate. The performance criteria are shown in Table 2a. The top of the fair band is a point above 2.1, which (with average sex ratios) is the replacement rate—a rate that can be sustained indefinitely without the population increasing or declining. Thus the good band is 2.1 or below. The fair band was set to less than half a child above replacement. Rates below replacement are not sustainable, but the excessively high scores they get have little effect on the health and population index because they are usually offset by lower health scores.

| band | top point on scale | child deaths per 1,000 live births | life expectancy [LE] (years) | healthy life expectancy [HLE] (years) | difference between HLE & LE | total fertility rate (children/woman) |
|---|---|---|---|---|---|---|
| good | 100 | 0 | 85 | 79 | -7.1% | 1.2 |
| fair | 80 | 22 | 75 | 69 | -8.0% | 2.2 |
| medium | 60 | 45 | 70 | 64 | -8.6% | 2.6 |
| poor | 40 | 90 | 60 | 54 | -10.0% | 3.4 |
| bad | 20 | 180 | 45 | 39 | -13.3% | 5.0 |
| base | 0 | 360 | 30 | 24 | -20.0% | 8.2 |

**Table 2a. Performance criteria for health and population indicators.**

# Table 3. Wealth Index; Household Wealth

| Country | Food note | Low food % | Stunt % | Under wt % | Low b wt % | Food score | Basic note | % with water | % with sanit. | Basic score | Need score | GDP/pers PPP$ | Inc. score | *HW score* | *NW score* | W index |
|---|---|---|---|---|---|---|---|---|---|---|---|---|---|---|---|---|
| **AMERICAS** | | | | | | | | | | | | | | | | |
| Antigua & Barbuda | --c | -- | -- | -- | 8 | 84 | -c | -- | 96 | 92 | 84 | 9277 | 57 | 70 | 66 | 68 |
| Argentina | hhc | 1 | 4.7 | 1.9 | 7 | 91 | cc | 71 | 68 | 44 | 44 | 12013 | 64 | 54 | 41 | 47 |
| Bahamas | --h | -- | -- | -- | h 7 | 86 | cc | 94 | 82 | 64 | 64 | 14614 | 69 | 66 | 50 | 58 |
| Barbados | hhc | -- | 7.0 | 5.9 | 10 | 86 | cc | 100 | 100 | 100 | 86 | 12001 | 64 | 75 | 46 | 60 |
| Belize | -hc | -- | -- | 6.2 | 4 | 88 | cc | 83 | 57 | 29 | 29 | 4566 | 37 | 33 | 31 | 32 |
| Bolivia | hcc | 23 | 26.8 | 10 | 5 | 51 | cc | 80 | 65 | 40 | 40 | 2269 | 22 | 31 | 13 | 22 |
| Brazil | hhc | 10 | 10.5 | 5.7 | 8 | 79 | cc | 76 | 70 | 47 | 47 | 6625 | 46 | 46 | 39 | 42 |
| Canada | --c | -- | -- | -- | 6 | 88 | | -- | -- | -- | 80* | 23582 | 84 | 82 | 72 | 77 |
| Chile | hhc | 5 | 2.4 | 0.9 | 5 | 90 | ch | 91 | 83 | 66 | 66 | 8787 | 55 | 60 | 51 | 55 |
| Colombia | hhc | 12 | 15.0 | 8.4 | 9 | 70 | cc | 85 | 85 | 70 | 70 | 6006 | 44 | 57 | 35 | 46 |
| Costa Rica | -hc | 7 | -- | 2.2 | 7 | 86 | cc | 96 | 84 | 68 | 68 | 5987 | 44 | 56 | 42 | 49 |
| Cuba | -cc | 19 | -- | 9 | 7 | 62 | cc | 93 | 66 | 41 | 41 | 3967 | 33 | 37 | 33 | 35 |
| Dominica | --c | -- | -- | -- | 10 | 80 | cc | 96 | 80 | 60 | 60 | 5102 | 40 | 50 | 36 | 43 |
| Dominican R | ccc | 26 | 11 | 6 | 13 | 52 | cc | 79 | 85 | 59 | 52 | 4598 | 37 | 44 | 41 | 42 |
| Ecuador | hhc | 5 | 34.0 | 16.5 | 13 | 41 | cc | 68 | 76 | 44 | 41 | 3003 | 27 | 34 | 23 | 28 |
| El Salvador | hhc | 10 | 23.1 | 11.2 | 11 | 56 | cc | 66 | 90 | 41 | 41 | 4036 | 34 | 37 | 47 | 42 |
| Grenada | --c | -- | -- | -- | 9 | 82 | | -- | -- | -- | 80* | 5838 | 43 | 61 | 39 | 50 |
| Guatemala | hhc | 17 | 49.7 | 26.6 | 15 | 20 | | 68 | 87 | 44 | 20 | 3505 | 30 | 25 | 35 | 30 |
| Guyana | ccc | 16 | 10 | 12 | 15 | 68 | | 91 | 88 | 76 | 68 | 3403 | 29 | 48 | 21 | 34 |
| Haiti | hhc | 61 | 31.9 | 27.5 | 15 | 16 | | 37 | 25 | 10 | 10 | 1383 | 14 | 12 | 20 | 16 |
| Honduras | hhc | 21 | 39.6 | 18.3 | 9 | 34 | | 78 | 74 | 52 | 34 | 2433 | 23 | 28 | 27 | 27 |
| Jamaica | hhc | 11 | 9.6 | 10.2 | 10 | 78 | | 86 | 89 | 72 | 72 | 3389 | 29 | 50 | 29 | 39 |
| Mexico | hhc | 6 | 22.8 | 14.2 | 7 | 56 | | 85 | 72 | 49 | 49 | 7704 | 51 | 50 | 44 | 47 |
| Nicaragua | chc | 31 | 25 | 11.9 | 9 | 45 | | 78 | 85 | 57 | 45 | 2142 | 21 | 33 | 20 | 26 |
| Panama | hcc | 17 | 9.9 | 7 | 8 | 66 | | 93 | 83 | 66 | 66 | 5249 | 41 | 53 | 31 | 42 |
| Paraguay | chc | 13 | 17 | 3.7 | 5 | 66 | | 60 | 41 | 16 | 16 | 4288 | 35 | 25 | 43 | 34 |
| Peru | hhc | 19 | 25.8 | 7.8 | 11 | 52 | | 67 | 72 | 43 | 43 | 4282 | 35 | 39 | 32 | 35 |
| St Kitts & Nevis | --c | -- | -- | -- | 9 | 82 | | 100 | 100 | 100 | 82 | 10672 | 61 | 71 | 56 | 63 |
| St Lucia | --c | -- | -- | -- | 8 | 84 | | 85 | -- | 70 | 70 | 5183 | 41 | 55 | 41 | 48 |
| St Vincent & Grenadines | --c | -- | -- | -- | 8 | 84 | | 89 | 98 | 78 | 78 | 4692 | 38 | 58 | 26 | 42 |
| Suriname | --c | 9 | -- | -- | 13 | 82 | hh | 72 | 56 | 28 | 28 | 5161 | 41 | 34 | 50 | 42 |
| Trinidad & Tobago | hhc | 11 | 4.8 | 6.7 | 10 | 78 | ch | 97 | 56 | 28 | 28 | 7485 | 50 | 39 | 46 | 42 |
| United States | hhc | -- | 2.1 | 1.4 | 7 | 96 | | -- | -- | -- | 80* | 29605 | 90 | 85 | 83 | 84 |
| Uruguay | ccc | 4 | 8 | 5 | 8 | 84 | hh | 83 | 82 | 64 | 64 | 8623 | 54 | 59 | 45 | 52 |
| Venezuela | hhc | 15 | 13.2 | 4.5 | 9 | 70 | | 79 | 59 | 32 | 32 | 5808 | 43 | 37 | 32 | 34 |
| **AFRICA** | | | | | | | | | | | | | | | | |
| Algeria | hhc | 5 | 18.3 | 12.8 | 9 | 63 | | 90 | 91 | 80 | 63 | 4792 | 39 | 51 | 28 | 39 |
| Angola | ccc | 43 | 53 | 42 | 19 | 19 | | 31 | 40 | 12 | 12 | 1821 | 18 | 15 | 12 | 13 |
| Benin | hh- | 15 | 25.0 | 29.2 | -- | 48 | | 56 | 27 | 11 | 11 | 867 | 9 | 10 | 17 | 13 |
| Botswana | ccc | 25 | 29 | 17 | 11 | 48 | | 90 | 55 | 27 | 27 | 6103 | 44 | 35 | 49 | 42 |
| Burkina Faso | cc | 30 | 29 | 30 | 21 | 47 | | 42 | 37 | 15 | 15 | 870 | 9 | 12 | 11 | 11 |
| Burundi | ch- | 63 | 43 | 37.5 | -- | 15 | | 52 | 51 | 21 | 15 | 570 | 6 | 10 | 4 | 7 |
| Cameroon | ccc | 32 | 29 | 22 | 13 | 44 | | 54 | 89 | 25 | 25 | 1474 | 15 | 20 | 10 | 15 |
| Cape Verde | ccc | -- | 16 | 14 | 9 | 68 | | 65 | 27 | 11 | 11 | 3233 | 28 | 19 | 35 | 27 |
| Central African R | ccc | 42 | 34 | 27 | 15 | 31 | | 38 | 27 | 11 | 11 | 1118 | 11 | 11 | 10 | 10 |
| Chad | cch | 46 | 40 | 39 | h 20 | 25 | | 54 | 27 | 11 | 11 | 856 | 9 | 10 | 13 | 11 |
| Comoros | hhc | -- | 33.8 | 25.8 | 8 | 42 | | 53 | 23 | 9 | 9 | 1398 | 14 | 11 | 15 | 13 |
| Congo, DR | hhc | 55 | 45.2 | 34.4 | 15 | 18 | | 42 | 18 | 7 | 7 | 822 | 8 | 7 | 5 | 6 |
| Congo, R | rural;hhc | 34 | 27.5 | 23.9 | 16 | 41 | | 34 | 69 | 14 | 14 | 995 | 10 | 12 | 7 | 9 |
| Côte d'Ivoire | hhc | 15 | 24.4 | 23.8 | 12 | 54 | | 42 | 39 | 16 | 16 | 1598 | 16 | 16 | 13 | 14 |
| Djibouti | ccc | -- | 26 | 18 | 11 | 52 | | 90 | 55 | 27 | 27 | 1266 | 13 | 20 | 23 | 21 |
| Egypt | chc | 4 | 25 | 12.4 | 10 | 53 | | 87 | 88 | 74 | 53 | 3041 | 27 | 40 | 34 | 37 |
| Equatorial Guinea | --h | -- | -- | -- | h 12 | 76 | | 95 | 54 | 25 | 25 | 1817 | 18 | 21 | 15 | 18 |
| Eritrea | hhc | 67 | 38.4 | 43.7 | 13 | 13 | | 22 | 13 | 5 | 5 | 833 | 8 | 6 | 32 | 19 |
| Ethiopia | rural;hhc | 51 | 64.2 | 47.7 | 16 | 14 | | 25 | 19 | 8 | 8 | 574 | 6 | 7 | 4 | 5 |
| Gabon | --- | 8 | -- | -- | -- | 84 | ch | 67 | 76 | 43 | 43 | 6353 | 45 | 44 | 30 | 37 |
| Gambia | cc- | 25 | 30 | 26 | -- | 47 | | 69 | 37 | 15 | 15 | 1453 | 14 | 14 | 18 | 16 |
| Ghana | hhc | 11 | 25.9 | 27.3 | 8 | 50 | | 65 | 32 | 13 | 13 | 1735 | 17 | 15 | 22 | 18 |
| Guinea | c-c | 31 | 29 | -- | 13 | 45 | | 46 | 31 | 12 | 12 | 1782 | 18 | 15 | 16 | 15 |
| Guinea-Bissau | --c | -- | -- | -- | 20 | 60 | | 43 | 46 | 17 | 17 | 616 | 6 | 11 | 4 | 7 |
| Kenya | hhc | 41 | 33.6 | 22.5 | 16 | 32 | | 44 | 85 | 18 | 18 | 980 | 10 | 14 | 17 | 15 |
| Lesotho | ccc | 28 | 44 | 16 | 11 | 28 | | 62 | 38 | 15 | 15 | 1626 | 16 | 15 | 24 | 19 |
| Liberia | --- | 42 | -- | -- | -- | 31 | | 46 | 30 | 12 | 12 | 843 | 8 | 10 | 5 | 7 |
| Libyan Arab J | hhc | 1 | 15.1 | 4.7 | 7 | 70 | | 97 | 98 | 94 | 70 | 6697 | 47 | 58 | 58 | 58 |
| Madagascar | hcc | 39 | 49.8 | 40 | 5 | 20 | | 40 | 40 | 16 | 16 | 756 | 8 | 12 | 7 | 9 |
| Malawi | hhc | 37 | 48.3 | 29.9 | 20 | 22 | | 47 | 3 | 1 | 1 | 523 | 5 | 3 | 10 | 6 |
| Mali | hhc | 29 | 30.1 | 40.0 | 16 | 33 | | 66 | 6 | 2 | 2 | 681 | 7 | 4 | 8 | 6 |

158

| Country | Food note | Low food % | Stunt % | Under wt % | Low b wt % | Food score | Basic note | % with water | % with sanit. | Basic score | Need score | GDP/pers PPP$ | Inc. score | *HW* score | *NW* score | W index |
|---|---|---|---|---|---|---|---|---|---|---|---|---|---|---|---|---|
| Mauritania | hhc | 13 | 44.0 | 23.0 | 11 | 28 | | 37 | 57 | 15 | 15 | 1563 | 16 | 15 | 12 | 13 |
| Mauritius | hcc | 6 | 9.7 | 16 | 13 | 68 | | 98 | 100 | 96 | 68 | 8312 | 53 | 60 | 49 | 54 |
| Morocco | chc | 5 | 23 | 9.5 | 9 | 56 | | 65 | 58 | 31 | 31 | 3305 | 29 | 30 | 31 | 30 |
| Mozambique | ccc | 63 | 36 | 26 | 20 | 15 | | 46 | 34 | 14 | 14 | 782 | 8 | 11 | 5 | 8 |
| Namibia | hhc | 30 | 28.5 | 26.2 | 16 | 47 | | 83 | 62 | 36 | 36 | 5176 | 41 | 38 | 44 | 41 |
| Niger | ccc | 39 | 41 | 50 | 15 | 20 | | 61 | 19 | 8 | 8 | 739 | 7 | 7 | 8 | 7 |
| Nigeria | hcc | 8 | 42.7 | 36 | 16 | 30 | | 49 | 41 | 16 | 16 | 795 | 8 | 12 | 12 | 12 |
| Rwanda | ccc | 37 | 42 | 27 | 17 | 31 | | -- | -- | -- | 31 | 660 | 7 | 19 | 5 | 12 |
| São Tomé & Príncipe | hhc | -- | 25.9 | 16.6 | 7 | 52 | | 82 | 35 | 14 | 14 | 1469 | 15 | 14 | 10 | 12 |
| Senegal | hhc | 17 | 24.7 | 22.2 | 4 | 54 | | 81 | 65 | 40 | 40 | 1307 | 13 | 26 | 18 | 22 |
| Seychelles | chc | -- | 23 | 5.7 | 10 | 56 | hh96 | 83 | 98 | 66 | 56 | 10600 | 61 | 58 | 41 | 49 |
| Sierra Leone | hhc | 43 | 34.7 | 28.7 | 11 | 29 | | 34 | 11 | 4 | 4 | 458 | 5 | 4 | 3 | 3 |
| Somalia | --c | 73 | -- | -- | 16 | 11 | | 31 | 43 | 12 | 11 | 712 | 7 | 9 | 5 | 7 |
| South Africa | hh- | -- | 22.8 | 9.2 | -- | 56 | | 87 | 87 | 74 | 56 | 8488 | 54 | 55 | 49 | 52 |
| Sudan | hhc | 20 | 34.3 | 33.9 | 15 | 41 | | 73 | 51 | 21 | 21 | 1394 | 14 | 17 | 9 | 13 |
| Swaziland | hhc | 14 | 30.3 | 9.7 | 10 | 46 | | 50 | 59 | 20 | 20 | 3816 | 32 | 26 | 47 | 36 |
| Tanzania | ccc | 40 | 42 | 27 | 14 | 31 | | 66 | 86 | 41 | 31 | 480 | 5 | 18 | 3 | 10 |
| Togo | hhc | 23 | 29.2 | 24.5 | 20 | 48 | | 55 | 37 | 15 | 15 | 1372 | 14 | 14 | 18 | 16 |
| Tunisia | hhc | 1 | 22.5 | 9.0 | 8 | 57 | | 98 | 80 | 60 | 57 | 5405 | 42 | 49 | 38 | 43 |
| Uganda | hhc | 28 | 38.3 | 25.5 | 13 | 36 | | 46 | 57 | 18 | 18 | 1074 | 11 | 14 | 11 | 12 |
| Zambia | hhc | 45 | 42.4 | 23.5 | 13 | 27 | | 38 | 71 | 15 | 15 | 719 | 7 | 11 | 5 | 8 |
| Zimbabwe | chc | 39 | 32 | 15.5 | 10 | 35 | | 79 | 52 | 23 | 23 | 2669 | 24 | 23 | 26 | 24 |
| EUROPE | | | | | | | | | | | | | | | | |
| Albania | --c | -- | -- | -- | 7 | 86 | | -- | -- | -- | 80* | 2804 | 25 | 52 | 26 | 39 |
| Austria | --c | -- | -- | -- | 6 | 88 | | -- | -- | -- | 80* | 23166 | 83 | 81 | 77 | 79 |
| Belarus | --- | -- | -- | -- | -- | -- | | -- | -- | -- | -- | 6319 | 45 | 45 | 41 | 43 |
| Belgium | --c | -- | -- | -- | 6 | 88 | | -- | -- | -- | 80* | 23223 | 83 | 81 | 68 | 74 |
| Bosnia & Herzegovina | --- | -- | -- | -- | -- | -- | | -- | -- | -- | -- | # 1720 | 17 | 17 | 13 | 15 |
| Bulgaria | --c | -- | -- | -- | 6 | 88 | | -- | -- | -- | 80* | 4809 | 39 | 59 | 31 | 45 |
| Croatia | hh- | -- | 0.8 | 0.6 | -- | 98 | hh | 96 | 68 | 44 | 44 | 6749 | 47 | 45 | 49 | 47 |
| Czech R | hhc | -- | 1.9 | 1.0 | 6 | 96 | | -- | -- | -- | 80* | 12362 | 65 | 72 | 51 | 61 |
| Denmark | --c | -- | -- | -- | 6 | 88 | hh | 100 | 100 | 100 | 88 | 24218 | 84 | 86 | 81 | 83 |
| Estonia | --- | -- | -- | -- | -- | -- | | -- | -- | -- | -- | 7682 | 51 | 51 | 50 | 50 |
| Finland | --c | -- | -- | -- | 4 | 92 | hh | 100 | 100 | 100 | 92 | 20847 | 81 | 86 | 74 | 80 |
| France | --c | -- | -- | -- | 5 | 90 | | -- | -- | -- | 80* | 21175 | 81 | 80 | 70 | 75 |
| Germany | --h | -- | -- | -- | h 6 | 88 | | -- | -- | -- | 80* | 22169 | 82 | 81 | 72 | 76 |
| Greece | --c | -- | -- | -- | 6 | 88 | | -- | -- | -- | 80* | 13943 | 68 | 74 | 59 | 66 |
| Hungary | hhc | -- | 2.9 | 2.2 | 9 | 94 | | -- | -- | -- | 80* | 10232 | 60 | 70 | 46 | 58 |
| Iceland | --h | -- | -- | -- | h 3 | 94 | -h | -- | 95 | 90 | 90 | 25110 | 85 | 87 | 82 | 84 |
| Ireland | --c | -- | -- | -- | 4 | 92 | | -- | -- | -- | 80* | 21482 | 81 | 80 | 77 | 78 |
| Italy | --c | -- | -- | -- | 5 | 90 | | -- | -- | -- | 80* | 20585 | 81 | 80 | 63 | 71 |
| Latvia | --h | -- | -- | -- | h 5 | 90 | | -- | -- | -- | 80* | 5728 | 43 | 61 | 53 | 57 |
| Lithuania | --h | -- | -- | -- | h 4 | 92 | | -- | -- | -- | 80* | 6436 | 46 | 63 | 51 | 57 |
| Luxembourg | --h | -- | -- | -- | h 4 | 92 | | -- | -- | -- | 80* | 33505 | 93 | 86 | 93 | 89 |
| Macedonia, FYR | --- | -- | -- | -- | -- | -- | | -- | -- | -- | -- | 4254 | 35 | 35 | 22 | 28 |
| Malta | --h | -- | -- | -- | h 6 | 88 | | -- | -- | -- | 80* | 16447 | 73 | 76 | 60 | 68 |
| Moldova | --c | -- | -- | -- | 4 | 92 | | 55 | 50 | 20 | 20 | 1947 | 19 | 19 | 30 | 24 |
| Netherlands | --h | -- | -- | -- | h 4 | 92 | hh | 100 | 100 | 100 | 92 | 22176 | 82 | 87 | 78 | 82 |
| Norway | --c | -- | -- | -- | 4 | 92 | | -- | -- | -- | 80* | 26342 | 86 | 83 | 84 | 83 |
| Poland | --h | -- | -- | -- | h 8 | 84 | | -- | -- | -- | 80* | 7619 | 50 | 65 | 47 | 56 |
| Portugal | --c | -- | -- | -- | 5 | 90 | | -- | -- | -- | 80* | 14701 | 69 | 74 | 70 | 72 |
| Romania | hhc | -- | 7.8 | 5.7 | 7 | 84 | -h | -- | 49 | 20 | 20 | 5648 | 43 | 31 | 34 | 32 |
| Slovakia | --h | -- | -- | -- | h 6 | 88 | -h | -- | 51 | 21 | 21 | 9699 | 59 | 40 | 51 | 45 |
| Slovenia | --h | -- | -- | -- | h 6 | 88 | -h | -- | 89 | 78 | 78 | 14293 | 69 | 73 | 63 | 68 |
| Spain | --c | -- | -- | -- | 4 | 92 | hh | 99 | 97 | 94 | 92 | 16212 | 72 | 82 | 60 | 71 |
| Sweden | --c | -- | -- | -- | 5 | 90 | | -- | -- | -- | 80* | 20659 | 81 | 80 | 76 | 78 |
| Switzerland | --c | -- | -- | -- | 5 | 90 | | -- | -- | -- | 80* | 25512 | 85 | 82 | 81 | 81 |
| Ukraine | --h | -- | -- | -- | h 6 | 88 | hh | 96 | 49 | 20 | 20 | 3194 | 28 | 24 | 39 | 31 |
| United Kingdom | --c | -- | -- | -- | 7 | 86 | hh | 100 | 96 | 92 | 86 | 20336 | 80 | 83 | 78 | 80 |
| Yugoslavia | hh- | -- | 6.8 | 1.6 | -- | 86 | | 76 | 69 | 45 | 45 | # 2300 | 22 | 33 | 21 | 27 |
| RUSSIAN FEDERATION | hhc | -- | 12.7 | 3.0 | 6 | 75 | | -- | -- | -- | 75 | 6460 | 46 | 60 | 37 | 48 |
| ASIA | | | | | | | | | | | | | | | | |
| Afghanistan | ccc | 62 | 52 | 48 | 20 | 15 | | 6 | 10 | 2 | 2 | 800 | 8 | 5 | 8 | 6 |
| Armenia | --c | -- | -- | -- | 7 | 86 | | -- | -- | -- | 80* | 2072 | 20 | 50 | 32 | 41 |
| Azerbaijan | hhc | -- | 22.2 | 10.1 | 6 | 57 | | -- | -- | -- | 57 | 2175 | 21 | 39 | 48 | 43 |
| Bahrain | hcc | -- | 9.9 | 9 | 6 | 80 | | 94 | 97 | 88 | 80 | 13111 | 66 | 73 | 48 | 60 |
| Bangladesh | hhc | 37 | 54.6 | 56.3 | 50 | 17 | | 95 | 43 | 17 | 17 | 1361 | 14 | 15 | 33 | 24 |
| Bhutan | hh- | -- | 56.1 | 37.9 | -- | 18 | | 58 | 70 | 31 | 18 | 1536 | 15 | 16 | 32 | 24 |
| Brunei Darussalam | --h | -- | -- | -- | h 5 | 90 | | -- | -- | -- | 80* | 16765 | 73 | 76 | 60* | 68 |
| Cambodia | cch | 33 | 56 | 52 | h 18 | 18 | | 30 | 19 | 8 | 8 | 1257 | 13 | 10 | 17 | 13 |

159

| Country | Food note | Low food % | Stunt % | Under wt % | Low b wt % | Food score | Basic note | % with water | % with sanit. | Basic score | Need score | GDP/pers PPP$ | Inc. score | *HW score* | *NW score* | **W index** |
|---|---|---|---|---|---|---|---|---|---|---|---|---|---|---|---|---|
| China | ccc | 13 | 34 | 16 | 9 | 41 | | 67 | 24 | 10 | 10 | 3105 | 27 | 18 | 50 | 34 |
| Cyprus | --h | -- | -- | -- | h 9 | 82 | | 100 | -- | 100 | 82 | 17482 | 75 | 78 | 70 | 74 |
| Georgia | --- | -- | -- | -- | -- | -- | | -- | -- | -- | -- | 3353 | 29 | 29 | 41 | 35 |
| India | hhc | 22 | 52.0 | 53.4 | 33 | 19 | | 81 | 29 | 12 | 12 | 2077 | 20 | 16 | 26 | 21 |
| Indonesia | hhc | 6 | 42.2 | 34.0 | 8 | 30 | | 74 | 53 | 24 | 24 | 2651 | 24 | 24 | 17 | 20 |
| Iran | hhc | 6 | 18.9 | 15.7 | 10 | 62 | | 95 | 64 | 39 | 39 | 5121 | 40 | 39 | 46 | 42 |
| Iraq | ccc | 15 | 31 | 23 | 15 | 45 | | 81 | 75 | 53 | 45 | 3197 | 28 | 36 | 28 | 32 |
| Israel | --c | -- | -- | -- | 7 | 86 | hh | 99 | 70 | 47 | 47 | 17301 | 75 | 61 | 63 | 62 |
| Japan | --c | -- | -- | -- | 7 | 86 | | 97 | -- | 94 | 86 | 23257 | 83 | 84 | 74 | 79 |
| Jordan | hcc | 3 | 15.8 | 5 | 10 | 68 | | 97 | 99 | 94 | 68 | 3347 | 29 | 48 | 20 | 34 |
| Kazakhstan | hhc | -- | 15.8 | 8.3 | 9 | 68 | | 93 | 99 | 86 | 68 | 4378 | 36 | 52 | 44 | 48 |
| Korea, DPR | cc- | 48 | 60 | 60 | -- | 16 | | 100 | 99 | 98 | 16 | 4058 | 34 | 25 | 34 | 29 |
| Korea, R | --c | 1 | -- | -- | 9 | 98 | | 93 | 100 | 86 | 86 | 13478 | 67 | 76 | 59 | 67 |
| Kuwait | hhc | 3 | 12.2 | 6.4 | 7 | 76 | | -- | -- | -- | 76 | 25314 | 85 | 80 | 76 | 78 |
| Kyrgyzstan | ccc | -- | 25 | 11 | 6 | 53 | | 79 | 100 | 59 | 53 | 2317 | 22 | 37 | 30 | 33 |
| Lao PDR | hhc | 33 | 47.3 | 40.0 | 18 | 24 | | 44 | 18 | 7 | 7 | 1734 | 17 | 12 | 17 | 14 |
| Lebanon | hhc | 2 | 12.2 | 3.0 | 10 | 76 | | 94 | 63 | 37 | 37 | 4326 | 35 | 36 | 23 | 29 |
| Malaysia | -cc | 2 | -- | 19 | 8 | 62 | | 78 | 94 | 57 | 57 | 8137 | 52 | 54 | 54 | 54 |
| Maldives | ccc | -- | 27 | 43 | 13 | 29 | | 60 | 44 | 18 | 18 | 4083 | 34 | 26 | 36 | 31 |
| Mongolia | ccc | 48 | 22 | 10 | 7 | 23 | | 45 | 87 | 18 | 18 | 1541 | 15 | 16 | 20 | 18 |
| Myanmar | hcc | 7 | 44.6 | 39 | 24 | 27 | | 60 | 43 | 17 | 17 | 1199 | 12 | 14 | 12 | 13 |
| Nepal | hh- | 21 | 48.8 | 46.9 | -- | 22 | | 71 | 16 | 6 | 6 | 1157 | 12 | 9 | 23 | 16 |
| Oman | ccc | -- | 23 | 23 | 8 | 56 | | 85 | 78 | 57 | 56 | 9960 | 60 | 58 | 52 | 55 |
| Pakistan | hhc | 19 | 49.6 | 38.2 | 25 | 20 | | 79 | 56 | 28 | 20 | 1715 | 17 | 18 | 23 | 20 |
| Philippines | ccc | 22 | 30 | 28 | 9 | 47 | | 85 | 87 | 70 | 47 | 3555 | 30 | 38 | 33 | 35 |
| Qatar | hh- | -- | 8.1 | 5.5 | -- | 84 | hc | 100 | 97 | 94 | 84 | 20987 | 81 | 82 | 60* | 71 |
| Saudi Arabia | --c | 4 | -- | -- | 7 | 92 | | -- | -- | -- | 80* | 10158 | 60 | 70 | 64 | 67 |
| Singapore | --c | -- | -- | -- | 7 | 86 | hh | 100 | 100 | 100 | 86 | 24210 | 84 | 85 | 78 | 81 |
| Sri Lanka | hcc | 25 | 23.8 | 34 | 25 | 41 | | 57 | 63 | 29 | 29 | 2979 | 26 | 27 | 30 | 28 |
| Syrian Arab R | ccc | 1 | 21 | 13 | 7 | 59 | | 86 | 67 | 43 | 43 | 2892 | 26 | 34 | 23 | 28 |
| Tajikistan | --h | -- | -- | -- | h 8 | 84 | ch | 60 | 62 | 33 | 33 | 1041 | 10 | 21 | 18 | 19 |
| Thailand | ccc | 24 | 16 | 19 | 6 | 55 | | 81 | 96 | 62 | 55 | 5456 | 42 | 48 | 41 | 44 |
| Turkey | hhc | 2 | 20.5 | 10.4 | 8 | 59 | | 49 | 80 | 20 | 20 | 6422 | 46 | 33 | 29 | 31 |
| Turkmenistan | --c | -- | -- | -- | 5 | 90 | | 74 | 91 | 52 | 52 | 2550 | 24 | 38 | 18 | 28 |
| United Arab Emirates | ccc | 1 | 17 | 14 | 6 | 66 | | 97 | 92 | 84 | 66 | 17719 | 75 | 70 | 76 | 73 |
| Uzbekistan | hh- | -- | 31.3 | 18.8 | -- | 45 | | 90 | 100 | 80 | 45 | 2053 | 20 | 32 | 30 | 31 |
| Viet Nam | ccc | 19 | 44 | 41 | 17 | 28 | | 45 | 29 | 12 | 12 | 1689 | 17 | 14 | 18 | 16 |
| Yemen | ccc | 37 | 52 | 46 | 19 | 19 | | 61 | 66 | 35 | 19 | 719 | 7 | 13 | 13 | 13 |
| PACIFIC | | | | | | | | | | | | | | | | |
| Australia | --c | -- | -- | -- | 6 | 88 | | -- | -- | -- | 80* | 22452 | 82 | 81 | 79 | 80 |
| Fiji | hhc | -- | 2.7 | 7.9 | 12 | 84 | | 77 | 92 | 56 | 56 | 4231 | 35 | 45 | 46 | 45 |
| New Zealand | --c | -- | -- | -- | 6 | 88 | | 97 | -- | 94 | 88 | 17288 | 75 | 81 | 74 | 77 |
| Papua New Guinea | rural;hhc | 24 | 43.2 | 29.9 | 23 | 29 | | 41 | 83 | 16 | 16 | 2359 | 22 | 19 | 25 | 22 |
| Samoa | --c | -- | -- | -- | 6 | 88 | | 68 | -- | 44 | 44 | 3832 | 32 | 38 | 31 | 34 |
| Solomon Is | hhc | -- | 27.3 | 21.3 | 20 | 50 | | -- | -- | -- | 50 | 1940 | 19 | 34 | 35 | 34 |
| Tonga | h-c | -- | 1.3 | -- | 2 | 97 | | 95 | 95 | 90 | 90 | w 4281 | 35 | 62 | 37 | 49 |
| Vanuatu | hhc | -- | 19.1 | 19.7 | 7 | 61 | | 77 | 28 | 11 | 11 | 3120 | 27 | 19 | 42 | 30 |

**Notes**

The wealth index (**W index**) is the unweighted average of a household wealth index (*HW score*) and a national wealth index (*NW score*). The household wealth index is shown here. The national wealth index is shown in Table 4.

The household wealth index is the average of two unweighted indicators (column heading in parentheses):

Needs (Need score), the lower score of two indicators—

Food sufficiency (Food score), represented by the percentage of population with insufficient food (Low food %), prevalence of stunting in children under five years of age (Stunt %), prevalence of low weight-for-age in children under five years (Under wt %), whichever gave the lowest score. If data were not available on these indicators, percentage of babies whose birth weight is less than 2500 grams (Low b wt %) was used instead.

Basic services (Basic score), represented by the percentage of population with access to safe water (% with water) or the percentage of population with access to basic sanitation (% with sanit), whichever gave the lower score.

Income (Inc score), represented by Gross Domestic Product per person, in current international purchasing-power-parity dollars ($PPP).

The food sufficiency indicators are not strictly comparable. The percentage of the population with insufficient food is a measure of food supply. The other indicators are measures of physiological condition, and are influenced by health and sanitation as well as food supply. The percentage of babies with low birth weight is especially affected by other factors.

Food note = sources and other notes for the Stunt % (left letter), Under wt % (center letter), and Low b wt % (right letter) columns.

Low food % = percentage of the population with insufficient food. Insufficient food means food consumption below minimum energy requirement. Data are for 1995-1997 and are from FAO (1999b). They were estimated from food supply data (derived from production and trade data) and household surveys (FAO 1996a).

Stunt % = prevalence of stunting = percentage of children under five years with low height-for-age. Data are for the latest year available and are from Onis & Blössner (1997), if indicated by the letter h in the Food note column, or UNICEF (1999b), if indicated by the letter c. The World Health Organization (WHO) regards height-for-age as the best indicator for monitoring child growth, because it measures cumulative deficient growth associated with long term factors, including chronic insufficient daily food intake, frequent infection, and poor feeding practices (Visschedjik & Siméant 1998; World Health Organization 1998b).

Under wt % = prevalence of low weight-for-age in children under five years. Data are for the latest year available and are from Onis & Blössner (1997), if indicated by the letter h in the Food note column, or UNICEF (1999b), if indicated by the letter c.

Low b wt % = babies whose birth weight is less than 2500 grams, as a percentage of babies born alive. Data are for the latest year in the period 1990-1997 and are from UNICEF (1999b), if indicated by the letter c in the Food note column, or World Health Organization (1996-1998a), if indicated by the latter h.

Food score = food sufficiency score. The performance criteria for the food indicators are shown in Table 3a. For insufficient food, the top of the fair band corresponds to the 1996 World Food Summit target to halve the number of hungry people by 2015, from 20% of the total population of developing countries to under 10% (FAO 1999b). For stunting, the top of the medium band corresponds to the WHO target of less than 20% in all countries by 2010 (World Health Organization 1998b; Visschedjik & Siméant 1998). For low weight-for-age children and low birth-weight babies, the top of the fair band corresponds to the general target of WHO's General Strategy for Health of no more than 10% (United Nations 1996). The criteria for percentage of the population with insufficient food match those for the other food indicators.

Basic note = sources for % with water (left) and % with sanit. (right) columns, if not the main source.

% with water = percentage of population with access to safe water. Data are for the latest year in the period 1990-1998 and are from UNICEF (1999b), except those marked with the letter h in the Basic note column, which are for a single year in the period 1991-1993 or for the year in the Basic note column, and are from World Health Organization (1996-1998a).

% with sanit. = percentage of population with access to basic sanitation. Data are for the latest year in the period 1990-1998 and are from UNICEF (1999b), except those marked with the letter h in the Basic note column, which are for a single year in the period 1991-1993 or for the year in the Basic note column, and are from World Health Organization (1996-1998a).

Basic score = basic services score = the lower of the water and sanitation scores. The performance criteria are shown in Table 3a. The top of the good band matches the UN target of 100% set by the International Conference on Population and Development (Cairo, 1994), the World Summit for Social Development (Copenhagen, 1995), the Fourth World Conference on Women (Beijing, 1995), and the Second World Conference on Human Settlements (Habitat II, Istanbul, 1996) (United Nations Population Division 1997; Office of the UN System Support and Services 1996).

Need score = needs score, the lower of the food sufficiency and basic services scores.

GDP/pers $PPP = Gross Domestic Product per person, in current international purchasing power parity dollars, except where marked with the symbol #, which is in current US dollars. GDP is the total economic activity of a country, regardless of who owns the productive assets (*The Economist* 1997). Data are for 1998 and are from United Nations Development Programme (2000), except where marked with the symbol #, which are for 1997 and are from United Nations Statistical Division (1999), or the letter w, which are for 1999 Gross National Product and are from World Bank (2000a).

Inc score = income score. The performance criteria are shown in Table 3a. The bands are based on the relationship between income and performance on health and population, knowledge, and community, as described in the section on income in Chapter 2 and shown in Table 3b.

| band | top point on scale | % population with not enough food | prevalence of stunting in children under 5 (%) | prevalence of underweight children under 5 (%) | prevalence of babies with low birth-weight (%) | % population with safe water & basic sanitation | Gross Domestic Product per person $PPP |
|---|---|---|---|---|---|---|---|
| good | 100 | 0 | 0 | 0 | 0 | 100 | 40,000 |
| fair | 80 | 10 | 10 | 10 | 10 | 90 | 20,000 |
| medium | 60 | 20 | 20 | 20 | 20 | 80 | 10,000 |
| poor | 40 | 35 | 35 | 35 | 35 | 75 | 5,000 |
| bad | 20 | 50 | 50 | 50 | 50 | 50 | 2,000 |
| base | 0 | 100 | 100 | 100 | 100 | 0 | 0 |

Table 3a. Performance criteria for indicators of food sufficiency, basic services, and income (GDP per person).

| income group | good | fair | medium | poor | bad |
|---|---|---|---|---|---|
| PPP$20.1-40.0 | 15 | 5 | 1 | 1 | 0 |
| PPP$10.1-20.0 | 1 | 12 | 5 | 1 | 1 |
| PPP$5.1-10.0 | 0 | 13 | 16 | 6 | 0 |
| PPP$2.1-5.0 | 0 | 1 | 22 | 21 | 4 |
| PPP$0.1-2.0 | 0 | 0 | 2 | 18 | 35 |

Table 3b. Numbers of countries with good, fair, medium, poor or bad scores for a combination of health and population, knowledge, and community in different income groups (GDP per person in PPP$000s).

* A score with an asterisk has been reduced in accordance with the insufficient data rule. To prevent high scores resulting merely from lack of data, a good score is allowed only if it is based on all applicable components (data in an indicator, indicators in an index), and a fair score only if it is based on at least half the components. Good and fair scores (100-61) based on fewer than half the applicable components have been reduced to 60. Good scores (100-81) based on more than half but not all the applicable components have been reduced to 80.

# Table 4. National Wealth

| Country | Size score | IU note | Inflation % | Unem-ployed % | IU score | Debt note | Debt serv % export | Debt serv % GNP | ST debt: reserve | Pub debt % GDP | Def/sur % GDP | Debt score | NW score |
|---|---|---|---|---|---|---|---|---|---|---|---|---|---|
| **AMERICAS** | | | | | | | | | | | | | |
| Antigua & Barbuda | 57 | 91 | 4.5 | 6.0 | 70 | -- | -- | -- | 0.11 | -- | -- | 80* | 66 |
| Argentina | 64 | 96 | 0.2 | 16.3 | 37 | 96-98;97 | 424 | 53 | 1.65 | -- | -1.5 | 1 | 41 |
| Bahamas | 69 | 97 | 0.5 | 9.8 | 61 | s98 | -- | -- | 40.15 | -- | -1.9 | 0 | 50 |
| Barbados | 64 | 97 | 3.6 | 14.5 | 42 | 96-98 | 44 | 29 | 4.96 | -- | -- | 15 | 46 |
| Belize | 37 | 97 | 1.1 | 12.7 | 49 | 96-98;95 | 88 | 48 | 18.86 | -- | -5.0 | 0 | 31 |
| Bolivia | 22 | 96 | 89.1 | 4.2 | 0 | 96-98;98 | 336 | 63 | 1.68 | -- | -2.3 | 9 | 13 |
| Brazil | 46 | 97 | 6.9 | 7.8 | 55 | 96-98;93 | 347 | 28 | 1.22 | -- | -9.4 | 8 | 39 |
| Canada | 84 | 98 | 1.0 | 8.3 | 67 | 98 | -- | -- | -- | 89.8 | 0.3 | 55 | 72 |
| Chile | 55 | 98 | 5.1 | 7.2 | 66 | 96-98;98 | 179 | 53 | 0.50 | -- | 0.4 | 29 | 51 |
| Colombia | 44 | 98 | 18.7 | 15.0 | 33 | 96-98;98 | 215 | 32 | 0.70 | -- | -4.7 | 21 | 35 |
| Costa Rica | 44 | 98 | 11.7 | 5.6 | 39 | 96-98;96 | 63 | 40 | 0.77 | -- | -3.8 | 40 | 42 |
| Cuba | 33 | s98 | 2.7 | | | -- | -- | -- | -- | -- | -- | -- | 33 |
| Dominica | 40 | 97 | 2.4 | 23.1 | 24 | 96-98 | 56 | 35 | 1.91 | -- | -- | 42 | 36 |
| Dominican R | 37 | 97 | 8.3 | 15.9 | 38 | 96-98;97 | 51 | 30 | 1.44 | -- | 0.4 | 51 | 41 |
| Ecuador | 27 | 98 | 36.1 | 11.5 | 19 | 96-98;94 | 228 | 79 | 0.71 | -- | 0.0 | 19 | 23 |
| El Salvador | 34 | 97 | 4.5 | 8.0 | 68 | 96-98;96 | 84 | 29 | 0.56 | -- | -0.5 | 54 | 47 |
| Grenada | 43 | 96 | 2.8 | 17.0 | 36 | 96-98;95 | 95 | 52 | 0.41 | -- | 2.3 | 34 | 39 |
| Guatemala | 30 | 98 | 6.6 | -- | -- | 96-98;97 | 117 | 25 | 1.10 | -- | -0.7 | 44 | 35 |
| Guyana | 29 | 92 | 28.2 | 11.7 | 25 | 96-98 | 151 | 163 | 0.24 | -- | -- | 0 | 21 |
| Haiti | 14 | 98 | 10.0 | -- | -- | 96-98 | 171 | 19 | -- | -- | -- | 31 | 20 |
| Honduras | 23 | 98 | 13.7 | 3.9 | 37 | 96-98 | 147 | 72 | 0.37 | -- | -- | 24 | 27 |
| Jamaica | 29 | 99 | 6.3 | 15.8 | 38 | 96-98 | 91 | 80 | 1.44 | -- | -- | 20 | 29 |
| Mexico | 51 | 98 | 15.9 | 2.3 | 35 | 96-98;97 | 121 | 44 | 0.90 | -- | -1.1 | 38 | 44 |
| Nicaragua | 21 | 98 | 13.1 | 13.3 | 37 | 96-98;95 | 601 | 313 | 0.25 | -- | -0.6 | 0 | 20 |
| Panama | 41 | 98 | 0.6 | 13.9 | 44 | 96-98;98 | 71 | 82 | 12.97 | -- | 0.2 | 0 | 31 |
| Paraguay | 35 | 96 | 9.8 | 8.2 | 41 | 96-98;93 | 48 | 23 | 0.69 | -- | 1.2 | 62 | 43 |
| Peru | 35 | 98 | 7.3 | 7.7 | 53 | 96-98;98 | 380 | 55 | 0.76 | -- | -0.2 | 5 | 32 |
| St Kitts & Nevis | 61 | 98 | 3.6 | -- | -- | 96-98;94 | 65 | 36 | 0.04 | -- | 1.1 | 45 | 56 |
| St Lucia | 41 | 97 | 0.0 | 20.5 | 29 | 96-98 | 42 | 29 | 0.95 | -- | -- | 54 | 41 |
| St Vincent & Grenadines | 38 | 91 | 5.5 | 19.8 | 30 | 96-98;98 | 248 | 139 | 10.86 | -- | -8.2 | 0 | 26 |
| Suriname | 41 | 97 | 7.2 | 10.5 | 54 | -- | -- | -- | 0.84 | -- | -- | 66 | 50 |
| Trinidad & Tobago | 50 | 98 | 5.7 | 14.2 | 43 | 96-98;95 | 73 | 39 | 1.21 | -- | 0.2 | 41 | 46 |
| United States | 90 | 98 | 1.6 | 4.5 | 82 | s98 | -- | -- | -- | 57.4 | 0.9 | 70 | 83 |
| Uruguay | 54 | 98 | 10.9 | 10.1 | 39 | 96-98;98 | 162 | 38 | 1.81 | -- | -0.8 | 33 | 45 |
| Venezuela | 43 | 97 | 50.0 | 11.4 | 8 | 96-98;98 | 150 | 46 | 0.41 | -- | -2.8 | 36 | 32 |
| **AFRICA** | | | | | | | | | | | | | |
| Algeria | 39 | 97 | 5.7 | 28.7 | 13 | 96-98;96 | 206 | 66 | 0.48 | -- | 2.9 | 23 | 28 |
| Angola | 18 | 98 | 107.4 | -- | -- | 96-98 | 236 | 276 | -- | -- | -- | 0 | 12 |
| Benin | 9 | 98 | 5.8 | -- | -- | 96-98 | 159 | 48 | 0.27 | -- | -- | 34 | 17 |
| Botswana | 44 | 95 | 10.5 | 21.5 | 27 | 96-98;96 | 14 | 9 | 0.00 | -- | 8.4 | 80* | 49 |
| Burkina Faso | 9 | 98 | 5.0 | -- | -- | 96-98 | 274 | 33 | 0.35 | -- | -- | 15 | 11 |
| Burundi | 6 | 98 | 12.5 | -- | -- | 96-98;97 | 806 | 69 | 1.13 | -- | -5.5 | 0 | 4 |
| Cameroon | 15 | 98 | 0.0 | -- | -- | 96-98;95 | 356 | 97 | 321.75 | -- | 0.2 | 0 | 10 |
| Cape Verde | 28 | 98 | 4.4 | -- | -- | 96-98 | 75 | 32 | 0.32 | -- | -- | 50 | 35 |
| Central African R | 11 | 98 | -1.9 | -- | -- | 96-98 | 358 | 56 | 0.27 | -- | -- | 7 | 10 |
| Chad | 9 | 98 | 4.4 | -- | -- | 96-98;91 | 211 | 40 | 0.19 | -- | -7.1 | 22 | 13 |
| Comoros | 14 | 98 | 1.0 | -- | -- | 96-98 | 268 | 67 | 0.19 | -- | -- | 16 | 15 |
| Congo, DR | 8 | 98 | 29.2 | -- | -- | 96-98;97 | 774 | 678 | -- | -- | -0.8 | 0 | 5 |
| Congo, R | 10 | 98 | 1.8 | -- | -- | 96-98;97 | 286 | 84 | 16.41 | -- | -8.6 | 0 | 7 |
| Côte d'Ivoire | 16 | 98 | 4.5 | -- | -- | 96-98;98 | 246 | 129 | 2.17 | -- | -1.3 | 8 | 13 |
| Djibouti | 13 | 98 | 2.0 | -- | -- | 96-98 | 85 | 38 | 0.99 | -- | -- | 42 | 23 |
| Egypt | 27 | 95 | 9.4 | 11.3 | 43 | 96-98;97 | 129 | 32 | 0.33 | -- | -2.0 | 41 | 34 |
| Equatorial Guinea | 18 | 98 | 3.0 | -- | -- | 96-98 | 72 | 73 | 6.00 | -- | -- | 10 | 15 |
| Eritrea | 8 | 98 | 16.6 | -- | -- | 96-98 | 27 | 11 | -- | -- | -- | 80* | 32 |
| Ethiopia | 6 | 98 | 3.7 | -- | -- | 96-98;93 | 898 | 140 | 0.09 | -- | -5.9 | 0 | 4 |
| Gabon | 45 | 98 | 2.3 | -- | -- | 96-98;91 | 143 | 94 | 32.56 | -- | -1.7 | 0 | 30 |
| Gambia | 14 | 98 | 1.1 | -- | -- | 96-98;93 | 111 | 68 | 0.25 | -- | 3.7 | 26 | 18 |
| Ghana | 17 | 98 | 19.3 | -- | -- | 96-98;93 | 172 | 57 | 1.86 | -- | -2.6 | 31 | 22 |
| Guinea | 18 | 98 | 5.1 | -- | -- | 96-98;98 | 306 | 68 | 0.83 | -- | -4.1 | 12 | 16 |
| Guinea-Bissau | 6 | 98 | 8.0 | -- | -- | 96-98 | 1733 | 299 | 0.60 | -- | -- | 0 | 4 |
| Kenya | 10 | 98 | 6.6 | -- | -- | 96-98;96 | 174 | 51 | 1.05 | -- | -0.9 | 30 | 17 |
| Lesotho | 16 | 98 | 7.8 | -- | -- | 96-98;98 | 73 | 41 | 0.30 | -- | -4.1 | 39 | 24 |
| Liberia | 8 | s97 | 11.0 | -- | -- | 95-97 | 388 | 121 | 4914.0 | -- | -- | 0 | 5 |
| Libyan Arab J | 47 | 98 | 7.0 | -- | -- | -- | -- | -- | 0.04 | -- | -- | 80* | 58 |
| Madagascar | 8 | 98 | 6.2 | -- | -- | 96-98;96 | 396 | 90 | 0.79 | -- | -1.3 | 4 | 7 |
| Malawi | 5 | 98 | 29.8 | -- | -- | 96-98 | 226 | 62 | 0.19 | -- | -- | 19 | 10 |
| Mali | 7 | 98 | 4.1 | -- | -- | 96-98 | 322 | 85 | 0.42 | -- | -- | 11 | 8 |

162

| Country | Size score | IU note | Inflation % | Unem-ployed % | IU score | Debt note | Debt serv % export | Debt serv % GNP | ST debt: reserve | Pub debt % GDP | Def/sur % GDP | Debt score | NW score |
|---|---|---|---|---|---|---|---|---|---|---|---|---|---|
| Mauritania | 16 | 98 | 8.0 | -- | -- | 96-98 | 318 | 141 | 0.69 | -- | -- | 5 | 12 |
| Mauritius | 53 | 95 | 6.1 | 9.8 | 59 | 96-98;98 | 92 | 60 | 1.43 | -- | 0.9 | 30 | 49 |
| Morocco | 29 | 96 | 3.0 | 17.8 | 34 | 96-98;95 | 157 | 55 | 0.44 | -- | -4.4 | 32 | 31 |
| Mozambique | 8 | 98 | 0.6 | -- | -- | 96-98 | 539 | 85 | 0.44 | -- | -- | 0 | 5 |
| Namibia | 41 | 98 | 6.2 | -- | -- | 93 | -- | -- | 0.19 | -- | -4.5 | 51 | 44 |
| Niger | 7 | 98 | 4.6 | -- | -- | 96-98 | 340 | 58 | 0.85 | -- | -- | 9 | 8 |
| Nigeria | 8 | 98 | 10.0 | -- | -- | 96-98 | 184 | 81 | 0.14 | -- | -- | 20 | 12 |
| Rwanda | 7 | 98 | 6.8 | -- | -- | 96-98;93 | 554 | 39 | 0.22 | -- | -7.4 | 0 | 5 |
| São Tomé & Principe | 15 | 98 | 42.1 | -- | -- | 96-98 | 1268 | 375 | 1.09 | -- | -- | 0 | 10 |
| Senegal | 13 | 98 | 2.5 | -- | -- | 96-98 | 187 | 60 | 0.75 | -- | -- | 27 | 18 |
| Seychelles | 61 | 98 | 1.0 | -- | -- | 96-98;98 | 47 | 33 | 17.00 | -- | 1.4 | 0 | 41 |
| Sierra Leone | 5 | 98 | 35.5 | -- | -- | 96-98;97 | 745 | 105 | 0.21 | -- | -6.0 | 0 | 3 |
| Somalia | 7 | s98 | 16.0 | -- | -- | 95-97 | 3090 | 341 | -- | -- | -- | 0 | 5 |
| South Africa | 54 | 96 | 7.4 | 5.1 | 53 | 96-98;98 | 66 | 17 | 2.31 | -- | -2.9 | 37 | 49 |
| Sudan | 14 | 98 | 17.1 | -- | -- | 96-98 | 2448 | 195 | 1.68 | -- | -- | 0 | 9 |
| Swaziland | 32 | 98 | 8.1 | -- | -- | 96-98 | 17 | 14 | 0.14 | -- | -- | 77 | 47 |
| Tanzania | 5 | 98 | 12.6 | -- | -- | 96-98 | 484 | 81 | 0.22 | -- | -- | 0 | 3 |
| Togo | 14 | 98 | 1.0 | -- | -- | 96-98 | 143 | 68 | 0.98 | -- | -- | 26 | 18 |
| Tunisia | 42 | 98 | 3.1 | -- | -- | 96-98;96 | 118 | 57 | 0.83 | -- | -3.1 | 31 | 38 |
| Uganda | 11 | 98 | 5.8 | -- | -- | 96-98 | 311 | 37 | 0.10 | -- | -- | 12 | 11 |
| Zambia | 7 | 98 | 24.5 | -- | -- | 96-98;96 | 438 | 166 | 2.07 | -- | 0.7 | 0 | 5 |
| Zimbabwe | 24 | 98 | 32.3 | -- | -- | 96-98;97 | 140 | 55 | 3.12 | -- | -5.0 | 29 | 26 |
| EUROPE | | | | | | | | | | | | | |
| Albania | 25 | u98 | 20.7 | 17.6 | 31 | 96-98;98 | 79 | 22 | 0.12 | -- | -8.5 | 24 | 26 |
| Austria | 83 | 98 | 0.8 | 4.2 | 83 | e99 | -- | -- | -- | 65.2 | -2.1 | 60 | 77 |
| Belarus | 45 | 98 | 73.0 | 2.3 | 0 | 96-98;98 | 14 | 5 | 0.46 | -- | -0.9 | 75 | 41 |
| Belgium | 83 | 98 | 0.9 | 9.1 | 64 | e99 | -- | -- | -- | 116.1 | -0.7 | 41 | 68 |
| Bosnia & Herzegovina | 17 | u97 | 14.0 | 72.5 | 0 | 95-97 | 234 | 38 | -- | -- | -- | 19 | 13 |
| Bulgaria | 39 | u98 | 22.3 | 12.2 | 30 | 96-98;98 | 150 | 91 | 0.13 | -- | 0.0 | 17 | 31 |
| Croatia | 47 | 98 | 5.7 | 11.4 | 54 | 96-98;98 | 74 | 33 | 0.51 | -- | 0.6 | 49 | 49 |
| Czech R | 65 | 98 | 10.6 | 7.5 | 39 | 96-98;98 | 77 | 46 | 0.44 | -- | -1.6 | 37 | 51 |
| Denmark | 84 | 98 | 1.8 | 5.5 | 78 | e99 | -- | -- | -- | 52.6 | 2.8 | 77 | 81 |
| Estonia | 51 | 98 | 8.2 | 9.6 | 49 | 96-98;98 | 18 | 14 | 1.53 | -- | -0.1 | 49 | 50 |
| Finland | 81 | 98 | 1.3 | 11.3 | 55 | e99 | -- | -- | -- | 46.6 | 1.9 | 78 | 74 |
| France | 81 | 98 | 0.7 | 11.8 | 53 | e99 | -- | -- | -- | 58.9 | -1.8 | 64 | 70 |
| Germany | 82 | 98 | 0.6 | 9.7 | 61 | e99 | -- | -- | -- | 61.1 | -1.4 | 64 | 72 |
| Greece | 68 | 97 | 5.4 | 10.3 | 59 | e99 | -- | -- | -- | 104.6 | -1.8 | 43 | 59 |
| Hungary | 60 | 98 | 14.3 | 7.8 | 37 | 96-98;98 | 118 | 64 | 0.65 | -- | -6.1 | 28 | 46 |
| Iceland | 85 | 98 | 1.7 | 3.9 | 84 | s98;97 | -- | -- | -- | 48.3 | 0.4 | 73 | 82 |
| Ireland | 81 | 98 | 2.2 | 7.8 | 69 | e99 | -- | -- | -- | 50.1 | 1.9 | 76 | 77 |
| Italy | 81 | 98 | 1.8 | 12.2 | 51 | e99 | -- | -- | -- | 115.1 | -1.9 | 39 | 63 |
| Latvia | 43 | 98 | 4.7 | 13.8 | 45 | 96-98;98 | 24 | 12 | 0.37 | -- | 0.1 | 80* | 53 |
| Lithuania | 46 | 98 | 5.1 | 13.5 | 46 | 96-98;98 | 37 | 20 | 0.57 | -- | -0.4 | 67 | 51 |
| Luxembourg | 93 | 98 | 1.0 | 2.5 | 90 | e99 | -- | -- | -- | 6.0 | 4.4 | 98 | 93 |
| Macedonia, FYR | 35 | u98 | -0.1 | 41.4 | 0 | 96-98 | 148 | 84 | 0.21 | -- | -- | 19 | 22 |
| Malta | 73 | 97 | 3.1 | 5.0 | 79 | 95-97;97 | 30 | 29 | 0.95 | -- | -9.8 | 15 | 60 |
| Moldova | 19 | u98 | 7.7 | 1.9 | 51 | 96-98 | 93 | 53 | 0.14 | -- | -- | 33 | 30 |
| Netherlands | 82 | 98 | 2.0 | 4.4 | 82 | e99 | -- | -- | -- | 62.9 | 1.0 | 68 | 78 |
| Norway | 86 | 98 | 2.3 | 3.3 | 85 | s98;97 | -- | -- | -- | 33.4 | 0.7 | 80 | 84 |
| Poland | 50 | 98 | 11.8 | 10.5 | 39 | 96-98;98 | 103 | 30 | 0.32 | -- | -1.0 | 49 | 47 |
| Portugal | 69 | 98 | 2.2 | 5.0 | 80 | e99 | -- | -- | -- | 55.8 | -2.0 | 64 | 70 |
| Romania | 43 | 98 | 59.1 | 6.3 | 1 | 96-98;97 | 97 | 28 | 0.54 | -- | -3.9 | 51 | 34 |
| Slovakia | 59 | 98 | 6.7 | 11.9 | 52 | 96-98 | 75 | 47 | 0.63 | -- | -- | 36 | 51 |
| Slovenia | 69 | 98 | 8.0 | 7.7 | 50 | 95-97 | 36 | 21 | 0.24 | -- | -- | 65 | 63 |
| Spain | 72 | 98 | 1.8 | 18.8 | 32 | e99 | -- | -- | -- | 63.7 | -1.1 | 63 | 60 |
| Sweden | 81 | 98 | -0.1 | 6.5 | 74 | e99 | -- | -- | -- | 65.7 | 1.9 | 69 | 76 |
| Switzerland | 85 | 98 | 0.1 | 3.6 | 86 | s98;97 | -- | -- | -- | 48.0 | -1.3 | 70 | 81 |
| Ukraine | 28 | 98 | 10.6 | 11.3 | 39 | 96-98 | 64 | 24 | 0.92 | -- | -- | 60 | 39 |
| United Kingdom | 80 | 98 | 2.7 | 6.1 | 76 | e99 | -- | -- | -- | 45.7 | 1.3 | 76 | 78 |
| Yugoslavia | 22 | su97 | 9.0 | 25.6 | 19 | -- | -- | -- | -- | -- | -- | -- | 21 |
| RUSSIAN FEDERATION | 46 | 98 | 27.7 | 13.3 | 26 | 96-98;95 | 166 | 45 | 1.43 | -- | -4.7 | 32 | 37 |
| ASIA | | | | | | | | | | | | | |
| Afghanistan | 8 | s98 | 14.0 | -- | -- | -- | -- | -- | -- | -- | -- | -- | 8 |
| Armenia | 20 | 98 | 8.7 | 9.3 | 46 | 96-98 | 121 | 33 | 0.17 | -- | -- | 43 | 32 |
| Azerbaijan | 21 | 98 | -0.8 | 1.1 | 96 | 96-98;98 | 54 | 15 | 0.09 | -- | -3.9 | 55 | 48 |
| Bahrain | 66 | 98 | -0.4 | -- | -- | 98 | -- | -- | 5.60 | -- | -5.8 | 12 | 48 |
| Bangladesh | 14 | 96 | 4.5 | 2.5 | 70 | 96-98 | 151 | 24 | 0.17 | -- | -- | 36 | 33 |
| Bhutan | 15 | 98 | 7.0 | -- | -- | 96-98;98 | 56 | 21 | 0.01 | -- | -0.4 | 65 | 32 |
| Brunei Darussalam | 73 | s98 | 0.0 | -- | -- | -- | -- | -- | -- | -- | -- | -- | 60* |
| Cambodia | 13 | 98 | 14.8 | -- | -- | 96-98 | 202 | 58 | 0.11 | -- | -- | 24 | 17 |

| Country | Size score | IU note | Inflation % | Unem-ployed % | IU score | Debt note | Debt serv % export | Debt serv % GNP | ST debt: reserve | Pub debt % GDP | Def/sur % GDP | Debt score | *NW score* |
|---|---|---|---|---|---|---|---|---|---|---|---|---|---|
| China | 27 | 98 | -0.8 | 3.1 | 88 | 96-98;97 | 67 | 15 | 0.15 | -- | -1.5 | 60 | 50 |
| Cyprus | 75 | 98 | 2.2 | 3.3 | 85 | 97 | -- | -- | 1.67 | -- | -5.3 | 45 | 70 |
| Georgia | 29 | u98 | 3.6 | 4.2 | 76 | 96-98;98 | 170 | 26 | -- | -- | -2.5 | 31 | 41 |
| India | 20 | 98 | 13.2 | -- | -- | 96-98;98 | 147 | 20 | 0.30 | -- | -5.2 | 37 | 26 |
| Indonesia | 24 | 98 | 58.0 | 5.5 | 2 | 96-98;98 | 238 | 84 | 0.79 | -- | -2.4 | 18 | 17 |
| Iran | 40 | 98 | 20.0 | -- | -- | 96-98;98 | 71 | 13 | -- | -- | 0.3 | 58 | 46 |
| Iraq | 28 | s98 | 45.0 | -- | -- | -- | -- | -- | -- | -- | -- | -- | 28 |
| Israel | 75 | 98 | 5.4 | 8.6 | 64 | w96;98 | -- | -- | 0.19 | 118.8 | -1.2 | 38 | 63 |
| Japan | 83 | 98 | 0.6 | 4.1 | 84 | s98;93 | -- | -- | -- | 99.9 | -1.5 | 46 | 74 |
| Jordan | 29 | 98 | 3.1 | -- | -- | 96-98;97 | 145 | 150 | 0.30 | -- | -3.3 | 2 | 20 |
| Kazakhstan | 36 | 98 | 7.3 | 13.7 | 45 | 96-98 | 74 | 25 | 0.41 | -- | -- | 58 | 44 |
| Korea, DPR | 34 | s98 | 5.0 | -- | -- | -- | -- | -- | -- | -- | -- | -- | 34 |
| Korea, R | 67 | 98 | 7.5 | 6.8 | 52 | 96-98;97 | 83 | 31 | 0.62 | -- | -1.3 | 51 | 59 |
| Kuwait | 85 | 98 | 0.5 | -- | -- | -- | -- | -- | 1.09 | -- | -- | 58 | 76 |
| Kyrgyzstan | 22 | u98 | 10.3 | 3.1 | 40 | 96-98 | 133 | 48 | 0.27 | -- | -- | 36 | 30 |
| Lao PDR | 17 | 98 | 81.0 | -- | -- | 96-98 | 246 | 70 | 0.10 | -- | -- | 18 | 17 |
| Lebanon | 35 | 98 | 4.6 | -- | -- | 96-98;98 | 159 | 44 | 0.42 | -- | -15.1 | 0 | 23 |
| Malaysia | 52 | 97 | 2.7 | 2.5 | 82 | 96-98;97 | 54 | 55 | 0.30 | -- | 2.9 | 32 | 54 |
| Maldives | 34 | 98 | 5.0 | -- | -- | 96-98;98 | 29 | 42 | 0.22 | -- | -5.3 | 39 | 36 |
| Mongolia | 15 | 98 | 9.4 | 5.7 | 43 | 96-98;98 | 86 | 49 | 0.19 | -- | -10.8 | 9 | 20 |
| Myanmar | 12 | 98 | 10.0 | -- | -- | 96-98;97 | 309 | 3 | 0.61 | -- | -0.9 | 12 | 12 |
| Nepal | 12 | 98 | 8.4 | -- | -- | 96-98;98 | 118 | 31 | 0.05 | -- | -4.7 | 44 | 23 |
| Oman | 60 | 98 | -0.9 | -- | -- | 96-98;98 | 49 | 23 | 1.25 | -- | -6.6 | 37 | 52 |
| Pakistan | 17 | 97 | 11.8 | 6.1 | 39 | 96-98;98 | 220 | 42 | 1.79 | -- | -6.3 | 20 | 23 |
| Philippines | 30 | 98 | 9.7 | 9.6 | 41 | 96-98;97 | 102 | 57 | 0.69 | -- | 0.1 | 31 | 33 |
| Qatar | 81 | 98 | 2.9 | -- | -- | -- | -- | -- | -- | -- | -- | -- | 60* |
| Saudi Arabia | 60 | 98 | -0.2 | -- | -- | -- | -- | -- | 0.73 | -- | -- | 71 | 64 |
| Singapore | 84 | 98 | -0.3 | 3.2 | 87 | w97;97 | -- | -- | 1.04 | 74.2 | 11.7 | 59 | 78 |
| Sri Lanka | 26 | 98 | 9.4 | 10.6 | 43 | 96-98;98 | 97 | 43 | 0.59 | -- | -8.0 | 27 | 30 |
| Syrian Arab R | 26 | 91 | 19.0 | 6.8 | 33 | 96-98;97 | 349 | 129 | -- | -- | -0.2 | 8 | 23 |
| Tajikistan | 10 | u98 | 43.2 | 2.9 | 13 | 96-98 | 122 | 42 | -- | -- | -- | 39 | 18 |
| Thailand | 42 | 98 | 8.1 | 3.4 | 49 | 96-98;98 | 116 | 58 | 0.48 | -- | -3.5 | 31 | 41 |
| Turkey | 46 | 98 | 84.6 | 6.2 | 0 | 96-98;97 | 176 | 52 | 1.06 | -- | -8.4 | 25 | 29 |
| Turkmenistan | 24 | u95 | 1005.2 | 3.0 | 0 | 96-98 | 186 | 67 | -- | -- | -- | 26 | 18 |
| United Arab Emirates | 75 | 98 | 2.0 | -- | -- | 98 | -- | -- | 0.46 | -- | -0.3 | 79 | 76 |
| Uzbekistan | 20 | u98 | 29.0 | 0.4 | 25 | 96-98 | 81 | 13 | -- | -- | -- | 55 | 30 |
| Viet Nam | 17 | 98 | 7.8 | -- | -- | 96-98;98 | 181 | 81 | 0.36 | -- | -1.1 | 20 | 18 |
| Yemen | 7 | 98 | 11.2 | -- | -- | 96-98;98 | 91 | 69 | 0.13 | -- | -2.6 | 25 | 13 |
| PACIFIC | | | | | | | | | | | | | |
| Australia | 82 | 98 | 0.9 | 8.0 | 68 | s98;98 | -- | -- | -- | 37.0 | 2.8 | 84 | 79 |
| Fiji | 35 | 95 | 5.2 | 5.4 | 65 | 96-98;96 | 15 | 10 | 0.04 | -- | -4.9 | 48 | 46 |
| New Zealand | 75 | 98 | 1.6 | 7.5 | 70 | s98;98 | -- | -- | -- | 38.7 | 0.5 | 78 | 74 |
| Papua New Guinea | 22 | 98 | 13.6 | -- | -- | 96-98;94 | 94 | 56 | 1.01 | -- | -4.1 | 32 | 25 |
| Samoa | 32 | 98 | 2.2 | -- | -- | 96-98 | 84 | 59 | 0.53 | -- | -- | 30 | 31 |
| Solomon Is | 19 | 98 | 12.4 | -- | -- | 96-98 | 30 | 19 | 0.18 | -- | -- | 68 | 35 |
| Tonga | 35 | 98 | 2.9 | -- | -- | 96-98;91 | 83 | 23 | 0.08 | -- | -5.8 | 42 | 37 |
| Vanuatu | 27 | 98 | 3.2 | -- | -- | 96-98 | 24 | 16 | 0.63 | -- | -- | 73 | 42 |

**Notes**

The national wealth index (*NW score*) is the average of three weighted indicators (column heading in parentheses) [weight in brackets]:

Size of the economy (Size score) [2], represented by Gross Domestic Product (GDP) per person.

Inflation and unemployment (IU score) [1], represented by the annual inflation rate or the annual unemployment rate for the same period, whichever gives the lower score.

Debt (Debt score) [1], represented by an external debt indicator or a public debt indicator, whichever gives the lower score.

Size was given a higher weight than the other indicators, because it is more comprehensive.

Size score = size of economy score, based on GDP/person, in current international purchasing power parity dollars (or, exceptionally, in current US dollars). Data are in Table 3. Performance criteria are the same as for income and are given in Table 3a.

IU note = the applicable year for the inflation and unemployment data. Where both indicators are available, the latest common year was chosen. Where only inflation data are available, the year is usually 1998.

Inflation % = the annual percentage change in the consumer price index (CPI), the cost to the average consumer of buying a fixed basket of goods and services. Because the basket varies from country to country (as does household and income group coverage), the CPI may not be as reliable an indicator for international comparisons of inflation as the GDP deflator (annual GDP at current prices divided by the value of GDP at constant prices), which reflects changes in prices in all components of GDP (such as government consumption, capital formation, and international trade) and not just private consumption. However, the CPI is the inflation measurement used for monetary policy and is more suitable for comparison with the unemployment rate. It is also more familiar than the GDP deflator. Data are from International Monetary Fund (2000), except where marked with the letter s in the IU note column, which are from International Institute for Strategic Studies (1999a).

Unemployed % = total unemployment as a percentage of the total labor force. Data are from International Labour Office (ILO 2000), except where marked with the letter u in the IU note column, which are from United Nations Economic Commission for Europe (UNECE 2000). ILO data are usually from national labor force surveys. UNECE data are from national employment office statistics and usually cover only registered unemployment, which tends to be less than total unemployment.

IU score = the lower of the inflation and unemployment scores. The performance criteria are shown in Table 4a. For inflation, the tops of the good and fair bands match the lowest and highest rates respectively in the range of inflation targets of the central banks of Australia, Canada, England, the Euro area, New Zealand, and Sweden; and the top of poor reflects the general view that inflation of 10% or more is harmful (*The Economist* 1999). Negative inflation (deflation) signals a contracting economy, and very low rates of inflation are a symptom of stagnation. However, stagnation and contraction are generally accompanied by increasing unemployment, which usually would prevent a country from getting a high score. It is harder to achieve low rates of unemployment than of inflation, and zero unemployment is probably impossible. High employment drives up prices, and during the 1990s only ten countries have achieved rates of inflation *and* unemployment below 4.0% (Azerbaijan, China, Cyprus, Iceland, Japan, Luxembourg, Malaysia, Norway, Singapore, Switzerland). Accordingly, the performance criteria for unemployment are less stringent than for inflation: the tops of the fair and medium bands are slightly above those for inflation.

Debt note = the applicable year for the debt data. A range of years refers to debt service data; a single year to public debt and deficit/surplus data.

Debt serv % export = the present value of debt service (the sum of principal repayments and interest payments on total external debt) as a percentage of exports of all goods and services. The present value of debt service is the discounted sum of all debt service payments due over the life of existing loans (discount rates are the rates charged by OECD countries for officially supported export credits). Total external debt is the sum of all disbursed and outstanding (at year-end) public and publicly guaranteed long-term debt, private non-guaranteed long-term debt, the use of IMF credit, and short-term debt due by all borrowers in a country to all non-resident creditors. Data for the period 1996-1998 are from World Bank (2000b); data for 1995-1997 are from World Bank (1999b).

Debt serv % GNP = the present value of debt service (the sum of principal repayments and interest payments on total external debt) as a percentage of Gross National Product. Data for the period 1996-1998 are from World Bank (2000b); data for 1995-1997 are from World Bank (1999b).

ST debt: reserve = the ratio of short-term debt to international reserves. Short-term debt is defined as external debt with an original maturity of one year or less, plus repayments due within the next 12 months on debt with an original maturity of over a year, plus arrears. It comprises liabilities to banks, debt securities (money market instruments, bonds and notes) issued in international markets by both public and private sector borrowers, and official and officially-guaranteed non-bank export credits. Because liabilities to banks and debt securities overlap, short-term debt may be overestimated. International reserves are gross reserves and comprise special drawing rights, reserves of International Monetary Fund (IMF) members held by the IMF, and holdings of foreign exchange under the control of monetary authorities. Reserves may be underestimated because they exclude monetary gold. Data are for 1999 and are from BIS/IMF/OECD/World Bank (2000).

Pub debt % GDP = gross public debt (general government gross financial liabilities) as a percentage of GDP. Data are for the year indicated in the Debt note column and are from the source indicated in the same column: e = Eurostat (2000); s = International Institute for Strategic Studies (1999a); w = World Bank (1999a).

Def/sur % GDP = central government overall budget deficit or surplus (current and capital revenue and official grants received, less total expenditure and lending minus repayments) as a percentage of the Gross Domestic Product in the national currency. Data are for the year indicated in the Debt notes column and are from World Bank (2000a), except where the year is preceded by the letter e, which are from Eurostat (2000).

Debt score = the lower of the external debt and public debt scores. The external debt score is of the lowest score of present value of external debt service as a % of exports of goods and services, or present value of external debt service as a % of GNP, or the ratio of short-term debt to international reserves. The public debt score is the weighted average [weights in brackets] of the scores for gross public debt as % of GDP [2] and annual central government deficit/surplus as % of GDP [1]. The performance criteria are shown in Table 4a. For the two debt service indicators, the tops of bad and poor match the points at which the World Bank classifies a country as severely and moderately indebted respectively (World Bank 2000b). For the ratio of short-term debt to international reserves, the top of medium is the benchmark suggested by IMF Policy Development and Review Department (2000) for the reverse indicator—the ratio of international reserves to short-term debt. The benchmark is less applicable to economies (such as those of industrialized countries), in which much of the private sector has unrestricted access to international capital markets, and which typically have ratios that would qualify as poor or bad according to these criteria. In less open or well regulated markets, the benchmark (a ratio of 1.0) matches the point above which a country is vulnerable to creditor panic, according to Sachs & Woo (1999). For the public debt and deficit indicators, the top of medium matches the Treaty of Maastricht's criteria of no more than 60% for an acceptable ratio of government debt to GDP and no more than 3% for an acceptable budget deficit (Black 1997).

| band | top point on scale | inflation rate (%) | unemploy-ment rate (%) | debt service as % of exports | debt service as % of GNP | ratio of short-term debt to reserves | public debt as % of GDP | deficit/ surplus as % of GDP |
|------|------|------|------|------|------|------|------|------|
| good | 100 | 0 | 0 | 0 | 0 | 0.0 | 1 | 2.9 |
| fair | 80 | 3 | 5 | 33 | 12 | 0.5 | 31 | -0.1 |
| medium | 60 | 6 | 10 | 66 | 24 | 1.0 | 61 | -3.1 |
| poor | 40 | 10 | 15 | 132 | 48 | 2.0 | 91 | -6.1 |
| bad | 20 | 35 | 25 | 220 | 80 | 4.0 | 121 | -9.1 |
| base | 0 | 60 | 35 | 440 | 160 | 8.0 | 151 | -12.1 |

**Table 4a. Performance criteria for indicators of inflation, unemployment, and debt.**

* A score with an asterisk has been reduced in accordance with the insufficient data rule. To prevent high scores resulting merely from lack of data, a good score is allowed only if it is based on all applicable components (data in an indicator, indicators in an index), and a fair score only if it is based on at least half the components. Good and fair scores (100-61) based on fewer than half the applicable components have been reduced to 60. Good scores (100-81) based on more than half but not all the applicable components have been reduced to 80.

## Table 5. Knowledge

| Country | Ed note | 1st net % | 2nd net % | 1st2nd score | 3rd/ 10k | 3rd score | E score | Tel note | Main lines/ 100 | Cell subs/ 100 | Phone total | Ph score | Fault/ 100 l/yr | Fault score | Tel score | Internet users/ 10k | I net score | C score | K index |
|---|---|---|---|---|---|---|---|---|---|---|---|---|---|---|---|---|---|---|---|
| **AMERICAS** | | | | | | | | | | | | | | | | | | | |
| Antigua & Barbuda | | -- | -- | -- | -- | -- | -- | s96 | 46.80 | 1.89 | 48.69 | 79 | 59.0 | 36 | 36 | 412.94 | 67 | 51 | 51 |
| Argentina | t94 | 99.9 | 76.9 | 78 | 311.7 | 82 | 80 | f97 | 20.27 | 7.81 | 28.08 | 62 | 19.7 | 68 | 62 | 83.05 | 22 | 42 | 67 |
| Bahamas | t95 | 94.6 | 84.6 | 73 | 233.1 | 73 | 73 | | 35.23 | 2.67 | 37.90 | 70 | -- | -- | 70 | 405.41 | 67 | 68 | 71 |
| Barbados | t95 | 97.4 | 85.7 | 80 | 253.5 | 76 | 78 | f95 | 42.40 | 4.48 | 46.88 | 77 | 9.6 | 84 | 77 | 186.57 | 45 | 61 | 72 |
| Belize | -- | 99.9 | 63.6 | 72 | -- | -- | 72 | | 13.75 | 1.49 | 15.24 | 45 | 69.5 | 32 | 32 | 434.78 | 69 | 50 | 65 |
| Bolivia | t91 | 97.4 | 40.0 | 58 | 212.2 | 70 | 64 | t97 f93 | 6.88 | 2.74 | 9.62 | 32 | 28.0 | 58 | 32 | 12.57 | 3 | 17 | 48 |
| Brazil | t96 | 97.1 | 65.9 | 67 | 142.4 | 60 | 63 | f97 | 12.05 | 4.68 | 16.73 | 47 | 3.8 | 94 | 47 | 180.89 | 44 | 45 | 57 |
| Canada | t95 | 99.9 | 95.2 | 95 | 595.3 | 100 | 97 | | 63.39 | 17.56 | 80.95 | 92 | -- | -- | 80* | 2475.21 | 100 | 90 | 95 |
| Chile | t97 | 90.3 | 85.2 | 65 | 260.2 | 77 | 71 | | 20.55 | 6.50 | 27.05 | 62 | 52.0 | 39 | 39 | 202.37 | 47 | 43 | 62 |
| Colombia | t96 | 89.4 | 76.4 | 57 | 164.0 | 63 | 60 | | 17.35 | 4.91 | 22.26 | 56 | 56.0 | 38 | 38 | 46.32 | 12 | 25 | 48 |
| Costa Rica | t94 | 91.8 | 55.8 | 52 | 283.0 | 80 | 66 | | 17.18 | 2.83 | 20.01 | 52 | 42.1 | 46 | 46 | 260.35 | 55 | 50 | 61 |
| Cuba | t96 | 99.9 | 69.9 | 75 | 101.3 | 49 | 62 | | 3.49 | 0.04 | 3.53 | 12 | 14.3 | 76 | 12 | 22.49 | 6 | 9 | 44 |
| Dominica | -- | -- | -- | -- | -- | -- | -- | tf96 | 25.23 | 0.86 | 26.09 | 61 | 12.0 | 80 | 61 | 264.03 | 55 | 58 | 58 |
| Dominican R | t96 | 91.3 | 78.5 | 61 | 222.3 | 72 | 66 | f92 | 9.28 | 3.11 | 12.39 | 41 | 133.2 | 13 | 13 | 24.30 | 6 | 9 | 47 |
| Ecuador | t90 | 99.9 | 50.9 | 67 | 201.2 | 69 | 68 | | 7.83 | 2.53 | 10.36 | 34 | 82.0 | 27 | 27 | 12.32 | 3 | 15 | 50 |
| El Salvador | t96 | 89.1 | 36.4 | 41 | 193.5 | 68 | 54 | f96 | 8.00 | 1.76 | 9.76 | 32 | 36.7 | 51 | 32 | 49.73 | 13 | 22 | 43 |
| Grenada | -- | -- | -- | -- | -- | -- | -- | | 26.28 | 1.35 | 27.63 | 62 | 9.0 | 85 | 62 | 191.26 | 45 | 53 | 53 |
| Guatemala | t95 | 73.8 | 34.9 | 28 | 80.4 | 43 | 35 | t97 f93 | 4.08 | 1.03 | 5.11 | 17 | 45.2 | 44 | 17 | 46.29 | 12 | 14 | 28 |
| Guyana | t96 | 92.8 | 74.9 | 63 | 107.1 | 51 | 57 | | 7.05 | 0.17 | 7.22 | 24 | -- | -- | 24 | 23.53 | 6 | 15 | 43 |
| Haiti | -- | 19.4 | 34.2 | 11 | -- | -- | 11 | tf97 | 0.80 | -- | 0.80 | 3 | 108.0 | 18 | 3 | 0.82 | 0 | 1 | 8 |
| Honduras | t94 | 87.5 | 36.0 | 39 | 98.5 | 48 | 43 | | 3.81 | 0.53 | 4.34 | 14 | 36.0 | 51 | 14 | 27.49 | 7 | 10 | 32 |
| Jamaica | t95 | 95.6 | 69.8 | 66 | 76.8 | 42 | 54 | t97 s96 f93 | 16.57 | 2.17 | 18.74 | 50 | 70.0 | 32 | 32 | 197.01 | 46 | 39 | 49 |
| Mexico | t96 | 99.9 | 66.1 | 73 | 173.9 | 65 | 69 | f95 | 10.36 | 3.50 | 13.86 | 43 | 4.6 | 92 | 43 | 140.87 | 38 | 40 | 59 |
| Nicaragua | t97 | 78.6 | 50.5 | 36 | 120.9 | 54 | 45 | f94 | 3.13 | 0.45 | 3.58 | 12 | 7.0 | 88 | 12 | 33.58 | 9 | 10 | 33 |
| Panama | t96 | 89.9 | 71.3 | 55 | 302.5 | 82 | 68 | f95 | 15.13 | 2.89 | 18.02 | 49 | 97.0 | 21 | 21 | 108.42 | 29 | 25 | 54 |
| Paraguay | t96 | 96.3 | 61.1 | 63 | 94.8 | 47 | 55 | | 5.53 | 4.12 | 9.65 | 32 | -- | -- | 32 | 19.15 | 5 | 18 | 43 |
| Peru | t97 | 93.8 | 83.9 | 71 | 269.9 | 79 | 75 | f97 | 6.67 | 3.00 | 9.67 | 32 | 33.6 | 53 | 32 | 80.65 | 21 | 26 | 59 |
| St Kitts & Nevis | t95 | -- | -- | -- | 102.4 | 49 | 49 | t97 | 41.83 | 1.07 | 42.90 | 74 | -- | -- | 74 | 364.52 | 64 | 69 | 56 |
| St Lucia | t95 | -- | -- | -- | 72.5 | 41 | 41 | | 26.79 | 1.29 | 28.08 | 62 | -- | -- | 62 | 135.64 | 36 | 49 | 44 |
| St Vincent & Grenadines | -- | -- | -- | -- | -- | -- | -- | f93 | 18.79 | 0.67 | 19.46 | 51 | 16.3 | 73 | 51 | 178.57 | 44 | 47 | 47 |
| Suriname | t90 | 99.9 | -- | 80* | 112.4 | 52 | 66 | | 15.23 | 1.36 | 16.59 | 47 | 47.5 | 42 | 42 | 163.71 | 42 | 42 | 58 |
| Trinidad & Tobago | t96 | 99.9 | 71.5 | 75 | 78.7 | 42 | 58 | f97 | 20.58 | 2.05 | 22.63 | 56 | 75.0 | 30 | 30 | 155.88 | 41 | 35 | 50 |
| United States | t95 | 99.9 | 96.3 | 96 | 534.1 | 98 | 97 | f97 | 66.13 | 25.60 | 91.73 | 97 | 13.4 | 78 | 78 | 2219.16 | 100 | 89 | 94 |
| Uruguay | t96 | 94.3 | 83.8 | 72 | 245.8 | 75 | 73 | f97 | 25.04 | 5.96 | 31.00 | 65 | 95.3 | 22 | 22 | 699.30 | 83 | 52 | 66 |
| Venezuela | t91 | 82.5 | 48.9 | 39 | 275.7 | 79 | 59 | f97 | 11.67 | 8.67 | 20.34 | 53 | 3.5 | 94 | 53 | 21.51 | 6 | 29 | 49 |
| **AFRICA** | | | | | | | | | | | | | | | | | | | |
| Algeria | t95 | 96.0 | 68.5 | 66 | 123.8 | 55 | 60 | | 5.32 | 0.06 | 5.38 | 18 | 50.0 | 40 | 18 | 0.66 | 0 | 9 | 43 |
| Angola | t91 | 34.7 | 31.2 | 14 | 6.6 | 4 | 9 | f97 | 0.60 | 0.08 | 0.68 | 2 | 7.0 | 88 | 2 | 2.07 | 1 | 1 | 6 |
| Benin | t96 | 67.6 | 28.2 | 23 | 25.6 | 15 | 19 | f95 | 0.66 | 0.11 | 0.77 | 3 | 76.0 | 30 | 3 | 3.46 | 1 | 2 | 13 |
| Botswana | t96 | 80.1 | 88.8 | 59 | 58.7 | 33 | 46 | f97 | 6.50 | 1.46 | 7.96 | 26 | 37.2 | 50 | 26 | 63.69 | 17 | 21 | 38 |
| Burkina Faso | 96 | 32.3 | 12.8 | 7 | 8.3 | 5 | 6 | | 0.36 | 0.02 | 0.38 | 1 | 70.9 | 32 | 1 | 0.88 | 0 | 0 | 4 |
| Burundi | t92 | 35.6 | 17.1 | 9 | 7.4 | 4 | 6 | | 0.29 | 0.01 | 0.30 | 1 | 32.4 | 54 | 1 | 0.23 | 0 | 0 | 4 |
| Cameroon | t90 | 61.7 | 39.8 | 24 | 28.9 | 16 | 20 | tsf97 | 0.54 | 0.03 | 0.57 | 2 | 73.0 | 31 | 2 | 1.40 | 0 | 1 | 14 |
| Cape Verde | -- | 99.9 | 36.6 | 62 | -- | -- | 62 | | 9.80 | 0.25 | 10.05 | 33 | 39.7 | 48 | 33 | 49.02 | 13 | 23 | 49 |
| Central African R | t91 | 46.2 | 19.0 | 13 | 12.2 | 7 | 10 | f96 | 0.27 | 0.02 | 0.29 | 1 | 61.9 | 35 | 1 | 0.57 | 0 | 0 | 7 |
| Chad | t95 | 47.9 | 17.9 | 13 | 5.1 | 3 | 8 | f97 | 0.12 | -- | 0.12 | 0 | 80.2 | 28 | 0 | 0.46 | 0 | 0 | 5 |
| Comoros | t95 | 50.1 | 35.7 | 19 | 5.7 | 3 | 11 | | 0.95 | -- | 0.95 | 3 | 84.8 | 26 | 3 | 3.04 | 1 | 2 | 8 |
| Congo, DR | t94 | 58.2 | 37.1 | 22 | 21.2 | 12 | 17 | ts97 f95 | 0.04 | 0.02 | 0.06 | 0 | 7.0 | 88 | 0 | 0.04 | 0 | 0 | 11 |
| Congo, R | t92 | 78.3 | 84.1 | 53 | 58.7 | 33 | 43 | f90 | 0.79 | 0.12 | 0.91 | 3 | 60.5 | 36 | 3 | 0.36 | 0 | 1 | 29 |
| Côte d'Ivoire | t94 | 58.3 | 34.1 | 21 | 56.8 | 32 | 26 | | 1.19 | 0.64 | 1.83 | 6 | 99.0 | 20 | 6 | 7.00 | 2 | 4 | 19 |
| Djibouti | t96 | 31.9 | 19.6 | 9 | 2.6 | 1 | 5 | | 1.27 | 0.04 | 1.31 | 4 | 98.0 | 21 | 4 | 8.03 | 2 | 3 | 4 |
| Egypt | t95 | 95.2 | 75.1 | 68 | 189.5 | 67 | 67 | | 6.02 | 0.14 | 6.16 | 20 | -- | -- | 20 | 15.16 | 4 | 12 | 49 |
| Equatorial Guinea | t90 | 79.3 | 68.5 | 43 | 16.4 | 9 | 26 | | 1.29 | 0.07 | 1.36 | 4 | 62.0 | 35 | 4 | 10.90 | 3 | 3 | 18 |
| Eritrea | t97 | 29.3 | 37.9 | 15 | 9.0 | 5 | 10 | | 0.67 | -- | 0.67 | 2 | 64.0 | 34 | 2 | 0.84 | 0 | 1 | 7 |
| Ethiopia | t96 | 35.2 | 24.8 | 12 | 7.4 | 4 | 8 | f97 | 0.28 | -- | 0.28 | 1 | 187.0 | 3 | 1 | 1.01 | 0 | 0 | 5 |
| Gabon | t90 | -- | -- | -- | 44.9 | 26 | 26 | tsf97 | 3.27 | 0.83 | 4.10 | 14 | 67.0 | 33 | 14 | 17.14 | 5 | 9 | 20 |

166

| Country | Ed note | 1st net % | 2nd net % | 1st2nd score | 3rd/10k | 3rd score | E score | Tel note | Main lines/100 | Cell subs/100 | Phone total | Ph score | Fault/100 l/yr | Fault score | Tel score | Internet users/10k | I net score | C score | K index |
|---|---|---|---|---|---|---|---|---|---|---|---|---|---|---|---|---|---|---|---|
| Gambia | t94 | 65.9 | 33.3 | 24 | 14.8 | 8 | 16 | f96 | 2.08 | 0.41 | 2.49 | 8 | 76.0 | 30 | 8 | 20.34 | 5 | 6 | 13 |
| Ghana | t90 | -- | -- | -- | 12.6 | 7 | 7 | sf97 | 0.75 | 0.12 | 0.87 | 3 | 86.0 | 26 | 3 | 3.13 | 1 | 2 | 5 |
| Guinea | t96 | 45.6 | 14.6 | 11 | 11.2 | 6 | 8 | | 0.48 | 0.28 | 0.76 | 2 | 70.7 | 32 | 2 | 0.65 | 0 | 1 | 6 |
| Guinea-Bissau | -- | 52.3 | 24.1 | 16 | -- | -- | 16 | | 0.71 | -- | 0.71 | 2 | 33.3 | 53 | 2 | 2.65 | 1 | 1 | 11 |
| Kenya | t90 | 65.0 | 61.1 | 33 | 14.2 | 8 | 20 | tsf97 | 0.92 | 0.02 | 0.94 | 3 | 192.7 | 1 | 1 | 5.17 | 1 | 1 | 14 |
| Lesotho | t96 | 68.6 | 72.9 | 41 | 23.4 | 13 | 27 | | 0.97 | 0.48 | 1.45 | 5 | -- | -- | 5 | 0.97 | 0 | 2 | 19 |
| Liberia | -- | -- | -- | -- | -- | -- | -- | tf97 | 0.22 | -- | 0.22 | 1 | 144.0 | 11 | 1 | 0.38 | 0 | 0 | 0 |
| Libyan Arab J | t91 | 99.9 | 99.9 | 100 | 161.0 | 63 | 81 | f92 | 8.36 | 0.33 | 8.69 | 29 | 230.0 | 0 | 0 | -- | -- | 0 | 54 |
| Madagascar | t96 | 58.7 | -- | 19 | 18.8 | 11 | 15 | | 0.29 | 0.08 | 0.37 | 1 | 91.9 | 23 | 1 | 1.83 | 0 | 0 | 10 |
| Malawi | t95 | 98.5 | 72.6 | 73 | 5.8 | 3 | 38 | | 0.35 | 0.10 | 0.45 | 1 | -- | -- | 1 | 1.86 | 0 | 0 | 25 |
| Mali | t97 | 38.1 | 17.9 | 10 | 13.3 | 8 | 9 | | 0.25 | 0.04 | 0.29 | 1 | -- | -- | 1 | 0.94 | 0 | 0 | 6 |
| Mauritania | t95 | 62.9 | -- | 23 | 36.5 | 21 | 22 | | 0.58 | -- | 0.58 | 2 | 138.0 | 12 | 2 | 3.95 | 1 | 1 | 15 |
| Mauritius | t97 | 96.5 | 68.0 | 67 | 56.7 | 32 | 49 | | 21.37 | 5.27 | 26.64 | 61 | 64.0 | 34 | 34 | 108.85 | 29 | 31 | 43 |
| Morocco | t96 | 76.6 | 37.7 | 31 | 118.0 | 54 | 42 | f97 | 5.44 | 0.42 | 5.86 | 19 | 46.0 | 43 | 19 | 14.35 | 4 | 11 | 32 |
| Mozambique | t96 | 39.6 | 22.4 | 12 | 4.0 | 2 | 7 | | 0.40 | 0.04 | 0.44 | 1 | 61.0 | 36 | 1 | 1.85 | 0 | 0 | 5 |
| Namibia | t95 | 91.4 | 80.7 | 63 | 73.5 | 41 | 52 | f96 | 6.86 | 1.17 | 8.03 | 27 | 76.0 | 30 | 27 | 30.12 | 8 | 17 | 40 |
| Niger | t91 | 24.4 | 9.4 | 4 | 5.6 | 3 | 3 | f93 | 0.18 | 0.01 | 0.19 | 1 | 80.0 | 28 | 1 | 0.30 | 0 | 0 | 2 |
| Nigeria | t93 | -- | -- | -- | 41.0 | 23 | 23 | f92 | 0.38 | 0.02 | 0.40 | 1 | 327.0 | 0 | 0 | 0.38 | 0 | 0 | 15 |
| Rwanda | p97 s91 | 78.3 | 8.0 | 21 | -- | -- | 21 | | 0.16 | 0.08 | 0.24 | 1 | 17.0 | 72 | 1 | 1.21 | 0 | 0 | 14 |
| São Tomé & Principe | -- | -- | -- | -- | -- | -- | -- | | 2.21 | -- | 2.21 | 7 | 67.0 | 33 | 7 | 28.37 | 8 | 7 | 7 |
| Senegal | t94 | 59.5 | 19.8 | 16 | 29.7 | 17 | 16 | | 1.55 | 0.25 | 1.80 | 6 | 23.4 | 62 | 6 | 8.33 | 2 | 4 | 12 |
| Seychelles | -- | -- | -- | -- | -- | -- | -- | f95 | 24.35 | 4.89 | 29.24 | 63 | 43.0 | 46 | 46 | 256.90 | 54 | 50 | 50 |
| Sierra Leone | t90 | 44.0 | -- | 12 | 11.9 | 7 | 9 | | 0.38 | -- | 0.38 | 1 | 23.0 | 63 | 1 | 10.95 | 3 | 2 | 7 |
| Somalia | -- | -- | -- | -- | -- | -- | -- | | 0.14 | -- | 0.14 | 0 | -- | -- | 0 | 0 | 0 | 0 | 0 |
| South Africa | t95 | 99.9 | 94.9 | 95 | 184.1 | 66 | 80 | | 11.46 | 5.64 | 17.10 | 48 | 48.8 | 41 | 41 | 285.75 | 58 | 49 | 70 |
| Sudan | t90 | -- | -- | -- | 27.2 | 15 | 15 | | 0.57 | 0.03 | 0.60 | 2 | 12.0 | 80 | 2 | 0.18 | 0 | 1 | 10 |
| Swaziland | t96 | 94.6 | 81.5 | 70 | 63.0 | 36 | 53 | f95 | 3.05 | 0.49 | 3.54 | 12 | 189.0 | 2 | 2 | 10.50 | 3 | 2 | 36 |
| Tanzania | t97 | 47.4 | -- | 14 | 5.7 | 3 | 8 | f96 | 0.38 | 0.12 | 0.50 | 2 | 175.0 | 5 | 2 | 0.93 | 0 | 1 | 6 |
| Togo | t96 | 82.3 | 58.3 | 42 | 31.5 | 18 | 30 | | 0.71 | 0.17 | 0.88 | 3 | 60.0 | 36 | 3 | 170.57 | 43 | 23 | 28 |
| Tunisia | t96 | 99.9 | 74.3 | 77 | 134.1 | 58 | 67 | | 8.06 | 0.42 | 8.48 | 28 | 48.0 | 42 | 28 | 10.71 | 3 | 15 | 50 |
| Uganda | t96 | -- | -- | -- | 17.9 | 10 | 10 | | 0.28 | 0.15 | 0.43 | 1 | 80.0 | 28 | 1 | 7.30 | 2 | 1 | 7 |
| Zambia | t94 | 72.4 | 42.2 | 30 | 23.8 | 14 | 22 | | 0.88 | 0.06 | 0.94 | 3 | 139.2 | 12 | 3 | 3.42 | 1 | 2 | 15 |
| Zimbabwe | t96 | 93.1 | 59.2 | 55 | 66.1 | 38 | 46 | tf97 | 1.72 | 0.43 | 2.15 | 7 | 223.0 | 0 | 0 | 7.88 | 2 | 1 | 31 |
| **EUROPE** | | | | | | | | | | | | | | | | | | | |
| Albania | p95 t96 | 96.0 | -- | 80* | 108.7 | 51 | 65 | | 3.05 | 0.15 | 3.20 | 11 | 14.0 | 77 | 11 | 2.72 | 1 | 6 | 45 |
| Austria | t96 | 99.9 | 97.3 | 97 | 298.8 | 81 | 89 | f97 | 49.10 | 28.17 | 77.27 | 91 | 7.2 | 88 | 88 | 1351.35 | 100 | 94 | 91 |
| Belarus | p95 t96 | 97.0 | -- | 80* | 316.8 | 83 | 81 | | 24.14 | 0.12 | 24.26 | 59 | 8.2 | 86 | 59 | 7.27 | 2 | 30 | 64 |
| Belgium | t95 | 99.9 | 99.9 | 100 | 355.1 | 85 | 92 | | 50.02 | 17.32 | 67.34 | 87 | 4.7 | 92 | 87 | 788.88 | 86 | 86 | 90 |
| Bosnia & Herzegovina | -- | -- | -- | -- | -- | -- | -- | | 9.07 | 0.69 | 9.76 | 32 | -- | -- | 32 | 1.29 | 0 | 16 | 16 |
| Bulgaria | t96 | 97.9 | 77.6 | 75 | 311.0 | 82 | 78 | f97 | 32.89 | 1.52 | 34.41 | 67 | 5.9 | 90 | 67 | 179.94 | 44 | 55 | 70 |
| Croatia | t96 | 99.9 | 72.4 | 76 | 191.1 | 67 | 71 | f97 | 34.77 | 4.07 | 38.84 | 71 | 12.9 | 79 | 71 | 446.33 | 70 | 70 | 71 |
| Czech R | t96 | 99.9 | 99.9 | 100 | 200.9 | 69 | 84 | | 36.39 | 9.39 | 45.78 | 77 | 32.4 | 54 | 54 | 389.03 | 66 | 60 | 76 |
| Denmark | t95 | 99.9 | 94.8 | 95 | 334.9 | 84 | 89 | | 65.97 | 36.44 | 102.41 | 100 | -- | -- | 80* | 1887.04 | 100 | 90 | 89 |
| Estonia | t96 | 99.9 | 86.1 | 86 | 296.5 | 81 | 83 | | 34.29 | 16.99 | 51.28 | 80 | 26.4 | 59 | 59 | 1031.75 | 94 | 76 | 81 |
| Finland | t96 | 99.9 | 95.4 | 95 | 441.8 | 92 | 93 | | 55.39 | 57.18 | 112.57 | 100 | 8.4 | 86 | 86 | 2857.97 | 100 | 93 | 93 |
| France | t96 | 99.9 | 98.7 | 98 | 354.1 | 85 | 91 | f96 | 56.97 | 18.78 | 75.75 | 90 | 5.9 | 90 | 90 | 335.10 | 62 | 76 | 86 |
| Germany | t96 | 99.9 | 95.3 | 95 | 260.3 | 77 | 86 | f95 | 56.68 | 16.97 | 73.65 | 89 | 8.7 | 85 | 85 | 731.38 | 84 | 84 | 85 |
| Greece | t96 | 99.9 | 91.4 | 91 | 344.8 | 85 | 88 | | 52.22 | 19.41 | 71.63 | 89 | 27.0 | 58 | 58 | 330.19 | 62 | 60 | 79 |
| Hungary | t95 | 97.5 | 96.9 | 92 | 190.3 | 67 | 79 | f97 | 33.59 | 10.50 | 44.09 | 75 | 16.8 | 73 | 73 | 294.35 | 59 | 66 | 75 |
| Iceland | t96 | 99.9 | 87.5 | 87 | 291.8 | 81 | 84 | | 64.65 | 33.14 | 97.79 | 99 | -- | -- | 80* | 3623.19 | 100 | 90 | 86 |
| Ireland | t96 | 99.9 | 99.9 | 100 | 370.3 | 86 | 93 | f92 | 43.47 | 25.70 | 69.17 | 88 | 38.0 | 50 | 50 | 815.00 | 87 | 68 | 85 |
| Italy | t96 | 99.9 | 95.0 | 95 | 329.9 | 84 | 89 | | 45.07 | 35.53 | 80.60 | 92 | 16.2 | 73 | 73 | 520.29 | 75 | 74 | 84 |
| Latvia | t96 | 99.9 | 80.6 | 80 | 224.9 | 72 | 76 | | 30.16 | 6.81 | 36.97 | 70 | 56.8 | 37 | 37 | 406.77 | 67 | 52 | 68 |
| Lithuania | t96 | -- | -- | -- | 225.1 | 72 | 72 | | 29.96 | 7.23 | 37.19 | 70 | 21.8 | 65 | 65 | 215.98 | 49 | 57 | 67 |
| Luxembourg | -- | -- | -- | -- | -- | -- | -- | | 69.17 | 30.80 | 99.97 | 100 | 10.1 | 83 | 83 | 1180.08 | 99 | 91 | 80* |
| Macedonia, FYR | p95 s95 t96 | 85.0 | 51.0 | 42 | 155.7 | 62 | 52 | t97 f96 | 19.87 | 1.53 | 21.40 | 54 | 21.3 | 66 | 54 | 100.05 | 27 | 40 | 48 |
| Malta | t96 | 99.9 | 85.2 | 85 | 218.3 | 71 | 78 | | 49.88 | 5.87 | 55.75 | 82 | 35.1 | 52 | 52 | 520.83 | 75 | 63 | 73 |
| Moldova | t96 | -- | -- | -- | 214.3 | 71 | 71 | | 15.02 | 0.16 | 15.18 | 45 | 79.0 | 28 | 28 | 7.51 | 2 | 15 | 52 |
| Netherlands | t96 | 99.9 | 99.9 | 100 | 301.8 | 82 | 91 | | 59.31 | 21.29 | 80.60 | 92 | 2.7 | 95 | 92 | 1016.37 | 94 | 93 | 92 |
| Norway | t96 | 99.9 | 97.6 | 97 | 423.9 | 90 | 93 | f97 | 66.01 | 47.39 | 113.40 | 100 | 14.0 | 77 | 77 | 2249.21 | 100 | 88 | 91 |
| Poland | t95 | 99.4 | 86.5 | 85 | 186.5 | 67 | 76 | | 22.76 | 4.98 | 27.74 | 62 | 26.0 | 59 | 59 | 408.34 | 67 | 63 | 72 |
| Portugal | t95 | 99.9 | 89.7 | 89 | 324.2 | 83 | 86 | f97 | 41.35 | 30.89 | 72.24 | 89 | 35.9 | 51 | 51 | 602.57 | 80 | 65 | 79 |

| Country | Ed note | 1st net % | 2nd net % | 1st2nd score | 3rd/10k | 3rd score | E score | Tel note | Main lines/100 | Cell subs/100 | Phone total | Ph score | Fault/100 l/yr | Fault score | Tel score | Internet users/10k | I net score | C score | K index |
|---|---|---|---|---|---|---|---|---|---|---|---|---|---|---|---|---|---|---|---|
| Romania | t96 | 99.9 | 75.8 | 78 | 181.9 | 66 | 72 | f96 | 16.24 | 2.86 | 19.10 | 51 | 88.3 | 25 | 25 | 66.74 | 18 | 21 | 55 |
| Slovakia | t96 | -- | -- | -- | 189.7 | 67 | 67 | | 28.63 | 8.65 | 37.28 | 70 | 27.3 | 58 | 58 | 929.89 | 91 | 74 | 69 |
| Slovenia | p95 t96 | 99.9 | -- | 80* | 265.7 | 78 | 79 | | 37.48 | 8.36 | 45.84 | 77 | -- | -- | 77 | 1003.51 | 93 | 85 | 81 |
| Spain | t96 | 99.9 | 91.9 | 92 | 425.4 | 90 | 91 | | 41.37 | 17.91 | 59.28 | 84 | 1.2 | 98 | 84 | 440.17 | 69 | 76 | 86 |
| Sweden | t96 | 99.9 | 99.9 | 100 | 311.6 | 82 | 91 | f95 | 67.37 | 46.40 | 113.77 | 100 | 8.4 | 86 | 86 | 3952.87 | 100 | 93 | 92 |
| Switzerland | t95 | 99.9 | 83.7 | 83 | 207.2 | 70 | 76 | f95 | 67.54 | 23.52 | 91.06 | 96 | 8.1 | 86 | 86 | 1406.15 | 100 | 93 | 82 |
| Ukraine | t95 | -- | -- | -- | 299.6 | 81 | 80* | f97 | 19.07 | 0.23 | 19.30 | 51 | 42.5 | 46 | 46 | 29.49 | 8 | 27 | 62 |
| United Kingdom | t96 | 99.9 | 91.8 | 92 | 323.7 | 83 | 87 | f97 | 55.69 | 25.23 | 80.92 | 92 | 3.7 | 94 | 92 | 1357.17 | 100 | 96 | 90 |
| Yugoslavia, | t96 | -- | -- | -- | 162.5 | 63 | 63 | | 21.81 | 2.26 | 24.07 | 59 | -- | -- | 59 | 94.03 | 25 | 42 | 56 |
| RUSSIAN FED. | t94 | 99.9 | 87.6 | 87 | 300.6 | 81 | 84 | | 19.66 | 0.51 | 20.17 | 53 | 38.4 | 49 | 49 | 67.71 | 18 | 33 | 67 |
| **ASIA** | | | | | | | | | | | | | | | | | | | |
| Afghanistan | t90 | 49.7 | 21.9 | 15 | 16.5 | 9 | 12 | | 0.14 | -- | 0.14 | 0 | -- | -- | 0 | -- | -- | 0 | 8 |
| Armenia | t96 | -- | -- | -- | 99.6 | 48 | 48 | | 15.72 | 0.20 | 15.92 | 46 | 20.0 | 68 | 46 | 11.31 | 3 | 24 | 40 |
| Azerbaijan | t96 | -- | -- | -- | 151.3 | 62 | 62 | | 8.87 | 0.85 | 9.72 | 32 | 75.0 | 30 | 30 | 1.24 | 0 | 15 | 46 |
| Bahrain | t93 | 98.2 | 87.2 | 83 | 144.4 | 61 | 72 | | 24.55 | 14.34 | 38.89 | 71 | 18.0 | 71 | 71 | 311.45 | 61 | 66 | 70 |
| Bangladesh | t90 | 75.1 | 21.6 | 24 | 39.7 | 23 | 23 | | 0.30 | 0.06 | 0.36 | 1 | 17.3 | 72 | 1 | 0.10 | 0 | 0 | 15 |
| Bhutan | -- | 13.2 | -- | 0 | -- | -- | 0 | f93 | 1.64 | -- | 1.64 | 5 | 67.0 | 33 | 5 | -- | -- | 5 | 2 |
| Brunei Darussalam | t95 | 87.9 | 81.9 | 60 | 51.6 | 29 | 44 | | 24.68 | 15.60 | 40.28 | 72 | 86.2 | 25 | 25 | 317.46 | 61 | 43 | 44 |
| Cambodia | t97 | 99.9 | 38.8 | 63 | 8.5 | 5 | 34 | f97 | 0.23 | 0.57 | 0.80 | 3 | 35.1 | 52 | 3 | 0.67 | 0 | 1 | 23 |
| China | t97 | 99.9 | 70.0 | 75 | 48.8 | 28 | 51 | | 6.96 | 1.90 | 8.86 | 29 | -- | -- | 29 | 24.79 | 7 | 18 | 40 |
| Cyprus | p95 s95 t96 | 96.0 | 93.0 | 85 | 132.3 | 58 | 71 | | 58.51 | 16.83 | 75.34 | 90 | 23.2 | 63 | 63 | 433.71 | 69 | 66 | 69 |
| Georgia | t96 | 89.0 | 75.9 | 57 | 314.9 | 82 | 69 | f92 | 11.55 | 1.10 | 12.65 | 41 | 43.1 | 45 | 41 | 9.18 | 2 | 21 | 53 |
| India | t96 | 77.2 | 59.7 | 38 | 63.8 | 36 | 37 | f97 | 2.20 | 0.12 | 2.32 | 8 | 174.0 | 5 | 5 | 5.09 | 1 | 3 | 26 |
| Indonesia | t96 | 99.2 | 56.1 | 67 | 115.7 | 53 | 60 | f97 | 2.70 | 0.52 | 3.22 | 11 | 13.2 | 78 | 11 | 14.54 | 4 | 7 | 42 |
| Iran | t96 | 90.0 | 81.2 | 61 | 176.3 | 65 | 63 | | 11.18 | 0.59 | 11.77 | 39 | 2.6 | 96 | 39 | 15.21 | 4 | 21 | 49 |
| Iraq | -- | 74.6 | 42.9 | 32 | -- | -- | 32 | | 3.10 | -- | 3.10 | 10 | -- | -- | 10 | -- | -- | 10 | 25 |
| Israel | t95 | -- | -- | -- | 357.1 | 85 | 80* | f95 | 47.11 | 35.88 | 82.99 | 93 | 12.0 | 80 | 80 | 752.01 | 85 | 82 | 81 |
| Japan | t94 | 99.9 | 99.9 | 100 | 313.1 | 82 | 91 | f95 | 50.26 | 37.38 | 87.64 | 95 | 1.7 | 97 | 95 | 1323.42 | 100 | 97 | 93 |
| Jordan | p95 t94 | 89.0 | -- | 58 | 213.6 | 70 | 64 | | 8.55 | 1.18 | 9.73 | 32 | 58.0 | 37 | 32 | 101.81 | 27 | 29 | 52 |
| Kazakhstan | t95 | -- | -- | -- | 285.9 | 80 | 80 | f95 | 10.36 | 0.17 | 10.53 | 35 | 405.0 | 0 | 0 | 11.67 | 3 | 1 | 54 |
| Korea, DPR | -- | -- | -- | -- | -- | -- | -- | f93 | 4.71 | -- | 4.71 | 16 | 50.0 | 40 | 16 | -- | -- | 16 | 16 |
| Korea, R | t97 | 99.9 | 99.9 | 100 | 610.6 | 100 | 100 | f97 | 43.27 | 30.19 | 73.46 | 89 | 15.0 | 75 | 75 | 668.32 | 82 | 78 | 93 |
| Kuwait | t96 | 65.2 | 63.2 | 34 | 174.0 | 65 | 49 | | 23.59 | 13.80 | 37.39 | 70 | 30.0 | 56 | 56 | 331.31 | 62 | 59 | 52 |
| Kyrgyzstan | t95 | 99.5 | 77.8 | 78 | 108.8 | 51 | 64 | f94 | 7.64 | 0.03 | 7.67 | 26 | 37.0 | 50 | 26 | 5.41 | 1 | 13 | 47 |
| Lao PDR | t96 | 73.0 | 63.4 | 38 | 26.0 | 15 | 26 | | 0.55 | 0.12 | 0.67 | 2 | -- | -- | 2 | -- | -- | 2 | 18 |
| Lebanon | t95 | 76.1 | -- | 36 | 271.2 | 79 | 57 | | 19.43 | 15.67 | 35.10 | 68 | -- | -- | 68 | 313.38 | 61 | 64 | 59 |
| Malaysia | t95 | 99.9 | 64.0 | 72 | 104.8 | 50 | 61 | f97 | 19.76 | 9.92 | 29.68 | 64 | 39.0 | 49 | 49 | 360.66 | 64 | 56 | 59 |
| Maldives | -- | -- | -- | -- | -- | -- | -- | | 7.05 | 0.56 | 7.61 | 25 | 69.6 | 32 | 25 | 5.93 | 2 | 13 | 13 |
| Mongolia | t97 | 85.1 | 55.9 | 43 | 200.9 | 69 | 56 | tsf97 | 3.66 | 0.08 | 3.74 | 12 | 18.0 | 71 | 12 | 5.03 | 1 | 6 | 39 |
| Myanmar | t94 | 99.3 | 54.2 | 66 | 59.0 | 34 | 50 | | 0.52 | 0.02 | 0.54 | 2 | 169.0 | 6 | 2 | -- | -- | 2 | 34 |
| Nepal | t96 | 78.4 | 54.6 | 37 | 48.5 | 28 | 32 | f94 | 0.85 | -- | 0.85 | 3 | 200.0 | 0 | 0 | 5.69 | 1 | 0 | 21 |
| Oman | t97 | 67.7 | 66.6 | 37 | 69.5 | 40 | 38 | f96 | 9.23 | 4.33 | 13.56 | 42 | 1.8 | 97 | 42 | 83.96 | 22 | 32 | 36 |
| Pakistan | t91 | -- | -- | -- | 30.1 | 17 | 17 | | 1.94 | 0.14 | 2.08 | 7 | 98.6 | 21 | 7 | 4.35 | 1 | 4 | 13 |
| Philippines | t95 | 99.9 | 77.8 | 79 | 295.8 | 81 | 80 | f97 | 3.70 | 2.19 | 5.89 | 20 | 5.2 | 91 | 20 | 20.56 | 5 | 12 | 57 |
| Qatar | t96 | 83.3 | 73.3 | 50 | 151.8 | 62 | 56 | f97 | 25.99 | 11.36 | 37.35 | 70 | 15.5 | 75 | 70 | 345.42 | 63 | 66 | 59 |
| Saudi Arabia | t96 | 60.1 | 58.7 | 29 | 145.5 | 61 | 45 | | 14.26 | 3.11 | 17.37 | 48 | 2.8 | 95 | 48 | 9.91 | 3 | 25 | 38 |
| Singapore | t96 | 91.4 | 75.6 | 61 | 273.0 | 79 | 70 | | 56.20 | 34.60 | 90.80 | 96 | 4.3 | 93 | 93 | 2370.79 | 100 | 96 | 79 |
| Sri Lanka | t95 | 99.9 | 76.0 | 78 | 47.4 | 27 | 52 | f97 | 2.84 | 0.94 | 3.78 | 13 | 15.2 | 75 | 13 | 10.84 | 3 | 8 | 37 |
| Syrian Arab R | t94 | 94.7 | 42.3 | 53 | 155.9 | 62 | 57 | | 9.54 | -- | 9.54 | 32 | 50.0 | 40 | 32 | 6.52 | 2 | 17 | 44 |
| Tajikistan | t96 | -- | -- | -- | 189.5 | 67 | 67 | | 3.68 | 0.01 | 3.69 | 12 | 121.8 | 16 | 12 | -- | -- | 12 | 49 |
| Thailand | t96 | 88.0 | 47.6 | 44 | 225.2 | 72 | 58 | | 8.35 | 3.25 | 11.60 | 39 | 26.4 | 59 | 39 | 33.17 | 9 | 24 | 47 |
| Turkey | t96 | 99.9 | 58.4 | 69 | 230.1 | 73 | 71 | | 25.41 | 5.25 | 30.66 | 64 | 56.1 | 38 | 38 | 67.43 | 18 | 28 | 57 |
| Turkmenistan | t90 | -- | -- | -- | 207.2 | 70 | 70 | | 8.22 | 0.07 | 8.29 | 28 | 46.3 | 43 | 28 | -- | -- | 28 | 56 |
| United Arab Emirates | t96 | 82.0 | 77.8 | 51 | 80.1 | 43 | 47 | f93 | 38.90 | 20.96 | 59.86 | 84 | 1.1 | 98 | 84 | 849.98 | 88 | 86 | 60 |
| Uzbekistan | t91 | -- | -- | -- | 304.8 | 82 | 80* | f97 | 6.47 | 0.07 | 6.54 | 22 | 104.2 | 19 | 19 | 4.21 | 1 | 10 | 57 |
| Viet Nam | t96 | 99.9 | 55.1 | 68 | 67.8 | 39 | 53 | | 2.58 | 0.24 | 2.82 | 9 | -- | -- | 9 | 1.29 | 0 | 4 | 37 |
| Yemen | t96 | -- | -- | -- | 41.9 | 24 | 24 | t97 f93 | 1.34 | 0.11 | 1.45 | 5 | 20.0 | 68 | 5 | 2.37 | 1 | 3 | 17 |
| **PACIFIC** | | | | | | | | | | | | | | | | | | | |
| Australia | t97 | 99.9 | 96.0 | 96 | 568.2 | 100 | 98 | | 51.21 | 28.55 | 79.76 | 92 | -- | -- | 80* | 1603.51 | 100 | 90 | 95 |
| Fiji | t91 | 99.9 | 84.2 | 84 | 107.9 | 51 | 67 | | 9.68 | 1.01 | 10.69 | 36 | 153.0 | 9 | 9 | 62.81 | 17 | 13 | 49 |

| Country | Ed note | 1st net % | 2nd net % | 1st2nd score | 3rd/ 10k | 3rd score | *E score* | Tel note | Main lines/ 100 | Cell subs/ 100 | Phone total | Ph score | Fault/ 100 l/yr | Fault score | Tel score | Internet users/ 10k | I net score | *C score* | K index |
|---|---|---|---|---|---|---|---|---|---|---|---|---|---|---|---|---|---|---|---|
| New Zealand | t97 | 99.9 | 92.9 | 93 | 451.1 | 92 | 92 | | 47.91 | 20.26 | 68.17 | 87 | 46.0 | 43 | 43 | 1538.86 | 100 | 71 | 85 |
| Papua New Guinea | t95 | 78.9 | -- | 39 | 31.8 | 18 | 28 | ts96 f95 | 1.14 | 0.07 | 1.21 | 4 | 10.1 | 83 | 4 | 0.12 | 0 | 2 | 19 |
| Samoa | p97 s95 | 96.5 | 45.0 | 58 | -- | -- | 58 | | 4.87 | 1.72 | 6.59 | 22 | 29.0 | 57 | 22 | 22.99 | 6 | 14 | 43 |
| Solomon Is | -- | -- | -- | -- | -- | -- | -- | | 1.89 | 0.17 | 2.06 | 7 | 5.0 | 92 | 7 | 47.96 | 13 | 10 | 10 |
| Tonga | -- | -- | -- | -- | -- | -- | -- | tsf96 | 7.90 | 0.31 | 8.21 | 27 | 761.0 | 0 | 0 | 16.24 | 4 | 2 | 2 |
| Vanuatu | -- | 71.3 | 42.8 | 29 | -- | -- | 29 | f95 | 2.84 | 0.12 | 2.96 | 10 | 56.0 | 38 | 10 | 5.75 | 1 | 5 | 21 |

**Notes**

The knowledge index (**K index**) is the average of two weighted indicators (column heading in parentheses) [weight in brackets]: an education score (*E score*) [2]; and a communication score (*C score*) [1]. Education has a higher weight than communication because the quality of communication depends on education.

The education score is the average of two unweighted indicators:

Primary and secondary school enrollment (1st2nd score), the unweighted average score of the net primary school enrollment rate and the net secondary enrollment rate.

Tertiary school enrollment per 10,000 population (3rd score).

Enrollment rates are more reliable than other available indicators of education, notably the adult literacy rate (the percentage of adults aged 15 years and over who are literate)—see the section on education in Chapter 2. Net enrollment rates are preferable to gross enrollment rates because the latter include late entrants and repeaters. A gross enrollment rate of 100% can mean good or not good performance depending on how much late entry and repetition is involved.

Ed note = education note: a year after the letter p or s is the year of the primary or secondary enrollment data other than 1997; a year after the letter t is the year of the tertiary enrollment data.

1st net % = net primary school enrollment rate = the percentage of children of primary school-age who are enrolled in primary school. Data are for 1997, except where noted otherwise in the Ed note column, and are from UNESCO (1999b).

2nd net % = net secondary school enrollment rate = the percentage of children of secondary school-age enrolled in secondary school. Data are for 1997, except where noted otherwise in the Ed note column, and are from UNESCO (1999b).

1st 2nd score = the average of the scores for the net primary and net secondary enrollment rates. The performance criteria are shown in Table 5a. The United Nations' target is for universal primary education by 2015 (World Summit for Social Development [Copenhagen 1995] and the Fourth World Conference on Women [Beijing 1995] [United Nations Population Division 1997; Office of the UN System Support and Services 1996]). Hence the top of the good band was set at 100% and the top of fair at 95%. No UN target exists for secondary education, but since it is almost as basic as primary, the top of the good band was set at 100%, with progressively lower standards for the other bands.

3rd/10k = tertiary school students per 10,000 population. Data are for the year given in the Ed note column (after the letter t) and are from UNESCO (1999c).

3rd score = tertiary enrollment score. The performance criteria are shown in Table 5a. They have been set so that the good band includes the lowest rates of countries with the largest proportions of highly literate adults (Sweden, Canada and the United States).

The communication score is the average score of two unweighted indicators:

A telephone indicator (Tel score), represented by the lower score of main telephone lines + cellular phone subscribers per 100 persons (Ph score), and Faults per 100 main telephone lines per year (Fault score).

Internet users per 10,000 persons (I net score).

Tel note: a year after the letter f is the year of the faults data (if not 1998); a year after the letter s, the year of the cell phone data (if not 1998); a year after the letter t, the year of the main line data (if not 1998).

Main lines/100 = main telephone lines per 100 persons. Data are for 1998 [unless noted otherwise in the Tel note column] and are from International Telecommunication Union (1997, 1998 & 2000).

Cell subs/100 = cellular mobile phone subscribers per 100 persons. Data are for 1998, unless noted otherwise in the Tel note column, and are from International Telecommunication Union (1997, 1998 & 2000).

Ph score = phone score. The performance criteria are shown in Table 5a. The top of fair is the point where (in general) 95% of households have a main line.

Fault/100 l/yr = faults per 100 main telephone lines per year. Data are for 1998, unless noted otherwise in the Tel note column, and are from International Telecommunication Union (1997, 1998 & 1999).

Fault score. The performance criteria are shown in Table 5a. The top of bad was set at one fault per main line per year.

Internet users/10k = Internet per 10,000 persons. Data are for 1998 and are from International Telecommunication Union (2000).

I net score = Internet score. The performance criteria are shown in Table 5a. They encompass the range of performance of 92% of countries but otherwise are arbitrary.

| band | top point on scale | net primary school enrollment (%) | net secondary school enrollment (%) | tertiary school enrollment per 10,000 population | main telephone lines + cellular phones per 100 persons | faults per 100 main telephone lines | Internet users per 10,000 population |
|---|---|---|---|---|---|---|---|
| good | 100 | 100 | 100 | 560 | 100 | 0 | 1200 |
| fair | 80 | 95 | 90 | 280 | 50 | 12 | 600 |
| medium | 60 | 90 | 80 | 140 | 25 | 25 | 300 |
| poor | 40 | 80 | 60 | 70 | 12 | 50 | 150 |
| bad | 20 | 60 | 30 | 35 | 6 | 100 | 75 |
| base | 0 | 20 | 0 | 0 | 0 | 200 | 0 |

**Table 5a. Performance criteria for indicators of education and communication.**

* A score with an asterisk has been reduced in accordance with the insufficient data rule. To prevent high scores resulting merely from lack of data, a good score is allowed only if it is based on all applicable components (data in an indicator, indicators in an index), and a fair score only if it is based on at least half the components. Good and fair scores (100-61) based on fewer than half the applicable components have been reduced to 60. Good scores (100-81) based on more than half but not all the applicable components have been reduced to 80.

# Table 6. Community Index; Freedom and Governance; Peace

| Country | F&G note | PRR | CLR | PFR | CPI | F&G score | Armed conflicts | Def% GDP | Peace score | Crime score | P&O score | C index |
|---|---|---|---|---|---|---|---|---|---|---|---|---|
| AMERICAS | | | | | | | | | | | | |
| Antigua & Barbuda | | 45 | 60 | 44 | -- | 50 | | 0.6 | 94 | -- | 80* | 50 |
| Argentina | | 75 | 60 | 49 | 35 | 55 | | 1.8 | 82 | -- | 80* | 55 |
| Bahamas | | 90 | 90 | 91 | -- | 80* | | 0.6 | 94 | 14 | 54 | 54 |
| Barbados | | 90 | 90 | 79 | -- | 80* | | 0.5 | 95 | 42 | 68 | 68 |
| Belize | | 90 | 90 | 67 | -- | 80* | | 2.6 | 74 | -- | 74 | 74 |
| Bolivia | | 90 | 60 | 71 | 27 | 62 | T[98-] ? | 1.8 | 40 | 35 | 37 | 37 |
| Brazil | | 60 | 45 | 57 | 39 | 50 | | 3.2 | 68 | -- | 68 | 50 |
| Canada | | 90 | 90 | 81 | 92 | 88 | | 1.1 | 89 | 55 | 72 | 72 |
| Chile | | 75 | 75 | 64 | 74 | 72 | | 3.7 | 63 | 58 | 60 | 60 |
| Colombia | | 45 | 45 | 33 | 32 | 39 | [63-] 1190 + [94-95] ? | 3.2 | 20 | 31 | 25 | 25 |
| Costa Rica | | 90 | 75 | 79 | 54 | 74 | | 0.7 | 93 | 55 | 74 | 74 |
| Cuba | | 0 | 0 | 5 | -- | 2 | | 5.3 | 53 | -- | 53 | 2 |
| Dominica | | 90 | 90 | 79 | -- | 80* | | -- | -- | -- | -- | 80 |
| Dominican R | | 75 | 60 | 60 | -- | 65 | | 1.1 | 89 | -- | 80* | 65 |
| Ecuador | | 75 | 60 | 46 | 26 | 52 | [95-98] ? | 2.6 | 40 | 52 | 46 | 46 |
| El Salvador | | 75 | 60 | 50 | 41 | 56 | [79-95] 4410 | 1.7 | 12 | -- | 12 | 12 |
| Grenada | | 90 | 75 | 73 | -- | 79 | | -- | -- | -- | -- | 79 |
| Guatemala | CPI99 | 60 | 45 | 37 | 32 | 43 | [68-96] 5170 | 1.2 | 11 | -- | 11 | 11 |
| Guyana | | 75 | 75 | 71 | -- | 74 | | 1.0 | 90 | -- | 80* | 74 |
| Haiti | | 30 | 30 | 34 | -- | 31 | [91-95] 600 | 2.4 | 28 | -- | 28 | 28 |
| Honduras | CPI99 | 60 | 60 | 42 | 18 | 45 | | 2.0 | 80 | -- | 80 | 45 |
| Jamaica | CPI99 | 75 | 75 | 85 | 38 | 68 | | 0.9 | 91 | 24 | 57 | 57 |
| Mexico | | 60 | 45 | 40 | 33 | 44 | [94-] 830 | 1.0 | 23 | -- | 23 | 23 |
| Nicaragua | CPI99 | 60 | 60 | 50 | 31 | 50 | [82-98] 1770 | 1.1 | 18 | 31 | 24 | 24 |
| Panama | | 90 | 75 | 60 | -- | 75 | | 1.3 | 87 | 53 | 70 | 70 |
| Paraguay | CPI99 | 45 | 60 | 39 | 20 | 41 | T[99-] ? | 1.4 | 40 | -- | 40 | 40 |
| Peru | | 30 | 45 | 26 | 44 | 36 | [81-95] 2000 + [95-98] ? + T[95-] ? | 1.6 | 18 | 62 | 40 | 36 |
| St Kitts & Nevis | | 90 | 75 | 76 | -- | 80 | | -- | -- | 61 | 61 | 61 |
| St Lucia | | 90 | 75 | 83 | -- | 80* | | -- | -- | -- | -- | 80 |
| St Vincent & Grenadines | | 75 | 90 | 79 | -- | 80* | | -- | -- | 37 | 37 | 37 |
| Suriname | | 60 | 60 | 59 | -- | 60 | | 4.2 | 59 | -- | 59 | 59 |
| Trinidad & Tobago | | 90 | 75 | 63 | -- | 76 | | 0.7 | 93 | 47 | 70 | 70 |
| United States | CL: Northern Marianas | 90 | 75 | 83 | 78 | 81 | | 3.2 | 68 | 49 | 58 | 58 |
| Uruguay | CPI99 | 90 | 75 | 61 | 44 | 67 | | 2.3 | 77 | 55 | 66 | 66 |
| Venezuela | | 45 | 45 | 56 | 27 | 43 | [94-95] ? | 1.5 | 40 | 48 | 44 | 43 |
| AFRICA | | | | | | | | | | | | |
| Algeria | | 15 | 30 | 14 | -- | 20 | [92-] 10000 | 4.8 | 0 | -- | 0 | 0 |
| Angola | | 15 | 15 | 16 | 17 | 16 | [92-] 1880 + [97-] 1670 + [98-] 4500 | 11.7 | 4 | -- | 4 | 4 |
| Benin | | 75 | 60 | 60 | -- | 65 | | 1.4 | 86 | -- | 80* | 65 |
| Botswana | | 75 | 75 | 63 | 60 | 68 | | 6.5 | 47 | 44 | 45 | 45 |
| Burkina Faso | | 45 | 45 | 50 | 30 | 42 | | 2.5 | 75 | -- | 75 | 42 |
| Burundi | | 15 | 15 | 14 | -- | 15 | [93-] 29430 | 7.2 | 0 | -- | 0 | 0 |
| Cameroon | | 0 | 15 | 18 | 20 | 13 | [94-95] 2500 | 2.9 | 17 | -- | 17 | 13 |
| Cape Verde | | 90 | 75 | 58 | -- | 74 | | 1.6 | 84 | -- | 80* | 74 |
| Central African R | | 60 | 45 | 32 | -- | 46 | [96-97] 500 | 4.7 | 30 | -- | 30 | 30 |
| Chad | | 15 | 30 | 22 | -- | 22 | [94-] 170 + T[98-] ? | 5.6 | 37 | -- | 37 | 22 |
| Comoros | | 15 | 45 | 50 | -- | 37 | [97-] ? | -- | 40 | -- | 40 | 37 |
| Congo, DR | | 0 | 15 | 8 | -- | 8 | [96-] 21000 + [97-] 1670 + [98-] 4500 | 6.6 | 0 | -- | 0 | 0 |
| Congo, R | | 15 | 30 | 18 | -- | 21 | [98-] 6000 | 3.9 | 9 | -- | 9 | 9 |
| Côte d'Ivoire | | 15 | 45 | 21 | 27 | 27 | | 0.9 | 91 | -- | 80* | 27 |
| Djibouti | | 45 | 15 | 30 | -- | 30 | | 5.1 | 54 | -- | 54 | 30 |
| Egypt | | 15 | 30 | 25 | 31 | 25 | | 4.1 | 59 | 97 | 78 | 25 |
| Equatorial Guinea | | 0 | 0 | 18 | -- | 6 | | 1.5 | 85 | -- | 80* | 6 |
| Eritrea | | 0 | 30 | 26 | -- | 19 | [95-]? + [98-] 8000 | 35.8 | 0 | -- | 0 | 0 |
| Ethiopia | | 30 | 30 | 30 | 32 | 30 | [98-] 8000 + [97-] 670 + T[96-] ? | 6.0 | 3 | 84 | 43 | 30 |
| Gabon | | 30 | 45 | 36 | -- | 37 | | 2.2 | 78 | -- | 78 | 37 |
| Gambia | | 0 | 30 | 24 | -- | 18 | | 3.6 | 64 | -- | 64 | 18 |
| Ghana | | 60 | 60 | 31 | 35 | 46 | | 1.4 | 86 | -- | 80* | 46 |
| Guinea | | 15 | 30 | 23 | -- | 23 | | 1.8 | 82 | -- | 80* | 23 |
| Guinea-Bissau | | 60 | 30 | 35 | -- | 42 | [98-99] 1000 | 5.5 | 20 | -- | 20 | 20 |
| Kenya | | 15 | 30 | 24 | 21 | 22 | T[96-] 250 | 3.1 | 35 | -- | 35 | 22 |
| Lesotho | | 45 | 45 | 35 | -- | 42 | [98-] ? | 3.5 | 40 | -- | 40 | 40 |
| Liberia | | 45 | 30 | 26 | -- | 34 | [89-96] 1880 | 3.9 | 18 | -- | 18 | 18 |

| Country | F&G note | PRR | CLR | PFR | CPI | F&G score | Armed conflicts | Def % GDP | Peace score | Crime score | P&O score | C index |
|---|---|---|---|---|---|---|---|---|---|---|---|---|
| Libyan Arab J | | 0 | 0 | 8 | -- | 3 | T[96-] | 5.3 | 40 | -- | 40 | 3 |
| Madagascar | | 75 | 45 | 58 | -- | 59 | | 0.9 | 91 | 98 | 94 | 59 |
| Malawi | | 60 | 60 | 38 | 41 | 50 | | 1.2 | 88 | -- | 80* | 50 |
| Mali | | 60 | 60 | 65 | -- | 62 | | 2.0 | 80 | -- | 80 | 62 |
| Mauritania | | 15 | 30 | 26 | -- | 24 | | 2.2 | 78 | -- | 78 | 24 |
| Mauritius | | 90 | 75 | 77 | 47 | 72 | | 2.1 | 79 | 66 | 72 | 72 |
| Morocco | PR;CL: Western Sahara | 15 | 30 | 41 | 47 | 33 | | 4.6 | 57 | 86 | 71 | 33 |
| Mozambique | | 60 | 45 | 42 | 22 | 42 | [76-95] 2500 | 3.9 | 17 | -- | 17 | 17 |
| Namibia | | 75 | 60 | 56 | 54 | 61 | T[99] ? | 3.6 | 40 | -- | 40 | 40 |
| Niger | | 30 | 30 | 30 | -- | 30 | [91-96] ? + T[99-] ? | 1.5 | 40 | -- | 40 | 30 |
| Nigeria | | 45 | 60 | 38 | 12 | 39 | [94-95] 2500 + T[96-] ? | 4.3 | 17 | -- | 17 | 17 |
| Rwanda | | 0 | 15 | 22 | -- | 12 | [90-] 81100 + [97-] 3000 | 6.9 | 0 | 61 | 30 | 12 |
| São Tomé & Principe | | 90 | 75 | 64 | -- | 76 | | -- | -- | 9 | 9 | 9 |
| Senegal | | 45 | 45 | 57 | 35 | 45 | [98-] 500 | 1.7 | 30 | -- | 30 | 30 |
| Seychelles | | 60 | 60 | 40 | -- | 53 | | 2.9 | 71 | 56 | 63 | 53 |
| Sierra Leone | | 60 | 30 | 12 | -- | 34 | [91-99] 4440 | 3.3 | 12 | -- | 12 | 12 |
| Somalia | | 0 | 0 | 10 | -- | 3 | [91-] 39440 + [97-] 670 | 4.7 | 0 | -- | 0 | 0 |
| South Africa | | 90 | 75 | 67 | 50 | 70 | T[94-] 330 + T[98-] ? | 1.6 | 33 | -- | 33 | 33 |
| Sudan | | 0 | 0 | 12 | -- | 4 | [83-] 2940 + [95-] 1000 + [95-] 200 | 4.8 | 13 | 86 | 49 | 4 |
| Swaziland | | 15 | 30 | 18 | -- | 21 | | -- | -- | 6 | 6 | 6 |
| Tanzania | | 45 | 45 | 41 | 25 | 39 | | 3.7 | 63 | -- | 63 | 39 |
| Togo | | 30 | 30 | 21 | -- | 27 | | 2.4 | 76 | -- | 76 | 27 |
| Tunisia | | 15 | 30 | 21 | 52 | 29 | | 1.8 | 82 | -- | 80* | 29 |
| Uganda | | 30 | 30 | 50 | 23 | 33 | [95-] 200 + [93-] 430 + [97-] 3000 | 3.1 | 14 | -- | 14 | 14 |
| Zambia | | 30 | 45 | 30 | 34 | 35 | T[99-] ? | 1.9 | 40 | 55 | 47 | 35 |
| Zimbabwe | | 15 | 30 | 26 | 30 | 25 | | 5.0 | 55 | 38 | 46 | 25 |
| EUROPE | | | | | | | | | | | | |
| Albania | CPI99 | 45 | 30 | 35 | 23 | 33 | [97] 2000 | 6.6 | 18 | -- | 18 | 18 |
| Austria | | 90 | 90 | 84 | 77 | 85 | | 0.8 | 92 | 71 | 81 | 81 |
| Belarus | | 15 | 15 | 16 | 41 | 22 | | 3.2 | 68 | 66 | 67 | 22 |
| Belgium | | 90 | 75 | 88 | 61 | 78 | | 1.5 | 85 | 74 | 79 | 78 |
| Bosnia & Herzegovina | | 30 | 30 | 35 | -- | 32 | [92-95] 22500 | 8.1 | 0 | -- | 0 | 0 |
| Bulgaria | | 75 | 60 | 60 | 35 | 57 | | 3.7 | 63 | 64 | 63 | 57 |
| Croatia | | 45 | 45 | 30 | 37 | 39 | [91-95] 2000 | 8.3 | 18 | 79 | 48 | 39 |
| Czech R | | 90 | 75 | 73 | 43 | 70 | | 2.1 | 79 | 73 | 76 | 70 |
| Denmark | | 90 | 90 | 88 | 98 | 91 | | 1.6 | 84 | 65 | 74 | 74 |
| Estonia | | 90 | 75 | 73 | 57 | 74 | | 1.3 | 87 | 38 | 62 | 62 |
| Finland | | 90 | 90 | 80 | 100 | 90 | | 1.5 | 85 | 56 | 70 | 70 |
| France | PR: New Caledonia | 75 | 75 | 68 | 67 | 71 | | 2.8 | 72 | 67 | 69 | 69 |
| Germany | | 90 | 75 | 83 | 76 | 81 | | 1.5 | 85 | 65 | 75 | 75 |
| Greece | | 90 | 60 | 60 | 49 | 65 | T[75-] ? | 4.8 | 40 | 86 | 63 | 63 |
| Hungary | | 90 | 75 | 60 | 52 | 69 | | 1.4 | 86 | 76 | 81 | 69 |
| Iceland | | 90 | 90 | 84 | 91 | 89 | | -- | -- | -- | -- | 80* |
| Ireland | | 90 | 90 | 72 | 72 | 81 | | 1.0 | 90 | -- | 80* | 80 |
| Italy | | 90 | 75 | 64 | 46 | 69 | | 2.0 | 80 | 78 | 79 | 69 |
| Latvia | | 90 | 75 | 68 | 34 | 67 | | 2.5 | 75 | 62 | 68 | 67 |
| Lithuania | | 90 | 75 | 73 | 41 | 70 | | 1.3 | 87 | 67 | 77 | 70 |
| Luxembourg | | 90 | 90 | 87 | 86 | 88 | | 0.9 | 91 | 65 | 78 | 78 |
| Macedonia, FYR | CPI99 | 60 | 60 | 48 | 33 | 50 | T[97-] ? | 9.9 | 35 | 89 | 62 | 50 |
| Malta | | 90 | 90 | 77 | -- | 80* | | 0.9 | 91 | 90 | 90 | 80 |
| Moldova | PR;CL: Transdniester | 45 | 30 | 34 | 26 | 34 | [92-97] 170 | 4.3 | 37 | 69 | 53 | 34 |
| Netherlands | PR: Aruba; CL: Netherlands Antilles | 82 | 82 | 81 | 89 | 83 | | 1.8 | 82 | 52 | 67 | 67 |
| Norway | | 90 | 90 | 93 | 91 | 91 | | 2.2 | 78 | 76 | 77 | 77 |
| Poland | | 90 | 75 | 75 | 41 | 70 | | 2.2 | 78 | 77 | 77 | 70 |
| Portugal | | 90 | 90 | 77 | 64 | 80 | | 2.3 | 77 | 65 | 71 | 71 |
| Romania | | 75 | 75 | 46 | 29 | 56 | | 2.3 | 77 | 77 | 77 | 56 |
| Slovakia | | 75 | 75 | 60 | 35 | 61 | | 2.0 | 80 | 82 | 81 | 61 |
| Slovenia | | 90 | 75 | 64 | 55 | 71 | | 1.7 | 83 | 74 | 78 | 71 |
| Spain | | 90 | 75 | 76 | 70 | 78 | T[59-] 20 | 1.3 | 40 | 80 | 60 | 60 |
| Sweden | | 90 | 90 | 85 | 94 | 90 | | 2.5 | 75 | 46 | 60 | 60 |
| Switzerland | | 90 | 90 | 89 | 86 | 89 | | 1.4 | 86 | 85 | 85 | 85 |
| Ukraine | | 60 | 45 | 32 | 15 | 38 | | 2.9 | 71 | 68 | 69 | 38 |
| United Kingdom | PR;CL: Northern Ireland | 75 | 67 | 73 | 87 | 75 | T[69-] 100 | 2.8 | 38 | 67 | 52 | 52 |
| Yugoslavia | PR;CL: Kosovo | 22 | 22 | 15 | 13 | 18 | [98-99] 7500 + [99] 1000 | 9.1 | 3 | 82 | 42 | 18 |

| Country | F&G note | PRR | CLR | PFR | CPI | F&G score | Armed conflicts | Def% GDP | Peace score | Crime score | P&O score | C index |
|---|---|---|---|---|---|---|---|---|---|---|---|---|
| RUSSIAN FEDERATION | PR;CL: Chechnya | 30 | 22 | 32 | 21 | 26 | [94-96] 11670 + [91-96] 170 + T[96-] ? | 5.2 | 0 | 53 | 26 | 26 |
| ASIA | | | | | | | | | | | | |
| Afghanistan | | 0 | 0 | 8 | -- | 3 | [92-] 8250 | 14.5 | 4 | -- | 4 | 3 |
| Armenia | PR;CL: Nagorno-Karabakh; CPI 99 | 37 | 30 | 34 | 25 | 31 | | 8.4 | 39 | 76 | 57 | 31 |
| Azerbaijan | CL: Nagorno-Karabakh | 15 | 30 | 24 | 15 | 21 | | 4.6 | 57 | 80 | 68 | 21 |
| Bahrain | | 0 | 15 | 20 | -- | 12 | | 6.7 | 46 | 63 | 54 | 12 |
| Bangladesh | | 60 | 45 | 32 | -- | 46 | [82-98] 180 | 1.9 | 36 | -- | 36 | 36 |
| Bhutan | | 0 | 15 | 19 | -- | 11 | | 4.5 | 57 | -- | 57 | 11 |
| Brunei Darussalam | | 0 | 30 | 21 | -- | 17 | | 6.9 | 45 | -- | 45 | 17 |
| Cambodia | | 15 | 15 | 31 | -- | 20 | [97-98] 500 | 4.2 | 30 | -- | 30 | 20 |
| China | CL: Tibet | 0 | 7 | 16 | 31 | 13 | T[91-] 110 | 5.3 | 38 | 92 | 65 | 13 |
| Cyprus | ave. Greek & Turk | 67 | 82 | 79 | -- | 76 | | 5.5 | 52 | 87 | 69 | 69 |
| Georgia | PR;CL: Abkhazia | 37 | 37 | 43 | 23 | 35 | [92-94] 2000 + [90-96] 140 | 2.5 | 17 | 73 | 45 | 35 |
| India | PR;CL: Kashmir | 45 | 37 | 48 | 28 | 39 | [89-] 2000 + [84-] 60 + T[89-] 270 + T[96-] ? | 3.0 | 17 | 74 | 45 | 39 |
| Indonesia | PR; CL: West Papua | 30 | 37 | 41 | 17 | 31 | [75-] 8000 + [65-] 860 + [97-] 1330 + T[91-] 220 + T[98-] ? | 2.6 | 0 | 97 | 48 | 31 |
| Iran | | 15 | 15 | 26 | -- | 19 | [79-] 710 + [79-] 620 | 6.5 | 19 | -- | 19 | 19 |
| Iraq | | 0 | 0 | 2 | -- | 1 | [88-] 5000 + [91-] 3440 + T[93-] ? | 7.3 | 3 | -- | 3 | 1 |
| Israel | PR;CL: Israeli-administered territories | 52 | 52 | 60 | 66 | 57 | [78-] 1320 + T[93-] ? | 11.6 | 19 | 68 | 43 | 43 |
| Japan | | 90 | 75 | 75 | 64 | 76 | | 1.0 | 90 | 94 | 92 | 76 |
| Jordan | | 45 | 45 | 34 | 46 | 42 | | 7.7 | 41 | 74 | 57 | 42 |
| Kazakhstan | | 15 | 30 | 26 | 30 | 25 | | 2.2 | 78 | 58 | 68 | 25 |
| Korea, DPR | | 0 | 0 | 0 | -- | 0 | | 14.3 | 24 | -- | 24 | 0 |
| Korea, R | | 75 | 75 | 64 | 40 | 63 | | 3.1 | 69 | 72 | 70 | 63 |
| Kuwait | | 45 | 30 | 42 | -- | 39 | | 12.9 | 28 | 46 | 37 | 37 |
| Kyrgyzstan | CPI99 | 30 | 30 | 31 | 22 | 28 | | 3.6 | 64 | 64 | 64 | 28 |
| Lao PDR | | 0 | 15 | 27 | -- | 14 | | 3.7 | 63 | -- | 63 | 14 |
| Lebanon | | 15 | 30 | 31 | -- | 25 | [78-] 1320 | 3.6 | 19 | -- | 19 | 19 |
| Malaysia | | 30 | 30 | 24 | 48 | 33 | | 3.7 | 63 | 88 | 75 | 33 |
| Maldives | | 15 | 30 | 28 | -- | 24 | | -- | -- | 73 | 73 | 24 |
| Mongolia | CPI99 | 75 | 60 | 61 | 43 | 60 | | 2.1 | 79 | -- | 79 | 60 |
| Myanmar | | 0 | 0 | 0 | -- | 0 | [85-] 600 | 6.8 | 28 | 87 | 57 | 0 |
| Nepal | | 60 | 45 | 33 | -- | 46 | T[97-] 330 | 0.7 | 33 | 94 | 63 | 46 |
| Oman | | 15 | 15 | 23 | -- | 18 | | 13.6 | 26 | -- | 26 | 18 |
| Pakistan | CPI99 | 0 | 30 | 29 | 22 | 20 | [89-] 2000 + [84-] 60 + T[90-] 100 + T[98-] ? | 6.5 | 17 | -- | 17 | 17 |
| Philippines | | 75 | 60 | 60 | 28 | 56 | [68-97] 2500 | 2.3 | 17 | 75 | 46 | 46 |
| Qatar | | 15 | 15 | 30 | -- | 20 | | 12.0 | 30 | 82 | 56 | 20 |
| Saudi Arabia | | 0 | 0 | 8 | -- | 3 | | 15.7 | 21 | -- | 21 | 3 |
| Singapore | | 30 | 30 | 27 | 91 | 44 | | 5.0 | 55 | 89 | 72 | 44 |
| Sri Lanka | | 60 | 45 | 24 | -- | 43 | [83-] 3410 | 6.1 | 15 | 63 | 39 | 39 |
| Syrian Arab R | | 0 | 0 | 22 | -- | 7 | | 7.3 | 43 | 97 | 70 | 7 |
| Tajikistan | | 15 | 15 | 5 | -- | 12 | [92-97] 8500 | 8.3 | 3 | 90 | 46 | 12 |
| Thailand | | 75 | 60 | 60 | 32 | 57 | | 1.5 | 85 | 74 | 79 | 57 |
| Turkey | | 45 | 30 | 34 | 38 | 37 | [84-] 2440 + T[77-] ? | 4.4 | 17 | 89 | 53 | 37 |
| Turkmenistan | | 0 | 0 | 11 | -- | 4 | | 2.8 | 72 | -- | 72 | 4 |
| United Arab Emirates | | 15 | 30 | 19 | -- | 21 | | 6.5 | 47 | -- | 47 | 21 |
| Uzbekistan | | 0 | 15 | 14 | 24 | 13 | T[99-] ? | 5.4 | 40 | -- | 40 | 13 |
| Viet Nam | | 0 | 0 | 20 | 25 | 11 | | 3.4 | 66 | -- | 66 | 11 |
| Yemen | | 30 | 15 | 26 | -- | 24 | T[98-] ? | 6.6 | 40 | -- | 40 | 24 |
| PACIFIC | | | | | | | | | | | | |
| Australia | PR;CL: Christmas I | 75 | 82 | 87 | 83 | 82 | | 1.9 | 81 | 59 | 70 | 70 |
| Fiji | | 75 | 60 | 34 | -- | 56 | | 1.6 | 84 | -- | 80* | 56 |
| New Zealand | CL: Cook Is | 90 | 82 | 89 | 94 | 89 | | 1.5 | 85 | -- | 80* | 80 |
| Papua New Guinea | | 75 | 60 | 63 | -- | 66 | [88-98] 910 | 1.0 | 22 | -- | 22 | 22 |
| Samoa | | 75 | 75 | 56 | -- | 69 | | -- | -- | 76 | 76 | 69 |
| Solomon Is | | 90 | 75 | 76 | -- | 80 | | -- | -- | -- | -- | 80 |
| Tonga | | 30 | 60 | 54 | -- | 48 | | -- | -- | 49 | 49 | 48 |
| Vanuatu | | 90 | 60 | 46 | -- | 65 | | -- | -- | 68 | 68 | 65 |

**Notes**

The community index (**C index**) is the lower of a freedom and governance index (***F&G score***) and a peace and order index (***P&O score***).

The freedom and governance index is the average of four unweighted indicators (column heading in parentheses):

Political rights rating (PRR).

Civil liberties rating (CLR).

Press freedom rating (PFR).

Corruption perceptions index (CPI).

The PFR and CPI overlap with the CLR, which includes press freedom and corruption. However, all four indicators are used because each has its own strengths. The PRR and CLR together cover almost all aspects of human rights and freedoms, but the basis of each rating is not disclosed. The PFR and CPI cover only one aspect each, but the basis of each rating is fully described.

The peace and order index is the average of two unweighted indicators:

Peace (Peace score), represented by deaths from armed conflicts per year or military expenditure as a percentage of Gross Domestic Product, whichever gives the lower score.

Crime (Crime score), represented by the unweighted average of the homicide rate and other violent crimes. Crime data and scores are shown in Table 7.

F&G note = notes on adjustments to the PRR and CLR and on different years for the CPI. Countries with a PR or CL note here have had their PRR or CLR reduced because of a lower rating for a related or disputed territory. The reduced rating is the average of the country's rating and the territory's rating. The territory concerned is indicated after PR, CL or both. For example—PR;CL: Christmas I. Countries with a CPI note here have a CPI for 1997-1999 rather than 1998-2000.

PRR = Freedom House's political rights rating for 1999 (Freedom House 2000a). Freedom House converts raw points to ratings of 1-7. In general, it classifies ratings of 1 or 2 as "free", 3, 4 or 5 as "partly free", and 6 or 7 as "not free". The ratings were converted to the Barometer scale (Table 6a) as follows: 1=90; 2=75; 3=60; 4=45; 5=30; 6=15; 7=0.

CLR = Freedom House's civil liberties rating for 1999 (Freedom House 2000a). Freedom House converts raw points to ratings of 1-7. In general, it classifies ratings of 1 or 2 as "free", 3, 4 or 5 as "partly free", and 6 or 7 as "not free". The ratings were converted to the Barometer scale (Table 6a) as follows: 1=90; 2=75; 3=60; 4=45; 5=30; 6=15; 7=0.

PFR = Freedom House's press freedom rating for 1999 (Freedom House 2000b). Freedom House gives separate ratings for the print and broadcast media, with respect to laws and regulations that influence media content, political pressures and controls on media content, economic influences over media content, and repressive actions (killing journalists, physical violence, censorship, self-censorship, arrests, etc.). The resulting total number of points can range from 0 (complete freedom) to 100 (complete repression). Freedom House classifies 0-30 points as "free", 31-60 points as "partly free", and 61-100 points as "not free". The performance criteria in Table 6a were based on this classification.

CPI = Transparency International's corruption perceptions index. The index is for 1998-2000 and from Transparency International (2000), unless noted CPI99 in the F&G note column, in which case it is for 1997-1999 and from Transparency International (1999). Transparency International used 17 surveys from 10 independent institutions to assess a country's performance for its 1999 CPI (Transparency International 1999), and 16 surveys for its 2000 CPI (Transparency International 2000). At least three surveys were required for a country to be included in the 1999 or 2000 CPI. The CPI reflects perceptions of the degree of corruption as seen by business people, risk analysts and the general public and ranges from 10 (highly clean) to 0 (highly corrupt). The 10 to 0 scale was placed directly onto the Barometer scale (Table 6a).

Armed conflicts = international or internal armed conflict in at least one year in the period 1995-1999. The number in brackets is the year or years. The number outside the brackets is the average number of deaths per year since the conflict started (which may have been before 1995). ? = number of deaths not estimated. T = active terrorism. Data are from International Institute for Strategic Studies (1999b).

Def % GDP = defence expenditure as a percentage of Gross Domestic Product. Defence expenditure = military expenditure = the cash outlays of central or federal government to meet the costs of national armed forces. Armed forces include strategic land, naval, air, command, administration and support forces, and also paramilitary forces such as the *gendarmerie*, customs service and border guard if these are trained in military tactics, equipped as a military force and operate under military authority in the event of war. Costs include operating costs, procurement and construction, and research and development. Data are for 1998 and are from International Institute for Strategic Studies (1999a).

Peace score = the lower of the armed conflicts and military expenditure scores. If more than one armed conflict is recorded for a country, the armed conflicts score is based on the total number of deaths per year. If the number of deaths has not been estimated (that is, if the only entry is ?), it is assumed to be 10. Otherwise, a ? is ignored. For example— Uzbekistan: ? = 10; but Turkey: 2440 + ? = 2440. The performance criteria are shown in Table 6a.

Crime score: see Table 7 for data. The performance criteria are shown in Table 6a.

| band | top point on scale | political rights rating | civil liberties rating | press freedom rating | corruption perceptions index | deaths from armed conflicts per year | military expenditure as % of GDP | homicides per 100,000 population | rapes per 100,000 population | robberies per 100,000 population | assaults per 100,000 population |
|---|---|---|---|---|---|---|---|---|---|---|---|
| good | 100 | 100 | 100 | 0 | 10 | -- | 0 | 0 | 0 | 0 | 0 |
| fair | 80 | 80 | 80 | 15 | 8 | -- | 2 | 5 | 10 | 20 | 40 |
| medium | 60 | 60 | 60 | 30 | 6 | -- | 4 | 10 | 20 | 40 | 80 |
| poor | 40 | 40 | 40 | 50 | 4 | 0 | 8 | 20 | 40 | 80 | 160 |
| bad | 20 | 20 | 20 | 75 | 2 | 1000 | 16 | 40 | 80 | 160 | 320 |
| base | 0 | 0 | 0 | 100 | 0 | 10000 | 32 | 80 | 160 | 320 | 640 |

**Table 6a. Performance criteria for indicators of freedom and governance and peace and order.**

* A score with an asterisk has been reduced in accordance with the insufficient data rule. To prevent high scores resulting merely from lack of data, a good score is allowed only if it is based on all applicable components (data in an indicator, indicators in an index), and a fair score only if it is based on at least half the components. Good and fair scores (100-61) based on fewer than half the applicable components have been reduced to 60. Good scores (100-81) based on more than half but not all the applicable components have been reduced to 80.

## Table 7. Crime

| Country | Year | Homicides (ho) | | | Rapes (ra) | | | Robberies (ro) | | | Assaults (as) | | | OVC score | Crime score |
|---|---|---|---|---|---|---|---|---|---|---|---|---|---|---|---|
| | | number | rate | score | number | rate | score | number | rate | score | number | rate | score | | |
| AMERICAS | | | | | | | | | | | | | | | |
| Antigua & Barbuda | -- | -- | -- | -- | -- | -- | -- | -- | -- | -- | -- | -- | -- | -- | -- |
| Argentina | -- | -- | -- | -- | -- | -- | -- | -- | -- | -- | -- | -- | -- | -- | -- |
| Bahamas | 94asm | 227 | 82.8 | 0 | 215 | 78.5 | 21 | 544 | 198.5 | 15 | 335 | 122.3 | 49 | 28 | 14 |
| Barbados | 90 | 30 | 11.5 | 57 | 71 | 27.3 | 53 | 339 | 130.4 | 27 | 1736 | 667.7 | 0 | 27 | 42 |
| Belize | -- | -- | -- | -- | -- | -- | -- | -- | -- | -- | -- | -- | -- | -- | -- |
| Bolivia | 94 | 1687 | 23.3 | 37 | 2261 | 31.2 | 49 | 11543 | 159.5 | 20 | -- | -- | -- | 34 | 35 |
| Brazil | -- | -- | -- | -- | -- | -- | -- | -- | -- | -- | -- | -- | -- | -- | -- |
| Canada | 98 | 555 | 1.8 | 93 | 25493 | 84.1 | 19 | 28952 | 95.6 | 36 | 223260 | 736.8 | 0 | 18 | 55 |
| Chile | 94 | 626 | 4.5 | 82 | 961 | 6.9 | 86 | 72058 | 514.9 | 0 | 45383 | 324.3 | 20 | 35 | 58 |
| Colombia | 94 | 27130 | 78.6 | 1 | 1930 | 5.6 | 89 | 28486 | 82.5 | 39 | 28748 | 83.3 | 59 | 62 | 31 |
| Costa Rica | 94 | 298 | 9.7 | 61 | 294 | 9.6 | 81 | 16067 | 523.2 | 0 | 2052 | 66.8 | 67 | 49 | 55 |
| Cuba | -- | -- | -- | -- | -- | -- | -- | -- | -- | -- | -- | -- | -- | -- | -- |
| Dominica | -- | -- | -- | -- | -- | -- | -- | -- | -- | -- | -- | -- | -- | -- | -- |
| Dominican R | -- | -- | -- | -- | -- | -- | -- | -- | -- | -- | -- | -- | -- | -- | -- |
| Ecuador | 94 | 2073 | 18.5 | 43 | 935 | 8.3 | 83 | 21814 | 194.4 | 16 | 2958 | 26.4 | 87 | 62 | 52 |
| El Salvador | -- | -- | -- | -- | -- | -- | -- | -- | -- | -- | -- | -- | -- | -- | -- |
| Grenada | -- | -- | -- | -- | -- | -- | -- | -- | -- | -- | -- | -- | -- | -- | -- |
| Guatemala | -- | -- | -- | -- | -- | -- | -- | -- | -- | -- | -- | -- | -- | -- | -- |
| Guyana | -- | -- | -- | -- | -- | -- | -- | -- | -- | -- | -- | -- | -- | -- | -- |
| Haiti | -- | -- | -- | -- | -- | -- | -- | -- | -- | -- | -- | -- | -- | -- | -- |
| Honduras | -- | -- | -- | -- | -- | -- | -- | -- | -- | -- | -- | -- | -- | -- | -- |
| Jamaica | 94 | 743 | 29.8 | 30 | 1070 | 42.9 | 38 | 5461 | 218.8 | 13 | 13855 | 555.1 | 5 | 19 | 24 |
| Mexico | -- | -- | -- | -- | -- | -- | -- | -- | -- | -- | -- | -- | -- | -- | -- |
| Nicaragua | 94 | 1128 | 25.6 | 34 | 1323 | 30.1 | 50 | 13325 | 302.8 | 2 | 8991 | 204.3 | 34 | 29 | 31 |
| Panama | 94 | 323 | 12.5 | 55 | 290 | 11.2 | 78 | 3662 | 141.8 | 25 | 2763 | 107.0 | 53 | 52 | 53 |
| Paraguay | -- | -- | -- | -- | -- | -- | -- | -- | -- | -- | -- | -- | -- | -- | -- |
| Peru | 90 | 1289 | 6.0 | 76 | -- | -- | -- | 54130 | 250.7 | 9 | 5738 | 26.6 | 87 | 48 | 62 |
| St Kitts & Nevis | 90 | 2 | 5.0 | 80 | 19 | 47.5 | 36 | 4 | 10.0 | 90 | 236 | 590.0 | 3 | 43 | 61 |
| St Lucia | -- | -- | -- | -- | -- | -- | -- | -- | -- | -- | -- | -- | -- | -- | -- |
| St Vincent & Grenadines | 94asm | 16 | 14.4 | 51 | 123 | 110.8 | 12 | 44 | 39.6 | 60 | 1163 | 1047.7 | 0 | 24 | 37 |
| Suriname | -- | -- | -- | -- | -- | -- | -- | -- | -- | -- | -- | -- | -- | -- | -- |
| Trinidad & Tobago | 90 | 94 | 7.6 | 70 | 220 | 17.7 | 65 | 3116 | 251.3 | 9 | 18435 | 1486.7 | 0 | 25 | 47 |
| United States | 97 | 18210 | 6.8 | 73 | 96120 | 35.9 | 44 | 497950 | 186.1 | 17 | 1022490 | 382.0 | 16 | 26 | 49 |
| Uruguay | 94hoi | 186 | 5.9 | 76 | -- | -- | -- | 3072 | 97.0 | 36 | 6981 | 220.4 | 32 | 34 | 55 |
| Venezuela | 90 | 2474 | 12.7 | 55 | 2928 | 15.0 | 70 | 38728 | 198.6 | 15 | 29621 | 151.9 | 42 | 42 | 48 |
| AFRICA | | | | | | | | | | | | | | | |
| Algeria | -- | -- | -- | -- | -- | -- | -- | -- | -- | -- | -- | -- | -- | -- | -- |
| Angola | -- | -- | -- | -- | -- | -- | -- | -- | -- | -- | -- | -- | -- | -- | -- |
| Benin | -- | -- | -- | -- | -- | -- | -- | -- | -- | -- | -- | -- | -- | -- | -- |
| Botswana | 90 | 152 | 11.9 | 56 | 614 | 48.0 | 36 | 523 | 40.9 | 60 | 10414 | 813.6 | 0 | 32 | 44 |
| Burkina Faso | -- | -- | -- | -- | -- | -- | -- | -- | -- | -- | -- | -- | -- | -- | -- |
| Burundi | -- | -- | -- | -- | -- | -- | -- | -- | -- | -- | -- | -- | -- | -- | -- |
| Cameroon | -- | -- | -- | -- | -- | -- | -- | -- | -- | -- | -- | -- | -- | -- | -- |
| Cape Verde | -- | -- | -- | -- | -- | -- | -- | -- | -- | -- | -- | -- | -- | -- | -- |
| Central African R | -- | -- | -- | -- | -- | -- | -- | -- | -- | -- | -- | -- | -- | -- | -- |
| Chad | -- | -- | -- | -- | -- | -- | -- | -- | -- | -- | -- | -- | -- | -- | -- |
| Comoros | -- | -- | -- | -- | -- | -- | -- | -- | -- | -- | -- | -- | -- | -- | -- |
| Congo, DR | -- | -- | -- | -- | -- | -- | -- | -- | -- | -- | -- | -- | -- | -- | -- |
| Congo, R | -- | -- | -- | -- | -- | -- | -- | -- | -- | -- | -- | -- | -- | -- | -- |
| Côte d'Ivoire | -- | -- | -- | -- | -- | -- | -- | -- | -- | -- | -- | -- | -- | -- | -- |
| Djibouti | -- | -- | -- | -- | -- | -- | -- | -- | -- | -- | -- | -- | -- | -- | -- |
| Egypt | 94 | 871 | 1.5 | 94 | 9 | 0.0 | 100 | 375 | 0.6 | 99 | 108 | 0.2 | 100 | 100 | 97 |
| Equatorial Guinea | -- | -- | -- | -- | -- | -- | -- | -- | -- | -- | -- | -- | -- | -- | -- |
| Eritrea | -- | -- | -- | -- | -- | -- | -- | -- | -- | -- | -- | -- | -- | -- | -- |
| Ethiopia | 90 | 3601 | 7.6 | 70 | 289 | 0.6 | 99 | 33 | 0.1 | 100 | 2955 | 6.2 | 97 | 99 | 84 |
| Gabon | -- | -- | -- | -- | -- | -- | -- | -- | -- | -- | -- | -- | -- | -- | -- |
| Gambia | -- | -- | -- | -- | -- | -- | -- | -- | -- | -- | -- | -- | -- | -- | -- |
| Ghana | -- | -- | -- | -- | -- | -- | -- | -- | -- | -- | -- | -- | -- | -- | -- |
| Guinea | -- | -- | -- | -- | -- | -- | -- | -- | -- | -- | -- | -- | -- | -- | -- |
| Guinea-Bissau | -- | -- | -- | -- | -- | -- | -- | -- | -- | -- | -- | -- | -- | -- | -- |
| Kenya | -- | -- | -- | -- | -- | -- | -- | -- | -- | -- | -- | -- | -- | -- | -- |
| Lesotho | -- | -- | -- | -- | -- | -- | -- | -- | -- | -- | -- | -- | -- | -- | -- |
| Liberia | -- | -- | -- | -- | -- | -- | -- | -- | -- | -- | -- | -- | -- | -- | -- |
| Libyan Arab J | -- | -- | -- | -- | -- | -- | -- | -- | -- | -- | -- | -- | -- | -- | -- |
| Madagascar | 94 | 63 | 0.4 | 98 | 50 | 0.3 | 99 | 31 | 0.2 | 100 | 1158 | 8.1 | 96 | 98 | 98 |
| Malawi | -- | -- | -- | -- | -- | -- | -- | -- | -- | -- | -- | -- | -- | -- | -- |
| Mali | -- | -- | -- | -- | -- | -- | -- | -- | -- | -- | -- | -- | -- | -- | -- |

| Country | Year | Homicides (ho) | | | Rapes (ra) | | | Robberies (ro) | | | Assaults (as) | | | OVC score | Crime score |
|---|---|---|---|---|---|---|---|---|---|---|---|---|---|---|---|
| | | number | rate | score | number | rate | score | number | rate | score | number | rate | score | | |
| Mauritania | -- | -- | -- | -- | -- | -- | -- | -- | -- | -- | -- | -- | -- | -- | -- |
| Mauritius | 94 | 36 | 3.3 | 87 | 34 | 3.1 | 94 | 767 | 69.5 | 45 | 12862 | 1165.0 | 0 | 46 | 66 |
| Morocco | 94 | 472 | 1.8 | 93 | 932 | 3.5 | 93 | -- | -- | -- | 2396 | 9.0 | 95 | 80* | 86 |
| Mozambique | -- | -- | -- | -- | -- | -- | -- | -- | -- | -- | -- | -- | -- | -- | -- |
| Namibia | -- | -- | -- | -- | -- | -- | -- | -- | -- | -- | -- | -- | -- | -- | -- |
| Niger | -- | -- | -- | -- | -- | -- | -- | -- | -- | -- | -- | -- | -- | -- | -- |
| Nigeria | -- | -- | -- | -- | -- | -- | -- | -- | -- | -- | -- | -- | -- | -- | -- |
| Rwanda | 90 | 926 | 13.2 | 54 | 721 | 10.3 | 79 | 2747 | 39.3 | 61 | 4762 | 68.1 | 66 | 69 | 61 |
| São Tomé & Principe | 94hoi | 178 | 142.4 | 0 | -- | -- | -- | -- | -- | -- | 414 | 331.2 | 19 | 19 | 9 |
| Senegal | -- | -- | -- | -- | -- | -- | -- | -- | -- | -- | -- | -- | -- | -- | -- |
| Seychelles | 90 | 5 | 7.1 | 72 | 32 | 45.7 | 37 | 11 | 15.7 | 84 | 584 | 834.3 | 0 | 40 | 56 |
| Sierra Leone | -- | -- | -- | -- | -- | -- | -- | -- | -- | -- | -- | -- | -- | -- | -- |
| Somalia | -- | -- | -- | -- | -- | -- | -- | -- | -- | -- | -- | -- | -- | -- | -- |
| South Africa | -- | -- | -- | -- | -- | -- | -- | -- | -- | -- | -- | -- | -- | -- | -- |
| Sudan | 94asm | 1002 | 3.5 | 86 | 610 | 2.1 | 96 | 846 | 2.9 | 97 | 17836 | 61.6 | 69 | 87 | 86 |
| Swaziland | 90 | 874 | 118.1 | 0 | 558 | 75.4 | 22 | 1514 | 204.6 | 14 | 9183 | 1240.9 | 0 | 12 | 6 |
| Tanzania | -- | -- | -- | -- | -- | -- | -- | -- | -- | -- | -- | -- | -- | -- | -- |
| Togo | -- | -- | -- | -- | -- | -- | -- | -- | -- | -- | -- | -- | -- | -- | -- |
| Tunisia | -- | -- | -- | -- | -- | -- | -- | -- | -- | -- | -- | -- | -- | -- | -- |
| Uganda | -- | -- | -- | -- | -- | -- | -- | -- | -- | -- | -- | -- | -- | -- | -- |
| Zambia | 94asm | 1456 | 15.8 | 48 | 337 | 3.7 | 93 | 3287 | 35.7 | 64 | 22056 | 239.8 | 30 | 62 | 55 |
| Zimbabwe | 94 | 1779 | 16.0 | 48 | 3091 | 27.7 | 52 | 12378 | 111.0 | 32 | 67598 | 606.3 | 2 | 29 | 38 |
| EUROPE | | | | | | | | | | | | | | | |
| Albania | -- | -- | -- | -- | -- | -- | -- | -- | -- | -- | -- | -- | -- | -- | -- |
| Austria | 94 | 283 | 3.5 | 86 | 553 | 6.9 | 86 | 2442 | 30.4 | 70 | 33667 | 419.2 | 14 | 57 | 71 |
| Belarus | 94 | 1029 | 9.9 | 60 | 672 | 6.5 | 87 | 7013 | 67.7 | 46 | 3221 | 31.1 | 84 | 72 | 66 |
| Belgium | 94 | 343 | 3.4 | 86 | 899 | 8.9 | 82 | 1448 | 14.4 | 86 | 33329 | 330.6 | 19 | 62 | 74 |
| Bosnia & Herzegovina | -- | -- | -- | -- | -- | -- | -- | -- | -- | -- | -- | -- | -- | -- | -- |
| Bulgaria | 94 | 948 | 11.2 | 58 | 903 | 10.7 | 79 | 6597 | 78.1 | 41 | 1079 | 12.8 | 94 | 71 | 64 |
| Croatia | 94 | 367 | 8.1 | 68 | 94 | 2.1 | 96 | 389 | 8.6 | 91 | 1168 | 25.9 | 87 | 91 | 79 |
| Czech R | 90 | -- | -- | -- | 890 | 8.6 | 83 | 3855 | 37.4 | 63 | -- | -- | -- | 73 | 73 |
| Denmark | 94 | 263 | 5.1 | 80 | 481 | 9.2 | 82 | 4880 | 93.8 | 36 | 9881 | 189.8 | 36 | 51 | 65 |
| Estonia | 94 | 385 | 25.7 | 34 | 2981 | 198.9 | 0 | -- | -- | -- | 411 | 27.4 | 86 | 43 | 38 |
| Finland | 94 | 533 | 10.5 | 59 | 387 | 7.6 | 85 | 2122 | 41.6 | 59 | 19836 | 389.3 | 16 | 53 | 56 |
| France | 94hoiasm | 2696 | 4.7 | 81 | 6526 | 11.3 | 77 | 73310 | 127.0 | 28 | 63435 | 109.8 | 53 | 53 | 67 |
| Germany | FRG90 | 2995 | 4.9 | 80 | 5112 | 8.3 | 83 | 35111 | 57.3 | 51 | 213481 | 348.1 | 18 | 51 | 65 |
| Greece | 94 | 298 | 2.9 | 88 | 258 | 2.5 | 95 | 812 | 7.8 | 92 | 7566 | 72.6 | 64 | 84 | 86 |
| Hungary | 94 | 477 | 4.6 | 82 | 828 | 8.1 | 84 | 2570 | 25.0 | 75 | 11077 | 108.0 | 53 | 71 | 76 |
| Iceland | -- | -- | -- | -- | -- | -- | -- | -- | -- | -- | -- | -- | -- | -- | -- |
| Ireland | -- | -- | -- | -- | -- | -- | -- | -- | -- | -- | -- | -- | -- | -- | -- |
| Italy | 94 | 3040 | 5.3 | 79 | 869 | 1.5 | 97 | 29981 | 52.4 | 54 | 20873 | 36.5 | 82 | 78 | 78 |
| Latvia | 94 | 412 | 16.2 | 48 | 129 | 5.1 | 90 | 1142 | 44.8 | 58 | 1059 | 41.6 | 79 | 76 | 62 |
| Lithuania | 94 | 560 | 15.0 | 50 | 165 | 4.4 | 91 | 806 | 21.7 | 78 | 956 | 25.7 | 87 | 85 | 67 |
| Luxembourg | 90 | -- | -- | -- | 28 | 7.4 | 85 | 23 | 6.1 | 94 | 1452 | 382.1 | 16 | 65 | 65 |
| Macedonia, FYR | 94 | 80 | 3.7 | 85 | 38 | 1.8 | 96 | 132 | 6.2 | 94 | 527 | 24.6 | 88 | 93 | 89 |
| Malta | 94 | 11 | 3.0 | 88 | 10 | 2.7 | 95 | 33 | 9.1 | 91 | 83 | 22.8 | 89 | 92 | 90 |
| Moldova | 94 | 414 | 9.5 | 62 | 267 | 6.1 | 88 | 2288 | 52.6 | 54 | 1291 | 29.7 | 85 | 76 | 69 |
| Netherlands | 90 | 2206 | 14.8 | 50 | 1321 | 8.8 | 82 | 11946 | 79.9 | 40 | 22079 | 147.7 | 43 | 55 | 52 |
| Norway | 90 | 128 | 3.0 | 88 | 376 | 8.9 | 82 | 1047 | 24.7 | 75 | 7949 | 187.4 | 37 | 65 | 76 |
| Poland | 90 | -- | -- | -- | 1840 | 4.8 | 90 | 16217 | 42.5 | 59 | 14350 | 37.6 | 81 | 77 | 77 |
| Portugal | 90 | 725 | 7.3 | 71 | 315 | 3.2 | 94 | 4709 | 47.7 | 56 | 26621 | 269.7 | 26 | 59 | 65 |
| Romania | 94 | 1732 | 7.6 | 70 | 1391 | 6.1 | 88 | 4161 | 18.3 | 82 | 6733 | 29.6 | 85 | 85 | 77 |
| Slovakia | 94 | 205 | 3.8 | 85 | 213 | 4.0 | 92 | 1244 | 23.3 | 77 | -- | -- | -- | 80 | 82 |
| Slovenia | 94 | 111 | 5.7 | 77 | 240 | 12.4 | 75 | 294 | 15.1 | 85 | 1816 | 93.5 | 57 | 72 | 74 |
| Spain | 94hoi | 641 | 1.6 | 94 | 1211 | 3.1 | 94 | 55678 | 142.2 | 24 | 12129 | 31.0 | 84 | 67 | 80 |
| Sweden | 94 | 1050 | 12.0 | 56 | 1812 | 20.6 | 59 | 5331 | 60.7 | 50 | 53665 | 611.2 | 2 | 37 | 46 |
| Switzerland | 94hoi | 161 | 2.3 | 91 | 275 | 3.9 | 92 | 1954 | 27.9 | 72 | 3612 | 51.6 | 74 | 79 | 85 |
| Ukraine | 94asm | 5008 | 9.6 | 62 | 1715 | 3.3 | 93 | 32553 | 62.7 | 49 | 17091 | 32.9 | 83 | 75 | 68 |
| United Kingdom | 94 | 1180 | 2.0 | 92 | 5844 | 10.0 | 80 | 66629 | 114.5 | 31 | 219861 | 377.7 | 16 | 42 | 67 |
| Yugoslavia | 90 | 559 | 5.5 | 78 | 364 | 3.6 | 93 | 509 | 5.0 | 95 | 6128 | 60.3 | 70 | 86 | 82 |
| RUSSIAN FEDERATION | 94as90 | 34302 | 23.2 | 37 | 13956 | 9.4 | 81 | 148546 | 100.4 | 35 | 16514 | 11.2 | 94 | 70 | 53 |
| ASIA | | | | | | | | | | | | | | | |
| Afghanistan | -- | -- | -- | -- | -- | -- | -- | -- | -- | -- | -- | -- | -- | -- | -- |
| Armenia | 90 | 238 | 7.1 | 72 | 34 | 1.0 | 98 | 371 | 11.1 | 89 | -- | -- | -- | 80* | 76 |
| Azerbaijan | 94 | 667 | 8.9 | 64 | 77 | 1.0 | 98 | 295 | 3.9 | 96 | 418 | 5.6 | 97 | 97 | 80 |
| Bahrain | 90as89 | 5 | 1.0 | 96 | 18 | 3.7 | 93 | 3372 | 688.2 | 0 | 3050 | 622.4 | 1 | 31 | 63 |
| Bangladesh | -- | -- | -- | -- | -- | -- | -- | -- | -- | -- | -- | -- | -- | -- | -- |
| Bhutan | -- | -- | -- | -- | -- | -- | -- | -- | -- | -- | -- | -- | -- | -- | -- |
| Brunei Darussalam | -- | -- | -- | -- | -- | -- | -- | -- | -- | -- | -- | -- | -- | -- | -- |
| Cambodia | -- | -- | -- | -- | -- | -- | -- | -- | -- | -- | -- | -- | -- | -- | -- |

| Country | Year | Homicides (ho) | | | Rapes (ra) | | | Robberies (ro) | | | Assaults (as) | | | OVC score | Crime score |
|---|---|---|---|---|---|---|---|---|---|---|---|---|---|---|---|
| | | number | rate | score | number | rate | score | number | rate | score | number | rate | score | | |
| China | 90 | 23199 | 2.0 | 92 | 50331 | 4.4 | 91 | 105132 | 9.1 | 91 | 57498 | 5.0 | 97 | 93 | 92 |
| Cyprus | 94 | 12 | 1.6 | 94 | 7 | 1.0 | 98 | 14 | 1.9 | 98 | 976 | 133.0 | 47 | 81 | 87 |
| Georgia | 94 | 788 | 14.4 | 51 | 49 | 0.9 | 98 | 328 | 6.0 | 94 | 573 | 10.5 | 95 | 96 | 73 |
| India | 94 | 72543 | 7.9 | 68 | 13208 | 1.4 | 97 | 23933 | 2.6 | 97 | -- | -- | -- | 80* | 74 |
| Indonesia | 94hoi | 1517 | 0.8 | 97 | 1678 | 0.9 | 98 | 6777 | 3.5 | 96 | 10062 | 5.2 | 97 | 97 | 97 |
| Iran | -- | -- | -- | -- | -- | -- | -- | -- | -- | -- | -- | -- | -- | -- | -- |
| Iraq | -- | -- | -- | -- | -- | -- | -- | -- | -- | -- | -- | -- | -- | -- | -- |
| Israel | 94 | 389 | 7.2 | 71 | 550 | 10.2 | 80 | 450 | 8.4 | 92 | 15351 | 285.2 | 24 | 65 | 68 |
| Japan | 94 | 1746 | 1.4 | 94 | 1616 | 1.3 | 97 | 2684 | 2.2 | 98 | 24032 | 19.3 | 90 | 95 | 94 |
| Jordan | 94 | 298 | 5.7 | 77 | 36 | 0.7 | 99 | 500 | 9.6 | 90 | 14946 | 287.5 | 24 | 71 | 74 |
| Kazakhstan | 94 | 2664 | 15.6 | 49 | 1862 | 10.9 | 78 | 11919 | 70.0 | 45 | 6088 | 35.8 | 82 | 68 | 58 |
| Korea, DPR | -- | -- | -- | -- | -- | -- | -- | -- | -- | -- | -- | -- | -- | -- | -- |
| Korea, R | 94asm | 4514 | 10.2 | 60 | 6173 | 13.9 | 72 | 4580 | 10.3 | 90 | 5495 | 12.4 | 94 | 85 | 72 |
| Kuwait | 94 | 940 | 58.0 | 11 | 9 | 0.6 | 99 | 162 | 10.0 | 90 | 1523 | 94.0 | 56 | 82 | 46 |
| Kyrgyzstan | 94 | 564 | 12.3 | 55 | 400 | 8.7 | 83 | 1987 | 43.2 | 58 | 1790 | 38.9 | 80 | 74 | 64 |
| Lao PDR | -- | -- | -- | -- | -- | -- | -- | -- | -- | -- | -- | -- | -- | -- | -- |
| Lebanon | -- | -- | -- | -- | -- | -- | -- | -- | -- | -- | -- | -- | -- | -- | -- |
| Malaysia | 94hoi | 377 | 1.9 | 92 | 965 | 5.0 | 90 | 6072 | 31.2 | 69 | 2846 | 14.6 | 93 | 84 | 88 |
| Maldives | 90 | 14 | 6.4 | 74 | 2 | 0.9 | 98 | 28 | 12.7 | 87 | 474 | 215.4 | 33 | 73 | 73 |
| Mongolia | -- | -- | -- | -- | -- | -- | -- | -- | -- | -- | -- | -- | -- | -- | -- |
| Myanmar | 90 | 1786 | 4.3 | 83 | 780 | 1.9 | 96 | 384 | 0.9 | 99 | 16244 | 38.9 | 80 | 92 | 87 |
| Nepal | 90 | 484 | 2.5 | 90 | 112 | 0.6 | 99 | 183 | 0.9 | 99 | 1141 | 5.9 | 97 | 98 | 94 |
| Oman | -- | -- | -- | -- | -- | -- | -- | -- | -- | -- | -- | -- | -- | -- | -- |
| Pakistan | -- | -- | -- | -- | -- | -- | -- | -- | -- | -- | -- | -- | -- | -- | -- |
| Philippines | 94asm | 6338 | 9.5 | 62 | 2494 | 3.7 | 93 | 9169 | 13.7 | 86 | 17883 | 26.7 | 87 | 89 | 75 |
| Qatar | 94ro90 | 12 | 2.2 | 91 | 14 | 2.6 | 95 | 315 | 65.6 | 47 | 222 | 41.1 | 79 | 74 | 82 |
| Saudi Arabia | -- | -- | -- | -- | -- | -- | -- | -- | -- | -- | -- | -- | -- | -- | -- |
| Singapore | 94 | 51 | 1.7 | 93 | 81 | 2.8 | 94 | 812 | 27.7 | 72 | 601 | 20.5 | 90 | 85 | 89 |
| Sri Lanka | 90 | 2353 | 13.7 | 53 | 369 | 2.1 | 96 | 5702 | 33.1 | 67 | 15093 | 87.6 | 58 | 74 | 63 |
| Syrian Arab R | 94 | 174 | 1.3 | 95 | 100 | 0.7 | 99 | 18 | 0.1 | 100 | 72 | 0.5 | 100 | 100 | 97 |
| Tajikistan | 90 | 177 | 3.3 | 87 | 123 | 2.3 | 95 | 738 | 13.9 | 86 | 289 | 5.5 | 97 | 93 | 90 |
| Thailand | 90 | 5586 | 10.0 | 60 | 2514 | 4.5 | 91 | 3396 | 6.1 | 94 | 21752 | 39.1 | 80 | 88 | 74 |
| Turkey | 94 | 1794 | 2.9 | 88 | 503 | 0.8 | 98 | 1542 | 2.5 | 97 | 32245 | 52.7 | 74 | 90 | 89 |
| Turkmenistan | -- | -- | -- | -- | -- | -- | -- | -- | -- | -- | -- | -- | -- | -- | -- |
| United Arab Emirates | -- | -- | -- | -- | -- | -- | -- | -- | -- | -- | -- | -- | -- | -- | -- |
| Uzbekistan | -- | -- | -- | -- | -- | -- | -- | -- | -- | -- | -- | -- | -- | -- | -- |
| Viet Nam | -- | -- | -- | -- | -- | -- | -- | -- | -- | -- | -- | -- | -- | -- | -- |
| Yemen | -- | -- | -- | -- | -- | -- | -- | -- | -- | -- | -- | -- | -- | -- | -- |
| PACIFIC | | | | | | | | | | | | | | | |
| Australia | 94asm90 | 875 | 4.9 | 80 | 14027 | 78.2 | 21 | 14370 | 80.1 | 40 | 17963 | 106.4 | 53 | 38 | 59 |
| Fiji | -- | -- | -- | -- | -- | -- | -- | -- | -- | -- | -- | -- | -- | -- | -- |
| New Zealand | -- | -- | -- | -- | -- | -- | -- | -- | -- | -- | -- | -- | -- | -- | -- |
| Papua New Guinea | -- | -- | -- | -- | -- | -- | -- | -- | -- | -- | -- | -- | -- | -- | -- |
| Samoa | 94 | 10 | 6.1 | 76 | 9 | 5.5 | 89 | 2 | 1.2 | 99 | 242 | 147.6 | 43 | 77 | 76 |
| Solomon Is | -- | -- | -- | -- | -- | -- | -- | -- | -- | -- | -- | -- | -- | -- | -- |
| Tonga | 90 | 24 | 24.0 | 36 | 11 | 11.0 | 78 | 3 | 3.0 | 97 | 433 | 433.0 | 13 | 63 | 49 |
| Vanuatu | 90 | 1 | 0.7 | 97 | 30 | 20.0 | 60 | -- | -- | -- | 530 | 353.3 | 18 | 39 | 68 |

**Notes**

The crime score is the average of two unweighted indicators: homicide rate (homicide score); and other violent crimes (OVC score)—the unweighted average of scores for the rape rate, robbery rate, and assault rate. Homicides are distinguished from other violent crimes because they are more serious and are reported less inconsistently. Homicides include intentional homicides (murder) and unintentional homicides (manslaughter, except as a result of traffic accidents). Rape is sexual intercourse without valid consent. Robbery is the use of force or the threat of force to steal property. Assault is physical attack against the body of another person, other than rape or robbery. All data are from United Nations Crime Prevention and Criminal Justice Division (1997 & 1999), except for Canada, which are from Canadian Centre for Justice Statistics (1999), and the United States which are from Federal Bureau of Investigation (1999). Rates are per 100,000 population. Performance criteria for the scores are shown in Table 6a.

Year = the applicable year. A year following the code—as (assaults), ho (homicides), ra (rapes) or ro (robberies)—indicates a different year for that category; asm = major assaults only; hoi = intentional homicides only; FRG = the former Federal Republic of Germany (West Germany).

* A score with an asterisk has been reduced in accordance with the insufficient data rule. To prevent high scores resulting merely from lack of data, a good score is allowed only if it is based on all applicable components (data in an indicator, indicators in an index), and a fair score only if it is based on at least half the components. Good and fair scores (100-61) based on fewer than half the applicable components have been reduced to 60. Good scores (100-81) based on more than half but not all the applicable components have been reduced to 80.

# Table 8. Equity

| Country | HE year | H inc ratio | *HE score* | G inc ratio | G&W score | 1st F%M | 2nd F%M | 3rd F%M | F or M | Ave diff | G&K score | F % govt | F % parl | G&C score | *GE score* | E index |
|---|---|---|---|---|---|---|---|---|---|---|---|---|---|---|---|---|
| **AMERICAS** | | | | | | | | | | | | | | | | |
| Antigua & Barbuda | -- | -- | -- | -- | -- | -- | -- | -- | -- | -- | -- | 26.7 | 5.3 | 11 | 11 | 11 |
| Argentina | #92 | 10.8 | 35 | 3.4 | 36 | 100.0 | 107.7 | -- | =f- | 3.9 | 80* | 5.2 | 28.0 | 56 | 57 | 46 |
| Bahamas | #93 | 13.4 | 29 | 1.5 | 80 | 113.0 | 130.3 | -- | ff= | 21.7 | 38 | 30.3 | 15.0 | 30 | 49 | 39 |
| Barbados | -- | -- | -- | 1.6 | 76 | 94.6 | 94.1 | 137.7 | mmf | 16.3 | 47 | 25.5 | 10.7 | 21 | 48 | 48 |
| Belize | -- | -- | -- | 4.3 | 27 | 100.0 | 97.1 | -- | =m- | 1.5 | 80* | 6.0 | 6.9 | 14 | 40 | 40 |
| Bolivia | 90 | 8.6 | 42 | 2.7 | 46 | 95.0 | 86.5 | -- | mm- | 9.3 | 63 | 7.3 | 11.5 | 23 | 44 | 43 |
| Brazil | 96 | 25.5 | 9 | 2.5 | 50 | 94.4 | 103.4 | 115.9 | mff | 8.3 | 67 | 13.7 | 5.7 | 11 | 43 | 26 |
| Canada | 94 | 5.2 | 59 | 1.6 | 76 | 100.0 | 98.3 | 111.7 | =mf | 4.5 | 82 | 17.7 | 19.9 | 40 | 66 | 62 |
| Chile | 94 | 17.4 | 19 | 3.4 | 36 | 97.5 | 104.8 | 83.6 | mfm | 7.9 | 68 | 10.3 | 10.8 | 22 | 42 | 30 |
| Colombia | 96 | 20.3 | 16 | 2.0 | 60 | 100.0 | 104.7 | 105.3 | =ff | 3.3 | 87 | 20.5 | 11.8 | 24 | 57 | 36 |
| Costa Rica | 96 | 12.9 | 30 | 2.8 | 44 | 101.6 | 103.8 | 81.7 | ffm | 7.9 | 68 | 27.2 | 19.3 | 39 | 50 | 40 |
| Cuba | -- | -- | -- | 2.1 | 58 | 100.0 | 108.0 | 152.1 | =ff | 20.0 | 40 | 9.1 | 27.6 | 55 | 51 | 51 |
| Dominica | -- | -- | -- | -- | -- | -- | -- | -- | -- | -- | -- | 25 | 9.4 | 19 | 19 | 19 |
| Dominican R | 96 | 12.5 | 31 | 2.9 | 42 | 105.1 | 109.3 | 139.9 | fff | 18.1 | 44 | 9.8 | 16.1 | 32 | 39 | 35 |
| Ecuador | 95 | 9.2 | 39 | 4.1 | 29 | 100.0 | 101.4 | -- | =f- | 0.7 | 80* | 3.4 | 17.4 | 35 | 48 | 43 |
| El Salvador | 96 | 16.6 | 21 | 1.9 | 64 | 100.0 | 101.7 | 97.2 | =fm | 1.5 | 94 | 26.8 | 16.7 | 33 | 64 | 42 |
| Grenada | -- | -- | -- | -- | -- | -- | -- | -- | -- | -- | -- | 22.5 | 26.7 | 53 | 53 | 53 |
| Guatemala | -- | -- | -- | 3.3 | 37 | 90.9 | 83.4 | -- | mm- | 12.9 | 54 | 16.7 | 7.1 | 14 | 35 | 35 |
| Guyana | 93 | 7.4 | 48 | 2.7 | 46 | 100.4 | 104.1 | 100.4 | fff | 1.6 | 94 | 14.6 | 18.5 | 37 | 59 | 53 |
| Haiti | -- | -- | -- | 1.8 | 68 | 105.3 | 94.6 | -- | fm- | 5.4 | 78 | 22.2 | 3.6 | 7 | 51 | 51 |
| Honduras | 96 | 17.1 | 20 | 2.9 | 42 | 102.5 | 110.8 | 79.3 | ffm | 11.3 | 57 | 14.1 | 9.4 | 19 | 39 | 29 |
| Jamaica | 96 | 6.3 | 53 | 1.6 | 76 | 100.2 | 106.7 | 72.5 | ffm | 11.5 | 57 | 14.3 | 13.3 | 27 | 53 | 53 |
| Mexico | 95 | 16.2 | 22 | 2.8 | 44 | 100.0 | 93.8 | 89.6 | =mm | 5.5 | 78 | 7.5 | 18.2 | 36 | 53 | 37 |
| Nicaragua | 93 | 13.1 | 30 | 2.4 | 52 | 104.2 | 108.5 | 109.6 | fff | 7.4 | 70 | 17.4 | 9.7 | 19 | 47 | 38 |
| Panama | 97 | 14.7 | 26 | 2.4 | 52 | 100.7 | 101.1 | 149.1 | fff | 17.0 | 46 | 9.4 | 9.7 | 19 | 39 | 32 |
| Paraguay | 95 | 27.1 | 7 | 3.1 | 39 | 101.4 | 96.8 | 106.0 | fmf | 3.5 | 86 | 4.3 | 2.5 | 5 | 43 | 25 |
| Peru | 96 | 11.6 | 33 | 3.1 | 39 | 99.0 | 93.5 | -- | mm- | 3.8 | 80* | 13.2 | 10.8 | 22 | 47 | 40 |
| St Kitts & Nevis | -- | -- | -- | -- | -- | -- | -- | -- | -- | -- | -- | 16.7 | 13.3 | 27 | 27 | 27 |
| St Lucia | 95 | 9.3 | 39 | -- | -- | -- | -- | -- | -- | -- | -- | 5.0 | 11.1 | 22 | 22 | 30 |
| St Vincent & Grenadines | -- | -- | -- | -- | -- | -- | -- | -- | -- | -- | -- | 19.2 | 4.8 | 10 | 10 | 10 |
| Suriname | -- | -- | -- | 2.7 | 46 | 100.0 | -- | -- | =-- | 0.0 | 60* | 11.3 | 15.7 | 31 | 46 | 46 |
| Trinidad & Tobago | 92 | 8.3 | 43 | 2.6 | 48 | 100.0 | 102.1 | 71.9 | =fm | 10.1 | 60 | 13.8 | 11.1 | 22 | 43 | 43 |
| United States | 97 | 8.9 | 40 | 1.6 | 76 | 100.0 | 99.6 | 121.3 | =mf | 7.2 | 71 | 33.1 | 13.3 | 27 | 58 | 49 |
| Uruguay | -- | -- | -- | 2.0 | 60 | 101.1 | 112.1 | -- | ff- | 6.6 | 74 | 13.7 | 12.1 | 24 | 53 | 53 |
| Venezuela | 96 | 14.4 | 26 | 2.5 | 50 | 102.7 | 123.7 | -- | ff- | 13.2 | 54 | 14.5 | 12.1 | 24 | 43 | 34 |
| **AFRICA** | | | | | | | | | | | | | | | | |
| Algeria | 95 | 6.1 | 54 | 3.6 | 34 | 93.3 | 87.9 | 68.2 | mmm | 16.9 | 46 | 4.8 | 3.2 | 6 | 29 | 41 |
| Angola | -- | -- | -- | 1.5 | 80 | 96.6 | 81.6 | -- | mm- | 10.9 | 58 | 4.9 | 15.5 | 31 | 56 | 56 |
| Benin | -- | -- | -- | 1.4 | 84 | 59.4 | 47.8 | 22.7 | mmm | 56.7 | 12 | 14.9 | 6.0 | 12 | 36 | 36 |
| Botswana | -- | -- | -- | 2.3 | 54 | 106.3 | 105.8 | 86.5 | ffm | 8.5 | 66 | 13.5 | 17.0 | 34 | 51 | 51 |
| Burkina Faso | 94 | 10.0 | 37 | 1.4 | 84 | 64.3 | 58.0 | 29.5 | mmm | 49.4 | 15 | 11.5 | 8.1 | 16 | 38 | 37 |
| Burundi | 92 | 5.3 | 58 | 1.4 | 84 | 85.9 | 69.8 | 33.9 | mmm | 36.8 | 23 | 5.4 | 6.0 | 12 | 40 | 49 |
| Cameroon | -- | -- | -- | 2.3 | 54 | 91.9 | 77.3 | -- | mm- | 15.4 | 49 | 4.5 | 5.6 | 11 | 38 | 38 |
| Cape Verde | -- | -- | -- | 2.5 | 50 | 100.0 | 93.9 | -- | =m- | 3.1 | 80* | 11.1 | 11.1 | 22 | 51 | 51 |
| Central African R | 93 | 32.5 | 1 | 1.6 | 76 | 69.0 | 49.6 | 16.2 | mmm | 55.1 | 12 | 4.9 | 7.3 | 15 | 34 | 17 |
| Chad | -- | -- | -- | 1.7 | 72 | 58.1 | 36.5 | 14.4 | mmm | 63.7 | 8 | 4.3 | 2.4 | 5 | 28 | 28 |
| Comoros | -- | -- | -- | 1.9 | 64 | 83.0 | 82.4 | 40.2 | mmm | 31.5 | 28 | 2.7 | -- | -- | 46 | 46 |
| Congo, DR | -- | -- | -- | 1.8 | 68 | 69.8 | 62.6 | -- | mm- | 33.8 | 26 | 3.4 | -- | -- | 47 | 47 |
| Congo, R | -- | -- | -- | 1.8 | 68 | 93.8 | 78.8 | 21.8 | mmm | 35.2 | 25 | 6.5 | 12.0 | 24 | 39 | 39 |
| Côte d'Ivoire | 95 | 6.2 | 54 | 2.7 | 46 | 76.0 | 53.0 | 30.5 | mmm | 46.8 | 17 | 7.1 | 8.0 | 16 | 26 | 40 |
| Djibouti | -- | -- | -- | -- | -- | 75.3 | 66.1 | 76.7 | mmm | 27.3 | 33 | 0.9 | 0.0 | 0 | 16 | 16 |
| Egypt | 95 | 4.0 | 70 | 2.8 | 44 | 90.7 | 87.7 | 63.5 | mmm | 19.4 | 41 | 4.0 | 2.0 | 4 | 30 | 50 |
| Equatorial Guinea | -- | -- | -- | 2.5 | 50 | 102.0 | 90.0 | 14.0 | fmm | 32.7 | 27 | 4.9 | 5.0 | 10 | 29 | 29 |
| Eritrea | -- | -- | -- | 1.9 | 64 | 90.6 | 82.9 | 15.2 | mmm | 37.1 | 23 | 7.8 | 14.7 | 29 | 39 | 39 |
| Ethiopia | 95 | 6.7 | 51 | 2.0 | 60 | 62.1 | 54.7 | 25.4 | mmm | 52.6 | 14 | 8.9 | 2.0 | 4 | 26 | 38 |
| Gabon | -- | -- | -- | 1.7 | 72 | -- | -- | -- | -- | -- | -- | 7.7 | 8.3 | 17 | 44 | 44 |
| Gambia | 92 | 12.0 | 32 | 1.7 | 72 | 79.1 | 60.3 | 55.2 | mmm | 35.1 | 25 | 18.9 | 2.0 | 4 | 34 | 33 |
| Ghana | 97 | 5.0 | 60 | 1.3 | 88 | -- | -- | 26.6 | --m | 73.4 | 3 | 9.6 | 9.0 | 18 | 36 | 48 |
| Guinea | 94 | 7.4 | 48 | 1.5 | 80 | 57.5 | 31.1 | 12.1 | mmm | 66.4 | 7 | 13.0 | 8.8 | 18 | 35 | 41 |
| Guinea-Bissau | 91 | 28.0 | 6 | 2.1 | 58 | 59.0 | 51.3 | -- | mm- | 44.9 | 17 | 11.9 | 7.8 | 16 | 30 | 18 |
| Kenya | 94 | 10.0 | 37 | 1.6 | 76 | 105.0 | 88.6 | 38.5 | fmm | 26.0 | 34 | 5.8 | 3.6 | 7 | 39 | 38 |
| Lesotho | -- | -- | -- | 2.3 | 54 | 117.7 | 122.2 | 115.2 | fff | 18.4 | 43 | 14.6 | 3.8 | 8 | 35 | 35 |
| Liberia | -- | -- | -- | -- | -- | -- | -- | -- | -- | -- | -- | 7.0 | -- | -- | -- | -- |
| Libyan Arab J | -- | -- | -- | 4.3 | 27 | 100.0 | 100.0 | 92.2 | ==m | 2.6 | 90 | 3.4 | -- | -- | 58 | 58 |
| Madagascar | 93 | 10.2 | 37 | 1.7 | 72 | 102.1 | -- | 80.4 | f-m | 10.9 | 58 | 1.8 | 8.0 | 16 | 49 | 43 |
| Malawi | -- | -- | -- | 1.4 | 84 | 102.5 | 59.4 | 42.0 | fmm | 33.7 | 26 | 4.3 | 8.3 | 17 | 42 | 42 |
| Mali | 94 | 12.2 | 32 | 1.6 | 76 | 69.5 | 56.3 | 24.2 | mmm | 50.0 | 15 | 6.2 | 12.2 | 24 | 38 | 35 |

| Country | HE year | H inc ratio | HE score | G inc ratio | G&W score | 1st F%M | 2nd F%M | 3rd F%M | F or M | Ave diff | G&K score | F % govt | F % parl | G&C score | GE score | E index |
|---|---|---|---|---|---|---|---|---|---|---|---|---|---|---|---|---|
| Mauritania | 95 | 7.4 | 48 | 1.8 | 68 | 91.0 | -- | 20.7 | m-m | 44.2 | 18 | 5.4 | 3.8 | 8 | 31 | 39 |
| Mauritius | #91 | 8.4 | 43 | 2.8 | 44 | 100.2 | 105.6 | 100.5 | fff | 2.1 | 92 | 9.8 | 7.6 | 15 | 50 | 46 |
| Morocco | 98-- | 7.2 | 49 | 2.5 | 50 | 78.4 | 73.5 | 69.9 | mmm | 26.1 | 34 | 0.9 | 0.6 | 1 | 28 | 38 |
| Mozambique | 96-97 | 7.2 | 49 | 1.4 | 84 | 76.4 | 61.7 | 31.1 | mmm | 43.6 | 18 | 12.8 | 25.2 | 50 | 51 | 50 |
| Namibia | -- | -- | -- | 2.0 | 60 | 105.7 | 108.4 | 153.7 | fff | 22.6 | 37 | 11.4 | 25.0 | 50 | 49 | 49 |
| Niger | 95 | 20.5 | 16 | 1.7 | 72 | 60.9 | 52.8 | 100.0 | mm= | 28.8 | 31 | 10.9 | 1.2 | 2 | 35 | 25 |
| Nigeria | 96-97 | 12.7 | 31 | 2.3 | 54 | -- | -- | -- | -- | -- | -- | 6.2 | 2.5 | 5 | 29 | 30 |
| Rwanda | -- | -- | -- | 1.5 | 80 | 101.0 | 77.8 | -- | fm- | 11.6 | 57 | 10.7 | 17.1 | 34 | 57 | 57 |
| São Tomé & Principe | -- | -- | -- | -- | -- | -- | -- | -- | -- | -- | -- | 7.7 | 9.1 | 18 | 18 | 18 |
| Senegal | 95 | 7.5 | 47 | 1.9 | 64 | 82.1 | 64.6 | 32.3 | mmm | 40.3 | 20 | 5.6 | 12.1 | 24 | 36 | 41 |
| Seychelles | -- | -- | -- | -- | -- | -- | -- | -- | -- | -- | -- | 20.8 | 23.5 | 47 | 47 | 47 |
| Sierra Leone | -- | -- | -- | 2.4 | 52 | 79.0 | -- | -- | m-- | 21.0 | 39 | 5.9 | 8.8 | 18 | 36 | 36 |
| Somalia | -- | -- | -- | -- | -- | -- | -- | -- | -- | -- | -- | 0.0 | -- | -- | -- | -- |
| South Africa | 93-94 | 22.3 | 13 | 2.3 | 54 | 100.0 | 104.3 | 89.7 | =fm | 4.9 | 80 | 7.0 | 30.0 | 60 | 65 | 39 |
| Sudan | -- | -- | -- | 3.3 | 37 | -- | -- | 86.9 | --m | 13.1 | 54 | 1.7 | -- | -- | 45 | 45 |
| Swaziland | 94 | 23.9 | 11 | 2.4 | 52 | 101.6 | 93.5 | 99.1 | fmm | 3.0 | 88 | 7.5 | 3.1 | 6 | 49 | 30 |
| Tanzania | 93 | 6.7 | 51 | 1.4 | 84 | 101.9 | -- | 23.9 | f-m | 39.0 | 21 | 9.6 | 16.4 | 33 | 46 | 48 |
| Togo | -- | -- | -- | 2.1 | 58 | 74.4 | 52.2 | 20.6 | mmm | 50.9 | 14 | 3.0 | 1.2 | 2 | 25 | 25 |
| Tunisia | 90 | 7.8 | 46 | 2.9 | 42 | 100.0 | 95.0 | 82.1 | =mm | 7.6 | 70 | 7.9 | 11.5 | 23 | 45 | 45 |
| Uganda | 92-93 | 7.0 | 50 | 1.5 | 80 | -- | -- | 49.2 | --mm | 50.8 | 15 | 8.9 | 17.9 | 36 | 44 | 47 |
| Zambia | 96 | 13.0 | 30 | 1.7 | 72 | 98.1 | 70.8 | 39.4 | mmm | 30.6 | 29 | 8.4 | 10.1 | 20 | 40 | 35 |
| Zimbabwe | 90-91 | 15.6 | 23 | 1.7 | 72 | 98.1 | 90.5 | 41.1 | mmm | 23.4 | 37 | 11.6 | 14.0 | 28 | 46 | 34 |
| **EUROPE** | | | | | | | | | | | | | | | | |
| Albania | -- | -- | -- | 1.8 | 68 | 102.1 | -- | 136.7 | f-f | 19.4 | 41 | 11.8 | 5.2 | 10 | 40 | 40 |
| Austria | -- | -- | -- | 2.2 | 56 | 100.0 | 99.5 | 91.3 | =mm | 3.1 | 88 | 6.8 | 26.8 | 54 | 66 | 66 |
| Belarus | 98 | 2.9 | 81 | 1.6 | 76 | 96.9 | -- | 110.3 | m-f | 6.7 | 73 | 6.6 | 4.5 | 9 | 53 | 67 |
| Belgium | 92 | 3.6 | 74 | 1.9 | 64 | 100.0 | 100.0 | 95.6 | ==m | 1.5 | 94 | 6.6 | 23.3 | 47 | 68 | 71 |
| Bosnia & Herzegovina | -- | -- | -- | -- | -- | -- | -- | -- | -- | -- | -- | 2.8 | 28.6 | 57 | 57 | 57 |
| Bulgaria | 95 | 4.4 | 66 | 1.6 | 76 | 102.6 | 94.7 | 151.4 | fmf | 19.8 | 40 | 14.6 | 10.8 | 22 | 46 | 56 |
| Croatia | 98 | 3.9 | 71 | 1.8 | 68 | 100.0 | 101.7 | 96.7 | =fm | 1.7 | 93 | 19.0 | 20.5 | 41 | 67 | 69 |
| Czech R | 96 | 3.5 | 75 | 1.6 | 76 | 100.0 | 100.0 | 89.1 | ==m | 3.6 | 86 | 10.6 | 15.0 | 30 | 64 | 69 |
| Denmark | 92 | 3.6 | 74 | 1.4 | 84 | 100.0 | 101.3 | 114.4 | =ff | 5.2 | 79 | 13.9 | 37.4 | 75 | 79 | 76 |
| Estonia | 95 | 6.7 | 51 | 1.6 | 76 | 100.0 | 102.9 | 101.8 | =ff | 1.6 | 94 | 14.3 | 17.8 | 36 | 69 | 60 |
| Finland | 91 | 3.6 | 74 | 1.5 | 80 | 100.0 | 101.8 | 106.4 | =ff | 2.7 | 89 | 20.4 | 37.0 | 74 | 81 | 77 |
| France | 95 | 5.6 | 57 | 1.6 | 76 | 100.0 | 99.9 | 116.1 | =mf | 5.4 | 78 | 10.8 | 10.9 | 22 | 59 | 58 |
| Germany | 94 | 4.7 | 63 | 1.9 | 64 | 100.0 | 99.3 | 80.2 | =mm | 6.8 | 73 | 6.1 | 30.9 | 62 | 66 | 64 |
| Greece | 93 | 5.4 | 58 | 2.1 | 58 | 100.0 | 103.6 | 89.3 | =fm | 4.8 | 81 | 8.9 | 6.3 | 13 | 51 | 54 |
| Hungary | 96 | 4.5 | 65 | 1.8 | 68 | 98.5 | 102.7 | 104.4 | mff | 2.9 | 88 | 6.9 | 8.3 | 17 | 58 | 61 |
| Iceland | -- | -- | -- | 1.3 | 88 | 100.0 | 101.4 | 142.0 | =ff | 14.5 | 51 | 8.2 | 34.9 | 70 | 70 | 70 |
| Ireland | -- | -- | -- | 2.6 | 48 | 100.0 | 100.0 | 105.2 | ==f | 1.7 | 93 | 11.7 | 12.0 | 24 | 55 | 55 |
| Italy | 95 | 4.2 | 68 | 2.3 | 54 | 100.0 | 102.0 | 110.7 | =ff | 4.2 | 83 | 7.1 | 11.1 | 22 | 53 | 60 |
| Latvia | 98 | 5.3 | 58 | 1.3 | 88 | 100.0 | 99.6 | 124.8 | =mf | 8.4 | 66 | 17.6 | 17.0 | 34 | 63 | 60 |
| Lithuania | 96 | 5.2 | 59 | 1.6 | 76 | -- | -- | 130.4 | --f | 30.4 | 30 | 7.3 | 17.5 | 35 | 47 | 53 |
| Luxembourg | 94 | 3.9 | 71 | 2.6 | 48 | -- | -- | -- | -- | -- | -- | 17.8 | 16.7 | 33 | 40 | 55 |
| Macedonia, FYR | -- | -- | -- | 1.8 | 68 | 97.7 | 102.0 | 119.5 | mff | 7.9 | 68 | 20.0 | 7.5 | 15 | 50 | 50 |
| Malta | -- | -- | -- | 3.7 | 33 | 100.0 | 95.7 | 106.8 | =mf | 3.7 | 85 | 3.0 | 9.2 | 18 | 45 | 45 |
| Moldova | 92 | 6.0 | 55 | 1.5 | 80 | -- | -- | 111.4 | --f | 11.4 | 57 | 4.3 | 8.9 | 18 | 52 | 53 |
| Netherlands | 94 | 5.5 | 57 | 2.0 | 60 | 100.0 | 100.0 | 91.0 | ==m | 3.0 | 88 | 16.7 | 36.0 | 72 | 73 | 65 |
| Norway | 95 | 3.7 | 73 | 1.4 | 84 | 100.0 | 100.8 | 126.1 | =ff | 9.0 | 64 | 24.1 | 36.4 | 73 | 74 | 73 |
| Poland | 96 | 5.3 | 58 | 1.6 | 76 | 99.8 | 104.6 | 123.3 | mff | 9.4 | 62 | 9.8 | 13.0 | 26 | 55 | 56 |
| Portugal | 94-95 | 5.9 | 55 | 1.9 | 64 | 100.0 | 102.9 | 120.6 | =ff | 7.8 | 69 | 17.1 | 18.7 | 37 | 57 | 56 |
| Romania | 94 | 4.2 | 68 | 1.7 | 72 | 100.0 | 101.3 | 108.7 | =ff | 3.3 | 87 | 3.3 | 7.3 | 15 | 58 | 63 |
| Slovakia | 92 | 2.6 | 84 | 1.5 | 80 | -- | -- | 96.1 | --m | 3.9 | 60* | 15.6 | 12.7 | 25 | 55 | 69 |
| Slovenia | 95 | 4.2 | 68 | 1.6 | 76 | 99.0 | -- | 119.5 | m-f | 10.3 | 59 | 16.9 | 7.8 | 16 | 50 | 59 |
| Spain | 90 | 5.4 | 58 | 2.4 | 52 | 100.0 | 102.3 | 107.5 | =ff | 3.3 | 87 | 15.4 | 21.6 | 43 | 61 | 59 |
| Sweden | 92 | 3.6 | 74 | 1.2 | 92 | 100.0 | 100.0 | 123.9 | ==f | 8.0 | 68 | 30.8 | 42.7 | 85 | 82 | 78 |
| Switzerland | 92 | 5.8 | 56 | 2.0 | 60 | 100.0 | 92.4 | 59.0 | =mm | 16.2 | 48 | 7.1 | 23.0 | 46 | 51 | 53 |
| Ukraine | 96 | 4.8 | 62 | 1.8 | 68 | -- | -- | 111.4 | --f | 11.4 | 57 | 1.7 | 7.8 | 16 | 47 | 54 |
| United Kingdom | 91 | 6.5 | 52 | 1.7 | 72 | 100.0 | 103.0 | 103.3 | =ff | 2.1 | 92 | 6.9 | 18.4 | 37 | 67 | 59 |
| Yugoslavia | #90 | 5.3 | 58 | -- | -- | -- | -- | 115.0 | --f | 15.0 | 50 | 7.3 | 5.1 | 10 | 30 | 44 |
| **RUSSIAN FEDERATION** | 98 | 12.2 | 32 | 1.6 | 76 | 100.0 | 107.2 | 111.4 | =ff | 6.2 | 75 | 2.6 | 7.7 | 15 | 55 | 43 |
| **ASIA** | | | | | | | | | | | | | | | | |
| Afghanistan | -- | -- | -- | -- | -- | 49.7 | 45.8 | 47.3 | mmm | 52.4 | 14 | 0.0 | -- | -- | 14 | 14 |
| Armenia | -- | -- | -- | 1.5 | 80 | -- | -- | 121.0 | --f | 21.0 | 39 | 2.1 | 3.1 | 6 | 42 | 42 |
| Azerbaijan | -- | -- | -- | 1.7 | 72 | -- | -- | 94.1 | --m | 5.9 | 60* | 7.1 | 12.0 | 24 | 52 | 52 |
| Bahrain | -- | -- | -- | 4.0 | 30 | 101.2 | 108.2 | 187.4 | fff | 32.3 | 28 | 0.0 | -- | -- | 29 | 29 |
| Bangladesh | 95-96 | 4.9 | 61 | 2.6 | 48 | 86.6 | 57.6 | 19.8 | mmm | 45.3 | 17 | 1.9 | 9.1 | 18 | 28 | 44 |
| Bhutan | -- | -- | -- | 2.0 | 60 | 87.9 | -- | -- | m-- | 12.1 | 56 | 5.3 | 2.0 | 4 | 40 | 40 |
| Brunei Darussalam | -- | -- | -- | 2.2 | 56 | 101.4 | 104.8 | 155.9 | fff | 20.7 | 39 | 2.3 | -- | -- | 47 | 47 |
| Cambodia | 97 | 6.9 | 50 | 1.2 | 92 | 100.0 | 66.3 | 22.5 | =mm | 37.1 | 23 | 2.4 | 8.2 | 16 | 44 | 47 |

| Country | HE year | H inc ratio | *HE* score | G inc ratio | G&W score | 1st F%M | 2nd F%M | 3rd F%M | F or M | Ave diff | G&K score | F % govt | F % parl | G&C score | *GE* score | E index |
|---|---|---|---|---|---|---|---|---|---|---|---|---|---|---|---|---|
| China | 98 | 7.9 | 45 | 1.5 | 80 | 100.0 | 87.5 | 53.6 | =mm | 19.6 | 41 | 4.3 | 21.8 | 44 | 55 | 50 |
| Cyprus | -- | -- | -- | 2.5 | 50 | 100.0 | 103.3 | 125.2 | =ff | 9.5 | 62 | 5.3 | 5.4 | 11 | 41 | 41 |
| Georgia | -- | -- | -- | 1.6 | 76 | 99.1 | 98.6 | 97.8 | mmm | 1.5 | 94 | 3.4 | 7.2 | 14 | 61 | 61 |
| India | 97 | 5.7 | 56 | 2.7 | 46 | 85.5 | 68.0 | 60.9 | mmm | 28.5 | 31 | 5.8 | 9.0 | 18 | 32 | 44 |
| Indonesia | 96 | 5.6 | 57 | 2.0 | 60 | 98.7 | 90.8 | 53.3 | mmm | 19.1 | 42 | 1.9 | 8.0 | 16 | 39 | 48 |
| Iran | -- | -- | -- | 3.8 | 32 | 98.2 | 87.8 | 59.5 | mmm | 18.2 | 44 | 0.4 | 4.9 | 10 | 29 | 29 |
| Iraq | -- | -- | -- | 5.5 | 18 | 87.5 | 65.5 | -- | mm- | 23.5 | 36 | 0.0 | 6.4 | 13 | 22 | 22 |
| Israel | 92 | 6.2 | 54 | 2.0 | 60 | -- | -- | 108.0 | --f | 8.0 | 60* | 10.6 | 11.7 | 23 | 48 | 51 |
| Japan | 93 | 3.4 | 76 | 2.3 | 54 | 100.0 | 100.0 | 75.8 | ==m | 8.1 | 68 | 9.3 | 4.6 | 9 | 44 | 60 |
| Jordan | 97 | 5.8 | 56 | 3.7 | 33 | 100.0 | -- | -- | =-- | 0.0 | 60* | 3.4 | 0.0 | 0 | 31 | 43 |
| Kazakhstan | 96 | 6.3 | 53 | 1.6 | 76 | -- | -- | 118.1 | --f | 18.1 | 44 | 2.1 | 10.4 | 21 | 47 | 50 |
| Korea, DPR | -- | -- | -- | -- | -- | -- | -- | -- | -- | -- | -- | 0.8 | 20.1 | 40 | 40 | 40 |
| Korea, R | 93 | 5.2 | 59 | 2.2 | 56 | 100.0 | 100.0 | 61.2 | ==m | 12.9 | 54 | 1.0 | 3.7 | 7 | 39 | 49 |
| Kuwait | -- | -- | -- | 2.7 | 46 | 96.4 | 100.2 | 169.4 | mff | 24.4 | 36 | 4.9 | 0.0 | 0 | 27 | 27 |
| Kyrgyzstan | 97 | 7.5 | 47 | 1.5 | 80 | 99.7 | 102.5 | 105.6 | mff | 2.8 | 89 | 11.4 | 1.4 | 3 | 57 | 52 |
| Lao PDR | 92 | 4.2 | 68 | 1.5 | 80 | 90.3 | 71.8 | 43.9 | mmm | 31.3 | 29 | 3.7 | 21.2 | 42 | 50 | 59 |
| Lebanon | -- | -- | -- | 3.4 | 36 | 97.0 | -- | 92.2 | m-m | 5.4 | 78 | 0.0 | 2.3 | 5 | 40 | 40 |
| Malaysia | 95 | 12.0 | 32 | 2.6 | 48 | 100.4 | 114.5 | 90.6 | ffm | 8.1 | 68 | 8.1 | 7.3 | 15 | 44 | 38 |
| Maldives | -- | -- | -- | 1.7 | 72 | -- | -- | -- | -- | -- | -- | 13.0 | 6.0 | 12 | 42 | 42 |
| Mongolia | 95 | 5.6 | 57 | 1.5 | 80 | 105.7 | 132.2 | 215.8 | fff | 51.2 | 14 | 1.7 | 7.9 | 16 | 37 | 47 |
| Myanmar | -- | -- | -- | 1.4 | 84 | 98.6 | 95.7 | 155.5 | mmf | 20.4 | 40 | 0.0 | -- | -- | 62 | 62 |
| Nepal | 95-96 | 5.9 | 55 | 1.9 | 64 | 67.1 | 58.2 | 31.6 | mmm | 47.7 | 16 | 0.0 | 5.9 | 12 | 31 | 43 |
| Oman | -- | -- | -- | 6.2 | 14 | 97.2 | 95.6 | 91.3 | mmm | 5.3 | 79 | 3.6 | -- | -- | 46 | 46 |
| Pakistan | 96-97 | 4.3 | 67 | 3.3 | 37 | -- | -- | 58.5 | --m | 41.5 | 19 | 2.6 | -- | -- | 28 | 47 |
| Philippines | 97 | 7.6 | 47 | 1.8 | 68 | 100.0 | 101.8 | 133.2 | =ff | 11.7 | 57 | 22.8 | 12.4 | 25 | 50 | 48 |
| Qatar | -- | -- | -- | 4.3 | 27 | 102.9 | 96.6 | 531.3 | fmf | 145.9 | 0 | 0.0 | -- | -- | 13 | 13 |
| Saudi Arabia | -- | -- | -- | 6.1 | 15 | 93.1 | 82.4 | 109.4 | mmf | 11.3 | 57 | 0.0 | -- | -- | 36 | 36 |
| Singapore | -- | -- | -- | 2.0 | 60 | 98.0 | 97.9 | 80.7 | mmm | 7.8 | 69 | 7.2 | 4.3 | 9 | 46 | 46 |
| Sri Lanka | 95 | 5.3 | 58 | 2.1 | 58 | 100.0 | 108.8 | 69.2 | =fm | 13.2 | 54 | 10.2 | 4.9 | 10 | 41 | 49 |
| Syrian Arab R | -- | -- | -- | 3.7 | 33 | 91.8 | 87.2 | 71.6 | mmm | 16.5 | 47 | 3.9 | 10.4 | 21 | 34 | 34 |
| Tajikistan | -- | -- | -- | 1.7 | 72 | -- | -- | 46.8 | --m | 53.2 | 13 | 3.8 | 2.8 | 6 | 30 | 30 |
| Thailand | 98 | 7.6 | 47 | 1.6 | 76 | 102.6 | 97.1 | 111.1 | fmf | 5.5 | 78 | 2.1 | 5.6 | 11 | 55 | 51 |
| Turkey | 94 | 8.2 | 44 | 1.7 | 72 | 98.2 | 7.2.0 | 55.5 | mmm | 24.9 | 35 | 5.0 | 4.2 | 8 | 38 | 41 |
| Turkmenistan | 98 | 7.8 | 46 | 1.6 | 76 | -- | -- | -- | -- | -- | -- | 2.2 | 26.0 | 52 | 64 | 55 |
| United Arab Emirates | -- | -- | -- | 4.6 | 24 | 98.3 | 105.4 | 608.5 | fmm | 171.9 | 0 | 0.0 | 0.0 | 0 | 8 | 8 |
| Uzbekistan | 93 | 5.5 | 57 | 1.5 | 80 | -- | -- | -- | -- | -- | -- | 1.3 | 6.8 | 14 | 47 | 52 |
| Viet Nam | 98 | 5.6 | 57 | 1.4 | 84 | 100.0 | 97.0 | -- | =m- | 1.5 | 94 | 5.3 | 26.0 | 52 | 77 | 67 |
| Yemen | 92 | 7.6 | 47 | 3.6 | 34 | -- | -- | 14.4 | --m | 85.6 | 0 | 0.0 | 0.7 | 1 | 12 | 29 |
| PACIFIC | | | | | | | | | | | | | | | | |
| Australia | 94 | 7.0 | 50 | 1.5 | 80 | 100.0 | 100.0 | 101.9 | ==f | 0.6 | 98 | 22.6 | 22.4 | 45 | 74 | 62 |
| Fiji | -- | -- | -- | 3.1 | 39 | 100.0 | 100.4 | -- | =f- | 0.2 | 80* | 14.5 | 11.3 | 23 | 47 | 47 |
| New Zealand | 91 | 17.4 | 19 | 1.5 | 80 | 100.0 | 102.3 | 130.2 | =ff | 10.8 | 58 | 26.4 | 29.2 | 58 | 65 | 42 |
| Papua New Guinea | 96 | 12.6 | 31 | 1.7 | 72 | 85.0 | -- | 49.8 | m-m | 32.6 | 27 | 4.3 | 1.8 | 4 | 34 | 32 |
| Samoa | -- | -- | -- | 3.4 | 36 | 101.0 | 114.3 | -- | ff- | 7.7 | 69 | 9.1 | 8.2 | 16 | 40 | 40 |
| Solomon Is | -- | -- | -- | 1.4 | 84 | -- | -- | -- | -- | -- | -- | 0.0 | 2.0 | 4 | 44 | 44 |
| Tonga | -- | -- | -- | -- | -- | -- | -- | -- | -- | -- | -- | -- | 0.0 | 0 | 0 | 0 |
| Vanuatu | -- | -- | -- | -- | -- | 94.5 | 83.6 | -- | mm- | 11.0 | 58 | 0.0 | 0.0 | 0 | 29 | 29 |

**Notes**

The equity index (**E index**) is the unweighted average of a household equity index (***HE score***) and a gender equity index (***GE score***).

The household equity index consists of a single indicator: the ratio of the richest 20%'s income share to the poorest 20%'s. This indicator is used instead of the Gini index because it is easier for the layperson to grasp, and the Gini index does not distinguish between inequality among the rich, inequality among the poor, or inequality between rich and poor.

The gender equity index is the average of three unweighted indicators:

Gender and wealth, represented by the ratio of male income to female income.

Gender and knowledge, represented by the average difference between the male and female school enrollment rates (average of the differences in net primary enrollment rate, net secondary enrollment rate, and tertiary enrollment rate).

Gender and community, represented by the percentage of women in the national parliament.

HE year = the year of the household equity data.

H inc ratio = household income ratio = the ratio of the income share of the richest fifth of the population to that of the poorest fifth. Data are from World Bank (2000a), except where marked # in the HE year column which are from World Bank (1998). Income means either income or consumption expenditure.

***HE score*** = household equity index = household income ratio score. The performance criteria are shown in Table 8a.

G inc ratio = gender income ratio = the ratio of male income to female income. Income is represented by Gross Domestic Product per person in international purchasing power parity dollars. Data are for the latest year available (usually 1998) and are from United Nations Development Programme (2000). The indicator has several drawbacks. First, it ignores the pivotal role of women in maintaining the unpaid economy—for example, in rural Africa where women run households, fetch fuel and water, work in fields and gardens (but men dominate wage earning). Second, even within the context of the wage economy, the indicator does not show whether women have equal access to high paying jobs or are paid the same rate as equally qualified men. Third, the information is derived from data on the ratio of the average female wage to the average male wage and the female and male proportions of the economically active population aged 15 above, using complex manipulation to try to overcome the many data gaps.

G&W score = gender and wealth score. The performance criteria are shown in Table 8a.

1st F%M = the female net primary school enrollment rate as a percentage of the male net primary school enrollment rate. Data are for 1997 (except New Caledonia which are for 1991) and are from UNESCO (1999b).

2nd F%M = the female net secondary school enrollment rate as a percentage of the male net secondary school enrollment rate. Data are for 1997 (except Rwanda and New Caledonia which are for 1991) and are from UNESCO (1999b).

3rd F%M = the female tertiary school enrollment rate as a percentage of the male tertiary school enrollment rate. The rate is defined as the number of students per 100,000 population. Data are for the latest year available (years are shown in Table 5) and are from UNESCO (1999c).

F or M = whether the enrollment rates are equal (=), the female rate is higher (f), or the male rate is higher (m), shown in order of primary, secondary, and tertiary.

Ave diff = the average percentage difference between the female and male enrollment rates.

G&K score = gender and knowledge score, based on the average percentage difference between the female and male school enrollment rates. The performance criteria are shown in Table 8a. The top of good matches the United Nations' target of 0% difference by 2005 (World Summit for Social Development [Copenhagen 1995] and the Fourth World Conference on Women [Beijing 1995] [United Nations Population Division 1997; Office of the UN System Support and Services 1996]).

F % govt = percentage of women in ministerial or subministerial posts in the central or federal government. Data are for 1996 and are from United Nations Division for the Advancement of Women (1996). The indicator is not used here because it is not as representative of a society's attitudes and practices as the percentage of women in parliament, and the data are not as current. It is included in the table for comparison with the parliamentary indicator.

F % parl = percentage of women in the national parliament (lower or single house). Data are for 1999 and are from Inter-Parliamentary Union (2000).

G&C score = gender and community score. The performance criteria are shown in Table 8a.

| band | top point on scale | ratio of richest 20%'s income share to poorest 20%'s | ratio of male income to female income | average % difference between male & female school enrollment rates | % of seats held by women in the national parliament |
|---|---|---|---|---|---|
| good | 100 | 1:1 | 1:1 | 0 | 50 |
| fair | 80 | 3:1 | 1.5:1 | 5 | 40 |
| medium | 60 | 5:1 | 2:1 | 10 | 30 |
| poor | 40 | 9:1 | 3:1 | 20 | 20 |
| bad | 20 | 17:1 | 5:1 | 40 | 10 |
| base | 0 | 33:1 | 9:1 | 80 | 0 |

**Table 8a. Performance criteria for indicators of equity.**

* A score with an asterisk has been reduced in accordance with the insufficient data rule. To prevent high scores resulting merely from lack of data, a good score is allowed only if it is based on all applicable components (data in an indicator, indicators in an index), and a fair score only if it is based on at least half the components. Good and fair scores (100-61) based on fewer than half the applicable components have been reduced to 60. Good scores (100-81) based on more than half but not all the applicable components have been reduced to 80.

# Table 9. Ecosystem Wellbeing Index

| Country | Land | Water | Air | Spp & genes | Res use | EWI + RU | EWI - RU | RU diff | EWI | Foot ha/p | Foot score | Ebal ha/p | Ebal score | EF score | EF diff |
|---|---|---|---|---|---|---|---|---|---|---|---|---|---|---|---|
| AMERICAS | | | | | | | | | | | | | | | |
| Antigua & Barbuda | 55 | 60* | 0 | 47 | 44 | 41 | 40 | 1 | 40 | -- | -- | -- | -- | -- | -- |
| Argentina | 51 | 38 | 47 | 23 | 69 | 46 | 40 | 6 | 40 | 3.8 | 62 | 0.8 | 76 | 62 | 22 |
| Bahamas | 50 | -- | 20 | 27 | 57 | 38 | 32 | 6 | 32 | -- | -- | -- | -- | -- | -- |
| Barbados | 17 | 20 | 43 | 64 | 14 | 32 | 36 | -4 | 32 | -- | -- | -- | -- | -- | -- |
| Belize | 67 | 60* | 76 | 52 | 66 | 64 | 64 | 0 | 64 | -- | -- | -- | -- | -- | -- |
| Bolivia | 52 | 80* | 80* | 39 | 77 | 66 | 63 | 3 | 63 | 1.3 | 87 | 11.8 | 100 | 87 | 24 |
| Brazil | 48 | 23 | 51 | 22 | 74 | 44 | 36 | 8 | 36 | 2.6 | 74 | 8.6 | 100 | 74 | 38 |
| Canada | 73 | 50 | 12 | 41 | 40 | 43 | 44 | -1 | 43 | 7.7 | 23 | 2.4 | 87 | 23 | -20 |
| Chile | 59 | 21 | 23 | 18 | 65 | 37 | 30 | 7 | 30 | 3.4 | 66 | -1.8 | 36 | 36 | 6 |
| Colombia | 57 | 10 | 75 | 27 | 72 | 48 | 42 | 6 | 42 | 1.9 | 81 | 3.5 | 92 | 81 | 39 |
| Costa Rica | 10 | 80* | 40 | 33 | 74 | 47 | 41 | 6 | 41 | 2.8 | 72 | -1.0 | 40 | 40 | -1 |
| Cuba | 38 | 60 | 55 | 29 | 67 | 50 | 45 | 5 | 45 | 2.1 | 79 | -1.3 | 38 | 38 | -7 |
| Dominica | 71 | 60* | 77 | 51 | 70 | 66 | 65 | 1 | 65 | -- | -- | -- | -- | -- | -- |
| Dominican R | 57 | 47 | 55 | 25 | 63 | 49 | 46 | 3 | 46 | 1.4 | 86 | -0.5 | 50 | 50 | 4 |
| Ecuador | 64 | 80* | 47 | 33 | 81 | 61 | 56 | 5 | 56 | 2.3 | 77 | 1.4 | 82 | 77 | 21 |
| El Salvador | 13 | 47 | 74 | 49 | 47 | 46 | 46 | 0 | 46 | 1.5 | 85 | -1.1 | 39 | 39 | -7 |
| Grenada | 40 | 33 | 73 | 53 | 47 | 49 | 50 | -1 | 49 | -- | -- | -- | -- | -- | -- |
| Guatemala | 26 | 80* | 33 | 37 | 68 | 49 | 44 | 5 | 44 | 1.4 | 86 | 0.2 | 64 | 64 | 20 |
| Guyana | 30 | 80* | 72 | 71 | 85 | 68 | 63 | 5 | 63 | -- | -- | -- | -- | -- | -- |
| Haiti | 2 | 80* | 80 | 11 | 52 | 45 | 43 | 2 | 43 | 0.8 | 92 | -0.6 | 48 | 48 | 5 |
| Honduras | 27 | 72 | 35 | 47 | 77 | 52 | 45 | 7 | 45 | 1.4 | 86 | 0.6 | 72 | 72 | 27 |
| Jamaica | 28 | 58 | 45 | 9 | 45 | 37 | 35 | 2 | 35 | 2.7 | 73 | -2.3 | 33 | 33 | -2 |
| Mexico | 43 | 5 | 17 | 20 | 67 | 30 | 21 | 9 | 21 | 2.7 | 73 | -1.4 | 38 | 38 | 17 |
| Nicaragua | 41 | 80* | 18 | 57 | 79 | 55 | 49 | 6 | 49 | 1.3 | 87 | 2.8 | 89 | 87 | 38 |
| Panama | 20 | 77 | 25 | 27 | 75 | 45 | 37 | 8 | 37 | 2.4 | 76 | 1.5 | 82 | 76 | 39 |
| Paraguay | 47 | 33 | 80* | 24 | 80 | 53 | 46 | 7 | 46 | 2.8 | 72 | 2.3 | 86 | 72 | 26 |
| Peru | 38 | 80* | 80* | 51 | 80 | 66 | 62 | 4 | 62 | 1.3 | 87 | 7.7 | 100 | 87 | 25 |
| St Kitts & Nevis | 60 | -- | 40 | 59 | 57 | 54 | 53 | 1 | 53 | -- | -- | -- | -- | -- | -- |
| St Lucia | 46 | -- | 68 | 42 | 49 | 51 | 52 | -1 | 51 | -- | -- | -- | -- | -- | -- |
| St Vincent & Grenadines | 42 | -- | 80* | 43 | 53 | 54 | 55 | -1 | 54 | -- | -- | -- | -- | -- | -- |
| Suriname | 45 | 78 | 45 | 64 | 70 | 60 | 58 | 2 | 58 | -- | -- | -- | -- | -- | -- |
| Trinidad & Tobago | 15 | 60* | 11 | 46 | 29 | 32 | 33 | -1 | 32 | 2.4 | 76 | -2.0 | 35 | 35 | 3 |
| United States | 51 | 46 | 6 | 23 | 35 | 32 | 31 | 1 | 31 | 12.3 | 0 | -8.4 | 3 | 0 | -31 |
| Uruguay | 44 | 64 | 53 | 47 | 66 | 55 | 52 | 3 | 52 | 4.9 | 51 | -0.4 | 52 | 51 | -1 |
| Venezuela | 71 | 56 | 15 | 43 | 57 | 48 | 46 | 2 | 46 | 2.9 | 71 | 2.6 | 88 | 71 | 25 |
| AFRICA | | | | | | | | | | | | | | | |
| Algeria | 31 | 50 | 56 | 41 | 66 | 49 | 44 | 5 | 44 | 1.8 | 82 | -1.5 | 37 | 37 | -7 |
| Angola | 56 | 80* | 80 | 54 | 87 | 71 | 67 | 4 | 67 | 0.8 | 92 | 1.8 | 84 | 84 | 17 |
| Benin | 54 | 80* | 80* | 69 | 73 | 71 | 71 | 0 | 71 | 1.0 | 90 | 0.4 | 68 | 68 | -3 |
| Botswana | 65 | 80* | 70 | 77 | 48 | 68 | 73 | -5 | 68 | 1.7 | 83 | 0.0 | 60 | 60 | -8 |
| Burkina Faso | 31 | 55 | 80* | 65 | 68 | 60 | 58 | 2 | 58 | 0.9 | 91 | -0.2 | 56 | 56 | -2 |
| Burundi | 23 | 80* | 80* | 56 | 71 | 62 | 60 | 2 | 60 | 0.8 | 92 | -0.4 | 52 | 52 | -8 |
| Cameroon | 46 | 80* | 80* | 52 | 77 | 67 | 64 | 3 | 64 | 0.9 | 91 | 3.2 | 91 | 91 | 27 |
| Cape Verde | 10 | 60* | 80 | 40 | 71 | 52 | 47 | 5 | 47 | -- | -- | -- | -- | -- | -- |
| Central African R | 65 | 60* | 80* | 60 | 88 | 71 | 66 | 5 | 66 | 1.1 | 89 | 13.2 | 100 | 89 | 23 |
| Chad | 53 | 60* | 80* | 44 | 79 | 63 | 59 | 4 | 59 | 0.8 | 92 | 0.7 | 74 | 74 | 15 |
| Comoros | 11 | -- | 80* | 40 | 82 | 53 | 44 | 9 | 44 | -- | -- | -- | -- | -- | -- |
| Congo, DR | 62 | 80* | 80 | 37 | 79 | 68 | 65 | 3 | 65 | 0.7 | 93 | 6.2 | 100 | 93 | 28 |
| Congo, R | 56 | 80* | 80* | 74 | 69 | 72 | 72 | 0 | 72 | 1.2 | 88 | 18.7 | 100 | 88 | 16 |
| Côte d'Ivoire | 48 | 31 | 80* | 68 | 74 | 60 | 57 | 3 | 57 | 1.0 | 90 | 0.9 | 78 | 78 | 21 |
| Djibouti | 43 | 60* | 80 | 58 | 66 | 61 | 60 | 1 | 60 | -- | -- | -- | -- | -- | -- |
| Egypt | 54 | 0 | 66 | 54 | 58 | 46 | 43 | 3 | 43 | 1.7 | 83 | -1.3 | 38 | 38 | -5 |
| Equatorial Guinea | 43 | 60* | 80 | 66 | 86 | 67 | 62 | 5 | 62 | -- | -- | -- | -- | -- | -- |
| Eritrea | 42 | 80* | -- | 59 | 81 | 65 | 60 | 5 | 60 | 0.3 | 97 | -0.2 | 56 | 56 | -4 |
| Ethiopia | 46 | 80* | 80* | 51 | 76 | 67 | 64 | 3 | 64 | 0.9 | 91 | -0.3 | 54 | 54 | -10 |
| Gabon | 50 | 80* | 60 | 59 | 64 | 63 | 62 | 1 | 62 | 2.1 | 79 | 31.4 | 100 | 79 | 17 |
| Gambia | 34 | 60* | 80* | 75 | 66 | 63 | 62 | 1 | 62 | 1.0 | 90 | -0.7 | 46 | 46 | -16 |
| Ghana | 40 | 0 | 49 | 65 | 73 | 45 | 38 | 7 | 38 | 1.1 | 89 | -0.1 | 58 | 58 | 20 |
| Guinea | 39 | 80* | 80* | 67 | 83 | 70 | 66 | 4 | 66 | 0.8 | 92 | 0.6 | 72 | 72 | 6 |
| Guinea-Bissau | 31 | 80* | 80 | 74 | 84 | 70 | 66 | 4 | 66 | 0.8 | 92 | 2.0 | 85 | 85 | 19 |
| Kenya | 54 | 36 | 80* | 36 | 66 | 54 | 51 | 3 | 51 | 1.2 | 88 | -0.7 | 46 | 46 | -5 |
| Lesotho | 32 | 80* | 80 | 61 | 33 | 57 | 63 | -6 | 57 | 0.7 | 93 | -0.3 | 54 | 54 | -3 |
| Liberia | 39 | 80* | 80 | 60 | 79 | 68 | 65 | 3 | 65 | 1.2 | 88 | 3.8 | 94 | 88 | 23 |
| Libyan Arab J | 22 | 0 | 16 | 60 | 53 | 30 | 24 | 6 | 24 | 4.4 | 56 | -4.4 | 23 | 23 | -1 |
| Madagascar | 37 | 80* | 80* | 4 | 85 | 57 | 50 | 7 | 50 | 0.9 | 91 | 1.9 | 84 | 84 | 34 |
| Malawi | 47 | 70 | 80* | 51 | 81 | 66 | 62 | 4 | 62 | 0.9 | 91 | -0.2 | 56 | 56 | -6 |

| Country | Land | Water | Air | Spp & genes | Res use | EWI + RU | EWI - RU | RU diff | EWI | Foot ha/p | Foot score | Ebal ha/p | Ebal score | EF score | EF diff |
|---|---|---|---|---|---|---|---|---|---|---|---|---|---|---|---|
| Mali | 32 | 10 | 80* | 56 | 81 | 52 | 44 | 8 | 44 | 0.9 | 91 | 0.3 | 66 | 66 | 22 |
| Mauritania | 22 | 0 | 80* | 59 | 71 | 46 | 40 | 6 | 40 | 1.2 | 88 | -0.8 | 44 | 44 | 4 |
| Mauritius | 41 | 67 | 68 | 13 | 33 | 44 | 47 | -3 | 44 | 2.5 | 75 | -0.5 | 50 | 50 | 6 |
| Morocco | 28 | 4 | 61 | 37 | 76 | 41 | 32 | 9 | 32 | 1.6 | 84 | -0.8 | 44 | 44 | 12 |
| Mozambique | 50 | 59 | 80* | 31 | 82 | 60 | 55 | 5 | 55 | 0.8 | 92 | 0.3 | 66 | 66 | 11 |
| Namibia | 68 | 18 | 80 | 52 | 59 | 55 | 54 | 1 | 54 | 0.7 | 93 | 1.1 | 80 | 80 | 26 |
| Niger | 21 | 71 | 80* | 53 | 61 | 57 | 56 | 1 | 56 | 1.0 | 90 | -0.7 | 46 | 46 | -10 |
| Nigeria | 36 | 78 | 59 | 53 | 65 | 58 | 56 | 2 | 56 | 1.3 | 87 | -0.6 | 48 | 48 | -8 |
| Rwanda | 24 | 76 | 80 | 49 | 61 | 58 | 57 | 1 | 57 | 0.9 | 91 | -0.6 | 48 | 48 | -9 |
| São Tomé & Principe | 29 | 60* | 80 | 44 | 54 | 53 | 53 | 0 | 53 | -- | -- | -- | -- | -- | -- |
| Senegal | 46 | 31 | 80* | 60 | 75 | 58 | 54 | 4 | 54 | 1.1 | 89 | -0.3 | 54 | 54 | 0 |
| Seychelles | 59 | -- | 64 | 25 | 64 | 53 | 49 | 4 | 49 | -- | -- | -- | -- | -- | -- |
| Sierra Leone | 27 | 80* | 80 | 67 | 76 | 66 | 63 | 3 | 63 | 0.7 | 93 | 0.6 | 72 | 72 | 9 |
| Somalia | 41 | 73 | 80 | 54 | 67 | 63 | 62 | 1 | 62 | 1.0 | 90 | -0.4 | 52 | 52 | -10 |
| South Africa | 33 | 18 | 32 | 27 | 50 | 32 | 27 | 5 | 27 | 4.0 | 60 | -3.2 | 29 | 29 | 2 |
| Sudan | 50 | 0 | 80* | 55 | 84 | 54 | 46 | 8 | 46 | 1.1 | 89 | 0.5 | 70 | 70 | 24 |
| Swaziland | 40 | 57 | 80* | 45 | 49 | 54 | 55 | -1 | 54 | -- | -- | -- | -- | -- | -- |
| Tanzania | 60 | 60 | 80* | 16 | 84 | 60 | 54 | 6 | 54 | 1.0 | 90 | 0.2 | 64 | 64 | 10 |
| Togo | 38 | 75 | 80* | 73 | 72 | 68 | 66 | 2 | 66 | 0.8 | 92 | -0.1 | 58 | 58 | -8 |
| Tunisia | 27 | 25 | 39 | 37 | 65 | 39 | 32 | 7 | 32 | 2.3 | 77 | -1.4 | 38 | 38 | 6 |
| Uganda | 41 | 19 | 80* | 35 | 80 | 51 | 44 | 7 | 44 | 0.9 | 91 | 0.0 | 60 | 60 | 16 |
| Zambia | 52 | 0 | 80* | 39 | 71 | 48 | 43 | 5 | 43 | 1.2 | 88 | 2.9 | 89 | 88 | 45 |
| Zimbabwe | 56 | 75 | 42 | 47 | 75 | 59 | 55 | 4 | 55 | 1.5 | 85 | -1.0 | 40 | 40 | -15 |
| EUROPE | | | | | | | | | | | | | | | |
| Albania | 17 | 37 | 80 | 52 | 72 | 52 | 46 | 6 | 46 | 1.9 | 81 | -0.7 | 46 | 46 | 0 |
| Austria | 57 | 23 | 34 | 55 | 41 | 42 | 42 | 0 | 42 | 5.4 | 46 | -2.0 | 35 | 35 | -7 |
| Belarus | 33 | 80* | 40 | 49 | 62 | 53 | 50 | 3 | 50 | 5.3 | 47 | -2.5 | 32 | 32 | -18 |
| Belgium | 30 | 5 | 25 | 48 | 9 | 23 | 27 | -4 | 23 | 6.1 | 39 | -4.6 | 22 | 22 | -1 |
| Bosnia & Herzegovina | 21 | 60* | 73 | 31 | 42 | 45 | 46 | -1 | 45 | 1.3 | 87 | -0.1 | 58 | 58 | 13 |
| Bulgaria | 29 | 29 | 28 | 37 | 52 | 35 | 31 | 4 | 31 | 3.8 | 62 | -2.3 | 33 | 33 | 2 |
| Croatia | 24 | 13 | 51 | 44 | 60 | 38 | 33 | 5 | 33 | 2.4 | 76 | -0.5 | 50 | 50 | 17 |
| Czech R | 49 | 17 | 20 | 50 | 29 | 33 | 34 | -1 | 33 | 6.3 | 37 | -4.2 | 24 | 24 | -9 |
| Denmark | 29 | 22 | 23 | 50 | 37 | 32 | 31 | 1 | 31 | 10.5 | 0 | -6.3 | 13 | 0 | -31 |
| Estonia | 40 | 19 | 18 | 61 | 43 | 36 | 34 | 2 | 34 | 7.1 | 29 | -4.1 | 24 | 24 | -10 |
| Finland | 52 | 45 | 23 | 63 | 38 | 44 | 46 | -2 | 44 | 8.4 | 16 | 0.2 | 64 | 16 | -28 |
| France | 35 | 12 | 29 | 40 | 41 | 31 | 29 | 2 | 29 | 7.3 | 27 | -4.0 | 25 | 25 | -4 |
| Germany | 54 | 17 | 25 | 55 | 31 | 36 | 38 | -2 | 36 | 6.3 | 37 | -4.6 | 22 | 22 | -14 |
| Greece | 23 | 43 | 34 | 33 | 46 | 36 | 33 | 3 | 33 | 5.5 | 45 | -4.0 | 25 | 25 | -8 |
| Hungary | 31 | 18 | 41 | 43 | 48 | 36 | 33 | 3 | 33 | 5.1 | 49 | -2.7 | 31 | 31 | -2 |
| Iceland | 31 | 80* | 34 | 45 | 27 | 43 | 47 | -4 | 43 | 5.6 | 44 | 1.5 | 82 | 44 | 1 |
| Ireland | 30 | 23 | 26 | 51 | 53 | 37 | 32 | 5 | 32 | 9.5 | 5 | -4.1 | 24 | 5 | -27 |
| Italy | 27 | 22 | 27 | 45 | 39 | 32 | 30 | 2 | 30 | 5.5 | 45 | -4.3 | 23 | 23 | -7 |
| Latvia | 38 | 27 | 57 | 62 | 56 | 48 | 46 | 2 | 46 | 3.7 | 63 | -0.2 | 56 | 56 | 10 |
| Lithuania | 32 | 35 | 52 | 59 | 53 | 46 | 44 | 2 | 44 | 4.8 | 52 | -1.7 | 36 | 36 | -8 |
| Luxembourg | 31 | 14 | 8 | 54 | 15 | 24 | 27 | -3 | 24 | 6.1 | 39 | -4.6 | 22 | 22 | -2 |
| Macedonia, FYR | 34 | 60* | 43 | 33 | 50 | 44 | 42 | 2 | 42 | 3.2 | 68 | -2.5 | 32 | 32 | -10 |
| Malta | 15 | 0 | 2 | 48 | 3 | 14 | 16 | -2 | 14 | -- | -- | -- | -- | -- | -- |
| Moldova | 14 | 0 | 68 | 59 | 72 | 43 | 35 | 8 | 35 | 2.5 | 75 | -1.1 | 39 | 39 | 4 |
| Netherlands | 34 | 18 | 0 | 45 | 11 | 22 | 24 | -2 | 22 | 6.0 | 40 | -4.4 | 23 | 23 | 1 |
| Norway | 55 | 54 | 14 | 49 | 43 | 43 | 43 | 0 | 43 | 6.1 | 39 | -0.8 | 44 | 39 | -4 |
| Poland | 30 | 4 | 29 | 57 | 52 | 34 | 30 | 4 | 30 | 5.4 | 46 | -3.8 | 26 | 26 | -4 |
| Portugal | 26 | 21 | 46 | 31 | 51 | 35 | 31 | 4 | 31 | 5.0 | 50 | -3.4 | 28 | 28 | -3 |
| Romania | 30 | 12 | 36 | 43 | 56 | 35 | 30 | 5 | 30 | 3.5 | 65 | -1.6 | 37 | 37 | 7 |
| Slovakia | 46 | 18 | 37 | 60 | 59 | 44 | 40 | 4 | 40 | 3.9 | 61 | -2.5 | 32 | 32 | -8 |
| Slovenia | 32 | 33 | 34 | 40 | 46 | 37 | 35 | 2 | 35 | 5.4 | 46 | -3.5 | 27 | 27 | -8 |
| Spain | 31 | 14 | 23 | 14 | 53 | 27 | 20 | 7 | 20 | 5.5 | 45 | -3.7 | 26 | 26 | 6 |
| Sweden | 50 | 51 | 43 | 55 | 46 | 49 | 50 | -1 | 49 | 7.5 | 25 | -0.5 | 50 | 25 | -24 |
| Switzerland | 45 | 32 | 42 | 62 | 32 | 43 | 45 | -2 | 43 | 6.6 | 34 | -5.2 | 19 | 19 | -24 |
| Ukraine | 14 | 20 | 35 | 35 | 53 | 31 | 26 | 5 | 26 | 4.8 | 52 | -3.1 | 29 | 29 | 3 |
| United Kingdom | 38 | 21 | 30 | 41 | 20 | 30 | 32 | -2 | 30 | 6.3 | 37 | -5.3 | 18 | 18 | -12 |
| Yugoslavia | 25 | 60* | 38 | 27 | 61 | 42 | 37 | 5 | 37 | 3.9 | 61 | -2.4 | 33 | 33 | -4 |
| RUSSIAN FEDERATION | 58 | 48 | 27 | 37 | 54 | 45 | 42 | 3 | 42 | 5.4 | 46 | -2.0 | 35 | 35 | -7 |
| ASIA | | | | | | | | | | | | | | | |
| Afghanistan | 27 | 42 | 80 | 45 | 72 | 53 | 48 | 5 | 48 | 0.6 | 94 | -0.3 | 54 | 54 | 6 |
| Armenia | 49 | 52 | 80 | 38 | 75 | 59 | 55 | 4 | 55 | 1.2 | 88 | -0.6 | 48 | 48 | -7 |
| Azerbaijan | 35 | 0 | 51 | 27 | 57 | 34 | 28 | 6 | 28 | 2.2 | 78 | -1.8 | 36 | 36 | 8 |
| Bahrain | 23 | 0 | 0 | 56 | 8 | 17 | 20 | -3 | 17 | -- | -- | -- | -- | -- | -- |
| Bangladesh | 9 | 50 | 80* | 45 | 51 | 47 | 46 | 1 | 46 | 0.6 | 94 | -0.6 | 48 | 48 | 2 |
| Bhutan | 70 | 80* | 80 | 37 | 77 | 69 | 67 | 2 | 67 | 0.8 | 92 | 1.7 | 83 | 83 | 16 |

| Country | Land | Water | Air | Spp & genes | Res use | EWI + RU | EWI - RU | RU diff | EWI | Foot ha/p | Foot score | Ebal ha/p | Ebal score | EF score | EF diff |
|---|---|---|---|---|---|---|---|---|---|---|---|---|---|---|---|
| Brunei Darussalam | 35 | 80* | 10 | 59 | 28 | 42 | 46 | -4 | 42 | -- | -- | -- | -- | -- | -- |
| Cambodia | 36 | 80* | 80 | 31 | 80 | 61 | 57 | 4 | 57 | 0.8 | 92 | 2.2 | 86 | 86 | 29 |
| China | 37 | 23 | 22 | 31 | 64 | 35 | 28 | 7 | 28 | 1.8 | 82 | -1.2 | 39 | 39 | 11 |
| Cyprus | 45 | 47 | 13 | 51 | 36 | 38 | 39 | -1 | 38 | -- | -- | -- | -- | -- | -- |
| Georgia | 36 | 19 | 80* | 31 | 71 | 47 | 41 | 6 | 41 | 1.1 | 89 | -0.1 | 58 | 58 | 17 |
| India | 24 | 21 | 25 | 40 | 59 | 34 | 27 | 7 | 27 | 1.1 | 89 | -0.5 | 50 | 50 | 23 |
| Indonesia | 61 | 2 | 80* | 50 | 72 | 53 | 48 | 5 | 48 | 1.5 | 85 | 1.5 | 82 | 82 | 34 |
| Iran | 33 | 23 | 33 | 40 | 53 | 36 | 32 | 4 | 32 | 2.5 | 75 | -2.0 | 35 | 35 | 3 |
| Iraq | 18 | 13 | 51 | 41 | 58 | 36 | 31 | 5 | 31 | 1.7 | 83 | -1.6 | 37 | 37 | 6 |
| Israel | 37 | 18 | 0 | 54 | 18 | 25 | 27 | -2 | 25 | 5.4 | 46 | -5.4 | 18 | 18 | -7 |
| Japan | 34 | 27 | 29 | 11 | 27 | 26 | 25 | 1 | 25 | 5.9 | 41 | -5.8 | 16 | 16 | -9 |
| Jordan | 29 | 5 | 20 | 58 | 56 | 34 | 28 | 6 | 28 | 1.7 | 83 | -1.7 | 36 | 36 | 8 |
| Kazakhstan | 38 | 9 | 34 | 47 | 62 | 38 | 32 | 6 | 32 | 4.4 | 56 | -3.0 | 30 | 30 | -2 |
| Korea, DPR | 37 | 59 | 23 | 65 | 41 | 45 | 46 | -1 | 45 | 1.9 | 81 | -1.5 | 37 | 37 | -8 |
| Korea, R | 33 | 27 | 7 | 43 | 27 | 27 | 27 | 0 | 27 | 5.6 | 44 | -5.6 | 17 | 17 | -10 |
| Kuwait | 44 | 0 | 0 | 70 | 11 | 25 | 28 | -3 | 25 | 10.3 | 0 | -11.1 | 0 | 0 | -25 |
| Kyrgyzstan | 36 | 0 | 80 | 54 | 83 | 51 | 42 | 9 | 42 | 1.9 | 81 | -0.6 | 48 | 48 | 6 |
| Lao PDR | 46 | 80* | 80* | 45 | 88 | 68 | 63 | 5 | 63 | 0.9 | 91 | 6.3 | 100 | 91 | 28 |
| Lebanon | 17 | 55 | 22 | 57 | 33 | 37 | 38 | -1 | 37 | 3.2 | 68 | -2.9 | 30 | 30 | -7 |
| Malaysia | 47 | 0 | 35 | 50 | 59 | 38 | 33 | 5 | 33 | 3.7 | 63 | -0.2 | 56 | 56 | 23 |
| Maldives | 27 | 60* | 80* | 20 | 48 | 47 | 47 | 0 | 47 | -- | -- | -- | -- | -- | -- |
| Mongolia | 58 | 80* | 59 | 44 | 68 | 62 | 60 | 2 | 60 | 4.3 | 57 | 0.8 | 76 | 57 | -3 |
| Myanmar | 28 | 36 | 80* | 52 | 82 | 56 | 49 | 7 | 49 | 1.1 | 89 | 1.5 | 82 | 82 | 33 |
| Nepal | 50 | 71 | 80* | 56 | 75 | 66 | 64 | 2 | 64 | 1.0 | 90 | -0.2 | 56 | 56 | -8 |
| Oman | 25 | 15 | 20 | 52 | 40 | 30 | 28 | 2 | 28 | 3.4 | 66 | -3.1 | 29 | 29 | 1 |
| Pakistan | 26 | 13 | 80* | 57 | 59 | 47 | 44 | 3 | 44 | 1.1 | 89 | -0.6 | 48 | 48 | 4 |
| Philippines | 29 | 29 | 39 | 30 | 66 | 39 | 32 | 7 | 32 | 1.4 | 86 | -0.7 | 46 | 46 | 14 |
| Qatar | 37 | 0 | 0 | 66 | 19 | 24 | 26 | -2 | 24 | -- | -- | -- | -- | -- | -- |
| Saudi Arabia | 30 | 0 | 17 | 46 | 23 | 23 | 23 | 0 | 23 | 6.1 | 39 | -6.6 | 12 | 12 | -11 |
| Singapore | 32 | 52 | 0 | 71 | 7 | 32 | 39 | -7 | 32 | 12.3 | 0 | -13.8 | 0 | 0 | -32 |
| Sri Lanka | 43 | 61 | 80* | 43 | 63 | 58 | 57 | 1 | 57 | 1.0 | 90 | -0.6 | 48 | 48 | -9 |
| Syrian Arab R | 18 | 0 | 22 | 62 | 63 | 33 | 25 | 8 | 25 | 2.6 | 74 | -1.8 | 36 | 36 | 11 |
| Tajikistan | 40 | 0 | 80 | 36 | 76 | 46 | 39 | 7 | 39 | 0.9 | 91 | -0.6 | 48 | 48 | 9 |
| Thailand | 18 | 2 | 39 | 33 | 60 | 30 | 23 | 7 | 23 | 2.7 | 73 | -1.7 | 36 | 36 | 13 |
| Turkey | 22 | 0 | 51 | 39 | 71 | 37 | 28 | 9 | 28 | 2.7 | 73 | -1.6 | 37 | 37 | 9 |
| Turkmenistan | 43 | 0 | 35 | 44 | 51 | 35 | 30 | 5 | 30 | 3.6 | 64 | -3.1 | 29 | 29 | -1 |
| United Arab Emirates | 26 | 0 | 0 | 42 | 14 | 16 | 17 | -1 | 16 | 16.0 | 0 | -17.5 | 0 | 0 | -16 |
| Uzbekistan | 33 | 0 | 50 | 36 | 60 | 36 | 30 | 6 | 30 | 2.7 | 73 | -2.1 | 34 | 34 | 4 |
| Viet Nam | 28 | 37 | 80* | 50 | 72 | 53 | 49 | 4 | 49 | 1.0 | 90 | -0.4 | 52 | 52 | 3 |
| Yemen | 41 | 31 | 80 | 53 | 65 | 54 | 51 | 3 | 51 | 0.7 | 93 | -0.5 | 50 | 50 | -1 |
| PACIFIC | | | | | | | | | | | | | | | |
| Australia | 55 | 21 | 11 | 25 | 42 | 31 | 28 | 3 | 28 | 8.5 | 15 | -0.2 | 56 | 15 | -13 |
| Fiji | 36 | 45 | 80* | 25 | 72 | 52 | 46 | 6 | 46 | -- | -- | -- | -- | -- | -- |
| New Zealand | 59 | 39 | 32 | 23 | 50 | 41 | 38 | 3 | 38 | 9.6 | 4 | 5.0 | 100 | 4 | -34 |
| Papua New Guinea | 53 | 43 | 80* | 35 | 69 | 56 | 53 | 3 | 53 | 1.4 | 86 | 30.0 | 100 | 86 | 33 |
| Samoa | 30 | 60* | 77 | 32 | 67 | 53 | 50 | 3 | 50 | -- | -- | -- | -- | -- | -- |
| Solomon Is | 40 | 80* | 80* | 43 | 76 | 64 | 61 | 3 | 61 | -- | -- | -- | -- | -- | -- |
| Tonga | 9 | -- | 80 | 0 | 59 | 37 | 30 | 7 | 30 | -- | -- | -- | -- | -- | -- |
| Vanuatu | 34 | -- | 80 | 36 | 80 | 57 | 50 | 7 | 50 | -- | -- | -- | -- | -- | -- |

**Notes**

The Ecosystem Wellbeing Index (**EWI**) is the lower of the EWI including resource use (EWI + RU) and the EWI excluding resource use (EWI - RU). The former is the unweighted average of indices of land, water, air, species and genes, and resource use. The latter is the unweighted average of indices of land, water, air, and species and genes. Taking the lower version of the EWI prevents resource use (a set of indicators of human pressure on the ecosystem) from offsetting poor performance in the other ecosystem dimensions (primarily sets of indicators of the state of the ecosystem).

Land = land index (Table 10).

Water = water (inland waters) index (Table 14).

Air = air index (Table 17).

Spp & genes = species and genes index (Table 19).

Res use = resource use index (Table 22).

EWI + RU = EWI including resource use.

EWI - RU = EWI excluding resource use.

RU diff = resource use difference = difference in points between the EWI excluding resource use and the EWI including resource use (minus means that inclusion of resource use lowers the EWI).

Foot ha/p = ecological footprint in hectares per person. Data are for 1996 and are from Wackernagel *et al.* (2000). The footprint is the estimated amount of productive land and sea a country requires to produce the renewable resources it consumes and absorb its emissions of carbon dioxide from fossil fuels, divided by the country's population. Productivity is based on an average for the world, not an estimate of actual productivity in the country.

Foot score = ecological footprint score. The performance criteria are shown in Table 9a. I have set the top of fair at a little below the world average ecological footprint of 2.2 hectares/person.

Ebal ha/p = ecological balance in hectares per person. The ecological balance is the difference between a country's footprint and its national productive area. A positive number indicates a surplus: the footprint is smaller than the country's productive capacity. A negative number indicates a deficit: the footprint is bigger than the country's productive capacity. Data are for 1996 and are from Wackernagel *et al.* (2000).

Ebal score = ecological balance score. The performance criteria are shown in Table 9a. I have set the top of medium at 0 and the top of fair at 1, so that a surplus of 0.1-1.0 gets a fair score, a surplus greater than 1.0 gets a good score, and a deficit gets a medium, poor or bad score depending on its size.

EF score = Ecological Footprint score, the lower of the ecological footprint score and the ecological balance score.

EF diff = difference between the EF score and the EWI. A positive number is the amount by which the EF score is higher than the EWI. A negative number is the amount by which it is lower.

Correlations between the EWI, its main components (dimensions and elements) and income are shown in Table 9b.

| band | top point on scale | ecological footprint (ha/person) | ecological balance (ha/person) |
|------|------|------|------|
| good | 100 | 0 | 5 |
| fair | 80 | 2 | 1 |
| medium | 60 | 4 | 0 |
| poor | 40 | 6 | -1 |
| bad | 20 | 8 | -5 |
| base | 0 | 10 | -9 |

**Table 9a. Performance criteria for the Ecological Footprint .**

| | EWI | income | land div | land quality | Land | Water | global atmos | local air | Air | wild div | domes div | Species & genes | energy | res sectors | Res use |
|---|---|---|---|---|---|---|---|---|---|---|---|---|---|---|---|
| EWI | 1 | | | | | | | | | | | | | | |
| income | -0.537 | 1 | | | | | | | | | | | | | |
| land diversity | 0.334 | 0.012 | 1 | | | | | | | | | | | | |
| land quality | 0.164 | 0.215 | 0.029 | 1 | | | | | | | | | | | |
| Land | 0.423 | 0.066 | *0.712* | 0.540 | 1 | | | | | | | | | | |
| Water | *0.775* | -0.302 | 0.218 | -0.005 | 0.172 | 1 | | | | | | | | | |
| global atmosphere | *0.730* | *-0.751* | 0.047 | -0.029 | 0.088 | 0.393 | 1 | | | | | | | | |
| local air quality | 0.196 | 0.556 | 0.046 | 0.503 | 0.326 | -0.070 | -0.451 | 1 | | | | | | | |
| Air | *0.758* | *-0.711* | 0.027 | 0.023 | 0.089 | 0.382 | **0.933** | 0.103 | 1 | | | | | | |
| wild diversity | 0.325 | 0.007 | 0.065 | 0.013 | 0.052 | 0.084 | 0.037 | 0.253 | 0.043 | 1 | | | | | |
| domesticated diversity | 0.188 | -0.129 | -0.100 | 0.139 | -0.070 | 0.014 | 0.040 | 0.234 | 0.075 | 0.292 | 1 | | | | |
| Species & genes | 0.323 | -0.017 | 0.048 | 0.074 | 0.055 | 0.065 | 0.018 | 0.278 | 0.027 | **0.935** | 0.635 | 1 | | | |
| energy | *0.644* | **-0.817** | 0.116 | -0.130 | 0.080 | 0.355 | **0.843** | -0.543 | 0.793 | 0.010 | 0.024 | -0.013 | 1 | | |
| resource sectors | 0.370 | -0.369 | 0.261 | 0.154 | 0.321 | 0.221 | 0.372 | -0.174 | 0.310 | -0.085 | -0.122 | -0.100 | 0.448 | 1 | |
| Resource use | *0.628* | *-0.754* | 0.198 | -0.030 | 0.197 | 0.352 | *0.775* | -0.454 | *0.712* | -0.030 | -0.035 | -0.052 | **0.921** | *0.760* | 1 |

**Table 9b. Correlations between the EWI, ecosystem dimensions and elements, and income (GDP per person).** Correlations of 0.8 (or -0.8) and above are shown in **bold**; those between 0.6 and 0.8 (or -0.6 and -0.8) are shown in *italic*.

\* A score with an asterisk has been reduced in accordance with the insufficient data rule. To prevent high scores resulting merely from lack of data, a good score is allowed only if it is based on all applicable components (data in an indicator, indicators in an index), and a fair score only if it is based on at least half the components. Good and fair scores (100-61) based on fewer than half the applicable components have been reduced to 60. Good scores (100-81) based on more than half but not all the applicable components have been reduced to 80.

# Table 10. Land Index; Basic Data; Native Forest Change

| Country | Total area 000 ha | Land area 000 ha | 1995 ha/p | 2000 ha/p | Forest note | Native forest 80 000 ha | Native forest 95 000 ha | Ch 80-95 %/yr | Fch score | Conv score | Nat score | LMC score | LP score | LD score | LQ score | Land index |
|---|---|---|---|---|---|---|---|---|---|---|---|---|---|---|---|---|
| **AMERICAS** | | | | | | | | | | | | | | | | |
| Antigua & Barbuda | 44 | 44 | 0.7 | 0.6 | | 10.0 | 8.7 | -0.9 | 40 | 75 | 11 | 42 | 80* | 55 | -- | 55 |
| Argentina | 278040 | 273669 | 7.9 | 7.4 | | 36135.6 | 33394.5 | -0.5 | 50 | 84 | 55 | 63 | 28 | 51 | 54 | 51 |
| Bahamas | 1388 | 1001 | 3.6 | 3.3 | | 238.1 | 158.3 | -2.7 | 19 | 94 | 45 | 53 | 45 | 50 | 100 | 50 |
| Barbados | 43 | 43 | 0.2 | 0.2 | | 0 | 0 | -- | -- | 42 | 9 | 25 | 0 | 17 | -- | 17 |
| Belize | 2296 | 2280 | 10.7 | 9.5 | | 2046.5 | 1959.5 | -0.3 | 55 | 95 | 19 | 56 | 90 | 67 | 72 | 67 |
| Bolivia | 109858 | 108438 | 14.6 | 13.0 | | 55450.5 | 48281.7 | -0.9 | 40 | 96 | 53 | 63 | 70 | 65 | 52 | 52 |
| Brazil | 854740 | 845651 | 5.3 | 5.0 | | 591496.9 | 546239.0 | -0.5 | 50 | 88 | 54 | 64 | 48 | 59 | 48 | 48 |
| Canada | 997061 | 922097 | 31.1 | 29.6 | t 80/94 | 244571 | 244571 | 0.0 | 80 | 94 | 69 | 81 | 57 | 73 | 96 | 73 |
| Chile | 75663 | 74880 | 5.3 | 4.9 | | 7616.5 | 6876.6 | -0.7 | 45 | 93 | 50 | 63 | 77 | 68 | 59 | 59 |
| Colombia | 113891 | 103870 | 2.7 | 2.5 | | 57733.8 | 52861.5 | -0.6 | 48 | 90 | 61 | 66 | 69 | 67 | 57 | 57 |
| Costa Rica | 5110 | 5106 | 1.4 | 1.3 | | 1925.4 | 1220.0 | -3.0 | 17 | 81 | 24 | 41 | 85 | 56 | 10 | 10 |
| Cuba | 11086 | 10982 | 1.0 | 1.0 | | 1972.9 | 1596.7 | -1.4 | 34 | 50 | 4 | 29 | 55 | 38 | 52 | 38 |
| Dominica | 75 | 75 | 1.1 | 1.1 | | 45.5 | 45.5 | 0.0 | 80 | 75 | 43 | 66 | 80* | 71 | -- | 71 |
| Dominican R | 4873 | 4838 | 0.6 | 0.6 | | 1424.0 | 1574.9 | 0.7 | 98 | 55 | 4 | 57 | 90 | 65 | 57 | 57 |
| Ecuador | 28356 | 27684 | 2.4 | 2.2 | | 14169.9 | 11091.6 | -1.6 | 31 | 85 | 56 | 57 | 79 | 64 | 65 | 64 |
| El Salvador | 2104 | 2072 | 0.4 | 0.3 | | 154.6 | 101.1 | -2.8 | 18 | 49 | 2 | 23 | 2 | 16 | 13 | 13 |
| Grenada | 34 | 34 | 0.4 | 0.4 | | 3.6 | 3.6 | 0.0 | 80 | 59 | 41 | 60 | 0 | 40 | -- | 40 |
| Guatemala | 10889 | 10843 | 1.1 | 1.0 | | 5037.8 | 3813.4 | -1.8 | 29 | 75 | 35 | 46 | 79 | 57 | 26 | 26 |
| Guyana | 21497 | 19685 | 23.7 | 22.9 | # | 18651.9 | 18569.2 | 0.0 | 70 | 97 | 92 | 86 | 2 | 61 | 30 | 30 |
| Haiti | 2775 | 2756 | 0.4 | 0.3 | | 38.0 | 12.5 | -7.1 | 0 | 56 | 0 | 19 | 3 | 14 | 2 | 2 |
| Honduras | 11209 | 11189 | 2.0 | 1.7 | | 5693.4 | 4111.6 | -2.1 | 25 | 78 | 28 | 44 | 51 | 46 | 27 | 27 |
| Jamaica | 1099 | 1083 | 0.4 | 0.4 | | 507.4 | 159.5 | -7.4 | 0 | 64 | 11 | 25 | 35 | 28 | 53 | 28 |
| Mexico | 195820 | 190869 | 2.1 | 1.9 | | 63564.8 | 55278.3 | -0.9 | 40 | 79 | 36 | 52 | 35 | 46 | 43 | 43 |
| Nicaragua | 13000 | 12140 | 2.7 | 2.4 | | 7251.4 | 5545.9 | -1.8 | 29 | 71 | 25 | 42 | 60 | 48 | 41 | 41 |
| Panama | 7552 | 7443 | 2.8 | 2.6 | | 3746.3 | 2794.4 | -1.9 | 28 | 87 | 36 | 50 | 89 | 63 | 20 | 20 |
| Paraguay | 40675 | 39730 | 8.2 | 7.2 | | 16899.6 | 11518.2 | -2.5 | 20 | 88 | 52 | 53 | 35 | 47 | 59 | 47 |
| Peru | 128522 | 128000 | 5.4 | 5.0 | | 70609.9 | 67378.3 | -0.3 | 55 | 94 | 71 | 73 | 46 | 64 | 38 | 38 |
| St Kitts & Nevis | 26 | 26 | 0.6 | 0.7 | | 11.2 | 11.2 | 0.0 | 80 | 65 | 35 | 60 | 59 | 60 | -- | 60 |
| St Lucia | 62 | 61 | 0.4 | 0.4 | | 7.4 | 4.6 | -3.1 | 16 | 65 | 34 | 38 | 63 | 46 | -- | 46 |
| St Vincent & Grenadines | 39 | 39 | 0.4 | 0.3 | | 12.5 | 10.5 | -1.2 | 36 | 64 | 28 | 43 | 41 | 42 | -- | 42 |
| Suriname | 16326 | 15600 | 38.1 | 37.4 | | 14848.7 | 14712.9 | -0.1 | 60 | 99 | 94 | 84 | 21 | 63 | 45 | 45 |
| Trinidad & Tobago | 513 | 513 | 0.4 | 0.4 | | 191.8 | 148.3 | -1.7 | 30 | 66 | 51 | 49 | 13 | 37 | 15 | 15 |
| United States | 936352 | 915912 | 3.4 | 3.3 | t 92 | -- | 203646 | -- | -- | 64 | 25 | 44 | 65 | 51 | 70 | 51 |
| Uruguay | 17741 | 17481 | 5.4 | 5.2 | | 667.4 | 658.0 | -0.1 | 60 | 83 | 50 | 64 | 3 | 44 | 86 | 44 |
| Venezuela | 91205 | 88205 | 4.0 | 3.6 | | 51720.7 | 43742.1 | -1.1 | 38 | 92 | 44 | 58 | 98 | 71 | 72 | 71 |
| **AFRICA** | | | | | | | | | | | | | | | | |
| Algeria | 238174 | 238174 | 8.5 | 7.6 | | 1974.1 | 1376.4 | -2.4 | 21 | 94 | 83 | 66 | 55 | 62 | 31 | 31 |
| Angola | 124670 | 124670 | 11.4 | 9.7 | | 25245.0 | 22079.6 | -0.9 | 40 | 94 | 53 | 62 | 52 | 59 | 56 | 56 |
| Benin | 11262 | 11062 | 2.1 | 1.8 | | 5649.9 | 4611.2 | -1.3 | 35 | 83 | 13 | 44 | 74 | 54 | 69 | 54 |
| Botswana | 58173 | 56673 | 38.4 | 34.9 | | 15011.7 | 13915.6 | -0.5 | 50 | 99 | 44 | 64 | 81 | 70 | 65 | 65 |
| Burkina Faso | 27400 | 27360 | 2.6 | 2.3 | | 4735.0 | 4251.2 | -0.7 | 45 | 83 | 12 | 47 | 63 | 52 | 31 | 31 |
| Burundi | 2783 | 2568 | 0.4 | 0.4 | | 246.7 | 225.3 | -0.6 | 48 | 42 | 0 | 30 | 18 | 26 | 23 | 23 |
| Cameroon | 47544 | 46540 | 3.5 | 3.1 | | 21667.5 | 19581.6 | -0.7 | 45 | 83 | 15 | 48 | 43 | 46 | 50 | 46 |
| Cape Verde | 403 | 403 | 1.1 | 0.9 | | 6.4 | 6.4 | 0.0 | 80 | 74 | 0 | 51 | 0 | 34 | 10 | 10 |
| Central African R | 62298 | 62298 | 18.9 | 17.2 | | 31851.2 | 29923.6 | -0.4 | 53 | 96 | 44 | 64 | 68 | 65 | 91 | 65 |
| Chad | 128400 | 125920 | 18.8 | 16.5 | | 12319.6 | 11021.1 | -0.7 | 45 | 94 | 54 | 64 | 34 | 54 | 53 | 53 |
| Comoros | 223 | 223 | 0.4 | 0.3 | | 16.5 | 9.0 | -4.0 | 11 | 38 | 0 | 16 | 0 | 11 | 50 | 11 |
| Congo, DR | 234486 | 226705 | 5.0 | 4.4 | | 120681.2 | 109203.1 | -0.7 | 45 | 95 | 45 | 62 | 63 | 62 | 82 | 62 |
| Congo, R | 34200 | 34150 | 13.3 | 11.6 | | 20091.5 | 19500.0 | -0.2 | 58 | 98 | 51 | 69 | 29 | 56 | 87 | 56 |
| Côte d'Ivoire | 32246 | 31800 | 2.4 | 2.2 | | 7144.2 | 5403.1 | -1.8 | 29 | 70 | 21 | 40 | 63 | 48 | 87 | 48 |
| Djibouti | 2320 | 2318 | 3.9 | 3.6 | | 22.4 | 22.4 | 0.0 | 80 | 99 | 7 | 62 | 4 | 43 | 70 | 43 |
| Egypt | 100145 | 99545 | 1.6 | 1.5 | | 0.0 | 0.0 | -- | -- | 93 | 79 | 80* | 2 | 54 | 63 | 54 |
| Equatorial Guinea | 2805 | 2805 | 7.0 | 6.2 | | 1893.9 | 1778.1 | -0.4 | 53 | 91 | 49 | 64 | 0 | 43 | 97 | 43 |
| Eritrea | 11760 | 10100 | 3.2 | 2.6 | | 233.0 | 233.0 | 0.0 | 80 | 90 | 2 | 57 | 18 | 44 | 42 | 42 |
| Ethiopia | 110430 | 100000 | 1.8 | 1.6 | | 14338.6 | 13439.2 | -0.4 | 53 | 85 | 5 | 47 | 63 | 52 | 46 | 46 |
| Gabon | 26767 | 25767 | 23.9 | 21.0 | | 19398.3 | 17838.0 | -0.6 | 48 | 96 | 65 | 69 | 13 | 50 | 76 | 50 |
| Gambia | 1129 | 1000 | 0.9 | 0.8 | | 104.5 | 89.9 | -1.0 | 39 | 72 | 11 | 41 | 20 | 34 | 75 | 34 |
| Ghana | 23854 | 22754 | 1.3 | 1.1 | | 10929.7 | 8969.3 | -1.3 | 35 | 72 | 2 | 36 | 48 | 40 | 71 | 40 |
| Guinea | 24586 | 24572 | 3.4 | 3.3 | | 7563.1 | 6363.1 | -1.1 | 38 | 88 | 30 | 52 | 12 | 39 | 89 | 39 |
| Guinea-Bissau | 3612 | 2812 | 2.6 | 2.3 | | 2452.3 | 2307.9 | -0.4 | 53 | 85 | 1 | 46 | 0 | 31 | 71 | 31 |
| Kenya | 58037 | 56914 | 2.1 | 1.9 | | 1255.4 | 1173.8 | -0.3 | 55 | 86 | 43 | 61 | 67 | 63 | 54 | 54 |
| Lesotho | 3035 | 3035 | 1.6 | 1.4 | | 0.0 | 0.0 | -- | -- | 79 | 1 | 40 | 16 | 32 | 32 | 32 |
| Liberia | 11137 | 9632 | 4.6 | 3.1 | | 4887.1 | 4501.3 | -0.5 | 50 | 93 | 13 | 52 | 14 | 39 | 93 | 39 |
| Libyan Arab J | 175954 | 175954 | 35.4 | 31.4 | | 190.0 | 190.0 | 0.0 | 80 | 98 | 82 | 87 | 1 | 58 | 22 | 22 |
| Madagascar | 58704 | 58154 | 4.2 | 3.6 | | 17088.6 | 14889.1 | -0.9 | 40 | 89 | 15 | 48 | 18 | 38 | 37 | 37 |

| Country | Total area 000 ha | Land area 000 ha | 1995 ha/p | 2000 ha/p | Forest note | Native forest 80 000 ha | Native forest 95 000 ha | Ch 80-95 %/yr | Fch score | Conv score | Nat score | LMC score | LP score | *LD score* | *LQ score* | Land index |
|---|---|---|---|---|---|---|---|---|---|---|---|---|---|---|---|---|
| Malawi | 11848 | 9408 | 1.0 | 0.9 | | 4168.9 | 3212.9 | -1.7 | 30 | 73 | 4 | 36 | 69 | 47 | 84 | 47 |
| Mali | 124019 | 122019 | 12.3 | 10.9 | | 13224.2 | 11571.0 | -0.9 | 40 | 93 | 67 | 67 | 21 | 52 | 32 | 32 |
| Mauritania | 102552 | 102522 | 44.0 | 38.4 | | 554.0 | 554.0 | 0.0 | 80 | 99 | 84 | 88 | 19 | 65 | 22 | 22 |
| Mauritius | 204 | 203 | 0.2 | 0.2 | | 2.8 | 2.8 | 0.0 | 80 | 26 | 0 | 35 | 52 | 41 | 90 | 41 |
| Morocco | 44655 | 44630 | 1.7 | 1.6 | | 3787.2 | 3514.4 | -0.5 | 50 | 70 | 1 | 40 | 5 | 28 | 76 | 28 |
| Mozambique | 80159 | 78409 | 4.5 | 4.0 | | 18321.1 | 16833.9 | -0.6 | 48 | 91 | 35 | 58 | 33 | 50 | 82 | 50 |
| Namibia | 82429 | 82329 | 53.3 | 47.7 | | 13000.0 | 12374.1 | -0.3 | 55 | 98 | 54 | 69 | 80 | 73 | 68 | 68 |
| Niger | 126700 | 126670 | 13.8 | 11.8 | | 2550.0 | 2550.0 | 0.0 | 80 | 95 | 69 | 81 | 45 | 69 | 21 | 21 |
| Nigeria | 92377 | 91077 | 0.9 | 0.8 | | 15636.4 | 13629.2 | -0.9 | 40 | 56 | 3 | 33 | 41 | 36 | 40 | 36 |
| Rwanda | 2634 | 2467 | 0.5 | 0.3 | | 167.8 | 162.4 | -0.2 | 58 | 40 | 0 | 32 | 78 | 47 | 24 | 24 |
| São Tomé & Principe | 96 | 96 | 0.7 | 0.7 | | 56.0 | 56.0 | 0.0 | 80 | 50 | 1 | 44 | 0 | 29 | 91 | 29 |
| Senegal | 19672 | 19253 | 2.3 | 2.0 | | 8091.0 | 7269.2 | -0.7 | 45 | 82 | 1 | 43 | 59 | 48 | 46 | 46 |
| Seychelles | 45 | 45 | 0.6 | 0.6 | | 3.3 | 3.3 | 0.0 | 80 | 73 | 2 | 52 | 73 | 59 | -- | 59 |
| Sierra Leone | 7174 | 7162 | 1.7 | 1.5 | | 1919.1 | 1303.0 | -2.5 | 20 | 86 | 3 | 36 | 9 | 27 | 64 | 27 |
| Somalia | 63766 | 62734 | 7.6 | 6.2 | | 781.5 | 749.8 | -0.3 | 55 | 96 | 32 | 61 | 2 | 41 | 58 | 41 |
| South Africa | 122104 | 122104 | 3.3 | 3.0 | | 7420.7 | 7203.8 | -0.2 | 58 | 77 | 27 | 54 | 48 | 52 | 33 | 33 |
| Sudan | 250581 | 237600 | 8.9 | 8.1 | | 47695.8 | 41410.0 | -0.9 | 40 | 88 | 30 | 53 | 45 | 50 | 50 | 50 |
| Swaziland | 1736 | 1720 | 2.0 | 1.7 | | 74.0 | 74.0 | 0.0 | 80 | 76 | 0 | 52 | 16 | 40 | 91 | 40 |
| Tanzania | 94509 | 88359 | 3.0 | 2.6 | | 38102.5 | 32356.2 | -1.1 | 38 | 90 | 41 | 56 | 78 | 63 | 60 | 60 |
| Togo | 5678 | 5439 | 1.3 | 1.2 | | 1562.9 | 1223.7 | -1.6 | 31 | 51 | 1 | 28 | 59 | 38 | 46 | 38 |
| Tunisia | 16361 | 15536 | 1.7 | 1.6 | | 429.2 | 353.9 | -1.3 | 35 | 62 | 18 | 38 | 6 | 27 | 37 | 27 |
| Uganda | 24104 | 19965 | 1.1 | 0.9 | | 6991.1 | 6083.5 | -0.9 | 40 | 60 | 22 | 41 | 75 | 52 | 41 | 41 |
| Zambia | 75261 | 74339 | 9.1 | 8.1 | | 35854.2 | 31354.6 | -0.9 | 40 | 88 | 71 | 66 | 80 | 71 | 52 | 52 |
| Zimbabwe | 39076 | 38685 | 3.6 | 3.3 | | 9524.4 | 8625.8 | -0.7 | 45 | 86 | 18 | 50 | 67 | 56 | 73 | 56 |
| **EUROPE** | | | | | | | | | | | | | | | | |
| Albania | 2875 | 2740 | 0.9 | 0.9 | t 57/95 | 1196 | 928 | -0.5 | 50 | 61 | 3 | 38 | 17 | 31 | 17 | 17 |
| Austria | 8386 | 8273 | 1.0 | 1.0 | t 90/96 | 3794 | 3840 | 0.2 | 85 | 76 | 1 | 52 | 70 | 59 | 57 | 57 |
| Belarus | 20760 | 20748 | 2.0 | 2.0 | t 97 | -- | 7670 | -- | -- | 65 | 1 | 33 | 34 | 33 | 77 | 33 |
| Belgium | 3052 | 3028 | 0.3 | 0.3 | t 82/97 | 362 | 352 | -0.2 | 58 | 42 | 0 | 33 | 23 | 30 | 57 | 30 |
| Bosnia & Herzegovina | 5113 | 5100 | 1.5 | 1.3 | t | -- | 22219 | -- | -- | 80 | 0 | 40 | 6 | 29 | 21 | 21 |
| Bulgaria | 11091 | 11055 | 1.3 | 1.3 | t | -- | 2621 | -- | -- | 42 | 2 | 22 | 44 | 29 | 46 | 29 |
| Croatia | 5654 | 5592 | 1.2 | 1.3 | t 96 | -- | 1728 | -- | -- | 67 | 1 | 34 | 49 | 39 | 24 | 24 |
| Czech R | 7886 | 7728 | 0.7 | 0.8 | t 86/95 | 2625 | 2630 | 0.0 | 80 | 49 | 0 | 43 | 66 | 51 | 49 | 49 |
| Denmark | 4309 | 4243 | 0.8 | 0.8 | t 90 | -- | 104 | -- | -- | 29 | 1 | 15 | 57 | 29 | 93 | 29 |
| Estonia | 4510 | 4227 | 2.8 | 3.0 | t 96 | -- | 1711 | -- | -- | 63 | 1 | 32 | 57 | 40 | 86 | 40 |
| Finland | 33814 | 30459 | 6.0 | 5.9 | t 89/96 | 21812 | 21720 | -0.1 | 60 | 90 | 13 | 54 | 47 | 52 | 84 | 52 |
| France | 55150 | 55010 | 0.9 | 0.9 | t 97 | -- | 14195 | -- | -- | 55 | 0 | 27 | 50 | 35 | 83 | 35 |
| Germany | 35698 | 34927 | 0.4 | 0.4 | t 61/87 | 10162 | 10740 | 0.2 | 85 | 52 | 0 | 46 | 70 | 54 | 68 | 54 |
| Greece | 13196 | 12890 | 1.2 | 1.2 | t 92 | -- | 3239 | -- | -- | 61 | 0 | 30 | 10 | 23 | 57 | 23 |
| Hungary | 9303 | 9234 | 0.9 | 0.9 | t | -- | 1675 | -- | -- | 37 | 0 | 18 | 58 | 31 | 51 | 31 |
| Iceland | 10300 | 10025 | 37.4 | 35.7 | t 98 | -- | 18 | -- | -- | 98 | 40 | 69 | 50 | 63 | 31 | 31 |
| Ireland | 7028 | 6889 | 1.9 | 1.8 | t 96 | -- | 1 | -- | -- | 64 | 1 | 32 | 25 | 30 | 98 | 30 |
| Italy | 30127 | 29406 | 0.5 | 0.5 | t | -- | 9724 | -- | -- | 48 | 1 | 24 | 33 | 27 | 59 | 27 |
| Latvia | 6460 | 6205 | 2.4 | 2.6 | t 97 | -- | 2741 | -- | -- | 65 | 0 | 32 | 51 | 38 | 61 | 38 |
| Lithuania | 6520 | 6480 | 1.7 | 1.8 | t 96 | -- | 1694 | -- | -- | 46 | 0 | 23 | 51 | 32 | 77 | 32 |
| Luxembourg | 257 | 257 | 0.6 | 0.6 | t 97 | -- | 47 | -- | -- | 47 | 0 | 23 | 47 | 31 | 66 | 31 |
| Macedonia, FYR | 2571 | 2543 | 1.3 | 1.3 | t | -- | 876 | -- | -- | 66 | 0 | 33 | 64 | 43 | 34 | 34 |
| Malta | 32 | 32 | 0.1 | 0.1 | t 96 | -- | 0 | -- | -- | 44 | 0 | 22 | 0 | 15 | -- | 15 |
| Moldova | 3370 | 3297 | 0.8 | 0.8 | t 97 | -- | 323 | -- | -- | 26 | 0 | 13 | 17 | 14 | 49 | 14 |
| Netherlands | 4084 | 3392 | 0.2 | 0.2 | t 96 | -- | 239 | -- | -- | 50 | 0 | 25 | 53 | 34 | 80 | 34 |
| Norway | 32388 | 30683 | 7.1 | 6.9 | t 96 | -- | 8410 | -- | -- | 94 | 30 | 62 | 41 | 55 | 93 | 55 |
| Poland | 32325 | 30442 | 0.8 | 0.8 | t 96 | -- | 8903 | -- | -- | 43 | 1 | 22 | 46 | 30 | 42 | 30 |
| Portugal | 9198 | 9150 | 0.9 | 0.9 | t | -- | 2549 | -- | -- | 43 | 1 | 22 | 35 | 26 | 52 | 26 |
| Romania | 23839 | 23034 | 1.0 | 1.0 | t 97 | -- | 6210 | -- | -- | 50 | 1 | 25 | 41 | 30 | 39 | 30 |
| Slovakia | 4901 | 4808 | 0.9 | 0.9 | t 96 | -- | 2001 | -- | -- | 62 | 0 | 31 | 76 | 46 | 54 | 46 |
| Slovenia | 2025 | 2012 | 1.0 | 1.0 | t 96 | -- | 1098 | -- | -- | 81 | 2 | 41 | 57 | 46 | 32 | 32 |
| Spain | 50599 | 49944 | 1.3 | 1.3 | t 90 | -- | 11605 | -- | -- | 52 | 0 | 26 | 40 | 31 | 66 | 31 |
| Sweden | 44996 | 41162 | 4.7 | 4.6 | t 96 | -- | 26695 | -- | -- | 89 | 21 | 55 | 41 | 50 | 64 | 50 |
| Switzerland | 4129 | 3955 | 0.6 | 0.5 | t 97 | -- | 1169 | -- | -- | 79 | 0 | 39 | 57 | 45 | 82 | 45 |
| Ukraine | 60370 | 57935 | 1.1 | 1.1 | t 96 | -- | 5033 | -- | -- | 28 | 0 | 14 | 15 | 14 | 37 | 14 |
| United Kingdom | 24410 | 24160 | 0.4 | 0.4 | t | -- | 1069 | -- | -- | 51 | 0 | 25 | 64 | 38 | 78 | 38 |
| Yugoslavia | 10217 | 10200 | 1.0 | 1.0 | t | -- | 2855 | -- | -- | 53 | 0 | 26 | 22 | 25 | 28 | 25 |
| **RUSSIAN FEDERATION** | 1707540 | 1688850 | 11.4 | 11.5 | t 88/93 | 804529 | 799198 | -0.1 | 60 | 90 | 66 | 72 | 31 | 58 | 76 | 58 |
| **ASIA** | | | | | | | | | | | | | | | | |
| Afghanistan | 65209 | 65209 | 3.3 | 2.9 | | 1984.7 | 1390.1 | -2.3 | 23 | 81 | 17 | 40 | 2 | 27 | 68 | 27 |
| Armenia | 2980 | 2820 | 0.8 | 0.8 | t 96 | -- | 321 | -- | -- | 70 | 13 | 41 | 66 | 49 | 88 | 49 |
| Azerbaijan | 8660 | 8660 | 1.1 | 1.1 | t 88 | -- | 916 | -- | -- | 70 | 6 | 38 | 29 | 35 | 77 | 35 |
| Bahrain | 69 | 69 | 0.1 | 0.1 | | 0.0 | 0.0 | -- | -- | 68 | 0 | 34 | 0 | 23 | -- | 23 |

| Country | Total area 000 ha | Land area 000 ha | 1995 ha/p | 2000 ha/p | Forest note | Native forest 80 000 ha | Native forest 95 000 ha | Ch 80-95 %/yr | Fch score | Conv score | Nat score | LMC score | LP score | *LD score* | *LQ score* | Land index |
|---|---|---|---|---|---|---|---|---|---|---|---|---|---|---|---|---|
| Bangladesh | 14400 | 13017 | 0.1 | 0.1 | | 1117.5 | 699.7 | -3.1 | 16 | 24 | 0 | 13 | 2 | 9 | 23 | 9 |
| Bhutan | 4700 | 4700 | 2.5 | 2.2 | | 2974.2 | 2748.0 | -0.5 | 50 | 94 | 29 | 58 | 94 | 70 | 91 | 70 |
| Brunei Darussalam | 576 | 527 | 1.8 | 1.6 | | 482.7 | 433.9 | -0.7 | 45 | 96 | 59 | 67 | 96 | 77 | 35 | 35 |
| Cambodia | 18103 | 17652 | 1.8 | 1.6 | | 12025.3 | 9822.8 | -1.3 | 35 | 75 | 22 | 44 | 67 | 52 | 36 | 36 |
| China | 959805 | 932742 | 0.8 | 0.7 | | 105907.0 | 99522.5 | -0.4 | 53 | 71 | 22 | 48 | 56 | 51 | 37 | 37 |
| Cyprus | 925 | 924 | 1.2 | 1.2 | t 96 | -- | 90 | -- | -- | 77 | 3 | 40 | 56 | 45 | 57 | 45 |
| Georgia | 6970 | 6970 | 1.3 | 1.4 | t | -- | 2788 | -- | -- | 75 | 8 | 41 | 27 | 36 | 93 | 36 |
| India | 328759 | 297319 | 0.3 | 0.3 | | 55081.6 | 50384.8 | -0.6 | 48 | 28 | 2 | 26 | 20 | 24 | 40 | 24 |
| Indonesia | 190457 | 181157 | 0.9 | 0.9 | | 121815.0 | 103665.7 | -1.1 | 38 | 73 | 51 | 54 | 76 | 61 | 86 | 61 |
| Iran | 163319 | 162200 | 2.6 | 2.4 | | 1975.9 | 1464.5 | -2.0 | 26 | 83 | 6 | 38 | 37 | 38 | 33 | 33 |
| Iraq | 43832 | 43737 | 2.2 | 1.9 | | 69.0 | 69.0 | 0.0 | 80 | 84 | 25 | 63 | 0 | 42 | 18 | 18 |
| Israel | 2106 | 2062 | 0.4 | 0.3 | t 97 | -- | 31 | -- | -- | 60 | 1 | 30 | 50 | 37 | 95 | 37 |
| Japan | 37780 | 37652 | 0.3 | 0.3 | t | -- | 13382 | -- | -- | 43 | 8 | 25 | 53 | 34 | 98 | 34 |
| Jordan | 8921 | 8893 | 1.6 | 1.3 | | 35.0 | 22.4 | -2.9 | 18 | 91 | 50 | 53 | 13 | 40 | 29 | 29 |
| Kazakhstan | 271730 | 267073 | 16.2 | 16.5 | t 93 | -- | 10499 | -- | -- | 81 | 7 | 44 | 26 | 38 | 41 | 38 |
| Korea, DPR | 12054 | 12041 | 0.5 | 0.5 | | 4700.0 | 4700.0 | 0.0 | 80 | 62 | 1 | 48 | 14 | 37 | 79 | 37 |
| Korea, R | 9926 | 9873 | 0.2 | 0.2 | | 6304.0 | 6226.0 | -0.1 | 60 | 63 | 0 | 41 | 17 | 33 | 98 | 33 |
| Kuwait | 1782 | 1782 | 1.1 | 0.9 | | 0.0 | 0.0 | -- | -- | 94 | 33 | 63 | 7 | 44 | 66 | 44 |
| Kyrgyzstan | 19850 | 19180 | 4.2 | 4.1 | t 88 | -- | 672 | -- | -- | 86 | 7 | 46 | 17 | 36 | 94 | 36 |
| Lao PDR | 23680 | 23080 | 4.8 | 4.2 | | 14467.1 | 12430.7 | -1.0 | 39 | 95 | 17 | 50 | 38 | 46 | 79 | 46 |
| Lebanon | 1040 | 1023 | 0.3 | 0.3 | | 65.3 | 39.0 | -3.4 | 14 | 59 | 1 | 25 | 2 | 17 | 86 | 17 |
| Malaysia | 32975 | 32855 | 1.6 | 1.5 | | 21704.1 | 15371.1 | -2.3 | 23 | 73 | 41 | 45 | 56 | 49 | 47 | 47 |
| Maldives | 30 | 30 | 0.1 | 0.1 | | 0.0 | 0.0 | -- | -- | 80 | 0 | 40 | 0 | 27 | -- | 27 |
| Mongolia | 156650 | 156650 | 63.9 | 58.8 | | 9406.0 | 9406.0 | 0.0 | 80 | 98 | 60 | 79 | 78 | 79 | 58 | 58 |
| Myanmar | 67658 | 65755 | 1.5 | 1.4 | | 32890.2 | 26875.0 | -1.3 | 35 | 81 | 7 | 41 | 3 | 28 | 80 | 28 |
| Nepal | 14718 | 14300 | 0.7 | 0.6 | | 5565.6 | 4766.1 | -1.0 | 39 | 70 | 21 | 43 | 64 | 50 | 76 | 50 |
| Oman | 21246 | 21246 | 9.9 | 8.4 | | 0.0 | 0.0 | -- | -- | 99 | 77 | 80* | 80* | 80 | 25 | 25 |
| Pakistan | 79009 | 77088 | 0.6 | 0.5 | | 2608.8 | 1580.3 | -3.3 | 15 | 62 | 5 | 27 | 23 | 26 | 28 | 26 |
| Philippines | 30000 | 29817 | 0.4 | 0.4 | | 10815.5 | 6562.8 | -3.3 | 15 | 60 | 9 | 28 | 39 | 32 | 29 | 29 |
| Qatar | 1100 | 1100 | 2.0 | 1.8 | | 0.0 | 0.0 | -- | -- | 95 | 16 | 55 | 1 | 37 | 73 | 37 |
| Saudi Arabia | 214969 | 214969 | 11.8 | 9.9 | | 262.0 | 220.9 | -1.1 | 38 | 96 | 69 | 67 | 80* | 71 | 30 | 30 |
| Singapore | 62 | 61 | 0.0 | 0.0 | | 4.7 | 4.0 | -1.1 | 38 | 44 | 0 | 27 | 42 | 32 | 61 | 32 |
| Sri Lanka | 6561 | 6463 | 0.4 | 0.3 | | 2009.3 | 1657.1 | -1.3 | 35 | 60 | 0 | 32 | 66 | 43 | 74 | 43 |
| Syrian Arab R | 18518 | 18378 | 1.3 | 1.1 | | 162.9 | 92.2 | -3.7 | 13 | 61 | 9 | 27 | 0 | 18 | 46 | 18 |
| Tajikistan | 14310 | 14060 | 2.4 | 2.3 | t | -- | 390 | -- | -- | 89 | 10 | 49 | 22 | 40 | 94 | 40 |
| Thailand | 51311 | 51089 | 0.9 | 0.8 | | 17858.5 | 11100.8 | -3.1 | 16 | 53 | 8 | 26 | 72 | 41 | 18 | 18 |
| Turkey | 77482 | 76963 | 1.3 | 1.2 | t 96 | -- | 8100 | -- | -- | 54 | 2 | 28 | 10 | 22 | 34 | 22 |
| Turkmenistan | 48810 | 46993 | 11.5 | 10.5 | t | -- | 3742 | -- | -- | 92 | 12 | 52 | 24 | 43 | 93 | 43 |
| United Arab Emirates | 8360 | 8360 | 3.8 | 3.4 | | 0.0 | 0.0 | -- | -- | 94 | 77 | 80* | 0 | 53 | 26 | 26 |
| Uzbekistan | 44740 | 41424 | 1.8 | 1.7 | t 88 | -- | 1609 | -- | -- | 80 | 2 | 41 | 18 | 33 | 70 | 33 |
| Viet Nam | 33169 | 32549 | 0.4 | 0.4 | | 9658.2 | 7646.8 | -1.5 | 33 | 66 | 2 | 33 | 19 | 28 | 51 | 28 |
| Yemen | 52797 | 52797 | 3.5 | 2.9 | | 9.0 | 9.0 | 0.0 | 80 | 93 | 14 | 62 | 0 | 41 | 55 | 41 |
| **PACIFIC** | | | | | | | | | | | | | | | | |
| Australia | 774122 | 768230 | 42.8 | 40.7 | t 94 | -- | 155835 | -- | -- | 92 | 12 | 52 | 60 | 55 | 85 | 55 |
| Fiji | 1827 | 1827 | 2.4 | 2.2 | | 811.0 | 757.0 | -0.5 | 50 | 77 | 4 | 44 | 20 | 36 | 100 | 36 |
| New Zealand | 27053 | 26799 | 7.3 | 6.9 | t 96 | -- | 6398 | -- | -- | 75 | 9 | 42 | 92 | 59 | 79 | 59 |
| Papua New Guinea | 46284 | 45286 | 10.5 | 9.4 | | 38558.4 | 36908.5 | -0.3 | 55 | 98 | 63 | 72 | 14 | 53 | 98 | 53 |
| Samoa | 284 | 283 | 1.7 | 1.6 | | 151.0 | 127.0 | -1.1 | 38 | 51 | 1 | 30 | 30 | 30 | -- | 30 |
| Solomon Is | 2890 | 2799 | 7.4 | 6.3 | | 2439.6 | 2370.6 | -0.2 | 58 | 96 | 26 | 60 | 0 | 40 | 75 | 40 |
| Tonga | 75 | 72 | 0.7 | 0.7 | | 0.0 | 0.0 | -- | -- | 26 | 0 | 13 | 0 | 9 | -- | 9 |
| Vanuatu | 1219 | 1219 | 7.2 | 6.4 | | 1007.0 | 893.0 | -0.8 | 43 | 89 | 20 | 50 | 1 | 34 | 100 | 34 |

**Notes**

The **Land index** is the lower of a land diversity index (*LD score*) and a land quality index (*LQ score*).

    The land diversity index is the average of two weighted indicators (column heading in parentheses) [weight in brackets]:

        Land modification and conversion (LMC score) [2].

        Land protection (LP score) [1]. See Table 12 for data.

    Protected area coverage was given a lower weight because it measures a policy response, not the actual state of land diversity.

    Land modification and conversion is the average of three unweighted indicators:

        Converted land as % of total land (Conv score). The converted land area comprises cultivated land and built land. See Table 11 for data.

        Natural land as % of total land (Nat score). See Table 11 for data.

        % annual change in native forest area (Fch score). Ideally, forests would be differentiated within the converted land and natural land indicators, and changes in the area of native forest would be shown by changes within those indicators. This cannot be done with available data. See this table for data.

    Total area is the total surface area (land + inland waters) in thousands of hectares. Data refer to 1997 and are from FAO (1999), except for Belgium and Luxembourg which are from OECD (1999). China includes Hong Kong and Macao.

    Land area is in thousands of hectares. Data refer to 1997 and are from FAO (1999), except for Belgium and Luxembourg which are from OECD (1999). China includes Hong Kong and Macao.

1995 ha/p = land hectares per person in 1995, on the basis of population data from United Nations Population Division (1998b).

2000 ha/p = land hectares per person in 2000, on the basis of population data from United Nations Population Division (1998b).

Forest note = see Native forest below. # indicates a score for a decline of less than 0.05%.

Native forest = forest composed of tree species known to be indigenous to the area, or non-plantation forest. Areas are in thousand hectares (000 ha). Data are for 1980 and 1995, except where a different year is indicated in the Forest note column. If two years are given (e.g., 88/93), the first is instead of 1980, the second instead of 1995. All data are from FAO (1997a), except where indicated by the letter t in the Forest note column, which are from UNECE & FAO (2000).

Ch 80-95 %/yr = average annual percentage change in native forest area between 1980 and 1995 (or the applicable years).

Fch score = score for % annual change in native forest area. The performance criteria are shown in Table 10a. The tops of the fair and medium bands have been set so that an increase in forest area gets a good score, a decline of 0.1% or more a medium score or worse, and zero change (stability) a fair score. If the forest area is reported to be exactly the same size at the end of the reporting period as at the beginning (exactly 0.0 change), the score is 80. If there is a decline of less than 0.05%, the score is reduced to 70—indicated by # (Guyana is the only case).

Conv score = score for converted land as % of total land. The performance criteria are shown in Table 10a. The top of the medium band is based on the landscape pattern theory that habitat becomes dissected into isolated patches below 60% coverage (see Nat score below).

Nat score = score for natural land as % of total land. The performance criteria are shown in Table 10a. Fair performance is defined as better than 60, on the basis of landscape pattern theory, which suggests that if habitat coverage is reduced to less than 59.28% the landscape becomes dissected into isolated patches (O'Neill et al. 1995), which in turn leads to a loss of species.

LMC score = land modification and conversion score, the average of the above three scores.

LP score = land protection score. See Table 12 for data and performance criteria.

*LD score* = land diversity index, the weighted average of the land modification score and the land protection score.

*LQ score* = land quality index. See Table 13 for data and performance criteria.

| band | top point on scale | converted land as % of total land | natural land as % of total land | % annual change in forest area |
|--------|------|-----|-----|------|
| good | 100 | 0 | 100 | 0.8 |
| fair | 80 | 20 | 80 | 0.0 |
| medium | 60 | 40 | 60 | -0.1 |
| poor | 40 | 60 | 40 | -0.9 |
| bad | 20 | 80 | 20 | -2.5 |
| base | 0 | 100 | 0 | -5.7 |

**Table 10a. Performance criteria for indicators of land modification and conversion.**

* A score with an asterisk has been reduced in accordance with the insufficient data rule. To prevent high scores resulting merely from lack of data, a good score is allowed only if it is based on all applicable components (data in an indicator, indicators in an index), and a fair score only if it is based on at least half the components. Good and fair scores (100-61) based on fewer than half the applicable components have been reduced to 60. Good scores (100-81) based on more than half but not all the applicable components have been reduced to 80.

# Table 11. Natural, Modified, Cultivated, and Built Land

| Country | Natural note | Cultivated [Built] notes | Natural 000 ha | Nat % | Mod 000 ha | Mod % | Cult 000 ha | Cult % | Built 000 ha | Built % | Nat score | Conv score |
|---|---|---|---|---|---|---|---|---|---|---|---|---|
| **AMERICAS** | | | | | | | | | | | | |
| Antigua & Barbuda | d | C8+F0+P0 | 5 | 11.4 | 28 | 63.6 | 8 | 18.2 | 3 | 6.8 | 11 | 75 |
| Argentina | d | C27200+F547+ P14200 | 149970 | 54.8 | 79639 | 29.1 | 41947 | 15.3 | 2113 | 0.8 | 55 | 84 |
| Bahamas | d | C10+F0+P0 | 452 | 45.2 | 493 | 49.3 | 10 | 1.0 | 46 | 4.6 | 45 | 94 |
| Barbados | d | C17+F0+P0 | 4 | 9.3 | 14 | 32.6 | 17 | 39.5 | 8 | 18.6 | 9 | 42 |
| Belize | d | C89+F2+P5 | 440 | 19.3 | 1731 | 75.9 | 96 | 4.2 | 13 | 0.6 | 19 | 95 |
| Bolivia | d | C2100+F28+ P2100 | 57037 | 52.6 | 46717 | 43.1 | 4228 | 3.9 | 456 | 0.4 | 53 | 96 |
| Brazil | d | C65300+F4900+P18500 | 460666 | 54.5 | 286593 | 33.9 | 88700 | 10.5 | 9692 | 1.1 | 54 | 88 |
| Canada | r | C45700+Ft0+ Pe2688 [u86] | 640558 | 69.5 | 226653 | 24.6 | 48388 | 5.2 | 6498 | 0.7 | 69 | 94 |
| Chile | d | C2297+F1015+P1290 | 37421 | 50.0 | 31992 | 42.7 | 4602 | 6.1 | 865 | 1.2 | 50 | 93 |
| Colombia | d | C4430+F126+ P4008 | 63024 | 60.7 | 30318 | 29.2 | 8564 | 8.2 | 1964 | 1.9 | 61 | 90 |
| Costa Rica | d | C505+F28+ P234 | 1251 | 24.5 | 2905 | 56.9 | 767 | 15.0 | 183 | 3.6 | 24 | 81 |
| Cuba | d | C4450+F245+ P217 | 462 | 4.2 | 5057 | 46.0 | 4912 | 44.7 | 551 | 5.0 | 4 | 50 |
| Dominica | d | C15+F0+P0 | 32 | 42.7 | 24 | 32.0 | 15 | 20.0 | 4 | 5.3 | 43 | 75 |
| Dominican R | d | C1500+F45+ P209 | 179 | 3.7 | 2507 | 51.8 | 1754 | 36.3 | 398 | 8.2 | 4 | 55 |
| Ecuador | d | C3001+F45+ P509 | 15613 | 56.4 | 7931 | 28.6 | 3555 | 12.8 | 585 | 2.1 | 56 | 85 |
| El Salvador | d321a | C816+F4+P59 | 45 | 2.2 | 974 | 47.0 | 879 | 42.4 | 174 | 8.4 | 2 | 49 |
| Grenada | d | C11+F0+P0 | 14 | 41.2 | 6 | 17.6 | 11 | 32.4 | 3 | 8.8 | 41 | 59 |
| Guatemala | d | C1905+F28+ P260 | 3779 | 34.9 | 4359 | 40.2 | 2193 | 20.2 | 512 | 4.7 | 35 | 75 |
| Guyana | d | C496+F8+P#56 | 18111 | 92.0 | 964 | 4.9 | 560 | 2.8 | 50 | 0.3 | 92 | 97 |
| Haiti | d102a | C910+F8+P50 | 0 | 0.0 | 1557 | 56.5 | 968 | 35.1 | 231 | 8.4 | 0 | 56 |
| Honduras | d | C2045+F3+ P154 | 3106 | 27.8 | 5590 | 50.0 | 2202 | 19.7 | 291 | 2.6 | 28 | 78 |
| Jamaica | d | C274+F15+P26 | 119 | 11.0 | 574 | 53.0 | 315 | 29.1 | 75 | 6.9 | 11 | 64 |
| Mexico | d | C27300+F109+Pe7950 | 69396 | 36.4 | 81478 | 42.7 | 35359 | 18.5 | 4636 | 2.4 | 36 | 79 |
| Nicaragua | d | C2746+F14+ P482 | 3028 | 24.9 | 5642 | 46.5 | 3242 | 26.7 | 228 | 1.9 | 25 | 71 |
| Panama | d | C655+F6+P147 | 2668 | 35.8 | 3833 | 51.5 | 808 | 10.9 | 134 | 1.8 | 36 | 87 |
| Paraguay | d | C2285+F9+ P2170 | 20659 | 52.0 | 14310 | 36.0 | 4464 | 11.2 | 297 | 0.7 | 52 | 88 |
| Peru | d | C4200+F184+ P2712 | 91136 | 71.2 | 28571 | 22.3 | 7096 | 5.5 | 1197 | 0.9 | 71 | 94 |
| St Kitts & Nevis | d | C7+F0+P0 | 9 | 34.6 | 8 | 30.8 | 7 | 26.9 | 2 | 7.7 | 35 | 65 |
| St Lucia | d | C17+F0+P0 | 21 | 34.4 | 19 | 31.1 | 17 | 27.9 | 4 | 6.6 | 34 | 65 |
| St Vincent & Grenadines | d | C11+F0+P0 | 11 | 28.2 | 14 | 35.9 | 11 | 28.2 | 3 | 7.7 | 28 | 64 |
| Suriname | d | C67+F8+P2 | 14657 | 94.0 | 841 | 5.4 | 77 | 0.5 | 25 | 0.2 | 94 | 99 |
| Trinidad & Tobago | d295a | C122+F13+P1 | 264 | 51.5 | 75 | 14.6 | 136 | 26.5 | 38 | 7.4 | 51 | 66 |
| United States | r | C179000+ Ft13687+ Pe23925 [u87] | 230838 | 25.2 | 359070 | 39.2 | 216612 | 23.6 | 109392 | 11.9 | 25 | 64 |
| Uruguay | d | C1307+F156+ P1307 | 8740 | 50.0 | 5776 | 33.0 | 2770 | 15.8 | 195 | 1.1 | 50 | 83 |
| Venezuela | d | C3490+F253+ P1824 | 38700 | 43.9 | 42599 | 48.3 | 5567 | 6.3 | 1339 | 1.5 | 44 | 92 |
| **AFRICA** | | | | | | | | | | | | |
| Algeria | c | C8040+F485+ P3163 | 197680 | 83.0 | 27083 | 11.4 | 11688 | 4.9 | 1723 | 0.7 | 83 | 94 |
| Angola | c | C3500+F120+ P3500 | 66070 | 53.0 | 50913 | 40.8 | 7120 | 5.7 | 567 | 0.5 | 53 | 94 |
| Benin | c | C1595+F14+ P44 | 1440 | 13.0 | 7695 | 69.6 | 1653 | 14.9 | 274 | 2.5 | 13 | 83 |
| Botswana | m | C346+F1+P346 | 24940 | 44.0 | 30949 | 54.6 | 693 | 1.2 | 91 | 0.2 | 44 | 99 |
| Burkina Faso | c | C3440+F20+ P600 | 3280 | 12.0 | 19485 | 71.2 | 4060 | 14.8 | 535 | 2.0 | 12 | 83 |
| Burundi | c | C1100+F92+ P#96 | 0 | 0.0 | 1092 | 42.5 | 1288 | 50.2 | 188 | 7.3 | 0 | 42 |
| Cameroon | c | C7160+F16+ P200 | 6980 | 15.0 | 31507 | 67.7 | 7376 | 15.8 | 677 | 1.5 | 15 | 83 |
| Cape Verde | s | C41+F40+P3 | 0 | 0.0 | 300 | 74.4 | 84 | 20.8 | 19 | 4.7 | 0 | 74 |
| Central African R | m | C2020+F6+ P300 | 27410 | 44.0 | 32394 | 52.0 | 2326 | 3.7 | 168 | 0.3 | 44 | 96 |
| Chad | c | C3256+F4+ P3256 | 68000 | 54.0 | 51059 | 40.5 | 6516 | 5.2 | 345 | 0.3 | 54 | 94 |
| Comoros | F0+R1 | C118+F0+P2 | 1 | 0.4 | 83 | 37.2 | 120 | 53.8 | 19 | 8.5 | 0 | 38 |
| Congo, DR | c | C7880+F42+ P1500 | 102020 | 45.0 | 112924 | 49.8 | 9422 | 4.2 | 2339 | 1.0 | 45 | 95 |
| Congo, R | m | C185+F37+ P185 | 17420 | 51.0 | 16191 | 47.4 | 407 | 1.2 | 132 | 0.4 | 51 | 98 |
| Côte d'Ivoire | m | C7350+F66+ P1300 | 6680 | 21.0 | 15713 | 49.4 | 8716 | 27.4 | 691 | 2.2 | 21 | 70 |
| Djibouti | F0+R154 | 0 | 154 | 6.6 | 2133 | 92.0 | 0 | 0.0 | 31 | 1.3 | 7 | 99 |
| Egypt | c | C3300+F34+P0 | 78640 | 79.0 | 14396 | 14.5 | 3334 | 3.3 | 3175 | 3.2 | 79 | 93 |
| Equatorial Guinea | m | C230+F3+P10 | 1375 | 49.0 | 1166 | 41.6 | 243 | 8.7 | 21 | 0.7 | 49 | 91 |
| Eritrea | F0+R161 | C393+F49+ P393 | 161 | 1.6 | 8939 | 88.5 | 835 | 8.3 | 165 | 1.6 | 2 | 90 |
| Ethiopia | F134+R4777 | C10500+F140+P2000 | 4911 | 4.9 | 79610 | 79.6 | 12640 | 12.6 | 2839 | 2.8 | 5 | 85 |
| Gabon | m | C495+F21+ P470 | 16750 | 65.0 | 7965 | 30.9 | 986 | 3.8 | 66 | 0.3 | 65 | 96 |
| Gambia | m | C200+F1+P20 | 110 | 11.0 | 611 | 61.1 | 221 | 22.1 | 58 | 5.8 | 11 | 72 |
| Ghana | c | C4550+F53+ P840 | 460 | 2.0 | 15943 | 70.1 | 5443 | 23.9 | 908 | 4.0 | 2 | 72 |
| Guinea | m | C1485+F4+ P1070 | 7370 | 30.0 | 14279 | 58.1 | 2559 | 10.4 | 364 | 1.5 | 30 | 88 |
| Guinea-Bissau | F23+R0 | C350+F1+P#10 | 23 | 0.8 | 2372 | 84.4 | 361 | 12.8 | 56 | 2.0 | 1 | 85 |
| Kenya | c | C4520+F118+ P2130 | 24470 | 43.0 | 24283 | 42.7 | 6768 | 11.9 | 1393 | 2.4 | 43 | 86 |
| Lesotho | F0+R18 | C325+F6+P200 | 18 | 0.6 | 2387 | 78.6 | 531 | 17.5 | 99 | 3.3 | 1 | 79 |
| Liberia | m | C327+F6+P200 | 1250 | 13.0 | 7739 | 80.3 | 533 | 5.5 | 110 | 1.1 | 13 | 93 |
| Libyan Arab J | c158360a | C2115+F210+ P1330 | 144544 | 82.1 | 27450 | 15.6 | 3655 | 2.1 | 305 | 0.2 | 82 | 98 |
| Madagascar | c | C3108+F217+ P2400 | 8720 | 15.0 | 43000 | 73.9 | 5725 | 9.8 | 709 | 1.2 | 15 | 89 |

| Country | Natural note | Cultivated [Built] notes | Natural 000 ha | Nat % | Mod 000 ha | Mod % | Cult 000 ha | Cult % | Built 000 ha | Built % | Nat score | Conv score |
|---|---|---|---|---|---|---|---|---|---|---|---|---|
| Malawi | c | C1710+F126+ P184 | 380 | 4.0 | 6516 | 69.3 | 2020 | 21.5 | 492 | 5.2 | 4 | 73 |
| Mali | c | C4650+F14+ P3000 | 81750 | 67.0 | 32096 | 26.3 | 7664 | 6.3 | 509 | 0.4 | 67 | 93 |
| Mauritania | c93300a | C502+F2+P500 | 85857 | 83.7 | 15541 | 15.2 | 1004 | 1.0 | 120 | 0.1 | 84 | 99 |
| Mauritius | F0+R0 | C106+F9+P1 | 0 | 0.0 | 53 | 26.1 | 116 | 57.1 | 34 | 16.7 | 0 | 26 |
| Morocco | c | C9595+F321+ P2100 | 450 | 1.0 | 30843 | 69.1 | 12016 | 26.9 | 1321 | 3.0 | 1 | 70 |
| Mozambique | c | C3180+F28+ P3180 | 27440 | 35.0 | 43683 | 55.7 | 6388 | 8.1 | 898 | 1.1 | 35 | 91 |
| Namibia | m | C820+F0+P820 | 44460 | 54.0 | 36134 | 43.9 | 1640 | 2.0 | 95 | 0.1 | 54 | 98 |
| Niger | c95000a | C5000+F12+ P1044 | 87948 | 69.4 | 32193 | 25.4 | 6056 | 4.8 | 473 | 0.4 | 69 | 95 |
| Nigeria | c | C30738+F151+P4000 | 2730 | 3.0 | 48387 | 53.1 | 34889 | 38.3 | 5071 | 5.6 | 3 | 56 |
| Rwanda | c | C1150+F88+ P70 | 0 | 0.0 | 995 | 40.3 | 1308 | 53.0 | 164 | 6.6 | 0 | 40 |
| São Tomé & Principe | F1+R0 | C41+F0+P#0 | 1 | 1.0 | 47 | 49.0 | 41 | 42.7 | 7 | 7.3 | 1 | 50 |
| Senegal | c | C2266+F112+ P570 | 190 | 1.0 | 15688 | 81.5 | 2948 | 15.3 | 427 | 2.2 | 1 | 82 |
| Seychelles | F0+R1 | C7+F1+P0 | 1 | 2.2 | 32 | 71.1 | 8 | 17.8 | 4 | 8.9 | 2 | 73 |
| Sierra Leone | F13+R203 | C546+F6+P220 | 216 | 3.0 | 5960 | 83.2 | 772 | 10.8 | 214 | 3.0 | 3 | 86 |
| Somalia | c | C1061+F4+ P1061 | 20070 | 32.0 | 40115 | 63.9 | 2126 | 3.4 | 423 | 0.7 | 32 | 96 |
| South Africa | c | C16300+F1295+P8150 | 32970 | 27.0 | 61483 | 50.4 | 25745 | 21.1 | 1906 | 1.6 | 27 | 77 |
| Sudan | m | C16900+F203+ P11000 | 71280 | 30.0 | 136859 | 57.6 | 28103 | 11.8 | 1358 | 0.6 | 30 | 88 |
| Swaziland | F0+R4 | C180+F72+ P115 | 4 | 0.2 | 1304 | 75.8 | 367 | 21.3 | 45 | 2.6 | 0 | 76 |
| Tanzania | c | C4000+F154+ P3500 | 36230 | 41.0 | 42940 | 48.6 | 7654 | 8.7 | 1535 | 1.7 | 41 | 90 |
| Togo | F12+R41 | C2430+F21+ P20 | 53 | 1.0 | 2706 | 49.8 | 2471 | 45.4 | 209 | 3.8 | 1 | 51 |
| Tunisia | c | C4900+F201+ P310 | 2800 | 18.0 | 6871 | 44.2 | 5411 | 34.8 | 454 | 2.9 | 18 | 62 |
| Uganda | m | C6810+F20+ P180 | 4390 | 22.0 | 7592 | 38.0 | 7010 | 35.1 | 973 | 4.9 | 22 | 60 |
| Zambia | m | C5265+F44+ P3000 | 52780 | 71.0 | 12831 | 17.3 | 8309 | 11.2 | 419 | 0.6 | 71 | 88 |
| Zimbabwe | c | C3210+F84+ P1720 | 6960 | 18.0 | 26159 | 67.6 | 5014 | 13.0 | 552 | 1.4 | 18 | 86 |
| **EUROPE** | | | | | | | | | | | | |
| Albania | F85+W0+R4 | C702+Ft102+ P42 [ea90] | 89 | 3.2 | 1578 | 57.6 | 846 | 30.9 | 227 | 8.3 | 3 | 61 |
| Austria | F34+W84+R7 | C1479+Ft0+ Pe194 [e90] | 125 | 1.5 | 6193 | 74.9 | 1681 | 20.3 | 274 | 3.3 | 1 | 76 |
| Belarus | F43+W0+R92 | C6319+Ft195+ P297 | 135 | 0.7 | 13283 | 64.0 | 6811 | 32.8 | 519 | 2.5 | 1 | 65 |
| Belgium | F0+W0+R0 | C870+Ft294+ Pe55 [e95] | 0 | 0.0 | 1273 | 42.0 | 1219 | 40.3 | 536 | 17.7 | 0 | 42 |
| Bosnia & Herzegovina | F0+W0+R16 | C650+Ft57+ P120 | 16 | 0.3 | 4086 | 80.1 | 827 | 16.2 | 171 | 3.4 | 0 | 80 |
| Bulgaria | F256+W0+R0 | C4411+Ft969+ P180 [e94] | 256 | 2.3 | 4403 | 39.8 | 5560 | 50.3 | 836 | 7.6 | 2 | 42 |
| Croatia | F2+W33+R20 | C1442+Ft47+ P109 | 55 | 1.0 | 3715 | 66.4 | 1598 | 28.6 | 224 | 4.0 | 1 | 67 |
| Czech R | F0+W0+R0 | C3331+Ft0+ Pe95 | 0 | 0.0 | 3786 | 49.0 | 3426 | 44.3 | 516 | 6.7 | 0 | 49 |
| Denmark | F0+W10+R16 | C2373+Ft341+ Pe32 | 26 | 0.6 | 1209 | 28.5 | 2746 | 64.7 | 262 | 6.2 | 1 | 29 |
| Estonia | F2+W0+R34 | C1143+Ft305+ P31 | 36 | 0.9 | 2639 | 62.4 | 1479 | 35.0 | 73 | 1.7 | 1 | 63 |
| Finland | F1263+W408+R2388 | C2129+Ft0+ Pe10 [e90] | 4059 | 13.3 | 23322 | 76.6 | 2139 | 7.0 | 939 | 3.1 | 13 | 90 |
| France | F30+W0+R53 | C19468+Ft961+Pe1208 [e95] | 83 | 0.2 | 30335 | 55.1 | 21637 | 39.3 | 2955 | 5.4 | 0 | 55 |
| Germany | F0+W0+R0 | C12060+Ft0+ Pe527 | 0 | 0.0 | 18245 | 52.2 | 12587 | 36.0 | 4095 | 11.7 | 0 | 52 |
| Greece | F0+W0+R0 | C3915+Ft120+ Pe#508 [ea80] | 0 | 0.0 | 7810 | 60.6 | 4543 | 35.2 | 537 | 4.2 | 0 | 61 |
| Hungary | F0+W0+R7 | C5047+Ft136+ Pe115 | 7 | 0.1 | 3419 | 37.0 | 5298 | 57.4 | 510 | 5.5 | 0 | 37 |
| Iceland | F0+W0+ R4043 | C6+Ft12+Pe6 [e95] | 4043 | 40.3 | 5823 | 58.1 | 24 | 0.2 | 135 | 1.3 | 40 | 98 |
| Ireland | F1+W0+R38 | C1346+Ft590+ Pe352 | 39 | 0.6 | 4380 | 63.6 | 2288 | 33.2 | 182 | 2.6 | 1 | 64 |
| Italy | F6+W197+R0 | C10927+Ft133+Pe#454 [e90] | 203 | 0.7 | 13802 | 46.9 | 11514 | 39.2 | 3887 | 13.2 | 1 | 48 |
| Latvia | F4+W0+R11 | C1830+Ft143+ P80 | 15 | 0.2 | 4012 | 64.7 | 2053 | 33.1 | 125 | 2.0 | 0 | 65 |
| Lithuania | F12+W0+R16 | C3006+Ft284+ P50 [ea95] | 28 | 0.4 | 2936 | 45.3 | 3340 | 51.5 | 176 | 2.7 | 0 | 46 |
| Luxembourg | F0+W0+R0 | C67+Ft39+Pe8 | 0 | 0.0 | 122 | 47.5 | 114 | 44.4 | 21 | 8.2 | 0 | 47 |
| Macedonia, FYR | F0+W0+R2 | C658+Ft30+P64 | 2 | 0.1 | 1690 | 66.5 | 752 | 29.6 | 99 | 3.9 | 0 | 66 |
| Malta | F0+W0+R0 | C11+Ft0+P0 [e95] | 0 | 0.0 | 14 | 43.8 | 11 | 34.4 | 7 | 21.9 | 0 | 44 |
| Moldova | F0+W0+R0 | C2183+Ft1+P37 | 0 | 0.0 | 857 | 26.0 | 2221 | 67.4 | 219 | 6.6 | 0 | 26 |
| Netherlands | F0+W0+R0 | C935+Ft100+ Pe103 [e93] | 0 | 0.0 | 1693 | 49.9 | 1138 | 33.5 | 561 | 16.5 | 0 | 50 |
| Norway | F250+W329+ R8533 | C902+Ft300+ Pe14 | 9112 | 29.7 | 19655 | 64.1 | 1216 | 4.0 | 700 | 2.3 | 30 | 94 |
| Poland | F198+W0+R0 | C14424+Ft39+ Pe409 [e95] | 198 | 0.7 | 13063 | 42.9 | 14872 | 48.9 | 2309 | 7.6 | 1 | 43 |
| Portugal | F55+W44+R0 | C2900+Ft834+ Pe100 [e90] | 99 | 1.1 | 3803 | 41.6 | 3834 | 41.9 | 1414 | 15.5 | 1 | 43 |
| Romania | F233+W0+R0 | C9900+Ft91+ P487 | 233 | 1.0 | 11191 | 48.6 | 10478 | 45.5 | 1132 | 4.9 | 1 | 50 |
| Slovakia | F20+W0+R0 | C1605+Ft15+ Pe84 [e95] | 20 | 0.4 | 2955 | 61.5 | 1704 | 35.4 | 129 | 2.7 | 0 | 62 |
| Slovenia | F50+W0+R0 | C285+Ft1+P50 [e95] | 50 | 2.5 | 1577 | 78.4 | 336 | 16.7 | 49 | 2.4 | 2 | 81 |
| Spain | F5+W3+R0 | C19164+Ft1904+Pe1069 [e90] | 8 | 0.0 | 25870 | 51.8 | 22137 | 44.3 | 1929 | 3.9 | 0 | 52 |
| Sweden | F5177+ W2854+R455 | C2799+Ft569+ Pe58 [e90] | 8486 | 20.6 | 28078 | 68.2 | 3426 | 8.3 | 1172 | 2.8 | 21 | 89 |
| Switzerland | F7+W0+R9 | C444+Ft4+ Pe111 [ba80] | 16 | 0.4 | 3099 | 78.4 | 559 | 14.1 | 281 | 7.1 | 0 | 79 |
| Ukraine | F59+W6+R43 | C34081+Ft4425+P750 | 108 | 0.2 | 16008 | 27.6 | 39256 | 67.8 | 2563 | 4.4 | 0 | 28 |
| United Kingdom | F0+W0+R0 | C6425+Ft1400+Pe1101 | 0 | 0.0 | 12312 | 51.0 | 8926 | 36.9 | 2922 | 12.1 | 0 | 51 |
| Yugoslavia | F4+W12+R6 | C4058+Ft39+ P212 | 22 | 0.2 | 5339 | 52.3 | 4309 | 42.2 | 530 | 5.2 | 0 | 53 |
| **RUSSIAN FEDERATION** | F749198+ W70000+ R288669 | C127962+ Ft17340+ Pe8814 | 1107867 | 65.6 | 417994 | 24.8 | 154116 | 9.1 | 8873 | 0.5 | 66 | 90 |
| **ASIA** | | | | | | | | | | | | |
| Afghanistan | c | C8054+F8+ P3000 | 11090 | 17.0 | 42039 | 64.5 | 11062 | 17.0 | 1018 | 1.6 | 17 | 81 |

190

| Country | Natural note | Cultivated [Built] notes | Natural 000 ha | Nat % | Mod 000 ha | Mod % | Cult 000 ha | Cult % | Built 000 ha | Built % | Nat score | Conv score |
|---|---|---|---|---|---|---|---|---|---|---|---|---|
| Armenia | F284+W41+ R30 | C559+Ft13+P69 [e95] | 355 | 12.6 | 1631 | 57.8 | 641 | 22.7 | 193 | 6.8 | 13 | 70 |
| Azerbaijan | F400+W15+ R128 | C1935+Ft20+ P220 | 543 | 6.3 | 5562 | 64.2 | 2175 | 25.1 | 380 | 4.4 | 6 | 70 |
| Bahrain | F0+R0 | C5+F0+P0 | 0 | 0.0 | 47 | 68.1 | 5 | 7.2 | 17 | 24.6 | 0 | 68 |
| Bangladesh | c | C8241+F310+ P60 | 0 | 0.0 | 3200 | 24.6 | 8611 | 66.2 | 1206 | 9.3 | 0 | 24 |
| Bhutan | c | C160+F8+P27 | 1365 | 29.0 | 3045 | 64.8 | 195 | 4.1 | 95 | 2.0 | 29 | 94 |
| Brunei Darussalam | i | C7+F0+P1 | 310 | 58.8 | 194 | 36.8 | 8 | 1.5 | 15 | 2.8 | 59 | 96 |
| Cambodia | c | C3807+F7+ P150 | 3880 | 22.0 | 9296 | 52.7 | 3964 | 22.5 | 512 | 2.9 | 22 | 75 |
| China | c | C135371+ F33800+ P40000 | 205200 | 22.0 | 456408 | 48.9 | 209171 | 22.4 | 61963 | 6.6 | 22 | 71 |
| Cyprus | F0+W0+R28 | C145+Ft27+P0 [e95] | 28 | 3.0 | 684 | 74.0 | 172 | 18.6 | 40 | 4.3 | 3 | 77 |
| Georgia | F550+W0+R8 | C1066+Ft200+ P189 | 558 | 8.0 | 4698 | 67.4 | 1455 | 20.9 | 259 | 3.7 | 8 | 75 |
| India | c | C169850+ F14620+ P1130 | 5950 | 2.0 | 77269 | 26.0 | 185600 | 62.4 | 28500 | 9.6 | 2 | 28 |
| Indonesia | m | C30987+F6125+P1195 | 93150 | 51.4 | 39638 | 21.9 | 38307 | 21.1 | 10062 | 5.6 | 51 | 73 |
| Iran | c | C19400+F79+ P4400 | 9730 | 6.0 | 125418 | 77.3 | 23879 | 14.7 | 3173 | 2.0 | 6 | 83 |
| Iraq | c | C5540+F14+ P400 | 10930 | 25.0 | 25814 | 59.0 | 5954 | 13.6 | 1039 | 2.4 | 25 | 84 |
| Israel | F0+W0+R21 | C437+Ft91+P15 | 21 | 1.0 | 1212 | 58.8 | 543 | 26.3 | 286 | 13.9 | 1 | 60 |
| Japan | F3061+W0+ R0 | C4295+Ft10682+Pe65 | 3061 | 8.1 | 13261 | 35.2 | 15042 | 40.0 | 6288 | 16.7 | 8 | 43 |
| Jordan | c | C390+F23+P79 | 4450 | 50.0 | 3654 | 41.1 | 492 | 5.5 | 297 | 3.3 | 50 | 91 |
| Kazakhstan | F0+W0+ R19312 | C30135+Ft5+ P18682 | 19312 | 7.2 | 197953 | 74.1 | 48822 | 18.3 | 986 | 0.4 | 7 | 81 |
| Korea, DPR | F47+R27 | C2000+F1470+P5 | 74 | 0.6 | 7362 | 61.1 | 3475 | 28.9 | 1130 | 9.4 | 1 | 62 |
| Korea, R | c | C1924+F†363+Pe#0 | 0 | 0.0 | 6226 | 63.1 | 2287 | 23.2 | 1360 | 13.8 | 0 | 63 |
| Kuwait | c | C7+F5+P7 | 588 | 33.0 | 1091 | 61.2 | 19 | 1.1 | 84 | 4.7 | 33 | 94 |
| Kyrgyzstan | F100+W0+ R1325 | C1425+Ft57+ P900 | 1425 | 7.4 | 15143 | 79.0 | 2382 | 12.4 | 230 | 1.2 | 7 | 86 |
| Lao PDR | i | C852+F4+P80 | 3830 | 16.6 | 18069 | 78.3 | 936 | 4.1 | 245 | 1.1 | 17 | 95 |
| Lebanon | F0+R11 | C308+F13+P2 | 11 | 1.1 | 597 | 58.4 | 323 | 31.6 | 92 | 9.0 | 1 | 59 |
| Malaysia | c | C7605+F99+ P28 | 13470 | 41.0 | 10626 | 32.3 | 7732 | 23.5 | 1027 | 3.1 | 41 | 73 |
| Maldives | F0+R0 | C3+F0+P0 | 0 | 0.0 | 24 | 80.0 | 3 | 10.0 | 3 | 10.0 | 0 | 80 |
| Mongolia | c | C1320+F0+ P1320 | 93990 | 60.0 | 59870 | 38.2 | 2640 | 1.7 | 150 | 0.1 | 60 | 98 |
| Myanmar | c | C10151+F276+P35 | 4600 | 7.0 | 48523 | 73.8 | 10462 | 15.9 | 2170 | 3.3 | 7 | 81 |
| Nepal | c | C2968+F56+ P176 | 3000 | 21.0 | 7010 | 49.0 | 3200 | 22.4 | 1090 | 7.6 | 21 | 70 |
| Oman | c | C63+F0+P63 | 16360 | 77.0 | 4626 | 21.8 | 126 | 0.6 | 134 | 0.6 | 77 | 99 |
| Pakistan | c | C21600+F168+P500 | 3850 | 5.0 | 43967 | 57.0 | 22268 | 28.9 | 7003 | 9.1 | 5 | 62 |
| Philippines | i | C9520+F203+ P128 | 2590 | 8.7 | 15279 | 51.2 | 9851 | 33.0 | 2097 | 7.0 | 9 | 60 |
| Qatar | F0+R181 | C17+F0+P5 | 181 | 16.5 | 869 | 79.0 | 22 | 2.0 | 28 | 2.5 | 16 | 95 |
| Saudi Arabia | c178420a | C3830+F1+ P3830 | 149301 | 69.5 | 56877 | 26.5 | 7661 | 3.6 | 1130 | 0.5 | 69 | 96 |
| Singapore | F0+R0 | C1+F0+P0 [i] | 0 | 0.0 | 27 | 44.3 | 1 | 1.6 | 33 | 54.1 | 0 | 44 |
| Sri Lanka | F0+R18 | C1888+F139+ P44 | 18 | 0.3 | 3831 | 59.3 | 2071 | 32.0 | 543 | 8.4 | 0 | 60 |
| Syrian Arab R | c | C5521+F127+ P830 | 1650 | 9.0 | 9521 | 51.8 | 6478 | 35.2 | 729 | 4.0 | 9 | 61 |
| Tajikistan | F21+W18+ R1337 | C890+Ft10+ P355 | 1376 | 9.8 | 11137 | 79.2 | 1255 | 8.9 | 292 | 2.1 | 10 | 89 |
| Thailand | c | C20445+F529+P80 | 4090 | 8.0 | 22986 | 45.0 | 21054 | 41.2 | 2959 | 5.8 | 8 | 53 |
| Turkey | F186+W144+ R888 | C29162+Ft1854+Pe1238 | 1218 | 1.6 | 40374 | 52.5 | 32254 | 41.9 | 3117 | 4.0 | 2 | 54 |
| Turkmenistan | F0+W0+ R5668 | C1695+Ft12+ P1695 | 5668 | 12.1 | 37715 | 80.3 | 3402 | 7.2 | 208 | 0.4 | 12 | 92 |
| United Arab Emirates | c7440a | C81+F60+P29 | 6474 | 77.4 | 1354 | 16.2 | 170 | 2.0 | 362 | 4.3 | 77 | 94 |
| Uzbekistan | F200+W0+ R636 | C4850+Ft300+ P2080 | 836 | 2.0 | 32216 | 77.8 | 7230 | 17.5 | 1142 | 2.8 | 2 | 80 |
| Viet Nam | c | C7202+F1470+P33 | 650 | 2.0 | 20939 | 64.3 | 8705 | 26.7 | 2255 | 6.9 | 2 | 66 |
| Yemen | F0+R7564 | C1555+F0+ P1555 | 7564 | 14.3 | 41339 | 78.3 | 3110 | 5.9 | 784 | 1.5 | 14 | 93 |
| PACIFIC | | | | | | | | | | | | |
| Australia | F18836+ W29472+ R40538 | C26100+ Ft1043+ Pe30000 | 88846 | 11.6 | 618250 | 80.5 | 57143 | 7.4 | 3991 | 0.5 | 12 | 92 |
| Fiji | F38+R36 | C285+F78+P17 | 74 | 4.1 | 1334 | 73.0 | 380 | 20.8 | 39 | 2.1 | 4 | 77 |
| New Zealand | F1599+W0+ R907 | C3280+Ft1542+Pe1317 | 2506 | 9.4 | 17559 | 65.5 | 6139 | 22.9 | 595 | 2.2 | 9 | 75 |
| Papua New Guinea | c | C670+F30+P9 | 28530 | 63.0 | 15827 | 34.9 | 709 | 1.6 | 220 | 0.5 | 63 | 98 |
| Samoa | F4+R0 | C122+F9+P0 | 4 | 1.4 | 140 | 49.5 | 131 | 46.3 | 8 | 2.8 | 1 | 51 |
| Solomon Is | F711+R20 | C60+F18+P4 | 731 | 26.1 | 1966 | 70.2 | 82 | 2.9 | 20 | 0.7 | 26 | 96 |
| Tonga | F0+R0 | C48+F0+P0 | 0 | 0.0 | 19 | 26.4 | 48 | 66.7 | 5 | 6.9 | 0 | 26 |
| Vanuatu | F232+R16 | C120+F7+P3 | 248 | 20.3 | 832 | 68.3 | 130 | 10.7 | 9 | 0.7 | 20 | 89 |

**Notes**

The land modification and conversion indicator measures the converted and natural proportions of a country's land area. All data are in thousand hectares (000 ha), and all percentages are in terms of land area (Table 10).

Natural note = sources of data in the natural land column. A single lower-case letter (c, d, i, m, r, or s) indicates a source. If it is followed by a number and a lower-case letter a (e.g., d321a), it means that the estimate of natural land has been adjusted to avoid excessive conflict with the estimates of degraded land in Table 13. The original estimate is the number between the source letter and the a. ("Excessive conflict" arises when the area of degraded land exceeds the combined area of cultivated and modified land, in which case the area of natural land was adjusted so as to increase the area of modified land until the combined area of cultivated and modified land equals 100% of the area of degraded land.) Combinations of upper-case letters and numbers show the estimated area of natural land that is forest (F), other woodland (W), and remaining unconverted land (R). For more explanation, see Natural land below.

Cultivated [Built] notes = sources of data in the cultivated and built columns. For explanation, see Cultivated land and Built land below.

Natural/Nat = natural land = land that is negligibly to lightly human-influenced. Estimates of natural land area are extremely rough and different sources often differ greatly. The sources are given in the Natural note column:

Americas (except Canada and United States): Dinerstein, Olson, Graham *et al.* (1995), indicated by the letter d.

191

Canada and USA: Ricketts, Dinerstein, Olson *et al.* (1998), indicated by the letter r.

Africa (except Cape Verde, Comoros, Djibouti, Eritrea, Ethiopia, Guinea-Bissau, Lesotho, Mauritius, São Tomé & Principe, Seychelles, Sierra Leone, Swaziland, Togo): Conservation International (1996), indicated by the letter c; or MacKinnon & MacKinnon (1986a), indicated by the letter m. In the event of a conflict between these sources, the lower estimate was chosen.

Cape Verde: Stuart & Adams (1990), indicated by the letter s.

Europe: UNECE & FAO (2000), indicated by the F+W+R figures. F = the reported area of native forest that is undisturbed. W = the reported area of other woodland that is undisturbed. R = a *Wellbeing of Nations* (WoN) estimate of the area of remaining unconverted land that is natural.

Asia (except Armenia, Azerbaijan, Bahrain, Cyprus, Georgia, Israel, Japan, Kazakhstan, DPR Korea, Kyrgyzstan, Lebanon, Maldives, Qatar, Singapore, Sri Lanka, Tajikistan, Turkey, Turkmenistan, Uzbekistan, Yemen): Conservation International (1996), indicated by the letter c; Asian Bureau for Conservation & World Conservation Monitoring Centre (1997), indicated by the letter i; or MacKinnon & MacKinnon (1986b), indicated by the letter m. In the event of a conflict among these sources, the lowest estimate was chosen, except in the cases of Brunei Darussalam, Lao PDR, and Philippines. For these countries, Asian Bureau for Conservation & World Conservation Monitoring Centre (1997) was chosen as the source, because it provided more detailed assessment that clearly distinguished between natural and modified components of remaining original habitat.

Russian Federation, Armenia, Azerbaijan, Cyprus, Georgia, Israel, Japan, Kazakhstan, Kyrgyzstan, Tajikistan, Turkey, Turkmenistan, Uzbekistan: UNECE & FAO (2000), indicated by the F+W+R figures. F = the reported area of native forest that is undisturbed. W = the reported area of other woodland that is undisturbed. R = a WoN estimate of the area of remaining unconverted land that is natural.

Australia and New Zealand: UNECE & FAO (2000), indicated by the F+W+R figures. F = the reported area of native forest that is undisturbed. W = the reported area of other woodland that is undisturbed. R = a WoN estimate of the area of remaining unconverted land that is natural.

Papua New Guinea: Conservation International (1996), indicated by the letter c.

All other countries: WoN estimates, indicated by F+R figures (as for UNECE & FAO [2000] but without the W figure). F = the estimated area of natural forest that is natural. R = the estimated area of remaining unconverted land that is natural.

Dinerstein, Olson, Graham *et al.* (1995) used satellite imagery, maps and assessments by regional experts to define and map Latin American and Caribbean ecoregions and estimate habitat loss and fragmentation for each ecoregion. Table 11a shows my interpretations of their estimates to determine the percentage of each ecoregion that is intact or natural. Dinerstein, Olson, Graham *et al.* (1995) did not provide country-by-country estimates of habitat loss and fragmention. To do this, WoN overlaid their ecoregion maps with national boundaries to allocate ecoregions to countries. For ecoregions shared by more than one country, this implies that the percentage of intact habitat is evenly distributed throughout the ecoregion. This may not be true: an ecoregion estimated to be 50% intact and shared equally by two countries could be 75% intact in one country and 25% intact in the other. WoN's interpretations of the method of Dinerstein, Olson, Graham *et al.* (1995) produced some apparent overestimates of natural land area (for example, Trinidad & Tobago) but no obvious underestimate.

Ricketts, Dinerstein, Olson *et al.* (1998) used satellite imagery and assessments by national experts to define and map North American ecoregions and estimate the intact percentage of each. WoN overlaid their ecoregion map with national boundaries to allocate ecoregions to Canada or the United States, and estimate how much of the land area of each country is natural (= intact).

Conservation International (1996) was a global-scale analysis that used maps and satellite imagery to obtain country-by-country estimates of areas that were undisturbed, partially disturbed, or human dominated. The method is described in Hannah *et al.* (1994) and Hannah, Carr & Lankerani (1995). The smallest area mapped was 40,000 ha, and the smallest area recognized as undisturbed was 100,000 ha. The method tended to overestimate the undisturbed percentage in large, sparsely populated countries, and to underestimate it in small, densely populated countries. WoN interpreted undisturbed as equivalent to natural.

MacKinnon & MacKinnon (1986a &1986b) used maps and satellite imagery to estimate the percentage of original habitat remaining in subSaharan African countries (MacKinnon & MacKinnon 1986a) and South and Southeast Asian countries (MacKinnon & MacKinnon 1986b). Asian Bureau for Conservation & World Conservation Monitoring Centre (1997) used the same approach to update MacKinnon & MacKinnon (1986b). The term "original habitat remaining" is misleading, implying that the habitat is natural although some or much of it may be modified.

Stuart & Adams (1990) reported of Cape Verde: "Original vegetation unknown, and in any case long since destroyed through over-grazing and erosion."

The *Temperate and Boreal Forest Resources Assessment 2000* (UNECE & FAO 2000) contains national estimates by countries in North America, Europe and Asia-Pacific of the percentages of their native forest and other woodland that are undisturbed. WoN interpreted undisturbed as equivalent to natural.

WoN estimates assumed: 1% of native forest land (F) for each 0.2 ha F per person (up to 20 ha F per person) + 1% of remaining unconverted land (R) for each 0.1 ha R per person (up to 10 ha R per person). Exceptionally, for Finland, Iceland, Norway, Russia, Kazakhstan, Turkmenistan, Australia, and New Zealand—countries with low population densities (more than 5.0 ha/person) and natural forest and woodland data from UNECE & FAO (2000)—WoN assumed 50% of R was natural. WoN estimates were made in any of the following circumstances: (a) no other estimate was available; (b) to supplement UNECE & FAO (2000), which covers only forests and other woodland; (c) a Conservation International (1996) estimate of 0% seemed too low.

Mod = modified land = land that is moderately to heavily human-influenced, but not cultivated or built. Uncultivated permanent pasture is counted as modified. Otherwise this category is a residual obtained as follows: total land - natural land - cultivated land - built land = modified land.

Cult = cultivated land = cropland + plantation forest + cultivated pasture. The areas of cropland (C), plantation forest (F) and cultivated pasture (P) are given in the Cultivated [Built] notes column.

Cropland (C) = land under permanent or temporary agricultural crops, including temporary meadows for mowing or pasture, land under market and kitchen gardens, and land temporarily fallow (under five years). Data are for 1997 and are from FAO (1999a), except for Belgium and Luxembourg which are from Organisation for Economic Co-operation and Development (1999).

Plantation forest (F) = forests that have been established artificially, usually consisting of non-indigenous species or stocks. Data are for 1995 and are from FAO (1997a), except where indicated by the letter t which are for different years (given in the forest note column of Table 10) and are from UNECE & FAO (2000). † indicates a conflict between the reported area of forest and other reported areas in R Korea, resolved by reducing the area of plantation forest (in 000 ha) from 1,400 to 363.

Cultivated pasture (P) = sown (not wild) meadows and pastures. Except for Australia, data are WoN estimates, and are either 10% of the area of permanent pasture (land used for five years or more for wild or cultivated herbaceous forage crops) or the same area as cropland, whichever is smaller. Permanent pasture data are for 1994—the last year for which FAO has compiled pasture data—and are from FAO (1999a), except where indicated by the letter e which are for 1997 and are from Organisation for Economic Co-operation and Development (1999). In the case of Australia, FAO and OECD figures for arable land include 30 million ha of cultivated grassland. This has been subtracted from cropland and recorded separately as cultivated pasture. The FAO and OECD figures for permanent pasture are assumed to be all uncultivated. # indicates a conflict between the reported area of permanent pasture and other reported areas—resolved by reducing the area of permanent pasture as follows (in 000 ha): Guyana from 1230 to 562; Burundi from 1,090 to 963; Guinea-Bissau from 1,080 to 107; São Tomé & Principe from 1 to 0; Greece from 5217 to 5079; Italy from 4558 to 4538; R Korea from 90 to 0.

Built = built land = land occupied by buildings, transport infrastructure (roads, railways, docks, airports, etc.) and other human structures, including mines and quarries, waste tips, derelict land, and urban and suburban parks and gardens. Data are WoN estimates for 1996 except where indicated by a note in brackets (e.g., [u86]) in the Cultivated [Built] notes column as follows:

b Beeler (1992).

e Eurostat, European Commission, & the European Environment Agency (1998).

i Asian Bureau for Conservation & World Conservation Monitoring Centre (1997).

u United Nations Statistical Commission & Economic Commission for Europe (1992).

The applicable year is indicated in brackets. Data for years before 1990 have been adjusted to 1996 (indicated by the letter a) on the basis of population. Data for 1990 onwards have not been adjusted. Lithuania's built area, reported as an exceptionally low 17,600 ha, has been adjusted to 176,000 ha.

WoN estimates of built land draw on the data from the above sources to derive an average of 0.05 ha built land per person, except as follows:

Countries with a population density of 0.0-0.2 ha per person and a real Gross Domestic Product (GDP) of purchasing power parity (PPP) $0-PPP$5,000 (Bangladesh, Maldives): 0.01 ha built land per person.

Countries with a population density of 0.0-0.2 ha per person and a real GDP of PPP$10,200-PPP$20,000 (Barbados, Mauritius, Bahrain, R Korea): 0.03 ha built land per person.

Countries with a population density of 3.3-6.4 ha per person and a real GDP of PPP$5,100-PPP$10,000 (Brazil, Chile, Uruguay, Venezuela): 0.06 ha built land per person.

Countries with a population density of 3.3-6.4 ha per person and a real GDP of PPP$10,200-PPP$20,000 (Bahamas, United Arab Emirates): 0.16 ha built land per person.

Countries with a population density of 6.5-102.4 ha per person and a real GDP of PPP$2,500-PPP$10,000 (Argentina, Belize, Bolivia, Guyana, Paraguay, Suriname, Algeria, Botswana, Gabon, Libyan Arab J, Namibia, Russian Federation, Kazakhstan, Mongolia, Oman, Saudi Arabia): 0.06 ha built land per person.

Countries with a population density of 6.5-12.8 ha per person and a real GDP of PPP$10,200-PPP$20,000 (New Zealand): 0.16 ha built land per person.

Countries with a population density of 25.7-102.4 ha per person and a real GDP of PPP$10,200-PPP$20,000 (Australia): 0.22 ha built land per person.

Nat score = score for natural land as % of total land. See Table 10a for performance criteria.

Conv score = score for converted (cultivated + built) land as % of total land. See Table 10a for performance criteria.

| Categories of Dinerstein, Olson, Graham et al. (1995) | | | WoN interpretations |
|---|---|---|---|
| habitat loss | habitat block size | habitat fragmentation | |
| 0-10% lost | very large | relatively contiguous | 95% intact |
| 0-10% lost | all others | all others | 90% intact |
| 10-24% lost | very large | relatively contiguous | 85% intact |
| 10-24% lost | large or very large | low fragmentation | 80% intact |
| 10-24% lost | all others | all others | 75% intact |
| 24-49% lost | very large | relatively contiguous | 70% intact |
| 24-49% lost | large or very large | low fragmentation | 60% intact |
| 24-49% lost | all others | all others | 50% intact |
| 50-89% lost | very large | relatively contiguous | 40% intact |
| 50-89% lost | large or very large | low fragmentation | 25% intact |
| 50-89% lost | all others | all others | 10% intact |
| more than 90% lost | all | all | 0% intact |
| no data | all | all | 0% intact |

Table 11a. Intact percentages of ecoregions of Latin America and the Caribbean. *Wellbeing of Nations* (WoN) interpretations of Dinerstein and colleagues' categories of habitat loss, habitat block size, and habitat fragmentation.

# Table 12. Land Protection

| Country | Total area 000 ha | MTP 000 ha | MTP % | ITP 000 ha | ITP % | LTP 000 ha | LTP % | KTP 000 ha | KTP % | PP 000 ha | PP % | Wtd tot % | Size score | No & type unit | Ave % TP | Ave % PP | Ave % totP | Wtd % | Div score | LP score |
|---|---|---|---|---|---|---|---|---|---|---|---|---|---|---|---|---|---|---|---|---|
| **AMERICAS** | | | | | | | | | | | | | | | | | | | | |
| Antigua & Barbuda | 44 | 0 | 0 | 0 | 0 | 0 | 0 | 4 | 9.1 | 0 | 0 | 22.7 | 83 | -- | -- | -- | -- | -- | -- | 80* |
| Argentina | 278040 | 0 | 0 | 1793 | 0.6 | 1235 | 0.4 | 145 | 0.1 | 5939 | 2.1 | 2.9 | 23 | 12 ft | -- | -- | 6.3 | 4.7 | 38 | 28 |
| Bahamas | 1388 | 0 | 0 | 0 | 0 | 95 | 6.8 | 3 | 0.2 | 1 | 0.1 | 14.0 | 68 | 5 mez | 0.0 | 0.0 | 0.0 | 0.0 | 0 | 45 |
| Barbados | 43 | 0 | 0 | 0 | 0 | 0 | 0 | 0 | 0 | 0 | 0 | 0 | 0 | 2 ft | -- | -- | 0.0 | 0.0 | 0 | 0 |
| Belize | 2296 | 0 | 0 | 108 | 4.7 | 69 | 3.0 | 21 | 0.9 | 630 | 27.4 | 32.9 | 93 | 3 mez | 11.8 | 26.7 | 38.5 | 25.1 | 85 | 90 |
| Bolivia | 109858 | 8060 | 7.3 | 1895 | 1.7 | 189 | 0.2 | 0 | 0 | 7674 | 7.0 | 25.5 | 86 | 14 ez | 2.9 | 3.8 | 6.7 | 4.8 | 38 | 70 |
| Brazil | 854740 | 7415 | 0.9 | 12202 | 1.4 | 2229 | 0.3 | 320 | 0 | 30296 | 3.5 | 7.3 | 49 | 18 ez | 3.1 | 6.7 | 9.8 | 6.4 | 46 | 48 |
| Canada | 997061 | 22293 | 2.2 | 16022 | 1.6 | 3847 | 0.4 | 816 | 0.1 | 51789 | 5.2 | 12.0 | 64 | 8 ft | -- | -- | 7.6 | 5.7 | 43 | 57 |
| Chile | 75663 | 6728 | 8.9 | 1429 | 1.9 | 510 | 0.7 | 54 | 0.1 | 5406 | 7.1 | 30.7 | 91 | 4 ft | -- | -- | 9.6 | 7.2 | 49 | 77 |
| Colombia | 113891 | 2372 | 2.1 | 5858 | 5.1 | 751 | 0.7 | 31 | 0 | 349 | 0.3 | 16.7 | 73 | 17 ez | 6.3 | 8.3 | 14.6 | 10.4 | 61 | 69 |
| Costa Rica | 5110 | 0 | 0 | 194 | 3.8 | 336 | 6.6 | 51 | 1.0 | 617 | 12.1 | 30.3 | 90 | 5 mez | 12.9 | 7.2 | 20.1 | 16.5 | 73 | 85 |
| Cuba | 11086 | 0 | 0 | 0 | 0 | 116 | 1.0 | 33 | 0.3 | 1750 | 15.8 | 9.7 | 59 | 5 mez | 4.6 | 5.2 | 9.8 | 7.2 | 49 | 55 |
| Dominica | 75 | 0 | 0 | 0 | 0 | 0 | 0 | 7 | 9.3 | 9 | 12.0 | 29.2 | 89 | -- | -- | -- | -- | -- | -- | 80* |
| Dominican R | 4873 | 0 | 0 | 694 | 14.2 | 249 | 5.1 | 6 | 0.1 | 299 | 6.1 | 48.9 | 100 | 4 mez | 14.5 | 0.8 | 15.3 | 14.9 | 70 | 90 |
| Ecuador | 28356 | 0 | 0 | 3642 | 12.8 | 261 | 0.9 | 0 | 0 | 3645 | 12.9 | 33.4 | 93 | 13 ez | 6.7 | 1.0 | 7.7 | 7.2 | 49 | 79 |
| El Salvador | 2104 | 0 | 0 | 0 | 0 | 0 | 0 | 3 | 0.1 | 2 | 0.1 | 0.3 | 2 | 3 mez | 0.2 | 0.2 | 0.4 | 0.3 | 2 | 2 |
| Grenada | 34 | 0 | 0 | 0 | 0 | 0 | 0 | 0 | 0 | 0 | 0 | 0 | 0 | -- | -- | -- | -- | -- | -- | 0 |
| Guatemala | 10889 | 0 | 0 | 1267 | 11.6 | 527 | 4.8 | 27 | 0.2 | 344 | 3.2 | 32.2 | 92 | 6 mez | 8.1 | 0.7 | 8.8 | 8.4 | 54 | 79 |
| Guyana | 21497 | 0 | 0 | 0 | 0 | 59 | 0.3 | 0 | 0 | 0 | 0 | 0.4 | 3 | 5 ez | 0.0 | 0.0 | 0.0 | 0.0 | 0 | 2 |
| Haiti | 2775 | 0 | 0 | 0 | 0 | 0 | 0 | 7 | 0.3 | 2 | 0.1 | 0.5 | 4 | 5 mez | 0.1 | 0.0 | 0.1 | 0.1 | 1 | 3 |
| Honduras | 11209 | 0 | 0 | 332 | 3.0 | 327 | 2.9 | 21 | 0.2 | 449 | 4.0 | 12.5 | 65 | 5 mez | 1.2 | 3.2 | 4.4 | 2.8 | 22 | 51 |
| Jamaica | 1099 | 0 | 0 | 0 | 0 | 0 | 0 | 0 | 0 | 82 | 7.5 | 3.8 | 30 | 5 mez | 0.0 | 11.4 | 11.4 | 5.7 | 43 | 35 |
| Mexico | 195820 | 0 | 0 | 1338 | 0.7 | 543 | 0.3 | 64 | 0 | 12635 | 6.5 | 5.1 | 40 | 9 mez | 1.8 | 2.9 | 4.7 | 3.2 | 26 | 35 |
| Nicaragua | 13000 | 0 | 0 | 295 | 2.3 | 34 | 0.3 | 10 | 0.1 | 1244 | 9.6 | 9.9 | 60 | 4 mez | 5.5 | 10.9 | 16.4 | 10.9 | 62 | 60 |
| Panama | 7552 | 0 | 0 | 1185 | 15.7 | 145 | 1.9 | 22 | 0.3 | 181 | 2.4 | 44.7 | 100 | 4 mez | 10.5 | 7.4 | 17.9 | 14.2 | 68 | 89 |
| Paraguay | 40675 | 0 | 0 | 1160 | 2.9 | 196 | 0.5 | 9 | 0 | 35 | 0.1 | 6.7 | 47 | 5 ez | 1.4 | 0.4 | 1.8 | 1.6 | 13 | 35 |
| Peru | 128522 | 1533 | 1.2 | 1274 | 1.0 | 171 | 0.1 | 22 | 0 | 3760 | 2.9 | 6.7 | 47 | 16 ez | 4.8 | 2.2 | 7.0 | 5.9 | 44 | 46 |
| St Kitts & Nevis | 26 | 0 | 0 | 0 | 0 | 0 | 0 | 3 | 11.5 | 0 | 0 | 28.7 | 89 | 1 ft | -- | -- | 0.0 | 0.0 | 0 | 59 |
| St Lucia | 62 | 0 | 0 | 0 | 0 | 0 | 0 | 1 | 1.6 | 6 | 9.7 | 8.8 | 55 | 5 ft | -- | -- | 25.7 | 19.3 | 79 | 63 |
| St Vincent & Grenadines | 39 | 0 | 0 | 0 | 0 | 0 | 0 | 0 | 0 | 4 | 10.3 | 5.2 | 41 | -- | -- | -- | -- | -- | -- | 41 |
| Suriname | 16326 | 0 | 0 | 0 | 0 | 0 | 0 | 8 | 0 | 796 | 4.9 | 2.5 | 20 | 3 ez | 0.3 | 5.1 | 5.4 | 2.8 | 22 | 21 |
| Trinidad & Tobago | 513 | 0 | 0 | 0 | 0 | 0 | 0 | 2 | 0.4 | 17 | 3.3 | 2.4 | 19 | 2 mez | 0.1 | 0.0 | 0.1 | 0.1 | 1 | 13 |
| United States | 936352 | 31542 | 3.4 | 29443 | 3.1 | 8127 | 0.9 | 1742 | 0.2 | 59548 | 6.4 | 19.5 | 79 | 8 ft | -- | -- | 6.6 | 4.8 | 38 | 65 |
| Uruguay | 17741 | 0 | 0 | 0 | 0 | 14 | 0.1 | 1 | 0 | 31 | 0.2 | 0.3 | 2 | 4 ft | -- | -- | 1.0 | 0.7 | 6 | 3 |
| Venezuela | 91205 | 10650 | 11.7 | 7425 | 8.1 | 1128 | 1.2 | 53 | 0.1 | 36781 | 40.3 | 67.5 | 100 | 16 ez | 23.8 | 20.9 | 44.7 | 34.2 | 94 | 98 |
| **AFRICA** | | | | | | | | | | | | | | | | | | | | |
| Algeria | 238174 | 5640 | 2.4 | 0 | 0 | 98 | 0 | 24 | 0 | 129 | 0.1 | 6.1 | 44 | 4 ft | -- | -- | 23.6 | 17.7 | 75 | 55 |
| Angola | 124670 | 2960 | 2.4 | 2400 | 1.9 | 63 | 0.1 | 0 | 0 | 2758 | 2.2 | 11.1 | 62 | 9 ez | 0.2 | 7.4 | 7.6 | 3.9 | 31 | 52 |
| Benin | 11262 | 0 | 0 | 777 | 6.9 | 0 | 0 | 0 | 0 | 485 | 4.3 | 16.0 | 72 | 4 ez | 13.1 | 10.6 | 23.7 | 18.4 | 77 | 74 |
| Botswana | 58173 | 3823 | 6.6 | 728 | 1.3 | 0 | 0 | 0 | 0 | 5945 | 10.2 | 24.2 | 84 | 5 ez | 17.1 | 1.5 | 18.6 | 17.8 | 76 | 81 |
| Burkina Faso | 27400 | 0 | 0 | 478 | 1.7 | 57 | 0.2 | 0 | 0 | 2321 | 8.5 | 8.0 | 52 | 4 ez | 1.1 | 33.3 | 34.4 | 25.8 | 86 | 63 |
| Burundi | 2783 | 0 | 0 | 0 | 0 | 0 | 0 | 0 | 0 | 144 | 5.2 | 2.6 | 21 | 3 ez | 0.0 | 2.9 | 2.9 | 1.4 | 11 | 18 |
| Cameroon | 47544 | 0 | 0 | 1026 | 2.2 | 0 | 0 | 6 | 0 | 1066 | 2.2 | 5.5 | 42 | 8 ez | 5.0 | 2.2 | 7.2 | 6.1 | 44 | 43 |
| Cape Verde | 403 | 0 | 0 | 0 | 0 | 0 | 0 | 0 | 0 | 0 | 0 | 0 | 0 | -- | -- | -- | -- | -- | -- | 0 |
| Central African R | 62298 | 2810 | 4.5 | 292 | 0.5 | 86 | 0.1 | 0 | 0 | 2258 | 3.6 | 14.3 | 69 | 5 ez | 5.3 | 15.7 | 21.0 | 13.1 | 66 | 68 |
| Chad | 128400 | 0 | 0 | 414 | 0.3 | 0 | 0 | 0 | 0 | 11080 | 8.6 | 4.9 | 39 | 7 ez | 0.4 | 5.3 | 5.7 | 3.0 | 24 | 34 |
| Comoros | 223 | 0 | 0 | 0 | 0 | 0 | 0 | 0 | 0 | 0 | 0 | 0 | 0 | -- | -- | -- | -- | -- | -- | 0 |
| Congo, DR | 234486 | 7285 | 3.1 | 2632 | 1.1 | 0 | 0 | 0 | 0 | 0 | 0 | 9.9 | 60 | 10 ez | 13.5 | 1.2 | 14.7 | 14.1 | 68 | 63 |
| Congo, R | 34200 | 0 | 0 | 513 | 1.5 | 0 | 0 | 0 | 0 | 1187 | 3.5 | 4.8 | 38 | 2 ez | 0.2 | 1.9 | 2.1 | 1.1 | 9 | 29 |
| Côte d'Ivoire | 32246 | 1150 | 3.6 | 574 | 1.8 | 158 | 0.5 | 8 | 0 | 102 | 0.3 | 13.4 | 67 | 3 ez | 7.9 | 1.5 | 9.4 | 8.6 | 54 | 63 |
| Djibouti | 2320 | 0 | 0 | 0 | 0 | 10 | 0.4 | 0 | 0 | 0 | 0 | 0.8 | 6 | 2 ft | -- | -- | 0.0 | 0.0 | 0 | 4 |
| Egypt | 100145 | 0 | 0 | 0 | 0 | 30 | 0 | 7 | 0 | 695 | 0.7 | 0.3 | 2 | 2 ft | -- | -- | 0.0 | 0.0 | 0 | 2 |
| Equatorial Guinea | 2805 | 0 | 0 | 0 | 0 | 0 | 0 | 0 | 0 | 0 | 0 | 0 | 0 | 3 ez | 0.0 | 0.0 | 0.0 | 0.0 | 0 | 0 |
| Eritrea | 11760 | 0 | 0 | 0 | 0 | 0 | 0 | 0 | 0 | 501 | 4.3 | 2.2 | 18 | 8 ez | 0.0 | 4.6 | 4.6 | 2.3 | 18 | 18 |
| Ethiopia | 110430 | 0 | 0 | 2797 | 2.5 | 233 | 0.2 | 5 | 0 | 15664 | 14.2 | 12.4 | 65 | 11 ez | 2.7 | 14.7 | 17.4 | 10.0 | 60 | 63 |
| Gabon | 26767 | 0 | 0 | 0 | 0 | 15 | 0.1 | 0 | 0 | 708 | 2.6 | 1.5 | 12 | 2 ez | 0.0 | 3.7 | 3.7 | 1.8 | 14 | 13 |
| Gambia | 1129 | 0 | 0 | 0 | 0 | 11 | 1.0 | 7 | 0.6 | 3 | 0.3 | 3.1 | 25 | 2 ez | 0.9 | 0.7 | 1.6 | 1.2 | 10 | 20 |
| Ghana | 23854 | 0 | 0 | 1014 | 4.3 | 75 | 0.3 | 8 | 0 | 171 | 0.7 | 9.3 | 57 | 3 ez | 3.2 | 1.1 | 4.3 | 3.7 | 30 | 48 |
| Guinea | 24586 | 0 | 0 | 112 | 0.5 | 51 | 0.2 | 0 | 0 | 0 | 0 | 1.3 | 10 | 5 ez | 0.5 | 3.0 | 3.5 | 2.0 | 16 | 12 |

194

| Country | Total area 000 ha | MTP 000 ha | MTP % | ITP 000 ha | ITP % | LTP 000 ha | LTP % | KTP 000 ha | KTP % | PP 000 ha | PP % | Wtd tot % | Size score | No & type unit | Ave % TP | Ave % PP | Ave % totP | Wtd % | Div score | LP score |
|---|---|---|---|---|---|---|---|---|---|---|---|---|---|---|---|---|---|---|---|---|
| Guinea-Bissau | 3612 | 0 | 0 | 0 | 0 | 0 | 0 | 0 | 0 | 0 | 0 | 0 | 0 | 3 ez | 0.0 | 0.0 | 0.0 | 0.0 | 0 | 0 |
| Kenya | 58037 | 1175 | 2.0 | 1658 | 2.9 | 589 | 1.0 | 22 | 0 | 1013 | 1.7 | 13.2 | 66 | 13 ez | 10.3 | 7.9 | 18.2 | 14.2 | 68 | 67 |
| Lesotho | 3035 | 0 | 0 | 0 | 0 | 0 | 0 | 0 | 0 | 7 | 0.2 | 0.1 | 1 | 1 ft | -- | -- | 8.7 | 6.5 | 46 | 16 |
| Liberia | 11137 | 0 | 0 | 129 | 1.2 | 0 | 0 | 0 | 0 | 0 | 0 | 2.4 | 19 | 3 ez | 0.4 | 0.0 | 0.4 | 0.4 | 3 | 14 |
| Libyan Arab J | 175954 | 0 | 0 | 0 | 0 | 50 | 0 | 1 | 0 | 122 | 0.1 | 0.1 | 1 | 1 ft | -- | -- | 0.0 | 0.0 | 0 | 1 |
| Madagascar | 58704 | 0 | 0 | 152 | 0.3 | 589 | 1.0 | 3 | 0 | 486 | 0.8 | 2.5 | 20 | 9 ez | 1.5 | 0.4 | 1.9 | 1.7 | 14 | 18 |
| Malawi | 11848 | 0 | 0 | 545 | 4.6 | 142 | 1.2 | 9 | 0.1 | 362 | 3.1 | 12.6 | 65 | 3 ez | 11.4 | 13.3 | 24.7 | 18.0 | 76 | 69 |
| Mali | 124019 | 0 | 0 | 750 | 0.6 | 0 | 0 | 0 | 0 | 3782 | 3.0 | 2.7 | 22 | 5 ez | 0.8 | 3.0 | 3.8 | 2.3 | 18 | 21 |
| Mauritania | 102552 | 1173 | 1.1 | 310 | 0.3 | 13 | 0 | 0 | 0 | 250 | 0.2 | 3.4 | 27 | 3 ez | 0.3 | 0.0 | 0.3 | 0.3 | 2 | 19 |
| Mauritius | 204 | 0 | 0 | 0 | 0 | 0 | 0 | 7 | 3.4 | 5 | 2.5 | 8.1 | 52 | -- | -- | -- | -- | -- | -- | 52 |
| Morocco | 44655 | 0 | 0 | 0 | 0 | 0 | 0 | 9 | 0 | 307 | 0.7 | 0.3 | 2 | 3 ft | -- | -- | 1.6 | 1.2 | 10 | 5 |
| Mozambique | 80159 | 0 | 0 | 1575 | 2.0 | 0 | 0 | 0 | 0 | 5012 | 6.3 | 7.2 | 49 | 7 ez | 0.0 | 0.0 | 0.0 | 0.0 | 0 | 33 |
| Namibia | 82429 | 8843 | 10.7 | 831 | 1.0 | 97 | 0.1 | 4 | 0 | 1435 | 1.7 | 29.9 | 90 | 4 ez | 8.9 | 2.7 | 11.6 | 10.2 | 60 | 80 |
| Niger | 126700 | 1280 | 1.0 | 220 | 0.2 | 0 | 0 | 0 | 0 | 8194 | 6.5 | 6.2 | 45 | 4 ez | 4.2 | 3.6 | 7.8 | 6.0 | 44 | 45 |
| Nigeria | 92377 | 0 | 0 | 2226 | 2.4 | 49 | 0.1 | 0 | 0 | 745 | 0.8 | 5.4 | 42 | 8 ez | 5.0 | 0.7 | 5.7 | 5.3 | 41 | 41 |
| Rwanda | 2634 | 0 | 0 | 250 | 9.5 | 14 | 0.5 | 0 | 0 | 132 | 5.0 | 27.3 | 87 | 3 ez | 8.1 | 3.4 | 11.5 | 9.8 | 59 | 78 |
| São Tomé & Principe | 96 | 0 | 0 | 0 | 0 | 0 | 0 | 0 | 0 | 0 | 0 | 0 | 0 | 2 ft | -- | -- | 0.0 | 0.0 | 0 | 0 |
| Senegal | 19672 | 0 | 0 | 913 | 4.6 | 92 | 0.5 | 7 | 0 | 1228 | 6.2 | 13.1 | 66 | 5 ez | 4.1 | 3.4 | 7.5 | 5.8 | 43 | 59 |
| Seychelles | 45 | 0 | 0 | 0 | 0 | 0 | 0 | 3 | 6.7 | 0 | 0 | 16.7 | 73 | -- | -- | -- | -- | -- | -- | 73 |
| Sierra Leone | 7174 | 0 | 0 | 0 | 0 | 0 | 0 | 0 | 0 | 153 | 2.1 | 1.0 | 8 | 4 ez | 0.0 | 3.1 | 3.1 | 1.5 | 12 | 9 |
| Somalia | 63766 | 0 | 0 | 0 | 0 | 0 | 0 | 0 | 0 | 524 | 0.8 | 0.4 | 3 | 6 ez | 0.0 | 0.1 | 0.1 | 0.0 | 0 | 2 |
| South Africa | 122104 | 1962 | 1.6 | 1738 | 1.4 | 528 | 0.4 | 34 | 0 | 2135 | 1.7 | 8.3 | 53 | 16 ez | 2.9 | 3.9 | 6.8 | 4.8 | 38 | 48 |
| Sudan | 250581 | 7480 | 3.0 | 890 | 0.4 | 103 | 0 | 0 | 0 | 3750 | 1.5 | 9.1 | 56 | 16 ez | 2.1 | 1.4 | 3.5 | 2.8 | 22 | 45 |
| Swaziland | 1736 | 0 | 0 | 0 | 0 | 0 | 0 | 0 | 0 | 60 | 3.5 | 1.8 | 14 | 1 ft | -- | -- | 3.2 | 2.4 | 19 | 16 |
| Tanzania | 94509 | 2771 | 2.9 | 1156 | 1.2 | 167 | 0.2 | 5 | 0 | 22162 | 23.4 | 21.7 | 82 | 10 ez | 10.0 | 11.5 | 21.5 | 15.7 | 71 | 78 |
| Togo | 5678 | 0 | 0 | 356 | 6.3 | 0 | 0 | 2 | 0 | 71 | 1.3 | 16.4 | 73 | 3 ez | 3.1 | 2.0 | 5.1 | 4.1 | 33 | 59 |
| Tunisia | 16361 | 0 | 0 | 0 | 0 | 29 | 0.2 | 15 | 0.1 | 0 | 0 | 0.4 | 3 | 3 ft | -- | -- | 2.1 | 1.6 | 13 | 6 |
| Uganda | 24104 | 0 | 0 | 716 | 3.0 | 157 | 0.7 | 3 | 0 | 4036 | 16.7 | 15.4 | 71 | 9 ez | 4.9 | 34.3 | 39.2 | 22.0 | 82 | 75 |
| Zambia | 75261 | 2240 | 3.0 | 3781 | 5.0 | 322 | 0.4 | 20 | 0 | 16283 | 21.6 | 28.9 | 89 | 4 ez | 5.3 | 12.3 | 17.6 | 11.4 | 63 | 80 |
| Zimbabwe | 39076 | 1465 | 3.7 | 1057 | 2.7 | 180 | 0.5 | 2 | 0 | 2289 | 5.9 | 18.5 | 77 | 4 ez | 4.8 | 3.8 | 8.6 | 6.7 | 47 | 67 |
| EUROPE | | | | | | | | | | | | | | | | | | | | |
| Albania | 2875 | 0 | 0 | 0 | 0 | 0 | 0 | 38 | 1.3 | 56 | 1.9 | 2.9 | 23 | 2 ft | -- | -- | 0.9 | 0.7 | 6 | 17 |
| Austria | 8386 | 0 | 0 | 0 | 0 | 27 | 0.3 | 8 | 0.1 | 2344 | 28.0 | 14.8 | 70 | 2 ft | -- | -- | 20.6 | 15.4 | 71 | 70 |
| Belarus | 20760 | 0 | 0 | 0 | 0 | 304 | 1.5 | 0 | 0 | 561 | 2.7 | 3.7 | 30 | 2 ft | -- | -- | 7.2 | 5.4 | 42 | 34 |
| Belgium | 3052 | 0 | 0 | 0 | 0 | 0 | 0 | 0 | 0 | 78 | 2.6 | 1.3 | 10 | 2 ft | -- | -- | 9.0 | 6.7 | 47 | 23 |
| Bosnia & Herzegovina | 5113 | 0 | 0 | 0 | 0 | 17 | 0.3 | 0 | 0 | 8 | 0.2 | 0.7 | 6 | 2 ft | -- | -- | 0.9 | 0.7 | 6 | 6 |
| Bulgaria | 11091 | 0 | 0 | 108 | 1.0 | 126 | 1.1 | 57 | 0.5 | 200 | 1.8 | 5.0 | 40 | 2 ft | -- | -- | 10.6 | 7.9 | 52 | 44 |
| Croatia | 5654 | 0 | 0 | 0 | 0 | 56 | 1.0 | 32 | 0.6 | 288 | 5.1 | 5.4 | 42 | 2 ft | -- | -- | 15.0 | 11.2 | 62 | 49 |
| Czech R | 7886 | 0 | 0 | 0 | 0 | 69 | 0.9 | 17 | 0.2 | 1137 | 14.4 | 9.3 | 57 | 2 ft | -- | -- | 32.6 | 24.4 | 84 | 66 |
| Denmark | 4309 | 0 | 0 | 0 | 0 | 10 | 0.2 | 20 | 0.5 | 1335 | 31.0 | 16.7 | 73 | 2 ft | -- | -- | 4.2 | 3.1 | 25 | 57 |
| Estonia | 4510 | 0 | 0 | 112 | 2.5 | 66 | 1.5 | 0 | 0 | 330 | 7.3 | 13.0 | 66 | 2 ft | -- | -- | 6.3 | 4.7 | 38 | 57 |
| Finland | 33814 | 0 | 0 | 801 | 2.4 | 169 | 0.5 | 95 | 0.3 | 1710 | 5.1 | 8.4 | 54 | 1 ft | -- | -- | 5.8 | 4.3 | 34 | 47 |
| France | 55150 | 0 | 0 | 0 | 0 | 272 | 0.5 | 12 | 0 | 5084 | 9.2 | 5.4 | 42 | 3 ft | -- | -- | 17.2 | 12.9 | 66 | 50 |
| Germany | 35698 | 0 | 0 | 0 | 0 | 34 | 0.1 | 3 | 0 | 8843 | 24.8 | 12.6 | 65 | 2 ft | -- | -- | 27.9 | 20.9 | 81 | 70 |
| Greece | 13196 | 0 | 0 | 0 | 0 | 47 | 0.4 | 36 | 0.3 | 149 | 1.1 | 1.5 | 12 | 4 ft | -- | -- | 1.2 | 0.9 | 7 | 10 |
| Hungary | 9303 | 0 | 0 | 0 | 0 | 159 | 1.7 | 0 | 0 | 470 | 5.1 | 5.9 | 44 | 2 ft | -- | -- | 35.1 | 26.3 | 86 | 58 |
| Iceland | 10300 | 0 | 0 | 160 | 1.6 | 28 | 0.3 | 16 | 0.2 | 769 | 7.5 | 7.6 | 50 | -- | -- | -- | -- | -- | -- | 50 |
| Ireland | 7028 | 0 | 0 | 0 | 0 | 43 | 0.6 | 5 | 0.1 | 13 | 0.2 | 1.5 | 12 | 2 ft | -- | -- | 10.8 | 8.1 | 52 | 25 |
| Italy | 30127 | 0 | 0 | 0 | 0 | 356 | 1.2 | 13 | 0 | 1768 | 5.9 | 4.8 | 38 | 4 ft | -- | -- | 3.9 | 2.9 | 23 | 33 |
| Latvia | 6460 | 0 | 0 | 0 | 0 | 45 | 0.7 | 7 | 0.1 | 736 | 11.4 | 7.3 | 49 | 2 ft | -- | -- | 11.1 | 8.3 | 53 | 51 |
| Lithuania | 6520 | 0 | 0 | 0 | 0 | 143 | 2.2 | 29 | 0.4 | 474 | 7.3 | 8.7 | 55 | 2 ft | -- | -- | 7.5 | 5.6 | 42 | 51 |
| Luxembourg | 257 | 0 | 0 | 0 | 0 | 0 | 0 | 0 | 0 | 36 | 14.0 | 7.0 | 48 | 2 ft | -- | -- | 8.6 | 6.4 | 46 | 47 |
| Macedonia, FYR | 2571 | 0 | 0 | 0 | 0 | 149 | 5.8 | 14 | 0.5 | 17 | 0.7 | 12.7 | 65 | 2 ft | -- | -- | 13.8 | 10.3 | 61 | 64 |
| Malta | 32 | 0 | 0 | 0 | 0 | 0 | 0 | 0 | 0 | 0 | 0 | 0 | 0 | -- | -- | -- | -- | -- | -- | 0 |
| Moldova | 3370 | 0 | 0 | 0 | 0 | 0 | 0 | 19 | 0.6 | 21 | 0.6 | 1.2 | 10 | 1 ft | -- | -- | 5.4 | 4.0 | 32 | 17 |
| Netherlands | 4084 | 0 | 0 | 0 | 0 | 0 | 0 | 74 | 1.8 | 404 | 9.9 | 7.6 | 50 | 2 ft | -- | -- | 12.6 | 9.4 | 58 | 53 |
| Norway | 32388 | 0 | 0 | 1041 | 3.2 | 385 | 1.2 | 159 | 0.5 | 490 | 1.5 | 9.5 | 58 | 2 ft | -- | -- | 1.0 | 0.7 | 6 | 41 |
| Poland | 32325 | 0 | 0 | 0 | 0 | 101 | 0.3 | 65 | 0.2 | 2746 | 8.5 | 4.9 | 39 | 2 ft | -- | -- | 13.8 | 10.3 | 61 | 46 |
| Portugal | 9198 | 0 | 0 | 0 | 0 | 70 | 0.8 | 13 | 0.1 | 512 | 5.6 | 4.6 | 37 | 2 ft | -- | -- | 5.4 | 4.0 | 32 | 35 |
| Romania | 23839 | 0 | 0 | 580 | 2.4 | 421 | 1.8 | 37 | 0.2 | 35 | 0.1 | 7.8 | 51 | 6 ft | -- | -- | 3.4 | 2.5 | 20 | 41 |
| Slovakia | 4901 | 0 | 0 | 0 | 0 | 198 | 4.0 | 5 | 0.1 | 844 | 17.2 | 16.8 | 74 | 2 ft | -- | -- | 29.6 | 22.2 | 82 | 76 |
| Slovenia | 2025 | 0 | 0 | 0 | 0 | 84 | 4.1 | 0 | 0 | 31 | 1.5 | 9.0 | 56 | 2 ft | -- | -- | 12.5 | 9.4 | 58 | 57 |
| Spain | 50599 | 0 | 0 | 0 | 0 | 195 | 0.4 | 29 | 0.1 | 3991 | 7.9 | 4.7 | 38 | 6 ft | -- | -- | 7.9 | 5.9 | 44 | 40 |
| Sweden | 44996 | 0 | 0 | 1061 | 2.4 | 800 | 1.8 | 174 | 0.4 | 1585 | 3.5 | 9.7 | 59 | 2 ft | -- | -- | 0.9 | 0.7 | 6 | 41 |

| Country | Total area 000 ha | MTP 000 ha | MTP % | ITP 000 ha | ITP % | LTP 000 ha | LTP % | KTP 000 ha | KTP % | PP 000 ha | PP % | Wtd tot % | Size score | No & type unit | Ave % TP | Ave % PP | Ave % totP | Wtd % | Div score | LP score |
|---|---|---|---|---|---|---|---|---|---|---|---|---|---|---|---|---|---|---|---|---|
| Switzerland | 4129 | 0 | 0 | 0 | 0 | 17 | 0.4 | 0 | 0 | 696 | 16.9 | 9.2 | 57 | 4 ft | -- | -- | 12.9 | 9.7 | 59 | 57 |
| Ukraine | 60370 | 0 | 0 | 261 | 0.4 | 479 | 0.8 | 25 | 0 | 173 | 0.3 | 2.2 | 18 | 2 ft | -- | -- | 1.6 | 1.2 | 10 | 15 |
| United Kingdom | 24410 | 0 | 0 | 0 | 0 | 0 | 0 | 0 | 0 | 4943 | 20.2 | 10.1 | 60 | 2 ft | -- | -- | 22.0 | 16.5 | 73 | 64 |
| Yugoslavia | 10217 | 0 | 0 | 0 | 0 | 130 | 1.3 | 14 | 0.1 | 183 | 1.8 | 3.0 | 24 | 2 ft | -- | -- | 3.0 | 2.2 | 18 | 22 |
| RUSSIAN FED. | 1707540 | 19028 | 1.1 | 14833 | 0.9 | 2616 | 0.2 | 41 | 0 | 14264 | 0.8 | 5.3 | 41 | 4 ft | -- | -- | 1.7 | 1.3 | 10 | 31 |
| ASIA | | | | | | | | | | | | | | | | | | | | |
| Afghanistan | 65209 | 0 | 0 | 0 | 0 | 41 | 0.1 | 0 | 0 | 177 | 0.3 | 0.4 | 3 | 2 ft | -- | -- | 0.0 | 0.0 | 0 | 2 |
| Armenia | 2980 | 0 | 0 | 150 | 5.0 | 63 | 2.1 | 0 | 0 | 0 | 0 | 16.7 | 73 | 1 ft | -- | -- | 10.0 | 7.5 | 50 | 66 |
| Azerbaijan | 8660 | 0 | 0 | 0 | 0 | 151 | 1.7 | 41 | 0.5 | 284 | 3.3 | 5.8 | 43 | 1 ft | -- | -- | 0.0 | 0.0 | 0 | 29 |
| Bahrain | 69 | 0 | 0 | 0 | 0 | 0 | 0 | 0 | 0 | 0 | 0 | 0 | 0 | -- | -- | -- | -- | -- | -- | 0 |
| Bangladesh | 14400 | 0 | 0 | 0 | 0 | 0 | 0 | 0 | 0 | 98 | 0.7 | 0.3 | 2 | 3 ez | 0.0 | 0.0 | 0.0 | 0.0 | 0 | 2 |
| Bhutan | 4700 | 0 | 0 | 520 | 11.1 | 237 | 5.0 | 0 | 0 | 241 | 5.1 | 40.3 | 100 | 4 ez | 19.3 | 7.0 | 26.3 | 22.8 | 83 | 94 |
| Brunei Darussalam | 576 | 0 | 0 | 0 | 0 | 85 | 14.8 | 30 | 5.2 | 0 | 0 | 47.4 | 100 | 6 H | 24.7 | 7.1 | 31.8 | 28.2 | 88 | 96 |
| Cambodia | 18103 | 0 | 0 | 644 | 3.6 | 87 | 0.5 | 5 | 0 | 2531 | 14.0 | 15.0 | 70 | 6 ez | 4.4 | 11.3 | 15.7 | 10.0 | 60 | 67 |
| China | 959805 | 45037 | 4.7 | 3516 | 0.4 | 930 | 0.1 | 81 | 0 | 18653 | 1.9 | 13.7 | 67 | 6 ft | -- | -- | 5.3 | 4.0 | 32 | 56 |
| Cyprus | 925 | 0 | 0 | 0 | 0 | 0 | 0 | 9 | 1.0 | 66 | 7.1 | 5.5 | 42 | 1 ft | -- | -- | 33.4 | 25.0 | 85 | 56 |
| Georgia | 6970 | 0 | 0 | 0 | 0 | 143 | 2.1 | 52 | 0.7 | 0 | 0 | 5.2 | 41 | 2 ft | -- | -- | 0.0 | 0.0 | 0 | 27 |
| India | 328759 | 0 | 0 | 1720 | 0.5 | 1595 | 0.5 | 87 | 0 | 10811 | 3.3 | 3.4 | 27 | 26 ez | 0.4 | 0.9 | 1.3 | 0.8 | 6 | 20 |
| Indonesia | 190457 | 6687 | 3.5 | 6152 | 3.2 | 1420 | 0.7 | 168 | 0.1 | 19133 | 10.0 | 21.3 | 81 | 17 ez | 11.2 | 2.6 | 13.8 | 12.5 | 65 | 76 |
| Iran | 163319 | 0 | 0 | 884 | 0.5 | 182 | 0.1 | 16 | 0 | 7218 | 4.4 | 3.4 | 27 | 1 ft | -- | -- | 12.0 | 9.0 | 56 | 37 |
| Iraq | 43832 | 0 | 0 | 0 | 0 | 0 | 0 | 0 | 0 | 0 | 0 | 0 | 0 | -- | -- | -- | -- | -- | -- | 0 |
| Israel | 2106 | 0 | 0 | 0 | 0 | 0 | 0 | 3 | 0.1 | 305 | 14.5 | 7.5 | 50 | -- | -- | -- | -- | -- | -- | 50 |
| Japan | 37780 | 0 | 0 | 777 | 2.1 | 527 | 1.4 | 17 | 0 | 1230 | 3.3 | 7.9 | 52 | 2 ft | -- | -- | 12.1 | 9.1 | 56 | 53 |
| Jordan | 8921 | 0 | 0 | 0 | 0 | 0 | 0 | 1 | 0 | 297 | 3.3 | 1.6 | 13 | -- | -- | -- | -- | -- | -- | 13 |
| Kazakhstan | 271730 | 0 | 0 | 801 | 0.3 | 467 | 0.2 | 0 | 0 | 6069 | 2.2 | 2.0 | 16 | 3 ft | -- | -- | 8.3 | 6.2 | 45 | 26 |
| Korea, DPR | 12054 | 0 | 0 | 0 | 0 | 124 | 1.0 | 37 | 0.3 | 154 | 1.3 | 2.4 | 19 | 3 ft | -- | -- | 0.7 | 0.5 | 4 | 14 |
| Korea, R | 9926 | 0 | 0 | 0 | 0 | 0 | 0 | 0 | 0 | 364 | 3.7 | 1.9 | 15 | 1 ft | -- | -- | 3.4 | 2.5 | 20 | 17 |
| Kuwait | 1782 | 0 | 0 | 0 | 0 | 0 | 0 | 2 | 0.1 | 25 | 1.4 | 0.9 | 7 | -- | -- | -- | -- | -- | -- | 7 |
| Kyrgyzstan | 19850 | 0 | 0 | 0 | 0 | 272 | 1.4 | 27 | 0.1 | 389 | 2.0 | 3.2 | 26 | 2 ft | -- | -- | 0.1 | 0.1 | 1 | 17 |
| Lao PDR | 23680 | 0 | 0 | 0 | 0 | 0 | 0 | 0 | 0 | 2756 | 11.6 | 5.8 | 43 | 5 ez | 0.0 | 7.3 | 7.3 | 3.6 | 29 | 38 |
| Lebanon | 1040 | 0 | 0 | 0 | 0 | 0 | 0 | 3 | 0.3 | 0 | 0 | 0.4 | 3 | 1 ft | -- | -- | 0.0 | 0.0 | 0 | 2 |
| Malaysia | 32975 | 0 | 0 | 574 | 1.7 | 225 | 0.7 | 105 | 0.3 | 601 | 1.8 | 5.6 | 42 | 6 ez | 13.9 | 19.7 | 33.6 | 23.7 | 84 | 56 |
| Maldives | 30 | 0 | 0 | 0 | 0 | 0 | 0 | 0 | 0 | 0 | 0 | 0 | 0 | -- | -- | -- | -- | -- | -- | 0 |
| Mongolia | 156650 | 10407 | 6.6 | 4957 | 3.2 | 696 | 0.4 | 19 | 0 | 50 | 0 | 23.5 | 84 | 2 ft | -- | -- | 18.2 | 13.6 | 67 | 78 |
| Myanmar | 67658 | 0 | 0 | 161 | 0.2 | 0 | 0 | 0 | 0 | 13 | 0 | 0.4 | 3 | 10 ez | 0.2 | 0.0 | 0.2 | 0.2 | 2 | 3 |
| Nepal | 14718 | 0 | 0 | 791 | 5.4 | 226 | 1.5 | 0 | 0 | 253 | 1.7 | 14.0 | 68 | 12 ez | 6.5 | 4.6 | 11.1 | 8.8 | 55 | 64 |
| Oman | 21246 | 3400 | 16.0 | 0 | 0 | 0 | 0 | 0 | 0 | 28 | 0.1 | 40.1 | 100 | -- | -- | -- | -- | -- | -- | 80* |
| Pakistan | 79609 | 0 | 0 | 868 | 1.1 | 0 | 0 | 14 | 0 | 2857 | 3.6 | 4.0 | 32 | 12 ez | 0.3 | 0.9 | 1.2 | 0.7 | 6 | 23 |
| Philippines | 30000 | 0 | 0 | 320 | 1.1 | 117 | 0.4 | 0 | 0 | 775 | 2.6 | 4.1 | 33 | 5 ez | 0.9 | 13.6 | 14.5 | 7.7 | 51 | 39 |
| Qatar | 1100 | 0 | 0 | 0 | 0 | 0 | 0 | 0 | 0 | 2 | 0.2 | 0.1 | 1 | -- | -- | -- | -- | -- | -- | 1 |
| Saudi Arabia | 214969 | 1220 | 0.6 | 1327 | 0.6 | 60 | 0 | 0 | 0 | 79714 | 37.1 | 21.2 | 81 | -- | -- | -- | -- | -- | -- | 80* |
| Singapore | 62 | 0 | 0 | 0 | 0 | 0 | 0 | 0 | 0 | 3 | 4.8 | 2.4 | 19 | 3 H | 24.2 | 4.1 | 28.3 | 26.2 | 86 | 42 |
| Sri Lanka | 6561 | 0 | 0 | 0 | 0 | 445 | 6.8 | 85 | 1.3 | 298 | 4.5 | 17.9 | 76 | 5 ez | 4.7 | 4.5 | 9.2 | 6.9 | 48 | 66 |
| Syrian Arab R | 18518 | 0 | 0 | 0 | 0 | 0 | 0 | 0 | 0 | 0 | 0 | 0 | 0 | 1 ft | -- | -- | 0.0 | 0.0 | 0 | 0 |
| Tajikistan | 14310 | 0 | 0 | 0 | 0 | 86 | 0.6 | 1 | 0 | 500 | 3.5 | 2.7 | 22 | -- | -- | -- | -- | -- | -- | 22 |
| Thailand | 51311 | 0 | 0 | 1668 | 3.3 | 2545 | 5.0 | 119 | 0.2 | 2741 | 5.3 | 17.0 | 74 | 6 ez | 10.2 | 6.8 | 17.0 | 13.6 | 67 | 72 |
| Turkey | 77482 | 0 | 0 | 0 | 0 | 377 | 0.5 | 40 | 0.1 | 866 | 1.1 | 1.5 | 12 | 1 ft | -- | -- | 1.2 | 0.9 | 7 | 10 |
| Turkmenistan | 48810 | 0 | 0 | 545 | 1.1 | 274 | 0.6 | 2 | 0 | 1156 | 2.4 | 4.3 | 34 | 2 ft | -- | -- | 0.4 | 0.3 | 2 | 24 |
| United Arab Emirates | 8360 | 0 | 0 | 0 | 0 | 0 | 0 | 0 | 0 | 0 | 0 | 0 | 0 | -- | -- | -- | -- | -- | -- | 0 |
| Uzbekistan | 44740 | 0 | 0 | 575 | 1.3 | 230 | 0.5 | 14 | 0 | 0 | 0 | 3.4 | 27 | 2 ft | -- | -- | 0.0 | 0.0 | 0 | 18 |
| Viet Nam | 33169 | 0 | 0 | 0 | 0 | 188 | 0.6 | 15 | 0 | 792 | 2.4 | 2.1 | 17 | 8 ez | 0.7 | 4.2 | 4.9 | 2.8 | 22 | 19 |
| Yemen | 52797 | 0 | 0 | 0 | 0 | 0 | 0 | 0 | 0 | 0 | 0 | 0 | 0 | -- | -- | -- | -- | -- | -- | 0 |
| PACIFIC | | | | | | | | | | | | | | | | | | | | |
| Australia | 774122 | 14597 | 1.9 | 22903 | 3.0 | 7092 | 0.9 | 1962 | 0.3 | 12276 | 1.6 | 13.2 | 66 | 11 ft | -- | -- | 9.2 | 6.9 | 48 | 60 |
| Fiji | 1827 | 0 | 0 | 0 | 0 | 11 | 0.6 | 8 | 0.4 | 0 | 0 | 1.8 | 14 | 4 ft | -- | -- | 5.2 | 3.9 | 31 | 20 |
| New Zealand | 27053 | 1257 | 4.6 | 1656 | 6.1 | 764 | 2.8 | 304 | 1.1 | 1578 | 5.8 | 31.9 | 92 | 1 ft | -- | -- | 43.8 | 32.8 | 93 | 92 |
| Papua New Guinea | 46284 | 0 | 0 | 0 | 0 | 0 | 0 | 7 | 0 | 1026 | 2.2 | 1.1 | 9 | 6 ez | 0.1 | 5.9 | 6.0 | 3.0 | 24 | 14 |
| Samoa | 284 | 0 | 0 | 0 | 0 | 0 | 0 | 3 | 1.1 | 9 | 3.2 | 3.8 | 30 | -- | -- | -- | -- | -- | -- | 30 |
| Solomon Is | 2890 | 0 | 0 | 0 | 0 | 0 | 0 | 0 | 0 | 0 | 0 | 0 | 0 | 2 ft | -- | -- | 0.0 | 0.0 | 0 | 0 |
| Tonga | 75 | 0 | 0 | 0 | 0 | 0 | 0 | 0 | 0 | 0 | 0 | 0 | 0 | -- | -- | -- | -- | -- | -- | 0 |
| Vanuatu | 1219 | 0 | 0 | 0 | 0 | 0 | 0 | 0 | 0 | 3 | 0.2 | 0.1 | 1 | -- | -- | -- | -- | -- | -- | 1 |

**Notes**

Land protection is the average of two weighted indicators (column heading in parentheses) [weights in brackets]:

Protected area size (Size score) [2]—protected area as % of total area, weighted for size.

Protected area diversity (Div score) [1]—protected area as % of total area, weighted for diversity.

Protected area diversity was given a lower weight than protected area size because the data are less reliable.

The protected area size indicator measures how much of a country's land and inland water area is protected, weighted according to degree of protection and size of the protected areas. All data are in thousand hectares (000 ha), and all percentages are in terms of total (land + inland water) area. Data are for 1997 and are from the *United Nations list of protected areas 1997* (IUCN World Commission on Protected Areas & World Conservation Monitoring Centre 1998). Marine protected areas were excluded because information on them is weak and incomplete.

TP = totally protected areas: IUCN Category I, Strict Nature Reserve/Wilderness Area; Category II, National Park; and Category III, Natural Monument (IUCN CNPPA 1994). Totally protected areas have been grouped into four size classes:

MTP = 1 million hectares and above
ITP = 100,000-999,999 hectares
LTP = 10,000-99,999 hectares
KTP = 1,000-9,999 hectares, or entire islands less than 1,000 hectares

PP = partially protected areas: IUCN Category IV, Habitat/Species Management Area; Category V, Protected Landscape/Seascape; and Category VI, Managed Resource Protected Area (IUCN CNPPA 1994).

As defined by IUCN - World Conservation Union, totally protected areas are maintained in a natural state and are closed to extractive uses. Partially protected areas are managed for specific uses (e.g., recreation) or to provide optimum conditions for certain species or ecological communities. Totally protected areas are more likely to protect a wide range of natural ecological communities. For such communities to persist and evolve "naturally", buffered as far as possible against human activities, the areas need to be large. The bigger the area, the more protective it will be (Reid & Miller 1989).

Wtd tot % = weighted total percentage. Protected areas qualify as large on a sliding scale, which recognizes that it is as great an achievement for a country of 80,000 ha to protect 8,000 ha as it is for a country of 80 million ha to protect 8 million ha. Each 1% of protected area (as a percentage of total area) was multiplied by one of the factors in Table 12a. The factors vary depending on whether the areas are totally or partially protected, their size, and the size of the country.

Size score = protected area size score. The performance criteria are shown in Table 12b. The top of the medium band is set at 10% because international targets are for full protection of 10% of each major ecological region (IUCN/UNEP/WWF 1991) or 10% of each biome (Recommendation 16 of the IVth World Congress on National Parks and Protected Areas [McNeely 1993]).

The protected area diversity indicator (Div score) is intended to measure how much of each major ecosystem type occurs within protected areas. Ideally, it would use a classification of major ecosystem types that distinguished either the main vegetation types or the main groups of ecological communities. The classification needs to be consistent across countries and regions and at a scale that would provide adequate detail for small countries but not unmanageable detail for large countries. World Wildlife Fund has developed such a classification for the Americas (Dinerstein, Olson, Graham *et al*. 1995; Ricketts, Dinerstein, Olson *et al*. 1998) and has used it to assess protected area coverage of ecosystem diversity. However, the assessment was by ecoregion only, not by country and ecoregion, and so could not be used here. Asian Bureau for Conservation & World Conservation Monitoring Centre (1997) cover Southern Asia and Papua New Guinea thoroughly but in a non-standard way, particularly their treatment of totally and partially protected areas. The two assessments used here (World Conservation Monitoring Centre [1997] and Iremonger, Ravilious, & Quinton [1997]) reviewed coverage of ecosystem diversity by country and ecosystem type. World Conservation Monitoring Centre's ecofloristic zone classification is not as detailed as World Wildlife Fund's ecoregion classification. However, the detail is adequate, except for Central America and the Caribbean where only major ecofloristic zones are identifed. The forest type classification covers a narrower array of ecosystem types, and the types are crudely defined. In many countries remarkably few types are recognized (for example, only one in New Zealand). The ecofloristic zone assessment distinguishes between totally and partially protected areas; the forest type assessment does not.

No & type unit = the number of ecosystem units identified by the assessment of the country concerned, and the type of ecosystem classification used:

ez = ecofloristic zone; mez = major ecofloristic zone. Data are from World Conservation Monitoring Centre (1997)

ft = forest type. Data are from Iremonger, Ravilious, & Quinton (1997)

Ave % TP = the average percentage of the ecosystem type that is totally protected = the totally protected area of each ecosystem unit as a percentage of the total area of that unit, added together and divided by the number of units.

Ave % PP = the average percentage of the ecosystem type that is partially protected = the partially protected area of each ecosystem unit as a percentage of the total area of that unit, added together and divided by the number of units.

Ave % totP = the average percentage of the ecosystem type that is protected. In the case of ecofloristic zones (and major ecofloristic zones), this is the sum of totally and partially protected percentages. In the case of forest types, all degrees of protection are lumped together.

Wtd % = weighted total percentage, obtained by multiplying the totally protected percentage by 1, the partially protected percentage by 0.5, and adding them together. When only a total percentage was available (forest types), it was multiplied by 0.75.

Div score = protected area diversity score. The performance criteria are the same as for protected area size (Table 12b).

| area category | country 10 million+ ha | country 1 million+ ha | country 100,000+ ha | country 10,000+ ha |
|---|---|---|---|---|
| MTP (1 million+ ha) | 2.5 | -- | -- | -- |
| ITP (100,000+ ha) | 2.0 | 2.5 | -- | -- |
| LTP (10,000+ ha | 1.5 | 2.0 | 2.5 | -- |
| KTP (1,000+ ha) | 1.0 | 1.5 | 2.0 | 2.5 |
| PP | 0.5 | 0.5 | 0.5 | 0.5 |

**Table 12a. Factors for multiplying each 1% of protected area (as a percentage of total area), depending on whether the areas are totally protected (TP) or partially protected (PP), their size (M, I, L, or K), and the size of the country.**

| band | top point on scale | protected area as % of total area |
|---|---|---|
| good | 100 | 40 |
| fair | 80 | 20 |
| medium | 60 | 10 |
| poor | 40 | 5 |
| bad | 20 | 2.5 |
| base | 0 | 0 |

**Table 12b. Performance criteria for indicators of land protection.**

## Table 13. Land Quality

| Country | Cultivated 000 ha | Modified 000 ha | Total 000 ha | Light 000 ha | L % | Moderate 000 ha | M % | Strong 000 ha | S % | Extreme 000 ha | E % | Weighted total % | LQ score |
|---|---|---|---|---|---|---|---|---|---|---|---|---|---|
| AMERICAS | | | | | | | | | | | | | |
| Antigua & Barbuda | 8 | 28 | 36 | -- | -- | -- | -- | -- | -- | -- | -- | -- | -- |
| Argentina | 41947 | 79639 | 121586 | 44482 | 36.6 | 8528 | 7.0 | 197 | 0.2 | 0 | 0 | 25.6 | 54 |
| Bahamas | 10 | 493 | 503 | 0 | 0 | 0 | 0 | 0 | 0 | 0 | 0 | 0 | 100 |
| Barbados | 17 | 14 | 31 | -- | -- | -- | -- | -- | -- | -- | -- | -- | -- |
| Belize | 96 | 1731 | 1827 | 0 | 0 | 253 | 13.8 | 0 | 0 | 0 | 0 | 13.8 | 72 |
| Bolivia | 4228 | 46717 | 50945 | 1386 | 2.7 | 9004 | 17.7 | 3068 | 6.0 | 0 | 0 | 28.1 | 52 |
| Brazil | 88700 | 286593 | 375293 | 43181 | 11.5 | 75101 | 20.0 | 16445 | 4.4 | 0 | 0 | 32.3 | 48 |
| Canada | 48388 | 226653 | 275041 | 4472 | 1.6 | 2956 | 1.1 | 0 | 0 | 0 | 0 | 1.9 | 96 |
| Chile | 4602 | 31992 | 36594 | 3486 | 9.5 | 2630 | 7.2 | 2139 | 5.8 | 0 | 0 | 20.6 | 59 |
| Colombia | 8564 | 30318 | 38882 | 7775 | 20.0 | 4991 | 12.8 | 0 | 0 | 0 | 0 | 22.8 | 57 |
| Costa Rica | 767 | 2905 | 3672 | 0 | 0 | 917 | 25.0 | 2284 | 62.2 | 0 | 0 | 118.3 | 10 |
| Cuba | 4912 | 5057 | 9969 | 991 | 9.9 | 2245 | 22.5 | 0 | 0 | 0 | 0 | 27.5 | 52 |
| Dominica | 15 | 24 | 39 | -- | -- | -- | -- | -- | -- | -- | -- | -- | -- |
| Dominican R | 1754 | 2507 | 4261 | 53 | 1.2 | 929 | 21.8 | 19 | 0.4 | 0 | 0 | 23.0 | 57 |
| Ecuador | 3555 | 7931 | 11486 | 1120 | 9.8 | 887 | 7.7 | 369 | 3.2 | 0 | 0 | 17.4 | 65 |
| El Salvador | 879 | 974 | 1853 | 2 | 0.1 | 1493 | 80.6 | 358 | 19.3 | 0 | 0 | 109.6 | 13 |
| Grenada | 11 | 6 | 17 | -- | -- | -- | -- | -- | -- | -- | -- | -- | -- |
| Guatemala | 2193 | 4359 | 6552 | 21 | 0.3 | 3966 | 60.5 | 324 | 4.9 | 0 | 0 | 68.0 | 26 |
| Guyana | 560 | 964 | 1524 | 907 | 59.5 | 464 | 30.4 | 0 | 0 | 0 | 0 | 60.2 | 30 |
| Haiti | 968 | 1557 | 2525 | 0 | 0 | 0 | 0 | 2525 | 100 | 0 | 0 | 150.0 | 2 |
| Honduras | 2202 | 5590 | 7792 | 34 | 0.4 | 4191 | 53.8 | 638 | 8.2 | 0 | 0 | 66.3 | 27 |
| Jamaica | 315 | 574 | 889 | 87 | 9.8 | 195 | 21.9 | 0 | 0 | 0 | 0 | 26.8 | 53 |
| Mexico | 35359 | 81478 | 116837 | 575 | 0.5 | 17449 | 14.9 | 16584 | 14.2 | 0 | 0 | 36.5 | 43 |
| Nicaragua | 3242 | 5642 | 8884 | 237 | 2.7 | 3293 | 37.1 | 24 | 0.3 | 0 | 0 | 38.9 | 41 |
| Panama | 808 | 3833 | 4641 | 197 | 4.2 | 895 | 19.3 | 1841 | 39.7 | 0 | 0 | 80.9 | 20 |
| Paraguay | 4464 | 14310 | 18774 | 102 | 0.5 | 2266 | 12.1 | 1101 | 5.9 | 0 | 0 | 21.2 | 59 |
| Peru | 7096 | 28571 | 35667 | 1892 | 5.3 | 12774 | 35.8 | 1407 | 3.9 | 0 | 0 | 44.3 | 38 |
| St Kitts & Nevis | 7 | 8 | 15 | -- | -- | -- | -- | -- | -- | -- | -- | -- | -- |
| St Lucia | 17 | 19 | 36 | -- | -- | -- | -- | -- | -- | -- | -- | -- | -- |
| St Vincent & Grenadines | 11 | 14 | 25 | -- | -- | -- | -- | -- | -- | -- | -- | -- | -- |
| Suriname | 77 | 841 | 918 | 198 | 21.6 | 218 | 23.7 | 0 | 0 | 0 | 0 | 34.5 | 45 |
| Trinidad & Tobago | 136 | 75 | 211 | 9 | 4.3 | 202 | 95.7 | 0 | 0 | 0 | 0 | 97.8 | 15 |
| United States | 216612 | 359070 | 575682 | 12171 | 2.1 | 79244 | 13.8 | 1254 | 0.2 | 0 | 0 | 15.2 | 70 |
| Uruguay | 2770 | 5776 | 8546 | 400 | 4.7 | 402 | 4.7 | 0 | 0 | 0 | 0 | 7.0 | 86 |
| Venezuela | 5567 | 42599 | 48166 | 3401 | 7.1 | 4206 | 8.7 | 515 | 1.1 | 0 | 0 | 13.9 | 72 |
| AFRICA | | | | | | | | | | | | | |
| Algeria | 11688 | 27083 | 38771 | 11633 | 30.0 | 13083 | 33.7 | 2508 | 6.5 | 0 | 0 | 58.5 | 31 |
| Angola | 7120 | 50913 | 58033 | 2473 | 4.3 | 939 | 1.6 | 7654 | 13.2 | 0 | 0 | 23.5 | 56 |
| Benin | 1653 | 7695 | 9348 | 691 | 7.4 | 1058 | 11.3 | 25 | 0.3 | 0 | 0 | 15.4 | 69 |
| Botswana | 693 | 30949 | 31642 | 761 | 2.4 | 2568 | 8.1 | 1761 | 5.6 | 0 | 0 | 17.7 | 65 |
| Burkina Faso | 4060 | 19485 | 23545 | 2767 | 11.8 | 2757 | 11.7 | 6316 | 26.8 | 0 | 0 | 57.8 | 31 |
| Burundi | 1288 | 1092 | 2380 | 56 | 2.4 | 1734 | 72.9 | 0 | 0 | 0 | 0 | 74.1 | 23 |
| Cameroon | 7376 | 31507 | 38883 | 3767 | 9.7 | 1284 | 3.3 | 5673 | 14.6 | 0 | 0 | 30.0 | 50 |
| Cape Verde | 84 | 300 | 384 | 0 | 0 | 0 | 0 | 302 | 78.6 | 0 | 0 | 117.9 | 10 |
| Central African R | 2326 | 32394 | 34720 | 998 | 2.9 | 719 | 2.1 | 232 | 0.7 | 0 | 0 | 4.6 | 91 |
| Chad | 6516 | 51059 | 57575 | 15361 | 26.7 | 7011 | 12.2 | 317 | 0.6 | 0 | 0 | 26.5 | 53 |
| Comoros | 120 | 83 | 203 | 0 | 0 | 0 | 0 | 40 | 19.7 | 0 | 0 | 29.5 | 50 |
| Congo, DR | 9422 | 112924 | 122346 | 8294 | 6.8 | 3252 | 2.7 | 2171 | 1.8 | 0 | 0 | 8.8 | 82 |
| Congo, R | 407 | 16191 | 16598 | 1351 | 8.1 | 25 | 0.2 | 234 | 1.4 | 0 | 0 | 6.3 | 87 |
| Côte d'Ivoire | 8716 | 15713 | 24429 | 1827 | 7.5 | 0 | 0 | 461 | 1.9 | 0 | 0 | 6.6 | 87 |
| Djibouti | 0 | 2133 | 2133 | 418 | 19.6 | 0 | 0 | 70 | 3.3 | 0 | 0 | 14.8 | 70 |
| Egypt | 3334 | 14396 | 17730 | 473 | 2.7 | 3004 | 16.9 | 0 | 0 | 0 | 0 | 18.3 | 63 |
| Equatorial Guinea | 243 | 1166 | 1409 | 47 | 3.3 | 0 | 0 | 0 | 0 | 0 | 0 | 1.6 | 97 |
| Eritrea | 835 | 8939 | 9774 | 963 | 9.9 | 154 | 1.6 | 1145 | 11.7 | 672 | 6.9 | 37.9 | 42 |
| Ethiopia | 12640 | 79610 | 92250 | 6758 | 7.3 | 9773 | 10.6 | 8512 | 9.2 | 2642 | 2.9 | 33.9 | 46 |
| Gabon | 986 | 7965 | 8951 | 633 | 7.1 | 733 | 8.2 | 0 | 0 | 0 | 0 | 11.8 | 76 |
| Gambia | 221 | 611 | 832 | 154 | 18.5 | 28 | 3.4 | 0 | 0 | 0 | 0 | 12.7 | 75 |
| Ghana | 5443 | 15943 | 21386 | 618 | 2.9 | 1264 | 5.9 | 1043 | 4.9 | 0 | 0 | 14.7 | 71 |
| Guinea | 2559 | 14279 | 16838 | 1351 | 8.0 | 280 | 1.7 | 0 | 0 | 0 | 0 | 5.7 | 89 |
| Guinea-Bissau | 361 | 2372 | 2733 | 423 | 15.5 | 188 | 6.9 | 0 | 0 | 0 | 0 | 14.7 | 71 |
| Kenya | 6768 | 24283 | 31051 | 2127 | 6.9 | 2683 | 8.6 | 2914 | 9.4 | 10 | 0 | 26.2 | 54 |
| Lesotho | 531 | 2387 | 2918 | 0 | 0 | 413 | 14.2 | 795 | 27.2 | 0 | 0 | 55.0 | 32 |
| Liberia | 533 | 7739 | 8272 | 211 | 2.6 | 193 | 2.3 | 0 | 0 | 0 | 0 | 3.6 | 93 |
| Libyan Arab J | 3655 | 27450 | 31105 | 14870 | 47.8 | 16235 | 52.2 | 0 | 0 | 0 | 0 | 76.1 | 22 |
| Madagascar | 5725 | 43000 | 48725 | 372 | 0.8 | 7511 | 15.4 | 8896 | 18.3 | 454 | 0.9 | 45.0 | 37 |
| Malawi | 2020 | 6516 | 8536 | 1310 | 15.3 | 6 | 0.1 | 8 | 0.1 | 0 | 0 | 7.9 | 84 |

| Country | Cultivated 000 ha | Modified 000 ha | Total 000 ha | Light 000 ha | L % | Moderate 000 ha | M % | Strong 000 ha | S % | Extreme 000 ha | E % | Weighted total % | LQ score |
|---|---|---|---|---|---|---|---|---|---|---|---|---|---|
| Mali | 7664 | 32096 | 39760 | 11456 | 28.8 | 14905 | 37.5 | 856 | 2.2 | 0 | 0 | 55.2 | 32 |
| Mauritania | 1004 | 15541 | 16545 | 9367 | 56.6 | 5590 | 33.8 | 1588 | 9.6 | 0 | 0 | 76.5 | 22 |
| Mauritius | 116 | 53 | 169 | 16 | 9.5 | 0 | 0 | 0 | 0 | 0 | 0 | 4.8 | 90 |
| Morocco | 12016 | 30843 | 42859 | 1733 | 4.0 | 2357 | 5.5 | 1262 | 2.9 | 0 | 0 | 11.9 | 76 |
| Mozambique | 6388 | 43683 | 50071 | 7839 | 15.7 | 395 | 0.8 | 128 | 0.3 | 0 | 0 | 9.1 | 82 |
| Namibia | 1640 | 36134 | 37774 | 2348 | 6.2 | 4098 | 10.8 | 517 | 1.4 | 0 | 0 | 16.0 | 68 |
| Niger | 6056 | 32193 | 38249 | 17972 | 47.0 | 18947 | 49.5 | 1330 | 3.5 | 0 | 0 | 78.3 | 21 |
| Nigeria | 34889 | 48387 | 83276 | 1666 | 2.0 | 9645 | 11.6 | 15539 | 18.7 | 0 | 0 | 40.7 | 40 |
| Rwanda | 1308 | 995 | 2303 | 47 | 2.0 | 1626 | 70.6 | 0 | 0 | 0 | 0 | 71.6 | 24 |
| São Tomé & Principe | 41 | 47 | 88 | 8 | 9.1 | 0 | 0 | 0 | 0 | 0 | 0 | 4.6 | 91 |
| Senegal | 2948 | 15688 | 18636 | 2676 | 14.4 | 963 | 5.2 | 2704 | 14.5 | 0 | 0 | 34.2 | 46 |
| Seychelles | 8 | 32 | 40 | -- | -- | -- | -- | -- | -- | -- | -- | -- | -- |
| Sierra Leone | 772 | 5960 | 6732 | 268 | 4.0 | 1069 | 15.9 | 0 | 0 | 0 | 0 | 17.9 | 64 |
| Somalia | 2126 | 40115 | 42241 | 10206 | 24.2 | 804 | 1.9 | 830 | 2.0 | 1033 | 2.4 | 21.8 | 58 |
| South Africa | 25745 | 61483 | 87228 | 334 | 0.4 | 6893 | 7.9 | 27151 | 31.1 | 0 | 0 | 54.8 | 33 |
| Sudan | 28103 | 136859 | 164962 | 17155 | 10.4 | 36282 | 22.0 | 3446 | 2.1 | 0 | 0 | 30.4 | 50 |
| Swaziland | 367 | 1304 | 1671 | 0 | 0 | 0 | 0 | 52 | 3.1 | 0 | 0 | 4.7 | 91 |
| Tanzania | 7654 | 42940 | 50594 | 4960 | 9.8 | 4770 | 9.4 | 1653 | 3.3 | 136 | 0.3 | 19.9 | 60 |
| Togo | 2471 | 2706 | 5177 | 36 | 0.7 | 1062 | 20.5 | 433 | 8.4 | 0 | 0 | 33.5 | 46 |
| Tunisia | 5411 | 6871 | 12282 | 7767 | 63.2 | 1867 | 15.2 | 0 | 0 | 0 | 0 | 46.8 | 37 |
| Uganda | 7010 | 7592 | 14602 | 248 | 1.7 | 3167 | 21.7 | 1269 | 8.7 | 242 | 1.7 | 39.0 | 41 |
| Zambia | 8309 | 12831 | 21140 | 4622 | 21.9 | 2721 | 12.9 | 537 | 2.5 | 0 | 0 | 27.6 | 52 |
| Zimbabwe | 5014 | 26159 | 31173 | 95 | 0.3 | 3700 | 11.9 | 352 | 1.1 | 0 | 0 | 13.7 | 73 |
| EUROPE | | | | | | | | | | | | | |
| Albania | 846 | 1578 | 2424 | 48 | 2.0 | 906 | 37.4 | 835 | 34.4 | 0 | 0 | 90.0 | 17 |
| Austria | 1681 | 6193 | 7874 | 199 | 2.5 | 1714 | 21.8 | 0 | 0 | 0 | 0 | 23.0 | 57 |
| Belarus | 6811 | 13283 | 20094 | 3254 | 16.2 | 634 | 3.2 | 0 | 0 | 0 | 0 | 11.3 | 77 |
| Belgium | 1219 | 1273 | 2492 | 434 | 17.4 | 182 | 7.3 | 123 | 4.9 | 0 | 0 | 23.4 | 57 |
| Bosnia & Herzogovina | 827 | 4086 | 4913 | 73 | 1.5 | 1132 | 23.0 | 1789 | 36.4 | 0 | 0 | 78.3 | 21 |
| Bulgaria | 5560 | 4403 | 9963 | 181 | 1.8 | 3275 | 32.9 | 17 | 0.2 | 0 | 0 | 34.1 | 46 |
| Croatia | 1598 | 3715 | 5313 | 536 | 10.1 | 1909 | 35.9 | 1085 | 20.4 | 0 | 0 | 71.6 | 24 |
| Czech R | 3426 | 3786 | 7212 | 48 | 0.7 | 2231 | 30.9 | 0 | 0 | 0 | 0 | 31.3 | 49 |
| Denmark | 2746 | 1209 | 3955 | 275 | 7.0 | 0 | 0 | 0 | 0 | 0 | 0 | 3.5 | 93 |
| Estonia | 1479 | 2639 | 4118 | 522 | 12.7 | 20 | 0.5 | 0 | 0 | 0 | 0 | 6.8 | 86 |
| Finland | 2139 | 23322 | 25461 | 2922 | 11.5 | 623 | 2.4 | 0 | 0 | 0 | 0 | 8.2 | 84 |
| France | 21637 | 30335 | 51972 | 6351 | 12.2 | 1255 | 2.4 | 17 | 0 | 0 | 0 | 8.5 | 83 |
| Germany | 12587 | 18245 | 30832 | 6432 | 20.9 | 1334 | 4.3 | 245 | 0.8 | 0 | 0 | 15.9 | 68 |
| Greece | 4543 | 7810 | 12353 | 2954 | 23.9 | 1213 | 9.8 | 65 | 0.5 | 0 | 0 | 22.5 | 57 |
| Hungary | 5298 | 3419 | 8717 | 1270 | 14.6 | 1724 | 19.8 | 109 | 1.3 | 0 | 0 | 29.1 | 51 |
| Iceland | 24 | 5823 | 5847 | 1159 | 19.8 | 2777 | 47.5 | 0 | 0 | 0 | 0 | 57.4 | 31 |
| Ireland | 2288 | 4380 | 6668 | 0 | 0 | 76 | 1.1 | 0 | 0 | 0 | 0 | 1.1 | 98 |
| Italy | 11514 | 13802 | 25316 | 2952 | 11.7 | 2872 | 11.3 | 591 | 2.3 | 58 | 0.2 | 21.0 | 59 |
| Latvia | 2053 | 4012 | 6065 | 743 | 12.3 | 820 | 13.5 | 0 | 0 | 0 | 0 | 19.6 | 61 |
| Lithuania | 3340 | 2936 | 6276 | 776 | 12.4 | 341 | 5.4 | 0 | 0 | 0 | 0 | 11.6 | 77 |
| Luxembourg | 114 | 122 | 236 | 19 | 8.1 | 31 | 13.1 | 0 | 0 | 0 | 0 | 17.2 | 66 |
| Macedonia, FYR | 752 | 1690 | 2442 | 106 | 4.3 | 555 | 22.7 | 443 | 18.1 | 0 | 0 | 52.0 | 34 |
| Malta | 11 | 14 | 25 | -- | -- | -- | -- | -- | -- | -- | -- | -- | -- |
| Moldova | 2221 | 857 | 3078 | 31 | 1.0 | 930 | 30.2 | 7 | 0.2 | 0 | 0 | 31.0 | 49 |
| Netherlands | 1138 | 1693 | 2831 | 471 | 16.6 | 0 | 0 | 32 | 1.1 | 0 | 0 | 9.9 | 80 |
| Norway | 1216 | 19655 | 20871 | 326 | 1.6 | 535 | 2.6 | 0 | 0 | 0 | 0 | 3.4 | 93 |
| Poland | 14872 | 13063 | 27935 | 4442 | 15.9 | 8267 | 29.6 | 0 | 0 | 0 | 0 | 37.5 | 42 |
| Portugal | 3834 | 3803 | 7637 | 974 | 12.8 | 1659 | 21.7 | 0 | 0 | 0 | 0 | 28.1 | 52 |
| Romania | 10478 | 11191 | 21669 | 323 | 1.5 | 6822 | 31.5 | 1485 | 6.9 | 0 | 0 | 42.6 | 39 |
| Slovakia | 1704 | 2955 | 4659 | 94 | 2.0 | 1158 | 24.9 | 0 | 0 | 0 | 0 | 25.9 | 54 |
| Slovenia | 336 | 1577 | 1913 | 29 | 1.5 | 424 | 22.2 | 425 | 22.2 | 0 | 0 | 56.3 | 32 |
| Spain | 22137 | 25870 | 48007 | 3733 | 7.8 | 5192 | 10.8 | 755 | 1.6 | 0 | 0 | 17.1 | 66 |
| Sweden | 3426 | 28078 | 31504 | 1863 | 5.9 | 4753 | 15.1 | 0 | 0 | 0 | 0 | 18.1 | 64 |
| Switzerland | 559 | 3099 | 3658 | 219 | 6.0 | 206 | 5.6 | 2 | 0.1 | 0 | 0 | 8.8 | 82 |
| Ukraine | 39256 | 16008 | 55264 | 5002 | 9.1 | 18875 | 34.2 | 174 | 0.3 | 1750 | 3.2 | 45.6 | 37 |
| United Kingdom | 8926 | 12312 | 21238 | 742 | 3.5 | 1880 | 8.9 | 69 | 0.3 | 0 | 0 | 11.1 | 78 |
| Yugoslavia | 4309 | 5339 | 9648 | 498 | 5.2 | 2074 | 21.5 | 2573 | 26.7 | 0 | 0 | 64.2 | 28 |
| RUSSIAN FEDERATION | 154116 | 417994 | 572110 | 20062 | 3.5 | 56561 | 9.9 | 62 | 0 | 830 | 0.1 | 11.8 | 76 |
| ASIA | | | | | | | | | | | | | |
| Afghanistan | 11062 | 42039 | 53101 | 11800 | 22.2 | 2600 | 4.9 | 0 | 0 | 0 | 0 | 16.0 | 68 |
| Armenia | 641 | 1631 | 2272 | 56 | 2.5 | 104 | 4.6 | 0 | 0 | 0 | 0 | 5.8 | 88 |
| Azerbaijan | 2175 | 5562 | 7737 | 115 | 1.5 | 829 | 10.7 | 0 | 0 | 0 | 0 | 11.4 | 77 |
| Bahrain | 5 | 47 | 52 | -- | -- | -- | -- | -- | -- | -- | -- | -- | -- |
| Bangladesh | 8611 | 3200 | 11811 | 10317 | 87.4 | 1157 | 9.8 | 1494 | 12.6 | 48 | 0.4 | 73.2 | 23 |
| Bhutan | 195 | 3045 | 3240 | 301 | 9.3 | 0 | 0 | 0 | 0 | 0 | 0 | 4.7 | 91 |

| Country | Cultivated 000 ha | Modified 000 ha | Total 000 ha | Light 000 ha | L % | Moderate 000 ha | M % | Strong 000 ha | S % | Extreme 000 ha | E % | Weighted total % | LQ score |
|---|---|---|---|---|---|---|---|---|---|---|---|---|---|
| Brunei Darussalam | 8 | 194 | 202 | 0 | 0 | 52 | 25.7 | 32 | 15.8 | 0 | 0 | 49.4 | 35 |
| Cambodia | 3964 | 9296 | 13260 | 10199 | 76.9 | 1079 | 8.1 | 49 | 0.4 | 0 | 0 | 47.2 | 36 |
| China | 209171 | 456408 | 665579 | 236264 | 35.5 | 58203 | 8.7 | 82548 | 12.4 | 280 | 0 | 45.1 | 37 |
| Cyprus | 172 | 684 | 856 | 0 | 0 | 194 | 22.7 | 0 | 0 | 0 | 0 | 22.7 | 57 |
| Georgia | 1455 | 4698 | 6153 | 145 | 2.4 | 142 | 2.3 | 0 | 0 | 0 | 0 | 3.5 | 93 |
| India | 185600 | 77269 | 262869 | 61872 | 23.5 | 52536 | 20.0 | 9812 | 3.7 | 3925 | 1.5 | 40.3 | 40 |
| Indonesia | 38307 | 39638 | 77945 | 5753 | 7.4 | 2064 | 2.6 | 292 | 0.4 | 0 | 0 | 6.9 | 86 |
| Iran | 23879 | 125418 | 149297 | 38369 | 25.7 | 51555 | 34.5 | 7039 | 4.7 | 0 | 0 | 54.4 | 33 |
| Iraq | 5954 | 25814 | 31768 | 904 | 2.8 | 11843 | 37.3 | 10649 | 33.5 | 0 | 0 | 89.0 | 18 |
| Israel | 543 | 1212 | 1755 | 4 | 0.2 | 39 | 2.2 | 0 | 0 | 0 | 0 | 2.3 | 95 |
| Japan | 15042 | 13261 | 28303 | 559 | 2.0 | 0 | 0 | 0 | 0 | 0 | 0 | 1.0 | 98 |
| Jordan | 492 | 3654 | 4146 | 2057 | 49.6 | 1525 | 36.8 | 0 | 0 | 0 | 0 | 61.6 | 29 |
| Kazakhstan | 48822 | 197953 | 246775 | 39650 | 16.1 | 39650 | 16.1 | 24800 | 10.0 | 0 | 0 | 39.2 | 41 |
| Korea, DPR | 3475 | 7362 | 10837 | 2289 | 21.1 | 0 | 0 | 0 | 0 | 0 | 0 | 10.6 | 79 |
| Korea, R | 2287 | 6226 | 8513 | 205 | 2.4 | 0 | 0 | 0 | 0 | 0 | 0 | 1.2 | 98 |
| Kuwait | 19 | 1091 | 1110 | 374 | 33.7 | 0 | 0 | 0 | 0 | 0 | 0 | 16.9 | 66 |
| Kyrgyzstan | 2382 | 15143 | 17525 | 64 | 0.4 | 481 | 2.7 | 0 | 0 | 0 | 0 | 2.9 | 94 |
| Lao PDR | 936 | 18069 | 19005 | 1655 | 8.7 | 1103 | 5.8 | 51 | 0.3 | 0 | 0 | 10.6 | 79 |
| Lebanon | 323 | 597 | 920 | 0 | 0 | 63 | 6.8 | 0 | 0 | 0 | 0 | 6.8 | 86 |
| Malaysia | 7732 | 10626 | 18358 | 5296 | 28.8 | 3335 | 18.2 | 99 | 0.5 | 0 | 0 | 33.4 | 47 |
| Maldives | 3 | 24 | 27 | -- | -- | -- | -- | -- | -- | -- | -- | -- | -- |
| Mongolia | 2640 | 59870 | 62510 | 7702 | 12.3 | 10057 | 16.1 | 0 | 0 | 0 | 0 | 22.3 | 58 |
| Myanmar | 10462 | 48523 | 58985 | 5576 | 9.5 | 2959 | 5.0 | 0 | 0 | 0 | 0 | 9.8 | 80 |
| Nepal | 3200 | 7010 | 10210 | 1361 | 13.3 | 389 | 3.8 | 49 | 0.5 | 49 | 0.5 | 12.2 | 76 |
| Oman | 126 | 4626 | 4752 | 2515 | 52.9 | 2073 | 43.6 | 0 | 0 | 0 | 0 | 70.1 | 25 |
| Pakistan | 22268 | 43967 | 66235 | 26734 | 40.4 | 17036 | 25.7 | 7462 | 11.3 | 0 | 0 | 62.9 | 28 |
| Philippines | 9851 | 15279 | 25130 | 3298 | 13.1 | 4197 | 16.7 | 3748 | 14.9 | 1999 | 8.0 | 61.6 | 29 |
| Qatar | 22 | 869 | 891 | 198 | 22.2 | 21 | 2.4 | 0 | 0 | 0 | 0 | 13.5 | 73 |
| Saudi Arabia | 7661 | 56877 | 64538 | 52532 | 81.4 | 12006 | 18.6 | 0 | 0 | 0 | 0 | 59.3 | 30 |
| Singapore | 1 | 27 | 28 | 5 | 17.9 | 0 | 0 | 2 | 7.1 | 0 | 0 | 19.6 | 61 |
| Sri Lanka | 2071 | 3831 | 5902 | 1541 | 26.1 | 0 | 0 | 0 | 0 | 0 | 0 | 13.1 | 74 |
| Syrian Arab R | 6478 | 9521 | 15999 | 512 | 3.2 | 4928 | 30.8 | 150 | 0.9 | 0 | 0 | 33.7 | 46 |
| Tajikistan | 1255 | 11137 | 12392 | 465 | 3.8 | 132 | 1.1 | 0 | 0 | 0 | 0 | 3.0 | 94 |
| Thailand | 21054 | 22986 | 44040 | 2682 | 6.1 | 34393 | 78.1 | 0 | 0 | 996 | 2.3 | 85.8 | 18 |
| Turkey | 32254 | 40374 | 72628 | 331 | 0.5 | 17745 | 24.4 | 12827 | 17.7 | 0 | 0 | 51.2 | 34 |
| Turkmenistan | 3402 | 37715 | 41117 | 339 | 0.8 | 1184 | 2.9 | 0 | 0 | 0 | 0 | 3.3 | 93 |
| United Arab Emirates | 170 | 1354 | 1524 | 1005 | 65.9 | 519 | 34.1 | 0 | 0 | 0 | 0 | 67.1 | 26 |
| Uzbekistan | 7230 | 32216 | 39446 | 362 | 0.9 | 5786 | 14.7 | 0 | 0 | 0 | 0 | 15.1 | 70 |
| Viet Nam | 8705 | 20939 | 29644 | 6829 | 23.0 | 4257 | 14.4 | 547 | 1.8 | 0 | 0 | 28.6 | 51 |
| Yemen | 3110 | 41339 | 44449 | 11698 | 26.3 | 5104 | 11.5 | 0 | 0 | 0 | 0 | 24.6 | 55 |
| PACIFIC | | | | | | | | | | | | | |
| Australia | 57143 | 618250 | 675393 | 88016 | 13.0 | 3027 | 0.4 | 2743 | 0.4 | 0 | 0 | 7.5 | 85 |
| Fiji | 380 | 1334 | 1714 | 0 | 0 | 0 | 0 | 0 | 0 | 0 | 0 | 0 | 100 |
| New Zealand | 6139 | 17559 | 23698 | 3965 | 16.7 | 456 | 1.9 | 0 | 0 | 0 | 0 | 10.3 | 79 |
| Papua New Guinea | 709 | 15827 | 16536 | 314 | 1.9 | 25 | 0.2 | 0 | 0 | 0 | 0 | 1.1 | 98 |
| Samoa | 131 | 140 | 271 | -- | -- | -- | -- | -- | -- | -- | -- | -- | -- |
| Solomon Is | 82 | 1966 | 2048 | 504 | 24.6 | 0 | 0 | 0 | 0 | 0 | 0 | 12.3 | 75 |
| Tonga | 48 | 19 | 67 | -- | -- | -- | -- | -- | -- | -- | -- | -- | -- |
| Vanuatu | 130 | 832 | 962 | 0 | 0 | 0 | 0 | 0 | 0 | 0 | 0 | 0 | 100 |

## Notes

The land quality index (*LQ score*) consists of one indicator: the area of degraded land as a percentage of the area of cultivated + modified land, weighted according to severity of degradation. All data are in thousand hectares (000 ha), and all percentages are in terms of the combined cultivated and modified land area.

Cultivated = cultivated land area. Data are for 1997 and are from Table 11.

Modified = modified land area. Data are for 1990-1998 and are from Table 11. Note that the estimated area of modified land is a residual, derived from estimates of cultivated, built, and natural land. The reliability of these estimates is uncertain.

Total = total area of cultivated + modified land.

Light (L); Moderate (M); Strong (S); Extreme (E) = areas affected by degrees of soil degradation as defined in Table 13a. Data are for 1990 and are from GLASOD—the Global Assessment of the Status of Human-induced Soil Degradation (Oldeman 1993; Oldeman, Hakkeling, & Sombroek 1991; UNEP/ISRIC 1990)—except for: Iran, which are from FAO, UNDP & UNEP (1994); Kazakhstan, which are for the mid-1990s and are from Baitullin & Bekturova (1997); and Bangladesh, Bhutan, Cambodia, China, India, Indonesia, Korea DPR, Korea R, Lao PDR, Malaysia, Myanmar, Nepal, Pakistan, Philippines, Sri Lanka, Thailand, and Viet Nam, which are for the mid-1990s and are from ASSOD—the Assessment of the Status of Human-induced Soil Degradation in South and Southeast Asia (van Lynden & Oldeman 1997).

Weighted total % = the percentages of light, moderate, strong, and extreme degradation multiplied by the factors given in the points column of Table 13a. Percentages of light + modified + strong + extreme degradation may total more than 100% due to estimation problems discussed below and because estimates of cultivated area, modified area, and degraded area come from different sources. The weighted total percentages of Costa Rica, El Salvador, Haiti and Cape Verde also exceed 100% due to the effect of the weights.

*LQ score* = land quality index (degraded land score). The performance criteria are shown in Table 13c. The top of the good band is 0%, the background rate of human-induced soil degradation on natural land.

The data from ASSOD and for Iran were expressed as areas or percentages of the land areas of the countries concerned. These data were used directly without change. The data for Kazakhstan were given as area of "strong desertification" and area of "other desertification". The area of "strong desertification" was adopted as the area of strong land degradation. The area of "other desertification" was divided into equal areas of low and moderate degradation.

GLASOD's *World Map on Status of Human-induced Soil Degradation* distinguished the four degrees of soil degradation defined in Table 13a, and five extents of soil degradation defined in Table 13b. To produce the GLASOD map, groups of soil scientists gave their expert opinion on the types, degree and extent of soil degradation in 21 regions. They classified map units by type of degradation (if any) and by degree and extent of each type. A map unit may be affected by more than one type of degradation. For example, one part of the unit may be compacted while another part may have lost soil to water erosion.

As a regional assessment, GLASOD was not intended for use at country level. However, some regions consist of one or two countries (Argentina, Paraguay, Mexico, United States, Canada, China, Japan, the two Koreas) and many countries are as big as (or bigger than) the smallest region (Uruguay). Although inaccurate for small countries, GLASOD provides a good idea of the extent and severity of land degradation in countries of 10 million hectares and above.

To obtain country data, *The Wellbeing of Nations* (WoN) superimposed national boundaries on the GLASOD map using Map Maker, which then calculated the percentages of each map unit in each country. These percentages were used to estimate how much of each country is affected by each degree of degradation. GLASOD's ranges were converted to averages, as shown in the WoN average column of Table 13b. Where two types of land degradation affect a map unit, it was assumed that they do not overlap. In such cases, the percentages may exaggerate the area affected by degradation, particularly if both types of degradation are very frequent or dominant in extent.

The main problem with all the sources is that their information comes from expert opinion rather than from monitoring representative conditions on the ground. Kazakhstan illustrates the difference between one expert opinion and another. Using GLASOD's estimates, Kazakhstan's weighted total percentage of degraded land is 7.6%, similar to those of Kyrgyzstan (2.9%), Tajikistan (3.0%), Turkmenistan (3.3%) and Uzbekistan (15.1%). Using estimates by national scientists (Baitullin & Bekturova 1997), Kazakhstan's weighted total percentage is much higher: 39.2%.

The main problem with WoN's interpretation of the sources is that the estimates of soil degradation are denominated in terms of the cultivated + modified land area. As noted above, there is great uncertainty about the estimates of modified land. If they are too high, the weighted total percentage will be lower than it should be, and vice versa. One alternative would be to use the total land area as the denominator. However, this would favor countries with large areas of little used land, such as Canada and Russia. It would also detract from an important function of the indicator, which is to show the condition of the land that supports the essential resource sectors of agriculture and timber production. The other alternative is to use the cultivated area alone as the denominator, since this is better known and more reliable than the modified area. However, in many countries large areas of uncultivated land are degraded by grazing (and to a lesser extent timber production). Consequently, the degraded land area is often larger than the cultivated land area. The ideal would be to show degradation of cultivated land and of modified land separately, but this is not yet possible. Since the ideal is out of reach, none of the alternatives is satisfactory, and cultivated and modified land are both important, I chose to keep the focus on both.

| degree | definition | points |
|---|---|---|
| Light | Land with somewhat reduced agricultural suitability; restoration to full productivity possible by modifying management; original biotic functions still largely intact. | $\% \times 0.5$ |
| Moderate | Land with greatly reduced agricultural suitability; major improvements required to restore productivity; original biotic functions partly destroyed. | $\% \times 1.0$ |
| Strong | Land non-reclaimable at farm level; major engineering works required for restoration; original biotic functions destroyed. | $\% \times 1.5$ |
| Extreme | Land unreclaimable and beyond restoration; original biotic functions fully destroyed. | $\% \times 2.0$ |

**Table 13a. Degrees of soil degradation.** The percentage of each type was multiplied by the factor in the points column to obtain the weighted total percentage.

| extent of map unit affected | | |
|---|---|---|
| | GLASOD range (%) | WoN average (%) |
| 1. infrequent | 1-5 | 3 |
| 2. common | 6-10 | 8 |
| 3. frequent | 11-25 | 18 |
| 4. very frequent | 26-50 | 38 |
| 5. dominant | >50 | 75 |

**Table 13b. Extents of soil degradation.** GLASOD's estimated ranges of the extent of degraded land were converted to the average percentages shown in the WoN average column.

| band | top point on scale | degraded land as weighted % of cultivated + modified land |
|---|---|---|
| good | 100 | 0 |
| fair | 80 | 10 |
| medium | 60 | 20 |
| poor | 40 | 40 |
| bad | 20 | 80 |
| base | 0 | 160 |

**Table 13c. Performance criteria for land quality.**

# Table 14. Water Index; River Conversion; Water Withdrawal

| Country | Note | Gross cap GWh/y | Used cap GWh/y | Used %G | Tot supply km³/y | Dam cap km³ | Dam %TS | RC score | Int supply km³/y | WW km³/y | WW %IS | WW score | WQ score | IW score |
|---|---|---|---|---|---|---|---|---|---|---|---|---|---|---|
| **AMERICAS** | | | | | | | | | | | | | | |
| Antigua & Barbuda | ff90 | -- | -- | -- | 0.05 | -- | -- | -- | 0.05 | 0.005 | 10.0 | 80 | -- | 60* |
| Argentina | ff95 | 535000 | 30576 | 5.7 | 814.00 | -- | -- | 89 | 276.00 | 28.58 | 10.4 | 79 | 38 | 38 |
| Bahamas | -- | -- | -- | -- | -- | -- | -- | -- | -- | -- | -- | -- | -- | -- |
| Barbados | ff96 | -- | -- | -- | 0.08 | -- | -- | -- | 0.08 | 0.08 | 100.0 | 20 | -- | 20 |
| Belize | ff93 | 2000 | -- | -- | 18.55 | -- | -- | -- | 16.00 | 0.10 | 0.6 | 99 | -- | 60* |
| Bolivia | fs90 | 178000 | 1760 | 1.0 | 622.53 | -- | -- | 98 | 303.53 | 1.38 | 0.5 | 99 | -- | 80* |
| Brazil | ff92 | 3020000 | 311073 | 10.3 | 8233.0 | -- | -- | 79 | 5418.0 | 54.87 | 1.0 | 98 | 23 | 23 |
| Canada | ss90 | 1332000 | 353618 | 26.5 | 3460.0 | -- | -- | 53 | 3290.0 | 51.20 | 1.6 | 97 | 50 | 50 |
| Chile | fs90 | 227000 | 16676 | 7.3 | 922.00 | -- | -- | 85 | 884.00 | 21.40 | 2.4 | 95 | 21 | 21 |
| Colombia | ff96 | 1000000 | 34650 | 3.5 | 2132.0 | -- | -- | 93 | 2112.0 | 8.94 | 0.4 | 99 | 10 | 10 |
| Costa Rica | ff97 | 223000 | 3375 | 1.5 | 112.40 | -- | -- | 97 | 112.40 | 5.77 | 5.1 | 90 | -- | 80* |
| Cuba | ff95 | 2000 | 104 | 5.2 | 38.12 | -- | -- | 90 | 38.12 | 5.21 | 13.7 | 73 | 60* | 60 |
| Dominica | f96 | 200 | 17 | 8.5 | -- | -- | -- | 83 | -- | 0.02 | -- | -- | -- | 60* |
| Dominican R | ff94 | 50000 | 790 | 1.6 | 20.99 | -- | -- | 97 | 20.99 | 8.34 | 39.7 | 47 | -- | 47 |
| Ecuador | ff97 | 115000 | 5560 | 4.8 | 432.00 | -- | -- | 90 | 432.00 | 16.99 | 3.9 | 92 | -- | 80* |
| El Salvador | ff92 | 7000 | 2280 | 32.6 | 25.25 | -- | -- | 47 | 17.77 | 0.73 | 4.1 | 92 | -- | 47 |
| Grenada | -- | | 38 | 18 | 47.4 | -- | -- | 33 | -- | -- | -- | -- | -- | 33 |
| Guatemala | ff92 | 95000 | 2275 | 2.4 | 111.27 | -- | -- | 95 | 109.20 | 1.16 | 1.1 | 98 | -- | 80* |
| Guyana | ff92 | 8000 | 5 | 0.1 | 241.00 | -- | -- | 100 | 241.00 | 1.46 | 0.6 | 99 | -- | 80* |
| Haiti | ff91 | 4000 | 160 | 4.0 | 14.02 | -- | -- | 92 | 13.01 | 0.98 | 7.5 | 85 | -- | 80* |
| Honduras | ff92 | 16000 | 2230 | 13.9 | 95.93 | -- | -- | 72 | 95.93 | 1.52 | 1.6 | 97 | -- | 72 |
| Jamaica | ff93 | 450 | 100 | 22.2 | 9.40 | -- | -- | 58 | 9.40 | 0.90 | 9.6 | 81 | -- | 58 |
| Mexico | ff98 | 155000 | 31442 | 20.3 | 457.22 | -- | -- | 60 | 409.00 | 77.81 | 19.0 | 62 | 5 | 5 |
| | mm95 | | | | 475.26 | | | | 426.34 | 73.50 | 17.2 | | | |
| Nicaragua | ff98 | 33000 | 375 | 1.1 | 196.69 | -- | -- | 98 | 189.74 | 1.29 | 0.7 | 99 | -- | 80* |
| Panama | ff90 | 26000 | 2975 | 11.4 | 147.98 | -- | -- | 77 | 147.42 | 1.64 | 1.1 | 98 | -- | 77 |
| Paraguay | ff87 | 111000 | 51680 | 46.6 | 336.00 | -- | -- | 33 | 94.00 | 0.43 | 0.5 | 99 | -- | 33 |
| Peru | ss90 | 1812000 | 14400 | 0.8 | 1913.0 | -- | -- | 98 | 1616.0 | 18.97 | 1.2 | 97 | -- | 80* |
| St Kitts & Nevis | f | -- | -- | -- | 0.02 | -- | -- | -- | 0.02 | -- | -- | -- | -- | -- |
| St Lucia | f97 | -- | -- | -- | -- | -- | -- | -- | -- | 0.01 | -- | -- | -- | -- |
| St Vincent & Grenadines | f95 | -- | 20 | -- | -- | -- | -- | -- | -- | 0.01 | -- | -- | -- | -- |
| Suriname | fs90 | 12840 | 1435 | 11.2 | 128.00 | -- | -- | 78 | 88.00 | 0.49 | 0.6 | 99 | -- | 78 |
| Trinidad & Tobago | ff97 | -- | -- | -- | 3.84 | -- | -- | -- | 3.84 | 0.30 | 7.8 | 84 | -- | 60* |
| United States | ss90 | 4485000 | 354946 | 7.9 | 2956.0 | -- | -- | 84 | 2810.0 | 489.0 | 17.4 | 65 | 46 | 46 |
| Uruguay | fs90 | 32000 | 5767 | 18.0 | 139.00 | -- | -- | 64 | 59.00 | 4.2 | 7.1 | 86 | -- | 64 |
| Venezuela | ff70 | 345000 | 82169 | 23.8 | 1233.2 | -- | -- | 56 | 722.45 | 4.1 | 0.6 | 99 | -- | 56 |
| **AFRICA** | | | | | | | | | | | | | | |
| Algeria | ff90 f92 | 12000 | 135 | 1.1 | 14.33 | 4.30 | 30.0 | 50 | 13.90 | 4.50 | 32.4 | 52 | -- | 50 |
| Angola | ff87 | 150000 | 940 | 0.6 | 184.00 | -- | -- | 99 | 184.00 | 0.48 | 0.3 | 99 | -- | 80* |
| Benin | ff94 f94 | 2500 | -- | -- | 25.80 | 0.03 | 0.1 | 100 | 10.30 | 0.15 | 1.5 | 97 | -- | 80* |
| Botswana | ff92 f92 | -- | -- | -- | 14.70 | 0.40 | 2.7 | 95 | 2.90 | 0.11 | 3.8 | 92 | -- | 80* |
| Burkina Faso | ff92 f94 | 800 | 84 | 10.5 | 17.50 | 4.30 | 24.6 | 55 | 17.50 | 0.38 | 2.2 | 96 | -- | 55 |
| Burundi | ff87 | 6000 | 98 | 1.6 | 3.60 | -- | -- | 97 | 3.60 | 0.10 | 2.8 | 94 | -- | 80* |
| Cameroon | ff87 | 294000 | 2645 | 0.9 | 268.00 | -- | -- | 98 | 268.00 | 0.40 | 0.1 | 100 | -- | 80* |
| Cape Verde | ff90 | | | | 0.30 | -- | -- | -- | 0.30 | 0.03 | 10.0 | 80 | -- | 60* |
| Central African R | ff87 | -- | 76 | -- | 141.00 | -- | -- | -- | 141.00 | 0.07 | 0.0 | 100 | -- | 60* |
| Chad | fs90 | 150 | -- | -- | 43.00 | -- | -- | -- | 15.00 | 0.19 | 1.3 | 97 | -- | 60* |
| Comoros | f | -- | 2 | -- | 1.02 | -- | -- | -- | 1.02 | -- | -- | -- | -- | -- |
| Congo, DR | ff90 | 1397000 | 5420 | 0.4 | 1019.0 | -- | -- | 99 | 935.00 | 0.36 | 0.0 | 100 | -- | 80* |
| Congo, R | ff87 | 50000 | 435 | 0.9 | 832.00 | -- | -- | 98 | 222.00 | 0.04 | 0.0 | 100 | -- | 80* |
| Côte d'Ivoire | ff87 f93 | 46000 | 1190 | 2.6 | 77.70 | 38.10 | 49.0 | 31 | 76.70 | 0.71 | 0.9 | 98 | -- | 31 |
| Djibouti | ff85 | -- | -- | -- | 2.30 | -- | -- | -- | 0.30 | 0.01 | 3.3 | 93 | -- | 60* |
| Egypt | ff93 f94 | 50000 | 11564 | 23.1 | 68.50 | 169.0 | 246.7 | 0 | 1.80 | 53.10 | 2950 | 0 | -- | 0 |
| Equatorial Guinea | ff87 | -- | 2 | -- | 30.00 | -- | -- | -- | 30.00 | 0.01 | 0.0 | 100 | -- | 60* |
| Eritrea | ff87# f93 | -- | -- | -- | 8.80 | 0.03 | 0.3 | 99 | 2.80 | 0.13 | 4.6 | 91 | -- | 80* |
| Ethiopia | ff87# | 650000 | 1981 | 0.3 | 110.00 | -- | -- | 99 | 110.00 | 2.07 | 1.9 | 96 | -- | 80* |
| Gabon | ff87 | 80000 | 720 | 0.9 | 164.00 | -- | -- | 98 | 164.00 | 0.06 | 0.0 | 100 | -- | 80* |
| Gambia | fs90 | -- | -- | -- | 8.00 | -- | -- | -- | 3.00 | 0.03 | 1.0 | 98 | -- | 60* |
| Ghana | ff70 f94 | 13000 | 6040 | 46.5 | 53.20 | 148.5 | 279.1 | 0 | 30.30 | 0.30 | 1.0 | 98 | 6 | 0 |
| Guinea | ff87 | 26000 | 185 | 0.7 | 226.00 | -- | -- | 99 | 226.00 | 0.74 | 0.3 | 99 | -- | 80* |
| Guinea-Bissau | ff91 f94 | 300 | -- | -- | 27.00 | 0.00 | 0.0 | 100 | 16.00 | 0.02 | 0.1 | 100 | -- | 80* |
| Kenya | ff90 f92 | 9000 | 3183 | 35.4 | 30.20 | 4.10 | 13.6 | 73 | 20.20 | 2.05 | 10.1 | 80 | 36 | 36 |
| Lesotho | ff87 f94 | 2000 | 6 | 0.3 | 5.23 | 0.01 | 0.2 | 100 | 5.23 | 0.05 | 1.0 | 98 | -- | 80* |
| Liberia | ff87 | 11000 | 180 | 1.6 | 232.00 | -- | -- | 97 | 200.00 | 0.13 | 0.1 | 100 | -- | 80* |
| Libyan Arab J | ff94 f92 | -- | -- | -- | 0.60 | 0.39 | 65.0 | 17 | 0.60 | 4.60 | 766.7 | 0 | -- | 0 |
| Madagascar | fs90 | 321000 | 350 | 0.1 | 337.00 | -- | -- | 100 | 337.00 | 19.70 | 5.8 | 88 | -- | 80* |
| Malawi | ff94 f94 | 6000 | 890 | 14.8 | 18.68 | 0.10 | 0.5 | 70 | 17.54 | 0.94 | 5.4 | 89 | -- | 70 |

| Country | Note | Gross cap GWh/y | Used cap GWh/y | Used % G | Tot supply km³/y | Dam cap km³ | Dam % TS | RC score | Int supply km³/y | WW km³/y | WW % IS | WW score | WQ score | IW score |
|---|---|---|---|---|---|---|---|---|---|---|---|---|---|---|
| Mali | fs90 f92 | 5000 | 210 | 4.2 | 100.00 | 11.00 | 11.0 | 78 | 60.00 | 1.49 | 2.5 | 95 | 10 | 10 |
| Mauritania | fs90 f94 | -- | 25 | -- | 11.40 | 0.90 | 7.9 | 84 | 0.40 | 1.63 | 407.5 | 0 | -- | 0 |
| Mauritius | ff74 f94 | 150 | 145 | 96.7 | 2.21 | 0.07 | 3.2 | 94 | 2.21 | 0.36 | 16.3 | 67 | -- | 67 |
| Morocco | ff91 f92 | 4700 | 2338 | 49.7 | 30.00 | 11.00 | 36.7 | 43 | 30.00 | 11.05 | 36.8 | 49 | 4 | 4 |
| Mozambique | ff92 f87 | 72000 | 579 | 0.8 | 208.00 | 44.60 | 21.4 | 59 | 97.00 | 0.61 | 0.6 | 99 | -- | 59 |
| Namibia | ff91 f92 | 9000 | 815 | 9.1 | 45.50 | 0.90 | 2.0 | 96 | 6.20 | 0.25 | 4.0 | 92 | 18 | 18 |
| Niger | fs90 f90 | 1330 | -- | -- | 32.50 | 0.10 | 0.3 | 99 | 3.50 | 0.50 | 14.3 | 71 | -- | 71 |
| Nigeria | fs90 f93 | 91000 | 5450 | 6.0 | 280.00 | 30.3 | 10.8 | 78 | 221.00 | 4.00 | 1.8 | 96 | -- | 78 |
| Rwanda | ff93 | 3000 | 175 | 5.8 | 6.30 | -- | -- | 88 | 6.30 | 0.77 | 12.2 | 76 | -- | 76 |
| São Tomé & Principe | f f80 | -- | 8 | -- | 2.18 | 0.04 | 1.8 | 96 | 2.18 | -- | -- | -- | -- | 60* |
| Senegal | fs90 f94 | 4000 | 1000 | 25.0 | 39.40 | 1.60 | 4.1 | 92 | 26.40 | 1.50 | 5.7 | 89 | 31 | 31 |
| Seychelles | -- | -- | -- | -- | -- | -- | -- | -- | -- | -- | -- | -- | -- | -- |
| Sierra Leone | ff87 | 6800 | 10 | 0.1 | 160.00 | -- | -- | 100 | 160.00 | 0.37 | 0.2 | 100 | -- | 80* |
| Somalia | ff87 | 600 | 16 | 2.7 | 13.50 | -- | -- | 95 | 6.00 | 0.81 | 13.5 | 73 | -- | 73 |
| South Africa | ff90 f90 | | 529 | -- | 50.00 | 26.90 | 53.8 | 26 | 44.80 | 13.31 | 29.7 | 53 | 18 | 18 |
| Sudan | ff95 f95 | 19000 | 935 | 4.9 | 154.00 | 8.80 | 5.7 | 89 | 35.00 | 17.80 | 50.9 | 40 | 0 | 0 |
| Swaziland | ff80 f89 | 3800 | 120 | 3.2 | 4.51 | 0.20 | 4.4 | 91 | 2.64 | 0.66 | 25.0 | 57 | -- | 57 |
| Tanzania | ff94 | 190000 | 1730 | 0.9 | 89.00 | -- | -- | 98 | 80.00 | 1.17 | 1.5 | 97 | 60* | 60 |
| Togo | ff87 f94 | 1700 | 5 | 0.3 | 12.00 | 1.50 | 12.5 | 75 | 11.50 | 0.09 | 0.8 | 98 | -- | 75 |
| Tunisia | ff90 f91 | 1000 | 45 | 4.5 | 3.94 | 1.50 | 38.1 | 42 | 3.52 | 3.08 | 87.5 | 25 | -- | 25 |
| Uganda | ff70 | 13000 | 985 | 7.6 | 66.00 | -- | -- | 85 | 39.00 | 0.20 | 0.5 | 99 | 19 | 19 |
| Zambia | ff94 f94 | 28750 | 7116 | 24.8 | 116.00 | 200.00 | 172.4 | 0 | 80.20 | 1.71 | 2.1 | 96 | -- | 0 |
| Zimbabwe | ff87 | 18500 | 2275 | 12.3 | 20.00 | -- | -- | 75 | 14.10 | 1.22 | 8.7 | 83 | -- | 75 |
| EUROPE | | | | | | | | | | | | | | |
| Albania | ss90 | 13000 | 5573 | 42.9 | 23.80 | -- | -- | 37 | 18.60 | 0.34 | 1.8 | 96 | 60* | 37 |
| Austria | oo93 | 75000 | 36890 | 49.2 | 84.00 | -- | -- | 31 | 55.00 | 2.25 | 4.1 | 92 | 23 | 23 |
| Belarus | ff90 f91 | 7600 | 19 | 0.3 | 58.00 | 3.08 | 5.3 | 89 | 37.20 | 2.73 | 7.3 | 85 | -- | 80* |
| Belgium | oo94 | 1750 | 234 | 13.4 | 17.00 | -- | -- | 73 | 12.00 | 7.01 | 58.4 | 37 | 5 | 5 |
| Bosnia & Herzegovina | -- | 28000 | 1240 | 4.4 | -- | -- | -- | 91 | -- | -- | -- | -- | -- | 60* |
| Bulgaria | re88 | 26400 | 1840 | 7.0 | 205.00 | -- | -- | 86 | 18.00 | 11.00 | 61.1 | 36 | 29 | 29 |
| Croatia | re90 | 20000 | 7153 | 35.8 | -- | -- | -- | 44 | 61.40 | 0.56 | 0.9 | 98 | 13 | 13 |
| Czech R | oo97 | 13100 | 1969 | 15.0 | 16.00 | -- | -- | 70 | 15.00 | 2.49 | 16.6 | 67 | 17 | 17 |
| Denmark | oo96 | 120 | 16 | 13.3 | 6.00 | -- | -- | 73 | 6.00 | 0.96 | 16.0 | 68 | 22 | 22 |
| Estonia | ff95 f95 | 2000 | 2 | 0.1 | 12.81 | 0.00 | 0.0 | 100 | 12.71 | 0.16 | 1.3 | 97 | 19 | 19 |
| Finland | oo94 | 46000 | 11785 | 25.6 | 110.00 | -- | -- | 54 | 107.00 | 2.44 | 2.3 | 95 | 45 | 45 |
| France | so94 | 200000 | 62800 | 31.4 | 183.00 | -- | -- | 49 | 168.00 | 40.67 | 24.2 | 57 | 12 | 12 |
| Germany | oo95 | 120000 | 18207 | 15.2 | 178.00 | -- | -- | 70 | 107.00 | 43.37 | 40.5 | 46 | 17 | 17 |
| Greece | oo97 | 80000 | 4300 | 5.4 | 72.00 | -- | -- | 89 | 60.00 | 8.70 | 14.5 | 71 | 43 | 43 |
| Hungary | oo96 | 7000 | 156 | 2.2 | 120.00 | -- | -- | 96 | 76.00 | 6.01 | 7.9 | 84 | 18 | 18 |
| Iceland | oo97 | 184000 | 5564 | 3.0 | 170.00 | -- | -- | 94 | 170.00 | 0.16 | 0.1 | 100 | -- | 80* |
| Ireland | oo94 | 1400 | 727 | 51.9 | 46.00 | -- | -- | 28 | 43.00 | 1.18 | 2.7 | 95 | 23 | 23 |
| Italy | ss90 | 340000 | 44880 | 13.2 | 185.00 | -- | -- | 74 | 185.00 | 54.60 | 29.5 | 54 | 22 | 22 |
| Latvia | ff94 f88 | 6000 | 1862 | 31.0 | 35.45 | 1.05 | 3.0 | 94 | 16.74 | 0.29 | 1.7 | 97 | 27 | 27 |
| Lithuania | ff95 f91 | 5000 | 373 | 7.5 | 24.90 | 1.82 | 7.3 | 85 | 15.56 | 0.25 | 1.6 | 97 | 35 | 35 |
| Luxembourg | oo95 | 125 | 64 | 51.2 | 1.60 | -- | -- | 29 | 0.90 | 0.06 | 6.7 | 87 | 14 | 14 |
| Macedonia, FYR | -- | 9000 | 740 | 8.2 | -- | -- | -- | 84 | -- | -- | -- | -- | -- | 60* |
| Malta | ff95 f93 | -- | -- | -- | 0.02 | 0.00 | 1.0 | 98 | 0.02 | 0.06 | 300.0 | 0 | -- | 0 |
| Moldova | ff92 f94 | 2100 | 285 | 13.6 | 11.65 | 2.02 | 17.3 | 65 | 1.00 | 2.96 | 296.0 | 0 | 18 | 0 |
| Netherlands | oo96 | 1000 | 80 | 8.0 | 91.00 | -- | -- | 84 | 11.00 | 4.43 | 40.3 | 46 | 18 | 18 |
| Norway | oo94 | 600000 | 104067 | 17.3 | 393.00 | -- | -- | 65 | 382.00 | 2.59 | 0.7 | 99 | 54 | 54 |
| Poland | so97 | 23000 | 2062 | 9.0 | 56.20 | -- | -- | 82 | 49.50 | 11.80 | 23.8 | 57 | 4 | 4 |
| Portugal | so91 | 33000 | 13740 | 41.6 | 53.00 | -- | -- | 38 | 18.50 | 8.60 | 46.5 | 42 | 21 | 21 |
| Romania | rr94 | 70000 | 18950 | 27.1 | 208.00 | -- | -- | 53 | 37.00 | 26.00 | 70.3 | 32 | 12 | 12 |
| Slovakia | oo97 | 8000 | 4912 | 61.4 | 83.00 | -- | -- | 19 | 13.00 | 1.31 | 10.1 | 80 | 18 | 18 |
| Slovenia | ee90 | 12500 | 3758 | 30.1 | 18.70 | -- | -- | 50 | -- | 0.50 | 2.7 | 95 | 33 | 33 |
| Spain | so97 | 138000 | 41041 | 29.7 | 108.00 | -- | -- | 50 | 108.00 | 40.86 | 37.8 | 48 | 14 | 14 |
| Sweden | so95 | 176000 | 51000 | 29.0 | 176.20 | -- | -- | 51 | 164.00 | 2.71 | 1.7 | 97 | 57 | 51 |
| Switzerland | oo94 | 144000 | 28219 | 19.6 | 53.00 | -- | -- | 61 | 40.00 | 2.60 | 6.5 | 87 | 32 | 32 |
| Ukraine | ff92 | 45000 | 8611 | 19.1 | 139.55 | -- | -- | 62 | 53.10 | 25.99 | 48.9 | 41 | 20 | 20 |
| United Kingdom | oe94 | 8000 | 3317 | 41.5 | 147.00 | -- | -- | 38 | 145.00 | 14.24 | 9.8 | 80 | 21 | 21 |
| Yugoslavia | -- | 118000 | 14526 | 12.3 | -- | -- | -- | 75 | -- | -- | -- | -- | -- | 60* |
| RUSSIAN FEDERATION | fo97 f92 | 2400000 | 191412 | 8.0 | 4498.2 | 360.0 | 8.0 | 84 | 4312.7 | 87.37 | 2.0 | 96 | 48 | 48 |
| ASIA | | | | | | | | | | | | | | |
| Afghanistan | ff87 | -- | 455 | -- | 65.00 | -- | -- | -- | 55.00 | 26.11 | 47.5 | 42 | -- | 42 |
| Armenia | ff94 f93 | 21800 | 3450 | 15.8 | 10.53 | 1.16 | 11.0 | 78 | 9.07 | 2.93 | 32.3 | 52 | -- | 52 |
| Azerbaijan | ff95 f91 | 43500 | 2300 | 5.3 | 30.27 | 21.45 | 70.9 | 14 | 8.11 | 16.53 | 203.8 | 0 | -- | 0 |
| Bahrain | ff91 | -- | -- | -- | 0.12 | | -- | -- | 0.004 | 0.24 | 6000 | 0 | -- | 0 |
| Bangladesh | ff90 f91 | 1000 | 740 | 74.0 | 1210.6 | 20.30 | 1.7 | 97 | 105.00 | 14.64 | 13.9 | 72 | 50 | 50 |
| Bhutan | ff87 | 70000 | 1685 | 2.4 | 95.00 | -- | -- | 95 | 95.00 | 0.02 | 0.0 | 100 | -- | 80* |

| Country | Note | Gross cap GWh/y | Used cap GWh/y | Used %G | Tot supply km³/y | Dam cap km³ | Dam %TS | RC score | Int supply km³/y | WW km³/y | WW %IS | WW score | WQ score | IW score |
|---|---|---|---|---|---|---|---|---|---|---|---|---|---|---|
| Brunei Darussalam | ff94 f95 | -- | -- | -- | 8.50 | 0.05 | 0.6 | 99 | 8.50 | 0.09 | 1.1 | 98 | -- | 80* |
| Cambodia | ff87 | 83000 | 74 | 0.1 | 476.11 | -- | -- | 100 | 120.57 | 0.52 | 0.4 | 99 | -- | 80* |
| China | ff93 f95 | 5922000 | 186900 | 3.2 | 2829.6 | 480.0 | 17.0 | 66 | 2812.4 | 525.5 | 18.7 | 63 | 23 | 23 |
| Cyprus | ff93 f94 | 23500 | 1 | 0.0 | 0.90 | 0.30 | 33.3 | 47 | 0.90 | 0.21 | 23.3 | 58 | -- | 47 |
| Georgia | ff90 f96 | 139000 | 6010 | 4.3 | 63.33 | 3.18 | 5.0 | 90 | 58.13 | 3.47 | 6.0 | 88 | 19 | 19 |
| India | ff90 f96 | 2638000 | 69070 | 2.6 | 1907.8 | 250.0 | 13.1 | 74 | 1260.5 | 500.0 | 39.7 | 47 | 21 | 21 |
| Indonesia | ff90 f95 | 2147000 | 21400 | 1.0 | 2838.0 | 15.80 | 0.6 | 99 | 2838.0 | 74.35 | 2.6 | 95 | 2 | 2 |
| Iran | ff93 f93 | 176000 | 7376 | 4.2 | 137.51 | 39.20 | 28.5 | 51 | 128.50 | 70.03 | 54.5 | 38 | 23 | 23 |
| Iraq | ff90 f92 | 90000 | 690 | 0.8 | 75.42 | 50.20 | 66.6 | 17 | 35.20 | 42.80 | 121.6 | 16 | 13 | 13 |
| Israel | rr89 | -- | 9 | -- | 2.20 | -- | -- | -- | 1.70 | 1.85 | 108.8 | 18 | -- | 18 |
| Japan | ff92 f93 | 718000 | 81668 | 11.4 | 430.00 | 28.98 | 6.7 | 87 | 430.00 | 91.40 | 21.3 | 59 | 27 | 27 |
| Jordan | ff93 f93 | 100 | 22 | 22.0 | 0.88 | 0.14 | 15.9 | 68 | 0.68 | 0.98 | 144.1 | 11 | 5 | 5 |
| Kazakhstan | ff93 f94 | 110000 | 9200 | 8.4 | 109.61 | 88.75 | 81.0 | 9 | 75.42 | 33.67 | 44.6 | 44 | 13 | 9 |
| Korea, DPR | ff87 | -- | 23760 | -- | 77.13 | -- | -- | -- | 67.00 | 14.16 | 21.1 | 59 | -- | 59 |
| Korea, R | fo97 f94 | 72000 | 2424 | 3.4 | 69.70 | 16.20 | 23.2 | 57 | 64.85 | 24.80 | 38.2 | 48 | 27 | 27 |
| Kuwait | ff94 | -- | -- | -- | 0.02 | -- | -- | -- | 0.00 | 0.54 | 54000 | 0 | -- | 0 |
| Kyrgyzstan | ff94 f94 | 163000 | 12660 | 7.8 | 20.58 | 21.50 | 104.5 | 0 | 46.45 | 10.09 | 21.7 | 59 | -- | 0 |
| Lao PDR | ff87 f95 | 232000 | 1040 | 0.4 | 331.55 | 7.30 | 2.2 | 96 | 190.42 | 0.99 | 0.5 | 99 | -- | 80* |
| Lebanon | ff94 f95 | 1000 | 890 | 89.0 | 4.41 | 0.25 | 5.7 | 89 | 4.80 | 1.29 | 26.9 | 55 | -- | 55 |
| Malaysia | ff95 | 230000 | 6770 | 2.9 | 580.00 | -- | -- | 94 | 580.00 | 12.73 | 2.2 | 96 | 0 | 0 |
| Maldives | ff87 | -- | -- | -- | 0.03 | -- | -- | -- | 0.03 | 0.003 | 10.0 | 80 | -- | 60* |
| Mongolia | ff93 | 6000 | 1 | 0.0 | 34.80 | -- | -- | 100 | 34.80 | 0.43 | 1.2 | 98 | -- | 80* |
| Myanmar | ff87 | 366000 | 1615 | 0.4 | 1045.6 | -- | -- | 99 | 880.60 | 3.96 | 0.4 | 99 | 36 | 36 |
| Nepal | ff94 f95 | 727000 | 2828 | 0.4 | 210.20 | 0.09 | 0.0 | 100 | 198.20 | 28.95 | 14.6 | 71 | -- | 71 |
| Oman | ff91 f96 | -- | -- | -- | 0.98 | 0.06 | 6.1 | 88 | 0.98 | 1.22 | 124.5 | 15 | -- | 15 |
| Pakistan | ff91 | 262000 | 24540 | 9.4 | 418.27 | -- | -- | 81 | 248.00 | 155.6 | 62.7 | 35 | 13 | 13 |
| Philippines | ff95 f95 | 46800 | 5699 | 12.2 | 479.00 | 4.75 | 1.0 | 98 | 479.00 | 55.42 | 11.6 | 77 | 29 | 29 |
| Qatar | ff94 | -- | -- | -- | 0.05 | -- | -- | -- | 0.05 | 0.28 | 560.0 | 0 | -- | 0 |
| Saudi Arabia | ff92 f93 | -- | -- | -- | 2.40 | 0.48 | 20.0 | 60 | 2.40 | 17.02 | 709.2 | 0 | -- | 0 |
| Singapore | rr75 | -- | -- | -- | 0.60 | -- | -- | -- | 0.60 | 0.19 | 31.7 | 52 | -- | 52 |
| Sri Lanka | ff90 f96 | 7000 | 4540 | 64.9 | 50.00 | 5.94 | 11.9 | 76 | 50.00 | 9.77 | 19.5 | 61 | -- | 61 |
| Syrian Arab R | ff93 f94 | 5000 | 3496 | 69.9 | 26.26 | 15.80 | 60.2 | 20 | 7.00 | 14.41 | 205.9 | 0 | -- | 0 |
| Tajikistan | ff94 f94 | 527000 | 16120 | 3.1 | 15.98 | 28.97 | 181.3 | 0 | 66.30 | 11.87 | 17.9 | 64 | -- | 0 |
| Thailand | ff90 f95 | 55500 | 8366 | 15.1 | 409.94 | 85.00 | 20.7 | 59 | 210.00 | 33.13 | 15.8 | 68 | 2 | 2 |
| Turkey | fo97 f92 | 433000 | 49575 | 11.4 | 183.76 | 206.0 | 112.1 | 0 | 196.00 | 35.55 | 18.1 | 64 | 15 | 0 |
| Turkmenistan | ff94 f94 | 23900 | 5 | -- | 24.72 | 2.89 | 11.7 | 77 | 1.36 | 23.78 | 1749 | 0 | -- | 0 |
| United Arab Emirates | ff95 f95 | -- | -- | -- | 0.15 | 0.08 | 53.3 | 27 | 0.15 | 2.11 | 1407 | 0 | -- | 0 |
| Uzbekistan | ff94 f94 | 88000 | 6900 | 7.8 | 50.41 | 19.00 | 37.7 | 42 | 16.34 | 58.05 | 355.3 | 0 | 0 | 0 |
| Viet Nam | ff90 | 300000 | 10900 | 3.6 | 891.21 | -- | -- | 93 | 366.50 | 54.33 | 14.8 | 70 | 37 | 37 |
| Yemen | ff90 f95 | -- | -- | -- | 4.10 | 0.18 | 4.4 | 91 | 4.10 | 2.93 | 71.5 | 31 | -- | 31 |
| **PACIFIC** | | | | | | | | | | | | | | |
| Australia | so94 | 264000 | 15212 | 5.8 | 352.00 | -- | -- | 88 | 352.00 | 15.06 | 4.3 | 91 | 21 | 21 |
| Fiji | rr87 | 1090 | 385 | 35.3 | 28.60 | -- | -- | 45 | 28.60 | 0.03 | 0.1 | 100 | -- | 45 |
| New Zealand | so93 | 152000 | 26395 | 17.4 | 313.00 | -- | -- | 65 | 313.00 | 2.00 | 0.6 | 99 | 39 | 39 |
| Papua New Guinea | ff87 | 175000 | 570 | 0.3 | 801.00 | -- | -- | 99 | 801.00 | 0.10 | 0.0 | 100 | 43 | 43 |
| Samoa | -- | 140 | 25 | 17.9 | -- | -- | -- | 64 | -- | -- | -- | -- | -- | 60* |
| Solomon Is | rr87 | 1000 | 46 | 4.6 | 44.70 | -- | -- | 91 | 44.70 | 0.00 | 0.0 | 100 | -- | 80* |
| Tonga | -- | -- | -- | -- | -- | -- | -- | -- | -- | -- | -- | -- | -- | -- |
| Vanuatu | -- | -- | -- | -- | -- | -- | -- | -- | -- | -- | -- | -- | -- | -- |

**Notes**

In the absence of adequate data on marine waters, the water index is an inland waters index (*IW score*)—the lowest score of three sub-elements (column heading in parentheses): inland water diversity (RC score) and water withdrawal (WW score), covered in this table; and inland water quality (WQ score), covered in Tables 15 and 16.

Inland water diversity is represented by river conversion by dams, measured by dam capacity as % of total water supply or, if unavailable, river flow dammed for hydropower as a percentage of dammable flow. Hydropower includes large (more than 10 megawatts) and small (under 10 megawatts) schemes. Hydropower data are for the end of 1996 and are from World Energy Council (1999).

Note = sources of data on water supply and water withdrawal (in regular type), and dam capacity (*in italics*). In an entry in regular type (e.g., ff90), the first letter indicates the source for water supply (both total supply and internal supply), the second letter the source for water withdrawal, and the number the year to which the water withdrawal data refer. In an entry in italics (e.g., *f95*), the letter indicates the source for dam capacity, the number the applicable year. The sources are:

e   Eurostat, European Commission & the European Environment Agency (1998)

f   Food and Agriculture Organization of the United Nations (1995a, 1997b, 1997c, 1997d, 1999c, 2000b)

m   Instituto Nacional de Estadística, Geografía e Informática (1998)

o   Organisation for Economic Co-operation and Development (1999)

r   World Resources Institute *et al.* (1998)

s   Shiklomanov (1997)

\#     Eritrea's and Ethiopia's shares of the former Ethiopia's withdrawal were estimated on the basis of population

Gross cap = gross theoretical hydropower capability, measured in gigawatt hours per year (GWh/y). This is the annual energy potentially available in a country if all natural flows were harnessed with 100% efficiency by turbines down to sea level or to the water level at the border with neighboring countries. It is the maximum river flow that is potentially dammable for hydropower, and is usually estimated on the basis of precipitation and run-off. If gross theoretical capability is not known, the technically exploitable capability (the amount of energy potentially available within the limits of current technology) was used instead.

Used cap = electrical energy in gigawatt hours per year (GWh/y) generated by operational hydropower schemes plus the probable amount to be generated by schemes under construction.

Used % G = used capacity as a percentage of gross capacity.

Tot supply = total renewable water resources in cubic kilometers per year (km³/y) = water available to a country from precipitation within its borders plus river flows from neighboring countries. *In North Africa (Algeria, Djibouti, Egypt, Libya, Mauritania, Morocco, Somalia, Sudan, Tunisia), Malta, and much of West Asia (Afghanistan, Bahrain, Cyprus, Iran, Iraq, Jordan, Kuwait, Kyrgyzstan, Lebanon, Oman, Pakistan, Qatar, Saudi Arabia, Syria, Tajikistan, Turkey, Turkmenistan, United Arab Emirates, Yemen), the data are for* actual *renewable water resources = total renewable water resources minus the quantity of flows reserved to upstream and downstream countries through formal or informal agreements or treaties.*

Dam cap = dam capacity = the total cumulative capacity of all dams in cubic kilometres (km³).

Dam % TS = dam capacity as % of total supply.

RC score = river conversion score. The performance criteria are shown in Table 14a. They are intended to reflect the objective of maintaining all major riverine ecosystems in large units.

Int supply = internal renewable supply in cubic kilometers per year (km³/y) = water available to a country from precipitation within its borders (excluding river flows from neighboring countries).

WW = water withdrawal = annual withdrawals of ground and surface water for domestic, agricultural and industrial uses, in cubic kilometers per year (km³/y).

WW % IS = water withdrawal as a percentage of internal renewable supply. The indicator takes no account of annual or seasonal shortages which can be marked.

WW score = water withdrawal score. The performance criteria are shown in Table 14a. The top of bad (100%) matches a point that is clearly unsustainable.

| band | top point on scale | flow dammed for hydropower as % of dammable flow | dam capacity as % of total water supply | water withdrawal as % of internal renewable supply |
|------|------|------|------|------|
| good | 100 | 0 | 0 | 0 |
| fair | 80 | 10 | 10 | 10 |
| medium | 60 | 20 | 20 | 20 |
| poor | 40 | 40 | 40 | 50 |
| bad | 20 | 60 | 60 | 100 |
| base | 0 | 100 | 100 | 200 |

**Table 14a. Performance criteria for river conversion and water withdrawal indicators.**

\* A score with an asterisk has been reduced in accordance with the insufficient data rule. To prevent high scores resulting merely from lack of data, a good score is allowed only if it is based on all applicable components (data in an indicator, indicators in an index), and a fair score only if it is based on at least half the components. Good and fair scores (100-61) based on fewer than half the applicable components have been reduced to 60. Good scores (100-81) based on more than half but not all the applicable components have been reduced to 80.

# Table 15. Inland Water Quality: Score, Oxygen Balance, Nutrients, and Acidification

| Country | Basin | Station | Sources & years | Score | Based on | DO mg/l | BOD mg/l | COD mg/l | N mg/l | P mg/l | Alk. mg/l | pH |
|---|---|---|---|---|---|---|---|---|---|---|---|---|
| **AMERICAS** | | | | | | | | | | | | |
| Argentina | La Plata | R Paraná at Puerto Libertad | g 94 | 19 | HM: Cu | 9.9 | -- | -- | 0.45 | 0.073 | 18.2 | 7.3 |
| | | R Paraná at Corrientes | g 94 | 20 | F coli | 7.8 | -- | -- | 0.14 | 0.031 | 20.5 | 7.4 |
| | | R Paraná at Rosario | g 94 | 32 | HM: Hg | 7.3 | 1.0 | 8.0 | 0.05 | -- | 34.4 | 7.4 |
| | | average | | 24 | | | | | | | | |
| | N Mar Argentino | L Nahuel Huapi at Bariloche | g 94 | 53 | Acid | 10.6 | -- | | 0.02 | 0.002 | 12.7 | 6.7 |
| | country average | | | 38 | | | | | | | | |
| | not covered: Argentine interior, Subpolar SE Pacific, Chubut, S Mar Argentino; Groundwater | | | | | | | | | | | |
| Brazil | Amazon | R Amazon mouth | a 90 | 60* | P | -- | -- | -- | 0.17 | 0.020 | -- | -- |
| | | R Tocantins mouth | a 90 | 60* | SS | -- | -- | -- | 0.02 | 0.003 | -- | -- |
| | | average | | 60 | | | | | | | | |
| | São Francisco | R Capibaribe | g 88-90 | 0 | F coli; HM: Cd | 5.5 | 6.0 | -- | -- | -- | 86.6 | 7.1 |
| | | R São Francisco at Petrolandia | g 88-90 | 0 | HM: Cd, Pb | 8.4 | 3.0 | -- | -- | -- | 38.5 | 6.6 |
| | | average | | 0 | | | | | | | | |
| | L tropical W Atlantic | R Paraguaçu at Pedra do Cavalo | g 88-90 | 8 | HM: Cr | 5.5 | 2.0 | -- | 0.60 | 0.058 | 53.9 | 6.7 |
| | | R Paraiba do Sul at Barra Mansa | g 88-90 | 29 | HM: Pb | 7.5 | 2.0 | 26.0 | 0.80 | 0.084 | 15.3 | 7.0 |
| | | average | | 18 | | | | | | | | |
| | La Plata | B Guarapiranga | g 88-90 | 16 | HM: Cd, Cu | 7.9 | 3.0 | 10.0 | 0.70 | 0.031 | 16.1 | 6.9 |
| | country average | | | 23 | | | | | | | | |
| | not covered: Guianan tropical W Atlantic, Intertropical W Atlantic, Parnaíba; Groundwater | | | | | | | | | | | |
| Canada | Mackenzie | R Mackenzie mouth | o 94-96 | 29 | P | -- | -- | -- | -- | 0.090 | -- | -- |
| | | R Great Bear | g 91-92 | 60 | HM: Pb | -- | -- | -- | 0.16 | -- | -- | 7.8 |
| | | average | | 44 | | | | | | | | |
| | L subpolar NE Pacific | R Skeena | g 91 | 42 | HM: Hg | -- | -- | -- | 0.13 | 0.016 | -- | 7.9 |
| | U temperate NE Pacific | R Fraser at Hope | g 91 | 19 | P | -- | -- | -- | 0.12 | 0.171 | -- | 8.0 |
| | Columbia | R Columbia df | o 95-97 | 60 | HM: Cd | -- | -- | -- | 0.10 | 0.010 | -- | -- |
| | Churchill | R Churchill | g 94-96 | 80 | HM: Cu | 11.0 | -- | -- | -- | 0.008 | -- | 7.5 |
| | Nelson | R Nelson at Gillam | g 94-96 | 60 | HM: Cr | -- | -- | -- | -- | 0.017 | -- | 7.8 |
| | | R Saskatchewan mouth | o 94-96 | 47 | P | 9.5 | -- | -- | 0.13 | 0.041 | -- | -- |
| | | R Roseau | g 94-96 | 37 | P | 7.4 | -- | -- | -- | 0.063 | -- | 7.8 |
| | | average | | 48 | | | | | | | | |
| | St Lawrence | L Ontario mid lake | g 94-96 | 60* | Acid | 12.3 | -- | -- | -- | -- | -- | 8.4 |
| | | L Superior mid lake | g 96 | 80* | Acid | 13.3 | -- | -- | -- | 0.003 | -- | 7.2 |
| | | average | | 70 | | | | | | | | |
| | Fundy & Maine | R St John mouth | o 93-95 | 35 | HM: Cd | -- | -- | -- | 0.20 | 0.021 | -- | -- |
| | country average | | | 50 | | | | | | | | |
| | not covered: Arctic—W Beaufort Sea, E Beaufort Sea, Arctic Archipelagic Seas, Lincoln Sea & Nares Strait, W Baffin Bay; Pacific—E Bering Sea, Gulf of Alaska; Atlantic—Foxe Basin, NW Hudson Bay, S Hudson Bay, James Bay, E Hudson Bay, Hudson Strait & Ungava Bay, Labrador Sea, U temperate NW Atlantic; Groundwater | | | | | | | | | | | |
| Chile | Subtropical SE Pacific | R Maipo at El Manzano | g 88 | 34 | F coli | 11.0 | 1.0 | 4.0 | 0.19 | 0.000 | 75.0 | 8.3 |
| | Groundwater | G pozo Panamericana 1377 | g 88 | 9 | N | 4.4 | 0 | -- | 12.52 | 0.000 | 219.0 | 7.3 |
| | country average | | | 21 | | | | | | | | |
| | not covered: Titicaca/Poopó/Atacama, Temperate SE Pacific, Subpolar SE Pacific, S Mar Argentino | | | | | | | | | | | |
| Colombia | Magdalena | R Magdalena mouth | a 90 | 21 | P | -- | -- | -- | 0.25 | 0.120 | -- | -- |
| | | R Cauca at Juanchito | g 88 | 0 | F coli | 5.5 | 1.0 | 20.0 | 0.60 | 0.010 | 20.3 | 6.8 |
| | country average | | | 10 | | | | | | | | |
| | not covered: L tropical E Pacific, Intertropical E Pacific, W Caribbean, S Caribbean, Orinoco, Amazon; Groundwater | | | | | | | | | | | |
| Cuba | N Caribbean | B Damuji | g 94 | 61 | N | 7.7 | -- | -- | 0.72 | 0.004 | -- | 8.2 |
| | | B Hanabanilla | g 94-95 | 58 | P | 8.5 | -- | 2.0 | 0.53 | 0.028 | -- | 7.5 |
| | | average | | 59 | | | | | | | | |
| | Groundwater | G Aguada del Cura | g 94 | 80* | Acid | -- | -- | -- | 0.05 | -- | -- | 7.0 |
| | country average | | | 60* | | | | | | | | |
| | not covered: E Gulf of Mexico, U tropical W Atlantic, S Caribbean | | | | | | | | | | | |
| Mexico | Colorado | R Colorado | g 94-96 | 0 | F strep | 8.4 | 2.0 | 19.0 | 0.40 | 0.067 | 191.4 | 7.9 |
| | Grande de Santiago | L de Chapala | g 94-96 | 8 | F coli | 6.7 | 2.0 | 32.0 | 6.03 | 0.567 | 296.4 | 8.7 |
| | | R Lerma | g 94-96 | 0 | P; F coli | 1.3 | 23.0 | 107.0 | 5.64 | 1.383 | 8.0 | 7.0 |
| | | average | | 4 | | | | | | | | |
| | U tropical E Pacific | R Balsas at Balsas | g 94-96 | 0 | F coli | 6.4 | 38.0 | 76.0 | 0.09 | 0.219 | 144.5 | 7.4 |

| Country | Basin | Station | Sources & years | Score | Based on | DO mg/l | BOD mg/l | COD mg/l | N mg/l | P mg/l | Alk. mg/l | pH |
|---|---|---|---|---|---|---|---|---|---|---|---|---|
| | Bravo del Norte (Grande) | R Bravo at Matamoros | g 94-96 | 5 | HM: Cu | 7.7 | 4.0 | 34.0 | 0.50 | 0.160 | 164.0 | 8.1 |
| | | R Bravo at Presa de la Amistad | g 94-96 | 22 | N | 8.3 | 12.0 | 33.0 | 2.39 | | 125.3 | 6.9 |
| | | R Conchos at Ojinaga | g 94-96 | 6 | F coli | 8.3 | 5.0 | 17.0 | 3.11 | 0.254 | 264.8 | 6.0 |
| | | average | | 11 | | | | | | | | |
| | SW Gulf of Mexico | R Pánuco | g 94-96 | 10 | HM: Cu | 7.6 | 1.0 | 27.0 | 0.30 | 0.066 | 165.4 | 7.9 |
| | | R Coatzacoalcos | g 94-96 | 0 | F coli | 6.1 | 2.0 | 59.0 | 0.83 | 0.110 | 62.3 | 7.0 |
| | | average | | 5 | | | | | | | | |
| | SE Gulf of Mexico | R Grijalva | g 94-96 | 0 | F coli | 5.4 | 4.0 | 18.0 | 2.80 | 0.104 | 110.2 | 7.9 |
| | | R Usumacinta | g 94-96 | 9 | F coli | 7.6 | 3.0 | 16.0 | 1.85 | 0.063 | 138.2 | 8.2 |
| | | average | | 4 | | | | | | | | |
| | Groundwater | G pozo Aguascalientes | g 94-96 | 16 | N | -- | 1.0 | -- | 3.00 | 0.020 | 365.7 | 7.0 |
| | | G pozo Hacienda Tahdzibichen | g 94-96 | 9 | F coli | 4.8 | 3.0 | 17.0 | 6.98 | 0.016 | 336.9 | 7.1 |
| | | average | | 12 | | | | | | | | |
| | country average | | | 5 | | | | | | | | |
| | not covered: Mexican interior, U subtropical NE Pacific, W Gulf of California, E Gulf of California, W Caribbean | | | | | | | | | | | |
| United States | E Bering Sea | R Yukon at Pilot Station | g 94-95 | 26 | P | 10.1 | -- | -- | 0.15 | 0.102 | 88.0 | 7.8 |
| | Gulf of Alaska | R Talkeetna at Talkeetna | g 94-96 | 49 | P | 11.3 | -- | -- | 0.28 | 0.039 | 38.1 | 7.8 |
| | Columbia | R Columbia at Bonneville | g 94 | 60 | P | 10.0 | -- | -- | 0.17 | 0.025 | -- | 8.1 |
| | U subtropical NE Pacific | R Sacramento at Sacramento | g 94-96 | 44 | P | 9.2 | -- | -- | 0.13 | 0.045 | 0.0 | 7.6 |
| | Colorado | R Colorado at Hoover Dam | g 94-96 | 58 | HM: Cr | 7.2 | -- | -- | 0.36 | 0.012 | -- | 7.9 |
| | St Lawrence | R St Lawrence df | g 94 | 76 | Acid | 8.8 | -- | -- | 0.33 | 0.010 | 92.0 | 7.9 |
| | | R Niagara at L Ontario | g 94 | 58 | HM: Cr | 12.0 | -- | -- | 0.69 | 0.010 | -- | 8.0 |
| | | average | | 67 | | | | | | | | |
| | L temperate NW Atlantic | R Hudson at Troy | g 94 | 34 | F coli | 11.8 | -- | -- | 0.88 | 0.045 | 76.0 | 8.1 |
| | | R Delaware at Trenton | g 94 | 34 | P | 10.4 | 2.0 | -- | 0.95 | 0.074 | 30.2 | 7.8 |
| | | average | | 34 | | | | | | | | |
| | Chesapeake Bay | R Susquehanna at Harrisburg | g 94-95 | 39 | P | 10.0 | -- | -- | 0.95 | 0.053 | 29.8 | 7.5 |
| | | R Potomac at Washington | g 94-96 | 25 | P | 10.1 | -- | -- | 1.37 | 0.106 | -- | 7.8 |
| | | average | | 32 | | | | | | | | |
| | NE Gulf of Mexico | R Apalachicola at Chattahoochee | g 94-95 | 52 | F coli | 9.8 | -- | -- | 0.44 | 0.033 | -- | 7.7 |
| | Mississippi | R Mississippi mouth | o 93-95 | 19 | P | 9.0 | 1.5 | -- | 1.43 | 0.200 | -- | -- |
| | | R Arkansas at Little Rock | g 94-96 | 32 | P | 8.7 | -- | -- | 0.36 | 0.081 | -- | 7.8 |
| | | R Missouri at Hermann | g 94-96 | 17 | P | 9.3 | -- | -- | 1.25 | 0.269 | 154.1 | 7.9 |
| | | R Ohio at New Grand Chain | g 94-95 | 24 | P | 8.1 | -- | -- | 0.92 | 0.111 | -- | 7.6 |
| | | average | | 23 | | | | | | | | |
| | Bravo del Norte (Grande) | R Grande at Brownsville | g 94-96 | 20 | P | 7.4 | 4.0 | -- | 0.10 | 0.131 | -- | 8.2 |
| | country average | | | 46 | | | | | | | | |
| | not covered: US interior, E Chukchi Sea, W Beaufort Sea, L subpolar NE Pacific, U temperate NE Pacific, Oceanic NE Pacific, Fundy & Maine, Subtropical NW Atlantic, Brazos, Texas Colorado; Groundwater | | | | | | | | | | | |
| AFRICA | | | | | | | | | | | | |
| Ghana | W Gulf of Guinea | R Pra at Daboase | g 94 DO g 91-93 | 0 | HM: As, Cd | 7.7 | -- | -- | 3.00 | -- | 53.7 | 7.1 |
| | Volta | R Volta at B Kpong | g 94-95 | 12 | HM: Cu, Zn | 5.2 | 4.0 | -- | 0.25 | -- | 38.0 | 7.0 |
| | | R White Volta at Nawuni | g 94-95 | 13 | HM: Zn | 7.2 | 3.0 | -- | 1.32 | -- | 41.5 | 7.0 |
| | | average | | 12 | | | | | | | | |
| | country average | | | 6 | | | | | | | | |
| | not covered: Groundwater | | | | | | | | | | | |
| Kenya | U intertropical W Indian | R Tana | g 88 | 32 | P | -- | -- | -- | 0.01 | 0.080 | 74.0 | 7.5 |
| | Shebelli-Juba | L Naivasha | g 88 | 40 | P | -- | -- | -- | -- | 0.050 | 188.0 | 8.8 |
| | country average | | | 36 | | | | | | | | |
| | not covered: Rift Valley; Groundwater | | | | | | | | | | | |
| Mali | Niger | R Niger at Bamako | g 94-96 | 15 | P | 8.5 | -- | -- | 0.50 | 0.405 | 19.2 | 6.9 |
| | | R Niger at Koulikoro (06) | g 94-96 | 7 | P | 8.1 | -- | -- | 0.53 | 0.833 | 19.2 | 7.2 |
| | | average | | 11 | | | | | | | | |
| | Groundwater | G forage Bamako (05) | g 94-96 | 4 | P | -- | -- | -- | 0.44 | 1.050 | 51.0 | 5.9 |
| | | G forage Nossombougou (8) | g 96 | 15 | P | -- | -- | -- | 0.72 | 0.400 | 161.0 | 7.7 |
| | | average | | 9 | | | | | | | | |
| | country average | | | 10 | | | | | | | | |
| | not covered: Sahara, Senegal, Volta | | | | | | | | | | | |
| Morocco | SW Mediterranean | R Moulouya | g 94-96 | 0 | HM: Hg, Pb | 8.3 | 2.0 | 2.0 | 0.06 | 0.380 | 227.5 | 7.8 |
| | U subtropical NE Atlantic | R Sebou at Kenitra | g 94-96 | 0 | F coli | 4.9 | 19.0 | 87.0 | 0.83 | 0.340 | 176.7 | 8.1 |
| | | R Bou Regreg at Barrage Sidi Mohamed Ben Abdella | g 94-96 | 14 | N | 5.8 | 2.0 | -- | 8.98 | 0.204 | 117.4 | 8.1 |
| | | R er Rbia at Sidi Daoui | g 94-96 | 0 | F coli | 8.3 | 3.0 | 20.0 | 0.23 | 0.200 | 161.7 | 8.3 |

| Country | Basin | Station | Sources & years | Score | Based on | DO mg/l | BOD mg/l | COD mg/l | N mg/l | P mg/l | Alk. mg/l | pH |
|---------|-------|---------|-----------------|-------|----------|---------|----------|----------|--------|--------|-----------|-----|
| | | average | | 5 | | | | | | | | |
| | Groundwater | G puits artesien Ire 4/125 | g 94-96 | 14 | O | 2.4 | -- | -- | 2.16 | -- | 218.1 | 7.2 |
| | | G puits Mamora Ire 442/13 | g 94-96 | 0 | N | 5.7 | -- | -- | 25.62 | -- | 312.9 | 7.2 |
| | | average | | 7 | | | | | | | | |
| | country average | | | 4 | | | | | | | | |
| | not covered: Sahara | | | | | | | | | | | |
| Namibia | Orange | R Orange mouth | a 90 | 18 | | -- | -- | -- | 0.72 | -- | -- | -- |
| | not covered: Etosha, Okavango, Cunene, L Subtropical SE Atlantic; Groundwater | | | | | | | | | | | |
| Senegal | Senegal | R Senegal at St Louis | g 95 COD g 91-93 | 0 | O | -- | -- | 185.0 | 1.06 | -- | 90.0 | 7.2 |
| | | R Senegal at Podor | g 95 | 18 | F coli | -- | -- | -- | 0.19 | -- | 60.0 | 8.0 |
| | | average | | 9 | | | | | | | | |
| | Groundwater | G forage 2 Fatick | g 93 | 60* | N | -- | -- | -- | 0.18 | -- | 400.0 | 8.0 |
| | | G forage 3 Ziguinchor bis | g 93 | 47 | N | -- | -- | -- | 1.24 | -- | 320.0 | 7.8 |
| | | average | | 53 | | | | | | | | |
| | country average | | | 31 | | | | | | | | |
| | not covered: L subtropical NE Atlantic | | | | | | | | | | | |
| South Africa | Orange | R Orange mouth | a 90 | 18 | | -- | -- | -- | 0.72 | -- | -- | -- |
| | not covered: L Subtropical SE Atlantic, L subtropical W Indian, U subtropical W Indian; Groundwater | | | | | | | | | | | |
| Sudan | Nile | R Blue Nile at Khartoum | g 91-92 | 0 | P | 7.6 | 4.0 | -- | 1.02 | 1.418 | 114.7 | 7.7 |
| | | R White Nile at Jebel Aulia | g 91-92 | 0 | P | 8.1 | 5.0 | -- | 0.44 | 2.085 | 104.7 | 8.2 |
| | country average | | | 0 | | | | | | | | |
| | not covered: Sahara, Rift Valley, W Red Sea; Groundwater | | | 0 | | | | | | | | |
| Tanzania | Nile | R Kagera at Nyakanyasi | g 91 | 69 | Acid | -- | -- | -- | 0.12 | -- | 42.0 | 7.8 |
| | | L Victoria at South Port | g 91-92 | 60* | O | 6.0 | 4.0 | -- | -- | -- | 67.3 | 7.5 |
| | | average | | 67 | | | | | | | | |
| | U intertropical W Indian | R Ruvu at Mlandizi | g 92-93 | 63 | F coli | 8.5 | -- | -- | -- | -- | 74.5 | 8.0 |
| | Groundwater | G Makutopora Basin at Dodoma | g 91-93 | 60* | Acid | -- | -- | -- | -- | -- | 244.7 | 8.4 |
| | | G Sakina borehole | g 91-92 | 60* | Acid | -- | -- | -- | -- | -- | 148.0 | 8.7 |
| | | average | | 60 | | | | | | | | |
| | country average | | | 60* | | | | | | | | |
| | not covered: Rift Valley, Congo, Zambezi, Ruvuma, Rufiji | | | | | | | | | | | |
| Uganda | Nile | L Albert | a 90 | 19 | P | -- | -- | -- | 0.02 | 0.160 | -- | -- |
| | not covered: Rift Valley; Groundwater | | | | | | | | | | | |
| **EUROPE** | | | | | | | | | | | | |
| Albania | Adriatic | R Semani at Mbrostar | e 90 | 60* | N | 6.6 | 3.4 | 3.3 | 0.50 | 0.000 | -- | -- |
| | not covered: Ionian; Groundwater | | | | | | | | | | | |
| Austria | Danube | R Danube df | o 95-97 | 21 | N | 11.0 | 3.1 | -- | 2.45 | 0.092 | -- | -- |
| | | R Inn df | o 95-97 | 26 | P | 11.3 | 2.5 | -- | 1.52 | 0.101 | -- | -- |
| | country average | | | 23 | | | | | | | | |
| | not covered: German Bight (Elbe), Rhine; Groundwater | | | | | | | | | | | |
| Belgium | Rhine | R Meuse df 94-96 | o 94-96 | 10 | P | 10.5 | 2.2 | -- | 2.57 | 0.707 | -- | -- |
| | | R Meuse at Lanaye/ Ternaaien 91-92 | g 91-92 | 0 | F coli | 8.1 | 4.0 | 21.0 | 3.31 | 0.566 | 140.1 | 7.6 |
| | | latest | | 10 | | | | | | | | |
| | SE North Sea | R Schelde (Escaut) df 94-96 | o 94-96 | 0 | P | 7.4 | 4.2 | -- | 9.19 | 1.320 | -- | -- |
| | | R Schelde at Doel 91 | g 91 | 12 | P | 4.0 | 2.0 | 68.0 | 6.13 | 0.569 | 167.7 | 7.5 |
| | | latest | | 0 | | | | | | | | |
| | country average | | | 5 | | | | | | | | |
| | not covered: Groundwater | | | | | | | | | | | |
| Bulgaria | Aegean | R Arda df | oc 93 | 59 | N | 7.8 | -- | -- | 0.77 | -- | -- | -- |
| | | R Maritza at Svilengrad | e 91 | 17 | N | 7.2 | 4.5 | -- | 6.10 | -- | -- | -- |
| | | average | | 38 | | | | | | | | |
| | Danube | R Jantra mouth | oc 93 | 20 | N | 8.1 | -- | -- | 2.81 | -- | -- | -- |
| | | R Osam mouth | oc 93 | 20 | N | 9.8 | -- | -- | 2.88 | -- | -- | -- |
| | | average | | 20 | | | | | | | | |
| | country average | | | 29 | | | | | | | | |
| | not covered: W Black Sea; Groundwater | | | | | | | | | | | |
| Croatia | Danube | R Danube at Borovo | e 90 | 17 | P | 10.3 | 1.8 | 3.9 | 2.70 | 0.300 | -- | -- |
| | | R Sava at Zupanja | e 90 | 10 | P | 7.6 | 3.3 | 28.2 | 3.60 | 0.700 | -- | -- |
| | country average | | | 13 | | | | | | | | |
| | not covered: Adriatic; Groundwater | | | | | | | | | | | |
| Czech R | Oder | R Oder (Odra) df | o 95-97 | 15 | P | 9.4 | 5.4 | -- | 5.03 | 0.430 | -- | -- |
| | German Bight | R Elbe (Labe) df | o 95-97 | 18 | N | 10.3 | 3.7 | -- | 4.99 | 0.186 | -- | -- |
| | Danube | R Morava df | o 95-97 | 18 | N, P | 11.3 | 4.9 | -- | 4.23 | 0.264 | -- | -- |
| | country average | | | 17 | | | | | | | | |
| | not covered: Groundwater | | | | | | | | | | | |

| Country | Basin | Station | Sources & years | Score | Based on | DO mg/l | BOD mg/l | COD mg/l | N mg/l | P mg/l | Alk. mg/l | pH |
|---|---|---|---|---|---|---|---|---|---|---|---|---|
| Denmark | SW Baltic | R Sus mouth | o 95-97 | 17 | P | -- | 2.1 | -- | 1.93 | 0.278 | -- | -- |
| | | R Odense mouth | o 95-97 | 19 | N | -- | 1.9 | -- | 3.86 | 0.134 | -- | -- |
| | | average | | 18 | | | | | | | | |
| | S Skagerrak & W Kattegat | R Guden mouth | o 95-97 | 27 | P | -- | 2.6 | -- | 1.44 | 0.098 | -- | -- |
| | NE North Sea | R Skjern mouth | o 95-97 | 20 | N | 10.0 | 1.7 | -- | 2.61 | 0.064 | -- | -- |
| | country average | | | 22 | | | | | | | | |
| | not covered: N Baltic; Groundwater | | | | | | | | | | | |
| Estonia | S Gulf of Finland | R Narva 10 km from mouth | e 85-90 | 19 | N | 10.4 | 2.1 | 27.0 | 3.90 | 0.100 | -- | -- |
| | | R Narva at L Vörtsjäry | e 91 | 22 | N | -- | -- | -- | 2.40 | 0.043 | -- | 7.8 |
| | | average | | 20 | | | | | | | | |
| | SE Baltic | R Pärnu 1 km from mouth | e 85-90 | 18 | N | 11.9 | 1.7 | 33.9 | 4.30 | 0.200 | -- | -- |
| | country average | | | 19 | | | | | | | | |
| | not covered: Groundwater | | | | | | | | | | | |
| Finland | W Barents Sea | L Inari (151) | g 94-96 | 51 | Acid | 11.7 | -- | -- | 0.01 | 0.003 | 8.1 | 7.1 |
| | Gulf of Bothnia | R Tornionjoki (14100) | g 94-96 | 56 | Acid | 11.8 | -- | -- | 0.01 | 0.018 | 14.0 | 7.0 |
| | | L Yli-Kitka (144) | g 94-96 | 56 | Acid | 9.9 | -- | -- | 0.01 | 0.006 | 13.0 | 7.1 |
| | | R Kokernaenjoki mouth | o 95-97 | 15 | HM: Cu | 10.7 | -- | -- | 0.66 | 0.048 | -- | -- |
| | | average | | 42 | | | | | | | | |
| | N Gulf of Finland | R Kalkkinen (4800) | g 94-96 | 40 | HM: Hg | 11.4 | -- | -- | 0.01 | 0.006 | 9.4 | 7.1 |
| | | R Kymijoki (5610) | g 94-96 | 42 | HM: Hg | 11.2 | -- | -- | 0.03 | 0.022 | 11.5 | 6.9 |
| | | average | | 41 | | | | | | | | |
| | country average | | | 45 | | | | | | | | |
| | not covered: Groundwater | | | | | | | | | | | |
| France | La Manche | R Seine mouth 94-96 | o 94-96 | 4 | P | 5.7 | 4.5 | -- | 6.51 | 1.003 | -- | -- |
| | | R Seine at Paris 91-93 | g 91-93 | 0 | F coli | 8.9 | 4.0 | 24.0 | 19.28 | 0.573 | -- | 7.8 |
| | | latest | | 4 | | | | | | | | |
| | Loire | R Loire mouth | o 94-96 | 17 | P | 10.0 | 5.0 | -- | 2.67 | 0.282 | -- | -- |
| | | R Loire at Ingrandes | g 94 | 2 | N | 10.8 | 5.0 | 34.0 | 22.62 | 0.314 | -- | 8.0 |
| | | average | | 9 | | | | | | | | |
| | Bay of Biscay | R Garonne mouth | o 94-96 | 22 | P | 9.8 | 1.4 | -- | 2.15 | 0.119 | -- | -- |
| | | R Garonne at Valence d'Agen | g 94-95 | 14 | N | 10.0 | 2.0 | 8.0 | 9.36 | 0.136 | -- | 8.1 |
| | | average | | 18 | | | | | | | | |
| | N Mediterranean | R Rhone mouth | o 94-96 | 19 | P | 10.1 | 2.0 | -- | 1.55 | 0.179 | -- | -- |
| | | R Rhone at St Vallier | g 94 | 14 | F coli | 10.1 | 1.0 | 35.0 | 6.88 | 0.122 | -- | 8.1 |
| | | average | | 16 | | | | | | | | |
| | country average | | | 12 | | | | | | | | |
| | not covered: Rhine, SE North Sea, Ligurian & Tyrrhenian Seas; Groundwater | | | | | | | | | | | |
| Germany | German Bight | R Elbe mouth 95-97 | o 95-97 | 18 | N, P | 11.2 | -- | -- | 4.46 | 0.220 | -- | -- |
| | | R Elbe at Geesthacht 88-90 | g 88-90 | 5 | HM: Cd | 8.8 | 5.0 | 38.0 | 4.15 | 0.399 | 2.0 | 7.6 |
| | | R Weser mouth 95-97 | o 95-97 | 18 | N,P | 10.2 | 3.3 | -- | 4.78 | 0.210 | -- | -- |
| | | R Weser at Intschede 88-90 | g 88-90 | 16 | P | 9.1 | 5.0 | 17.0 | 3.86 | 0.325 | -- | 7.8 |
| | | average (latest) | | 18 | | | | | | | | |
| | Rhine | R Rhine df | o 95-97 | 19 | N | 9.9 | -- | -- | 3.41 | 0.137 | -- | -- |
| | | R Rhine at Kleve/Bimmen | g 88-90 | 0 | HM: Zn | 9.6 | 3.0 | 14.0 | 3.23 | 0.718 | 262.8 | 7.6 |
| | | R Rhine at Koblenz | g 88-90 | 16 | P | 9.0 | 2.0 | 15.0 | 2.70 | 0.326 | 332.7 | 7.8 |
| | | R Moselle at Koblenz | g 88-90 | 15 | P | 9.4 | 2.0 | 15.0 | 3.17 | 0.420 | 278.2 | 7.8 |
| | | average | | 12 | | | | | | | | |
| | Danube | R Danube df 95-97 | o 95-97 | 21 | N | 11.1 | 2.4 | -- | 2.43 | 0.096 | -- | -- |
| | | R Danube at Jochenstein 88-90 | g 88-90 | 20 | P | 10.9 | 3.0 | 15.0 | 1.57 | 0.137 | -- | 7.9 |
| | | latest | | 21 | | | | | | | | |
| | country average | | | 17 | | | | | | | | |
| | not covered: Oder, SW Baltic; Groundwater | | | | | | | | | | | |
| Greece | Adriatic | L Mikri Prespa | o 92 | 59 | N | -- | -- | -- | 0.10 | 0.026 | -- | -- |
| | Ionian | R Akeloos mouth | o 93-95 | 56 | HM: Cd | 11.3 | -- | -- | -- | -- | -- | -- |
| | Aegean | R Axios mouth | o 93-95 | 9 | P | 11.5 | -- | -- | 2.11 | 0.764 | -- | -- |
| | | R Strimonas mouth | o 93-95 | 20 | P | 11.0 | -- | -- | 1.62 | 0.131 | -- | -- |
| | | average | | 14 | | | | | | | | |
| | country average | | | 43 | | | | | | | | |
| | not covered: Groundwater | | | | | | | | | | | |
| Hungary | Danube | R Danube df | o 93-95 | 19 | HM: Cu | 9.5 | 2.4 | -- | 2.53 | 0.126 | -- | -- |
| | | R Danube at Budapest | g 91-92 | 15 | F coli | 11.0 | 5.0 | 24.0 | 2.56 | 0.211 | 156.7 | 7.8 |
| | | R Tisza at Szolnok | g 91-92 | 15 | P | 8.4 | 3.0 | -- | 2.15 | 0.402 | 2.5 | 7.9 |
| | | R Tisza df | o 93-95 P o 95 | 17 | P | 11.9 | 2.0 | -- | 1.16 | 0.310 | -- | -- |
| | | average | | 16 | | | | | | | | |
| | Groundwater | G deep well Pest County | g 91 | 20 | N | -- | -- | -- | 2.74 | -- | 12.1 | -- |
| | country average | | | 18 | | | | | | | | |
| | not covered: none | | | | | | | | | | | |
| Ireland | Celtic Sea | R Blackwater mouth | o 95-97 | 20 | N, P | 10.6 | 1.9 | -- | 2.68 | 0.138 | -- | -- |

| Country | Basin | Station | Sources & years | Score | Based on | DO mg/l | BOD mg/l | COD mg/l | N mg/l | P mg/l | Alk. mg/l | pH |
|---|---|---|---|---|---|---|---|---|---|---|---|---|
| | | R Barrow mouth | o 95-97 | 18 | N | 11.2 | 2.2 | -- | 4.62 | 0.118 | -- | -- |
| | | average | | 19 | | | | | | | | |
| | Irish Sea | R Boyne mouth | o 95-97 | 19 | N | 11.0 | 1.8 | -- | 3.15 | 0.113 | -- | -- |
| | Scottish & Irish Atlantic | R Clare mouth | o 95-97 | 31 | P | 10.6 | 1.5 | -- | 1.77 | 0.082 | -- | -- |
| | country average | | | 23 | | | | | | | | |
| | not covered: Groundwater | | | | | | | | | | | |
| Italy | Ligurian & Tyrrhenian | R Arno mouth | o 93-95 | 19 | N | 8.4 | -- | -- | 3.17 | 0.143 | -- | -- |
| | Adriatic | R Adige mouth | o 94-96 | 33 | P | 10.9 | 9.7 | -- | 1.78 | 0.075 | -- | -- |
| | | R Po mouth | o 94-96 | 19 | P | 6.9 | 3.4 | -- | 2.73 | 0.180 | -- | -- |
| | | average | | 26 | | | | | | | | |
| | country average | | | 22 | | | | | | | | |
| | not covered: N Mediterranean, Ionian, SE Mediterranean, Danube; Groundwater | | | | | | | | | | | |
| Latvia | SE Baltic | R Gauja at Sigulda | e 91 | 27 | P | 12.8 | 1.6 | 31.0 | 1.20 | 0.100 | -- | -- |
| | | R Daugava at Jekabpils | e 91 | 27 | P | 8.7 | 2.1 | 36.5 | 1.30 | 0.100 | -- | -- |
| | country average | | | 27 | | | | | | | | |
| | not covered: S Gulf of Finland; Groundwater | | | | | | | | | | | |
| Lithuania | SE Baltic | R Nemunas | e 91 | 60* | O | 10.4 | 3.9 | -- | -- | -- | -- | -- |
| | Groundwater | G Juodkrante | g 94-96 | 18 | P | 6.9 | 2.0 | 18.0 | 1.01 | 0.222 | 132.5 | 7.0 |
| | | G Marijanpole | g 94-96 | 11 | HM: Zn | 2.1 | 2.0 | 17.0 | 2.57 | 0.053 | 386.7 | 7.2 |
| | | G Panevezys | g 94-96 | 0 | HM: Zn | 3.6 | 1.0 | 10.0 | 0.69 | 0.014 | 272.2 | 7.5 |
| | | G Varena | g 94-96 | 16 | N | 2.7 | 2.0 | 2.0 | 6.60 | 0.052 | 167.5 | 7.5 |
| | | average | | 11 | | | | | | | | |
| | country average | | | 35 | | | | | | | | |
| | not covered: none | | | | | | | | | | | |
| Luxembourg | Rhine | R Sûre df | o 93-95 | 14 | P | 10.4 | 3.5 | -- | 5.08 | 0.449 | -- | -- |
| | not covered: Groundwater | | | | | | | | | | | |
| Moldova | Danube | R Prut at Ungheni | e 91 | 19 | P | 11.8 | 1.9 | 24.0 | 1.70 | 0.200 | -- | -- |
| | N Black Sea | R Dnestr at Bender | e 91 | 18 | N | 10.1 | 2.5 | 22.2 | 4.30 | 0.200 | -- | -- |
| | country average | | | 18 | | | | | | | | |
| | not covered: Groundwater | | | | | | | | | | | |
| Netherlands | Rhine | L Ijsselmeer | g 94-95 BOD & COD g 91-93 | 19 | P | 12.2 | 3.0 | 28.0 | 2.25 | 0.156 | -- | 8.7 |
| | | R Rhine Ijssel arm | g 94-95 BOD & COD g 91-93 | 17 | P | 8.6 | 2.0 | 21.0 | 4.34 | 0.304 | -- | 8.1 |
| | | R Rhine Ijssel-Kampen | o 94-96 | 17 | P | 9.0 | -- | -- | 4.10 | 0.273 | -- | -- |
| | | R Rijn/Maas delta | o 94-96 | 19 | N, P | 11.2 | -- | -- | 3.29 | 0.208 | -- | -- |
| | country average | | | 18 | | | | | | | | |
| | not covered: German Bight, SE North Sea; Groundwater | | | | | | | | | | | |
| Norway | Norwegian Sea | R Altaelva at Alta | g 91-93 | 60 | HM: Cu | -- | -- | -- | -- | 0.011 | -- | -- |
| | | R Vefsna at Mosjøen | g 91-93 | 60 | HM: Cu | -- | -- | -- | -- | 0.005 | -- | -- |
| | | R Orkla at Vormstad | g 91-93 | 19 | HM: Cu | -- | -- | -- | -- | 0.005 | -- | -- |
| | | R Suldalslaagen at Sand | g 91-93 | 60* | HM: Hg | -- | -- | -- | -- | 0.004 | -- | -- |
| | | average | | 50 | | | | | | | | |
| | N Skagerrak & E Kattegat | R Otra mouth | o 95-97 | 60* | HM: Pb | -- | -- | -- | 0.17 | 0.004 | -- | -- |
| | | R Skienselva mouth | o 95-97 | 70 | HM: Cu | -- | 0.4 | -- | 0.23 | 0.004 | -- | -- |
| | | R Numedalslaagen at Bommestad | g 91-93 | 47 | HM: Cu | -- | -- | -- | -- | 0.010 | -- | -- |
| | | R Drammenselva mouth | o 95-97 | 60* | HM: Pb | -- | -- | -- | 0.30 | 0.006 | -- | -- |
| | | R Glåma mouth | o 95-97 | 59 | HM: Cu | -- | -- | -- | 0.41 | 0.025 | -- | -- |
| | | average | | 59 | | | | | | | | |
| | country average | | | 54 | | | | | | | | |
| | not covered: W Barents Sea; Groundwater | | | | | | | | | | | |
| Poland | Wisla | R Wisla mouth | o 95-97 | 19 | P | 10.6 | 4.2 | -- | 1.88 | 0.194 | -- | -- |
| | | R Wisla at Kiezmark | g 94-95 | 0 | F coli | 10.8 | 4.0 | 26.0 | 3.58 | 0.226 | 159.5 | 8.2 |
| | | R Wisla at Warszawa | g 94-95 | 9 | F coli | 10.8 | 7.0 | 38.0 | 4.35 | 0.238 | -- | 8.4 |
| | | R Wisla at Krakow | g 94-95 | 0 | F coli, HM: Zn | 8.2 | 8.0 | 33.0 | 8.70 | 0.592 | -- | 7.6 |
| | | average | | 7 | | | | | | | | |
| | Oder | R Oder mouth | o 95-97 | 17 | P | 10.0 | 4.4 | -- | 2.55 | 0.318 | -- | -- |
| | | R Oder (Odra) at Krajnik | g 94-95 | 0 | F coli | 10.6 | 5.0 | 44.0 | 4.39 | 0.311 | 140.9 | 8.2 |
| | | R Oder (Odra) at Wroclaw | g 94-95 | 0 | F coli | 10.0 | 7.0 | 25.0 | 5.88 | 0.313 | 2.2 | 7.9 |
| | | R Oder (Odra) at Chalupki | g 94-95 | 0 | F coli | 8.7 | 8.0 | 25.0 | 8.12 | 0.429 | 2.1 | 7.5 |
| | | average | | 4 | | | | | | | | |
| | Groundwater | G Pomeranian Lake District | g 94-95 | 1 | HM: Zn | -- | -- | -- | 12.44 | 0.300 | -- | 7.5 |
| | country average | | | 4 | | | | | | | | |

| Country | Basin | Station | Sources & years | Score | Based on | DO mg/l | BOD mg/l | COD mg/l | N mg/l | P mg/l | Alk. mg/l | pH |
|---|---|---|---|---|---|---|---|---|---|---|---|---|
| | not covered: German Bight (Elbe) | | | | | | | | | | | |
| Portugal | L temperate NE Atlantic | R Douro mouth | o 92-93 | 32 | P | 9.7 | 2.3 | -- | 0.90 | 0.080 | -- | -- |
| | | R Tejo at Santarem | g 91-92 | 18 | P | 7.4 | 2.0 | 18.0 | 1.00 | 0.256 | 142.5 | 7.4 |
| | | average | | 25 | | | | | | | | |
| | U subtropical NE Atlantic | R Guadiana mouth | o 92-93 | 18 | P | 7.7 | 4.9 | -- | 1.02 | 0.242 | -- | -- |
| | country average | | | 21 | | | | | | | | |
| | not covered: Groundwater | | | | | | | | | | | |
| Romania | Danube | R Danube at Bazias | e 91 | 15 | N, P | 10.0 | 4.4 | 30.9 | 7.60 | 0.400 | -- | -- |
| | | R Oltul at Isbiceni | e 91 | 10 | P | 10.3 | -- | 54.1 | 3.60 | 0.700 | -- | -- |
| | | R Muresul at Nadlac | e 91 | 12 | N | 8.8 | 6.1 | 7.4 | 11.00 | 0.100 | -- | -- |
| | country average | | | 12 | | | | | | | | |
| | not covered: Groundwater | | | | | | | | | | | |
| Slovakia | Danube | R Maly Dunaj (Danube) df | o 95-97 | 17 | P | 9.7 | 3.1 | -- | 2.66 | 0.274 | -- | -- |
| | | R Hornad df | o 95-97 | 18 | P | 9.7 | 5.9 | -- | 3.64 | 0.222 | -- | -- |
| | | R Hron mouth | o 95-97 | 19 | P | 10.7 | 3.4 | -- | 2.15 | 0.194 | -- | -- |
| | | R Vah mouth | o 95-97 | 19 | P | 10.0 | 3.8 | -- | 2.88 | 0.201 | -- | -- |
| | country average | | | 18 | | | | | | | | |
| | not covered: Wisla; Groundwater | | | | | | | | | | | |
| Slovenia | Danube | R Sava at Brezice | e 90 | 19 | P | 9.2 | 6.3 | 35.0 | 1.70 | 0.200 | -- | -- |
| | | R Drava at Ormoz | e 91 | 48 | N | 10.2 | 2.5 | 9.7 | 1.20 | 0.000 | -- | -- |
| | country average | | | 33 | | | | | | | | |
| | not covered: Adriatic; Groundwater | | | | | | | | | | | |
| Spain | L temperate NE Atlantic | R Duero df | o 95-97 | 15 | P | 7.3 | 3.5 | -- | 1.85 | 0.392 | -- | -- |
| | U subtropical NE Atlantic | R Guadiana mouth | o 95-97 | 17 | P | 9.9 | 4.1 | -- | 1.94 | 0.316 | -- | -- |
| | | R Guadalquivir mouth | o 94-96 | 7 | P | 6.5 | 22.4 | -- | 2.19 | 0.838 | -- | -- |
| | | average | | 12 | | | | | | | | |
| | NW Mediterranean | R Ebro mouth | o 95-97 | 14 | P | 9.7 | 8.1 | -- | 3.32 | 0.444 | -- | -- |
| | country average | | | 14 | | | | | | | | |
| | not covered: Bay of Biscay, N Mediterranean; Groundwater | | | | | | | | | | | |
| Sweden | N Skagerrak & E Kattegat | L Vanern | o 95-97 pH e 90 | 58 | N | -- | -- | -- | 0.83 | 0.007 | -- | 7.4 |
| | N Baltic | R Mörrumsan mouth | o 95-97 | 60* | P | -- | -- | -- | 0.18 | 0.020 | -- | -- |
| | | R Ronneaan mouth | o 95-97 | 38 | N | -- | -- | -- | 1.62 | 0.037 | -- | -- |
| | | L Vattern | o 95-97 pH e 90 | 59 | N | -- | -- | -- | 0.77 | 0.005 | -- | 7.5 |
| | | average | | 52 | | | | | | | | |
| | Gulf of Bothnia | R Dalalven mouth | o 95-97 | 60* | P | -- | -- | -- | 0.14 | 0.017 | -- | -- |
| | | R Rane mouth | o 95-97 | 60* | P | -- | -- | -- | 0.05 | 0.016 | -- | -- |
| | | average | | 60 | | | | | | | | |
| | country average | | | 57 | | | | | | | | |
| | not covered: Groundwater | | | | | | | | | | | |
| Switzerland | Rhine | R Rhine at Basel | g 94-96 | 37 | P | 10.7 | -- | -- | 1.60 | 0.060 | 137.4 | 8.1 |
| | | R Rhine at Diepoldsau | g 94-96 | 10 | HM: Cr | 11.4 | -- | -- | 0.57 | 0.083 | 98.1 | 8.2 |
| | | R Aare at Brugg | g 94-96 | 31 | N | 10.5 | -- | -- | 1.95 | 0.066 | 153.6 | 8.0 |
| | | average | | 26 | | | | | | | | |
| | N Mediterranean | R Rhone at Chancy | g 94-96 | 13 | HM: Cr | 10.8 | -- | -- | 0.60 | 0.074 | 98.7 | 8.2 |
| | | R Rhone at Porte du Scex | g 94-96 | 23 | P | 11.3 | -- | -- | 0.60 | 0.113 | 74.0 | 8.2 |
| | | average | | 18 | | | | | | | | |
| | Adriatic | R Ticino at Riazzino | g 91 | 52 | P | 11.5 | -- | -- | 1.01 | 0.035 | 52.2 | 7.9 |
| | country average | | | 32 | | | | | | | | |
| | not covered: Danube; Groundwater | | | | | | | | | | | |
| Ukraine | N Black Sea | R Dnestr at Mogiliv-Podilskiy | e 89-91 | 19 | P | 12.8 | 3.1 | 23.5 | 2.30 | 0.200 | -- | -- |
| | Dnepr | R Dnepr at Kherson | e 89-91 | 27 | P | 9.6 | 3.0 | 32.3 | 0.50 | 0.100 | -- | -- |
| | Don | R Severskiy Donez at Krujilivka | e 91 | 14 | P | 3.4 | 1.5 | -- | 1.00 | 0.400 | -- | -- |
| | country average | | | 20 | | | | | | | | |
| | not covered: Wisla, Danube, Azov Sea; Groundwater | | | | | | | | | | | |
| United Kingdom | W North Sea | R Leven | g 94-96 | 40 | HM: Pb | 10.9 | 2.0 | -- | 0.43 | -- | 12.1 | 7.0 |
| | | R Tweed above Galafoot | g 94-96 | 51 | N | 11.3 | 2.0 | -- | 1.10 | -- | -- | 7.8 |
| | | R Trent at Nottingham | g 94-96 | 14 | N | 10.6 | 3.0 | -- | 9.34 | -- | 161.1 | 8.0 |
| | | R Thames at London | g 94-96 | 15 | N | 10.2 | 2.0 | -- | 7.85 | -- | 187.1 | 8.1 |
| | | average | | 30 | | | | | | | | |
| | English Channel | R Exe at Exeter | g 94-96 | 20 | N | 11.1 | 2.0 | -- | 2.82 | -- | 39.6 | 7.8 |
| | Celtic Sea | R Severn mouth | o 94-96 | 7 | P | 10.7 | 2.2 | -- | 6.59 | 0.832 | -- | -- |
| | | R Avon at Bristol | g 94-96 | 15 | N | 9.6 | 3.0 | -- | 7.96 | -- | 219.9 | 8.1 |
| | | average | | 11 | | | | | | | | |
| | Irish Sea | R Dee | g 94-96 | 20 | N | 10.5 | 1.0 | -- | 2.52 | -- | -- | 7.6 |
| | | R Mersey | g 94-96 | 15 | N | 7.7 | 4.0 | -- | 8.10 | -- | 102.9 | 7.4 |
| | | R Clyde mouth | o 94-96 | 11 | N | 8.4 | 3.7 | -- | 3.06 | 0.621 | -- | -- |
| | | average | | 15 | | | | | | | | |
| | Scottish & Irish Atlantic | R Carron | g 94-96 | 35 | HM: Cd | 11.3 | 1.0 | -- | 0.06 | -- | -- | 6.5 |

| Country | Basin | Station | Sources & years | Score | Based on | DO mg/l | BOD mg/l | COD mg/l | N mg/l | P mg/l | Alk. mg/l | pH |
|---|---|---|---|---|---|---|---|---|---|---|---|---|
| | | Lower Bann mouth | o 95-97 | 19 | P | 9.2 | 3.4 | -- | 1.12 | 0.161 | -- | -- |
| | | average | | 27 | | | | | | | | |
| | country average | | | 21 | | | | | | | | |
| | not covered: Groundwater | | | | | | | | | | | |
| RUSSIAN FEDERATION | Volga | R Volga at Narimanov | g 94 | 64 | N | 9.7 | 2.0 | -- | 0.66 | -- | 115.5 | 8.0 |
| | | R Volga at B Cheboksarskoye (201) | g 94 | 19 | P | 10.4 | 3.0 | -- | 2.20 | 0.168 | 192.8 | 7.6 |
| | | R Belaya at Ufa (203) | g 94 | 34 | P | 11.4 | 2.0 | -- | 1.37 | 0.074 | 129.6 | 7.9 |
| | | average | | 39 | | | | | | | | |
| | Severnaya Dvina | R Severnaya Dvina at Ust-Pinega (213) | g 94 | 58 | P | 8.3 | 2.0 | -- | 0.18 | 0.027 | 105.4 | 7.8 |
| | White Sea | R Mezen at Borovo | g 94 | 60 | P | 8.0 | 2.0 | -- | 0.05 | 0.025 | 60.7 | 7.1 |
| | E Barents Sea | R Pechora at Nar'jan-Mar | g 94 | 47 | P | 8.2 | 2.0 | -- | 0.16 | 0.041 | 60.3 | 7.2 |
| | Ob | R Ob at Salehard (011) | g 94 | 57 | N | 7.9 | 2.0 | -- | 0.85 | -- | 81.0 | 7.1 |
| | | R Tom at Tomsk (204) | g 94 | 39 | HM: Hg | 8.5 | 2.0 | -- | 1.13 | -- | 79.8 | 7.5 |
| | | R Irtysh at Krasnyi Jar (205) | g 94 | 18 | P | 9.7 | 3.0 | -- | 0.65 | 0.235 | 53.2 | 7.7 |
| | | average | | 38 | | | | | | | | |
| | Yenisey | R Yenisei at Igarka (210) | g 94 | 20 | HM: Zn | 8.6 | 1.0 | -- | 0.00 | 0.021 | 88.1 | 7.4 |
| | | L Baikal mid-lake (024) | g 91-93 | 40 | HM: Hg | 11.1 | 1.0 | -- | 0.11 | 0.021 | 60.9 | 7.8 |
| | | R Selenga mouth | g 94 | 60 | HM: Pb | 9.7 | 2.0 | -- | 0.07 | 0.015 | 110.6 | 7.5 |
| | | average | | 40 | | | | | | | | |
| | Lena | R Lena delta (028) | g 94 | 59 | P | 11.1 | 1.0 | -- | 0.07 | 0.026 | 61.7 | 7.5 |
| | Kolyma | R Kolyma at Kolymskoe | g 94 | 63 | Acid | 9.7 | 2.0 | -- | 0.06 | 0.021 | 25.5 | 7.1 |
| | Neva | L Onezhskoye (Onega) | g 94 | 59 | Acid | 10.3 | 2.0 | -- | 0.28 | 0.014 | 16.5 | 7.0 |
| | Don | R Don at Bagaevskij | g 94 | 30 | P | 15.5 | 4.0 | -- | 0.07 | 0.087 | 202.3 | 6.9 |
| | Azov Sea | R Kuban mouth | g 94 | 17 | N | 10.9 | 2.0 | -- | 5.83 | 0.066 | 124.7 | 7.8 |
| | Amur | R Amur mouth | g 94 | 61 | N | 10.2 | 4.0 | -- | 0.73 | -- | 31.2 | 7.2 |
| | country average | | | 48 | | | | | | | | |
| | not covered: Interior—N Caspian; Arctic—W Barents Sea, W Kara Sea, Pyasina, Taimyr, Khatanga, Anabar, Olenek, Yana, Indigirka, W Chukchi Sea; Atlantic—N Gulf of Finland, S Gulf of Finland, SE Baltic, Dnepr, E Black Sea; Pacific—W Bering Sea, U temperate NW Pacific, Sea of Okhotsk; Groundwater | | | | | | | | | | | |
| **ASIA** | | | | | | | | | | | | |
| Bangladesh | Ganges | R Meghna at Ashuganj | g 94-95 | 16 | P | 6.6 | 2.0 | -- | 4.89 | 0.376 | 82.6 | 7.3 |
| | | R Padma at Bheramara | g 94-95 | 46 | F coli | 7.3 | 3.0 | -- | -- | -- | 60.1 | 7.3 |
| | | R Brahmaputra at Fulchhari | g 94-95 | 49 | F coli | 7.1 | 2.0 | -- | -- | -- | 88.9 | 7.2 |
| | | average | | 37 | | | | | | | | |
| | NE Bay of Bengal | R Karnaphuli at Rangunia | g 95 | 38 | N | 6.6 | 1.0 | 16.0 | 1.61 | -- | 75.6 | 7.4 |
| | | L Kaptai at Kaptai | g 94-95 | 41 | N | 6.8 | 1.0 | 9.0 | 1.48 | -- | 40.2 | 7.4 |
| | | average | | 39 | | | | | | | | |
| | Groundwater | G tube well (07) | g 94-95 | 77 | O, Acid | 6.2 | 1.0 | -- | -- | -- | 130.2 | 7.3 |
| | | G tube well (09) | g 94-95 | 71 | Acid | 6.3 | 0.0 | -- | -- | -- | 79.7 | 7.2 |
| | | average | | 74 | | | | | | | | |
| | country average | | | 50 | | | | | | | | |
| | not covered: none | | | | | | | | | | | |
| China | Bo Hai | R Huang (Yellow) at Jinan | g 94-96 | 0 | SS, F coli | 8.9 | 3.0 | 3.0 | 3.40 | 0.833 | 177.1 | 8.0 |
| | Chang | R Chang (Yangtze) at Wuhan | g 94-96 | 20 | HM: Cd | 8.3 | 2.0 | 3.0 | 1.07 | 0.115 | 109.2 | 7.9 |
| | | L Tai | g 94-96 | 27 | P | 9.5 | 2.0 | 4.0 | 1.16 | 0.100 | 50.0 | 8.1 |
| | | average | | 23 | | | | | | | | |
| | Xi | R Xi (Pearl) at Zhaoqing | g 94-96 | 28 | F coli | 7.7 | 1.0 | 3.0 | 1.04 | 0.092 | 90.8 | 7.9 |
| | Chinese South China Sea | L Plover Cove (19), Hong Kong | g 94-96 | 40 | N | 8.0 | -- | -- | 1.50 | 0.016 | 23.2 | 7.9 |
| | country average | | | 23 | | | | | | | | |
| | not covered: E Asian interior, Balkhash, Tarim, Indus, Ganges, Irrawaddy, Salween, Amur, W Sea of Japan, E Yellow Sea, Liaodong Wan, SW Yellow Sea, East China Sea, Gulf of Tonkin, Mekong; Groundwater | | | | | | | | | | | |
| Georgia | S Caspian | R Kura at Rustavi | e 89 | 19 | N | 9.3 | 2.9 | 14.2 | 3.10 | -- | -- | -- |
| | E Black Sea | R Rioni at Poti | e 89 | 20 | N | 9.5 | 2.4 | 7.9 | 2.60 | 0.100 | -- | -- |
| | country average | | | 19 | | | | | | | | |
| | not covered: Groundwater | | | | | | | | | | | |
| India | Gulfs of Kachchh & Khambhat | R Sabarmati at Ahmedabad | g 95-96 | 0 | O, N, F coli | 1.1 | 78.0 | 220.0 | 32.80 | 1.067 | 429.8 | 7.6 |
| | | R Mahi at Vasad | g 95-96 | 18 | P | 9.6 | 2.0 | 10.0 | 3.41 | 0.216 | 181.9 | 8.3 |
| | | R Narmada near Garudeshwar | g 95-96 | 18 | N | 8.1 | 3.0 | 10.0 | 4.86 | 0.119 | 168.4 | 8.1 |
| | | R Tapti near Burhanpur | g 95-96 | 17 | P | 7.5 | 2.0 | 28.0 | 1.57 | 0.320 | 197.1 | 7.6 |
| | | average | | 13 | | | | | | | | |
| | Malabar Coast | R Chaliyar at Kalpalli | g 95-96 | 19 | F coli | 6.6 | 1.0 | 10.0 | 0.43 | -- | 28.0 | 7.0 |
| | | R Periyar near Alwaye | g 95-96 | 20 | F coli | 7.2 | 1.0 | 10.0 | 1.91 | -- | 8.4 | 6.7 |

| Country | Basin | Station | Sources & years | Score | Based on | DO mg/l | BOD mg/l | COD mg/l | N mg/l | P mg/l | Alk. mg/l | pH |
|---|---|---|---|---|---|---|---|---|---|---|---|---|
| | | R Kallada at Panamthottam | g 95-96 | 17 | F coli | 8.0 | 1.0 | 8.0 | 1.03 | -- | 11.9 | 7.2 |
| | | average | | 19 | | | | | | | | |
| | Coromandel Coast | R Cauvery near Musiri | g 95-96 | 17 | F coli | 6.8 | 1.0 | 17.0 | 3.49 | -- | 166.2 | 7.6 |
| | | R Pennar near Nellore | g 95-96 | 42 | P | 6.1 | 3.0 | 15.0 | 0.45 | 0.047 | 223.0 | 8.0 |
| | | average | | 29 | | | | | | | | |
| | Krishna | R Krishna near Vijayawada | g 95-96 | 28 | P | 7.4 | 2.0 | 9.0 | 1.16 | 0.096 | 141.5 | 8.0 |
| | | R Krishna at Gadwal | g 95-96 | 26 | N | 7.2 | 2.0 | 11.0 | 2.21 | 0.022 | 134.8 | 7.7 |
| | | R Tungabhadra at Ullanuru | g 95-96 | 18 | N | 7.2 | 1.0 | 29.0 | 5.10 | 0.047 | 154.5 | 8.5 |
| | | R Bhima near Takali | g 95-96 | 19 | P | 6.2 | 5.0 | 27.0 | 2.10 | 0.173 | 172.6 | 8.1 |
| | | average | | 23 | | | | | | | | |
| | Godavari | R Godavari near Polavaram | g 95-96 | 50 | P | 7.2 | 1.0 | 9.0 | 0.43 | 0.037 | 84.8 | 7.4 |
| | | R Godavari near Mancheral | g 95-96 | 19 | P | 7.7 | 2.0 | 12.0 | 0.52 | 0.198 | 182.3 | 8.0 |
| | | R Wainganga near Ashti | g 95-96 | 19 | N, P | 6.1 | 5.0 | 23.0 | 3.23 | 0.177 | 186.6 | 8.1 |
| | | average | | 29 | | | | | | | | |
| | NW Bay of Bengal | R Mahanadi mouth | a 90 | 24 | SS | -- | -- | -- | -- | -- | -- | -- |
| | | R Subarnarekha at Jamshedpur | g 95-96 | 26 | F coli | 6.4 | 3.0 | 40.0 | 0.50 | -- | 63.4 | 7.7 |
| | | average | | 25 | | | | | | | | |
| | Ganges | R Ganga df | a 90 | 17 | SS | -- | -- | -- | 0.86 | 0.075 | -- | -- |
| | Groundwater | G well Ahmedabad | g 95-96 | 17 | N | 5.7 | 1.0 | 7.0 | 5.98 | 0.055 | 406.2 | 7.9 |
| | | G well Baroda | g 95 | 19 | N | 7.5 | 1.0 | 9.0 | 4.02 | 0.048 | 417.6 | 8.0 |
| | | G well Kalpalli | g 95-96 | 19 | F coli | 5.7 | 0.0 | 4.0 | 2.16 | -- | 31.2 | 6.8 |
| | | G well Eluru (Alwaye) | g 95-96 | 20 | N | 4.8 | 1.0 | 9.0 | 2.78 | -- | 13.5 | 7.0 |
| | | G well Musiri | g 95-96 | 19 | N | 4.6 | 1.0 | 16.0 | 3.10 | -- | 202.5 | 7.5 |
| | | G well Vijayawada | g 95-96 | 0 | N | 4.2 | 3.0 | 13.0 | 50.96 | 0.655 | 345.3 | 7.5 |
| | | average | | 16 | | | | | | | | |
| | country average | | | 21 | | | | | | | | |
| | not covered: Rajasthan, Indus, Maharashtra Coast, Lakshadweep Sea, Mannar, NE Bay of Bengal, Irrawaddy, Andaman Sea | | | | | | | | | | | |
| Indonesia | U intertropical E Indian (Java) | R Garang 91-93 | g 91-93 | 0 | F coli | 6.2 | 4.0 | 12.0 | 1.23 | 0.112 | 107.0 | 7.6 |
| | | R Garang 94 | g 94 | 17 | HM: Cu | 4.6 | -- | 14.0 | 0.32 | 0.180 | 88.0 | 7.8 |
| | | lower | | 0 | | | | | | | | |
| | Java Sea & Karimata Strait (Sumatra) | R Musi at Palembang | g 91-93 | 5 | HM: Zn | 4.6 | 4.0 | 22.0 | 0.41 | 0.129 | 26.7 | 6.7 |
| | Java Sea (Java) | R Banjir Kanal 91-93 | g 91-93 | 0 | F coli | 1.4 | 14.0 | 26.0 | 2.75 | 0.243 | 58.6 | 6.9 |
| | | R Banjir Kanal 94 | g 94 | 1 | HM: Zn | 2.6 | 7.0 | 8.0 | 1.39 | 0.409 | 45.1 | 6.7 |
| | | R Sunter 91-93 | g 91-93 | 0 | F coli, HM: Pb, Zn | 0.8 | 24.0 | 48.0 | 6.13 | 0.546 | 98.8 | 7.1 |
| | | R Sunter 94 | g 94 | 6 | HM: Cd | 1.8 | 9.0 | 37.0 | 0.96 | 0.263 | 54.3 | 6.7 |
| | | R Citarum 91-93 | g 91-93 | 0 | F coli, HM: Pb | 1.3 | 18.0 | 44.0 | 3.70 | 0.415 | 84.7 | 7.5 |
| | | R Citarum 94 | g 94 | 0 | HM: Cd | 3.1 | 8.0 | 12.0 | 0.30 | 1.347 | 39.0 | 7.3 |
| | | R Surabaya 91-93 | g 91-93 | 0 | F coli, HM: Pb | 2.9 | 18.0 | 51.0 | 1.84 | 0.185 | 142.6 | 7.4 |
| | | B Saguling 91-93 | g 91-93 | 0 | F coli, HM: Pb | 6.6 | 4.0 | 14.0 | 1.52 | 0.196 | 65.9 | 8.2 |
| | | B Saguling 94 | g 94 | 11 | P | 4.5 | 5.0 | 13.0 | 0.00 | 0.649 | 48.0 | 7.6 |
| | | average 91-93 | | 0 | | | | | | | | |
| | Groundwater (Java) | G well Senayan Jakarta | g 91-93 | 11 | HM: Zn | 0.0 | -- | 6.0 | 0.33 | 0.198 | 179.4 | 8.3 |
| | | G well Pulogadung Jakarta | g 91-93 | 0 | HM: Zn | 0.0 | -- | 6.0 | 0.22 | 0.598 | 202.4 | 7.3 |
| | | G well Cibeureum | g 91-93 | 0 | HM: Pb | 3.7 | 1.0 | 3.0 | 0.99 | 0.136 | 122.6 | 7.5 |
| | | average | | 4 | | | | | | | | |
| | country average | | | 2 | | | | | | | | |
| | not covered: Strait of Malacca, W Sumatra, U intertropical E Indian (Bali-Alor), N Timor & Arafura Seas, Sulu & Celebes Seas, Makassar Strait, Java Sea & Karimata Strait (Kalimantan), Bali & Flores Seas, Molucca & Halmahera Seas, Ceram & Banda Seas, New Guinea tropical, New Guinea intertropical, Bismarck & Solomon Seas, N Coral Sea | | | | | | | | | | | |
| Iran | Shatt-al-Arab | Shatt-al-Arab mouth | a 90 | 13 | SS | -- | -- | -- | -- | 0.010 | -- | -- |
| | Groundwater | G well 7 Tabriz | g 91-92 | 33 | P | 10.5 | 1.0 | 7.0 | 0.30 | 0.000 | 136.6 | 7.1 |
| | country average | | | 23 | | | | | | | | |
| | not covered: S Caspian, Iranian interior, Helmand, Hari Rud & Murgab, Baluchistan, N Persian Gulf & Gulf of Oman, Makran Coast | | | | | | | | | | | |
| Iraq | Shatt-al-Arab | Shatt-al-Arab mouth | a 90 | 13 | SS | -- | -- | -- | -- | 0.010 | -- | -- |
| | not covered: Groundwater | | | | | | | | | | | |
| Japan | L temperate NW Pacific (Honshu) | R Kyu-Kitakami at Kanomata | g 92-93 | 29 | P | 9.8 | 2.0 | 4.0 | 0.53 | 0.090 | 26.2 | 6.8 |
| | | R Tone at Tone-Ozeki | g 94-96 | 16 | HM: Cd | 9.8 | 2.0 | 3.0 | 2.40 | 0.135 | 31.0 | 7.2 |
| | | R Sagami at Samukawa | g 94-96 | 20 | F coli | 9.0 | 2.0 | 2.0 | 1.98 | 0.063 | 53.5 | 7.7 |

213

| Country | Basin | Station | Sources & years | Score | Based on | DO mg/l | BOD mg/l | COD mg/l | N mg/l | P mg/l | Alk. mg/l | pH |
|---|---|---|---|---|---|---|---|---|---|---|---|---|
| | | R Kiso at Inuyama | g 94-96 | 37 | F coli | 10.4 | 1.0 | -- | 0.68 | 0.029 | 18.5 | 7.3 |
| | | average | | 25 | | | | | | | | |
| | U subtropical NW Pacific (Honshu) | L Biwa south center | g 94-96 | 65 | P | 10.1 | 1.0 | -- | 0.15 | 0.021 | -- | 8.1 |
| | | R Yodo at Hirakata Bridge | g 91-92 | 16 | P | 8.9 | 2.0 | -- | 1.34 | 0.356 | 30.8 | 7.4 |
| | | average | | 40 | | | | | | | | |
| | U subtropical NW Pacific (Shikoku) | R Yoshino at Takase | g 94-96 | 19 | N | 9.4 | 1.0 | -- | 3.51 | 0.016 | 32.3 | 7.4 |
| | U subtropical NW Pacific (Kyushu) | R Chikugo at Senoshita | g 94-96 | 29 | P | 9.8 | 2.0 | -- | 1.19 | 0.093 | -- | 7.7 |
| | | R Kuma at Yokoishi | g 94-95 | 40 | F coli | 9.6 | 1.0 | -- | 0.86 | 0.030 | 34.6 | 7.9 |
| | | average | | 34 | | | | | | | | |
| | E Sea of Japan (Honshu) | R Shinano at Kyuzogoya | g 94-95 | 37 | HM: Pb | 10.1 | 1.0 | -- | 0.88 | -- | 23.1 | 7.2 |
| | E Sea of Japan (Hokkaido) | R Ishikari at Ishikari | g 94-96 | 22 | F coli | 11.3 | 1.0 | -- | 0.79 | 0.068 | 37.1 | 7.3 |
| | Groundwater (Honshu) | G Suginami filtration plant | g 94-96 | 15 | N | 7.3 | 1.0 | -- | 8.47 | -- | 41.2 | 6.2 |
| | country average | | | 27 | | | | | | | | |
| | not covered: Sea of Okhotsk, L temperate NW Pacific (Hokkaido), U subtropical NW Pacific (Ryukyu Is) | | | | | | | | | | | |
| Jordan | Rift Valley | R Zarqua at King Talal Dam | g 94-96 | 0 | O, N, HM: Pb | -- | 74.0 | 165.0 | 45.85 | -- | -- | 7.5 |
| | Groundwater | G Awajan well 23 | g 96 | 0 | N | -- | -- | -- | 63.74 | -- | -- | 7.0 |
| | | G Azraq well 2 | g 95-96 | 20 | N | 10.5 | -- | -- | 2.82 | -- | -- | 7.5 |
| | | G Rahme well Wadi Araba | g 94-96 | 13 | N | -- | -- | -- | 9.85 | -- | -- | 7.2 |
| | | average | | 11 | | | | | | | | |
| | country average | | | 5 | | | | | | | | |
| | not covered: Arabian interior, E Red Sea | | | | | | | | | | | |
| Kazakhstan | Aral Sea | R Syr Darya mouth | a 90 | 13 | SS | -- | -- | -- | -- | -- | -- | -- |
| | not covered: N Caspian, Balkhash, Turgay, E Asian interior, Ob; Groundwater | | | | | | | | | | | |
| Korea, R | Korea Strait | R NakDong | o 95-97 | 25 | N | 9.1 | 1.1 | -- | 2.26 | 0.047 | -- | -- |
| | | R YoungSan | o 95-97 | 20 | P | 11.3 | 1.5 | -- | 1.76 | 0.127 | -- | -- |
| | | average | | 22 | | | | | | | | |
| | E Yellow Sea | R Han mouth OECD 95-97 | o 95-97 | -- | -- | 10.6 | 1.4 | -- | 1.76 | 0.039 | -- | -- |
| | | R Han GEMS 94-96 | g 94-96 | 21 | HM: Cu | 10.3 | 1.0 | -- | 0.23 | -- | 43.4 | 7.7 |
| | | R Keum | o 95-97 | 45 | N | 9.2 | 1.3 | -- | 1.33 | 0.033 | -- | -- |
| | | average | | 33 | | | | | | | | |
| | country average | | | 27 | | | | | | | | |
| | not covered: W Sea of Japan; Groundwater | | | | | | | | | | | |
| Malaysia | Strait of Malacca | R Klang | g 92 | 0 | F coli | 4.7 | 4.0 | 43.0 | 3.99 | 0.297 | -- | 7.1 |
| | | R Linggi | g 92 | 0 | F coli | 4.3 | 2.0 | 53.0 | 1.66 | -- | -- | 6.3 |
| | | R Sekudai | g 92 | 0 | F coli, HM: Cu | 4.6 | 1.0 | 28.0 | 1.92 | 0.016 | -- | 6.4 |
| | country average | | | 0 | | | | | | | | |
| | not covered: Malay/Thai South China Sea, Borneo South China Sea, Sulu & Celebes Seas; Groundwater | | | | | | | | | | | |
| Myanmar | Irrawaddy | R Irrawaddy | a 90 | 36 | SS | -- | -- | -- | -- | -- | -- | -- |
| | not covered: NE Bay of Bengal, Salween, Andaman Sea, Mekong; Groundwater | | | | | | | | | | | |
| Pakistan | Indus | R Indus at Kotri | g 94-96 | 0 | SS, HM: Cr, Cu | 5.3 | 6.0 | 17.0 | 5.99 | 0.436 | 133.9 | 7.4 |
| | | R Ravi below Lahore | g 94-96 | 0 | F coli | 7.4 | 3.0 | 37.0 | 6.33 | 0.234 | 144.6 | 7.8 |
| | | R Ravi above Lahore | g 94-96 | 0 | F coli | 7.0 | 2.0 | 27.0 | 7.06 | 0.140 | 127.7 | 7.8 |
| | | R Chenab Gujra branch | g 94-96 | 0 | F coli | 7.2 | 2.0 | 27.0 | 5.49 | 0.023 | 123.1 | 7.8 |
| | | average | | 0 | | | | | | | | |
| | Groundwater | G Lahore | g 94-96 | 27 | P | -- | -- | 8.0 | 0.36 | 0.100 | 242.5 | 7.6 |
| | country average | | | 13 | | | | | | | | |
| | not covered: Baluchistan, Makran Coast | | | | | | | | | | | |
| Philippines | Philippine South China Sea (Luzon) | B La Mesa | g 94-95 | 28 | F coli | 8.4 | 1.0 | -- | -- | -- | 64.5 | 7.5 |
| | L subtropical NW Pacific | R Cagayan | g 94-96 | 30 | F coli | 8.1 | 3.0 | -- | -- | -- | 49.7 | 7.8 |
| | country average | | | 29 | | | | | | | | |
| | not covered: U tropical W Pacific, Sulu & Celebes Seas; Groundwater | | | | | | | | | | | |
| Thailand | Chao Phraya | R Chao Phraya at Bangkok | g 91-93 | 0 | F coli | 1.7 | 5.0 | -- | 1.56 | 0.320 | 120.3 | 7.4 |
| | | R Chao Phraya below Nakhon Sawan | g 91-93 | 0 | F coli | 3.7 | 1.0 | -- | 0.12 | 0.227 | 70.9 | 7.9 |
| | | R Prasak at Kaeng Khoi | g 91-92 | 0 | F coli | 4.1 | 1.0 | -- | 0.12 | 0.075 | 145.3 | 7.7 |
| | | average | | 0 | | | | | | | | |
| | E Gulf of Thailand | R Bang at Pa Kong | g 91-93 | 0 | F coli, HM: Pb | 3.8 | 2.0 | -- | 0.41 | 0.351 | 60.5 | 7.1 |
| | Mekong | R Mun at Ubon Ratchathani | g 91-93 | 7 | P | 0.0 | 2.0 | -- | 1.10 | 0.837 | 45.0 | 7.3 |
| | country average | | | 2 | | | | | | | | |

| Country | Basin | Station | Sources & years | Score | Based on | DO mg/l | BOD mg/l | COD mg/l | N mg/l | P mg/l | Alk. mg/l | pH |
|---|---|---|---|---|---|---|---|---|---|---|---|---|
| | not covered: Salween, Andaman Sea, Strait of Malacca, Malay/Thai South China Sea, W Gulf of Thailand; Groundwater | | | | | | | | | | | |
| Turkey | S Black Sea | R Yesilirmak mouth | o 95-97 | 17 | P | 9.8 | 1.8 | -- | 2.91 | 0.270 | -- | -- |
| | | R Sakarya mouth | o 95-97 | 12 | P | 9.0 | 3.7 | -- | 1.70 | 0.490 | -- | -- |
| | | average | | 14 | | | | | | | | |
| | Aegean | R Gediz mouth | o 95-97 | 17 | P | 4.5 | 11.7 | -- | 0.87 | 0.287 | -- | -- |
| | country average | | | 15 | | | | | | | | |
| | not covered: Turkish interior, S Caspian, W Black Sea, E Black Sea, E Mediterranean, Shatt-al-Arab; Groundwater | | | | | | | | | | | |
| Uzbekistan | Aral Sea | R Amu Darya mouth | a 90 | 0 | SS | -- | -- | -- | -- | -- | -- | -- |
| | not covered: Groundwater | | | | | | | | | | | |
| Viet Nam | Gulf of Tonkin | R Hong (Red) mouth | a 90 | 19 | SS | -- | -- | -- | -- | -- | -- | -- |
| | Mekong | R Mekong mouth | a 90 | 56 | SS | -- | -- | -- | -- | -- | -- | -- |
| | country average | | | 37 | | | | | | | | |
| | not covered: Vietnamese South China Sea; Groundwater | | | | | | | | | | | |
| PACIFIC | | | | | | | | | | | | |
| Australia | Murray-Darling | R Murray-Darling mouth Atlas | a 90 | 0 | SS | -- | -- | -- | 0.03 | 0.100 | -- | -- |
| | | R Murray-Darling mouth OECD lower | o 92 | 31 | P | -- | -- | -- | 0.01 | 0.085 | -- | -- |
| | | | | 0 | | | | | | | | |
| | W Coral Sea | R Burdekin mouth | a 90 | 52 | SS | -- | -- | -- | -- | -- | -- | -- |
| | Subpolar SW Pacific | R Derwent mouth | o 93 | 10 | N | -- | -- | -- | 13.30 | 0.006 | -- | -- |
| | country average | | | 21 | | | | | | | | |
| | not covered: Gulf of Carpentaria, S Arafura & Timor Seas, L intertropical E Indian, W Australian subtropical, U temperate E Indian, L temperate E Indian, Subpolar E Indian, W Tasman Sea, Bass Strait; Groundwater | | | | | | | | | | | |
| New Zealand | E Tasman Sea (South I) | R Oreti at Riverton highway bridge | g 94-96 | 56 | N | 11.2 | 0 | -- | 0.91 | 0.025 | -- | 7.6 |
| | | R Waiau at Tuatapere | g 94-96 | 72 | P | 11.4 | 0 | -- | 0.24 | 0.016 | -- | 7.7 |
| | | R Haast at Roaring Billy | g 94-96 | 28 | P | 11.6 | 0 | -- | 0.07 | 0.096 | -- | 7.7 |
| | | R Grey at Dobson | g 94-96 | 65 | P | 10.9 | 0 | -- | 0.16 | 0.021 | -- | 7.3 |
| | | R Buller at Te Huha | g 94-96 | 59 | P | 11.1 | 0 | -- | 0.11 | 0.026 | -- | 7.6 |
| | | R Motueka at Woodstock | g 94-96 | 59 | P | 11.2 | 0 | -- | 0.18 | 0.026 | -- | 8.0 |
| | | average | | 56 | | | | | | | | |
| | E Tasman Sea (North I) | R Manawatu at Opiki bridge | g 94-96 | 19 | P | 10.5 | 2.0 | -- | 1.00 | 0.161 | -- | 7.7 |
| | | R Rangitikei at Kakariki | g 94-96 | 28 | P | 10.8 | 1.0 | -- | 0.27 | 0.096 | -- | 8.0 |
| | | R Wanganui at Paetawa | g 94-96 | 19 | P | 10.3 | 1.0 | -- | 0.46 | 0.158 | -- | 7.6 |
| | | R Waingongoro at SH45 | g 94-96 | 20 | P | 10.8 | 1.0 | -- | 2.00 | 0.128 | -- | 7.9 |
| | | R Waitara at Bertrand road | g 94-96 | 19 | P | 10.6 | 1.0 | -- | 0.60 | 0.168 | -- | 7.6 |
| | | R Waikato at Rangiriri | g 94-96 | 36 | P | 9.3 | 1.0 | -- | 0.70 | 0.065 | -- | 7.5 |
| | | R Hoteo at Gubbs | g 94-96 | 34 | P | 8.9 | 1.0 | -- | 0.80 | 0.072 | -- | 7.3 |
| | | average | | 25 | | | | | | | | |
| | Temperate SW Pacific (North I) | R Waitangi at Wakelins | g 94-96 | 63 | P | 9.7 | 0 | -- | 0.44 | 0.023 | -- | 7.5 |
| | | R Waihou at Te Aroha bridge | g 94-96 | 24 | P | 9.3 | 1.0 | -- | 1.34 | 0.109 | -- | 7.2 |
| | | R Tarawera at Awakaponga | g 94-96 | 21 | P | 6.9 | 2.0 | -- | 0.49 | 0.122 | -- | 7.2 |
| | | R Rangitaiki at Te Teko | g 94-96 | 49 | P | 10.7 | 1.0 | -- | 0.41 | 0.039 | -- | 7.1 |
| | | R Motu at Houpoto | g 94-96 | 24 | P | 10.5 | 0 | -- | 0.12 | 0.111 | -- | 7.7 |
| | | R Mohaka at Raupunga | g 94-96 | 19 | P | 10.9 | 1.0 | -- | 0.17 | 0.156 | -- | 8.3 |
| | | R Ngaruroro at Chesterhope | g 94-96 | 46 | P | 10.7 | 0 | -- | 0.13 | 0.042 | -- | 8.2 |
| | | R Tukituki at Red bridge | g 94-96 | 54 | P | 11.7 | 1.0 | -- | 0.84 | 0.033 | -- | 8.6 |
| | | R Ruamahanga at Waiaenga | g 94-96 | 31 | P | 10.6 | 1.0 | -- | 0.68 | 0.082 | -- | 7.6 |
| | | R Hutt at Boulcott | g 94-96 | 71 | P | 10.9 | 0 | -- | 0.34 | 0.017 | -- | 7.3 |
| | | average | | 40 | | | | | | | | |
| | Temperate SW Pacific (South I) | R Wairau at Tuamarina | g 94-96 | 26 | P | 10.7 | 0 | -- | 0.14 | 0.104 | -- | 7.7 |
| | | R Hurunui at Shi bridge | g 94-96 | 30 | P | 10.9 | 0 | -- | 0.32 | 0.089 | -- | 7.9 |
| | | R Waimakariri above old highway bridge | g 94-96 | 19 | P | 10.5 | 0 | -- | 0.13 | 0.178 | -- | 7.8 |
| | | R Opihi at Waipopo | g 94-96 | 36 | P | 11.1 | 0 | -- | 0.68 | 0.064 | -- | 7.6 |
| | | R Waitaki at Shi bridge | g 94-96 | 40 | P | 11.0 | 0 | -- | 0.14 | 0.050 | -- | 7.6 |
| | | R Taieri at Outram | g 94-96 | 51 | P | 11.6 | 1.0 | -- | 0.30 | 0.036 | -- | 7.6 |
| | | R Clutha at Balclutha | g 94-96 | 53 | P | 11.0 | 0 | -- | 0.15 | 0.034 | -- | 7.7 |
| | | R Mataura at Seaward Downs | g 94-96 | 39 | P | 10.8 | 1.0 | -- | 1.14 | 0.054 | -- | 7.2 |
| | | average | | 37 | | | | | | | | |
| | country average | | | 39 | | | | | | | | |
| | not covered: Groundwater | | | | | | | | | | | |
| Papua New Guinea | Bismarck & Solomon Seas | R Sepik mouth | a 90 | 60* | SS | -- | -- | -- | -- | -- | -- | -- |
| | N Coral Sea | R Fly mouth | a 90 | 27 | SS | -- | -- | -- | -- | -- | -- | -- |
| | country average | | | 43 | | | | | | | | |
| | not covered: New Guinea intertropical; Groundwater | | | | | | | | | | | |

**Notes**

The inland water quality score is the average score of drainage basins in each country. Each basin score is the lowest score of six indicators: oxygen balance, nutrients, acidification, suspended solids, microbial pollution, and arsenic and heavy metals. This table gives the basin and country scores, the indicator that determines each basin score, and data on oxygen balance, nutrients, and acidification. Table 16 gives data on suspended solids, microbial pollution, and arsenic and heavy metals.

Countries use different methods for measuring pollutants, so the data are not strictly comparable. All data are annual mean values at the location indicated in the Station column. Data are for the years and from the sources indicated in the Sources & years column.

Basin = drainage basin. Surface water basins are defined in Appendix 6. Groundwater is treated as if it were a single basin. Basins and groundwater not covered are noted at the end of each country section. Parts of basin names are abbreviated as follows: E = east; L = lower; N = north; S = south; U = upper; W = west.

Station = monitoring station (the point where the data are collected). Stations were chosen to meet the following criteria:

At least one station per country basin (portion of a basin in a country) near the mouth or downstream frontier (df).

In long coastal basins drained by many short rivers, additional stations to represent groups of rivers along the coast.

In large (100,000 km$^2$ or more) river basins, additional stations to represent sub-basins, preferably near the confluence with the main river or at or below major centers of population.

If the flow is interrupted by a large lake or reservoir, an additional station near the entrance to the lake or reservoir.

Groundwater stations at intervals throughout the country.

It was seldom possible to met these criteria in full. Four types of station are identified by a letter before the name of the water body concerned: B = built reservoir; G = groundwater; L = lake; R = river.

Sources & years = data sources, applicable years, and exceptions. Sources are indicated as follows:

a     National Water Research Institute (1996)

e     Eurostat *et al.* (1995)

g     Global Environmental Monitoring System (GEMS)/WATER data summaries and database (UNEP & WHO GEMS/Water Collaborating Centre 1988-1990, 1991-1993, 1999)

o     Organisation for Economic Co-operation and Development (1997 & 1999)

oc     OECD Centre for Co-operation with the Economies in Transition (1996)

When a single year is given, all data are for that year (unless otherwise noted in the Sources column). When a period is given (e.g., 94-96), all data are annual averages for that period (unless otherwise noted in the Sources column). If data for one of the indicators are for a different year, the indicator, source and year are noted after the indicator code. For example—o 95-97; pH e 90—means that data are from OECD and are for 1995-1997, except for acidity (pH) which are from Eurostat *et al.* and are for 1990. The codes used are: BOD = biochemical oxygen demand; COD = chemical oxygen demand; DO = dissolved oxygen; N = total nitrogen; P = total phosphorus.

Score = water quality score, the lowest score of the six indicators. Country scores are the average of basin scores (with groundwater treated as a single basin), which are the average of station scores.

Based on = the indicator that determines the station score (the indicator with the lowest score):

Acid = acidification, the average score of of alkalinity and acidity (pH) (this table)

F coli = fecal coliforms (microbial pollution) (Table 16)

HM = arsenic and heavy metals, the lowest score of arsenic (As), zinc (Zn), chromium (Cr), copper (Cu), nickel (Ni), lead (Pb), cadmium (Cd) and mercury (Hg) (Table 16)

N = total nitrogen (this table)

O = oxygen balance, the average of scores for dissolved oxygen, biochemical oxygen demand and chemical oxygen demand (this table)

P = total phosphorus (this table)

SS = total suspended solids (Table 16)

When two or more indicators are listed, their scores are the same.

The performance criteria are shown in Tables 15a and 15b. For convenience, the same criteria have been used for flowing surface waters (rivers), still surface waters (lakes), and groundwater, although ideally they should be different since natural conditions differ among them. For example, dissolved oxygen is naturally higher in rivers than in lakes, and concentrations of heavy metals are naturally higher in groundwater than in surface waters.

For dissolved oxygen (DO), the tops of the good and fair bands correspond to the range of 9-12 mg/l (depending on temperature) for 100% oxygen saturation of natural running waters (National Water Research Institute 1996). The tops of the medium, poor and bad bands match the draft quality classes of the United Nations Economic Commission for Europe (1990).

For biochemical oxygen demand (BOD), chemical oxygen demand (COD), total nitrogen (N), total phosphorus (P), alkalinity, acidity (pH) and microbial pollution (fecal coliforms), the tops of the fair, medium, poor and bad bands match the draft quality classes of the United Nations Economic Commission for Europe (1990): the good band corresponds to Class I (excellent), the fair band to Class II (good), the medium band to Class III (fair), the poor band to Class IV (poor), the bad band to Class V (bad).

For total suspended solids (TSS), the top of the bad band (1000 mg/l) is the point at which suspended solids start to limit light penetration and may shorten the life of reservoirs through sedimentation (National Water Research Institute 1996).

For arsenic and heavy metals, the tops of medium, poor and bad match the draft quality classes of the United Nations Economic Commission for Europe (1990): the good band corresponds to Class I (excellent), the fair band to Class II (good), the medium band to Class III (fair), the poor band to Class IV (poor), the bad band to Class V (bad).

DO = dissolved oxygen in milligrams of oxygen per liter (mg/l).

BOD = biochemical oxygen demand in milligrams of oxygen per liter (mg/l).

COD = chemical oxygen demand in milligrams of oxygen per liter (mg/l).

N = total nitrogen in milligrams of nitrogen per liter (mg/l). Few countries report total nitrogen. Most entries are various combinations of organic nitrogen, ammonia ($NH_3$), nitrates ($NO_3$) and nitrites ($NO_2$), one or more of which may be missing. Hence, nitrogen levels are usually understated, which is why the score for nutrients is the lower of the N score and P score.

P = total phosphorus in milligrams of phosphorus per liter (mg/l), but sometimes only phosphate ($PO_4$).

Alk. = alkalinity, measured as milligrams of calcium carbonate ($CaCO_3$) per liter (mg/l).

Ph = acidity in Ph units. The pH scale is logarithmic: 7.0 is neutral and each whole unit of the scale represents a multiplication factor of 10 (so 6.0 is 10 times more acid than 7.0, and 5.0 is 100 times more acid).

| band | top point on scale | DO mg O₂/l | BOD mg O₂/l | COD mg O₂/l | N mg/l | P mg/l | alkalinity mg CaCO₃/l | pH | TSS mg/l | no. fecal coliforms/ 100 ml |
|---|---|---|---|---|---|---|---|---|---|---|
| good | 100 | 12 | 0 | 0 | 0 | 0 | 400 | 8.5 | 0 | 0 |
| fair | 80 | 9 | 3 | 3 | 0.30 | 0.010 | 200 | 6.5 | 125 | 10 |
| medium | 60 | 6 | 5 | 10 | 0.75 | 0.025 | 100 | 6.3 | 250 | 30 |
| poor | 40 | 4 | 9 | 20 | 1.50 | 0.050 | 20 | 6.0 | 500 | 100 |
| bad | 20 | 3 | 15 | 30 | 2.50 | 0.125 | 10 | 5.3 | 1000 | 1000 |
| base | 0 | 1 | 30 | 60 | 25.00 | 1.250 | 0 | 4.5 | 2000 | 10000 |

**Table 15a. Performance criteria for dissolved oxygen (DO), biochemical oxygen demand (BOD), chemical oxygen demand (COD), total nitrogen (N), total phosphorus (P), alkalinity, acidity (pH), total suspended solids (TSS), and microbial pollution (fecal coliforms).**

| band | top point on scale | As µg/l | Zn µg/l | Cr µg/l | Cu µg/l | Ni µg/l | Pb µg/l | Cd µg/l | Hg µg/l |
|---|---|---|---|---|---|---|---|---|---|
| good | 100 | 0 | 0 | 0 | 0 | 0 | 0 | 0 | 0 |
| fair | 80 | 5 | 22 | 0.5 | 1.0 | 7.5 | 0.05 | 0.03 | 0.002 |
| medium | 60 | 10 | 45 | 1.0 | 2.0 | 15.0 | 0.10 | 0.07 | 0.003 |
| poor | 40 | 50 | 59 | 11.0 | 6.5 | 88.0 | 1.30 | 0.70 | 0.012 |
| bad | 20 | 100 | 65 | 16.0 | 9.2 | 790.0 | 34.00 | 1.80 | 2.400 |
| base | 0 | 200 | 260 | 80.0 | 92.0 | 800.0 | 68.00 | 18.00 | 2.500 |

**Table 15b. Performance criteria for arsenic and heavy metals.**

\* A score with an asterisk has been reduced in accordance with the insufficient data rule. To prevent high scores resulting merely from lack of data, a good score is allowed only if it is based on all applicable components (in this case, all indicators in a station score, all stations in a basin score, all basins in a country score), and a fair score only if it is based on at least half the components. Good and fair scores (100-61) based on fewer than half the applicable components have been reduced to 60. Good scores (100-81) based on more than half but not all the applicable components have been reduced to 80.

# Table 16. Inland Water Quality: Suspended Solids, Microbial Pollution, and Arsenic and Heavy Metals

| Country | Basin | Station | Sources & years | TSS mg/l | F coli/ 100 ml | As µg/l | Zn µg/l | Cr µg/l | Cu µg/l | Ni µg/l | Pb µg/l | Cd µg/l | Hg µg/l |
|---|---|---|---|---|---|---|---|---|---|---|---|---|---|
| **AMERICAS** | | | | | | | | | | | | | |
| Argentina | La Plata | R Paraná at Puerto Libertad | g 94 | -- | 250 | 10.0 | 42 | 5.0 | 15.0 | -- | 6.0 | 1.00 | -- |
| | | R Paraná at Corrientes | g 94 | 39 | 1204 | -- | -- | -- | -- | -- | -- | -- | -- |
| | | R Paraná at Rosario | g 94 | -- | 246 | -- | -- | -- | 2.0 | -- | -- | -- | 1.020 |
| Brazil | Amazon | R Amazon mouth | a 90 | 186 | -- | -- | -- | -- | -- | -- | -- | -- | -- |
| | | R Tocantins mouth | a 90 | 202 | -- | -- | -- | -- | -- | -- | -- | -- | -- |
| | São Francisco | R Capibaribe | g 88-90 | 44 | 21000 | -- | 55 | -- | 14.0 | -- | 48.0 | 37.00 | 0.748 |
| | | R São Francisco at Petrolandia | g 88-90 | 10 | 1000 | -- | 55 | -- | 10.0 | -- | 76.0 | 28.00 | 0.030 |
| | L tropical W Atlantic | R Paraguaçu at Pedra do Cavalo | g 88-90 | 8 | 295 | -- | 151 | 56.0 | 45.0 | -- | -- | -- | -- |
| | | R Paraiba do Sul at Barra Mansa | g 88-90 | 25 | 12 | -- | 11 | -- | 7.0 | -- | 20.0 | -- | 0.076 |
| | La Plata | B Guarapiranga | g 88-90 | 4 | 95 | -- | 78 | -- | 26.0 | -- | -- | 5.00 | -- |
| Canada | Mackenzie | R Mackenzie mouth | o 94-96 | -- | -- | -- | -- | 1.5 | 3.9 | -- | 1.5 | 0.25 | -- |
| | | R Great Bear | g 91-92 | 1 | -- | -- | 1 | -- | 1.0 | 1.0 | 1.0 | -- | -- |
| | L subpolar NE Pacific | R Skeena | g 91 | -- | -- | -- | -- | -- | -- | -- | -- | -- | 0.011 |
| | U temperate NE Pacific | R Fraser at Hope | g 91 | -- | -- | -- | -- | -- | -- | -- | -- | -- | 0.010 |
| | Columbia | R Columbia df | o 95-97 | -- | -- | -- | -- | 0.3 | 1.6 | -- | 0.9 | 0.08 | -- |
| | Churchill | R Churchill | g 94-96 | 3 | -- | -- | 3 | -- | 1.0 | -- | -- | -- | -- |
| | Nelson | R Nelson at Gillam | g 94-96 | 9 | -- | -- | 2 | 1.0 | 2.0 | 1.0 | -- | -- | -- |
| | | R Saskatchewan mouth | o 94-96 | -- | -- | -- | -- | 1.1 | 2.7 | -- | 0.7 | 0.32 | -- |
| | | R Roseau | g 94-96 | 40 | 37 | 1.0 | 5 | -- | 3.0 | 1.0 | 1.0 | -- | -- |
| | Fundy & Maine | R St John mouth | o 93-95 | -- | -- | -- | -- | -- | 2.0 | -- | 2.0 | 1.00 | -- |
| Chile | Subtropical SE Pacific | R Maipo at El Manzano | g 88 | 430 | 380 | 26.0 | -- | -- | 3.0 | -- | -- | -- | -- |
| | Groundwater | G pozo Panamericana 1377 | g 88 | 7 | 2 | -- | -- | -- | 25.0 | -- | -- | -- | -- |
| Colombia | Magdalena | R Magdalena mouth | a 90 | 928 | -- | -- | -- | -- | -- | -- | -- | -- | -- |
| | | R Cauca at Juanchito | g 88 | 118 | 130000 | -- | 99 | -- | 77.0 | -- | -- | -- | -- |
| Cuba | Groundwater | G Aguada del Cura | g 94 | -- | 2 | -- | -- | -- | -- | -- | -- | -- | -- |
| Mexico | Colorado | R Colorado | g 94-96 | 30 | 82000 | -- | -- | -- | -- | -- | -- | -- | -- |
| | Grande de Santiago | L de Chapala | g 94-96 | 31 | 6601 | -- | -- | -- | -- | -- | -- | -- | -- |
| | | R Lerma | g 94-96 | 90 | 1100000 | -- | -- | -- | -- | -- | -- | -- | -- |
| | U tropical E Pacific | R Balsas at Balsas | g 94-96 | 1334 | 110000 | -- | -- | -- | -- | -- | -- | -- | -- |
| | Bravo del Norte (Grande) | R Bravo at Matamoros | g 94-96 | 80 | -- | -- | 95 | -- | 70.0 | -- | -- | -- | -- |
| | | R Bravo at Presa de la Amistad | g 94-96 | 16 | 34 | -- | -- | -- | -- | -- | -- | -- | -- |
| | | R Conchos at Ojinaga | g 94-96 | 105 | 7300 | -- | -- | -- | -- | -- | -- | -- | -- |
| | SW Gulf of Mexico | R Pánuco | g 94-96 | 133 | 303 | -- | 20 | -- | 50.0 | -- | -- | -- | -- |
| | | R Coatzacoalcos | g 94-96 | 42 | 23000 | -- | -- | -- | -- | -- | -- | -- | -- |
| | SE Gulf of Mexico | R Grijalva | g 94-96 | 45 | 33000 | -- | -- | -- | -- | -- | -- | -- | -- |
| | | R Usumacinta | g 94-96 | 77 | 5960 | -- | -- | -- | -- | -- | -- | -- | -- |
| | Groundwater | G pozo Aguascalientes | g 94-96 | 6 | 3 | -- | -- | -- | -- | -- | -- | -- | -- |
| | | G pozo Hacienda Tahdzibichen | g 94-96 | 3 | 6118 | -- | -- | -- | -- | -- | -- | -- | -- |
| United States | E Bering Sea | R Yukon at Pilot Station | g 94-95 | -- | 3 | -- | -- | -- | -- | 2.0 | -- | -- | -- |
| | Gulf of Alaska | R Talkeetna at Talkeetna | g 94-96 | -- | 11 | -- | -- | -- | -- | -- | -- | -- | -- |
| | Columbia | R Columbia at Bonneville | g 94 | -- | 2 | 1.0 | 3 | 1.0 | 2.0 | 1.0 | -- | -- | -- |
| | U subtropical NE Pacific | R Sacramento at Sacramento | g 94-96 | -- | 80 | 1.0 | 1 | 1.0 | 1.0 | 1.0 | -- | -- | -- |
| | Colorado | R Colorado at Hoover Dam | g 94-96 | -- | 1 | 2.0 | 2 | 2.0 | 2.0 | 2.0 | -- | -- | -- |
| | St Lawrence | R St Lawrence df | g 94 | -- | 2 | -- | -- | -- | -- | -- | -- | -- | -- |
| | | R Niagara at L Ontario | g 94 | -- | 17 | -- | -- | 2.0 | -- | -- | -- | -- | -- |
| | L temperate NW Atlantic | R Hudson at Troy | g 94 | -- | 389 | -- | -- | -- | -- | -- | -- | -- | -- |
| | | R Delaware at Trenton | g 94-96 | -- | 92 | 1.0 | 21 | -- | 2.0 | 1.0 | 2.0 | -- | -- |
| | Chesapeake Bay | R Susquehanna at Harrisburg | g 94-95 | -- | 53 | -- | -- | -- | -- | 5.0 | -- | -- | -- |
| | | R Potomac at Washington | g 94-96 | -- | 37 | -- | 2 | 2.0 | 2.0 | 1.0 | -- | -- | -- |
| | NE Gulf of Mexico | R Apalachicola at Chattahoochee | g 94-95 | -- | 58 | -- | -- | -- | -- | -- | -- | -- | -- |
| | Mississippi | R Mississippi mouth | o 93-95 | -- | -- | -- | -- | 2.1 | 9.8 | -- | 5.9 | 1.00 | -- |
| | | R Arkansas at Little Rock | g 94-96 | -- | 79 | 1.0 | 3 | 2.0 | 2.0 | 2.0 | -- | 1.00 | -- |
| | | R Missouri at Hermann | g 94-96 | -- | 939 | 2.0 | 2 | 2.0 | 2.0 | 3.0 | -- | -- | -- |

| Country | Basin | Station | Sources & years | TSS mg/l | F coli/ 100 ml | As µg/l | Zn µg/l | Cr µg/l | Cu µg/l | Ni µg/l | Pb µg/l | Cd µg/l | Hg µg/l |
|---|---|---|---|---|---|---|---|---|---|---|---|---|---|
| | | R Ohio at New Grand Chain | g 94-95 | -- | 252 | -- | -- | -- | -- | | 2.0 | -- | -- |
| | Bravo del Norte (Grande) | R Grande at Brownsville | g 94-96 | -- | 388 | 4.0 | 3 | 2.0 | 2.0 | 2.0 | | -- | -- |
| **AFRICA** | | | | | | | | | | | | | |
| Ghana | W Gulf of Guinea | R Pra at Daboase | g 94 TSS & HM g 91-93 | 66 | 12 | 428.0 | 55 | -- | -- | -- | -- | 37.00 | -- |
| | Volta | R Volta at B Kpong | g 94-95 HM g 91-93 | 5 | 0 | -- | 143 | -- | 43.0 | -- | -- | -- | -- |
| | | R White Volta at Nawuni | g 94-95 HM g 91-93 | 185 | 16 | -- | 133 | -- | -- | -- | -- | -- | -- |
| Mali | Niger | R Niger at Bamako | g 94-96 | -- | 40 | -- | -- | -- | -- | -- | -- | -- | -- |
| | | R Niger at Koulikoro (06) | g 94-96 | -- | 24 | -- | -- | -- | -- | -- | -- | -- | -- |
| | Groundwater | G forage Bamako (05) | g 94-96 | -- | 1 | -- | -- | -- | -- | -- | -- | -- | -- |
| | | G forage Nossombougou (8) | g 96 | -- | 10 | -- | -- | -- | -- | -- | -- | -- | -- |
| Morocco | SW Mediterranean | R Moulouya | g 94-96 | 25 | 5967 | -- | 18 | 6.0 | 9.0 | 89.0 | 72.0 | 1.00 | 5.426 |
| | U subtropical NE Atlantic | R Sebou at Kenitra | g 94-96 | 200 | 19000 | 6.0 | 55 | 4.0 | 16.0 | 129.0 | 62.0 | 2.00 | 0.208 |
| | | R Bou Regreg at Barrage Sidi Mohamed Ben Abdella | g 94-96 | 21 | 259 | 7.0 | 27 | 2.0 | 11.0 | -- | 9.0 | 1.00 | -- |
| | | R er Rbia at Sidi Daoui | g 94-96 | 50 | 81000 | 5.0 | 37 | 5.0 | 11.0 | 54.0 | 51.0 | 2.00 | 0.619 |
| | Groundwater | G puits artesien Ire 4/125 | g 94-96 | -- | 0 | -- | 63 | 2.0 | -- | -- | -- | -- | -- |
| | | G puits Mamora Ire 442/13 | g 94-96 | -- | 0 | 1.0 | 24 | 1.0 | 4.0 | -- | 3.0 | 1.00 | -- |
| Namibia | Orange | R Orange mouth | a 90 | 1111 | -- | -- | -- | -- | -- | -- | -- | -- | -- |
| Senegal | Senegal | R Senegal at St Louis | g 95 Fcoli = Fstrep | -- | 200 | -- | -- | -- | -- | -- | -- | -- | -- |
| | | R Senegal at Podor | g 95 | -- | 1800 | -- | -- | -- | -- | -- | -- | -- | -- |
| South Africa | Orange | R Orange mouth | a 90 | 1111 | -- | -- | -- | -- | -- | -- | -- | -- | -- |
| Sudan | Nile | R Blue Nile at Khartoum | g 91-92 | 1106 | -- | -- | -- | -- | -- | -- | -- | -- | -- |
| | | R White Nile at Jebel Aulia | g 91-92 | 77 | -- | -- | -- | -- | -- | -- | -- | -- | -- |
| Tanzania | U intertropical W Indian | R Ruvu at Mlandizi | g 92-93 | -- | 17 | -- | -- | -- | -- | -- | -- | -- | -- |
| **EUROPE** | | | | | | | | | | | | | |
| Austria | Danube | R Danube df | o 95-97 | -- | -- | -- | -- | 0.4 | 2.4 | -- | 1.0 | 0.01 | -- |
| | | R Inn df | o 95-97 | -- | -- | -- | -- | 0.8 | 2.6 | -- | 1.3 | 0.01 | -- |
| Belgium | Rhine | R Meuse df 94-96 | o 94-96 | -- | -- | -- | -- | -- | 2.1 | -- | 3.2 | -- | -- |
| | | R Meuse at Lanaye/Ternaaien | g 91-92 | 10 | 14023 | 3.0 | 77 | 8.0 | 18.0 | 6.0 | 7.0 | 1.00 | 0.045 |
| | SE North Sea | R Schelde (Escaut) df | o 94-96 | -- | -- | -- | -- | 2.4 | 12.0 | -- | 7.2 | 0.39 | -- |
| | | R Schelde at Doel | g 91 | 52 | 1069 | 7.0 | 68 | 10.0 | 16.0 | 8.0 | 6.0 | 1.00 | 0.000 |
| Czech R | Oder | R Oder (Odra) df | o 95-97 | -- | -- | -- | -- | 7.3 | 8.3 | -- | 14.1 | 2.55 | -- |
| | German Bight | R Elbe (Labe) df | o 95-97 | -- | -- | -- | -- | 2.6 | 9.5 | -- | 2.4 | 0.27 | -- |
| | Danube | R Morava df | o 95-97 | -- | -- | -- | -- | 3.2 | 3.9 | -- | 3.4 | 2.09 | -- |
| Finland | Gulf of Bothnia | R Tornionjoki (14100) | g 94-96 | 4 | -- | | | | | | | | |
| | | R Kokernaenjoki mouth | o 95-97 | -- | -- | -- | -- | 1.8 | 28.4 | -- | 1.0 | 0.10 | -- |
| | N Gulf of Finland | R Kalkkinen (4800) | g 94-96 | 1 | -- | -- | -- | -- | -- | -- | -- | -- | 0.013 |
| | | R Kymijoki (5610) | g 94-96 | 5 | -- | -- | -- | -- | -- | -- | -- | -- | 0.011 |
| France | La Manche | R Seine at Paris | g 91-93 | 39 | 140000 | 5.0 | 96 | 3.0 | 11.0 | 5.0 | 6.0 | 1.00 | 0.200 |
| | Loire | R Loire mouth | o 94-96 | -- | -- | -- | -- | -- | -- | -- | -- | 0.40 | -- |
| | | R Loire at Ingrandes | g 94 Fcoli g 91-93 | 41 | 4012 | 5.0 | 64 | 3.0 | 13.0 | -- | 3.0 | 318.00 | 0.246 |
| | Bay of Biscay | R Garonne mouth | o 94-96 | -- | -- | -- | -- | 2.9 | 5.3 | -- | 1.5 | 0.27 | -- |
| | | R Garonne at Valence d'Agen | g 94-95 | 27 | -- | -- | 14 | 1.0 | 12.0 | -- | 2.0 | -- | 0.000 |
| | N Mediterranean | R Rhône mouth | a 90 HM o 94 | 626 | -- | -- | -- | -- | 10.0 | -- | -- | 0.14 | -- |
| | | R Rhône at St Vallier | g 94 Fcoli g 91-93 | 19 | 3785 | 10.0 | 50 | 10.0 | 10.0 | 10.0 | 10.0 | 144.00 | 0.083 |
| Germany | German Bight | R Elbe mouth | a 90 HM o 95 | 37 | -- | -- | -- | 1.0 | 2.1 | -- | -- | 0.39 | -- |
| | | R Elbe at Geesthacht | g 88-90 | 21 | 1953 | -- | -- | -- | -- | -- | -- | 14.00 | 0.465 |
| | | R Weser mouth | o 95-97 TSS a 90 | 31 | -- | -- | -- | 2.0 | 4.9 | -- | 4.3 | 0.20 | -- |

| Country | Basin | Station | Sources & years | TSS mg/l | F coli/ 100 ml | As µg/l | Zn µg/l | Cr µg/l | Cu µg/l | Ni µg/l | Pb µg/l | Cd µg/l | Hg µg/l |
|---|---|---|---|---|---|---|---|---|---|---|---|---|---|
| | | R Weser at Intschede | g 88-90 Fcoli = tot coli ÷ 10 | -- | 1205 | -- | -- | -- | -- | -- | -- | 1.00 | 0.041 |
| | Rhine | R Rhine df | o 95-97 | -- | -- | -- | -- | 3.2 | 7.7 | -- | 3.2 | 0.20 | -- |
| | | R Rhine at Kleve/Bimmen | g 88-90 | -- | 3592 | 2.0 | 1154 | 9.0 | 11.0 | 7.0 | 8.0 | -- | 0.130 |
| | | R Rhine at Koblenz | g 88-90 | -- | -- | 2.0 | -- | 4.0 | 7.0 | 5.0 | 6.0 | -- | 0.968 |
| | | R Moselle at Koblenz | g 88-90 | -- | -- | 2.0 | 34 | 4.0 | 5.0 | 5.0 | 7.0 | -- | 0.251 |
| | Danube | R Danube df | o 95-97 | -- | -- | -- | -- | 1.0 | 3.4 | -- | 1.4 | -- | -- |
| | | R Danube at Jochenstein | g 88-90 | -- | 769 | -- | -- | -- | -- | -- | -- | -- | 0.176 |
| Greece | Ionian | R Akeloos mouth | o 93-95 | -- | -- | -- | -- | -- | -- | -- | -- | 0.20 | -- |
| | Aegean | R Axios mouth | o 93-95 | -- | -- | -- | -- | -- | -- | -- | -- | 0.23 | -- |
| | | R Strimonas mouth | o 93-95 | -- | -- | -- | -- | -- | -- | -- | -- | 0.23 | -- |
| Hungary | Danube | R Danube df | o 93-95 HM o 95 | -- | -- | -- | -- | 8.6 | 14.7 | -- | 12.0 | 2.00 | -- |
| | | R Danube at Budapest | g 91-92 | -- | 3346 | -- | -- | 5.0 | -- | -- | 14.0 | 1.00 | -- |
| | | R Tisza at Szolnok | g 91-92 | 42 | 47 | -- | 77 | -- | 22.0 | -- | 10.0 | -- | 0.357 |
| | Groundwater | G deep well Pest County | g 91 | -- | 0 | | | | | | | | |
| Italy | Ligurian & Tyrrhenian | R Arno mouth | o 93-95 HM o 92-94 | | | | | | | | | 0.32 | |
| | Adriatic | R Adige mouth | o 94-96 HM o 92-94 | -- | -- | -- | -- | -- | -- | -- | -- | 1.00 | -- |
| | | R Po mouth | a 90 | 278 | -- | -- | -- | -- | -- | -- | -- | -- | -- |
| Lithuania | Groundwater | G Juodkrante | g 94-96 | -- | -- | -- | 78 | -- | 2.0 | 1.0 | 1.0 | -- | -- |
| | | G Marijanpole | g 94-96 | -- | -- | -- | 154 | -- | 19.0 | 1.0 | 2.0 | -- | -- |
| | | G Panevezys | g 94-96 | -- | -- | -- | 467 | -- | 1.0 | 1.0 | 1.0 | -- | -- |
| | | G Varena | g 94-96 | -- | -- | -- | 56 | -- | 3.0 | 1.0 | 1.0 | -- | -- |
| Luxembourg | Rhine | R Sûre df | o 93-95 Pb o 95 | -- | -- | -- | -- | 1.3 | 3.0 | -- | 6.0 | 0.12 | -- |
| Netherlands | Rhine | L Ijsselmeer | g 94-95 Fcoli g 91-93 | 34 | 16 | -- | 16 | 3.0 | 3.0 | 3.0 | 2.0 | -- | 0.020 |
| | | R Rhine Ijssel arm | g 94-95 Fcoli g 91-93 | 25 | 111 | -- | 39 | 3.0 | 5.0 | 3.0 | 3.0 | -- | 0.026 |
| | | R Rhine Ijssel-Kampen | o 94-96 | -- | -- | -- | -- | 2.8 | 5.3 | -- | 3.0 | 0.09 | -- |
| | | R Rijn/Maas delta | o 94-96 | -- | -- | -- | -- | 2.9 | 3.4 | -- | 2.4 | 0.23 | -- |
| Norway | Norwegian Sea | R Altaelva at Alta | g 91-93 | -- | -- | -- | 2 | -- | 2.0 | -- | -- | -- | 0.002 |
| | | R Vefsna at Mosjøen | g 91-93 | -- | -- | -- | 4 | -- | 2.0 | -- | -- | -- | 0.002 |
| | | R Orkla at Vormstad | g 91-93 | -- | -- | -- | 27 | -- | 12.0 | -- | -- | -- | 0.002 |
| | | R Suldalslaagen at Sand | g 91-93 | -- | -- | -- | 3 | -- | -- | -- | -- | -- | 0.002 |
| | N Skagerrak & E Kattegat | R Otra mouth | o 95-97 | -- | -- | -- | -- | 0.5 | 0.6 | -- | 0.3 | 0.03 | -- |
| | | R Skienselva mouth | o 95-97 | -- | -- | -- | -- | 0.5 | 1.5 | -- | 0.1 | 0.03 | -- |
| | | R Numedalslaagen at Bommestad | g 91-93 | -- | -- | -- | 18 | -- | 5.0 | -- | 1.0 | -- | 0.002 |
| | | R Drammenselva mouth | o 95-97 | -- | -- | -- | -- | 0.5 | 1.0 | -- | 0.2 | 0.02 | -- |
| | | R Glåma mouth | o 95-97 | -- | -- | -- | -- | 0.5 | 2.3 | -- | 0.7 | 0.05 | -- |
| Poland | Wisla | R Wisla mouth | o 95-97 TSS a 90 | 79 | -- | -- | -- | 0.3 | 1.4 | -- | 0.9 | 0.09 | -- |
| | | R Wisla at Kiezmark | g 94-95 | 21 | 17000 | -- | 12 | 1.0 | 2.0 | 2.0 | 2.0 | -- | 0.154 |
| | | R Wisla at Warszawa | g 94-95 | 33 | 6000 | -- | 68 | 3.0 | 8.0 | 6.0 | 8.0 | 1.00 | 0.400 |
| | | R Wisla at Krakow | g 94-95 | 28 | 34000 | -- | 305 | 5.0 | 24.0 | 41.0 | 34.0 | 7.00 | 0.699 |
| | Oder | R Oder mouth | o 95-97 | -- | -- | -- | -- | 0.4 | 3.0 | -- | 1.7 | 0.11 | -- |
| | | R Oder (Odra) at Krajnik | g 94-95 | 23 | 32000 | -- | 23 | 1.0 | 4.0 | 3.0 | 3.0 | -- | 0.200 |
| | | R Oder (Odra) at Wroclaw | g 94-95 | 26 | 50000 | -- | 102 | 7.0 | 5.0 | 15.0 | 10.0 | 4.00 | 0.358 |
| | | R Oder (Odra) at Chalupki | g 94-95 | 22 | 110000 | -- | 234 | 7.0 | 6.0 | 15.0 | 7.0 | 4.00 | 0.356 |
| | Groundwater | G Pomeranian Lake District | g 94-95 | -- | -- | -- | 255 | -- | -- | -- | -- | -- | -- |
| Portugal | L temperate NE Atlantic | R Tejo at Santarem | g 91-92 | 12 | 1258 | 26.0 | 29 | 8.0 | 13.0 | -- | -- | -- | 0.139 |
| | U subtropical NE Atlantic | R Guadiana mouth | o 92-93 | -- | -- | -- | -- | -- | -- | -- | -- | 1.90 | -- |
| Slovakia | Danube | R Maly Dunaj (Danube) df | o 95-97 | -- | -- | -- | -- | 0.6 | 7.8 | -- | 1.8 | 0.03 | -- |
| | | R Hornad df | o 95-97 | -- | -- | -- | -- | 3.1 | -- | -- | 9.7 | 1.54 | -- |
| | | R Vah mouth | o 95-97 | -- | -- | -- | -- | 0.7 | 2.1 | -- | 0.9 | 0.08 | -- |
| Spain | L temperate NE Atlantic | R Duero df | o 95-97 | -- | -- | -- | -- | 0.0 | 0.2 | -- | -- | 0.70 | -- |
| | U subtropical NE Atlantic | R Guadalquivir mouth | o 94-96 | -- | -- | -- | -- | 4.5 | 4.4 | -- | 2.6 | 1.40 | -- |

| Country | Basin | Station | Sources & years | TSS mg/l | F coli/100 ml | As µg/l | Zn µg/l | Cr µg/l | Cu µg/l | Ni µg/l | Pb µg/l | Cd µg/l | Hg µg/l |
|---|---|---|---|---|---|---|---|---|---|---|---|---|---|
| | NW Mediterranean | R Ebro mouth | o 95-97 TSS a 90 | 86 | -- | -- | -- | 0.6 | 1.8 | -- | 0.6 | 0.11 | -- |
| Sweden | N Baltic | R Mörrumsan mouth | o 95-97 | -- | -- | -- | -- | 0.4 | 1.5 | -- | 0.4 | 0.01 | -- |
| | | R Ronneaan mouth | o 95-97 | -- | -- | -- | -- | 0.6 | 1.4 | -- | 0.3 | 0.02 | -- |
| | Gulf of Bothnia | R Dalalven mouth | o 95-97 | -- | -- | -- | -- | 0.3 | 1.4 | -- | 0.4 | 0.02 | -- |
| | | R Rane mouth | o 95-97 | -- | -- | -- | -- | 0.1 | 1.4 | -- | 0.2 | 0.01 | -- |
| Switzerland | Rhine | R Rhine at Basel | g 94-96 | 17 | -- | -- | 6 | 1.0 | 1.0 | 1.0 | 1.0 | -- | 0.012 |
| | | R Rhine at Diepoldsau | g 94-96 HM g 91-93 | 119 | -- | -- | -- | 49.0 | -- | -- | -- | -- | -- |
| | | R Aare at Brugg | g 94-96 HM g 91-93 | 19 | -- | -- | 8 | -- | 2.0 | -- | 1.0 | -- | -- |
| | N Mediterranean | R Rhone at Chancy | g 94-96 HM g 91-93 | 29 | -- | -- | -- | 38.0 | -- | -- | -- | -- | -- |
| | | R Rhone at Porte du Scex | g 94-96 | 119 | -- | -- | 11 | -- | 3.0 | -- | 3.0 | -- | 0.019 |
| United Kingdom | W North Sea | R Leven | g 94-96 | 3 | -- | -- | 4 | 1.0 | 1.0 | 1.0 | 2.0 | -- | -- |
| | | R Tweed above Galafoot | g 94-96 | 5 | -- | -- | 2 | 1.0 | 4.0 | 1.0 | 1.0 | -- | -- |
| | | R Trent at Nottingham | g 94-96 | 18 | -- | 2.0 | 47 | 4.0 | 10.0 | 27.0 | 7.0 | -- | 0.035 |
| | | R Thames at London | g 94-96 | 14 | -- | 1.0 | 22 | 2.0 | 6.0 | 5.0 | 3.0 | -- | 0.016 |
| | English Channel | R Exe at Exeter | g 94-96 | 10 | -- | 1.0 | 8 | 1.0 | 2.0 | 4.0 | 1.0 | -- | 0.016 |
| | Celtic Sea | R Severn mouth | o 94-96 | -- | -- | -- | -- | 2.1 | 5.3 | -- | 4.3 | 0.13 | -- |
| | | R Avon at Bristol | g 94-96 | 21 | -- | -- | 28 | 2.0 | 5.0 | 7.0 | 8.0 | 1.00 | 0.036 |
| | Irish Sea | R Dee | g 94-96 | 11 | -- | 2.0 | 16 | 2.0 | 2.0 | 4.0 | 3.0 | -- | 0.013 |
| | | R Mersey | g 94-96 | 11 | -- | 2.0 | 27 | 5.0 | 7.0 | 8.0 | 5.0 | -- | 0.088 |
| | | R Clyde mouth | o 94-96 | -- | -- | -- | -- | 17.0 | 6.1 | -- | 7.3 | 0.50 | -- |
| | Scottish & Irish Atlantic | R Carron | g 94-96 | 1 | -- | -- | 4 | 1.0 | 1.0 | 2.0 | 2.0 | 1.00 | 0.030 |
| | | Lower Bann mouth | o 95-97 | -- | -- | -- | -- | 1.0 | 3.3 | -- | 0.5 | 0.10 | -- |
| RUSSIAN FEDERATION | Volga | R Volga at Narimanov | g 94 | 18 | -- | -- | 36 | -- | -- | -- | -- | -- | -- |
| | | R Volga at B Cheboksarskoye (201) | g 94 | 14 | -- | -- | 14 | -- | -- | -- | -- | -- | -- |
| | | R Belaya at Ufa (203) | g 94 | 80 | -- | -- | 8 | -- | -- | -- | -- | -- | 0.008 |
| | Severnaya Dvina | R Severnaya Dvina at Ust-Pinega (213) | g 94 | 8 | -- | -- | 8 | -- | -- | -- | -- | -- | -- |
| | White Sea | R Mezen at Borovo | g 94 | 4 | -- | -- | 8 | -- | -- | -- | -- | -- | -- |
| | E Barents Sea | R Pechora at Nar'jan-Mar | g 94 | 6 | -- | -- | 10 | -- | -- | -- | -- | -- | -- |
| | Ob | R Ob at Salehard (011) | g 94 | 9 | -- | -- | 41 | -- | -- | -- | -- | -- | -- |
| | | R Tom at Tomsk (204) | g 94 | 18 | -- | -- | -- | -- | -- | -- | -- | -- | 0.104 |
| | | R Irtysh at Krasnyi Jar (205) | g 94 | 16 | -- | -- | 21 | -- | -- | -- | -- | -- | -- |
| | Yenisey | R Yenisei at Igarka (210) | g 94 | 2 | -- | -- | 65 | -- | -- | -- | -- | -- | -- |
| | | L Baikal mid-lake (024) | g 91-93 | 0 | -- | -- | 9 | -- | -- | -- | -- | -- | 0.018 |
| | | R Selenga mouth | g 94 | 33 | -- | -- | 2 | -- | -- | -- | 1.0 | -- | -- |
| | Lena | R Lena delta (028) | g 94 | 35 | -- | -- | 7 | -- | -- | -- | -- | -- | -- |
| | Kolyma | R Kolyma at Kolymskoe | g 94 | 21 | -- | -- | 9 | -- | -- | -- | -- | -- | -- |
| | Neva | L Onezhskoye (Onega) | g 94 | 0 | -- | -- | 14 | -- | -- | -- | 1.0 | -- | -- |
| | Don | R Don at Bagaevskij | g 94 | 137 | -- | -- | 9 | -- | -- | -- | -- | -- | -- |
| | Azov Sea | R Kuban mouth | g 94 | 44 | -- | -- | 10 | -- | -- | -- | -- | -- | -- |
| | Amur | R Amur mouth | g 94 | 18 | -- | -- | 13 | -- | -- | -- | -- | -- | -- |
| ASIA | | | | | | | | | | | | | |
| Bangladesh | Ganges | R Meghna at Ashuganj | g 94-95 Fcoli = tot coli. ÷ 10 | 39 | 76 | -- | -- | -- | -- | -- | -- | -- | -- |
| | | R Padma at Bheramara | g 94-95 Fcoli = tot coli ÷ 10 | 212 | 80 | -- | -- | -- | -- | -- | -- | -- | -- |
| | | R Brahmaputra at Fulchhari | g 94-95 Fcoli = tot coli ÷ 10 | 34 | 67 | -- | -- | -- | -- | -- | -- | -- | -- |
| | NE Bay of Bengal | R Karnaphuli at Rangunia | g 95 | 54 | -- | -- | -- | -- | -- | -- | -- | -- | -- |
| | | L Kaptai at Kaptai | g 94-95 Fcoli = tot coli ÷ 10 | 25 | 56 | -- | -- | -- | -- | -- | -- | -- | -- |
| | Groundwater | G tube well (07) | g 94-95 | 56 | 0 | -- | -- | -- | -- | -- | -- | -- | -- |
| | | G tube well (09) | g 94-95 | 21 | 0 | -- | -- | -- | -- | -- | -- | -- | -- |
| China | Bo Hai | R Huang (Yellow) at Jinan | g 94-96 | 8470 | 45000 | 9.0 | 50 | 6.0 | 1.0 | -- | 1.0 | -- | -- |
| | Chang | R Chang (Yangtze) at Wuhan | g 94-96 | 140 | 161 | -- | 25 | -- | 4.0 | -- | 19.0 | 2.00 | -- |
| | | L Tai | g 94-96 | -- | 6 | 2.0 | 31 | 8.0 | 3.0 | -- | 1.0 | -- | -- |
| | Xi | R Xi (Pearl) at Zhaoqing | g 94-96 | 65 | 650 | 9.0 | 42 | 1.0 | 8.0 | -- | 2.0 | -- | 0.078 |

| Country | Basin | Station | Sources & years | TSS mg/l | F coli/ 100 ml | As µg/l | Zn µg/l | Cr µg/l | Cu µg/l | Ni µg/l | Pb µg/l | Cd µg/l | Hg µg/l |
|---|---|---|---|---|---|---|---|---|---|---|---|---|---|
| | Chinese South China Sea | L Plover Cove (19), Hong Kong | g 94-96 | -- | 5 | -- | -- | -- | -- | -- | -- | -- | -- |
| India | Gulfs of Kachchh & Khambhat | R Sabarmati at Ahmedabad | g 95-96 | -- | 380000 | -- | -- | -- | -- | -- | -- | -- | -- |
| | | R Mahi at Vasad | g 95-96 | -- | 82 | -- | -- | -- | -- | -- | -- | -- | -- |
| | | R Narmada near Garudeshwar | g 95-96 | -- | 177 | -- | -- | -- | -- | -- | -- | -- | -- |
| | | R Tapti near Burhanpur | g 95-96 | 0 | 20 | -- | -- | -- | -- | -- | -- | -- | -- |
| | Malabar Coast | R Chaliyar at Kalpalli | g 95-96 | -- | 1239 | -- | -- | -- | -- | -- | -- | -- | -- |
| | | R Periyar near Alwaye | g 95-96 | -- | 1062 | -- | -- | -- | -- | -- | -- | -- | -- |
| | | R Kallada at Panamthottam | g 95-96 | -- | 2331 | -- | -- | -- | -- | -- | -- | -- | -- |
| | Coromandel Coast | R Cauvery near Musiri | g 95-96 | 0 | 2535 | -- | -- | -- | -- | -- | -- | -- | -- |
| | | R Pennar near Nellore | g 95-96 | 0 | -- | -- | -- | -- | -- | -- | -- | -- | -- |
| | Krishna | R Krishna near Vijayawada | g 95-96 | 0 | 89 | -- | -- | -- | -- | -- | -- | -- | -- |
| | | R Krishna at Gadwal | g 95-96 | 0 | 0 | -- | -- | -- | -- | -- | -- | -- | -- |
| | | R Tungabhadra at Ullanuru | g 95-96 | 0 | 918 | -- | -- | -- | -- | -- | -- | -- | -- |
| | | R Bhima near Takali | g 95-96 | -- | 11 | -- | -- | -- | -- | -- | -- | -- | -- |
| | Godavari | R Godavari near Polavaram | g 95-96 | 0 | 0 | -- | -- | -- | -- | -- | -- | -- | -- |
| | | R Godavari near Mancheral | g 95-96 | 0 | 0 | -- | -- | -- | -- | -- | -- | -- | -- |
| | | R Wainganga near Ashti | g 95-96 | -- | 7 | -- | -- | -- | -- | -- | -- | -- | -- |
| | NW Bay of Bengal | R Mahanadi mouth | a 90 | 909 | -- | -- | -- | -- | -- | -- | -- | -- | -- |
| | | R Subarnarekha at Jamshedpur | g 95-96 | -- | 708 | -- | -- | -- | -- | -- | -- | -- | -- |
| | Ganges | R Ganga df | a 90 | 1130 | -- | -- | -- | -- | -- | -- | -- | -- | -- |
| | Groundwater | G well Ahmedabad | g 95-96 | -- | 3 | -- | -- | -- | -- | -- | -- | -- | -- |
| | | G well Baroda | g 95 | -- | 3 | -- | -- | -- | -- | -- | -- | -- | -- |
| | | G well Kalpalli | g 95-96 | -- | 1379 | -- | -- | -- | -- | -- | -- | -- | -- |
| | | G well Eluru (Alwaye) | g 95-96 | -- | 526 | -- | -- | -- | -- | -- | -- | -- | -- |
| | | G well Musiri | g 95-96 | 0 | 815 | -- | -- | -- | -- | -- | -- | -- | -- |
| | | G well Vijayawada | g 95-96 | -- | 97 | -- | -- | -- | -- | -- | -- | -- | -- |
| Indonesia | U intertropical E Indian (Java) | R Garang | g 91-93 | 97 | 280000 | -- | 67 | 48.0 | -- | 15.0 | -- | -- | -- |
| | | R Garang | g 94 | -- | -- | -- | -- | -- | 20.0 | -- | -- | -- | -- |
| | Java Sea & Karimata Strait (Sumatra) | R Musi at Palembang | g 91-93 | 77 | 4327 | -- | 211 | 30.0 | 22.0 | -- | -- | 10.00 | -- |
| | Java Sea (Java) | R Banjir Kanal | g 91-93 | 105 | 740000 | -- | 154 | 30.0 | 22.0 | -- | 66.0 | 6.00 | -- |
| | | R Banjir Kanal | g 94 | 58 | -- | -- | 253 | -- | 31.0 | 11.0 | -- | 10.00 | -- |
| | | R Sunter | g 91-93 | 125 | 850000 | -- | 295 | 31.0 | 27.0 | 16.0 | 74.0 | 10.00 | -- |
| | | R Sunter | g 94 | 288 | -- | -- | 202 | -- | 43.0 | 112.0 | -- | 13.00 | -- |
| | | R Citarum | g 91-93 | 215 | 570000 | -- | 113 | 28.0 | 46.0 | 35.0 | 128.0 | 12.00 | -- |
| | | R Citarum | g 94 | 236 | -- | -- | 3 | 50.0 | -- | -- | -- | 18.00 | -- |
| | | R Surabaya | g 91-93 | 297 | 78000 | -- | 87 | -- | 29.0 | -- | 99.0 | 8.00 | -- |
| | | B Saguling | g 91-93 | 54 | 12000 | -- | 135 | 28.0 | 25.0 | -- | 112.0 | 9.00 | -- |
| | | B Saguling | g 94 | 282 | -- | -- | -- | -- | -- | -- | -- | -- | -- |
| | Groundwater (Java) | G well Senayan Jakarta | g 91-93 | 23 | -- | -- | 156 | -- | -- | -- | -- | -- | -- |
| | | G well Pulogadung Jakarta | g 91-93 | 13 | -- | -- | 504 | -- | -- | -- | -- | -- | -- |
| | | G well Cibeureum | g 91-93 | 5 | 0 | -- | 194 | -- | 18.0 | -- | 194.0 | 11.00 | -- |
| Iran | Shatt-al-Arab | Shatt-al-Arab mouth | a 90 | 1364 | -- | -- | -- | -- | -- | -- | -- | -- | -- |
| | Groundwater | G well 7 Tabriz | g 91-92 | 0 | 0 | -- | -- | -- | -- | -- | -- | -- | -- |
| Iraq | Shatt-al-Arab | Shatt-al-Arab mouth | a 90 | 1364 | -- | -- | -- | -- | -- | -- | -- | -- | -- |
| Japan | L temperate NW Pacific (Honshu) | R Kyu-Kitakami at Kanomata | g 92-93 | 19 | 91 | -- | 15 | 4.0 | -- | 10.0 | -- | -- | -- |
| | | R Tone at Tone-Ozeki | g 94-96 | 21 | 1993 | 4.0 | 21 | -- | 6.0 | 8.0 | 5.0 | 5.00 | -- |
| | | R Sagami at Samukawa | g 94-96 | 145 | 1086 | -- | 5 | -- | -- | -- | -- | -- | 0.000 |
| | | R Kiso at Inuyama | g 94-96 | 4 | 225 | 1.0 | 9 | 1.0 | 1.0 | 1.0 | 1.0 | -- | -- |
| | U subtropical NW Pacific (Honshu) | L Biwa south center | g 94-96 | 10 | 1 | -- | -- | -- | -- | -- | -- | -- | -- |
| | | R Yodo at Hirakata Bridge | g 91-92 Fcoli = tot coli ÷ 10 | 19 | 2279 | -- | 13 | -- | 10.0 | -- | -- | -- | -- |
| | U subtropical NW Pacific (Shikoku) | R Yoshino at Takase | g 94-96 | 3 | 54 | -- | 5 | -- | -- | -- | -- | -- | -- |
| | U subtropical NW Pacific (Kyushu) | R Chikugo at Senoshita | g 94-96 | 11 | 217 | | | | | | | | |
| | | R Kuma at Yokoishi | g 94-95 | 5 | 103 | -- | 8 | -- | -- | -- | -- | -- | -- |
| | E Sea of Japan (Honshu) | R Shinano at Kyuzogoya | g 94-95 | 26 | 200 | -- | 10 | 1.0 | 4.0 | -- | 6.0 | -- | -- |

| Country | Basin | Station | Sources & years | TSS mg/l | F coli/ 100 ml | As µg/l | Zn µg/l | Cr µg/l | Cu µg/l | Ni µg/l | Pb µg/l | Cd µg/l | Hg µg/l |
|---|---|---|---|---|---|---|---|---|---|---|---|---|---|
| | E Sea of Japan (Hokkaido) | R Ishikari at Ishikari | g 94-96 Fcoli = tot coli ÷ 10 | 34 | 904 | 1.0 | 6 | 551.0 | -- | -- | 1.0 | -- | -- |
| | Groundwater (Honshu) | G Suginami filtration plant | g 94-96 | 1 | 1 | -- | 6 | -- | -- | -- | -- | -- | -- |
| Jordan | Rift Valley | R Zarqua at King Talal Dam | g 94-96 | 60 | 1858 | -- | 24 | 26.0 | 13.0 | 7.0 | 87.0 | 14.00 | -- |
| | Groundwater | G Awajan well 23 | g 96 | -- | 1 | -- | 18 | 17.0 | 8.0 | -- | 1.0 | -- | -- |
| | | G Azraq well 2 | g 95-96 | -- | 2 | -- | 4 | 1.0 | -- | 29.0 | 6.0 | -- | -- |
| | | G Rahme well Wadi Araba | g 94-96 | 120 | 2 | -- | 65 | 16.0 | 7.0 | -- | 2.0 | -- | -- |
| Kazakhstan | Aral Sea | R Syr Darya mouth | a 90 | 1364 | -- | -- | -- | -- | -- | -- | -- | -- | -- |
| Korea, R | E Yellow Sea | R Han GEMS | g 94-96 | 5 | 260 | -- | 9 | -- | 9.0 | -- | -- | -- | -- |
| Malaysia | Strait of Malacca | R Klang | g 92 | 311 | 430000 | 24.0 | 41 | 17.0 | -- | -- | 28.0 | 10.00 | 0.002 |
| | | R Linggi | g 92 | 420 | 160000 | 12.0 | 24 | 36.0 | -- | -- | 41.0 | 10.00 | 0.002 |
| | | R Sekudai | g 92 | 163 | 120000 | 1.0 | 91 | -- | 214.0 | -- | 60.0 | -- | 0.001 |
| Myanmar | Irrawaddy | R Irrawaddy | a 90 | 607 | -- | -- | -- | -- | -- | -- | -- | -- | -- |
| Pakistan | Indus | R Indus at Kotri | g 94-96 | 3417 | 2216 | -- | -- | 257.0 | 167.0 | -- | -- | -- | -- |
| | | R Ravi below Lahore | g 94-96 | 304 | 12144 | -- | -- | -- | -- | -- | -- | -- | -- |
| | | R Ravi above Lahore | g 94-96 | 348 | 19000 | -- | -- | 13.0 | -- | -- | -- | -- | -- |
| | | R Chenab Gujra branch | g 94-96 | 467 | 16000 | -- | -- | -- | -- | -- | -- | -- | -- |
| | Groundwater | G Lahore | g 94-96 | 1 | 0 | -- | -- | -- | -- | -- | -- | -- | -- |
| Philippines | Philippine South China Sea (Luzon) | B La Mesa | g 94-95 | 7 | 659 | -- | -- | -- | -- | -- | -- | -- | -- |
| | L subtropical NW Pacific | R Cagayan | g 94-96 Fcoli = tot coli ÷ 10 | 68 | 540 | | | | | | | | |
| Thailand | Chao Phraya | R Chao Phraya at Bangkok | g 91-93 | -- | 230000 | -- | 175 | 38.0 | 23.0 | -- | 53.0 | 4.00 | 0.416 |
| | | R Chao Phraya below Nakhon Sawan | g 91-93 | -- | 54000 | -- | 157 | 8.0 | 5.0 | -- | 16.0 | 1.00 | 0.217 |
| | | R Prasak at Kaeng Khoi | g 91-92 | -- | 12980 | -- | 152 | 9.0 | 10.0 | -- | 25.0 | 1.00 | 0.000 |
| | E Gulf of Thailand | R Bang at Pa Kong | g 91-93 | -- | 18000 | -- | 206 | 67.0 | 23.0 | -- | 115.0 | 10.00 | 0.192 |
| | Mekong | R Mun at Ubon Ratchathani | g 91-93 | -- | 2067 | -- | 92 | 3.0 | 13.0 | -- | 20.0 | -- | 0.400 |
| Turkey | S Black Sea | R Yesilirmak mouth | o 95-97 HM o 95 | -- | -- | -- | -- | -- | 7.0 | -- | -- | -- | -- |
| | | R Sakarya mouth | o 95-97 | -- | -- | -- | -- | 3.3 | 12.3 | -- | 10.3 | 3.33 | -- |
| | Aegean | R Gediz mouth | o 95-97 HM o 95 | -- | -- | -- | -- | 5.0 | -- | -- | 12.0 | -- | -- |
| Uzbekistan | Aral Sea | R Amu Darya mouth | a 90 | 3275 | -- | -- | -- | -- | -- | -- | -- | -- | -- |
| Viet Nam | Gulf of Tonkin | R Hong (Red) mouth | a 90 | 1057 | -- | -- | -- | -- | -- | -- | -- | -- | -- |
| | Mekong | R Mekong mouth | a 90 | 294 | -- | -- | -- | -- | -- | -- | -- | -- | -- |
| **PACIFIC** | | | | | | | | | | | | | |
| Australia | Murray-Darling | R Murray-Darling mouth Atlas | a 90 | 3797 | -- | -- | -- | 5.0 | 6.3 | -- | 2.5 | -- | -- |
| | W Coral Sea | R Burdekin mouth | a 90 | 355 | -- | -- | -- | -- | -- | -- | -- | -- | -- |
| Papua New Guinea | Bismarck & Solomon Seas | R Sepik mouth | a 90 | 68 | -- | -- | -- | -- | -- | -- | -- | -- | -- |
| | N Coral Sea | R Fly mouth | a 90 | 816 | -- | -- | -- | -- | -- | -- | -- | -- | -- |

**Notes**

This table gives data on suspended solids, microbial pollution, and arsenic and heavy metals. Countries use different methods for measuring pollutants, so the data are not strictly comparable. All data are annual mean values at the location indicated in the Station column. Data are for the years indicated in the Sources & years column.

Basin = drainage basin. Surface water basins are defined in Appendix 6. Groundwater is treated as if it were a single basin. Parts of basin names are abbreviated as follows: E = east; L = lower; N = north; S = south; U = upper; W = west.

Station = monitoring station (the point where the data are collected).

Sources & years = data sources, applicable years, and exceptions. Sources are indicated as follows:

a  National Water Research Institute (1996)

e  Eurostat *et al.* (1995)

g  Global Environmental Monitoring System (GEMS)/WATER data summaries and database (UNEP & WHO GEMS/Water Collaborating Centre 1988-1990, 1991-1993, 1999)

o  Organisation for Economic Co-operation and Development (1997 & 1999)

oc  OECD Centre for Co-operation with the Economies in Transition (1996)

When a single year is given, all data are for that year (unless otherwise noted in the Sources column). When a period is given (e.g., 94-96), all data are annual averages for that period (unless otherwise noted in the Sources column). If data for one of the indicators are for a different year, the indicator, source and year are noted after the indicator code. For example—o 95-97 TSS a 90—means that data are from OECD and are for 1995-1997, except for total suspended solids (TSS) which are from National Water Research Institute and are for 1990. The codes used are: F coli = fecal coliforms; HM = arsenic and heavy metals; Pb = lead; TSS = total suspended solids.

TSS = total suspended solids in milligrams per liter (mg/l).

F coli = microbial pollution, measured by the mean number of fecal coliforms per 100 milliliters (ml). Where fecal streptococci are measured instead (indicated in the Sources & years column), they are treated as equivalent to fecal coliforms. Where total coliforms are measured instead (also indicated in the Sources & years column), the number has been divided by 10 to approximate an equivalent level of fecal coliforms.

As = arsenic in micrograms per liter ($\mu$g/l).

Zn = zinc in micrograms per liter ($\mu$g/l).

Cr = chromium in micrograms per liter ($\mu$g/l).

Cu = copper in micrograms per liter ($\mu$g/l).

Ni = nickel in micrograms per liter ($\mu$g/l).

Pb = lead in micrograms per liter ($\mu$g/l).

Cd = cadmium in micrograms per liter ($\mu$g/l).

Hg = mercury in micrograms per liter ($\mu$g/l).

GEMS/WATER data on arsenic and on heavy metals except mercury, originally recorded in milligrams, were converted to micrograms. Since data recorded as 0.000 mg may mask quite high levels in micrograms (e.g., 0.5 $\mu$g of cadmium), they were treated as null values (--).

Cadmium values for the Loire in France reported to GEMS/WATER are much higher than for other stations in France, and much higher than the values reported to OECD. They have been excluded from the score for the Loire (Table 15).

# Table 17. Air Index; Global Atmosphere

| Country | CO₂ 000 mt C | CO₂/ha kg C | CO₂/p kg C | GG score | ODS year | ODS mt odp | ODS/ha g odp | ODS/p g odp | ODS score | GA score | LA score | Air index |
|---|---|---|---|---|---|---|---|---|---|---|---|---|
| **AMERICAS** | | | | | | | | | | | | |
| Antigua & Barbuda | 92 | 2091 | 1384 | 45 | 98 | 27 | 613.6 | 403.9 | 0 | 0 | -- | 0 |
| Argentina | 37629 | 135 | 1055 | 54 | 98 | 1894 | 6.8 | 52.4 | 59 | 54 | 47 | 47 |
| Bahamas | 475 | 342 | 1633 | 40 | 98 | 60 | 43.2 | 202.6 | 20 | 20 | -- | 20 |
| Barbados | 245 | 5698 | 918 | 57 | 98 | 25 | 581.4 | 93.2 | 43 | 43 | -- | 43 |
| Belize | 106 | 46 | 473 | 76 | 97 | 5 | 2.2 | 22.3 | 82 | 76 | -- | 76 |
| Bolivia | 2952 | 27 | 380 | 81 | 97 | 47 | 0.4 | 6 | 95 | 81 | -- | 80* |
| Brazil | 78666 | 92 | 481 | 76 | 97 | 10315 | 12.1 | 63 | 55 | 55 | 51 | 51 |
| Canada | 133890 | 134 | 4425 | 12 | 98 | 989 | 1 | 32.4 | 74 | 12 | 65 | 12 |
| Chile | 15884 | 210 | 1086 | 53 | 98 | 1090 | 14.4 | 73.5 | 51 | 51 | 23 | 23 |
| Colombia | 18551 | 163 | 463 | 77 | 98 | 1262 | 11.1 | 30.9 | 75 | 75 | -- | 75 |
| Costa Rica | 1355 | 265 | 362 | 82 | 98 | 344 | 67.3 | 89.5 | 44 | 44 | 40 | 40 |
| Cuba | 6854 | 618 | 619 | 69 | 97 | 685 | 61.8 | 61.9 | 55 | 55 | 60 | 55 |
| Dominica | 22 | 293 | 311 | 84 | 97 | 2 | 26.7 | 28.2 | 77 | 77 | -- | 77 |
| Dominican R | 3609 | 741 | 446 | 78 | 98 | 509 | 104.5 | 61.8 | 55 | 55 | -- | 55 |
| Ecuador | 5549 | 196 | 465 | 77 | 98 | 369 | 13 | 30.3 | 76 | 76 | 47 | 47 |
| El Salvador | 1489 | 708 | 252 | 87 | 98 | 199 | 94.6 | 33 | 74 | 74 | -- | 74 |
| Grenada | 50 | 1471 | 539 | 73 | -- | -- | -- | -- | -- | 73 | -- | 73 |
| Guatemala | 2097 | 193 | 199 | 90 | 97 | 382 | 35.1 | 36.3 | 71 | 71 | 33 | 33 |
| Guyana | 279 | 13 | 331 | 83 | 98 | 30 | 1.4 | 35.3 | 72 | 72 | -- | 72 |
| Haiti | 379 | 137 | 48 | 98 | -- | -- | -- | -- | -- | 80* | -- | 80 |
| Honduras | 1129 | 101 | 189 | 90 | 98 | 116 | 10.3 | 18.9 | 85 | 85 | 35 | 35 |
| Jamaica | 2928 | 2664 | 1164 | 51 | 98 | 222 | 202 | 87.5 | 45 | 45 | -- | 45 |
| Mexico | 99893 | 510 | 1060 | 53 | P98 | 5491 | 28 | 57.3 | 57 | 53 | 17 | 17 |
| Nicaragua | 831 | 64 | 178 | 91 | 98 | 41 | 3.2 | 8.5 | 93 | 91 | 18 | 18 |
| Panama | 2089 | 277 | 767 | 62 | 98 | 361 | 47.8 | 130.5 | 34 | 34 | 25 | 25 |
| Paraguay | 1041 | 26 | 205 | 90 | 98 | 113 | 2.8 | 21.6 | 83 | 83 | -- | 80* |
| Peru | 7818 | 61 | 321 | 84 | 98 | 337 | 2.6 | 13.6 | 89 | 84 | -- | 80* |
| St Kitts & Nevis | 28 | 1077 | 712 | 64 | 97 | 4 | 153.8 | 101.7 | 40 | 40 | -- | 40 |
| St Lucia | 54 | 871 | 364 | 82 | 98 | 6 | 96.8 | 39.9 | 68 | 68 | -- | 68 |
| St Vincent & Grenadines | 36 | 923 | 323 | 84 | 98 | 2 | 51.3 | 17.8 | 86 | 84 | -- | 80* |
| Suriname | 576 | 35 | 1398 | 45 | -- | -- | -- | -- | -- | 45 | -- | 45 |
| Trinidad & Tobago | 5995 | 11686 | 4695 | 11 | 98 | 215 | 419.1 | 167.6 | 26 | 11 | -- | 11 |
| United States | 1480881 | 1582 | 5449 | 6 | P98 | 32228 | 34.4 | 117.6 | 36 | 6 | 53 | 6 |
| Uruguay | 1469 | 83 | 450 | 77 | 98 | 218 | 12.3 | 66.3 | 53 | 53 | -- | 53 |
| Venezuela | 51144 | 561 | 2245 | 32 | P97 | 5752 | 63.1 | 252.5 | 15 | 15 | -- | 15 |
| **AFRICA** | | | | | | | | | | | | |
| Algeria | 25974 | 109 | 884 | 58 | 98 | 1785 | 7.5 | 59.3 | 56 | 56 | -- | 56 |
| Angola | 1409 | 11 | 120 | 94 | -- | -- | -- | -- | -- | 80* | -- | 80 |
| Benin | 203 | 18 | 36 | 98 | 97 | 14 | 1.2 | 2.5 | 98 | 98 | -- | 80* |
| Botswana | 916 | 16 | 595 | 70 | 97 | 16 | 0.3 | 10.4 | 92 | 70 | -- | 70 |
| Burkina Faso | 265 | 10 | 24 | 99 | 98 | 37 | 1.4 | 3.3 | 97 | 97 | -- | 80* |
| Burundi | 61 | 22 | 10 | 99 | 98 | 64 | 23 | 9.9 | 92 | 92 | -- | 80* |
| Cameroon | 647 | 14 | 46 | 98 | 97 | 286 | 6 | 20.5 | 84 | 84 | -- | 80* |
| Cape Verde | 33 | 82 | 83 | 96 | -- | -- | -- | -- | -- | 80* | -- | 80 |
| Central African R | 66 | 1 | 19 | 99 | 97 | 0 | 0 | 0 | 100 | 99 | -- | 80* |
| Chad | 30 | 0 | 4 | 100 | 98 | 38 | 0.3 | 5.2 | 96 | 96 | -- | 80* |
| Comoros | 18 | 81 | 28 | 99 | 98 | 4 | 17.9 | 6.1 | 95 | 95 | -- | 80* |
| Congo, DR | 637 | 3 | 13 | 99 | -- | -- | -- | -- | -- | 80* | -- | 80 |
| Congo, R | 496 | 15 | 183 | 91 | 95 | 15 | 0.4 | 5.9 | 95 | 91 | -- | 80* |
| Côte d'Ivoire | 3568 | 111 | 254 | 87 | 97 | 158 | 4.9 | 11.2 | 91 | 87 | -- | 80* |
| Djibouti | 100 | 43 | 162 | 92 | -- | -- | -- | -- | -- | 80* | -- | 80 |
| Egypt | 29829 | 298 | 461 | 77 | 98 | 2816 | 28.1 | 42.7 | 66 | 66 | -- | 66 |
| Equatorial Guinea | 167 | 60 | 397 | 80 | -- | -- | -- | -- | -- | 80 | -- | 80 |
| Eritrea | -- | -- | -- | -- | -- | -- | -- | -- | -- | -- | -- | -- |
| Ethiopia | 930 | 8 | 16 | 99 | 98 | 62 | 0.6 | 1 | 99 | 99 | -- | 80* |
| Gabon | 909 | 34 | 799 | 60 | 98 | 14 | 0.5 | 12 | 90 | 60 | -- | 60 |
| Gambia | 59 | 52 | 50 | 97 | 98 | 11 | 9.7 | 9 | 93 | 93 | -- | 80* |
| Ghana | 1106 | 46 | 59 | 97 | 98 | 54 | 2.3 | 2.8 | 98 | 97 | 49 | 49 |
| Guinea | 298 | 12 | 41 | 98 | 98 | 42 | 1.7 | 5.7 | 95 | 95 | -- | 80* |
| Guinea-Bissau | 63 | 17 | 55 | 97 | -- | -- | -- | -- | -- | 80* | -- | 80 |
| Kenya | 1813 | 31 | 64 | 97 | 97 | 534 | 9.2 | 18.8 | 85 | 85 | -- | 80* |
| Lesotho | -- | -- | -- | -- | 98 | 3 | 1 | 1.5 | 99 | 80* | -- | 80 |
| Liberia | 91 | 8 | 38 | 98 | -- | -- | -- | -- | -- | 80* | -- | 80 |
| Libyan Arab J | 11386 | 65 | 2185 | 33 | 97 | 1234 | 7 | 236.8 | 16 | 16 | -- | 16 |
| Madagascar | 328 | 6 | 22 | 99 | 97 | 132 | 2.2 | 9 | 93 | 93 | -- | 80* |
| Malawi | 198 | 17 | 20 | 99 | 98 | 184 | 15.5 | 17.8 | 86 | 86 | -- | 80* |
| Mali | 131 | 1 | 13 | 99 | 97 | 115 | 0.9 | 11 | 91 | 91 | -- | 80* |

| Country | CO$_2$ 000 mt C | CO$_2$/ha kg C | CO$_2$/p kg C | GG score | ODS year | ODS mt odp | ODS/ha g odp | ODS/p g odp | ODS score | GA score | LA score | Air index |
|---|---|---|---|---|---|---|---|---|---|---|---|---|
| Mauritania | 805 | 8 | 327 | 84 | 97 | 7 | 0.1 | 2.8 | 98 | 84 | -- | 80* |
| Mauritius | 465 | 2279 | 410 | 79 | 98 | 45 | 220.6 | 39.4 | 68 | 68 | -- | 68 |
| Morocco | 8702 | 195 | 324 | 84 | 97 | 1295 | 29 | 48.2 | 61 | 61 | -- | 61 |
| Mozambique | 303 | 4 | 16 | 99 | 96 | 43 | 0.5 | 2.4 | 98 | 98 | -- | 80* |
| Namibia | -- | -- | -- | -- | 97 | 33 | 0.4 | 20.3 | 84 | 80* | -- | 80 |
| Niger | 302 | 2 | 31 | 98 | 97 | 61 | 0.5 | 6.2 | 95 | 95 | -- | 80* |
| Nigeria | 22435 | 243 | 216 | 89 | 98 | 5476 | 59.3 | 51.5 | 59 | 59 | -- | 59 |
| Rwanda | 135 | 51 | 23 | 99 | -- | -- | -- | -- | -- | 80* | -- | 80 |
| São Tomé & Principe | 21 | 219 | 152 | 92 | -- | -- | -- | -- | -- | 80* | -- | 80 |
| Senegal | 855 | 43 | 97 | 95 | 98 | 138 | 7 | 15.3 | 88 | 88 | -- | 80* |
| Seychelles | 54 | 1200 | 720 | 64 | 97 | 2 | 44.4 | 26.7 | 79 | 64 | -- | 64 |
| Sierra Leone | 127 | 18 | 29 | 99 | -- | -- | -- | -- | -- | 80* | -- | 80 |
| Somalia | 4 | 0 | 0 | 100 | -- | -- | -- | -- | -- | 80* | -- | 80 |
| South Africa | 86532 | 709 | 2232 | 32 | 98 | 1022 | 8.4 | 26 | 79 | 32 | 42 | 32 |
| Sudan | 988 | 4 | 36 | 98 | 97 | 315 | 1.3 | 11.4 | 91 | 91 | -- | 80* |
| Swaziland | 109 | 63 | 118 | 94 | 97 | 18 | 10.4 | 19.5 | 84 | 84 | -- | 80* |
| Tanzania | 673 | 7 | 21 | 99 | 97 | 225 | 2.4 | 7.2 | 94 | 94 | -- | 80* |
| Togo | 219 | 39 | 51 | 97 | 95 | 50 | 8.8 | 12.3 | 90 | 90 | -- | 80* |
| Tunisia | 4541 | 278 | 493 | 75 | 98 | 974 | 59.5 | 104.3 | 39 | 39 | -- | 39 |
| Uganda | 297 | 12 | 15 | 99 | 98 | 14 | 0.6 | 0.7 | 99 | 99 | -- | 80* |
| Zambia | 670 | 9 | 78 | 96 | 97 | 63 | 0.8 | 7.3 | 94 | 94 | -- | 80* |
| Zimbabwe | 4968 | 127 | 443 | 78 | 97 | 1051 | 26.9 | 93.7 | 42 | 42 | -- | 42 |
| EUROPE | | | | | | | | | | | | |
| Albania | 432 | 150 | 138 | 93 | -- | -- | -- | -- | -- | 80* | -- | 80 |
| Austria | 16557 | 1974 | 2044 | 34 | 98 | 454 | 54.1 | 55.8 | 58 | 34 | 66 | 34 |
| Belarus | 16757 | 807 | 1619 | 40 | 98 | 268 | 12.9 | 26 | 79 | 40 | 58 | 40 |
| Belgium | 28127 | 9216 | 2778 | 25 | 98 | 565 | 185.1 | 55.7 | 58 | 25 | 58 | 25 |
| Bosnia & Herzegovina | 1211 | 237 | 344 | 83 | 91 | 145 | 28.4 | 33.1 | 73 | 73 | -- | 73 |
| Bulgaria | 13452 | 1213 | 1603 | 40 | 98 | 39 | 3.5 | 4.7 | 96 | 40 | 28 | 28 |
| Croatia | 5190 | 918 | 1157 | 51 | 98 | 121 | 21.4 | 27 | 78 | 51 | 59 | 51 |
| Czech R | 33495 | 4247 | 3252 | 20 | 97 | 19 | 2.4 | 1.8 | 99 | 20 | 58 | 20 |
| Denmark | 15380 | 3569 | 2926 | 23 | 98 | 294 | 68.2 | 55.8 | 58 | 23 | 62 | 23 |
| Estonia | 5151 | 1142 | 3559 | 18 | 98 | 57 | 12.6 | 39.9 | 68 | 18 | -- | 18 |
| Finland | 15307 | 453 | 2977 | 23 | 98 | 287 | 8.5 | 55.7 | 58 | 23 | 66 | 23 |
| France | 92878 | 1684 | 1588 | 40 | P98 | 9184 | 166.5 | 156.5 | 29 | 29 | 55 | 29 |
| Germany | 227364 | 6369 | 2771 | 25 | 98 | 4573 | 128.1 | 55.7 | 58 | 25 | 61 | 25 |
| Greece | 22027 | 1669 | 2084 | 34 | P98 | 1277 | 96.8 | 120.5 | 36 | 34 | 43 | 34 |
| Hungary | 15874 | 1706 | 1563 | 41 | 98 | 123 | 13.2 | 12.2 | 90 | 41 | 59 | 41 |
| Iceland | 572 | 56 | 2091 | 34 | 98 | 7 | 0.7 | 25.4 | 80 | 34 | 69 | 34 |
| Ireland | 9936 | 1414 | 2717 | 26 | 98 | 205 | 29.2 | 55.7 | 58 | 26 | 60 | 26 |
| Italy | 111323 | 3695 | 1940 | 36 | P97 | 8004 | 265.7 | 139.5 | 32 | 32 | 27 | 27 |
| Latvia | 2224 | 344 | 904 | 57 | 97 | 43 | 6.7 | 17.5 | 86 | 57 | -- | 57 |
| Lithuania | 4027 | 618 | 1087 | 53 | 98 | 111 | 17 | 30.1 | 76 | 53 | 52 | 52 |
| Luxembourg | 2154 | 8381 | 5164 | 8 | 98 | 23 | 89.5 | 54.5 | 58 | 8 | 60 | 8 |
| Macedonia, FYR | 2917 | 1135 | 1468 | 43 | 98 | 80 | 31.1 | 40 | 68 | 43 | -- | 43 |
| Malta | 480 | 15000 | 1259 | 48 | 98 | 144 | 4500 | 375.3 | 2 | 2 | -- | 2 |
| Moldova | 2835 | 841 | 648 | 68 | 98 | 40 | 11.9 | 9.1 | 93 | 68 | -- | 68 |
| Netherlands | 44256 | 10836 | 2834 | 25 | P98 | 17082 | 4182.7 | 1089.5 | 0 | 0 | 57 | 0 |
| Norway | 18470 | 570 | 4202 | 14 | 98 | 52 | 1.6 | 11.8 | 91 | 14 | 58 | 14 |
| Poland | 95413 | 2952 | 2466 | 29 | 97 | 443 | 13.7 | 11.4 | 91 | 29 | 63 | 29 |
| Portugal | 13522 | 1470 | 1371 | 46 | 98 | 550 | 59.8 | 55.7 | 58 | 46 | 50 | 46 |
| Romania | 29390 | 1233 | 1303 | 47 | 98 | 2670 | 112 | 118.8 | 36 | 36 | 43 | 36 |
| Slovakia | 10046 | 2050 | 1870 | 37 | 97 | 10 | 2 | 1.9 | 98 | 37 | 65 | 37 |
| Slovenia | 4109 | 2029 | 2059 | 34 | 97 | 9 | 4.4 | 4.5 | 96 | 34 | -- | 34 |
| Spain | 66584 | 1316 | 1681 | 39 | P97 | 7354 | 145.3 | 185.6 | 23 | 23 | 51 | 23 |
| Sweden | 12945 | 288 | 1462 | 43 | 98 | 495 | 11 | 55.8 | 58 | 43 | 73 | 43 |
| Switzerland | 11102 | 2689 | 1531 | 42 | 97 | 8 | 1.9 | 1.1 | 99 | 42 | 63 | 42 |
| Ukraine | 100427 | 1664 | 1967 | 35 | 98 | 3949 | 65.4 | 77.6 | 49 | 35 | -- | 35 |
| United Kingdom | 142096 | 5821 | 2427 | 30 | P98 | 4630 | 189.7 | 78.9 | 48 | 30 | 55 | 30 |
| Yugoslavia | 13416 | 1313 | 1262 | 48 | 91 | 1142 | 111.8 | 108.8 | 38 | 38 | -- | 38 |
| RUSSIAN FEDERATION | 390616 | 229 | 2645 | 27 | P97 | 15848 | 9.3 | 107.3 | 38 | 27 | 48 | 27 |
| ASIA | | | | | | | | | | | | |
| Afghanistan | 299 | 5 | 14 | 99 | -- | -- | -- | -- | -- | 80* | -- | 80 |
| Armenia | 758 | 254 | 213 | 89 | -- | -- | -- | -- | -- | 80* | -- | 80 |
| Azerbaijan | 8693 | 1004 | 1138 | 51 | 97 | 228 | 26.3 | 29.8 | 76 | 51 | -- | 51 |
| Bahrain | 4052 | 58725 | 6956 | 0 | 98 | 22 | 318.8 | 37 | 70 | 0 | -- | 0 |
| Bangladesh | 6683 | 464 | 54 | 97 | 97 | 841 | 58.4 | 6.9 | 94 | 94 | -- | 80* |
| Bhutan | 107 | 23 | 55 | 97 | -- | -- | -- | -- | -- | 80* | -- | 80 |
| Brunei Darussalam | 1475 | 2561 | 4783 | 10 | 98 | 65 | 112.8 | 206.3 | 19 | 10 | -- | 10 |
| Cambodia | 140 | 8 | 13 | 99 | -- | -- | -- | -- | -- | 80* | -- | 80 |

| Country | CO$_2$ 000 mt C | CO$_2$/ha kg C | CO$_2$/p kg C | GG score | ODS year | ODS mt odp | ODS/ha g odp | ODS/p g odp | ODS score | *GA score* | *LA score* | Air index |
|---|---|---|---|---|---|---|---|---|---|---|---|---|
| China | 917997 | 956 | 734 | 63 | P97 | 98053 | 102.2 | 78.4 | 49 | 49 | 22 | 22 |
| Cyprus | 1489 | 1610 | 1951 | 36 | 98 | 207 | 223.8 | 268.4 | 13 | 13 | -- | 13 |
| Georgia | 1205 | 173 | 235 | 88 | 98 | 27 | 3.9 | 5.3 | 96 | 88 | -- | 80* |
| India | 279899 | 851 | 290 | 85 | P97 | 31855 | 96.9 | 33 | 74 | 74 | 25 | 25 |
| Indonesia | 65103 | 342 | 320 | 84 | 98 | 4484 | 23.5 | 21.7 | 83 | 83 | -- | 80* |
| Iran | 78585 | 481 | 1216 | 50 | 98 | 8938 | 54.7 | 135.9 | 33 | 33 | -- | 33 |
| Iraq | 24916 | 568 | 1176 | 51 | -- | -- | -- | -- | -- | 51 | -- | 51 |
| Israel | 15581 | 7398 | 2659 | 27 | P97 | 14138 | 6713.2 | 2412.6 | 0 | 0 | -- | 0 |
| Japan | 316164 | 8369 | 2508 | 29 | P97 | 8414 | 222.7 | 66.8 | 53 | 29 | 55 | 29 |
| Jordan | 3831 | 429 | 625 | 69 | 97 | 1239 | 138.9 | 202.3 | 20 | 20 | -- | 20 |
| Kazakhstan | 33471 | 123 | 2044 | 34 | -- | -- | -- | -- | -- | 34 | -- | 34 |
| Korea, DPR | 68794 | 5707 | 2994 | 23 | 97 | 509 | 42.2 | 22.1 | 82 | 23 | -- | 23 |
| Korea, R | 116701 | 11757 | 2552 | 28 | 97 | 15273 | 1538.7 | 334 | 7 | 7 | 53 | 7 |
| Kuwait | 13653 | 7662 | 7882 | 0 | 97 | 616 | 345.7 | 355.6 | 4 | 0 | 38 | 0 |
| Kyrgyzstan | 1776 | 89 | 384 | 81 | -- | -- | -- | -- | -- | 80* | -- | 80 |
| Lao PDR | 96 | 4 | 19 | 99 | 92 | 4 | 0.2 | 0.9 | 99 | 99 | -- | 80* |
| Lebanon | 4300 | 4135 | 1368 | 46 | 98 | 602 | 578.8 | 188.6 | 22 | 22 | -- | 22 |
| Malaysia | 35710 | 1083 | 1702 | 39 | 98 | 2639 | 80 | 123.3 | 35 | 35 | -- | 35 |
| Maldives | 83 | 2767 | 315 | 84 | 98 | 1 | 33.3 | 3.7 | 97 | 84 | -- | 80* |
| Mongolia | 2103 | 13 | 829 | 59 | 98 | 20 | 0.1 | 7.8 | 94 | 59 | -- | 59 |
| Myanmar | 2318 | 34 | 53 | 97 | 98 | 52 | 0.8 | 1.2 | 99 | 97 | -- | 80* |
| Nepal | 553 | 38 | 25 | 99 | 97 | 31 | 2.1 | 1.4 | 99 | 99 | -- | 80* |
| Oman | 4850 | 228 | 2104 | 34 | 94 | 414 | 19.5 | 199.4 | 20 | 20 | -- | 20 |
| Pakistan | 25588 | 321 | 178 | 91 | 97 | 2089 | 26.2 | 14.5 | 88 | 88 | -- | 80* |
| Philippines | 20249 | 675 | 283 | 86 | 97 | 2991 | 99.7 | 41.9 | 66 | 66 | 39 | 39 |
| Qatar | 10348 | 9407 | 18197 | 0 | 98 | 135 | 122.7 | 233.1 | 17 | 0 | -- | 0 |
| Saudi Arabia | 72616 | 338 | 3728 | 17 | 96 | 3440 | 16 | 182.7 | 23 | 17 | -- | 17 |
| Singapore | 21909 | 353371 | 6393 | 0 | 98 | 123 | 1983.9 | 35.4 | 72 | 0 | -- | 0 |
| Sri Lanka | 2096 | 319 | 115 | 94 | 98 | 314 | 47.9 | 17 | 86 | 86 | -- | 80* |
| Syrian Arab R | 13011 | 703 | 870 | 58 | 97 | 2805 | 151.5 | 187.6 | 22 | 22 | -- | 22 |
| Tajikistan | 1519 | 106 | 256 | 87 | -- | -- | -- | -- | -- | 80* | -- | 80 |
| Thailand | 56992 | 1111 | 954 | 56 | 98 | 4593 | 89.5 | 76.2 | 49 | 49 | 39 | 39 |
| Turkey | 54042 | 697 | 852 | 59 | 97 | 4656 | 60.1 | 73.4 | 51 | 51 | 52 | 51 |
| Turkmenistan | 8397 | 172 | 1984 | 35 | 96 | 31 | 0.6 | 7.5 | 94 | 35 | -- | 35 |
| United Arab Emirates | 21697 | 2595 | 9404 | 0 | 97 | 693 | 82.9 | 300.4 | 10 | 0 | -- | 0 |
| Uzbekistan | 27936 | 624 | 1204 | 50 | 97 | 58 | 1.3 | 2.5 | 98 | 50 | -- | 50 |
| Viet Nam | 11595 | 350 | 152 | 92 | 97 | 792 | 23.9 | 10.4 | 92 | 92 | -- | 80* |
| Yemen | 4411 | 84 | 271 | 86 | 97 | 416 | 7.9 | 25.5 | 80 | 80 | -- | 80 |
| **PACIFIC** | | | | | | | | | | | | |
| Australia | 86336 | 112 | 4709 | 11 | 98 | 26 | 0 | 1.4 | 99 | 11 | 66 | 11 |
| Fiji | 206 | 113 | 262 | 87 | 97 | 14 | 7.7 | 17.8 | 86 | 86 | -- | 80* |
| New Zealand | 8492 | 314 | 2258 | 32 | 97 | 83 | 3.1 | 22.1 | 82 | 32 | 80 | 32 |
| Papua New Guinea | 659 | 14 | 146 | 93 | 97 | 39 | 0.8 | 8.7 | 93 | 93 | -- | 80* |
| Samoa | 36 | 127 | 209 | 90 | 97 | 5 | 17.6 | 29.1 | 77 | 77 | -- | 77 |
| Solomon Is | 44 | 15 | 109 | 94 | 97 | 2 | 0.7 | 4.9 | 96 | 94 | -- | 80* |
| Tonga | 33 | 440 | 338 | 83 | -- | -- | -- | -- | -- | 80* | -- | 80 |
| Vanuatu | 17 | 14 | 96 | 95 | -- | -- | -- | -- | -- | 80* | -- | 80 |

**Notes**

The **Air index** is the lower of a global atmosphere index (*GA score*), covered in this table, and a local air quality index (*LA score*), covered in Table 18

The global atmosphere index is the lower score of two indicators (column heading in parentheses):

Greenhouse gases, represented by carbon dioxide emissions per person (GG score).

Use—production or consumption, whichever is higher—of ozone depleting substances per person (ODS score).

CO$_2$ = total carbon dioxide emissions from fossil-fuel burning, cement manufacture, and gas flaring, in thousands of metric tons of carbon (000 mt C). Data are for 1997—except for R Congo which are for 1996 (because the 1997 figure of 72,000 mt is much lower than previous years)—and are from the Carbon Dioxide Information Analysis Center (CDIAC) (Marland *et al.* 2000). CDIAC derives its estimates from the energy statistics of the United Nations Statistical Division (supplemented with gas flaring data from the US Department of Energy's Energy Information Administration) and cement production estimates compiled by the US Department of Interior's Bureau of Mines.

CO$_2$/ha = carbon dioxide emissions per hectare of total (land + inland waters) area, in kilograms of carbon (kg C).

CO$_2$/p = carbon dioxide emissions per person, in kilograms of carbon (kg C).

GG score = the score for carbon dioxide emissions per person. The performance criteria are shown in Table 17a. The top of the fair band matches the point below which carbon emissions per person must fall to keep atmospheric concentrations at less than double the pre-industrial level. Dangerous climate change could occur above this level (Corner House 1997). To stay below it, global emissions would have to be cut from 6.6 billion metric tons of carbon in 1997 to between 3.7 and 4.9 billion metric tons. If the intermediate amount of 4.3 billion were shared equally by the world population of 10.8 billion projected for 2050 (UN's "medium variant" projection [United Nations Population Division 1998c]), each person would have an emissions allowance of just under 400 kilograms.

ODS year = the applicable year of the data on ozone depleting substances (ODS). The letter P before the year indicates that the data for that country refer to production. Data for all other countries refer to consumption. Production was chosen whenever it was higher than consumption, as it better reflects the reliance on ODS of the countries concerned. Consumption means net consumption, after subtracting amounts that were destroyed.

Consumption by members of the European Community (EC), which is reported for the EC as a whole and not for individual countries, was allocated to those countries (Austria, Belgium, Denmark, Finland, France, Germany, Greece, Ireland, Italy, Luxembourg, Netherlands, Portugal, Spain, Sweden, United Kingdom) on the basis of population. Production data are reported for individual countries.

ODS = annual use of ozone depleting substances (ODS) in metric tons of ozone depleting potential (mt odp). ODS include chlorofluorocarbons (CFCs), halons, other fully halogenated CFCs, carbon tetrachloride, methyl chloroform, HCFCs, and methyl bromide. These substances are used in automobile and truck air conditioning units, domestic and commercial refrigeration and air conditioning/heat pump equipment, aerosol products, portable fire extinguishers, pre-polymers, and insulation boards, panels and pipe covers (Ozone Secretariat, United Nations Environment Programme 1997). Data are from Ozone Secretariat, United Nations Environment Programme (1999) and United Nations Environment Programme (1998).

ODS/ha = use of ozone depleting substances per hectare of total (land + inland waters) area in grams of ozone depleting potential (g odp).

ODS/p = use of ozone depleting substances per person in grams of ozone depleting potential (g odp).

ODS score = the score for use of ozone depleting substances per person. The performance criteria are shown in Table 17a. The top of the good band (zero consumption/production) corresponds to international agreements to eliminate ODS.

| band | top point on scale | $CO_2$ emissions per person (kilograms carbon) | use of ozone depleting substances per person (grams) |
|------|------|------|------|
| good | 100 | 0 | 0 |
| fair | 80 | 400 | 25 |
| medium | 60 | 800 | 50 |
| poor | 40 | 1600 | 100 |
| bad | 20 | 3200 | 200 |
| base | 0 | 6400 | 400 |

**Table 17a Performance criteria for carbon dioxide emissions and use (consumption or production) of ozone depleting substances.**

\* A score with an asterisk has been reduced in accordance with the insufficient data rule. To prevent high scores resulting merely from lack of data, a good score is allowed only if it is based on all applicable components (data in an indicator, indicators in an index), and a fair score only if it is based on at least half the components. Good and fair scores (100-61) based on fewer than half the applicable components have been reduced to 60. Good scores (100-81) based on more than half but not all the applicable components have been reduced to 80.

# Table 18. Local Air Quality

| Country | City | Site | Year | SO₂ mean | SO₂ days | NO₂ mean | NO₂ days | O₃ days | CO days | SPM mean | PM10 mean | Pb mean | *LA score* | Based on |
|---|---|---|---|---|---|---|---|---|---|---|---|---|---|---|
| AMERICAS | | | | | | | | | | | | | | |
| Argentina | Córdoba | 1I | 91 | -- | -- | 102 | 70 | -- | -- | 324 | -- | -- | 24 | SPM |
| | | 2B | 91 | -- | -- | 93 | -- | -- | -- | 128 | -- | -- | 37 | NO₂ |
| | | 3R | 91 | -- | -- | 97 | 90 | -- | -- | 101 | -- | -- | 28 | NO₂ |
| | | ave | | | | | | | | | | | 30 | |
| | Mendoza | 1I | 94 | 2.6 | -- | 22.6 | -- | -- | -- | -- | -- | 0.2 | 77 | NO₂ |
| | | 2C | 94 | 2.6 | -- | 84.6 | -- | -- | -- | -- | -- | 0.4 | 39 | NO₂ |
| | | 3R | 94 | 2.6 | -- | 20.7 | -- | -- | -- | -- | -- | 0.2 | 79 | NO₂ |
| | | ave | | | | | | | | | | | 65 | |
| | average | | | | | | | | | | | | 47 | |
| Brazil | Osasco | 1M | 95 | 23 | -- | -- | -- | -- | -- | 131 | 95 | -- | 42 | PM10 |
| | Porto Alegre | 1I | 96 | 40 | -- | -- | -- | -- | -- | 110.4 | -- | -- | 55 | SPM |
| | | 2B | 96 | 30.5 | -- | -- | -- | -- | -- | 81.2 | -- | -- | 60* | SPM |
| | | ave | | | | | | | | | | | 57 | |
| | Rio de Janeiro | 1I | 96 | -- | -- | -- | -- | -- | -- | 274 | -- | -- | 30 | SPM |
| | | 2C | 96 | -- | -- | -- | -- | -- | -- | 136 | -- | -- | 50 | SPM |
| | | 3BR | 96 | -- | -- | -- | -- | -- | -- | 82 | -- | -- | 60* | SPM |
| | | ave | | | | | | | | | | | 47 | |
| | São Paulo | 1M | 95 | 17 | 19 | -- | -- | -- | 1 | -- | 90 | -- | 44 | PM10 |
| | | 2C | 95 | 34 | 24 | -- | -- | -- | 50 | 116 | 89 | -- | 44 | PM10 |
| | | 3BR | 95 | 16 | 2 | -- | -- | -- | 28 | -- | 61 | -- | 56 | PM10 |
| | | ave | | | | | | | | | | | 48 | |
| | Vitória | 2C | 96 | 18 | -- | -- | -- | -- | -- | 66 | -- | -- | 71 | SPM |
| | | 3C | 96 | 12 | -- | -- | -- | -- | -- | 67 | -- | -- | 70 | SPM |
| | | 4C | 96 | 20 | -- | -- | -- | -- | -- | 154 | -- | -- | 46 | SPM |
| | | ave | | | | | | | | | | | 62 | |
| | average | | | | | | | | | | | | 51 | |
| Canada | Hamilton | 0 | 95o | 21.0 | -- | 36.3 | -- | -- | -- | 65.6 | -- | 0.03 | 64 | NO₂ |
| | Montréal | 0 | 95o | 10.1 | -- | 34.6 | -- | -- | -- | 34.1 | -- | 0.025 | 65 | NO₂ |
| | Vancouver | 0 | 95o | 10.6 | -- | 34.7 | -- | -- | -- | 24.2 | -- | 0.01 | 65 | NO₂ |
| | average | | | | | | | | | | | | 65 | |
| Chile | Santiago | 1C | 95 | 34 | 3 | 75 | 96 | 14 | 21 | -- | 95 | -- | 26 | NO₂ |
| | | 2C | 95 | 23 | 0 | 86 | 104 | 0 | 20 | -- | 91 | -- | 23 | NO₂ |
| | | 3R | 95 | -- | -- | -- | -- | 114 | -- | -- | 73 | -- | 20 | O₃ |
| | average | | | | | | | | | | | | 23 | |
| Costa Rica | Heredia | 1C | 96 | 55.2 | 5 | 28 | 0 | 0 | 5 | -- | 76.5 | -- | 49 | PM10 |
| | San José | 2C | 96 | 40.4 | 2 | 41 | 0 | 0 | 6 | 271.7 | 97.3 | -- | 30 | SPM |
| | | 3C | 96 | 24.6 | 2 | 40 | 0 | 0 | 5 | 246.7 | 54.2 | -- | 33 | SPM |
| | | 4C | 96 | 40 | 2 | 52 | 0 | 0 | 17 | 242 | 55 | 0.38 | 33 | SPM |
| | | ave | | | | | | | | | | | 32 | |
| | average | | | | | | | | | | | | 40 | |
| Cuba | Habana | 1C | 94 | 0.6 | -- | 4.9 | -- | -- | -- | -- | -- | -- | 60* | NO₂ |
| Ecuador | Guayaquil | 1C | 95 | -- | -- | -- | -- | -- | -- | 127.3 | -- | -- | 52 | SPM |
| | Quito | 1I | 95 | 39.6 | 0 | -- | -- | -- | -- | 196 | -- | -- | 38 | SPM |
| | | 2B | 95 | 22.3 | 0 | -- | -- | -- | -- | 154 | 56.9 | -- | 46 | SPM |
| | | ave | | | | | | | | | | | 42 | |
| | average | | | | | | | | | | | | 47 | |
| Guatemala | Guatemala | 1I | 97 | -- | -- | 87 | -- | -- | -- | 370 | 111 | 0.1 | 19 | SPM |
| | | 2C | 96 | -- | -- | 52 | 0 | 0 | -- | 322 | 94 | 0.08 | 24 | SPM |
| | | 3R | 97 | -- | -- | 45 | -- | -- | -- | 110 | 40 | 0.22 | 56 | SPM |
| | average | | | | | | | | | | | | 33 | |
| Honduras | Tegucigalpa | 1C | 97 | -- | -- | 48 | -- | -- | -- | 495 | 124 | 0.11 | 12 | SPM |
| | | 2R | 96 | -- | -- | 14 | 0 | 30 | -- | -- | 22 | -- | 59 | O₃ |
| | average | | | | | | | | | | | | 35 | |
| Mexico | Guadalajara | 0 | 97o[S96] | 27.5 | -- | 210.3 | -- | -- | -- | -- | 107.7 | -- | 14 | NO₂ |
| | México | 0 | 97o | 41.1 | -- | 239.8 | -- | -- | -- | -- | 148.0 | -- | 10 | NO₂ |
| | | 2I | 96 | 55.1 | 20 | 73.4 | 81 | 154 | 0 | 365 | 126.4 | 0.455 | 12 | O₃ |
| | | 3B | 96 | 52.5 | 23 | 80.9 | 132 | 254 | 5 | 180 | 60.6 | 0.236 | 0 | O₃ |
| | | 5R | 96 | 36.7 | 0 | 79 | 107 | 246 | 3 | 227 | 56.7 | 0.173 | 0 | O₃ |
| | average of 2I, 3B, 5R | | | | | | | | | | | | 4 | |
| | Monterrey | 0 | 97o | 21.9 | -- | 103.9 | -- | -- | -- | -- | 67.2 | -- | 34 | NO₂ |
| | average | | | | | | | | | | | | 17 | |
| Nicaragua | Managua | 1C | 97 | -- | -- | 42 | -- | -- | -- | 393 | 79 | -- | 18 | SPM |
| | | 2R | 96 | -- | -- | 27 | 0 | 120 | -- | -- | 44 | 0 | 19 | O₃ |
| | average | | | | | | | | | | | | 18 | |
| Panama | Panamá | 1I | 97 | -- | -- | 40 | -- | -- | -- | 70 | -- | 1.2 | 36 | Pb |
| | | 2C | 96 | -- | -- | 59 | 0 | -- | -- | -- | 99 | 2.7 | 13 | Pb |

| Country | City | | Site | Year | SO₂ mean | SO₂ days | NO₂ mean | NO₂ days | O₃ days | CO days | SPM mean | PM10 mean | Pb mean | *LA* score | Based on |
|---|---|---|---|---|---|---|---|---|---|---|---|---|---|---|---|
| | | | 3R | 97 | -- | -- | 46 | -- | -- | -- | -- | 67 | 1.7 | 26 | Pb |
| | | average | | | | | | | | | | | | 25 | |
| United States | Chicago | | 0 | 97o | 12.1 | -- | 52.0 | -- | -- | -- | -- | 25.9 | 0.053 | 54 | NO₂ |
| | Denver | | 0 | 97o | 13.0 | -- | 54.3 | -- | -- | -- | -- | 20.9 | -- | 53 | NO₂ |
| | Los Angeles | | 0 | 97o | 6.0 | -- | 63.6 | -- | -- | -- | -- | 38.0 | 0.034 | 48 | NO₂ |
| | New York | | 0 | 97o | 17.0 | -- | 55.9 | -- | -- | -- | -- | 27.9 | 0.045 | 52 | NO₂ |
| | Washington-Baltimore | | 0 | 97o | -- | -- | 43.2 | -- | -- | -- | -- | 22.0 | 0.009 | 58 | NO₂ |
| | | average | | | | | | | | | | | | 53 | |
| Venezuela | Caracas | | 1I | 95 | -- | -- | 56 | -- | -- | -- | 53 | -- | 0.8 | 48 | Pb |
| | | | 2B | 95 | -- | -- | 79 | -- | -- | -- | 63 | -- | 1.7 | 26 | Pb |
| | | | 3R | 95 | -- | -- | 37 | -- | -- | -- | 43 | -- | 0.7 | 52 | Pb |
| | | average | | | | | | | | | | | | 42 | |
| **AFRICA** | | | | | | | | | | | | | | | |
| Ghana | Accra | | 1I | 90 | -- | -- | -- | -- | -- | -- | 149 | -- | -- | 47 | SPM |
| | | | 2R | 90 | -- | -- | -- | -- | -- | -- | 130 | -- | -- | 51 | SPM |
| | | average | | | | | | | | | | | | 49 | |
| South Africa | Cape Town | | 2C | 95 | -- | -- | 72 | 160 | 22 | -- | -- | 27 | -- | 11 | NO₂ |
| | Durban | | 1I | 95 | 53 | -- | -- | -- | -- | -- | -- | -- | -- | 59 | SO₂ |
| | | | 2B | 94 | 26 | -- | -- | -- | -- | -- | -- | -- | 0.61 | 56 | Pb |
| | | | 3R | 95 | 10 | -- | -- | -- | -- | -- | -- | -- | -- | 60* | SO₂ |
| | | ave | | | | | | | | | | | | 58 | |
| | Johannesburg | | 1C | 94 | -- | -- | 39 | 0 | 0 | 0 | -- | -- | 0.42 | 61 | NO₂ |
| | | | 2B | 95 | 21.5 | -- | 39.7 | -- | -- | -- | 106.3 | -- | 1.28 | 34 | Pb |
| | | | 3R | 95 | 17.2 | -- | 23.2 | -- | 14 | -- | 62.7 | -- | 0.27 | 72 | SPM |
| | | ave | | | | | | | | | | | | 56 | |
| | | average | | | | | | | | | | | | 42 | |
| **EUROPE** | | | | | | | | | | | | | | | |
| Austria | Graz | | 0 | 97o | 10.9 | -- | 34.0 | -- | -- | -- | 46.0 | -- | -- | 66 | NO₂ |
| | Linz | | 0 | 97o | 6.9 | -- | 27.0 | -- | -- | -- | 36.2 | -- | -- | 73 | NO₂ |
| | Wien [score based | | 0 | 97o[N96] | 14.0 | -- | 42.0 | -- | -- | -- | 43.9 | -- | -- | 59 | NO₂ |
| | on 0; 1I, 2C, 3R | | 1I | 96 | 17 | 1 | 32 | 0 | -- | 0 | -- | -- | -- | 68 | NO² |
| | shown here for | | 2C | 96 | 17 | 0 | -- | -- | 14 | 0 | -- | 36 | -- | 71 | PM10 |
| | comparison] | | 3R | 96 | 19 | 1 | 33 | 0 | 27 | 0 | -- | 36 | -- | 61 | O₃ |
| | | average | | | | | | | | | | | | 66 | |
| Belarus | Minsk | | 1I | 95 | -- | -- | 30 | -- | -- | -- | 50 | -- | -- | 60* | NO₂ |
| | | | 3C | 95 | -- | -- | 26 | -- | -- | -- | -- | -- | -- | 60* | NO₂ |
| | | | 5R | 95 | -- | -- | 54 | -- | -- | -- | 21 | -- | -- | 53 | NO₂ |
| | | average | | | | | | | | | | | | 58 | |
| Belgium | Antwerpen | | 0 | 97o[P95] | 23.1 | -- | 52.9 | -- | -- | -- | 75.5 | -- | 0.06 | 54 | NO₂ |
| | Brussel/Bruxelles | | 0 | 97o[P95] | 12.1 | -- | 47.8 | -- | -- | -- | 78.2 | -- | 0.099 | 56 | NO₂ |
| | Liège | | 0 | 97o[P95] | 12.0 | -- | 37.2 | -- | -- | -- | 82.3 | -- | 0.11 | 63 | NO₂ |
| | | average | | | | | | | | | | | | 58 | |
| Bulgaria | Plovdiv | | 1I | 96 | 79 | -- | 48 | -- | -- | -- | 155.8 | -- | 0.2 | 45 | SPM |
| | | | 2C | 96 | 111.4 | -- | 72.1 | -- | -- | -- | 352.3 | -- | 0.51 | 21 | SPM |
| | | | 3R | 96 | 100.8 | -- | 44.3 | -- | -- | -- | 156.7 | -- | 0.225 | 40 | SO₂ |
| | | ave | | | | | | | | | | | | 35 | |
| | Sofija | | 1I | 96 | 32.1 | -- | 144.5 | -- | -- | -- | 188.3 | -- | 0.175 | 24 | NO₂ |
| | | | 2C | 96 | 38.7 | -- | 207.8 | -- | -- | -- | 307.5 | -- | 0.45 | 14 | NO₂ |
| | | | 3R | 96 | 26.2 | -- | 125.7 | -- | -- | -- | 185 | -- | 0.125 | 29 | NO₂ |
| | | ave | | | | | | | | | | | | 22 | |
| | | average | | | | | | | | | | | | 28 | |
| Croatia | Zagreb | | 1I | 95 | 40 | 3 | -- | -- | -- | -- | -- | -- | -- | 60* | SO₂ |
| | | | 2C | 95 | 30 | 0 | -- | -- | -- | -- | 78 | -- | 0.52 | 59 | Pb |
| | | | 3R | 95 | 24 | 0 | -- | -- | -- | -- | 63 | -- | 0.52 | 59 | Pb |
| | | average | | | | | | | | | | | | 59 | |
| Czech R | Brno | | 0 | 97 [P95] | 12.8 | -- | 26.9 | -- | -- | -- | 50.2 | -- | 0.06 | 73 | NO₂ |
| | Hradec Králove | | 0 | 97o[P94] | 15.8 | -- | 36.0 | -- | -- | -- | 30.2 | -- | 0.051 | 64 | NO₂ |
| | Olomouc | | 0 | 97o [P95] | 34.0 | -- | 53.9 | -- | -- | -- | 39.3 | -- | 0.043 | 53 | NO₂ |
| | Ostrava | | 0 | 97o[P95] | 26.9 | -- | 44.2 | -- | -- | -- | 65.5 | -- | 0.068 | 58 | NO₂ |
| | Praha | | 0 | 97o[P95] | 23.8 | -- | 79.3 | -- | -- | -- | 58.8 | -- | 0.059 | 40 | NO₂ |
| | Ustí nad Labem | | 0 | 97o[P95] | 24.0 | -- | 38.7 | -- | -- | -- | 53.2 | -- | 0.029 | 61 | NO₂ |
| | | average | | | | | | | | | | | | 58 | |
| Denmark | Ålborg | | 0 | 97o | 2.8 | -- | 34.0 | -- | -- | -- | 53.9 | -- | 0.013 | 66 | NO₂ |
| | København | | 0 | 97o | 4.6 | -- | 42.9 | -- | -- | -- | 46.6 | -- | 0.016 | 59 | NO₂ |
| | | average | | | | | | | | | | | | 62 | |
| Finland | Helsinki | | 0 | 97o | 4.1 | -- | 32.0 | -- | -- | -- | 40.9 | -- | 0.01 | 68 | NO₂ |
| | Oulu | | 0 | 97o | 2.0 | -- | 22.9 | -- | -- | -- | -- | 16.0 | -- | 77 | NO₂ |
| | Tampere | | 0 | 97o | 2.0 | -- | -- | -- | -- | -- | 85.4 | -- | -- | 60* | SPM |

| Country | City | Site | Year | SO$_2$ mean | SO$_2$ days | NO$_2$ mean | NO$_2$ days | O$_3$ days | CO days | SPM mean | PM10 mean | Pb mean | *LA score* | Based on |
|---|---|---|---|---|---|---|---|---|---|---|---|---|---|---|
| | Turku | 0 | 97o | 6.0 | -- | 36.1 | -- | -- | -- | -- | -- | -- | 60* | NO$_2$ |
| | average | | | | | | | | | | | | 66 | |
| France | Aix-en-Provence | 1C | 95 | 22 | -- | 53 | -- | -- | -- | -- | -- | -- | 53 | NO$_2$ |
| | Marseille | 1C | 96 | 19 | -- | 66 | -- | -- | -- | -- | -- | -- | 47 | NO$_2$ |
| | | 2C | 96 | 25 | -- | 69 | -- | -- | -- | -- | -- | -- | 45 | NO$_2$ |
| | | 3C | 96 | 30 | -- | 82 | -- | -- | -- | -- | -- | -- | 39 | NO$_2$ |
| | | ave | | | | | | | | | | | 44 | |
| | Nantes | 0 | 95o[P93] | 8.0 | -- | 37.1 | -- | -- | -- | 16.9 | -- | -- | 63 | NO$_2$ |
| | Paris | 1 | 96 | 22 | -- | 62 | -- | -- | -- | 17 | -- | -- | 49 | NO$_2$ |
| | | 2 | 96 | 18 | -- | 49 | -- | -- | -- | 21 | -- | -- | 55 | NO$_2$ |
| | | 3 | 96 | 15 | -- | 51 | -- | -- | -- | 30 | -- | -- | 54 | NO$_2$ |
| | | ave | | | | | | | | | | | 53 | |
| | Rouen | 0 | 95o | 25.2 | -- | 38.7 | -- | -- | -- | 21.0 | -- | -- | 61 | NO$_2$ |
| | Strasbourg | 1C | 96 | 20 | 0 | 46 | 0 | 21 | -- | -- | 29 | -- | 57 | NO$_2$ |
| | average | | | | | | | | | | | | 55 | |
| Germany | Berlin | 0 | 97o | 10.7 | -- | 29.8 | -- | -- | -- | 43.4 | -- | -- | 70 | NO$_2$ |
| | Dortmund | 1M | 96 | 14 | 0 | 38 | 0 | 5 | 0 | 56 | -- | -- | 62 | NO$_2$ |
| | | 2IR | 96 | 15 | 0 | 38 | 1 | -- | 0 | 55 | -- | -- | 62 | NO$_2$ |
| | | ave | | | | | | | | | | | 62 | |
| | Duisburg | 1IR | 96 | 22 | 2 | 38 | 0 | -- | 0 | 42 | -- | -- | 62 | NO$_2$ |
| | | 2C | 96 | 22 | 2 | 40 | 1 | -- | 0 | 63 | -- | -- | 60 | NO$_2$ |
| | | 4R | 96 | 20 | 0 | 38 | 0 | -- | 0 | 53 | -- | -- | 62 | NO$_2$ |
| | | ave | | | | | | | | | | | 61 | |
| | Frankfurt | 0 | 97o | 11.0 | -- | 52.0 | -- | -- | -- | 37.8 | -- | -- | 54 | NO$_2$ |
| | Freiburg | 0 | 97o | 6.9 | -- | 27.2 | -- | -- | -- | 13.0 | -- | 0.02 | 73 | NO$_2$ |
| | Gelsenkirchen | 0 | 97o | 14.8 | -- | 39.2 | -- | -- | -- | 57.0 | -- | 0.041 | 61 | NO$_2$ |
| | Köln | 1BR | 96 | 14 | 0 | 40 | 0 | 2 | 0 | 43 | -- | -- | 60 | NO$_2$ |
| | | 2R | 96 | 13 | 0 | 38 | 0 | 6 | 0 | 52 | -- | -- | 62 | NO$_2$ |
| | | ave | | | | | | | | | | | 61 | |
| | Leipzig | 0 | 97o | 11.3 | -- | 53.1 | -- | -- | -- | 56.5 | -- | -- | 53 | NO$_2$ |
| | München | 0 | 97o | 7.0 | -- | 47.9 | -- | -- | -- | 50.9 | -- | -- | 56 | NO$_2$ |
| | average | | | | | | | | | | | | 61 | |
| Greece | Athína | 0 | 97o | 27.3 | -- | 55.8 | -- | -- | -- | -- | -- | 0.218 | 52 | NO$_2$ |
| | | 1I | 95 | 22 | 0 | 50 | 26 | 66 | 1 | -- | -- | -- | 36 | O$_3$ |
| | | 2C | 95 | 44 | 3 | 95 | 54 | 0 | 44 | -- | -- | -- | 36 | NO$_2$ |
| | | 3R | 95 | 36 | 7 | 48 | 12 | 30 | 1 | -- | -- | -- | 56 | NO$_2$ |
| | average of 1I, 2C, 3R | | | | | | | | | | | | 43 | |
| Hungary | Budapest | 0 | 97o[Pb94] | 19.9 | -- | 36.2 | -- | -- | -- | -- | 63.1 | 0.211 | 55 | PM10 |
| | | 1I | 96 | 46 | 2 | 25 | -- | -- | -- | 79 | -- | -- | 63 | SO$_2$ |
| | | 2R | 96 | 34 | 0 | 35 | -- | -- | -- | 55 | -- | -- | 65 | NO$_2$ |
| | | 3C | 96 | 60 | 13 | 99 | -- | -- | -- | 65 | -- | -- | 35 | NO$_2$ |
| | average of 1I, 2R, 3C | | | | | | | | | | | | 54 | |
| | Debrecen | 0 | 97o[Pb94] | 11.7 | -- | 30.3 | -- | -- | -- | -- | -- | 0.342 | 70 | NO$_2$ |
| | Győr | 0 | 97o[Pb94] | 11.1 | -- | 78.3 | -- | -- | -- | 23.4 | -- | 0.06 | 41 | NO$_2$ |
| | Miskolc | 0 | 97o[P96] | 25.5 | -- | 30.1 | -- | -- | -- | -- | 43.7 | -- | 65 | PM10 |
| | Pécs | 0 | 97o[Pb94] | 7.2 | -- | 33.2 | -- | -- | -- | 21.1 | -- | 0.342 | 67 | NO$_2$ |
| | average | | | | | | | | | | | | 59 | |
| Iceland | Reykjavík | 0 | 97o[Pb96] | 3.9 | -- | 30.5 | -- | -- | -- | -- | 27.1 | 0.028 | 69 | NO$_2$ |
| Ireland | Cork | 0 | 93o | 12.0 | -- | -- | -- | -- | -- | -- | -- | -- | 60* | SO$_2$ |
| | Dublin | 0 | 93o | 19.6 | -- | -- | -- | -- | -- | -- | -- | -- | 60* | SO$_2$ |
| | average | | | | | | | | | | | | 60 | |
| Italy | Milano | 0 | 93o [N92] | 30.9 | -- | 248.4 | -- | -- | -- | 77.3 | -- | -- | 9 | NO$_2$ |
| | Torino | 0 | 93o | -- | -- | -- | -- | -- | -- | 151.1 | -- | -- | 46 | SPM |
| | average | | | | | | | | | | | | 27 | |
| Lithuania | Kaunas | 1I | 96 | 1 | -- | 30 | -- | -- | -- | 100 | -- | 0.017 | 58 | SPM |
| | | 2C | 96 | 1 | -- | 40 | -- | -- | -- | 200 | -- | -- | 38 | SPM |
| | | 3R | 96 | 0.9 | -- | 20 | -- | -- | -- | 100 | -- | -- | 58 | SPM |
| | | ave | | | | | | | | | | | 51 | |
| | Klaipėda | 1I | 96 | 8 | -- | 30 | -- | -- | -- | 100 | -- | -- | 58 | SPM |
| | | 2C | 96 | 2 | -- | 20 | -- | -- | -- | 99 | -- | 0.015 | 58 | SPM |
| | | 3R | 96 | 2 | -- | 20 | -- | -- | -- | 99 | -- | -- | 58 | SPM |
| | | ave | | | | | | | | | | | 58 | |
| | Šiauliai | 1C | 96 | 2 | -- | 50 | -- | -- | -- | 200 | -- | -- | 38 | SPM |
| | | 2R | 96 | 3 | -- | 20 | -- | -- | -- | 100 | -- | -- | 58 | SPM |
| | | ave | | | | | | | | | | | 48 | |
| | Vilnius | 1I | 96 | 3 | -- | 40 | -- | -- | -- | 200 | -- | -- | 38 | SPM |
| | | 2C | 96 | 4 | -- | 40 | -- | -- | -- | 100 | -- | 0.012 | 58 | SPM |
| | | 3R | 96 | 2 | -- | 30 | -- | -- | -- | 100 | -- | 0.023 | 58 | SPM |
| | | ave | | | | | | | | | | | 51 | |

| Country | City | Site | Year | SO₂ mean | SO₂ days | NO₂ mean | NO₂ days | O₃ days | CO days | SPM mean | PM10 mean | Pb mean | *LA score* | Based on |
|---|---|---|---|---|---|---|---|---|---|---|---|---|---|---|
| | average | | | | | | | | | | | | 52 | |
| Luxembourg | Esch-sur-Alzette | 0 | 97o | 11.0 | -- | 34.1 | -- | -- | -- | -- | 28.0 | 0.12 | 66 | NO₂ |
| | Luxembourg | 0 | 97o | 16.5 | -- | 52.2 | -- | -- | -- | -- | 26.0 | 0.079 | 54 | NO₂ |
| | average | | | | | | | | | | | | 60 | |
| Netherlands | Den Haag | 0 | 97o | 8.9 | -- | 41.0 | -- | -- | -- | -- | 42.0 | -- | 59 | NO₂ |
| | Rotterdam | 0 | 97o | 10.9 | -- | 47.9 | -- | -- | -- | -- | 43.9 | -- | 56 | NO₂ |
| | Vlaardingen | 0 | 97o | 15.1 | -- | 45.9 | -- | -- | -- | -- | 47.1 | 0.02 | 57 | NO₂ |
| | average | | | | | | | | | | | | 57 | |
| Norway | Bergen | 0 | 97o[Pb92] | -- | -- | 40.0 | -- | -- | -- | -- | -- | 0.029 | 60 | NO₂ |
| | Drammen | 0 | 97o[Pb92] | -- | -- | 45.0 | -- | -- | -- | -- | -- | 0.23 | 57 | NO₂ |
| | Oslo | 0 | 97o[Pb92] | -- | -- | 43.2 | -- | -- | -- | 22.8 | -- | 0.108 | 58 | NO₂ |
| | average | | | | | | | | | | | | 58 | |
| Poland | Kraków | 0 | 97o | 30.0 | -- | 30.3 | -- | -- | -- | -- | 37.5 | -- | 70 | NO₂ |
| | Łódź | 0 | 97o | 14.0 | -- | 41.9 | -- | -- | -- | -- | -- | 0.112 | 59 | NO₂ |
| | Warszawa | 0 | 97o | 11.9 | -- | 30.2 | -- | -- | -- | -- | -- | -- | 60* | NO₂ |
| | average | | | | | | | | | | | | 63 | |
| Portugal | Barreiro | 0 | 96o | 11.9 | -- | 25.9 | -- | -- | -- | -- | 86.5 | -- | 45 | PM10 |
| | Lisboa | 0 | 96o | 10.1 | -- | 50.0 | -- | -- | -- | -- | 41.8 | -- | 55 | NO₂ |
| | average | | | | | | | | | | | | 50 | |
| Romania | Bucureşti | 1I | 96 | 6 | -- | -- | -- | -- | -- | 16 | -- | 0.75 | 50 | Pb |
| | | 2C | 95 | 17 | -- | 79 | 48 | -- | -- | 87 | -- | 1.36 | 33 | Pb |
| | | 3R | 96 | 3.7 | -- | 69.3 | -- | -- | -- | 70.7 | 81 | -- | 45 | NO₂ |
| | average | | | | | | | | | | | | 43 | |
| Slovakia | Banská Bystrica | 0 | 97o | 26.2 | -- | 49.0 | -- | -- | -- | -- | -- | -- | 55 | NO₂ |
| | Bratislava | 0 | 97o | 21.9 | -- | 33.8 | -- | -- | -- | 38.2 | -- | -- | 66 | NO₂ |
| | Košice | 0 | 97o | 23.0 | -- | 9.1 | -- | -- | -- | 58.2 | -- | -- | 74 | SPM |
| | average | | | | | | | | | | | | 65 | |
| Spain | Barcelona | 1 | 96 | -- | -- | 66.7 | -- | -- | -- | -- | -- | -- | 47 | NO₂ |
| | | 2 | 96 | 12.2 | -- | 45 | -- | -- | -- | -- | -- | -- | 57 | NO₂ |
| | | 3 | 96 | 12.5 | -- | 50.3 | -- | -- | -- | -- | -- | -- | 55 | NO₂ |
| | | ave | | | | | | | | | | | 53 | |
| | Madrid | 0 | 97o | 15.7 | -- | 66.2 | -- | -- | -- | -- | 32.8 | -- | 47 | NO₂ |
| | Valladolid | 0 | 97o | -- | -- | 55.3 | -- | -- | -- | -- | -- | -- | 52 | NO₂ |
| | average | | | | | | | | | | | | 51 | |
| Sweden | Göteborg | 0 | 96o | 4.5 | -- | 30.1 | -- | -- | -- | -- | 7.0 | -- | 70 | NO₂ |
| | Stockholm | 0 | 96o | 4.0 | -- | 23.0 | -- | -- | -- | -- | 4.0 | -- | 77 | NO₂ |
| | average | | | | | | | | | | | | 73 | |
| Switzerland | Basel | 0 | 96o | 6.8 | -- | 26.8 | -- | -- | -- | 36.0 | -- | 0.05 | 73 | NO₂ |
| | Genève | 1C | 95 | 13 | 0 | 58 | 0 | 0 | 0 | -- | -- | -- | 51 | NO₂ |
| | Zürich | 0 | 96o | 10.0 | -- | 36.0 | -- | -- | -- | 34.0 | -- | 0.041 | 64 | NO₂ |
| | average | | | | | | | | | | | | 63 | |
| United Kingdom | Birmingham | 1C | 95 | 18 | 4 | 45 | 5 | 10 | 0 | -- | 23 | -- | 57 | NO₂ |
| | Edinburgh | 1C | 95 | 21 | 0 | 49 | 2 | 1 | 0 | -- | 20 | -- | 55 | NO₂ |
| | Glasgow | 0 | 97o | -- | -- | 50.2 | -- | -- | -- | -- | -- | 0.041 | 55 | NO₂ |
| | Liverpool | 1C | 95 | 24 | 4 | 49 | 0 | 7 | 0 | -- | 27 | -- | 55 | NO₂ |
| | London | 0 | 97o[S96] | 28.1 | -- | 61.0 | -- | -- | -- | -- | -- | 0.09 | 49 | NO₂ |
| | Manchester | 0 | 97o | -- | -- | 52.3 | -- | -- | -- | -- | -- | -- | 54 | NO₂ |
| | Newcastle | 0 | 97o [S96] | 22.0 | -- | 40.0 | -- | -- | -- | -- | -- | -- | 60 | NO₂ |
| | Sheffield | 1I | 95 | -- | -- | 49 | 1 | -- | 0 | -- | -- | -- | 55 | NO₂ |
| | average | | | | | | | | | | | | 55 | |
| RUSSIAN FEDERATION | Moskva | 0 | 92o | 1.0 | -- | 79.8 | -- | -- | -- | 100.5 | -- | -- | 40 | NO₂ |
| | Novosibirsk | 0 | 93o | 5.0 | -- | 50.1 | -- | -- | -- | 111.0 | -- | -- | 55 | NO₂ |
| | Omsk | 0 | 93o | 10.0 | -- | 30.0 | -- | -- | -- | 99.4 | -- | -- | 58 | SPM |
| | S Peterburg | 0 | 93o | 9.9 | -- | 80.0 | -- | -- | -- | 100.0 | -- | -- | 40 | NO₂ |
| | average | | | | | | | | | | | | 48 | |
| **ASIA** | | | | | | | | | | | | | | |
| China | Beijing | 1I | 94 | 115 | -- | -- | -- | -- | -- | 485 | -- | -- | 13 | SPM |
| | | 2B | 94 | 89.9 | -- | -- | -- | -- | -- | 343 | -- | -- | 22 | SPM |
| | | 3R | 94 | 110 | -- | -- | -- | -- | -- | 322 | -- | -- | 24 | SPM |
| | | ave | | | | | | | | | | | 20 | |
| | Chongqing | 1 | 94 | 330 | -- | 60 | -- | -- | -- | 340 | -- | -- | 7 | SO₂ |
| | Guangzhou | 1I | 94 | 66.7 | -- | -- | -- | -- | -- | 400 | -- | -- | 18 | SPM |
| | | 2B | 94 | 75.4 | -- | -- | -- | -- | -- | 359 | -- | -- | 20 | SPM |
| | | 3R | 94 | 62.4 | -- | -- | -- | -- | -- | 339 | -- | -- | 22 | SPM |
| | | ave | | | | | | | | | | | 20 | |
| | Hong Kong | 1I | 96 | 19 | 0 | 65 | 9 | -- | -- | 99 | 59 | 0.078 | 47 | NO₂ |
| | | 2C | 96 | 18 | 0 | 62 | 7 | -- | -- | 101 | 59 | 0.083 | 49 | NO₂ |
| | | 3R | 96 | 15 | 0 | 47 | 1 | 5 | -- | 87 | 52 | 0.083 | 56 | NO₂ |
| | | ave | | | | | | | | | | | 51 | |

| Country | City | Site | Year | SO₂ mean | SO₂ days | NO₂ mean | NO₂ days | O₃ days | CO days | SPM mean | PM10 mean | Pb mean | *LA* score | Based on |
|---|---|---|---|---|---|---|---|---|---|---|---|---|---|---|
| | Shanghai | 1I | 94 | 67 | -- | -- | -- | -- | -- | 232 | -- | -- | 34 | SPM |
| | | 2B | 94 | 79.2 | -- | -- | -- | -- | -- | 289 | -- | -- | 28 | SPM |
| | | 3R | 94 | 62.4 | -- | -- | -- | -- | -- | 235 | -- | -- | 34 | SPM |
| | | ave | | | | | | | | | | | 32 | |
| | Shenyang | 1I | 94 | 256 | -- | -- | -- | -- | -- | 539 | -- | -- | 10 | SPM |
| | | 2B | 94 | 98 | -- | -- | -- | -- | -- | 449 | -- | -- | 15 | SPM |
| | | 3R | 94 | 64 | -- | -- | -- | -- | -- | 428 | -- | -- | 16 | SPM |
| | | ave | | | | | | | | | | | 14 | |
| | Xi'an | 1I | 94 | 63 | -- | -- | -- | -- | -- | 459 | -- | -- | 14 | SPM |
| | | 2B | 94 | 79.7 | -- | -- | -- | -- | -- | 503 | -- | -- | 12 | SPM |
| | | 3R | 94 | 44.9 | -- | -- | -- | -- | -- | 482 | -- | -- | 13 | SPM |
| | | ave | | | | | | | | | | | 13 | |
| | average | | | | | | | | | | | | 22 | |
| India | Ahmadabad | 1I | 96 | 31 | -- | 13 | -- | -- | -- | 234 | 158 | 0.058 | 28 | PM10 |
| | | 2C | 96 | 18 | -- | 15 | -- | -- | -- | 306 | 194 | -- | 21 | PM10 |
| | | 3R | 96 | 12 | -- | 9 | -- | -- | -- | 187 | 92 | -- | 39 | SPM |
| | | ave | | | | | | | | | | | 29 | |
| | Calcutta | 1I | 96 | 26 | 4 | 35 | 4 | -- | -- | 541 | 544 | 0.266 | 0 | PM10 |
| | | 2C | 96 | 31 | 4 | 35 | 4 | -- | -- | 542 | 378 | -- | 2 | PM10 |
| | | 3R | 96 | 9 | 1 | 15 | 1 | -- | -- | 420 | 362 | -- | 4 | PM10 |
| | | ave | | | | | | | | | | | 2 | |
| | Hyderabad | 1I | 96 | 13 | -- | 10 | -- | -- | -- | 67 | 75 | 0.069 | 50 | PM10 |
| | | 2C | 96 | 34 | 1 | 35 | 1 | -- | -- | 234 | 178 | -- | 24 | PM10 |
| | | 3R | 96 | 16 | 1 | 15 | 1 | -- | -- | 150 | 98 | -- | 41 | PM10 |
| | | ave | | | | | | | | | | | 38 | |
| | Jaipur | 1I | 96 | 12 | 1 | 44 | 8 | -- | -- | 355 | 315 | 0.078 | 8 | PM10 |
| | | 2C | 96 | 7 | -- | 27 | 7 | -- | -- | 220 | 184 | -- | 23 | PM10 |
| | | 3R | 96 | 7 | -- | 20 | 2 | -- | -- | 226 | 172 | -- | 26 | PM10 |
| | | ave | | | | | | | | | | | 19 | |
| | Kanpur | 1I | 96 | 8 | -- | 20 | -- | -- | -- | 434 | 219 | 0.96 | 16 | SPM |
| | | 2C | 96 | 8 | -- | 21 | -- | -- | -- | 368 | 190 | -- | 20 | SPM |
| | | 3R | 96 | 6 | -- | 14 | -- | -- | -- | 233 | 131 | -- | 34 | PM10 |
| | | ave | | | | | | | | | | | 23 | |
| | Mumbai | 1I | 96 | 25 | 4 | 32 | 3 | -- | -- | 244 | 136 | 0.057 | 33 | PM10 |
| | | 2B | 96 | 18 | 3 | 54 | 8 | -- | -- | 194 | 90 | -- | 38 | SPM |
| | | 3R | 96 | 13 | 1 | 21 | 2 | -- | -- | 195 | 111 | -- | 38 | PM10 |
| | | ave | | | | | | | | | | | 36 | |
| | Nagpur | 1I | 96 | 8 | -- | 15 | -- | -- | -- | 161 | 82 | 0.087 | 44 | SPM |
| | | 2C | 96 | 6 | -- | 13 | -- | -- | -- | 226 | 132 | -- | 34 | PM10 |
| | | 3R | 96 | 6 | -- | 12 | -- | -- | -- | 133 | 64 | -- | 50 | SPM |
| | | ave | | | | | | | | | | | 43 | |
| | New Delhi | 1I | 96 | 17 | -- | 40 | -- | -- | -- | 498 | 216 | 0.332 | 12 | SPM |
| | | 2C | 96 | 24 | 2 | 77 | 7 | -- | -- | 459 | 246 | -- | 14 | SPM |
| | | 3R | 96 | 11 | -- | 46 | 3 | -- | -- | 299 | 275 | -- | 12 | PM10 |
| | | ave | | | | | | | | | | | 13 | |
| | average | | | | | | | | | | | | 25 | |
| Japan | Kawasaki | 0 | 96o | 24.1 | -- | 64.9 | -- | -- | -- | -- | 47.1 | 0.11 | 48 | NO₂ |
| | Matsue | 0 | 96o | -- | -- | 10.0 | -- | -- | -- | -- | 25.0 | 0.03 | 80 | PM10 |
| | Osaka | 1I | 94 | 20.9 | 0 | 65.8 | -- | -- | 0 | -- | 46 | 0.06 | 47 | NO₂ |
| | | 2B | 94 | 18.7 | 0 | 62 | -- | -- | 0 | -- | 40 | 0.06 | 49 | NO₂ |
| | | 3R | 94 | 18.3 | 0 | 60.2 | -- | -- | -- | -- | 47 | 0.06 | 50 | NO₂ |
| | | ave | | | | | | | | | | | 49 | |
| | Tokyo | 0 | 96o | 18.9 | -- | 69.0 | -- | -- | -- | -- | 47.9 | 0.09 | 45 | NO₂ |
| | average | | | | | | | | | | | | 55 | |
| Korea, R | Inch'ŏn | 0 | 97o | 34.0 | -- | 48.9 | -- | -- | -- | 85.4 | -- | 0.171 | 56 | NO₂ |
| | Kwangyu | 0 | 97o | 23.5 | -- | 39.5 | -- | -- | -- | 74.7 | -- | 0.033 | 60 | NO₂ |
| | Pusan | 0 | 97o | 46.7 | -- | 52.8 | -- | -- | -- | 84.6 | -- | 0.084 | 54 | NO₂ |
| | Sŏul | 0 | 97o | 29.3 | -- | 60.2 | -- | -- | -- | 71.3 | -- | 0.11 | 50 | NO₂ |
| | Taegu | 0 | 97o | 41.9 | -- | 45.1 | -- | -- | -- | 62.7 | -- | 0.03 | 57 | NO₂ |
| | Taejŏn | 0 | 97o | 28.5 | -- | 41.4 | -- | -- | -- | 66.5 | -- | 0.181 | 59 | NO₂ |
| | Ulsan | 1I | 96 | 80 | 64 | 29 | 0 | 1 | 0 | 121 | -- | -- | 37 | SO₂ |
| | average | | | | | | | | | | | | 53 | |
| Kuwait | Kuwait | 1 | 96 | 44.4 | 9 | 61.5 | 30 | 61 | 9 | -- | -- | -- | 38 | O₃ |
| Philippines | Manila | 1I | 95 | -- | -- | -- | -- | -- | -- | 296 | -- | -- | 27 | SPM |
| | | 3B | 95 | -- | -- | -- | -- | -- | -- | 210 | -- | -- | 37 | SPM |
| | | 4R | 95 | -- | -- | -- | -- | -- | -- | 118 | -- | -- | 54 | SPM |
| | average | | | | | | | | | | | | 39 | |
| Thailand | Bangkok | 1I | 95 | -- | -- | -- | -- | -- | -- | 385 | -- | 0.19 | 19 | SPM |
| | | 2B | 95 | -- | -- | -- | -- | -- | -- | 138 | -- | 0.14 | 49 | SPM |

| Country | City | Site | Year | SO₂ mean | SO₂ days | NO₂ mean | NO₂ days | O₃ days | CO days | SPM mean | PM10 mean | Pb mean | *LA score* | Based on |
|---|---|---|---|---|---|---|---|---|---|---|---|---|---|---|
| | | 3R | 95 | -- | -- | -- | -- | -- | -- | 146 | -- | 0.08 | 48 | SPM |
| | average | | | | | | | | | | | | 39 | |
| Turkey | Ankara | 0 | 97o | 41.9 | -- | 45.2 | -- | -- | -- | -- | 53.4 | -- | 57 | NO₂ |
| | Eskişehir | 0 | 97o [N95] | 71.0 | -- | 7.0 | -- | -- | -- | -- | -- | -- | 52 | SO₂ |
| | Istanbul | 0 | 97o | 83.2 | -- | -- | -- | -- | -- | -- | -- | -- | 47 | SO₂ |
| | Izmir | 0 | 97o | 64.1 | -- | -- | -- | -- | -- | -- | -- | -- | 54 | SO₂ |
| | average | | | | | | | | | | | | 52 | |
| PACIFIC | | | | | | | | | | | | | | |
| Australia | Melbourne | 1I | 95 | 1 | 0 | 22 | 0 | 1 | 0 | -- | 18 | 0.07 | 78 | NO₂ |
| | | 2C | 95 | 0 | 0 | 40 | 0 | 0 | -- | -- | 21 | 0.11 | 60 | NO₂ |
| | | 3R | 95 | 0 | 0 | 29 | 0 | 0 | 0 | -- | 17 | 0.1 | 71 | NO₂ |
| | | ave | | | | | | | | | | | 70 | |
| | Perth | 1I | 95 | 5 | 0 | 8 | 0 | -- | -- | -- | -- | -- | 60* | NO₂ |
| | | 2C | 95 | -- | -- | 36 | 0 | -- | 2 | -- | 24 | 0.26 | 64 | NO₂ |
| | | 3R | 95 | -- | -- | 12 | 0 | 6 | -- | 38 | 19 | 0.1 | 80* | SPM |
| | | ave | | | | | | | | | | | 68 | |
| | Sydney | 2B | 95 | -- | -- | -- | -- | -- | 39 | 70 | 31 | 0.2 | 52 | CO |
| | | 3R | 95 | -- | -- | 33 | 0 | 0 | -- | 38 | 16 | 0.1 | 67 | NO₂ |
| | | ave | | | | | | | | | | | 59 | |
| | average | | | | | | | | | | | | 66 | |
| New Zealand | Auckland | 1I | 96 | 6.5 | 0 | 20.4 | 0 | -- | -- | 33 | 25 | 0.05 | 80 | PM10 |
| | | 2B | 96 | -- | -- | 16.1 | 0 | -- | -- | 12 | -- | 0.03 | 80* | NO₂ |
| | | ave | | | | | | | | | | | 80 | |
| | Christchurch | 1BR | 95 | 6 | 0 | 17.1 | -- | -- | -- | 34 | 21.8 | 0.11 | 80* | NO₂ |
| | average | | | | | | | | | | | | 80 | |

**Notes**

The local air quality index (*LA score*) is the average of city scores in each country, each city score being the lowest score of six indicators: sulfur dioxide, nitrogen dioxide, ground-level ozone, carbon monoxide, particulates, and lead.

Site = monitoring site. 0 indicates an average of several sites. 1, 2, 3, etc., indicate an individual site. The type of location is shown by a letter: B = business district; C = city center; I = industrial; M = mixed; R = residential.

Year = the year of the data. All data are from World Health Organization (1998c), unless the year is annotated with the letter o, in which case they are from Organisation for Economic Co-operation and Development (1999), supplemented by OECD Centre for Co-operation with the Economies in Transition (1996). Exceptions are indicated in brackets: N= nitrogen dioxide; P = particulates; Pb = lead; S = sulfur dioxide.

$SO_2$ = sulfur dioxide, recorded as annual average ambient air concentration of sulfur dioxide ($SO_2$ mean) in micrograms per cubic meter ($\mu g/m^3$) and as number of days per year in which ambient air concentrations of $SO_2$ exceeded World Health Organization (WHO) guidelines ($SO_2$ days).

$NO_2$ = nitrogen dioxide, recorded as annual average ambient air concentration of nitrogen dioxide ($NO_2$ mean) in micrograms per cubic meter ($\mu g/m^3$) and as number of days per year in which ambient air concentrations of $NO_2$ exceeded WHO guidelines ($NO_2$ days).

$O_3$ days = number of days per year in which ambient air concentrations of ground-level ozone exceeded WHO guidelines.

CO days = number of days per year in which ambient air concentrations of carbon monoxide exceeded WHO guidelines.

SPM mean = annual average ambient air concentration of suspended particulate matter in micrograms per cubic meter ($\mu g/m^3$).

PM10 mean = annual average ambient air concentration of fine particulates 10 micrometers or less in diameter in micrograms per cubic meter ($\mu g/m^3$). A micrometer is 500 times smaller than the period at the end of this sentence. The smaller the particles the more dangerous they are. The smallest particles (2.5 micrometers or less) can remain in the air for days or weeks and penetrate deep into the lungs.

Pb mean = annual average ambient air concentration of lead in micrograms per cubic meter ($\mu g/m^3$).

*LA score* = the local air quality index, the lowest score of the above indicators. The performance criteria are shown in Table 18a. For annual ambient air concentrations of sulfur dioxide ($SO_2$), nitrogen dioxide ($NO_2$), suspended particulate matter (SPM) and lead (Pb), the top of the medium band matches WHO guidelines (World Health Organization 1998d). WHO has issued no guidelines for fine particulates because there is no threshold for morbidity and mortality (Junker & Schwela 1998). The tops of the fair and medium bands represent 2% and 4% increases in daily mortality from PM10. For number of days per year in which ambient air concentrations of sulfur dioxide ($SO_2$), nitrogen dioxide ($NO_2$), ozone ($O_3$) or carbon monoxide (CO) exceeded WHO guidelines, the performance criteria reflect personal judgment.

Based on = the indicator that determines the site score (the indicator with the lowest score). Scores for $SO_2$ and $NO_2$ are for annual average ambient air concentration or for number of days per year WHO guidelines were exceeded, whichever gives the lower score.

| band | top point on scale | SO₂ µg/m³ | SO₂ no. days >WHO | NO₂ µg/m³ | NO₂ no. days >WHO | O₃ no. days >WHO | CO no. days >WHO | SPM µg/m³ | PM10 µg/m³ | Pb µg/m³ |
|---|---|---|---|---|---|---|---|---|---|---|
| good | 100 | 0 | 0 | 0 | 0 | 0 | 0 | 0 | 0 | 0 |
| fair | 80 | 25 | 14 | 20 | 14 | 14 | 14 | 45 | 25 | 0.25 |
| medium | 60 | 50 | 28 | 40 | 28 | 28 | 28 | 90 | 50 | 0.50 |
| poor | 40 | 100 | 56 | 80 | 56 | 56 | 56 | 180 | 100 | 1.00 |
| bad | 20 | 200 | 112 | 160 | 112 | 112 | 112 | 360 | 200 | 2.00 |
| base | 0 | 400 | 224 | 320 | 224 | 224 | 224 | 720 | 400 | 4.00 |

**Table 18a. Performance criteria for air pollutants.** No. days >WHO = number of days when ambient air concentrations exceeded WHO guidelines.

* A score with an asterisk has been reduced in accordance with the insufficient data rule. To prevent high scores resulting merely from lack of data, a good score is allowed only if it is based on all applicable components (data in an indicator, indicators in an index), and a fair score only if it is based on at least half the components. Good and fair scores (100-61) based on fewer than half the applicable components have been reduced to 60. Good scores (100-81) based on more than half but not all the applicable components have been reduced to 80.

# Table 19. Species and Genes Index; Wild Species Rank; Wild Plant Species

| Country | W spp rank | Flowering plants | | | Gymnosperms | | | Pteridophytes | | | Ave % | #G | PS score | AS score | *WD score* | *DD score* | S&G index |
|---|---|---|---|---|---|---|---|---|---|---|---|---|---|---|---|---|---|
| | | Tot | Thr | % | Tot | Thr | % | Tot | Thr | % | | | | | | | |
| AMERICAS | | | | | | | | | | | | | | | | | |
| Antigua & Barbuda | 166= | 766 | 3 | 0.4 | 1 | -- | -- | 33 | -- | -- | 0.4 | 1 | 60* | 35 | 47 | -- | 47 |
| Argentina | 18 | 9000 | 233 | 2.6 | 13 | 9 | 69.2 | 359 | 5 | 1.4 | 24.4 | 3 | 9 | 44 | 26 | 17 | 23 |
| Bahamas | 155 | 1065 | 29 | 2.7 | 3 | 2 | 66.7 | 43 | 0 | 0 | 23.1 | 3 | 11 | 12 | 11 | 60 | 27 |
| Barbados | 179 | 542 | 2 | 0.4 | 0 | 0 | 0 | 30 | -- | -- | 0.4 | 2 | 80* | 52 | 66 | 60 | 64 |
| Belize | 61 | 2750 | 52 | 1.9 | 10 | 4 | 40.0 | 134 | 1 | 0.8 | 14.2 | 3 | 24 | 81 | 52 | -- | 52 |
| Bolivia | 13 | 16500 | 222 | 1.4 | 17 | 4 | 23.5 | 850 | 1 | 0.1 | 8.3 | 3 | 39 | 56 | 47 | 22 | 39 |
| Brazil | 5 | 55000 | 1352 | 2.5 | 15 | 3 | 20.0 | 1200 | 3 | 0.3 | 7.6 | 3 | 42 | 25 | 33 | 1 | 22 |
| Canada | 51 | 3172 | 251 | 7.9 | 33 | 3 | 9.1 | 65 | 18 | 27.7 | 14.9 | 3 | 23 | 58 | 40 | 42 | 41 |
| Chile | 59 | 5125 | 285 | 5.6 | 9 | 9 | 100 | 150 | 35 | 23.3 | 43.0 | 3 | 0 | 23 | 11 | 33 | 18 |
| Colombia | 4 | 50000 | 688 | 1.4 | 20 | 11 | 55.0 | 1200 | 13 | 1.1 | 19.2 | 3 | 16 | 43 | 29 | 24 | 27 |
| Costa Rica | 23 | 11000 | 502 | 4.6 | 9 | 6 | 66.7 | 1110 | 19 | 1.7 | 24.3 | 3 | 10 | 57 | 33 | -- | 33 |
| Cuba | 68 | 6004 | 879 | 14.6 | 23 | 8 | 34.8 | 495 | 1 | 0.2 | 16.5 | 3 | 19 | 11 | 15 | 57 | 29 |
| Dominica | 157 | 1027 | 56 | 5.5 | 1 | -- | -- | 200 | 1 | 0.5 | 3.0 | 2 | 70 | 33 | 51 | -- | 51 |
| Dominican R | 78 | 5000 | 130 | 2.6 | 7 | 3 | 42.9 | 650 | 3 | 0.5 | 15.3 | 3 | 22 | 18 | 20 | 35 | 25 |
| Ecuador | 8= | 18250 | 813 | 4.5 | 12 | 2 | 16.7 | 1100 | 9 | 0.8 | 7.3 | 3 | 43 | 43 | 43 | 12 | 33 |
| El Salvador | 62 | 2500 | 38 | 1.5 | 11 | 4 | 36.4 | 400 | -- | -- | 19.0 | 2 | 16 | 82 | 49 | -- | 49 |
| Grenada | 159 | 919 | 8 | 0.9 | 1 | -- | -- | 148 | -- | -- | 0.9 | 1 | 60* | 46 | 53 | -- | 53 |
| Guatemala | 21= | 8000 | 338 | 4.2 | 29 | 15 | 51.7 | 652 | 2 | 0.3 | 18.7 | 3 | 17 | 82 | 49 | 14 | 37 |
| Guyana | 36 | 6000 | 149 | 2.5 | 2 | -- | -- | 407 | 3 | 0.7 | 1.6 | 2 | 80* | 75 | 77 | 60 | 71 |
| Haiti | 88= | 4685 | 95 | 2.0 | 7 | 3 | 42.9 | 550 | 2 | 0.4 | 15.1 | 3 | 22 | 0 | 11 | -- | 11 |
| Honduras | 30 | 5000 | 88 | 1.8 | 30 | 8 | 26.7 | 650 | -- | -- | 14.3 | 2 | 24 | 70 | 47 | -- | 47 |
| Jamaica | 103 | 2746 | 737 | 26.8 | 4 | 3 | 75.0 | 558 | 4 | 0.7 | 34.2 | 3 | 0 | 18 | 9 | -- | 9 |
| Mexico | 3 | 25000 | 1473 | 5.9 | 71 | 71 | 100 | 1000 | 14 | 1.4 | 35.8 | 3 | 0 | 35 | 17 | 26 | 20 |
| Nicaragua | 25 | 7000 | 93 | 1.3 | 14 | 4 | 28.6 | 576 | 1 | 0.2 | 10.0 | 3 | 35 | 80 | 57 | -- | 57 |
| Panama | 17 | 9000 | 1274 | 14.2 | 15 | 11 | 73.3 | 900 | 17 | 1.9 | 29.8 | 3 | 3 | 51 | 27 | -- | 27 |
| Paraguay | 34 | 7500 | 128 | 1.7 | 1 | 1 | 100 | 350 | -- | -- | 50.9 | 2 | 0 | 63 | 31 | 11 | 24 |
| Peru | 6 | 17121 | 878 | 5.1 | 24 | 1 | 4.2 | 1100 | 27 | 2.5 | 3.9 | 3 | 61 | 37 | 49 | 54 | 51 |
| St Kitts & Nevis | 171 | 533 | 4 | 0.8 | 0 | 0 | 0 | 126 | -- | -- | 0.8 | 2 | 80* | 39 | 59 | -- | 59 |
| St Lucia | 163= | 909 | 5 | 0.6 | -- | 1 | -- | 119 | -- | -- | 0.6 | 1 | 60* | 25 | 42 | -- | 42 |
| St Vincent & Grenadines | 156 | 1000 | 9 | 0.9 | 1 | -- | -- | 165 | -- | -- | 0.9 | 1 | 60* | 26 | 43 | -- | 43 |
| Suriname | 37 | 4700 | 103 | 2.2 | 3 | -- | -- | 315 | -- | -- | 2.2 | 1 | 60* | 68 | 64 | -- | 64 |
| Trinidad & Tobago | 85 | 1982 | 19 | 1.0 | 1 | 1 | 100 | 277 | 1 | 0.4 | 33.8 | 3 | 0 | 78 | 39 | 60 | 46 |
| United States | 8= | 18956 | 4539 | 24.0 | 113 | 46 | 40.7 | 404 | 84 | 20.8 | 28.5 | 3 | 4 | 36 | 20 | 30 | 23 |
| Uruguay | 115 | 2184 | 15 | 0.7 | 1 | -- | -- | 93 | -- | -- | 0.7 | 1 | 60* | 51 | 55 | 30 | 47 |
| Venezuela | 10 | 20000 | 410 | 2.1 | 14 | 4 | 28.6 | 1059 | 12 | 1.1 | 10.6 | 3 | 33 | 54 | 43 | 42 | 43 |
| AFRICA | | | | | | | | | | | | | | | | | |
| Algeria | 93 | 3100 | 138 | 4.5 | 18 | 3 | 16.7 | 46 | -- | -- | 10.6 | 2 | 33 | 39 | 36 | 50 | 41 |
| Angola | 28 | 5000 | 23 | 0.5 | -- | 1 | -- | 185 | -- | -- | 0.5 | 1 | 60* | 61 | 60 | 43 | 54 |
| Benin | 83 | 2000 | 4 | 0.2 | 1 | -- | -- | 200 | -- | -- | 0.2 | 1 | 60* | 80* | 70 | 68 | 69 |
| Botswana | 73 | 2136 | 7 | 0.3 | 0 | 0 | 0 | 15 | -- | -- | 0.3 | 2 | 80* | 80 | 80 | 72 | 77 |
| Burkina Faso | 106 | 1100 | -- | -- | 0 | 0 | 0 | -- | -- | -- | -- | 0 | -- | 75 | 75 | 45 | 65 |
| Burundi | 79= | 2500 | -- | -- | -- | -- | -- | -- | -- | -- | -- | 0 | -- | 72 | 72 | 23 | 56 |
| Cameroon | 31 | 8000 | 82 | 1.0 | 3 | -- | -- | 257 | 7 | 2.7 | 1.9 | 2 | 80* | 44 | 62 | 31 | 52 |
| Cape Verde | 178 | 740 | 1 | 0.1 | 0 | 0 | 0 | 34 | -- | -- | 0.1 | 2 | 80* | 0 | 40 | -- | 40 |
| Central African R | 53 | 3600 | 1 | 0 | 2 | -- | -- | -- | -- | -- | 0.0 | 1 | 60* | 70 | 65 | 50 | 60 |
| Chad | 97= | 1600 | 12 | 7.9 | -- | -- | -- | -- | -- | -- | 7.9 | 1 | 40 | 47 | 43 | 45 | 44 |
| Comoros | 162 | 660 | 4 | 0.6 | 1 | -- | -- | 60 | -- | -- | 0.6 | 2 | 60* | 21 | 40 | -- | 40 |
| Congo, DR | 20 | 11000 | 75 | 0.7 | 7 | 3 | 42.9 | -- | -- | -- | 21.8 | 2 | 13 | 49 | 31 | 50 | 37 |
| Congo, R | 50 | 4350 | 3 | 0.1 | 7 | -- | -- | -- | -- | -- | 0.1 | 1 | 60* | 69 | 64 | 93 | 74 |
| Côte d'Ivoire | 43 | 3517 | 92 | 2.6 | 0 | 0 | 0 | 143 | 2 | 1.4 | 2.0 | 3 | 80 | 57 | 68 | 68 | 68 |
| Djibouti | 165 | 635 | 2 | 0.3 | 2 | -- | -- | 4 | -- | -- | 0.3 | 1 | 60* | 60* | 60 | 55 | 58 |
| Egypt | 118 | 2066 | 82 | 4.0 | 4 | -- | -- | 6 | -- | -- | 4.0 | 1 | 60 | 48 | 54 | 54 | 54 |
| Equatorial Guinea | 60 | 3000 | 3 | 0.1 | 0 | 0 | 0 | 250 | 8 | 3.2 | 1.7 | 3 | 83 | 56 | 69 | 60 | 66 |
| Eritrea | 84 | -- | -- | -- | -- | -- | -- | -- | -- | -- | -- | 0 | -- | 53 | 53 | 70 | 59 |
| Ethiopia | 42 | 6500 | 163 | 2.5 | 3 | -- | -- | 100 | -- | -- | 2.5 | 1 | 60* | 42 | 51 | 50 | 51 |
| Gabon | 54 | 6500 | 91 | 1.4 | 1 | -- | -- | 150 | -- | -- | 1.4 | 1 | 60* | 58 | 59 | 60 | 59 |
| Gambia | 135= | 966 | 1 | 0.1 | 0 | 0 | 0 | 8 | -- | -- | 0.1 | 2 | 80* | 80* | 80 | 66 | 75 |
| Ghana | 56 | 3600 | 101 | 2.8 | 1 | -- | -- | 124 | 2 | 1.6 | 2.2 | 2 | 78 | 65 | 71 | 52 | 65 |
| Guinea | 55 | 3000 | 37 | 1.2 | 0 | 0 | 0 | -- | 2 | -- | 1.2 | 2 | 80* | 60 | 70 | 60 | 67 |
| Guinea-Bissau | 131 | 1000 | -- | -- | 0 | 0 | 0 | -- | -- | -- | -- | 0 | -- | 80* | 80 | 61 | 74 |
| Kenya | 24 | 6000 | 231 | 3.9 | 6 | 4 | 66.7 | 500 | 5 | 1.0 | 23.9 | 3 | 10 | 40 | 25 | 59 | 36 |
| Lesotho | 174 | 1576 | 21 | 1.3 | 0 | 0 | 0 | 15 | 0 | 0 | 0.7 | 3 | 93 | 44 | 68 | 48 | 61 |
| Liberia | 64 | 2200 | 25 | 1.1 | 0 | 0 | 0 | -- | -- | -- | 1.1 | 2 | 80* | 52 | 66 | 48 | 60 |
| Libyan Arab J | 140 | 1800 | 57 | 3.2 | 10 | -- | -- | 15 | -- | -- | 3.2 | 1 | 60* | 48 | 54 | 72 | 60 |
| Madagascar | 45 | 9000 | 259 | 2.9 | 5 | 5 | 100 | 500 | 42 | 8.4 | 37.1 | 3 | 0 | 2 | 1 | 11 | 4 |
| Malawi | 44 | 3600 | 59 | 1.6 | 4 | 1 | 25.0 | 161 | -- | -- | 13.3 | 2 | 27 | 72 | 49 | 54 | 51 |
| Mali | 100 | 1741 | 15 | 0.9 | 0 | -- | -- | -- | -- | -- | 0.9 | 1 | 60* | 53 | 56 | 56 | 56 |

235

| Country | W spp rank | Flowering plants | | | Gymnosperms | | | Pteridophytes | | | Ave % | #G | PS score | AS score | *WD* score | *DD* score | S&G index |
|---|---|---|---|---|---|---|---|---|---|---|---|---|---|---|---|---|---|
| | | Tot | Thr | % | Tot | Thr | % | Tot | Thr | % | | | | | | | |
| Mauritania | 152= | 1100 | 3 | 0.3 | 0 | 0 | 0 | -- | -- | -- | 0.3 | 2 | 80* | 39 | 59 | 58 | 59 |
| Mauritius | 170 | 572 | 291 | 50.9 | 0 | 0 | 0 | 178 | 3 | 1.7 | 26.3 | 3 | 7 | 0 | 3 | 33 | 13 |
| Morocco | 81 | 3600 | 182 | 5.1 | 19 | 4 | 21.1 | 56 | -- | -- | 13.1 | 2 | 27 | 38 | 32 | 47 | 37 |
| Mozambique | 38 | 5500 | 78 | 1.4 | 10 | 10 | 100 | 183 | 2 | 1.1 | 34.2 | 3 | 0 | 53 | 26 | 42 | 31 |
| Namibia | 76 | 3128 | 74 | 2.4 | 1 | -- | -- | 45 | 1 | 2.2 | 2.3 | 2 | 77 | 53 | 65 | 27 | 52 |
| Niger | 125 | 1178 | -- | -- | 0 | 0 | 0 | 8 | -- | -- | -- | 0 | -- | 58 | 58 | 42 | 53 |
| Nigeria | 40 | 4614 | 37 | 0.8 | 1 | -- | -- | 100 | -- | -- | 0.8 | 1 | 60* | 55 | 57 | 45 | 53 |
| Rwanda | 77 | 2288 | -- | -- | 2 | -- | -- | -- | -- | -- | -- | 0 | -- | 67 | 67 | 14 | 49 |
| São Tomé & Principe | 158 | 744 | 2 | 0.3 | 1 | -- | -- | 150 | 1 | 0.7 | 0.5 | 2 | 80* | 8 | 44 | -- | 44 |
| Senegal | 96 | 2062 | 31 | 1.5 | 0 | -- | -- | 24 | -- | -- | 1.5 | 1 | 60* | 62 | 61 | 57 | 60 |
| Seychelles | 160 | 1139 | 78 | 6.9 | 1 | -- | -- | -- | 1 | -- | 6.9 | 1 | 45 | 5 | 25 | -- | 25 |
| Sierra Leone | 75 | 2090 | 29 | 1.4 | 0 | 0 | 0 | -- | -- | -- | 1.4 | 2 | 80* | 56 | 68 | 66 | 67 |
| Somalia | 71 | 3000 | 103 | 3.4 | 2 | -- | -- | 26 | -- | -- | 3.4 | 1 | 60* | 48 | 54 | -- | 54 |
| South Africa | 15 | 23000 | 2168 | 9.4 | 40 | 38 | 95.0 | 380 | 9 | 2.4 | 35.6 | 3 | 0 | 34 | 17 | 48 | 27 |
| Sudan | 39 | 3132 | 10 | 0.3 | 5 | -- | -- | -- | -- | -- | 0.3 | 1 | 60* | 56 | 58 | 49 | 55 |
| Swaziland | 82 | 2636 | 35 | 1.3 | 8 | 7 | 87.5 | 71 | -- | -- | 44.4 | 2 | 0 | 56 | 28 | 80 | 45 |
| Tanzania | 19 | 10000 | 429 | 4.3 | 8 | 5 | 62.5 | -- | 2 | -- | 33.4 | 2 | 0 | 39 | 19 | 9 | 16 |
| Togo | 74 | 2000 | 4 | 0.2 | 1 | -- | -- | 200 | -- | -- | 0.2 | 1 | 60* | 77 | 68 | 83 | 73 |
| Tunisia | 120 | 2150 | 23 | 1.1 | 10 | 1 | 10.0 | 36 | -- | -- | 5.6 | 2 | 52 | 40 | 46 | 19 | 37 |
| Uganda | 29 | 5000 | 12 | 0.2 | 6 | 3 | 50.0 | 400 | -- | -- | 25.1 | 2 | 9 | 68 | 38 | 28 | 35 |
| Zambia | 48 | 4600 | 10 | 0.2 | 1 | 1 | 100 | 146 | 1 | 0.7 | 33.6 | 3 | 0 | 70 | 35 | 48 | 39 |
| Zimbabwe | 33 | 4200 | 95 | 2.3 | 6 | 3 | 50.0 | 234 | 2 | 0.9 | 17.7 | 3 | 18 | 74 | 46 | 48 | 47 |
| **EUROPE** | | | | | | | | | | | | | | | | | |
| Albania | 99 | 2965 | 77 | 2.6 | 21 | 2 | 9.5 | 45 | -- | -- | 6.1 | 2 | 49 | 58 | 53 | 50 | 52 |
| Austria | 95 | 2950 | 22 | 0.8 | 12 | -- | -- | 66 | 1 | 1.5 | 1.2 | 2 | 80* | 51 | 65 | 34 | 55 |
| Belarus | 151 | -- | 1 | -- | -- | -- | -- | -- | -- | -- | -- | 0 | -- | 54 | 54 | 40 | 49 |
| Belgium | 143 | 1400 | 2 | 0.1 | 2 | -- | -- | 50 | -- | -- | 0.1 | 1 | 60* | 35 | 47 | 51 | 48 |
| Bosnia & Herzegovina | 119 | -- | 62 | -- | -- | 1 | -- | -- | 1 | -- | -- | 0 | -- | 25 | 25 | 43 | 31 |
| Bulgaria | 90 | 3505 | 105 | 3.0 | 15 | 1 | 6.7 | 52 | -- | -- | 4.9 | 2 | 55 | 35 | 45 | 22 | 37 |
| Croatia | 111 | -- | 5 | -- | -- | -- | -- | -- | 1 | -- | -- | 0 | -- | 47 | 47 | 37 | 44 |
| Czech R | 130 | -- | -- | -- | -- | -- | -- | -- | -- | -- | -- | 0 | -- | 54 | 54 | 41 | 50 |
| Denmark | 150 | 1200 | 2 | 0.2 | 2 | -- | -- | 50 | -- | -- | 0.2 | 1 | 60* | 49 | 54 | 43 | 50 |
| Estonia | 132 | 1630 | 2 | 0.1 | 40 | -- | -- | 4 | -- | -- | 0.1 | 1 | 60* | 58 | 59 | 65 | 61 |
| Finland | 144 | 1040 | 5 | 0.5 | 4 | -- | -- | 58 | 1 | 1.7 | 1.1 | 2 | 80* | 52 | 66 | 58 | 63 |
| France | 70 | 4500 | 168 | 3.7 | 20 | -- | -- | 110 | 7 | 6.4 | 5.1 | 2 | 54 | 35 | 44 | 33 | 40 |
| Germany | 101 | 2600 | 13 | 0.5 | 10 | -- | -- | 72 | 1 | 1.4 | 1.0 | 2 | 80* | 38 | 59 | 47 | 55 |
| Greece | 72 | 4900 | 565 | 11.5 | 21 | 3 | 14.3 | 71 | 3 | 4.2 | 10.0 | 3 | 35 | 39 | 37 | 24 | 33 |
| Hungary | 113 | 2148 | 30 | 1.4 | 8 | -- | -- | 58 | -- | -- | 1.4 | 1 | 60* | 43 | 51 | 28 | 43 |
| Iceland | 173 | 340 | 1 | 0.3 | 1 | -- | -- | 36 | -- | -- | 0.3 | 1 | 60* | 6 | 33 | 70 | 45 |
| Ireland | 161 | 892 | -- | -- | 2 | -- | -- | 56 | 1 | 1.8 | 1.8 | 1 | 60* | 34 | 47 | 58 | 51 |
| Italy | 67 | 5463 | 306 | 5.6 | 29 | 2 | 6.9 | 106 | 3 | 2.8 | 5.1 | 3 | 54 | 36 | 45 | 46 | 45 |
| Latvia | 133 | 1153 | -- | -- | 4 | -- | -- | 48 | -- | -- | -- | 0 | -- | 65 | 65 | 56 | 62 |
| Lithuania | 154 | 1200 | 1 | 0.1 | -- | -- | -- | -- | -- | -- | 0.1 | 1 | 60* | 58 | 59 | 58 | 59 |
| Luxembourg | 149 | 1200 | 1 | 0.1 | 4 | -- | -- | 42 | -- | -- | 0.1 | 1 | 60* | 51 | 55 | 51 | 54 |
| Macedonia, FYR | 126 | -- | -- | -- | -- | -- | -- | -- | -- | -- | -- | 0 | -- | 24 | 24 | 50 | 33 |
| Malta | 166= | 900 | 14 | 1.6 | 3 | 1 | 33.3 | 11 | -- | -- | 17.5 | 2 | 18 | 46 | 32 | 80 | 48 |
| Moldova | 152= | -- | 5 | -- | -- | -- | -- | -- | -- | -- | -- | 0 | -- | 57 | 57 | 63 | 59 |
| Netherlands | 146 | 1170 | 1 | 0.1 | 3 | -- | -- | 48 | -- | -- | 0.1 | 1 | 60* | 34 | 47 | 40 | 45 |
| Norway | 139 | 1650 | 11 | 0.7 | 4 | -- | -- | 61 | 1 | 1.6 | 1.2 | 2 | 80* | 36 | 58 | 30 | 49 |
| Poland | 105 | 2300 | 25 | 1.1 | 10 | 1 | 10.0 | 62 | 1 | 1.6 | 4.2 | 3 | 59 | 36 | 47 | 76 | 57 |
| Portugal | 107 | 2500 | 260 | 10.4 | 8 | 2 | 25.0 | 65 | 7 | 10.8 | 15.4 | 3 | 21 | 24 | 22 | 48 | 31 |
| Romania | 88= | 3175 | 97 | 3.2 | 11 | 1 | 9.1 | 62 | 1 | 1.6 | 4.6 | 3 | 57 | 33 | 45 | 38 | 43 |
| Slovakia | 123 | -- | -- | -- | -- | -- | -- | -- | -- | -- | -- | 0 | -- | 50 | 50 | 79 | 60 |
| Slovenia | 124 | -- | 12 | -- | -- | -- | -- | -- | 1 | -- | -- | 0 | -- | 46 | 46 | 27 | 40 |
| Spain | 69 | 4916 | 970 | 19.7 | 18 | 6 | 33.3 | 114 | 9 | 7.9 | 20.3 | 3 | 15 | 20 | 17 | 8 | 14 |
| Sweden | 128 | 1650 | 12 | 0.7 | 4 | -- | -- | 60 | 1 | 1.7 | 1.2 | 2 | 80* | 44 | 62 | 40 | 55 |
| Switzerland | 102 | 2927 | 29 | 1.0 | 16 | -- | -- | 87 | 1 | 1.2 | 1.1 | 2 | 80* | 58 | 69 | 48 | 62 |
| Ukraine | 92 | -- | 49 | -- | -- | 3 | -- | -- | -- | -- | -- | 0 | -- | 35 | 35 | 36 | 35 |
| United Kingdom | 141 | 1550 | 17 | 1.1 | 3 | -- | -- | 70 | 1 | 1.4 | 1.3 | 2 | 80* | 29 | 54 | 14 | 41 |
| Yugoslavia | 91 | -- | -- | -- | -- | -- | -- | -- | -- | -- | -- | 0 | -- | 28 | 28 | 26 | 27 |
| **RUSSIAN FEDERATION** | 35 | -- | 207 | -- | -- | 5 | -- | -- | 2 | -- | -- | 0 | -- | 33 | 33 | 44 | 37 |
| **ASIA** | | | | | | | | | | | | | | | | | |
| Afghanistan | 86 | 3500 | 4 | 0.1 | -- | 2 | -- | -- | -- | -- | 0.1 | 1 | 60* | 42 | 51 | 32 | 45 |
| Armenia | 117 | -- | 31 | -- | -- | -- | -- | -- | -- | -- | -- | 0 | -- | 37 | 37 | 40 | 38 |
| Azerbaijan | 104 | -- | 27 | -- | -- | 1 | -- | -- | -- | -- | -- | 0 | -- | 24 | 24 | 33 | 27 |
| Bahrain | 177 | 195 | -- | -- | -- | -- | -- | -- | -- | -- | -- | 0 | -- | 56 | 56 | -- | 56 |
| Bangladesh | 63 | 5000 | 23 | 0.5 | -- | -- | -- | -- | 1 | -- | 0.5 | 1 | 60* | 30 | 45 | 46 | 45 |
| Bhutan | 57= | 5446 | 17 | 0.3 | 22 | 5 | 22.7 | -- | 1 | -- | 11.5 | 2 | 31 | 32 | 31 | 48 | 37 |
| Brunei Darussalam | 57= | 3000 | 25 | 0.8 | -- | 0 | -- | -- | -- | -- | 0.8 | 1 | 60* | 58 | 59 | -- | 59 |
| Cambodia | 66 | -- | 3 | -- | -- | 2 | -- | -- | -- | -- | -- | 0 | -- | 32 | 32 | 29 | 31 |

236

| Country | W spp rank | Flowering plants | | | Gymnosperms | | | Pteridophytes | | | Ave % | #G | PS score | AS score | WD score | DD score | S&G index |
|---|---|---|---|---|---|---|---|---|---|---|---|---|---|---|---|---|---|
| | | Tot | Thr | % | Tot | Thr | % | Tot | Thr | % | | | | | | | |
| China | 2 | 30000 | 196 | 0.7 | 200 | 99 | 49.5 | 2000 | 17 | 0.9 | 17.0 | 3 | 19 | 28 | 23 | 48 | 31 |
| Cyprus | 147 | 1650 | 50 | 3.0 | 12 | 1 | 8.3 | 20 | -- | -- | 5.7 | 2 | 51 | 44 | 47 | 58 | 51 |
| Georgia | 97= | -- | 28 | -- | -- | 1 | -- | -- | -- | -- | -- | 0 | -- | 21 | 21 | 52 | 31 |
| India | 7 | 15000 | 1207 | 8.1 | -- | 9 | -- | 1000 | 30 | 3.0 | 5.6 | 2 | 52 | 19 | 35 | 49 | 40 |
| Indonesia | 1 | 27500 | 208 | 0.8 | -- | 14 | -- | 1875 | 42 | 2.2 | 1.5 | 2 | 80* | 15 | 47 | 57 | 50 |
| Iran | 46= | 6500 | -- | -- | 33 | 2 | 6.1 | -- | -- | -- | 6.1 | 1 | 49 | 34 | 41 | 37 | 40 |
| Iraq | 112 | 2914 | -- | -- | 7 | -- | -- | 16 | -- | -- | -- | 0 | -- | 46 | 46 | 32 | 41 |
| Israel | 116 | 2294 | 32 | 1.4 | 8 | -- | -- | 15 | -- | -- | 1.4 | 1 | 60* | 38 | 49 | 64 | 54 |
| Japan | 41 | 4700 | 617 | 13.1 | 42 | 15 | 35.7 | 630 | 75 | 11.9 | 20.2 | 3 | 15 | 17 | 16 | 2 | 11 |
| Jordan | 145 | 2088 | 9 | 0.4 | 6 | -- | -- | 6 | -- | -- | 0.4 | 1 | 60* | 48 | 54 | 65 | 58 |
| Kazakhstan | 79= | -- | 71 | -- | -- | 0 | -- | -- | -- | -- | -- | 0 | -- | 35 | 35 | 71 | 47 |
| Korea, DPR | 127 | 2898 | -- | -- | -- | 5 | -- | -- | -- | -- | -- | 0 | -- | 65 | 65 | -- | 65 |
| Korea, R | 142 | 2898 | 63 | 2.2 | -- | 2 | -- | -- | 1 | -- | 2.2 | 1 | 60* | 19 | 39 | 52 | 43 |
| Kuwait | 168 | 280 | -- | -- | 1 | -- | -- | 1 | -- | -- | -- | 0 | -- | 76 | 76 | 58 | 70 |
| Kyrgyzstan | 134 | -- | 33 | -- | -- | 1 | -- | -- | -- | -- | -- | 0 | -- | 58 | 58 | 47 | 54 |
| Lao PDR | 49 | -- | 1 | -- | -- | 1 | -- | -- | -- | -- | -- | 0 | -- | 37 | 37 | 62 | 45 |
| Lebanon | 129 | 2000 | 5 | 0.3 | 12 | -- | | 40 | -- | -- | 0.3 | 1 | 60* | 52 | 56 | 60 | 57 |
| Malaysia | 16 | 15000 | 462 | 3.1 | -- | 16 | -- | 500 | 12 | 2.4 | 2.8 | 2 | 72 | 32 | 52 | 45 | 50 |
| Maldives | 180 | 260 | -- | -- | 2 | -- | -- | 15 | -- | -- | -- | 0 | -- | 0 | 0 | 60 | 20 |
| Mongolia | 109 | 2272 | -- | -- | -- | 1 | -- | -- | -- | -- | -- | 0 | -- | 37 | 37 | 58 | 44 |
| Myanmar | 21= | 7000 | 22 | 0.3 | -- | 10 | -- | -- | -- | -- | 0.3 | 1 | 60* | 38 | 49 | 57 | 52 |
| Nepal | 32 | 6500 | 19 | 0.3 | 23 | 1 | 4.4 | 450 | -- | -- | 2.4 | 2 | 76 | 36 | 56 | 56 | 56 |
| Oman | 148 | 1182 | 30 | 2.5 | 3 | -- | -- | 14 | -- | -- | 2.5 | 1 | 60* | 37 | 48 | 60 | 52 |
| Pakistan | 46= | 5309 | 13 | 0.3 | 21 | 1 | 4.8 | 137 | -- | -- | 2.6 | 2 | 74 | 42 | 58 | 55 | 57 |
| Philippines | 27 | 8000 | 313 | 3.9 | 31 | 6 | 19.4 | 900 | 41 | 4.6 | 9.3 | 3 | 37 | 11 | 24 | 42 | 30 |
| Qatar | 176 | 305 | -- | -- | 1 | -- | -- | 0 | 0 | 0 | -- | 0 | -- | 66 | 66 | -- | 66 |
| Saudi Arabia | 114 | 1998 | 7 | 0.4 | 8 | -- | -- | 22 | -- | -- | 0.4 | 1 | 60* | 49 | 54 | 31 | 46 |
| Singapore | 138 | 2000 | 28 | 1.4 | 2 | -- | -- | 166 | 1 | 0.6 | 1.0 | 2 | 80* | 62 | 71 | -- | 71 |
| Sri Lanka | 65 | 3000 | 421 | 14.0 | -- | -- | -- | 314 | 34 | 10.8 | 12.4 | 2 | 29 | 27 | 28 | 73 | 43 |
| Syrian Arab R | 122 | 2000 | 7 | 0.4 | 12 | 1 | 8.3 | 40 | -- | -- | 4.4 | 2 | 58 | 63 | 60 | 67 | 62 |
| Tajikistan | 121 | -- | 49 | -- | -- | 1 | -- | -- | -- | -- | -- | 0 | -- | 33 | 33 | 42 | 36 |
| Thailand | 14 | 11000 | 382 | 3.5 | 25 | 3 | 12.0 | 600 | -- | -- | 7.8 | 2 | 41 | 40 | 40 | 19 | 33 |
| Turkey | 52 | 8543 | 1875 | 22.0 | 22 | -- | -- | 85 | 1 | 1.2 | 11.6 | 2 | 31 | 31 | 31 | 54 | 39 |
| Turkmenistan | 94 | -- | 17 | -- | -- | -- | -- | -- | -- | -- | -- | 0 | -- | 28 | 28 | 75 | 44 |
| United Arab Emirates | 163= | 340 | -- | -- | 2 | -- | -- | 5 | -- | -- | -- | 0 | -- | 42 | 42 | -- | 42 |
| Uzbekistan | 108 | -- | 40 | -- | -- | 1 | -- | -- | -- | -- | -- | 0 | -- | 32 | 32 | 45 | 36 |
| Viet Nam | 26 | 10500 | 326 | 3.1 | -- | 18 | -- | -- | 14 | -- | 3.1 | 1 | 60* | 33 | 46 | 57 | 50 |
| Yemen | 135= | 1620 | 148 | 9.1 | 2 | -- | -- | 28 | 1 | 3.6 | 6.4 | 2 | 48 | 54 | 51 | 57 | 53 |
| PACIFIC | | | | | | | | | | | | | | | | | |
| Australia | 11 | 15148 | 2170 | 14.3 | 90 | 29 | 32.2 | 400 | 46 | 11.5 | 19.3 | 3 | 16 | 22 | 19 | 38 | 25 |
| Fiji | 137 | 1197 | 66 | 5.5 | 11 | 5 | 45.5 | 310 | 3 | 1.0 | 17.3 | 3 | 18 | 0 | 9 | 57 | 25 |
| New Zealand | 110 | 2160 | 202 | 9.4 | 22 | 2 | 9.1 | 200 | 7 | 3.5 | 7.3 | 3 | 43 | 0 | 21 | 28 | 23 |
| Papua New Guinea | 12 | 10000 | 26 | 0.3 | 44 | 5 | 11.4 | 1500 | 61 | 4.1 | 5.3 | 3 | 53 | 20 | 36 | 32 | 35 |
| Samoa | 169 | 514 | 18 | 3.5 | 0 | 0 | 0 | 223 | -- | -- | 3.5 | 2 | 65 | 0 | 32 | -- | 32 |
| Solomon Is | 87 | 2780 | 38 | 1.4 | 22 | 2 | 9.1 | 370 | 2 | 0.5 | 3.7 | 3 | 63 | 7 | 35 | 60 | 43 |
| Tonga | 172 | 360 | 1 | 0.3 | 1 | 1 | 100 | 102 | -- | -- | 50.2 | 2 | 0 | 0 | 0 | -- | 0 |
| Vanuatu | 175 | 870 | 23 | 2.6 | -- | 3 | -- | -- | -- | -- | 2.6 | 1 | 60* | 13 | 36 | -- | 36 |

**Notes**

The species and genes index (**S&G index**) is the weighted average [weights in brackets] of a wild diversity index (**WD score**) [2] and a domesticated diversity index (**DD score**) [1]. Wild diversity has a higher weight because it is measured in terms of species, the extinction of which represents a greater genetic loss than the extinction of breeds and varieties, the measurement units for domesticated diversity.

The wild diversity index is the average of two unweighted indicators (column heading in parentheses):

Threatened wild plant species in a group as % of total wild plant species in that group (PS score). See this table for data.

Threatened wild animal species in a group as % of total wild animal species in that group (AS score). See Table 20 for data.

Data for the domesticated diversity index are given in Tables 20 and 21.

W spp rank = wild species rank. This is the average rank of each of the 180 countries in total numbers of wild native species in seven groups: three plant groups (flowering plants, gymnosperms, pteridophytes); and four animal groups (mammals, breeding birds, reptiles, amphibians). Countries were ranked separately for each group, and the average taken of the ranks.

The wild plant species indicator covers wild higher plants in three groups:

Flowering Plants = angiosperms
Gymnosperms = conifers, cycads, and gnetophytes
Pteridophytes = ferns, horsetails, and clubmosses

Tot = total native species.

Thr = threatened native species. Threatened means critically endangered (high risk of extinction in the immediate future), endangered (high risk of extinction in the near future) or vulnerable (high risk of extinction in the medium-term future). Full definitions are in IUCN Species Survival Commission (1994). Data are for 1998 and are from the UNEP World Conservation Monitoring Centre Threatened Plants Database (WCMC 1998a).

% = threatened native species as a percentage of total native species in the group concerned.

Ave % = the average percentage of the three groups.

#G = the number of groups covered. If all three groups are covered, then the indicator for that country is complete. If fewer than three are covered, then the result may be due to the lack of data. If the group does not exist in the country (for example, gymnosperms in Côte d'Ivoire), it is included in the number in brackets but is not counted in the calculation of the average percentage.

PS score = wild plant species score. The performance criteria are shown in Table 19a. The background extinction rate is estimated to be less than 0.01% of species per century (Reid & Miller 1989). I have assumed that the background percentage of threatened species is less than 100 times the extinction rate, or less than 1%. Therefore, the top of the good band was set at 0%, and the top of the fair band at 2%.

AS score = wild animal species score. The performance criteria are shown in Table 19a. They are identical to those for threatened plant species and have the same rationale.

| band | top point on scale | threatened wild plant species in a group as % of total wild plant species in that group | threatened wild animal species in a group as % of total wild animal species in that group |
|---|---|---|---|
| good | 100 | 0 | 0 |
| fair | 80 | 2 | 2 |
| medium | 60 | 4 | 4 |
| poor | 40 | 8 | 8 |
| bad | 20 | 16 | 16 |
| base | 0 | 32 | 32 |

**Table 19a Performance criteria for wild diversity indicators.**

* A score with an asterisk has been reduced in accordance with the insufficient data rule. To prevent high scores resulting merely from lack of data, a good score is allowed only if it is based on all applicable components (data in an indicator, indicators in an index), and a fair score only if it is based on at least half the components. Good and fair scores (100-61) based on fewer than half the applicable components have been reduced to 60. Good scores (100-81) based on more than half but not all the applicable components have been reduced to 80.

# Table 20. Wild Animal Species; Domesticated Diversity

| Country | Mammals | | | Birds | | | Reptiles | | | Amphibians | | | MB % | MB RA% | #cl | AS score | BrD mean | BrD score | Thbr mean | Thbr score | DD score |
|---|---|---|---|---|---|---|---|---|---|---|---|---|---|---|---|---|---|---|---|---|---|
| | Total | Thr | % | Total | Thr | % | Total | Thr | % | Total | Thr | % | | | | | | | | | |
| **AMERICAS** | | | | | | | | | | | | | | | | | | | | | |
| Antigua & Barbuda | 7 | 0 | 0.0 | 49 | 1 | 2.0 | 13 | 5 | 38.5 | 2 | 0 | 0.0 | 1.0 | 10.1 | 4 | 35 | -- | -- | -- | -- | -- |
| Argentina | 320 | 32 | 10.0 | 897 | 37 | 4.1 | 220 | 6 | 2.7 | 145 | 5 | 3.4 | 7.1 | 5.1 | 4 | 44 | 0.1 | 2 | 0.67 | 33 | 17 |
| Bahamas | 12 | 5 | 41.7 | 88 | 3 | 3.4 | 35 | 5 | 14.3 | 2 | 0 | 0.0 | 22.5 | 14.9 | 4 | 12 | -- | -- | 0.00 | 60* | 60 |
| Barbados | 6 | 0 | 0.0 | 24 | 0 | 0.0 | 9 | 2 | 22.2 | 1 | 0 | 0.0 | 0.0 | 5.6 | 4 | 52 | -- | -- | 0.00 | 60* | 60 |
| Belize | 125 | 4 | 3.2 | 356 | 2 | 0.6 | 107 | 4 | 3.7 | 32 | 0 | 0.0 | 1.9 | 1.9 | 4 | 81 | -- | -- | -- | -- | -- |
| Bolivia | 316 | 23 | 7.3 | 1170 | 27 | 2.3 | 208 | 2 | 1.0 | 112 | 1 | 0.9 | 4.8 | 2.9 | 4 | 56 | 0.6 | 12 | 0.67 | 33 | 22 |
| Brazil | 394 | 79 | 20.1 | 1492 | 112 | 7.5 | 470 | 22 | 4.7 | 505 | 6 | 1.2 | 13.8 | 8.4 | 4 | 25 | 0.1 | 2 | 2.29 | 0 | 1 |
| Canada | 193 | 14 | 7.3 | 426 | 7 | 1.6 | 41 | 2 | 4.9 | 41 | 1 | 2.4 | 4.4 | 4.1 | 4 | 58 | 4.2 | 55 | 0.75 | 30 | 42 |
| Chile | 91 | 21 | 23.1 | 296 | 19 | 6.4 | 72 | 0 | 0.0 | 41 | 3 | 7.3 | 14.8 | 9.2 | 4 | 23 | 0.8 | 16 | 0.33 | 51 | 33 |
| Colombia | 359 | 36 | 10.0 | 1695 | 76 | 4.5 | 585 | 13 | 2.2 | 585 | 0 | 0.0 | 7.3 | 4.2 | 4 | 43 | 0.3 | 6 | 0.45 | 43 | 24 |
| Costa Rica | 205 | 14 | 6.8 | 600 | 13 | 2.2 | 214 | 7 | 3.3 | 162 | 1 | 0.6 | 4.5 | 3.2 | 4 | 57 | -- | -- | -- | -- | -- |
| Cuba | 31 | 11 | 35.5 | 137 | 14 | 10.2 | 102 | 7 | 6.9 | 48 | 0 | 0.0 | 22.9 | 13.1 | 4 | 11 | 1.7 | 34 | 0.00 | 80* | 57 |
| Dominica | 12 | 1 | 8.3 | 52 | 3 | 5.8 | 14 | 4 | 28.6 | 2 | 0 | 0.0 | 7.1 | 10.7 | 4 | 33 | -- | -- | -- | -- | -- |
| Dominican R | 20 | 5 | 25.0 | 136 | 14 | 10.3 | 105 | 10 | 9.5 | 35 | 1 | 2.9 | 17.6 | 11.9 | 4 | 18 | 0.5 | 10 | 0.00 | 60* | 35 |
| Ecuador | 302 | 31 | 10.3 | 1388 | 61 | 4.4 | 374 | 10 | 2.7 | 402 | 0 | 0.0 | 7.3 | 4.3 | 4 | 43 | 0.2 | 4 | 1.00 | 20 | 12 |
| El Salvador | 135 | 2 | 1.5 | 251 | 0 | 0.0 | 73 | 4 | 5.5 | 23 | 0 | 0.0 | 0.8 | 1.8 | 4 | 82 | -- | -- | -- | -- | -- |
| Grenada | 15 | 0 | 0.0 | 50 | 1 | 2.0 | 16 | 4 | 25.0 | 3 | 0 | 0.0 | 1.0 | 6.8 | 4 | 46 | -- | -- | -- | -- | -- |
| Guatemala | 250 | 6 | 2.4 | 458 | 5 | 1.1 | 231 | 8 | 3.5 | 99 | 0 | 0.0 | 1.8 | 1.8 | 4 | 82 | 0.4 | 8 | 1.00 | 20 | 14 |
| Guyana | 193 | 9 | 4.7 | 678 | 2 | 0.3 | -- | 6 | -- | -- | 0 | -- | 2.5 | 2.5 | 2 | 75 | -- | -- | 0.00 | 60* | 60 |
| Haiti | 4 | 4 | 100 | 75 | 13 | 17.3 | 102 | 7 | 6.9 | 46 | 1 | 2.2 | 58.7 | 31.6 | 4 | 0 | -- | -- | -- | -- | -- |
| Honduras | 173 | 9 | 5.2 | 422 | 4 | 0.9 | 152 | 6 | 3.9 | 56 | 0 | 0.0 | 3.0 | 2.5 | 4 | 70 | -- | -- | -- | -- | -- |
| Jamaica | 24 | 5 | 20.8 | 113 | 9 | 8.0 | 36 | 8 | 22.2 | 21 | 4 | 19.0 | 14.4 | 17.5 | 4 | 18 | -- | -- | -- | -- | -- |
| Mexico | 450 | 69 | 15.3 | 769 | 38 | 4.9 | 687 | 18 | 2.6 | 285 | 4 | 1.4 | 10.1 | 6.1 | 4 | 35 | 0.1 | 2 | 0.33 | 51 | 26 |
| Nicaragua | 200 | 6 | 3.0 | 482 | 4 | 0.8 | 161 | 7 | 4.3 | 59 | 0 | 0.0 | 1.9 | 2.0 | 4 | 80 | -- | -- | -- | -- | -- |
| Panama | 218 | 20 | 9.2 | 732 | 16 | 2.2 | 226 | 7 | 3.1 | 164 | 0 | 0.0 | 5.7 | 3.6 | 4 | 51 | -- | -- | -- | -- | -- |
| Paraguay | 305 | 9 | 3.0 | 556 | 24 | 4.3 | 120 | 2 | 1.7 | 85 | 0 | 0.0 | 3.7 | 2.3 | 4 | 63 | 0.1 | 2 | 1.00 | 20 | 11 |
| Peru | 344 | 47 | 13.7 | 1538 | 71 | 4.6 | 298 | 6 | 2.0 | 315 | 1 | 0.3 | 9.1 | 5.2 | 4 | 37 | 0.4 | 8 | 0.00 | 100 | 54 |
| St Kitts & Nevis | 7 | 0 | 0.0 | 32 | 1 | 3.1 | 10 | 3 | 30.0 | 1 | 0 | 0.0 | 1.5 | 8.3 | 4 | 39 | -- | -- | -- | -- | -- |
| St Lucia | 9 | 1 | 11.1 | 50 | 5 | 10.0 | 17 | 6 | 35.3 | 2 | 0 | 0.0 | 10.6 | 14.1 | 4 | 25 | -- | -- | -- | -- | -- |
| St Vincent & Grenadines | 8 | 2 | 25.0 | 108 | 2 | 1.9 | 16 | 4 | 25.0 | 3 | 0 | 0.0 | 13.4 | 13.0 | 4 | 26 | -- | -- | -- | -- | -- |
| Suriname | 180 | 11 | 6.1 | 603 | 1 | 0.2 | 151 | 6 | 4.0 | 95 | 0 | 0.0 | 3.2 | 2.6 | 4 | 68 | -- | -- | -- | -- | -- |
| Trinidad & Tobago | 100 | 1 | 1.0 | 260 | 2 | 0.8 | 70 | 5 | 7.1 | 26 | 0 | 0.0 | 0.9 | 2.2 | 4 | 78 | -- | -- | 0.00 | 60* | 60 |
| United States | 428 | 37 | 8.6 | 650 | 55 | 8.5 | 280 | 27 | 9.6 | 233 | 25 | 10.7 | 8.6 | 9.4 | 4 | 36 | 0.9 | 18 | 0.46 | 43 | 30 |
| Uruguay | 81 | 6 | 7.4 | 237 | 10 | 4.2 | -- | 3 | -- | -- | 0 | -- | 5.8 | 5.8 | 2 | 51 | 1.0 | 20 | 0.50 | 40 | 30 |
| Venezuela | 305 | 25 | 8.2 | 1181 | 24 | 2.0 | 259 | 12 | 4.6 | 199 | 0 | 0.0 | 5.1 | 3.7 | 4 | 54 | 0.2 | 4 | 0.00 | 80* | 42 |
| **AFRICA** | | | | | | | | | | | | | | | | | | | | | |
| Algeria | 92 | 13 | 14.1 | 192 | 5 | 2.6 | -- | 2 | -- | -- | 0 | -- | 8.4 | 8.4 | 2 | 39 | 0.5 | 10 | 0.05 | 90 | 50 |
| Angola | 276 | 18 | 6.5 | 765 | 10 | 1.3 | -- | 4 | -- | -- | 0 | -- | 3.9 | 3.9 | 2 | 61 | 1.3 | 26 | 0.00 | 60* | 43 |
| Benin | 188 | 7 | 3.7 | 307 | 0 | 0.0 | -- | 1 | -- | -- | 0 | -- | 1.9 | 1.9 | 2 | 80* | 1.8 | 36 | 0.00 | 100 | 68 |
| Botswana | 164 | 5 | 3.0 | 386 | 4 | 1.0 | 157 | 0 | 0.0 | 38 | 0 | 0.0 | 2.0 | 1.0 | 4 | 80 | 6.5 | 66 | 0.11 | 78 | 72 |
| Burkina Faso | 147 | 7 | 4.8 | 335 | 1 | 0.3 | -- | 1 | -- | -- | 0 | -- | 2.5 | 2.5 | 2 | 75 | 0.5 | 10 | 0.00 | 80* | 45 |
| Burundi | 107 | 5 | 4.7 | 451 | 4 | 0.9 | -- | 0 | -- | -- | 0 | -- | 2.8 | 2.8 | 2 | 72 | 3.0 | 47 | 2.00 | 0 | 23 |
| Cameroon | 297 | 37 | 12.5 | 690 | 12 | 1.7 | -- | 1 | -- | -- | 1 | -- | 7.1 | 7.1 | 2 | 44 | 0.7 | 14 | 0.36 | 49 | 31 |
| Cape Verde | 5 | 3 | 60.0 | 38 | 2 | 5.3 | 12 | 0 | 0.0 | 0 | 0 | 0 | 32.7 | 21.8 | 4 | 0 | -- | -- | -- | -- | -- |
| Central African R | 209 | 12 | 5.7 | 537 | 1 | 0.2 | -- | 1 | -- | -- | 0 | -- | 3.0 | 3.0 | 2 | 70 | 1.0 | 20 | 0.00 | 80* | 50 |
| Chad | 134 | 17 | 12.7 | 370 | 1 | 0.3 | -- | 1 | -- | -- | 0 | -- | 6.5 | 6.5 | 2 | 47 | 2.0 | 40 | 0.33 | 51 | 45 |
| Comoros | 12 | 2 | 16.7 | 50 | 7 | 14.0 | 22 | 2 | 9.1 | -- | 0 | -- | 15.4 | 13.3 | 3 | 21 | -- | -- | -- | -- | -- |
| Congo, DR | 415 | 40 | 9.6 | 929 | 24 | 2.6 | -- | 2 | -- | -- | 0 | -- | 6.1 | 6.1 | 2 | 49 | 3.0 | 47 | 0.30 | 53 | 50 |
| Congo, R | 200 | 12 | 6.0 | 449 | 1 | 0.2 | -- | 1 | -- | -- | 0 | -- | 3.1 | 3.1 | 2 | 69 | 13.0 | 86 | 0.00 | 100 | 93 |
| Côte d'Ivoire | 230 | 17 | 7.4 | 535 | 9 | 1.7 | -- | 2 | -- | -- | 1 | -- | 4.6 | 4.6 | 2 | 57 | 1.8 | 36 | 0.00 | 100 | 68 |
| Djibouti | -- | 4 | -- | 126 | 1 | 0.8 | -- | 0 | -- | -- | 0 | -- | 0.8 | 0.8 | 1 | 60* | 3.7 | 51 | 0.00 | 60* | 55 |
| Egypt | 98 | 12 | 12.2 | 153 | 1 | 0.7 | 83 | 6 | 7.2 | 6 | 0 | 0.0 | 6.4 | 5.0 | 4 | 48 | 1.5 | 30 | 0.11 | 78 | 54 |
| Equatorial Guinea | 184 | 15 | 8.2 | 273 | 4 | 1.5 | -- | 2 | -- | -- | 1 | -- | 4.8 | 4.8 | 2 | 56 | -- | -- | 0.00 | 60* | 60 |
| Eritrea | 112 | 12 | 10.7 | 319 | 0 | 0.0 | -- | 6 | -- | -- | 0 | -- | 5.3 | 5.3 | 2 | 53 | 2.1 | 41 | 0.00 | 100 | 70 |
| Ethiopia | 255 | 34 | 13.3 | 626 | 12 | 1.9 | -- | 1 | -- | -- | 0 | -- | 7.6 | 7.6 | 2 | 42 | 0.3 | 6 | 0.03 | 94 | 50 |
| Gabon | 190 | 15 | 7.9 | 466 | 3 | 0.6 | -- | 1 | -- | -- | 0 | -- | 4.3 | 4.3 | 2 | 58 | -- | -- | 0.00 | 60* | 60 |
| Gambia | 108 | 3 | 2.8 | 280 | 0 | 0.0 | -- | 1 | -- | -- | 0 | -- | 1.4 | 1.4 | 2 | 80* | 4.0 | 53 | 0.00 | 80* | 66 |
| Ghana | 222 | 13 | 5.9 | 529 | 6 | 1.1 | -- | 2 | -- | -- | 0 | -- | 3.5 | 3.5 | 2 | 65 | 1.3 | 26 | 0.11 | 78 | 52 |
| Guinea | 190 | 11 | 5.8 | 409 | 9 | 2.2 | -- | 1 | -- | -- | 1 | -- | 4.0 | 4.0 | 2 | 60 | 1.0 | 20 | 0.00 | 100 | 60 |
| Guinea-Bissau | 108 | 2 | 1.9 | 243 | 0 | 0.0 | -- | 1 | -- | -- | 0 | -- | 0.9 | 0.9 | 2 | 80* | 2.5 | 43 | 0.00 | 80* | 61 |
| Kenya | 359 | 51 | 14.2 | 844 | 18 | 2.1 | 187 | 5 | 2.7 | 88 | 0 | 0.0 | 8.1 | 4.8 | 4 | 40 | 1.6 | 32 | 0.07 | 86 | 59 |

239

| Country | Mammals | | | Birds | | | Reptiles | | | Amphibians | | | MB % | MB RA% | #cl | AS score | BrD mean | BrD score | Thbr mean | Thbr score | DD score |
|---|---|---|---|---|---|---|---|---|---|---|---|---|---|---|---|---|---|---|---|---|---|
| | Total | Thr | % | Total | Thr | % | Total | Thr | % | Total | Thr | % | | | | | | | | | |
| Lesotho | 33 | 3 | 9.1 | 58 | 3 | 5.2 | -- | 0 | -- | -- | 0 | -- | 7.2 | 7.2 | 2 | 44 | 1.8 | 36 | 0.00 | 60* | 48 |
| Liberia | 193 | 16 | 8.3 | 372 | 10 | 2.7 | 62 | 2 | 3.2 | 38 | 0 | 0.0 | 5.5 | 3.5 | 4 | 52 | 4.5 | 57 | 0.50 | 40 | 48 |
| Libyan Arab J | 76 | 9 | 11.8 | 91 | 1 | 1.1 | -- | 3 | -- | -- | 0 | -- | 6.4 | 6.4 | 2 | 48 | 2.6 | 44 | 0.00 | 100 | 72 |
| Madagascar | 105 | 50 | 47.6 | 202 | 27 | 13.4 | 252 | 18 | 7.1 | 144 | 2 | 1.4 | 30.5 | 17.4 | 4 | 2 | 0.1 | 2 | 1.00 | 20 | 11 |
| Malawi | 195 | 8 | 4.1 | 521 | 8 | 1.5 | 124 | 0 | 0.0 | 69 | 0 | 0.0 | 2.8 | 1.4 | 4 | 72 | 1.4 | 28 | 0.00 | 80* | 54 |
| Mali | 137 | 13 | 9.5 | 397 | 1 | 0.3 | 16 | 1 | 6.3 | -- | 0 | -- | 4.9 | 5.4 | 3 | 53 | 0.6 | 12 | 0.00 | 100 | 56 |
| Mauritania | 61 | 10 | 16.4 | 273 | 1 | 0.4 | -- | 2 | -- | -- | 0 | -- | 8.4 | 8.4 | 2 | 39 | 0.8 | 16 | 0.00 | 100 | 58 |
| Mauritius | 4 | 4 | 100 | 27 | 10 | 37.0 | 11 | 4 | 36.4 | 0 | 0 | 0 | 68.5 | 57.8 | 4 | 0 | -- | -- | 0.67 | 33 | 33 |
| Morocco | 105 | 16 | 15.2 | 210 | 4 | 1.9 | -- | 2 | -- | -- | 0 | -- | 8.6 | 8.6 | 2 | 38 | 2.6 | 44 | 0.33 | 51 | 47 |
| Mozambique | 179 | 15 | 8.4 | 498 | 12 | 2.4 | -- | 5 | -- | 62 | 0 | 0.0 | 5.4 | 3.6 | 3 | 53 | 3.8 | 52 | 0.67 | 33 | 42 |
| Namibia | 154 | 14 | 9.1 | 469 | 7 | 1.5 | -- | 3 | -- | 32 | 1 | 3.1 | 5.3 | 4.6 | 3 | 53 | 0.7 | 14 | 0.50 | 40 | 27 |
| Niger | 131 | 11 | 8.4 | 299 | 1 | 0.3 | -- | 0 | -- | -- | 0 | -- | 4.3 | 4.3 | 2 | 58 | 1.7 | 34 | 0.33 | 51 | 42 |
| Nigeria | 274 | 25 | 9.1 | 681 | 6 | 0.9 | >135 | 2 | 1.5 | >109 | 0 | 0.0 | 5.0 | 2.9 | 4 | 55 | 0.2 | 4 | 0.07 | 86 | 45 |
| Rwanda | 151 | 8 | 5.3 | 513 | 6 | 1.2 | -- | 0 | -- | -- | 0 | -- | 3.3 | 3.3 | 2 | 67 | 1.4 | 28 | 2.00 | 0 | 14 |
| São Tomé & Principe | 8 | 3 | 37.5 | 63 | 9 | 14.3 | 16 | 1 | 6.3 | 9 | 0 | 0.0 | 25.9 | 14.5 | 4 | 8 | -- | -- | -- | -- | -- |
| Senegal | 155 | 11 | 7.1 | 384 | 2 | 0.5 | -- | 6 | -- | -- | 0 | -- | 3.8 | 3.8 | 2 | 62 | 0.7 | 14 | 0.00 | 100 | 57 |
| Seychelles | -- | 4 | -- | 38 | 9 | 23.7 | 15 | 4 | 26.7 | 12 | 4 | 33.3 | 23.7 | 27.9 | 3 | 5 | -- | -- | -- | -- | -- |
| Sierra Leone | 147 | 11 | 7.5 | 466 | 9 | 1.9 | -- | 3 | -- | -- | 0 | -- | 4.7 | 4.7 | 2 | 56 | 3.9 | 53 | 0.00 | 80* | 66 |
| Somalia | 171 | 19 | 11.1 | 422 | 6 | 1.4 | 193 | 2 | 1.0 | 27 | 0 | 0.0 | 6.3 | 3.4 | 4 | 48 | -- | -- | -- | -- | -- |
| South Africa | 247 | 41 | 16.6 | 596 | 25 | 4.2 | 299 | 19 | 6.4 | 95 | 9 | 9.5 | 10.4 | 9.2 | 4 | 34 | 0.7 | 14 | 0.09 | 82 | 48 |
| Sudan | 267 | 24 | 9.0 | 680 | 2 | 0.3 | -- | 2 | -- | -- | 0 | -- | 4.7 | 4.7 | 2 | 56 | 0.3 | 6 | 0.04 | 92 | 49 |
| Swaziland | 47 | 4 | 8.5 | 364 | 3 | 0.8 | 102 | 0 | 0.0 | 40 | 0 | 0.0 | 4.7 | 2.3 | 4 | 56 | 5.3 | 61 | 0.00 | 100 | 80 |
| Tanzania | 316 | 43 | 13.6 | 822 | 28 | 3.4 | 284 | 5 | 1.8 | 124 | 0 | 0.0 | 8.5 | 4.7 | 4 | 39 | 0.2 | 4 | 1.25 | 15 | 9 |
| Togo | 196 | 9 | 4.6 | 391 | 0 | 0.0 | -- | 2 | -- | -- | 0 | -- | 2.3 | 2.3 | 2 | 77 | 6.7 | 67 | 0.00 | 100 | 83 |
| Tunisia | 78 | 11 | 14.1 | 173 | 3 | 1.7 | -- | 3 | -- | -- | 0 | -- | 7.9 | 7.9 | 2 | 40 | 0.9 | 18 | 1.00 | 20 | 19 |
| Uganda | 338 | 19 | 5.6 | 830 | 7 | 0.8 | 149 | 0 | 0.0 | 50 | 0 | 0.0 | 3.2 | 1.6 | 4 | 68 | 0.8 | 16 | 0.50 | 40 | 28 |
| Zambia | 229 | 12 | 5.2 | 605 | 5 | 0.8 | -- | 0 | -- | 83 | 0 | 0.0 | 3.0 | 2.0 | 4 | 70 | 1.8 | 36 | 0.00 | 60* | 48 |
| Zimbabwe | 270 | 12 | 4.4 | 532 | 4 | 0.8 | 153 | 0 | 0.0 | 120 | 0 | 0.0 | 2.6 | 1.3 | 4 | 74 | 2.2 | 41 | 0.28 | 55 | 48 |
| EUROPE | | | | | | | | | | | | | | | | | | | | | |
| Albania | 68 | 3 | 4.4 | 230 | 1 | 0.4 | 31 | 4 | 12.9 | 13 | 0 | 0.0 | 2.4 | 4.4 | 4 | 58 | 6.3 | 65 | 0.62 | 35 | 50 |
| Austria | 83 | 9 | 10.8 | 213 | 2 | 0.9 | 14 | 0 | 0.0 | 20 | 0 | 0.0 | 5.8 | 2.9 | 4 | 51 | 3.5 | 50 | 1.12 | 18 | 34 |
| Belarus | 57 | 5 | 8.8 | 221 | 3 | 1.4 | 7 | 0 | 0.0 | 13 | 0 | 0.0 | 5.1 | 2.5 | 4 | 54 | 1.8 | 36 | 0.44 | 44 | 40 |
| Belgium | 58 | 11 | 19.0 | 180 | 1 | 0.6 | 8 | 0 | 0.0 | 17 | 0 | 0.0 | 9.8 | 4.9 | 4 | 35 | 9.5 | 78 | 0.88 | 25 | 51 |
| Bosnia & Herzegovina | 72 | 10 | 13.9 | -- | 2 | -- | 27 | 1 | 3.7 | 16 | 1 | 6.3 | 13.9 | 8.0 | 3 | 25 | 2.9 | 46 | 0.50 | 40 | 43 |
| Bulgaria | 81 | 15 | 18.5 | 240 | 4 | 1.7 | 33 | 2 | 6.1 | 17 | 0 | 0.0 | 10.1 | 6.6 | 4 | 35 | 1.4 | 28 | 1.17 | 17 | 22 |
| Croatia | 76 | 9 | 11.8 | 224 | 3 | 1.3 | 29 | 1 | 3.4 | 20 | 1 | 5.0 | 6.6 | 5.4 | 4 | 47 | 6.0 | 64 | 1.50 | 10 | 37 |
| Czech R | 81 | 8 | 9.9 | 199 | 1 | 0.5 | 10 | 0 | 0.0 | 19 | 0 | 0.0 | 5.2 | 2.6 | 4 | 54 | 11.3 | 83 | 2.03 | 0 | 41 |
| Denmark | 43 | 5 | 11.6 | 196 | 1 | 0.5 | 5 | 0 | 0.0 | 14 | 0 | 0.0 | 6.1 | 3.0 | 4 | 49 | 8.0 | 72 | 1.26 | 15 | 43 |
| Estonia | 65 | 5 | 7.7 | 213 | 2 | 0.9 | 5 | 0 | 0.0 | 11 | 0 | 0.0 | 4.3 | 2.2 | 4 | 58 | 6.3 | 65 | 0.17 | 66 | 65 |
| Finland | 60 | 6 | 10.0 | 248 | 3 | 1.2 | 5 | 0 | 0.0 | 5 | 0 | 0.0 | 5.6 | 2.8 | 4 | 52 | 3.6 | 51 | 0.17 | 66 | 58 |
| France | 93 | 18 | 19.4 | 269 | 2 | 0.7 | 32 | 3 | 9.4 | 32 | 1 | 3.1 | 10.1 | 8.1 | 4 | 35 | 1.8 | 36 | 0.74 | 30 | 33 |
| Germany | 76 | 12 | 15.8 | 239 | 3 | 1.3 | 12 | 0 | 0.0 | 20 | 0 | 0.0 | 8.6 | 4.3 | 4 | 38 | 2.8 | 45 | 0.36 | 49 | 47 |
| Greece | 95 | 14 | 14.7 | 251 | 2 | 0.8 | 51 | 6 | 11.8 | 15 | 1 | 6.7 | 7.8 | 8.5 | 4 | 39 | 1.0 | 20 | 0.79 | 28 | 24 |
| Hungary | 72 | 9 | 12.5 | 205 | 4 | 2.0 | 15 | 1 | 6.7 | 17 | 0 | 0.0 | 7.3 | 5.3 | 4 | 43 | 2.4 | 43 | 1.31 | 14 | 28 |
| Iceland | 11 | 6 | 54.5 | 88 | 0 | 0.0 | 0 | 0 | 0 | 0 | 0 | 0 | 27.3 | 27.3 | 4 | 6 | 2.1 | 41 | 0.00 | 100 | 70 |
| Ireland | 25 | 5 | 20.0 | 142 | 1 | 0.7 | 1 | 0 | 0.0 | 3 | 0 | 0.0 | 10.4 | 5.2 | 4 | 34 | 1.0 | 20 | 0.02 | 96 | 58 |
| Italy | 90 | 14 | 15.6 | 234 | 2 | 0.9 | 40 | 4 | 10.0 | 34 | 4 | 11.8 | 8.3 | 9.6 | 4 | 36 | 4.3 | 59 | 0.75 | 33 | 46 |
| Latvia | 83 | 5 | 6.0 | 217 | 2 | 0.9 | 7 | 0 | 0.0 | 13 | 0 | 0.0 | 3.5 | 1.7 | 4 | 65 | 6.3 | 65 | 0.39 | 47 | 56 |
| Lithuania | 68 | 5 | 7.4 | 202 | 3 | 1.5 | 7 | 0 | 0.0 | 13 | 0 | 0.0 | 4.4 | 2.2 | 4 | 58 | 9.9 | 80 | 0.58 | 37 | 58 |
| Luxembourg | 55 | 6 | 10.9 | 126 | 1 | 0.8 | 7 | 0 | 0.0 | 14 | 0 | 0.0 | 5.8 | 2.9 | 4 | 51 | 9.5 | 78 | 0.88 | 25 | 51 |
| Macedonia, FYR | 77 | 11 | 14.3 | -- | 3 | -- | 24 | 2 | 8.3 | 12 | 0 | 0.0 | 14.3 | 7.5 | 3 | 24 | 3.5 | 50 | 0.33 | 51 | 50 |
| Malta | 22 | 3 | 13.6 | 26 | 0 | 0.0 | 8 | 0 | 0.0 | 1 | 0 | 0.0 | 6.8 | 3.4 | 4 | 46 | -- | -- | 0.00 | 80* | 80 |
| Moldova | 68 | 3 | 4.4 | 177 | 5 | 2.8 | 9 | 1 | 11.1 | 13 | 0 | 0.0 | 3.6 | 4.6 | 4 | 57 | 3.4 | 49 | 0.11 | 78 | 63 |
| Netherlands | 55 | 11 | 20.0 | 191 | 1 | 0.5 | 7 | 0 | 0.0 | 16 | 0 | 0.0 | 10.3 | 5.1 | 4 | 34 | 1.2 | 24 | 0.24 | 57 | 40 |
| Norway | 54 | 10 | 18.5 | 243 | 2 | 0.8 | 5 | 0 | 0.0 | 5 | 0 | 0.0 | 9.6 | 4.8 | 4 | 36 | 1.5 | 30 | 0.73 | 31 | 30 |
| Poland | 84 | 15 | 17.9 | 227 | 3 | 1.3 | 9 | 0 | 0.0 | 18 | 0 | 0.0 | 9.6 | 4.8 | 4 | 36 | 11.4 | 83 | 0.15 | 70 | 76 |
| Portugal | 63 | 17 | 27.0 | 207 | 4 | 1.9 | 29 | 0 | 0.0 | 17 | 1 | 5.9 | 14.4 | 8.7 | 4 | 24 | 3.1 | 47 | 0.37 | 49 | 48 |
| Romania | 84 | 17 | 20.2 | 247 | 3 | 1.2 | 25 | 2 | 8.0 | 19 | 0 | 0.0 | 10.7 | 7.3 | 4 | 33 | 0.7 | 14 | 0.19 | 62 | 38 |
| Slovakia | 85 | 9 | 10.6 | 209 | 3 | 1.4 | 14 | 1 | 7.1 | 18 | 0 | 0.0 | 6.0 | 4.8 | 4 | 50 | 4.9 | 59 | 0.00 | 100 | 79 |
| Slovenia | 69 | 9 | 13.0 | 207 | 1 | 0.5 | 21 | 0 | 0.0 | 20 | 1 | 5.0 | 6.8 | 4.6 | 4 | 46 | 4.1 | 54 | 1.94 | 1 | 27 |
| Spain | 82 | 24 | 29.3 | 278 | 6 | 2.2 | 53 | 6 | 11.3 | 25 | 3 | 12.0 | 15.8 | 13.7 | 4 | 20 | 0.8 | 16 | 1.97 | 1 | 8 |
| Sweden | 60 | 8 | 13.3 | 249 | 2 | 0.8 | 6 | 0 | 0.0 | 13 | 0 | 0.0 | 7.1 | 3.5 | 4 | 44 | 3.9 | 53 | 0.81 | 28 | 40 |
| Switzerland | 75 | 6 | 8.0 | 193 | 1 | 0.5 | 14 | 0 | 0.0 | 18 | 0 | 0.0 | 4.3 | 2.1 | 4 | 58 | 4.0 | 53 | 0.46 | 43 | 48 |
| Ukraine | 97 | 17 | 17.5 | 263 | 6 | 2.3 | 24 | 2 | 8.3 | 21 | 0 | 0.0 | 9.9 | 7.0 | 4 | 35 | 1.0 | 20 | 0.30 | 53 | 36 |
| United Kingdom | 50 | 12 | 24.0 | 230 | 1 | 0.4 | 8 | 0 | 0.0 | 7 | 0 | 0.0 | 12.2 | 6.1 | 4 | 29 | 1.1 | 22 | 1.69 | 6 | 14 |
| Yugoslavia | 86 | 11 | 12.8 | -- | 4 | -- | 33 | 1 | 3.0 | 21 | 0 | 0.0 | 12.8 | 5.3 | 3 | 28 | 1.3 | 26 | 0.84 | 26 | 26 |

| Country | Mammals | | | Birds | | | Reptiles | | | Amphibians | | | MB % | MB RA% | #cl | AS score | BrD mean | BrD score | Thbr mean | Thbr score | DD score |
|---|---|---|---|---|---|---|---|---|---|---|---|---|---|---|---|---|---|---|---|---|---|
| | Total | Thr | % | Total | Thr | % | Total | Thr | % | Total | Thr | % | | | | | | | | | |
| RUSSIAN FEDERATION | 269 | 42 | 15.6 | 628 | 35 | 5.6 | 58 | 6 | 10.3 | 23 | 0 | 0.0 | 10.6 | 7.9 | 4 | 33 | 2.7 | 45 | 0.46 | 43 | 44 |
| ASIA | | | | | | | | | | | | | | | | | | | | | |
| Afghanistan | 123 | 13 | 10.6 | 235 | 4 | 1.7 | 103 | 1 | 1.0 | 6 | 1 | 16.7 | 6.2 | 7.5 | 4 | 42 | 0.2 | 4 | 0.00 | 60* | 32 |
| Armenia | 77 | 7 | 9.1 | -- | 3 | -- | 51 | 5 | 9.8 | 6 | 0 | 0.0 | 9.1 | 6.3 | 3 | 37 | 3.5 | 50 | 0.75 | 30 | 40 |
| Azerbaijan | 91 | 13 | 14.3 | -- | 3 | -- | 54 | 5 | 9.3 | 10 | 0 | 0.0 | 14.3 | 7.9 | 3 | 24 | 1.4 | 28 | 0.56 | 38 | 33 |
| Bahrain | 17 | 1 | 5.9 | 28 | 1 | 3.6 | 25 | 0 | 0.0 | 1 | 0 | 0.0 | 4.8 | 2.4 | 4 | 56 | -- | -- | -- | -- | -- |
| Bangladesh | 109 | 21 | 19.3 | 295 | 13 | 4.4 | 119 | 21 | 17.6 | 19 | 0 | 0.0 | 11.9 | 10.3 | 4 | 30 | 0.4 | 8 | 0.08 | 84 | 46 |
| Bhutan | 99 | 20 | 20.2 | 448 | 10 | 2.2 | 19 | 0 | 0.0 | 24 | 0 | 0.0 | 11.2 | 5.6 | 4 | 32 | 4.6 | 57 | 0.50 | 40 | 48 |
| Brunei Darussalam | 157 | 9 | 5.7 | 359 | 11 | 3.1 | 44 | 3 | 6.8 | 76 | 0 | 0.0 | 4.4 | 3.9 | 4 | 58 | -- | -- | -- | -- | -- |
| Cambodia | 123 | 21 | 17.1 | 307 | 15 | 4.9 | 82 | 10 | 12.2 | 28 | 0 | 0.0 | 11.0 | 8.6 | 4 | 32 | 0.9 | 18 | 0.50 | 40 | 29 |
| China | 394 | 76 | 19.3 | 1100 | 64 | 5.8 | 340 | 31 | 9.1 | 263 | 1 | 0.4 | 12.6 | 8.6 | 4 | 28 | 0.2 | 4 | 0.04 | 92 | 48 |
| Cyprus | 21 | 3 | 14.3 | 79 | 0 | 0.0 | 23 | 3 | 13.0 | 4 | 0 | 0.0 | 7.2 | 6.8 | 4 | 44 | 6.7 | 60* | 0.25 | 57 | 58 |
| Georgia | 89 | 14 | 15.7 | -- | 3 | -- | 50 | 7 | 14.0 | 14 | 1 | 7.1 | 15.7 | 12.3 | 3 | 21 | 6.1 | 64 | 0.49 | 41 | 52 |
| India | 316 | 86 | 27.2 | 923 | 56 | 6.1 | 390 | 25 | 6.4 | 197 | 3 | 1.5 | 16.6 | 10.3 | 4 | 19 | 0.3 | 6 | 0.04 | 92 | 49 |
| Indonesia | 436 | 140 | 32.1 | 1519 | 108 | 7.1 | 511 | 28 | 5.5 | 270 | 0 | 0.0 | 19.6 | 11.2 | 4 | 15 | 1.6 | 32 | 0.09 | 82 | 57 |
| Iran | 140 | 23 | 16.4 | 323 | 6 | 1.9 | 164 | 8 | 4.9 | 11 | 2 | 18.2 | 11.0 | 10.4 | 4 | 34 | 1.5 | 30 | 0.44 | 44 | 37 |
| Iraq | 81 | 10 | 12.3 | 172 | 2 | 1.2 | 81 | 2 | 2.5 | 6 | 0 | 0.0 | 6.8 | 4.0 | 4 | 46 | 0.7 | 14 | 0.33 | 51 | 32 |
| Israel | 92 | 14 | 15.2 | 180 | 4 | 2.2 | -- | 4 | -- | -- | 0 | -- | 8.7 | 8.7 | 2 | 38 | 3.3 | 49 | 0.00 | 80* | 64 |
| Japan | 132 | 37 | 28.0 | >250 | 20 | 8.0 | 66 | 11 | 16.7 | 52 | 10 | 19.2 | 18.0 | 18.0 | 4 | 17 | 0.2 | 4 | 3.50 | 0 | 2 |
| Jordan | 71 | 8 | 11.3 | 141 | 2 | 1.4 | -- | 1 | -- | -- | 0 | -- | 6.3 | 6.3 | 2 | 48 | 1.5 | 30 | 0.00 | 100 | 65 |
| Kazakhstan | 178 | 18 | 10.1 | -- | 12 | -- | 49 | 2 | 4.1 | 12 | 1 | 8.3 | 10.1 | 7.5 | 3 | 35 | 2.3 | 42 | 0.00 | 100 | 71 |
| Korea, DPR | -- | 13 | -- | 115 | 4 | 3.5 | 19 | 0 | 0.0 | 14 | 0 | 0.0 | 3.5 | 1.2 | 3 | 65 | -- | -- | -- | -- | -- |
| Korea, R | 49 | 13 | 26.5 | 112 | 8 | 7.1 | 25 | 0 | 0.0 | 14 | 0 | 0.0 | 16.8 | 8.4 | 4 | 19 | 1.2 | 24 | 0.00 | 80* | 52 |
| Kuwait | 21 | 1 | 4.8 | 20 | 0 | 0.0 | 29 | 1 | 3.4 | 2 | 0 | 0.0 | 2.4 | 2.1 | 4 | 76 | 4.5 | 57 | 0.00 | 60* | 58 |
| Kyrgyzstan | -- | 7 | -- | -- | 3 | -- | 23 | 2 | 8.7 | 3 | 0 | 0.0 | -- | 4.4 | 2 | 58 | 2.5 | 43 | 0.33 | 51 | 47 |
| Lao PDR | 172 | 27 | 15.7 | 487 | 13 | 2.7 | 66 | 12 | 18.2 | 37 | 0 | 0.0 | 9.2 | 9.1 | 4 | 37 | 1.2 | 24 | 0.00 | 100 | 62 |
| Lebanon | 54 | 6 | 11.1 | 154 | 0 | 0.0 | -- | 1 | -- | -- | 0 | -- | 5.6 | 5.6 | 2 | 52 | -- | -- | 0.00 | 60* | 60 |
| Malaysia | 286 | 47 | 16.4 | 501 | 29 | 5.8 | 268 | 21 | 7.8 | 158 | 0 | 0.0 | 11.1 | 7.5 | 4 | 32 | 2.9 | 46 | 0.44 | 44 | 45 |
| Maldives | 3 | 0 | 0.0 | 23 | 0 | 0.0 | 2 | 2 | 100 | 0 | 0 | 0 | 0.0 | 33.3 | 4 | 0 | -- | -- | 0.00 | 60* | 60 |
| Mongolia | 134 | 12 | 9.0 | -- | 11 | -- | 21 | 0 | 0.0 | 8 | 0 | 0.0 | 9.0 | 3.0 | 3 | 37 | 0.8 | 16 | 0.00 | 100 | 58 |
| Myanmar | 251 | 36 | 14.3 | 867 | 26 | 3.0 | 203 | 20 | 9.9 | 75 | 0 | 0.0 | 8.6 | 6.8 | 4 | 38 | 0.7 | 14 | 0.00 | 100 | 57 |
| Nepal | 167 | 27 | 16.2 | 611 | 16 | 2.6 | 80 | 5 | 6.3 | 36 | 0 | 0.0 | 9.4 | 6.3 | 4 | 36 | 0.6 | 12 | 0.00 | 100 | 56 |
| Oman | 56 | 9 | 16.1 | 107 | 2 | 1.9 | 64 | 4 | 6.3 | -- | 0 | -- | 9.0 | 8.1 | 3 | 37 | 6.3 | 60* | 0.00 | 60* | 60 |
| Pakistan | 151 | 18 | 11.9 | 375 | 12 | 3.2 | 172 | 9 | 5.2 | 17 | 0 | 0.0 | 7.6 | 5.1 | 4 | 42 | 0.5 | 10 | 0.00 | 100 | 55 |
| Philippines | 153 | 50 | 32.7 | 395 | 57 | 14.4 | 190 | 8 | 4.2 | 67 | 22 | 32.8 | 23.5 | 21.0 | 4 | 11 | 0.2 | 4 | 0.00 | 80* | 42 |
| Qatar | 11 | 0 | 0.0 | 23 | 1 | 4.3 | 17 | 1 | 5.9 | -- | 0 | -- | 2.2 | 3.4 | 3 | 66 | -- | -- | -- | -- | -- |
| Saudi Arabia | 77 | 7 | 9.1 | 155 | 5 | 3.2 | 84 | 2 | 2.4 | -- | 0 | -- | 6.2 | 4.9 | 3 | 49 | 0.1 | 2 | 0.00 | 60* | 31 |
| Singapore | 45 | 3 | 6.7 | 118 | 1 | 0.8 | -- | 3 | -- | -- | 0 | -- | 3.8 | 3.8 | 2 | 62 | -- | -- | -- | -- | -- |
| Sri Lanka | 88 | 20 | 22.7 | 250 | 9 | 3.6 | 144 | 8 | 5.6 | 39 | 0 | 0.0 | 13.1 | 8.0 | 4 | 27 | 3.1 | 47 | 0.00 | 100 | 73 |
| Syrian Arab R | 63 | 4 | 6.3 | 204 | 2 | 1.0 | -- | 3 | -- | -- | 0 | -- | 3.7 | 3.7 | 2 | 63 | 1.7 | 34 | 0.00 | 100 | 67 |
| Tajikistan | 84 | 9 | 10.7 | -- | 5 | -- | 44 | 1 | 2.3 | 2 | 0 | 0.0 | 10.7 | 4.3 | 3 | 33 | 1.7 | 34 | 0.33 | 51 | 42 |
| Thailand | 265 | 34 | 12.8 | 616 | 20 | 3.2 | 298 | 18 | 6.0 | 107 | 0 | 0.0 | 8.0 | 5.5 | 4 | 40 | 0.3 | 6 | 0.67 | 33 | 19 |
| Turkey | 116 | 17 | 14.7 | 302 | 7 | 2.3 | 102 | 12 | 11.8 | 18 | 3 | 16.7 | 8.5 | 11.4 | 4 | 31 | 0.4 | 8 | 0.00 | 100 | 54 |
| Turkmenistan | 103 | 13 | 12.6 | -- | 3 | -- | 82 | 2 | 2.4 | 5 | 0 | 0.0 | 12.6 | 5.0 | 3 | 28 | 63.5 | 100 | 0.33 | 51 | 75 |
| United Arab Emirates | 25 | 3 | 12.0 | 67 | 2 | 3.0 | 37 | 1 | 2.7 | -- | 0 | -- | 7.5 | 5.9 | 3 | 42 | -- | -- | -- | -- | -- |
| Uzbekistan | 97 | 11 | 11.3 | -- | 7 | -- | 64 | 1 | 1.6 | 2 | 0 | 0.0 | 11.3 | 4.3 | 3 | 32 | 1.2 | 24 | 0.17 | 66 | 45 |
| Viet Nam | 213 | 37 | 17.4 | 535 | 20 | 3.7 | 180 | 24 | 13.3 | 80 | 1 | 1.3 | 10.6 | 8.9 | 4 | 33 | 0.7 | 14 | 0.00 | 100 | 57 |
| Yemen | 66 | 4 | 6.1 | 143 | 6 | 4.2 | 77 | 2 | 2.6 | -- | 0 | -- | 5.2 | 4.3 | 3 | 54 | 0.7 | 14 | 0.00 | 100 | 57 |
| PACIFIC | | | | | | | | | | | | | | | | | | | | | |
| Australia | 252 | 63 | 25.0 | 649 | 33 | 5.1 | 748 | 39 | 5.2 | 205 | 25 | 12.2 | 15.1 | 11.9 | 4 | 22 | 1.7 | 34 | 0.46 | 43 | 38 |
| Fiji | 4 | 5 | 100 | 74 | 12 | 16.2 | 25 | 6 | 24.0 | 2 | 1 | 50.0 | 58.1 | 47.5 | 4 | 0 | 4.3 | 55 | 0.00 | 60* | 57 |
| New Zealand | 10 | 8 | 80.0 | 150 | 62 | 41.3 | 42 | 11 | 26.2 | 3 | 1 | 33.3 | 60.7 | 45.2 | 4 | 0 | 1.2 | 24 | 0.67 | 33 | 28 |
| Papua New Guinea | 214 | 58 | 27.1 | 644 | 32 | 5.0 | 280 | 9 | 3.2 | 197 | 0 | 0.0 | 16.0 | 8.8 | 4 | 20 | 0.7 | 14 | 0.33 | 51 | 32 |
| Samoa | 3 | 3 | 100 | 40 | 6 | 15.0 | 8 | 1 | 12.5 | -- | 0 | -- | 57.5 | 42.5 | 3 | 0 | -- | -- | -- | -- | -- |
| Solomon Is | 53 | 21 | 39.6 | 163 | 22 | 13.5 | 61 | 4 | 6.6 | 17 | 0 | 0.0 | 26.5 | 14.9 | 4 | 7 | -- | -- | 0.00 | 60* | 60 |
| Tonga | 1 | 1 | 100 | 37 | 3 | 8.1 | 6 | 2 | 33.3 | 0 | 0 | 0 | 54.0 | 47.1 | 4 | 0 | -- | -- | -- | -- | -- |
| Vanuatu | 12 | 4 | 33.3 | 76 | 8 | 10.5 | 20 | 2 | 10.0 | 0 | 0 | 0 | 21.9 | 17.9 | 4 | 13 | -- | -- | -- | -- | -- |

**Notes**

The wild animal species indicator covers four higher animal classes:

Mammals (excluding oceanic mammals).

Birds. Birds include only species that breed in the country concerned, because of widely differing standards in recording vagrants, accidentals, and irregular migrants. The number of breeding bird species in Bolivia was extrapolated from the number of total bird species.

Reptiles.

Amphibians.

Total = total native species. Data are from the UNEP World Conservation Monitoring Centre Threatened Animals Database (WCMC 1998b).

Thr = threatened native species. Threatened means critically endangered (high risk of extinction in the immediate future), endangered (high risk of extinction in the near future) or vulnerable (high risk of extinction in the medium-term future). Full definitions are in IUCN Species Survival Commission (1994). Data are for 2000 and are from the IUCN Species Survival Commission (2000), except for data on threatened breeding bird species which are from BirdLife International (2000).

% = threatened native species as a percentage of total native species in the class concerned.

MB % = the average percentage of mammals and birds.

MBRA % = the average percentage of mammals, birds, reptiles and amphibians.

#cl = the number of classes covered. If all four classes are covered, then the indicator for that country is complete. If fewer than four are covered, then the result may be due to the lack of data. If the class does not exist in the country (for example, reptiles in Iceland), it is included in the number in brackets but is not counted in the calculation of the average percentage.

AS score = wild animal species score. This is based on either the average percentage of mammals and birds or the average percentage of mammals, birds, reptiles and amphibians, whichever gives the lower score. The mammal and bird data are more reliable than the data on reptiles and amphibians, and ideally the indicator would be based on these two classes alone. However, the reptile and amphibian data are no worse than the plant data, and excluding them would give misleadingly high scores to several countries, such as Barbados and Turkey. Scores are based on mammals and birds alone in 160 countries, and on the four classes in 23 countries (11 in the Americas, 2 in Africa, 4 in Europe, 6 in Asia). The performance criteria are shown in Table 19a.

The domesticated diversity index (**DD score**) is the average of two unweighted indicators (column heading in parentheses):

Breed diversity (BrD mean), represented by the number of not at risk breeds per million head of a species.

Threatened breeds (Thbr mean), represented by the ratio of threatened to not at risk breeds of a species.

Belgium and Luxembourg: in this table and Table 21, domesticated diversity entries for Belgium and Luxembourg refer to the two countries together, because FAO (2000a) does not provide data on them separately.

BrD mean = mean breed diversity = the number of not at risk breeds per million head of a species, taking the average of three domesticated mammal species: the most numerous species and the next two most numerous or best assessed species in the country concerned. Data are in Table 21. *Note: this indicator is not applied to species of fewer than 100,000 head and only one not at risk breed, to prevent such cases from inflating the score.*

BrD score = breed diversity score. The performance criteria are shown in Table 20a.

Thbr mean = mean threatened breeds = the ratio of threatened to not at risk breeds of a species, taking the average of the three species chosen for mean breed diversity. Data are in Table 21.

Thbr score = mean threatened breeds score. The performance criteria are shown in Table 20a. The tops of the poor, medium and fair bands (0.5, 0.2 and 0.1 threatened breeds per one not at risk breed) correspond to 1 threatened breed per 2, 5 and 10 not at risk breeds respectively.

| band | top point on scale | number of not at risk breeds per million head of a species | ratio of threatened to not at risk breeds of a species |
|---|---|---|---|
| good | 100 | 20 | 0.0 |
| fair | 80 | 10 | 0.1 |
| medium | 60 | 5 | 0.2 |
| poor | 40 | 2 | 0.5 |
| bad | 20 | 1 | 1.0 |
| base | 0 | 0 | 2.0 |

**Table 20a Performance criteria for domesticated diversity indicators.**

* A score with an asterisk has been reduced in accordance with the insufficient data rule. To prevent high scores resulting merely from lack of data, a good score is allowed only if it is based on all applicable components (data in an indicator, indicators in an index), and a fair score only if it is based on at least half the components. Good and fair scores (100-61) based on fewer than half the applicable components have been reduced to 60. Good scores (100-81) based on more than half but not all the applicable components have been reduced to 80.

# Table 21. Domesticated Diversity (continued)

| Country | Sp | Head 000 | Br tot | Br thr | Br tm | Br ok | Br div | Thr rat | Sp | Head 000 | Br tot | Br thr | Br tm | Br ok | Br div | Thr rat | Sp | Head 000 | Br tot | Br thr | Br tm | Br ok | Br div | Thr rat |
|---|---|---|---|---|---|---|---|---|---|---|---|---|---|---|---|---|---|---|---|---|---|---|---|---|
| **AMERICAS** | | | | | | | | | | | | | | | | | | | | | | | | |
| Antigua & Barbuda | Bos | 15.7 | 1 | -- | -- | -- | -- | -- | Cap | 11.8 | 1 | -- | -- | -- | -- | -- | Ovi | 12.2 | 0 | -- | -- | -- | -- | -- |
| Argentina | Bos | 55000.0 | 4 | 1 | 0 | 1 | 0.0 | 1.00 | Eqc | 3300.0 | 2 | 1 | 0 | 1 | 0.3 | 1.00 | Ovi | 14000.0 | 3 | 0 | 0 | 2 | 0.1 | 0.00 |
| Bahamas | Cap | 14.5 | 0 | -- | -- | -- | -- | -- | Ovi | 5.7 | 2 | 0 | 0 | 1 | -- | 0.00 | Sus | 5.8 | 0 | -- | -- | -- | -- | -- |
| Barbados | Ovi | 41.0 | 1 | 0 | 0 | 1 | -- | 0.00 | Bos | 23.0 | 1 | -- | -- | -- | -- | -- | Sus | 33.0 | 0 | -- | -- | -- | -- | -- |
| Belize | Bos | 58.0 | 0 | -- | -- | -- | -- | -- | Eqc | 5.0 | 0 | -- | -- | -- | -- | -- | Sus | 23.0 | 1 | -- | -- | -- | -- | -- |
| Bolivia | Ovi | 8574.5 | 1 | 0 | 0 | 1 | 0.1 | 0.00 | Bos | 6556.0 | 3 | 2 | 0 | 1 | 0.2 | 2.00 | Lam | 1900.0 | 3 | 0 | 0 | 3 | 1.6 | 0.00 |
| Brazil | Bos | 163470.0 | 27 | 1 | 3 | 13 | 0.1 | 0.19 | Ovi | 18300.0 | 7 | 2 | 0 | 3 | 0.2 | 0.67 | Sus | 27425.0 | 12 | 6 | 0 | 0 | 0.0 | 6.00 |
| Canada | Bos | 12981.0 | 14 | 2 | 1 | 6 | 0.5 | 0.42 | Eqc | 508.0 | 12 | 2 | 0 | 6 | 11.8 | 0.33 | Sus | 12402.7 | 5 | 3 | 0 | 2 | 0.2 | 1.50 |
| Chile | Bos | 4134.0 | 1 | 0 | 0 | 1 | 0.2 | 0.00 | Eqc | 590.0 | 1 | 1 | 0 | 0 | 1.7 | 1.00 | Ovi | 4116.0 | 2 | 0 | 0 | 2 | 0.5 | 0.00 |
| Colombia | Bos | 25614.2 | 10 | 4 | 1 | 5 | 0.2 | 0.90 | Ovi | 2195.6 | 3 | 0 | 0 | 1 | 0.5 | 0.00 | Sus | 2764.6 | 4 | -- | -- | -- | -- | -- |
| Costa Rica | Bos | 1617.0 | 2 | -- | -- | -- | -- | -- | Eqc | 114.5 | 0 | -- | -- | -- | -- | -- | Sus | 290.0 | 1 | -- | -- | -- | -- | -- |
| Cuba | Bos | 4650.0 | 6 | 0 | 0 | 1 | 0.2 | 0.00 | Eqc | 620.0 | 1 | -- | -- | -- | -- | -- | Ovi | 310.0 | 1 | 0 | 0 | 1 | 3.2 | 0.00 |
| Dominica | Bos | 13.4 | 1 | -- | -- | -- | -- | -- | Cap | 9.7 | 1 | -- | -- | -- | -- | -- | Ovi | 7.6 | 0 | -- | -- | -- | -- | -- |
| Dominican R | Bos | 1904.4 | 4 | 0 | 0 | 1 | 0.5 | 0.00 | Cap | 163.5 | 1 | -- | -- | -- | -- | -- | Sus | 539.6 | 0 | -- | -- | -- | -- | -- |
| Ecuador | Bos | 5534.0 | 2 | 1 | 0 | 1 | 0.2 | 1.00 | Ovi | 2180.2 | 1 | -- | -- | -- | -- | -- | Sus | 2786.3 | 0 | -- | -- | -- | -- | -- |
| El Salvador | Bos | 1141.5 | 0 | -- | -- | -- | -- | -- | Eqc | 95.8 | 0 | -- | -- | -- | -- | -- | Sus | 335.1 | 1 | -- | -- | -- | -- | -- |
| Grenada | Ovi | 13.0 | 0 | -- | -- | -- | -- | -- | Bos | 4.4 | 1 | -- | -- | -- | -- | -- | Cap | 7.0 | 1 | -- | -- | -- | -- | -- |
| Guatemala | Bos | 2300.0 | 2 | 1 | 0 | 1 | 0.4 | 1.00 | Ovi | 551.3 | 1 | -- | -- | -- | -- | -- | Sus | 825.0 | 1 | -- | -- | -- | -- | -- |
| Guyana | Bos | 220.0 | 0 | -- | -- | -- | -- | -- | Ovi | 130.0 | 1 | 0 | 0 | 1 | 7.7 | 0.00 | Sus | 20.0 | 1 | -- | -- | -- | -- | -- |
| Haiti | Cap | 1618.2 | 1 | -- | -- | -- | -- | -- | Bos | 1300.0 | 1 | -- | -- | -- | -- | -- | Sus | 800.0 | 0 | -- | -- | -- | -- | -- |
| Honduras | Bos | 2060.8 | 0 | -- | -- | -- | -- | -- | Eqc | 178.0 | 0 | -- | -- | -- | -- | -- | Sus | 700.0 | 1 | -- | -- | -- | -- | -- |
| Jamaica | Cap | 440.0 | 0 | -- | -- | -- | -- | -- | Bos | 400.0 | 6 | -- | -- | -- | -- | -- | Sus | 180.0 | 0 | -- | -- | -- | -- | -- |
| Mexico | Bos | 30293.1 | 5 | 0 | 0 | 1 | 0.0 | 0.00 | Ovi | 5900.0 | 5 | 0 | 0 | 1 | 0.2 | 0.00 | Sus | 13854.9 | 3 | 1 | 0 | 0 | 0.1 | 1.00 |
| Nicaragua | Bos | 1693.0 | 1 | -- | -- | -- | -- | -- | Eqc | 245.0 | 1 | -- | -- | -- | -- | -- | Sus | 700.0 | 1 | -- | -- | -- | -- | -- |
| Panama | Bos | 1400.0 | 0 | -- | -- | -- | -- | -- | Eqc | 165.0 | 0 | -- | -- | -- | -- | -- | Sus | 251.8 | 1 | -- | -- | -- | -- | -- |
| Paraguay | Bos | 9863.0 | 1 | 1 | 0 | 0 | 0.1 | 1.00 | Eqc | 400.0 | 0 | -- | -- | -- | -- | -- | Sus | 2500.0 | 0 | -- | -- | -- | -- | -- |
| Peru | Ovi | 13700.0 | 2 | 0 | 0 | 2 | 0.1 | 0.00 | Bos | 4898.3 | 1 | 0 | 0 | 1 | 0.2 | 0.00 | Lam | 4147.0 | 4 | 0 | 0 | 4 | 1.0 | 0.00 |
| St Kitts & Nevis | Cap | 14.5 | 1 | -- | -- | -- | -- | -- | Bos | 3.6 | 1 | -- | -- | -- | -- | -- | Ovi | 8.0 | 0 | -- | -- | -- | -- | -- |
| St Lucia | Sus | 14.8 | 0 | -- | -- | -- | -- | -- | Bos | 12.4 | 1 | -- | -- | -- | -- | -- | Ovi | 12.5 | 0 | -- | -- | -- | -- | -- |
| St Vincent & Grenadines | Ovi | 13.0 | 0 | -- | -- | -- | -- | -- | Bos | 6.2 | 1 | -- | -- | -- | -- | -- | Cap | 6.0 | 1 | -- | -- | -- | -- | -- |
| Suriname | Bos | 102.0 | 0 | -- | -- | -- | -- | -- | Ovi | 10.6 | 0 | -- | -- | -- | -- | -- | Sus | 25.0 | 0 | -- | -- | -- | -- | -- |
| Trinidad & Tobago | Cap | 59.0 | 1 | -- | -- | -- | -- | -- | Bos | 34.0 | 2 | -- | -- | -- | -- | -- | Ovi | 12.0 | 1 | 0 | 0 | 1 | -- | 0.00 |
| United States | Bos | 98521.5 | 34 | 4 | 0 | 11 | 0.1 | 0.36 | Eqc | 6180.0 | 33 | 6 | 0 | 16 | 2.6 | 0.38 | Sus | 62206.0 | 18 | 5 | 0 | 8 | 0.1 | 0.63 |
| Uruguay | Ovi | 15500.0 | 2 | 1 | 0 | 1 | 0.1 | 1.00 | Bos | 10700.0 | 0 | -- | -- | -- | -- | -- | Eqc | 500.0 | 1 | 0 | 0 | 1 | 2.0 | 0.00 |
| Venezuela | Bos | 15992.4 | 6 | 0 | 0 | 3 | 0.2 | 0.00 | Cap | 4000.0 | 1 | 0 | 0 | 1 | 0.3 | 0.00 | Ovi | 781.0 | 3 | -- | -- | -- | -- | -- |
| **AFRICA** | | | | | | | | | | | | | | | | | | | | | | | | |
| Algeria | Ovi | 18200.0 | 8 | 1 | 0 | 7 | 0.4 | 0.14 | Bos | 1650.0 | 1 | 0 | 0 | 1 | 0.6 | 0.00 | Cap | 3400.0 | 6 | 0 | 0 | 2 | 0.6 | 0.00 |
| Angola | Bos | 3900.0 | 7 | 0 | 0 | 5 | 1.3 | 0.00 | Cap | 2000.0 | 0 | -- | -- | -- | -- | -- | Ovi | 336.0 | 4 | -- | -- | -- | -- | -- |
| Benin | Bos | 1345.0 | 4 | 0 | 0 | 4 | 3.0 | 0.00 | Cap | 1087.0 | 2 | 0 | 0 | 1 | 0.9 | 0.00 | Ovi | 634.0 | 3 | 0 | 0 | 1 | 1.6 | 0.00 |
| Botswana | Bos | 2380.0 | 9 | 2 | 0 | 6 | 2.5 | 0.33 | Cap | 1835.0 | 2 | 0 | 0 | 2 | 1.1 | 0.00 | Ovi | 250.0 | 4 | 0 | 0 | 4 | 16.0 | 0.00 |
| Burkina Faso | Cap | 7950.0 | 4 | -- | -- | -- | -- | -- | Bos | 4550.0 | 4 | 0 | 0 | 4 | 0.9 | 0.00 | Ovi | 6350.0 | 3 | 0 | 0 | 1 | 0.2 | 0.00 |
| Burundi | Cap | 593.7 | 0 | -- | -- | -- | -- | -- | Bos | 329.0 | 2 | 2 | 0 | 0 | 3.0 | 2.00 | Ovi | 165.0 | 0 | -- | -- | -- | -- | -- |
| Cameroon | Bos | 5900.0 | 12 | 5 | 0 | 7 | 1.2 | 0.71 | Cap | 3850.0 | 1 | 0 | 0 | 1 | 0.3 | 0.00 | Ovi | 3880.0 | 4 | -- | -- | -- | -- | -- |
| Cape Verde | Sus | 636.0 | 0 | -- | -- | -- | -- | -- | Bos | 22.0 | 0 | -- | -- | -- | -- | -- | Cap | 112.0 | 0 | -- | -- | -- | -- | -- |
| Central African R | Bos | 2992.1 | 5 | 0 | 0 | 5 | 1.7 | 0.00 | Cap | 2350.0 | 1 | 0 | 0 | 1 | 0.4 | 0.00 | Sus | 622.0 | 0 | -- | -- | -- | -- | -- |
| Chad | Bos | 5582.1 | 4 | 2 | 0 | 2 | 0.4 | 1.00 | Cam | 700.0 | 3 | 0 | 0 | 3 | 4.3 | 0.00 | Ovi | 2431.6 | 6 | 0 | 0 | 3 | 1.2 | 0.00 |
| Comoros | Cap | 129.0 | 0 | -- | -- | -- | -- | -- | Bos | 50.0 | 0 | -- | -- | -- | -- | -- | Ovi | 20.0 | 0 | -- | -- | -- | -- | -- |
| Congo, DR | Cap | 4500.0 | 4 | 0 | 0 | 2 | 0.4 | 0.00 | Bos | 900.0 | 10 | 3 | 0 | 5 | 5.6 | 0.60 | Ovi | 930.0 | 3 | -- | -- | -- | -- | -- |
| Congo, R | Cap | 285.0 | 1 | 0 | 0 | 1 | 3.5 | 0.00 | Bos | 75.0 | 2 | 0 | 0 | 2 | 26.7 | 0.00 | Ovi | 115.0 | 1 | 0 | 0 | 1 | 8.7 | 0.00 |
| Côte d'Ivoire | Ovi | 1370.0 | 2 | 0 | 0 | 2 | 1.5 | 0.00 | Bos | 1330.0 | 4 | 0 | 0 | 4 | 3.0 | 0.00 | Cap | 1070.0 | 1 | 0 | 0 | 1 | 0.9 | 0.00 |
| Djibouti | Cap | 511.0 | 0 | -- | -- | -- | -- | -- | Bos | 269.0 | 1 | 0 | 0 | 1 | 3.7 | 0.00 | Ovi | 463.0 | 0 | -- | -- | -- | -- | -- |
| Egypt | Ovi | 4400.0 | 8 | 0 | 0 | 7 | 1.6 | 0.00 | Bub | 3180.0 | 4 | 1 | 0 | 3 | 0.9 | 0.33 | Cap | 3261.0 | 7 | 0 | 0 | 7 | 2.1 | 0.00 |
| Equatorial Guinea | Ovi | 36.0 | 0 | -- | -- | -- | -- | -- | Bos | 4.8 | 1 | -- | -- | -- | -- | -- | Cap | 8.1 | 1 | 0 | 0 | 1 | -- | 0.00 |
| Eritrea | Cap | 1700.0 | 2 | 0 | 0 | 1 | 0.6 | 0.00 | Bos | 1550.0 | 4 | 0 | 0 | 4 | 2.6 | 0.00 | Ovi | 1570.0 | 6 | 0 | 0 | 5 | 3.2 | 0.00 |
| Ethiopia | Bos | 35095.2 | 23 | 1 | 0 | 12 | 0.4 | 0.00 | Cap | 16950.0 | 6 | 0 | 0 | 4 | 0.2 | 0.00 | Ovi | 22000.0 | 13 | 0 | 0 | 9 | 0.4 | 0.00 |
| Gabon | Sus | 212.0 | 0 | -- | -- | -- | -- | -- | Cap | 90.0 | 1 | 0 | 0 | 1 | -- | 0.00 | Ovi | 195.0 | 0 | -- | -- | -- | -- | -- |
| Gambia | Bos | 360.0 | 1 | 0 | 0 | 1 | 2.8 | 0.00 | Cap | 265.0 | 1 | -- | -- | -- | -- | -- | Ovi | 190.0 | 1 | 0 | 0 | 1 | 5.3 | 0.00 |
| Ghana | Cap | 2739.4 | 1 | 0 | 0 | 1 | 0.4 | 0.00 | Bos | 1272.9 | 4 | 1 | 0 | 3 | 2.4 | 0.33 | Ovi | 2516.5 | 4 | 0 | 0 | 3 | 1.2 | 0.00 |
| Guinea | Bos | 2368.0 | 1 | 0 | 0 | 1 | 0.4 | 0.00 | Cap | 864.0 | 1 | 0 | 0 | 1 | 1.2 | 0.00 | Ovi | 687.0 | 1 | 0 | 0 | 1 | 1.5 | 0.00 |
| Guinea-Bissau | Bos | 520.0 | 1 | 0 | 0 | 1 | 1.9 | 0.00 | Cap | 315.0 | 1 | 0 | 0 | 1 | 3.2 | 0.00 | Sus | 340.0 | 0 | -- | -- | -- | -- | -- |

| Country | Sp | Head 000 | Br tot | Br thr | Br tm | Br ok | Br div | Thr rat | Sp | Head 000 | Br tot | Br thr | Br tm | Br ok | Br div | Thr rat | Sp | Head 000 | Br tot | Br thr | Br tm | Br ok | Br div | Thr rat |
|---|---|---|---|---|---|---|---|---|---|---|---|---|---|---|---|---|---|---|---|---|---|---|---|---|
| Kenya | Bos | 13392.0 | 16 | 2 | 0 | 10 | 0.7 | 0.20 | Cam | 830.0 | 3 | 0 | 0 | 3 | 3.6 | 0.00 | Cap | 7600.0 | 4 | 0 | 0 | 3 | 0.4 | 0.00 |
| Lesotho | Ovi | 720.0 | 0 | -- | -- | -- | -- | -- | Bos | 510.0 | 2 | -- | -- | -- | -- | -- | Cap | 560.0 | 2 | 0 | 0 | 1 | 1.8 | 0.00 |
| Liberia | Cap | 220.0 | 1 | 0 | 0 | 1 | 4.5 | 0.00 | Bos | 36.0 | 2 | 1 | 0 | 1 | -- | 1.00 | Ovi | 210.0 | 0 | -- | -- | -- | -- | -- |
| Libyan Arab J | Ovi | 6400.0 | 3 | 0 | 0 | 1 | 0.2 | 0.00 | Bos | 142.0 | 1 | 0 | 0 | 1 | 7.0 | 0.00 | Cap | 2200.0 | 1 | 0 | 0 | 1 | 0.5 | 0.00 |
| Madagascar | Bos | 10353.0 | 2 | 1 | 0 | 1 | 0.1 | 1.00 | Ovi | 790.0 | 1 | -- | -- | -- | -- | -- | Sus | 1700.0 | 0 | -- | -- | -- | -- | -- |
| Malawi | Cap | 1260.0 | 2 | 0 | 0 | 2 | 1.6 | 0.00 | Bos | 750.0 | 1 | 0 | 0 | 1 | 1.3 | 0.00 | Ovi | 110.0 | 1 | -- | -- | -- | -- | -- |
| Mali | Cap | 8524.6 | 3 | 0 | 0 | 1 | 0.1 | 0.00 | Bos | 6058.0 | 4 | 0 | 0 | 4 | 0.7 | 0.00 | Ovi | 5975.4 | 8 | 0 | 0 | 6 | 1.0 | 0.00 |
| Mauritania | Ovi | 6200.0 | 4 | 0 | 0 | 2 | 0.3 | 0.00 | Cam | 1185.0 | 2 | 0 | 0 | 2 | 1.7 | 0.00 | Cap | 4133.0 | 6 | 0 | 0 | 2 | 0.5 | 0.00 |
| Mauritius | Cap | 93.0 | 1 | 0 | 0 | 1 | -- | 0.00 | Bos | 27.0 | 2 | 0 | 0 | 1 | -- | 0.00 | Ovi | 7.2 | 3 | 2 | 0 | 1 | -- | 2.00 |
| Morocco | Ovi | 16576.4 | 24 | 0 | 0 | 6 | 0.4 | 0.00 | Bos | 2559.8 | 3 | 0 | 0 | 2 | 0.8 | 0.00 | Eqc | 150.0 | 1 | 1 | 0 | 0 | 6.7 | 1.00 |
| Mozambique | Bos | 1310.0 | 3 | 1 | 0 | 1 | 0.8 | 1.00 | Cap | 390.0 | 3 | 1 | 0 | 1 | 2.6 | 1.00 | Ovi | 124.0 | 4 | 0 | 0 | 1 | 8.1 | 0.00 |
| Namibia | Ovi | 2100.0 | 2 | 0 | 0 | 2 | 1.0 | 0.00 | Bos | 2000.0 | 6 | 1 | 0 | 0 | 0.5 | 1.00 | Cap | 1700.0 | 2 | -- | -- | -- | -- | -- |
| Niger | Cap | 6469.0 | 3 | 0 | 0 | 2 | 0.3 | 0.00 | Bos | 217.0 | 3 | 1 | 0 | 1 | 4.6 | 1.00 | Ovi | 4312.0 | 3 | 0 | 0 | 1 | 0.2 | 0.00 |
| Nigeria | Cap | 24300.0 | 9 | 0 | 0 | 2 | 0.1 | 0.00 | Bos | 19850.0 | 15 | 2 | 0 | 9 | 0.4 | 0.00 | Ovi | 20500.0 | 8 | 0 | 0 | 1 | 0.0 | 0.00 |
| Rwanda | Bos | 725.5 | 2 | 2 | 0 | 0 | 1.4 | 2.00 | Cap | 634.0 | 0 | -- | -- | -- | -- | -- | Ovi | 290.0 | 0 | -- | -- | -- | -- | -- |
| São Tomé & Principe | Cap | 4.8 | 0 | -- | -- | -- | -- | -- | Bos | 4.0 | 0 | -- | -- | -- | -- | -- | Ovi | 2.5 | 0 | -- | -- | -- | -- | -- |
| Senegal | Ovi | 4300.0 | 5 | 0 | 0 | 4 | 0.9 | 0.00 | Bos | 2955.0 | 3 | 0 | 0 | 3 | 1.0 | 0.00 | Cap | 3595.0 | 1 | 0 | 0 | 1 | 0.3 | 0.00 |
| Seychelles | Sus | 18.2 | 1 | -- | -- | -- | -- | -- | Bos | 1.4 | 0 | -- | -- | -- | -- | -- | Cap | 5.2 | 0 | -- | -- | -- | -- | -- |
| Sierra Leone | Bos | 400.0 | 1 | 0 | 0 | 1 | 2.5 | 0.00 | Cap | 190.0 | 1 | 0 | 0 | 1 | 5.3 | 0.00 | Ovi | 350.0 | 0 | -- | -- | -- | -- | -- |
| Somalia | Ovi | 13000.0 | 3 | -- | -- | -- | -- | -- | Bos | 5000.0 | 6 | -- | -- | -- | -- | -- | Cap | 12000.0 | 8 | -- | -- | -- | -- | -- |
| South Africa | Ovi | 28680.3 | 22 | 2 | 1 | 15 | 0.5 | 0.17 | Bos | 13565.0 | 16 | 1 | 1 | 14 | 1.0 | 0.11 | Cap | 6457.1 | 4 | 0 | 0 | 3 | 0.5 | 0.00 |
| Sudan | Ovi | 42500.0 | 14 | 0 | 0 | 13 | 0.3 | 0.00 | Bos | 35000.0 | 14 | 1 | 0 | 9 | 0.3 | 0.11 | Cap | 37500.0 | 7 | 0 | 0 | 6 | 0.2 | 0.00 |
| Swaziland | Bos | 652.0 | 4 | 0 | 0 | 4 | 6.1 | 0.00 | Cap | 438.0 | 2 | 0 | 0 | 2 | 4.6 | 0.00 | Ovi | 26.0 | 2 | 0 | 0 | 2 | -- | 0.00 |
| Tanzania | Bos | 14350.0 | 11 | 7 | 0 | 4 | 0.3 | 1.75 | Cap | 9900.0 | 1 | 0 | 0 | 1 | 0.1 | 0.00 | Ovi | 4150.0 | 5 | 2 | 0 | 1 | 0.2 | 2.00 |
| Togo | Cap | 1110.0 | 1 | 0 | 0 | 1 | 0.9 | 0.00 | Bos | 222.8 | 4 | 0 | 0 | 4 | 18.0 | 0.00 | Sus | 850.0 | 1 | 0 | 0 | 1 | 1.2 | 0.00 |
| Tunisia | Ovi | 6600.0 | 5 | 0 | 0 | 4 | 0.6 | 0.00 | Bos | 780.0 | 1 | 1 | 0 | 0 | 1.3 | 1.00 | Eqc | 56.2 | 3 | 2 | 0 | 1 | -- | 2.00 |
| Uganda | Bos | 5700.0 | 10 | 6 | 0 | 4 | 0.7 | 1.50 | Cap | 3650.0 | 3 | 0 | 0 | 3 | 0.8 | 0.00 | Ovi | 1970.0 | 2 | 0 | 0 | 2 | 1.0 | 0.00 |
| Zambia | Bos | 2273.0 | 4 | 0 | 0 | 4 | 1.8 | 0.00 | Cap | 1069.0 | 1 | -- | -- | -- | -- | -- | Sus | 324.0 | 0 | -- | -- | -- | -- | -- |
| Zimbabwe | Bos | 5500.0 | 3 | 1 | 0 | 2 | 0.4 | 0.50 | Cap | 2770.0 | 1 | 0 | 0 | 1 | 0.4 | 0.00 | Ovi | 525.0 | 4 | 1 | 0 | 3 | 5.7 | 0.33 |
| EUROPE | | | | | | | | | | | | | | | | | | | | | | | | |
| Albania | Ovi | 1941.0 | 11 | 2 | 0 | 9 | 4.6 | 0.22 | Bos | 720.0 | 5 | 3 | 0 | 2 | 2.8 | 1.50 | Cap | 1120.0 | 15 | 2 | 0 | 13 | 11.6 | 0.15 |
| Austria | Sus | 3810.0 | 0 | -- | -- | -- | -- | -- | Bos | 2172.0 | 10 | 0 | 6 | 4 | 1.8 | 0.75 | Ovi | 383.7 | 7 | 1 | 4 | 2 | 5.2 | 1.50 |
| Belarus | Bos | 4515.0 | 5 | 1 | 0 | 3 | 0.7 | 0.33 | Eqc | 233.2 | 2 | 1 | 0 | 1 | 4.3 | 1.00 | Sus | 3608.0 | 2 | 0 | 0 | 1 | 0.3 | 0.00 |
| Belgium | Sus | 7632.0 | 3 | 0 | 0 | 3 | 0.4 | 0.00 | Bos | 3185.0 | 8 | 1 | 0 | 7 | 2.2 | 0.14 | Ovi | 155.0 | 14 | 10 | 0 | 4 | 25.8 | 2.50 |
| Bosnia & Herzegovina | Bos | 350.0 | 1 | 0 | 0 | 1 | 2.9 | 0.00 | Eqc | 50.0 | 1 | 1 | 0 | 0 | -- | 1.00 | Ovi | 285.0 | 3 | -- | -- | -- | -- | -- |
| Bulgaria | Ovi | 2774.0 | 9 | 3 | 0 | 6 | 2.2 | 0.50 | Bos | 671.0 | 2 | 2 | 0 | 0 | 1.5 | 2.00 | Sus | 1721.0 | 1 | 1 | 0 | 0 | 0.6 | 1.00 |
| Croatia | Sus | 1361.6 | 5 | 3 | 1 | 1 | 0.7 | 3.50 | Bos | 438.5 | 7 | 1 | 2 | 4 | 9.1 | 0.50 | Ovi | 488.5 | 6 | 2 | 0 | 4 | 8.2 | 0.50 |
| Czech R | Sus | 4001.0 | 5 | 2 | 0 | 3 | 0.7 | 0.67 | Bos | 1657.0 | 8 | 5 | 1 | 2 | 1.2 | 2.75 | Ovi | 93.6 | 11 | 8 | 0 | 3 | 32.1 | 2.67 |
| Denmark | Sus | 11991.0 | 6 | 1 | 2 | 3 | 0.3 | 0.67 | Bos | 1968.0 | 14 | 1 | 3 | 9 | 4.6 | 0.28 | Ovi | 156.0 | 14 | 8 | 1 | 3 | 19.2 | 2.83 |
| Estonia | Sus | 326.4 | 2 | 0 | 0 | 2 | 6.1 | 0.00 | Bos | 307.5 | 3 | 1 | 0 | 2 | 6.5 | 0.50 | Ovi | 30.8 | 2 | 0 | 0 | 2 | -- | 0.00 |
| Finland | Sus | 1540.7 | 2 | 0 | 0 | 2 | 1.3 | 0.00 | Bos | 1100.6 | 4 | 0 | 2 | 2 | 1.8 | 0.50 | Ovi | 128.3 | 1 | 0 | 0 | 1 | 7.8 | 0.00 |
| France | Bos | 20214.0 | 37 | 1 | 11 | 25 | 1.2 | 0.26 | Ovi | 10240.0 | 51 | 3 | 6 | 42 | 4.1 | 0.14 | Sus | 16190.0 | 11 | 3 | 5 | 3 | 0.2 | 1.83 |
| Germany | Sus | 26294.0 | 13 | 2 | 3 | 8 | 0.3 | 0.44 | Bos | 14942.0 | 29 | 2 | 10 | 17 | 1.1 | 0.41 | Ovi | 2298.0 | 23 | 0 | 7 | 16 | 7.0 | 0.22 |
| Greece | Ovi | 9290.0 | 11 | 3 | 0 | 8 | 0.9 | 0.38 | Bos | 577.0 | 3 | 2 | 0 | 1 | 1.7 | 2.00 | Cap | 5520.0 | 2 | 0 | 0 | 2 | 0.4 | 0.00 |
| Hungary | Sus | 5479.0 | 7 | 4 | 1 | 2 | 0.4 | 2.25 | Bos | 873.0 | 6 | 3 | 0 | 3 | 3.4 | 1.00 | Ovi | 909.0 | 6 | 1 | 2 | 3 | 3.3 | 0.67 |
| Iceland | Ovi | 477.0 | 1 | 0 | 0 | 1 | 2.1 | 0.00 | Bos | 74.8 | 1 | 0 | 0 | 1 | -- | 0.00 | Eqc | 79.8 | 1 | 0 | 0 | 1 | -- | 0.00 |
| Ireland | Bos | 7093.0 | 9 | 0 | 1 | 8 | 1.1 | 0.06 | Ovi | 5624.0 | 5 | 0 | 0 | 5 | 0.9 | 0.00 | Sus | 1801.0 | 2 | 0 | 0 | 2 | 1.1 | 0.00 |
| Italy | Ovi | 10770.0 | 47 | 15 | 3 | 29 | 2.7 | 0.57 | Bos | 7150.0 | 31 | 0 | 11 | 20 | 2.8 | 0.28 | Cap | 1365.0 | 24 | 14 | 0 | 10 | 7.3 | 1.40 |
| Latvia | Sus | 403.4 | 4 | 0 | 1 | 3 | 7.4 | 0.17 | Bos | 375.7 | 4 | 0 | 2 | 2 | 5.3 | 0.50 | Eqc | 23.3 | 2 | 0 | 1 | 1 | -- | 0.50 |
| Lithuania | Sus | 1167.7 | 2 | 0 | 1 | 1 | 0.9 | 0.50 | Bos | 927.7 | 4 | 0 | 2 | 2 | 2.2 | 0.50 | Eqc | 74.8 | 4 | 1 | 1 | 2 | 26.7 | 0.75 |
| Luxembourg | Sus | 7632.0 | 3 | 0 | 0 | 3 | 0.4 | 0.00 | Bos | 3185.0 | 8 | 1 | 0 | 7 | 2.2 | 0.14 | Ovi | 155.0 | 14 | 10 | 0 | 4 | 25.8 | 2.50 |
| Macedonia, FYR | Ovi | 1550.0 | 3 | 0 | 0 | 3 | 1.9 | 0.00 | Bos | 290.0 | 1 | 0 | 0 | 1 | 3.4 | 0.00 | Sus | 196.8 | 1 | 1 | 0 | 0 | 5.1 | 1.00 |
| Malta | Sus | 69.0 | -- | -- | -- | -- | -- | -- | Bos | 21.0 | 1 | 0 | 0 | 1 | -- | 0.00 | Ovi | 16.0 | 1 | 0 | 0 | 1 | -- | 0.00 |
| Moldova | Ovi | 940.0 | 2 | 0 | 0 | 1 | 1.1 | 0.00 | Bos | 525.0 | 4 | 1 | 0 | 3 | 5.7 | 0.33 | Cap | 95.0 | 1 | 0 | 0 | 1 | -- | 0.00 |
| Netherlands | Sus | 13418.0 | 2 | 0 | 0 | 2 | 0.1 | 0.00 | Bos | 4184.0 | 5 | 0 | 2 | 3 | 0.7 | 0.33 | Ovi | 1465.0 | 7 | 0 | 3 | 4 | 2.7 | 0.38 |
| Norway | Ovi | 2399.0 | 6 | 1 | 0 | 5 | 2.1 | 0.20 | Bos | 1041.6 | 3 | 0 | 2 | 1 | 1.0 | 1.00 | Sus | 689.6 | 2 | 1 | 0 | 1 | 1.5 | 1.00 |
| Poland | Sus | 18537.6 | 9 | 0 | 3 | 6 | 0.3 | 0.25 | Bos | 6555.0 | 4 | 0 | 0 | 4 | 0.6 | 0.00 | Ovi | 392.1 | 18 | 0 | 5 | 13 | 33.2 | 0.19 |
| Portugal | Ovi | 5850.0 | 10 | 0 | 0 | 10 | 1.7 | 0.00 | Bos | 1270.0 | 10 | 1 | 0 | 9 | 7.1 | 0.11 | Sus | 2341.0 | 2 | 1 | 0 | 1 | 0.4 | 1.00 |
| Romania | Ovi | 8409.0 | 5 | 0 | 0 | 5 | 0.6 | 0.00 | Bos | 3143.0 | 5 | 0 | 2 | 3 | 1.0 | 0.33 | Sus | 7194.0 | 6 | 0 | 2 | 4 | 0.6 | 0.25 |
| Slovakia | Sus | 1592.6 | 3 | 0 | 0 | 2 | 1.3 | 0.00 | Bos | 704.8 | 3 | 0 | 0 | 3 | 4.3 | 0.00 | Ovi | 326.2 | 3 | 0 | 0 | 3 | 9.2 | 0.00 |
| Slovenia | Sus | 592.4 | 6 | 4 | 1 | 1 | 1.7 | 4.50 | Bos | 453.1 | 4 | 1 | 0 | 3 | 6.6 | 0.33 | Ovi | 72.4 | 2 | 1 | 0 | 1 | -- | 1.00 |
| Spain | Ovi | 23751.0 | 26 | 4 | 1 | 18 | 0.8 | 0.25 | Bos | 6065.0 | 32 | 12 | 9 | 10 | 1.6 | 1.65 | Sus | 21600.0 | 12 | 6 | 4 | 2 | 0.1 | 4.00 |
| Sweden | Sus | 2321.0 | 2 | 1 | 0 | 0 | 0.4 | 1.00 | Bos | 1757.0 | 9 | 2 | 3 | 3 | 1.7 | 1.17 | Ovi | 420.0 | 5 | 1 | 0 | 4 | 9.5 | 0.25 |
| Switzerland | Bos | 1615.0 | 6 | 1 | 1 | 4 | 2.5 | 0.38 | Ovi | 490.0 | 9 | 1 | 4 | 4 | 8.2 | 0.75 | Sus | 1420.0 | 3 | 0 | 1 | 2 | 1.4 | 0.25 |
| Ukraine | Bos | 11722.0 | 10 | 2 | 0 | 5 | 0.4 | 0.40 | Ovi | 1198.0 | 10 | 0 | 0 | 3 | 2.5 | 0.00 | Sus | 10083.0 | 7 | 1 | 0 | 2 | 0.2 | 0.50 |
| United Kingdom | Ovi | 44656.0 | 56 | 3 | 9 | 40 | 0.9 | 0.19 | Bos | 11423.0 | 34 | 8 | 2 | 23 | 2.0 | 0.39 | Sus | 7284.0 | 13 | 9 | 0 | 2 | 0.3 | 4.50 |

| Country | Sp | Head 000 | Br tot | Br thr | Br tm | Br ok | Br div | Thr rat | Sp | Head 000 | Br tot | Br thr | Br tm | Br ok | Br div | Thr rat | Sp | Head 000 | Br tot | Br thr | Br tm | Br ok | Br div | Thr rat |
|---|---|---|---|---|---|---|---|---|---|---|---|---|---|---|---|---|---|---|---|---|---|---|---|---|
| Yugoslavia | Sus | 4372.0 | 11 | 6 | 0 | 5 | 1.1 | 1.20 | Bos | 1831.0 | 7 | 4 | 0 | 3 | 1.6 | 1.33 | Ovi | 2392.0 | 9 | 0 | 0 | 3 | 1.3 | 0.00 |
| RUSSIAN FED. | Bos | 28634.0 | 28 | 5 | 1 | 17 | 0.6 | 0.32 | Eqc | 2000.0 | 35 | 13 | 1 | 14 | 7.0 | 0.96 | Sus | 17300.0 | 18 | 1 | 0 | 11 | 0.6 | 0.09 |
| ASIA | | | | | | | | | | | | | | | | | | | | | | | | |
| Afghanistan | Ovi | 14300.0 | 10 | 0 | 0 | 3 | 0.2 | 0.00 | Bos | 1500.0 | 5 | -- | -- | -- | -- | -- | Cap | 2200.0 | 3 | -- | -- | -- | -- | -- |
| Armenia | Ovi | 575.0 | 8 | 1 | 0 | 2 | 3.5 | 0.50 | Bos | 512.0 | 0 | -- | -- | -- | -- | -- | Cap | 12.5 | 1 | 1 | 0 | 0 | -- | 1.00 |
| Azerbaijan | Ovi | 5131.9 | 10 | 2 | 0 | 3 | 0.6 | 0.67 | Bos | 1909.8 | 2 | 0 | 0 | 2 | 1.0 | 0.00 | Cap | 370.9 | 1 | 1 | 0 | 0 | 2.7 | 1.00 |
| Bahrain | Ovi | 17.1 | 1 | -- | -- | -- | -- | -- | Bos | 13.0 | 0 | -- | -- | -- | -- | -- | Cap | 16.0 | 0 | -- | -- | -- | -- | -- |
| Bangladesh | Cap | 33500.0 | 1 | 0 | 0 | 1 | 0.0 | 0.00 | Bos | 23400.0 | 6 | 1 | 0 | 4 | 0.2 | 0.25 | Ovi | 1110.0 | 1 | 0 | 0 | 1 | 0.9 | 0.00 |
| Bhutan | Bos | 435.0 | 3 | 1 | 0 | 2 | 4.6 | 0.50 | Ovi | 58.5 | 0 | -- | -- | -- | -- | -- | Sus | 74.9 | 1 | -- | -- | -- | -- | -- |
| Brunei Darussalam | Bub | 6.0 | 0 | -- | -- | -- | -- | -- | Cap | 3.3 | 0 | -- | -- | -- | -- | -- | Sus | 4.5 | 0 | -- | -- | -- | -- | -- |
| Cambodia | Bos | 2820.8 | 2 | 1 | 0 | 0 | 0.4 | 1.00 | Bub | 693.7 | 2 | 0 | 0 | 1 | 1.4 | 0.00 | Sus | 2438.3 | 0 | -- | -- | -- | -- | -- |
| China | Sus | 429211.6 | 114 | 10 | 0 | 79 | 0.2 | 0.13 | Cap | 141956.4 | 31 | 0 | 0 | 28 | 0.2 | 0.00 | Ovi | 127163.4 | 34 | 0 | 0 | 29 | 0.2 | 0.00 |
| Cyprus | Sus | 436.4 | 0 | -- | -- | -- | -- | -- | Bos | 62.5 | 3 | 0 | 1 | 0 | -- | 0.50 | Cap | 300.0 | 3 | 0 | 0 | 2 | 6.7 | 0.00 |
| Georgia | Bos | 1051.0 | 7 | 1 | 0 | 3 | 2.9 | 0.33 | Ovi | 550.0 | 14 | 1 | 0 | 7 | 12.7 | 0.14 | Sus | 365.9 | 2 | 1 | 0 | 1 | 2.7 | 1.00 |
| India | Bos | 214877.0 | 63 | 3 | 1 | 26 | 0.1 | 0.13 | Cap | 122530.0 | 26 | 0 | 0 | 11 | 0.1 | 0.00 | Ovi | 57600.0 | 57 | 0 | 0 | 35 | 0.6 | 0.00 |
| Indonesia | Cap | 15197.8 | 7 | 1 | 0 | 5 | 0.3 | 0.20 | Bos | 12239.3 | 16 | 1 | 0 | 15 | 1.2 | 0.07 | Bub | 3145.1 | 10 | 0 | 0 | 10 | 3.2 | 0.00 |
| Iran | Ovi | 53900.0 | 25 | 0 | 0 | 3 | 0.1 | 0.00 | Bos | 8047.4 | 9 | 1 | 0 | 3 | 0.4 | 0.33 | Eqc | 250.0 | 11 | 1 | 0 | 0 | 4.0 | 1.00 |
| Iraq | Ovi | 6000.0 | 8 | 0 | 0 | 3 | 0.5 | 0.00 | Bos | 1100.0 | 6 | 0 | 0 | 1 | 0.9 | 0.00 | Cap | 1300.0 | 3 | 1 | 0 | 1 | 0.8 | 1.00 |
| Israel | Ovi | 340.0 | 2 | -- | -- | -- | -- | -- | Bos | 300.0 | 3 | 0 | 0 | 1 | 3.3 | 0.00 | Cap | 73.0 | 4 | 0 | 0 | 1 | -- | 0.00 |
| Japan | Sus | 9879.0 | 0 | -- | -- | -- | -- | -- | Bos | 4658.0 | 7 | 1 | 0 | 0 | 0.2 | 1.00 | Eqc | 27.0 | 8 | 5 | 2 | 1 | -- | 6.00 |
| Jordan | Ovi | 2000.0 | 1 | 0 | 0 | 1 | 0.5 | 0.00 | Bos | 65.0 | 1 | 0 | 0 | 1 | -- | 0.00 | Cap | 795.0 | 2 | 0 | 0 | 2 | 2.5 | 0.00 |
| Kazakhstan | Ovi | 9000.0 | 17 | 0 | 0 | 10 | 1.1 | 0.00 | Bos | 3957.9 | 4 | 0 | 0 | 3 | 0.8 | 0.00 | Eqc | 986.3 | 6 | 0 | 0 | 5 | 5.1 | 0.00 |
| Korea, DPR | Sus | 2970.0 | 1 | -- | -- | -- | -- | -- | Bos | 565.0 | 0 | -- | -- | -- | -- | -- | Cap | 1900.0 | 0 | -- | -- | -- | -- | -- |
| Korea, R | Sus | 7863.7 | 0 | -- | -- | -- | -- | -- | Bos | 2486.5 | 2 | 0 | 0 | 1 | 0.4 | 0.00 | Cap | 500.0 | 1 | 0 | 0 | 1 | 2.0 | 0.00 |
| Kuwait | Ovi | 445.0 | 3 | 0 | 0 | 2 | 4.5 | 0.00 | Bos | 20.0 | 0 | -- | -- | -- | -- | -- | Cap | 150.0 | 0 | -- | -- | -- | -- | -- |
| Kyrgyzstan | Ovi | 3400.0 | 5 | 0 | 0 | 3 | 0.9 | 0.00 | Bos | 825.0 | 4 | 0 | 0 | 3 | 3.6 | 0.00 | Eqc | 320.0 | 2 | 1 | 0 | 1 | 3.1 | 1.00 |
| Lao PDR | Sus | 1936.5 | 4 | 0 | 0 | 4 | 2.1 | 0.00 | Bos | 1497.0 | 1 | 0 | 0 | 1 | 0.7 | 0.00 | Bub | 1286.0 | 1 | 0 | 0 | 1 | 0.8 | 0.00 |
| Lebanon | Cap | 460.0 | 2 | -- | -- | -- | -- | -- | Bos | 82.0 | 2 | 0 | 0 | 1 | -- | 0.00 | Ovi | 162.0 | 1 | -- | -- | -- | -- | -- |
| Malaysia | Sus | 2961.0 | 1 | 1 | 0 | 0 | 0.3 | 1.00 | Bos | 713.0 | 6 | 1 | 0 | 3 | 4.2 | 0.33 | Cap | 235.0 | 3 | 0 | 0 | 1 | 4.3 | 0.00 |
| Maldives | Cap | -- | 1 | 0 | 0 | 1 | -- | 0.00 | -- | -- | -- | -- | -- | -- | -- | -- | -- | -- | -- | -- | -- | -- | -- | -- |
| Mongolia | Ovi | 14694.2 | 16 | 0 | 0 | 15 | 1.0 | 0.00 | Bos | 3725.8 | 5 | 0 | 0 | 4 | 1.1 | 0.00 | Cap | 11061.9 | 4 | 0 | 0 | 4 | 0.4 | 0.00 |
| Myanmar | Bos | 10739.5 | 6 | 0 | 0 | 6 | 0.6 | 0.00 | Bub | 2391.0 | 2 | 0 | 0 | 2 | 0.8 | 0.00 | Sus | 3715.0 | 3 | 0 | 0 | 3 | 0.8 | 0.00 |
| Nepal | Bos | 7030.7 | 8 | 0 | 0 | 5 | 0.7 | 0.00 | Bub | 3470.6 | 4 | 0 | 0 | 3 | 0.9 | 0.00 | Cap | 6204.6 | 5 | 0 | 0 | 2 | 0.3 | 0.00 |
| Oman | Cap | 728.0 | 0 | -- | -- | -- | -- | -- | Bos | 148.0 | 0 | -- | -- | -- | -- | -- | Ovi | 160.0 | 1 | 0 | 0 | 1 | 6.3 | 0.00 |
| Pakistan | Cap | 49700.0 | 28 | 0 | 0 | 25 | 0.5 | 0.00 | Bub | 21300.0 | 4 | 0 | 0 | 4 | 0.2 | 0.00 | Ovi | 31300.0 | 32 | 0 | 0 | 29 | 0.9 | 0.00 |
| Philippines | Sus | 10390.0 | 2 | -- | -- | -- | -- | -- | Bub | 3006.0 | 2 | 0 | 0 | 1 | 0.3 | 0.00 | Cap | 6780.0 | 2 | 0 | 0 | 1 | 0.1 | 0.00 |
| Qatar | Ovi | 207.0 | 0 | -- | -- | -- | -- | -- | Cam | 47.8 | 0 | -- | -- | -- | -- | -- | Cap | 177.0 | 0 | -- | -- | -- | -- | -- |
| Saudi Arabia | Ovi | 8300.0 | 7 | 0 | 0 | 1 | 0.1 | 0.00 | Cam | 428.0 | 0 | -- | -- | -- | -- | -- | Cap | 4500.0 | 4 | -- | -- | -- | -- | -- |
| Singapore | Sus | 190.0 | 0 | -- | -- | -- | -- | -- | Bos | 0.2 | 0 | -- | -- | -- | -- | -- | Cap | 0.3 | 0 | -- | -- | -- | -- | -- |
| Sri Lanka | Bos | 1599.0 | 4 | 0 | 0 | 2 | 1.3 | 0.00 | Bub | 720.7 | 3 | 0 | 0 | 3 | 4.2 | 0.00 | Cap | 519.3 | 2 | 0 | 0 | 2 | 3.9 | 0.00 |
| Syrian Arab R | Ovi | 15000.0 | 3 | 0 | 0 | 2 | 0.1 | 0.00 | Bos | 905.0 | 3 | 0 | 0 | 3 | 3.3 | 0.00 | Cap | 1200.0 | 3 | 0 | 0 | 2 | 1.7 | 0.00 |
| Tajikistan | Ovi | 1620.0 | 6 | 0 | 0 | 4 | 2.5 | 0.00 | Bos | 911.5 | 4 | 0 | 0 | 1 | 1.1 | 0.00 | Cap | 625.0 | 3 | 1 | 0 | 1 | 1.6 | 1.00 |
| Thailand | Sus | 7200.0 | 4 | 2 | 0 | 1 | 0.1 | 2.00 | Bos | 5677.0 | 4 | 0 | 0 | 3 | 0.5 | 0.00 | Bub | 3500.0 | 1 | 0 | 0 | 1 | 0.3 | 0.00 |
| Turkey | Ovi | 30238.0 | 23 | 0 | 0 | 13 | 0.4 | 0.00 | Bos | 11185.0 | 12 | 0 | 0 | 5 | 0.4 | 0.00 | Cap | 8376.0 | 7 | 0 | 0 | 3 | 0.4 | 0.00 |
| Turkmenistan | Ovi | 5650.0 | 3 | 0 | 0 | 1 | 0.2 | 0.00 | Cap | 375.0 | 3 | 1 | 0 | 1 | 2.7 | 1.00 | Eqc | 16.0 | 3 | 0 | 0 | 3 | 187.5 | 0.00 |
| United Arab Emirates | Cap | 1050.0 | 0 | -- | -- | -- | -- | -- | Cam | 195.0 | 0 | -- | -- | -- | -- | -- | Ovi | 440.0 | 0 | -- | -- | -- | -- | -- |
| Uzbekistan | Ovi | 8000.0 | 8 | 0 | 0 | 3 | 0.4 | 0.00 | Bos | 5225.2 | 2 | 0 | 0 | 1 | 0.2 | 0.00 | Cap | 697.9 | 4 | 1 | 0 | 2 | 2.9 | 0.50 |
| Viet Nam | Sus | 18885.8 | 8 | 0 | 0 | 8 | 0.4 | 0.00 | Bos | 4063.6 | 7 | 0 | 0 | 6 | 1.5 | 0.00 | Bub | 2955.7 | 1 | 0 | 0 | 1 | 0.3 | 0.00 |
| Yemen | Ovi | 4595.1 | 11 | 0 | 0 | 1 | 0.2 | 0.00 | Bos | 1288.8 | 2 | 0 | 0 | 1 | 0.8 | 0.00 | Cap | 4150.2 | 7 | 0 | 0 | 5 | 1.2 | 0.00 |
| PACIFIC | | | | | | | | | | | | | | | | | | | | | | | | |
| Australia | Ovi | 119600.0 | 26 | 3 | 1 | 9 | 0.1 | 0.39 | Bos | 26710.0 | 17 | 0 | 0 | 10 | 0.4 | 0.00 | Eqc | 220.0 | 2 | 1 | 0 | 1 | 4.5 | 1.00 |
| Fiji | Bos | 344.6 | 0 | -- | -- | -- | -- | -- | Cap | 235.0 | 1 | 0 | 0 | 1 | 4.3 | 0.00 | Sus | 111.7 | 0 | -- | -- | -- | -- | -- |
| New Zealand | Ovi | 46100.0 | 13 | 0 | 0 | 3 | 0.1 | 0.00 | Eqc | 85.0 | 2 | 1 | 0 | 0 | -- | 1.00 | Sus | 413.0 | 1 | 1 | 0 | 0 | 2.4 | 1.00 |
| Papua New Guinea | Sus | 1500.0 | 1 | 0 | 0 | 1 | 0.7 | 0.00 | Bos | 86.0 | 1 | 1 | 0 | 0 | -- | 1.00 | Ovi | 6.0 | 1 | 0 | 0 | 1 | -- | 0.00 |
| Samoa | Sus | 178.8 | 1 | -- | -- | -- | -- | -- | Bos | 26.0 | 0 | -- | -- | -- | -- | -- | Eqa | 7.0 | 0 | -- | -- | -- | -- | -- |
| Solomon Is | Sus | 58.0 | 1 | 0 | 0 | 1 | -- | 0.00 | Bos | 10.0 | 0 | -- | -- | -- | -- | -- | Eqc | 0.1 | 0 | -- | -- | -- | -- | -- |
| Tonga | Sus | 80.9 | 0 | -- | -- | -- | -- | -- | Bos | 13.9 | 0 | -- | -- | -- | -- | -- | Eqc | 11.4 | 0 | -- | -- | -- | -- | -- |
| Vanuatu | Bos | 151.0 | 0 | -- | -- | -- | -- | -- | Sus | 62.0 | 0 | -- | -- | -- | -- | -- | Cap | 12.0 | 0 | -- | -- | -- | -- | -- |

**Notes**

This table gives the data for the domesticated diversity index (Table 20).

Sp = the chosen species, abbreviated as follows:

Bos = cattle and kin = all domesticated forms of the genus *Bos*: cattle (*Bos primigenius*), Bali cattle (domesticated *Bos javanicus*), mithun (domesticated *Bos gaurus*) and yak (domesticated *Bos mutus*)

Bub = water buffalo (domesticated *Bubalus arnee*)

Cam = camels = both domesticated forms of the genus *Camelus*: Bactrian camel (*Camelus bactrianus* [domesticated *Camelus ferus*]) and dromedary (*Camelus dromedarius*)

Cap = goat (*Capra hircus*)

Eqa = ass (*Equus asinus*)

Eqc = horse (*Equus caballus*)

Lam = both domesticated species of the genus *Lama*: alpaca (*Lama pacos*) and llama (*Lama glama*)

Ovi = sheep (*Ovis aries*)

Sus = pig (*Sus domesticus*)

Head 000 = the estimated stock of the species, in thousands of head. Data are for 1999 and are from Food and Agriculture Organization of the United Nations (2000a).

Br tot = number of established breeds in DAD-IS = number of breeds in the Domesticated Animal Diversity Information System (DAD-IS) of the FAO Global Strategy for the Management of Farm Animal Genetic Resources, *excluding wild species, feral populations (descendants of domesticated stock, now living in the wild), and—if possible to ascertain—not yet established breeds (recent imports, experimental lines, breeds under development)*. Wild species are excluded to avoid duplication of the wild animal species indicator. Feral populations are excluded because they are often a threat to wild species and natural ecosystems. Recent imports, experimental lines and breeds under development are excluded because they are not an established part of a particular agro-ecosystem. Data are for 1998-1999 and are from FAO Initiative for Domesticated Animal Diversity (1998, 1999) and Rege (1999).

Br thr = number of established breeds that are threatened with extinction = number of African cattle breeds assessed by Rege (1999) as threatened, or number of all other breeds assessed by the FAO Initiative for Domesticated Animal Diversity (1998) as "critical" or "endangered" (excluding wild species, feral populations and not yet established breeds). FAO criteria for threatened breeds are given in Scherf (1985). A breed is "critical" if:

> *either* total number of breeding females is less than 100
>
> *or* total number of breeding males is 5 or less
>
> *or* total population is slightly above 100 and decreasing, and less than 80% of females are bred pure.

A breed is "endangered" if:

> *either* total number of breeding females is between 100 and 1000
>
> *or* total number of breeding males is more than 5 but no more than 20
>
> *or* total population is slightly below 1000 but increasing, and more than 80% of females are bred pure
>
> *or* total population is slightly above 1000 and decreasing, and less than 80% of females are bred pure.

In the event of a conflict between Rege (1999) and FAO Initiative for Domesticated Animal Diversity (1998), I followed Rege, because his assessment of "threatened" takes account of the impact of crossbreeding and interbreeding. Because the FAO criteria do not include the degree of incrossing from other breeds (and also because they do not apply species-specific estimates of effective population size), they tend to understate the number of threatened breeds (Simon 1999).

Br tm = number of established breeds that are threatened but maintained = number of breeds assessed by the FAO Initiative for Domesticated Animal Diversity (1998) as "critical" or "endangered" (excluding wild species, feral populations and not yet established breeds) but for which active conservation programs are in place.

Br ok = number of established breeds that are not at risk of extinction = number of breeds assessed by the FAO Initiative for Domesticated Animal Diversity (1998) as "not at risk" (excluding wild species and feral populations). Breeds "not at risk" are considered by definition to be established, unless they are explicitly noted as experimental or under development, in which case they are excluded. A breed is "not at risk" if:

> *either* total number of breeding females is more than 1000 and total number of breeding males is more than 20
>
> *or* total population approaches 1000 and is increasing, and close to 100% of females are bred pure.

The difference between Br tot and Br thr + Br tm + Br ok is the number of breeds in DAD-IS that have not been assessed. For example, of Brazil's 27 cattle breeds in DAD-IS, 10 have not been assessed.

Br div = breed diversity = the number of breeds assessed as "not at risk" per million head of the species. If no breed is assessed as not at risk, it is assumed that the number of not at risk breeds is 1 (given the stock sizes concerned, it could not be less than this). For example, Malaysia has 2,961,000 pigs (Sus), but the breed columns show 1 breed in DAD-IS, 1 threatened breed, and 0 not at risk breeds. The not at risk figure is obviously incomplete, so it is assumed there is at least one not at risk breed.

Thr rat = threatened breeds ratio = the ratio of threatened (thr) and threatened but maintained (tm) breeds to not at risk breeds. In calculating the ratio, threatened but maintained breeds count as half a breed. For example, of Brazil's cattle breeds, 1 is threatened, 3 are threatened but maintained, and 13 are not at risk. The ratio is therefore $(1 + [3 \div 2]) \div 13 = 0.19$ (0.19 threatened breeds per 1 not at risk breed). If no breed is assessed as not at risk, it is assumed that the number of not at risk breeds is 1 (given the stock sizes concerned, it could not be less than this).

Note the number of established breeds in DAD-IS may be much smaller than the number that exists, and many of the breeds in DAD-IS have not been assessed. *Consequently, the indicators reflect the state of knowledge as much as of the actual level and condition of domesticated animal diversity.*

# Table 22. Resource Use Index; Energy; Timber

| Country | EC total | EC/ha | EC/p | *E* score | Timber note | Volume 000 m³ | NAI 000 m³ | Felling 000 m³ | Prod 000 m³ | Imp 000 m³ | F+I % NAI | P+I % vol | Timb score | Ag score | Fish score | *RS* score | RU index |
|---|---|---|---|---|---|---|---|---|---|---|---|---|---|---|---|---|---|
| **AMERICAS** | | | | | | | | | | | | | | | | | |
| Antigua & Barbuda | 5 | 113.6 | 75.2 | 52 | x90 | 600 | -- | -- | 0 | 15 | -- | 2.5 | 75 | 12 | 20 | 36 | 44 |
| Argentina | 2404 | 8.6 | 67.4 | 66 | z90 | 3720700 | -- | -- | 11427 | 397 | -- | 0.3 | 97 | 60 | 60 | 72 | 69 |
| Bahamas | 24 | 17.3 | 82.5 | 59 | x90 | 11600 | -- | -- | 117 | 101 | -- | 1.9 | 81 | 12 | 74 | 56 | 57 |
| Barbados | 15 | 348.8 | 56.2 | 18 | x90 | 0 | -- | -- | 5 | 75 | -- | 8000 | 0 | 18 | 13 | 10 | 14 |
| Belize | 10 | 4.4 | 44.6 | 78 | y90 | 100100 | -- | -- | 188 | 5 | -- | 0.2 | 98 | 48 | 16 | 54 | 66 |
| Bolivia | 150 | 1.4 | 19.3 | 90 | y90 | 3650500 | -- | -- | 1989 | 1 | -- | 0.1 | 99 | 76 | 20 | 65 | 77 |
| Brazil | 6787 | 7.9 | 41.5 | 79 | y90 | 65486000 | -- | -- | 197816 | 448 | -- | 0.3 | 97 | 60 | 49 | 69 | 74 |
| Canada | 10410 | 10.4 | 344.0 | 18 | vi94 r95 | 29364059 | 442030 | 214128 | 191178 | 9254 | 50.5 | 0.7 | 88 | 42 | 57 | 62 | 40 |
| Chile | 912 | 12.1 | 62.4 | 69 | z90 | 1491100 | -- | -- | 31670 | 0 | -- | 2.1 | 79 | 45 | 62 | 62 | 65 |
| Colombia | 1129 | 9.9 | 28.2 | 86 | y90 | 6018100 | -- | -- | 18618 | 55 | -- | 0.3 | 97 | 60 | 16 | 58 | 72 |
| Costa Rica | 113 | 22.1 | 30.1 | 85 | y90 | 149100 | -- | -- | 5311 | 20 | -- | 3.6 | 64 | 64 | 62 | 63 | 74 |
| Cuba | 444 | 40.1 | 40.1 | 80 | y90 | 104400 | -- | -- | 2756 | 20 | -- | 2.7 | 73 | 49 | 43 | 55 | 67 |
| Dominica | 1 | 13.3 | 14.1 | 93 | x90 | 2700 | -- | -- | 0 | 15 | -- | 0.6 | 94 | 37 | 14 | 48 | 70 |
| Dominican R | 209 | 42.9 | 25.8 | 78 | x90 | 44200 | -- | -- | 562 | 374 | -- | 2.1 | 79 | 59 | 6 | 48 | 63 |
| Ecuador | 355 | 12.5 | 29.7 | 85 | y90 | 1310200 | -- | -- | 11340 | 8 | -- | 0.9 | 91 | 69 | 75 | 78 | 81 |
| El Salvador | 139 | 66.1 | 23.5 | 67 | y90 | 5800 | -- | -- | 5129 | 25 | -- | 88.9 | 0 | 51 | 33 | 28 | 47 |
| Grenada | 3 | 88.2 | 32.3 | 58 | x90 | 400 | -- | -- | 0 | 14 | -- | 3.5 | 65 | 25 | 17 | 36 | 47 |
| Guatemala | 266 | 24.4 | 25.3 | 87 | y90 | 416600 | -- | -- | 12995 | 16 | -- | 3.1 | 69 | 62 | 19 | 50 | 68 |
| Guyana | 22 | 1.0 | 26.1 | 87 | x90 | 3241200 | -- | -- | 442 | 0 | -- | 0.0 | 100 | 70 | 79 | 83 | 85 |
| Haiti | 83 | 29.9 | 10.6 | 85 | x90 | 1000 | -- | -- | 6397 | 19 | -- | 641.6 | 0 | 52 | 8 | 20 | 52 |
| Honduras | 124 | 11.1 | 20.7 | 90 | y90 | 345800 | -- | -- | 7176 | 25 | -- | 2.1 | 79 | 58 | 58 | 65 | 77 |
| Jamaica | 150 | 136.5 | 59.6 | 46 | y90 | 24400 | -- | -- | 343 | 141 | -- | 2.0 | 80 | 48 | 8 | 45 | 45 |
| Mexico | 5658 | 28.9 | 60.0 | 70 | y90 | 1856800 | -- | -- | 23866 | 1812 | -- | 1.4 | 86 | 57 | 49 | 64 | 67 |
| Nicaragua | 109 | 8.4 | 23.3 | 88 | y90 | 651000 | -- | -- | 4198 | 8 | -- | 0.6 | 94 | 64 | 52 | 70 | 79 |
| Panama | 90 | 11.9 | 33.1 | 83 | y90 | 440400 | -- | -- | 1098 | 16 | -- | 0.3 | 97 | 58 | 48 | 68 | 75 |
| Paraguay | 133 | 3.3 | 26.1 | 87 | y90 | 347500 | -- | -- | 8097 | 2 | -- | 2.3 | 77 | 70 | 76 | 74 | 80 |
| Peru | 571 | 4.4 | 23.4 | 88 | y90 | 10599800 | -- | -- | 9157 | 55 | -- | 0.1 | 99 | 61 | 56 | 72 | 80 |
| St Kitts & Nevis | 2 | 76.9 | 50.8 | 61 | x90 | 800 | -- | -- | 0 | 7 | -- | 0.9 | 91 | 20 | 51 | 54 | 57 |
| St Lucia | 3 | 48.4 | 20.2 | 76 | x90 | 300 | -- | -- | 0 | 28 | -- | 9.3 | 37 | 17 | 12 | 22 | 49 |
| St Vincent & Grenadines | 2 | 51.3 | 17.9 | 74 | x90 | 700 | -- | -- | 0 | 37 | -- | 5.3 | 53 | 40 | 7 | 33 | 53 |
| Suriname | 26 | 1.6 | 63.1 | 68 | y90 | 2806600 | -- | -- | 183 | 0 | -- | 0.0 | 100 | 50 | 69 | 73 | 70 |
| Trinidad & Tobago | 375 | 731.0 | 293.7 | 0 | y90 | 20800 | -- | -- | 60 | 69 | -- | 0.6 | 94 | 19 | 60 | 58 | 29 |
| United States | 95075 | 101.5 | 349.8 | 18 | v 92 i87-92 f92 | 45180000 | 761000 | 734000 | 490618 | 56638 | 103.9 | 1.2 | 54 | 42 | 60 | 52 | 35 |
| Uruguay | 118 | 6.7 | 36.1 | 82 | z90 | 114200 | -- | -- | 6163 | 67 | -- | 5.5 | 52 | 41 | 56 | 50 | 66 |
| Venezuela | 3277 | 35.9 | 143.9 | 44 | y90 | 4923800 | -- | -- | 2038 | 71 | -- | 0.0 | 100 | 51 | 62 | 71 | 57 |
| **AFRICA** | | | | | | | | | | | | | | | | | |
| Algeria | 1459 | 6.1 | 49.6 | 75 | z90 | 110700 | -- | -- | 2735 | 768 | -- | 3.2 | 68 | 39 | 67 | 58 | 66 |
| Angola | 89 | 0.7 | 7.6 | 96 | y90 | 861200 | -- | -- | 6472 | 6 | -- | 0.8 | 92 | 64 | 79 | 78 | 87 |
| Benin | 65 | 5.8 | 11.5 | 94 | y90 | 109800 | -- | -- | 5994 | 1 | -- | 5.5 | 52 | 62 | 44 | 53 | 73 |
| Botswana | 134 | 2.3 | 87.0 | 58 | x90 | 287400 | -- | -- | 1673 | 0 | -- | 0.6 | 94 | 15 | 7 | 39 | 48 |
| Burkina Faso | 116 | 4.2 | 10.5 | 95 | y90 | 169400 | -- | -- | 10794 | 0 | -- | 6.4 | 48 | 57 | 18 | 41 | 68 |
| Burundi | 51 | 18.3 | 8.0 | 91 | y90 | 12400 | -- | -- | 1799 | 0 | -- | 14.5 | 24 | 69 | 62 | 52 | 71 |
| Cameroon | 185 | 3.9 | 13.3 | 93 | y90 | 3867700 | -- | -- | 15172 | 1 | -- | 0.4 | 96 | 65 | 24 | 62 | 77 |
| Cape Verde | 2 | 5.0 | 5.0 | 97 | x90 | 400 | -- | -- | 0 | 9 | -- | 2.3 | 77 | 21 | 38 | 45 | 71 |
| Central African R | 32 | 0.5 | 9.4 | 95 | y90 | 3087200 | -- | -- | 3518 | 0 | -- | 0.1 | 99 | 68 | 80* | 82 | 88 |
| Chad | 42 | 0.3 | 5.9 | 97 | x90 | 343000 | -- | -- | 1919 | 18 | -- | 0.6 | 94 | 58 | 34 | 62 | 79 |
| Comoros | 1 | 4.5 | 1.6 | 98 | x90 | 1000 | -- | -- | 0 | 3 | -- | 0.3 | 97 | 41 | 62 | 67 | 82 |
| Congo, DR | 531 | 2.3 | 11.1 | 94 | y90 | 23113100 | -- | -- | 49534 | 0 | -- | 0.2 | 98 | 68 | 28 | 65 | 79 |
| Congo, R | 49 | 1.4 | 18.1 | 91 | y90 | 4652200 | -- | -- | 4314 | 0 | -- | 0.1 | 99 | 44 | 2 | 48 | 69 |
| Côte d'Ivoire | 216 | 6.7 | 15.4 | 92 | y90 | 2079200 | -- | -- | 13283 | 0 | -- | 0.6 | 94 | 60 | 15 | 56 | 74 |
| Djibouti | 5 | 2.2 | 8.1 | 96 | x90 | 400 | -- | -- | 0 | 4 | -- | 1.0 | 90 | 11 | 8 | 36 | 66 |
| Egypt | 1613 | 16.1 | 24.9 | 87 | z90 | 3400 | -- | -- | 2829 | 3020 | -- | 172.0 | 0 | 48 | 43 | 30 | 58 |
| Equatorial Guinea | 6 | 2.1 | 14.3 | 93 | z90 | 374600 | -- | -- | 811 | 0 | -- | 0.2 | 98 | -- | 68 | 80* | 86 |
| Eritrea | 29 | 2.5 | 8.4 | 96 | -- | -- | -- | -- | 2196 | 61 | -- | -- | -- | 53 | 80* | 66 | 81 |
| Ethiopia | 487 | 4.4 | 8.4 | 96 | y90 | 979900 | -- | -- | 50148 | 24 | -- | 5.1 | 54 | 58 | 60 | 57 | 76 |
| Gabon | 76 | 2.8 | 66.8 | 67 | y90 | 4269600 | -- | -- | 5332 | 1 | -- | 0.1 | 99 | 41 | 47 | 62 | 64 |
| Gambia | 14 | 12.4 | 11.8 | 94 | x90 | 4700 | -- | -- | 813 | 3 | -- | 17.4 | 18 | 32 | 63 | 38 | 66 |
| Ghana | 315 | 13.2 | 16.9 | 91 | y90 | 480400 | -- | -- | 21905 | 1 | -- | 4.6 | 57 | 68 | 39 | 55 | 73 |
| Guinea | 62 | 2.5 | 8.5 | 96 | z90 | 341700 | -- | -- | 8650 | 9 | -- | 2.5 | 75 | 61 | 78 | 71 | 83 |
| Guinea-Bissau | 7 | 1.9 | 6.2 | 97 | x90 | 72800 | -- | -- | 589 | 0 | -- | 0.8 | 92 | 62 | 58 | 71 | 84 |
| Kenya | 527 | 9.1 | 18.5 | 91 | y90 | 92100 | -- | -- | 29377 | 4 | -- | 31.9 | 0 | 61 | 65 | 42 | 66 |
| Lesotho | 175 | 57.7 | 86.8 | 58 | z90 | 700 | -- | -- | 1594 | 0 | -- | 227.7 | 0 | 23 | 0 | 8 | 33 |

247

| Country | EC total | EC/ha | EC/p | E score | Timber note | Volume 000 m³ | NAI 000 m³ | Felling 000 m³ | Prod 000 m³ | Imp 000 m³ | F+I % NAI | P+I % vol | Timb score | Ag score | Fish score | RS score | RU index |
|---|---|---|---|---|---|---|---|---|---|---|---|---|---|---|---|---|---|
| Liberia | 52 | 4.7 | 21.6 | 89 | y90 | 704800 | -- | -- | 3021 | 0 | -- | 0.4 | 96 | 52 | 59 | 69 | 79 |
| Libyan Arab J | 547 | 3.1 | 105.0 | 54 | z90 | 26000 | -- | -- | 651 | 167 | -- | 3.1 | 69 | 25 | 63 | 52 | 53 |
| Madagascar | 115 | 2.0 | 7.9 | 96 | y90 | 930400 | -- | -- | 9517 | 10 | -- | 1.0 | 90 | 73 | 62 | 75 | 85 |
| Malawi | 105 | 8.9 | 10.4 | 95 | y90 | 269000 | -- | -- | 9692 | 1 | -- | 3.6 | 64 | 63 | 78 | 68 | 81 |
| Mali | 72 | 0.6 | 6.9 | 96 | x90 | 364300 | -- | -- | 6437 | 1 | -- | 1.8 | 82 | 54 | 63 | 66 | 81 |
| Mauritania | 40 | 0.4 | 16.3 | 92 | z90 | 16800 | -- | -- | 15 | 1 | -- | 0.1 | 99 | 25 | 25 | 50 | 71 |
| Mauritius | 36 | 176.5 | 31.8 | 38 | y90 | 1300 | -- | -- | 15 | 91 | -- | 8.2 | 39 | 17 | 28 | 28 | 33 |
| Morocco | 379 | 8.5 | 14.1 | 93 | z90 | 191500 | -- | -- | 1746 | 964 | -- | 1.4 | 86 | 56 | 35 | 59 | 76 |
| Mozambique | 186 | 2.3 | 10.1 | 95 | y90 | 644200 | -- | -- | 18018 | 0 | -- | 2.8 | 72 | 68 | 66 | 69 | 82 |
| Namibia | 141 | 1.7 | 86.9 | 58 | x90 | 253300 | -- | -- | 0 | 0 | -- | 0.0 | 100 | 18 | 66 | 61 | 59 |
| Niger | 72 | 0.6 | 7.4 | 96 | y90 | 36200 | -- | -- | 6460 | 1 | -- | 17.8 | 18 | 52 | 8 | 26 | 61 |
| Nigeria | 1570 | 17.0 | 15.1 | 91 | y90 | 1017400 | -- | -- | 98514 | 13 | -- | 9.7 | 36 | 66 | 17 | 40 | 65 |
| Rwanda | 60 | 22.8 | 10.1 | 89 | y90 | 19800 | -- | -- | 3000 | 10 | -- | 15.2 | 22 | 53 | 24 | 33 | 61 |
| São Tomé & Principe | 1 | 10.4 | 7.2 | 95 | -- | | -- | -- | 9 | 0 | -- | -- | -- | 24 | 3 | 13 | 54 |
| Senegal | 89 | 4.5 | 10.1 | 95 | y90 | 264300 | -- | -- | 4909 | 62 | -- | 1.9 | 81 | 58 | 26 | 55 | 75 |
| Seychelles | 3 | 66.7 | 40.0 | 67 | z90 | 400 | -- | -- | 0 | 2 | -- | 0.5 | 95 | 11 | 77 | 61 | 64 |
| Sierra Leone | 36 | 5.0 | 8.1 | 96 | y90 | 111700 | -- | -- | 3315 | 1 | -- | 3.0 | 70 | 62 | 37 | 56 | 76 |
| Somalia | 94 | 1.5 | 10.7 | 95 | x90 | 37700 | -- | -- | 7955 | 1 | -- | 21.1 | 14 | -- | 67 | 40 | 67 |
| South Africa | 3366 | 27.6 | 86.8 | 58 | z90 | 809900 | -- | -- | 33171 | 416 | -- | 4.1 | 59 | 54 | 14 | 42 | 50 |
| Sudan | 201 | 0.8 | 7.3 | 96 | y90 | 1379500 | -- | -- | 9486 | 52 | -- | 0.7 | 93 | 58 | 67 | 73 | 84 |
| Swaziland | 80 | 46.1 | 86.5 | 58 | z90 | 10900 | -- | -- | 1494 | 0 | -- | 13.7 | 26 | 57 | -- | 41 | 49 |
| Tanzania | 394 | 4.2 | 12.5 | 94 | y90 | 2155500 | -- | -- | 39022 | 2 | -- | 1.8 | 82 | 67 | 74 | 74 | 84 |
| Togo | 32 | 5.6 | 7.5 | 96 | y90 | 62700 | -- | -- | 1182 | 4 | -- | 1.9 | 81 | 56 | 10 | 49 | 72 |
| Tunisia | 273 | 16.7 | 29.6 | 85 | z90 | 33700 | -- | -- | 2807 | 471 | -- | 9.7 | 36 | 56 | 46 | 46 | 65 |
| Uganda | 165 | 6.8 | 8.2 | 96 | y90 | 255300 | -- | -- | 15649 | 0 | -- | 6.1 | 49 | 73 | 73 | 65 | 80 |
| Zambia | 187 | 2.5 | 21.8 | 89 | y90 | 813500 | -- | -- | 8042 | 2 | -- | 1.0 | 90 | 61 | 7 | 53 | 71 |
| Zimbabwe | 302 | 7.7 | 26.9 | 86 | y90 | 286300 | -- | -- | 8378 | 12 | -- | 2.9 | 71 | 48 | 74 | 64 | 75 |
| EUROPE | | | | | | | | | | | | | | | | | |
| Albania | 41 | 14.3 | 13.1 | 93 | vif95 | 83455 | 1004 | 740 | 409 | 30 | 76.7 | 0.5 | 81 | 56 | 18 | 52 | 72 |
| Austria | 1180 | 140.7 | 145.7 | 44 | vif92-96 | 1097307 | 27837 | 19821 | 14033 | 6837 | 95.8 | 1.9 | 65 | 50 | 1 | 39 | 41 |
| Belarus | 1040 | 50.1 | 100.5 | 55 | vi94 f96 | 1201310 | 24960 | 9550 | 17745 | 29 | 38.4 | 1.5 | 91 | 40 | 80* | 70 | 62 |
| Belgium | 2162 | 708.4 | 213.5 | 0 | v97 i82-97 f86-95 | 141033 | 5176 | 4400 | 3970 | 5756 | 196.2 | 6.9 | 4 | 48 | 2 | 18 | 9 |
| Bosnia & Herzegovina | 689 | 134.8 | 195.8 | 35 | vif95 | 250360 | 5480 | 1200 | 40 | 41 | 22.6 | 0.0 | 95 | 44 | 11 | 50 | 42 |
| Bulgaria | 824 | 74.3 | 98.2 | 55 | vif95 | 467345 | 11972 | 4852 | 3041 | 39 | 40.9 | 0.7 | 90 | 47 | 14 | 50 | 52 |
| Croatia | 310 | 54.8 | 69.1 | 65 | v96 if86-96 | 356302 | 7423 | 4600 | 3398 | 351 | 66.7 | 1.1 | 84 | 44 | 38 | 55 | 60 |
| Czech R | 1696 | 215.1 | 164.6 | 33 | vif95 | 683806 | 13369 | 16345 | 13781 | 1240 | 131.5 | 2.2 | 20 | 49 | 7 | 25 | 29 |
| Denmark | 762 | 176.8 | 145.0 | 38 | vi90 f96 | 55200 | 3200 | 2194 | 2129 | 3927 | 191.3 | 11.0 | 5 | 46 | 61 | 37 | 37 |
| Estonia | 267 | 59.2 | 184.5 | 37 | vif96 | 314537 | 7452 | 4028 | 6061 | 559 | 61.6 | 2.1 | 85 | 33 | 29 | 49 | 43 |
| Finland | 1183 | 35.0 | 230.1 | 31 | vif91-96 | 1940000 | 73666 | 54300 | 53670 | 9691 | 86.9 | 3.3 | 74 | 36 | 24 | 45 | 38 |
| France | 9971 | 180.8 | 170.5 | 37 | vif97 f96 | 2891777 | 93211 | 60174 | 42770 | 5976 | 71.0 | 1.7 | 82 | 41 | 16 | 46 | 41 |
| Germany | 13819 | 387.1 | 168.4 | 16 | v87 i95 f96 | 2880000 | 88998 | 46270 | 39052 | 11573 | 65.0 | 1.8 | 84 | 46 | 8 | 46 | 31 |
| Greece | 1130 | 85.6 | 106.9 | 53 | vir92 | 151788 | 3813 | 2408 | 1692 | 1583 | 104.7 | 2.2 | 53 | 45 | 19 | 39 | 46 |
| Hungary | 1062 | 114.2 | 104.6 | 51 | vif96 | 314667 | 10344 | 6049 | 4167 | 1390 | 71.9 | 1.8 | 82 | 51 | 3 | 45 | 48 |
| Iceland | 60 | 5.8 | 219.3 | 33 | vi98 f96 | 800 | 58 | 0 | 0 | 119 | 205.2 | 14.9 | 1 | 14 | 52 | 22 | 27 |
| Ireland | 505 | 71.9 | 138.1 | 45 | vif96 | 44000 | 3500 | 2330 | 2266 | 814 | 89.8 | 7.0 | 71 | 37 | 79 | 62 | 53 |
| Italy | 7042 | 233.7 | 122.7 | 31 | vif95 | 1428742 | 30507 | 8746 | 9550 | 14210 | 75.2 | 1.7 | 81 | 48 | 14 | 48 | 39 |
| Latvia | 191 | 29.6 | 77.6 | 61 | v97 if96 | 502000 | 13200 | 8010 | 10030 | 138 | 61.7 | 2.0 | 85 | 37 | 34 | 52 | 56 |
| Lithuania | 379 | 58.1 | 102.3 | 54 | vi96 f92-96 | 362637 | 9808 | 5570 | 4879 | 370 | 60.6 | 1.4 | 85 | 46 | 29 | 53 | 53 |
| Luxembourg | 134 | 521.4 | 321.3 | 7 | vi85-97 r92-94 | 20377 | 667 | 360 | 345 | 501 | 129.1 | 4.2 | 22 | 48 | 2 | 24 | 15 |
| Macedonia, FYR | 131 | 51.0 | 65.9 | 67 | vif95 | 63420 | 1010 | 999 | 774 | 82 | 107.0 | 1.3 | 48 | 49 | 2 | 33 | 50 |
| Malta | 22 | 687.5 | 57.7 | 0 | vif96 | 0 | 0 | 0 | 0 | 53 | 5300 | 5300 | 0 | 16 | 3 | 6 | 3 |
| Moldova | 198 | 58.8 | 45.2 | 71 | vif97 | 41600 | 1035 | 483 | 406 | 45 | 51.0 | 1.1 | 87 | 52 | 80* | 73 | 72 |
| Netherlands | 3507 | 858.7 | 224.6 | 0 | vif91-95 | 54209 | 2328 | 1561 | 1023 | 5858 | 318.7 | 12.7 | 0 | 48 | 18 | 22 | 11 |
| Norway | 1027 | 31.7 | 233.6 | 31 | vif94-96 | 771448 | 24391 | 11632 | 7985 | 4781 | 67.3 | 1.7 | 83 | 28 | 56 | 56 | 43 |
| Poland | 4193 | 129.7 | 108.4 | 48 | vif92-96 | 1908019 | 42871 | 31617 | 23300 | 1333 | 76.9 | 1.3 | 81 | 50 | 40 | 57 | 52 |
| Portugal | 690 | 75.0 | 70.0 | 62 | vif96 | 275760 | 14312 | 11500 | 8978 | 2436 | 97.4 | 4.1 | 64 | 40 | 17 | 40 | 51 |
| Romania | 1730 | 72.6 | 76.7 | 62 | vi84 f93-97 | 1341465 | 31878 | 13600 | 11649 | 162 | 43.2 | 0.9 | 89 | 54 | 11 | 51 | 56 |
| Slovakia | 668 | 136.3 | 124.3 | 46 | vif96 | 510948 | 13858 | 7400 | 5532 | 545 | 57.3 | 1.2 | 86 | 54 | 80* | 73 | 59 |
| Slovenia | 262 | 129.4 | 131.3 | 47 | vif96 | 310577 | 6339 | 2300 | 2133 | 545 | 44.9 | 0.9 | 89 | 43 | 4 | 45 | 46 |
| Spain | 3947 | 78.0 | 99.6 | 55 | vi90 f94 | 594111 | 30092 | 12639 | 15631 | 5869 | 61.5 | 3.6 | 85 | 44 | 26 | 52 | 53 |
| Sweden | 2051 | 45.6 | 231.6 | 31 | vif92-96 | 2928117 | 94122 | 66510 | 58100 | 10148 | 81.4 | 2.3 | 80 | 45 | 58 | 61 | 46 |
| Switzerland | 1011 | 244.9 | 139.4 | 29 | v93-95 if85-95 | 394853 | 8848 | 7451 | 4546 | 1370 | 99.7 | 1.5 | 61 | 43 | 0 | 35 | 32 |
| Ukraine | 6506 | 107.8 | 127.4 | 48 | vif96 | 1695912 | 30357 | 11300 | 10052 | 342 | 38.4 | 0.6 | 91 | 58 | 25 | 58 | 53 |
| United Kingdom | 9402 | 385.2 | 160.6 | 16 | vif95 | 264000 | 13720 | 9000 | 7635 | 10613 | 143.0 | 6.9 | 17 | 40 | 17 | 25 | 20 |
| Yugoslavia | 616 | 60.3 | 58.0 | 70 | vi95 f91-95 | 322313 | 6858 | 3454 | 1320 | 532 | 58.1 | 0.6 | 86 | 54 | 17 | 52 | 61 |
| RUSSIAN FEDERATION | 24596 | 14.4 | 166.6 | 39 | vi93 f95 | 80676360 | 919700 | 150200 | 115600 | 477 | 16.4 | 0.1 | 96 | 57 | 58 | 70 | 54 |

| Country | EC total | EC/ha | EC/p | *E* score | Timber note | Volume 000 m³ | NAI 000 m³ | Felling 000 m³ | Prod 000 m³ | Imp 000 m³ | F+I % NAI | P+I % vol | Timb score | Ag score | Fish score | *RS* score | RU index |
|---|---|---|---|---|---|---|---|---|---|---|---|---|---|---|---|---|---|
| ASIA | | | | | | | | | | | | | | | | | |
| Afghanistan | 82 | 1.3 | 3.9 | 98 | z90 | 96100 | -- | -- | 8091 | 3 | -- | 8.4 | 39 | 53 | -- | 46 | 72 |
| Armenia | 73 | 24.5 | 20.6 | 88 | vif96 | 42740 | 360 | 200 | 36 | 0 | 55.6 | 0.1 | 86 | 32 | 71 | 63 | 75 |
| Azerbaijan | 465 | 53.7 | 60.8 | 70 | vif88 | 127440 | 1440 | 60000 | 0 | 316 | 4189 | 0.2 | 0 | 51 | 80* | 44 | 57 |
| Bahrain | 333 | 4826.1 | 571.6 | 0 | x90 | 0 | -- | -- | 0 | 64 | -- | 6400 | 0 | -- | 32 | 16 | 8 |
| Bangladesh | 742 | 51.5 | 6.0 | 74 | y90 | 78100 | -- | -- | 33058 | 89 | -- | 42.4 | 0 | 42 | 41 | 28 | 51 |
| Bhutan | 20 | 4.3 | 10.3 | 95 | y90 | 421900 | -- | -- | 1702 | 0 | -- | 0.4 | 96 | -- | -- | 60* | 77 |
| Brunei Darussalam | 101 | 175.3 | 327.5 | 19 | x90 | 124600 | -- | -- | 296 | 38 | -- | 0.3 | 97 | 7 | 7 | 37 | 28 |
| Cambodia | 75 | 4.1 | 7.2 | 96 | z90 | 1484600 | -- | -- | 8008 | 16 | -- | 0.5 | 95 | 63 | 34 | 64 | 80 |
| China | 37895 | 39.5 | 30.3 | 80 | z90 | 12972000 | -- | -- | 291886 | 18451 | -- | 2.4 | 76 | 41 | 27 | 48 | 64 |
| Cyprus | 68 | 73.5 | 89.1 | 58 | vi80-90 f86-95 | 5000 | 90 | 50 | 35 | 176 | 251.1 | 4.2 | 0 | 41 | 2 | 14 | 36 |
| Georgia | 96 | 13.8 | 18.7 | 91 | vif95 | 434000 | 4000 | 500 | 0 | 10 | 12.8 | 0.0 | 97 | 53 | 2 | 51 | 71 |
| India | 15026 | 45.7 | 15.6 | 77 | y90 | 2998300 | -- | -- | 299490 | 1783 | -- | 10.0 | 35 | 49 | 41 | 42 | 59 |
| Indonesia | 5379 | 28.2 | 26.4 | 86 | y90 | 19752300 | -- | -- | 193218 | 235 | -- | 1.0 | 90 | 54 | 34 | 59 | 72 |
| Iran | 4127 | 25.3 | 63.9 | 68 | z90 | 141100 | -- | -- | 6793 | 114 | -- | 4.9 | 55 | 46 | 17 | 39 | 53 |
| Iraq | 1064 | 24.3 | 50.2 | 75 | z90 | 4400 | -- | -- | 177 | 0 | -- | 4.0 | 60 | 39 | 28 | 42 | 58 |
| Israel | 660 | 313.4 | 112.6 | 21 | vif97 | 6000 | 380 | 120 | 124 | 978 | 288.9 | 18.4 | 0 | 43 | 2 | 15 | 18 |
| Japan | 19489 | 515.9 | 154.6 | 8 | v95 i90-95 f95 | 3482138 | 69205 | 29000 | 20093 | 27955 | 82.3 | 1.4 | 79 | 36 | 27 | 47 | 27 |
| Jordan | 172 | 19.3 | 28.1 | 86 | z90 | 3400 | -- | -- | 11 | 250 | -- | 7.7 | 41 | 41 | 0 | 27 | 56 |
| Kazakhstan | 1571 | 5.8 | 95.9 | 56 | vif93 | 369810 | 6140 | 1400 | 315 | 360 | 28.7 | 0.2 | 93 | 54 | 57 | 68 | 62 |
| Korea, DPR | 2852 | 236.6 | 124.1 | 30 | z90 | 404900 | -- | -- | 7000 | 14 | -- | 1.7 | 83 | 54 | 22 | 53 | 41 |
| Korea, R | 6264 | 631.1 | 137.0 | 1 | x90 | 460300 | -- | -- | 1822 | 5652 | -- | 1.6 | 84 | 33 | 41 | 53 | 27 |
| Kuwait | 683 | 383.3 | 394.3 | 15 | z90 | 500 | -- | -- | 0 | 147 | -- | 29.4 | 3 | 5 | 16 | 8 | 11 |
| Kyrgyzstan | 113 | 5.7 | 24.5 | 88 | v88 | 23000 | -- | -- | 42 | 67 | -- | 0.5 | 95 | 58 | 80* | 78 | 83 |
| Lao PDR | 53 | 2.2 | 10.5 | 95 | y90 | 1686500 | -- | -- | 4591 | 1 | -- | 0.3 | 97 | 67 | 80* | 81 | 88 |
| Lebanon | 199 | 191.3 | 63.3 | 36 | z90 | 3900 | -- | -- | 407 | 477 | -- | 22.7 | 12 | 44 | 37 | 31 | 33 |
| Malaysia | 1871 | 56.7 | 89.2 | 58 | y90 | 3774300 | -- | -- | 29297 | 668 | -- | 0.8 | 92 | 31 | 59 | 61 | 59 |
| Maldives | 4 | 133.3 | 15.2 | 47 | -- | -- | -- | -- | 0 | 4 | -- | -- | -- | 16 | 84 | 50 | 48 |
| Mongolia | 92 | 0.6 | 36.3 | 82 | x90 | 344100 | -- | -- | 631 | 18 | -- | 0.2 | 98 | 24 | 43 | 55 | 68 |
| Myanmar | 347 | 5.1 | 7.9 | 96 | y90 | 4206300 | -- | -- | 22430 | 4 | -- | 0.5 | 95 | 60 | 48 | 68 | 82 |
| Nepal | 289 | 19.6 | 13.0 | 90 | y90 | 281800 | -- | -- | 21474 | 0 | -- | 7.6 | 42 | 59 | 80* | 60 | 75 |
| Oman | 291 | 13.7 | 126.2 | 48 | x90 | 0 | -- | -- | 0 | 34 | -- | 3400 | 0 | -- | 64 | 32 | 40 |
| Pakistan | 2090 | 26.3 | 14.5 | 87 | y90 | 170200 | -- | -- | 33044 | 204 | -- | 19.5 | 16 | 45 | 35 | 32 | 59 |
| Philippines | 1571 | 52.4 | 22.0 | 74 | y90 | 1431200 | -- | -- | 42530 | 907 | -- | 3.0 | 70 | 62 | 42 | 58 | 66 |
| Qatar | 736 | 669.1 | 1294.2 | 0 | x90 | 0 | -- | -- | 0 | 55 | -- | 5500 | 0 | -- | 79 | 39 | 19 |
| Saudi Arabia | 3630 | 16.9 | 186.4 | 37 | z90 | 1700 | -- | -- | 0 | 1341 | -- | 78.9 | 0 | 17 | 10 | 9 | 23 |
| Singapore | 1037 | 16725.8 | 302.6 | 0 | x90 | 700 | -- | -- | 0 | 918 | -- | 131.1 | 0 | -- | 30 | 15 | 7 |
| Sri Lanka | 214 | 32.6 | 11.7 | 84 | y90 | 96600 | -- | -- | 10414 | 47 | -- | 10.8 | 33 | 45 | 50 | 43 | 63 |
| Syrian Arab R | 594 | 32.1 | 39.7 | 80 | z90 | 18000 | -- | -- | 50 | 298 | -- | 1.9 | 81 | 48 | 12 | 47 | 63 |
| Tajikistan | 140 | 9.8 | 23.6 | 88 | vif95 | 5620 | 82 | 10 | 0 | 59 | 84.1 | 1.0 | 77 | 38 | 80* | 65 | 76 |
| Thailand | 3610 | 70.4 | 60.4 | 65 | y90 | 827300 | -- | -- | 36302 | 1292 | -- | 4.5 | 57 | 56 | 56 | 56 | 60 |
| Turkey | 2590 | 33.4 | 40.8 | 80 | vif96 | 1349323 | 36601 | 17606 | 17668 | 1947 | 53.4 | 1.5 | 87 | 50 | 49 | 62 | 71 |
| Turkmenistan | 497 | 10.2 | 117.4 | 51 | vif95 | 14100 | 122 | 10 | 0 | 28 | 31.1 | 0.2 | 92 | 30 | 31 | 51 | 51 |
| United Arab Emirates | 1434 | 171.5 | 621.5 | 1 | z90 | 600 | -- | -- | 0 | 850 | -- | 141.7 | 0 | 8 | 73 | 27 | 14 |
| Uzbekistan | 1890 | 42.2 | 81.4 | 60 | v88 | 11000 | -- | -- | 0 | 343 | -- | 3.1 | 69 | 36 | 79 | 61 | 60 |
| Viet Nam | 849 | 25.6 | 11.1 | 87 | y90 | 1049100 | -- | -- | 36232 | 135 | -- | 3.5 | 65 | 43 | 63 | 57 | 72 |
| Yemen | 215 | 4.1 | 13.2 | 93 | x90 | 100 | -- | -- | 0 | 186 | -- | 186.0 | 0 | 31 | 80 | 37 | 65 |
| PACIFIC | | | | | | | | | | | | | | | | | |
| Australia | 4415 | 5.7 | 240.8 | 30 | vif94 | 15006651 | 339763 | 19560 | 22935 | 1026 | 6.1 | 0.2 | 99 | 49 | 16 | 55 | 42 |
| Fiji | 21 | 11.5 | 26.7 | 87 | y90 | 100200 | -- | -- | 594 | 3 | -- | 0.6 | 94 | 47 | 32 | 58 | 72 |
| New Zealand | 654 | 24.2 | 173.9 | 38 | vif96 | 2553000 | 33700 | 22730 | 15324 | 54 | 67.6 | 0.6 | 83 | 25 | 81 | 63 | 50 |
| Papua New Guinea | 96 | 2.1 | 21.3 | 89 | y90 | 6066600 | -- | -- | 8772 | 2 | -- | 0.1 | 99 | 44 | 8 | 50 | 69 |
| Samoa | 3 | 10.6 | 17.4 | 91 | y90 | 16200 | -- | -- | 131 | 4 | -- | 0.8 | 92 | 31 | 6 | 43 | 67 |
| Solomon Is | 6 | 2.1 | 14.8 | 93 | y90 | 277500 | -- | -- | 872 | 0 | -- | 0.3 | 97 | 36 | 47 | 60 | 76 |
| Tonga | 2 | 26.7 | 20.5 | 87 | x90 | 0 | -- | -- | 5 | 6 | -- | 1100 | 0 | 36 | 60 | 32 | 59 |
| Vanuatu | 1 | 0.8 | 5.6 | 97 | y90 | 99100 | -- | -- | 63 | 1 | -- | 0.1 | 99 | 48 | 41 | 63 | 80 |

**Notes**

The resource use index (**RU index**) is the unweighted average of an energy and materials index (*E score*) and a resource sectors index (*RS score*).

The energy and materials index is limited to an energy index because of a lack of data on consumption of materials and waste generation. It is the lower score of two indicators (column heading in parentheses):

Energy consumption per hectare of total area (EC/ha).

Energy consumption per person (EC/p).

**Energy consumption is production plus imports minus exports minus bunkers plus or minus stock changes of commercial energy (solid fuels, liquid fuels, gases, and electricity) and traditional fuels (such as fuelwood, charcoal, animal wastes, and plant wastes).**

EC total = total energy consumption in thousands of terajoules. Data are for 1997 and are from United Nations Energy Statistics Unit (2000). Consumption by Botswana, Lesotho, Namibia, Swaziland and South Africa is lumped under the South Africa Customs Union (which consists of these five countries). I have assumed each country's share of energy consumption to be the same as its share of the combined population of these countries. Data for Eritrea and Ethiopia were also lumped together and have been separated on the basis of each country's share of their combined population.

EC/ha = energy consumption per hectare of total area in gigajoules. Data on total area are from Table 10.

EC/p = energy consumption per person in gigajoules, calculated on the basis of the population in 1997 (population data from United Nations Population Division 1998b).

*E score* = energy index, the lower score of energy consumption per hectare of total area and energy consumption per person. The performance criteria are shown in Table 22a. In the absence of objective standards, Portugal was used as a benchmark because it has the best combination of high human wellbeing (HWI of 72) and relatively low energy consumption per hectare (75 GJ) and per person (70 GJ). The tops of the medium and fair bands were set so that Portugal's performance would fall in the fair band.

The resource sectors index is the unweighted average of three sub-elements (column heading in parentheses):

Agriculture (Ag score). See Table 23 for data, scores and performance criteria.

Fisheries (Fish score). See Tables 23 and 24 for data and scores, and Table 24a for performance criteria.

Timber (Timb score). See this table.

Timber is represented by a single indicator: fellings + imports as a % of net annual increment; or, if that is not available, production + imports as a % of volume.

Timber note: Data on production and imports are for 1998 and are from FAO (2000a). All other data are for the year indicated in this column. If the year is marked with the letters f, i, r or v, the data come from UNECE & FAO (2000): f = fellings; i = net annual increment; r = removals; v = volume of naturally regenerated forest + plantations. If the year is marked with the letters x, y or z, the data come from FAO (1993 & 1995c) and Pandey (1995): x = volume of naturally regenerated forest only; y = volume of naturally regenerated forest + industrial plantations; z = volume of naturally regenerated forest + industrial plantations + nonindustrial plantations.

Volume = volume of growing stock of forest in thousands of cubic meters (000 m³). Where the Notes column shows the letters v, y or z, plantations are included; where it shows the letter x, plantations are excluded.

NAI = net annual increment (including bark) in thousands of cubic meters (000 m³).

Felling = annual fellings (including bark) in thousands of cubic meters (000 m³). The letter r in the Notes column for Greece and Luxembourg indicates that the data refer to removals (fellings data being unavailable). The letter r in the Notes column for Canada indicates that removals data have been used instead of fellings, since the latter are reported to be 88,433,000 m³—substantially less than the reported removals of 214,128,000 m³, an impossibility unless a lot of wood was cut one year and removed the next.

Prod = roundwood production less bark, in thousands of cubic meters (000 m³). Production by Belgium and Luxembourg is lumped together by FAO. It has been separated here in the same proportions as their fellings.

Imp = imports of roundwood + sawnwood + wood-based panels (but not pulp or paper products), in thousands of cubic meters (000 m³). Imports by Belgium and Luxembourg are lumped together by FAO. They have been separated here in the same proportions as their fellings.

F+I % NAI = fellings plus imports as a percentage of net annual increment.

P+I % vol = production plus imports as a percentage of volume.

Timb score = timber score, the score of timber fellings + imports as % of net annual increment (NAI), or if unavailable, timber production + imports as % of volume. The performance criteria are shown in Table 22a. For fellings + imports as % of NAI, the top of the medium band was set to ensure that fair felling + import rates were at or below NAI. The performance criteria for production + imports as % of volume are intended to be at least as conservative as those for fellings + imports as % of NAI, but are not as well founded because the relationship between volume and net annual increment varies with forest age, species composition, productivity and environmental conditions.

| band | top point on scale | energy consumption per hectare (GJ) | energy consumption per person (GJ) | fellings + imports as % of net annual increment | timber production + imports as % of volume |
|------|------|------|------|------|------|
| good | 100 | 0 | 0 | 1 | 0 |
| fair | 80 | 40 | 40 | 81 | 2 |
| medium | 60 | 80 | 80 | 101 | 4 |
| poor | 40 | 160 | 160 | 111 | 8 |
| bad | 20 | 320 | 320 | 131 | 16 |
| base | 0 | 640 | 640 | 211 | 32 |

**Table 22a. Performance criteria for energy and timber indicators.**

\* A score with an asterisk has been reduced in accordance with the insufficient data rule. To prevent high scores resulting merely from lack of data, a good score is allowed only if it is based on all applicable components (data in an indicator, indicators in an index), and a fair score only if it is based on at least half the components. Good and fair scores (100-61) based on fewer than half the applicable components have been reduced to 60. Good scores (100-81) based on more than half but not all the applicable components have been reduced to 80.

# Table 23. Agriculture; Fish and Seafood Self-Reliance

| Country | H area 000 ha | Prod 000 mt | Fert 000 mt | Prod /ha | Prod score | Fert/ 000 ha | Fert score | AP score | Cereals | Stch roots | Sug swtn | Oils nuts | Pulse veg | Fruit | Meat eggs | D'ry | FP % S | ASR score | Ag score | F&S P%S | FSR score |
|---|---|---|---|---|---|---|---|---|---|---|---|---|---|---|---|---|---|---|---|---|---|
| **AMERICAS** | | | | | | | | | | | | | | | | | | | | | |
| Antigua & Barbuda | 2 | 11 | -- | 6.1 | 70 | -- | -- | 70 | 1 | 34 | 0 | 9 | 38 | 86 | 16 | 58 | 30 | 12 | 12 | 50 | 20 |
| Argentina | 45804 | 88232 | 840.0 | 1.9 | 38 | 18.3 | 82 | 60 | >100 | >100 | >100 | >100 | >100 | >100 | >100 | >100 | 100 | 100 | 60 | 100 | 100 |
| Bahamas | 61 | 111 | 0.4 | 1.8 | 36 | 6.5 | 93 | 64 | 1 | 9 | 79 | 0 | 57 | 57 | 28 | 5 | 29 | 12 | 12 | 100 | 100 |
| Barbados | 47 | 645 | 3.2 | 13.7 | 94 | 67.9 | 46 | 70 | 3 | 43 | >100 | 17 | 76 | 15 | 73 | 26 | 44 | 18 | 18 | 33 | 13 |
| Belize | 69 | 1498 | 4.2 | 21.8 | 100 | 61.2 | 49 | 74 | 61 | 57 | >100 | 73 | 79 | >100 | 68 | 27 | 71 | 48 | 48 | 100 | 100 |
| Bolivia | 2512 | 9383 | 9.1 | 3.7 | 57 | 3.6 | 96 | 76 | 83 | 100 | >100 | >100 | >100 | 99 | >100 | 69 | 94 | 88 | 76 | 49 | 20 |
| Brazil | 237066 | 511451 | 4846.5 | 2.1 | 41 | 20.4 | 80 | 60 | 85 | 100 | >100 | >100 | 92 | >100 | >100 | 89 | 96 | 92 | 60 | 79 | 59 |
| Canada | 32248 | 81033 | 2696.4 | 2.5 | 45 | 83.6 | 39 | 42 | >100 | >100 | 59 | >100 | 94 | 19 | >100 | >100 | 84 | 68 | 42 | 93 | 86 |
| Chile | 1897 | 14484 | 422.0 | 7.6 | 78 | 222.5 | 12 | 45 | 68 | 98 | 94 | 35 | >100 | >100 | 94 | 90 | 85 | 70 | 45 | 100 | 100 |
| Colombia | 24578 | 56694 | 573.0 | 2.3 | 43 | 23.3 | 77 | 60 | 50 | >100 | >100 | 88 | 91 | >100 | 94 | 98 | 90 | 80 | 60 | 40 | 16 |
| Costa Rica | 1593 | 8542 | 59.7 | 5.4 | 67 | 37.5 | 62 | 64 | 18 | >100 | >100 | 88 | >100 | >100 | >100 | >100 | 88 | 76 | 64 | 100 | 100 |
| Cuba | 2332 | 47064 | 239.0 | 20.2 | 100 | 102.5 | 34 | 67 | 20 | 97 | >100 | 30 | 74 | >100 | 80 | 76 | 72 | 49 | 49 | 67 | 43 |
| Dominica | 25 | 133 | 2.7 | 5.3 | 66 | 108.4 | 33 | 49 | 2 | >100 | 55 | 99 | 93 | >100 | 9 | 48 | 63 | 37 | 37 | 34 | 14 |
| Dominican R | 1460 | 9852 | 102.0 | 6.7 | 73 | 69.9 | 45 | 59 | 27 | >100 | >100 | 89 | >100 | >100 | 91 | 60 | 83 | 66 | 59 | 15 | 6 |
| Ecuador | 5015 | 18521 | 94.4 | 3.7 | 57 | 18.8 | 81 | 69 | 84 | >100 | 100 | 96 | >100 | >100 | 99 | 99 | 97 | 94 | 69 | 100 | 100 |
| El Salvador | 945 | 5931 | 88.0 | 6.3 | 71 | 93.1 | 37 | 54 | 63 | 89 | >100 | 53 | 76 | 73 | 70 | 64 | 73 | 51 | 51 | 72 | 49 |
| Grenada | 21 | 50 | -- | 2.4 | 44 | -- | -- | 44 | 1 | 84 | 57 | 86 | 75 | >100 | 25 | 5 | 54 | 25 | 25 | 43 | 17 |
| Guatemala | 2876 | 19831 | 172.0 | 6.9 | 74 | 59.8 | 50 | 62 | 67 | >100 | >100 | >100 | >100 | >100 | 88 | 74 | 91 | 62 | 62 | 47 | 19 |
| Guyana | 276 | 4225 | 15.0 | 15.3 | 98 | 54.4 | 53 | 75 | >100 | 88 | >100 | >100 | 75 | >100 | 82 | 32 | 85 | 70 | 70 | 100 | 100 |
| Haiti | 910 | 3676 | 5.0 | 4.0 | 60 | -- | -- | 60 | 39 | 100 | 89 | 38 | 94 | >100 | 79 | 56 | 74 | 52 | 52 | 21 | 8 |
| Honduras | 2631 | 7124 | 78.0 | 2.7 | 47 | 29.6 | 70 | 58 | 74 | 96 | >100 | 99 | >100 | >100 | 86 | 90 | 93 | 86 | 58 | 100 | 100 |
| Jamaica | 248 | 4106 | 25.0 | 16.6 | 100 | 100.8 | 35 | 67 | 1 | >100 | >100 | 82 | 95 | >100 | 57 | 37 | 71 | 48 | 48 | 20 | 8 |
| Mexico | 24705 | 107036 | 1325.0 | 4.3 | 61 | 53.6 | 53 | 57 | 73 | 93 | 99 | 40 | >100 | >100 | 86 | 80 | 84 | 68 | 57 | 100 | 100 |
| Nicaragua | 1063 | 5343 | 39.0 | 5.0 | 65 | 36.7 | 63 | 64 | 74 | 88 | >100 | 84 | >100 | >100 | >100 | >100 | 93 | 86 | 64 | 100 | 100 |
| Panama | 488 | 3497 | 38.0 | 7.2 | 76 | 77.8 | 41 | 58 | 45 | 98 | >100 | 35 | 99 | >100 | 95 | 89 | 83 | 66 | 58 | 100 | 100 |
| Paraguay | 3694 | 10894 | 33.0 | 2.9 | 49 | 8.9 | 91 | 70 | >100 | 100 | 100 | >100 | 92 | 97 | >100 | 86 | 97 | 94 | 70 | 88 | 76 |
| Peru | 3787 | 18825 | 165.0 | 5.0 | 65 | 43.6 | 58 | 61 | 45 | 98 | 98 | 77 | >100 | 99 | 97 | 70 | 85 | 70 | 61 | 100 | 100 |
| St Kitts & Nevis | 5 | 231 | 1.1 | 44.2 | 100 | 211.7 | 13 | 56 | 0 | 90 | >100 | 75 | 54 | 47 | 23 | 0 | 49 | 20 | 20 | 74 | 52 |
| St Lucia | 33 | 200 | 7.0 | 6.0 | 70 | 210 | 14 | 42 | 0 | 88 | 0 | >100 | 22 | >100 | 21 | 6 | 42 | 17 | 17 | 29 | 12 |
| St Vincent & Grenadines | 71 | 132 | 3.0 | 1.9 | 38 | 42.4 | 59 | 48 | 7 | >100 | 85 | 92 | 95 | >100 | 29 | 16 | 65 | 40 | 40 | 79 | 59 |
| Suriname | 90 | 390 | 7.3 | 4.3 | 61 | 80.8 | 40 | 50 | >100 | 57 | 86 | 74 | 91 | >100 | 58 | 50 | 77 | 56 | 50 | 100 | 100 |
| Trinidad & Tobago | 208 | 1746 | 10.0 | 8.4 | 81 | 48.1 | 56 | 68 | 4 | 26 | >100 | 27 | 46 | 92 | 71 | 8 | 47 | 19 | 19 | 87 | 74 |
| United States | 187405 | 607066 | 20200.1 | 3.2 | 52 | 107.8 | 33 | 42 | >100 | >100 | 97 | >100 | >100 | 84 | >100 | 96 | 97 | 94 | 42 | 87 | 74 |
| Uruguay | 1135 | 3291 | 119.0 | 2.9 | 49 | 104.9 | 34 | 41 | >100 | 85 | 69 | 99 | 79 | >100 | >100 | >100 | 91 | 82 | 41 | 100 | 100 |
| Venezuela | 3270 | 16161 | 292.0 | 4.9 | 64 | 89.3 | 38 | 51 | 54 | 93 | 95 | 74 | 85 | >100 | 96 | 68 | 83 | 66 | 51 | 85 | 70 |
| **AFRICA** | | | | | | | | | | | | | | | | | | | | | |
| Algeria | 5347 | 10507 | 59.0 | 2.0 | 40 | 11.0 | 89 | 64 | 52 | 91 | 0 | 54 | 93 | 97 | 90 | 33 | 64 | 39 | 39 | 89 | 78 |
| Angola | 2543 | 4866 | 10.0 | 1.9 | 38 | 3.9 | 96 | 67 | 56 | 100 | 79 | 88 | 92 | 99 | 77 | 66 | 82 | 64 | 64 | 93 | 86 |
| Benin | 2237 | 4692 | 35.0 | 2.1 | 41 | 15.6 | 84 | 62 | 81 | >100 | 57 | >100 | 91 | 100 | 87 | 58 | 84 | 68 | 62 | 75 | 53 |
| Botswana | 293 | 206 | 3.3 | 0.7 | 14 | 11.4 | 89 | 51 | 33 | 34 | 0 | 23 | 45 | 19 | >100 | 47 | 38 | 15 | 15 | 17 | 7 |
| Burkina Faso | 4183 | 4356 | 24.1 | 1.0 | 20 | 5.8 | 94 | 57 | 99 | 99 | 98 | 99 | >100 | 100 | 100 | 91 | 98 | 96 | 57 | 48 | 19 |
| Burundi | 2180 | 4491 | 6.0 | 2.1 | 41 | 2.8 | 97 | 69 | 82 | 100 | 91 | 95 | 93 | 100 | 99 | 88 | 93 | 86 | 69 | 94 | 88 |
| Cameroon | 5844 | 10804 | 34.0 | 1.8 | 36 | 5.8 | 94 | 65 | 90 | >100 | 95 | >100 | 99 | >100 | 99 | 85 | 96 | 92 | 65 | 53 | 24 |
| Cape Verde | 39 | 67 | -- | 1.7 | 34 | -- | -- | 34 | 13 | 66 | 52 | 32 | 75 | 73 | 62 | 34 | 51 | 21 | 21 | 100 | 100 |
| Central African R | 934 | 1812 | 1.2 | 1.9 | 38 | 1.3 | 99 | 68 | 83 | 100 | 94 | 98 | 95 | 100 | 100 | 99 | 96 | 92 | 68 | 95 | 90 |
| Chad | 2475 | 2458 | 10.5 | 1.0 | 20 | 4.2 | 96 | 58 | 91 | 100 | 96 | 86 | 100 | 100 | >100 | 96 | 96 | 92 | 58 | 99 | 98 |
| Comoros | 84 | 231 | 0.1 | 2.7 | 47 | 1.2 | 99 | 73 | 27 | 100 | 0 | >100 | 92 | 100 | 48 | 65 | 66 | 41 | 41 | 91 | 82 |
| Congo, DR | 9616 | 27937 | 10.0 | 2.9 | 49 | 1.0 | 99 | 74 | 79 | 96 | 96 | 99 | 95 | 100 | 90 | 17 | 84 | 68 | 68 | 56 | 28 |
| Congo, R | 449 | 1806 | 3.0 | 4.0 | 60 | 6.7 | 93 | 76 | 15 | 100 | >100 | 88 | 89 | 99 | 47 | 4 | 68 | 44 | 44 | 6 | 2 |
| Côte d'Ivoire | 10162 | 14090 | 70.0 | 1.4 | 28 | 6.9 | 93 | 60 | 62 | 100 | >100 | >100 | 93 | >100 | 95 | 7 | 82 | 64 | 60 | 38 | 15 |
| Djibouti | 4 | 22 | -- | 5.2 | 66 | -- | -- | 66 | 0 | 0 | 0 | 0 | 85 | 7 | 87 | 35 | 27 | 11 | 11 | 21 | 8 |
| Egypt | 5998 | 53499 | 1194.0 | 8.9 | 82 | 199.1 | 15 | 48 | 66 | >100 | 96 | 55 | >100 | >100 | 84 | 90 | 86 | 72 | 48 | 67 | 43 |
| Equatorial Guinea | -- | -- | -- | -- | -- | -- | -- | -- | -- | -- | -- | -- | -- | -- | -- | -- | -- | -- | -- | -- | -- |
| Eritrea | 496 | 408 | 5.0 | 0.8 | 16 | 10.1 | 90 | 53 | 25 | 100 | 0 | >100 | 90 | 100 | 100 | 83 | 75 | 53 | 53 | 100 | 100 |
| Ethiopia | 13126 | 18489 | 154.2 | 1.4 | 28 | 11.8 | 88 | 58 | >100 | >100 | >100 | 96 | >100 | >100 | >100 | 99 | 99 | 98 | 58 | 95 | 90 |
| Gabon | 234 | 1032 | 0.4 | 4.4 | 62 | 1.7 | 98 | 80 | 21 | 99 | 100 | 86 | 65 | 98 | 53 | 5 | 66 | 41 | 41 | 70 | 47 |
| Gambia | 261 | 218 | 0.8 | 0.8 | 16 | 3.1 | 97 | 56 | 49 | 80 | 0 | >100 | 29 | 86 | 91 | 34 | 59 | 32 | 32 | 100 | 100 |
| Ghana | 6167 | 17640 | 13.0 | 2.9 | 49 | 2.1 | 98 | 73 | 87 | >100 | 47 | >100 | 97 | >100 | 86 | 52 | 84 | 68 | 68 | 97 | 94 |
| Guinea | 3450 | 4334 | 2.8 | 1.2 | 24 | 0.8 | 99 | 61 | 68 | 100 | 81 | 99 | 95 | >100 | 89 | 68 | 87 | 74 | 61 | 96 | 92 |
| Guinea-Bissau | 388 | 490 | 0.8 | 1.3 | 26 | 2.1 | 98 | 62 | 64 | 100 | 70 | >100 | 91 | >100 | 97 | 83 | 88 | 76 | 62 | 100 | 100 |
| Kenya | 3862 | 12813 | 120.0 | 3.3 | 53 | 31.1 | 69 | 61 | 75 | 100 | 99 | 47 | >100 | >100 | 97 | 100 | 90 | 80 | 61 | 100 | 100 |
| Lesotho | 249 | 419 | 7.1 | 1.7 | 34 | 28.3 | 72 | 53 | 56 | 91 | 0 | 1 | 55 | 45 | 85 | 81 | 52 | 23 | 23 | 0 | 0 |
| Liberia | 327 | 1040 | -- | 3.2 | 52 | -- | -- | -- | 23 | 100 | 98 | 99 | 88 | 99 | 88 | 17 | 76 | 55 | 52 | 80 | 60 |

| Country | H area 000 ha | Prod 000 mt | Fert 000 mt | Prod /ha | Prod score | Fert/ 000 ha | Fert score | AP score | Cer- eals | Stch roots | Sug swtn | Oils nuts | Pulse veg | Fruit | Meat eggs | D'ry | FP % S | ASR score | Ag score | F&S P%S | FSR score |
|---|---|---|---|---|---|---|---|---|---|---|---|---|---|---|---|---|---|---|---|---|---|
| Libyan Arab J | 751 | 1431 | 71.0 | 1.9 | 38 | 94.6 | 36 | 37 | 16 | 96 | 0 | 35 | 70 | 92 | 93 | 30 | 54 | 25 | 25 | 86 | 72 |
| Madagascar | 2992 | 8993 | 13.2 | 3.0 | 50 | 4.4 | 96 | 73 | 91 | >100 | 99 | 77 | >100 | >100 | 100 | 97 | 95 | 90 | 73 | 100 | 100 |
| Malawi | 2486 | 5988 | 41.0 | 2.4 | 44 | 16.5 | 83 | 63 | 96 | >100 | >100 | 91 | >100 | 100 | 98 | 71 | 94 | 88 | 63 | 96 | 92 |
| Mali | 3999 | 3423 | 32.0 | 0.8 | 16 | 8.0 | 92 | 54 | 91 | 95 | 89 | >100 | 99 | 96 | 100 | 89 | 95 | 90 | 54 | 99 | 98 |
| Mauritania | 373 | 277 | 5.0 | 0.7 | 14 | 13.4 | 87 | 50 | 45 | 47 | 0 | 13 | 57 | 87 | 95 | 85 | 54 | 25 | 25 | 100 | 100 |
| Mauritius | 106 | 5994 | 34.5 | 56.3 | 100 | 324.2 | 0 | 50 | 0 | 45 | >100 | 7 | 78 | 37 | 59 | 18 | 43 | 17 | 17 | 56 | 28 |
| Morocco | 8737 | 22938 | 298.0 | 2.6 | 46 | 34.1 | 66 | 56 | >100 | >100 | 89 | 75 | >100 | >100 | 96 | 86 | 93 | 86 | 56 | 100 | 100 |
| Mozambique | 3959 | 8052 | 11.0 | 2.0 | 40 | 2.8 | 97 | 68 | 75 | 100 | 92 | >100 | 98 | >100 | 91 | 60 | 89 | 78 | 68 | 83 | 66 |
| Namibia | 366 | 351 | -- | 0.9 | 18 | -- | -- | 18 | 38 | 100 | 0 | 20 | 34 | 25 | >100 | 100 | 52 | 23 | 18 | 100 | 100 |
| Niger | 10256 | 3613 | 11.0 | 0.3 | 6 | 1.1 | 99 | 52 | 89 | 100 | 85 | 82 | >100 | 93 | 100 | 92 | 93 | 86 | 52 | 64 | 39 |
| Nigeria | 71339 | 122847 | 135.0 | 1.7 | 34 | 1.9 | 98 | 66 | 94 | 100 | 55 | 100 | 100 | 100 | 95 | 27 | 84 | 68 | 66 | 53 | 24 |
| Rwanda | 1150 | 4348 | 0.1 | 3.8 | 58 | 0.1 | 100 | 79 | 38 | 100 | 58 | 26 | 85 | 100 | 100 | 93 | 75 | 53 | 53 | 75 | 53 |
| São Tomé & Principe | 76 | 91 | -- | 1.2 | 24 | -- | -- | 24 | 25 | 99 | 0 | >100 | 91 | 100 | 82 | 5 | 63 | 37 | 24 | 84 | 68 |
| Senegal | 2791 | 3177 | 15.0 | 1.1 | 22 | 5.4 | 95 | 58 | 54 | 80 | 93 | 82 | 83 | 98 | 95 | 47 | 79 | 59 | 58 | 100 | 100 |
| Seychelles | 6 | 15 | -- | 2.4 | 44 | -- | -- | 44 | 0 | 7 | 0 | 70 | 36 | 34 | 73 | 2 | 28 | 11 | 11 | 100 | 100 |
| Sierra Leone | 1134 | 1613 | 3.0 | 1.4 | 28 | 2.6 | 97 | 62 | 52 | >100 | 71 | 98 | 95 | 100 | 93 | 68 | 85 | 70 | 62 | 100 | 100 |
| Somalia | -- | -- | 0.5 | -- | -- | -- | -- | -- | -- | -- | -- | -- | -- | -- | -- | -- | -- | -- | -- | -- | -- |
| South Africa | 11421 | 49835 | 780.0 | 4.4 | 62 | 68.3 | 46 | 54 | >100 | 97 | >100 | 85 | 99 | >100 | 91 | >100 | 96 | 92 | 54 | 36 | 14 |
| Sudan | 13039 | 15317 | 92.0 | 1.2 | 24 | 7.1 | 93 | 58 | >100 | 100 | >100 | >100 | 96 | >100 | >100 | 99 | 99 | 98 | 58 | 95 | 90 |
| Swaziland | 159 | 4647 | 6.0 | 29.2 | 100 | 37.9 | 62 | 81 | 64 | 51 | >100 | >100 | 54 | >100 | 80 | 75 | 78 | 57 | 57 | -- | -- |
| Tanzania | 10157 | 19388 | 38.0 | 1.9 | 38 | 3.7 | 96 | 67 | 92 | >100 | 98 | >100 | 99 | >100 | 96 | 98 | 98 | 96 | 67 | 100 | 100 |
| Togo | 1865 | 2432 | 17.6 | 1.3 | 26 | 9.4 | 91 | 58 | >100 | >100 | 0 | >100 | 95 | 99 | 93 | 32 | 77 | 56 | 56 | 24 | 10 |
| Tunisia | 5451 | 7896 | 86.1 | 1.4 | 28 | 15.8 | 84 | 56 | 82 | 90 | 57 | >100 | >100 | >100 | 99 | 90 | 90 | 80 | 56 | 100 | 100 |
| Uganda | 8189 | 21706 | 3.4 | 2.6 | 46 | 0.4 | 100 | 73 | 85 | 100 | 99 | 99 | 97 | >100 | 95 | 98 | 97 | 94 | 73 | 100 | 100 |
| Zambia | 1384 | 4620 | 41.0 | 3.3 | 53 | 29.6 | 70 | 61 | 96 | 100 | >100 | 98 | >100 | 96 | 100 | 91 | 98 | 96 | 61 | 90 | 80 |
| Zimbabwe | 3195 | 7577 | 174.4 | 2.4 | 44 | 54.6 | 53 | 48 | >100 | 90 | >100 | 100 | 99 | 96 | 91 | >100 | 97 | 94 | 48 | 87 | 74 |
| **EUROPE** | | | | | | | | | | | | | | | | | | | | | |
| Albania | 424 | 1409 | 7.0 | 3.3 | 53 | 16.5 | 83 | 68 | 47 | 87 | 55 | 67 | 99 | 76 | 87 | 98 | 77 | 56 | 56 | 45 | 18 |
| Austria | 2140 | 11897 | 229.9 | 5.6 | 68 | 107.4 | 33 | 50 | >100 | 87 | 98 | 68 | 60 | 65 | >100 | >100 | 85 | 70 | 50 | 2 | 1 |
| Belarus | 4360 | 19685 | 747.0 | 4.5 | 62 | 171.3 | 19 | 40 | 69 | >100 | 75 | 54 | 98 | 70 | >100 | >100 | 83 | 66 | 40 | 100 | 100 |
| Belgium | 3096 | 16300 | 310.0 | 5.3 | 66 | 100.1 | 35 | 50 | 57 | 64 | >100 | 25 | 90 | 32 | >100 | >100 | 71 | 48 | 48 | 6 | 2 |
| Bosnia & Herzegovina | 650 | 2008 | 16.0 | 3.1 | 51 | 24.6 | 75 | 63 | 74 | 97 | 9 | 50 | 97 | 72 | 59 | 84 | 68 | 44 | 44 | 28 | 11 |
| Bulgaria | 4011 | 7759 | 185.0 | 1.9 | 38 | 46.1 | 57 | 47 | 74 | 66 | 31 | >100 | 98 | >100 | >100 | >100 | 84 | 68 | 47 | 86 | 72 |
| Croatia | 1374 | 6074 | 186.4 | 4.4 | 62 | 135.7 | 26 | 44 | 99 | 99 | 93 | 73 | 78 | 75 | 96 | 79 | 86 | 72 | 44 | 100 | 100 |
| Czech R | 3362 | 17379 | 367.7 | 5.2 | 66 | 109.4 | 33 | 49 | 97 | >100 | >100 | 97 | 78 | 47 | 97 | >100 | 89 | 78 | 49 | 18 | 7 |
| Denmark | 2587 | 17122 | 437.0 | 6.6 | 73 | 168.9 | 19 | 46 | >100 | >100 | >100 | 42 | 75 | 14 | >100 | >100 | 79 | 59 | 46 | 100 | 100 |
| Estonia | 472 | 1277 | 22.0 | 2.7 | 47 | 46.7 | 57 | 52 | 76 | 94 | 9 | 24 | 73 | 26 | 76 | >100 | 60 | 33 | 33 | 100 | 100 |
| Finland | 1948 | 6510 | 331.7 | 3.3 | 53 | 170.3 | 19 | 36 | >100 | 84 | 93 | 46 | 63 | 20 | >100 | >100 | 76 | 55 | 36 | 53 | 24 |
| France | 29584 | 143486 | 5065.0 | 4.8 | 64 | 171.2 | 19 | 41 | >100 | 91 | >100 | >100 | >100 | 81 | >100 | >100 | 96 | 92 | 41 | 41 | 16 |
| Germany | 21536 | 112382 | 2818.9 | 5.2 | 66 | 130.9 | 27 | 46 | >100 | >100 | >100 | 43 | 46 | 43 | 87 | >100 | 77 | 56 | 46 | 21 | 8 |
| Greece | 7787 | 20771 | 560.0 | 2.7 | 47 | 71.9 | 44 | 45 | 93 | 86 | 98 | 91 | >100 | >100 | 67 | 68 | 88 | 76 | 45 | 47 | 19 |
| Hungary | 5823 | 24239 | 456.6 | 4.2 | 61 | 78.4 | 41 | 51 | >100 | >100 | >100 | >100 | >100 | >100 | >100 | >100 | 100 | 100 | 51 | 8 | 3 |
| Iceland | 8 | 19 | 20.4 | 2.3 | 43 | 2425.7 | 0 | 21 | 0 | 40 | 31 | 1 | 19 | 0 | >100 | 100 | 36 | 14 | 14 | 100 | 100 |
| Ireland | 808 | 5783 | 691.0 | 7.1 | 75 | 854.8 | 0 | 37 | 92 | 88 | >100 | 13 | 66 | 7 | >100 | >100 | 71 | 48 | 37 | 100 | 100 |
| Italy | 23760 | 82370 | 1819.5 | 3.5 | 55 | 76.6 | 42 | 48 | 86 | 72 | 99 | 73 | >100 | >100 | 85 | 68 | 85 | 70 | 48 | 35 | 14 |
| Latvia | 698 | 2620 | 127.0 | 3.8 | 58 | 182.1 | 17 | 37 | 82 | 100 | 85 | 37 | 84 | 50 | 71 | >100 | 76 | 55 | 37 | 100 | 100 |
| Lithuania | 1505 | 6289 | 166.0 | 4.2 | 61 | 110.3 | 32 | 46 | 9 | 100 | 99 | 81 | >100 | >100 | >100 | >100 | 86 | 72 | 46 | 96 | 92 |
| Luxembourg | B | B | B | 5.3 | 66 | 100.1 | 35 | 50 | 57 | 64 | >100 | 25 | 90 | 32 | >100 | >100 | 71 | 48 | 48 | 6 | 2 |
| Macedonia, FYR | 583 | 1860 | 38.0 | 3.2 | 52 | 65.2 | 47 | 49 | 84 | 96 | 60 | 64 | >100 | >100 | 63 | 88 | 82 | 64 | 49 | 6 | 2 |
| Malta | 16 | 152 | 1.0 | 9.3 | 83 | 61.6 | 49 | 66 | 4 | 91 | 0 | 0 | 90 | 39 | 61 | 46 | 41 | 16 | 16 | 7 | 3 |
| Moldova | 2333 | 7105 | 116.0 | 3.0 | 50 | 49.7 | 55 | 52 | 95 | 86 | >100 | >100 | 80 | >100 | >100 | >100 | 95 | 90 | 52 | 100 | 100 |
| Netherlands | 6669 | 25856 | 504.0 | 3.9 | 59 | 75.6 | 42 | 50 | 31 | 83 | >100 | 22 | >100 | 32 | >100 | >100 | 71 | 48 | 48 | 46 | 18 |
| Norway | 795 | 2344 | 203.0 | 2.9 | 49 | 255.2 | 8 | 28 | 72 | 82 | 3 | 16 | 57 | 21 | 96 | >100 | 56 | 28 | 28 | 100 | 100 |
| Poland | 13875 | 84744 | 1634.0 | 6.1 | 70 | 117.8 | 31 | 50 | 96 | >100 | >100 | 53 | >100 | >100 | >100 | >100 | 94 | 88 | 50 | 70 | 47 |
| Portugal | 4845 | 9650 | 275.0 | 2.0 | 40 | 56.8 | 52 | 46 | 44 | 56 | 11 | 41 | >100 | 83 | 87 | 98 | 65 | 40 | 40 | 42 | 17 |
| Romania | 10792 | 30609 | 428.0 | 2.8 | 48 | 39.7 | 60 | 54 | 86 | 99 | 91 | >100 | 98 | >100 | >100 | 99 | 97 | 94 | 54 | 27 | 11 |
| Slovakia | 1585 | 7942 | 113.0 | 5.0 | 65 | 71.3 | 44 | 54 | >100 | 92 | 98 | >100 | 96 | 52 | >100 | >100 | 92 | 84 | 54 | 100 | 100 |
| Slovenia | 402 | 2185 | 66.2 | 5.4 | 67 | 164.9 | 19 | 43 | 53 | 96 | 82 | 11 | 61 | 75 | 99 | >100 | 72 | 49 | 43 | 9 | 4 |
| Spain | 30748 | 74540 | 2163.9 | 2.4 | 44 | 70.4 | 45 | 44 | 99 | 58 | 99 | 79 | >100 | >100 | >100 | 83 | 90 | 80 | 44 | 58 | 31 |
| Sweden | 2116 | 11417 | 304.0 | 5.4 | 67 | 143.7 | 24 | 45 | >100 | 77 | 100 | 45 | 49 | 12 | 98 | 96 | 72 | 49 | 45 | 100 | 100 |
| Switzerland | 829 | 4962 | 116.0 | 6.0 | 70 | 139.9 | 25 | 47 | 70 | 81 | 87 | 28 | 44 | 45 | 80 | >100 | 67 | 43 | 43 | 1 | 0 |
| Ukraine | 20988 | 80958 | 906.0 | 3.8 | 58 | 43.2 | 58 | 58 | 85 | 100 | >100 | >100 | >100 | 100 | >100 | >100 | 98 | 96 | 58 | 68 | 44 |
| United Kingdom | 10079 | 58222 | 2221.0 | 5.8 | 69 | 220.4 | 12 | 40 | >100 | 93 | 95 | 47 | 68 | 6 | 83 | 91 | 73 | 51 | 40 | 43 | 17 |
| Yugoslavia | 4825 | 16198 | 241.0 | 3.3 | 53 | 50.0 | 55 | 54 | 98 | >100 | >100 | 89 | 98 | 99 | 99 | 98 | 98 | 96 | 54 | 42 | 17 |
| RUSSIAN FEDERATION | 69599 | 148036 | 1850.0 | 2.1 | 41 | 26.6 | 73 | 57 | 93 | 94 | 85 | 97 | 91 | 58 | 79 | 100 | 87 | 74 | 57 | 100 | 100 |
| **ASIA** | | | | | | | | | | | | | | | | | | | | | |
| Afghanistan | 8054 | 5007 | 50.0 | 0.6 | 12 | 6.2 | 94 | 53 | 96 | 99 | 39 | 76 | >100 | >100 | >100 | 98 | 88 | 76 | 53 | -- | -- |

| Country | H area 000 ha | Prod 000 mt | Fert 000 mt | Prod /ha | Prod score | Fert/ 000 ha | Fert score | AP score | Cer-eals | Stch roots | Sug swtn | Oils nuts | Pulse veg | Fruit | Meat eggs | D'ry | FP % S | ASR score | Ag score | F&S P%S | FSR score |
|---|---|---|---|---|---|---|---|---|---|---|---|---|---|---|---|---|---|---|---|---|---|
| Armenia | 316 | 1549 | 8.0 | 4.9 | 64 | 25.3 | 75 | 69 | 42 | 100 | 2 | 4 | 96 | 95 | 50 | 87 | 59 | 32 | 32 | 100 | 100 |
| Azerbaijan | 1550 | 2973 | 39.0 | 1.9 | 38 | 25.2 | 75 | 56 | 62 | 92 | 2 | 88 | 98 | 88 | 60 | 95 | 73 | 51 | 51 | 100 | 100 |
| Bahrain | -- | -- | 0.6 | -- | -- | -- | -- | -- | -- | -- | -- | -- | -- | -- | -- | -- | -- | -- | -- | -- | -- |
| Bangladesh | 9193 | 34634 | 1259.4 | 3.8 | 58 | 137.0 | 26 | 42 | 89 | 99 | >100 | 47 | 93 | 98 | 93 | 90 | 89 | 78 | 42 | 100 | 100 |
| Bhutan | -- | -- | 0.1 | -- | -- | -- | -- | -- | -- | -- | -- | -- | -- | -- | -- | -- | -- | -- | -- | -- | -- |
| Brunei Darussalam | 12 | 16 | 5.0 | 1.3 | 26 | 405.9 | 0 | 13 | 1 | 39 | 0 | 2 | 30 | 25 | 40 | 0 | 17 | 7 | 7 | 17 | 7 |
| Cambodia | 2214 | 3532 | 12.8 | 1.6 | 32 | 5.8 | 94 | 63 | >100 | 100 | 87 | 79 | 100 | 100 | 100 | 51 | 90 | 80 | 63 | 100 | 100 |
| China | 221710 | 1027765 | 36505.0 | 4.6 | 63 | 164.7 | 19 | 41 | 94 | 99 | 98 | 89 | >100 | 100 | >100 | 92 | 96 | 92 | 41 | 87 | 74 |
| Cyprus | 268 | 923 | 31.0 | 3.4 | 54 | 115.7 | 31 | 42 | 19 | >100 | 2 | 15 | >100 | >100 | >100 | 92 | 66 | 41 | 41 | 6 | 2 |
| Georgia | 990 | 2542 | 37.0 | 2.6 | 46 | 37.4 | 63 | 54 | 54 | 99 | 3 | 51 | 98 | >100 | >100 | 92 | 75 | 53 | 53 | 53 | 24 |
| India | 296783 | 670289 | 14308.2 | 2.3 | 43 | 48.2 | 56 | 49 | >100 | >100 | >100 | >100 | 100 | >100 | >100 | 100 | 100 | 100 | 49 | 100 | 100 |
| Indonesia | 83421 | 165601 | 2688.7 | 2.0 | 40 | 32.2 | 68 | 54 | 91 | >100 | 99 | >100 | 98 | >100 | 99 | 54 | 93 | 86 | 54 | 100 | 100 |
| Iran | 14785 | 46709 | 1139.8 | 3.2 | 52 | 77.1 | 41 | 46 | 74 | 100 | 86 | 66 | >100 | >100 | 95 | 95 | 89 | 78 | 46 | 43 | 17 |
| Iraq | 4156 | 8235 | 349.0 | 2.0 | 40 | 84.0 | 39 | 39 | 74 | 79 | 21 | 22 | 97 | >100 | 96 | 87 | 72 | 49 | 39 | 100 | 100 |
| Israel | 863 | 4156 | 104.0 | 4.8 | 64 | 120.5 | 30 | 47 | 7 | >100 | 5 | 41 | >100 | >100 | 84 | 97 | 67 | 43 | 43 | 6 | 2 |
| Japan | 13235 | 49264 | 1563.0 | 3.7 | 57 | 118.1 | 30 | 43 | 25 | 79 | 78 | 20 | 84 | 60 | 68 | 80 | 62 | 36 | 36 | 55 | 27 |
| Jordan | 427 | 2063 | 20.0 | 4.8 | 64 | 46.9 | 56 | 60 | 6 | 99 | 0 | 62 | >100 | 95 | 90 | 79 | 66 | 41 | 41 | 0 | 0 |
| Kazakhstan | 19034 | 14565 | 124.0 | 0.8 | 16 | 6.5 | 93 | 54 | >100 | 99 | 55 | 89 | >100 | >100 | >100 | 99 | 93 | 86 | 54 | 100 | 100 |
| Korea, DPR | 3477 | 11354 | 170.1 | 3.3 | 53 | 48.9 | 56 | 54 | 72 | 100 | 0 | 88 | 100 | 100 | 99 | 100 | 82 | 64 | 54 | 100 | 100 |
| Korea, R | 7240 | 24108 | 932.5 | 3.3 | 53 | 128.8 | 28 | 40 | 29 | 32 | 41 | 23 | 96 | 83 | 88 | 92 | 60 | 33 | 33 | 95 | 90 |
| Kuwait | 3 | 90 | 1.0 | 26.7 | 100 | 297.4 | 3 | 51 | 0 | 4 | 0 | 0 | 29 | 3 | 55 | 10 | 13 | 5 | 5 | 39 | 16 |
| Kyrgyzstan | 924 | 2804 | 31.0 | 3.0 | 50 | 33.6 | 66 | 58 | 94 | >100 | 75 | 90 | >100 | >100 | >100 | 98 | 95 | 90 | 58 | 100 | 100 |
| Lao PDR | 829 | 1733 | 6.1 | 2.1 | 41 | 7.4 | 93 | 67 | 84 | 100 | 82 | >100 | 100 | 100 | 100 | 31 | 87 | 74 | 67 | 98 | 96 |
| Lebanon | 419 | 3128 | 50.0 | 7.5 | 77 | 119.3 | 30 | 53 | 7 | 99 | 77 | 51 | 91 | >100 | 75 | 42 | 68 | 44 | 44 | 100 | 100 |
| Malaysia | 94221 | 62403 | 1146.0 | 0.7 | 14 | 12.2 | 88 | 51 | 26 | 49 | 61 | >100 | 36 | >100 | 93 | 3 | 58 | 31 | 31 | 89 | 78 |
| Maldives | 8 | 56 | -- | 7.3 | 76 | -- | -- | 76 | 0 | 74 | 0 | 85 | 76 | 54 | 22 | 0 | 39 | 16 | 16 | 100 | 100 |
| Mongolia | 298 | 298 | 4.0 | 1.0 | 20 | 13.4 | 87 | 53 | 50 | 82 | 0 | 0 | 96 | 1 | >100 | 96 | 53 | 24 | 24 | 67 | 43 |
| Myanmar | 14607 | 22981 | 172.0 | 1.6 | 32 | 11.8 | 88 | 60 | >100 | 100 | >100 | 99 | >100 | >100 | 100 | 94 | 99 | 98 | 60 | 100 | 100 |
| Nepal | 4434 | 9999 | 103.0 | 2.2 | 42 | 23.2 | 77 | 59 | >100 | 99 | >100 | 83 | >100 | 98 | 99 | 99 | 97 | 94 | 59 | 100 | 100 |
| Oman | -- | -- | 12.0 | -- | -- | -- | -- | -- | -- | -- | -- | -- | -- | -- | -- | -- | -- | -- | -- | -- | -- |
| Pakistan | 35921 | 89203 | 2409.0 | 2.5 | 45 | 67.1 | 46 | 45 | >100 | 99 | 99 | 70 | 94 | >100 | 97 | 99 | 95 | 90 | 45 | 100 | 100 |
| Philippines | 19490 | 74231 | 646.1 | 3.8 | 58 | 33.1 | 67 | 62 | 88 | 95 | 99 | >100 | 98 | >100 | 95 | 2 | 85 | 70 | 62 | 81 | 62 |
| Qatar | -- | -- | 0.9 | -- | -- | -- | -- | -- | -- | -- | -- | -- | -- | -- | -- | -- | -- | -- | -- | -- | -- |
| Saudi Arabia | 852 | 5683 | 323.0 | 6.7 | 73 | 379.3 | 0 | 36 | 18 | 81 | 0 | 4 | 77 | 65 | 67 | 31 | 43 | 17 | 17 | 25 | 10 |
| Singapore | -- | -- | 4.9 | -- | -- | -- | -- | -- | -- | -- | -- | -- | -- | -- | -- | -- | -- | -- | -- | -- | -- |
| Sri Lanka | 1874 | 7191 | 204.4 | 3.8 | 58 | 109.0 | 33 | 45 | 51 | 90 | 83 | >100 | 79 | 99 | 90 | 46 | 80 | 60 | 45 | 75 | 53 |
| Syrian Arab R | 6558 | 12880 | 305.9 | 2.0 | 40 | 46.6 | 57 | 48 | >100 | >100 | 69 | 98 | >100 | >100 | 99 | 97 | 95 | 90 | 48 | 30 | 12 |
| Tajikistan | 917 | 1610 | 69.0 | 1.7 | 34 | 75.3 | 42 | 38 | 32 | 78 | 2 | 84 | >100 | >100 | 80 | 94 | 71 | 48 | 38 | 100 | 100 |
| Thailand | 27655 | 119871 | 1566.8 | 4.3 | 61 | 56.7 | 52 | 56 | >100 | >100 | >100 | 96 | >100 | >100 | >100 | 21 | 90 | 80 | 56 | 100 | 100 |
| Turkey | 27696 | 91403 | 1798.7 | 3.3 | 53 | 64.9 | 48 | 50 | 94 | >100 | >100 | 90 | >100 | >100 | 93 | 99 | 97 | 94 | 50 | 84 | 68 |
| Turkmenistan | 1332 | 1815 | 141.0 | 1.4 | 28 | 105.8 | 33 | 30 | 44 | 65 | 4 | 69 | 99 | >100 | 87 | 95 | 70 | 47 | 30 | 100 | 100 |
| United Arab Emirates | 52 | 1064 | 35.0 | 20.6 | 100 | 679.2 | 0 | 50 | 1 | 5 | 0 | 0 | 65 | 39 | 46 | 14 | 21 | 8 | 8 | 100 | 100 |
| Uzbekistan | 7166 | 10663 | 530.0 | 1.5 | 30 | 74.0 | 43 | 36 | 64 | 86 | 2 | >100 | >100 | >100 | 81 | 99 | 79 | 59 | 36 | 100 | 100 |
| Viet Nam | 11122 | 46352 | 1544.0 | 4.2 | 61 | 138.8 | 25 | 43 | >100 | >100 | 99 | >100 | >100 | >100 | 99 | 10 | 88 | 76 | 43 | 100 | 100 |
| Yemen | 1081 | 1886 | 12.0 | 1.7 | 34 | 11.1 | 89 | 61 | 24 | 100 | 0 | 22 | 85 | 97 | 85 | 48 | 58 | 31 | 31 | 98 | 96 |
| PACIFIC | | | | | | | | | | | | | | | | | | | | | |
| Australia | 23408 | 93821 | 1924.0 | 4.0 | 60 | 82.2 | 39 | 49 | >100 | 95 | >100 | >100 | >100 | >100 | >100 | 99 | 98 | 49 | 41 | 16 |
| Fiji | 177 | 5197 | 19.0 | 29.4 | 100 | 107.4 | 33 | 66 | 11 | 91 | >100 | 96 | 52 | 80 | 62 | 68 | 70 | 47 | 47 | 98 | 96 |
| New Zealand | 1150 | 3460 | 661.0 | 3.0 | 50 | 574.9 | 0 | 25 | 83 | 88 | 13 | 4 | >100 | >100 | >100 | >100 | 73 | 51 | 25 | 100 | 100 |
| Papua New Guinea | 2957 | 5472 | 13.0 | 1.8 | 36 | 4.4 | 96 | 66 | 1 | 100 | 99 | >100 | 98 | 99 | 48 | 1 | 68 | 44 | 44 | 21 | 8 |
| Samoa | -- | -- | -- | -- | -- | -- | -- | -- | 0 | >100 | 0 | >100 | 100 | >100 | 38 | 25 | 58 | 31 | 31 | 14 | 6 |
| Solomon Is | 293 | 519 | -- | 1.8 | 36 | -- | -- | 36 | 0 | 100 | 0 | >100 | 93 | 96 | 82 | 34 | 63 | 37 | 36 | 100 | 100 |
| Tonga | -- | -- | -- | -- | -- | -- | -- | -- | 0 | >100 | 0 | >100 | 100 | 100 | 29 | 67 | 62 | 36 | 36 | 100 | 100 |
| Vanuatu | 86 | 362 | -- | 4.2 | 61 | -- | -- | 61 | 5 | 89 | 0 | >100 | >100 | 97 | >100 | 78 | 71 | 48 | 48 | 66 | 41 |

**Notes**

Agriculture (Ag score) is the lower score of agricultural productivity (AP score) and agricultural self-reliance (ASR score). All data are for 1996, except Samoa and Tonga which are for 1992, and are from the food balance sheets and commodities database in FAO (1998a). Luxembourg is included with Belgium (B).

H area = harvested area (food crops only) in thousands of hectares (000 ha); except Haiti, Liberia, Rwanda, Bosnia & Herzegovina and Afghanistan, which is cropland area in thousands of hectares (from Table 11).

Prod = food crop production in thousands of metric tons (000 mt).

Fert = fertilizer use in thousands of metric tons (000 mt). Although the harvested area and production figures refer to the same set of food crops, the fertilizer data apply to non-food crops as well.

Prod/ha = metric tons of food crop production per harvested hectare.

Prod score = score of one of the agricultural productivity indicators: food produced per harvested hectare. The performance criteria are shown in Table 23a.

Fert/000 ha = metric tons of fertilizer used per 1000 harvested hectares.

Fert score = score of the other agricultural productivity indicator: fertilizer used per 1000 harvested hectares. The performance criteria are shown in Table 23a.

253

AP score = agricultural productivity score, the unweighted average score of food produced per harvested hectare (Prod score) and fertilizer used per 1000 harvested hectares (Fert score).

The remaining columns give production as a % of supply for eight categories of food: cereals; starchy roots (Stch roots); sugar crops and sweeteners (Sug swtn); oil crops, plant oils and tree nuts (Oils nuts); pulses and vegetables (Pulse veg); fruit; meat, offal, animal fats [except butter, cream, and fish oils] and eggs (Meat eggs); and dairy products [milk, butter, cream, cheese and other milk products] (D'ry). Production means total domestic production. Supply means the amount available for consumption, which is production + imports - exports ± stock changes. >100 indicates that production exceeds supply, the balance being exported.

FP % S = food production as a percentage of supply, the average of the eight groups, cereals through dairy products. >100 is counted as 100.

ASR score = agricultural self-reliance score, the score of food production as % of supply. The performance criteria are shown in Table 23a. They mirror the performance criteria for food sufficiency.

Ag score = the lower of the AP score and the ASR score.

F&SP%S = fish and seafood production as a percentage of supply. Fish and seafood include seaweeds and fish oils. Production means the domestic catch + aquaculture. Supply means the amount available for consumption, which is production + imports - exports ± stock changes. Data are for 1996 and are from the food balance sheets and commodities database in FAO (1998a).

FSR score = fish and seafood self-reliance, the score of fish and seafood production as % of supply. The performance criteria are shown in Table 24a. They are the same as for agricultural self-reliance (Table 23a).

| band | top point on scale | food produced per harvested hectare (mt) | fertilizer used per 1000 harvested hectares (mt) | food production as % of supply |
|---|---|---|---|---|
| good | 100 | 16 | 0 | 100 |
| fair | 80 | 8 | 20 | 90 |
| medium | 60 | 4 | 40 | 80 |
| poor | 40 | 2 | 80 | 65 |
| bad | 20 | 1 | 160 | 50 |
| base | 0 | 0 | 320 | 0 |

**Table 23a. Performance criteria for agriculture indicators.**

* A score with an asterisk has been reduced in accordance with the insufficient data rule. To prevent high scores resulting merely from lack of data, a good score is allowed only if it is based on all applicable components (data in an indicator, indicators in an index), and a fair score only if it is based on at least half the components. Good and fair scores (100-61) based on fewer than half the applicable components have been reduced to 60. Good scores (100-81) based on more than half but not all the applicable components have been reduced to 80.

# Table 24. Fisheries

| Country | Spp tot | Spp ass | ODR | ODR% | Spp score | mib | Marine catch mt | Inland water catch mt | Total catch mt | Shelf 000 km² | S/I 000 km² | Decked vessels grt | Undeck vessels number | Fleet capacity grt | t cap/km² | Area score | mt catch/t cap | Catch score | FP score | FSR score | Fish score |
|---|---|---|---|---|---|---|---|---|---|---|---|---|---|---|---|---|---|---|---|---|---|
| **AMERICAS** | | | | | | | | | | | | | | | | | | | | | |
| Antigua & Barbuda | -- | -- | -- | -- | -- | m | 470 | 0 | -- | 35 | -- | -- | 150 | 450 | 0.01 | 100 | 1.04 | 21 | 60 | 20 | 20 |
| Argentina | 13 | 11 | 5 | 45 | 27 | m | 1135452 | 11863 | -- | 835 | -- | 220954 | 2300 | 227854 | 0.27 | 89 | 4.98 | 65 | 60 | 100 | 60 |
| Bahamas | 1 | 1 | 0 | 0 | 100 | m | 9557 | 0 | -- | 65 | -- | 6400 | *510* | 6910 | 0.11 | 96 | 1.38 | 28 | 74 | 100 | 74 |
| Barbados | 1 | 1 | 0 | 0 | 100 | m | 3284 | 0 | -- | 1 | -- | 2584 | 7750 | 4834 | 4.83 | 16 | 0.68 | 14 | 43 | 13 | 13 |
| Belize | -- | -- | -- | -- | -- | m | 1229 | [94] 1 | -- | 25 | -- | 67221 | 900 | 69921 | 2.80 | 32 | 0.02 | 0 | 16 | 100 | 16 |
| Bolivia | -- | -- | -- | -- | -- | -- | -- | 5692 | -- | NA | -- | -- | -- | -- | -- | -- | -- | -- | -- | 20 | 20 |
| Brazil | 10 | 4 | 4 | 100 | 0 | b | 587600 | 183180 | 770780 | 905 | 996 | 84200 | 44000 | 216200 | 0.22 | 91 | 3.56 | 56 | 49 | 59 | 49 |
| Canada | 35 | 35 | 8 | 23 | 56 | m | 829878 | 38208 | -- | 2875 | -- | 596060 | 20470 | 657470 | 0.23 | 91 | 1.26 | 25 | 57 | 86 | 57 |
| Chile | 13 | 11 | 7 | 64 | 14 | m | 7433864 | [94] 5 | -- | 295 | -- | 178618 | 12000 | 214618 | 0.73 | 71 | 34.64 | 100 | 62 | 100 | 62 |
| Colombia | 3 | 0 | 0 | -- | -- | m | 106926 | 23524 | | 105 | -- | 20950 | 6000 | 38950 | 0.37 | 85 | 2.75 | 47 | 66 | 16 | 16 |
| Costa Rica | -- | -- | -- | -- | -- | m | 20106 | 1087 | -- | 45 | -- | 8650 | *2950* | 11600 | 0.26 | 90 | 1.73 | 35 | 62 | 100 | 62 |
| Cuba | 12 | 11 | 2 | 18 | 64 | m | 71202 | 2142 | -- | 135 | -- | 150680 | -- | 150680 | 1.12 | 58 | 0.47 | 9 | 44 | 43 | 43 |
| Dominica | -- | -- | -- | -- | -- | m | 838 | 0 | -- | 20 | -- | -- | 895 | 2685 | 0.13 | 95 | 0.31 | 6 | 50 | 14 | 14 |
| Dominican R | 2 | 1 | 0 | 0 | 80* | b | 15817 | 2160 | 17977 | 35 | 35 | -- | 3550 | 10650 | 0.30 | 88 | 1.69 | 34 | 67 | 6 | 6 |
| Ecuador | 6 | 3 | 0 | 0 | 80* | m | 505095 | 300 | -- | 95 | -- | 70200 | *1600* | 71800 | 0.76 | 70 | 7.03 | 75 | 75 | 100 | 75 |
| El Salvador | -- | -- | -- | -- | -- | b | 10208 | 4325 | 14533 | 35 | 35 | 7862 | 10000 | 37862 | 1.08 | 58 | 0.38 | 8 | 33 | 49 | 33 |
| Grenada | 2 | 1 | 0 | 0 | 80* | m | 1486 | 0 | -- | 30 | -- | -- | *730* | 730 | 0.02 | 99 | 2.03 | 40 | 73 | 17 | 17 |
| Guatemala | -- | -- | -- | -- | -- | b | 4228 | 4025 | 8253 | 25 | 25 | 4700 | 2900 | 13400 | 0.54 | 78 | 0.61 | 12 | 45 | 19 | 19 |
| Guyana | 1 | 0 | 0 | -- | -- | b | 43730 | 700 | 44430 | 35 | 53 | 4300 | 1600 | 9100 | 0.17 | 93 | 4.88 | 64 | 79 | 100 | 79 |
| Haiti | 1 | 0 | 0 | -- | -- | b | 5000 | 500 | 5500 | 35 | 35 | 280 | *3000* | 3280 | 0.09 | 96 | 1.68 | 34 | 65 | 8 | 8 |
| Honduras | 1 | 1 | 0 | 0 | 100 | m | 19626 | 127 | -- | 25 | -- | 25600 | *700* | 26300 | 1.05 | 59 | 0.75 | 15 | 58 | 100 | 58 |
| Jamaica | -- | -- | -- | -- | -- | b | 9827 | 710 | 10537 | 45 | 45 | 874 | 7150 | 22324 | 0.50 | 80 | 0.47 | 9 | 44 | 8 | 8 |
| Mexico | 15 | 8 | 2 | 25 | 53 | m | 1175184 | 113665 | -- | 555 | -- | 435163 | 71641 | 650086 | 1.17 | 57 | 1.81 | 36 | 49 | 100 | 49 |
| Nicaragua | -- | -- | -- | -- | -- | m | 10457 | 538 | -- | 125 | -- | 18100 | 120 | 21700 | 0.17 | 93 | 0.48 | 10 | 52 | 100 | 52 |
| Panama | 3 | 3 | 0 | 0 | 100 | m | 176014 | 130 | -- | 95 | -- | 267400 | *3000* | 270400 | 2.85 | 32 | 0.65 | 13 | 48 | 100 | 48 |
| Paraguay | -- | -- | -- | -- | -- | -- | -- | 17810 | -- | NA | -- | -- | -- | -- | -- | -- | -- | -- | -- | 76 | 76 |
| Peru | 7 | 7 | 4 | 57 | 17 | m | 8886553 | 50789 | -- | 135 | -- | 199900 | -- | 199900 | 1.48 | 50 | 44.45 | 100 | 56 | 100 | 56 |
| St Kitts & Nevis | -- | -- | -- | -- | -- | m | 218 | 0 | -- | e 11 | -- | -- | 270 | 810 | 0.07 | 97 | 0.27 | 5 | 51 | 52 | 51 |
| St Lucia | -- | -- | -- | -- | -- | m | 1176 | 0 | -- | 1 | -- | -- | 489 | 1467 | 1.47 | 51 | 0.80 | 16 | 33 | 12 | 12 |
| St Vincent & Grenadines | -- | -- | -- | -- | -- | m | 1320 | 0 | -- | 8 | -- | 41650 | 430 | 42940 | 5.37 | 13 | 0.03 | 1 | 7 | 59 | 7 |
| Suriname | -- | -- | -- | -- | -- | b | 12860 | 139 | 12999 | 35 | 42 | 2300 | 1150 | 5750 | 0.14 | 94 | 2.26 | 43 | 69 | 100 | 69 |
| Trinidad & Tobago | -- | -- | -- | -- | -- | m | 13250 | 0 | -- | 15 | -- | 2451 | 1450 | 6801 | 0.45 | 82 | 1.95 | 39 | 60 | 74 | 60 |
| United States | 74 | 59 | 14 | 24 | 55 | m | 5187877 | 36690 | -- | 2325 | -- | 1401586 | 72000 | 1617586 | 0.70 | 72 | 3.21 | 52 | 60 | 74 | 60 |
| Uruguay | 6 | 6 | 4 | 67 | 13 | m | 125597 | 849 | -- | 85 | -- | 23297 | -- | 23297 | 0.27 | 89 | 5.39 | 67 | 56 | 100 | 56 |
| Venezuela | 10 | 7 | 0 | 0 | 80* | m | 440065 | 59753 | -- | 95 | -- | 117002 | *12683* | 129685 | 1.37 | 53 | 3.39 | 54 | 62 | 70 | 62 |
| **AFRICA** | | | | | | | | | | | | | | | | | | | | | |
| Algeria | 5 | 5 | 0 | 0 | 100 | m | 105872 | 15 | -- | 15 | -- | 27898 | -- | 27898 | 1.86 | 43 | 3.79 | 58 | 67 | 78 | 67 |
| Angola | 2 | 2 | 0 | 0 | 100 | m | 87847 | 6000 | -- | 85 | -- | 24710 | *4200* | 28910 | 0.34 | 86 | 3.04 | 50 | 79 | 86 | 79 |
| Benin | 1 | 0 | 0 | -- | -- | b | 7000 | 37449 | 44449 | 15 | 17 | 668 | *23100* | 23768 | 1.40 | 52 | 1.87 | 37 | 44 | 53 | 44 |
| Botswana | -- | -- | -- | -- | -- | i | -- | 2000 | -- | NA | 15 | -- | 1000 | 3000 | 0.20 | 92 | 0.67 | 13 | 52 | 7 | 7 |
| Burkina Faso | -- | -- | -- | -- | -- | i | -- | 8000 | -- | NA | 0 | -- | 3000 | 9000 | -- | -- | 0.89 | 18 | 18 | 19 | 18 |
| Burundi | -- | -- | -- | -- | -- | i | -- | 21051 | -- | NA | 2 | -- | 1000 | 3000 | 1.50 | 50 | 7.02 | 75 | 62 | 88 | 62 |
| Cameroon | 4 | 3 | 2 | 67 | 13 | b | 64740 | 21000 | 85740 | 15 | 25 | 7900 | 7100 | 29200 | 1.17 | 57 | 2.94 | 49 | 40 | 24 | 24 |
| Cape Verde | 1 | 1 | 1 | 100 | 0 | m | 8495 | 0 | -- | 35 | -- | 3550 | 1250 | 7300 | 0.21 | 92 | 1.16 | 23 | 38 | 100 | 38 |
| Central African R | -- | -- | -- | -- | -- | -- | -- | 12900 | -- | NA | -- | -- | -- | -- | -- | -- | -- | -- | -- | 90 | 80* |
| Chad | -- | -- | -- | -- | -- | i | -- | 90000 | -- | NA | 25 | -- | 19100 | 57300 | 2.29 | 37 | 1.57 | 31 | 34 | 98 | 34 |
| Comoros | 2 | 1 | 0 | 0 | 80* | m | 13200 | 0 | -- | 35 | -- | -- | 4450 | 13350 | 0.38 | 85 | 0.99 | 20 | 62 | 82 | 62 |
| Congo, DR | -- | -- | -- | -- | -- | b | 3876 | 154001 | 157877 | 1 | 79 | 5383 | 16500 | 54883 | 0.69 | 72 | 2.88 | 49 | 61 | 28 | 28 |
| Congo, R | -- | -- | -- | -- | -- | b | 17000 | 19820 | 36820 | 15 | 16 | 8760 | 550 | 10410 | 0.65 | 74 | 3.54 | 55 | 64 | 2 | 2 |
| Côte d'Ivoire | 5 | 3 | 1 | 33 | 43 | m | 58854 | 11335 | -- | 55 | -- | 10582 | *3600* | 14182 | 0.26 | 90 | 4.15 | 61 | 65 | 15 | 15 |
| Djibouti | -- | -- | -- | -- | -- | -- | 350 | 0 | -- | 4 | -- | -- | -- | -- | -- | -- | -- | -- | -- | 8 | 8 |
| Egypt | 8 | 4 | 1 | 25 | 53 | b | 78296 | 171133 | 249429 | 65 | 71 | -- | 36401 | 109203 | 1.54 | 49 | 2.28 | 43 | 48 | 43 | 43 |
| Equatorial Guinea | 1 | 0 | 0 | -- | -- | b | 3000 | 380 | 3380 | 25 | 25 | 650 | *1100* | 1750 | 0.07 | 97 | 1.93 | 39 | 68 | -- | 68 |
| Eritrea | -- | -- | -- | -- | -- | -- | 3670 | 0 | -- | 75 | -- | -- | -- | -- | -- | -- | -- | -- | -- | 100 | 80* |
| Ethiopia | -- | -- | -- | -- | -- | i | -- | 6325 | -- | NA | 104 | -- | 1835 | 5505 | 0.05 | 98 | 1.15 | 23 | 60 | 90 | 60 |
| Gabon | 1 | 1 | 1 | 100 | 0 | b | 32789 | 7606 | 40395 | 55 | 65 | 4381 | 1600 | 9181 | 0.01 | 100 | 4.40 | 62 | 54 | 47 | 47 |
| Gambia | 1 | 0 | 0 | -- | -- | b | 20598 | 2500 | 23098 | 4 | 5 | -- | 1600 | 4800 | 0.96 | 62 | 4.81 | 64 | 63 | 100 | 63 |
| Ghana | 12 | 5 | 2 | 40 | 33 | b | 293322 | 60000 | 353322 | 55 | 66 | 63985 | 25000 | 138985 | 2.11 | 39 | 2.54 | 45 | 39 | 94 | 39 |
| Guinea | -- | -- | -- | -- | -- | b | 64760 | 4000 | 68760 | 35 | 35 | 4516 | 2300 | 11416 | 0.33 | 87 | 6.02 | 70 | 78 | 92 | 78 |

255

| Country | Spp tot | Spp ass | ODR | ODR% | Spp score | m i b | Marine catch mt | Inland water catch mt | Total catch mt | Shelf 000 km² | S/I 000 km² | Decked vessels grt | Undeck vessels number | Fleet capacity grt | t cap/ km² | Area score | mt catch/ t cap | Catch score | FP score | FSR score | Fish score |
|---|---|---|---|---|---|---|---|---|---|---|---|---|---|---|---|---|---|---|---|---|---|
| Guinea-Bissau | 1 | 0 | 0 | -- | -- | b | 6079 | 250 | 6329 | 55 | 63 | 2760 | 1150 | 6210 | 0.10 | 96 | 1.02 | 20 | 58 | 100 | 58 |
| Kenya | 1 | 0 | 0 | -- | -- | b | 5465 | 187241 | 192706 | 25 | 36 | 4198 | 10124 | 34570 | 0.96 | 62 | 5.57 | 68 | 65 | 100 | 65 |
| Lesotho | -- | -- | -- | -- | -- | -- | -- | 26 | -- | NA | -- | -- | -- | -- | -- | -- | -- | -- | -- | 0 | 0 |
| Liberia | -- | -- | -- | -- | -- | m | 5232 | 4000 | -- | 45 | -- | 2500 | 770 | 4810 | 0.11 | 96 | 1.09 | 22 | 59 | 60 | 59 |
| Libyan Arab J | -- | -- | -- | -- | -- | m | 34232 | 0 | -- | 35 | -- | 12700 | 650 | 14650 | 0.42 | 83 | 2.34 | 43 | 63 | 72 | 63 |
| Madagascar | 2 | 1 | 0 | 0 | 80* | b | 84640 | 30000 | 114640 | 195 | 201 | 9800 | 28507 | 95321 | 0.47 | 81 | 1.20 | 24 | 62 | 100 | 62 |
| Malawi | -- | -- | -- | -- | -- | i | -- | 53664 | -- | NA | 24 | 306 | 2807 | 8727 | 0.36 | 86 | 6.15 | 71 | 78 | 92 | 78 |
| Mali | -- | -- | -- | -- | -- | i | -- | 132900 | -- | NA | 20 | -- | 7700 | 23100 | 1.16 | 57 | 5.75 | 69 | 63 | 98 | 63 |
| Mauritania | 4 | 4 | 4 | 100 | 0 | m | 84500 | 5500 | -- | 25 | -- | 38000 | 3500 | 48500 | 1.94 | 41 | 1.74 | 35 | 25 | 100 | 25 |
| Mauritius | 1 | 0 | 0 | -- | -- | m | 16872 | [93] 3 | -- | 95 | -- | 2663 | 2056 | 8831 | 0.09 | 96 | 1.91 | 38 | 67 | 28 | 28 |
| Morocco | 16 | 9 | 4 | 44 | 28 | m | 842791 | 1500 | -- | 65 | -- | 225377 | 6500 | 244877 | 3.77 | 22 | 3.44 | 54 | 35 | 100 | 35 |
| Mozambique | 3 | 2 | 0 | 0 | 80* | b | 21740 | 5093 | 26833 | 185 | 203 | 7620 | 17200 | 24820 | 0.12 | 95 | 1.08 | 22 | 66 | 66 | 66 |
| Namibia | 10 | 9 | 2 | 22 | 57 | m | 290782 | 1195 | -- | 125 | -- | 67122 | 10 | 67152 | 0.54 | 78 | 4.33 | 62 | 66 | 100 | 66 |
| Niger | -- | -- | -- | -- | -- | i | -- | 3541 | -- | NA | 0 | -- | 3000 | 9000 | -- | -- | 0.39 | 8 | 8 | 39 | 8 |
| Nigeria | 9 | 2 | 2 | 100 | 0 | b | 231579 | 117903 | 349482 | 65 | 78 | 40267 | 77067 | 271468 | 3.48 | 25 | 1.29 | 26 | 17 | 24 | 17 |
| Rwanda | -- | -- | -- | -- | -- | i | -- | 3300 | -- | NA | 2 | -- | 1700 | 5100 | 2.55 | 35 | 0.65 | 13 | 24 | 53 | 24 |
| São Tomé & Principe | -- | -- | -- | -- | -- | m | 2800 | 0 | -- | 1 | -- | 1450 | 2700 | 9550 | 9.55 | 0 | 0.29 | 6 | 3 | 68 | 3 |
| Senegal | 11 | 5 | 5 | 100 | 0 | m | 323617 | 35000 | -- | 15 | -- | 40500 | 10251 | 71253 | 4.75 | 16 | 4.54 | 63 | 26 | 100 | 26 |
| Seychelles | -- | -- | -- | -- | -- | m | 3982 | 0 | -- | 45 | -- | -- | 383 | 1149 | 0.03 | 99 | 3.46 | 55 | 77 | 100 | 77 |
| Sierra Leone | 4 | 2 | 2 | 100 | 0 | b | 47313 | 15000 | 62313 | 25 | 25 | 5850 | 5650 | 22800 | 0.91 | 64 | 2.73 | 47 | 37 | 100 | 37 |
| Somalia | -- | -- | -- | -- | -- | m | 15200 | 300 | -- | 165 | -- | 6600 | 1550 | 8150 | 0.05 | 98 | 1.86 | 37 | 67 | -- | 67 |
| South Africa | 12 | 10 | 2 | 20 | 60 | m | 573558 | 800 | -- | 255 | -- | 78430 | 2600 | 81030 | 0.32 | 87 | 7.08 | 75 | 74 | 14 | 14 |
| Sudan | -- | -- | -- | -- | -- | b | 4000 | 40000 | 44000 | 95 | 225 | -- | 7665 | 22995 | 0.10 | 96 | 1.91 | 38 | 67 | 90 | 67 |
| Swaziland | -- | -- | -- | -- | -- | -- | -- | 60 | -- | NA | -- | -- | -- | -- | -- | -- | -- | -- | -- | -- | -- |
| Tanzania | 2 | 1 | 0 | 0 | 80* | b | 42771 | 317029 | 359800 | 65 | 127 | 2900 | 23550 | 73550 | 0.58 | 77 | 4.89 | 64 | 74 | 100 | 74 |
| Togo | 2 | 0 | 0 | -- | -- | b | 7203 | 4998 | 12201 | 1 | 3 | 449 | 1700 | 5549 | 1.85 | 43 | 2.20 | 42 | 42 | 10 | 10 |
| Tunisia | 10 | 10 | 4 | 40 | 33 | b | 82915 | 440 | 83355 | 55 | 63 | 3022 | 14450 | 46372 | 0.74 | 70 | 1.80 | 36 | 46 | 100 | 46 |
| Uganda | -- | -- | -- | -- | -- | i | -- | 208789 | -- | NA | 41 | -- | 10000 | 30000 | 0.73 | 71 | 6.96 | 75 | 73 | 100 | 73 |
| Zambia | -- | -- | -- | -- | -- | i | -- | 66465 | -- | NA | 9 | 2200 | 28850 | 88750 | 9.86 | 0 | 0.75 | 15 | 7 | 80 | 7 |
| Zimbabwe | -- | -- | -- | -- | -- | i | -- | 16405 | -- | NA | 4 | -- | 840 | 2520 | 0.63 | 75 | 6.51 | 73 | 74 | 74 | 74 |
| **EUROPE** | | | | | | | | | | | | | | | | | | | | | |
| Albania | -- | -- | -- | -- | -- | m | 1160 | 219 | -- | 12 | -- | 300 | -- | 300 | 0.03 | 99 | 3.87 | 59 | 79 | 18 | 18 |
| Austria | -- | -- | -- | -- | -- | i | -- | 400 | -- | NA | 1 | -- | 300 | 900 | 0.90 | 64 | 0.44 | 9 | 36 | 1 | 1 |
| Belarus | -- | -- | -- | -- | -- | -- | -- | 256 | -- | NA | -- | -- | -- | -- | -- | -- | -- | -- | -- | 100 | 80* |
| Belgium | -- | -- | -- | -- | -- | m | 35088 | 511 | -- | 3 | -- | 23262 | -- | 23262 | 7.75 | 1 | 1.51 | 30 | 16 | 2 | 2 |
| Bosnia & Herzegovina | -- | -- | -- | -- | -- | -- | 0 | 2500 | -- | 5 | -- | -- | -- | -- | -- | -- | -- | -- | -- | 11 | 11 |
| Bulgaria | 2 | 2 | 2 | 100 | 0 | m | 10444 | 2293 | -- | 15 | -- | 34373 | -- | 34373 | 2.29 | 37 | 0.30 | 6 | 14 | 72 | 14 |
| Croatia | -- | -- | -- | -- | -- | b | 14782 | 364 | 15146 | 55 | 56 | 7905 | 11409 | 42132 | 0.75 | 70 | 0.36 | 7 | 38 | 100 | 38 |
| Czech R | -- | -- | -- | -- | -- | -- | -- | 3929 | -- | NA | -- | -- | -- | -- | -- | -- | -- | -- | -- | 7 | 7 |
| Denmark | 7 | 6 | 3 | 50 | 20 | m | 1998769 | 264 | -- | 105 | -- | 95208 | 896 | 97896 | 0.93 | 63 | 20.42 | 100 | 61 | 100 | 61 |
| Estonia | -- | -- | -- | -- | -- | m | 129662 | 2366 | -- | 45 | -- | 98083 | 16000 | 114083 | 2.54 | 35 | 1.14 | 23 | 29 | 100 | 29 |
| Finland | -- | -- | -- | -- | -- | m | 119048 | 48436 | -- | 55 | -- | 19994 | 44 | 20126 | 0.37 | 85 | 5.92 | 70 | 78 | 24 | 24 |
| France | 19 | 16 | 6 | 38 | 36 | m | 597195 | 4500 | -- | 175 | -- | 178807 | 7/21 | 178828 | 1.02 | 60 | 3.34 | 53 | 50 | 16 | 16 |
| Germany | 2 | 1 | 1 | 100 | 0 | m | 216864 | 22889 | -- | 35 | -- | 78779 | 850 | 81329 | 2.32 | 37 | 2.67 | 47 | 28 | 8 | 8 |
| Greece | 23 | 20 | 11 | 55 | 18 | m | 147757 | 17585 | -- | 125 | -- | 118492 | 1953 | 124351 | 0.99 | 60 | 1.19 | 24 | 34 | 19 | 19 |
| Hungary | -- | -- | -- | -- | -- | -- | -- | 13506 | -- | NA | -- | -- | -- | -- | -- | -- | -- | -- | -- | 3 | 3 |
| Iceland | 6 | 5 | 4 | 80 | 8 | m | 1611809 | 739 | -- | 105 | -- | 123988 | 1150 | 127438 | 1.21 | 56 | 12.65 | 92 | 52 | 100 | 52 |
| Ireland | 4 | 3 | 0 | 0 | 80* | m | 381595 | 3761 | -- | 145 | -- | 57884 | 2 | 57890 | 0.40 | 84 | 6.59 | 73 | 79 | 100 | 79 |
| Italy | 28 | 22 | 13 | 59 | 16 | m | 383985 | 10035 | -- | 205 | -- | 250000 | 1000 | 253000 | 1.23 | 55 | 1.52 | 30 | 34 | 14 | 14 |
| Latvia | 3 | 3 | 2 | 67 | 13 | m | 148680 | 514 | -- | 35 | -- | 62248 | -- | 62248 | 1.78 | 44 | 2.39 | 44 | 34 | 100 | 34 |
| Lithuania | 3 | 2 | 0 | 0 | 80* | m | 46536 | 1260 | -- | 8 | -- | 142693 | -- | 142693 | 17.84 | 0 | 0.33 | 7 | 29 | 92 | 29 |
| Luxembourg | -- | -- | -- | -- | -- | -- | -- | 0 | -- | NA | -- | -- | -- | -- | -- | -- | -- | -- | -- | 2 | 2 |
| Macedonia, FYR | -- | -- | -- | -- | -- | -- | -- | 208 | -- | NA | -- | -- | -- | -- | -- | -- | -- | -- | -- | 2 | 2 |
| Malta | -- | -- | -- | -- | -- | m | 854 | 0 | -- | 8 | -- | 19220 | 750 | 21470 | 2.68 | 33 | 0.04 | 1 | 17 | 3 | 3 |
| Moldova | -- | -- | -- | -- | -- | -- | -- | 5 | -- | 1 | -- | -- | -- | -- | -- | -- | -- | -- | -- | 100 | 80* |
| Netherlands | 3 | 2 | 1 | 50 | 20 | m | 433985 | 4107 | -- | 65 | -- | 180606 | 1 | 180609 | 2.78 | 32 | 2.40 | 44 | 32 | 18 | 18 |
| Norway | 12 | 11 | 5 | 45 | 27 | m | 2524665 | 413 | -- | 435 | -- | 338923 | 8000 | 362923 | 0.83 | 67 | 6.96 | 75 | 56 | 100 | 56 |
| Poland | 4 | 4 | 1 | 25 | 53 | m | 401346 | 24889 | -- | 30 | -- | 136897 | 870 | 139507 | 4.65 | 17 | 2.88 | 49 | 40 | 47 | 40 |
| Portugal | 9 | 8 | 3 | 38 | 36 | m | 260519 | -- | -- | 25 | -- | 123279 | 2803 | 131688 | 5.27 | 14 | 1.98 | 40 | 30 | 17 | 17 |
| Romania | 3 | 3 | 2 | 67 | 13 | m | 40227 | 9048 | -- | 25 | -- | 13445 | 3768 | 24749 | 0.99 | 60 | 1.63 | 33 | 35 | 11 | 11 |
| Slovakia | -- | -- | -- | -- | -- | -- | -- | 1948 | -- | NA | -- | -- | -- | -- | -- | -- | -- | -- | -- | 100 | 80* |
| Slovenia | -- | -- | -- | -- | -- | m | 1849 | 292 | -- | 1 | -- | 905 | 41 | 1028 | 1.03 | 59 | 1.80 | 36 | 48 | 4 | 4 |
| Spain | 51 | 46 | 19 | 41 | 32 | m | 1134331 | 9489 | -- | 125 | -- | 656216 | 3239 | 665933 | 5.33 | 13 | 1.70 | 34 | 26 | 31 | 26 |
| Sweden | 2 | 2 | 1 | 50 | 20 | m | 402643 | 1943 | -- | 180 | -- | 57000 | 3000 | 66000 | 0.37 | 85 | 6.10 | 70 | 58 | 100 | 58 |
| Switzerland | -- | -- | -- | -- | -- | i | -- | 1588 | -- | NA | 2 | -- | 600 | 1800 | 0.90 | 64 | 0.88 | 18 | 41 | 0 | 0 |

| Country | Spp tot | Spp ass | ODR | ODR% | Spp score | m/i/b | Marine catch mt | Inland water catch mt | Total catch mt | Shelf 000 km² | S/I 000 km² | Decked vessels grt | Undeck vessels number | Fleet capacity grt | t cap/km² | Area score | mt catch/t cap | Catch score | FP score | FSR score | Fish score |
|---|---|---|---|---|---|---|---|---|---|---|---|---|---|---|---|---|---|---|---|---|---|
| Ukraine | 14 | 13 | 4 | 31 | 45 | m | 371667 | 6847 | -- | 75 | -- | 411384 | -- | 411384 | 5.49 | 13 | 0.90 | 18 | 25 | 44 | 25 |
| United Kingdom | 6 | 6 | 2 | 33 | 43 | m | 907756 | 2146 | -- | 535 | -- | 247407 | 205 | 248022 | 0.46 | 82 | 3.66 | 57 | 60 | 17 | 17 |
| Yugoslavia | -- | -- | -- | -- | -- | b | 364 | 4766 | 5130 | 1 | 1 | 461 | 188 | 1025 | 1.03 | 59 | 5.00 | 65 | 62 | 17 | 17 |
| RUSSIAN FED | 41 | 31 | 4 | 13 | 74 | m | 4098935 | 212874 | -- | 4385 | -- | 2991912 | -- | 2991912 | 0.68 | 73 | 1.37 | 27 | 58 | 100 | 58 |
| ASIA | | | | | | | | | | | | | | | | | | | | | |
| Afghanistan | -- | -- | -- | -- | -- | -- | -- | 1300 | -- | NA | -- | -- | -- | -- | -- | -- | -- | -- | -- | -- | -- |
| Armenia | -- | -- | -- | -- | -- | i | -- | 520 | -- | NA | 2 | 101 | 30 | 191 | 0.10 | 96 | 2.72 | 47 | 71 | 100 | 71 |
| Azerbaijan | -- | -- | -- | -- | -- | m | -- | 9271 | -- | NA | -- | -- | -- | -- | -- | -- | -- | -- | -- | 100 | 80* |
| Bahrain | -- | -- | -- | -- | -- | m | 9388 | 0 | -- | 4 | -- | 2800 | 1720 | 7960 | 1.99 | 40 | 1.18 | 24 | 32 | -- | 32 |
| Bangladesh | 3 | 1 | 0 | 0 | 60* | b | 264650 | 586712 | 851362 | 75 | 89 | 11600 | 117317 | 363551 | 4.08 | 20 | 2.34 | 43 | 41 | 100 | 41 |
| Bhutan | -- | -- | -- | -- | -- | -- | -- | 310 | -- | NA | -- | -- | -- | -- | -- | -- | -- | -- | -- | -- | -- |
| Brunei Darussalam | -- | -- | -- | -- | -- | m | 4712 | 7 | -- | 8 | -- | 1132 | 843 | 3661 | 0.46 | 82 | 1.29 | 26 | 54 | 7 | 7 |
| Cambodia | -- | -- | -- | -- | -- | b | 30500 | 72499 | 102999 | 60 | 65 | -- | 33476 | 100428 | 1.55 | 49 | 1.02 | 20 | 34 | 100 | 34 |
| China | 14 | 9 | 4 | 44 | 28 | m | 11151924 | 1607385 | -- | 980 | -- | 5548449 | 5608 | 5565273 | 5.68 | 12 | 2.00 | 40 | 27 | 74 | 27 |
| Cyprus | 2 | 2 | 1 | 50 | 20 | m | 2528 | 65 | 2593 | 15 | 15 | 1153 | 491 | 2626 | 0.18 | 93 | 0.99 | 20 | 44 | 2 | 2 |
| Georgia | -- | -- | -- | -- | -- | m | 2822 | 219 | -- | -- | -- | 32870 | -- | 32870 | -- | -- | 0.08 | 2 | 2 | 24 | 2 |
| India | 38 | 12 | 0 | 0 | 60* | m | 2596205 | 623378 | -- | 585 | -- | 1078000 | 181505 | 1622515 | 2.77 | 32 | 1.60 | 32 | 41 | 100 | 41 |
| Indonesia | 38 | 16 | 2 | 13 | 60* | m | 3174069 | 335358 | 3509427 | 3285 | 378 | 539505 | 544879 | 2174142 | 5.75 | 11 | 1.61 | 32 | 34 | 100 | 34 |
| Iran | 1 | 1 | 0 | 0 | 100 | b | 251000 | 88800 | 339800 | 105 | 116 | 60600 | 8700 | 86700 | 0.75 | 70 | 3.92 | 59 | 76 | 17 | 17 |
| Iraq | -- | -- | -- | -- | -- | b | 2000 | 9900 | 11900 | 1 | 2 | 2237 | 1700 | 7337 | 3.67 | 23 | 1.62 | 32 | 28 | 100 | 28 |
| Israel | 1 | 1 | 1 | 100 | 0 | b | 2374 | 2715 | 5089 | 4 | 4 | 4765 | 210 | 5395 | 1.35 | 53 | 0.94 | 19 | 24 | 2 | 2 |
| Japan | 66 | 44 | 11 | 25 | 53 | m | 5875835 | 91455 | -- | 775 | -- | 1508316 | 25320 | 1584276 | 2.04 | 40 | 3.71 | 57 | 50 | 27 | 27 |
| Jordan | -- | -- | -- | -- | -- | b | 2 | 350 | 352 | 1 | 1 | -- | 71 | 213 | 0.21 | 92 | 1.65 | 33 | 62 | 0 | 0 |
| Kazakhstan | -- | -- | -- | -- | -- | i | -- | 48402 | -- | NA | 47 | 26500 | 120 | 26860 | 0.57 | 77 | 1.80 | 36 | 57 | 100 | 57 |
| Korea, DPR | -- | -- | -- | -- | -- | m | 1660550 | 104000 | -- | 95 | -- | 721000 | 10000 | 731000 | 7.69 | 2 | 2.27 | 43 | 22 | 100 | 22 |
| Korea, R | 35 | 26 | 7 | 27 | 51 | m | 2310282 | 9646 | -- | 225 | -- | 825994 | -- | 825994 | 3.67 | 23 | 2.80 | 48 | 41 | 90 | 41 |
| Kuwait | 1 | 0 | 0 | -- | -- | m | 8616 | 0 | -- | 10 | -- | 11623 | -- | 11623 | 1.16 | 57 | 0.74 | 15 | 36 | 16 | 16 |
| Kyrgyzstan | -- | -- | -- | -- | -- | -- | -- | 185 | -- | NA | -- | -- | -- | -- | -- | -- | -- | -- | -- | 100 | 80* |
| Lao PDR | -- | -- | -- | -- | -- | -- | -- | 25850 | -- | NA | -- | -- | -- | -- | -- | -- | -- | -- | -- | 96 | 80* |
| Lebanon | -- | -- | -- | -- | -- | b | 4065 | 20 | 4085 | 4 | 4 | 700 | 1300 | 4600 | 1.15 | 57 | 0.89 | 18 | 37 | 100 | 37 |
| Malaysia | 38 | 10 | 0 | 0 | 60* | m | 1108436 | 3939 | -- | 385 | -- | 302250 | 12989 | 341067 | 0.89 | 64 | 3.25 | 52 | 59 | 78 | 59 |
| Maldives | 3 | 2 | 0 | 0 | 80* | m | 104566 | 0 | -- | e 959 | -- | 299 | 5084 | 15551 | 0.02 | 99 | 6.72 | 74 | 84 | 100 | 84 |
| Mongolia | -- | -- | -- | -- | -- | | | 158 | -- | NA | -- | -- | -- | -- | -- | -- | -- | -- | -- | 43 | 43 |
| Myanmar | 1 | 0 | 0 | -- | -- | b | 606466 | 151748 | 758214 | 235 | 254 | 11600 | 110000 | 341600 | 1.34 | 53 | 2.22 | 42 | 48 | 100 | 48 |
| Nepal | -- | -- | -- | -- | -- | -- | -- | 11230 | -- | NA | -- | -- | -- | -- | -- | -- | -- | -- | -- | 100 | 80* |
| Oman | 4 | 1 | 0 | 0 | 60* | m | 139864 | 0 | -- | 75 | -- | 8120 | 11350 | 42170 | 0.56 | 78 | 3.32 | 53 | 64 | -- | 64 |
| Pakistan | 13 | 4 | 0 | 0 | 60* | m | 405444 | 121405 | -- | 55 | -- | 189700 | 29193 | 277279 | 5.04 | 15 | 1.46 | 29 | 35 | 100 | 35 |
| Philippines | 24 | 9 | 2 | 22 | 57 | b | 1675927 | 186000 | 1861927 | 605 | 607 | 79100 | 400000 | 1279100 | 2.11 | 39 | 1.45 | 29 | 42 | 62 | 42 |
| Qatar | -- | -- | -- | -- | -- | m | 4271 | 0 | -- | 15 | -- | -- | 350 | 1050 | 0.07 | 97 | 4.07 | 60 | 79 | -- | 79 |
| Saudi Arabia | 3 | 1 | 0 | 0 | 60* | m | 45691 | 0 | -- | 135 | -- | 4728 | 7278 | 26562 | 0.20 | 92 | 1.72 | 34 | 62 | 10 | 10 |
| Singapore | 1 | 0 | 0 | -- | -- | m | 10102 | [94] 23 | -- | 1 | -- | 4010 | 170 | 4520 | 4.52 | 17 | 2.23 | 42 | 30 | -- | 30 |
| Sri Lanka | 5 | 2 | 0 | 0 | 60* | b | 217500 | 12000 | 229500 | 55 | 56 | 12550 | 27269 | 94357 | 1.68 | 46 | 2.43 | 44 | 50 | 53 | 50 |
| Syrian Arab R | -- | -- | -- | -- | -- | b | 1940 | 3560 | 5500 | 1 | 2 | 120 | 1250 | 1370 | 0.69 | 72 | 4.01 | 60 | 66 | 12 | 12 |
| Tajikistan | -- | -- | -- | -- | -- | -- | -- | 260 | -- | NA | -- | -- | -- | -- | -- | -- | -- | -- | -- | 100 | 80* |
| Thailand | 39 | 17 | 1 | 6 | 60* | m | 3013733 | 188617 | -- | 275 | -- | 428000 | 39000 | 545000 | 1.98 | 40 | 5.53 | 68 | 56 | 100 | 56 |
| Turkey | 12 | 11 | 7 | 64 | 14 | m | 582610 | 47976 | -- | 95 | -- | 83000 | 2254 | 89762 | 0.94 | 62 | 6.49 | 72 | 49 | 68 | 49 |
| Turkmenistan | -- | -- | -- | -- | -- | i | -- | 9490 | -- | NA | 18 | 22517 | -- | 22517 | 1.25 | 55 | 0.42 | 8 | 31 | 100 | 31 |
| United Arab Emirates | 9 | 2 | 0 | 0 | 60* | m | 105884 | 0 | -- | 80 | -- | 19000 | -- | 19000 | 0.24 | 90 | 5.57 | 68 | 73 | 100 | 73 |
| Uzbekistan | -- | -- | -- | -- | -- | i | -- | 3611 | -- | NA | 33 | -- | 294 | 882 | 0.03 | 99 | 4.09 | 60 | 79 | 100 | 79 |
| Viet Nam | 3 | 1 | 0 | 0 | 60* | b | 751900 | 136700 | 888600 | 465 | 471 | 24561 | 85000 | 279561 | 0.59 | 76 | 3.18 | 52 | 63 | 100 | 63 |
| Yemen | 2 | 0 | 0 | -- | -- | m | 102964 | 1000 | -- | 155 | -- | 6000 | 3468 | 9468 | 0.06 | 98 | 10.87 | 87 | 80* | 96 | 80 |
| PACIFIC | | | | | | | | | | | | | | | | | | | | | |
| Australia | 21 | 13 | 1 | 8 | 80* | m | 203247 | 1724 | -- | 2315 | -- | 48390 | 2000 | 54390 | 0.02 | 99 | 3.74 | 57 | 79 | 16 | 16 |
| Fiji | 2 | 0 | 0 | -- | -- | b | 30811 | 3586 | 34397 | 125 | 125 | -- | 42870 | 128610 | 1.03 | 59 | 0.27 | 5 | 32 | 96 | 32 |
| New Zealand | 20 | 17 | 0 | 0 | 80* | m | 543128 | 1114 | -- | 325 | -- | 75300 | 1200 | 78900 | 0.24 | 90 | 6.88 | 74 | 81 | 100 | 81 |
| Papua New Guinea | 1 | 1 | 0 | 0 | 100 | b | 12500 | 13500 | 26000 | 595 | 605 | 3500 | 3100 | 12800 | 0.02 | 99 | 2.03 | 40 | 80 | 8 | 8 |
| Samoa | -- | -- | -- | -- | -- | m | 1100 | 0 | -- | 35 | -- | -- | 2680 | 8040 | 0.23 | 91 | 0.14 | 3 | 47 | 6 | 6 |
| Solomon Is | -- | -- | -- | -- | -- | m | 70600 | 0 | -- | 175 | -- | 2900 | 30000 | 92900 | 0.53 | 79 | 0.76 | 15 | 47 | 100 | 47 |
| Tonga | -- | -- | -- | -- | -- | m | 2596 | 0 | -- | 55 | -- | -- | 780 | 2340 | 0.04 | 98 | 1.11 | 22 | 60 | 100 | 60 |
| Vanuatu | -- | -- | -- | -- | -- | m | 2727 | 0 | -- | 125 | -- | -- | 120 | 360 | 0.00 | 100 | 7.57 | 78 | 80* | 41 | 41 |

**Notes**

Fisheries (Fish score) is the lower score of two indicators (column heading in parentheses):

Fishing pressure (FP score), the unweighted average score of depleted species + overexploited species as % of assessed species (Spp score), fish catching capacity per unit of fish producing area (Area score), and weight of catch per unit of fish catching capacity (Catch score).

Fish and seafood self-reliance (FSR score), represented by fish and seafood production as % of supply.

Spp tot = number of fishery species or species groups that are the subject of a major fishery, in which the country concerned is one of the main participants. All data in this and the Spp ass and ODR columns are for 1994 and are from FAO Marine Resources Service, Fishery Resources Division (1997).

Spp ass = number of the above fishery species whose status has been assessed by FAO.

ODR = number of assessed fishery species estimated to be overexploited (O), depleted (D), or depleted but recovering (R). Overexploited species are being fished at above a level that is believed to be sustainable, with a high risk of stock collapse or depletion. Catches of depleted species are well below historical levels, irrespective of the amount of fishing effort. Catches of recovering species are increasing after a collapse from a previous high. Non-ODR species are classified as underexploited or undeveloped, moderately exploited, or fully exploited. Underexploited or undeveloped species are believed to have a significant potential for expanded production. Moderately exploited species are believed to have limited potential for expanded production. Fully exploited species are being fished at or close to an optimal yield level, with no room expected for further expansion.

ODR % = overexploited species + depleted species + depleted but recovering species as a percentage of assessed species.

Spp score = species score = score for ODR %. The performance criteria are shown in Table 24a. The tops of the fair and medium bands were set at five times those for the wild species indicators (Table 19), since depleted and overexploited species are not necessarily threatened.

mib = whether the fisheries covered in the catch and area columns are marine (m), inland water (i), or both (b). Catch and area are identifiably marine or inland, but the fishing fleet may be either or both. In countries with an exclusively marine or inland fishery the fleet is obviously marine or inland. This is not so in countries with both types of fishery. In general, most decked vessels can be assumed to be marine (FAO Fishery Information, Data and Statistics Unit 1996). However, the undecked vessels may be part of either fishery. To reduce the risk of comparing fishing capacity with too small or too big a fishing area, marine coastal countries labeled m were assessed on the basis of their marine catch and area alone, and their fishing fleet was treated as entirely marine. Marine coastal countries labeled b have an inland water catch greater than their marine catch or an undecked vessel capacity greater than their decked vessel capacity, and were assessed on the basis of their total (marine + inland water) catch, with their fishing fleet treated as a combination of marine and inland water. Iran (with an inland water catch and undecked vessel capacity that do not meet these criteria) was also assessed on the basis of total catch, because the inland fishery was assumed to be entirely on the Caspian Sea. Countries labeled i are landlocked and therefore have exclusively inland fisheries.

Catch data are in metric tons (mt) and are from FAO (1998b). All data are for 1995, except where indicated otherwise in brackets. Total (marine + inland water) catch is given only for countries assessed on the basis of their combined marine and inland water catches.

Shelf = continental shelf area in thousands of square kilometers (000 km$^2$), except if marked with the letter e where it is the exclusive economic zone. Data are based on estimates by FAO Fishery Resources Division (1996). NA = not applicable (landlocked country).

S/I = shelf area + inland water area in thousands of square kilometers (000 km$^2$) if the country is assessed on both, or inland water area if the country is landlocked. The inland water area is whatever remains after subtracting the land area from the total area in Table 10.

Decked vessels/Undeck vessels: Fishing fleet capacity is in gross registered tons (grt) for decked vessels and in numbers for undecked [undeck] vessels. Data are for 1995 and are from FAO Fishery Information, Data and Statistics Unit (1998). In the undecked vessels column, numbers in regular type refer to powered vessels only; numbers in *italics*, to powered and unpowered vessels.

Fleet capacity = total of decked + undecked capacities in gross registered tons (grt). Numbers of undecked vessels were converted to tons at 3 tons per vessel (following Garcia & Newton 1994) for powered vessels only (in regular type in the undecked vessels column), and at 1 ton per vessel for fleets of powered and unpowered vessels (in *italics* in the undecked vessels column).

t cap/km$^2$ = tons of fishing fleet capacity per square kilometer of fish producing area (continental shelf area, inland water area or shelf + inland water area, as appropriate).

Area score = the score for weight of fish catching capacity per unit of fish producing area. The performance criteria are shown in Table 24a and are explained under Catch score below.

mt catch/t cap = metric tons of catch (marine, inland waters or both, as appropriate) per ton of fishing fleet capacity.

Catch score = the score for weight of catch per unit of fish catching capacity. The performance criteria are shown in Table 24a. The criteria for this indicator and for fish catching capacity per unit of fish producing area are based on the following calculations. Garcia and Newton (1994) estimate that the global maximum sustainable yield (MSY) of marine fisheries is 82.8 million tons taken by a world fleet of 42.0 million corrected gross registered tons (grt). Corrected grt is the actual grt of 26.2 million in 1989 multiplied by a technology coefficient of 1.59. The technology coefficient takes account of improvements in the technology of the fishing fleet. Assuming the technology coefficient continued to increase at an annual rate of 0.059 (the rate during the 1980s), it would have been 1.94 in 1995. Thus an efficient MSY fleet would have an actual grt of 21.6 million (42.0 million divided by 1.94). This would produce a global MSY average of 3.8 tons of catch per ton of capacity. Grainger and Garcia (1996) estimate the global average potential catch per km$^2$ of continental shelf (the main producing area of marine fisheries) to be 3.0-4.5 tons (the range is due to different methods of calculation). The mid-point figure of 3.75 tons/km$^2$ of shelf is convenient, being close to the figure of 3.8 tons of catch per ton of capacity. Global MSY is likely to be higher than what is sustainable in some areas, and lower than the locally sustainable level in others. Furthermore, MSY may not be sustainable in any case if the fishery's impact on the ecosystem has not been adequately taken into account. Accordingly, global MSY was used conservatively to set the top of the medium bands for both indicators. For tons of catch per ton of capacity, the top of the medium band was set at 4 tons of catch per ton of capacity, slightly higher (and therefore more conservative) than the estimated global MSY average of 3.8 tons. For tons of fishing capacity per km$^2$ of fish producing area, the top of the medium band was set at 1 ton of capacity per km$^2$ of producing area. This roughly corresponds to the 4 tons of catch per ton of capacity, since 1 ton of capacity is estimated to take 3.8 tons of catch at the global MSY average, and 3.8 tons is within the range of the global average potential catch per km$^2$ of continental shelf. Since the estimated potential catch per km$^2$ of fish producing area is based on continental shelf area, it is applicable to marine fisheries but not necessarily to inland water fisheries. Of the 157 countries covered by these indicators, 93 were rated on marine fisheries alone, 46 countries (where marine and inland water fleets could not be distinguished) were rated on marine and inland water fisheries together, and 18 landlocked countries were rated on inland water fisheries alone. The performance criteria may be less valid for the 46 countries rated on both fisheries, and may not be suitable for the 18 countries rated on inland water fisheries.

FP score = fishing pressure score, the unweighted average of the species, area and catch scores.

FSR score = fish and seafood self-reliance, the score of fish and seafood production as % of supply. See Table 23 for data. The performance criteria are shown in Table 24a. They are the same as for agricultural self-reliance (Table 23a).

| band | top point on scale | depleted + overexploited species as % of assessed species | tons of fish catching capacity per km$^2$ of fish producing area | tons of catch per ton of fish catching capacity | fish & seafood production as % of supply |
|---|---|---|---|---|---|
| good | 100 | 0 | 0.0 | 16 | 100 |
| fair | 80 | 10 | 0.5 | 8 | 90 |
| medium | 60 | 20 | 1.0 | 4 | 80 |
| poor | 40 | 35 | 2.0 | 2 | 65 |
| bad | 20 | 50 | 4.0 | 1 | 50 |
| base | 0 | 100 | 8.0 | 0 | 0 |

**Table 24a. Performance criteria for fisheries indicators.**

# Table 25. Wellbeing Index and Wellbeing/Stress Index

| Country | HWI | EWI | ESI | HWI - ESI | WI | WSI | WSI score | GJ/$k | Pop/ha | Spp/ha | WI rank | WSI rank | HWI rank | EWI rank |
|---|---|---|---|---|---|---|---|---|---|---|---|---|---|---|
| **AMERICAS** | | | | | | | | | | | | | | |
| Antigua & Barbuda | 49 | 40 | 60 | -11 | 44.5 | 0.82 | 33 | 7.8 | 1.55 | 19.80 | 70 | 68 | 61= | 109= |
| Argentina | 55 | 40 | 60 | -5 | 47.5 | 0.92 | 37 | 6.5 | 0.13 | 0.04 | 55 | 53= | 43= | 109= |
| Bahamas | 54 | 32 | 68 | -14 | 43.0 | 0.79 | 32 | 4.9 | 0.22 | 0.90 | 78 | 73= | 46= | 131= |
| Barbados | 62 | 32 | 68 | -6 | 47.0 | 0.91 | 36 | 4.7 | 6.28 | 14.23 | 59 | 57= | 32= | 131= |
| Belize | 50 | 64 | 36 | 14 | 57.0 | 1.39 | 48 | 10.4 | 0.10 | 1.53 | 9 | 6 | 55= | 13= |
| Bolivia | 34 | 63 | 37 | -3 | 48.5 | 0.92 | 37 | 6.7 | 0.08 | 0.17 | 50 | 53= | 109= | 17= |
| Brazil | 45 | 36 | 64 | -19 | 40.5 | 0.70 | 28 | 6.4 | 0.20 | 0.07 | 92 | 84= | 72= | 120= |
| Canada | 78 | 43 | 57 | 21 | 60.5 | 1.37 | 47 | 15.3 | 0.03 | 0.00 | 7= | 9= | 10= | 94= |
| Chile | 55 | 30 | 70 | -15 | 42.5 | 0.79 | 32 | 4.9 | 0.20 | 0.08 | 79 | 73= | 43= | 146= |
| Colombia | 43 | 42 | 58 | -15 | 42.5 | 0.74 | 30 | 4.1 | 0.37 | 0.48 | 81 | 79= | 79= | 101= |
| Costa Rica | 56 | 41 | 59 | -3 | 48.5 | 0.95 | 38 | 4.5 | 0.79 | 2.60 | 48 | 46= | 41= | 107= |
| Cuba | 40 | 45 | 55 | -15 | 42.5 | 0.73 | 29 | 12.9 | 1.01 | 0.62 | 82 | 82 | 90= | 81= |
| *Dominica* | *56* | *65* | *35* | *21* | *60.5* | *1.60* | *52* | *3.3* | *0.95* | *17.44* | *6* | *1* | *41=* | *10=* |
| Dominican R | 49 | 46 | 54 | -5 | 47.5 | 0.91 | 36 | 5.4 | 1.74 | 1.22 | 56 | 57= | 61= | 72= |
| Ecuador | 43 | 56 | 44 | -1 | 49.5 | 0.98 | 39 | 6.0 | 0.45 | 0.77 | 41 | 40= | 79= | 40= |
| El Salvador | 36 | 46 | 54 | -18 | 41.0 | 0.67 | 27 | 8.2 | 2.98 | 1.61 | 90 | 90= | 102= | 72= |
| *Grenada* | *55* | *49* | *51* | *4* | *52.0* | *1.08* | *42* | *6.6* | *2.76* | *33.88* | *26* | *23=* | *43=* | *62=* |
| Guatemala | 23 | 44 | 56 | -33 | 33.5 | 0.41 | 16 | 6.2 | 1.05 | 0.89 | 148 | 143= | 131= | 85= |
| Guyana | 51 | 63 | 37 | 14 | 57.0 | 1.38 | 48 | 8.1 | 0.04 | 0.34 | 10 | 7= | 54 | 17= |
| Haiti | 19 | 43 | 57 | -38 | 31.0 | 0.33 | 13 | 8.3 | 2.96 | 1.97 | 166 | 160 | 145= | 94= |
| Honduras | 33 | 45 | 55 | -22 | 39.0 | 0.60 | 24 | 9.3 | 0.58 | 0.58 | 103 | 104 | 112 | 81= |
| Jamaica | 54 | 35 | 65 | -11 | 44.5 | 0.83 | 33 | 17.3 | 2.35 | 3.19 | 68 | 65= | 46= | 122= |
| Mexico | 45 | 21 | 79 | -34 | 33.0 | 0.57 | 23 | 7.2 | 0.50 | 0.14 | 150 | 108 | 72= | 176 |
| Nicaragua | 28 | 49 | 51 | -23 | 38.5 | 0.55 | 22 | 11.7 | 0.39 | 0.65 | 110= | 111= | 118= | 62= |
| Panama | 52 | 37 | 63 | -11 | 44.5 | 0.83 | 33 | 4.6 | 0.38 | 1.49 | 69 | 65= | 51= | 117= |
| Paraguay | 35 | 46 | 54 | -19 | 40.5 | 0.65 | 26 | 6.6 | 0.14 | 0.22 | 93 | 94= | 107= | 72= |
| Peru | 44 | 62 | 38 | 6 | 53.0 | 1.16 | 43 | 5.0 | 0.20 | 0.16 | 19 | 16 | 76= | 21= |
| *St Kitts & Nevis* | *52* | *53* | *47* | *5* | *52.5* | *1.11* | *42* | *6.3* | *1.46* | *27.27* | *21* | *19* | *51=* | *51=* |
| *St Lucia* | *53* | *51* | *49* | *4* | *52.0* | *1.08* | *42* | *3.7* | *2.48* | *17.84* | *25* | *23=* | *49=* | *55=* |
| *St Vincent & Grenadines* | *41* | *54* | *46* | *-5* | *47.5* | *0.89* | *36* | *4.2* | *2.92* | *33.36* | *57* | *60=* | *87=* | *46=* |
| Suriname | 52 | 58 | 42 | 10 | 55.0 | 1.24 | 45 | 12.2 | 0.03 | 0.37 | 15 | 12 | 51= | 33= |
| Trinidad & Tobago | 53 | 32 | 68 | -15 | 42.5 | 0.78 | 31 | 42.9 | 2.52 | 5.29 | 80 | 77= | 49= | 131= |
| United States | 73 | 31 | 69 | 4 | 52.0 | 1.06 | 41 | 12.1 | 0.30 | 0.02 | 27 | 27= | 18= | 141= |
| Uruguay | 61 | 52 | 48 | 13 | 56.5 | 1.27 | 45 | 3.9 | 0.19 | 0.15 | 11 | 11 | 35= | 54 |
| Venezuela | 43 | 46 | 54 | -11 | 44.5 | 0.80 | 32 | 16.2 | 0.27 | 0.25 | 73 | 72 | 79= | 72= |
| **AFRICA** | | | | | | | | | | | | | | |
| Algeria | 29 | 44 | 56 | -27 | 36.5 | 0.52 | 21 | 11.1 | 0.13 | 0.01 | 130 | 118= | 117 | 85= |
| Angola | 8 | 67 | 33 | -25 | 37.5 | 0.24 | 10 | 5.3 | 0.10 | 0.05 | 123 | 171= | 175 | 4= |
| Benin | 27 | 71 | 29 | -2 | 49.0 | 0.93 | 37 | 9.1 | 0.54 | 0.24 | 47 | 49= | 124= | 2 |
| Botswana | 34 | 68 | 32 | 2 | 51.0 | 1.06 | 41 | 11.3 | 0.03 | 0.05 | 35 | 27= | 109= | 3 |
| Burkina Faso | 17 | 58 | 42 | -25 | 37.5 | 0.40 | 16 | 10.4 | 0.44 | 0.06 | 122 | 146= | 151= | 33= |
| Burundi | 6 | 60 | 40 | -34 | 33.0 | 0.15 | 6 | 12.7 | 2.41 | 1.10 | 156 | 178 | 177= | 28= |
| Cameroon | 15 | 64 | 36 | -21 | 39.5 | 0.42 | 17 | 7.0 | 0.32 | 0.19 | 101 | 138= | 157= | 13= |
| Cape Verde | 47 | 47 | 53 | -6 | 47.0 | 0.89 | 36 | 1.7 | 1.06 | 2.06 | 60 | 60= | 65= | 70= |
| Central African R | 16 | 66 | 34 | -18 | 41.0 | 0.47 | 19 | 7.1 | 0.06 | 0.07 | 91 | 127= | 153= | 6= |
| Chad | 13 | 59 | 41 | -28 | 36.0 | 0.32 | 13 | 6.1 | 0.06 | 0.02 | 134 | 161= | 164= | 32 |
| Comoros | 20 | 44 | 56 | -36 | 32.0 | 0.36 | 14 | 1.0 | 3.11 | 3.61 | 161 | 156= | 141= | 85= |
| Congo, DR | 7 | 65 | 35 | -28 | 36.0 | 0.20 | 8 | 12.6 | 0.22 | 0.05 | 135 | 175 | 176 | 10= |
| Congo, R | 15 | 72 | 28 | -13 | 43.5 | 0.54 | 22 | 11.2 | 0.09 | 0.15 | 77 | 114 | 157= | 1 |
| Côte d'Ivoire | 20 | 57 | 43 | -23 | 38.5 | 0.47 | 19 | 8.4 | 0.46 | 0.14 | 112= | 127= | 141= | 35= |
| Djibouti | 18 | 60 | 40 | -22 | 39.0 | 0.45 | 18 | 6.4 | 0.28 | 0.28 | 106 | 133 | 147= | 28= |
| Egypt | 39 | 43 | 57 | -18 | 41.0 | 0.68 | 27 | 8.2 | 0.68 | 0.02 | 89 | 89 | 94= | 94= |
| Equatorial Guinea | 15 | 62 | 38 | -23 | 38.5 | 0.39 | 16 | 7.9 | 0.16 | 1.32 | 114 | 148= | 157= | 21= |
| Eritrea | 10 | 60 | 40 | -30 | 35.0 | 0.25 | 10 | 10.2 | 0.33 | -- | 140 | 169= | 171= | 28= |
| Ethiopia | 13 | 64 | 36 | -23 | 38.5 | 0.36 | 14 | 16.5 | 0.57 | 0.07 | 115 | 156= | 164= | 13= |
| Gabon | 28 | 62 | 38 | -10 | 45.0 | 0.74 | 30 | 8.8 | 0.05 | 0.27 | 66 | 79= | 118= | 21= |
| Gambia | 16 | 62 | 38 | -22 | 39.0 | 0.42 | 17 | 8.0 | 1.16 | 1.21 | 107 | 138= | 153= | 21= |
| Ghana | 22 | 38 | 62 | -40 | 30.0 | 0.35 | 14 | 10.3 | 0.85 | 0.19 | 168 | 159 | 133= | 114= |
| Guinea | 15 | 66 | 34 | -19 | 40.5 | 0.44 | 18 | 4.5 | 0.30 | 0.15 | 95 | 134= | 157= | 6= |
| Guinea-Bissau | 13 | 66 | 34 | -21 | 39.5 | 0.38 | 15 | 7.2 | 0.34 | 0.37 | 102 | 150= | 164= | 6= |
| Kenya | 18 | 51 | 49 | -31 | 34.5 | 0.37 | 15 | 15.5 | 0.52 | 0.14 | 143 | 153= | 147= | 55= |
| Lesotho | 24 | 57 | 43 | -19 | 40.5 | 0.56 | 22 | 46.7 | 0.71 | 0.55 | 94 | 109= | 127= | 35= |
| *Liberia* | *9* | *65* | *35* | *-26* | *37.0* | *0.26* | *10* | *25.6* | *0.28* | *0.26* | *126* | *168* | *174* | *10=* |
| Libyan Arab J | 38 | 24 | 76 | -38 | 31.0 | 0.50 | 20 | 15.7 | 0.03 | 0.01 | 164 | 122= | 96= | 169= |
| Madagascar | 24 | 50 | 50 | -26 | 37.0 | 0.48 | 19 | 8.5 | 0.27 | 0.17 | 124 | 126 | 127= | 58= |
| Malawi | 22 | 62 | 38 | -16 | 42.0 | 0.58 | 23 | 14.6 | 0.92 | 0.39 | 88 | 106= | 133= | 21= |

259

| Country | HWI | EWI | ESI | HWI - ESI | WI | WSI | WSI score | GJ/$k | Pop/ha | Spp/ha | WI rank | WSI rank | HWI rank | EWI rank |
|---|---|---|---|---|---|---|---|---|---|---|---|---|---|---|
| Mali | 21 | 44 | 56 | -35 | 32.5 | 0.38 | 15 | 9.3 | 0.09 | 0.02 | 157 | 150= | 137= | 85= |
| Mauritania | 17 | 40 | 60 | -43 | 28.5 | 0.28 | 11 | 9.4 | 0.03 | 0.01 | 174 | 164= | 151= | 109= |
| Mauritius | 54 | 44 | 56 | -2 | 49.0 | 0.96 | 38 | 3.4 | 5.68 | 3.88 | 45 | 45 | 46= | 85= |
| Morocco | 36 | 32 | 68 | -32 | 34.0 | 0.53 | 21 | 4.3 | 0.63 | 0.09 | 146 | 115= | 102= | 131= |
| Mozambique | 11 | 55 | 45 | -34 | 33.0 | 0.24 | 10 | 13.6 | 0.25 | 0.08 | 155 | 171= | 169= | 43= |
| Namibia | 34 | 54 | 46 | -12 | 44.0 | 0.74 | 30 | 17.3 | 0.02 | 0.05 | 75 | 79= | 109= | 46= |
| Niger | 11 | 56 | 44 | -33 | 33.5 | 0.25 | 10 | 8.7 | 0.08 | 0.01 | 149 | 169= | 169= | 40= |
| Nigeria | 16 | 56 | 44 | -28 | 36.0 | 0.36 | 14 | 16.4 | 1.21 | 0.06 | 133 | 156= | 153= | 40= |
| Rwanda | 12 | 57 | 43 | -31 | 34.5 | 0.28 | 11 | 15.3 | 2.94 | 1.12 | 144 | 164= | 168 | 35= |
| *São Tomé & Principe* | *10* | *53* | *47* | *-37* | *31.5* | *0.21* | *8* | *3.9* | *1.53* | *10.32* | *163* | *174* | *171=* | *51=* |
| Senegal | 20 | 54 | 46 | -26 | 37.0 | 0.43 | 17 | 5.8 | 0.48 | 0.13 | 125 | 136= | 141= | 46= |
| *Seychelles* | *50* | *49* | *51* | *-1* | *49.5* | *0.98* | *39* | *4.9* | *1.71* | *25.33* | *40* | *40=* | *55=* | *62=* |
| Sierra Leone | 6 | 63 | 37 | -31 | 34.5 | 0.16 | 6 | 19.8 | 0.68 | 0.38 | 145 | 177 | 177= | 17= |
| *Somalia* | *3* | *62* | *38* | *-35* | *32.5* | *0.08* | *3* | *15.0* | *0.16* | *0.06* | *158* | *180* | *180* | *21=* |
| South Africa | 43 | 27 | 73 | -30 | 35.0 | 0.59 | 24 | 11.8 | 0.33 | 0.20 | 136 | 105 | 79= | 161= |
| Sudan | 13 | 46 | 54 | -41 | 29.5 | 0.24 | 10 | 4.7 | 0.12 | 0.02 | 171 | 171= | 164= | 72= |
| Swaziland | 24 | 54 | 46 | -22 | 39.0 | 0.52 | 21 | 25.8 | 0.58 | 1.88 | 104 | 118= | 127= | 46= |
| Tanzania | 18 | 54 | 46 | -28 | 36.0 | 0.39 | 16 | 21.6 | 0.35 | 0.12 | 132 | 148= | 147= | 46= |
| Togo | 21 | 66 | 34 | -13 | 43.5 | 0.62 | 25 | 5.0 | 0.82 | 0.49 | 76 | 103 | 137= | 6= |
| Tunisia | 44 | 32 | 68 | -24 | 38.0 | 0.65 | 26 | 5.6 | 0.59 | 0.15 | 116= | 94= | 76= | 131= |
| Uganda | 10 | 44 | 56 | -46 | 27.0 | 0.18 | 7 | 7.1 | 0.90 | 0.28 | 177 | 176 | 171= | 85= |
| Zambia | 16 | 43 | 57 | -41 | 29.5 | 0.28 | 11 | 22.7 | 0.12 | 0.08 | 170 | 164= | 153= | 94= |
| Zimbabwe | 23 | 55 | 45 | -22 | 39.0 | 0.51 | 21 | 11.4 | 0.30 | 0.14 | 105 | 120= | 131= | 43= |
| EUROPE | | | | | | | | | | | | | | |
| Albania | 38 | 46 | 54 | -16 | 42.0 | 0.70 | 28 | 6.2 | 1.08 | 1.17 | 86 | 84= | 96= | 72= |
| Austria | 80 | 42 | 58 | 22 | 61.0 | 1.38 | 48 | 6.6 | 0.98 | 0.40 | 5 | 7= | 4= | 101= |
| Belarus | 46 | 50 | 50 | -4 | 48.0 | 0.92 | 37 | 20.7 | 0.49 | -- | 53 | 53= | 68= | 58= |
| Belgium | 80 | 23 | 77 | 3 | 51.5 | 1.04 | 41 | 9.4 | 3.33 | 0.56 | 34 | 31= | 4= | 172= |
| *Bosnia & Herzegovina* | *24* | *45* | *55* | *-31* | *34.5* | *0.44* | *18* | *113.8* | *0.78* | *--* | *141* | *134=* | *127=* | *81=* |
| Bulgaria | 58 | 31 | 69 | -11 | 44.5 | 0.84 | 34 | 24.5 | 0.74 | 0.36 | 67 | 64 | 39 | 141= |
| Croatia | 57 | 33 | 67 | -10 | 45.0 | 0.85 | 34 | 14.1 | 0.79 | -- | 64 | 63 | 40 | 126= |
| Czech R | 70 | 33 | 67 | 3 | 51.5 | 1.04 | 41 | 15.7 | 1.30 | -- | 30= | 31= | 24= | 126= |
| Denmark | 81 | 31 | 69 | 12 | 56.0 | 1.17 | 43 | 6.1 | 1.23 | 0.35 | 13 | 15 | 2= | 141= |
| Estonia | 62 | 34 | 66 | -4 | 48.0 | 0.94 | 38 | 35.2 | 0.31 | 0.44 | 51 | 48 | 32= | 125 |
| Finland | 81 | 44 | 56 | 25 | 62.5 | 1.45 | 49 | 11.4 | 0.15 | 0.04 | 2 | 3 | 2= | 85= |
| France | 75 | 29 | 71 | 4 | 52.0 | 1.06 | 41 | 7.7 | 1.07 | 0.09 | 29 | 27= | 16 | 154 |
| Germany | 77 | 36 | 64 | 13 | 56.5 | 1.20 | 44 | 7.9 | 2.30 | 0.08 | 12 | 13 | 13= | 120= |
| Greece | 70 | 33 | 67 | 3 | 51.5 | 1.04 | 41 | 8.5 | 0.81 | 0.41 | 30= | 31= | 24= | 126= |
| Hungary | 65 | 33 | 67 | -2 | 49.0 | 0.97 | 39 | 14.5 | 1.08 | 0.27 | 44 | 43= | 30= | 126= |
| Iceland | 80 | 43 | 57 | 23 | 61.5 | 1.40 | 48 | 9.7 | 0.03 | 0.05 | 4 | 5 | 4= | 94= |
| Ireland | 76 | 32 | 68 | 8 | 54.0 | 1.12 | 42 | 6.7 | 0.53 | 0.16 | 17 | 18 | 15 | 131= |
| Italy | 74 | 30 | 70 | 4 | 52.0 | 1.06 | 41 | 6.0 | 1.90 | 0.20 | 28 | 27= | 17 | 146= |
| Latvia | 62 | 46 | 54 | 8 | 54.0 | 1.15 | 43 | 19.7 | 0.36 | 0.24 | 16 | 17 | 32= | 72= |
| Lithuania | 61 | 44 | 56 | 5 | 52.5 | 1.09 | 42 | 24.2 | 0.56 | 0.23 | 22 | 21= | 35= | 85= |
| Luxembourg | 77 | 24 | 76 | 1 | 50.5 | 1.01 | 41 | 10.4 | 1.68 | 5.63 | 37 | 37 | 13= | 169= |
| Macedonia, FYR | 46 | 42 | 58 | -12 | 44.0 | 0.79 | 32 | 20.5 | 0.79 | -- | 74 | 73= | 68= | 101= |
| Malta | 70 | 14 | 86 | -16 | 42.0 | 0.81 | 33 | 4.4 | 12.16 | 30.34 | 84 | 69= | 24= | 180 |
| Moldova | 41 | 35 | 65 | -24 | 38.0 | 0.63 | 25 | 30.1 | 1.30 | -- | 118 | 99= | 87= | 122= |
| Netherlands | 78 | 22 | 78 | 0 | 50.0 | 1.00 | 40 | 10.6 | 3.87 | 0.36 | 38= | 38= | 10= | 175 |
| Norway | 82 | 43 | 57 | 25 | 62.5 | 1.44 | 49 | 9.6 | 0.14 | 0.06 | 3 | 4 | 1 | 94= |
| Poland | 65 | 30 | 70 | -5 | 47.5 | 0.93 | 37 | 16.6 | 1.20 | 0.08 | 54 | 49= | 30= | 146= |
| Portugal | 72 | 31 | 69 | 3 | 51.5 | 1.04 | 41 | 4.9 | 1.07 | 0.31 | 32 | 31= | 22 | 141= |
| Romania | 50 | 30 | 70 | -20 | 40.0 | 0.71 | 28 | 17.8 | 0.94 | 0.15 | 97 | 83 | 55= | 146= |
| Slovakia | 61 | 40 | 60 | 1 | 50.5 | 1.02 | 41 | 15.7 | 1.10 | -- | 36 | 36 | 35= | 109= |
| Slovenia | 71 | 35 | 65 | 6 | 53.0 | 1.09 | 42 | 11.1 | 0.98 | -- | 20 | 21= | 23 | 122= |
| Spain | 73 | 20 | 80 | -7 | 46.5 | 0.91 | 36 | 6.3 | 0.78 | 0.11 | 61 | 57= | 18= | 177 |
| Sweden | 79 | 49 | 51 | 28 | 64.0 | 1.55 | 51 | 11.7 | 0.20 | 0.05 | 1 | 2 | 8= | 62= |
| Switzerland | 78 | 43 | 57 | 21 | 60.5 | 1.37 | 47 | 5.5 | 1.79 | 0.81 | 7= | 9= | 10= | 94= |
| Ukraine | 47 | 26 | 74 | -27 | 36.5 | 0.64 | 26 | 58.2 | 0.84 | -- | 128 | 98 | 65= | 164 |
| United Kingdom | 73 | 30 | 70 | 3 | 51.5 | 1.04 | 41 | 7.7 | 2.41 | 0.08 | 33 | 31= | 18= | 146= |
| Yugoslavia | 42 | 37 | 63 | -21 | 39.5 | 0.67 | 27 | 25.2 | 1.04 | -- | 100 | 90= | 85= | 117= |
| RUSSIAN FEDERATION | 48 | 42 | 58 | -10 | 45.0 | 0.83 | 33 | 38.1 | 0.09 | -- | 65 | 65= | 63= | 101= |
| ASIA | | | | | | | | | | | | | | |
| *Afghanistan* | *6* | *48* | *52* | *-46* | *27.0* | *0.12* | *5* | *4.9* | *0.35* | *0.06* | *178* | *179* | *177=* | *68=* |
| Armenia | 45 | 55 | 45 | 0 | 50.0 | 1.00 | 40 | 8.7 | 1.18 | -- | 38= | 38= | 72= | 43= |
| Azerbaijan | 42 | 28 | 72 | -30 | 35.0 | 0.58 | 23 | 39.2 | 0.89 | -- | 137 | 106= | 85= | 155= |
| *Bahrain* | *46* | *17* | *83* | *-37* | *31.5* | *0.55* | *22* | *34.6* | *8.94* | *3.86* | *162* | *111=* | *68=* | *178* |
| Bangladesh | 27 | 46 | 54 | -27 | 36.5 | 0.50 | 20 | 5.7 | 8.97 | 0.38 | 131 | 122= | 124= | 72= |
| Bhutan | 14 | 67 | 33 | -19 | 40.5 | 0.42 | 17 | 7.0 | 0.45 | 1.29 | 96 | 138= | 163 | 4= |

| Country | HWI | EWI | ESI | HWI - ESI | WI | WSI | WSI score | GJ/$k | Pop/ha | Spp/ha | WI rank | WSI rank | HWI rank | EWI rank |
|---|---|---|---|---|---|---|---|---|---|---|---|---|---|
| Brunei Darussalam | 47 | 42 | 58 | -11 | 44.5 | 0.81 | 32 | 11.0 | 0.57 | 6.31 | 72 | 69= | 65= | 101= |
| Cambodia | 20 | 57 | 43 | -23 | 38.5 | 0.47 | 19 | 5.6 | 0.62 | -- | 112= | 127= | 141= | 35= |
| China | 36 | 28 | 72 | -36 | 32.0 | 0.50 | 20 | 9.7 | 1.34 | 0.04 | 160 | 122= | 102= | 155= |
| Cyprus | 67 | 38 | 62 | 5 | 52.5 | 1.08 | 42 | 6.3 | 0.85 | 1.96 | 23 | 23= | 27= | 114= |
| Georgia | 48 | 41 | 59 | -11 | 44.5 | 0.81 | 32 | 9.5 | 0.71 | -- | 71 | 69= | 63= | 107= |
| India | 31 | 27 | 73 | -42 | 29.0 | 0.42 | 17 | 9.3 | 3.08 | 0.05 | 172 | 138= | 114= | 161= |
| Indonesia | 36 | 48 | 52 | -16 | 42.0 | 0.69 | 28 | 7.6 | 1.11 | 0.17 | 87 | 87= | 102= | 68= |
| Iran | 38 | 32 | 68 | -30 | 35.0 | 0.56 | 22 | 11.0 | 0.41 | 0.04 | 138 | 109= | 96= | 131= |
| Iraq | 19 | 31 | 69 | -50 | 25.0 | 0.28 | 11 | 15.7 | 0.53 | 0.07 | 180 | 164= | 145= | 141= |
| Israel | 59 | 25 | 75 | -16 | 42.0 | 0.79 | 32 | 6.2 | 2.95 | 1.23 | 85 | 73= | 38 | 165= |
| Japan | 80 | 25 | 75 | 5 | 52.5 | 1.07 | 41 | 6.4 | 3.35 | 0.16 | 24 | 26 | 4= | 165= |
| Jordan | 38 | 28 | 72 | -34 | 33.0 | 0.53 | 21 | 8.1 | 0.75 | 0.26 | 151 | 115= | 96= | 155= |
| Kazakhstan | 43 | 32 | 68 | -25 | 37.5 | 0.63 | 25 | 26.9 | 0.06 | -- | 120 | 99= | 79= | 131= |
| *Korea, DPR* | *21* | *45* | *55* | *-34* | *33.0* | *0.38* | *15* | *30.6* | *1.99* | *0.24* | *153* | *150=* | *137=* | *81=* |
| Korea, R | 67 | 27 | 73 | -6 | 47.0 | 0.92 | 37 | 10.1 | 4.72 | 0.31 | 58 | 53= | 27= | 161= |
| Kuwait | 50 | 25 | 75 | -25 | 37.5 | 0.67 | 27 | 15.6 | 1.11 | 0.20 | 119 | 90= | 55= | 165= |
| Kyrgyzstan | 38 | 42 | 58 | -20 | 40.0 | 0.66 | 26 | 10.9 | 0.24 | -- | 98 | 93 | 96= | 101= |
| Lao PDR | 15 | 63 | 37 | -22 | 39.0 | 0.41 | 16 | 8.1 | 0.23 | -- | 108 | 143= | 157= | 17= |
| Lebanon | 40 | 37 | 63 | -23 | 38.5 | 0.63 | 25 | 10.7 | 3.16 | 2.17 | 109 | 99= | 90= | 117= |
| Malaysia | 46 | 33 | 67 | -21 | 39.5 | 0.69 | 28 | 11.0 | 0.67 | 0.51 | 99 | 87= | 68= | 126= |
| *Maldives* | *22* | *47* | *53* | *-31* | *34.5* | *0.42* | *17* | *4.1* | *9.53* | *10.17* | *142* | *138=* | *133=* | *70=* |
| Mongolia | 39 | 60 | 40 | -1 | 49.5 | 0.98 | 39 | 27.7 | 0.02 | 0.01 | 42 | 40= | 94= | 28= |
| Myanmar | 21 | 49 | 51 | -30 | 35.0 | 0.41 | 16 | 6.6 | 0.67 | 0.12 | 139 | 143= | 137= | 62= |
| Nepal | 28 | 64 | 36 | -8 | 46.0 | 0.78 | 31 | 11.9 | 1.63 | 0.53 | 63 | 77= | 118= | 13= |
| Oman | 31 | 28 | 72 | -41 | 29.5 | 0.43 | 17 | 12.7 | 0.12 | 0.07 | 169 | 136= | 114= | 155= |
| Pakistan | 18 | 44 | 56 | -38 | 31.0 | 0.32 | 13 | 9.3 | 1.97 | 0.08 | 167 | 161= | 147= | 85= |
| Philippines | 44 | 32 | 68 | -24 | 38.0 | 0.65 | 26 | 6.3 | 2.53 | 0.32 | 116= | 94= | 76= | 131= |
| *Qatar* | *40* | *24* | *76* | *-36* | *32.0* | *0.53* | *21* | *61.7* | *0.54* | *0.32* | *159* | *115=* | *90=* | *169=* |
| Saudi Arabia | 31 | 23 | 77 | -46 | 27.0 | 0.40 | 16 | 18.4 | 0.10 | 0.01 | 176 | 146= | 114= | 172= |
| Singapore | 66 | 32 | 68 | -2 | 49.0 | 0.97 | 39 | 10.6 | 57.53 | 37.60 | 43 | 43= | 29 | 131= |
| Sri Lanka | 40 | 57 | 43 | -3 | 48.5 | 0.93 | 37 | 4.7 | 2.87 | 0.58 | 49 | 49= | 90= | 35= |
| Syrian Arab R | 28 | 25 | 75 | -47 | 26.5 | 0.37 | 15 | 12.2 | 0.87 | 0.13 | 179 | 153= | 118= | 165= |
| Tajikistan | 28 | 39 | 61 | -33 | 33.5 | 0.46 | 18 | 21.0 | 0.43 | -- | 147 | 131= | 118= | 113 |
| Thailand | 50 | 23 | 77 | -27 | 36.5 | 0.65 | 26 | 9.0 | 1.20 | 0.25 | 127 | 94= | 55= | 172= |
| Turkey | 45 | 28 | 72 | -27 | 36.5 | 0.63 | 25 | 6.4 | 0.86 | 0.12 | 129 | 99= | 72= | 155= |
| Turkmenistan | 32 | 30 | 70 | -38 | 31.0 | 0.46 | 18 | 55.7 | 0.09 | -- | 165 | 131= | 113 | 146= |
| United Arab Emirates | 41 | 16 | 84 | -43 | 28.5 | 0.49 | 20 | 32.5 | 0.29 | 0.06 | 173 | 125 | 87= | 179 |
| Uzbekistan | 36 | 30 | 70 | -34 | 33.0 | 0.51 | 21 | 32.2 | 0.54 | -- | 152 | 120= | 102= | 146= |
| Viet Nam | 28 | 49 | 51 | -23 | 38.5 | 0.55 | 22 | 6.8 | 2.41 | 0.35 | 110= | 111= | 118= | 62= |
| Yemen | 15 | 51 | 49 | -34 | 33.0 | 0.31 | 12 | 16.3 | 0.34 | 0.04 | 154 | 163 | 157= | 55= |
| **PACIFIC** | | | | | | | | | | | | | | |
| Australia | 79 | 28 | 72 | 7 | 53.5 | 1.10 | 42 | 11.9 | 0.02 | 0.02 | 18 | 20 | 8= | 155= |
| Fiji | 50 | 46 | 54 | -4 | 48.0 | 0.93 | 37 | 6.7 | 0.45 | 0.89 | 52 | 49= | 55= | 72= |
| New Zealand | 73 | 38 | 62 | 11 | 55.5 | 1.18 | 44 | 10.0 | 0.14 | 0.10 | 14 | 14 | 18= | 114= |
| Papua New Guinea | 22 | 53 | 47 | -25 | 37.5 | 0.47 | 19 | 8.0 | 0.10 | 0.28 | 121 | 127= | 133= | 51= |
| Samoa | 43 | 50 | 50 | -7 | 46.5 | 0.86 | 34 | 4.9 | 0.63 | 2.77 | 62 | 62 | 79= | 58= |
| *Solomon Is* | *37* | *61* | *39* | *-2* | *49.0* | *0.95* | *38* | *6.4* | *0.15* | *1.20* | *46* | *46=* | *101* | *27* |
| *Tonga* | *26* | *30* | *70* | *-44* | *28.0* | *0.37* | *15* | *9.8* | *1.32* | *6.76* | *175* | *153=* | *126* | *146=* |
| Vanuatu | 35 | 50 | 50 | -15 | 42.5 | 0.70 | 28 | 1.6 | 0.16 | 0.80 | 83 | 84= | 107= | 58= |

**Notes**

The Wellbeing Index(WI) is the point on the Barometer of Sustainability where the Human Wellbeing Index (HWI) and Ecosystem Wellbeing Index (EWI) intersect. The Wellbeing/Stress Index (WSI) is the ratio of human wellbeing to ecosystem stress, calculated by dividing the HWI by the Ecosystem Stress Index (ESI).

*Countries in italics were rated on less than two-thirds of the human or ecosystem sub-elements.*

HWI = Human Wellbeing Index (Table 1).

EWI = Ecosystem Wellbeing Index (Table 9).

ESI = Ecosystem Stress Index = 100 minus the EWI.

HWI - ESI = Human Wellbeing Index minus Ecosystem Stress Index.

WI = Wellbeing Index (expressed as the average of the HWI and the EWI).

WSI = Wellbeing/Stress Index = the HWI divided by the ESI.

WSI score = score for Wellbeing/Stress Index. See Table 25a for performance criteria.

GJ/$k = gigajoules of energy consumed per PPP$1000 of Gross Domestic Product (GDP). Energy data are for 1997 and are from United Nations Energy Statistics Unit (2000). GDP data are also for 1997 and are from World Bank (1999a) and United Nations Development Programme (1999)

Pop/ha = population per hectare of land + inland water. Population data are estimates for 2000 and from United Nations Population Division (1998b). Area data are from FAO (1999), except for Belgium and Luxembourg which are from OECD (1999).

Spp/ha = the estimated number of wild species per hectare of land + inland water. Species are native wild species of higher plants (angiosperms, gymnosperms and pteridophytes), mammals, breeding birds, reptiles and amphibians. Species data are from the World Conservation Monitoring Centre Threatened Plants Database (WCMC 1998a) and Threatened Animals Database (WCMC 1998b). Area data are from FAO (1999), except for Belgium and Luxembourg which are from OECD (1999).

WI rank = average Wellbeing Index rank.
WSI rank = Wellbeing/Stress Index rank
HWI rank = Human Wellbeing Index rank.
EWI rank = Ecosystem Wellbeing Index rank.
Correlations between income (GDP per person) and the HWI, ESI, human elements and ecosystem elements are shown in Table 25b.

Correlations between the WSI, income (GDP per person), education, freedom and governance, and education and freedom and governance combined, are shown in Table 25c.

| band | top point on scale | ratio of human wellbeing to ecosystem stress |
|------|-----------|-----------|
| good | 100 | 8.0 |
| fair | 80 | 4.0 |
| medium | 60 | 2.0 |
| poor | 40 | 1.0 |
| bad | 20 | 0.5 |
| base | 0 | 0.0 |

**Table 25a. Performance criteria for the Wellbeing/Stress Index.**

| | HWI | health | population | household wealth | national wealth | knowledge | freedom & governance | peace & order | ESI | global atmosphere | local air quality | energy |
|---|---|---|---|---|---|---|---|---|---|---|---|---|
| income | **0.824** | **0.902** | **0.851** | **0.895** | **0.871** | **0.948** | *0.740* | 0.560 | 0.537 | *-0.751* | 0.556 | **-0.817** |

**Table 25b. Correlations between income and the Human Wellbeing Index (HWI), human elements, the Ecosystem Stress Index (ESI) and ecosystem elements.** Only correlations above 0.5 (or -0.5) are shown; those of 0.8 (or -0.8) or above are shown in **bold**; those between 0.6 and 0.8 (or -0.6 and -0.8) in *italic*.

| | WSI | income | education | freedom & governance | education + freedom & governance |
|---|---|---|---|---|---|
| Wellbeing/Stress Index (WSI) | 1 | | | | |
| income | *0.640* | 1 | | | |
| education | *0.766* | *0.680* | 1 | | |
| freedom & governance | *0.771* | 0.571 | 0.539 | 1 | |
| education + freedom & governance | **0.883** | *0.728* | **0.887** | **0.834** | 1 |

**Table 25c. Correlations between the Wellbeing/Stress Index (WSI), income (GDP per person), education, freedom and governance, and education and freedom and governance combined.** Correlations of 0.8 and above are shown in **bold**; those between 0.6 and 0.8 are shown in *italic*.

# Table 26. Wellbeing Performance Groups

## Group 1: fair Wellbeing Index, medium Wellbeing/Stress Index

**Moderate ecosystem deficit**

| Country | HWI | EWI | ESI | HWI- ESI | WI | WSI | WSI score |
|---|---|---|---|---|---|---|---|
| Austria | 80 | 42 | 58 | 22 | 61.0 | 1.38 | 48 |
| Finland | 81 | 44 | 56 | 25 | 62.5 | 1.45 | 49 |
| Iceland | 80 | 43 | 57 | 23 | 61.5 | 1.40 | 48 |
| Norway | 82 | 43 | 57 | 25 | 62.5 | 1.44 | 49 |
| Sweden | 79 | 49 | 51 | 28 | 64.0 | 1.55 | 51 |

## Group 2: medium Wellbeing Index, medium Wellbeing/Stress Index

**Moderate ecosystem deficit**

| Country | HWI | EWI | ESI | HWI- ESI | WI | WSI | WSI score |
|---|---|---|---|---|---|---|---|
| Canada | 78 | 43 | 57 | 21 | 60.5 | 1.37 | 47 |
| Latvia | 62 | 46 | 54 | 8 | 54.0 | 1.15 | 43 |
| Lithuania | 61 | 44 | 56 | 5 | 52.5 | 1.09 | 42 |
| Switzerland | 78 | 43 | 57 | 21 | 60.5 | 1.37 | 47 |
| Uruguay | 61 | 52 | 48 | 13 | 56.5 | 1.27 | 45 |

**Moderate human deficit**

| Country | HWI | EWI | ESI | HWI- ESI | WI | WSI | WSI score |
|---|---|---|---|---|---|---|---|
| Belize | 50 | 64 | 36 | 14 | 57.0 | 1.39 | 48 |
| *Dominica* | *56* | *65* | *35* | *21* | *60.5* | *1.60* | *52* |
| Guyana | 51 | 63 | 37 | 14 | 57.0 | 1.38 | 48 |
| Peru | 44 | 62 | 38 | 6 | 53.0 | 1.16 | 43 |

**Moderate double deficit**

| Country | HWI | EWI | ESI | HWI- ESI | WI | WSI | WSI score |
|---|---|---|---|---|---|---|---|
| *Grenada* | *55* | *49* | *51* | *4* | *52.0* | *1.08* | *42* |
| *St Kitts & Nevis* | *52* | *53* | *47* | *5* | *52.5* | *1.11* | *42* |
| *St Lucia* | *53* | *51* | *49* | *4* | *52.0* | *1.08* | *42* |
| Suriname | 52 | 58 | 42 | 10 | 55.0 | 1.24 | 45 |

**High ecosystem deficit**

| Country | HWI | EWI | ESI | HWI- ESI | WI | WSI | WSI score |
|---|---|---|---|---|---|---|---|
| Australia | 79 | 28 | 72 | 7 | 53.5 | 1.10 | 42 |
| Belgium | 80 | 23 | 77 | 3 | 51.5 | 1.04 | 41 |
| Cyprus | 67 | 38 | 62 | 5 | 52.5 | 1.08 | 42 |
| Czech R | 70 | 33 | 67 | 3 | 51.5 | 1.04 | 41 |
| Denmark | 81 | 31 | 69 | 12 | 56.0 | 1.17 | 43 |
| France | 75 | 29 | 71 | 4 | 52.0 | 1.06 | 41 |
| Germany | 77 | 36 | 64 | 13 | 56.5 | 1.20 | 44 |
| Greece | 70 | 33 | 67 | 3 | 51.5 | 1.04 | 41 |
| Ireland | 76 | 32 | 68 | 8 | 54.0 | 1.12 | 42 |
| Italy | 74 | 30 | 70 | 4 | 52.0 | 1.06 | 41 |
| Japan | 80 | 25 | 75 | 5 | 52.5 | 1.07 | 41 |
| Luxembourg | 77 | 24 | 76 | 1 | 50.5 | 1.01 | 41 |
| New Zealand | 73 | 38 | 62 | 11 | 55.5 | 1.18 | 44 |
| Portugal | 72 | 31 | 69 | 3 | 51.5 | 1.04 | 41 |
| Slovakia | 61 | 40 | 60 | 1 | 50.5 | 1.02 | 41 |
| Slovenia | 71 | 35 | 65 | 6 | 53.0 | 1.09 | 42 |
| United Kingdom | 73 | 30 | 70 | 3 | 51.5 | 1.04 | 41 |
| United States | 73 | 31 | 69 | 4 | 52.0 | 1.06 | 41 |

**High human deficit**

| Country | HWI | EWI | ESI | HWI- ESI | WI | WSI | WSI score |
|---|---|---|---|---|---|---|---|
| Botswana | 34 | 68 | 32 | 2 | 51.0 | 1.06 | 41 |

## Group 3: medium Wellbeing Index, poor or bad Wellbeing/Stress Index

**Moderate double deficit**

| Country | HWI | EWI | ESI | HWI- ESI | WI | WSI | WSI score |
|---|---|---|---|---|---|---|---|
| Armenia | 45 | 55 | 45 | 0 | 50.0 | 1.00 | 40 |
| Belarus | 46 | 50 | 50 | -4 | 48.0 | 0.92 | 37 |
| Brunei Darussalam | 47 | 42 | 58 | -11 | 44.5 | 0.81 | 32 |

| Country | HWI | EWI | ESI | HWI- ESI | WI | WSI | WSI score |
|---|---|---|---|---|---|---|---|
| Cape Verde | 47 | 47 | 53 | -6 | 47.0 | 0.89 | 36 |
| Colombia | 43 | 42 | 58 | -15 | 42.5 | 0.74 | 30 |
| Costa Rica | 56 | 41 | 59 | -3 | 48.5 | 0.95 | 38 |
| Dominican R | 49 | 46 | 54 | -5 | 47.5 | 0.91 | 36 |
| Ecuador | 43 | 56 | 44 | -1 | 49.5 | 0.98 | 39 |
| Fiji | 50 | 46 | 54 | -4 | 48.0 | 0.93 | 37 |
| Georgia | 48 | 41 | 59 | -11 | 44.5 | 0.81 | 32 |
| Macedonia, FYR | 46 | 42 | 58 | -12 | 44.0 | 0.79 | 32 |
| Mauritius | 54 | 44 | 56 | -2 | 49.0 | 0.96 | 38 |
| RUSSIAN FEDERATION | 48 | 42 | 58 | -10 | 45.0 | 0.83 | 33 |
| Samoa | 43 | 50 | 50 | -7 | 46.5 | 0.86 | 34 |
| *Seychelles* | *50* | *49* | *51* | *-1* | *49.5* | *0.98* | *39* |
| *St Vincent & Grenadines* | *41* | *54* | *46* | *-5* | *47.5* | *0.89* | *36* |
| Venezuela | 43 | 46 | 54 | -11 | 44.5 | 0.80 | 32 |

**High ecosystem deficit**

| Country | HWI | EWI | ESI | HWI- ESI | WI | WSI | WSI score |
|---|---|---|---|---|---|---|---|
| Barbados | 62 | 32 | 68 | -6 | 47.0 | 0.91 | 36 |
| Estonia | 62 | 34 | 66 | -4 | 48.0 | 0.94 | 38 |
| Hungary | 65 | 33 | 67 | -2 | 49.0 | 0.97 | 39 |
| Korea, R | 67 | 27 | 73 | -6 | 47.0 | 0.92 | 37 |
| Malta | 70 | 14 | 86 | -16 | 42.0 | 0.81 | 33 |
| Netherlands | 78 | 22 | 78 | 0 | 50.0 | 1.00 | 40 |
| Poland | 65 | 30 | 70 | -5 | 47.5 | 0.93 | 37 |
| Singapore | 66 | 32 | 68 | -2 | 49.0 | 0.97 | 39 |
| Spain | 73 | 20 | 80 | -7 | 46.5 | 0.91 | 36 |

**High human deficit**

| Country | HWI | EWI | ESI | HWI- ESI | WI | WSI | WSI score |
|---|---|---|---|---|---|---|---|
| Benin | 27 | 71 | 29 | -2 | 49.0 | 0.93 | 37 |
| Bolivia | 34 | 63 | 37 | -3 | 48.5 | 0.92 | 37 |
| Central African R | 16 | 66 | 34 | -18 | 41.0 | 0.47 | 19 |
| Congo, R | 15 | 72 | 28 | -13 | 43.5 | 0.54 | 22 |
| Gabon | 28 | 62 | 38 | -10 | 45.0 | 0.74 | 30 |
| Malawi | 22 | 62 | 38 | -16 | 42.0 | 0.58 | 23 |
| Nepal | 28 | 64 | 36 | -8 | 46.0 | 0.78 | 31 |
| *Solomon Is* | *37* | *61* | *39* | *-2* | *49.0* | *0.95* | *38* |
| Togo | 21 | 66 | 34 | -13 | 43.5 | 0.62 | 25 |

**High double deficit, ecosystem worse**

| Country | HWI | EWI | ESI | HWI- ESI | WI | WSI | WSI score |
|---|---|---|---|---|---|---|---|
| Antigua & Barbuda | 49 | 40 | 60 | -11 | 44.5 | 0.82 | 33 |
| Argentina | 55 | 40 | 60 | -5 | 47.5 | 0.92 | 37 |
| Bahamas | 54 | 32 | 68 | -14 | 43.0 | 0.79 | 32 |
| Bulgaria | 58 | 31 | 69 | -11 | 44.5 | 0.84 | 34 |
| Chile | 55 | 30 | 70 | -15 | 42.5 | 0.79 | 32 |
| Croatia | 57 | 33 | 67 | -10 | 45.0 | 0.85 | 34 |
| Israel | 59 | 25 | 75 | -16 | 42.0 | 0.79 | 32 |
| Jamaica | 54 | 35 | 65 | -11 | 44.5 | 0.83 | 33 |
| Panama | 52 | 37 | 63 | -11 | 44.5 | 0.83 | 33 |
| Trinidad & Tobago | 53 | 32 | 68 | -15 | 42.5 | 0.78 | 31 |

**High double deficit, people worse**

| Country | HWI | EWI | ESI | HWI- ESI | WI | WSI | WSI score |
|---|---|---|---|---|---|---|---|
| Albania | 38 | 46 | 54 | -16 | 42.0 | 0.70 | 28 |
| Cuba | 40 | 45 | 55 | -15 | 42.5 | 0.73 | 29 |
| Egypt | 39 | 43 | 57 | -18 | 41.0 | 0.68 | 27 |
| El Salvador | 36 | 46 | 54 | -18 | 41.0 | 0.67 | 27 |
| Indonesia | 36 | 48 | 52 | -16 | 42.0 | 0.69 | 28 |
| Mongolia | 39 | 60 | 40 | -1 | 49.5 | 0.98 | 39 |
| Namibia | 34 | 54 | 46 | -12 | 44.0 | 0.74 | 30 |
| Sri Lanka | 40 | 57 | 43 | -3 | 48.5 | 0.93 | 37 |
| Vanuatu | 35 | 50 | 50 | -15 | 42.5 | 0.70 | 28 |

## Group 4: poor Wellbeing Index, poor Wellbeing/Stress Index

### High double deficit, ecosystem worse

| Country | HWI | EWI | ESI | HWI- ESI | WI | WSI | WSI score |
|---|---|---|---|---|---|---|---|
| Azerbaijan | 42 | 28 | 72 | -30 | 35.0 | 0.58 | 23 |
| *Bahrain* | *46* | *17* | *83* | *-37* | *31.5* | *0.55* | *22* |
| Brazil | 45 | 36 | 64 | -19 | 40.5 | 0.70 | 28 |
| Kazakhstan | 43 | 32 | 68 | -25 | 37.5 | 0.63 | 25 |
| Kuwait | 50 | 25 | 75 | -25 | 37.5 | 0.67 | 27 |
| Malaysia | 46 | 33 | 67 | -21 | 39.5 | 0.69 | 28 |
| Mexico | 45 | 21 | 79 | -34 | 33.0 | 0.57 | 23 |
| Moldova | 41 | 35 | 65 | -24 | 38.0 | 0.63 | 25 |
| Philippines | 44 | 32 | 68 | -24 | 38.0 | 0.65 | 26 |
| Romania | 50 | 30 | 70 | -20 | 40.0 | 0.71 | 28 |
| South Africa | 43 | 27 | 73 | -30 | 35.0 | 0.59 | 24 |
| Thailand | 50 | 23 | 77 | -27 | 36.5 | 0.65 | 26 |
| Tunisia | 44 | 32 | 68 | -24 | 38.0 | 0.65 | 26 |
| Turkey | 45 | 28 | 72 | -27 | 36.5 | 0.63 | 25 |
| Ukraine | 47 | 26 | 74 | -27 | 36.5 | 0.64 | 26 |
| Yugoslavia | 42 | 37 | 63 | -21 | 39.5 | 0.67 | 27 |

### High double deficit, people worse

| Country | HWI | EWI | ESI | HWI- ESI | WI | WSI | WSI score |
|---|---|---|---|---|---|---|---|
| Algeria | 29 | 44 | 56 | -27 | 36.5 | 0.52 | 21 |
| Honduras | 33 | 45 | 55 | -22 | 39.0 | 0.60 | 24 |
| Kyrgyzstan | 38 | 42 | 58 | -20 | 40.0 | 0.66 | 26 |
| Lesotho | 24 | 57 | 43 | -19 | 40.5 | 0.56 | 22 |
| Nicaragua | 28 | 49 | 51 | -23 | 38.5 | 0.55 | 22 |
| Paraguay | 35 | 46 | 54 | -19 | 40.5 | 0.65 | 26 |
| Swaziland | 24 | 54 | 46 | -22 | 39.0 | 0.52 | 21 |
| Viet Nam | 28 | 49 | 51 | -23 | 38.5 | 0.55 | 22 |
| Zimbabwe | 23 | 55 | 45 | -22 | 39.0 | 0.51 | 21 |

### Extreme double deficit

| Country | HWI | EWI | ESI | HWI- ESI | WI | WSI | WSI score |
|---|---|---|---|---|---|---|---|
| Iran | 38 | 32 | 68 | -30 | 35.0 | 0.56 | 22 |
| Jordan | 38 | 28 | 72 | -34 | 33.0 | 0.53 | 21 |
| Lebanon | 40 | 37 | 63 | -23 | 38.5 | 0.63 | 25 |
| Morocco | 36 | 32 | 68 | -32 | 34.0 | 0.53 | 21 |
| *Qatar* | *40* | *24* | *76* | *-36* | *32.0* | *0.53* | *21* |
| Uzbekistan | 36 | 30 | 70 | -34 | 33.0 | 0.51 | 21 |

## Group 5: poor Wellbeing Index, bad Wellbeing/Stress Index

### High human deficit

| Country | HWI | EWI | ESI | HWI- ESI | WI | WSI | WSI score |
|---|---|---|---|---|---|---|---|
| Angola | 8 | 67 | 33 | -25 | 37.5 | 0.24 | 10 |
| Bhutan | 14 | 67 | 33 | -19 | 40.5 | 0.42 | 17 |
| Cameroon | 15 | 64 | 36 | -21 | 39.5 | 0.42 | 17 |
| Congo, DR | 7 | 65 | 35 | -28 | 36.0 | 0.20 | 8 |
| Equatorial Guinea | 15 | 62 | 38 | -23 | 38.5 | 0.39 | 16 |
| Ethiopia | 13 | 64 | 36 | -23 | 38.5 | 0.36 | 14 |
| Gambia | 16 | 62 | 38 | -22 | 39.0 | 0.42 | 17 |
| Guinea | 15 | 66 | 34 | -19 | 40.5 | 0.44 | 18 |
| Guinea-Bissau | 13 | 66 | 34 | -21 | 39.5 | 0.38 | 15 |
| Lao PDR | 15 | 63 | 37 | -22 | 39.0 | 0.41 | 16 |
| *Liberia* | *9* | *65* | *35* | *-26* | *37.0* | *0.26* | *10* |
| Sierra Leone | 6 | 63 | 37 | -31 | 34.5 | 0.16 | 6 |
| *Somalia* | *3* | *62* | *38* | *-35* | *32.5* | *0.08* | *3* |

### High double deficit, ecosystem worse

| Country | HWI | EWI | ESI | HWI- ESI | WI | WSI | WSI score |
|---|---|---|---|---|---|---|---|
| United Arab Emirates | 41 | 16 | 84 | -43 | 28.5 | 0.49 | 20 |

### High double deficit, people worse

| Country | HWI | EWI | ESI | HWI- ESI | WI | WSI | WSI score |
|---|---|---|---|---|---|---|---|
| *Afghanistan* | *6* | *48* | *52* | *-46* | *27.0* | *0.12* | *5* |
| Bangladesh | 27 | 46 | 54 | -27 | 36.5 | 0.50 | 20 |
| *Bosnia & Herzegovina* | *24* | *45* | *55* | *-31* | *34.5* | *0.44* | *18* |

| Country | HWI | EWI | ESI | HWI- ESI | WI | WSI | WSI score |
|---|---|---|---|---|---|---|---|
| Burkina Faso | 17 | 58 | 42 | -25 | 37.5 | 0.40 | 16 |
| Burundi | 6 | 60 | 40 | -34 | 33.0 | 0.15 | 6 |
| Cambodia | 20 | 57 | 43 | -23 | 38.5 | 0.47 | 19 |
| Chad | 13 | 59 | 41 | -28 | 36.0 | 0.32 | 13 |
| Comoros | 20 | 44 | 56 | -36 | 32.0 | 0.36 | 14 |
| Côte d'Ivoire | 20 | 57 | 43 | -23 | 38.5 | 0.47 | 19 |
| Djibouti | 18 | 60 | 40 | -22 | 39.0 | 0.45 | 18 |
| Eritrea | 10 | 60 | 40 | -30 | 35.0 | 0.25 | 10 |
| Guatemala | 23 | 44 | 56 | -33 | 33.5 | 0.41 | 16 |
| Haiti | 19 | 43 | 57 | -38 | 31.0 | 0.33 | 13 |
| Kenya | 18 | 51 | 49 | -31 | 34.5 | 0.37 | 15 |
| *Korea, DPR* | *21* | *45* | *55* | *-34* | *33.0* | *0.38* | *15* |
| Madagascar | 24 | 50 | 50 | -26 | 37.0 | 0.48 | 19 |
| *Maldives* | *22* | *47* | *53* | *-31* | *34.5* | *0.42* | *17* |
| Mali | 21 | 44 | 56 | -35 | 32.5 | 0.38 | 15 |
| Mozambique | 11 | 55 | 45 | -34 | 33.0 | 0.24 | 10 |
| Myanmar | 21 | 49 | 51 | -30 | 35.0 | 0.41 | 16 |
| Niger | 11 | 56 | 44 | -33 | 33.5 | 0.25 | 10 |
| Nigeria | 16 | 56 | 44 | -28 | 36.0 | 0.36 | 14 |
| Pakistan | 18 | 44 | 56 | -38 | 31.0 | 0.32 | 13 |
| Papua New Guinea | 22 | 53 | 47 | -25 | 37.5 | 0.47 | 19 |
| Rwanda | 12 | 57 | 43 | -31 | 34.5 | 0.28 | 11 |
| *São Tomé & Principe* | *10* | *53* | *47* | *-37* | *31.5* | *0.21* | *8* |
| Senegal | 20 | 54 | 46 | -26 | 37.0 | 0.43 | 17 |
| Sudan | 13 | 46 | 54 | -41 | 29.5 | 0.24 | 10 |
| Tanzania | 18 | 54 | 46 | -28 | 36.0 | 0.39 | 16 |
| Uganda | 10 | 44 | 56 | -46 | 27.0 | 0.18 | 7 |
| Yemen | 15 | 51 | 49 | -34 | 33.0 | 0.31 | 12 |
| Zambia | 16 | 43 | 57 | -41 | 29.5 | 0.28 | 11 |

**Extreme double deficit**

| Country | HWI | EWI | ESI | HWI- ESI | WI | WSI | WSI score |
|---|---|---|---|---|---|---|---|
| China | 36 | 28 | 72 | -36 | 32.0 | 0.50 | 20 |
| Ghana | 22 | 38 | 62 | -40 | 30.0 | 0.35 | 14 |
| India | 31 | 27 | 73 | -42 | 29.0 | 0.42 | 17 |
| Iraq | 19 | 31 | 69 | -50 | 25.0 | 0.28 | 11 |
| Libyan Arab J | 38 | 24 | 76 | -38 | 31.0 | 0.50 | 20 |
| Mauritania | 17 | 40 | 60 | -43 | 28.5 | 0.28 | 11 |
| Oman | 31 | 28 | 72 | -41 | 29.5 | 0.43 | 17 |
| Saudi Arabia | 31 | 23 | 77 | -46 | 27.0 | 0.40 | 16 |
| Syrian Arab R | 28 | 25 | 75 | -47 | 26.5 | 0.37 | 15 |
| Tajikistan | 28 | 39 | 61 | -33 | 33.5 | 0.46 | 18 |
| *Tonga* | *26* | *30* | *70* | *-44* | *28.0* | *0.37* | *15* |
| Turkmenistan | 32 | 30 | 70 | -38 | 31.0 | 0.46 | 18 |

**Notes**

Countries are in five groups, depending on their Wellbeing Index (WI) and Wellbeing/Stress Index (WSI). Each group is divided into up to eight sub-groups, depending on the combination of human and ecosystem wellbeing:

| | |
|---|---|
| moderate ecosystem deficit | = HWI good or fair, EWI medium |
| high ecosystem deficit | = HWI fair, EWI poor or bad |
| moderate human deficit | = HWI medium, EWI fair |
| high human deficit | = HWI poor or bad, EWI fair |
| moderate double deficit | = HWI and EWI both medium |
| high double deficit, ecosystem worse | = HWI medium, EWI poor or bad |
| high double deficit, people worse | = HWI poor or bad, EWI medium |
| extreme double deficit | = HWI and EWI both poor or bad |

Within each group, countries are listed by combination sub-group, and within each sub-group in alphabetical order.
*Countries in italics were rated on less than two-thirds of the human or ecosystem sub-elements.*
HWI = Human Wellbeing Index.
EWI = Ecosystem Wellbeing Index.
ESI = Ecosystem Stress Index  = 100 minus the EWI.
HWI - ESI = Human Wellbeing Index minus Ecosystem Stress Index.
WI = Wellbeing Index (expressed as the average of the HWI and the EWI).
WSI = Wellbeing/Stress Index = the HWI divided by the ESI.
WSI score = score for Wellbeing/Stress Index. See Table 25a for performance criteria.

# Table 27. Countries Ranked by Wellbeing Index

| Rank | Country | HWI | EWI | ESI | WI | WSI |
|---|---|---|---|---|---|---|
| 1 | Sweden | 79 | 49 | 51 | 64.0 | 1.55 |
| 2 | Finland | 81 | 44 | 56 | 62.5 | 1.45 |
| 3 | Norway | 82 | 43 | 57 | 62.5 | 1.44 |
| 4 | Iceland | 80 | 43 | 57 | 61.5 | 1.40 |
| 5 | Austria | 80 | 42 | 58 | 61.0 | 1.38 |
| 6 | Dominica | 56 | 65 | 35 | 60.5 | 1.60 |
| 7= | Canada | 78 | 43 | 57 | 60.5 | 1.37 |
| 7= | Switzerland | 78 | 43 | 57 | 60.5 | 1.37 |
| 9 | Belize | 50 | 64 | 36 | 57.0 | 1.39 |
| 10 | Guyana | 51 | 63 | 37 | 57.0 | 1.38 |
| 11 | Uruguay | 61 | 52 | 48 | 56.5 | 1.27 |
| 12 | Germany | 77 | 36 | 64 | 56.5 | 1.20 |
| 13 | Denmark | 81 | 31 | 69 | 56.0 | 1.17 |
| 14 | New Zealand | 73 | 38 | 62 | 55.5 | 1.18 |
| 15 | Suriname | 52 | 58 | 42 | 55.0 | 1.24 |
| 16 | Latvia | 62 | 46 | 54 | 54.0 | 1.15 |
| 17 | Ireland | 76 | 32 | 68 | 54.0 | 1.12 |
| 18 | Australia | 79 | 28 | 72 | 53.5 | 1.10 |
| 19 | Peru | 44 | 62 | 38 | 53.0 | 1.16 |
| 20 | Slovenia | 71 | 35 | 65 | 53.0 | 1.09 |
| 21 | St Kitts & Nevis | 52 | 53 | 47 | 52.5 | 1.11 |
| 22 | Lithuania | 61 | 44 | 56 | 52.5 | 1.09 |
| 23 | Cyprus | 67 | 38 | 62 | 52.5 | 1.08 |
| 24 | Japan | 80 | 25 | 75 | 52.5 | 1.07 |
| 25 | St Lucia | 53 | 51 | 49 | 52.0 | 1.08 |
| 26 | Grenada | 55 | 49 | 51 | 52.0 | 1.08 |
| 27 | United States | 73 | 31 | 69 | 52.0 | 1.06 |
| 28 | Italy | 74 | 30 | 70 | 52.0 | 1.06 |
| 29 | France | 75 | 29 | 71 | 52.0 | 1.06 |
| 30= | Czech R | 70 | 33 | 67 | 51.5 | 1.04 |
| 30= | Greece | 70 | 33 | 67 | 51.5 | 1.04 |
| 32 | Portugal | 72 | 31 | 69 | 51.5 | 1.04 |
| 33 | United Kingdom | 73 | 30 | 70 | 51.5 | 1.04 |
| 34 | Belgium | 80 | 23 | 77 | 51.5 | 1.04 |
| 35 | Botswana | 34 | 68 | 32 | 51.0 | 1.06 |
| 36 | Slovakia | 61 | 40 | 60 | 50.5 | 1.02 |
| 37 | Luxembourg | 77 | 24 | 76 | 50.5 | 1.01 |
| 38= | Armenia | 45 | 55 | 45 | 50.0 | 1.00 |
| 38= | Netherlands | 78 | 22 | 78 | 50.0 | 1.00 |
| 40 | Seychelles | 50 | 49 | 51 | 49.5 | 0.98 |
| 41 | Ecuador | 43 | 56 | 44 | 49.5 | 0.98 |
| 42 | Mongolia | 39 | 60 | 40 | 49.5 | 0.98 |
| 43 | Singapore | 66 | 32 | 68 | 49.0 | 0.97 |
| 44 | Hungary | 65 | 33 | 67 | 49.0 | 0.97 |
| 45 | Mauritius | 54 | 44 | 56 | 49.0 | 0.96 |
| 46 | Solomon Is | 37 | 61 | 39 | 49.0 | 0.95 |
| 47 | Benin | 27 | 71 | 29 | 49.0 | 0.93 |
| 48 | Costa Rica | 56 | 41 | 59 | 48.5 | 0.95 |
| 49 | Sri Lanka | 40 | 57 | 43 | 48.5 | 0.93 |
| 50 | Bolivia | 34 | 63 | 37 | 48.5 | 0.92 |
| 51 | Estonia | 62 | 34 | 66 | 48.0 | 0.94 |
| 52 | Fiji | 50 | 46 | 54 | 48.0 | 0.93 |
| 53 | Belarus | 46 | 50 | 50 | 48.0 | 0.92 |
| 54 | Poland | 65 | 30 | 70 | 47.5 | 0.93 |
| 55 | Argentina | 55 | 40 | 60 | 47.5 | 0.92 |
| 56 | Dominican R | 49 | 46 | 54 | 47.5 | 0.91 |
| 57 | St Vincent & Grenadines | 41 | 54 | 46 | 47.5 | 0.89 |
| 58 | Korea, R | 67 | 27 | 73 | 47.0 | 0.92 |
| 59 | Barbados | 62 | 32 | 68 | 47.0 | 0.91 |
| 60 | Cape Verde | 47 | 47 | 53 | 47.0 | 0.89 |
| 61 | Spain | 73 | 20 | 80 | 46.5 | 0.91 |
| 62 | Samoa | 43 | 50 | 50 | 46.5 | 0.86 |
| 63 | Nepal | 28 | 64 | 36 | 46.0 | 0.78 |
| 64 | Croatia | 57 | 33 | 67 | 45.0 | 0.85 |
| 65 | RUSSIAN FEDERATION | 48 | 42 | 58 | 45.0 | 0.83 |
| 66 | Gabon | 28 | 62 | 38 | 45.0 | 0.74 |
| 67 | Bulgaria | 58 | 31 | 69 | 44.5 | 0.84 |
| 68 | Jamaica | 54 | 35 | 65 | 44.5 | 0.83 |

| Rank | Country | HWI | EWI | ESI | WI | WSI |
|---|---|---|---|---|---|---|
| 69 | Panama | 52 | 37 | 63 | 44.5 | 0.83 |
| 70 | Antigua & Barbuda | 49 | 40 | 60 | 44.5 | 0.82 |
| 71 | Georgia | 48 | 41 | 59 | 44.5 | 0.81 |
| 72 | Brunei Darussalam | 47 | 42 | 58 | 44.5 | 0.81 |
| 73 | Venezuela | 43 | 46 | 54 | 44.5 | 0.80 |
| 74 | Macedonia, FYR | 46 | 42 | 58 | 44.0 | 0.79 |
| 75 | Namibia | 34 | 54 | 46 | 44.0 | 0.74 |
| 76 | Togo | 21 | 66 | 34 | 43.5 | 0.62 |
| 77 | Congo, R | 15 | 72 | 28 | 43.5 | 0.54 |
| 78 | Bahamas | 54 | 32 | 68 | 43.0 | 0.79 |
| 79 | Chile | 55 | 30 | 70 | 42.5 | 0.79 |
| 80 | Trinidad & Tobago | 53 | 32 | 68 | 42.5 | 0.78 |
| 81 | Colombia | 43 | 42 | 58 | 42.5 | 0.74 |
| 82 | Cuba | 40 | 45 | 55 | 42.5 | 0.73 |
| 83 | Vanuatu | 35 | 50 | 50 | 42.5 | 0.70 |
| 84 | Malta | 70 | 14 | 86 | 42.0 | 0.81 |
| 85 | Israel | 59 | 25 | 75 | 42.0 | 0.79 |
| 86 | Albania | 38 | 46 | 54 | 42.0 | 0.70 |
| 87 | Indonesia | 36 | 48 | 52 | 42.0 | 0.69 |
| 88 | Malawi | 22 | 62 | 38 | 42.0 | 0.58 |
| 89 | Egypt | 39 | 43 | 57 | 41.0 | 0.68 |
| 90 | El Salvador | 36 | 46 | 54 | 41.0 | 0.67 |
| 91 | Central African R | 16 | 66 | 34 | 41.0 | 0.47 |
| 92 | Brazil | 45 | 36 | 64 | 40.5 | 0.70 |
| 93 | Paraguay | 35 | 46 | 54 | 40.5 | 0.65 |
| 94 | Lesotho | 24 | 57 | 43 | 40.5 | 0.56 |
| 95 | Guinea | 15 | 66 | 34 | 40.5 | 0.44 |
| 96 | Bhutan | 14 | 67 | 33 | 40.5 | 0.42 |
| 97 | Romania | 50 | 30 | 70 | 40.0 | 0.71 |
| 98 | Kyrgyzstan | 38 | 42 | 58 | 40.0 | 0.66 |
| 99 | Malaysia | 46 | 33 | 67 | 39.5 | 0.69 |
| 100 | Yugoslavia | 42 | 37 | 63 | 39.5 | 0.67 |
| 101 | Cameroon | 15 | 64 | 36 | 39.5 | 0.42 |
| 102 | Guinea-Bissau | 13 | 66 | 34 | 39.5 | 0.38 |
| 103 | Honduras | 33 | 45 | 55 | 39.0 | 0.60 |
| 104 | Swaziland | 24 | 54 | 46 | 39.0 | 0.52 |
| 105 | Zimbabwe | 23 | 55 | 45 | 39.0 | 0.51 |
| 106 | Djibouti | 18 | 60 | 40 | 39.0 | 0.45 |
| 107 | Gambia | 16 | 62 | 38 | 39.0 | 0.42 |
| 108 | Lao PDR | 15 | 63 | 37 | 39.0 | 0.41 |
| 109 | Lebanon | 40 | 37 | 63 | 38.5 | 0.63 |
| 110= | Nicaragua | 28 | 49 | 51 | 38.5 | 0.55 |
| 110= | Viet Nam | 28 | 49 | 51 | 38.5 | 0.55 |
| 112= | Cambodia | 20 | 57 | 43 | 38.5 | 0.47 |
| 112= | Côte d'Ivoire | 20 | 57 | 43 | 38.5 | 0.47 |
| 114 | Equatorial Guinea | 15 | 62 | 38 | 38.5 | 0.39 |
| 115 | Ethiopia | 13 | 64 | 36 | 38.5 | 0.36 |
| 116= | Philippines | 44 | 32 | 68 | 38.0 | 0.65 |
| 116= | Tunisia | 44 | 32 | 68 | 38.0 | 0.65 |
| 118 | Moldova | 41 | 35 | 65 | 38.0 | 0.63 |
| 119 | Kuwait | 50 | 25 | 75 | 37.5 | 0.67 |
| 120 | Kazakhstan | 43 | 32 | 68 | 37.5 | 0.63 |
| 121 | Papua New Guinea | 22 | 53 | 47 | 37.5 | 0.47 |
| 122 | Burkina Faso | 17 | 58 | 42 | 37.5 | 0.40 |
| 123 | Angola | 8 | 67 | 33 | 37.5 | 0.24 |
| 124 | Madagascar | 24 | 50 | 50 | 37.0 | 0.48 |
| 125 | Senegal | 20 | 54 | 46 | 37.0 | 0.43 |
| 126 | Liberia | 9 | 65 | 35 | 37.0 | 0.26 |
| 127 | Thailand | 50 | 23 | 77 | 36.5 | 0.65 |
| 128 | Ukraine | 47 | 26 | 74 | 36.5 | 0.64 |
| 129 | Turkey | 45 | 28 | 72 | 36.5 | 0.63 |
| 130 | Algeria | 29 | 44 | 56 | 36.5 | 0.52 |
| 131 | Bangladesh | 27 | 46 | 54 | 36.5 | 0.50 |
| 132 | Tanzania | 18 | 54 | 46 | 36.0 | 0.39 |
| 133 | Nigeria | 16 | 56 | 44 | 36.0 | 0.36 |
| 134 | Chad | 13 | 59 | 41 | 36.0 | 0.32 |
| 135 | Congo, DR | 7 | 65 | 35 | 36.0 | 0.20 |
| 136 | South Africa | 43 | 27 | 73 | 35.0 | 0.59 |

| Rank | Country | HWI | EWI | ESI | WI | WSI |
|------|---------|-----|-----|-----|------|------|
| 137 | Azerbaijan | 42 | 28 | 72 | **35.0** | 0.58 |
| 138 | Iran | 38 | 32 | 68 | **35.0** | 0.56 |
| 139 | Myanmar | 21 | 49 | 51 | **35.0** | 0.41 |
| 140 | Eritrea | 10 | 60 | 40 | **35.0** | 0.25 |
| *141* | *Bosnia & Herzegovina* | *24* | *45* | *55* | ***34.5*** | *0.44* |
| *142* | *Maldives* | *22* | *47* | *53* | ***34.5*** | *0.42* |
| 143 | Kenya | 18 | 51 | 49 | **34.5** | 0.37 |
| 144 | Rwanda | 12 | 57 | 43 | **34.5** | 0.28 |
| 145 | Sierra Leone | 6 | 63 | 37 | **34.5** | 0.16 |
| 146 | Morocco | 36 | 32 | 68 | **34.0** | 0.53 |
| 147 | Tajikistan | 28 | 39 | 61 | **33.5** | 0.46 |
| 148 | Guatemala | 23 | 44 | 56 | **33.5** | 0.41 |
| 149 | Niger | 11 | 56 | 44 | **33.5** | 0.25 |
| 150 | Mexico | 45 | 21 | 79 | **33.0** | 0.57 |
| 151 | Jordan | 38 | 28 | 72 | **33.0** | 0.53 |
| 152 | Uzbekistan | 36 | 30 | 70 | **33.0** | 0.51 |
| *153* | *Korea, DPR* | *21* | *45* | *55* | ***33.0*** | *0.38* |
| 154 | Yemen | 15 | 51 | 49 | **33.0** | 0.31 |
| 155 | Mozambique | 11 | 55 | 45 | **33.0** | 0.24 |
| 156 | Burundi | 6 | 60 | 40 | **33.0** | 0.15 |
| 157 | Mali | 21 | 44 | 56 | **32.5** | 0.38 |
| *158* | *Somalia* | *3* | *62* | *38* | ***32.5*** | *0.08* |

| Rank | Country | HWI | EWI | ESI | WI | WSI |
|------|---------|-----|-----|-----|------|------|
| *159* | *Qatar* | *40* | *24* | *76* | ***32.0*** | *0.53* |
| 160 | China | 36 | 28 | 72 | **32.0** | 0.50 |
| 161 | Comoros | 20 | 44 | 56 | **32.0** | 0.36 |
| *162* | *Bahrain* | *46* | *17* | *83* | ***31.5*** | *0.55* |
| *163* | *São Tomé & Principe* | *10* | *53* | *47* | ***31.5*** | *0.21* |
| 164 | Libyan Arab J | 38 | 24 | 76 | **31.0** | 0.50 |
| 165 | Turkmenistan | 32 | 30 | 70 | **31.0** | 0.46 |
| 166 | Haiti | 19 | 43 | 57 | **31.0** | 0.33 |
| 167 | Pakistan | 18 | 44 | 56 | **31.0** | 0.32 |
| 168 | Ghana | 22 | 38 | 62 | **30.0** | 0.35 |
| 169 | Oman | 31 | 28 | 72 | **29.5** | 0.43 |
| 170 | Zambia | 16 | 43 | 57 | **29.5** | 0.28 |
| 171 | Sudan | 13 | 46 | 54 | **29.5** | 0.24 |
| 172 | India | 31 | 27 | 73 | **29.0** | 0.42 |
| 173 | United Arab Emirates | 41 | 16 | 84 | **28.5** | 0.49 |
| 174 | Mauritania | 17 | 40 | 60 | **28.5** | 0.28 |
| *175* | *Tonga* | *26* | *30* | *70* | ***28.0*** | *0.37* |
| 176 | Saudi Arabia | 31 | 23 | 77 | **27.0** | 0.40 |
| 177 | Uganda | 10 | 44 | 56 | **27.0** | 0.18 |
| *178* | *Afghanistan* | *6* | *48* | *52* | ***27.0*** | *0.12* |
| 179 | Syrian Arab R | 28 | 25 | 75 | **26.5** | 0.37 |
| 180 | Iraq | 19 | 31 | 69 | **25.0** | 0.28 |

**Notes**

Countries are ranked first by Wellbeing Index (WI) and then—among those with the same WI—by Wellbeing/Stress Index (WSI). Countries with the same three-digit WSI are differentiated by taking the WSI to four digits.

*Countries in italics were rated on less than two-thirds of the human or ecosystem sub-elements.*

HWI = Human Wellbeing Index.

EWI = Ecosystem Wellbeing Index.

ESI = Ecosystem Stress Index = 100 minus the EWI.

WI = Wellbeing Index (expressed as the average of the HWI and the EWI).

WSI = Wellbeing/Stress Index = the HWI divided by the ESI.

# Appendix A.
# Monetary and Physical Accounts

Monetary and physical accounts have indispensable but limited roles in the measurement of wellbeing and sustainability, providing detailed information on the market economy and the use of materials and energy. This appendix reviews the contributions and limitations of accounts, expanding on the summary in Chapter 1.

## Counting Money: The System of National Accounts

By far the most widely used method of measuring progress is the System of National Accounts (SNA). National accounts are the records of asset changes, income, and expenditure that governments compile routinely to track the activity of their national economy, analyze its structure and performance, decide economic policies, and compare the economies of different countries.

National accounting became important during and after the Second World War to help increase production for the war effort, then to rebuild shattered economies, and eventually to guide economic development in general. Work on a standard international method of compiling national accounts began in the 1940s. The method became the SNA, codified and adopted by the United Nations in 1953 and revised in 1968 and 1993.[1]

The SNA measures the performance not of the economy as a whole but of the market economy (the production of goods and services that are owned and traded and so have a monetary value) plus some arbitrarily chosen goods and services that are not traded but for which a market value can be inferred: goods produced by farmers for their own consumption, the equivalent rental value of owner-occupied dwellings, and government services.[2] Anything without a price—from parenting and education

to forests and air—is excluded, regardless of its importance for economic welfare.

This concentration on the market economy is what makes the SNA so useful for analysis and management. Market transactions are measured in money, and market prices are the most direct and reliable way of establishing monetary values. With money as the common unit of measurement, data on a vast number of disparate activities can be combined, taken apart, and recombined, transforming the bewildering minutiae of the inventory and cash register into intelligible indicators of production, consumption, capital formation, saving, balance of trade, inflation, employment, and other factors that are vital for diagnosis. Standardization around market values and a set of widely accepted accounting conventions ensure that the many different components of the accounts are treated consistently and have the same meaning in all contexts and countries.[3]

But devotion to price has its price. It limits the applicability of the SNA to only one part of the economy. The economy is everything that has value for use or exchange. As such it consists of three other economic spheres besides the market: the nonmarket, social, and natural economies. In none of these is price the measure. The nonmarket economy includes household work, parenting, family care of children and elders, voluntary work, and reciprocal exchange of food, products, and tasks. The social economy covers education, information sharing, structures of decision making, and the norms and organizations that regulate access to resources and the conduct of economic activities. The natural economy is the ecosystem, the source of all life support, raw materials, and energy.

The market economy depends on and affects these other economies, but because the SNA excludes them it cannot account for them. It portrays the market in an imaginary world where the rest of the economy has no real substance. The ecosystem is a convenient cornucopia, a limitless supplier of resources and absorber of wastes. Human beings are consumers, abstractions with no more flesh or blood than the invisible hand.

This would not matter if the limits of the SNA were widely recognized and its leading indicators were matched by equally appealing indicators of human wellbeing and the state of the ecosystem. But this is not the case.

The presumption that the market economy is the economy and not just a part of it sets up false conflicts between "economy" and "environment" and between "economy" and "society."[4] When commentators or politicians say that an environmental or social policy is "bad for the economy" because it will reduce the growth rate of the gross domestic product, they are mistaking a part of the economy for the whole. A policy that increases the value of nonmarket services (such as work in the home) or protects the environment could very well be good for the economy even if it means a somewhat lower level of market production.[5]

## Wrong Number: Gross Domestic Product

The gross domestic product (GDP) and gross national product (GNP) are much the most influential indicators derived from the national accounts. GDP measures the total value added of enterprises operating in the country concerned, regardless of whether owned by residents or nonresidents.[6] GNP measures the total value added of enterprises owned by residents of the country concerned, regardless of whether the money comes from domestic or foreign operations.[7]

Movements of these indicators are used to evaluate the overall performance of the economy and hence to judge the success or failure of economic policies pursued by governments. Politicians, analysts, bankers, investors, the business community, the media, and the public rely on them as general indicators of economic progress and even of overall wellbeing.[8]

GDP is an excellent measure of the size of the market economy, but it is a weak indicator of economic development and a completely misleading signal of welfare or wellbeing. As a measure of economic development, its main flaws (which also apply to GNP) are:[9]

- GDP does not show income distribution, so gains for the few appear as gains for all.

- GDP includes the value of depreciation of buildings, equipment, and machines instead of subtracting it.

- GDP goes up as the unpaid roles of families and communities are displaced by the paid service sector—as parenting is replaced by child care, home cooking by fast food joints, and good neighbors by alarm systems and security companies. Similarly, GDP rises in developing countries when the market displaces the nonmarket household economy as a major supplier of food, water, energy, and housing and destroys the social structure that goes with it.

- GDP takes no account of the depletion of natural resources, such as deforestation, depletion of fish stocks, reductions in fuel and mineral reserves, and losses of fertile soil.

- GDP either ignores environmental degradation or counts it as a benefit. Pollution can swell GDP several times: once when a factory produces it as a byproduct, again when industry or government spends money to clean it up, again when households or governments spend money to protect against it (buying filters or insulation, for example), and again to cope with the consequences such as medical bills for treatment of respiratory diseases. Environmental damage reduces GDP only if it directly reduces current production or increases its cost. If damage reduces future productivity or causes levels of pain and suffering that are not reflected in purchases, GDP overlooks it.

- GDP does not distinguish between costs and benefits, productive and destructive activities, or sustainable and unsustainable ones. Things most people would regard as bad—earthquakes, hurricanes, cancer, AIDS, crime, divorce—add to the GDP because dealing with them causes money to change hands. It is as if a business kept a balance sheet by merely adding up all transactions, without distinguishing between income and expenses, or between assets and liabilities.

These flaws lead GDP and GNP to exaggerate income and so encourage consumption and economic policies that cannot be sustained.[10] A country may be heading for bankruptcy—depleting its mineral reserves, destroying its forests, degrading its air and waters, and spending the proceeds on current consumption—and still be complacent about its economic performance because GDP growth looks so good.

GDP is not a measure of welfare (or even of total wealth), but it is treated as one. The common perception of GDP as a welfare indicator tilts government decisions toward expanding GDP as a major development objective, to the neglect or even at the expense of other aspects of development and the quality of life.[11]

One strategy for dealing with this problem is to remind people that GDP is simply a measure of market activity. But economists are constantly saying this. Politicians and everyone else need a general measure of progress, a clear guide through the welter of contradictory statistics. They will go on using GDP until they have something better.

## Better Bookkeeping: Greening the National Accounts

Attempts at better monetary accounts are often called green accounts, a misleading term since some do not go very far to correct the SNA's environmental omissions while others try to address its main social flaws as well. Some try to replace GDP with a single number, a statement of net benefit that includes both market and non-market goods and services, subtracting the losses in both from the gains in both. Others recognize that GDP is a pretty good indicator of the size of the market, but people need something more—another two or three pretty good indicators of environmental and social conditions that can put the GDP in perspective.

The 1993 revision of the SNA expanded its coverage of assets to include parts of the natural environment, as long as they have a market price and someone owns or controls them: crops and livestock but not wildlife; built and cultivated land but not other land; water in reservoirs but not water in rivers or lakes; and not the sea, air, or atmosphere. A tract of timber that is under economic control (owned or licensed) is now recognized as an economic asset, but not other wood in the forest, other goods obtained from the wild such as fruit and medicines, the plants and animals for which the forest is habitat, the forest's role in the water cycle, its storage of carbon, its influence on climate, or its cultural and spiritual value. These still are excluded.[12]

Instead, the 1993 revision recommends that the majority of environmental goods and services be covered in satellite accounts that are separate from but linked to the main (or core) accounts of the SNA. This prevents the core accounts from being corrupted by nonmarket values while allowing the compilers of environmental accounts the freedom to test various ways of putting a price on nature.

The United Nations Statistical Division has developed the System of Integrated Environmental and Economic Accounting (SEEA) as a framework for environmental accounts linked to the SNA. The framework provides a home for monetary and nonmonetary accounts of the flows of resources from the ecosystem to the economy, their transformation and movements within the economy, and the flows of pollutants and wastes back to the ecosystem. The accounts include detailed breakdowns of the conventional national accounts, monetary accounts using unconventional (nonmarket) methods, and physical accounts (stocks and flows expressed, for example, in weight). They are expected to enable countries to subtract depreciation of capital, depletion of natural resources, and degradation of the environment from GDP to obtain a statement of environmentally adjusted net domestic product, or eco domestic product (EDP).[13]

Several countries are working on bits and pieces of the SEEA, some have made partial adjustments to GDP, but none has attempted a comprehensive accounting.[14] The chief constraints are inadequate data and a lack of confidence in nonmarket methods of valuation. Norway (which with France probably has the most fully developed physical accounts) has ruled out calculation of an EDP on the grounds that it would entail "a long series of subjective assessments of values".[15]

The Index of Sustainable Economic Welfare (ISEW) is even more ambitious: an attempt at an economic measure of national wellbeing.[16] ISEWs have been calculated for Australia, Denmark, Germany, Netherlands, the United Kingdom, and the United States, where it is called the Genuine Progress Indicator (GPI).[17] The GPI starts with personal consumption expenditure (taken from the national accounts and treated with some misgiving as the core contributor to wellbeing). It adjusts this figure for income distribution and then adds several benefits that national accounts omit or don't count as benefits, such as the value of household work, parenting, and volunteer work. It makes a number of other adjustments and then subtracts a series of social and environmental costs, including crime, family breakdown, loss of leisure time, underemployment, commuting, automobile accidents, noise, air and water pollution, ozone depletion, radioactive wastes, soil degradation, depletion of nonrenewable energy resources, and loss of farmland, wetlands, and forests.[18]

Marginally less ambitious are the World Bank's estimates of national wealth and genuine saving. Wealth is defined as the stock of capital that is the basis of well-being and consists of things, people, and nature. Things (or "produced assets") are machinery, equipment, buildings, infrastructure, and urban land. People (or "human resources") are labor plus investment in education plus "social capital," which is roughly the norms and organizations through which people share information, coordinate activities, and make decisions. Nature (or "natural capital") is ostensibly the ecosystem and all its benefits but in practice includes only cropland, pastures, forests, protected areas, and minerals (including fossil fuels).

National wealth calculations try to estimate the use values of things, people, and nature but in practice measure only their money-making capacity. People get the gold. Things get the silver. Nature gets the bronze. Human resources account for more than 70% of wealth in 5 out of 12 regions. Natural capital accounts for less than 10% of wealth in 7 of the regions. Except in the oil-producing Middle East (where natural capital is big because oil is big), human resources make up 60–79% of wealth, produced assets supply 15–30%, and natural capital contributes 2–21%. In the Middle East the proportions are human resources 43%, produced assets 18%, and natural capital (mostly oil) 39%.[19]

The Genuine Saving Indicator attempts to show whether the stock of national wealth is growing or shrinking. It starts with conventional measures of saving, adds investment in education, and deducts estimates of resource depletion and environmental degradation. It can help to show whether, for example, the level of government expenditure is sustainable, tax and monetary policies encourage saving, resource royalties are consumed or invested (and if invested, how), and saving is sufficient to offset any cumulative effects of pollution.[20]

Monetary accounts have to cope with incomplete and low-quality social and environmental data, just as non-monetary assessments do. But they contend with the extra problem of converting the data to monetary units. This is not a problem with things that are traded: they use the market price. It is also fairly straightforward with things that are not traded but have equivalents that are— food for subsistence, for example, or minerals in proved but undeveloped reserves—since a price can be obtained

from the equivalent. However, for everything else they must use nonmarket values. Usually these are either "contingent" values or the costs of social and environmental damage.

Contingent values are obtained by asking people how much they would pay to secure a benefit or prevent damage (willingness to pay) or how much compensation they would accept if they were deprived of the benefit or suffered the damage (willingness to accept). Genuine saving takes account of the impacts of pollution on wellbeing by estimating people's willingness to pay to avoid pain, suffering, and death from pollution-linked disease. It would value rain forests on the basis of global willingness to pay for their preservation, but who do you ask? Even if you think you know who to ask, this is a fantasy market, a bit like asking what you would do if you won the lottery. It assumes that people have sufficient information about the benefit or damage concerned—the risk of suffering and death from pollution or the benefits of rain forests—and that they have the money to pay what they say they would pay. Another basic, if unsurprising, flaw is that people are willing to accept much more than they are willing to pay (which shows that they have more sense than money).[21]

Costs are calculated from expenditures on avoiding and treating damage (such as expenditures on crime prevention or medical bills that result from pollution). Since actual expenditures are often lower than the full costs of damage, so-called maintenance costs may be estimated as well. These are hypothetical expenditures—guesses about the costs that might have been incurred to maintain social and environmental quality.[22]

If values cannot be estimated in these ways, they are assigned arbitrarily. The GPI puts the costs of greenhouse gases and radioactive wastes at $1 per barrel-equivalent of fossil fuel and nuclear energy consumption. Genuine saving sets the damage from carbon dioxide at $20 per ton of carbon emitted. National wealth assumes that nontimber benefits of forests—such as recreation, tourism, medicines, and other wild products—come from 10% of the forested area and are worth $112–$145 per hectare. Protected areas are valued at the opportunity cost (the value of benefits that could have been obtained if the area were not protected) of not using them as pasture land.[23]

The use of a single measure—money—disguises the fact that a consistent method is not being used. The grand totals (Mexico's eco domestic product of 36.4

billion pesos, the United States' GPI per person of US$4,068, India's genuine saving of 8% of GNP, Italy's national wealth of US$257,000 per person) are constructed from various combinations of market values, contingent values, actual expenditures, hypothetical expenditures, and stabs in the dark. Furthermore, the money values mask the physical data on which they are based. They overlay the assumptions and judgments embedded in the physical data with another set of assumptions and judgments.

Outside market values, economists have the choice of no numbers or wrong numbers. To their credit, they sometimes opt for no numbers. The GPI's estimate of the cost of air pollution does not include damage to health or increased mortality. Genuine saving leaves out fisheries, soil erosion, and biodiversity, and its valuation of forests ignores nonwood products and services such as carbon storage and watershed protection. National wealth excludes water and "many of the critically important ecological and life-support functions provided by natural systems, as well as existence values and the aesthetic pleasure we derive from nature."[24]

Such omissions limit the imposition of questionable money values, but they expose another problem. Monetary approaches treat the major elements of their evaluations in highly unequal ways. A core element obtained from the national accounts—whether net domestic product, personal consumption expenditures, gross domestic investment, or produced assets—is covered comprehensively. Then certain social and environmental elements—social costs, resource depletion, environmental degradation, natural capital—are covered partially, sometimes skimpily. Since accounts are built from particulars and are designed to be complete (everything should add up), these omissions create huge distortions.

A more fundamental defect lies in measuring the condition of the ecosystem only as an adjustment of a measure of human wealth. Inevitably, ecological contributions are dwarfed by those of the economy. As value added rises, resources and the environment appear to diminish in importance, even though their contribution to human wellbeing does not change. In the national wealth estimates, 74% of Western Europe's US$237,000 of total wealth per person comes from human resources, 23% from produced assets, and 2% from natural capital (the ecosystem). Since this invites the conclusion that the ecosystem no longer matters, the World Bank authors feel obliged to point out that "even though natural capital is normally third in importance as a source of wealth behind human resources and produced assets, it does form the ecological basis for life and is a fundamental building block of national wealth."[25]

The situation is analogous to the relationship between the daily food energy people must consume to exist and the nonfood energy they may consume as they go about their existence: the 2,200 kilocalories of food energy are less than 1% of the 222,500 kilocalories of other energy consumed by the average North American. If food consumption dropped to zero, it would have a negligible effect on total energy consumption, except that we'd be dead. This is one reason why we don't lump food energy with commercial energy. If something is irreplaceable and essential for us, we need to know its condition and the stresses we are placing on it independently of some measure of our own condition.

The leading argument for greening the national accounts and reforming GDP is that money is the only language that the key economic ministries in any government understand. If social and environmental problems are not translated into monetary terms, they will not be taken into account, or at best they will play second and third fiddle to "the economy."[26]

This argument fails for two reasons. First, GDP is misleading not just because it includes bad things and omits good things but because it is a monetary indicator forced into a nonmonetary role. Money is not the measure of all things. No matter how meticulous the calculation, dollars trivialize much of what we value most. Second, although money is often a deciding factor in strategies—"How much will it cost?" "What is the most cost-effective way of doing this?"—it is seldom the deciding factor when choosing national objectives, such as reducing malnutrition and mortality rates and increasing school enrollment, literacy, and access to safe water and sanitation, all of which are set instead on the basis of a consensus on performance.

GDP is a good indicator of the size of the market, and national accounts are a proven source of this and other useful information for managing the market economy. They continue to need improvement to reflect resource depletion, environmental damage, and social costs. However, they lose credibility when their scope is extended beyond what can be valued convincingly with market prices. Assessments are better suited to measuring nonmarket aspects of human wellbeing and the condition of the ecosystem.

### Heavy Lifting: Physical Accounts

The nearest equivalents to national accounts in ecosystem assessment are natural resource accounts and material/energy balances. Both measure physical exchanges between the economy and the environment. Natural resource accounts record changes in the stocks of raw materials such as minerals or timber. Material/energy balances record the flows of materials and energy from the environment to the economy, through the economy, and back to the environment as pollution and wastes.[27]

Total material requirement (TMR) has been calculated for the United States, Austria, Germany, Netherlands, and Japan. It includes the natural resources that enter the economy as commodities for further processing, such as grain used in food manufacturing, petroleum sent to a refinery, minerals that go into metal products, and logs for lumber. It also includes materials that are displaced in the course of resource production or construction: for instance, soil erosion from agriculture, the rock and soil removed to reach an ore body, the portion of ore that is discarded to concentrate it, and material moved to build a highway or dredge a channel. The weight of all these materials is added up to obtain a country's TMR. For example, the TMR of the United States is 22 billion metric tons, and Japan's TMR per person is 45 metric tons.[28] Another study has calculated the total domestic output (TDO) of these countries: the amount of TMR that is returned to the national environment as pollutants of air, land, and water. For example, the TDO of the United States is 19 billion metric tons, and Japan's TDO per person is 14 metric tons.[29]

Physical accounts are highly informative but can capture only a limited set of people–ecosystem interactions. The natural world consists of countless visible and invisible parts that interact with each other at scales ranging from planetary to microscopic and are always changing. Millions of species of plants, animals, and other organisms have yet to be identified, let alone described.[30] The substances people take as resources and put back as wastes move through the system like shape-shifters, changing chemical composition and switching between solid, liquid, and gas. The small fraction of ecological goings-on that is captured by environmental statistics is recorded in

a jumble of incompatible units: weight, volume, area, energy, toxicity, population numbers, and so forth. Moreover, environmental conditions are extremely patchy: this stretch of river is filthy, that stretch of river is pristine. For these reasons, physical accounts are likely to be limited to what they do best: natural resource accounts and material/energy balances.

### Notes

1. Inter-Secretariat Working Group on National Accounts (1993).
2. United Nations Statistical Division (1993).
3. Hecht (n.d.).
4. Repetto et al. (1989).
5. Cobb, Halstead, & Rowe (1995a).
6. Value added is the value of the goods and services produced by an enterprise minus the value of the goods and services it buys. Total value added is the sum of the value added of all sectors of the market economy. GDP is calculated at factor cost or at market prices. GDP at factor cost is the total value added of enterprises operating in the country. GDP at market prices is GDP at factor cost plus indirect taxes minus government subsidies.
7. GNP is GDP at market prices plus (or minus) net factor income from abroad (total incomes received by residents of the country from activities carried on abroad—such as remittances from overseas workers, company profits, and interest from loans—minus any expenditure on similar items earned within the country by nonresidents). In countries where foreign debt or foreign ownership is high, GNP may be smaller than GDP.
8. Inter-Secretariat Working Group on National Accounts (1993).
9. Many economists and others have pointed out the defects of GDP and GNP. This list, which is not complete, draws mainly on Cobb, Halstead, & Rowe (1995a, 1995b); Daly & Cobb (1989); Repetto et al. (1989); Sheng (1995); Ahmad, El Sarafy, & Lutz (1989); and Lutz (1993).
10. Ahmad, El Sarafy, & Lutz (1989).
11. Sheng (1995).
12. United Nations Statistical Division (1993).
13. United Nations Statistical Division (1993).
14. For reviews, see Hamilton & Lutz (1996) and Sheng (1995).
15. Norway's Central Bureau of Statistics, quoted in Sheng (1995).
16. Daly & Cobb (1989).
17. Dieren (1995).
18. Cobb, Halstead, & Rowe (1995a).

19. Kunte et al. (1998); World Bank staff (1997).
20. Hamilton & Lutz (1996); World Bank staff (1997).
21. Munasinghe & McNeely (1995).
22. Atkinson & Hamilton (1996); Bartelmus & van Tongeren (1994); United Nations Statistical Division (1993).
23. Cobb, Halstead, & Rowe (1995a); Kunte et al. (1998); World Bank staff (1997).
24. World Bank staff (1997).
25. World Bank staff (1997).
26. United Nations Statistical Division (1993); World Bank staff (1997).
27. United Nations Statistical Division (1993).
28. Austria: Fischer-Kowalski, Haberl, & Payer (1997). United States, Germany, Netherlands, Japan: Adriaanse et al. (1997). Austrian data are for 1988. Data for the other countries are for 1994.
29. All five countries: Matthews et al. (2000). Data are for 1996 and exclude oxygen.
30. Wilson (1988); World Conservation Monitoring Centre (1992).

# Appendix B.
# Wellbeing Assessment

This appendix describes the Wellbeing Assessment method used in *The Wellbeing of Nations*, amplifying the summary in Chapter 1 (parts of which are repeated for completeness). It is intended to provide sufficient detail for readers to undertake their own assessments, as well as to understand how the book's findings were reached and rework them if they wish. Supplementary notes at the end of the appendix compare aspects of Wellbeing Assessment with alternatives offered by other methods.

Anyone interested in a course on the method should contact me. For a training kit, contact IUCN-The World Conservation Union.[1]

## *Scope and Origins of Wellbeing Assessment*

Wellbeing Assessment is a method of assessing the conditions and interactions of people and the environment. It provides a systematic and transparent way of deciding the main features of human and ecosystem wellbeing to be measured, and of choosing the most representative indicators of those features. It enables the indicators to be combined into indices of each feature and ultimately into a Human Wellbeing Index, an Ecosystem Wellbeing Index, a Wellbeing Index, and a Wellbeing/Stress Index (the ratio of human wellbeing to ecosystem stress). Together, these four indices provide a measurement of sustainable development.

The method conforms with the Bellagio principles for assessing sustainable development (Supplement 1). It is designed to be used at many geographical levels, including regional, national, provincial, and municipal, but is less suitable at very small scales (below 100 km²). Versions for local and corporate use are being developed.

Wellbeing Assessment began as a synthesis of approaches to assessment formulated by Tony Hodge,

Alejandro Imbach, and Diana Lee-Smith and my Barometer of Sustainability method. These approaches were tested and improved by teams in Colombia, Zimbabwe, and India and IUCN offices in Central America, Southern Africa, and Pakistan, during the first phase (1994–1996) of an IUCN project on assessing progress toward sustainability, supported by the International Development Research Centre (IDRC).[2] I further developed the method for the second phase of the IUCN/IDRC project (1997–1999) and for this book. Wellbeing Assessment will continue to evolve as others apply it in different environmental and societal contexts.

## *Framework: Equal Treatment of People and Ecosystem*

The underlying hypothesis of Wellbeing Assessment is that sustainable development is a combination of human wellbeing and ecosystem wellbeing. Human wellbeing is a requirement for sustainability because no rational person would want to perpetuate a low standard of living. Ecosystem wellbeing is a requirement because it is the ecosystem that supports life and makes possible any standard of living. The hypothesis is expressed in the metaphor of the Egg of Wellbeing (Figure B1). The ecosystem surrounds and supports people much as the white of an egg surrounds and supports the yolk. Just as an egg can be good only if both the yolk and white are good, so a society can be well and sustainable only if both people and the ecosystem are well.

To compare human development and ecosystem conservation and keep the focus on improving both, the wellbeing of people and the ecosystem are considered together but measured separately. Information is organized into two subsystems: people (human communities,

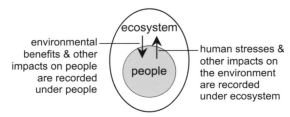

**Figure B1. The Egg of Wellbeing, showing treatment of interactions between people and ecosystem.**

economies, and artifacts); and ecosystem (ecological communities, processes, and resources). Interactions between the two are recorded under the receiving subsystem (Figure B1). Human stresses on the ecosystem (such as pollution and resource depletion)—as well as benefits to it from conservation—are recorded under *ecosystem*. Benefits from the ecosystem to people (from the supply of resources to spiritual comfort) are recorded under *people,* along with environmental stresses on people (such as the effects of natural disasters). For example, the impact of agriculture and fisheries on the land, water, air, and organisms is measured as part of ecosystem wellbeing; their impact on food supply, incomes, employment, health, and community stability is measured as part of human wellbeing.

Each subsystem is divided into five dimensions, pro-

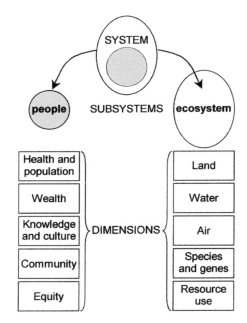

**Figure B2. Wellbeing Assessment framework.** Information is organized into two subsystems, each divided into five dimensions.

viding a common framework for all assessments using the Wellbeing Assessment method (Figure B2). The framework allows users to select their own indicators and produce assessments that are tailored to their conditions and needs yet broadly comparable with other well-

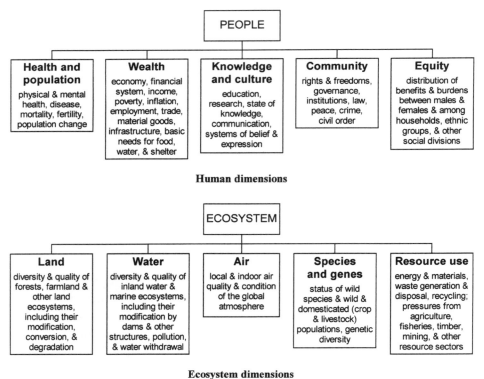

**Figure B3. Illustrative list of topics covered by the dimensions.**

being assessments. The dimensions are designed to combine a wide range of topics into a few major groups of roughly equal importance. They are comprehensive enough to accommodate most of the concerns of most societies: any issue regarded as significant for wellbeing and sustainable development has a place in one of them (Figure B3).

The background of the dimensions is described in Supplement 2; frameworks of other methods are discussed in Supplement 3.

## Six-Stage Cycle

Because it is impossible to measure human or ecosystem wellbeing directly, assessments must select indicators of the main features of each. Knowing the essential role of indicators, it is tempting to jump right in and choose them at once. However, it is seldom clear at the start of an assessment how well a given set of indicators represents a desirable combination of human and environmental conditions, what aspects are left out, how much the indicators overlap, or how they relate to each other. Since indicators require the collection and analysis of often large amounts of data, choosing the wrong indicators can be a costly mistake.

Consequently, it is necessary first to take apart the concepts of human and ecosystem wellbeing to identify the features to be measured—and then to unpack each feature to reveal aspects that are both representative and measurable. Wellbeing Assessment does this by going down the hierarchy in Figure B4, which provides a series of increasingly specific stepping stones from system and goal to indicators and performance criteria (standards of achievement). These steps ensure that the indicators are as representative as possible of the system as a whole and of people's goals for themselves and their environment. Even so, each indicator conveys information only about the particular element or subelement it represents. To provide a picture of the entire system and of progress toward the goals, the indicators need to be combined into indices. The steps taken to select the indicators are reversed to provide a logical and transparent procedure for combining them, going back up the hierarchy from indicators to system.

## Stage 1. Define the System and Goals

The system consists of the people and ecosystem of the area to be assessed. Defining it involves deciding and

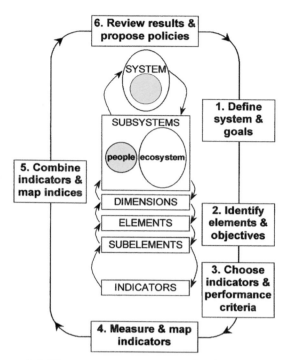

**Figure B4. Six-stage assessment cycle.** Starting on the right and moving clockwise, indicators are selected going down the hierarchy (center) and combined going up it.

mapping the boundaries of the assessment area and its differentiation units: the smallest units into which the area will be divided for the purposes of data collection and analysis and participation in the assessment. Differentiation units should be decision-making (administrative or political) units, such as nations, states, provinces, counties, and municipalities, because assessments are meant to aid decisions. (Because the ecosystem seldom respects political boundaries, it is also useful to divide the assessment area into ecological units, such as ecoregions or vegetation zones, and hydrological units, such as inland water and marine basins.) The finer the detail, the more the assessment will reveal local differences in human and environmental conditions but the more expensive and complicated it will be. For example, Italy consists of 20 regions, 103 provinces, and 8,102 municipalities.[3] Differentiating an Italian assessment by province would be more informative than by region and vastly more practical than by municipality.

Goals for the system and subsystems encapsulate a vision of sustainable development and provide the basis for deciding what the assessment will measure. For *The Wellbeing of Nations* (WoN), I defined the goal for the system as "sustainable and equitable combinations of human and ecosystem wellbeing," and goals for the sub-systems (people and ecosystem) as "a high level of human wellbeing" and "a high level of ecosystem wellbeing." Participants in other assessments would define system and subsystem goals themselves.

## Stage 2. Identify Elements and Objectives

Participants in an assessment decide which aspects of human and ecosystem wellbeing are to be measured by identifying elements and objectives. Elements are key subjects or concerns that must be considered to get an adequate sense of the state of each dimension. In WoN, I chose two for each dimension because the fewer the elements the clearer their role and the stronger their influence on the dimension index. The dimensions (Figures B2 and B3) are big conceptual boxes that accommodate concerns common to all societies (e.g., water, and knowledge and culture), without requiring them to address those of little interest to them (e.g., marine waters to Uzbekistan) or excluding those of interest to some but not all societies (e.g., the maintenance of Islamic values, which could go under knowledge and culture). Accordingly, there are many ways of dividing the dimensions into elements. Land, for example, could be divided into major ecosystems (forests, farmland, etc.). In WoN, however, I chose land diversity and land quality because these are the fundamental concerns for land management and result in fewer elements.

If an element is too broad to measure directly, it is split into subelements. If a suitable indicator can be chosen directly, the subelement level is skipped. Of the 20 elements in WoN, 2 were dropped for lack of suitable indicators, 11 were split into subelements, and 7 were not. Land quality, for example, could be measured directly by the indicator "degraded land as a percentage of cultivated + modified land." However, land diversity had to be split into two subelements—land modification and conversion and land protection—each providing a different perspective on how well the diversity of land ecosystems is maintained.

Objectives for the elements provide a logical bridge between the general goals for the system and subsystems and the specific performance criteria for the indicators. The objective "soil degradation close to background rates" translates the goal for the ecosystem ("a high level of ecosystem wellbeing") into a particular aim for land qual-

ity that succinctly expresses the point of the element and provides a basis for choosing performance criteria for the indicator: the percentages of degraded land that are desirable, acceptable, or unacceptable. Objectives for dimensions and subelements may also be identified but are not necessary (and were not defined in WoN).

Once the elements are identified, the scope of the data required for indicators will be evident. At this stage, it is useful to compile a meta-database: an inventory of sources of data on each element, including when and how the data are collected, where and how stored, and how they can be obtained—essential information for the choice of indicators.

## Stage 3. Choose Indicators and Performance Criteria

### INDICATORS

Indicators are measurable aspects of an element. Wellbeing Assessment distinguishes between primary and secondary indicators. *Primary* indicators are the chief means of measuring the condition of elements and subelements. Performance criteria are defined for them, and they are combined into higher-level indices. Consequently, they must be chosen with great care to avoid overlap and double-counting with other primary indicators. *Secondary* indicators are supplementary sources of information, which are not combined into indices. Hence, performance criteria are not needed, and the indicators can be chosen less rigorously. If the primary indicators of health are life expectancy at birth and child and maternal mortality rates, secondary indicators might be the incidence of particular diseases, the number of doctors and hospital beds per 1,000 persons, and the percentage of children immunized against infectious diseases. (WoN used only primary indicators.) Throughout this appendix, "indicator" means "primary indicator."

Assessment participants choose one or more indicators for each element (or subelement) on the basis of how fully the indicator represents the element or subelement concerned and how reliable and feasible it is (Figure B5).

An indicator is fully *representative* if it covers the most important aspects of the element or subelement concerned and shows trends over time and differences between places and groups of people. "Life expectancy at birth" comes close to being a fully representative indicator of health because it reflects all the causes of death, and

**Representative**
Covers the most important aspects of the element concerned. Shows trends over time & differences between places & groups of people.

**Reliable**
Directly reflects how far the objective concerned is met. Is well founded, accurate, & measured in a standardized way with sound & consistent sampling procedures.

**Feasible**
Depends on data that are readily available or obtainable at reasonable cost.

**Figure B5. Basis for indicator selection.** The ideal indicator is representative, reliable and feasible. Indicator selection is often a matter of balancing these qualities.

**Table B1. What to do with potential indicators in each of five quality classes.**

| Indicator Quality Class | What to Do with the Indicator |
| --- | --- |
| The indicator is representative, reliable and feasible. | Use it. |
| The indicator is reliable and feasible but not representative. | Try to find one or more additional indicators until the element or subelement is adequately represented. |
| The indicator is representative and feasible but not reliable. | Is it reliable enough to use if everyone is made aware of its flaws? If yes, use it and try to find one or more additional indicators that together could produce a more reliable picture. If no, drop it. |
| The indicator is feasible but not representative or reliable. | Drop it. |
| The indicator is representative and reliable but not feasible. | Can the element or subelement be represented reasonably by another indicator or set of indicators? If yes, drop it. If no, reexamine the indicator's feasibility. It may be cost-effective after all. |

the death rates from those causes, that a typical person would be exposed to throughout life. Even so, it is incomplete since it does not measure the number of years a person can expect to live with different degrees of disability or illness. "Healthy life expectancy," by contrast, is highly representative because it subtracts the number of years likely to be lost to illness and injury.

An indicator is more likely to be *reliable* if it is accurate, is measured in a standardized way with sound and consistent sampling procedures, is well founded, and directly reflects the objective concerned. "Well founded" means that its relationship to the element it represents is well established, scientifically valid, or is a defensible and testable hypothesis. For example, stunting (low height for age) in children is a well-founded indicator of lack of food, since many studies have demonstrated the relationship. An indicator directly reflects the objective concerned if it measures its actual achievement rather than factors that advance or impede its achievement. Healthy life expectancy at birth shows how well the objective "long lives in good health" has been attained, whereas immunization rates, health expenditure, and numbers of doctors are only contributing factors.

An indicator is *feasible* if it depends on data that are readily available or obtainable at reasonable cost. The data required for an assessment will be available in a variety of forms and from a variety of sources. For the purpose of determining feasibility, the crucial distinction is between (a) data that are already collected as a matter of course and are available as maps or statistics; and (b) uncollected

data. The meta-database (compiled in the previous stage) should show whether the data are collected.

Potential indicators fall into various quality classes depending on how well they meet the criteria of representativeness, reliability, and feasibility. Suggestions about what to do with indicators in each class are given in Table B1. If no indicator that adequately meets these criteria can be found, then the element or subelement should be excluded from the assessment and its exclusion clearly noted.

**PERFORMANCE CRITERIA**

Participants in an assessment choose performance criteria for each indicator. The criteria translate the objectives into measurable performance and enable different indicator measurements to be converted to scores so that they can be combined.

A large number of indicators is inevitable, given the broad scope of human and ecosystem wellbeing, but presents an enormous communication problem. Every indicator sends a signal. The more indicators, the more signals—

a perplexing cacophony of good, bad, and somewhere-in-between news. The problem is overcome by combining the indicators into indices. How to do this raises other obstacles, however, because a typical set of indicators is a mess of incompatible measurements: land condition in hectares, water pollution in milligrams per liter, species diversity in percentages of threatened species, health in years of life expectancy, income in money, education in school enrollment rates, freedom in the observation of rights, and so on.

Combining such different indicators mixes apples and oranges. To do this successfully requires finding a common unit that does not distort their qualities as apples or oranges ("citrus units" would favor oranges, "pome units" would favor apples). The common unit may be a physical unit, money, or a performance score. Because of the limitations of physical units and money (explained in Supplement 4), Wellbeing Assessment uses performance scores. Several scales for performance scores have been devised (described in Supplement 5). Wellbeing Assessment uses

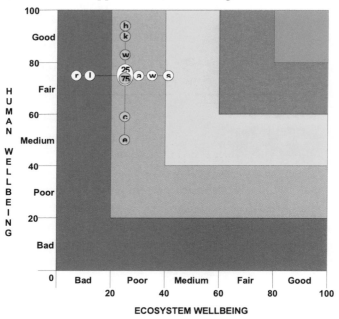

**Figure B6. Barometer of Sustainability.** The Wellbeing Index (WI) of a hypothetical country is shown on the Barometer. The Human Wellbeing Index (HWI) is in the yolk of the egg. The Ecosystem Wellbeing Index (EWI) is in the white. The WI is where the HWI and EWI intersect. Yellow circles (vertical axis) show the points on the scale of the human dimensions: c = community; e = equity; h = health and population; k = knowledge; w = wealth. White circles (horizontal axis) show points of the ecosystem dimenions: a = air; l = land; r = resource use; s = species and genes; w = water.

the Barometer of Sustainability (Figure B6) because it is the only performance scale designed to measure human and ecosystem wellbeing together without submerging one in the other. The Barometer's unique features are:

- Two axes: one for human wellbeing, the other for ecosystem wellbeing. This enables each set of indicators to be combined independently, keeping them separate to allow analysis of people–ecosystem interactions.

- The axis with the lower score overrides the other axis. This prevents a high score for human wellbeing from offsetting a low score for ecosystem wellbeing (or vice versa), reflecting the view that people and the ecosystem are equally important and that sustainable development must improve and maintain the wellbeing of both.

- Each axis is divided into five bands. This allows users to define not just the end points of the scale but intermediate points as well for greater flexibility and control of the scale.

Performance criteria enable an indicator measurement to be given a score by converting it to the scale of the Barometer. They define the rate of exchange between the indicator and the scale—the level of performance that is worth a given number of points (Table B2).

Choosing performance criteria involves defining the top point of each band on the basis of three factors:

- The range of performance is used to set the base and top of the scale. As a general rule, base–best (0–100) should encompass the range of performance. This may be current performance or a combination of past, current, and expected performance. For example, WoN's

**Table B2. The five bands of the Barometer of Sustainability.**

| Band | Points Range | Points Top | Definition |
|---|---|---|---|
| Good | 100–81 | 100 | Desirable performance, objective fully met |
| Fair | 80–61 | 80 | Acceptable performance, objective almost or barely met |
| Medium | 60–41 | 60 | Neutral or transitional performance |
| Poor | 40–21 | 40 | Undesirable performance |
| Bad | 20–1 | 20 | Unacceptable performance |
| Base | 0 | 0 | Base of scale |

base–best for life expectancy at birth (30–85 years) encompasses the lowest current performance of 34 years and the highest expected performance (by 2050) of 84 years. If outliers of extreme performance would make the scale unduly long, it can be cut off (at the bottom or at the top). For example, the scale for the indicator "tons of fertilizer per 1,000 harvested hectares" was cut off at 320 tons to prevent distortion by a few countries that use very much higher levels (up to 2,426 tons). In WoN, to prevent arbitrary shortening of the scale, base–best encompassed the range of performance of more than 90% of the countries in all cases except fecal coliforms.

- The objective of the element concerned guides the setting of the good band. For example, WoN's objective for the wild diversity element, "maintenance of all native wild species and reductions of extinctions to background rates," suggests that the good band of the threatened species indicators should be close to the background rate (estimated to be less than 0.01% of species per century).

- At least one of the following is used to set one or more bands:

  *Estimated sustainable rate.* For example, a sustainable rate of timber felling would be less than 100% of net annual increment.

  *Estimated background rate* ("natural" or "normal" performance). For example, the background rate of human-caused soil degradation on natural land is zero.

  *Other threshold.* For example, a single death represents the threshold between peace and armed conflict.

  *International (or national) standard.* For example, UN standards for water quality.

  *International (or national) target.* For example, a UN target for education is 100% primary education by 2015.

  *Expert opinion.* For example, Transparency International's Corruption Perceptions Index.

  *Derivation from a related indicator.* For example, in the absence of a UN target for secondary education, WoN used a less stringent version of the criteria for primary education.

*The judgment of participants.* If none of the preceding factors is available, the choice of performance criteria is entirely up to the judgment of participants. Performance criteria for 62 of WoN's 87 indicators were guided by the preceding factors; the remaining 25 were set on the basis of personal judgment.

Sustainable rates determine the top of the medium or fair band, depending on how much assessment participants want to apply the precautionary principle (that it is better to err on the side of caution). A highly precautionary approach would not allow even a slightly unsustainable rate to be considered fair (acceptable performance); a less precautionary approach might. In WoN, for instance, I took a highly precautionary approach to the indicator "timber fellings + imports as a percentage of net annual increment": fellings + imports had to be well below increment to qualify as good and not exceed it to qualify as fair. I was less precautionary in my treatment of "annual change in native forest area": the area must not decline at all to qualify as good but may shrink by up to 0.05% a year and still qualify as fair.

Background rates usually determine the top of the good band (best performance). The chief question to decide is how far from the background rate is still good (i.e., where to put the top of fair). This depends on what is at stake. In the case of the threatened species indicators (background extinction rate close to 0%), I set the top of fair at 2% because extinctions are irreparable. In the case of land degradation (background rate 0%), I set it at 10% of the cultivated and modified land area because the percentage is weighted, and 10% overall is equivalent to 20% light (easily reparable) degradation, 10% moderate (less easily reparable), 5% strong (barely reparable), or 2.5% extreme (irreparable) degradation.

The bands set by other thresholds depend on the threshold. If it is between clearly unacceptable performance on one side (armed conflict) and performance that ranges from neutral to desirable on the other (from military preparedness without conflict to complete peace), then the threshold sets the top of the poor or bad band. If it is between clearly desirable performance on one side (unfragmented habitats) and performance that ranges from neutral to unacceptable on the other (increasing fragmentation of habitats), the threshold sets the top of the medium or fair band.

Standards, targets, and expert opinion may determine several bands. The UN Economic Commission for Europe has defined five water quality classes (excellent, good, fair, poor, bad), which can be translated directly into the Barometer's good, fair, medium, poor, and bad bands. In WoN, a series of UN targets—60 years by 2000, more than 70 years by 2005, and more than 75 years by 2015—were used to set the tops of the poor, medium, and fair bands for life expectancy at birth. Single standards and targets set the top of the good, fair, or medium bands, depending on how ambitious they are. Targets such as universal primary education and elimination of ozone depleting substances cannot be bettered and form the top of the good band. The ambitiousness of less absolute targets can be judged from the range of performance: if few societies exceed them, they are put at the top of the fair band; if many exceed them, they are put at the top of the medium band. Sometimes other considerations may prevail: international targets set the top of the fair band of three of WoN's food sufficiency indicators but the top of the medium band of the fourth to aid interpretation by enabling the performance criteria of all four indicators to match.

For many indicators it is useful for the performance criteria to increase or decline exponentially (in doublings) from the best point, to reflect the increasing difficulty of improving performance as one approaches the ideal, or from the worst point, to reflect diminishing returns (Table B3). An exponential scale also accommodates a wide range of performance while keeping high standards for the good and fair bands. For example, child mortality rates range from 263 to 6 deaths per 1,000 live births. The UN target is for all countries to have rates below 45 deaths by 2015. An exponential scale from 0 to 360 accommodates the current range of performance and puts 45 at the top of the medium band, so that less than 45 is fair and half of 45 is good. A scale with bands of equal size could not do this. If it kept 45 at the top of medium, the base of the scale would be 112.5 deaths, which would exclude the performance of 44 countries. If the base of an equally divided scale were set at 265 to accommodate the current range of performance, the top of medium would rise to 106, and the top of fair (at 53) would be worse than the UN target of 45.

Choosing performance criteria is the most thought-provoking part of Wellbeing Assessment, demanding judgment throughout. This is all to the good. Pondering

## Table B3. Performance criteria for two indicators.

The child mortality criteria increase exponentially from the best point, the protected land criteria from the worst point.

| Band | Top Point on Scale | Child Deaths per 1,000 Live Births | Protected Land as % of Total Land |
|---|---|---|---|
| Good | 100 | 0 | 40 |
| Fair | 80 | 22 | 20 |
| Medium | 60 | 45 | 10 |
| Poor | 40 | 90 | 5 |
| Bad | 20 | 180 | 2.5 |
| Base | 0 | 360 | 0 |

and debating the specifics of what it will take to achieve high levels of human and ecosystem wellbeing are essential for building the consensus required to develop sustainably. The criteria chosen for WoN are summarized in Appendix C.

## Stage 4. Measure and Map Indicators

Having chosen the indicators, it is necessary to obtain the data for them. The assessment needs to set up its own database; make arrangements with sources of existing data to receive them regularly; and organize surveys and monitoring systems for any indicators requiring data not currently collected. The data should be linked to the base maps prepared as part of stage 1 to enable the indicators to be mapped by differentiation unit, as they are in WoN.

Data for many of the indicators will apply to the entire area of each differentiation unit. But data for some—notably water quality and local air quality—will be point data, specific to a particular measuring station. It is helpful to show the locations of these stations on maps so that users can judge the completeness of coverage. In addition, participants must decide whether to take the average of the stations or the worst measurement. If the monitoring agency is scrupulous in sampling only (or largely) those locations where air or water pollution is most likely to occur, then the average is probably the fairest reading. If it omits areas known to be polluted and includes many pristine spots, it may be more prudent to choose the worst-performing station. In WoN, I took the average of the worst pollutants at each location.

Data (indicator measurements) are given scores on the

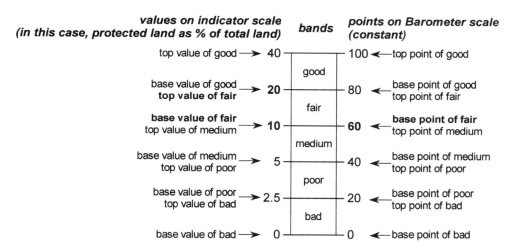

**Figure B7. Correspondence of values on an indicator scale to points on the Barometer scale when best performance is the highest value and worst the lowest.** The values on the indicator scale on the left—40, 20, 10, 5, 2.5, 0—are indicator specific. In this instance they define the performance bands for protected land as % of total land. The points on the Barometer scale on the right—100, 80, 60, 40, 20, 0—define the bands of the Barometer. They remain constant. See text and formula for explanation of how the values and points highlighted in bold are selected and used to calculate the score for Zimbabwe (protected land 15.8%).

basis of the performance criteria. The performance criteria define which band a given indicator measurement will go into and the indicator values that correspond to the top point and base point of that band. For example, using the performance criteria given in Table B3, Zimbabwe's protected land percentage of 18.5% would go into the fair band because it is between 20% and 10%: 20% on the indicator scale corresponds to 80 on the Barometer scale (the top point of the fair band), and 10% on the indicator scale corresponds to 60 on the Barometer scale (the base point of the fair band). Afghanistan's child mortality rate of 257 deaths per 1,000 live births would go into the bad band because it is between 180 and 360: 180 on the indicator scale corresponds to 20 on the Barometer scale (the top point of the bad band), and 360 on the indicator scale corresponds to 0 on the Barometer scale (the base point of the bad band). Note that the base point of each band on the Barometer scale is the same as the top point of the band below (Figures B7 and B8).

The indicator measurement's exact position in the band on the Barometer scale is determined by calculating its score. This is done in one of two ways, depending on whether: best performance is the highest value and worst performance is the lowest value (for example, protected land as a percentage of total land) or best performance is the lowest value and worst performance

is the highest value (for example, the child mortality rate).

When *best is the highest value and worst is the lowest*, the formula for calculating the score is:

> {[(actual indicator value – base indicator value) ÷ (top indicator value – base indicator value)] × 20} + base point of the band on the Barometer scale

The terms *top* and *base* always refer to the band in which the indicator measurement falls. The *actual indicator value* is the measurement of the indicator being scored. The *top indicator value* is the top value of the relevant band on the indicator scale, and the *base indicator value* is the base value of the band. The *base point of the band* is the base point of the relevant band on the Barometer scale (Figure B7).

Following the formula, the calculation for Zimbabwe's protected land percentage (18.5%) is:

> 18.5 (actual indicator value) – 10 (base indicator value) = 8.5
> 20 (top indicator value) – 10 (base indicator value) = 10
> 8.5 ÷ 10 = 0.85
> 0.85 × 20 = 17.0
> 17.0 + 60 (base point of band on the Barometer) = 77

When *best is the lowest value and worst is the highest*, the formula for calculating the score is:

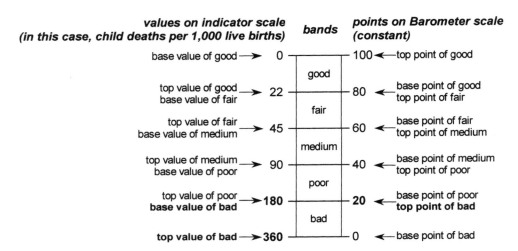

**Figure B8. Correspondence of values on an indicator scale to points on the Barometer scale when best performance is the lowest value and worst the highest.** The values on the indicator scale on the left—0, 22, 45, 90, 180, 360—are indicator specific. In this instance they define the performance bands for child deaths per 1,000 live births. The points on the Barometer scale on the right—100, 80, 60, 40, 20, 0—define the bands of the Barometer. They remain constant. Note that the base point of each band is still the top point of the band below. However, the base value now corresponds to the top point of the band; the top value, to the base point. See text and formula for explanation of how the values and points highlighted in bold are selected and used to calculate the score for Afghanistan (257 child deaths).

---

> top point of the band on the Barometer scale − {[(actual indicator value − base indicator value) ÷ (top indicator value − base indicator value)] × 20}

As before, the terms *top* and *base* always refer to the band in which the indicator measurement falls. Also as before, the *actual indicator value* is the measurement of the indicator being scored, the *top indicator value* is the top value of the band on the indicator scale, and the *base indicator value* is the base value of the band. The difference between this and the previous case is that the indicator scale goes in the opposite direction to the Barometer scale—from lowest to highest instead of from highest to lowest. Consequently, the top value of a band on the indicator scale corresponds to the *base* point of the band on the Barometer scale; and the base value of the band on the indicator scale corresponds to the *top* of the band on the Barometer scale (Figure B8). The other difference is that the final step in the calculation is to subtract from the top point of the band on the Barometer scale instead of adding to its base point.

Following the formula, the calculation for Afghanistan's child mortality rate of 257 deaths per 1,000 live births is:

> 257 (actual indicator value) − 180 (base indicator value) = 77
> 360 (top indicator value) − 180 (base indicator value) = 180
> 77 ÷ 180 = 0.428
> 0.428 × 20 = 8.56
> 20 (top point of band on the Barometer) − 8.56 = 11.44 = 11

In all cases, scores are rounded to the nearest whole point, with 0.5 rounded down.

Data availability is seldom uniform. While some differentiation units may have data on all the indicators, others may have data on only a selection of them. Such uneven coverage can seriously distort results. For example, if all units do well on water consumption and poorly on water quality, the ones that are rated only on consumption will appear to be better than they actually are. An "insufficient data rule" prevents high scores resulting merely from lack of data. A good score (81–100) is allowed only if it is based on all applicable components (e.g., data in an indicator, indicators in an element, elements in a dimension). A fair score (61–80) is allowed only if it is based on at least half the components. Potentially good scores based on more than half but not all the applicable components are reduced to 80 (the top of fair). Potentially good or fair scores based on fewer than half the applicable components are reduced to 60 (the top of medium). For example, a society with a score of 88 for water consumption but no data on water quality would have an overall water score of 80 rather than 88. If water were divided into three elements (water consumption, water quality, aquatic habitats) and data were available only for water consumption, the score would be reduced to 60.

## Stage 5. Combine Indicators and Map Indices

Once the indicators have been given a score, they can be combined back up the hierarchy (Figure B4), from indicators to system: indicator scores are combined into a subelement score, subelement scores into an element index, element indices into a dimension index, and dimension indices into a subsystem index.

Components (indicators, subelements, elements, or dimensions) are combined in one of three ways:

- *Unweighted average:* The components are added and averaged. For example, if one component has a score of 70 and another has a score of 30, the combined score is 50: 70 + 30 = 100 ÷ 2 = 50.

- *Weighted average:* The components are given different weights, then added and averaged. For example, if the component with the 70 score is given a weight of 1 and the component with the 30 score is given a weight of 2, then the combined score is 43: (70 × 1) + (30 × 2) = 130 ÷ 3 = 43.3. (Scores are multiplied by their weights and then the total score is divided by the total weight. In this case a weight of 1 plus a weight of 2 makes a total weight of 3.)

- *Veto:* A lower score overrides a higher score. For example, the component with the 30 score would override the component with the 70 score, resulting in an overall score of 30.

The choice of combining procedure is a matter of judging which most closely reflects the situation in relation to the goals and objectives. The following are guidelines, not hard-and-fast rules.

An *unweighted average* is used mainly when the components are judged to be roughly equal in importance *and* in the quality and coverage of their indicators. Strong performance in all components is desirable and weak performance in any of them undesirable, but not to the extent that bad performance in one component overrides better performance in the others. For these reasons, WoN used the unweighted average to combine the peace and crime subelements, household equity and gender equity, the water quality scores of different drainage basins, the scores for threatened plants and threatened animals, and the scores for agriculture, fisheries, and timber.

The human and ecosystem dimensions are a special case. They are equally important and should be equally well represented by their indicators, but even if they are

not, the unweighted average is used to combine them into indices (the HWI and EWI) to show their roles clearly, unobscured by technical manipulation such as weighting.

The unweighted average may also be used when one component contributes to another but taking the lower score is considered too drastic. For example, WoN divided household wealth into two subelements: income and needs. Since income contributes to the provision of needs, it would be better to take the subelement with the lower score to prevent double-counting. However, needs are reported less reliably in high-income than in low-income countries, and taking the lower score would result in the misleading impression that many of the former are as poor as the latter.

Sometimes components are weighted implicitly, and no explicit weighting is necessary. An example is crime, which WoN divided into homicides and "other violent crimes" (rapes, robberies, assaults), which tend to be less consistently reported. This implicitly gave homicides a weight of 3 and the other violent crimes weights of 1 each.

A *weighted average* is used to combine components that are considered to be unequal in importance or in the quality and coverage of the indicators. The weight reflects the difference in importance or in quality and coverage. In WoN, for example, education was given twice the weight of communication because the quality of communication depends on education. Similarly, wild diversity was given twice the weight of domesticated diversity because the loss of a wild species is more significant than the loss of a livestock breed or crop variety.

A *veto* is used mainly under three circumstances. First, when good performance is essential in both components of a pair. Sometimes success in one component may be at the expense of failure in the other, and the veto ensures that only success in both is rewarded: for example, health and population, inflation and unemployment, and agricultural productivity and agricultural self-reliance. Sometimes the components are halves of a whole, and good performance in one alone does not get the job done: for example, safe water and basic sanitation, telephone accessibility and telephone reliability, land diversity and land quality, global atmosphere and local air quality.

Second, when inferior performance in one component outweighs superior performance—no matter how good—in all the others. Examples are air and water pollutants: dangerous levels of one substance are not made less dangerous by safe levels of the others.

Third, to avoid counting the same feature more than once when it is represented by more than one component. Elements and subelements may have to be represented by more than one indicator to ensure adequate coverage (see Table B1 and the section on indicators). For example, WoN had to use three indicators of food sufficiency: percentage of population with insufficient food, prevalence of stunting in children, and prevalence of low weight for age in children. These indicators measure different symptoms of the same feature: lack of food. Some countries were covered by all three, some by two, some by one. To prevent double-counting, WoN used only the lowest score.

All combining procedures used in WoN are summarized in Appendix D.

The dimensions are combined into two subsystem indices: the Human Wellbeing Index (HWI) and the Ecosystem Wellbeing Index (EWI). The HWI is the lower of *either* the unweighted average of four human dimensions (all except equity) *or* the unweighted average of all five human dimensions (including equity). Whereas the other human dimensions measure human conditions—health and population, wealth, knowledge and culture, and community—equity is a modifier, measuring how fairly those conditions are shared. When the HWI with equity is *higher* than the HWI without equity, it is a sign that human development is inadequate throughout society, and only deprivation is being shared. Hence the inclusion of equity makes conditions look rosier than they are. When the HWI with equity is *lower* than the HWI without equity, it shows that the relatively high standard of living revealed by the other dimensions is unfairly distributed. Thus the inclusion of equity gives a more realistic picture of human wellbeing overall. Accordingly, equity is included only when it does not raise the HWI.

Similarly, the EWI is the lower of *either* the unweighted average of four ecosystem dimensions (all except resource use) *or* the unweighted average of all five ecosystem dimensions (including resource use). The other ecosystem dimensions measure the state of land, water, air, and species and genes. But resource use is a modifier, measuring activities that alter the state of land, water, air, and species and genes. If the EWI with resource use is *higher* than the EWI without resource use, it is a sign that

the resource use indicators understate the impacts of these activities. Hence the inclusion of resource use makes the state of the environment look better than it is. If the EWI with resource use is *lower* than the EWI without resource use, it shows that the other ecosystem dimensions understate the impacts of resource uses. Thus the inclusion of resource use better reflects the actual state of the ecosystem. Accordingly, resource use is included only when it does not raise the EWI.

The Wellbeing Index (WI) is the point on the Barometer of Sustainability where the HWI and the EWI intersect (Figure B6). It is a graphic index, and a single number does not do it justice. Taking the lower of the HWI and EWI discounts either the state of the environment or the condition of people (whichever is higher). For example:

| Society | HWI | EWI | Lower Score | Average Score |
|---|---|---|---|---|
| A | 75 | 25 | 25 | 50.0 |
| B | 25 | 75 | 25 | 50.0 |
| C | 25 | 25 | 25 | 25.0 |

The lower number masks a crucial difference between Society A and Society B: while they have as far to go to achieve sustainability, A's priority is to improve the ecosystem, B's to improve the condition of people. Worse, the lower number suggests that Society C is in the same position as A and B, although it is much weaker, with both a depressed standard of living and an impoverished environment. While the average of the HWI and EWI also hides differences between Societies A and B, it has the merit of expressing the distance to sustainability. Although their paths will differ, A and B are equally far from sustainability. Society C, by contrast, with an average of 25.0, has much further to travel. Hence, when it is desirable to express the WI as a single number (for example, to rank performance), it is better to use the average. But bear in mind that the true WI is the juxtaposition of human and ecosystem wellbeing shown on the Barometer of Sustainability.

The Wellbeing/Stress Index (WSI) measures the ratio of human wellbeing to ecosystem stress. It is produced in two steps. First the EWI is subtracted from 100 to convert it into an Ecosystem Stress Index (ESI)—the reverse of the EWI. Then the HWI is divided by the ESI.

It is useful to know how to calculate scores and combine indicators manually, but when an assessment has to cope with many indicators and indicator combinations for many differentiation units, the work becomes extremely tedious and time-consuming. Fortunately, software called Combo is available to do it electronically. Combo calculates scores on the basis of the user's performance criteria and is a valuable tool for testing the effects of different criteria. Combo also combines indicator components on the basis of combining procedures and weights chosen by the user.[4]

## Stage 6. Review Results and Propose Policies

The review links the assessment to action by:

- Analyzing the indicators and indices, the patterns of performance, and the data behind them.
- Determining the elements and areas where improvements are most needed.
- Proposing policies and actions to make the improvements.
- Planning the priority actions.
- Reviewing and revising policy, program, and project objectives and targets.

Participants examine links between indicators, patterns of performance, strengths, weaknesses, causal factors, opportunities, and obstacles. They analyze policy options for improving socioeconomic and environmental conditions, setting targets for the HWI, EWI, and WSI and for the dimensions and elements on which most progress could or should be made. They propose policies and actions (including new or revised sustainable development policies and action plans) to achieve the targets. The review also provides the diagnosis for designing programs and projects.

The Barometer of Sustainability provides a starting point, showing the HWI and EWI of each society being assessed (e.g., countries in a region, states or provinces in a country, communities in a district). By displaying each society's structure of wellbeing—the pattern of dimensions—it reveals the dimensions that most need improvement. These can be further analyzed to identify the elements and subelements requiring priority attention, how they are linked, the causes of the main problems, and what policies and actions are needed in response. The discussion in Chapter 4 illustrates the potential.

## Supplement 1. Bellagio Principles for Assessing Sustainable Development

In 1996, the International Institute for Sustainable Development convened an international group of assessment specialists to draw up the Bellagio principles for assessing sustainable development.[5] The principles express a consensus on best practice for both the content and process of assessment. Their essential points are:

The content of assessment should:

1. Be guided by a clear vision of sustainable development and goals that define that vision.
2. Review the condition and trend of the whole system, its socioeconomic and ecological parts, and interactions between the parts.
3. Consider equity and disparities within the current population and between present and future generations.
4. Combine long-term and short-term views and cover distant as well as local impacts on people and ecosystems.
5. Adopt an explicit framework to link the vision and goals to indicators and focus on a limited number of issues and indicators.

The process of assessment should:

6. Use an accessible method, make the data available to all, and make explicit all judgments, assumptions, and uncertainties in data and interpretations.
7. Communicate effectively to its intended audience, using a simple structure and clear and plain language.
8. Involve key groups to ensure recognition of different values and decision makers to make the link to policies and action.
9. Be done regularly to determine trends and improve collective learning and decision making, adjusting goals, frameworks, and indicators as new insights are gained.
10. Be supported by improved local and national capacities for assessment and data collection, maintenance, and documentation.

Wellbeing Assessment satisfies principle 1 through stage 1 of the assessment cycle: define the system and goals.

It fulfills principle 2 through the framework's equal treatment of people and the ecosystem and its provision for measuring interactions between them. It accords with principle 3 through equal treatment of people and the ecosystem, which is designed to cover equity between present and future generations, and through the equity dimension, which covers equity within the current population.

Wellbeing Assessment does not oblige users to combine long-term and short-term views or cover both distant and local impacts (principle 4), but it provides ample scope for doing so. For example, WoN addresses immediate human needs and long-term requirements to maintain ecosystem diversity. It measures global and local impacts (such as global atmosphere and local air quality) and accounts for the effects of food and timber consumption on both domestic and external ecosystems.

Wellbeing Assessment meets principle 5 via the hierarchy from system and goals to indicators and performance criteria (stages 1 through 3). Although some technicalities are unavoidable, the method is designed to be as accessible as possible for people with little training in measurement and limited mathematical skills (principle 6). Throughout WoN, I have tried to make explicit all judgments, assumptions, and uncertainties. The structure of Wellbeing Assessment is simple (principle 7), and maps and the Barometer of Sustainability are designed for effective communication.

The remaining three principles are the responsibility of participants in particular assessments and the managers of national and local assessment systems. Regular global assessment of wellbeing is planned, including the production of updated and improved editions of WoN.

## Supplement 2. Background of the Dimensions

The dimensions divide each subsystem into major components that meet five criteria:

- Limited in number (ideally four, certainly no more than five) because the fewer the components in an index, the stronger their effect.

- Equally important, allowing them to be combined into subsystem indices using unweighted averages (to keep the effect of each dimension on the HWI or EWI clear and simple).

- Specific enough to ensure that all assessments cover universally important aspects of human and ecosystem wellbeing.

- Broad and flexible enough to accommodate concerns common to all societies, without requiring or excluding coverage of issues that matter to some but not all.

- Easy to grasp—not dependent on a highly technical or abstract model of the human subsystem or the ecosystem—and simply expressed.

Fulfilling these criteria has been a challenge. Table B4

**Table B4. Evolution of the dimensions of Wellbeing Assessment from the first draft of the Barometer of Sustainability (BoS) to the present version of *The Wellbeing of Nations* (WoN).** The version is in parentheses: BoS drafts, April 1995 (BoS 95a), July 1995 (BoS 95b), 1996 (BoS 96); WoN drafts, 1997 (WoN 97), 1998 (WoN 98), 2000 (WoN 00).

| *Previous Dimensions* | *Current Dimensions* |
|---|---|
| Human health (BoS 95a) → | Health and population (BoS 95b) |
| Access to resources (BoS 95a) ↓ Wealth and livelihood (BoS 96) → | Wealth (WoN 97) |
| Knowledge (BoS 95a) → | Knowledge and culture (WoN 98) |
| Institutions (BoS 95a) ↓ Behavior and institutions (BoS 95b) ↓ Freedom and order (WoN 97) → | Community (WoN 98) |
| Part of the other human dimensions (BoS 95a) → | Equity (BoS 96) |
| Part of ecosystem naturalness and ecosystem quality (BoS 95a) → | Land (BoS 96) |
| Part of ecosystem naturalness and ecosystem quality (BoS 95a) → | Water (BoS 96) |
| Part of ecosystem quality (BoS 95a) → | Air (BoS 96) |
| Biodiversity maintenance (BoS 95a) ↓ Biodiversity (BoS 96) ↓ Species and populations (WoN 98) → | Species and genes (WoN 00) |
| Resource conservation (BoS 95a) → | Resource use (BoS 96) |

traces the evolution of the current set of five human and five ecosystem dimensions over the course of three drafts of the Barometer of Sustainability method (1995–1996) and three of *The Wellbeing of Nations* (1997–2000).

The four original human dimensions consisted of the three components of the Human Development Index (HDI)—human health, access to resources, and knowledge—plus institutions (not covered by the HDI).[6] Human health was soon expanded to health and population to cover both of these closely related concerns together. Access to resources was expanded to wealth and livelihood to cover all aspects of material and monetary wellbeing, later expressed more simply as wealth. Knowledge was eventually expanded to knowledge and culture to accommodate religious belief systems, societal values, the arts, and self- and community-expression—aspects neglected by assessments to date but for which undoubtedly there should be a place. Institutions was expanded to behavior and institutions to cover issues such as crime and conflict. The name was changed to freedom and order in an effort to clarify its scope. This was too limited, however, so the dimension was expanded to community to cover all aspects of governance, institutions, and community organization as well as human rights and interpersonal behavior (e.g., peace, crime). Equity was originally part of the other human dimensions but was distinguished as the fifth dimension to make it more visible.

The four original ecosystem dimensions were based on the three objectives of the *World Conservation Strategy:* maintenance of essential ecological processes and life-support systems, preservation of genetic diversity, and sustainable utilization of species and ecosystems.[7] Ecosystem naturalness and ecosystem quality corresponded to the first objective, biodiversity maintenance to the second, resource conservation to the third. This arrangement did not meet the criterion of "easy to grasp." Accordingly, ecosystem naturalness and ecosystem quality were replaced by three dimensions: land, water, and air. Biodiversity maintenance was simplified to biodiversity, and resource conservation to resource use. However, the new arrangement flouted the criterion "equally important." Putting ecosystem, species, and genetic diversity into one dimension—biodiversity—made it more important than any of the others while reducing the importance of land and water (since they could cover ecosystem quality but not the diversity of land and water ecosystems). Consequently,

biodiversity was split up by moving ecosystem diversity to land and water, and covering species and genetic diversity in a new dimension—species and populations—later renamed "species and genes" to clarify its scope.

## *Supplement 3. Assessment Frameworks*

Methods of assessing human and environmental conditions differ chiefly in the frameworks they use to organize information (covered in this supplement) and in whether and how they combine indicators (the next supplement).

Most assessment frameworks are dual, triple, or quadruple (Figure B9). Wellbeing Assessment employs a dual framework, dividing the system into two equal subsystems: people and ecosystem. Dual frameworks are also used by the UN Environment Programme's Global Environment Outlook ("human system" and "environmental system"), the World Resources Institute's approach to measuring environmental policy performance ("human subsystem" and "environmental subsystem"), and several other methods.[8]

Triple frameworks include the World Bank's estimates of national wealth (discussed in Appendix A), which distinguish three kinds of capital: produced assets (economy), human resources (society), and natural capital (environment). Similarly, the Consultative Group on Sustainable Development Indicators divides its Dashboard of Sustainability into economic performance, social health, and environmental quality.[9]

The UN Commission on Sustainable Development uses a quadruple framework for reporting on implementation of Agenda 21, the action plan of the 1992 United Nations Conference on Environment and Development: economic aspects, social aspects, institutional aspects, and environmental aspects.[10]

These differences are not trivial: the more the human subsystem is divided, the less the weight of the environment (Figure B9). The dual framework gives people and the environment equal weight. The triple framework reduces the weight of the environment to a third; the quadruple framework reduces it to a quarter.

| dual: | PEOPLE | | ENVIRONMENT | |
|---|---|---|---|---|
| triple: | ECONOMY | SOCIETY | ENVIRONMENT | |
| quadruple: | ECONOMY | SOCIETY | INSTITUTIONS | ENVIRONMENT |

**Figure B9. Three frameworks for assessing sustainable development.** The weight of the environment declines as the number of human domains increases.

## Supplement 4. Common Units for Combining Indicators

Many assessment methods do not combine their indicators, preventing them from showing overall human and environmental conditions, revealing major performance patterns, or communicating results succinctly.

Those that do combine their indicators start by converting their disparate indicator measurements to a common unit. The unit is either a physical unit, money, or a performance score.

Physical units can combine only a limited range of things. Materials can be combined on the basis of their weight, but this does not account for their different impacts: a ton of arsenic is more of a problem than a ton of old lace. Pollutants with similar effects can be combined according to their potential for that effect: greenhouse gas emissions can be combined according to the contribution of each gas to global warming, and heavy metals on the basis of their toxicity. But pollutants with different effects cannot be combined in this way. Uses of energy and renewable resources can be converted into the area of productive land and sea required to supply the resources and absorb carbon dioxide from fossil fuels, but area is not a suitable unit for measuring air quality or genetic diversity.[11] No single physical unit has been found that could combine all indicators of ecosystem wellbeing, let alone of human wellbeing.

Money is standard in all economic accounts. It is also used in some environmental assessments, such as the cost of remediation (COR) index, a measure of the cost of moving from the present state of environment to a more desirable level.[12] However, it too has serious weaknesses. It reflects the market price of apples and oranges, not their taste, nutritional content, or cultural value. It can measure the value of things that are traded in the market, but it distorts the value of anything not traded. The less tradable the item, the greater the distortion. Most items in an assessment of wellbeing and sustainability have no market price, so nonmarket values must be estimated from contingent values (asking people how much they would pay for a benefit or how much compensation they would accept if deprived of the benefit) or from expenditures on avoiding and treating damage. Using these techniques together is like combining real apples (market values), fake apples (contingent values), real oranges (actual expenditures), and fake oranges (hypothetical expenditures).

Faced with the drawbacks of physical units and money, performance scores have an overwhelming advantage. They measure how good an orange is at being an orange and how good an apple is as an apple—the distance between a standard level of performance and the actual performance recorded by an indicator measurement. On a 0–100 scale, best performance is 100 and worst 0. A given apple or orange would receive a score according to how good it was in relation to best and worst. Performance criteria for apples and oranges may be very different, but since their scores are calculated in the same way on the same scale, the scores can be combined.

Performance scores allow use of whatever yardstick is most appropriate to the issue concerned: income and value added are measured in money, health in disease and death rates, employment in jobs, species diversity in percentages of threatened species, land degradation as erosion rates, and so forth. Distortion is negligible because the original units in which the indicator is measured are kept intact.

Judgment is required to decide performance criteria, but judgment is also needed when using physical units or money. When the indicators are closely related (as in the equivalent effects of pollutants or the weight of material), the judgment is not great. But when they are far apart (as in the monetary value of biodiversity, human life, security, or community harmony), the judgment required is considerable.

## Supplement 5. Performance Scales

A performance scale—a scale for calculating performance scores—is set by defining *one end* of the scale (best performance), *both ends* (best and worst performance), the *midpoint* (average performance), or *bands* (both ends plus intermediate points). Definitions of these points are based either on *observed* performance (or a mixture of observed and expected performance) in a sample of societies or on *desired* performance, a specified objective (Table B5).

The Dutch Environmental Pressure index (EPI) is a *one-end* performance scale that combines compound indicators of six types of pollution (Table B6). A sustainability or no-major-effect level is defined for each type. The actual level of pollution is expressed as a percentage of the sustainability level, and the six percentages are added together to give a total index of environmental pressure. The scale goes from 0 (sustainability levels achieved for all issues) to more than 8,000 (the combined difference

**Table B5. Classification of selected performance scales according to the points on the scale that are defined and on what basis.**

| *What Is Defined* → <br><br> *On What Basis* ↓ | *One End* <br> *(best performance)* | *Both Ends* <br> *(best and worst performance)* | *Midpoint* <br> *(average performance)* | *Bands* <br> *(both ends + intermediate points)* |
|---|---|---|---|---|
| Observed and expected performance | | Human Development Index <br> Environmental Sustainability Index | Development Diamond <br> Environment Diamond | |
| Desired performance (objectives) | Environmental Pressure Index | | | Barometer of Sustainability |

between the sustainability level and performance in 1985).[13]

The Human Development Index (HDI) combines indicators of longevity, education, and standard of living (income). *Both ends* of its 0–1 scale are defined. The bottom end (0) is the lowest observed performance over the past 30 years (in the HDI's sample of 174 countries) and the top end (1) is the highest expected performance in the next 30 years (Table B7). Each indicator measurement gets a score of 0 to 1 depending on where it falls in relation to the lowest and highest performance for that indicator. The indicators are combined by adding their scores and taking the average.[14]

The Environmental Sustainability Index (ESI) combines indicators of 22 factors (which are at the level of Wellbeing Assessment's elements). Like the HDI, both

ends of its 0–100 scale are defined on the basis of the lowest and highest current performance for the indicator concerned.[15]

The development diamond exemplifies a scale for which the *midpoint* is defined. It has four axes, one for each indicator (Figure B10). The midpoint of each axis is defined as the average performance of a group of countries classified by income (high-income, upper-middle income, lower-middle income, low-income). The performance of a particular country is shown in relation to the average of its group. The indicators are combined visually by being displayed together but are not combined numerically. The Asian Development Bank's environment diamond is the same concept. Its four axes display compound indicators of air quality, water quality, land condition, and biodiversity. The performance of each of seven Asian countries is shown in relation to the average of the group.[16]

Polygons such as the development and environment diamonds can be effective at showing differences in performance among elements and indicators, but with one variable shown per axis (point of the polygon), they work

**Table B6. Environmental Pressure Index: types of pollution and their sustainability or no-major-effect levels.**

| *Compound Indicator:* <br> *Type of Pollution* | *Objective: Sustainability Level* |
|---|---|
| Greenhouse gases | Preindustrial levels (background rates) |
| Acidification | Level at which little damage occurs to vegetation on sensitive sites |
| Eutrophication | Soil: equilibrium fertilization (balance between nutrient addition and removal) <br> Water: zero (nutrient carrying capacity already reached or exceeded) |
| Toxic substances | Maximum acceptable risk (national standard) |
| Solid waste disposal | As low as possible |
| Nuisance from noise and odor | As low as possible |

**Table B7. Human Development Index: indicators and their end points.**

| *Element* | *Indicator* | *Top End = 1* | *Bottom End = 0* |
|---|---|---|---|
| Longevity | Life expectancy at birth | 85 years | 25 years |
| Education | Adult literacy rate | 100% | 0% |
| | Combined gross enrollment rate | 100% | 0% |
| Standard of living | Real GDP per capita | PPP$40,000 | PPP$100 |

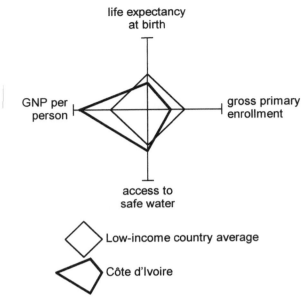

**Figure B10. Example of a development diamond.** Côte d'Ivoire has above average GNP per person and access to safe water, and below average life expectancy at birth and gross primary school enrollment, in relation to other low-income countries (World Bank 1995).

best when dealing with a few elements or indicators. (AMOEBA, used in the Dutch Water Management Plan, is a variable polygon with as many as 32 axes, which can be pretty confusing.)[17] Another drawback to polygons is that they are not convenient for showing change over time or the performance of more than one society per polygon.

The advantage of setting the scale on the basis of *observed* performance (as in the HDI and the development diamond) is that the range of past and present performance is a verifiable fact. The disadvantage is that the results merely show one society's performance in relation to others. It may be at the top, the bottom, or in the middle—but its rank is meaningless if everyone is doing well or badly. The Environmental Sustainability Index records where a country falls along a continuum of performance defined by the best-performing country at one end and the worst at the other; it does not show whether the best-performing country is close to sustainability or far from it.

Setting the scale on the basis of objectives or *desired* performance (as in the EPI and the Barometer of Sustainability) is more informative. The results can show not just whether a society is doing well or badly but how well or

badly—which also provides for a more meaningful comparison with other societies.

## Notes

1. Requests for courses should be sent to Robert Prescott-Allen, PADATA, 627 Aquarius Road, Victoria, British Columbia, V9C 4G5, Canada; fax +1 250 474 6976; e-mail rpa@wellbeing-of-nations.ca. The training kit can be obtained from IUCN Monitoring & Evaluation Initiative, Rue Mauverney 28, Gland, 1196, Switzerland; fax +41 22 999 0025; phone +41 22 999 0001; e-mail mail@hq.iucn.org.

2. Colombia team: Natalia Ortiz and Hernando Sanchez, Monitoring and Evaluation Unit, Fundación Pro Sierra Nevada de Santa Marta. Zimbabwe teams: Sam Chimbuya and Carmel Lue-Mbizvo, IUCN Assessment Team, IUCN Regional Office for Southern Africa; Elliot Mhaka, Cephas Chidenga, Douglas Chimhande, Joseph Chizororo, Peter Gambara, Davison Haukozi, Zii Masiye, John Mbetu, Peter Mfumu, John Mupingo, Constantine Mushure, Aaaron Tshabangu, and Unity Tshabangu, District Environmental Action Plan (DEAP) Core Team, Government of Zimbabwe. India team: Ashok Kumar, Vijay Pillay, V. A. Abraham, Subash Marcus, and George Varughese, Development Alternatives.

3. Italy's regions, provinces, and municipalities: Touring Club Italiano (1993).

4. At present Combo is available only in a 16-bit version, which does not work with all 32-bit applications, although it works well with the 32-bit version of Map Maker (Appendix E). Combo can be obtained from IUCN or from me (see note 1 for contact details). Improved software, called Wellbeing Barometers, is being developed.

5. Hardi & Zdan (1977). Requests for copies of the Bellagio principles should be sent to the International Institute for Sustainable Development (IISD), 161 Portage East, 6th Floor, Winnipeg, Manitoba, R3B 0Y4, Canada; fax +1 204 958 7710; e-mail: reception@iisdpost.iisd.ca.

6. UNDP (1990, 1994).

7. IUCN/UNEP/WWF (1980).

8. UNEP GEO model: Bakkes & van Woerden (1997), Swart & Bakkes (1995). World Resources Institute (WRI) approach: Hammond et al. (1995). Other methods: Corson (1996) uses a pair of indices—environmental sustainability (ecosystem) and socioeconomic sustainability (people)—to assess the sustainability of ten industrial nations. Hodge (1995) divides his essentially dual framework (people and ecosystems) into four domains: people, interactions between people and ecosystems, ecosystems, and synthesis.

9. Consultative Group on Sustainable Development Indicators (2000).
10. United Nations (1996).
11. Equivalent effects: Adriaanse (1993). Weight: Adriaanse et al. (1997). Area and Ecological Footprint (discussed further in Chapter 3): Wackernagel & Rees (1996); Wackernagel et al. (2000).
12. Appendix A describes economic accounts. The cost of remediation index adds the estimated costs of targets for reductions in pollution, erosion, waste generation, etc.:

Harvard University Environmental Systems Program (1996).
13. Adriaanse (1993).
14. UNDP (1990, 1994, 1997, 2000).
15. Global Leaders for Environment Tomorrow Task Force (2001).
16. Development diamond: World Bank (1998). Environment diamond: Harvard University Environmental Systems Program (1996).
17. Bakkes et al. (1994).

# *Appendix C.*
# Performance Criteria Chosen for
# *The Wellbeing of Nations*

In Wellbeing Assessment, performance criteria are chosen for each indicator to make the indicators more operational and to enable indicator measurements to be converted to a score so that they can be combined. Choosing performance criteria involves defining the levels of performance for the indicator concerned that correspond to the base and the tops of the bands of the Barometer of Sustainability (Table C1).

This appendix describes the types of performance criteria chosen for *The Wellbeing of Nations* (WoN) and the basis for selecting them. Table C2 gives examples of each type and the number of indicators per type. Table C3 gives examples of each basis for selection and the number of indicators per basis. Tables C4 (human indicators) and C5 (ecosystem indicators) list all the performance criteria and classify them by type and basis.

### Table C1. The five-band scale of the Barometer of Sustainability.
Performance criteria define levels of performance that correspond to the base of the scale and the top of each band.

| Band | Range of Points | Top Point | Definition of Band |
|------|-----------------|-----------|--------------------|
| Good | 100–81 | 100 | Desirable performance, objective fully met |
| Fair | 80–61 | 80 | Acceptable performance, objective almost or barely met |
| Medium | 60–41 | 60 | Neutral or transitional performance |
| Poor | 40–21 | 40 | Undesirable performance |
| Bad | 20–1 | 20 | Unacceptable performance |
| Base | 0 | 0 | Base of scale |

## *Types of Performance Criteria*

Indicators can be classified in five performance groups:

1. *Best possible performance is 0, 100%, or parity.* Examples are homicide rate (0), percentage of population with safe water and basic sanitation (100%), and female share of income (parity). What must be decided here is how far from best possible good performance becomes merely fair performance and at what point fair becomes medium.

2. *No limit to best possible performance but worst possible is 0 or 100%.* Examples are income ($0) and dissolved oxygen in running waters (100% saturation). What must be decided here is how far from worst possible bad performance becomes poor performance and at what point poor becomes medium.

3. *A sustainable level can be defined, on both sides of which conditions are unsustainable.* An example is the total fertility rate (TFR, the average number of children born alive by a woman in her lifetime). In this case, the sustainable rate is the replacement rate, or 2.1 (with average sex ratios). Populations will grow if their TFRs are above this rate and will decline if they are below it.

4. *A sustainable level can be defined, on only one side of which conditions are unsustainable.* An example is timber fellings as a percentage of net annual increment. In this case, the sustainable rate is 100% or (using the precautionary principle) less than 100%. If fellings are much less than 100% no harm is done because the forest will eventually reach a natural state with a high proportion of old trees.

5. *A range of good or bad performance can be broadly defined,* but no definite best possible, worst possible, or sustainable level. An example is energy consumption per person.

For many indicators it is useful for the performance criteria to increase or decline exponentially (in doublings) from the best point to reflect the increasing difficulty of improving performance as one approaches the ideal. An example is the threatened species indicator. Conversely, in a number of cases it makes sense for the performance criteria to increase or decline exponentially from the worst point to reflect diminishing returns (for example, income per person).

An exponential scale also accommodates a wide range of performance while keeping high standards for the good and fair bands. For example, child mortality rates range from 263 to 6 deaths per 1,000 live births. The United Nations (UN) target is for all countries to have rates below 45 deaths by 2015. An exponential scale from 0 to 360 accommodates the current range of performance and puts 45 at the top of the medium band, so that less than 45 is fair and half of 45 is good. A scale with bands of equal size could not do this. If it kept 45 at the top of medium, the base of the scale would be 112.5 deaths, which would exclude the performance of 44 countries. If the base of an equally divided scale were set at 265 to accommodate the current range of performance, the top of medium would rise to 106, and even the top of fair (at 53) would be worse performance than the UN target of 45.

Because of these advantages, WoN performance criteria are exponential except when bands are set at levels that make an exponential scale unnecessary, impractical, or excessively long. An example is life expectancy at birth. The range of current and projected performance is 34–84 years. UN targets are for countries to achieve 60 years by 2000, over 70 years by 2005, and over 75 years by 2015. If best is set at 85 years and the targets of 60, 70, and 75 years are used to define the tops of poor, medium, and fair respectively, an exponential scale is unnecessary.

In all, 10 types of performance criteria can be distinguished (Table C2), depending on which performance group the indicator is in and whether the criteria change exponentially.

## Basis for Choosing Performance Criteria

In Wellbeing Assessment, the base of the scale and the tops of the bands are defined on the basis of three factors:

*The range of performance.* As a general rule, base–best (0–100) should encompass the range of performance. However, if outliers of extreme performance would distort the scale, it can be cut off (at the bottom or at the top). For example, the scale for the indicator "tons of fertilizer per 1,000 harvested hectares" was cut off at 320 tons to prevent distortion by a few countries that use very much higher levels (up to 2,426 tons). In WoN, to prevent arbitrary shortening of the scale, base–best encompassed the range of performance of more than 90% of the countries in all cases except fecal coliforms.

*The objective of the element concerned.* For example, the objective of the peace and order element is "peaceful communities, protected from crime and violence," implying an absence of armed conflict and low levels of military expenditure and violent crime. This guided the setting of the good and fair bands of the peace and crime indicators.

*At least one of the following:*

A. *Estimated sustainable rate.* For example, a sustainable rate of timber felling would be less than 100% of net annual increment. In WoN, estimated sustainable rates were usually placed at the top of the medium band (rather than at the top of the fair band) for two reasons. First, to comply with the precautionary principle that use levels should be well within the calculated capacity of the target population and its supporting ecosystem. Second, to ensure that if local conditions call for a different rate, it is still likely to be sustainable. For example, a sustainable rate of 4 tons of fish catch per ton of fishing capacity was derived from an estimate of global maximum sustainable yield (MSY). The MSY of a national fishery could be substantially lower or higher. Putting the global rate at the top of medium ensured that a catch that exceeded a lower national MSY would not receive a good score.

B. *Estimated background rate* ("natural" or "normal" performance). For example, the background rate of human-caused land degradation is 0. In WoN, estimated background rates were usually placed at best, with the top of fair placed fairly close. In the case of land degradation, best was defined as 0% and the top of fair as 10%.

C. *Other threshold.* For example, a single death represents the threshold between peace and armed conflict.

D. *International standard.* For example, a UN standard for water quality is less than 30 milligrams of nitrogen per liter of water. In WoN, international standards were placed at best, the top of fair, or the top of medium, depending on the range of current performance. If a standard covers different levels of performance, these levels were placed at the tops of the appropriate bands. Thus the international standards for inland water quality define pollutant levels for excellent, good, fair, poor, and bad water quality classes. These were adopted to define the good, fair, medium, poor, and bad bands, respectively.

E. *International target.* For example, a UN target for education is 100% primary education by 2015. In WoN, international targets were placed at best, the top of fair, or the top of medium, depending on how ambitious they are. Targets such as universal primary education and elimination of ozone depleting substances cannot be bettered and formed the top of the good band. The ambitiousness of less absolute targets were judged from the range of performance: if few societies exceed them, they were put at the top of the fair band; if many, at the top of the medium band. Sometimes, however, other considerations prevailed: international targets set the top of the fair band of three of WoN's food sufficiency indicators but the top of the medium band of the fourth to aid interpretation by enabling the performance criteria of all four indicators to match.

F. *Expert opinion.* For example, the World Bank's classification of debt ratios and Freedom House's rating of press freedom.

G. *Derivation from a related indicator.* For example, in the absence of a specific UN target, the performance criteria for secondary education are a less stringent version of those for primary education.

H. *Personal judgment.* If none of the above factors is available, the bands are defined on the basis of personal judgment.

**Table C2. WoN performance criteria by type.** There are 10 types, depending on the indicator performance group and whether the scale is exponential or nonexponential.

| Indicator Performance Group | 1. Exponential Scale | | 2. Nonexponential Scale | |
| --- | --- | --- | --- | --- |
| | *No. of Indicators* | *Example* | *No. of Indicators* | *Example* |
| 1. Best possible performance is 0, 100%, or parity | 23 | Homicides per 100,000 population | 29 | Women's share of seats in parliament |
| 2. Worst possible performance is 0 or 100% | 4 | Tertiary school enrollment | 3 | Dissolved oxygen in inland waters |
| 3. Sustainable level, both sides of which are unsustainable | 0 | — | 1 | Total fertility rate |
| 4. Sustainable level, one side of which is unsustainable | 4 | Annual change in native forest area | 2 | Timber fellings + imports as a percentage of net annual increment |
| 5. Range of good or bad performance | 6 | Energy consumption per person | 15 | Life expectancy at birth |
| TOTAL | 37 | — | 50 | — |

**Table C3. WoN performance criteria by basis for selection** (in addition to the range of performance and the objective of the element concerned).

| Basis for Selection | No. of Indicators | Example |
|---|---|---|
| A. Estimated sustainable rate | 7 | Tons of catch per ton of fishing fleet capacity |
| B. Estimated background rate | 3 | Degraded land as a percentage of total cultivated + modified land |
| C. Other threshold | 6 | Deaths from armed conflict |
| D. International standard | 21 | Annual mean ambient air concentration of sulfur dioxide |
| E. International target | 13 | Life expectancy at birth |
| F. Expert opinion | 6 | Press freedom rating |
| G. Derivation from related indicator | 6 | Food production as a percentage of supply (derived from food sufficiency indicators) |
| H. Personal judgment | 25 | Ratio of richest 20%'s income share to poorest 20%'s |
| TOTAL | 87 | — |

**Table C4. Performance criteria for human indicators used in *The Wellbeing of Nations*.**

| Indicator | Unit | Base | Top of Bad | Top of Poor | Top of Medium | Top of Fair | Top of Good | Type of Performance Criteria and Basis for Selection |
|---|---|---|---|---|---|---|---|---|
| Life expectancy at birth | years | 30 | 45 | 60 | 70 | 75 | 85 | Type: 5.2. Basis: E. Base–best encompasses current range of 34–81 years and projected high of 84 years by 2050. Tops of poor, medium, and fair match UN targets of at least 60 years by 2000, >70 years by 2005, >75 years by 2015. |
| Healthy life expectancy at birth | years | 24 | 39 | 54 | 64 | 69 | 79 | Type: 5.2. Basis: G. Base–best encompasses current range of 26–75 years. Base and tops of poor, medium, fair, and good set at 6 points (or 7.1–20.0%) below the corresponding points for unadjusted life expectancy, close to the range of percentages of lifespan lost to disability (7.0–25.1%). |
| Child mortality rate [included for comparison but not counted as an indicator] | deaths/ 1,000 live births | 360 | 180 | 90 | 45 | 22 | 0 | Type: 1.1. Basis: E. Base–best encompasses current range of 263–6 deaths. Top of medium matches UN target of <45 deaths by 2015. |
| Total fertility rate | children/ woman | 8.2 | 5.0 | 3.4 | 2.6 | 2.2 | 1.2 | Type: 3.2. Basis: A. Base–best encompasses current range of 7.6–1.2 children. Top of fair is a point below the replacement rate of 2.1 children. |
| Population with insufficient food | % | 100 | 50 | 35 | 20 | 10 | 0 | Type: 1.2. Basis: E. Base–best encompasses current range of 73–1%. Top of fair matches World Food Summit target to halve the number of hungry people by 2015. |
| Prevalence of stunting (low height for age) in children under 5 | % | 100 | 50 | 35 | 20 | 10 | 0 | Type: 1.2. Basis: E. Base–best encompasses current range of 64–1%. Top of medium matches WHO target of <20% by 2020. |
| Prevalence of underweight (low weight for age) children under 5 | % | 100 | 50 | 35 | 20 | 10 | 0 | Type: 1.2. Basis: E. Base–best encompasses current range of 60–1%. Top of fair matches WHO target of not more than 10%. |
| Prevalence of babies with low birth weight | % | 100 | 50 | 35 | 20 | 10 | 0 | Type: 1.2. Basis: E. Base–best encompasses current range of 50–2%. Top of fair matches WHO target of not more than 10%. |
| Population with safe water and basic sanitation | % | 0 | 50 | 65 | 80 | 90 | 100 | Type: 1.2. Basis: E. Base–best encompasses current range of 3–100%. Best matches UN target of 100%. |
| Gross domestic product per person | $PPP | 0 | 2,000 | 5,000 | 10,000 | 20,000 | 40,000 | Type: 2.2. Basis: C. Base–best encompasses current range of PPP$460–33,505. Bands are based on the relationship between income and health, population, knowledge, and community. |
| Annual inflation rate | % | 60 | 35 | 10 | 6 | 3 | 0 | Type: 5.2. Basis: E. Current range is +1,005 to –2%. Base–best encompasses performance of 91% of countries. Tops of good and fair match the range of official inflation targets. Top of poor reflects the consensus that inflation of 10% or more is harmful. |

| Indicator | Unit | Base | Top of Bad | Top of Poor | Top of Medium | Top of Fair | Top of Good | Type of Performance Criteria and Basis for Selection |
|---|---|---|---|---|---|---|---|---|
| Annual unemployment rate | % | 35 | 25 | 15 | 10 | 5 | 0 | Type: 5.2. Basis: G. Current range is 72.5–0.4%. Base–best encompasses performance of 98% of countries. The tops of fair and medium are somewhat above the equivalent points for inflation. |
| Present value of debt service as a percentage of exports of goods and services | % | 440 | 220 | 132 | 66 | 33 | 0 | Type: 1.2. Basis: F. Current range is 3,090–14%. Base–best encompasses performance of 91% of countries. Tops of bad and poor match the points at which the World Bank classifies a country as severely and moderately indebted, respectively. |
| Present value of debt service as a percentage of gross national product | % | 160 | 80 | 48 | 24 | 12 | 0 | Type: 1.2. Basis: F. Current range is 678–3%. Base–best encompasses performance of 93% of countries. Tops of bad and poor match the points at which the World Bank classifies a country as severely and moderately indebted, respectively. |
| Ratio of short-term debt to international reserves | ratio | 8.0 | 4.0 | 2.0 | 1.0 | 0.5 | 0.0 | Type: 1.2. Basis: C. Current range is 4,914–0. Base–best encompasses performance of 93% of countries. Top of medium is the benchmark suggested by the International Monetary Fund for the reverse indicator (ratio of international reserves to short-term debt) and in poorly regulated markets is the point above which a country is vulnerable to creditor panic. |
| Gross public debt (general government gross financial liabilities) as a percentage of gross domestic product | % | 151 | 121 | 91 | 61 | 31 | 1 | Type: 5.2. Basis: E. Base–best encompasses current range of 118.8–6.0%. Top of medium matches the Treaty of Maastricht's standard of no more than 60% for an acceptable ratio of public debt to GDP. |
| Annual central government deficit/surplus as a percentage of gross domestic product | % | –12.1 | –9.1 | –6.1 | –3.1 | –0.1 | 2.9 | Type: 5.2. Basis: E. Current range is –15.1 to +11.7%. Base–best encompasses performance of 92% of countries. Top of medium matches the Treaty of Maastricht's standard of no more than 3% for an acceptable budget deficit. |
| Net primary school enrollment | % of age group | 20 | 60 | 80 | 90 | 95 | 100 | Type: 1.1. Basis: E. Current range is 13.2–99.9%. Base–best encompasses performance of 99% of countries. Best matches UN target of 100% by 2015. |
| Net secondary school enrollment | % of age group | 0 | 30 | 60 | 80 | 90 | 100 | Type: 1.2. Basis: G. Base–best encompasses current range of 8.0–99.9%. In the absence of a target, top of fair is set less stringently than for primary enrollment. |
| Tertiary school enrollment | per 10,000 population | 0 | 35 | 70 | 140 | 280 | 560 | Type: 2.1. Basis: C. Current range is 2.6–610.6 per 10,000. Base–best encompasses performance of 98% of countries. Good is set to include the lowest rates of countries with the largest proportions of highly literate adults. |
| Main telephone lines and cellular phones per 100 persons | % | 0 | 6 | 12 | 25 | 50 | 100 | Type: 2.1. Basis: H. Current range is 0.1–113.8%. Base–best encompasses performance of 98% of countries. Top of fair is point at which, in general, 95% of households have a main line. |
| Faults per 100 main telephone lines | % | 200 | 100 | 50 | 25 | 12 | 0 | Type: 1.1 Basis: H. Current range is 761.0–1.1%. Base–best encompasses performance of 97% of countries. Top of bad set at 1 fault/line/year. |
| Internet users | per 10,000 population | 0 | 75 | 150 | 300 | 600 | 1,200 | Type: 2.1. Basis: H. Current range is 0–3,953. Base–best encompasses performance of 92% of countries. |

| Indicator | Unit | Base | Top of Bad | Top of Poor | Top of Medium | Top of Fair | Top of Good | Type of Performance Criteria and Basis for Selection |
|---|---|---|---|---|---|---|---|---|
| Political rights rating | points | 0 | 20 | 40 | 60 | 80 | 100 | Type: 5.2. Basis: F. Base–best encompasses current range of 0–90 points. Freedom House points put on Barometer scale so that "free" = good or fair, "partly free" = medium, and "not free" = poor or bad. |
| Civil liberties rating | points | 0 | 20 | 40 | 60 | 80 | 100 | Type: 5.2. Basis: F. Base–best encompasses current range of 0–90 points. Freedom House points put on Barometer scale on same basis as political rights rating. |
| Press freedom rating | points | 100 | 75 | 50 | 30 | 15 | 0 | Type: 5.2. Basis: F. Base–best encompasses current range of 100–15. Freedom House points put on Barometer scale on same basis as political rights rating. |
| Corruption perceptions index | points | 0 | 2 | 4 | 6 | 8 | 10 | Type: 1.2. Basis: F. Base–best encompasses current range of 1.2–10 points. Transparency International's scale placed directly on the Barometer scale. |
| Deaths from armed conflicts per year | number | 10,000 | 1,000 | 0 | -- | -- | -- | Type: 1.2. Basis: C. Current range is 84,100–0 deaths. Base–best encompasses performance of 90% of countries. Bands set so that any armed conflict results in at least a poor score. |
| Military expenditure as a percentage of gross domestic product | % | 32 | 16 | 8 | 4 | 2 | 0 | Type: 1.1. Basis: H. Current range is 35.8–0.5%. Base–best encompasses performance of 99% of countries. |
| Homicides | per 100,000 population | 80 | 40 | 20 | 10 | 5 | 0 | Type: 1.1. Basis: H. Current range is 142–0.4 homicides/100,000. Base–best encompasses performance of 97% of countries. |
| Rapes | per 100,000 population | 160 | 80 | 40 | 20 | 10 | 0 | Type: 1.1. Basis: H. Current range is 199–0 rapes/100,000. Base–best encompasses performance of 99% of countries. |
| Robberies | per 100,000 population | 320 | 160 | 80 | 40 | 20 | 0 | Type: 1.1. Basis: H. Current range is 688–0.1 robberies/100,000. Base–best encompasses performance of 97% of countries. |
| Assaults | per 100,000 population | 640 | 320 | 160 | 80 | 40 | 0 | Type: 1.1. Basis: H. Current range is 1,487–0.2/assaults per 100,000. Base–best encompasses performance of 91% of countries. |
| Ratio of richest 20%'s income share to poorest 20%'s | ratio | 33:1 | 17:1 | 9:1 | 5:1 | 3:1 | 1:1 | Type: 1.1. Basis: H. Base–best encompasses current range of 32.5:1–2.6:1. |
| Ratio of male income to female income | ratio | 9:1 | 5:1 | 3:1 | 2:1 | 1.5:1 | 1:1 | Type: 1.1. Basis: H. Base–best encompasses current range of 6.2:1–1.2:1. |
| Average difference between male and female school enrollment rates | % | 80 | 40 | 20 | 10 | 5 | 0 | Type: 1.1. Basis: E. Current range is 170.7–0%. Base–best encompasses performance of 98% of countries. Best matches UN target of 0% by 2005. |
| Women's share of seats in parliament | % | 0 | 10 | 20 | 30 | 40 | 50 | Type: 1.2. Basis: H. Base–best encompasses current range of 0–36.8%. |

**Table C5. Performance criteria for ecosystem indicators used in *The Wellbeing of Nations*.**

| Indicator | Unit | Base | Top of Bad | Top of Poor | Top of Medium | Top of Fair | Top of Good | Type of Performance Criteria and Basis for Selection |
|---|---|---|---|---|---|---|---|---|
| Converted land as a percentage of total land | % | 100 | 80 | 60 | 40 | 20 | 0 | Type: 5.2. Basis: C. Base–best encompasses current range of 75.5–0.7%. Top of medium is based on the landscape pattern theory that habitat becomes dissected into isolated patches below 60% coverage (= 40% converted). |
| Natural land as a percentage of total land | % | 0 | 20 | 40 | 60 | 80 | 100 | Type: 5.2. Basis: C. Base–best encompasses current range of 0.0–94.0%. Top of medium is set on same basis as converted land. |
| Annual change in native forest area | % | –5.7 | –2.5 | –0.9 | –0.1 | 0.0 | 0.8 | Type: 4.1. Basis: A. Current range is –7.4 to +0.7%. Base–best encompasses performance of 98% of countries. Tops of fair and medium have been set so that an increase in forest area gets a good score and only stability or a decline of less than 0.05% gets a fair score. |
| Protected land (+ inland waters) as a percentage of total land (+ inland waters) | weighted % | 0 | 2.5 | 5 | 10 | 20 | 40 | Type: 2.1. Basis: E. Current range is 0–67.5 weighted %. Base–best encompasses performance of 97% of countries. Top of medium matches international target of full protection of 10% of each major ecosystem type. |
| Degraded land as a percentage of cultivated + modified land | weighted % | 160 | 80 | 40 | 20 | 10 | 0 | Type: 1.1. Basis: B. Base–best encompasses current range of 0–150 weighted %. Best matches the background rate of human-induced soil degradation on natural land. |
| Dam capacity as a percentage of total water supply | % | 100 | 60 | 40 | 20 | 10 | 0 | Type: 1.2. Basis: H. Current range is 279–0%. Base–best encompasses performance of 91% of countries. |
| Flow dammed for hydropower as a percentage of dammable flow | % | 100 | 60 | 40 | 20 | 10 | 0 | Type: 1.2. Basis: H. Base–best encompasses current range of 100–0%. |
| Dissolved oxygen in inland waters | mg/l | 1 | 3 | 4 | 6 | 9 | 12 | Type: 2.2. Basis: B and D. Current range is 0.0–15.5 mg/l. Base–best encompasses performance at 98% of stations. Best and top of fair correspond to the range for 100% oxygen saturation of natural running waters. Tops of medium, poor, and bad match UNECE quality classes. |
| Biochemical oxygen demand (BOD) | mg $O_2$/l | 30 | 15 | 9 | 5 | 3 | 0 | Type: 1.2. Basis: D. Current range is 78.0–0.0 mg/l. Base–best encompasses performance at 99% of stations. Tops of fair, medium, poor, and bad match UNECE quality classes. |
| Chemical oxygen demand (COD) | mg $O_2$/l | 60 | 30 | 20 | 10 | 3 | 0 | Type: 1.2. Basis: D. Current range is 220.0–2.0 mg/l. Base–best encompasses performance at 94% of stations. Tops of fair, medium, poor, and bad match UNECE quality classes. |
| Nitrogen in inland waters | mg N/l | 25.0 | 2.50 | 1.50 | 0.75 | 0.30 | 0 | Type: 1.2. Basis: D. Current range is 63.7–0.00 mg/l. Base–best encompasses performance at 99% of stations. Tops of fair, medium, poor, and bad match UNECE quality classes. |
| Phosphorus in inland waters | mg P/l | 1.25 | 0.125 | 0.050 | 0.025 | 0.010 | 0 | Type: 1.2. Basis: D. Current range is 2.085–0.00 mg/l. Base–best encompasses performance at 98% of stations. Tops of fair, medium, poor, and bad match UNECE quality classes. |
| Alkalinity of inland waters | mg $CaCO_3$/l | 0 | 10 | 20 | 100 | 200 | 400 | Type: 2.2. Basis: D. Current range is 0.0–429.8 mg/l. Base–best encompasses performance at 98% of stations. Tops of fair, medium, poor, and bad match UNECE quality classes. |
| Acidity of inland waters | pH | 4.5 | 5.3 | 6.0 | 6.3 | 6.5 | 8.5 | Type: 5.2. Basis: D. Current range is 5.9–8.8. Base–best encompasses performance at 97% of stations. Best and tops of fair, medium, poor, and bad match UNECE quality classes. |

| Indicator | Unit | Base | Top of Bad | Top of Poor | Top of Medium | Top of Fair | Top of Good | Type of Performance Criteria and Basis for Selection |
|---|---|---|---|---|---|---|---|---|
| Total suspended solids in inland waters | mg/l | 2,000 | 1,000 | 500 | 250 | 125 | 0 | Type: 5.1. Basis: D. Current range is 8,470–0 mg/l. Base–best encompasses performance at 98% of stations. Top of bad is point at which water quality is seriously reduced. |
| Fecal coliforms in inland waters | number/100 ml | 10,000 | 1,000 | 100 | 30 | 10 | 0 | Type: 5.2. Basis: D. Current range is 1,100,000–0/100 ml. Base–best encompasses performance at 78% of stations. Tops of fair, medium, poor, and bad match UNECE quality classes. |
| Arsenic in inland waters | micrograms (µg)/l | 200 | 100 | 50 | 10 | 5 | 0 | Type: 1.2. Basis: D. Current range is 428–1 µg/l. Base–best encompasses performance at 99% of stations. Tops of medium, poor, and bad match UNECE quality classes. |
| Cadmium in inland waters | µg/l | 18.0 | 1.8 | 0.7 | 0.07 | 0.03 | 0 | Type: 1.2. Basis: D. Current range is 37.0–0.01 µg/l. Base–best encompasses performance at 94% of stations. Tops of medium, poor, and bad match UNECE quality classes. |
| Chromium in inland waters | µg/l | 80 | 16 | 11 | 1 | 0.5 | 0 | Type: 1.2. Basis: D. Current range is 551–0 µg/l. Base–best encompasses performance at 98% of stations. Tops of medium, poor, and bad match UNECE quality classes. |
| Copper in inland waters | µg/l | 92 | 9.2 | 6.5 | 2 | 1 | 0 | Type: 1.2. Basis: D. Current range is 214.0–0.2 µg/l. Base–best encompasses performance at 99% of stations. Tops of medium, poor, and bad match UNECE quality classes. |
| Lead in inland waters | µg/l | 68 | 34 | 1.3 | 0.1 | 0.05 | 0 | Type: 1.2. Basis: D. Current range is 194.0–0.1 µg/l. Base–best encompasses performance at 93% of stations. Tops of medium, poor, and bad match UNECE quality classes. |
| Mercury in inland waters | µg/l | 2.5 | 2.4 | 0.012 | 0.003 | 0.002 | 0 | Type: 1.2. Basis: D. Current range is 5.426–0.000 µg/l. Base–best encompasses performance at 99% of stations. Tops of medium, poor, and bad match UNECE quality classes. |
| Nickel in inland waters | µg/l | 800 | 790 | 88 | 15 | 7.5 | 0 | Type: 1.2. Basis: D. Base–best encompasses current range of 129–1 µg/l. Tops of medium, poor, and bad match UNECE quality classes. |
| Zinc in inland waters | µg/l | 260 | 65 | 59 | 45 | 22 | 0 | Type: 1.2. Basis: D. Current range is 1,154–1 µg/l. Base–best encompasses performance at 97% of stations. Tops of medium, poor, and bad match UNECE quality classes. |
| Water withdrawal as a percentage of internal renewable supply | % | 200 | 100 | 50 | 20 | 10 | 0 | Type: 4.2. Basis: A. Current range is 54,000–0%. Base–best encompasses performance of 91% of countries. Top of bad matches a point that is clearly unsustainable. |
| Carbon dioxide emissions per person | kg carbon | 6,400 | 3,200 | 1,600 | 800 | 400 | 0 | Type: 4.1. Basis: A and B. Current range is 18,197–0 kg. Base–best encompasses performance of 98% of countries. Top of fair matches the point below which carbon emissions per person must fall to keep atmospheric concentrations at less than double the preindustrial level. |
| Use of ozone depleting substances (ODSs) per person | g ozone depleting potential | 400 | 200 | 100 | 50 | 25 | 0 | Type: 1.1. Basis: B and E. Current range is 2,413–0 g. Base–best encompasses performance of 98% of countries. Best matches international agreements to eliminate ODSs. |
| Annual mean ambient air concentration of sulfur dioxide | µg/m³ | 400 | 200 | 100 | 50 | 25 | 0 | Type: 1.1. Basis: D. Base–best encompasses current range of 330–0 µg/m³. Top of medium matches WHO guideline. Top of poor matches lowest observed effect level. |

| Indicator | Unit | Base | Top of Bad | Top of Poor | Top of Medium | Top of Fair | Top of Good | Type of Performance Criteria and Basis for Selection |
|---|---|---|---|---|---|---|---|---|
| Days ambient air concentration of sulfur dioxide exceeds WHO guideline | number | 224 | 112 | 56 | 28 | 14 | 0 | Type: 1.1. Basis: H. Base–best encompasses current recorded range of 64–0 days. |
| Annual mean ambient air concentration of nitrogen dioxide | µg/m³ | 320 | 160 | 80 | 40 | 20 | 0 | Type: 1.1. Basis: D. Base–best encompasses current range of 248.4–2.3 µg/m³. Top of medium matches WHO guideline. |
| Days ambient air concentration of nitrogen dioxide exceeds WHO guideline | number | 224 | 112 | 56 | 28 | 14 | 0 | Type: 1.1. Basis: H. Base–best encompasses current recorded range of 160–0 days. |
| Days ambient air concentration of ozone exceeds WHO guideline | number | 224 | 112 | 56 | 28 | 14 | 0 | Type: 1.1. Basis: H. Current range is 309–0 days. Base–best encompasses performance at 94% of stations. |
| Days ambient air concentration of carbon monoxide exceeds WHO guideline | number | 224 | 112 | 56 | 28 | 14 | 0 | Type: 1.1. Basis: H. Base–best encompasses current range of 50–0 days. |
| Annual mean ambient air concentration of suspended particulate matter (SPM) | µg/m³ | 720 | 360 | 180 | 90 | 45 | 0 | Type: 1.1. Basis: D. Base–best encompasses current range of 543–9.4 µg/m³. Top of medium matches WHO guideline. |
| Annual mean ambient air concentration of fine particulates 10 micrometers or less in diameter (PM10) | µg/m³ | 400 | 200 | 100 | 50 | 25 | 0 | Type: 1.1. Basis: H. Current range is 544–4 µg/m³. Base–best encompasses performance at 99% of stations. Tops of fair and medium represent 2% and 4% increases in daily mortality from PM10, respectively. |
| Annual mean ambient air concentration of lead | µg/m³ | 4 | 2 | 1 | 0.5 | 0.25 | 0 | Type: 1.1. Basis: D. Base–best encompasses current range of 2.7–0.0 µg/m³. Top of medium matches WHO guideline. |
| Threatened species in a group as a percentage of total species in that group: plants | % | 32 | 16 | 8 | 4 | 2 | 0 | Type: 1.1. Basis: B. Current range is 43.0–0.7%. Base–best encompasses performance of 91% of countries. Top of fair based on estimated background extinction rate of <0.01% per century. |
| Threatened species in a group as a percentage of total species in that group: animals | % | 32 | 16 | 8 | 4 | 2 | 0 | Type: 1.1. Basis: B. Current range is 68.5–0.8%. Base–best encompasses performance of 96% of countries. Top of fair based on estimated background extinction rate of <0.01% per century. |

| Indicator | Unit | Base | Top of Bad | Top of Poor | Top of Medium | Top of Fair | Top of Good | Type of Performance Criteria and Basis for Selection |
|---|---|---|---|---|---|---|---|---|
| Number of not-at-risk breeds per million head of a species | number | 0 | 1 | 2 | 5 | 10 | 20 | Type: 5.2. Basis: H. Current range is 0.1–63.5. Base–best encompasses performance of 99% of countries. |
| Ratio of threatened to not-at-risk breeds of a species | ratio | 2.0 | 1.0 | 0.5 | 0.2 | 0.1 | 0.0 | Type: 5.2. Basis: H. Current range is 3.5:1–0.0:1. Base–best encompasses performance of 98% of countries. |
| Energy consumption per hectare of total area | gigajoules (GJ) | 640 | 320 | 160 | 80 | 40 | 0 | Type: 5.1. Basis: H. Current range is 16,725.8–0.3 GJ. Base–best encompasses performance of 96% of countries. |
| Energy consumption per person | GJ | 640 | 320 | 160 | 80 | 40 | 0 | Type: 5.1. Basis: H. Current range is 1,294.2–1.6 GJ. Base–best encompasses performance of 99% of countries. |
| Food produced per harvested hectare | metric tons | 0 | 1 | 2 | 4 | 8 | 16 | Type: 5.1. Basis: H. Current range is 0.3–56.3 mt. Base–best encompasses performance of 95% of countries. |
| Fertilizer consumed per 1,000 harvested hectares | metric tons | 320 | 160 | 80 | 40 | 20 | 0 | Type: 5.1. Basis: H. Current range is 2,425.7–0.1 mt. Base–best encompasses performance of 96% of countries. |
| Food production as a percentage of supply | % | 0 | 50 | 65 | 80 | 90 | 100 | Type: 1.2. Basis: G. Base–best encompasses current range of 1–100%. Criteria mirror those for food sufficiency. |
| Depleted + overexploited fishery species as a percentage of assessed species | % | 100 | 50 | 35 | 20 | 10 | 0 | Type: 1.2. Basis: G. Base–best encompasses current range of 100–0%. Tops of fair and medium set at five times those for the threatened wild species indicators. |
| Tons of fishing fleet capacity per km$^2$ of continental shelf and/or inland water area | tons | 8 | 4 | 2 | 1 | 0.5 | 0 | Type: 4.1. Basis: A. Current range is 17.8–0 tons. Base–best encompasses performance of 98% of countries. Top of medium matches estimated capacity/area needed to catch estimated global maximum sustainable yield with current technology. |
| Tons of catch per ton of fishing fleet capacity | tons | 0 | 1 | 2 | 4 | 8 | 16 | Type: 4.1. Basis: A. Current range is 0.02–44.4 tons. Base–best encompasses performance of 98% of countries. Top of medium matches estimated global maximum sustainable yield. |
| Fish production as a percentage of supply | % | 0 | 50 | 65 | 80 | 90 | 100 | Type: 1.2. Basis: G. Base–best encompasses current range of 1–100%. Criteria mirror those for food sufficiency. |
| Timber fellings + imports as a percentage of net annual increment (NAI) | % | 211 | 131 | 111 | 101 | 81 | 1 | Type: 4.2. Basis: A. Current range is 5,300–6%. Base–best encompasses performance of 90% of countries. Top of medium ensures that only felling + import rates at or below NAI receive a fair score. |
| Timber production + imports as a percentage of volume | % | 32 | 16 | 8 | 4 | 2 | 0 | Type: 5.1. Basis: H. Current range is 8,000–0%. Base–best encompasses performance of 92% of countries. Bands based on a rough and possibly unrepresentative relationship between volume and NAI. |

# *Appendix D.*
# Summary of Combining Procedures Used in *The Wellbeing of Nations*

Sustainability is measured by the Wellbeing Index (WI) and the Wellbeing/Stress index (WSI).

The Wellbeing Index is a graphic index shown on the Barometer of Sustainability as the intersection of the Human Wellbeing Index (HWI) and the Ecosystem Wellbeing Index (EWI).

The Wellbeing/Stress Index measures the ratio of human wellbeing to ecosystem stress. It is obtained by subtracting the EWI from 100 to provide an Ecosystem Stress Index (ESI) and dividing the HWI by the ESI.

In *The Wellbeing of Nations,* the term *index* (plural *indices*) is reserved for system, subsystem, dimension, and element scores. Scores of subelements and indicators are called simply scores. Procedures used to combine indices and scores are summarized in the text below by subsystem and dimension and in Table D1 at the end by combining procedure.

## *Human Wellbeing Index*

The HWI is the unweighted average of five dimension indices:

Health and population.

Wealth.

Knowledge and culture.

Community.

Equity.

*Equity is included only if it lowers the HWI.*

## Health and Population

The health and population index is the lower of two element indices: a health index and a population index.

The health index consists of a single indicator: healthy life expectancy at birth.

The population index consists of a single indicator: total fertility rate.

## Wealth

The wealth index is the unweighted average of two element indices: a household wealth index and a national wealth index.

The household wealth index is the average of two unweighted subelements:

Needs, the lower score of two indicators: food sufficiency, represented by the percentage of the population with insufficient food, prevalence of stunting (low height for age) in children under 5 years, or prevalence of low weight for age in children under 5, whichever gives the lowest score (or, if these are not available, the percentage of babies with low birth weight); and basic services, represented by the percentage of the population with safe water or the percentage of the population with basic sanitation, whichever gives the lower score.

Income, represented by gross domestic product (GDP) per person.

The national wealth index is the average of three weighted subelements [weights in brackets]:

Size of the economy [2], represented by GDP per person.

Inflation and unemployment [1], represented by the annual inflation rate or the annual unemployment rate (for the same period), whichever gives the lower score.

Debt [1], represented by an external debt indicator (debt service as a percentage of exports, debt service as a percentage of GNP, or ratio of short-term debt to international reserves, whichever gives the lowest score) or a public debt indicator (the weighted average of general government gross financial liabilities as a percentage of GDP [2] and annual central government deficit or surplus as a percentage of GDP [1]), whichever gives the lower score.

## Knowledge and Culture

Because of inadequate information on culture, this dimension is limited to a knowledge element. The knowledge index is the average of two weighted subelements [weights in brackets]: education [2] and communication [1].

Education is the average of two unweighted indicators:

Primary and secondary school enrollment, the unweighted average of the net primary school enrollment rate and the net secondary school enrollment rate.

Tertiary school enrollment per 10,000 population.

Communication is the average of two unweighted indicators:

A telephone indicator, the lower score of main telephone lines + cellular phone subscribers per 100 persons and faults per 100 main telephone lines per year.

Internet users per 10,000 population.

## Community

The community index is the lower of two element indices: a freedom and governance index and a peace and order index.

The freedom and governance index is the average of four unweighted indicators:

A political rights rating.

A civil liberties rating.

A press freedom rating.

A corruption perceptions index.

The peace and order index is the average of two unweighted subelements:

Peace, represented by deaths from armed conflicts per year or military expenditure as a percentage of GDP, whichever gives the lower score.

Crime, represented by the unweighted average of the homicide rate and other violent crimes (the unweighted average of the rape rate, robbery rate, and assault rate).

## Equity

The equity index is the unweighted average of two element indices: a household equity index and a gender equity index.

The household equity index consists of a single indicator: the ratio of the income share of the richest fifth of the population to that of the poorest fifth.

The gender equity index is the average of three unweighted subelements:

Gender and wealth, represented by the ratio of male income to female income.

Gender and knowledge, represented by the average difference between male and female school enrollment rates.

Gender and community, represented by women's share of seats in parliament.

## *Ecosystem Wellbeing Index*

The EWI is the unweighted average of five dimension indices:

Land.

Water.

Air.

Species and genes.

Resource use.

*Resource use is included only if it lowers the EWI.*

## Land

The land index is the lower of two element indices: a land diversity index and a land quality index.

The land diversity index is the average of two weighted subelements [weights in brackets]:

Land modification and conversion [2], represented by the unweighted average of converted land as a percentage of total land, natural land as a percentage of total land, and percentage change in native forest area.

Land protection [1], represented by protected area as a percentage of land and inland water area (weighted according to degree of protection, size of the protected areas, and how much ecosystem diversity is protected).

The land quality index consists of a single indicator: degraded land as a percentage of cultivated + modified land, weighted according to severity of degradation [weights in brackets]: light [0.5], moderate [1.0], strong [1.5], extreme [2.0].

## Water

Because of inadequate information on the sea, this dimension is limited to an inland waters element. The inland waters index is the lowest of three subelements:

Inland water diversity, represented by river conversion by dams, measured by dam capacity as a percentage of total water supply or, if that is not available, river flow dammed for hydropower as a percentage of dammable flow.

Inland water quality, the unweighted average score of drainage basins in each country, each basin score being the lowest score of six indicators: oxygen balance, nutrients, acidification, suspended solids, microbial pollution, and arsenic and heavy metals.

Water withdrawal, represented by water withdrawal as a percentage of internal renewable supply.

## Air

The air index is the lower of two element indices: a global atmosphere index and a local air quality index.

The global atmosphere index is the lower score of two indicators:

Greenhouse gases, represented by carbon dioxide emissions per person.

Use (consumption or production, whichever is greater) of ozone depleting substances per person.

The local air quality index is the unweighted average of city scores in each country, each city score being the lowest score of six indicators: sulfur dioxide, nitrogen dioxide, ground-level ozone, carbon monoxide, particulates, and lead.

## Species and Genes

The species and genes index is the weighted average [weights in brackets] of two element indices: a wild diversity index [2] and a domesticated diversity index [1].

The wild diversity index is the average of two unweighted subelements:

Wild plant species, represented by threatened plant species in a group as a percentage of total plant species in that group, taking the average percentage of three groups: flowering plants, gymnosperms (conifers, cycads, and gnetophytes), and ferns and allies.

Wild animal species, represented by threatened animal species in a group as a percentage of total animal species in that group, taking the average percentage of either two groups (mammals and birds) or four groups (mammals, birds, reptiles, and amphibians), whichever gives the lower score.

The domesticated diversity index is the average of two unweighted indicators:

Number of not-at-risk breeds of a species per million head of that species, taking the average of the most numerous livestock species and the two next most numerous or best-assessed livestock species.

Ratio of threatened breeds of a species to not-at-risk breeds of that species, taking the average of the most numerous livestock species and the two next most numerous or best-assessed livestock species.

## Resource Use

The resource use index is the unweighted average of two element indices: an energy and materials index and a resource sectors index.

The energy and materials index covers only energy because of inadequate information on material flows. It is the lower score of two indicators: energy consumption per hectare of total area and energy consumption per person.

The resource sectors index is the unweighted average of three subelements: agriculture, fisheries, and timber.

Agriculture is the lower score of two unweighted indicators:

Agricultural productivity, the unweighted average score of tons of food crops produced per harvested hectare and tons of fertilizer used per 1,000 harvested hectares.

Agricultural self-reliance, represented by food production as a percentage of supply.

Fisheries is the lower score of two unweighted indicators:

Fishing pressure, the unweighted average score of depleted species + overexploited species as a percentage of assessed species, tons of fishing capacity per square kilometer of continental shelf (or inland waters in the case of freshwater fisheries), and tons of catch per ton of fishing capacity.

Fish and seafood self-reliance, represented by fish and seafood production as a percentage of supply.

Timber is represented by a single indicator: fellings + imports as a percentage of net annual increment or, if that is not available, production + imports as a percentage of volume.

**Table D1. Summary of indices and other compound indicators by level and combining procedure (unweighted average, weighted average, or lower/lowest score). The higher level is in bold.**

| Level | Unweighted Average | Weighted Average | Lower/Lowest Score |
|---|---|---|---|
| Dimensions → **subsystem** | human dimensions → **HWI** | | |
| | ecosystem dimensions → **EWI** | | |
| Elements → **dimension** | household wealth + national wealth → **wealth** | wild diversity + domesticated diversity → **species and genes** | health + population → **health and population** |
| | household equity + gender equity → **equity** | | freedom and governance + peace and order → **community** |
| | energy and materials + resource sectors → **resource use** | | land diversity + land quality → **land** |
| | | | global atmosphere + local air quality → **air** |
| Subelements → **element** | needs + income → **household wealth** | size of the economy + inflation and unemployment + debt → **national wealth** | inland water diversity + inland water quality + water withdrawal → **inland waters** |
| | peace + crime → **peace and order** | education + communication → **knowledge** | |
| | gender and wealth + gender and knowledge + gender and community → **gender equity** | land modification and conversion + land protection → **land diversity** | |
| | wild plant species + wild animal species → **wild diversity** | | |
| | agriculture + fisheries + timber → **resource sectors** | | |
| Indicators → **subelement or element** | primary and secondary school enrollment + tertiary school enrollment → **education** | protected area as a percentage of total area weighted for size + protected area as a percentage of total area weighted for diversity → **land protection** | food sufficiency + basic services → **needs** |
| | telephone indicator + Internet users per 10,000 population → **communication** | | annual inflation rate + annual unemployment rate → **inflation and unemployment** |
| | political rights rating + civil liberties rating + press freedom rating + corruption perceptions index → **freedom and governance** | | external debt + public debt → **debt** |

| Level | Unweighted Average | Weighted Average | Lower/Lowest Score |
|---|---|---|---|
| | homicide rate + other violent crimes → **crime** | | deaths from armed conflicts per year + military expenditure as a percentage of GDP → **peace** |
| | converted land as a percentage of total land + natural land as a percentage of total land + percentage change in native forest area → **land modification and conversion** | | carbon dioxide emissions per person + use of ozone depleting substances → **global atmosphere** |
| | water quality of drainage basins → **inland water quality** | | average percentage of threatened mammal and bird species + average percentage of threatened mammal, bird, reptile, and amphibian species → **wild animal species** |
| | air quality of cities → **local air quality** | | agricultural productivity + agricultural self-reliance → **agriculture** |
| | percentage of threatened flowering plant species + percentage of threatened gymnosperm species + percentage of threatened ferns and allied species → **wild plant species** | | fishing pressure + fish and seafood self-reliance → **fisheries** |
| | number of not-at-risk breeds of a species per million head of that species + ratio of threatened breeds of a species to not-at-risk breeds of that species → **domesticated diversity** | | |
| Component indicators → **indicator** | net primary school enrollment rate + net secondary school enrollment rate → **primary and secondary school enrollment** | general government gross financial liabilities as a percentage of GDP + annual central government deficit/surplus as a percentage of GDP → **public debt** | percentage of population with insufficient food + prevalence of stunting in children + prevalence of low weight for age in children → **food sufficiency** |
| | rape rate + robbery rate + assault rate → **other violent crimes** | percentages of total area in five protected area categories → **protected area as a percentage of total area weighted for size** | percentage of population with safe water + percentage of population with basic sanitation → **basic services** |
| | water quality at stations → **water quality of basins** | mean percentage of totally protected ecosystem types + mean percentage of partially protected ecosystem types → **protected area as a percentage of total area weighted for diversity** | debt service as a percentage of exports + debt service as a percentage of GNP + ratio of short-term debt to international reserves → **external debt** |
| | air quality at sites → **air quality of cities** | lightly degraded percentage of cultivated and modified land area + moderately degraded percentage + strongly degraded percentage + extremely degraded percentage → **degraded land as a percentage of cultivated + modified land (land quality)** | main telephone lines and cellular phone subscribers per 100 persons + faults per 100 main telephone lines per year → **telephone indicator** |
| | percentage of threatened mammal species + percentage of threatened bird species → **average percentage of threatened mammal and bird species** | | oxygen balance + nutrients + acidification + suspended solids + microbial pollution + arsenic and heavy metals → **water quality at station** |

| Level | Unweighted Average | Weighted Average | Lower/Lowest Score |
|---|---|---|---|
| | percentage of threatened mammal species + percentage of threatened bird species + percentage of threatened reptile species + percentage of threatened amphibian species → **average percentage of the four groups** | | consumption of ozone depleting substances per person + production of ozone depleting substances per person → **use of ozone depleting substances** |
| | tons of food crops produced per harvested hectare + tons of fertilizer used per 1,000 harvested hectares → **agricultural productivity** | | sulfur dioxide + nitrogen dioxide + ground-level ozone + carbon monoxide + particulates + lead → **air quality at sites** |
| | depleted species and overexploited species as a percentage of assessed species + tons of fishing capacity per km² of fish-producing area + tons of catch per ton of fishing capacity → **fishing pressure** | | |

# Appendix E.
# Map Maker Pro

## *The Map Processor for Windows*

Downloadable from the web: www.mapmaker.com

"Map Maker Pro combines the powerful features of map making software with the user-friendliness of Windows. It has the look and feel of an image production package, with drag-and-drop facilities, a tools palette and customizable tool boxes, but it will allow you to create and manipulate professional looking maps... I would not have thought of using my PC to create a map, but found the process quite fascinating... The end results are highly rewarding and the three dimensional terrain contouring is amazing."

—*Internet magazine,* Sept. 2000,
www.vnunet.com

"Map Maker is the sort of useful program to look out for ... Map Maker is a versatile tool ..."

—*New Scientist,* Sept. 28, 1996

"An excellent and inexpensive tool for dedicated map-making... Packs a lot of specialist equipment into a small footprint."

—*Personal Computer World,* Feb. 1997

"Making a map is straightforward with Map Maker Pro ... the program is fast—screen operations and other actions reflect lean code ... An impressive set of features and capabilities at a modest price."

—*GIS World,* June 1997

Maps are vital tools for virtually any project. Whether you are designing irrigation systems, facilitating social forestry schemes, managing urban infrastructure, battling for land rights, mapping disease vectors, or rapidly laying out a refugee camp, reliable and readily updatable maps are crucial. Until recently, computer-based mapping has been expensive and complicated. *Map Maker Pro* is a simple-to-use program that has been developed in the field especially for development projects.

Map Maker users are creating the entire range of maps, from world maps (such as those in this book) to detailed plans of landmine fields and experimental horticultural plots. Map Maker enables you to:

- Make your own maps from scratch.
- Use existing data from other geographic information systems and computer-aided design programs (e.g., ArcView, ArcInfo, MapInfo, and AutoCAD).
- Prepare maps from scanned images such as paper maps and aerial photographs.
- Measure distances and areas on the screen.
- Carry out sophisticated data analyses.
- Create three-dimensional terrain models.
- Measure gradients and derive contours.
- Annotate maps with existing symbols or design your own symbols to indicate water pumps, land use patterns, health posts, and so on.
- Import entire maps or map extracts into documents written in any Windows word processor.
- Create maps in the field on a laptop using global positioning satellite (GPS) or traditional survey techniques.
- Create large-scale wall maps on multiple sheets using Map Maker's poster print option and a standard printer. (Each sheet can be updated individually.)
- Combine field measurements with existing maps by using one of a wide variety of map projections.

*Map Maker Pro* runs on Windows 95, 98, NT4, and 2000. Although a high-specification computer will give more impressive results, *Map Maker Pro* runs easily on a computer with a 486 processor. The program can be downloaded for a 21-day evaluation period free of charge from http://www.mapmaker.com.

Add-on modules are available from the Web site. *Rubber Map* adjusts scanned images such as aerial photographs or historical maps so that they coincide with your vector data. *Prospect* creates three-dimensional images to help assess the visual impact of forestry schemes. More modules are on the way.

Launched in September 1996, *Map Maker Pro* has been purchased by customers in 95 countries.

The Web site includes a list of independent international trainers who offer on-site training courses in Map Maker.

Map Maker Ltd, Carradale, The Pier, Kintyre, Scotland, PA28 6SQ United Kingdom; phone: +44 (0) 1583 431 358; fax: +44 (0) 1583 431 728; e-mail: info@mapmaker.com.

# Appendix F.
# Initial Classification of Interior, Coastal, and Ocean Basins

This preliminary classification of basins was developed to aid the selection of a representative set of water quality monitoring stations.

Inland waters are grouped into receiving basins. Drainages with no outlet to the sea form interior basins, grouped by continent. Drainages to coastal waters form coastal basins, grouped by coastal realm. Oceanic islands are assigned to ocean basins, grouped by adjacent coastal realm. Coastal realms follow the classification of Hayden, Ray, & Dolan (1984). Interior basins are listed first; then coastal and ocean basins, roughly from west to east: North American Arctic, Eastern Pacific, Western Atlantic, Eurasian Arctic, Eastern Atlantic, Indian, and Western Pacific.

Drainages of 100,000 km² or more are identified in *italics* and their area given in square kilometers. Usually they are treated as basins in their own right, unless this would entail too fine a subdivision of the coastal body into which they flow.

| Realm & Basin | Extent | Country | Station |
|---|---|---|---|
| **Interior Americas** | | | |
| United States interior | Great Basin complex | United States | -- |
| Mexican interior | Casas Grandes, Nazas-Aguanaval, El Salado | Mexico | -- |
| Titicaca/Poopó/Atacama | *Titicaca-Poopó 114,000* | Bolivia, Chile, Peru | -- |
| Argentine interior | North-central Argentina | Argentina | -- |
| **Interior Africa** | | | |
| Sahara | Sahara desert | Algeria, Chad, Egypt, Libya, Mali, Mauritania, Morocco, Niger, Sudan, Tunisia, Western Sahara | -- |
| Lake Chad | *Lake Chad 2,381,635* | Algeria, Cameroon, Central African R, Chad, Niger, Nigeria, Sudan | -- |
| Etosha | South-central Angola & north-central Namibia | Angola, Namibia | -- |
| Kalahari-Makgadikgadi | Makgadikgadi pans & much of the Kalahari desert | Botswana, Namibia, Zimbabwe | -- |
| Okavango | *Okavango 323,192* | Angola, Botswana, Namibia | -- |
| Rift Valley | Rift Valley (Eritrea - Tanzania): Danakil; *Awash 112,030*; Central lakes; *Omo-Gibe (L Turkana) 199,952*; Southern lakes | Djibouti, Eritrea, Ethiopia, Kenya, Sudan, Tanzania, Uganda | -- |
| **Interior Asia** | | | |
| Turkish interior | Burdur lakes, Akarcay, Konya, Van Lake | Turkey | -- |
| Rift Valley | Jordan R | Jordan | R Zarqua at King Talal Dam |
| | | Israel, Lebanon, Syria | -- |
| Arabian | Arabian desert | Jordan, Oman, Saudi Arabia, United Arab Emirates, Yemen | -- |
| N Caspian Sea | C Tjulenij - Volga delta -Kazakhstan/Turkmenistan border; *Ural 270,000* | Azerbaijan, Kazakhstan, Russia | -- |
| Volga | *Volga 1,360,000* | Russia | R Volga at Narimanov |
| | | | R Volga at B Cheboksarskoye (201) |
| | | | R Belaya at Ufa (203) |
| S Caspian Sea | Kazakhstan/Turkmenistan border - C Tjulenij; *Kura 225,000* | Armenia, Azerbaijan, Iran, Turkey, Turkmenistan | -- |
| | | Georgia | R Kura at Rustavi |
| Iranian interior | Lake Orimiye; Central plateau | Iran | -- |
| Helmand | *Helmand 386,000* | Afghanistan, Iran | -- |
| Hari Rud & Murgab | Hari Rud & Murgab | Afghanistan, Iran, Turkmenistan | -- |
| Aral Sea | Aral Sea; *Amu Darya 653,000*; *Syr Darya 540,000* | Kazakhstan | R Syr Darya mouth |
| | | Uzbekistan | R Amu Darya mouth |
| | | Afghanistan, Kyrgyzstan, Tajikistan, Turkmenistan, | -- |
| Balkhash Lake | *Balkhash Lake 250,000 (Ili 176,000)* | China, Kazakhstan, Kyrgyzstan | -- |
| Tarim | Tarim desert; *Tarim 980,000* | China, Kyrgyzstan | -- |
| Muynkum | Muynkum desert | Kazakhstan, Kyrgyzstan | -- |
| E Asian interior | Lakes Ala, Tengiz, Aschchikol & Ghalkarteniz | China, Kazakhstan | -- |
| Turgay | *Turgay 157,000* | Kazakhstan | -- |
| Issyk | Lake Issyk | Kyrgyzstan | -- |
| Gobi | Gobi desert | Mongolia | -- |
| Baluchistan | Lake Gaz Murian - Kharan desert | Iran, Pakistan | -- |
| W Rajasthan | W Rajasthan | India | -- |
| **Interior Pacific** | | | |
| Australian interior | Australian interior | Australia | -- |
| **North American Arctic** | | | |
| E Chukchi Sea | Bering Strait & C Prince of Wales - P Barrow | United States | -- |
| W Beaufort Sea | P Barrow - Herschel I | Canada, United States | -- |

| Realm & Basin | Extent | Country | Station |
|---|---|---|---|
| Mackenzie | Mackenzie & Kugmallit Bays (Herschel I - Warren P); *Mackenzie 1,784,580* | Canada | R Mackenzie mouth |
| | | | R Great Bear |
| E Beaufort Sea | Warren P - C Bathurst - C Kellett (Banks I) - C Prince Alfred (Banks I) | Canada | -- |
| Arctic Archipelagic Seas | Amundsen Gulf, M'Clure Strait, Peary Channel & Nansen Sound - Jones Sound, Lancaster Scount & Gulf of Boothia, including intermediate waters & mainland & island drainages; *Back 106,920* | Canada | -- |
| Lincoln Sea & Nares Strait | C Aldrich (Ellesmere I) - Nares Strait & C Brevoort - C Morris Jesup; C Brevoort - C Isabella (Ellesmere I) & C Alexander | Canada, Greenland | -- |
| Wandel Sea | C Morris Jesup - Nordostrundingen | Greenland | -- |
| W Baffin Bay | C Isabella (Ellesmere I) - C Dyer (Baffin I) & Davis Strait | Canada | -- |
| E Baffin Bay | C Alexander - Kangaarsuk & Davis Strait | Greenland | -- |
| W Greenland Sea | Nordostrundingen - Uunarteq/C Tobin | Greenland | -- |
| W Denmark Strait | Uunarteq/C Tobin - C Wandel | Greenland | -- |
| **Northeast Pacific** | | | |
| E Bering Sea | C Prince of Wales - Aleutian Is; *Yukon 836,760* | United States | R Yukon at Yukon Station |
| | | Canada | -- |
| Gulf of Alaska | Aleutian Is - C Fox | United States | R Talkeetna at Talkeetna |
| | | Canada | -- |
| Lower subpolar NE Pacific | C Fox - C Scott & C Caution | United States | -- |
| | | Canada | R Skeena |
| Upper temperate NE Pacific | C Scott & C Caution - C Disappointment; *Fraser 232,170* | Canada | R Fraser at Hope |
| | | United States | -- |
| Columbia | C Disappointment - C Lookout; *Columbia 669,410* | United States | R Columbia at Bonneville |
| | | Canada | R Columbia df |
| Lower temperate NE Pacific | C Lookout - P Reyes | United States | -- |
| Upper subtropical NE Pacific | P Reyes - C San Lucas | United States | R Sacramento at Sacramento |
| | | Mexico | -- |
| W Gulf of California | C San Lucas - Colorado | Mexico | -- |
| Colorado | *Colorado 615,000* | United States | R Colorado at Hoover Dam |
| | | Mexico | R Colorado |
| E Gulf of California | Colorado - Mazatlán | Mexico, United States | -- |
| Grande de Santiago | Mazatlán - C Corrientes; *Grande de Santiago 125,000* | Mexico | L de Chapala |
| | | | R Lerma |
| Oceanic NE Pacific | Hawaiian Is | United States | -- |
| **Tropical East Pacific** | | | |
| Upper tropical E Pacific | C Corrientes (Mexico) - P Cosigüina (Nicaragua); *Balsas 106,000* | Mexico | R Balsas at Balsas |
| | | El Salvador, Guatemala, Honduras, Nicaragua | -- |
| Lower tropical E Pacific | P Cosigüina - C Corrientes (Colombia) | Colombia, Costa Rica, Nicaragua, Panama | -- |
| Intertropical E Pacific | C Corrientes - P Pariñas | Colombia, Ecuador, Peru | -- |
| **Southeast Pacific** | | | |
| Subtropical SE Pacific | P Pariñas - P Toro | Peru | -- |
| | | Chile | R Maipo at El Manzano |
| Temperate SE Pacific | P Toro - P Tres Montes | Chile | -- |
| Subpolar SE Pacific | P Tres Montes - C San Diego | Argentina, Chile | -- |
| **Northwest Atlantic** | | | |
| Foxe Basin | C Hallowell (Baffin I) - King Charles C (Baffin I) & C Englefield (Melville Peninsula) - Seahorse P (Southampton I) | Canada | -- |
| W Hudson Bay | Beach P (mainland) & C Munn (Southampton I) - C Churchill); *Thelon/Kazan 230,110; Churchill 280,470* | Canada | R Churchill |
| Nelson | C Churchill - Marsh P; *Nelson 1,129,360* | Canada | R Nelson at Gillam |
| | | | R Saskatchewan mouth |
| | | | R Roseau |
| | | United States | -- |
| S Hudson Bay | Marsh P - C Henrietta Maria; *Hayes 107,690; Severn 100,460* | Canada | -- |
| James Bay | C Henrietta Maria - C Iones; *Albany 133,520; Moose 108,210* | Canada | -- |
| E Hudson Bay | C Iones - C Wolstenholme | Canada | -- |
| Hudson Strait & Ungava Bay | King Charles C (Baffin I) - Resolution I & C Wolstenholme - Button Is; *Koksoak 133,000* | Canada | -- |
| Labrador Sea | C Dyer (Baffin I) - Resolution I & Button Is - North Head | Canada | -- |

| Realm & Basin | Extent | Country | Station |
|---|---|---|---|
| Southern Greenland | Kangaarsuk & Davis Strait - Uummannarsuaq/C Farvel - C Wandel | Greenland | -- |
| Upper temperate NW Atlantic | North Head - C Ray; C St Lawrence - C Sable | Canada | -- |
| Gulf of St Lawrence | C Ray - C St Lawrence; *St Lawrence 1,179,980* | Canada | L Ontario mid-lake |
| | | | L Superior mid-lake |
| | | United States | R St Lawrence df |
| | | | R Niagara at L Ontario |
| Bay of Fundy & Gulf of Maine | C Sable - C Cod | Canada | R St John mouth |
| | | United States | -- |
| Lower temperate NW Atlantic | C Cod - C Henlopen | United States | R Hudson at Troy |
| Chesapeake Bay | C Henlopen - C Hatteras/C Lookout | United States | R Delaware at Trenton |
| | | | R Susquehanna at Harrisburg |
| | | | R Potomac at Washington |
| Subtropical NW Atlantic | C Hatteras/C Lookout - Northwest Providence Channel - East C (FL) | Bahamas, United States | -- |
| NE Gulf of Mexico | East C - Dauphin I; *Mobile/Alabama 115,000* | United States | R Apalachicola at Chattahoochee |
| Mississippi | Dauphin I - Texas P; *Mississippi 3,250,000* | United States | R Mississippi mouth |
| | | | R Arkansas at Little Rock |
| | | | R Missouri at Hermann |
| | | | R Ohio at New Grand Chain |
| | | Canada | -- |
| Brazos | Texas P - Matagorda Bay; *Brazos 114,000* | United States | -- |
| Texas Colorado | Matagorda Bay - Port Isabel; *Colorado (Texas) 100,000* | United States | -- |
| Bravo del Norte/Grande | Port Isabel - Playa Lauro Villar; *Bravo del Norte (Grande) 550,000* | United States | R Grande at Brownsville |
| | | Mexico | R Bravo at Matamoros |
| | | | R Bravo at Presa de la Amistad |
| | | | R Conchos at Ojinaga |
| SW Gulf of Mexico | Playa Lauro Villar - Tupilco | Mexico | R Pánuco |
| | | | R Coatzacoalcos |
| SE Gulf of Mexico | Tupilco - C Catoche; *Grijalva/Usumacinta 120,000* | Mexico | R Grijalva |
| | | | R Usumacinta |
| | | Guatemala | -- |
| E Gulf of Mexico | C Corrientes - Varadero | Cuba | -- |
| **Tropical West Atlantic** | | | |
| Upper tropical W Atlantic | Northwest Providence Channel & Varadero (Cuba) - P de Quemados (Cuba) - C Engaño (Dominican R) - I de Vieques (Puerto Rico) | Bahamas, Cuba, Dominican R, Haiti, Puerto Rico, Turks & Caicos Is | -- |
| Antillean tropical W Atlantic & E Caribbean Sea | Virgin Passage (I de Vieques) - Grenada | Anguilla, Antigua & Barbuda, Barbados, British Virgin Is, Dominica, Grenada, Guadeloupe, Martinique, Montserrat, Netherlands Antilles (Saba, St Eustatius, St Maarten), St Kitts & Nevis, St Lucia, St Vincent & Grenadines, US Virgin Is | -- |
| N Caribbean Sea | C Corrientes (Cuba) - I de Vieques (Puerto Rico) | Cuba | B Damuji |
| | | | B Hanabanilla |
| | | Cayman Is, Dominican R, Haiti, Jamaica, Puerto Rico | -- |
| W Caribbean Sea | C Catoche - P S Bernardo | Belize, Colombia, Costa Rica, Guatemala, Honduras, Mexico, Nicaragua, Panama | -- |
| Magdalena | P San Bernardo - P Perret; *Magdalena 240,000* | Colombia | R Magdalena mouth |
| | | | R Cauca at Juanchito |
| S Caribbean Sea | P Perret - Península de Paria | Aruba, Colombia, Netherlands Antilles (Bonaire & Curaçao), Venezuela | -- |
| Orinoco | Península de Paria -Guyana/Venezuela border; *Orinoco 966,000* | Colombia, Trinidad & Tobago, Venezuela | -- |
| Essequibo | Guyana/Venezuela border - Georgetown; *Essequibo 147,000* | Guyana, Venezuela | -- |
| Guianan tropical W Atlantic | Georgetown - C do Norte | Brazil, French Guiana, Guyana, Suriname | -- |
| Amazon | C do Norte - C Gurupi; *Amazon 6,000,000* | Brazil | R Amazon mouth |
| | | | R Tocantins mouth |
| | | Bolivia, Colombia, Ecuador, Guyana, Peru, Venezuela | -- |
| Intertropical W Atlantic | C Gurupi - Parnaíba; Parnaíba - P Coconho; | Brazil | -- |
| Parnaíba | *Parnaíba 325,000* | Brazil | |
| São Francisco | P Coconho - P do Conselho; *São Francisco 600,000* | Brazil | R Capibaribe |
| | | | R São Francisco at Petrolandia |

| Realm & Basin | Extent | Country | Station |
|---|---|---|---|
| Lower tropical W Atlantic | P do Conselho - C Frio | Brazil | R Paraguaçu at Pedra do Cavalo |
| | | | R Pairaba do Sul at Barra Mansa |
| **Southwest Atlantic** | | | |
| Subtropical SW Atlantic | C Frio - P del Este | Brazil, Uruguay | -- |
| La Plata | P del Este - P Mogotes; *la Plata/Paraná/ Uruguay 3,200,000* | Argentina | R Paraná at Puerto Libertad |
| | | | R Paraná at Corrientes |
| | | | R Paraná at Rosario |
| | | Brazil | B Guarapiranga |
| | | Bolivia, Paraguay, Uruguay | -- |
| N Mar Argentino | P Mogotes - Pen. Valdés | Argentina | L Nahuel Huapi at Bariloche |
| Chubut | Pen. Valdés - C Tres Puntas; *Chubut 138,000* | Argentina | -- |
| S Mar Argentino | C Tres Puntas - C San Diego | Argentina | -- |
| **Eurasian Arctic** | | | |
| E Denmark Strait | Reykjanesta - Fontur (northern half of island) | Iceland | -- |
| W Barents Sea | Nordkapp - C Orlovskij | Finland | L Inari stn 151 |
| | | Norway, Russia | |
| Severnaya Dvina | Dvina Gulf; *Severnaya Dvina 358,000* | Russia | R Severnaya Dvina at Ust-Pinega (213) |
| White Sea | C Orlovskij - Dvina Gulf - C Kanin Nos | Russia | R Mezen at Borovo |
| E Barents Sea | C Kanin Nos - C Zelanija; *Pechora 322,000* | Russia | R Pechora at Nar'jan-Mar |
| W Kara Sea | C Zelanija - C Suberta; C Sokal'skogo - C Olenij | Russia | -- |
| Ob | Gulfs of Ob & Taz (C Suberta - C Sokal'skogo); *Ob 2,990,000; Pur 112,000; Taz 150,000* | Russia | R Ob at Salehard (011) |
| | | | R Tom at Tomsk (204) |
| | | | R Irtysh at Krasnyi Jar (205) |
| | | China, Kazakhstan | -- |
| Yenisey | C Olenij - Dikson I; *Yenisey 2,580,000* | Russia | R Yenisei at Igarka (210) |
| | | | L Baikal mid-lake (024) |
| | | | R Selenga mouth |
| | | Mongolia | -- |
| Pyasina | Dikson I - C Povorotnyi; *Pyasina 182,000* | Russia | -- |
| Taimyr | C Povorotnyi - C Celjuskin; *Taimyr 124,000* | Russia | -- |
| Khatanga | C Celjuskin - C Paksa; *Khatanga 422,000* | Russia | -- |
| Anabar | C Paksa - Terpjaj-Tumsa Pen.; *Anabar 100,000* | Russia | -- |
| Olenek | Terpjaj-Tumsa Pen. - Dzangylah I; *Olenek 219,000* | Russia | -- |
| Lena | Dzangylah I - C Buor Haja; *Lena 2,470,000* | Russia | R Lena delta (028) |
| Yana | C Buor-Haja - C Svjatoj Nos & C Anisij; *Yana (Jana) 238,000* | Russia | -- |
| Indigirka | C Svjatoj Nos & C Anisij - C Krestovskskij; *Indigirka 360,000* | Russia | -- |
| Kolyma | C Krestovskskij - C Billingsa; *Kolyma 647,000* | Russia | R Kolyma at Kolymskoe |
| W Chukchi Sea | C Billingsa - Bering Strait & C Dezneva | Russia | -- |
| **Northeast Atlantic** | | | |
| Icelandic Atlantic | Reykjanesta - Fontur (southern half of island) | Iceland | -- |
| Norwegian Sea | Nordkapp - Lindesnes | Norway | R Altaelva at Alta |
| | | | R Vefsna at Mosjøen |
| | | | R Orkla at Vormstad |
| | | | R Suldalslaagen at Sand |
| | | Faeroe Is | -- |
| N Skagerrak & E Kattegat | Lindesnes - Helsingborg | Norway | R Otra mouth |
| | | | R Skienselva mouth |
| | | | R Numedalslaagen at Bommestad |
| | | | R Drammenselva mouth |
| | | | R Glåma mouth |
| | | Sweden | L Vanern |
| N Baltic Sea | Helsingborg - Kappelskär (incl. Bornholm); Helsingør - Møns Klint | Sweden | R Mörrumsan mouth |
| | | | R Ronneaan mouth |
| | | | L Vattern |
| | | Denmark | -- |
| Gulf of Bothnia | Kappelskär - Hangö | Sweden | R Dalalven mouth |
| | | | R Rane mouth |
| | | Finland | R Tornionjoki stn 14100 |
| | | | L Yli-Kitka stn 144 |
| | | | R Kokernaenjoki mouth |
| N Gulf of Finland | Hangö - Neva | Finland | R Kalkkinen stn 4800 |
| | | | R Kymijoki stn 5610 |
| | | Russia | -- |
| Neva | *Neva 281,000* | Russia | L Onezhskoye (Onega) |
| S Gulf of Finland | Neva - N of Riguld (Estonia) | Estonia | R Narva 10 km from mouth |
| | | | R Narva at L Vörtsjäry |
| | | Latvia, Russia | -- |

| Realm & Basin | Extent | Country | Station |
|---|---|---|---|
| SE Baltic Sea | N of Riguld - Gdansk Bay | Estonia | R Pärnu 1 km from mouth |
| | | Latvia | R Gauja at Sigulda |
| | | | R Daugava at Jekabpils |
| | | Lithuania | R Nemunas |
| | | Russia | -- |
| Wisla | Gdansk Bay; *Wisla (Vistula) 193,000* | Poland | R Wisla mouth |
| | | | R Wisla at Kiezmark |
| | | | R Wisla at Warszawa |
| | | | R Wisla at Krakow |
| | | Belarus, Slovakia, Ukraine | -- |
| Oder (S Baltic Sea) | Gdansk Bay - C Arkona; *Oder 126,000* | Poland | R Oder mouth |
| | | | R Oder (Odra) at Krajnik |
| | | | R Oder (Odra) at Wroclaw |
| | | | R Oder (Odra) at Chalupki |
| | | Czech R | R Oder (Odra) df |
| | | Germany | -- |
| SW Baltic Sea | C Arkona - Samsø; Møns Klint - N of Kalundborg | Denmark | R Sus mouth |
| | | | R Odense mouth |
| | | Germany | -- |
| S Skagerrak & W Kattegat | Helsingør - N of Kalundborg - Hanstholm (Denmark) | Denmark | R Guden mouth |
| NE North Sea | Hanstholm - Sylt | Denmark | R Skjern mouth |
| German Bight | Sylt - Schiermonnikoog (Netherlands); *Elbe 144,500* | Germany | R Elbe mouth |
| | | | R Elbe at Geesthacht |
| | | | R Weser mouth |
| | | | R Weser at Intschede |
| | | Czech R | R Elbe (Labe) df |
| | | Austria, Netherlands, Poland | -- |
| Rhine | Schiermonnikoog - Schouwen (Netherlands); *Rhine 168,757* | Netherlands | L Ijsselmeer |
| | | | R Rhine Ijssel arm |
| | | | R Rhine Ijssel-Kampen |
| | | | R Rijn/Maas delta |
| | | Germany | R Rhine df |
| | | | R Rhine at Kleve/Bimmen |
| | | | R Rhine at Koblenz |
| | | | R Moselle at Koblenz |
| | | Belgium | R Meuse df |
| | | | R Meuse at Lanaye/ Ternaaien |
| | | Luxembourg | R Sûre df |
| | | Switzerland | R Rhine at Basel |
| | | | R Rhine at Diepoldsau |
| | | | R Aare at Brugg |
| | | Austria, France, Liechtenstein | -- |
| SE North Sea | Schouwen - C Nez (France) | Belgium | R Schelde (Escaut) df |
| | | | R Schelde at Doel |
| | | France, Netherlands | -- |
| W North Sea | Duncansby Head (Scotland) - South Foreland (England) | United Kingdom | R Leven |
| | | | R Tweed above Galafoot |
| | | | R Trent at Nottingham |
| | | | R Thames at London |
| N English Channel | South Foreland - Land's End (England) | United Kingdom | R Exe at Exeter |
| Celtic Sea | Land's End - St David's Head (Wales) & Carnsore P - Mizen Head (Ireland) | United Kingdom | R Severn mouth |
| | | | R Avon at Bristol |
| | | Ireland | R Blackwater mouth |
| | | | R Barrow mouth |
| Irish Sea | St David's Head - Mull of Kintyre (Scotland) & Carnsore P - Fair Head (N Ireland) | Ireland | R Boyne mouth |
| | | United Kingdom | R Dee |
| | | | R Mersey |
| | | | R Clyde mouth |
| | | I of Man | -- |
| Scottish & Irish Atlantic | Shetland & Orkney Is; Duncansby Head - Mull of Kintyre; Fair Head - Mizen Head | United Kingdom | R Carron |
| | | | Lower Bann mouth |
| | | Ireland | R Clare mouth |
| La Manche (S English Channel) | C Nez - I d'Ouessant | France | R Seine mouth |
| | | | R Seine at Paris |
| | | Channel Is | -- |
| Loire | I d'Ouessant - I de Noirmoutier; *Loire 120,000* | France | R Loire mouth |
| | | | R Loire at Ingrandes |
| Bay of Biscay | I de Noirmoutier - C Ortegal | France | R Garonne mouth |
| | | | R Garonne at Valence d'Agen |
| | | Andorra, Spain | -- |

| Realm & Basin | Extent | Country | Station |
|---|---|---|---|
| Lower temperate NE Atlantic | C Ortegal - C Espichel (Portugal) | Portugal | R Douro mouth |
| | | | R Tejo at Santarem |
| | | Spain | R Duero df |
| Upper subtropical NE Atlantic | C Espichel - P Marroquí (Spain) - Jbel Musa (Morocco) - Ras Nouâdhibou (Western Sahara/Mauritania) | Portugal | R Guadiana mouth |
| | | Spain | R Guadiana mouth |
| | | | R Guadalquivir mouth |
| | | Morocco | R Sebou at Kenitra |
| | | | R Bou Regreg at Barrage Sidi Mohamed Ben Abdella |
| | | | R er Rbia at Sidi Daoui |
| | | Western Sahara | -- |
| NW Mediterranean Sea | P Marroquí - C de Creus | Spain | R Ebro mouth |
| | | Andorra | -- |
| N Mediterranean Sea | C de Creus - C Ferrat - C Corse & C Pertusato (Corsica) - P Falcone & C Carbonara (Sardinia) | France | R Rhone mouth |
| | | | R Rhone at St Vallier |
| | | Switzerland | R Rhone at Chancy |
| | | | R Rhone at Porte du Scex |
| | | Spain, Italy | -- |
| Ligurian & Tyrrenhian Seas | C Ferrat - Scilla - P del Faro & C Boeo (Sicily) - C Carbonara - P Falcone - C Pertusato - C Corse | Italy | R Arno mouth |
| | | France | -- |
| Ionian Sea | C delle Correnti & P del Faro (Sicily) - Scilla - C d'Otranto & C i Gjuhes (Otranto Channel) - Akra Ténaro (Greece) | Italy, Albania | -- |
| | | Greece | R Akeloos mouth |
| Adriatic Sea | C d'Otranto (Italy) - C i Gjuhes (Albania) | Italy | R Adige mouth |
| | | | R Po mouth |
| | | Switzerland | R Ticino at Riazzino |
| | | Albania | R Semani at Mbrostar |
| | | Greece | L Mikri Prespa |
| | | Bosnia & Herzegovina, Croatia, Macedonia FYR, Slovenia, Yugoslavia | -- |
| Aegean Sea (including Sea of Marmara & Sea of Crete) | Akra Ténaro - Bosporus - Kas (Turkey) | Greece | R Axios mouth |
| | | | R Strimonas mouth |
| | | Bulgaria | R Arda df |
| | | | R Maritza at Svilengrad |
| | | Turkey | R Gediz mouth |
| | | Macedonia FYR, Yugoslavia | -- |
| W Black Sea | Bosporus - C Kaliakra | Bulgaria, Turkey | -- |
| Danube | C Kaliakra - L Sasyk; *Danube 796,250* | Romania | R Danube at Bazias |
| | | | R Oltul at Isbiceni |
| | | | R Muresul at Nadlac |
| | | Austria | R Danube df |
| | | | R Inn df |
| | | Bulgaria | R Jantra mouth |
| | | | R Osam mouth |
| | | Czech R | R Morava df |
| | | Germany | R Danube df |
| | | | R Danube at Jochenstein |
| | | Hungary | R Danube df |
| | | | R Danube at Budapest |
| | | | R Tisza at Szolnok |
| | | | R Tisza df |
| | | Moldova | R Prut at Ungheni |
| | | Slovakia | R Maly Dunaj (Danube) df |
| | | | R Hornad df |
| | | | R Hron mouth |
| | | | R Vah mouth |
| | | Italy, Switzerland, Ukraine, Yugoslavia | -- |
| N Black Sea | L Sasyk - Dnepr; Dnepr - Kerčenska Strait | Ukraine | R Dnestr at Mogiliv-Podilskiy |
| | | Moldova | R Dnestr at Bender |
| Dnepr | *Dnepr 558,000* | Ukraine | R Dnepr at Kherson |
| | | Belarus, Russia | -- |
| Don | *Don 422,000* | Ukraine | R Severskiy Donez at Krujilivka |
| | | Russia | R Don at Bagaevskij |
| Azov Sea (except Don) | Kerčenska Strait | Russia | R Kuban mouth |
| | | Ukraine | -- |
| E Black Sea | Kerčenska Strait - Trabzon (Turkey) | Georgia | R Rioni at Poti |
| | | Russia, Turkey | -- |
| S Black Sea | Trabzon - Bosporus | Turkey | R Yesilirmak mouth |
| | | | R Sakarya mouth |

| Realm & Basin | Extent | Country | Station |
|---|---|---|---|
| E Mediterranean Sea | Kas (Turkey) - Port Said (Egypt) | Cyprus, Egypt, Israel, Lebanon, Syria, Turkey | -- |
| Nile | Port Said - Alexandria; *Nile 3,112, 369* | Sudan | R Blue Nile at Khartoum |
| | | | R White Nile at Jebel Aulia |
| | | Tanzania | R Kagera at Nyakanyasi |
| | | | L Victoria at South Port |
| | | Uganda | L Albert |
| | | Burundi, DR Congo, Egypt, Eritrea, Ethiopia, Kenya, Rwanda | -- |
| SE Mediterranean Sea | Alexandria - C Bon (Tunisia) + C Boeo - C delle Correnti | Egypt, Italy, Libya, Malta, Tunisia | -- |
| SW Mediterranean Sea | C Bon - Jbel Musa | Morocco | R Moulouya |
| | | Algeria, Tunisia | -- |
| Senegal & Cape Verde | Ras Nouâdhibou - C Vert; *Senegal 484,181* | Senegal | R Senegal at St Louis |
| | | | R Senegal at Podor |
| | | Cape Verde, Guinea, Mali, Mauritania | -- |
| Lower subtropical NE Atlantic | C Vert -Guinea/Sierra Leone border | Gambia, Guinea, Guinea-Bissau, Senegal | -- |
| **Tropical East Atlantic** | | | |
| Upper tropical E Atlantic | Guinea/Sierra Leone border - C Palmas (Côte d'Ivoire) | Côte d'Ivoire, Guinea, Liberia, Sierra Leone | -- |
| W Gulf of Guinea | C Palmas - Volta; Volta - North Point (Nigeria) | Ghana | R Pra at Daboase |
| | | Benin, Burkina Faso, Côte d'Ivoire, Guinea, Nigeria, Togo | -- |
| Volta | *Volta 394,196* | Ghana | R Volta at B Kpong |
| | | | R White Volta at Nawuni |
| | | Benin, Burkina Faso, Côte d'Ivoire, Mali, Togo | -- |
| Niger | North Point - West Point (Nigeria); *Niger 2,273,946* | Mali | R Niger at Bamako |
| | | | R Niger at Koulikoro |
| | | Algeria, Benin, Burkina Faso, Cameroon, Chad, Côte d'Ivoire, Guinea, Niger, Nigeria | -- |
| E Gulf of Guinea (Intertropical E Atlantic) | West Point - C Lopez (Gabon); *Sanaga 135,000* | Cameroon, Central African R, Equatorial Guinea, Gabon, Nigeria, São Tomé & Principe | -- |
| **Southeast Atlantic** | | | |
| Upper subtropical SE Atlantic | C Lopez - Cabinda/DR Congo border; *Ogooué 220,270* | Angola, Cameroon, R Congo, Equatorial Guinea, Gabon | -- |
| Congo | Cabinda/DR Congo border - Soyo (Angola); *Congo 3,789,053* | Angola, Burundi, Cameroon, Central African R, DR Congo, R Congo, Rwanda, Tanzania, Zambia | -- |
| Cuanza | Soyo - Santa Maria; *Cuanza 149,000* | Angola | -- |
| Cunene | Santa Maria - C Fria (Namibia); *Cunene 112,000* | Angola, Namibia | -- |
| Lower subtropical SE Atlantic | C Fria - Orange; Orange - C Agulhas (South Africa) | Namibia, South Africa | -- |
| Orange | *Orange 896,368* | Namibia | R Orange mouth |
| | | South Africa | R Orange mouth |
| | | Botswana, Lesotho | -- |
| **Western Indian Ocean** | | | |
| Lower subtropical W Indian | C Agulhas - I Mariana (Mozambique) | Mozambique, South Africa, Swaziland | -- |
| Upper subtropical W Indian | I Mariana - P São Sebastião; *Limpopo 401,864* | Botswana, Mozambique, South Africa, Zimbabwe | -- |
| Madagascar subtropical | C Ankaboa - Tolanaro | Madagascar | -- |
| Save | P São Sebastião - Marromeu (Mozambique); *Save 103,000* | Mozambique, Zimbabwe | -- |
| Zambezi | Marromeu - I de Moçambique; *Zambezi 1,351,365* | Angola, Botswana, Malawi, Mozambique, Namibia, Zambia, Zimbabwe | -- |
| E Mozambique Channel (Inner Madagascar tropical) | C Ankaboa - C Vilanandro | Madagascar | -- |
| Outer Madagascar tropical | Tolanaro - C Angontsy | Madagascar, Mauritius, Réunion | -- |
| Lower intertropical W Indian | C Angotsy - C Vilanandro (Madagascar) - I de Moçambique - C Delgado (Mozambique) | Comoros, Madagascar, Mayotte, Mozambique | -- |
| Ruvuma | C Delgado - Songo Mnara (Tanzania); *Ruvuma 166,500* | Malawi, Mozambique, Tanzania | -- |
| Rufiji | Songo Mnara - Buyuni; *Rufiji 178,000* | Tanzania | -- |
| Upper intertropical W Indian | Buyuni - Kismaanyo (Somalia) | Tanzania | R Ruvu at Mlandizi |
| | | Kenya | R Tana |
| | | Somalia | -- |

| Realm & Basin | Extent | Country | Station |
|---|---|---|---|
| Shebelli-Juba | Kismaanyo-Mogadishu; *Shebelli-Juba 810,427* | Ethiopia, Somalia | -- |
| | | Kenya | L Naivasha |
| Horn of Africa & S Gulf of Aden | Mogadishu - Djibouti/Eritrea border | Djibouti, Ethiopia, Somalia | -- |
| W Red Sea | Djibouti/Eritrea border - Ra's Muhammad (Egypt) | Egypt, Eritrea, Sudan | -- |
| E Red Sea | Ra's Muhammad - Ra's Bab al-Mandab (Yemen) | Egypt, Israel, Jordan, Saudi Arabia, Yemen | -- |
| N Gulf of Aden & NW Arabian Sea | Ra's Bab al-Mandab - Ra's al Hadd (Oman) | Oman, United Arab Emirates, Yemen | -- |
| S Gulf of Oman & Persian Gulf | Ra's al Hadd - al Subiya (Kuwait) | Bahrain, Kuwait, Oman, Qatar, Saudi Arabia, United Arab Emirates | -- |
| Shatt-al-Arab | al Subiya - Ra's-e Abadan (Iran); *Shatt-al-Arab/ Tigris/Euphrates 884,000* | Iran | Shatt-al-Arab mouth |
| | | Iraq | Shatt-al-Arab mouth |
| | | Kuwait, Syria, Turkey | -- |
| N Persian Gulf & Gulf of Oman | Ra's-e Abadan - Ra's-e Faste | Iran | -- |
| Makran Coast | Ra's-e Faste - Ras Muari (Pakistan) | Iran, Pakistan | -- |
| Indus | Ras Muari - Pakistan/India border; *Indus 1,060,000* | Pakistan | R Indus at Kotri |
| | | | R Ravi below Lahore |
| | | | R Ravi above Lahore |
| | | | R Chenab Gujra branch |
| | | Afghanistan, China, India | -- |
| Gulfs of Kachchh & Khambhat | Pakistan/India border - Daman | India | R Sabarmati at Ahmedabad |
| | | | R Mahi at Vasad |
| | | | R Narmada near Garudeshwar |
| | | | R Tapti near Burhanpur |
| Maharashtra Coast | Daman - C Rama | India | -- |
| Malabar Coast | C Rama - C Comorin | India | R Chaliyar at Kalpalli |
| | | | R Periyar near Alwaye |
| | | | R Kallada at Panamthottam |
| Lakshadweep Sea | Lakshadweep Is & Maldives | India, Maldives | -- |
| Mannar | C Comorin - Matara (Sri Lanka) | India, Sri Lanka | -- |
| **Eastern Indian Ocean** | | | |
| Coromandel Coast | Matara - Krishna delta (India) | India | R Cauvery near Musiri |
| | | | R Pennar near Nellore |
| | | Sri Lanka | -- |
| Krishna | Krsihna delta - Machilpatnam; *Krishna 258,948* | India | R Krishna near Vijayawada |
| | | | R Krishna at Gadwal |
| | | | R Tungabhadra at Ullanuru |
| | | | R Bhima near Takali |
| Godavari | Machilpatnam - Pondicherry; *Godavari 312,812* | India | R Godavari near Polavaram |
| | | | R Godavari near Mancheral |
| | | | R Wainganga near Ashti |
| NW Bay of Bengal | Pondicherry - Orissa/West Bengal border (India); *Mahanadi 141,589* | India | R Mahanadi mouth |
| | | | R Subarnarekha at Jamshedpur |
| Ganges | Orissa/West Bengal border - Sandwip (Bangladesh); *Ganga/Brahmaputra/Meghna 1,652,318* | India (1,096,588) | R Ganga df |
| | | Bangladesh (121,070) | R Meghna at Ashuganj |
| | | | R Padma at Bheramara |
| | | | R Brahmaputra at Fulchhari |
| | | Bhutan (47,000), China (240,480), Nepal (147,180) | -- |
| NE Bay of Bengal | Sandwip - Mawdin (Myanmar) | Bangladesh, | R Karnaphuli at Rangunia |
| | | | L Kaptai at Kaptai |
| | | India, Myanmar | -- |
| Irrawaddy & Salween | Mawdin - Thongwa; *Irrawaddy 396,000* | Myanmar | R Irrawaddy |
| | | China, India | -- |
| Salween | Thongwa - Kyaikkami (Myanmar); *Salween 270,000* | Myanmar, China, Thailand | -- |
| Andaman Sea | Kyaikkami - Phuket (Thailand) - C Ba'u (Sumatra) + Andaman & Nicobar Is | India, Indonesia, Myanmar, Thailand | -- |
| Strait of Malacca | Phuket - Sungai Rengit (Malaysia); C Ba'u - Durian Strait (Sumatra) | Malaysia | R Klang |
| | | | R Linggi |
| | | | R Sekudai |
| | | Indonesia, Singapore, Thailand | -- |
| W Sumatra | C Ba'u - Sunda Strait | Indonesia | -- |
| Upper intertropical E Indian (Java) | Sunda Strait - Bali Strait (S Java) | Indonesia | R Garang |
| Upper intertropical E Indian (Bali-Alor) | Bali Strait - Ombai Strait | Indonesia | -- |
| N Timor & Arafura Seas | Timor - Tanjung Vais (New Guinea) - C Yubo (Papua New Guinea) | East Timor, Indonesia, Papua New Guinea | -- |
| Gulf of Carpentaria | C York - C Wilberforce; *Flinders 108,000* | Australia | -- |

| Realm & Basin | Extent | Country | Station |
|---|---|---|---|
| S Arafura & Timor Seas | C Wilberforce - C Voltaire | Australia | -- |
| Lower intertropical E Indian | C Voltaire - North West C | Australia | -- |
| W Australian subtropical | North West C - C Leeuwin | Australia | -- |
| Upper temperate E Indian | C Leeuwin - C du Couedic | Australia | -- |
| Murray-Darling | C du Couedic - C Jaffa; *Murray-Darling 1,060,000* | Australia | R Murray-Darling mouth |
| Lower temperate E Indian | C Jaffa - C Otway - Woolnorth P (Tasmania) | Australia | -- |
| Subpolar E Indian | Woolnorth P - South West C (Tasmania) | Australia | -- |
| **Northwest Pacific** | | | |
| W Bering Sea | C Dezneva - C Afrika; *Anadyr 191,000* | Russia | -- |
| Upper temperate NW Pacific | C Afrika - C Lopatka | Russia | -- |
| Sea of Okhotsk | C Lopatka - Kuril Is - Hokkaido (C Nosappu - C Soya) - E Sakhalin (C Kril'on - C Elizavety) - C Aleksandra | Japan, Russia | -- |
| Amur & Tatarskij Strait | C Aleksandra & C Elizavety - Amgu (Russia) & C Soya (Hokkaido); *Amur 1,855,000* | Russia | R Amur mouth |
| | | China, Mongolia | -- |
| Lower temperate NW Pacific (Hokkaido) | C Nosappu (Hokkaido) - C Esan (Hokkaido) | Japan | -- |
| Lower temperate NW Pacific (Honshu) | P Shiriya (Honshu) - C Shio-no (Honshu) | Japan | R Kyu-Kitakami at Kanomata |
| | | | R Tone at Tone-Ozeki |
| | | | R Sagami at Samukawa |
| | | | R Kiso at Inuyama |
| Upper subtropical NW Pacific (Honshu) | C Shio-no - Kanmon Strait (Honshu/Kyushu) | Japan | L Biwa south center |
| | | | R Yodo at Hirakata Bridge |
| Upper subtropical NW Pacific (Shikoku) | Shikoku | Japan | R Yoshino at Takase |
| Upper subtropical NW Pacific (Kyushu) | Kyushu | Japan | R Chikugo at Senoshita |
| | | | R Kuma at Yokoishi |
| Upper subtropical NW Pacific (Ryukyu Is) | Ryukyu Is | Japan | -- |
| E Sea of Japan (Honshu) | Kanmon Strait - P Shiriya | Japan | R Shinano at Kyuzogoya |
| E Sea of Japan (Hokkaido) | C Esan - C Soya | Japan | R Ishikari at Ishikari |
| W Sea of Japan | Amgu - Pusan (R Korea) | China, DR Korea, R Korea, Russia | -- |
| Korea Strait | Pusan - Chindo | R Korea | R NakDong |
| | | | R YoungSan |
| E Yellow Sea | Chindo - Lushun | R Korea | R Han mouth |
| | | | R Han |
| | | | R Keum |
| | | China, DR Korea | -- |
| Liaodong Wan | Lushun - Qinhuangdao; *Liao 228,960* | China | -- |
| Bo Hai | Qinhuangdao - Penglai *Huang (Yellow) 752,443* | China | R Huang (Yellow) at Jinan |
| SW Yellow Sea | Penglai - Qidong | China | -- |
| Chang | Qidong - Nanhui; *Chang (Yangtze) 2,077,783* | China | R Chang (Yangtze) at Wuhan |
| | | | L Tai |
| East China Sea | Nanhui - Nan'ao Dao | China | -- |
| Chinese South China Sea | Nan'ao Dao - Xi; Xi - Sanya  (Hainan) | China | L Plover Cove stn 19 Hong Kong |
| Xi | *Xi (Pearl) 442,100* | China | R Xi (Pearl) at Zhaoqing |
| | | Viet Nam | -- |
| Gulf of Tonkin | Sanya - C Doc (Viet Nam); *Hong (Red) 169,600* | Viet Nam | R Hong (Red) mouth |
| | | China, Lao | -- |
| Vietnamese South China Sea | C Doc - C Ky Van | Viet Nam | -- |
| Mekong | C Ky Van - C Nai  (Viet Nam/Cambodia border); *Mekong 786,000* | Viet Nam | R Mekong |
| | | Thailand | R Mun at Ubon Ratchathani |
| | | Cambodia, China, Lao, Myanmar | -- |
| E Gulf of Thailand | C Nai - Chao Phraya | Cambodia | -- |
| | | Thailand | R Bang at Pa Kong |
| Chao Phraya | *Chao Phraya 160,000* | Thailand | R Chao Phraya at Bangkok |
| | | | R Chao Phraya below Nakhon Sawan |
| | | | R Prasak at Kaeng Khoi |
| W Gulf of Thailand | Chao Phraya - Ko Samui | Thailand | -- |
| Malay/Thai South China Sea | Ko Samui - Sungai Rengit (Malaysia) | Malaysia, Thailand | -- |
| Borneo South China Sea | C Datu (Sarawak/Kalimantan border) - Tiga Tarok (Sabah) | Brunei Darussalam, Malaysia | -- |
| Philippine South China Sea | C Melville (Balabac) - Mayraira P (N Luzon) | Philippines | B La Mesa |
| Lower subtropical NW Pacific | Mayraira P - Yog P (Catanduanes) | Philippines | R Cagayan |
| **Tropical West Pacific** | | | |
| Upper tropical W Pacific | Yog P - Kalipagan (S Mindanao) | Philippines | -- |

| Realm & Basin | Extent | Country | Station |
|---|---|---|---|
| Sulu & Celebes Seas | rest of Philippines + Sabah E of Tiga Tarok + Kalimantan N of C Mangkalihat + N Sulawesi (C Dampelas - C Pulisan) | Indonesia, Malaysia, Philippines | -- |
| Makassar Strait | C Mangkalihat - C South (Kalimantan) & C Dampelas - Selayar I (Sulawesi) | Indonesia | -- |
| Java Sea & Karimata Strait (Kalimantan) | C South - C Datu | Indonesia | -- |
| Java Sea & Karimata Strait (Sumatra) | Sunda Strait - Durian Strait | Indonesia | R Musi at Palembang |
| Java Sea (Java) | Sunda Strait - Bali Strait (N Java) | Indonesia | R Banjir Kanal |
| | | | R Sunter |
| | | | R Citarum |
| | | | R Surabaya |
| | | | B Saguling |
| Bali & Flores Seas | Bali Strait - Ombai Strait | Indonesia | -- |
| Molucca & Halmahera Seas | C Pulisan (Sulawesi) - (Sula Is) + Halmahera | Indonesia | -- |
| Ceram & Banda Seas | C Dehekolano - Selayar I (Sulawesi) + Buru, Ambon, Seram, Tenggara Is & Aru | Indonesia | -- |
| New Guinea tropical | C Vais - C Memori (New Guinea) | Indonesia | -- |
| New Guinea intertropical | C Memori - C Girgir (Papua New Guinea) | Indonesia, Papua New Guinea | -- |
| Bismarck & Solomon Seas | C Girgir - Goschen Strait (PNG) + Bismarck Archipelago & Solomon Is | Papua New Guinea | R Sepik mouth |
| | | Indonesia, Solomon Is | -- |
| N Coral Sea | Goschen Strait - C Yubo (PNG) | Papua New Guinea | R Fly mouth |
| | | Indonesia | -- |
| E Coral Sea | Vanuatu - New Caledonia | New Caledonia, Vanuatu | -- |
| W Coral Sea | C York - Sandy C; *Burdekin 131,000; Fitzroy 143,000* | Australia | R Burdekin mouth |
| Oceanic tropical W Pacific | Micronesia | Guam, Kiribati, Marshall Is, Federated States of Micronesia, Nauru, Northern Mariana Is, Palau | -- |
| **Southwest Pacific** | | | |
| W Tasman Sea | Sandy C - C Howe | Australia | -- |
| Bass Strait | C Howe - C Otway; C Naturaliste - Woolnorth P (Tasmania) | Australia | -- |
| Subpolar SW Pacific | C Naturaliste - South West C (Tasmania) | Australia | R Derwent mouth |
| E Tasman Sea (South I) | Southwest C - Perano Head | New Zealand | R Oreti at Riverton hwy bridge |
| | | | R Waiau at Tuatapere |
| | | | R Haast at Roaring Billy |
| | | | R Grey at Dobson |
| | | | R Buller at Te Huha |
| | | | R Motueka at Woodstock |
| E Tasman Sea (North I) | C Terawhiti - C Reinga | New Zealand | R Manawatu at Opiki bridge |
| | | | R Rangitikei at Kakariki |
| | | | R Wanganui at Paetawa |
| | | | R Waingongoro at SH45 |
| | | | R Waitara at Bertrand road |
| | | | R Waikato at Rangiriri |
| | | | R Hoteo at Gubbs |
| Temperate SW Pacific (North I) | C Reinga - C Terawhiti | New Zealand | R Waitangi at Wakelins |
| | | | R Waihou at Te Aroha bridge |
| | | | R Tarawera at Awakaponga |
| | | | R Rangitaiki at Te Teko |
| | | | R Motu at Houpoto |
| | | | R Mohaka at Raupunga |
| | | | R Ngaruroro at Chesterhope |
| | | | R Tukituki at Red bridge |
| | | | R Ruamahanga at Waiaenga |
| | | | R Hutt at Boulcott |
| Temperate SW Pacific (South I) | Perano Head - Southwest C | New Zealand | R Wairau at Tuamarina |
| | | | R Hurunui at Shi bridge |
| | | | R Waimakariri above Old hwy bridge |
| | | | R Opihi at Waipopo |
| | | | R Waitaki at Shi bridge |
| | | | R Taieri at Outram |
| | | | R Clutha at Balclutha |
| | | | R Mataura at Seaward Downs |
| Oceanic SW Pacific | Fiji & Polynesia (except Hawaiian Is) | American Samoa, Cook Is, Fiji, French Polynesia, Samoa, Tokelau, Tonga, Tuvalu, Wallis & Futuna | -- |

B = reservoir; C = cape; df = downstream frontier; E = east; I = island; Is = islands; L = lake; N = north; NE = northeast; NW = northwest; P = point; R = river; S = south; SE = southeast; SW = southwest; W = west.

# References

Accademia Italiana della Cucina. 1995. I formaggi a denominazione di origine e tipici della Sardegna. [Origin-denominated and typical cheeses of Sardinia.] In: Accademia Italiana della Cucina. 1995. *1996 guide to the restaurants of Italy.*

Adriaanse, Albert. 1993. *Environmental policy performance indicators.* Sdu Uitgeverij Koninginnegracht, The Hague.

Adriaanse, Albert, Stefan Bringezu, Allen Hammond, Yuichi Moriguchi, Eric Rodenburg, Donald Rogich, and Helmut Schütz. 1997. *Resource flows: the material basis of industrial economies.* World Resources Institute, Washington, DC.

Ahmad, Y. J., S. El Sarafy, and E. Lutz (eds.). 1989. *Environmental accounting for sustainable development.* A United Nations Environment Programme–World Bank Symposium. The World Bank, Washington, DC.

Alderson, Lawrence. 1989. *The chance to survive.* A. H. Jolly (Editorial). Yelvertoft Manor, England.

Andreae, Meinrat O., and Robert E. Dickinson. 1995. Sustainability and the changing atmosphere: assessing changes in chemical and physical climate. In: Mohan Munasinghe and Walter Shearer (eds.). 1995. *Defining and measuring sustainability: the biogeophysical foundations.* The United Nations University and the World Bank, Washington, DC.

Asian Bureau for Conservation (ABC) and World Conservation Monitoring Centre (WCMC). 1997. *Protected area systems review of the Indo-Malayan Realm.* Asian Bureau for Conservation, Hong Kong (China) and Canterbury (England).

Associazione Nazionale Allevatori Bovini Razza Valdostana. 1995. Personal communication from the director, Dr. Piero Prola, May 1995, Associazione Nazionale Allevatori Bovini Razza Valdostana, Gressan, Valle d'Aosta, Italy.

Atkinson, Giles, and Kirk Hamilton. 1996. Accounting for progress: indicators for sustainable development. *Environment* 38(7).

Baitullin, I., and G. Bekturova. 1997. National strategy to combat desertification in the Republic of Kazakhstan. *Desertification Control Bulletin* 30: 19–27.

Bakkes, J. A., G. J. van den Born, J. C. Helder, R. J. Swart, C. W. Hope, and J. D. E. Parker. 1994. *An overview of environmental indicators: state of the art and perspectives.* United Nations Environment Programme (UNEP), Nairobi, and National Institute of Public Health and Environment (RIVM), Bilthoven, Netherlands.

Bakkes, Jan, and Jaap van Woerden (eds.). 1997. *The future of the global environment: a model-based analysis supporting UNEP's first global environment outlook.* National Institute of Public Health and Environment (RIVM), Bilthoven, Netherlands, and United Nations Environment Programme (UNEP), Nairobi.

Bangladesh Bureau of Statistics. 1999. *Bangladesh compendium of environment statistics 1997.* Bangladesh Bureau of Statistics, Statistics Division, Ministry of Planning, Government of the People's Republic of Bangladesh, Dhaka.

Bartelmus, Peter, and Jan van Tongeren. 1994. *Environmental accounting: an operational perspective.* DESIPA Working Paper Series 1. United Nations, New York.

Beeler, Giuseppe L. 1992. *Prontuario dello studioso.* [*Handbook for students.*] Istituto Editoriale Ticinese, Bellinzona, Switzerland.

BirdLife International. 2000. *Threatened birds of the world.* BirdLife International, Cambridge.

BIS/IMF/OECD/World Bank 2000. *Joint BIS-IMF-OECD-World Bank statistics on external debt.* Bank for International Settlements, International Monetary Fund, Organisation for Economic Co-operation and Development and The World Bank Group. www.oecd.org/dac/debt/htm.

Bixby, Donald E., Carolyn J. Christman, Cynthia J. Ehrman, and D. Phillip Sponenberg. 1994. *Taking stock: the North American livestock census.* McDonald and Woodward, Blacksburg, Virginia.

Black, John. 1997. *A dictionary of economics.* Oxford University Press, Oxford, England.

Boltvinik, Julio, and Enrique Hernández Laos. 1999. *Pobreza y distribución del ingreso en México. [Poverty and income distribution in Mexico.]* Siglo Veintuno Editores, México, DF.

Bryant, Dirk, Lauretta Burke, John McManus, and Mark Spalding. 1998. *Reefs at risk: a map-based indicator of threats to the world's coral reefs.* World Resources Institute (WRI), International Center for Living Aquatic Resources Management (ICLARM), World Conservation Monitoring Centre (WCMC), United Nations Environment Programme (UNEP), Washington, DC.

Canadian Centre for Justice Statistics. 1999. *Uniform crime reporting survey.* Statistics Canada, Ottawa.

Chichilnisky, Graciela. 1997. *The knowledge revolution.* Working Paper Series 9717, Faculty of Business and Law, Deakin University, Burwood, Victoria, Australia.

Chichilnisky, Graciela. 1998. *The knowledge revolution: its impact on consumption patterns and resource use.* Paper prepared for the Human Development Report 1998. United Nations Development Programme, New York.

Cobb, Clifford, Ted Halstead, and Jonathan Rowe. 1995a. *The Genuine Progress Indicator: summary of data and methodology.* Redefining Progress, San Francisco.

Cobb, Clifford, Ted Halstead, and Jonathan Rowe. 1995b. If the GDP is up, why is America down? *The Atlantic Monthly,* October 1995.

Collar, N. J., M. J. Crosby, and A. J. Stattersfield. 1994. *Birds to watch 2: the world list of threatened birds.* BirdLife International, Cambridge, England.

Conservation International. 1996. *Database on human disturbance of world ecosystems.* Conservation International, Washington, DC.

Consultative Group on Sustainable Development Indicators. 2000. *Dashboard of sustainability,* version 1.5. International Institute for Sustainable Development, Winnipeg.

Corner House, The. 1997. *Climate and equity after Kyoto.* Briefing 3. The Corner House, Sturminster Newton, England.

Corson, Walter H. 1996. Measuring sustainability: indicators, trends, and performance. In: Dennis C. Pirages (ed.). 1996. *Building sustainable societies: a blueprint for a post-industrial world.* M.E. Sharpe.

Cunningham, E. P., and O. Syrstad. 1987. *Crossbreeding* Bos indicus *and* Bos taurus *for milk production in the tropics.* FAO Animal Production and Health Paper 68, Food and Agriculture Organization of the United Nations, Rome.

Daly, Herman E., and John B. Cobb, Jr. 1989. *For the common good: redirecting the economy toward community, the environment and a sustainable future.* Beacon Press, Boston.

Dieren, Wouter van (ed.). 1995. *Taking nature into account: toward a sustainable national income.* A report to the Club of Rome. Springer-Verlag, New York.

Dinerstein, Eric, David M. Olson, Douglas J. Graham, Avis L. Webster, Steven A. Primm, Marnie P. Bookbinder, and George Ledec. 1995. *A conservation assessment of the terrestrial ecoregions of Latin America and the Caribbean.* The World Bank, Washington, DC.

*The Economist.* 1997. Guide to economic indicators. 3rd edition. Profile Books, London.

*The Economist.* 1999. The navigators [central banks]: a survey of the world economy. *The Economist,* 25 September 1999.

Eurostat. 1997. *Indicators of sustainable development: a pilot study following the methodology of the United Nations Commission on Sustainable Development.* European Communities, Luxembourg.

Eurostat. 2000. *GDP and government finances in the EU.* Eurostat, Luxembourg.

Eurostat, European Commission, and the European Environment Agency. 1998. *Europe's environment: statistical compendium for the second assessment.* European Communities, Luxembourg.

Eurostat, European Commission, European Environment Agency Task Force, DG XI and PHARE European Commission, United Nations Economic Commission for Europe, Organisation for Economic Cooperation and Development, and World Health Organization. 1995. *Europe's environment: statistical compendium for the Dobris assessment.* Office for Official Publications of the European Community, Luxembourg.

Fairbairn, Te'o I. J., Charles E. Morrison, Richard W. Baker, and Sheree A. Groves. 1991. *The Pacific Islands: politics, economics, and international relations.* East–West Center, University of Hawaii Press, Honolulu.

FAO Fishery Information, Data and Statistics Unit. 1998. Fishery fleet statistics on diskette. Food and Agriculture Organization of the United Nations, Rome.

FAO Initiative for Domesticated Animal Diversity. 1998. *Domesticated Animal Diversity Information System (DAD-IS) 2.0.* CD-ROM. Food and Agriculture Organization of the United Nations, Rome.

FAO Initiative for Domesticated Animal Diversity. 1999. Domesticated Animal Diversity Information System (DAD-IS) online. www.fao.org/dad-is/index.htm

FAO Marine Resources Service, Fishery Resources Division. 1997. *Review of the state of world fishery resources: marine fisheries.* FAO Fisheries Circular 920. Food and Agriculture Organization of the United Nations, Rome.

FAO, UNDP, and UNEP. 1994. *Land degradation in South Asia: its severity, causes and effects upon the people.* World Soil Resources Reports 78. Food and Agriculture Organization of the United Nations, Rome.

Federal Bureau of Investigation. 1999. *Uniform crime reports:*

crime in the United States 1997. Department of Justice, Washington, DC.

Fenwick, J. 1992. *International profiles on marine scientific research.* Woods Hole Oceanographic Institution, Massachusetts.

Fischer-Kowalski, Marina, Helmut Haberl, and Harald Payer. 1997. In: Bedrich Moldan and Suzanne Billharz. 1997. *Sustainability indicators: report of the project on indicators of sustainable development.* SCOPE 58. Wiley, New York.

Food and Agriculture Organization of the United Nations (FAO). 1993. *Forest resources assessment 1990. Tropical countries.* FAO Forestry Paper 112. Food and Agriculture Organization of the United Nations, Rome.

Food and Agriculture Organization of the United Nations (FAO). 1995a. *Irrigation in Africa in figures.* Water Reports 7. Food and Agriculture Organization of the United Nations, Rome.

Food and Agriculture Organization of the United Nations (FAO). 1995b. *Water resources of African countries: a review.* Food and Agriculture Organization of the United Nations, Rome.

Food and Agriculture Organization of the United Nations (FAO). 1995c. *Forest resources assessment 1990. Global synthesis.* FAO Forestry Paper 124. Food and Agriculture Organization of the United Nations, Rome.

Food and Agriculture Organization of the United Nations (FAO). 1996a. *The Sixth World Food Survey, 1996.* Food and Agriculture Organization of the United Nations, Rome.

Food and Agriculture Organization of the United Nations (FAO). 1996b. *Global databank for farm animal genetic resources.* Domestic Animal Diversity (DAD) database. Food and Agriculture Organization of the United Nations, Rome.

Food and Agriculture Organization of the United Nations (FAO). 1997a. *Statistical estimates for forest cover, Forest Resources Assessment Programme.* Food and Agriculture Organization of the United Nations, Rome.

Food and Agriculture Organization of the United Nations (FAO). 1997b. *Irrigation in the Near East region in figures.* Water Reports 9. Food and Agriculture Organization of the United Nations, Rome.

Food and Agriculture Organization of the United Nations (FAO). 1997c. *Irrigation in the countries of the former Soviet Union in figures.* Water Reports 15. Food and Agriculture Organization of the United Nations, Rome.

Food and Agriculture Organization of the United Nations (FAO). 1997d. *Irrigation potential in Africa.* FAO Land and Water Bulletin 4. Food and Agriculture Organization of the United Nations, Rome.

Food and Agriculture Organization of the United Nations (FAO). 1998a. FAOSTAT database. Food and Agriculture Organization of the United Nations, Rome.

Food and Agriculture Organization of the United Nations (FAO). 1998b. *FAO yearbook: fishery statistics, capture production: Vol. 82, 1996.* Food and Agriculture Organization of the United Nations, Rome.

Food and Agriculture Organization of the United Nations (FAO). 1999a. FAOSTAT database. Food and Agriculture Organization of the United Nations, Rome.

Food and Agriculture Organization of the United Nations (FAO). 1999b. *The state of food insecurity in the world.* Food and Agriculture Organization of the United Nations, Rome.

Food and Agriculture Organization of the United Nations (FAO). 1999c. *Irrigation in Asia in figures.* Water Reports 18. Food and Agriculture Organization of the United Nations, Rome.

Food and Agriculture Organization of the United Nations (FAO). 2000a. FAOSTAT database. Food and Agriculture Organization of the United Nations, Rome.

Food and Agriculture Organization of the United Nations (FAO). 2000b. *Irrigation in Latin America in figures.* Water Reports in press. Food and Agriculture Organization of the United Nations, Rome.

Freedom House. 1999a. *Freedom in the world, 1998–1999.* Freedom House, New York.

Freedom House. 1999b. *Press freedom survey, 1999.* Freedom House, New York.

Freedom House. 2000a. *Freedom in the world, 1999–2000.* Freedom House, New York.

Freedom House. 2000b. *Press freedom survey, 2000.* Freedom House, New York.

Gallopín, Gilberto Carlos. 1997. Indicators and their use: information for decision-making. Part 1: Introduction. In: Bedrich Moldan and Suzanne Billharz. 1997. *Sustainability indicators: report of the project on indicators of sustainable development.* SCOPE 58. Wiley, New York.

Garcia, S. M., and C. Newton. 1994. *Current situation, trends and prospects in world capture fisheries.* Paper presented at the Conference on Fisheries Management: Global Trends. Seattle, Washington, 14–16 June 1994. Fisheries Department, Food and Agriculture Organization of the United Nations, Rome.

Global Environmental Monitoring System (GEMS). 1988. *Assessment of freshwater quality.* United Nations Environment Programme, Nairobi, and World Health Organization, Geneva.

Global Leaders for Environment Tomorrow Task Force. 2001. *Pilot environmental sustainability index.* World Economic

Forum, in collaboration with Yale Center for Environmental Law and Policy, Yale University, and Center for International Earth Science Information Network, Columbia University, New York.

Goldsmith, Edward, Robert Allen, Michael Allaby, John Davoll, and Sam Lawrence. 1972. *Blueprint for survival.* Penguin, Harmondsworth, and Houghton Mifflin, Boston.

Grainger, R. J. R., and S. M. Garcia. 1996. *Chronicles of marine fishery landings (1950–1994). Trend analysis and fisheries potential.* FAO Fisheries Technical Paper 359. Food and Agriculture Organization of the United Nations, Rome.

Gutierrez Montes, Isabel Adriana. 1996. Aportes de un proyecto de manejo de vida silvestre a la calidad de vida de las poblaciones rurales—el caso de la Cooperativa Omar Baca, Cosigüina, Nicaragua. [*Contributions of a wildlife management project to the quality of life of rural populations—the case of the Omar Baca Cooperative, Cosigüina, Nicaragua.*] Centro Agronomico Tropical de Investigacion y Eseñanza (CATIE), Turrialba, Costa Rica.

Guveya, Emmanuel, Freddie Kachote, and Misael Kokwe. 1999. *A wellbeing assessment of Mangisai, Nyevera and Sedeya communities in Zimuto Communal Lands, Zimbabwe.* IUCN–The World Conservation Union Regional Office for Southern Africa, Harare, Zimbabwe.

Hamilton, Kirk, and Ernst Lutz. 1996. *Green national accounts: policy uses and empirical experience.* Environment Department Papers, Environmental Economics Series, Paper 39. The World Bank, Washington, DC.

Hammond, Allen, Albert Adriaanse, Eric Rodenburg, Dirk Bryant, and Richard Woodward. 1995. *Environmental indicators: a systematic approach to measuring and reporting on environmental policy performance in the context of sustainable development.* World Resources Institute, Washington, DC.

Hannah, Lee, John L. Carr, and Ali Lankerani. 1995. Human disturbance and natural habitat: a biome level analysis of a global data set. *Biodiversity and Conservation* 4: 128–155.

Hannah, Lee, David Lohse, Charles Hutchinson, John L. Carr, and Ali Lankerani. 1994. A preliminary inventory of human disturbance of world ecosystems. *Ambio* 23(4–5): 246–250.

Hardi, Peter, and Terence Zdan (eds.). 1997. *Assessing sustainable development: principles in practice.* International Institute for Sustainable Development, Winnipeg.

Harvard University Environmental Systems Program. 1996. *Measuring sustainable development in Asia: environmental quality indices.* Final Report. Asian Development Bank, Manila.

Hasnain, H. U. 1985. *Sheep and goats in Pakistan.* FAO Animal Production and Health Paper 56, Food and Agriculture Organization of the United Nations, Rome.

Hayden, Bruce P., G. Carleton Ray, and Robert Dolan. 1984.

Classification of coastal and marine environments. *Environmental Conservation* 11(3): 199–207.

Hecht, Joy E. No date. *Environmental accounting: what's it all about?* IUCN Green Accounting Initiative. IUCN–The World Conservation Union, Washington, DC.

Hodge, Tony. 1995. From theory to practice: assessing progress toward sustainable development in the Great Lakes Basin. In: Tony Hodge, Susan Holtz, Cameron Smith, and Kelly Hawke Baxter (eds.). 1995. *Pathways to sustainability: assessing our progress.* National Round Table on the Environment and the Economy, Ottawa.

Hodge, R. Anthony, and Robert Prescott-Allen. 1997. *Report on British Columbia's progress toward sustainability.* Ministry of Environment, Lands and Parks, Victoria, British Columbia.

Holling, C. S. 1995. Sustainability: the cross-scale dimension. In: Mohan Munasinghe and Walter Shearer (eds.). 1995. *Defining and measuring sustainability: the biogeophysical foundations.* The United Nations University and the World Bank, Washington, DC.

Humana, Charles. 1992. *World human rights guide,* 3rd edition. Oxford University Press, New York.

Hunter, M. L. Jr., G. L. Jacobson Jr., and T. Webb. 1988. Paleoecology and the coarse-filter approach to maintaining biological diversity. *Conservation Biology* (2): 375–383.

Imbach, Alejandro. 1996. *Participatory rural assessment and mapping.* IUCN–The World Conservation Union, Gland, Switzerland.

IMF Policy Development and Review Department. 2000. Debt- and reserve-related indicators of vulnerability. International Monetary Fund, Washington, DC.

IMO/FAO/UNESCO/WMO/WHO/IAEA/UN/UNEP Joint Group of Experts on the Scientific Aspects of Marine Pollution (GESAMP). 1990. *The state of the marine environment.* Reports and Studies GESAMP 39. United Nations Environment Programme, Nairobi.

Instituto Nacional de Estadística, Geografía e Informática. 1998. *Estadísticas del medio ambiente, México, 1997.* [*Environmental Statistics, México, 1997.*] Secretaría de Medio Ambiente, Recursos Naturales y Pesca, México.

Intergovernmental Panel on Climate Change, Working Group 1. 1996. *Climate change 1995: the science of climate change.* Cambridge University Press, Cambridge, England.

International Institute for Strategic Studies. 1996. *The military balance 1996/97.* Oxford University Press for the International Institute for Strategic Studies, London.

International Institute for Strategic Studies. 1997. *The military balance 1997/98.* Oxford University Press for the International Institute for Strategic Studies, London.

International Institute for Strategic Studies. 1999a. *The military balance 1999/2000.* Oxford University Press for the International Institute for Strategic Studies, London.

International Institute for Strategic Studies. 1999b. *The 1999 chart of armed conflict.* The International Institute for Strategic Studies, London.

International Labour Office (ILO). 1999. *Key indicators of the labour market 1999.* International Labour Office, Geneva.

International Labour Office. 2000. LABORSTA: Labour Statistcs Database. http://laborsta.ilo.org/.

International Monetary Fund (IMF). 2000. *World Economic Outlook (WEO) Database September 2000.* International Monetary Fund, Washington, DC.

International Telecommunication Union. 1997. *Yearbook of statistics: telecommunication services 1986–1995.* International Telecommunication Union, Geneva.

International Telecommunication Union. 1998. *World telecommunication development report 1998.* International Telecommunication Union, Geneva.

International Telecommunication Union. 1999. *World telecommunication development report 1999.* International Telecommunication Union, Geneva.

International Telecommunication Union. 2000. Data tables on basic indicators, cellular subscribers, and Internet indicators, January 2000. Personal communication, Telecommunication Development Bureau, International Telecommunication Union, Geneva.

Inter-Parliamentary Union. 2000. *Women in national parliaments.* www.ipu.org.

Inter-Secretariat Working Group on National Accounts. 1993. *System of national accounts.* United Nations, New York.

Iremonger, S., C. Ravilious, and T. Quinton (eds.). 1997. *A global overview of forest conservation.* CD-ROM. World Conservation Monitoring Centre (WCMC) and Center for International Forestry Research (CIFOR), Cambridge, England.

IUCN CNPPA. 1994. *Guidelines for protected area management categories.* Commission on National Parks and Protected Areas (CNPPA) [now World Commission on Protected Areas], IUCN–The World Conservation Union, Gland, Switzerland, and Cambridge, England.

IUCN Species Survival Commission. 1994. *IUCN Red List categories.* IUCN–The World Conservation Union, Gland, Switzerland.

IUCN Species Survival Commission. 2000. *The 2000 IUCN Red List of Threatened Species.* IUCN–World Conservation Union, Gland, Switzerland.

IUCN/UNEP/WWF. 1980. *World conservation strategy: living resource conservation for sustainable development.* International Union for Conservation of Nature and Natural Resources (IUCN), United Nations Environment Programme (UNEP), Nairobi, and World Wildlife Fund, Gland, Switzerland.

IUCN/UNEP/WWF. 1991. *Caring for the earth: a strategy for sustainable living.* IUCN–The World Conservation Union, United Nations Environment Programme (UNEP), Nairobi, and World Wildlife Fund, Gland, Switzerland.

IUCN World Commission on Protected Areas and World Conservation Monitoring Centre. 1998. *United Nations list of protected areas 1997.* IUCN–The World Conservation Union, Gland, Switzerland, and World Conservation Monitoring Centre, Cambridge, England.

Junker, Armin, and Dietrich Schwela. 1998. *Air quality guidelines, standards and risk considerations.* Contribution to the XI World Clean Air and Environment Congress, 13–18 September 1998, Durban, South Africa.

Kumar, Ashok. 1999. *A system assessment of Dasudi Gram Panchayat.* IUCN–The World Conservation Union, Gland, Switzerland.

Kunte, Arundhati, Kirk Hamilton, John Dixon, and Michael Clemens. 1998. *Estimating national wealth: methodology and results.* Environment Department Papers, Environmental Economics Series, Paper 57. The World Bank, Washington, DC.

Landes, David. 1999. *The wealth and poverty of nations.* Abacus, London.

Leroux, Guy. 1980. *La cuisine brésilienne* [Brazilian cuisine]. Les Editions du Pacifique, Papeete, Tahiti.

Levin, Simon A. 1995. Scale and sustainability: a population and community perspective. In: Mohan Munasinghe and Walter Shearer (eds.). 1995. *Defining and measuring sustainability: the biogeophysical foundations.* The United Nations University and the World Bank, Washington, DC.

Loh, Jonathan, Jørgen Randers, Alex MacGillivray, Val Kapos, Martin Jenkins, Brian Groombridge, Neil Cox, and Ben Warren. 1999. *Living planet report 1999.* WWF International, Gland, Switzerland.

Lopez, Alan D., Joshua Salomon, Omar Ahmad, Christopher J.L. Murray, and Doris Mafat. 2000. *Life tables for 191 countries: data, methods and results.* GPE Discussion Paper 9. World Health Organization, Geneva.

Lutz, E. (ed.) 1993. *Toward improved accounting for the environment.* An UNSTAT–World Bank Symposium. The World Bank, Washington, DC.

MacKinnon, John, and Kathy MacKinnon. 1986a. *Review of the protected areas system in the Afrotropical realm.* International Union for Conservation of Nature and Natural Resources, Gland, Switzerland, and United Nations Environment Programme (UNEP), Nairobi.

MacKinnon, John, and Kathy MacKinnon. 1986b. *Review of the protected areas system in the Indo-Malayan realm.* International Union for Conservation of Nature and Natural Resources, Gland, Switzerland, and United Nations Environment Programme (UNEP), Nairobi.

Manitoba Environment. 1997. *Moving toward sustainable development reporting: state of the environment report for Manitoba 1997.* SOE Reporting, Manitoba Environment, Winnipeg, Manitoba.

Marland, Gregg, Tom Boden, and Robert J. Andres. 2000 (6 September). *National $CO_2$ emissions from fossil-fuel burning, cement manufacture, and gas flaring 1751–1997.* Carbon Dioxide Information Analysis Center, Oak Ridge National Laboratory, Oak Ridge, Tennessee.

Mathers, Colin D., Ritu Sadana, Joshua A. Salomon, Christopher J.L. Murray, and Alan D. Lopez. 2000. *Estimates of DALE for 191 countries: methods and results.* Global Programme on Evidence for Health Policy Discussion Paper 16. World Health Organization, Geneva.

Matthews, Emily, Christof Amann, Stefan Bringezu, Marina Fischer-Kowalski, Walter Hüttler, René Kleijn, Yuichi Moriguchi, Christian Ottke, Eric Rodenburg, Don Rogich, Heinz Schandl, Helmut Schütz, Ester van der Voet, and Helga Weisz. 2000. *The weight of nations: material outflows from industrial economies.* World Resources Institute, Washington, DC.

McNeely, Jeffrey (ed.). 1993. *Parks for life: report of the IVth World Congress on National Parks and Protected Areas.* IUCN–The World Conservation Union, Gland, Switzerland.

Munasinghe, Mohan, and Jeffrey McNeely. 1995. Key concepts and terminology of sustainable development. In: Mohan Munasinghe and Walter Shearer (eds.). 1995. *Defining and measuring sustainability: the biogeophysical foundations.* The United Nations University and the World Bank, Washington, DC.

National Water Research Institute. 1996. *The Annotated Digital Atlas of Global Water Quality.* World Health Organization (WHO) and United Nations Environment Programme (UNEP) Global Environment Monitoring System (GEMS), Geneva

OECD Centre for Co-operation with the Economies in Transition. 1996. *Environmental information systems in the Russian Federation: an OECD assessment.* Organisation for Economic Co-operation and Development, Paris.

Office of the UN System Support and Services. 1996. *UN conference goals and commitments inter-related to the "DAC reflection."* United Nations Development Programme, New York.

Oldeman, L. R. 1993. *An international methodology for an assessment of soil degradation and georeferenced soils and terrain database.* International Soil Reference and Information Centre, Wageningen, Netherlands.

Oldeman, L. R., R. T. A. Hakkeling, and W. G. Sombroek. 1991. *World map of the status of human-induced soil degradation: an explanatory note,* 2nd revised edition. International Soil Reference and Information Centre, Wageningen, Netherlands, and United Nations Environment Programme, Nairobi.

O'Neill, R. V., C. T. Hunsaker, D. Jones, J. M. Klopatek, V. H. Dale, M. G. Turner, R. H. Gardner, and R. Graham. 1995. Sustainability and landscape and regional scales. In: Mohan Munasinghe and Walter Shearer (eds.). 1995. *Defining and measuring sustainability: the biogeophysical foundations.* The United Nations University and the World Bank, Washington, DC.

Onis, Mercedes de, and Monika Blössner. 1997. *WHO global database on child growth and malnutrition.* World Health Organization, Geneva.

Organisation for Economic Co-operation and Development. 1994. *Environmental indicators: OECD core set.* Organisation for Economic Co-operation and Development, Paris.

Organisation for Economic Co-operation and Development. 1997. *OECD environmental data: compendium 1997.* Organisation for Economic Co-operation and Development, Paris.

Organisation for Economic Co-operation and Development. 1999. *OECD environmental data: compendium 1999.* Organisation for Economic Co-operation and Development, Paris.

Organisation for Economic Co-operation and Development, Human Resources Development Canada, and Statistics Canada. 1997. *Literacy skills for the knowledge society: further results from the International Adult Literacy Survey.* Organisation for Economic Co-operation and Development, Paris, and Human Resources Development Canada and Statistics Canada, Ottawa.

Ozone Secretariat, United Nations Environment Programme. 1997. *Production and consumption of ozone depleting substances 1986–1995.* Ozone Secretariat, UNEP, Nairobi.

Ozone Secretariat, United Nations Environment Programme. 1999. *Production and consumption of ozone depleting substances 1986–1998.* Ozone Secretariat, UNEP, Nairobi.

Pajuoja, Heikki. 1995. *The outlook for the European forest resources and roundwood supply.* UNECE/FAO Timber and Forest Discussion Papers, ETTS V Working Paper ECE/TIM/DP/4. United Nations Economic Commission for Europe and Food and Agriculture Organization of the United Nations, New York and Geneva.

Palmer, Kara, and Richard Conlin. 1997. Sustainable Seattle: the indicators of sustainable community. In: Peter Hardi and Terence Zdan. 1997. *Assessing sustainable development: princi-*

*ples in practice.* International Institute for Sustainable Development, Winnipeg.

Pandey, Devendra. 1995. *Forest resources assessment 1990. Tropical forest plantation resources.* FAO Forestry Paper 128. Food and Agriculture Organization of the United Nations, Rome.

Pernetta, John, and Danny Elder. 1993. *Cross-sectoral, integrated coastal area planning (CICAP): guidelines and principles for coastal area development.* IUCN–The World Conservation Union, Gland, Switzerland.

Porter, Valerie. 1991. *Cattle: a handbook to the breeds of the world.* Christopher Helm, London.

Porter, Valerie. 1993. *Pigs: a handbook to the breeds of the world.* Helm Information, Mountfield, England.

Prescott-Allen, Robert. 1995. *Barometer of sustainability: a method of assessing progress toward sustainable societies,* 3rd draft. PADATA, Victoria, BC.

Prescott-Allen, Robert. 1997. *Barometer of sustainability: measuring and communicating wellbeing and sustainable development.* An Approach to Assessing Progress Toward Sustainability: Tools and Training Series. IUCN–The World Conservation Union, Gland, Switzerland.

Ray, G. Carleton. 1996a. Biodiversity is biogeography: implications for conservation. *Oceanography* 9(1): 50–59.

Ray, G. Carleton. 1996b. Coastal–marine discontinuities and synergisms: implications for biodiversity conservation. *Biodiversity and Conservation* 5: 1095–1108.

Redefining Progress. 1999. *Footprint of Nations ranking list (1995 data).* Updated 20 October 1999. Redefining Progress, San Francisco.

Rege, J. E. O. 1999. The state of African cattle genetic resources I. Classification framework and identification of threatened and extinct breeds. *Animal Genetic Resources Information* 25: 1–25.

Rege, J. E. O., G. S. Aboagye, and C. L. Tawah. 1994. Shorthorn cattle of west and central Africa I. Origin, distribution, classification and population statistics. *World Animal Review* 78(1): 2–13.

Rege, J. E. O., and C. L. Tawah. 1999. The state of African cattle genetic resources II. Geographical distribution, characteristics and uses of present-day breeds and strains. *Animal Genetic Resources Information* 26: 1–25.

Reid, Walter V., and Kenton R. Miller. 1989. *Keeping options alive: the scientific basis for conserving biodiversity.* World Resources Institute, Washington, DC.

Repetto, R., W. Magrath, M. Wells, C. Beer, and F. Rossini. 1989. *Wasting assets: natural resources in the national income accounts.* World Resources Institute, Washington, DC.

Ricketts, Taylor, Eric Dinerstein, David Olson, Colby Loucks, William Eichbaum, Kevin Kavanagh, Prashant Hedao, Patrick Hurley, Karen Carney, Robin Abell, and Steven Walters. 1998. *A conservation assessment of the terrestrial ecoregions of North America. Volume I: the United States and Canada* (prepublication draft). World Wildlife Fund, Washington, DC.

Sachs, Jeffrey D., and Wing Thye Woo. 1999. Executive summary: The Asian financial crisis: what happened, and what is to be done. *Asia competitiveness report 1999.* World Economic Forum, www.weforum.org.

Scherf, Beate D. (ed.). 1995. *World Watch list for domestic animal diversity,* 2nd edition. Food and Agriculture Organization of the United Nations, Rome.

Serageldin, Ismail, and Andrew Steer. 1994. Epilogue: expanding the capital stock. In: Ismail Serageldin and Andrew Steer (eds.). 1994. *Making development sustainable: from concepts to action.* Environmentally Sustainable Development Occasional Papers 2. The World Bank, Washington, DC.

Sheng, Fulai. 1995. *Real value for nature: an overview of global efforts to achieve true measures of economic progress.* World Wide Fund for Nature (WWF) International, Gland, Switzerland.

Sherman, Kenneth. 1995. Large marine ecosystems and fisheries. In: Mohan Munasinghe and Walter Shearer (eds.). 1995. *Defining and measuring sustainability: the biogeophysical foundations.* The United Nations University and the World Bank, Washington, DC.

Shiklomanov, I. A. 1997. *Comprehensive assessment of the freshwater resources of the world.* World Meteorological Organization, Geneva.

Simon, D. L. 1999. European approaches to conservation of farm animal genetic resources. *Animal Genetic Resources Information* 25: 79–99.

Smith, Adam. 1986 [1776]. *The wealth of nations. Books I–III.* Penguin Books, London.

Stuart, Simon N., and Richard J. Adams. 1990. *Biodiversity in Sub-Saharan Africa and its islands: conservation, management and sustainable use.* Occasional Papers of the IUCN Species Survival Commission 6. IUCN–The World Conservation Union, Gland, Switzerland.

Swart, Rob, and Jan Bakkes (eds.). 1995. *Scanning the global environment: a framework and methodology for integrated environmental reporting and assessment.* United Nations Environment Programme (UNEP), Nairobi, and National Institute of Public Health and Environment (RIVM), Bilthoven, Netherlands.

Third Ministerial Conference on the Protection of Forests in Europe. 1998. *Follow-up reports on the Ministerial Conferences on the Protection of Forests in Europe,* volume II. Ministry of Agriculture, Rural Development and Fisheries, Lisbon, Portugal.

Touring Club Italiano. 1993. *Annuario generale dei comuni e delle frazioni d'Italia.* [*Gazetteer of the municipalities and hamlets of Italy.*] Touring Club Italiano, Milan.

Transparency International. 1999. *1999 Corruption perceptions index.* http://www.gwdg.de/~uwvw/1999Data.html.

Transparency International. 2000. *The 2000 corruption perceptions index.* Transparency International, Berlin. www.transparancy.de/documents/cpi/2000/.

UNECE and FAO. 2000. *Temperate and boreal forest resource assessment 2000.* United Nations Economic Commission for Europe, Geneva, and Food and Agriculture Organization of the United Nations, Rome.

UNEP/ISRIC. 1990. *World map on status of human-induced soil degradation.* United Nations Environment Programme, Nairobi.

UNEP and WHO GEMS/Water Collaborating Centre. 1988–1990. *GEMS/Water data summary 1988–1990.* World Health Organization and United Nations Environment Programme. National Water Research Institute, Burlington, Ontario.

UNEP and WHO GEMS/Water Collaborating Centre. 1991–1993. *GEMS/Water data summary 1991–1993.* World Health Organization and United Nations Environment Programme. National Water Research Institute, Burlington, Ontario.

UNEP and WHO GEMS/Water Collaborating Centre. 1999. GEMS/Water database. World Health Organization and United Nations Environment Programme. National Water Research Institute, Burlington, Ontario.

UNESCO. 1999a. Illiteracy estimates and projections. Personal communication, UNESCO Institute for Statistics, United Nations Educational, Scientific and Cultural Organization, Paris.

UNESCO. 1999b. Net enrollment rates. Personal communication, UNESCO Institute for Statistics, United Nations Educational, Scientific and Cultural Organization, Paris.

UNESCO. 1999c. Number of tertiary students per 100,000 inhabitants. Personal communication, UNESCO Institute for Statistics, United Nations Educational, Scientific and Cultural Organization, Paris.

UNESCO. 1999d. *Statistical yearbook 1999.* United Nations Educational, Scientific and Cultural Organization, Paris, and Bernan Press, Lanham, MD.

UNICEF. 1999a. *The state of the world's children 1999.* Oxford University Press, Oxford, England.

UNICEF. 1999b. *The state of the world's children 2000.* www.unicef.org.

United Nations. 1992. *Agenda 21: programme of action for sustainable development.* United Nations, New York.

United Nations. 1995. *The world's women 1995: trends and statistics.* Social Statistics and Indicators Series K No. 12. United Nations, New York.

United Nations. 1996. *Indicators of sustainable development framework and methodologies.* United Nations, New York.

United Nations ACC Task Force on Basic Social Services for All. 1997. *Basic social services for all 1997.* United Nations, New York.

United Nations Crime Prevention and Criminal Justice Division. 1997. *4th UN survey of crime trends and operations of criminal justice systems.* United Nations, Vienna.

United Nations Crime Prevention and Criminal Justice Division. 1999. *5th UN survey of crime trends and operations of criminal justice systems.* United Nations, Vienna.

United Nations Development Programme. 1990. *Human development report 1990.* Oxford University Press, Oxford, England.

United Nations Development Programme. 1991. *Human development report 1991.* Oxford University Press, Oxford, England.

United Nations Development Programme. 1992. *Human development report 1992.* Oxford University Press, Oxford, England.

United Nations Development Programme. 1993. *Human development report 1993.* Oxford University Press, Oxford, England.

United Nations Development Programme. 1994. *Human development report 1994.* Oxford University Press, Oxford, England.

United Nations Development Programme. 1995. *Human development report 1995.* Oxford University Press, Oxford, England.

United Nations Development Programme. 1996. *Human development report 1996.* Oxford University Press, Oxford, England.

United Nations Development Programme. 1997. *Human development report 1997.* Oxford University Press, Oxford, England.

United Nations Development Programme. 1998. *Human development report 1998.* Oxford University Press, Oxford, England.

United Nations Development Programme. 1999. *Human development report 1999.* Oxford University Press, Oxford, England.

United Nations Development Programme. 2000. *Human development report 2000.* Oxford University Press, New York and Oxford.

United Nations Division for the Advancement of Women.

1996. *Fact sheet on women in government as at January 1996.* United Nations, New York.

United Nations Economic Commission for Europe. 1990. Draft ECE standard statistical classification of ecological freshwater quality. In: Statistical Office, Department of International Economic and Social Affairs. 1991. *Concepts and methods of environment statistics: statistics of the natural environment. A technical report.* Studies in Methods, series F, no. 57. United Nations, New York.

United Nations Economic Commission for Europe. 2000. Statistics on unemployment. www.unece.org/stats/data.htm.

United Nations Energy Statistics Unit. 2000. *1997 Energy statistics yearbook.* United Nations, New York.

United Nations Environment Programme. 1996. *Report of the Secretariat on information provided by the parties in accordance with articles 7 and 9 of the Montreal Protocol.* United Nations Environment Programme, Nairobi.

United Nations Environment Programme. 1998. *Report of the Secretariat on information provided by the parties in accordance with articles 7 and 9 of the Montreal Protocol.* United Nations Environment Programme, Nairobi.

United Nations Environment Programme. 1999. *Global environment outlook 2000.* United Nations Environment Programme, Nairobi.

United Nations Population Division. 1996. *World population prospects: the 1996 revision. Annex I: Demographic indicators.* United Nations, New York.

United Nations Population Division. 1997. *Information note: wall chart on basic social services for all, 1977.* United Nations, New York.

United Nations Population Division. 1998a. *World population prospects: the 1998 revision.* United Nations, New York.

United Nations Population Division. 1998b. *World population projections to 2150.* United Nations, New York.

United Nations Statistical Commission and Economic Commission for Europe. 1992. *The environment in Europe and North America: annotated statistics 1992.* United Nations, New York.

United Nations Statistical Division. 1993. *Integrated environmental and economic accounting: interim version. Handbook of national accounting.* Studies in Methods, Series F, 61. United Nations, New York.

United Nations Statistical Division. 1997. *Minimum national social data set (MNSDS).* Endorsed by the United Nations Statistical Commission at its 29th session, 11–14 February 1997. United Nations, New York.

United Nations Statistical Division. 1999. *Statistical yearbook.* United Nations, New York.

U.S. Bureau of the Census. 1999. *Current population survey.* U.S. Bureau of the Census, Washington, DC.

van Lynden, G. W. J., and L. R. Oldeman. 1997. *The assessment of the status of human-induced soil degradation in south and southeast Asia.* United Nations Environment Programme, Nairobi, Food and Agricultural Organization of the United Nations, Rome, and International Soil Reference and Information Centre, Wageningen, Netherlands.

Visschedjik, Jan, and Sylvère Siméant. 1998. Targets for health for all in the 21st century. *World Health Statistics Quarterly* 51(1): 56–67.

Vitousek, P. M., P. R. Ehrlich, A. H. Ehrlich, and P. A. Matson. 1986. Human appropriation of the products of photosynthesis. *BioScience* 36(6): 366–373.

Wackernagel, Mathis, Alejandro Callejas Linares, Diana Deumling, Niels B. Schulz, María Antonieta Vásquez Sánchez, Ina Susana López Falfán, and Jonathan Loh. 2000. *Ecological footprints and ecological capacities of 152 nations: the 1996 update.* Redefining Progress, San Francisco.

Wackernagel, Mathis, and William E. Rees. 1996. *Our ecological footprint: reducing human impact on the earth.* New Society Publishers, Gabriola Island, BC.

Weizsäcker, Ernst von, Amory B. Lovins, and L. Hunter Lovins. 1997. *Factor Four: doubling wealth-halving resource use.* Earthscan, London.

Welcomme, R. L. 1985. *River fisheries.* FAO Fisheries Technical Paper 262. Food and Agriculture Organization of the United Nations, Rome.

Wilson, E. O. 1988. The current state of biological diversity. In: E. O. Wilson (ed.). 1988. *Biodiversity.* National Academy Press, Washington, DC.

World Bank. 1998. *World development indicators 1998.* World development indicators on CD-ROM. The World Bank, Washington, DC.

World Bank. 1999a. *World development indicators 1999.* World development indicators on CD-ROM. The World Bank, Washington, DC.

World Bank. 1999b. *Global development finance 1999.* Global development finance on CD-ROM. The World Bank, Washington, DC.

World Bank. 2000a. *World development indicators 2000.* World development indicators on CD-ROM. The World Bank, Washington, DC.

World Bank. 2000b. *Global development finance 2000.* Global development finance on CD-ROM. The World Bank, Washington, DC.

World Bank staff. 1997. *Expanding the measure of wealth: indicators of environmentally sustainable development.* Environmentally Sustainable Development Studies and Monographs Series 17. The World Bank, Washington, DC.

World Commission on Environment and Development. 1987. *Our common future.* Oxford University Press, Oxford, England.

World Conservation Monitoring Centre. 1992. *Global biodiversity: status of the earth's living resources.* Chapman and Hall, London.

World Conservation Monitoring Centre. 1997. *Biodiversity conservation in the tropics: gaps in habitat protection and funding priorities.* WCMC Biodiversity Series 6. World Conservation Monitoring Centre, Cambridge, England.

World Conservation Monitoring Centre. 1998a. WCMC threatened plants database. World Conservation Monitoring Centre, Cambridge, England.

World Conservation Monitoring Centre. 1998b. WCMC threatened animals database. World Conservation Monitoring Centre, Cambridge, England.

World Energy Council. 1999. *Survey of energy resources.* World Energy Council, London.

World Health Organization (WHO). 1996–1998a. WHO Health-for-All database (data from WHO member states and regional offices). World Health Organization, Geneva.

World Health Organization (WHO). 1998b. *Health for all in the twenty-first century.* Document A51/5. World Health Organization, Geneva.

World Health Organization (WHO). 1998c. *Healthy cities air management information system.* AMIS 2.0, 1998. CD-ROM. World Health Organization, Geneva.

World Health Organization (WHO). 1998d. *Guidelines for air quality.* World Health Organization, Geneva.

World Health Organization (WHO). 2000. *World health report 2000.* World Health Organization, Geneva.

World Meteorological Organization. 1995. *Scientific assessment of ozone depletion: 1994.* WMO Global Ozone Research and Monitoring Project, Report 37. World Meteorological Organization, Geneva.

World Resources Institute, United Nations Environment Programme, United Nations Development Programme, and World Bank. 1998. *World Resources 1998–99.* Oxford University Press, Oxford, England.

# *Index*